Dictionary of Literary Biography

1. *The American Renaissance in New England,* edited by Joel Myerson (1978)
2. *American Novelists Since World War II,* edited by Jeffrey Helterman and Richard Layman (1978)
3. *Antebellum Writers in New York and the South,* edited by Joel Myerson (1979)
4. *American Writers in Paris, 1920-1939,* edited by Karen Lane Rood (1980)
5. *American Poets Since World War II,* 2 parts, edited by Donald J. Greiner (1980)
6. *American Novelists Since World War II, Second Series,* edited by James E. Kibler Jr. (1980)
7. *Twentieth-Century American Dramatists,* 2 parts, edited by John MacNicholas (1981)
8. *Twentieth-Century American Science-Fiction Writers,* 2 parts, edited by David Cowart and Thomas L. Wymer (1981)
9. *American Novelists, 1910-1945,* 3 parts, edited by James J. Martine (1981)
10. *Modern British Dramatists, 1900-1945,* 2 parts, edited by Stanley Weintraub (1982)
11. *American Humorists, 1800-1950,* 2 parts, edited by Stanley Trachtenberg (1982)
12. *American Realists and Naturalists,* edited by Donald Pizer and Earl N. Harbert (1982)
13. *British Dramatists Since World War II,* 2 parts, edited by Stanley Weintraub (1982)
14. *British Novelists Since 1960,* 2 parts, edited by Jay L. Halio (1983)
15. *British Novelists, 1930-1959,* 2 parts, edited by Bernard Oldsey (1983)
16. *The Beats: Literary Bohemians in Postwar America,* 2 parts, edited by Ann Charters (1983)
17. *Twentieth-Century American Historians,* edited by Clyde N. Wilson (1983)
18. *Victorian Novelists After 1885,* edited by Ira B. Nadel and William E. Fredeman (1983)
19. *British Poets, 1880-1914,* edited by Donald E. Stanford (1983)
20. *British Poets, 1914-1945,* edited by Donald E. Stanford (1983)
21. *Victorian Novelists Before 1885,* edited by Ira B. Nadel and William E. Fredeman (1983)
22. *American Writers for Children, 1900-1960,* edited by John Cech (1983)
23. *American Newspaper Journalists, 1873-1900,* edited by Perry J. Ashley (1983)
24. *American Colonial Writers, 1606-1734,* edited by Emory Elliott (1984)
25. *American Newspaper Journalists, 1901-1925,* edited by Perry J. Ashley (1984)
26. *American Screenwriters,* edited by Robert E. Morsberger, Stephen O. Lesser, and Randall Clark (1984)
27. *Poets of Great Britain and Ireland, 1945-1960,* edited by Vincent B. Sherry Jr. (1984)
28. *Twentieth-Century American-Jewish Fiction Writers,* edited by Daniel Walden (1984)
29. *American Newspaper Journalists, 1926-1950,* edited by Perry J. Ashley (1984)
30. *American Historians, 1607-1865,* edited by Clyde N. Wilson (1984)
31. *American Colonial Writers, 1735-1781,* edited by Emory Elliott (1984)
32. *Victorian Poets Before 1850,* edited by William E. Fredeman and Ira B. Nadel (1984)
33. *Afro-American Fiction Writers After 1955,* edited by Thadious M. Davis and Trudier Harris (1984)
34. *British Novelists, 1890-1929: Traditionalists,* edited by Thomas F. Staley (1985)
35. *Victorian Poets After 1850,* edited by William E. Fredeman and Ira B. Nadel (1985)
36. *British Novelists, 1890-1929: Modernists,* edited by Thomas F. Staley (1985)
37. *American Writers of the Early Republic,* edited by Emory Elliott (1985)
38. *Afro-American Writers After 1955: Dramatists and Prose Writers,* edited by Thadious M. Davis and Trudier Harris (1985)
39. *British Novelists, 1660-1800,* 2 parts, edited by Martin C. Battestin (1985)
40. *Poets of Great Britain and Ireland Since 1960,* 2 parts, edited by Vincent B. Sherry Jr. (1985)
41. *Afro-American Poets Since 1955,* edited by Trudier Harris and Thadious M. Davis (1985)
42. *American Writers for Children Before 1900,* edited by Glenn E. Estes (1985)
43. *American Newspaper Journalists, 1690-1872,* edited by Perry J. Ashley (1986)
44. *American Screenwriters, Second Series,* edited by Randall Clark, Robert E. Morsberger, and Stephen O. Lesser (1986)
45. *American Poets, 1880-1945, First Series,* edited by Peter Quartermain (1986)
46. *American Literary Publishing Houses, 1900-1980: Trade and Paperback,* edited by Peter Dzwonkoski (1986)
47. *American Historians, 1866-1912,* edited by Clyde N. Wilson (1986)
48. *American Poets, 1880-1945, Second Series,* edited by Peter Quartermain (1986)
49. *American Literary Publishing Houses, 1638-1899,* 2 parts, edited by Peter Dzwonkoski (1986)
50. *Afro-American Writers Before the Harlem Renaissance,* edited by Trudier Harris (1986)
51. *Afro-American Writers from the Harlem Renaissance to 1940,* edited by Trudier Harris (1987)
52. *American Writers for Children Since 1960: Fiction,* edited by Glenn E. Estes (1986)
53. *Canadian Writers Since 1960, First Series,* edited by W. H. New (1986)
54. *American Poets, 1880-1945, Third Series,* 2 parts, edited by Peter Quartermain (1987)
55. *Victorian Prose Writers Before 1867,* edited by William B. Thesing (1987)
56. *German Fiction Writers, 1914-1945,* edited by James Hardin (1987)
57. *Victorian Prose Writers After 1867,* edited by William B. Thesing (1987)
58. *Jacobean and Caroline Dramatists,* edited by Fredson Bowers (1987)
59. *American Literary Critics and Scholars, 1800-1850,* edited by John W. Rathbun and Monica M. Grecu (1987)
60. *Canadian Writers Since 1960, Second Series,* edited by W. H. New (1987)
61. *American Writers for Children Since 1960: Poets, Illustrators, and Nonfiction Authors,* edited by Glenn E. Estes (1987)
62. *Elizabethan Dramatists,* edited by Fredson Bowers (1987)
63. *Modern American Critics, 1920-1955,* edited by Gregory S. Jay (1988)

ST. PHILIP'S COLLEGE LIBRARY

64 *American Literary Critics and Scholars, 1850-1880,* edited by John W. Rathbun and Monica M. Grecu (1988)

65 *French Novelists, 1900-1930,* edited by Catharine Savage Brosman (1988)

66 *German Fiction Writers, 1885-1913,* 2 parts, edited by James Hardin (1988)

67 *Modern American Critics Since 1955,* edited by Gregory S. Jay (1988)

68 *Canadian Writers, 1920-1959, First Series,* edited by W. H. New (1988)

69 *Contemporary German Fiction Writers, First Series,* edited by Wolfgang D. Elfe and James Hardin (1988)

70 *British Mystery Writers, 1860-1919,* edited by Bernard Benstock and Thomas F. Staley (1988)

71 *American Literary Critics and Scholars, 1880-1900,* edited by John W. Rathbun and Monica M. Grecu (1988)

72 *French Novelists, 1930-1960,* edited by Catharine Savage Brosman (1988)

73 *American Magazine Journalists, 1741-1850,* edited by Sam G. Riley (1988)

74 *American Short-Story Writers Before 1880,* edited by Bobby Ellen Kimbel, with the assistance of William E. Grant (1988)

75 *Contemporary German Fiction Writers, Second Series,* edited by Wolfgang D. Elfe and James Hardin (1988)

76 *Afro-American Writers, 1940-1955,* edited by Trudier Harris (1988)

77 *British Mystery Writers, 1920-1939,* edited by Bernard Benstock and Thomas F. Staley (1988)

78 *American Short-Story Writers, 1880-1910,* edited by Bobby Ellen Kimbel, with the assistance of William E. Grant (1988)

79 *American Magazine Journalists, 1850-1900,* edited by Sam G. Riley (1988)

80 *Restoration and Eighteenth-Century Dramatists, First Series,* edited by Paula R. Backscheider (1989)

81 *Austrian Fiction Writers, 1875-1913,* edited by James Hardin and Donald G. Daviau (1989)

82 *Chicano Writers, First Series,* edited by Francisco A. Lomelí and Carl R. Shirley (1989)

83 *French Novelists Since 1960,* edited by Catharine Savage Brosman (1989)

84 *Restoration and Eighteenth-Century Dramatists, Second Series,* edited by Paula R. Backscheider (1989)

85 *Austrian Fiction Writers After 1914,* edited by James Hardin and Donald G. Daviau (1989)

86 *American Short-Story Writers, 1910-1945, First Series,* edited by Bobby Ellen Kimbel (1989)

87 *British Mystery and Thriller Writers Since 1940, First Series,* edited by Bernard Benstock and Thomas F. Staley (1989)

88 *Canadian Writers, 1920-1959, Second Series,* edited by W. H. New (1989)

89 *Restoration and Eighteenth-Century Dramatists, Third Series,* edited by Paula R. Backscheider (1989)

90 *German Writers in the Age of Goethe, 1789-1832,* edited by James Hardin and Christoph E. Schweitzer (1989)

91 *American Magazine Journalists, 1900-1960, First Series,* edited by Sam G. Riley (1990)

92 *Canadian Writers, 1890-1920,* edited by W. H. New (1990)

93 *British Romantic Poets, 1789-1832, First Series,* edited by John R. Greenfield (1990)

94 *German Writers in the Age of Goethe: Sturm und Drang to Classicism,* edited by James Hardin and Christoph E. Schweitzer (1990)

95 *Eighteenth-Century British Poets, First Series,* edited by John Sitter (1990)

96 *British Romantic Poets, 1789-1832, Second Series,* edited by John R. Greenfield (1990)

97 *German Writers from the Enlightenment to Sturm und Drang, 1720-1764,* edited by James Hardin and Christoph E. Schweitzer (1990)

98 *Modern British Essayists, First Series,* edited by Robert Beum (1990)

99 *Canadian Writers Before 1890,* edited by W. H. New (1990)

100 *Modern British Essayists, Second Series,* edited by Robert Beum (1990)

101 *British Prose Writers, 1660-1800, First Series,* edited by Donald T. Siebert (1991)

102 *American Short-Story Writers, 1910-1945, Second Series,* edited by Bobby Ellen Kimbel (1991)

103 *American Literary Biographers, First Series,* edited by Steven Serafin (1991)

104 *British Prose Writers, 1660-1800, Second Series,* edited by Donald T. Siebert (1991)

105 *American Poets Since World War II, Second Series,* edited by R. S. Gwynn (1991)

106 *British Literary Publishing Houses, 1820-1880,* edited by Patricia J. Anderson and Jonathan Rose (1991)

107 *British Romantic Prose Writers, 1789-1832, First Series,* edited by John R. Greenfield (1991)

108 *Twentieth-Century Spanish Poets, First Series,* edited by Michael L. Perna (1991)

109 *Eighteenth-Century British Poets, Second Series,* edited by John Sitter (1991)

110 *British Romantic Prose Writers, 1789-1832, Second Series,* edited by John R. Greenfield (1991)

111 *American Literary Biographers, Second Series,* edited by Steven Serafin (1991)

112 *British Literary Publishing Houses, 1881-1965,* edited by Jonathan Rose and Patricia J. Anderson (1991)

113 *Modern Latin-American Fiction Writers, First Series,* edited by William Luis (1992)

114 *Twentieth-Century Italian Poets, First Series,* edited by Giovanna Wedel De Stasio, Glauco Cambon, and Antonio Illiano (1992)

115 *Medieval Philosophers,* edited by Jeremiah Hackett (1992)

116 *British Romantic Novelists, 1789-1832,* edited by Bradford K. Mudge (1992)

117 *Twentieth-Century Caribbean and Black African Writers, First Series,* edited by Bernth Lindfors and Reinhard Sander (1992)

118 *Twentieth-Century German Dramatists, 1889-1918,* edited by Wolfgang D. Elfe and James Hardin (1992)

119 *Nineteenth-Century French Fiction Writers: Romanticism and Realism, 1800-1860,* edited by Catharine Savage Brosman (1992)

120 *American Poets Since World War II, Third Series,* edited by R. S. Gwynn (1992)

121 *Seventeenth-Century British Nondramatic Poets, First Series,* edited by M. Thomas Hester (1992)

122 *Chicano Writers, Second Series,* edited by Francisco A. Lomelí and Carl R. Shirley (1992)

123 *Nineteenth-Century French Fiction Writers: Naturalism and Beyond, 1860-1900,* edited by Catharine Savage Brosman (1992)

124 *Twentieth-Century German Dramatists, 1919-1992,* edited by Wolfgang D. Elfe and James Hardin (1992)

125 *Twentieth-Century Caribbean and Black African Writers, Second Series,* edited by Bernth Lindfors and Reinhard Sander (1993)

126 *Seventeenth-Century British Nondramatic Poets, Second Series,* edited by M. Thomas Hester (1993)

127 *American Newspaper Publishers, 1950-1990,* edited by Perry J. Ashley (1993)

128 *Twentieth-Century Italian Poets, Second Series,* edited by Giovanna Wedel De Stasio, Glauco Cambon, and Antonio Illiano (1993)

129 *Nineteenth-Century German Writers, 1841-1900,* edited by James Hardin and Siegfried Mews (1993)

130 *American Short-Story Writers Since World War II,* edited by Patrick Meanor (1993)

131 *Seventeenth-Century British Nondramatic Poets, Third Series,* edited by M. Thomas Hester (1993)

132 *Sixteenth-Century British Nondramatic Writers, First Series,* edited by David A. Richardson (1993)

133 *Nineteenth-Century German Writers to 1840,* edited by James Hardin and Siegfried Mews (1993)

134 *Twentieth-Century Spanish Poets, Second Series,* edited by Jerry Phillips Winfield (1994)

135 *British Short-Fiction Writers, 1880-1914: The Realist Tradition,* edited by William B. Thesing (1994)

136 *Sixteenth-Century British Nondramatic Writers, Second Series,* edited by David A. Richardson (1994)

137 *American Magazine Journalists, 1900-1960, Second Series,* edited by Sam G. Riley (1994)

138 *German Writers and Works of the High Middle Ages: 1170-1280,* edited by James Hardin and Will Hasty (1994)

139 *British Short-Fiction Writers, 1945-1980,* edited by Dean Baldwin (1994)

140 *American Book-Collectors and Bibliographers, First Series,* edited by Joseph Rosenblum (1994)

141 *British Children's Writers, 1880-1914,* edited by Laura M. Zaidman (1994)

142 *Eighteenth-Century British Literary Biographers,* edited by Steven Serafin (1994)

143 *American Novelists Since World War II, Third Series,* edited by James R. Giles and Wanda H. Giles (1994)

144 *Nineteenth-Century British Literary Biographers,* edited by Steven Serafin (1994)

145 *Modern Latin-American Fiction Writers, Second Series,* edited by William Luis and Ann González (1994)

146 *Old and Middle English Literature,* edited by Jeffrey Helterman and Jerome Mitchell (1994)

147 *South Slavic Writers Before World War II,* edited by Vasa D. Mihailovich (1994)

148 *German Writers and Works of the Early Middle Ages: 800-1170,* edited by Will Hasty and James Hardin (1994)

149 *Late Nineteenth- and Early Twentieth-Century British Literary Biographers,* edited by Steven Serafin (1995)

150 *Early Modern Russian Writers, Late Seventeenth and Eighteenth Centuries,* edited by Marcus C. Levitt (1995)

151 *British Prose Writers of the Early Seventeenth Century,* edited by Clayton D. Lein (1995)

152 *American Novelists Since World War II, Fourth Series,* edited by James and Wanda Giles (1995)

153 *Late-Victorian and Edwardian British Novelists, First Series,* edited by George M. Johnson (1995)

154 *The British Literary Book Trade, 1700-1820,* edited by James K. Bracken and Joel Silver (1995)

155 *Twentieth-Century British Literary Biographers,* edited by Steven Serafin (1995)

156 *British Short-Fiction Writers, 1880-1914: The Romantic Tradition,* edited by William F. Naufftus (1995)

157 *Twentieth-Century Caribbean and Black African Writers, Third Series,* edited by Bernth Lindfors and Reinhard Sander (1995)

158 *British Reform Writers, 1789-1832,* edited by Gary Kelly and Edd Applegate (1995)

159 *British Short-Fiction Writers, 1800-1880,* edited by John R. Greenfield (1996)

160 *British Children's Writers, 1914-1960,* edited by Donald R. Hettinga and Gary D. Schmidt (1996)

161 *British Children's Writers Since 1960, First Series,* edited by Caroline Hunt (1996)

162 *British Short-Fiction Writers, 1915-1945,* edited by John H. Rogers (1996)

163 *British Children's Writers, 1800-1880,* edited by Meena Khorana (1996)

164 *German Baroque Writers, 1580-1660,* edited by James Hardin (1996)

165 *American Poets Since World War II, Fourth Series,* edited by Joseph Conte (1996)

166 *British Travel Writers, 1837-1875,* edited by Barbara Brothers and Julia Gergits (1996)

167 *Sixteenth-Century British Nondramatic Writers, Third Series,* edited by David A. Richardson (1996)

168 *German Baroque Writers, 1661-1730,* edited by James Hardin (1996)

169 *American Poets Since World War II, Fifth Series,* edited by Joseph Conte (1996)

170 *The British Literary Book Trade, 1475-1700,* edited by James K. Bracken and Joel Silver (1996)

171 *Twentieth-Century American Sportswriters,* edited by Richard Orodenker (1996)

172 *Sixteenth-Century British Nondramatic Writers, Fourth Series,* edited by David A. Richardson (1996)

173 *American Novelists Since World War II, Fifth Series,* edited by James R. Giles and Wanda H. Giles (1996)

174 *British Travel Writers, 1876-1909,* edited by Barbara Brothers and Julia Gergits (1997)

175 *Native American Writers of the United States,* edited by Kenneth M. Roemer (1997)

176 *Ancient Greek Authors,* edited by Ward W. Briggs (1997)

177 *Italian Novelists Since World War II, 1945-1965* edited by Augustus Pallotta (1997)

178 *British Fantasy and Science-Fiction Writers Before World War I,* edited by Darren Harris-Fain (1997)

179 *German Writers of the Renaissance and Reformation, 1280-1580,* edited by James Hardin and Max Reinhart (1997)

180 *Japanese Fiction Writers, 1868-1945,* edited by Van C. Gessel (1997)

181 *South Slavic Writers Since World War II,* edited by Vasa D. Mihailovich (1997)

182 *Japanese Fiction Writers Since World War II,* edited by Van C. Gessel (1997)

183 *American Travel Writers, 1776-1864,* edited by James J. Schramer and Donald Ross (1997)

184 *Nineteenth-Century British Book-Collectors and Bibliographers,* edited by William Baker and Kenneth Womack (1997)

185 *American Literary Journalists, 1945-1995, First Series,* edited by Arthur J. Kaul (1998)

186 *Nineteenth-Century American Western Writers,* edited by Robert L. Gale (1998)

187 *American Book Collectors and Bibliographers, Second Series,* edited by Joseph Rosenblum (1998)

188 *American Book and Magazine Illustrators to 1920,* edited by Steven E. Smith, Catherine A. Hastedt, and Donald H. Dyal (1998)

189 *American Travel Writers, 1850-1915,* edited by Donald Ross and James J. Schramer (1998)

190 *British Reform Writers, 1832-1914,* edited by Gary Kelly and Edd Applegate (1998)

191 *British Novelists Between the Wars,* edited by George M. Johnson (1998)

192 *French Dramatists, 1789-1914,* edited by Barbara T. Cooper (1998)

193 *American Poets Since World War II, Sixth Series,* edited by Joseph Conte (1998)

194 *British Novelists Since 1960, Second Series,* edited by Merritt Moseley (1998)

195 *British Travel Writers, 1910-1939,* edited by Barbara Brothers and Julia Gergits (1998)

196 *Italian Novelists Since World War II, 1965-1995,* edited by Augustus Pallotta (1998)

Documentary Series

1 *Sherwood Anderson, Willa Cather, John Dos Passos, Theodore Dreiser, F. Scott Fitzgerald, Ernest Hemingway, Sinclair Lewis,* edited by Margaret A. Van Antwerp (1982)

2 *James Gould Cozzens, James T. Farrell, William Faulkner, John O'Hara, John Steinbeck, Thomas Wolfe, Richard Wright,* edited by Margaret A. Van Antwerp (1982)

3 *Saul Bellow, Jack Kerouac, Norman Mailer, Vladimir Nabokov, John Updike, Kurt Vonnegut,* edited by Mary Bruccoli (1983)

4 *Tennessee Williams,* edited by Margaret A. Van Antwerp and Sally Johns (1984)

5 *American Transcendentalists,* edited by Joel Myerson (1988)

6 *Hardboiled Mystery Writers: Raymond Chandler, Dashiell Hammett, Ross Macdonald,* edited by Matthew J. Bruccoli and Richard Layman (1989)

7 *Modern American Poets: James Dickey, Robert Frost, Marianne Moore,* edited by Karen L. Rood (1989)

8 *The Black Aesthetic Movement,* edited by Jeffrey Louis Decker (1991)

9 *American Writers of the Vietnam War: W. D. Ehrhart, Larry Heinemann, Tim O'Brien, Walter McDonald, John M. Del Vecchio,* edited by Ronald Baughman (1991)

10 *The Bloomsbury Group,* edited by Edward L. Bishop (1992)

11 *American Proletarian Culture: The Twenties and The Thirties,* edited by Jon Christian Suggs (1993)

12 *Southern Women Writers: Flannery O'Connor, Katherine Anne Porter, Eudora Welty,* edited by Mary Ann Wimsatt and Karen L. Rood (1994)

13 *The House of Scribner, 1846-1904,* edited by John Delaney (1996)

14 *Four Women Writers for Children, 1868-1918,* edited by Caroline C. Hunt (1996)

15 *American Expatriate Writers: Paris in the Twenties,* edited by Matthew J. Bruccoli and Robert W. Trogdon (1997)

16 *The House of Scribner, 1905-1930,* edited by John Delaney (1997)

17 *The House of Scribner, 1931-1984,* edited by John Delaney (1998)

Yearbooks

1980 edited by Karen L. Rood, Jean W. Ross, and Richard Ziegfeld (1981)

1981 edited by Karen L. Rood, Jean W. Ross, and Richard Ziegfeld (1982)

1982 edited by Richard Ziegfeld; associate editors: Jean W. Ross and Lynne C. Zeigler (1983)

1983 edited by Mary Bruccoli and Jean W. Ross; associate editor: Richard Ziegfeld (1984)

1984 edited by Jean W. Ross (1985)

1985 edited by Jean W. Ross (1986)

1986 edited by J. M. Brook (1987)

1987 edited by J. M. Brook (1988)

1988 edited by J. M. Brook (1989)

1989 edited by J. M. Brook (1990)

1990 edited by James W. Hipp (1991)

1991 edited by James W. Hipp (1992)

1992 edited by James W. Hipp (1993)

1993 edited by James W. Hipp, contributing editor George Garrett (1994)

1994 edited by James W. Hipp, contributing editor George Garrett (1995)

1995 edited by James W. Hipp, contributing editor George Garrett (1996)

1996 edited by Samuel W. Bruce and L. Kay Webster, contributing editor George Garrett (1997)

1997 edited by Matthew J. Bruccoli and George Garrett, with the assistance of L. Kay Webster (1998)

Concise Series

Concise Dictionary of American Literary Biography, 6 volumes (1988-1989): *The New Consciousness, 1941-1968; Colonization to the American Renaissance, 1640-1865; Realism, Naturalism, and Local Color, 1865-1917; The Twenties, 1917-1929; The Age of Maturity, 1929-1941; Broadening Views, 1968-1988.*

Concise Dictionary of British Literary Biography, 8 volumes (1991-1992): *Writers of the Middle Ages and Renaissance Before 1660; Writers of the Restoration and Eighteenth Century, 1660-1789; Writers of the Romantic Period, 1789-1832; Victorian Writers, 1832-1890; Late Victorian and Edwardian Writers, 1890-1914; Modern Writers, 1914-1945; Writers After World War II, 1945-1960; Contemporary Writers, 1960 to Present.*

Dictionary of Literary Biography® • Volume One Hundred Ninety-Six

Italian Novelists Since World War II, 1965–1995

Dictionary of Literary Biography® • Volume One Hundred Ninety-Six

Italian Novelists Since World War II, 1965–1995

Edited by
Augustus Pallotta
Syracuse University

A Bruccoli Clark Layman Book
Gale Research
Detroit, Washington, D.C., London

Advisory Board for
DICTIONARY OF LITERARY BIOGRAPHY

John Baker
William Cagle
Patrick O'Connor
George Garrett
Trudier Harris

Matthew J. Bruccoli and Richard Layman, Editorial Directors
C. E. Frazer Clark Jr., Managing Editor
Karen Rood, Senior Editor

Printed in the United States of America

The paper used in this publication meets the minimum requirements
of American National Standard for Information Sciences–Permanence
Paper for Printed Library Materials, ANSI Z39.48-1984. ™

This publication is a creative work fully protected by all applicable copyright laws, as well as by misappropriation, trade secret, unfair competition, and other applicable laws. The authors and editors of this work have added value to the underlying factual material herein through one or more of the following: unique and original selection, coordination, expression, arrangement, and classification of the information.

All rights to this publication will be vigorously defended.

Copyright © 1999 by Gale Research
27500 Drake Road
Farmington Hills, MI 48331

All rights reserved including the right of reproduction in
whole or in part in any form.

Library of Congress Cataloging-in-Publication Data

Italian novelists since World War II, 1965–1995 / edited by Augustus Pallotta.
  p. cm.–(Dictionary of literary biography; v. 196)
"A Bruccoli Clark Layman book."
Includes bibliographical references and index.
ISBN 0-7876-1851-9 (alk. paper)
1. Italian fiction–20th century–Bio-bibliography–Dictionaries. 2. Novelists, Italian–20th century–Biography–Dictionaries. I. Pallotta, Augustus. II. Series.
PQ4174.I85 1998
853'.9109'03–dc21   98-7896
[B]--DC21   CIP

---

10 9 8 7 6 5 4 3 2 1

To my wife Lucy and to my sons Sammy and Lee Richard

Contents

Plan of the Series xiii
Introduction xv

Alberto Arbasino (1930-) 3
Rosetta di Pace

Nanni Balestrini (1935-) 10
Ernesto Livorni

Maria Bellonci (1902-1986) 17
Angela M. Jeannet

Stefano Benni (1947-) 25
David Ward

Alberto Bevilacqua (1934-) 32
Eugenio Ragni

Gesualdo Bufalino (1920-1996) 41
Rosetta di Pace

Italo Calvino (1923-1985) 50
Franco Ricci

Ferdinando Camon (1935-) 68
Angela M. Jeannet

Gianni Celati (1937-) 77
Michael Hanne

Vincenzo Consolo (1933-) 86
Tom O'Neill

Franco Cordelli (1943-) 95
Simone Casini

Andrea De Carlo (1952-) 101
Antonella Francini

Daniele Del Giudice (1949-) 109
Christopher Concolino

Luca Desiato (1941-) 116
Nicoletta Tinozzi-Mehrmand

Francesca Duranti (1935-) 124
Jan Kozma

Umberto Eco (1932-) 132
Carl A. Rubino

Franco Ferrucci (1936-) 145
Tommasina Gabriele

Raffaele La Capria (1922-) 153
Monica Cristina Storini

Gina Lagorio (1922-) 160
Maria Rosaria Vitti-Alexander

Luigi Malerba (1927-) 167
Francesco Guardiani

Gianfranco Manfredi (1948-) 174
Anna Nelli

Giorgio Manganelli (1922-1990) 181
Rebecca West

Dacia Maraini (1936-) 189
Augustus Pallotta

Stanislao Nievo (1928-) 201
Gabriele Erasmi

Roberto Pazzi (1946-) 208
Franco Ricci

Giuseppe Pontiggia (1934-) 214
Daniela Marcheschi

Francesca Sanvitale (1928-) 220
Simona Wright

Carlo Sgorlon (1930-) 230
Mario Aste

Antonio Tabucchi (1943-) 236
Augustus Pallotta

Pier Vittorio Tondelli (1955-1991) 246
Christopher Concolino

Dante Troisi (1920-1989) 255
Patricia M. Gathercole and Augustus Pallotta

Ferruccio Ulivi (1912-) 261
Salvatore Cappelletti

Paolo Valesio (1939-) 268
Paul Colilli

Sebastiano Vassalli (1941-) 275
Deborah L. Contrada

Elémire Zolla (1926-) 283
Anna Botta

Books for Further Reading 293
Contributors 297
Cumulative Index 301

Plan of the Series

... Almost the most prodigious asset of a country, and perhaps its most precious possession, is its native literary product — when that product is fine and noble and enduring.

Mark Twain*

The advisory board, the editors, and the publisher of the *Dictionary of Literary Biography* are joined in endorsing Mark Twain's declaration. The literature of a nation provides an inexhaustible resource of permanent worth. We intend to make literature and its creators better understood and more accessible to students and the reading public, while satisfying the standards of teachers and scholars.

To meet these requirements, *literary biography* has been construed in terms of the author's achievement. The most important thing about a writer is his writing. Accordingly, the entries in *DLB* are career biographies, tracing the development of the author's canon and the evolution of his reputation.

The purpose of *DLB* is not only to provide reliable information in a convenient format but also to place the figures in the larger perspective of literary history and to offer appraisals of their accomplishments by qualified scholars.

The publication plan for *DLB* resulted from two years of preparation. The project was proposed to Bruccoli Clark by Frederick C. Ruffner, president of the Gale Research Company, in November 1975. After specimen entries were prepared and typeset, an advisory board was formed to refine the entry format and develop the series rationale. In meetings held during 1976, the publisher, series editors, and advisory board approved the scheme for a comprehensive biographical dictionary of persons who contributed to North American literature. Editorial work on the first volume began in January 1977, and it was published in 1978. In order to make *DLB* more than a reference tool and to compile volumes that individually have claim to status as literary history, it was decided to organize volumes by topic, period, or genre. Each of these freestanding volumes provides a biographical-bibliographical guide and overview for a particular area of literature. We are convinced that this organization—as opposed to a single alphabet method—constitutes a valuable innovation in the presentation of reference material. The volume plan necessarily requires many decisions for the placement and treatment of authors who might properly be included in two or three volumes. In some instances a major figure will be included in separate volumes, but with different entries emphasizing the aspect of his career appropriate to each volume. Ernest Hemingway, for example, is represented in *American Writers in Paris, 1920-1939* by an entry focusing on his expatriate apprenticeship; he is also in *American Novelists, 1910-1945* with an entry surveying his entire career, as well as in *American Short-Story Writers, 1910-1945, Second Series* with an entry concentrating on his short stories. Each volume includes a cumulative index of the subject authors and articles. Comprehensive indexes to the entire series are planned.

Since 1981 the series has been further augmented by the *DLB Yearbooks,* which update published entries and add new entries to keep the *DLB* current with contemporary activity. There have also been *DLB Documentary Series* volumes which provide biographical and critical source materials for figures whose work is judged to have particular interest for students. One of these companion volumes is entirely devoted to Tennessee Williams.

We define literature as the *intellectual commerce of a nation:* not merely as belles lettres but as that ample and complex process by which ideas are generated, shaped, and transmitted. *DLB* entries are not limited to "creative writers" but extend to other figures who in their time and in their way influenced the mind of a people. Thus the series encompasses historians, journalists, publishers, book collectors, and screenwriters. By this means readers of *DLB* may be aided to perceive literature not as cult scripture in the keeping of intellectual high priests but firmly positioned at the center of a nation's life.

---

*From an unpublished section of Mark Twain's autobiography, copyright by the Mark Twain Company

DLB includes the major writers appropriate to each volume and those standing in the ranks behind them. Scholarly and critical counsel has been sought in deciding which minor figures to include and how full their entries should be. Wherever possible, useful references are made to figures who do not warrant separate entries.

Each *DLB* volume has an expert volume editor responsible for planning the volume, selecting the figures for inclusion, and assigning the entries. Volume editors are also responsible for preparing, where appropriate, appendices surveying the major periodicals and literary and intellectual movements for their volumes, as well as lists of further readings. Work on the series as a whole is coordinated at the Bruccoli Clark Layman editorial center in Columbia, South Carolina, where the editorial staff is responsible for accuracy and utility of the published volumes.

One feature that distinguishes *DLB* is the illustration policy—its concern with the iconography of literature. Just as an author is influenced by his surroundings, so is the reader's understanding of the author enhanced by a knowledge of his environment. Therefore *DLB* volumes include not only drawings, paintings, and photographs of authors, often depicting them at various stages in their careers, but also illustrations of their families and places where they lived. Title pages are regularly reproduced in facsimile along with dust jackets for modern authors. The dust jackets are a special feature of *DLB* because they often document better than anything else the way in which an author's work was perceived in its own time. Specimens of the writers' manuscripts and letters are included when feasible.

Samuel Johnson rightly decreed that "The chief glory of every people arises from its authors." The purpose of the *Dictionary of Literary Biography* is to compile literary history in the surest way available to us—by accurate and comprehensive treatment of the lives and work of those who contributed to it.

The DLB Advisory Board

Introduction

As indicated in the introduction to *DLB 177: Italian Novelists Since World War II, 1945–1965,* Neorealism was the dominant expression through which, in the immediate aftermath of World War II, Italian writers and filmmakers sought to portray a realistic and poignant picture of Italian society. The country was emerging from two decades of authoritarian rule and a war that had left more than forty million people in a state of economic ruin, psychological dejection, and social disorientation. A decade of impressive economic growth proved to be the catalyst to a process of transformation so intense that by the early 1960s, novels, movies, and television programs had definitively left behind the images of a struggling society so vividly portrayed in the films of Vittorio De Sica and Roberto Rossellini. Yet the forces of democracy and capitalism that replaced Fascism had generated new problems: materialism, a less egalitarian distribution of wealth, social inequities, alienation, and political instability.

These problems came to a head in 1968 with widespread unrest that presaged drastic changes in the country's social, cultural, and eventually political landscape. Thus, the writers included in *DLB 196: Italian Novelists Since World War II, 1965–1995* deal with realities that are far more complex than the concerns addressed by the novelists in *DLB 177,* what follows is an overview of Italian narrative from 1965 to nearly the end of the twentieth century.

In literary circles of the early 1960s the novel became a battleground for postwar ideological disputes, often fought along generational lines. Reacting to social and technological changes taking place around them, younger writers challenged the traditional values exemplified by both the neorealist novel and the *romanzo medio*—a well-crafted and socially-conscious novel that was popular with middle-class readers. They pointed to the formal innovations and the psychological probing exemplified by the *nouveau roman* (new novel) and the so-called *école du regard* championed, among others, by Michel Butor and Natalie Sarraute. In the cinema too the socialist poetics of Neorealism had been superseded, and critical attention was given to such movies as Alain Resnais's *L'année dernière à Marienbad* (Last Year at Marienbad, 1961) and *Hiroshima, mon amour* (Hiroshima, My Love, 1962). In Italy, Federico Fellini had progressed from the realism of *La Strada* (The Road, 1954) to alienation and disorientation in *La dolce vita* (The Sweet Life, 1960). More representative of the unease felt at this time in Italian society are the movies of Michelangelo Antonioni, notably *L'avventura* (The Adventure, 1959) and *L'eclisse* (Eclipse, 1962). In addition the works of French intellectuals such as Claude Levi-Strauss, Roland Barthes, Michel Foucault, Jacques Lacan, and Jacques Derrida were sowing the seeds of a cultural revolution grounded in moral and philosophical relativism.

In contrast to the intellectual ferment that was taking place in France, Italian critics by and large were discussing whether Neorealism was still alive; the merits of yet another novel penned by Alberto Moravia; and the latest examples of romanzo medio written by Giovanni Arpino, Carlo Cassola, and Piero Chiara. Nonetheless changes were occurring, spurred in part by small and internally fractious avant-garde groups advocating new forms of expression through experimentation. An important voice in this regard was Luciano Anceschi, a student of avant-garde movements and editor of the periodical *Il Verri*. In 1963 a group of young and idealistic literati calling themselves simply Gruppo 63, encouraged by Anceschi, met at a literary congress in Palermo where they advocated a break with tradition once and for all. The group included several writers—Umberto Eco, Luigi Malerba, Giorgio Manganelli, and Sebastiano Vassalli—who in the course of time achieved national recognition and in the case of Eco, worldwide prominence.

Gruppo 63 had little immediate impact on the course of Italian narrative but succeeded fully in underscoring the necessity of change and innovation. They proposed a "young" narrative freed from the constraints of tradition, a narrative that would renew itself from within through the freedom to experiment and focus on language as its central means of elaboration. The tenets of innovation enunciated in the volume *Gruppo 63* (1964) did not come to fruition until the late 1970s by virtue of the works of the adherents themselves: Eco, Malerba, Vassalli and, to a lesser extent, Nanni Balestrini and Manganelli. In a larger context the ideology espoused by the group had social ramifications that became apparent only in retrospect.

In his comprehensive and penetrating study of recent Italian fiction, *Il romanzo di ritorno* (1990), Stefano Tani identifies the three pivotal tenets of Gruppo 63 as "rottura, provocazione, e trasgressione" (a break [with tradition], provocation, and transgression). As a social and cultural manifestation, then, the group foreshadows the explosive discontent with the social and political establishment that gripped the country in 1968. Indeed, Gruppo 63 represented much more than a literary phenomenon. It was made up of young, well-educated, middle-class youths attuned to social problems (most of them were Marxists at least in ideology if not by party affiliation), who were also cognizant of the remarkable technological advances that were shaping Italian society. They looked around and saw a new class of spirited entrepreneurs determined to forge a promising future for the Italian economy through innovation and modernization of the traditional structures of production and transacting commerce. As young intellectuals they were forward-looking, progressive minded, and ahead of their time, at least intuitively. In an idealistic fashion they sought to adapt the changes they saw in other areas of society to the institution of literature, albeit with little immediate success.

The resistance to change came from established writers, such as Moravia, Cassola, Vasco Pratolini, and Paolo Volponi, who, clinging to a Marxist vision of the world, centered their narratives around social stratifications, proletarian emancipation, social tensions, and all the perceived evils of a decadent and unredeemably greedy middle class. They remained stoic in their ideological positions even as they attempted to effect cosmetic innovations in their works. Arguably, the emblematic figure of this faction of Italian intellectuals within the areas of cinema and literature is Pier Paolo Pasolini, a well-meaning and multitalented artist who believed in the need for profound changes in class structure. He also stood for free artistic expression, as long as it remained within the confines of Marxism. Pasolini's dilemma—that is to say, his desire to remain faithful to an inflexible ideology and to be artistically innovative—is not evident in *Ragazzi di vita* (1955; translated as *The Ragazzi*, 1968) nor in his film *Il Vangelo secondo Matteo* (The Gospel According to Matthew, 1964), both of which have an internal coherence; however, it is apparent in *Uccellacci and uccellini* (Hawks and Sparrows, 1965), where the transparent effort to meld art and Marxism leaves readers cold and puzzled.

The resistance to change was also apparent in political institutions, which in Italy hold more than a casual relationship with cultural life. As cultural and political observer Elio Vittorini remarks in his *Diario in pubblico* (Public Diary, 1957), "Una storia della letteratura ha sempre in sé la storia della politica" (A history of literature always carries from within a history of politics). Firm in their unwillingness to relinquish the privileges attached to political power, a fractious, quarrelsome, and largely corrupt political class of all ideological stripes created a precarious situation of chronic instability. Until the day of final collapse in 1993, Italy was prevented from moving toward a political system that could provide the equilibrium of social and political forces that existed in most other European countries.

One of the significant writers who helped pave the way for a redefinition of the novel was Italo Calvino, who had been on the literary scene since the publication of his first novel, *Il sentiero dei nidi di ragno* (1947; translated as *The Path of the Nest of Spiders*, 1956). A major force in Italian letters until his death in 1985, Calvino was throughout his career a quiet and likable rebel. A partisan who fought against Fascism, he held on to Marxist ideas, but in 1957 he did not hesitate to distance himself from Soviet Communism. His work is a testament to an assiduous, persistent, and coherent experimentation consistent with his idea of the novel as a medium that mirrors scientific and technological progress in harmony with the evolving function of literature in society.

In a time-honored tradition of Italian art, Calvino regarded himself as an *artigiano* (craftsman) who never tired of reshaping and refining the art of telling a story. His originality is manifested in his uncanny ability to blend realism and fantasy. When describing an object or a physical structure, he combines imagination with scientific rigor and precision. Clearly the hallmark of his work is change and innovation, as attested by a self-definition inserted in the first chapter of *Se una notte d'inverno* (1979; translated as *If on a Winter's Night a Traveller*, 1981): "Si sa che è un autore che cambia molto da libro a libro. E proprio in questo cambiamento si riconosce che è lui" (It is well known that he is a writer who changes much from book to book. And precisely in such change one recognizes who he is).

Calvino's works are remarkable as well because they betray a measure of ideological and formal elasticity not found in his contemporaries. His evolution as a writer is marked by distinct phases: the juxtaposition of fantasy and neorealist description in *Ultimo viene il corvo* (1949; partly translated as *Adam, One Afternoon and Other Stories*, 1957) and *Marcovaldo* (1963); a commitment to ideology and social enlightenment through his use of fable in the trilogy *I nostri antenati* (Our Ancestors, 1960); the exploration of science and science fiction in *Le cosmicomiche* (1965; translated as *Cosmicomics*, 1968) and *Ti con zero* (1967; translated as *t zero*, 1969); experimentation with structuralist ideas and the conception of the novel as a sum of combinatory strategies in such works as *Il castello dei destini incrociati* (1969; translated as *The Castle of Crossed Destinies*, 1977); the bold innovation of *Le città invisibili* (1972; translated as *Invisible Cities*, 1974), the ultimate meaning of which is left to the subjective interpretation of the reader; and in his last work, *Se una notte d'inverno un viaggiatore* a successful and highly experimental formal structure of novels within the novel converging and interacting in the course of the narration.

No one would deny that the international success of Calvino—and later of Eco—has contributed in no small measure to the deprovincialization of Italian culture, a process that began during the first decade of the twentieth century with Giuseppe Prezzolini's periodical, *La Voce*. Many would argue, however, that the penchant for innovation has made the novel less socially relevant, that at some point the fantastic, the ludic, and the surreal should give way to concrete human experiences. Some critics, then, while conceding his brilliance, also argue that in the course of his evolution as a writer Calvino was instrumental in taking the novel too far from its historical function as an instrument through which society is better understood.

Close to Calvino in terms of a commitment to formal innovation and the experimental use of language is a group of writers—including Balestrini, Malerba, Manganelli, and Vassalli—directly associated with Gruppo 63 or supportive of their program. Balestrini's literary education was influenced by the father of linguistic experimentation in this century, Carlo Emilio Gadda, and by the works of Bertolt Brecht, James Joyce, Ezra Pound, and Alain Robbe-Grillet. Balestrini emphasizes language, not action or characterization, and relies heavily on a skillful use of the monologue learned from Joyce and Robbe-Grillet. The energy of language that flows through his novels brings to mind Filippo Marinetti's *lingua in azione* (language in action) of the early twentieth century. The leader of Italian Futurism, Marinetti saw language as a vital part of a dynamic culture.

Balestrini's forceful, at times aggressive, use of language finds correspondence in his political involvement, his solidarity with the working classes, and his leadership in a political party of the far Left, "Potere operaio" (Workers' Power). In the novel *Vogliamo tutto* (We Want Everything, 1971) he turns to the advocacy of force as a necessary and effective instrument in carrying out the proletarian revolution. Such advocacy becomes more explicit and forceful in the pamphlet published a year later that carried a telling and symptomatic title, one that binds literature to militant political action: *Prendiamoci tutto. Conferenza per un romanzo. Letteratura e lotta di classe* (Let's Take It All. Lecture for a Novel. Literature and Class Struggle, 1972). Here he remarks: "La violenza. L'organizzazione di massa della violenza proletaria, della violenza operaia. Il passaggio alla pratica diretta di appropriazione collettiva della ricchezza sociale: da 'vogliamo tutto' a 'prendiamoci tutto'" (Violence. Mass organization of proletarian violence. The transition to direct practice of collective appropriation of social wealth: from "We want it all" to "Let's take it all").

Malerba has remained faithful to his association with Gruppo 63 in his commitment to a vigorous and continual experimentation with language. As an example one may cite the linguistic deftness of the short story "L'Egemenone di Tch'u" (The Ruler of Tch'u) found in *Le rose imperiali* (The Imperial Roses, 1974) in which the main character's verbal skills are explained: "Pare che fosse insuperabile nell'artificio verbale, nelle perifrasi, nelle allusioni, nelle similitudini, nelle allegorie, insomma nell'usare tutte le vie traverse del discorso" (It seems that he was a master of verbal artifice, in his periphrases, allusions, similes, and allegories, in short, in using all the crossed paths of speech).

Much like Calvino, Malerba is skeptical of human reason and its capacity to explain, much less to solve, the conflicts that arise from a multilayered perception of reality. In an interview with JoAnn Cannon published in *Modern Language Notes* in January 1989 he remarks: "Credo di essere in assoluto lo scrittore che ha usato il maggior numero di punti interrogativi di tutta la storia italiana" (I believe I am by far the writer who has used the largest number of question marks in the entire history of Italian literature). In the end, however, no answer is apt to satisfy Malerba, who is resistant to both rational explanations and religious assurances. But he does believe in a close rapport between literature and science and in assigning to science greater significance in cultural matters. In the same interview he asserts, "Dal Seicento in poi è la scienza che ha offerto materia di riflessione alla letteratura e alla filosofia. . . . Con Calvino mi sono sempre trovato d'accordo sulla necessità per uno scrittore di tenere uno sguardo aperto sulla scienza" (Since the seventeenth century, it is science that has given to literature and philosophy material to reflect on. . . . I have always agreed with Calvino on the need for a writer to keep an open mind regarding science). He ends the interview with the assertion that a writer needs science and philosophy to expand his or her field of vision of the world.

There is, of course, greater generational continuity among writers whose work is devoted to more-traditional forms, such as the historical novel, which continues to yield narratives of high quality. However, even within this group the tendency is to look at history more inclusively than their predecessors and to do so with an equal desire for linguistic and structural innovation. Such writers as Vincenzo Consolo, Dacia Maraini, Vassalli, Roberto Pazzi, and Stanislao Nievo have contributed to the renewal of the historical narrative.

In *Il sorriso dell'ignoto marinaio* (The Smile of the Unknown Sailor, 1976) Consolo practices a narrative methodology entailing extensive historical research that harkens back to the nineteenth-century novelist Alessandro Manzoni. But the melange of documents and the use of standard Italian infused with Sicilian dialect render the work attuned to modern times. Consolo openly admits his purpose: "Scrivo del passato per dire del presente" (I write about the past to address the present). In this light one can read *Retablo* (1987), the story of an eighteenth-century Milanese nobleman who in traveling through Sicily is exposed to the backward socioeconomic conditions and the presence of violence, which cannot but bring to mind the realities of the postwar era.

In a similar fashion Maraini's *La lunga vita di Marianna Ucría* (1990; translated as *The Silent Duchess*, 1993) offers a masterful re-creation of society in eighteenth-century Sicily, marked by harsh differences in social life between the aristocracy and the proletarian class made up of farmhands, artisans, and domestic servants. The book opens with an arresting account of a young bandit's final hours in a cavernous prison before he is brought to the gallows in a central square in Palermo amid a large and festive crowd gathered for the occasion. As with Consolo, Maraini, a prominent feminist, calls attention to the present by re-creating the past, in this case by bringing to life the struggles and vicissitudes of Marianna Ucría, a deaf-mute noblewoman who is able to overcome her physical condition and the severe limits imposed on the women of the time. When appropariate, Maraini blends Italian with the Sicilian of the period to underscore the marginal literacy of the citizenry, especially among women of all classes.

A member of Gruppo 63, Vassalli has continued to write narratives outside of the literary mainstream and eschew political involvement. His early works, *Abitare il vento* (To Inhabit the Wind, 1980) and *Mareblù* (Blue Sea, 1982), bring to light social outcasts through whose experience and mindset the novelist projects an unflattering view of the late 1960s as a period of social rebellion marked by narcissism and a bankrupt ideology. His interest in history is coupled with a strong proletarian consciousness that filters and qualifies historical elements. Hence the demarcation between truth and fiction, history and invention is intentionally blurred, indeed deemed insignificant.

In the critically acclaimed *La chimera* (Chimera, 1990) Vassalli throws light on seventeenth-century Lombardy under Spanish rule through the story of a foundling named Antonia. The novel has called to mind another work set in the same region during the same period, Manzoni's *I promessi sposi* (1827; translated as *The Betrothed*, 1828). Some critics have viewed Vassalli's book as an effort to engage in a fruitful dialogue with Manzoni's classic novel.

Pazzi shares with Vassalli a narrative treatment marked by a strong interest in psychology and a less-than-rigorous use of historical sources. What distinguishes the two is Pazzi's interest in mysticism and religion as well as a less sanguine attachment to Marxism. His most successful novel to date, *Cercando l'imperatore* (Looking for the Emperor, 1985), focuses on the last days of Czar Nicholas II and his family before they were brutally killed by the Bolsheviks. The reader is offered a fictional reconstruction of the event through a compelling account of what goes through the minds of individual members of the royal family in their final hours. Nicholas II was a czar, but in Pazzi's treatment the czar moves the reader to empathy as a victim of his time and his social rank upon which he had no control. Indeed, Pazzi's sympathies lie with the victims of history whose suffering and personal tragedies are viewed as a source of moral instruction.

Stanislao Nievo is the great-grandnephew of Ippolito Nievo, the famous author of *Le confessioni di un italiano* (1867; translated as *The Castle of Fratta*, 1958) and a young officer in Giuseppe Garibaldi's volunteer army who died in a sea storm in 1861 at the age of thirty. In *Il prato in fondo al mare* (The Meadow at the Bottom of the Sea, 1974) Nievo combines fiction with historical documents in search of his ancestor's personal and ideological identity which, in a sense, is also his own. Clearly this is the sort of literary work that broadens substantially one's understanding of a significant historical period, in this case the Risorgimento, the movement of patriotic struggle that led to Italy's unification in 1860. Further, the novel owes its critical and popular success to both historical documentation and a literary craft that yields surreal and mythic images of surprising freshness.

Gianni Celati, Malerba, and Manganelli are linked by their sense of metaphysical malaise, which can be viewed as turn-of-the-century existentialism. They are from the same generation as Calvino with whom they share a penchant for experimentation and a mild disdain for the traditional novel. Celati, whose early novel *Comiche* (Comic Cuts, 1971) was inspired by the silent movies of Buster Keaton and the Marx brothers, is at his best when he portrays socially marginalized characters such as the mentally disturbed and the socially deviant or when his characters are engaged in an existential quest that takes them nowhere. In *Quattro novelle sulle apparenze* (Four Novellas on Appearances, 1987) the protagonists search for meaning behind the surfaces and appearances of everyday life only to find that their efforts uncover more surfaces and more appearances.

Manganelli, born in 1922, was one of the older writers drawn to Gruppo 63. He has entertained an ambivalent, often contradictory relationship with literature; occasionally he finds some redeeming value in it, but more often than not he views it as a cynical exercise in word elaboration at the service of the god of rhetoric. Faithful to the values of Gruppo 63, he has remained an experimental writer all his life. He has much in common with Calvino, for as Rebecca West points out in her article on Manganelli in this volume, he is "a master of formal elaboration, the artificer of landscapes built on pure abstractions." It is true that Manganelli's main interest lies in form and language, but his works also reflect a deep concern for finitude, mortality, and the ultimate meaning of human existence.

Postwar Italian feminism arose in the climate of social discontent that came to a head in 1968, taking the form of huge marches in most Italian cities organized by college students, women groups, and factory workers. Generally the protests were peaceful, but in a few instances militant participants confronted the police, causing violent clashes and bloodshed. Each of the three groups had its agenda: students demanded school reforms; women, the legalization of divorce and abortion; and factory workers, higher wages and better working conditions. As Grazia Sumeli Weinberg points out in her *Invito alla lettura di Dacia Maraini* (An Introduction to the Works of Dacia Maraini, 1993), the decision of the women to join workers and college students proved to be a winning strategy because it carried far-reaching implications:

É un dato accertato che il femminismo, aggregandosi al movimento studentesco del sessantotto, ne abbia condiviso la carica rivoluzionaria nella certezza che una trasformazione della società in uno stato di parità interclassista porti inevitabilmente all'appiattamento delle divergenze tra i ruoli tradizionali dei due sessi.

(It is a fact that Italian feminism, by joining the student movement of 1968, shared its revolutionary thrust, certain that a transformation of society to a condition of equality among social classes would lead inevitably to a leveling of the differences in the traditional roles between the two sexes.)

The standard-bearer of Italy's postwar feminism has been Maraini, who has earned a solid reputation as a novelist, poet, and playwright. Her second book of verses, *Donne mie* (Oh, My Women, 1974), contains a passionate appeal to women to break free from centuries-old stereotypes and social roles fashioned by men and assert themselves as responsible, independent individuals. Maraini's long-standing interest in the theater lies in her perception of drama as a social art form rather than aesthetic expression. "Il teatro," she says," è un fatto sociale legato alla società in cui si vive" (Theater is a social matter, tied to the society in which we live). It follows that virtually all the social questions associated with feminism, from abortion to patriarchy, are treated in such works as *Il manifesto* (The Manifesto, 1970), *Ricatto a teatro* (Blackmail on Stage, 1970), and *I sogni di Clitennestra* (Clytemnestra's Dreams, 1981).

It is, however, Maraini's narrative that has proven widely successful and strengthened her identity as a feminist writer. The most important work in this regard is *Donna in guerra* (1975; translated as *Woman at War,* 1984), a thought-provoking work in which a woman's yearning for self-fulfillment is objectively probed. The story documents the gradual disaffection in the relationship of a young couple: Giacomo, a kind but inflexible man who holds a traditional view of marriage, and Vannina, who grows weary of feigning happiness while accepting her gray existence with resigned indifference. The resolution of the crisis takes the form of an open break with tradition: the woman leaves her husband to start a new life.

La lunga vita di Marianna Ucría, the most successful of Maraini's works, is a remarkable novel attesting to a technical and stylistic mastery of the narrative craft after a long season of innovation and experimentation. While remaining essentially faithful to the tenets of feminism, Maraini deliberately goes beyond ideology to view her characters' existential condition in human terms and no longer through an exclusive male-female dichotomy.

Gina Lagorio, whose work is rich in psychological examinations of human interactions, changed from male to female protagonists in the mid 1970s. Beginning with *La spiaggia del lupo* (Wolf Beach, 1977), her women turn inward to find the strength to overcome crises instead of looking outside of themselves for aid. Introspection, solitude, and suffering, coupled with a *voglia di chiarezza* (desire for clarity), become, in Lagorio's narrative, sources of strength for women in their search for self-definition. In *La spiaggia del lupo* Angela reflects on ending her involvement with a man: "Essere sola non mi fa paura: mi fa paura sentirmi divisa, vivere a metà. Sono forte e mi basto; di questo soffro: che mi sono accorta di bastarmi" (To be alone does not scare me: what scares me is to feel divided, to live in half. I am strong and I am self-sufficient; I suffer for this: that I have become aware of being self-sufficient). Like Maraini in *Marianna Ucría,* Lagorio goes straight to the core of a person's humanity.

Francesca Duranti's novels confront problems to which many women can relate. In *Piazza, mia bella piazza* (My Town Square, My Beautiful Square, 1978) she probes a marriage that deteriorates when the husband obstructs his wife's strong desire to become a professional writer. She learns painfully that she can only rely on her inner strengths to become independent. In *Effetti personali* (Personal Effects, 1988) the protagonist, Lavinia, is left by her husband for another woman after ten years of marriage. When she meets another man and has to choose between her self-development and a man who is the antithesis of her former husband, she opts for independence and self-reliance as essential requisites for personal growth.

Eco has perhaps been more influential than Calvino with the generation of Italian writers who came of age in the 1970s. Having achieved prominence first as a critic and then as a novelist, Eco has had a twofold impact on younger novelists, providing them with both a theoretical framework and a successful expression of what has come to be known as the postindustrial or the postmodern novel. In such works as *Opera aperta* (1976; translated as *The Open Work*, 1989) and *Le forme del contenuto* (The Forms of Content, 1971), Eco examines markedly different approaches to literary analysis, informed by a solid knowledge of history, philosophy, and philology in addition to his expertise in the field of semiotics.

Eco's decision to give creative form to his ideas about texts and become a novelist has proven to be felicitous. The international acclaim that followed the publication of his first novel, *Il nome della rosa* (1980; translated as *The Name of the Rose*, 1983), can only be compared to the reception accorded in the early 1960s to Tomasi di Lampedusa's *Il Gattopardo* (1958; translated as *The Leopard*, 1960). The extraordinary success of the two works is doubtless due to a widely felt realization that each in its own way speaks to crucial turning points in the history of Western civilization: *Il Gattopardo* as a farewell to the aristocracy that had ruled Europe for centuries and *Il nome della rosa* as inaugurating the postmodern era, marked by new ways of thinking and new approaches to the reading, interpreting, and writing of literary texts. Indeed postmodern narratives are often called metafictions by experts because they differ markedly from traditional novels.

In *Il nome della rosa* and the novels that followed—*Il pendolo di Foucault* (1988; translated as *Foucault's Pendulum*, 1989) and *L'isola del giorno dopo* (1994; translated as *The Island of the Day Before*, 1995)—Eco shows a formidable knowledge of the past and the evolution of Western societies. It is, by design, a narrative that teaches and enlightens readers in addition to affording them a pleasurable experience (what Eco calls *dilettare*) inasmuch as his novels, through skillful intertextual references, allusions, and intimations, point to other important works of the past. Further, to keep the reader interested and even amused, Eco draws from a panoply of contemporary cultural forms such as the detective novel, science fiction, movies, and cartoons that bridge the gap between past and present.

In a 1996 interview titled *Dove va il romanzo?* (Where Is the Novel Going?) the writer Antonio Tabucchi was asked about the evolution of recent Italian fiction. He replied: "Io credo che quello che possiamo constatare è una caduta fortissima fra le divisioni dei vari generi letterari.... Ormai sono cadute le barriere tra romanzo, saggio, poesia, memorialista eccetera. E questa evoluzione sta avvenendo in tutta l'Europa e anche al di là dei confini europei" (I believe we are seeing a marked blurring among the various literary genres. The barriers among the novel, the essay, poetry, and memory-based narrative have fallen. And this gradual evolution is taking place throughout Europe and even beyond the European borders).

Among the writers included in *DLB 196* there are several who are also poets and playwrights; further, there are some who try to integrate, with uneven success, elements of other genres to the body of the narrative. Consolo's *Il sorriso di un ignoto marinaio*, for example, is a narrative with selections of verses and other composite elements; Manganelli's prose too on occasion shifts from narrative to become essayistic. Also interesting in this regard is Maraini's *Bagheria* (1993), which is misleadingly subtitled *Romanzo* (A Novel). In fact the book is the factual, largely autobiographical account of the author's return after a long absence to her native town of Bagheria, a few miles east of Palermo. The work is constructed with a twofold perspective: the landscape of Bagheria, with its impressive seventeenth-century villas, seen through the eyes of a child, and the discerning views of the mature Maraini who reflects upon a vastly changed Bagheria and environs ruined by real estate speculations and other commercial interests, often advanced by corrupt politicians and Mafia elements.

The writer that best exemplifies this mixing of genres is Franco Cordelli, who has written experimental plays, such as *L'antipasqua* (Before Easter, 1987) and *Lena* (1987), but is better known for his narrative. In three of his novels, *Procida* (1973), *Pinkerton* (1986), and *Guerre lontane* (Distant Wars, 1990), the production of a play is woven into the narrative texture in a way in which, as Simone Casini points out in this volume, readers of the text (as well as the spectators within the novel) are made "cognizant of a particular treatment of reality which carries the logic and the imprint of a play."

The so-called *la giovane narrativa* (new novel) began to draw attention in the mid 1970s, coinciding with a new phase of increased prosperity that, among other things, facilitated the expansion and consolidation of the publishing industry. Unlike past expectations of renewal and innovation that proved to be inflated, Italian narrative of the 1980s and early 1990s has indeed taken a significant turn. The question is whether the new novel points to the revitalization or the deterioration of Italian narrative. In either case *la giovane narrativa* is new because it represents a substantially different elaboration of the genre from the past and marks a decisive break with tradition in terms of the historical function in society of the novel and literature in general. According to Filippo La Porta, more than anything else, the young writers of the latter decades of the twentieth century reflect in their work "la consapevo-lezza che si è spezzato un legame con i modelli e le tradizioni del passato" (a consciousness that they have broken the ties with the models and the traditions of the past).

The most significant change, arguably, concerns the perception this younger generation of writers holds of their craft and their role in society. Following the fall of Fascism, Italian novelists were allied with progressive forces and, moved by the desire to partake in the effort to fashion a more egalitarian society, chose to shed light on a wide spectrum of social ills. Accordingly the novelist has been a socially conscious intellectual who valued ideology and ideals. A conservative reader could dislike the Marxist ideas of Pratolini, Volponi, or Pasolini while still respecting the writer's desire to contribute to a better society.

The ideological commitment that marks the work of so many Italian writers of the postwar period has come to an end with the demise of Marxism and the ideological reconfiguration—in some cases the metamorphosis—of political parties. Younger writers are for the most part indifferent to Marxism, uninterested in sociopolitical institutions as agents of change, and above all highly skeptical of what constituted the driving force of the preceding generations of committed writers, namely the belief that ideology or indeed literature can effect real changes in society. In other words the so-called postmodern novelists do not value writing as a socially redeeming endeavor. Their view of late-twentieth-century life is marked by skepticism, and quite often pessimism, toward not only politics but also such traditional concepts and institutions as love, marriage, family, and religion—what Italians call *il privato* and *la sfera del privato* (the private sphere of one's life).

What are the values that inform postmodern narrative? The question can be answered with a sense of historical consciousness by recognizing that in their existential outlook younger writers share a close kinship with the trenchant pessimism of Giacomo Leopardi (1798–1837) and the worldview of Luigi Pirandello (1867–1938), who sees life as being governed by relativism, chance, and a lack of certitudes. Indeed in Western societies relativism in matters of individual conduct and morality has come to dominate in the years since World War II. As opposed to more introspective literature of the 1960s and 1970s, recent narrative is concerned with the external, the adventurous, and the arcane. Recent novelists are nonreligious or derisive of religion in their approach to the supernatural. Deep down, theirs is a passive view of life that moves decidedly away from the battlegrounds of ideology, social relevance, and textual meaning of previous generations, and it moves toward a representation of reality in ludic, theatrical, and melodramatic keys. La Porta points out that the novelists of the 1990s focus on the external to convey to readers the realization that "dietro le apparenze non c'è nulla" (there is nothing behind external appearances); these writers show a penchant for a Pirandellian use of masks to underscore the fact that there is no authenticity in postmodern life.

Carlo Bo is a widely respected man of letters who has spent his life with books and has enjoyed a distinguished career as a book reviewer, critic, and cultural observer. His reflections on novelists carry a note of criticism veined with the sad realization that something central to the literary enterprise is slipping away at the turn of this century, as is clear from remarks in the 10 June 1989 "Tuttolibri" insert of *La Stampa*:

> I romanzi di questo tempo sono di testa, non di cuore. Non raccontano un sentimento vero, un'emozione vera, un problema vero. Gli scrittori al di sotto di quarant'anni sono tutti abilissimi, molto più di cinquant'anni fa, ma giocano con la forma, come pattinassero su una superficie linguistica. Sono scrittori manieristi, barocchi, freddi, e lucidi artigiani della manipolazione.
>
> (The novels published these days come from the head, not the heart. They do not tell stories, true feelings, true emotions, real problems. The novelists under forty are all very clever, much more so than the writers of fifty years ago, but they play with form as though they were skating on a linguistic surface. They are mannerist, baroque, cold and lucid artists of manipulation.)

When cultural conditions change drastically, as they have in Italy since the late 1960s, perceptions and attitudes toward cultural forms change as well. A case in point is the institution of literary prizes, which for three decades following World War II represented a legitimate recognition of merit in spite of the widely known fact that in the best Italian tradition the choice of finalists for the various categories was often influenced by ideological and personal considerations. In the late 1970s many cities, resort towns, and cultural entities, spurred by the blandishments of publishing houses and the limelight provided by the media, have made extraordinary efforts to vie for the sponsorship of literary prizes. As a result, prizes have become so numerous that the standards of quality have of necessity been lowered; having lost their original purpose, prizes have become an advertising tool for publishing houses.

A second and more pernicious development, in which publishers also play a pivotal role, is that the book, and especially the novel, is marketed with the same strategies used to sell soap detergents and body deodorants. This phenomenon is known variously in Italy as *consumo culturale* (cultural consumption), *il mercato delle lettere* (the literary market), and *l'industria del romanzo* (the industry of the novel). Some observers, such as Enzo Golino, writing in the daily *La Repubblica* of 1 September 1987, take a fatalist approach: "Piaccia o meno, la letteratura è entrata in un circuito comunicativo industriale complesso, non può essere trattata come un corpo separato della società. Anche l'immaginazione è una merce" (Whether we like it or not, literature has become part of a complex industrial network in the communications industry and, as such, it cannot be treated as a separate entity within society. Creativity too is a commodity).

While Golino correctly suggests that the nature of marketing literature has fundamentally changed, he is mistaken in implying that in the past, literature was treated as a separate entity of society. Since the invention of the printing press, books have been commercially produced, advertised, and sold. What is new today is that a potentially gifted writer who has a successful novel to his credit is treated much like an athlete or an actor. Writers often are appropriated by large publishing houses in the sense that they become attached through long-term, highly lucrative contracts and are then obliged to publish a new book every two years or so. As publishers have come to regard their books merely as products, the lack of distinction between a novel and sunbathing lotion has become more noticeable in marketing strategies that are offensive to the historical dignity of the book. An example of this phenomenon is illustrated by Luigi Monga in his review of Oriana Fallaci's *Insciallah* (1990) in the summer 1991 issue of *World Literature Today*:

> Oriana Fallaci's latest novel was launched in July 1990 with all the hullabaloo of what her publisher had intended to be: the literary event of 1990. Hoping to sell at least 400,000 hardcover copies, Rizzoli had commandeered its best-known literary critics to write glowing reviews in all the newspapers and magazines it controls; in some cases, first-page news had to move aside to make room for their favorable articles. Marketing experts had mapped an intenisve campaign; in early summer the walls of several cities had been papered with enormous posters and banners announcing the impending appearance of *Insciallah*. Conversely, Rizzoli's competitors unanimously issued acid reports on this *commedia all'italiana,* panning the novel as a dinosaur with few redeeming qualities. This shameless manipulation of the media continues on the dust jacket, with an unabashed quote from no less a literary authority than the president of Chicago's Columbia College, who views Fallaci as "one of the most widely read and beloved authors of the world."

In *Il romanzo di ritorno* Tani recognizes the risks of such practices: "La casa editrice si è fatta sempre più attiva e invadente alle spalle dello scrittore fino ad entrare di buon diritto come protagonista nell'immaginario narrativo" (Publishing houses have become increasingly more active and intrusive behind the writer's back to the point of acting as rightful protagonists in the creative sphere of the novel). The major drawback in this process of appropriation and intrusion is that publishers recruit young writers, in Tani's words, "con criteri orientati verso la novità e senza particolari preoccupazioni per la qualità o la rilevanza letteraria di quanto si presenta come nuovo" (with criteria pointing to novelty and without particular worries for quality or the literary relevance of what is promoted as new).

Among the first writers to chart a new course for the Italian narrative are Antonio Tabucchi, Andrea De Carlo, Pier Vittorio Tondelli, and Stefano Benni. Since 1985 Tabucchi has emerged as perhaps the most important Italian novelist after Calvino and Eco. Indeed he has much in common with Calvino: his approach to writing as a craft, his passion for storytelling, and his continual striving for formal innovation. This last attribute manifests itself as a remarkable resiliency to renew himself in nearly every book he has written. Thus his first novel, *Piazza d'Italia* (A Town Square in Italy, 1975), reaped considerable success because it marked a fresh approach to historical narrative: a century of Italian history told in a fluent, nimble prose that was distinguished by attributes dear to Calvino: lightness, swiftness, and simplicity.

Tabucchi turned to the short story with *Il gioco del rovescio* (1981; translated as a *Letter from Casablanca*, 1986), a collection based on the notion of reversal of roles and individual identity. These stories require the reader's active participation and creative ability to fill in the missing gaps in the story line. Tabucchi's affinity for the detective story comes to fruition in the novella *Notturno indiano* (1984; translated as *Indian Nocturne*, 1988), an ingenious study of a man's search for his alter ego carried on outside of the physical confines of European culture. In a second book of short stories, *Piccoli equivoci senza importanza* (1985; translated as *Little Misunderstandings of No Importance,* 1988), a quintessential expression of the postmodern aesthetic, Tabucchi depicts misunderstandings among intimates, revealing his characters' ambivalent motives and lack of certitude in nearly anything involving deep emotions, faith, trust, and the like. With *Sostiene Pereira. Una testimonianza* (1994; translated as *Pereira Declares. A True Account,* 1995) he returns to a more traditional narrative marked by linear development, well-developed characters, introspection, and a fresh focus on history and ideology.

De Carlo's *Treno di panna* (1981; translated as *Cream Train,* 1981) is generally mentioned as the earliest expression of the Italian postmodern novel. The work carries a foreword by Calvino that shows his support of a new generation of young writers engaged in formal experimentation. However, De Carlo's first novel gained attention mainly as the disquieting portrait of the restless and self-centered Italian youth in the early 1980s. The protagonist belongs to a generation without dreams and illusions, indifferent not just to the traditional values of his parents but to the ideals of social change and equality that had moved the previous generation to militant action. *Treno di panna* takes place in California, but it is not the mythic California found in Cesare Pavese's *La luna e i falò* (1950; translated as *The Moon and the Bonfire,* 1953); it is rather the distillation of De Carlo's travels through the United States in 1980. As does Calvino's fiction, De Carlo's novel betrays a strong interest in American popular culture and literature, especially in a group of contemporary writers known as minimalists.

Travel, restlessness, and a clear affinity with the works of Henry Miller, Jack Kerouac, and in particular the hard-boiled fiction of Raymond Chandler are among the main characteristics of the work of Tondelli, who died in 1991 at the age of thirty-six. Tondelli and De Carlo are authors of unengaged, outward-looking, youthful narratives. Their works reflect generational changes, fresh explorations of sensual gratification, and exposure to so-called alternate lifestyles that revolve around homosexuality and drugs. They present transgressive behaviors without apologies or explanations, with a cold realism that discounts moral scrutiny. Tondelli's and De Carlo's works complement one another in painting a vivid portrait of an egocentric, uncommitted generation that has become the hallmark of the postmodern world.

A talented and eclectic writer, Benni brings to his narrative resonances from disparate sources, including the work of Herman Melville, Carlo Emilio Gadda's macaronic prose, Hollywood movies, contemporary American fiction, and the ludic style in Calvino's *Le cosmicomiche* as well as his fantastic, fablelike narrations. Unlike Tondelli, who tends to be centrifugal, Benni is capable of tying together the various strands of his narrative and remaining focused, especially in *Comici spaventati guerrieri* (Comical and Frightened Warriors, 1986), which throws light on a corrupt political class and the intellectually sterile lifestyle of a consumer society that has turned its back even on the much maligned bourgeois values of yesteryear.

Thirty years after the debut of Gruppo 63, at a literary meeting in Palermo, a new group surfaced: it calls itself Gruppo 93, and it is made up of writers in their thirties or somewhat older. They too have published a sort of manifesto containing theoretical position papers and a sample of their work. *Gruppo 93. Le tendenze attuali della poesia e della narrativa* (Group 93. Present-day Trends in Poetry and the Narrative, 1993) includes a candid assessment of contemporary Italian literature by a respected critic, Romano Luperini, who is anything but conservative in matters of ideology and literary expression. Luperini finds the present cultural climate in Italy flat, lifeless, and stagnant. He adds that avant-garde expressions such as Gruppo 93 no longer make any sense in a climate dominated by postmodernism, which has co-opted the ideas that relate to the literary use of time and space around which many of the avant-garde battles of this century were fought: "Oggi l'avanguardia non è possibile perché è venuto a cadere il presupposto di fondo: divenendo norma non può essere rottura" (Today it is no longer possible to have an avant-garde because the main rationale for its being has gone: becoming part of the norm, avant-garde can no longer represent a break [with tradition]).

In the section of the volume called "Un autoritratto" (A Self-portrait), four exponents of the Gruppo 93, writing in unison, stake their position on two notions: *lateralità* (being on the sidelines) and *letteratura minore,* the latter term referring to "una letteratura minore nel senso più drammatico del termine: minoritaria e quasi marginale senza sbocchi evidenti, a tratti malata di epigonismo" (a literature with a small *l* in the most dramatic sense of the term: in the minority and nearly marginal, without apparent outlets, and at times afflicted with being second-rate imitation).

While it is disheartening to realize that many young writers in the 1990s have felt compelled to adopt a timid and defensive stance regarding their profession, even to the point of according a marginal place in society to a cultural institution that in the history of every civilization has held a central role, there is no need to be overly concerned. A century ago the work of Gabriele D'Annunzio, permeated with hedonism, narcissism, sensuality, and eroticism, was said to mark the end of the socially and spiritually redeeming function of literature. Today, D'Annunzio's works are collecting dust on library shelves. More important, within a short time Italian literature was renewed and revitalized through the works of Giuseppe Ungaretti, Eugenio Montale, and Pirandello. This editor believes firmly that the same pattern will reoccur in the early part of the next century.

—*Augustus Pallotta*

Acknowledgments

This book was produced by Bruccoli Clark Layman, Inc. Karen L. Rood is senior editor for the *Dictionary of Literary Biography* series. In-house editor is George P. Anderson. The publisher thanks Rosalind and Aldo Nesticó for their help in illustrating the volume.

Administrative support was provided by Ann M. Cheschi, Beverly Dill, and Tenesha S. Lee.

Bookkeeper is Joyce Fowler. Assistant bookkeepers are Carol Cheschi and Neil Senol.

Copyediting supervisor is Samuel W. Bruce. The copyediting staff includes Phyllis A. Avant, Charles Brower, Christine Copeland, Margo Dowling, Thom Harman, Jannette L. Giles, Nicole M. Nichols, and Raegan E. Quinn. Freelance copyeditors are Rebecca Mayo and Jennie Williamson.

Editorial associate is Jeff Miller.

Layout and graphics staff includes Janet E. Hill, Mark J. McEwan, and Alison Smith.

Office manager is Kathy Lawler Merlette.

Photography editors are Melissa D. Hinton, Margaret Meriwether, and Paul Talbot. Photographic copy work was performed by Joseph M. Bruccoli.

Production manager is Marie L. Parker.

SGML supervisor is Cory McNair. The SGML staff includes Linda Drake, Frank Graham, Jennifer Harwell, and Alex Snead.

Systems manager is Marie L. Parker.

Database manager is Javed Nurani. Kim Kelly performed data entry.

Typesetting supervisor is Kathleen M. Flanagan. The typesetting staff includes Pamela D. Norton, Karla Corley Price, and Patricia Flanagan Salisbury. Freelance typesetters include Deidre Murphy and Delores Plastow.

Walter W. Ross and Steven Gross did library research. They were assisted by the following librarians at the Thomas Cooper Library of the University of South Carolina: Linda Holderfield and the interlibrary-loan staff; reference-department head Virginia Weathers; reference librarians Marilee Birchfield, Stefanie Buck, Stefanie DuBose, Rebecca Feind, Karen Joseph, Donna Lehman, Charlene Loope, Anthony McKissick, Jean Rhyne, and Kwamine Simpson; circulation-department head Caroline Taylor; and acquisitions- searching supervisor David Haggard.

The editor of this volume wishes to thank Matthew J. Bruccoli and Antonio Illiano for their interest in the project; George Anderson for his meticulous work as in-house editor; L. Kay Webster and Kathy Lawler Merlette for their administrative assistance. The support these individuals have lent to the two volumes of *Italian Novelists Since World War II* has been valuable. I wish to thank as well the contributors to both volumes for their patience and generous collaboration. A special note of appreciation goes to Olga Ragusa, my former professor at Columbia, who has supported me in this and other professional endeavors.

Antonio Illiano, Professor of Romance Languages at the University of North Carolina is series editor for the Italian literature volumes in the *Dictionary of Literary Biography*.

Dictionary of Literary Biography® • Volume One Hundred Ninety-Six

Italian Novelists Since World War II, 1965–1995

Dictionary of Literary Biography

Alberto Arbasino
(22 January 1930 -)

Rosetta Di Pace
University of Oklahoma

BOOKS: *Le piccole vacanze* (Turin: Einaudi, 1957);
L'Anonimo Lombardo (Milan: Feltrinelli, 1959);
Parigi o cara (Milan: Feltrinelli, 1960);
Fratelli d'Italia (Milan: Feltrinelli, 1963; revised and enlarged, Turin: Einaudi, 1976; revised and enlarged, Milan: Adelphi, 1993);
La narcisata. La controra (Milan: Feltrinelli, 1964);
Certi romanzi (Milan: Feltrinelli, 1964); revised as *Certi romanzi: nuova edizione seguita da La Belle Époque per le scuole* (Turin: Einaudi, 1977);
Grazie per le magnifiche rose (Milan: Feltrinelli, 1965);
La maleducazione teatrale: strutturalismo e drammaturgia (Milan: Feltrinelli, 1966);
Le due orfanelle: Venezia e Firenze (Milan: Feltrinelli, 1968);
Off-off (Milan: Feltrinelli, 1968);
Super-Eliogabalo (Milan: Feltrinelli, 1969);
Sessanta posizioni (Milan: Feltrinelli, 1971);
I Turchi: codex Vindobonensis 8626 (Parma: Ricci, 1972);
La bella di Lodi (Turin: Einaudi, 1972);
Il principe costante (Turin: Einaudi, 1972);
Amate sponde; commedia italiana, by Arbasino and Mario Missiroli (Turin: Einaudi, 1974);
Le interviste impossibili, by Arbasino and others (Milan: Bompiani, 1975);
Specchio delle mie brame (Turin: Einaudi, 1975);
Nuove interviste impossibili, by Arbasino and others (Milan: Bompiani, 1976);
Fantasmi italiani (Rome: Cooperativa Scrittori, 1977);
In questo stato (Milan: Garzanti, 1978);
Un paese senza (Milan: Garzanti, 1980);
Il teatro italiano oggi, edited by Erminia Artese (Cosenza: Lerici, 1980);
Trans-Pacific Express (Milan: Garzanti, 1981);

Alberto Arbasino (photograph by Giovanni Giovannetti)

Matinée: un concerto di poesia (Milan: Garzanti, 1983);
Il meraviglioso, anzi (Milan: Garzanti, 1985);
La caduta dei tiranni (Palermo: Sellerio, 1990);
Paese senza (Milan: Garzanti, 1992);
Mekong (Milan: Adelphi, 1994);
Lettere da Londra (Milan: Adelphi, 1997);
Passeggiando tra i draghi addormentati (Milan: Adelphi, 1997).

OTHER: Ivy Compton-Burnett, *Più donne che uomini,* preface by Arbasino (Milan: Longanesi, 1974);
Oscar Wilde, *Salome,* preface by Arbasino (Milan: Rizzoli, 1974);

Carlo Dossi, *Vita di Alberto Pisani,* preface by Arbasino (Turin: Einaudi, 1974);

Favole su favole: fiabe e leggende, translated, transcribed, and transformed by Arbasino and others (Cosenza: Lerici, 1975);

Daniela Palazzoli, *I viaggi perduti,* introduction by Arbasino (Turin: Bompiani, 1985).

Alberto Arbasino's fiction is immersed in post–World War II Italian culture. Well known as a journalist and film, theater, and literary critic as well as a novelist, he brings to his work erudition, a mordant wit, and a remarkable verbal virtuosity. Drawing from modern and postmodern art, Arbasino is experimental in his writing though he rejects the antirational premise of much avant-garde writing. Throughout his career he has attempted the uneasy task of rendering his work both self-reflexive and connected to reality. His receptivity to the postmodern practices of assemblage, genre bending, and pastiche are exemplified by the role of the narrator in his work. Perhaps the key to Arbasino's work is the rational discourse maintained by the narrators who present his fictional world.

Arbasino was born on 22 January 1933 into a wealthy family in the provincial town of Voghera, in the northern region of Lombardy. His secondary education consisted of the humanities-based school that places a heavy emphasis on the study of the classics. In 1947, heeding the wishes of his family, he reluctantly enrolled at the University of Pavia as a medical student. He soon transferred to the University of Milan, where he received a degree in law and political sciences. From 1954 to 1956 he continued his studies at the Sorbonne in Paris and at the University of The Hague. In 1957 he was hired as an instructor at the University of Rome, a post he held until 1965.

In the 1950s Arbasino traveled extensively in Europe and the United States and began to contribute to such well-known journals as *Il Mondo, Il Ponte,* and *Il Verri.* The last, founded by Luciano Anceschi in 1950, became the main organ for Italian avant-garde writers of the 1960s who identified with Gruppo 63. Arbasino was one of this group's most articulate exponents in his rejection of Neorealism and its ideological affiliation with Marxism. Politically, he identified with the centrist, business-supported Republican Party, which he represented in Parliament in 1983.

Arbasino began his literary career in 1957 with a collection of short stories titled *Le piccole vacanze* (Short Vacations). Most of these stories were reprinted in his second work, *L'Anonimo Lombardo* (Anonymous Lombard, 1959), which also included *Il ragazzo perduto* (The Lost Young Man), a novel in epistolary form. The novella consists of forty-five letters addressed to Roberto, the narrator's lover, and to Emilio, his friend and confidant. The two interlocutors remain silent as no letters are ever answered. Yet the one-way correspondence keeps the monologue going, in the course of which the intellectual and sensual aspects of the narrator's relationship with Roberto are explored. There are clear echoes here of James Joyce's *Portrait of the Artist as a Young Man* (1916), but the narrator's rational grip on reality concedes no ground to the forces of the irrational and the subconscious. Even in this early work Arbasino conveys a sense of self-assurance and full acquaintance with his craft.

Il ragazzo perduto is a significant work because it manifests some of the key traits of Arbasino's fiction: avoidance of conventional plots and characters, use of repetition as well as surprise, and love of allusion. His use of the epistolary form allows him to do away with the traditional requisites of plot and character development. Further, the series of letters creates a spare narrative structure that follows a linear development at the expense of psychological introspection. The repetition of the letter form creates the impression that the story can go on indefinitely, poised as it is for the next letter, the next occurrence, the next surprise. The epistolary form allows for profuse ruminations on such recurrent events as short trips and parties. The prodigality of the monologue is due in large part to the writer's use of notes, footnotes, literary references, and allusions—all gathered from Arbasino's voluminous reading. He is indeed one of the best-read living writers in Italy.

However, the loquacity of the correspondent's intellectual discourse is undermined by a psychological opacity and muteness, which are constants in Arbasino's work. This lack of emotional insight goes hand in hand with the display of a camp sensibility. In *Il ragazzo perduto* the correspondent's snobbishness is paired with the license of the erudite libertine; the end result is that an elitist discourse is often yoked to trivial subjects. The man who reads *tous les livres* (all the books) can advise his lover nonchalantly on how to read Marcel Proust from the viewpoint of homosexual cruising. He can also go blithely on in another letter to give advice to a young admirer on the importance of impeccable taste in personal attire.

Fratelli d'Italia (Brothers of Italy, 1963), Arbasino's most ambitious work, is regarded by many critics as an expression of Gruppo 63. He draws a large-scale portrait of jetsetters in an early 1960s Italy caught in the throes of economic growth and cultural decline. Again, the responsibility for telling

Cover for the 1977 revision of Arbasino's 1964 book, in which he discusses the development of the Italian novel after World War II

the story, for structurally controlling it and for fashioning narrative strategies, is placed in the hands of an intellectual narrator who is a veiled stand-in for the author. In spite of Arbasino's often repeated intention of creating a *romanzo-conversazione* (conversation- novel), perhaps in the fashion of the English writer Ivy Compton-Burnett, whom he greatly admired, there is only one voice in *Fratelli d'Italia*–that of the jet-setting narrator.

The narrator's key interlocutors are Antonio, his lover (who becomes Andrea in the 1976 edition); the German musician Klaus; and the young Frenchman Jean-Claude. They share the narrator's attitudes, ideas, frayed nerves, and insatiable need to travel. In the course of the novel the narrator and his companions flit up and down the Italian peninsula from one musical festival to another, across Europe to see Bavarian castles, and to London to catch the shows and exhibits, do a bit of shopping, and dine in newly discovered restaurants. While Arbasino clearly identifies with the narrator and his doubles, he seems hostile to the other characters in the novel.

In *Fratelli d'Italia* it is the sovereign consciousness of the narrator that stands out. The text is anchored to the monologue, a structure that, as in *Il ragazzo perduto,* lets the reader hear Arbasino's unmistakable voice in all its brilliance, exclusiveness, and spleen. The use of conversation, as his earlier use of the epistolary form, is really only a pretext that enables the narrator to withdraw into his fierce monologue, which drowns all dialogue and is deaf to other possibilities.

The significance of the narrator in *Fratelli d'Italia* is also manifested by the running commentary spliced throughout the book. The heavy dose of quotations, literary references, and theoretical speculations in the novel spill over into Arbasino's critical volume, *Certi romanzi* (Certain Novels, 1964), which offers valuable observations on the development of the Italian novel after World War II and can also be read as a defense of *Fratelli d'Italia*. In the postface to the 1976 edition of *Fratelli d'Italia* Arbasino clearly indicates the link between the novel and the critical volume:

> Avevo progettato di corredare il già lungo romanzo di un suo journal di apprendimento saggistico . . . Ma non già fuori del romanzo, bensí del suo "cuore stesso." Ecco l'origine di *Certi romanzi*. . . . Solo le dimensioni raggiunte, insomma, hanno infine estromesso *Certi romanzi* dalla loro sede originaria, per una situazione in un volumetto separato.

> (I had planned to supply the already long novel with its own essay journal . . . Not, however, outside the novel, but in its "very heart." Here then is the origin of *Certi romanzi*. . . . Only the length it had reached took, in the end, *Certi romanzi* out of its original place, to find its ultimate destination in a small separate volume.)

Arbasino thus succeeds in blurring the line between creative and critical writing as his fictional narrator shares his own enthusiasm for theoretical discourse.

In *Fratelli d'Italia* Arbasino is more interested in writing per se than in the characters of his story. His writing betrays a close adherence to the formalist and structuralist ideas that were being debated at the time. In his postface Arbasino remembers the critical revelations that influenced his writing:

> Proprio in quella fase cosí pioneristica e sperimentale, la felicità della scoperta degli strumenti critici e tecnici proposti dal formalismo russo e dallo strutturalismo sospingeva a una intensa "progettualità"nella formalizzazione delle strutture narrative . . . Ah, quell'eccitazione creativa e critica nello smontare e rimontare il Giocattolo all'incrocio fra tante euforie.

> (In the midst of such pioneering experimental activity the happiness of discovering the critical and technical instruments proposed by Russian formalism and structuralism pushed one to intense projects in formalizing narrative structures . . . Ah, the creative and critical excitement in pulling apart and putting together again the Toy [i.e., the novel] amidst so much euphoria.)

Despite his enthusiasm for the new theories from abroad Arbasino was to follow them on the formal level only, for he adopted the structures of modern and postmodern fiction without following the implications of his theorizing to their ultimate conclusions. Arbasino's subversion of conventional narrative forms is thus not a result of the ontological crisis at the core of much contemporary art. He does not share the postmodern distrust of representing reality; his iconoclasm is not against realism but against its modes of representation. As much as Arbasino is a radical formalist, he remains a realist in practice. It would be hard to find in all contemporary Italian fiction a more thoroughgoing rationalistic discourse than Arbasino's.

The satiric narrative thrust of *Fratelli d'Italia* is directed at the antics of a handful of gossipy, chic drifters from the Lombard upper crust suffering mostly from the boredom of an affluent lifestyle. Although the narrator learns and matures as a result of his traveling, the same cannot be said of other characters, who travel to relieve their boredom. Events are described in midflight as the listless travelers go from one activity to another in a pervasive carnival atmosphere. One is struck by the absence of landscapes and open vistas as Arbasino keeps his focus relentlessly on social interaction.

A playful atmosphere also dominates in Arbasino's next novel, *Super-Eliogabalo* (Super Heliogabalus, 1969), a successful but controversial work in which he turns the historical novel into pastiche. The setting is the decadent imperial Rome of the third century A.D. under the reign of Heliogabalus. Arbasino draws from the historical figure of the boy emperor, remembered for his depravity and cruelty, but his protagonist is an anachronistic, hippie-punk character from the dissolute social order of Rome in the 1960s.

In *Super-Eliogabalo* Arbasino substitutes the pseudospace of the stage for a conventional "realistic" approach, a strategy that allows him to collapse time and history. The novel is written in the form of a screenplay in which the elements of spectacle, of show, predominate in a seemingly endless present. Shown by an impassive chronicler that acts as if he were a stage director, a series of skitlike scenes pass in front of the reader in which marionette-like characters appear, vanish, and then reappear. In the first scene a train of litters makes its way to a villa at Ostia where the imperial retinue is to spend a weekend.

Throughout Arbasino wittily flaunts glaring anachronisms, which bring down all historical barriers. The emperor is first seen as

> si cala fin sotto gli occhi un gran casco lucido da motociclista che reca la semplice sigla S-M e si adagia completamente disperato e disilluso in fondo a un cocchio pubblicitario tirato al trotto da una schiera di damine del

Settecento, tutte nei, cicisbei, crinoline, e bottoni elettorali della Famiglia Kennedy.

(he pulls down over his eyes a big shiny motorcycle helmet with the simple monogram S-M and lies down in complete despair and disillusion in the back of a publicity coach pulled by a trotting line of eighteenth-century female figurines, all beauty marks and serving cavaliers, crinolines, and Kennedy campaign buttons.)

Later in the story Heliogabalus reads biographical accounts of his own life from the contemporary Roman historian Dio Cassius, the fourteenth-century *Historia Augusta,* and from the French playwright Antonin Artaud's *Héliogabale, ou l'anarchiste couronné* (Heliogabalus, or the Crowned Anarchist, 1934), going from one to the other with great ease. At one point, annoyed by some of the opinions he reads about himself, he throws the *Historia Augusta* into a ditch.

Arbasino so comically exaggerates the mannerisms of the outlandish and freakish Heliogabalus that he resembles an "opera buffa" (Comic Opera) character. He gives his cartoonish caricature twentieth-century attitudes and expressions, thus revealing and brilliantly achieving his true intention, which is to parody the ethos and the style of the 1960s subculture, which he sees as a grotesque carnival. One may balk at the proliferation of so much arbitrary play, of so many grotesque images, but this frenzy is as controlled as its expressive language.

A partial sampling from a long list of the many causes for the present-day decadence of Italian society suggests how Arbasino is orderly even when representing disorder:

> L'accumulo?
> Lo sperpero?
> Il capriccio?
> Il bisogno?
> Il conformismo?
> La centralizzazione?
> La mancanza d'obbedienza?
> Lo spopolamento delle campagne?
> La lotta di classe?

> (Hoarding?
> Waste?
> Whim?
> Need?
> Conformism?
> Centralization?
> The lack of obedience?
> The depopulation of the countryside?
> The class war?)

Every item of this eye-catching catalogue in *Super-Eliogabalo,* a work ostensibly set in the ancient past, calls attention to a modern social phenomenon.

One of the prime targets of Arbasino's satire is the disorder in the madhouse of the imperial villa, which, being under perpetual remodeling, makes the emperor nervous:

> Lo staff appare stravolto dalla confusione. I cuochi, i masseurs, gli addetti alle salse, gli addetti alle orge, nonché l'assaggiatore, l'avvelenatore, l'aguzzino e il sicario, devono lavorare in piccolo o insieme, due o tre per stanza, perché i lavori in corso li hanno sloggiati dai loro uffici soliti.

> (The staff seems upset by such confusion. The cooks, the masseurs, the sauces experts, the orgies experts, no less than the taster, the poisoner, the jailer and the throat-cutter, have to work in small groups or together, two or three to a room, since the work in progress has driven them out of their usual offices.)

There is no surcease for the reader from Arbasino's comic inventiveness and the constant movement of grotesque characters as they engage in a busy round of murder and mayhem. But through it all one never loses the sense that Arbasino has a deliberate method to his madness.

Arbasino uses his playfulness as a vehicle of his satire and not as a means of participating in the randomness that underlies postmodern aesthetics. Generally the key target of Arbasino's satire is mass culture. The emergent model of social pluralism is as repugnant to Arbasino as it is to Heliogabalus, who laments intense legislative fervor:

> Quest'epoca deve finire al più presto. È opera di civismo etico oltre che di cinismo estetico aiutarla a cessare, rapidamente. Invece di continuare a fare dei ridicoli consigli della Corona cercando inutilmente di mettere d'accordo le correnti più mediocri dell'illuminismo regressivo, occorre tagliare in qualche modo la radice della perfida cultura fintaprogressiva.

> (This period has to end as soon as possible. It is a matter of ethical civic duty as well as of aesthetic cynicism, to help it end quickly. Instead of continuing to have such ridiculous councils to the Crown trying in vain to make work one of the most mediocre currents of a regressive Enlightenment, it is imperative to cut in some way at the roots of such wicked pseudoprogressive culture.)

Arbasino has never welcomed the postmodern embrace of popular art. One example of his satire of mass culture is Heliogabalus's decision to order an Eiffel Tower made of toothpicks for his Adrian villa at Tivoli. It is clear in this and other works that Arbasino's satire is a means of rejecting the garish forms and the vulgarity of popular culture together with its myth of progress.

Significantly, Arbasino's favorite verb is *franare* (to crumble), a word he usually attributes to the social disintegration that mass culture has brought about in postwar Italy. The final scene in *Super-Eliogabalo* takes place in the temple, which also functions as a supermarket. Here the emperor falls victim to the ambition of his four mothers (who are also his lovers), who want him to be the youngest god in the Roman Pantheon. In this apotheosis of "Apocalyptic Kitsch," in which the emperor becomes the sacrificial victim of a ritual killing, Rome remains eternal only in its decadence and its chaos.

From the costume drama of *Super-Eliogabalo* Arbasino turns to the drawing-room comedy of *La bella di Lodi* (The Beauty from Lodi, 1972), in which he continues to aim his satiric barbs at mass culture. The setting is the industrial region of Lombardy during the prosperous 1960s. Roberta, a rich woman with entrepreneurial savvy, and Franco, a mechanic, are manikins in a Cinderella story in reverse. The opposition to the breaking down of class lines is clear and testifies to Arbasino's conservative values. He has always been a writer who has gone out of his way to distance himself from the democratic Left. The only authors he has ever praised have been the high priests of modernism—Robert Musil, Thomas Mann, T. S. Eliot, and Carlo Emilio Gadda—all well-known conservative elites. With them Arbasino shares a nostalgia for the past and a similar attitude toward the petty bourgeoisie.

In *Fantasmi italiani* (Italian Ghosts, 1977), a collection of articles on the ills he sees afflicting contemporary Italy, Arbasino never tires of downgrading the lower middle class, even when he has to recognize "l'egemonia politica e culturale e di costume raggiunta ormai dal ceto piccolo-borghese" (the political and cultural and social hegemony reached by the petty bourgeoisie). Referring to the upper class as the "big world" and the lower class as the "little world," he adds: "Malgrado la difformità apparente delle 'posizioni' ideologiche, il Gran Mondo e il Piccolo Mondo (del tempo non solo di Goethe, ma ancora di Mann), ormai, davvero non si distinguono più." (In spite of the apparent differences of their ideological "positions," the Big World and the Little World [not only of Goethe's time, but even of Mann's time], can no longer be really distinguished.)

In *La bella di Lodi* Roberta and Franco are immersed in what Arbasino calls in *Fantasmi italiani* "il bagno di quella omogeneizzazione o emulsione che è lo studiatissimo prodotto terminale e madornale dell'Illuminismo depravato: la cultura di massa" (the bath of that homogenization or emulsion which is the much-studied final and engrossing product of the depraved Enlightenment: mass culture). Here the operative word is *depraved,* applied to the emancipatory forces of the Enlightenment. The petty bourgeoisie and the proletariat may be experiencing a phenomenal growth, but Arbasino finds their language and taste deplorable. Franco, however, acquires some of his girlfriend's excellent taste. Indeed, through Roberta's pragmatism, he is slowly absorbed into her upper-middle-class world. She overcomes her disdain for the working class and, moved by physical attraction, accepts the inevitability of class fusion by marrying Franco.

In his next two novels, *Il principe costante* (The Constant Prince, 1972) and *Specchio delle mie brame* (Mirror of My Desires, 1975), Arbasino, rather than debunking popular culture, seems interested in offering the reader a catalogue of sexual perversities. The gleeful relish with which such vices are described is unchecked by any moral frame. Given their limited scope, one is tempted to see the two books as nothing more than witty literary indulgences in which Arbasino trades his caustic sarcasm for a sort of sado-erotic gothicism mixing levity, wickedness, and horror.

The first of the two novels, *Il principe costante,* is based on Calderón de la Barca's seventeenth-century play of the same title. Arbasino reworks the play into a short novel that has little resemblance to the original text, save for historical references and general plotlines. The difference of emphasis in the two works could not be more striking. The Spanish playwright sought to portray Christian virtues personified in the devout, historical figure of a medieval Portuguese prince. Arbasino, on the other hand, lays the stress on the character's imprisonment and death. The stark dichotomy between gloomy events and the mood of farce and burlesque that surrounds them is vintage Arbasino. Instead of focusing like Calderón on Prince Ferdinand's experience in the conquest of Tangier which would lead to his death or on the transience of earthly life, Arbasino's emphasis is his character's indulgence in masochism.

The novel is not lacking in merriment. Arbasino portrays Fenix, the Moorish princess who in Calderón's play shares the author's deep melancholia, as a beautiful, willful woman "abbastanza neurotica, un pochino beffarda, lievemente Anni Trenta, ma tutt'altro che sciocca" (rather neurotic, a little mocking, slightly 1930s style, yet anything but a fool). With Fenix, Arbasino lets his comic imagination run free. Her duet with Ferdinand in the royal garden at Fez is a wonderful spoof of the same duet in Calderón's work. In the original play the characters, reflecting on the passing of time and the inevitability of death, compare human life to the short lifespan of flowers. Arbasino's Fenix interrupts the prince to tell him flatly that she despises analogies of any sort: "Ah, no, per favore, se anche i fiori cominciano a diventare simboli d'una cosa o metafore di un'altra, allora preferisco buttarli tutti subito nella spazzatura" (Oh no, please, if even flowers start becoming symbols of this and metaphors of that, then I would rather throw them all in the trash right now).

Arbasino often injects himself into the text, as in his description of a battle: "Tutta questa battaglia si svolge rapidissima e risulta quasi illeggibile, soprattutto a chi vi partecipa" (This whole battle takes place rapidly and is almost unreadable, especially to those who take part in it). He also uses anachronistic allusions, as when the prince introduces himself to a visitor in his cell: "Hey, you, my name is Mickey Mouse!" Such conscious manipulation of the text for the purpose of farce and parody gives way to the gloom in which the novel ends, a realistic description of the prince's torture, physical deterioration, and lingering death.

In *Specchio delle mie brame* Arbasino indulges in a decadent and sophisticated study of libido through the story of a Sicilian baroness and her sexual exploits at the turn of the twentieth century. It is a book that rightly belongs in the libertine tradition though it also sheds a faint light on the woes of the Italian South. The novel is patterned on *Snow White*, and there are characters and events that bear distinct similarities to the Grimm fairy tale. Arbasino, though, puts his own twist on the story. His Prince Charming, who comes to no one's rescue, is none other than Miss Judy Faggotty, a young Scottish governess who could have been drawn by D. H. Lawrence.

In the book Arbasino shows his marked distaste for the work of important Sicilian writers such as Giovanni Verga, Federico De Roberto, Luigi Pirandello, and Giuseppe Tomasi di Lampedusa by mocking and parodying their styles. This hostility is also found in Arbasino's critical writings, especially the revised 1977 edition of *Certi romanzi,* in which the author never tires of lambasting Italian authors from the turn of the century to the present, accusing them of provincialism and backwardness vis-à-vis their English and French counterparts. He is similarly disdainful of Italian theater in *Grazie per le magnifiche rose* (Thanks for the Beautiful Roses, 1965) and *La maleducazione teatrale* (The Unrefined Stage, 1966), complaining, among other shortcomings, about its resistance to innovation, the indifference of the actors, and the intrusiveness of the directors. In such criticism Arbasino stands out more as a polemicist than a critic in the sense that he readily points his castigating finger at whatever he dislikes but never makes the effort to be constructive.

La caduta dei tiranni (The Fall of the Tyrants, 1990) shows Arbasino's inexhaustible curiosity and, no less, his relentless critical spirit. The book was motivated by the political upheavals in central Europe in 1989. He travels from Berlin to Prague to Budapest, soon setting aside his observations on political events to turn to caustic criticism. In Prague he notices a new baroque spirit in the air as it shakes with rock music while Budapest remains the city of "super kitsch," lacking in elegance and sophistication. He prefers the Berlin described by W. H. Auden and Christopher Isherwood.

In *Mekong* (1994), a book on his recent travels to Cambodia in its post-Communist era, Arbasino is not insensitive to the sights of devastation and human suffering wrought by ideological folly. Nor does he fail to point out the contradictions, absurdities, and dilemmas in this war-ravaged part of Asia. By the same token Arbasino is not imbued with a missionary spirit: he reports things the way he sees them, empathy never having been his forte. Even in this book of reportage his prose sparkles when he has an aesthetic experience, such as when he discovers ancient temples in the heart of the jungle.

In 1993, thirty years after its initial publication, *Fratelli d'Italia* was revised and republished with great success. Yet Arbasino remains true to himself at the twilight of his career, enriching the text with the same narcissistic flavor that runs throughout his works. It can be said in sum that no other post–World War II Italian author has managed so well to remain attuned to the country's cultural and political ills.

Interviews:
Alberto Sinigaglia, *Vent'anni al Duemila* (Turin: E.R.I, 1982);
Graziella Pulce, *Lettura d'autore: conversazioni di critica e di letteratura con Giorgio Manganelli, Pietro Citati e Alberto Arbasino* (Rome: Bulzoni, 1988).

References:
Elisabetta Bolla, *Invito alla lettura di Arbasino* (Milan: Mursia, 1979);
Angelo Guglielmi, *La letteratura del risparmio* (Milan: Bompiani, 1973);
Maria Luisa Vecchi, *Arbasino* (Florence: La Nuova Italia, 1980).

Nanni Balestrini
(2 July 1935 -)

Ernesto Livorni
Yale University

BOOKS: *Il sasso appeso* (Milan: Scheiwiller, 1961);
Come si agisce (Milan: Feltrinelli, 1963);
Altri procedimenti 1964-1965 (Milan: Scheiwiller, 1965);
Tristano (Milan: Feltrinelli, 1966);
Ma noi facciamone un'altra: poesie 1964-1968 (Milan: Feltrinelli, 1968);
Vogliamo tutto (Milan: Feltrinelli, 1971);
Prendiamoci tutto. Conferenza per un romanzo. Letteratura e lotta di classe (Milan: Feltrinelli, 1971);
Le cinque giornate, by Dario Argento and Balestrini (Milan: Bompiani, 1974);
Ballate distese (Turin: Geiger, 1975);
Profondo thrilling, by Argento and Balestrini (Milan: Sonzongno, 1975);
La violenza illustrata (Turin: Einaudi, 1976);
Poesie pratiche 1954-1969 (Turin: Einaudi, 1976);
Ballate della signorina Richmond: primo libro (Rome: Cooperativa Scrittori, 1977);
Blackout (Milan: Feltrinelli, 1980);
Sulla neoavanguardia, by Balestrini and others (Foggia: Bastogi, 1983);
Ipocalisse: 49 sonetti, Provenza 1980-1983 (Milan: Scheiwiller, 1986);
Gli invisibili (Milan: Bompiani, 1987); translated by Liz Heron as *The Unseen* (London: Verso, 1989);
Il ritorno della signorina Richmond: terzo libro, 1984-1986 (Oderzo, Treviso: Becco Giallo, 1987);
Ut pictura poesis: "com la pintura, aixi és la poesia," by Balestrini and others (Barcelona: Fundacio Caxia de Pensions, 1988);
La signorina Richmond se ne va: secondo libro (Milan: Corpo 10, 1988);
Osservazioni sul volo degli uccelli. Poesie 1954-1956 (Milan: Scheiwiller, 1988);
L'orda d'oro 1968-1977; la grande ondata rivoluzionaria e creativa, politica ed esistenziale, by Ballestrini and Primo Moroni (Milan: SugarCo, 1988);
L'editore (Milan: Bompiani, 1989);
Il pubblico del labirinto: quarto libro della signorina Richmond, 1985-1989 (Milan: Scheiwiller, 1992);

Nanni Balestrini (photograph by Giovanni Giovannetti)

I furiosi (Milan: Bompiani, 1994);
Estremi rimedi (Lecce: Piero Manni, 1995);
Una mattina ci siam svegliati (Milan: Baldini & Castoldi, 1995).

OTHER: *Gruppo 63, la nuova letteratura; 34 scrittori, Palermo, ottobre, 1963,* edited by Balestrini and Alfredo Giuliani (Milan: Feltrinelli, 1964);

Gruppo 63: Il romanzo sperimentale: Palermo 1965, edited by Balestrini (Milan: Feltrinelli, 1966);

Jack London, *Martin Eden,* translated by Gastone Rossi, preface by Balestrini (Milan: Sonzogno, 1974);

"Linguaggio e opposizione," in *Critica e teoria,* edited by Renato Barilli and Angelo Guglielmi (Milan: Feltrinelli, 1976), pp. 77–79;

Alfonso Natella, *Come pesci nell'acqua inquinata,* preface by Balestrini (Milan: Librirossi, 1978);

Leon Battista Alberti, *Momo o del Principe,* edited by Rino Consolo, preface by Balestrini (Genoa: Costa & Nolan, 1987);

Ugo Foscolo, *Ugo Foscolo,* selected and introduced by Balestrini (Rome: Istituto Poligrafico e Zecca dello Stato, 1995).

TRANSLATIONS: Claude Simon, *Trittico* (Turin: Einaudi, 1975);

Jean-François Lyotard, *Il muro del Pacifico* (Milan: Multipla, 1986);

Samuel Beckett, *Soprassalti* (Carnago: SugarCo, 1992).

Nanni Balestrini's work represents one of the major expressions of the Neo-avant-garde movement that swept through Italian literature in the 1960s. Through his writing Balestrini strives to revive language in a world in which he believes the social structure, with its ever-increasing alienation of classes and compartmentalization of individual roles, has irremediably destroyed meaningful communication. To counter this trend Balestrini seeks to affirm language as the object of artistic expression. Hence the daring technical experimentations that mark his literary career: from the device of collage to the use of the computer Balestrini aims to create an art product that is new and revolutionary with respect to both its syntax and its affinity with the spoken language.

Born in Milan on 2 July 1935, Balestrini enrolled in the school of engineering at the Università Cattolica in that city. Later he broadened his interests by studying economics and political science. He was also reading the Dadaists as well as Guillaume Apollinaire, Bertolt Brecht, Ezra Pound, as well as Carlo Emilio Gadda and the writers of the *linea lombarda* (Lombard line), as Luciano Anceschi had come to define that literary tendency. Balestrini's collaboration with this Italian critic started officially in 1957, when some of his poems appeared in *Il Verri,* the journal that Anceschi had just founded. Balestrini also began serving as a member of the editorial board of the journal.

Il Verri soon became the promoting voice of the "Gruppo 63," the avant-garde group born in Milan under Anceschi's auspices. The group's dialectical relationship with the critic's thought is implied by the name coined by Edoardo Sanguineti for the five leaders of the group: *novissimi* (very new lyric poets), for Anceschi before had championed the *lirici nuovi* (new lyric poets). Balestrini, the youngest member of "Gruppo 63," held a well-articulated ideological position and organized the meetings and conferences of the writers.

In his essay "Linguaggio e opposizione" (Language and Opposition)–collected in the volume *Critica e teoria* (Criticism and Theory, 1976) edited by Renato Barilli and Angelo Guglielmi–Balestrini argues that language is at an impasse since "il bisogno di servirsi con immediatezza delle parole porta infatti a un'approssimazione per difetto o per eccesso rispetto al contenuto originario della comunicazione" (the need to use words with immediacy leads in fact to approximation due to deficiency or excess with respect to the original content of communication). He stresses the difference between spoken and written language; the latter, he states, "offre la possibilità di una stesura dilazionata" (offers the possibility of a periodic revision), whereas in the former "ciò che è detto è invece detto per sempre" (what is said, instead, is said once and for all). Balestrini proposes a new and fresh approach: "una poesia piú vicina all'articolarsi dell'emozione e del pensiero in linguaggio" (a poetry closer to the process in which emotion and thought take on linguistic form). According to such a project, "sarà una possibilità di *opporsi* efficacemente alla continua sedimentazione che ha come complice l'inerzia del linguaggio" (it may be possible to resist effectively continuous sedimentation to which the inertia of language contributes).

This program inspired Balestrini to write such experimental works as the book of poems *Come si agisce* (How to Act, 1963) and the novel *Tristano* (Tristan, 1966), the latter written after he moved to Rome in 1964. The title of the novel is part of Balestrini's innovative and polemic intent: the allusion to the hero of the German legend, whose love for Iseult is well known, is the extratextual reference that makes his variations on the original myth striking. In the opera by Wagner, for example, Tristan's love is marked by a sense of destiny and loss that leads to self-destruction; in Balestrini's novel, though, his love becomes a sign of freedom and allows him choices. There are indeed so many avenues offered to the protagonist that he gets lost in that existential openness of the text that owes much to James Joyce's interior monologue and Alain Robbe-Grillet's exterior monologue.

In "Linguaggio e opposizione" Balestrini points to a linguistic monologue in which the language itself is the main character. Accordingly, *Tristano* does not have a traditional plot and characters: the name given to the couple involved in the love story is *C,* and that same letter names the places where the couple happens to be:

> Dove sei stata. Inventa tutto. Il sermolino Thymus serpillum il papavero luteo delle Alpi Papaver alpinum var. achantopetala il ranuncolo amaro nordico Ranunculus acer borealis ne sopravvive qualche esemplare nelle Alpi il Thalictrum alpinum l'Atragene alpina var. sibirica. Fino ad averne abbastanza. In seguito questa parola era sufficiente a produrre la contrazione delle arterie. La sua voce normalmente bassa e velata tremava un po'. Avanzavano con grande rapidità e si trovarono ben presto a portata di voce. Cominciò a muoversi piú veloce. Partimmo un'ora dopo e a C scendemmo all'albergo. Ti telefono se vuoi. Mentre state al telefono pensate che il tempo fugge che avete un milione di cose da fare. Era certamente diverso da C. State sdraiata sul divano col telefono per terra e muovendovi in continuazione. Non può venire. Non mi hai mai scritto disse C. Si alzò aprí la porta. Tutt'a un tratto tornò a sedersi davanti allo specchio e aprí la bottiglietta. C vive sotto una tale pressione mentale che è virtualmente costretto a parlare ad alta voce per la maggior parte del tempo. I minuti scorrevano lenti. Camminò sul prato tra gli alberi. Era piena di gioia di vivere mentre chiacchierava con le due ragazze al suo fianco che ridevano a qualcosa che lei aveva appena detto. Ad un tratto stetti in apprensione per C e respirai di sollievo quando la rividi. Ritornò con una lettera che era arrivata mentre eravamo a C. Be' ti muovi. In questa veduta non sono stato capace di scorgere nulla piú di quanto avevo visto nella precedente. Quando lessi questi testi non solo li trovai insignificanti ma non riuscii a scorgere alcun elemento per il quale essi si riferissero al tema prescelto.

> (Where have you been. Invent everything. The thyme Thymus serpillum the luteous poppy of the Alps Papaver alpinum var. acantopetala the Nordic bitter ranunculus Ranunculus acer borealis of which some specimen survives in the Alps the Ghalictrum alpinum the alpine "Atragene" var. "sibirica". Until you have enough of it. Afterwards this word was sufficient to the contraction of the arteries. His/her voice usually low and muted was shaking a little. They were going forward with great swiftness and very soon they found themselves within call. S/he started to move more quickly. We left an hour later and in C we got off at the hotel. I'll telephone you if you wish. While you are on the phone you think that time runs away that you have a million things to do. S/he was certainly different than C. You are lying down on the sofa with the telephone on the floor and continuously moving. S/he cannot come. S/he never wrote to me said C. S/he got up opened the door. All of a sudden s/he went back to sit down before the mirror and opened the bottle. C lives under such mental pressure that he is virtually forced to speak in a loud voice most of the time. The minutes were flowing slowly. She walked in the meadow among the trees. She was full of joy of life while she was chatting with the two girls beside her who were laughing at something she had just said. All of a sudden I was concerned for C and I breathed with relief when I saw her again. She came back with a letter that had arrived while we were in C. Well do you move. In this view I have not been able to notice anything more than I had seen in the previous one. When I read these texts not only did I find them meaningless but I could not discern any element in which they referred to the selected topic.)

Relying on the technique of collage, Balestrini is able to assemble *laisses* (strophes) in which various stylistic devices converge in the creation of a deranged structure: the passage is deprived of any elegiac tone by the cold, objective effect of the botanical nomenclature, and the narrative voice alternates between the impersonal and the personal, between the singular and the plural, so that the boundaries between direct and indirect speech are eliminated. As a result the features of the characters are blended together to the point that they become a truly indissoluble couple. Finally, the refrain, constituted by some sentences that obsessively return throughout the ten chapters, contributes to the sense of stillness that prevails at the end of the novel.

The construction of such laisses—a technique that Balestrini exploited in all his novels—allows the author to reach a paradoxical effect. As he apparently builds at least the approximation of a plot of a traditional novel, his political and ideological intent is to destroy from within the logical and syntactic structures upon which the art of storytelling relies:

> Alzò gli occhi e lo vide venire verso la macchina. Rallentai lentamente entrando nell'abitato. Quando arrivano all'aeroporto mancano pochi minuti a mezzogiorno. Qui si ha nettamente l'impressione di un cielo al tramonto o all'aurora con il sole che splende attraverso zone oscure che fanno considerevole ombra strati orizzontali di nuvole con il sole dietro forse riflesso al fondo da un oggetto luminoso come una massa d'acqua. Ciò avviene in particolare modo quando il sole è vicino al livello dell'occhio un'ora circa dopo l'alba o prima del tramonto. È triste. In realtà le loro illusioni rivoluzionarie andavano a poco a poco chiarendosi come tali nel contatto con la realtà delle cose man mano cioè che essi venivano accorgendosi come l'anelito rinnovatore fosse già stato esaurorato nell'ultimo periodo resistenziale e definitivamente liquidato poi durante il 1945 dalle forze conservatrici che avevano già posto solide basi per la conservazione del vecchio stato. Lunga pausa. Tutti i miei amici sono rimasti uguali non sono cambiati nean-

che un po' ma le cose sono cambiate sono andate in un'altra direzione mentre noi discutevamo tanti bei programmi. C alza le apalle. Si alza stancamente. Questi successi sentono di doverli a una società che avrebbe dovuto crollare sotto il loro impulso rinnovatore e che invece si è risollevata a poco a poco senza di loro nonostante la loro opposizione anzi coinvolgendoli un po' alla volta in una serie di legami poco vincolanti all'apparenza ma presto divenuti indispensabili i nuovi impieghi le nuove prospettive di carriera i nuovi beni di consumo di un tenore di vita piú elevato. Squilla il telefono. Con sarcasmo. Ma senza troppo entusiasmo. Ride nervosamente.

(She looked up and saw him coming toward the car. I slowed down as I entered the inhabited place. When they arrive at the airport it is a few minutes before noon. Here there is the distinct impression of a sky at sunset or at dawn with the sun shining through dark zones that make a large shade horizontal strata of clouds with the sun behind perhaps reflected in the background by a bright object like a mass of water. This happens in particular when the sun is near the level of the eye about an hour after dawn or before sunset. It/S/he is sad. Actually little by little their revolutionary illusions were becoming clear as such upon contact with the reality of things that is as they were becoming aware as if the renovating yearning had already been deprived of authority in the last resistance period and then definitively liquidated during 1945 by the conservative forces which had already laid solid bases for the preservation of the old state. Long pause. All my friends are still the same they have not changed even a bit but things have changed they have gone in another direction while we were discussing many beautiful programs. C raises his/her shoulders. S/he gets up wearily. These successes they sense they owe them to a society that should have crumbled down under their renovating impulse and instead it has little by little risen again without them in spite of their opposition actually involving them little by little in a series of ties apparently slightly binding but soon become indispensable the new jobs the new perspectives of career the new consumer goods of a highly improved standard of living. The telephone rings. With sarcasm. But without too much enthusiasm. S/he laughs nervously.)

In 1967 Ballestrini founded the short-lived journal *Quindici,* which was published until its suspension in 1969 due to the irreconcilable political views of the editorial board members. The journal contributed significantly to intellectual life during its brief run, not only through its well-informed literary and art criticism but also through its articles on political events. Balestrini also founded another magazine, *Compagni* (Comrades), and was instrumental in establishing the left-wing, extraparliamentary political organization known as *Potere operaio* (Workers' Power). The writer's increased political involvement led him to publish another book of poems, *Ma noi facciamone un'altra* (But Let's Make An-

Cover for a 1990 edition of Balestrini's 1987 novel, which focuses on the militant leftist group Autonomia

other One, 1968), and the novel *Vogliamo tutto* (We Want It All, 1971).

After the release of his second novel Ballestrini gave a lecture in November 1971 that he soon published as a pamphlet, *Prendiamoci tutto. Conferenza per un romanzo. Letteratura e lotta di classe* (Let's Take It All. Lecture for a Novel. Literature and Class-Struggle, 1971). The title *Prediamoci tutto* summarizes the development of Balestrini's poetics, as he explains in his discussion of the final episode of the novel:

Perché in questa fase del capitalismo, l'unico sbocco che ha questa figura sociale che è l'operaio-massa, che chiede soldi indipendentemente dal lavoro, indipendentemente dalla produttività; l'unico suo sbocco collettivo è quello di chiedere ricchezza sulla base della forza e della contrapposizione, al livello dei rapporti di forza, con il potere. Vale a dire: la violenza. L'organizzazione di massa della violenza proletaria, della violenza operaia. Il passaggio alla pratica diretta di appropriazione collettiva della ricchezza sociale; da "vogliamo tutto" a "prendiamoci tutto."

(Because in this phase of capitalism, the only way out offered to this social figure which is the mass-worker, demanding money regardless of work, regardless of productivity; his only collective way out is that of demanding wealth on the basis of power and opposition at the level of power relationships, with the establishment. That is to say: violence. The mass organization of the proletarian violence, of the working-class violence. The transition to the direct practice of collective appropriation of the social wealth: from "we want it all" to "let's take it all.")

Balestrini's "language and opposition" has now become more specifically defined as "literature and class struggle": the development of this ideological consciousness marks the vicissitudes of the protagonist in the novel.

In *Vogliamo tutto* an anonymous worker leaves southern Italy to work first in Milan and then in the Fiat factories in Turin. The two parts into which the novel is structured stress the transition in the character's attitude: "Prima della Fiat politicamente ero un qualunquista" (Before Fiat I was politically a whichever-ist). This rite of passage is also signaled by the frequent use of the plural pronoun in the second part, in which, as Balestrini stresses in his lecture, the class struggle becomes the true protagonist:

Da quando il personaggio capisce la dimensione collettiva, quella della lotta, da quel momento in poi le cose di cui si parla sono solo quelle che servono per chiarire i livelli delle lotte, gli strumenti delle lotte. Di qui i capitoli del libro s'intitolano a questi livelli, a questi strumenti: il salario, che è il terreno su cui si lotta. I compagni, cioè il livello organizzativo minimo. L'autonomia, cioè il modo in cui si sviluppa il movimento. L'assemblea, cioè la forma di organizzazione di massa. E infine l'insurrezione, e cioè la forma della lotta. Il linguaggio diventa quello delle lotte, quello propriamente delle lotte: i volantini, i capannelli, le assemblee. E attraverso questo linguaggio c'è il racconto, giorno per giorno, delle lotte di Mirafiori, fino allo scontro finale, diretto, con le forze dello stato che esplode nella battaglia di corso Traiano.

(Once the character understands the collective dimension, that of the struggle, from that moment on the things we talk about are those needed to clarify the levels of the struggles, the instruments of the struggles. Hence the chapters of the book are titled according to these levels, to these instruments: the salary, which is the ground on which there is the struggle. The comrades, that is, the least organizational level. The autonomy, that is, the way in which the movement develops. The assembly, that is, the form of mass organization. And finally the insurrection, that is, the form of the struggle. The language becomes that of the struggles, that specifically of the struggles: the leaflets, the small crowds, the meetings. And through this language there is the tale, day by day, of the struggles at the Mirafiori factory, until the final, direct clash with the state which explodes in the battle of Corso Traiano.)

Each episode marks a step forward in the protagonist's class consciousness: from the professional night school he attends in his hometown to his seasonal jobs, from his brief work experience in the Alemagna factory in Milan to his attempt to earn some money selling his own blood (only to find out that he is supposed to donate it). The alternating dramatic and comic tones of the episodes build up the necessary tension for the depiction of the epic struggle in the second part of the novel.

Balestrini is aware that such a protagonist could easily lose his humanity and become a robot. In partial agreement with his critics, who noticed a current of fascism hidden in the character's attitude, Balestrini nevertheless points to the peculiarity of the protagonist, who he argues represents the worker in an ideal state, without the awareness of being shaped by party ideology. The protagonist seems to owe much to *Ragazzi di vita* (1955), Pier Paolo Pasolini's important novel about Roman street urchins in the 1950s. (Pasolini was the first intellectual to write an essay on the Neo-avant-garde writers; the 1957 essay was collected in his 1960 volume, *Passione e ideologia*.) Balestrini's protagonist may be seen to represent the next stage of the sub-proletarian condition at the end of the process of industrialization in the Italy of the 1960s.

Following the tragic death of Giangiacomo Feltrinelli in March 1972 while carrying out a terrorist act and the subsequent dissolution of the political organization Potere operaio, Balestrini left Feltrinelli publishers to join the staff of the Marsilio publishing firm. He also collaborated on screenplays, including Dario Argento's *Le cinque giornate* (The Five Days, 1974) and wrote poems dedicated to "signorina Richmond," which were collected as *Ballate distese* (Extended Ballads, 1975) and *Ballate della signorina Richmond: primo libro* (The Ballads of Miss Richmond, First Book, 1977).

Balestrini's third novel, *La violenza illustrata* (Violence Illustrated, 1976), is made up of ten chapters (just as were his two previous novels) that at first appear to be ten different short stories. The starting point of each story is the violent language of the newspapers: the language that represents and illustrates facts regarding well-known personalities such as Lt. William Calley and millionaire Aristotle Onassis or the crime news. More important, it is a language that reveals the hypocrisy of the media in presenting the political struggle of the workers. This apparently loose series of themes is connected by linguistic techniques that parallel the contemporary experiments in painting by Andy Warhol, such as decomposition and repetition. For example, in the first episode of *La violenza illustrata,* "Deposizione della madre di William Calley al processo per la strage di Song My Lai" (Deposition of William Calley's Mother at the Trial for the My Lai Massacre), Balestrini creates laisses that respect the syntactic construction while lacking punctuation, thus relying on the reader to impose a logical organization. In the second chapter, Balestrini mocks the hurried processes of the press by systematically transposing two lines in each laisse.

Remaining faithful to the views he expressed in "Language and Opposition," Balestrini counters the excesses and deficiencies of language programmed for immediate consumption. The final laisse in the second chapter offers a good example of the motives operating in the book:

> Un gradevole aumento di tensione fisica tutto il mio corpo vibra io sono molto eccitata le sensazioni sono tutte concentrate in un unico punto è una sensazione di leggerezza una scintilla quasi fremente sento una specie di elettricità. Poi gli operai dell'Autem la Autelco la Fargas e di tantissime altre fabbriche sempre più numerosi continuano a affluire gli studenti la polizia è completamente assente da tutta la zona il centro della città è completamente in mano agli operai in un'atmosfera entusiasmante. Una sensazione di vertigine di perdere me stessa come se non esistessi come corpo ma solo come sensazione come se ogni nervo del mio corpo diventasse vivo e cominciasse a pensare la sensazione di un nodo rigido che scoppia e fluttua improvvisamente e io apprezzo molto questa sensazione e sono piena di amore.
>
> (A pleasant increase of physical tension all my body vibrates I am very excited the sensations are all concentrated in one single point it is a sensation of lightness an almost quivering spark I feel a sort of electricity. Then the workers of the factories Autem Autelco Fargas and of so many other factories more and more numerous the students keep crowding the police is completely absent from the entire area the center of the city is completely in the hands of the workers in a thrilling atmosphere. A sensation of vertigo of losing myself as though I did not exist as a body but only as a sensation as though each nerve of my body became alive and started thinking the sensation of a rigid knot suddenly exploding and floating and I appreciate this sensation very much and I am full of love.)

In a modified stream of consciousness—a technique fully embraced in the first chapter that seems to be an homage to Joyce even in its content—the focus moves back and forth from the female subject to the workers' struggle in the streets. Balestrini thus deliberately frees his writing from the rules of grammar and syntax.

Among other political and intellectual activities in those years, Balestrini helped to found *Arena,* a short-lived center for publishing services that facilitated the distribution of the material of smaller publishing concerns. As the first issue of another ambitious project was ready for release—the magazine *Alfabeta,* which would be published the following year thanks to the efforts of Antonio Porta—a warrant was issued for the arrest of Balestrini and the other intellectual leaders of Autonomia (Autonomy), a militant leftist group. He was said to belong to an armed subversive group and charged with nineteen counts of murder, including one for the assassination of the former Italian prime minister Aldo Moro. Balestrini took refuge in Paris, where he worked for the prestigious publisher Gallimard. He chose to continue to live in exile in the French capital even after the so-called Trial of April 7 was held in 1984 and absolved him of any wrongdoing.

In the 1980s Balestrini continued to write and to be involved in cultural events despite his troubles with Italian authorities. In 1983 he founded another journal, *Change International,* and in 1984 he helped organize the international poetry festival at Cogolin, near Saint-Tropez. His works included the books of poems *Blackout* (1980) and *Ipocalisse: 49 sonetti, Provenza 1980–1983* (Hypocalypse, 1986), the latter being the first work he wrote after moving to Provence. He also returned to the series dedicated to "Signorina Richmond," publishing the second and third volumes, *La signorina Richmond se ne va: secondo libro* (Miss Richmond Leaves: Second Book, 1988) and *Il ritorno della signorina Richmond: terzo libro, 1984–1986* (The Return of Miss Richmond, Third Book, 1987).

In his fourth novel, *Gli invisibili* (1987; translated as *The Unseen,* 1989), Balestrini again makes wide use of the collage and laisses. Through the memories of the protagonist, a young man from the Milan hinterland involved in the Autonomia movement, he reviews the events of the second half of the 1970s, focusing on a few dramatic episodes: the occupation of an abandoned old castle called Cantinone and his arrest and interrogation. These episodes are interspersed within other narratives, including the revolt in the special prison where the protagonist and other political prisoners are kept, the confrontation with a feminist group, the internal conflict within the group that leads to the secession of some members, and the account of the experience of the isolation cell following the revolt.

Making use of the unpunctuated laisse he created for the first episode of *La violenza illustrata,* Balestrini in the first chapter frames the protagonist in the static impossibility of the present time of his trial. The reconstruction of the past is more fluid and has a conversational, though deranged, style and tone, especially in the most critical moments of the narrative:

> poi quando si è arrivati a quella riunione che ha deciso la rottura del nostro gruppo e che racconterò dopo dopo quella riunione di lui e di quelli che hanno preso la sua strada non si è saputo piú niente di lui di Valeriana di Cotogno e di Gelso se non dei volantini che rivendicavano le azioni armate che loro hanno fatto hanno fatto una serie di iniziative armate fino a questo carabiniere ma questo l'ho saputo solo dopo quando ero già dentro non hanno fatto morti hanno fatto rapine attentati qualche ferimento fino a questo carabiniere ma allora quando l'ho visto quella sera alla televisione con China non abbiamo pensato minimamente che potevano entrarci loro

> (then when we arrived to that meeting that decided the breaking off of our group and that I will tell later after that meeting of him and of those who took his way we would know nothing of him of wValeriana of Cotogno of Gelso but leaflets which claimed the armed actions which they have done they have done a series of armed initiatives until this carabineer but this I found out only later when I was already in prison they have killed nobody they have committed robbery attempts some woundings until this carabineer but then when I saw him that evening on television with China we did not think at all that they could be involved)

In 1988 Balestrini moved to Berlin, where he wrote *L'editore* (The Publisher, 1989), a novel in which he again analyzes political events in Italy in the 1970s, the decade of terrorism and profound social changes. The novel reconstructs the tragic death of the publisher Giangiacomo Feltrinelli (never mentioned by name), who was blown up by the dynamite he was apparently set to use in a terrorist act of his own. The somewhat detached tone of the investigation is justified by the intention of a few close friends of the publisher to write a screenplay for a film on his story. Among the friends a couple who separated just around the time of the accident play a major role. Political and private events intersect and condition each other throughout the narrative. The striking first chapter includes a detailed description of the autopsy, and several other chapters include newspaper clippings—either concerned with Feltrinelli or with current events. The last chapter offers a credible analysis of Feltrinelli's ambivalent life and a plausible reconstruction of his death.

With this novel Balestrini confirms not only his political engagement and his belief in the necessity of a full understanding of the historical events of the 1970s but also the essential role language plays in the search for epistemological as well as historical truth. Although his writing has moved away from the linguistic experimentation of *Tristano,* Balestrini remains one of the most interesting stylists in Italian letters.

Interview:
Monica Gemelli and Felice Piemontese, eds., *L'invenzione della realtà. Conversazioni sulla letteratura e altro* (Naples: Guida, 1994).

References:
Luciano Anceschi, "A proposito di un 'romanzo,'" *Il Verri,* no. 38 (1972): 88–93;

Renato Barilli, "Romanzi di tre 'Novissimi,'" in *L'azione e l'estasi* (Milan: Feltrinelli, 1967), pp. 161–177;

Filippo Bettini and Giorgio Patrizi, "*Vogliamo tutto:* neoavanguardia e ideologia letteraria in Nanni Balestrini," *Il Ponte* (December 1972): 1473–1485;

Giampaolo Borghello, *"Vogliamo tutto,"* Linea rossa. Intellettuali, letteratura e lotta di classe 1965–1975 (Venice: Marsilio, 1982), pp. 135–145;

Angelo Guglielmi, "Le tecniche di Balestrini," in *Vero e falso* (Milan: Feltrinelli, 1968), pp. 138–142;

Guglielmi, "Una favola primitiva," in *La letteratura del risparmio* (Milan: Bompiani, 1973), pp. 53–62;

Giorgio Manacorda, "Libello (su alcuni luoghi comuni della letteratura all'alba degli Anni Settanta)," *Nuovi Argomenti,* 27 (1972): 78–120;

Walter Pedullà, "Dopo la tragedia la farsa di Balestrini. . . . " and "Tristano parla chiaro. Il 'nuovo realismo' di Balestrini è una tigre di carta?," in *La letteratura del benessere* (Rome: Bulzoni, 1973), pp. 514–517; 522–526;

Pedullà, "Nanni Balestrini a cavallo della contestazione," in *Il morbo di Basedow ovvero dell'avanguardia* (Cosenza: Lerici, 1975), pp. 115–140;

Pedullà, "La teoria alla ricerca del significato," in *L'estrema funzione. La letteratura degli anni Settanta svela i propri segreti* (Venice & Padua: Marsilio, 1975), pp. 131–143;

Pedullà, "La violenza ha l'orgasmo con Balestrini," in *Miti, finzioni e buone maniere di fine millennio* (Milan: Rusconi, 1983), pp. 305–308;

Jacqueline Risset, "Forza della fiction," in *L'invenzione e il modello* (Rome: Bulzoni, 1972), pp. 210–212;

Risset, Preface, *Tristan,* French translation of *Tristano,* by Balestrini (Paris: Seuil, 1969);

Mario Spinella, Introduction, *Vogliamo tutto,* by Balestrini (Milan: Mondadori, 1988);

Francesco Varanini, "I frammenti ricomposti: romanzo della fabbrica e fabbrica del romanzo nell'Italia del boom e della crisi," in *Italianiatica,* nos. 2–3 (1982): 327–335.

Maria Bellonci
(3 November 1902 - 13 May 1986)

Angela M. Jeannet
Franklin and Marshall College

BOOKS: *Lucrezia Borgia, la sua vita e i suoi tempi* (Milan: Mondadori, 1939; translated and abridged by Bernard and Barbara Wall as *The Life and Times of Lucrezia Borgia* (New York: Harcourt, Brace, 1953; London: Weidenfeld & Nicolson, 1953);

Segreti dei Gonzaga (Milan: Mondadori, 1947); part 3, "Il duca nel labirinto," translated by Stuart Hood as *A Prince of Mantua: The Life and Times of Vencenzo Gonzaga* (London: Weidenfeld & Nicolson, 1956; New York: Harcourt, Brace, 1956);

Milano viscontea (Turin: Edizioni Radio Italiana, 1956);

Delitto di stato (Milan: Mondadori, 1961);

Pubblici segreti (Milan: Mondadori, 1965);

Piccolo romanzo di Dorotea Gonzaga, e altre prose, edited by Massimo Grillandi (Verona: Mondadori, 1968);

Come un racconto gli anni del Premio Strega (Milan: Mondadori, 1971);

Tu vipera gentile (Milan: Mondadori, 1972);

I Visconti a Milano, by Bellonci, Gian Alberto Dell'Acqua, and Carlo Perogalli (Milan: Cassa di risparmio delle provincie lombarde, 1977);

Rinascimento privato (Milan: Mondadori, 1985); translated by William Weaver as *Private Renaissance* (New York: Morrow, 1989);

Segni sul muro (Milan: Mondadori, 1988);

Pubblici segreti N.Z. (Milan: Mondadori, 1989).

Collection: *Opere,* edited by Ernesto Ferrero, 2 volumes (Milan: Mondadori, 1994–1997).

OTHER: Andrea Mantegna, *L'opera completa,* introduction by Bellonci (Milan: Rizzoli, 1979);

Gaspara Stampa, *Rime,* introduction by Bellonci (Milan: Rizzoli, 1994).

TRANSLATIONS: Emile Zola, *Nana* (Florence: Casini, 1955);

Stendhal, *Vanina Vanini e altre cronache italiane* (Milan: Mondadori, 1961);

Maria Bellonci (photograph by Paola Agosti)

Alexandre Dumas, *I tre moschettieri* (Florence: Giunti-Marzocco, 1977);

Marco Polo, *Il Milione* (Turin: ERI, 1982); translated by Teresa Waugh as *Marco Polo* (New York: Facts on File, 1984; London: Sidwick & Jackson, 1984);

Jules Verne, *Viaggio al centro della terra* (Florence: Giunti-Marzocco, 1983);

Stendhal, *La duchessa di Paliano* (Milan: Mondadori, 1994).

Active between 1930 and 1986, Maria Bellonci was a writer who met with considerable commercial success and was also the recipient of several literary prizes, including the coveted Premio Strega in 1985. Although she was fully aware of various trends in Italian literary life, she chose to follow her own path and fashioned a fictional form akin to the historical novel that might be called "document-based fiction." While scrupulously based on archival research, the books succeed as fiction because of Bellonci's deep understanding of her characters and her sensitivity to the flavor and atmosphere of the times in which they lived.

The historical period favored by Bellonci was the Italian Renaissance. She focused on the events, places, and characters of a society that is traditionally associated with the modern concept of political power and its penetration in all aspects of life. Her sight fixed on the fifteenth and sixteenth centuries, she depicted life at the courts of Italian princes and their struggles for hegemony on the peninsula. She explored various manifestations of power not in abstract terms but through the creation of complex characters. Her keenness of observation, empathy, and felicity of style are evident also in writings she devoted to twentieth-century figures, which may prompt readers to regret that she never wrote a fictional work set in her own times. Her interest in topics and characters drawn from the past was revived in the 1980s and 1990s among such women writers as Dacia Maraini, Francesca Sanvitale, Rosetta Loy, and Marta Morazzoni.

The oldest of four children, Bellonci was born Maria Villavecchia on 3 November 1902 in Rome to a family of the upper bourgeoisie that prided itself on its aristocratic roots. She would live all of her life in the Italian capital, whose charmed presence she evoked in many of her diaries and fictional works. Her father, Girolamo Vittorio Villavecchia, was a professor of chemistry at the University of Rome. Her mother, Felicita Bellucci Villavecchia, was much younger than her husband and devoted her life to the family. Bellonci's education was the standard one for many girls of her social class: excellent, thorough, and humanistic, with extensive grounding in the classics, music, and the arts. Her first literary effort was an unpublished novel titled "Clio e le amazzoni" (Clio and the Amazons), written when she was twenty and promptly discarded. The work occasioned her meeting Goffredo Bellonci, a prominent Italian critic and journalist whom she married in 1928. In the early years of their lifelong companionship Goffredo served as a literary mentor for his young wife.

Maria Bellonci's name is associated with the Premio Strega, the prestigious literary prize she helped found in 1944. During the final days of World War II, while the city of Rome was still in the throes of fighting and hunger, a group of literati began gathering every Sunday at the Bellonci residence. These "Amici della domenica" (Sunday friends), as they called themselves, formed the nucleus of the jury that henceforth voted to select the winner among works of fiction submitted by publishers and other sponsors. The Belloncis established the prize, which was funded by the Alberti family, producers of the well-known Strega liqueur. Maria Bellonci was director and manager of the prize for more than forty years. The authors who vied for the Premio Strega include the most important names in contemporary Italian letters.

Lucrezia Borgia, la sua vita e i suoi tempi (1939; translated as *The Life and Times of Lucrezia Borgia*, 1953), Bellonci's first published work, is a hefty volume whose central character is the famous daughter of Pope Alexander VI. The author pointed with pride to the rigorous research that enabled her to produce an eminently reliable biography as well as a popular book. Writing about Lucrezia, who lived from 1480 to 1519, Bellonci dissects the power struggles at the papal court with vivid detail, skillfully reconstructing the events and the passions that shaped the creation of the modern age.

At the beginning of the novel Lucrezia is a child and already promised in marriage to more than one nobleman by her politically motivated father. As an adolescent Lucrezia becomes a prized pawn in the power games being played by the Pope and other European potentates for the control of the Italian peninsula. She is first married to Giovanni Sforza, but the marriage is annulled. Her second husband, Alfonso of Aragon, is mysteriously murdered. Lucrezia learns to dissemble and dissimulate, exercising those forms of power that were a part of the ideal image of a Renaissance princess.

In her twenties Lucrezia is married to Alfonso d'Este of Ferrara. Bellonci portrays her as having become a woman without illusions, enduring "con la pazienza delle donne che hanno eletto per sé d'essere savie" (with the patience of women who have chosen to be wise). Neither the pleasures and magnificence of the brilliant Ferrara court nor the presence of an accomplished and well-educated young woman could dispel the continuous turmoil and the aura of deadly intrigues that haunted the powerful and the powerless alike. At the end, on her deathbed after yet another childbirth, she takes courage from every drop of blood she feels coursing through her veins and from every breath she is able

Dust jacket for Bellonci's 1961 novella, in which a Gonzaga family secret leads to a string of murders

to draw. Passion for life is her last form of resistance.

Bellonci provides a documented rather than a mythical portrait of Lucrezia and thereby rescues her from the lurid legends her life inspired. Rejecting the usual one-dimensional view of woman, she depicts this child of the Borgia not as a monster nor simply as a victim but as a complex participant in stories that involve powerful human passions: her darkly ambiguous bonds with father and brother; her thirst for elegance, wealth, pleasure, and power; and her conflicting feelings toward relatives, husbands, children, and lovers. Through it all Lucrezia's continuously refined ability to observe and adapt, to interpret and reflect, allowed her to construct a distinctive definition of herself in the midst of political and personal tragedy.

In *Segreti dei Gonzaga* (Secrets of the Gonzagas, 1947), another successful novel, the central figure is Vincenzo Gonzaga, who ruled Mantua in the last quarter of the sixteenth century. The book is comprised of three parts that are filled with dramatic events. Power politics is ubiquitous and invariably accompanied by intricate and dangerous love games set in the splendid, ostentatious courts of various princes. (The edition of the novel brought out in 1963 by Mondadori includes an appendix with a selection of love letters written by Gonzaga and an inventory of the jewels his family owned.)

The first part, titled "Principe a Mantova" (A Prince in Mantua), opens in 1562 with the birth of Vincenzo, son of the wise duke Guglielmo and a pious mother, Leonora of the house of Austria. The handsome and adventurous young prince is denied access to the government of the principality by his father. Kept away from power and finances, he becomes more and more capricious and irresponsible, giving his parents ever new reasons for displeasure and lack of trust. He is involved in adulterous affairs, duels, and several murders. The novelist introduces four women who are influential in Vincenzo's life: Barbara Sanseverino Sanvitale, an audacious, self-assured noblewoman who has a flirtatious friendship with the young man; Hippolita, who is the most devoted of his many lovers; Margherita Farnese, who is his first wife in a dramatic, unconsummated marriage; and Leonora, a member of the Medici family who becomes his second wife. The first part ends with the death of Duke Guglielmo.

The second part, "Duca nel labirinto" (The Duke in the Labyrinth), opens with Vincenzo's coronation and his effort to overcome the malaise he experiences when he assumes power. The Italian peninsula is the theater of never-ending rivalries among various small principalities that are fomented by the major European powers—Spain, Austria, and France—which use dissension and instability in Italy to their advantage. The new duke uses the strategic position of the two domains that make up his duchy, one in the region that is today Piedmont and the other in the lower Po Valley, to pursue his own political objectives. He is constantly negotiating acquisitions of land, fighting skirmishes with his neighbors and relatives, pursuing politically advantageous marriage contracts for his children, and engaging in military actions at the service of Austria or the papacy. Dreaming of wars that might revive the memory of the Crusades against the infidels, he fights three times to push back the Turkish advances in Hungary and Croatia.

Meanwhile, Vincenzo also has intense affairs with women whom Bellonci admirably brings to life. Leonora shows her keen political sense by orchestrating a court life that includes several children, the continuous flow of her husband's lovers, and all kinds of major and minor conflicts. Secure in her position as duchess and wife, she even governs the continuously endangered duchy when her husband is a prisoner or away from Mantua. Yet Bellonci records that Leonora wrote to her eleven-year-old sister Maria, who was destined to become queen of France, not to marry if she wished to avoid gathering the "bitter fruits" of marriage. Part two ends with the failure of the duke's dreams of glory and territorial expansion. However, he compensates for his disappointment by becoming one of the greatest patrons of the arts of the late Renaissance. He was a major sponsor of the *commedia dell'arte,* the innovative Italian dramatic genre characterized by improvisation that was destined to reap success all over Europe, especially in France, and as far away as Russia.

The third part, "Gonzaga solo" (The Duke Alone), treats the last years of Vincenzo's life. His palaces, by this time covered with precious frescoes and filled with artwork, attract even the great Flemish painter Peter Paul Rubens. Intrigues and dreams of expansion continue to occupy the duke's mind, but Leonora has become the true head of state, and the political intrigues leading to his son Francesco's marriage hold center stage. As Vincenzo lies dying, false accusations of treason and conspiracy cause a bloodbath in the neighboring principality of Piacenza, ruled by Ranuccio Farnese, and many among the duke's lovers and friends are tortured and executed. Providing a glimpse into the future, Bellonci indicates that with the imminent collapse of the Mantuan principality the art treasures gathered in the ducal palaces will be sold to the English king, and Austrian mercenaries will sack and pillage the flourishing city and its countryside. When they close the novel, readers realize that the word *segreti* (secrets)—a word frequently found in Bellonci's texts—does not refer simply to an aura of mystery but rather to the depths of human contradictions that cause the apparent inconsistencies of our actions and to the gaps and lies embedded in historical records.

Bellonci's stature as a writer of fiction and a cultural leader are complemented by the quality of her contributions to various periodical publications. *Pubblici segreti* (Public Secrets, 1965) is a collection of articles—book reviews, reports on cultural events, travel diaries, and reflections on contemporary issues—that appeared in the weekly *Il Punto* from 1958 to 1964. A second, posthumously published volume, *Pubblici segreti N.Z.* (1989), collects articles Bellonci wrote for *Il Messaggero* from 1964 to 1970. The title of the 1965 collection anticipates the title Bellonci was to give her major fictional work, *Rinascimento privato* (1985; translated as *Private Renaissance,* 1989). Bellonci's commentary and her coverage of public events reveal her intimate knowledge of the Italian cultural world. Her concise pieces demonstrate her consummate skill, attention to detail, and control of her medium. Their broad range attests to her intellectual curiosity, vast culture, and enthusiasm for life. The entire spectrum of Italian cultural life opens up, drawn by the inimitable pen of a woman who was a close observer of and often a participant in the significant events that took place from the 1930s to the 1980s.

Bellonci's reflections often cluster around three favorite subjects: the Italian situation during and after World War II (the Fascist period is curiously absent), the status of women, and the life of the senses, joyously evoked through the descriptions of human pleasures and the depictions of animals, landscapes, and cityscapes. Bellonci's sketches of women who excel in various fields—drawn with quick, colorful strokes that capture the individuality of the subjects—prove her to be a precursor of later feminists. She understood well the contradictions that fill women's lives, the power plays that define their destinies, and the inevitability of the triumph of what she calls women's "quiet revolution." The reader of these sketches would find it difficult to assert that Italian women were not influential during the first half of the twentieth century in fields such as literature, art, and politics.

Bellonci's book reviews and comments on literature are marked by keen insights, often revealed by a few swift lines. The literary life in Italy that emerges from her pages is active and intense. Her thoughts on literary matters, the results of experience with books, are sweeping. For instance, upon reading the letters of Honoré de Balzac, an author she admired, she writes: "Una dose d'ingenuità . . . è necessaria al narratore per credere alle proprie invenzioni—ed ecco perché oggi la nostra troppo scaltra narrativa produce libri freddi" (A narrator needs a bit of naiveté, if he is to believe his own inventions; that is the reason why our excessively clever fiction writers, today, produce frigid books). Another posthumous collection, *Segni sul muro* (Signs on the Wall, 1988), spans much of Bellonci's career and gathers materials that are in part fictional and in part journalistic. In addition to writing about some of her favorite places, such as Rome, Ferrara, Milan, and Mantua, she also comments on various writers, including Boccaccio, Carlo Goldoni, Virginia Woolf, Albert Camus, Anna Banti, and Primo Levi, whom she discusses in the context of their cultural backdrops.

Come un racconto gli anni del Premio Strega (The Years of the Strega Prize Told Like a Story, 1971) traces the events of a crucial part of Bellonci's life as a woman of letters. The history of the Premio Strega evokes the tragic atmosphere that pervaded Italy in 1944 and 1945 with its hardships and sorrows caused by the war. The elation over the end of the conflict is expressed in the moderate tones appropriate to someone who knows the price paid for peace and survival and also the regrets and remorse that inevitably follow any historical upheaval. Bellonci writes not only of the enthusiasm and energy that went into the establishment of a literary prize but also the fun that attended it. She also discusses the rivalries and excitement that surrounded the institution of the prize and the toll that such an intense activity took on her life. Clearly she made a crucial contribution to the revival of cultural life in Italy at a time when the country lay mortified by military defeat, torn by civil war, and weakened by physical devastation as well as economic ruin.

Tu vipera gentile (O, Noble Viper, 1972) is a collection of three of Bellonci's best novellas. The title refers to the coat of arms of the Visconti family that ruled the city of Milan for two centuries between the Middle Ages and the Renaissance; it shows a snake devouring an infant and is still widely recognized today as the logo of Alfa Romeo automobiles, which are built in Milan. In each of the stories, whether staged in Mantua or Milan, at the end of the Middle Ages or in the seventeenth century, the intricate political maneuvers of the Italian principalities are explored in all their complexity.

The first novella, "Delitto di stato" (Crime for Reasons of State), was originally published as a separate work in 1961 and in 1981 was adapted by Bellonci and Anna Maria Rinoaldi as a television drama. The work is composed of two parts, each told in the first person. The first part is a letter of confession written in the early 1600s by Count Tommaso Striggi, a learned and loyal courtier of the Gonzagas of Mantua. The second part is a letter by Paride Maffei, a young man who inherits Striggi's papers after his death and through them learns of a sequence of dramatic events. At the root of the drama is the accidental discovery of a lurid Gonzaga secret by a small party of people. To avoid the threat of a political scandal and to protect the honor of the Gonzaga family, Striggi perpetrated several murders. A chain of suicides and Striggi's assassination silenced all the witnesses to the family secret. In addition, Paride discovers two complicated love stories involving the Duke of Mantua, the deceased Count Striggi, and a beautiful girl, a sixteen-year-old singer named Flaminia. Before leaving Mantua forever, Paride hands to an abbot a written account of his tale of tragic and piteous events.

The title of the second novella, "Soccorso a Dorotea" (Help for Dorotea), is ironic because no help is forthcoming for the young Dorotea, daughter of Ludovico and Barbara Gonzaga, who ruled Mantua in the mid 1400s. She is jilted by Galeazzo Maria Sforza, heir to the duchy of Milan, and shortly thereafter dies. Her parents, already painfully tried by the physical handicaps that afflict some of their children, must cope with the cruelty of fate and the equally cruel reasons of state. They share with her the humiliation of rejection and then grieve her death.

With the third novella, which provides the collection with its title, Bellonci moves even further into the past. The story takes place in the 1320s, when the seat of the papacy was in Avignon. She tells the story of the Visconti rulers of Milan, from Ottone, who established the family's dynasty in 1277, to Filippo Maria, the last heir who died in 1447. In this celebration of the great city of Milan and its rulers Bellonci depicts a multitude of events that are as colorful as a fresco.

The novellas explore all aspects of our common human experience: love's secret passions

Dust jacket for Bellonci's 1965 collection of writings for Il Punto

bound with political transgressions, the fleeting movements of feigned emotions, the pain held inside in the face of pitiless onlookers, the questions asked in the secrecy of a conscience, and the mutual pacts made silently in conjugal love.

Bellonci's characters have the solidity and complexity of people the reader might know. Yet her clear presentation of the differences between the present and past centuries keeps the reader from a too facile and fallacious identification. The writer enters the recesses of individual consciences and personal relations, shedding light on the distinctive psychologies of individuals. She uncovers the hidden faces of greatness and shame and the existence of a peculiar logic that rules passions and emotions. The pride of the narrator/historian, as Bellonci explains in *Pubblici segreti,* is her ability to construct a universe out of elusive material: "quella sensazione temeraria di affacciarmi a panorami che sembrano aspettarmi—me sola—da secoli" (that reckless sensation of looking upon vistas that seem to have been waiting for me—only for me—for centuries).

In *Rinascimento privato* Bellonci chose a first-person narration to weave the story of yet another Renaissance noblewoman, Isabella d'Este. In order to explore every moment of her life, the author imagines the princess writing a journal in which she daydreams and speaks to herself, questioning her past actions and other people's motives and looking into the future. The first sentence of the book is one that could apply equally to both the princess and her twentieth-century interpreter: "Il mio segreto è una memoria che agisce a volte per terribilità" (My secret is a memory that works at times in awesome ways). Bellonci's exploration of the historical character of Isabella Gonzaga, who married into the Este family, was one of her most intriguing. Isabella appears briefly in every book Bellonci wrote, and this last novel, Bellonci's most powerfully constructed and most lovingly executed, is dedicated to her.

The Renaissance princess is depicted as a mature woman reflecting on her life and the events in which she played a large part. In the quiet of the "Clocks Room" in her palace she is poised at the center of a whirlwind of events. Still entangled with life's storms, she examines them from her study, which in a sense is her observatory. It is Isabella d'Este who utters the passionate words that convey

Bellonci's sense that the past is forever present: "Che cosa è il tempo, e perché deve considerarsi passato? Fino a quando viviamo esiste un solo tempo, il presente" (What is time, and why must it be considered past? As long as we are alive, there is only one time, the present).

Pride of action mingles in Isabella's spirit with the joy she finds in her sensuous lingering on the beauties of natural landscapes and her appreciation of the elegant magnificence of her rooms. Certainly a woman's condition is precarious, but as portrayed by Bellonci, Isabella's determination and lucidity distinguish her, even in an age such as the Renaissance that is peopled by exceptional individuals. Isabella has known rebellious urges and passionate love. She has shown obstinacy in political dealings and finesse in diplomatic matters. Yet she is also defined by tenderness, melancholy, compassion, hard-won wisdom, and a fierce sense of self in the context of family pride. She dared to assert herself, as the world threatened to annihilate her, by relying at times on her personal charm and her vanity, her elegant clothes and exquisite jewels.

The pleasures and torments as well as the friendships and rivalries that fill the lives of the women who were Isabella's contemporaries and peers have a nonstereotypical quality in Bellonci's novel. This Renaissance is private not because the novel confines women to the domestic sphere but because the writer redefines the era and what is womanly. The Renaissance, Bellonci says, is a complex phenomenon that includes not only public events but also the private dimension, including the details and emotions of everyday life that are such a major part of people's existence at all levels of society. Bellonci portrays women as diverse individuals endowed with many, and at times contradictory, qualities: gentleness and ambition, thirst for power and love of peace, determination, patience, and keen intelligence.

With *Rinascimento privato* Bellonci reaches the peak of her art, and Isabella reaches her fullest development. Readers feel this parallel in the intimacy that develops between the author and her creation as Bellonci mixes letters and diary entries to tell Isabella's story. The reader is aware of a double voice: Isabella meditates the events in which she was an agent as well as a clear-eyed witness, and Bellonci, more explicitly than at any other point in her career, creates through her character a means of self-exploration. Although all of Bellonci's female characters are articulate and literate, Isabella, like Bellonci, is a writer: the expression of her doings parallels Bellonci's passion for her own writing. It does not matter that ultimately the historical events were inimical to Isabella d'Este's political project and that she had to relinquish power to the hands of her ineffective son. Isabella's writing asserts her control over the brute forces of circumstance and time just as Bellonci's writing triumphs in rescuing the figure of Isabella d'Este from the prison of the past, the deformations of prejudice, and the threat of oblivion.

In Bellonci's writings written documentation consistently anchors her imagination. Yet the novelist has no fear that there might be a contradiction between the two, as is evident from her remark on the matter in *Segni sul muro:* "Ogni narratore è in realtà uno storico" (All narrators are actually historians). While she was thorough in her research, she also emphasizes her independence from the documents she consulted and her critical awareness that such data may tell a misleading and tendentious tale. A document cannot be trusted blindly since it inevitably eliminates, ignores, or downplays unpalatable truths, in short those things that make history the sum result of human complexities.

In Bellonci's view the novelist must tease out the secrets hidden in what is reported, as a detective does with the evidence; must reconstruct what was said and how, what was not said and why; and must use not only data, logic, clarity of vision, and critical acumen but also an understanding of human beings that includes at the same time distance and compassion. The writer's task consists of re-creating characters without doing violence to the logic of their psychologies, the givens of documentary evidence, and the spirit of the times. In addition, writing must be the expression of a living conscience for whom motives, contexts, and individual idiosyncracies are a daily experience, lived in the present. The writer's vision is truly comprehensive, and Bellonci sums up its most distinctive quality in a reflection on her trade in *Segni sul muro:* "Scoprire un segreto del passato significa sempre trovarsi di fronte ad un altro e più profondo segreto, legato per radici oscure alla nostra presente e comune qualità di viventi" (To uncover a secret of the past means to face another and more profound secret, which is connected through obscure roots to our shared humanity and our own present existence).

Bellonci's characters live in a context the author knows intimately and reproduces in its most minute particularities: it may be Mantua, the city where the writer spent much time consulting archival material, with its changing seasons as the backdrop for the tumultuous lives of the Gonzagas. Or it may be Rome in the light of the various hours of the day, not only as the place where Lucrezia Borgia moved as a young girl betrothed to princes and as a young woman weeping over murders but also as the sensuous city where Maria Bellonci hastened to meet her own bridegroom:

> L'estate romana è calda, ma ariosa: quando il cielo appare di un azzurro così teso che la speranza di una nuvola cade da sé contro quella purità arida e fonda, d'improvviso un vento, che ha l'arguzia e la velocità del fiato marino, guizza nei minimi angoli e nelle stradette della città, solleva le cose e gli animi con un movimento scherzoso, quasi un motivo musicale di fantasia.
>
> (The Roman summer is hot, but airy: When the sky hovers with a blue so intense that hopes of a cloud vanish against that deep and arid purity, suddenly a breath of air that is salty and fleeting like a sea breeze darts through the smallest corners and alleys of the city. It lifts objects and spirits with its playful movement, like a musical fantasy).

In her work Bellonci is commited to the principles that originated in the late nineteenth century and shaped early-twentieth-century literature. Writing for Bellonci is a life passion; literary creation is a willful construction; and literature is the field for the discovery of deep affinities among writers, across the centuries. For Bellonci, as for the great writers of Modernism, the act of writing is a statement of ethics and a special form of participation in epochal events. Writing has nothing to do with improvisation or instinct but is rather the expression of a well-trained intellect that rules over sensibility.

Bellonci appreciates the richness of female intelligence, which is never divorced from the senses and the real. Her clear-eyed commitment to literature places her in the company of Madame de Sévigné, Simone de Beauvoir, and Marguerite Yourcenar. Like her great contemporaries, Bellonci trusted written language even as she remained conscious of its weaknesses, flaws, and silences; she believed that through it one could truly "say everything." She reflected on language, perfected and elaborated it, fashioning it into a personal tool whose apparent spontaneity is the outcome of a long discipline.

In addition to her own writing Maria Bellonci translated Marco Polo's *Il Milione* and some French works. Except for what has been said in book reviews and occasional prefaces to her works, critical assessment of her writing is still lacking. She is practically unknown in the United States. However, the publication of her complete works in the Mondadori *I Meridiani* series confirms a continued interest in her work and her importance in Italian literature.

Interview:
Sandra Petrignani, "Maria Bellonci. L'indifferente," *Le signore della scrittura* (Milan: Mursia, 1984), pp. 47–56.

References:
Valeria Della Valle, "Una lingua moderna con una patina di antico," in *Rinascimento privato,* by Bellonci (Milan: Mondadori, 1989), pp. 561–570;

Massimo Grillandi, *Invito alla lettura di Maria Bellonci* (Milan: Mursia, 1983);

Angela M. Jeannet, "Maria Bellonci e i suoi segni," *Il Veltro,* 50 (January–April 1966): 149–153;

Carol Lazzaro-Weis, *From the Margins to the Mainstream* (Philadelphia: University of Pennsylvania Press, 1993), pp. 132–133;

Geno Pampaloni, *Storia della letteratura italiana: Il Novecento* (Milan: Garzanti, 1987), pp. 656–657.

Stefano Benni
(12 August 1947 -)

David Ward
Wellesley College

BOOKS: *Bar Sport* (Milan: Mondadori, 1976); revised as *Bar sport Duemila* (Milan: Feltrinelli, 1997);
La tribù di Moro seduto (Milan: Mondadori, 1977);
Non siamo Stato noi (Rome: Savelli, 1978);
Il Benni furioso (Rome: Il manifesto, 1979);
Spettacoloso (Milan: Mondadori, 1981);
Prima o poi l'amore arriva (Milan: Feltrinelli, 1981);
Terra! (Milan: Feltrinelli, 1983); translated by Annapaola Cancogni as *Terra!* (New York: Pantheon, 1985; London: Pluto, 1986);
I meravigliosi animali di Stranalandia, with drawings by Pirro Cuniberti (Milan: Feltrinelli, 1984);
Comici spaventati guerrieri: romanzo (Milan: Feltrinelli, 1986);
Il ritorno del Benni furioso (Rome: Il manifesto, 1986);
Il bar sotto il mare (Milan: Feltrinelli, 1987);
Baol: Una tranquilla notte di regime (Milan: Feltrinelli, 1990);
Ballate (Milan: Feltrinelli, 1991);
La compagnia dei Celestini (Milan: Feltrinelli, 1992);
L'ultima lacrima (Milan: Feltrinelli, 1994);
Elianto (Milan: Feltrinelli, 1996).

OTHER: Nicolas de Larmessin, *L'Arciboldo dei mestieri. Visioni fantastiche e costumi grotteschi nelle stampe di Nicolas De Larmessin,* preface by Benni (Milan: Gabriele Mazzotta, 1979);
Jacques Roubaud, *Il rapimento di Ortensia,* translated by Benni (Milan: Feltrinelli, 1988);
Francesco Tullio Altan, *Mix / Altan,* preface by Benni (Milan: Rizzoli Libri, 1990);
Coline Serreau, *Tuttosa e Chebestia,* translated by Benni (Genova: Marietti, 1993);
Philip K. Dick, *Se questo mondo vi sembra spietato, dovreste vedere cosa sono gli altri,* translated by Alberto Cristofori, introduction by Benni (Rome: Edizioni e/o, 1996).

Stefano Benni is considered by many to be the most innovative and talented of the group of young Italian writers including Aldo Busi, Andrea De Carlo, Pier Vittorio Tondelli, and Daniele Del Giudice whose work first came to critical light in the early 1980s. More than any of the others Benni has succeeded in blending together two of the functions that are conventionally attributed to narrative, for in his novels he both denounces the ills of society and experiments with the imaginative creation of new worlds. While funny and lexically inventive, Benni's novels, even when set in outer space, always address contemporary Italian issues. Deeply rooted in the recognizable political and cultural scene of contemporary Italy, they contain in disguised form bitingly satirical portraits of well-known politicians and businessmen.

Stefano Benni (photograph by Lucio Trevisan/Grazia Neri)

As even a cursory examination of Benni's novels reveals, he is above all a brilliantly imaginative comic writer. One of his sidelines, in fact, is to act as an unofficial script consultant to some of Italy's best-known comedians, such as Beppe Grillo, Paolo Rossi, and Dario Fo. Benni locates the beginnings of his comic talent in the solitary childhood he spent in the countryside around Bologna. This was an environment that enabled him to give full rein to his imagination. He was an avid reader of Anglo-American literature, and one of his childhood pastimes was to invent new and fantastic endings for novels, including Herman Melville's *Moby-Dick* (1851). This is a work that was to have an important influence on Benni's later writing, above all on the structuring of his narratives.

Benni has come to see the comedian not only as a purveyor of humor but also as an agent of political change. Free from institutional ties and consciously speaking from the margins of literary and cultural society, the comedian in Benni's view should consistently play the role of the thorn in the side of authority. This belief led Benni in his 1992 interview with Stefano Malatesta to express his disappointment with several promising comic talents whose compromises and television appearances have had the effect of blunting the revolutionary force and potential of their comedy.

As a comic writer Benni has been greatly influenced by the ludic style of Italo Calvino's *Le Cosmicomiche* (1965; translated as *Cosmicomics*, 1968) and by his friend Gianni Celati's early novels *Le avventure di Guiscardi* (The Adventures of Guizzardi, 1973) and *Lunario del paradiso* (Paradise Almanac, 1978). Going beyond the scope of his literary antecedents, Benni has taken the contemporary Italian novel further into postmodernist parody and pastiche. His novels draw on a bewildering array of precursors, his allusions ranging from Giovanni Boccaccio's *Decameron* of the fourteenth century to *Moby-Dick* of the nineteenth to contemporary Anglo-American popular culture.

Perhaps the greatest influence on Benni's writing from Italian literary tradition is the Lombardy-born novelist Carlo Emilio Gadda. Benni may be seen to be carrying on the plurilingual tradition associated primarily with the author of *Quer pasticciaccio brutto de Via Merulana.* (1957; translated as *That Awful Mess on Via Merulana,* 1965). However, whereas Gadda incorporates local dialects not usually associated with literary language into his novels, Benni's innovation lies in what might be called an "internationalization" of literary Italian. Hardly a page goes by in a Benni novel without coming across words or phrases drawn from Anglo-American pop culture such as references to titles and lyrics of British or American rock songs. Some of his modified translations of English words and phrases have found their way into contemporary Italian usage: "Policeman," for example, becomes "pulismano"; "manager" becomes "manàgero," which sounds like the Italian slang expression for "Dammit!" On other occasions Benni gives his readers long, Gaddaesque, lexically rich lists, such as the thirty-five names of fish he spells out in *Baol: Una tranquilla notte di regime* (Baol: A Quiet Night in the Regime, 1990) and the twenty-four varieties of discotheque at Rigolone Marina, Benni's invented name for the Adriatic seaside resort Rimini, in *La compagnia dei Celestini* (The Heavenly Company, 1992).

Another sign of Benni's inventiveness is in his renaming of well-known characters and things. "Coca-Cola," for example, is known as "Stracola," which could be translated as "Very-Cola." "Swatch" watches are called "Spatsch," a word that is similar to the Italian verb *spacciare* (to deal drugs). Some of Benni's novels contain entire sections that are either partly written in invented languages or are parodies of standard Italian. In one of his minor works, *I meravigliosi animali di Stranalandia* (The Wonderful Animals of Strangeland, 1984), Benni with the help of illustrations by Pirro Cuniberti describes the eccentric creatures and flora of a previously undiscovered land. He informs readers of the days of the week in "Strangelandese," the language spoken by the only inhabitant, Osvaldo. Monday (lunedì) in Strangelandese is either *luvedì*, the day one picks grapes (uva), or *lucidì*, when one chooses to wax (lucidare) the floor. Wednesday (mercoledì) is either *mermeldì*, the day one makes marmalade (marmelata), or *merdredì*, when because of bad weather or depression one wants to shout "shit!" (merda!).

Benni also finds new expressive potential in the supposedly degraded state of present-day Italian. In this he differs greatly from Pier Paolo Pasolini, a writer who feared that the inherent potential of the Italian language for poetic expression had been destroyed by linguistic contamination from the worlds of business and science as well as other languages. By writing ironically and wittily, Benni reclaims an expressive potential that Pasolini feared had been lost. An example of such reappropriation occurs in *Baol*, where Benni combines in one phrase of six words three monosyllabic imports from English and the world of advertising, describing the Bar Apocalypso as looking like "un set di spot di Brut"—a setting for a television commercial for Brut aftershave.

Born on 12 August 1947 in Bologna of working-class parents and brought up in the nearby countryside around Rioveggio, Benni moved back to the city in his mid teens to complete his high school educa-

Covers for four of Benni's books published in the 1990s

tion. In the 1970s he was drawn to the vitality of the night life of Bologna, which provided him with a source of comic inspiration. Benni's novels, especially his earlier ones, contain many elliptical references to the city, and readers who are not familiar with its bars, bowling alleys, and soccer culture may find some of his references hard to follow. For example, those who do not know that Helmut Haller and Turkylmaz were once special favorites with Bologna fans will be puzzled by Benni's unexplained references to them and to other doyens of local soccer. Benni has since become increasingly disenchanted with the embourgeoisement of Bologna and has spoken of the city as a little Switzerland, a city whose appearance of surface calm is belied by a rotten core. Nevertheless, Benni, a self-proclaimed "unmarried father" whose son was born in 1988, now divides his time between an apartment in the historic center of the city and a house in the country.

Benni's first book-length work, *Bar Sport* (Bar Sport, 1976), is an affectionate homage to the life that goes on in and around the kind of bar that can be found in almost any of the outlying quarters of Bologna. The book is structured around a series of mainly unconnected vignettes and stories that describe the eccentric locals and the events that take place there. A memorable character is the fake professor, who comically mistranslates Latin: "Fiat lux" (Let there be light), a phrase redolent of the Bible, becomes "Faccia lei" (You do it) and "Sine qua non" (Without which not), an expression used to denote something absolutely essential, becomes "siamo qua noi" (we're here).

Bar Sport is based on the same kind of short texts that Benni had previously freelance written for alternative left-wing daily newspapers such as *Il manifesto*, reviews such as *Foglio, Mago,* and *Linea d'ombra*, and for the weekly magazines *Mondo, Panorama,* and *Espresso,* the latter of which he left after a disagreement over its editorial policies. It was with such short pieces that Benni first made his name as a comic writer. Other short writings have been collected in *La tribù di Moro seduto* (The Tribe of Sitting Moro, 1977), the title alluding to Aldo Moro, a leading politician who was murdered by the Red Brigades in 1978; *Non siamo Stato noi* (We Are Not the State, 1978), which is a play on the expression "It's not our fault"; *Il Benni furioso* (The Furious Benni, 1979); *Spettacoloso* (Spectacular, 1981); and *Il ritorno del Benni furioso* (The Return of the Furious Benni, 1986). In the 1990s Benni has contributed infrequently to the satirical weekly *Cuore* until its demise in 1996.

Benni's first long novel, *Terra!* (1983; translated 1985), seems more akin to the structure of *Bar Sport* than to a conventional linear narrative. A science-fiction novel set in the year 2156 amid postnuclear-world-war desolation, it is the first of Benni's many experiments with literary form and genre. The larger narrative concerns the attempts to discover a new ecologically pure planet made by the spaceships of the three political alliances that are still contending for control of what remains of the earth. As in many of Benni's novels the major narrative thread is complemented by a parallel subplot. In this case it concerns the attempt of the old Chinese sage Fang and the nine-year-old child genius Frank Einstein to rediscover the Incan city of Cuzco, which is located in the center of the earth.

The most successful moments of the novel, though, come in the parentheses and meanderings that punctuate the main narratives and give the characters the chance to engage in long bouts of storytelling. The stories told by the astronauts and other characters include, for example, excursuses on why mice live underground and rabbits have long ears as well as on the strange names that have been given to equally strange planets by previous explorers. In a funny episode Benni recounts the attempts made by the captain of one of the spaceships to trap huge meteors. The whole interlude is played out as the twenty-second-century pastiche of a Melvillean whale-hunting story, with the meteors hurtling through space playing the part of the whales. In the seafaring story, one of Benni's favorite narrative models, extended storytelling is natural because sailors have vast amounts of time on their hands and tell stories to entertain themselves.

Although set in the suburban Italy of the present, Benni's second long novel, *Comici spaventati guerrieri: romanzo* (Frightened, Comic Guerrillas: A Novel, 1986), may be read as a companion piece to *Terra!* After experimenting with the science-fiction tale, Benni explores a second popular genre, the detective story, through which he pays an explicit homage to Gadda. The two novels have central characters with a similar relationship, Lucio Lucertola and his young assistant Lupetto paralleling Fang and Einstein of *Terra!* In both novels Benni's sympathies lie strongly with the disenfranchised who have lost out in the power game. In *Comici spaventati guerrieri* the victims are those who like Lupetto are confined to the margins of the vacuous consumerist culture that has replaced the humanistic ideals and values represented in the novel by Lucio Lucertola, the retired old-style high school teacher.

Lucio and Lupetto, believing themselves better detectives than incompetent police officers, set about solving the mystery of the murder of Leone, the young and promising soccer player and friend of Lupetto who is murdered outside a suburban condominium. Their investigation of the crime turns into a more general quest into the corruption of Italian society, which is represented by the inhabitants of the condominium. In a conventional detective story the mystery is finally revealed, but Stefano Tani notes that in Benni's novel in true postmodern parodic style "il giallo tradisce le aspettative del lettore, non offre cioè né soluzioni né giustizia" (readers' expectations are let down as the mystery story offers neither solution nor justice). Benni extends the responsibility for Leone's murder to the entire corrupt city and society.

With his third major work, the collection *Il bar sotto il mare* (The Bar Under the Sea, 1987), Benni earned the national reputation that was to establish him as a major figure in the Italian literary scene. While he remains faithful to the emphasis on storytelling that characterized the two earlier novels, Benni here exhibits a more sophisticated approach to narrative form. The work marks a watershed in his artistic development toward the more robust narrative framework of his later novels *Baol: Una tranquilla notte di regime* (Baol: A Tranquil Night in the Regime, 1990), *La compagnia dei Celestini* (The Heavenly Company, 1992), and *Elianto* (1996).

The retelling of already existing narratives provides the structural basis for the collection. The pretext for the series of stories that make up *Il bar sotto il mare* is furnished in the prologue. Walking along a beach one night, a character identified only as the Guest sees an old man enter the sea and disappear under the water. Following the old man, the Guest suddenly finds himself in a welcoming, warm, dry bar, frequented by bizarre characters who pass the time telling each other their stories. Benni offers no physical description of the storytellers, giving them only generic titles such as the "Man with the Hat," the "Sailor," the "Carpet Salesman," and the "Man with the Black Glasses." There is no standard approach in the twenty-four stories told. The longest is thirty pages, and the shortest, told by a flea in a black dog's coat, is just four-and-one-half lines.

Insofar as it illustrates the process of storytelling itself, the first story is of particular interest. Told by the "First Man with the Hat" and titled "L'anno del tempo matto" (The Year of Crazy Weather), it is the apocryphal account of a year in the life of the village of Sompazzo, a name that in Italian hides the phrase "sono pazzo" (I'm crazy). It tells of how one year the weather was so hot that apples turned to marmalade on the trees and eggs boiled before the hens could lay them (when they flapped their wings they produced already cooked omelettes). The story bears all the marks of a narrative that has gone through a series of retellings, for when a story is retold again and again new and exaggerated details are often added, extending it ever further into the realm of the hyperbolic.

Another story in the collection illustrates the same idea through a contest of insults. Told by the "Second Man with the Hat" and titled "Achille ed Ettore" (Achille and Ettore), this story concerns two lifelong friends who are unable to agree who should keep the racing bicycle that miraculously has fallen out of the sky. To decide who should keep it, they begin a competition to see who can insult the other more effectively. Gathering momentum, the insults build from the supposed secrets of unfaithful wives to involved descriptions of uselessness, sexual proclivities, and political views. The interest lies in the elaboration in language of harder-hitting, ever-longer, more-complex tirades, as when Achille attacks Ettore's right-wing politics:

> Carogna fetente di un fascistaccio più fascista di tutti i padroni fascisti della casa del fascio più fascista del peggio fascista che confronto a te Mussolini era un compagno che compagno a tresette ti ci vorrebbe Kappler e compagno a bocce il fuehrer che sei più fascista di un prete fascista e più democristiano di un treno di suore e fascista più di tutte le esseesse passate di qua e di tutti i dittatori del Vanzenzuela e di tutti i preti che c'è a Roma e di tutti i padroni che c'è al mondo.

> You stinking lump of dead meat of a lousy fascist more fascist than all the fascist bosses in the most fascist of all the fascist headquarters of the worst fascist, Mussolini was a communist compared to you; you deserve Kappler as your card-playing partner and Hitler to play bowls with; you're more fascist than a fascist priest and more Christian Democrat than a train load of nuns and more fascist than all the SS troops who passed this way during the war, more fascist than the dictator of Vanzenzuela, more fascist than all the priests in Rome and all the bosses in the world.

For Benni existing literary forms constitute a ready-made arena within which the renarration of stories can take place. Indeed, most of the stories in *Il bar sotto il mare* are recognizable as parodies of genres or styles if not of particular works: one story takes the form of the Faustus myth set in a Paris restaurant; another is a Melvillean seafaring story about a whale who falls in love with an English captain and lives happily ever after with him. There are also parodies of Edgar Allan Poe, Leo Tolstoy, American minimalist prose, Lewis Carroll's Jabberwocky-style language, Agatha Christie, and Oscar Wilde. Emerging from the text is the implication that renarration does not entail the elaboration of completely new forms but rather the appropriation and re-elaboration of existing ones. His appropriation of existing narrative forms suggests that the kind of renarration with which he is concerned is different from that of the strong poets or forgers of new vocabularies who have been in the forefront of recent critical theory. Benni's project is far less elitist, and he encourages the participation of his readers, just as he allowed the cover artist for *Il bar sotto il mare,* Giovanni Mulazzani, to interpret his narrators visually.

Mulazzani's cover captures the moment the Guest first enters the bar, thus subtly aligning him with the viewer or reader, for the storytellers are turned to regard their visitor(s). Thus, both guest and reader are invited to take part in the storytelling. Mulazzani has freely translated Benni's generic descriptions of his storytellers into recognizable figures, only some of which are motivated by textual details. The story told by the "Man with the Dark Glasses," for example, is introduced by a quotation by Vince Lombardi–"When the Going Gets Tough, the Tough Get Going"–which Benni wrongly attributes to John Belushi, a cult figure in Italy, particularly remembered for his role in John Landis's film *The Blues Brothers.* This explains why the "Man with the Dark Glasses" appears to be Belushi in the drawing. The "Man with the Cloak" is depicted as Edgar Allan Poe because his story is so obviously a parody of the type of horror story associated with the American writer.

On other occasions, however, Mulazzani makes independent interpretive choices by either choosing to draw a figure from his own stock of visual images or drawing them to resemble recognizable figures to whom there is no reference in the text. The storyteller called the "Blonde with the Red Dress" is drawn as a Marilyn Monroe figure; the "Sailor" looks as though he could have come from the set of Rainer Fassbinder's film *Querelle* (1982); the "Old Man," who is described only as wearing a gardenia in his lapel, is drawn to look a bit like Sigmund Freud. Mulazzani's various interpretive choices thus reinforce Benni's theme, the idea of narration as the ongoing retelling of stories.

The last of the stories is begun by the Guest, the stand-in for the reader, who must tell his story in order to exit the bar. The story he commences on the final page of the book and leaves unfinished exactly repeats the second paragraph of the prologue: "Camminavo una notte in riva al mare di Brigantes, dove le case sembrano navi affondate, immerse nella nebbia . . ." (I was walking one night along the sea shore in Brigantes, where the houses look like sunken ships, shrouded in fog . . .). How will the story continue? Will it replicate the text just read? Or will it be a renarration–like Mulazzani's drawing–that extends the text beyond its present borders? This is the question that Benni leaves with his reader, the new protagonist of the text-in-the-making.

Benni's next novel, *Baol: Una tranquilla notte di regime,* marked a successful return to the more linear narrative of his first two novels. Less dispersive than these early efforts yet no less funny or less bitingly satirical, *Baol* testifies to Benni's greater confidence and dexterity in negotiating the passage from short story to longer novel. Although his previous works certainly did not ignore the social realities of contemporary Italy, *Baol* reveals a more concerted effort not only to address specific issues such as the invasive nature of television in everyday life and the diminishing space for personal liberties but also to point an accusing finger at the responsible parties.

As in all of his texts, Benni in *Baol* draws on high as well as popular Anglo-American culture. The two most obvious subtexts are George Orwell's *1984* (1949) and Ridley Scott's film *Blade Runner* (1982), which was adapted from Philip K. Dick's novel *Do Androids Dream of Electric Sheep?* (1968). In *Baol* the role of Orwell's "Big Brother" is taken by an omniscient television company, based on Italian magnate Silvio Berlusconi's *Fininvest* empire, which includes television, publishing, and retailing interests and also owns one of Italy's top soccer teams. The television company employs a group of "reality composers" to reedit real film footage so that it can be used by the ruling regime for propaganda purposes.

Benni is especially concerned in the novel with the independence from institutional control that he believes a comic needs to fulfill a political function. The book and particularly the experience of Grapatax, an aging but inspirational comic, may be read as a kind of allegory for the uncompromised political role Benni has sought to create for himself. After the reality composers turn Grapatax's ridiculing of the regime's leader into apparent praise, the magician Bedoglian Baol–a figure clearly based on Decker, Harrison Ford's surly and cynical replicant hunter in *Blade Runner*–seeks to locate the genuine footage and broadcast it as inspiration to the Resistance. As in the film, where Decker must struggle with the question of what it is to be human, so in the final pages of the novel Bedoglian Baol is left with the fear that he may be no more than a piece of composed reality.

Benni's *La compagnia dei Celestini* was hailed by Alessandro Baricco in the May 1993 issue of *L'Indice* as "uno dei libri più importanti scritti da un italiano in questi ultimi anni" (one of the most important books written by an Italian in the last few years). A response to the Gulf War and the climate of increasing racial intolerance that has marked Italy in the 1990s, the novel is set in Gladonia, a name for Italy derived from the revelation of the existence of *Gladio,* a state-supported, underground, anti-Communist army that came to light at the beginning of the 1990s. It has been speculated that this group may have been involved in some of the terrorist atrocities that have taken place on Italian soil in the last twenty-five years. Many of the novel's most important characters are identified by their "Tesseraloggia" number, a reference to the P2, a rogue Freemasons' lodge that was involved not only in *Gladio* but also in many other political and economic scandals. One of the central characters, Mussolardi, is another caricatured portrait of Silvio Berlusconi, a consistent target for Benni's seething comic critiques.

Benni's novel tells of the attempts made by Mussolardi's giant television empire to discover the secret location of the world championships of "Pallastrada" (Street-Soccer), a game that is the emblem of clandestine, communal activity whose integrity would only be cheapened were it to open itself to the voracious appetite of the television cameras. In an unholy alliance between Mussolardi's company and the armed forces of a Norman Schwarzkopf-figure named John Buonommo (John Goodman), the high-tech but indiscriminate tactics of the Gulf War are used to bombard the site of the championship. For Benni the game's ability to escape the grasping hands of Mussolardi's television empire is also the measure of the extent to which Italian alternative society is able to resist the encroachments of a centralizing and hostile dominant culture currently sweeping Italy.

As in his previous work, Benni again places his hope for possible resistance in the hands of the disenfranchised. Like Pasolini, he believes in the vitality and inventiveness of those groups and individuals who have remained untouched by the process of embourgeoisement, the apotheosis of which is represented here by television. The heroes and heroines of *La compagnia dei Celestini* are a group of multiracial orphans who flee their orphanage in order to take part in the World Street Soccer Championship.

Like *Il bar sotto il mare*, *La compagnia dei Celestini* suggests that wit, inventiveness, linguistic dexterity, and the ability to tell stories are themselves tantamount to acts of resistance to the homogenizing effects of mass culture. To have and develop an ability to fantasize and create is for Benni to outsmart and therefore oppose the conformist nature of society. *La compagnia dei Celestini* offers an example of such inventiveness in a game called "Facciamo" (What if), which serves as a stand-in for Pallastrada when it cannot be played normally. In the new game both teams invent improbable scenarios that have to be equaled or bettered to win:

Facciamo che . . . il vostro campo era in salita e noi giocavamo in discesa . . .

Facciamo che viene il terremoto che pareggia il campo e si apre un crepaccio e voi ci cadete dentro e io sto per fare gol.

Facciamo che dal fondo del crepaccio viene su un geyser di vapore che a noi ci solleva in alto e a te ti bagna tutto così non puoi fare gol. . . .

(What if . . . your pitch sloped uphill and we were playing downhill . . .

What if there's an earthquake which levels the pitch, opens up a crater and you fall in it while I'm about to score.

What if a geyser comes up from the bottom of the crater, lifts us up and drenches you so you can't score. . . .)

Still only in his early fifties, Benni's future as one of Italy's leading contemporary novelists and humorists seems assured. His works have been translated into more than eighteen languages, including English. In his own country he is a best-selling novelist. *La compagnia dei Celestini,* for example, sold more than 250,000 copies, an enormous number by Italian standards. His recent work suggests that Benni has begun to envisage a more overtly political role for his fiction writing than he did at the beginning of his career. It seems likely that he will continue to celebrate imagination and individual creativity as themselves acts of rebellion and resistance to the reigning orthodoxy of mainstream culture.

Interview:

Stefano Malatesta, "Cari comici, siete a pezzi," *La Repubblica,* 14 October 1992.

References:

Alessandro Baricco, "Narratori italiani: Utopia nonostante la realtà," *L'Indice,* 10 (May 1993): 6–7;

Baricco, "Scrittori avari: cerchiamo il nuovo," *Tuttolibri,* 18 (July 1993);

Severino Cesari, Preface, *Il ritorno del Benni furioso,* by Benni (Rome: Il manifesto, 1986), pp. 7–14;

Stefano Tani, *Il romanzo di ritorno: Dal romanzo medio degli anni sessanta alla giovane narrativa degli anni ottanta* (Milan: Mursia, 1990), pp. 216–223.

Alberto Bevilacqua
(27 June 1934 -)

Eugenio Ragni
University of Rome "Roma Tre"

Translated by Augustus Pallotta

BOOKS: *La polvere sull'erba* (Caltanisetta: Sciascia, 1955);
L'amicizia perduta (Caltanisetta: Sciascia, 1961);
Una città in amore (Milan: Sugar, 1962; revised edition, Milan: Rizzoli, 1970);
La Califfa (Milan: Rizzoli, 1964); translated by Harvey Fergusson as *Califfa* (New York: Atheneum, 1969; London: Allen & Unwin, 1969);
Questa specie d'amore (Milan: Rizzoli, 1966);
L'occhio del gatto (Milan: Rizzoli, 1966);
Il viaggio misterioso (Milan: Rizzoli, 1972);
L'indignazione (Milan: Rizzoli, 1973);
Umana avventura (Milan: Garzanti, 1974);
Attenti al buffone: il racconto del film, saggi, altri racconti tematici (Milan: Garzanti, 1975);
La crudeltà (Milan: Garzanti, 1975);
Una scandalosa giovinezza (Milan: Rizzoli, 1978);
La festa parmigiana (Milan: Rizzoli, 1980);
Le rose di Danzica, edited by Cipriano Cavaliere (Turin: ERI, 1981);
Immagine e somiglianza. Poesie, 1955–1982 (Milan: Rizzoli, 1982);
Il curioso delle donne (Milan: Mondadori, 1983);
La donna delle meraviglie (Milan: Mondadori, 1984);
Vita mia (Milan: Mondadori, 1985);
La grande Giò (Milan: Mondadori, 1986);
Il corpo desiderato (Milan: Mondadori, 1988);
Una misteriosa felicità (Milan: Mondadori, 1988);
Il gioco delle passioni (Milan: Mondadori, 1989);
I sensi incantati (Milan: Mondadori, 1991);
Messaggi segreti (Milan: Mondadori, 1992);
Un cuore magico (Milan: Mondadori, 1993);
L'eros (Milan: Mondadori, 1994);
Lettera alla madre sulla felicità (Milan: Mondadori, 1995);
Anima amante (Milan: Mondadori, 1996);
Gialloparma (Milan: Mondadori, 1997).
Collection: *La mia Parma* (Milan: Rizzoli, 1982).

MOTION PICTURES: *La Califfa,* adapted from his novel and directed by Bevilacqua, 1970;

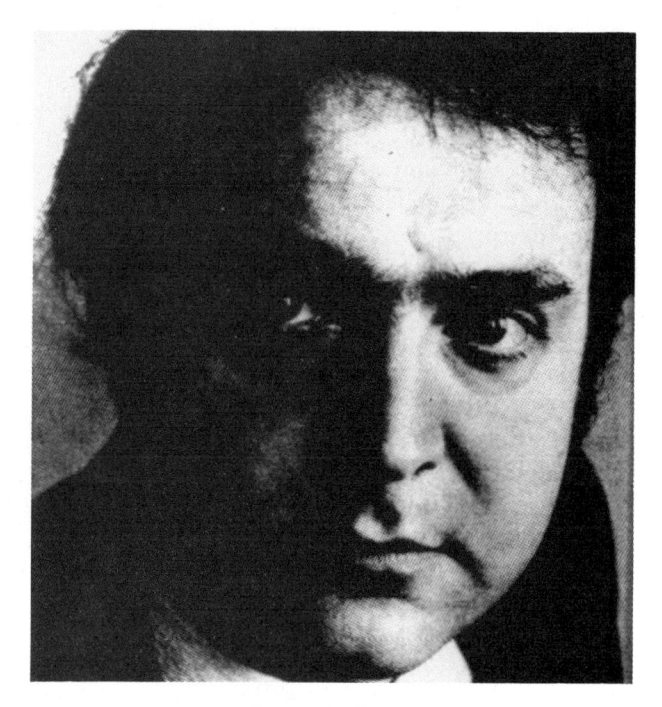

Alberto Bevilacqua

Attenti al buffone, written and directed by Bevilacqua, 1975;
Questa specie d'amore, adapted from his novel and directed by Bevilacqua, 1976;
Le rose di Danzica, written and directed by Bevilacqua, 1979;
Bosco d'amore, adapted from Giovanni Boccaccio's *Decameron* and directed by Bevilacqua, 1981.

OTHER: *I grandi comici,* edited by Bevilacqua (Milan: Rizzoli, 1965);
I grandi della risata, edited by Bevilacqua (Milan: Mondadori, 1995).

Alberto Bevilacqua's novels have the force and immediacy of experiences relived through memory. Although his dominating narrators often leave little room for the reader's involvement and interpretation and sometimes subject experiences to such intense psychological scrutiny that the progress of the plot is slowed, Bevilacqua draws readers into his work through the fluency and richness of his style, which seems especially engaging when he writes of his native city of Parma. He writes of marital relationships, existential crises, the inner life, and in his later works of paranormal phenomena. The enviable success of Bevilacqua's novels, from *Questa specie d'amore* (This Sort of Love, 1966) to *I sensi incantati* (Bewitched, 1991), can be attributed only in part to his fame as a television commentator and as a contributor to popular magazines. The clarity of his writing and his storytelling ability are appreciated by the educated middle- and upper-class readers who make up his audience. A prolific writer, Bevilacqua is the author of eighteen novels, seven volumes of poetry, and five collections of short stories. He has also written scores of articles and reviews for newspapers and magazines.

Most critics agree that Bevilacqua reached the high point of his career in the 1960s when he wrote *Una città in amore* (A City in Love, 1962), *La Califfa* (1964; translated as *Califfa*, 1969), and *Questa specie d'amore*, all of which he set in Parma. He republished these three and a fourth novel set in the city, *La festa parmigiana* (A Festive Parma, 1980), in a single volume appropriately titled *La mia Parma* (My Parma, 1982). The city is the author's fond projection of a lost paradise, a "città dell'anima" (a city of the soul). He presents the people of this city that opposed Fascism during World War II and prospered in the postwar economic boom as whimsical and sanguine, generous in giving as well as sinning.

Born on 27 June 1934, Bevilacqua was brought up in a neighborhood of Parma called Oltretorrente, a poor section of the city known for the rebellious spirit of its inhabitants, where even a factory worker was considered well off. Under Fascism, Oltretorrente was known as a "trouble spot"—"the most cursed parish in Italy"—and even the assistant bishop was afraid to venture there. It is said that he came once a year, on Palm Sunday, to celebrate a hasty mass. Bevilacqua spent his childhood and early youth in this environment; here he pursued his education, graduating from the law school of the University of Parma in 1956. In the course of his maturation the novelist established an intense love-hate relationship with his native city.

It is difficult to assess the novelist's relationship with his father, Mario Bevilacqua, who was called "Tano sulla moto rossa" (Tano with the red motorcycle) in Oltretorrente and widely known for taking part in dangerous sport activities such as acrobatic aviation. A confirmed antifascist, Mario Bevilacqua was, as his son recalls his childhood in a 1968 interview in *Il Pensiezo nazioale,* a husband and father too often absent from home: "Ebbi un padre che non vidi quasi mai e drammaticamente le poche volte che ci capitò d'incontrarci. L'ombra di questi fatti ha pesato sulla mia adolescenza, e dentro di me, e nelle pagine dei miei libri" (I hardly ever saw my father, and the few times I happened to see him, it was a dramatic experience. These circumstances have weighed heavily on my adolescence; they are within me and in my books). A father figure appears insistently in Bevilacqua's works; in *Questa specie d'amore* and some other works he is a recurring presence, both as a painful void and as an ideal projection.

On the other hand, Bevilacqua's relationship with his mother, Giuseppina Cantadori Bevilacqua, was close. She led a wretched and difficult life that resulted in her contracting a serious nervous disorder. Her presence in Bevilacqua's life and work is extraordinary, beginning with the first verses he wrote on a school day in 1947 which were later included in *L'indignazione* (Indignation, 1973): "Io cerco un ventre / orgoglioso e umiliato / per morirci teneramente / come ci sono nato" (I look for a womb / proud and humiliated / to die in it tenderly / as I was born).

By the time Bevilacqua's first book, *La polvere sull'erba* (Dust on the Grass), a collection of short stories, was published in 1955, the writer, who had just entered his twenties, had written poetry and acquired considerable experience as a newspaper contributor. Soon after his graduation from law school he began to work for the *Gazzetta di Parma,* first as a reporter and then as a contributor to the paper's biweekly literary supplement called *Il Raccoglitore*. Founded in 1951, this publication had become an important cultural organ thanks to the contributions of writers such as Attilio Bertolucci and Luigi Malerba, the scriptwriter Cesare Zavattini, and the publisher Ugo Guanda. Within a short time *Il Raccoglitore* drew the attention of important critics and intellectuals, among them Pier Paolo Pasolini, Giorgio Caproni, Oreste Macrí, and Aldo Borlenghi. Bevilacqua's poetry appeared in *Il Raccoglitore* as well as in *Botteghe oscure, L'Europa letteraria,* and *Paragone,* thanks in part to the encouragement provided by Bertolucci, who was Bevilacqua's art history teacher in high school.

Bevilacqua spoke of the foundation of his literary work in the April 1979 issue of *L'Informatore librario:* "Io nasco da una matrice lirica e quindi le mie componenti sono quelle della fantasia, del mistero, del verso" (My work issues from a lyrical matrix, and accordingly its constituent elements are imagination, mystery, and poetry). Clearly, Bevilacqua's poetry is an important part of his career as well as an influence on his fiction. The second notable feature of his fiction is the realism found in the novels that deal with the city of Parma and the surrounding plains of the Valle Padana (Po Valley)—the latter evoked by the youthful Bevilacqua as "terra di papaveri e di grano / . . . . promiscua / di violentate vite"; "terra dove si muore / lasciando sempre molti figli" (a fertile land of poppies and wheat / a land of violated lives / where people die / leaving always many children).

In Bevilacqua's youthful poetry the realism of familiar settings is softened while his poetic diction, expertly crafted and mildly colloquial, carries a personal imprint distinguished by a contemplative lyricism of nostalgic recollections. With remarkable stylistic awareness for so young a writer, the poet addresses his main themes: the painful and impenetrable mystery of life, his nagging doubts regarding the afterlife, emotions and relationships, and the representation of his native land as history, myth, landscape, and memory. Present throughout Bevilacqua's verses is his feeling of being unconnected to his time. Because he lives in an era foreign to his sensibilities, he views himself as the survivor of a shipwreck of ideas and ideals identified with an age that has come to an end. Both his poetic and narrative works betray an obstinate effort to return to traditional roots emotionally grounded in history, family, and region—an ideal setting where the writer is able to find individual fulfillment.

Bevilacqua has lived in Rome since 1956. In 1958 and 1959 he contributed regularly to *La Fiera letteraria,* and in 1960 he began to work for the Roman daily *Il Messaggero,* first as a crime reporter and then as a contributor to the cultural section of the paper. He has characterized the reporting experience as both formative and traumatic; perhaps for this reason the figure of the former journalist appears in *Questa specie d'amore* and *Umana avventura* (A Human Journey, 1974). Bevilacqua worked at *Il Messaggero* until 1966, when he was hired by Milan's prominent daily *Il Corriere della sera.* Introduced to the cinema by Cesare Zavattini in the early 1950s, he contributed to various scripts and began a long training as movie director that climaxed in his directing the movie versions of two of his novels, *La Califfa* in 1970 and *Questa specie d'amore* in 1976. In 1971 he married the poet Marianna Buccich.

In 1962 Bevilacqua published his first novel, *Una città in amore,* a work he revised and republished in 1970. In the December 1970 issue of *Uomini e libri* he wrote of his inspiration for the novel:

Parma, fin dai tempi in cui vivevo nei suoi borghi mi ha affascinato con il suo potere di evocazione poetica, dove il meraviglioso si fonde con il reale, con l'epopea, e anche la cronaca assume la suggestione della parabola. Potrei concludere che Parma diventa il teatro in cui inscenare con la massima evidenza le passioni del nostro secolo, il luogo in cui ai miei occhi si riflettono simbolicamente i luoghi della terra dove l'uomo è ancora uomo: con la sua rivolta contro la dittatura e la decadenza massificata e tecnologica, con il suo credere biologicamente, nella libertà, con i suoi amori di carne e ossa, le sue beffe, il suo humor. No, *Una città in amore* non è solo questo. È anche la storia (o la rivelazione) di Guido Picelli, una delle figure fondamentali del '900 politico europeo, rimasta per cause disparate ancora nell'ombra.

(As far back as the time I lived in her neighborhoods, Parma has fascinated me with her power of evoking poetic memories. It is a city where the wondrous fuses with the real and the epic, where daily living carries a creative aura. I can conclude by saying that Parma is the imaginary theater where one can stage with full evidence the major passions of this century, the place which, in my view, reflects symbolically the places on this earth where man is still man, with his opposition to dictatorships, to technological mass decadence, with his natural belief in freedom, his physical love, his jestful acts, and his humor. And yet *Una città in amore* is not limited to this. It is also the story (or the discovery) of Guido Picelli, one of the seminal political figures of the twentieth century, still ignored on account of disparate reasons.)

The novel reconstructs a barely known episode in the history of Parma: the resistance offered by the working-class district of Oltretorrente to the Fascist squads backing Mussolini's bid for power.

Following a legal strike called by the Socialist leader Filippo Turati, the Fascists in Parma destroyed the main offices of the newspapers and the leftist parties and sought through violence to occupy the town hall. The anti-Fascists of Oltretorrente resisted for five days by carrying out the tactics of urban guerrilla Guido Picelli. Eight persons died in the clash, but the superior forces led by Italo Balbo were unable to overcome the resistance of Oltretorrente residents and withdrew. The account of the heroism of that hot July 1922, in which Mussolini came to national power, is captured by a resident's retrospective remark: "Voi adesso dite abbasso i fascisti, Mussolini era un matto, ma è facile dirlo adesso. Noi lo abbiamo detto quando lui era duce, e a faccia franca lo abbiamo detto" (Now you say "Down with the Fascists!" or "Mussolini was crazy." It is easy to say it now; we said that when he was in power, and we said it without fear).

The novel's memorable characters include Alceste Dioguardi, called Bordino, and his son Benedetto, nicknamed Aile because according to him he had had a relationship "per un anno di seguito, ad Addis Abeba, con una ch'era stata la favorita di Aile Selassie" (for a full year at Addis Ababa with a woman who had been Haile Selassie's favorite mistress); Don Ersilio Campagna, a handsome and sinful priest known to his flock as "don Bell'Arma" (Reverend Handsome Weapon); the passionate couple Guido Picelli and Amelia Sampieri; and the youngster Giuseppe Ricasoli, alias José. Later, a thirty-year-old Ricasoli would fight "la guerra di Spagna, contro Franco" (against Franco in the Spanish Civil War). He remained in Spain to guard the tomb of Guido Picelli, killed in the battle of El Matoral by "una pallottola di un franchista, precisa sopra la sua bocca" (the bullet of a soldier in Franco's army, which hit him right above the mouth).

Narrated by an eyewitness of the Resistance, a stand-in for the author who tells the various tales of the armed struggle against Nazism and Fascism, the novel strikes a balance between compelling narrative and historical fact, between melodrama and civic passion. First- and third-person narration alternates in the book, the first person representing the author whose stories and vivid accounts were based on those told by his mother and grandmother. The Resistance is surely worthy of being brought to life and serves as well as an exemplary counterpoint to the squalid contemporary reality of a community no longer "in love," having lost the feeling of love and the passionate drive of "amori da scriverci sopra" (loves worth writing about). The Parma with which Bevilacqua identifies is removed not so much in time as in moral climate, suggesting the alienation he feels with the modern reality.

A comparison of the original edition of *Una città in amore* and the revised version shows a refinement of the framework of the novel. The revision is also notable for including local forms of speech and political documents omitted initially, according to the author, out of a fear of censorship. The improvements can be traced in part to Bevilacqua's artistic growth and maturity, for during the interim he published three of his most significant novels.

La Califfa, Bevilacqua's second novel, is centered on the story of Irene Corsini, known as Califfa. Bevilacqua explains in the 22 July 1964 issue of *Lavoro nuovo* that in much of the Po Valley in northern Italy the word *Califfa* identifies "donne (giovani, aggressive, belle) che riescono ad imporsi con il loro temperamento, con la loro idea della vita: un'idea anti-conformista—sia nell'amore che nei rapporti sociali—accompagnata da una purezza di fondo" (young women, aggressive and beautiful, who are able to assert themselves through their temperament and vision of life, a vision which is nonconformist in terms of social and emotional relationships and is accompanied by an element of innocence). Through Corsini's experiences Bevilacqua portrays an urban community divided into two parts by a river that also marks the social division of its inhabitants. On one side is the prosperous middle class made up of entrepreneurs and the owners of small and medium-sized industries, and on the other are the working-class people living in the less attractive sections of the city.

The discreetly private love affair between Califfa and a rich businessman, Annibale Doberdò, is a telling commentary on the economic prosperity of the late 1950s, a period when there were signs of possible cooperation between factory workers and management. According to Luigi Scorrano in his book on Bevilacqua, Califfa and her lover "riassumono tutte le altre presenze del proprio ambiente nel senso che ne hanno assorbito vizi e virtù in misura 'esemplare' e mentre vivono di vita propria rispecchiano quella di coloro che li circondano" (personify all the other human types of their environment in the sense that they have absorbed, in an exemplary fashion, their virtues and flaws, and while they lead their own lives, they also reflect the lives of people around them).

Singled out by Doberdò's binoculars at the Teatro Regio during a performance of *Aida,* Califfa a few days later "crosses the bridge" like so many attractive women of humble background—"povere cagne attratte dalle enormi immondizie di un benessere superfluo ... partono per un oscuro viaggio anche se non percorrono che poche decine di metri" (poor bitches drawn by the heaps of garbage of excessive prosperity ... they leave for an unknown voyage even though they only walk a few yards). But such women remain separated from the new world they desire; their struggle, besides being futile, "diventa un inferno individuale" (turns into a personal hell). Instinctive and sincere, Califfa is deeply troubled by her new life of secrecy:

> L'onestà di andare in fondo alle cose, chi ce l'ha in questa Italia lazzarona, dove tutti, i loro peccati li nascondono come beni di contrabbando, solo per puntare il dito contro le debolezze degli altri? .... Io, invece, una di quelle che badano all'apparenza e poi fanno i loro comodi allo scuro, non lo sono stata mai: l'Irene Corsini, detta Califfa, quello che ha dentro ce l'ha in faccia, e costi quel che costi!

> (Who is honest enough to go to the bottom of things in this wretched Italy where people hide their sins like contraband only to point a finger at the weaknesses of others? .... I have never been one of those who are careful

about appearances but do what they please in the dark. I, Irene Corsini called Califfa, I carry on my face what I feel inside, and let the chips fall where they may!)

The beautiful Califfa leaves behind a difficult life, but she is determined to face the obstacles erected by a social class that is clearly hostile to her. Her relationship with Doberdò starts as erotic flirting on the part of a newly enriched businessman, but it evolves gradually into a serious matter marked by love, understanding, and respect.

Engaged in an unscrupulous race for wealth, Doberdò rediscovers through Irene the meaning of love, charity, and solidarity—values that he, having become wealthy and powerful through marriage, had relegated into the recesses of his conscience. He had become

> simbolo vivente di una categoria sociale che il fascismo doveva arricchire senza poi travolgerla nel suo crollo, che i preti dovevano benedire anche nei suoi peccati e alla quale la guerra doveva offrire, dal desolato deserto, i fiori amari della speculazione.

> (a living symbol of a social class which Fascism was to enrich without taking it along when it collapsed, a class which was blessed by the priests along with its sins, to which the war was to offer, from the desolate desert, the bitter flowers of speculation.)

The understanding between the lovers, though, occurs between two individuals of the same class. The bridge that joins the two parts of the city remains only an illusory means of communication between the down-to-earth families of the workers and the well-to-do bourgeoisie, whose comforts have made them pregnant with falseness and egotism. As a class the wealthy are capable of transforming spontaneous emotions into calculation; they pigeonhole people into social roles and enforce rigid rules of behavior.

Irene's vitality and nonconformist lifestyle do not penetrate at all the shield of selfishness and class-conscious isolation carried by the people that move within Doberdò's social milieu. She is tolerated solely out of respect for what everyone regards as yet another erotic whim by the boss, and upon his sudden death Califfa is left with no choice but to cross the bridge once more to regain her former identity. The losers, however, are those she leaves behind in that inferno dressed as heaven which entices and destroys. One of the most contemptible of such beings bids her goodbye with these words:

> Quando penserà a me, a me e alle altre persone che ha conosciuto in questo ambiente, cerchi di non detestarci troppo.... Il mondo non lo abbiamo fatto noi, e se è vero che la vita è una bolgia, è giusto che ci siano anche i diavoli... Perchè se un santo dovrà nascere, nascerà anche per merito nostro, perchè ci siamo noi.

> (When you think about me and the other people you have met in this part of town, try not to hate us too much.... We did not make the world, and if it is true that life is hell, it stands to reason that there are devils... And if a saint is born, it is also our merit, because we are here.)

A comparison of *La Califfa* and *Una città in amore* underscores Bevilacqua's progress in style and narrative design. In both works he uses first- and third-person narration, alternating sections in which characters tell their own stories with those in which the narrator is a stand-in for the author, but there is a significant inversion: in *Una città in amore* the primary first-person narrator is an artifice, the authorial stand-in who connects and conveys the various narrative threads of the novel; in *La Califfa* it is the voice of the protagonist, Irene, that is present from the first page. She narrates firsthand the salient events of the story and communicates impulses, reflections, and intimate feelings with the immediacy and the color of experienced reality. In this fashion the second work preserves verisimilitude even in those passages that are marked by proletarian rhetoric and insistent psychological excursions. *La Califfa* offers a unified, harmonious work marked by two narrating voices—the passionate and impetuous voice of the female protagonist and the more terse and objective voice representing the author—that complement one another.

It is perhaps the contrast of the narrating voices, lending to *La Califfa* a flair of quasi-playful melodrama, that in addition to lightening the tone of the story enables Bevilacqua to avoid the trap of a facile and outdated sentimental representation of the poor. Equally evident is the novelist's considerable ease in fashioning dialogue, for every line answers a logical need. Exemplary in this regard is the dialogue between two religious figures, Monsignor Martinolli and the "Monsignor from Rome." In addition remarkable visual descriptions sustain group scenes, such as the workers' strike and the death of Irene's husband, Guido. It is not a coincidence that in 1970 Bevilacqua was asked to direct the movie adaptation of *La Califfa*.

La Califfa also has a greater symbolic relevance to society than does the first novel. The characters of *Una città in amore* remain tied to the Parma of 1922 as re-created fifty years later by a young man who saw his town as a paradise lost. In its broad outlines the city that serves as the setting for *La Califfa* is the same, but Bevilacqua blunts Parma's physical distinctiveness and instead sharpens its Manichaean division into "la città del popolo" (the city of common folks)—also called "il povr'almi" (the city of poor souls)—and "quella dei borghesi e degli agrari" (the city of the middle class and rich landowners). While still maintaining the conventions of the realistic novel Bevilacqua through this polarization is able to suggest fundamental questions of social and ethical significance. The work takes on a symbolic dimension and ultimately casts a harsh judgment on the economic prosperity of the late 1950s that widened the gap between the rich and the poor and deepened the crisis of moral values.

Questa specie d'amore, perhaps Bevilacqua's most representative novel because it brings together the themes treated in previous works, shows his gift for introspection as well as his mastery of narrative and his ability to balance historical events and fictional elaboration. The setting is again the Oltretorrente section of Parma, but here Bevilacqua focuses on a problematic marriage. The political situation of the 1960's disrupts the privacy of a family, affecting irrevocably its foundation.

The move to Rome by the main character, Federico, who is a reporter for a tabloid, sparks the long, analytical, and often merciless account of an apparently perfect marital relationship that is undermined at the base by a strong emotion disguised as love. The diary-letter that Federico writes to his wife becomes the balance sheet of a marriage that he feels lacks absolute commitment. He is completely absorbed by professional ambition to the point of forgetting and even denying his painful past. She, on the other hand, leads a sheltered life, protected first by her family and then by her husband "con l'intransigenza di chi intendeva proteggere in realtà il proprio egoismo, per cui la capacità a soffrire le si era atrofizzata" (with the intransigence of one who sought really to protect her egoism and as a result of which her ability to endure suffering had worn out). The two live together only in a physical sense, for their difference in social background and upbringing and, more importantly, their selfishness and the necessity of yielding to the hypocrisy of compromises have blocked real love.

Although the subject of a marital crisis was common in the 1960s when the end of Neorealism led to a focus on individual rather than social concerns—one recalls in particular the success of Giuseppe Berto's *Il male oscuro* (1964; translated as *Incubus,* 1966)—Bevilacqua's intent is quite different than those who focused on such a crisis per se. Without forsaking the social realities around him—the advent of the economic boom and the consumer society and the hard-fought referendum for the legalization of divorce, which led to a new law in 1969—Bevilacqua highlights the cultural and existential issues that had a profound effect on him; he thus creates a protagonist who stands as an emblem of the time. As he faces his own incipient physical deterioration, Federico comes to realize that life is a short-lived gift. In his diary he offers a clear account of his moral conduct through the lucid and somewhat masochistic analysis of his marriage. The roots of Federico's crisis, recollections of which he suppresses at first because they are painful, reach back to his native soil. These same memories return later, not as negative resonances but as models of felicitous existence.

Parma serves as a counterpoint to modern, sophisticated Rome, but here Parma is not the ideal of *Una città in amore* or the class-conscious city of *La Califfa*. Instead it is the home of Federico's parents, ordinary folks who were raised in a healthy, provincial environment and thus represent that part of society still capable of loving. Such people have endured suffering and social injustices, which has perhaps led them to believe in a life of moral values as opposed to one of compromises and shortcuts. Mother and father, "coppia di vecchi uccelli fedeli sopra un trespolo" (an old couple of faithful birds on a perch), are not symbols of a world that has receded in the past and is no longer viable; they are instead symbols of a vital world marked by real love, history, and certainties grounded in time-tested values. Their world stands in contrast to the presumption and illusory pursuits of a new generation that has built its future on shifting sands.

Less a study of a marital relationship than a quest for a lost dimension in personal life, *Questa specie d'amore* is perhaps best read as a book about the recovery of the father figure, "non di chi attacca, ma di chi si deve difendere, non di chi crea, ma di chi deve subire le conseguenze: padre che camminava a testa nuda sotto il sole, cranio rosso di fatica dove la prigionia e la guerra avevano distrutto per prima cosa i capelli" (not of an aggressive individual but one who is placed on the defensive; not one who causes consequences but one who must suffer them: a father who walked under the sun, his head bare and red from labor, a bald head attesting that the war and the years in prison had first wiped out his hair). It is not an accident that the scenes in which the father appears as the protagonist are—as is the case with other works by Bevilacqua—the most intense. In Bevilacqua's adaptation of the novel for film the father stands out as a figure who does not yield to facile lyricism and so becomes a painful symbol of authentic feelings.

The next novel, *L'occhio del gatto* (The Cat's Eye, 1966), confirms Bevilacqua's proclivity for an emblematic narrative anchored to historical reality. It too is a complex novel evolving around a marital crisis, but its main theme is clearly the violence of contemporary life, which Bevilacqua has confronted with increasing conviction in his later works. He believes that ever-present violence poisons and overwhelms people, forcing them into two groups: oppressors and oppressed. People seem to him to have a congenital need to ignore violence until they become victims and refuse to intervene and assume responsibility until something or someone forces them to open their eyes.

The protagonist is Marcello, a documentary filmmaker who becomes "enlightened" when he embarks on a trip to "uno dei tanti vulcani o inferni clandestini sui quali ora strepita il mondo" (one of those volcanoes or hidden hells present in our world today). In an unnamed Far Eastern country where people die like insects, the coldly objective Marcello captures with his camera dramatic impressions of the results of violence: houses in ruins and corpses of tortured men lying about. He becomes aware of the "cancer" that eats away human conscience and leads people to accept those who are driven by the thirst for power. Because Marcello's wife leaves him for a crude but wealthy man, Marcello assumes the detached, ironic look of a cat—hence the title—and attains "il potere di vedere e di giudicare prima che gli altri se ne accorgano" (the power to see and to judge before others become aware of it). Marcello's heightened perception of individual conduct leads him to see his wife and her lover as emblematic negative figures of contemporary life, marked by bad taste, insensitivity, and complicitous indifference.

Bevilacqua's book of verse *L'indignazione* (Indignation, 1973) shows his bitter recognition that man is incapable of eradicating evil or of stopping himself from promoting it. He suggests there is no answer to the eternal, anxiety-ridden question of *why?* in regard to the pain of existence other than the absence of God or his indifference toward a newly crucified, modern man for whom no resurrection is in store. The only ray of hope rests on friendship and solidarity among individuals who are aware of inhabiting a world on the verge of collapse and stand ready to combat the aberrations of a corrupt and corrupting age. In an interview given the same year of the publication of the volume, Bevilacqua remarked on the importance of writing poetry: "La poesia ha rappresentato il segreto *alter ego* del narratore. Essa non ha mai smesso di dare i suoi frutti accanto al suo partner creativo: anche se questi frutti sono rimasti nell'ombra" (Poetry has represented the secret *alter ego* of [my] activity as narrator. It has never stopped yielding fruits together with its creative partner even though such fruits lay in the shade).

In the poems collected in *La crudeltà* (Cruelty, 1975) Bevilacqua delves further into the existential condition, focusing on the relationship between life and death. Life is seen as a prison inside which the suffering poet questions himself; he becomes anxious realizing that he can offer nothing but commiseration to a humanity waiting for answers:

Mio fratello che di fronte mi siedi
per giorni; che mi parli con occhi
senza vista .
. . . .
          Ti ruoto intorno
col mio pensiero, più oltre non so andare
d'un faro sopra un mare di relitti.

(My brother seated opposite to me
for days on end; you speak to me with eyes
that don't see .
. . . .
          I surround you
with my thought, but I can go no farther
than a beacon on the waters of a shipwreck.)

Between these volumes of poetry Bevilacqua published his fifth novel, *Umana avventura* (1974), the story of a journey with allegorical undertones. Instead of a realistic approach Bevilacqua presents a series of "mirages," identified with the protagonist's mysterious, lyrically rendered, painful visionary experiences. On the most superficial level the work deals with an archaeologist and his discovery of a city at the bottom of the sea near the Greek island of Delos. He keeps the discovery secret even from his daughter, who intervenes to save him from drowning. The secret city touches the archaeologist deeply and sparks a process of spiritual awakening that leads him to seek redemption at all costs.

The journey to the city buried in the depths of the Aegean Sea is a quest for truth, and in this regard Bevilacqua's work shares clear analogies with Dante's *Divine Comedy*. As in Dante's work the protagonist of *Umana avventura* symbolizes the yearning of mankind to abandon the "forest" of the contemporary world and seek genuine meaning for human existence. Like Dante's pilgrim who has to go through the cleansing stage of Purgatory before he experiences revelation, the archaeologist is able to return to the underwater city only after a cathartic experience reveals to him the emptiness of his life. The archaeologist is the symbol of contemporary man, who has only his past to fall back upon, and his past is now in the depths of his subconscious.

In an interview with Stelio Cro, Bevilacqua discusses the larger meaning of his allegory:

> Protagonista di questo libro è l'Europa. Delo e le isole adiacenti sono usati come luoghi metaforici per indicare appunto una classicità distrutta, una classicità sprofondata nel marcio della storia. In un certo senso l'individuo contemporaneo nella sua visita, nella sua discesa agli inferi, addirittura esemplificata all'inizio dall'immersione, non può che scontrarsi con le regioni remote della sua storia. Quello che m'interessava era di esaminare il crollo della cultura europea.
>
> (The real protagonist of this book is Europe. Delos and the adjacent islands are metaphorical places identifying a classical civilization which has been destroyed, a civilization confined to the rotting depths of history. In a sense the contemporary individual in his journey to hell, clearly suggested at the beginning of the novel through the immersion in the sea, cannot but confront the distant regions of his history. What interested me was to examine the collapse of European culture.)

What Bevilacqua seems to convey in this book is that it is no longer possible to seek refuge in the past, to exhibit the past like a passport, as something valid and useful. In the allegorical framework of the novel the daughter seems to represent the elusive modern reality; Parma and Rome respectively symbolize ancient Jerusalem and Babylon; and the submerged city stands for both a lost cultural Eden and the womb capable of regenerating Western culture. Adolfo Bioy Casares asserts that *Umana avventura* marks "il punto più alto della narrativa di Bevilacqua, *su obra maestra*" (the highest point of Bevilacqua's work, his masterpiece).

The novels that follow *Umana avventura* are generally not as noteworthy and do not show any remarkable development. *Una scandalosa giovinezza* (A Scandalous Youth, 1978) presents a woman protagonist, Zelia Grossi, who has much in common with Califfa though she moves in a different social setting, the lower Po Valley, which is examined with meticulous attention. As in previous novels the main character takes on symbolic significance.

Much more successful is *La festa parmigiana* (A Festive Parma, 1980), which is made up of eccentric local stories from the past and recent times in which the common thread is love. Says a character: "Parma, ormai, è un'altra: un luogo del mondo come tanti, senza più solennità né pietà. Ha subito una flessione verso la violenza e la sopravvivenza" (Parma is no longer the same; it is a place like many others, having lost its solemn and religious atmosphere. It has experienced a bent for violence and survival). He goes on to compare the city to "una delle adolescenti di oggi: dal sesso tempestoso, ma senza felicità" (one of today's adolescents, given to passionate lovemaking devoid of happiness). According to Giuseppe Amoroso, Bevilacqua skillfully uses irony to chart moral and spiritual landscape familiar to his work.

In 1982, after nearly thirty years of writing poetry, Bevilacqua published *Immagine e somiglianza. Poesie, 1955-1982* (Image and Likeness), a text that combines previously published as well as new verses. In the preface the poet asserts that his poems are offered as "articolazioni interne di un itinerario che solo qui si presenta nella sua completezza e sostanziale omogeneneità" (inner expressions of a trajectory that stands out for its completeness and substantial unity). The volume was not conceived as a chronological document but as a "bilancio di lavoro" (balance sheet), providing a record of Bevilacqua's development and attesting to a fresh point of departure. From his scrupulous process of revision Bevilacqua's poetry emerges as better focused and more sharply defined than ever before. He uses irony to create a vision of the future that contains a ray of optimism:

> Un fondo
> di riso m'è rimasto in cuore
> non mio, chissà di quale
> smarrita felicità.
> . . . .
> Ora, fra poco,
> dovrò pur ritrovarla la lampada.
> Era qui
> un eterno fa.
>
> (A residue
> of laughter is left in my heart
> not mine, who knows of what
> strayed happiness.
> . . . .
> Now, shortly,
> I must find my lamp.
> It was here
> so very long ago.)

While Bevilacqua is known primarily as a novelist, his poetry does not deserve the label of "minor work" or to be considered subordinate to his fiction. In contrast to his prose Bevilacqua's verse attests to a process of harmonious synthesis and convergence; his collections unfold both as an autonomous and parallel activity with respect to the narrative.

In the novels *Il curioso delle donne* (The Strange Thing about Women, 1983) and *La donna delle meraviglie* (The Marvelous Woman, 1984) Bevilacqua returns to the theme of marital relationships. In the first of these he offers disparate portraits of women in an effort to capture the main expressions of womanhood, which is seen as ultimately elusive. Blending imagination and personal experience, Bevilacqua draws the women in his life to whom he felt most attracted. In the second novel a mysterious woman works her way into the home and the life of an itinerant storyteller whose lover abandons him for another man. But neither the skillful weaving of the story nor the element of suspense saves the work from being stifled by excessive reflections and psychological excursions.

In the late 1980s and the 1990s Bevilacqua has continued to explore familiar themes and to saturate his novels with introspection. *Il gioco delle passioni* (The Game of Passions, 1989) is set in an unlikely Veneto that serves as the emblem of national corruption. The narrative is saddled by moralistic chastisements, broad allusions lacking referential links to reality, and stylistic redundancies. *I sensi incantati* and *Un cuore magico* (A Magic Heart, 1993) are marked by the tired re-elaboration of familiar settings and themes–the Po Valley, marital crises, parents–and the recurrence of the theme of individual enlightenment, which here is debased to a mere narrative expedient.

In assessing Bevilacqua's contribution to Italian literature in nearly forty years, one cannot but acknowledge the substantial qualities of his work. He has given his readers a generous and erotic Parma and a Po Valley peopled by real characters who are neither preachers nor figurines of regional folklore. He has shown his readers a constant moral commitment that is direct, sincere, and unabashedly personal. "La mia opera," he told Stelio Cro, "più o meno è frutto non solo di una mia scelta, ma anche di una mia estrema sofferenza" (My work is essentially the product of both a personal choice and deep personal suffering). Bevilacqua searched deeply in history and personal memory and refused to make peace with the modern world which he considers rife with corruption and violence.

Interviews:

Elio Filippo Accrocca, *Ritratti su misura di scrittori italiani* (Venice: Sodalizio del Libro, 1960), pp. 73–74;

Accrocca, "Califfa si, Califfa no," *Il Lavoro nuovo,* 22 July 1964;

Claudio Toscani, "Dieci domande ad Alberto Bevilacqua," *Il Ragguaglio librario,* new series no. 36 (February 1969): 42–45;

"Umana avventura: un sogno della Storia," *Uomini e libri,* 6 (June–July 1970): 35–36;

"Bevilacqua: 'una città in amore,'" *Uomini e libri,* 6 (December 1970): 53–54;

Flora Vincenti, "Narrativa contemporanea: Orientamenti degli anni '70," *Uomini e libri* (June 1972): 14–15;

"A colloquio con Alberto Bevilacqua. La poesia come giovinezza," *La fiera letteraria,* 3 June 1973, pp. 14–15;

Stelio Cro, "Intervista con Alberto Bevilacqua," *Canadian Journal of Italian Studies,* 2 (Fall–Winter 1978–1979): 69–91;

Sira Testi, "A colloquio con Alberto Bevilacqua," *L'Informatore librario,* 9 (April 1979): 5–7.

References:

Giuseppe Amoroso, "Alberto Bevilacqua," in *Letteratura italiana contemporanea,* volume 4, edited by Gaetano Mariani & Mario Petrucciani (Rome: Lucarini, 1978), pp. 49–66;

Giuliano Manacorda, *Vent'anni di pazienza. Saggi sulla letteratura italiana contemporanea* (Florence: Nuova Italia, 1972), pp. 321–325;

Luigi Scorrano, *Alberto Bevilacqua* (Florence: Nuova Italia, 1982);

Scorrano, "Poesia di Alberto Bevilacqua," *Otto-Novecento,* 2, no. 1 (1978): 115–149;

Stefano Tani, *Il romanzo di ritorno* (Milan: Mursia, 1990), pp. 24–29;

Claudio Toscani, *Invito alla lettura di Alberto Bevilacqua* (Milan: Mursia, 1974).

Gesualdo Bufalino
(15 November 1920 – 14 June 1996)

Rosetta di Pace
University of Oklahoma

BOOKS: *Diceria dell'untore* (Palermo: Sellerio, 1981); translated by Stephen Sartarelli as *The Plague-Sower* (Hygiene, Colo.: Il poligrafico piemontese, 1988);

Museo d'ombre (Palermo: Sellerio, 1982);

L'amaro miele (Turin: Einaudi, 1982);

Dizionario dei personaggi di romanzo da Don Chisciotte all'Innominabile (Milan: Il Saggiatore, 1982);

Argo il cieco, ovvero i sogni della memoria (Palermo: Sellerio, 1984); translated by Patrick Creagh as *Blind Argus or The Fables of the Memory* (London: Collins Harvill, 1988);

Cere perse (Palermo: Sellerio, 1985);

Incontro con Pietro Palma: itinerario tra le isole, by Bufalino, Mario Monteverdi, and Enzo Papa (Siracusa: Ediprint, 1986);

L'uomo invaso e altre invenzioni (Milan: Bompiani, 1986);

Il malpensante. Lunario dell'anno che fu (Milan: Bompiani, 1987);

La luce e il lutto (Palermo: Sellerio, 1988);

Le menzogne della notte (Milan: Bompiani, 1988); translated by Creagh as *Night's Lies* (London: Collins Harvill, 1990);

Saline di Sicilia (Palermo: Sellerio, 1988);

Invito alle Fêtes galantes di Verlaine (Milan: Sciardelli, 1989);

Il matrimonio illustrato: testi d'ogni tempo e paese scelti per norma dei celibi e memoria dei coniugati, by Gesualdo Bufalino and Giovanna Bufalino (Milan: Bompiani, 1989);

Trittico, by Bufalino, Vincenzo Consolo, and Leonardo Sciascia, edited by Antonio Di Grado and Giuseppe Lazzaro Danzuso (Catania: Sanfilippo, 1989);

Saldi d'autunno (Milan: Bompiani, 1990);

Il guerrin meschino: frammento di un'opera di pupi (Catania: Girasole, 1991);

L'inchiostro del diavolo (Milan: Sciardelli, 1991);

Qui pro quo (Milan: Bompiani, 1991);

Calende greche: ricordi d'una vita immaginaria (Milan: Bompiani, 1992);

Gesualdo Bufalino (photgraph by Giovanni Giovannetti)

Il tempo in posa: immagini di una Sicilia perduta (Palermo: Sellerio, 1992);

Lamento del vecchio puparo (Rome: Edizioni dell'Elefante, 1992);

Cento Sicilie: testimonianze per un ritratto. Antologia di testi, by Bufalino and Nunzio Zago (Florence: Nuova Italia, 1993);

Bluff di parole (Milan: Bompiani, 1994);

Carteggio di gioventù: 1943–1950, by Bufalino and Angelo Romano, edited by Nunzio Zago (Valverde: Il girasole, 1994);

Il fiele ibleo (Cava dei Tirreni: Avagliano, 1995);

L'enfant du paradis: cinefilie (Comiso: Salarchi immagini, 1996);

Tommaso e il fotografo cieco, ovvero Il patatrac (Milan: Bompiani, 1996);

In corpore vili: autoritratto letterario: opera postuma (Massa e Cozzile: Gattopardo, 1997);

Collection: *Opere: 1981–1988,* edited by Maria Corti and Francesca Caputo (Milan: Bompiani, 1992).

OTHER: Gioacchino Iacono and Francesco Meli, *Comiso ieri: immagini di vita signorile e rurale,* edited by Bufalino (Palermo: Sellerio, 1978);

Ernest Renan and Jean Giraudaux, *Due preghiere,* edited by Bufalino (Palermo: Sellerio, 1981);

Gustave Flaubert, *Memorie di un pazzo,* preface by Bufalino (Florence: Passigli, 1983);

Giuseppe Leone, *L'isola nuda: aspetti del paesaggio siciliano,* text by Bufalino (Milan: Bompiani, 1988);

Bruno Caruso. Mitologia, text by Bufalino (Siracusa: Lombardi, 1989);

Salvatore Quasimodo, *Notturni del re silenzioso,* preface by Bufalino (Messina: Sicania, 1989);

Clemente Fava: Opere 1975–1990: Palazzo dei Diamanti, Centro Attività Visive 10 marzo–14 aprile 1991, text by Bufalino and Adriano Baccilieri (Bologna: Grafis Industrie Grafiche, 1991);

Enzo Leopardi, *Il signore delle isole,* preface by Bufalino (Catania: Prova d'autore, 1991);

Il colore della fede: la religiosità in Salvatore Fiume, text by Bufalino and others (Cinisello Balsamo: Edizioni paoline, 1992);

Sebastiano Gesu, ed., *La Sicilia e il cinema,* preface by Bufalino (Catania: Maimone, 1993);

Matteo Maria Boiardo, *Matteo Maria Boiardo,* selected and introduced by Bufalino (Rome: Istituto poligrafico e Zecca dello Stato, 1995);

Nino Genovese and Sebastiano Gesu, eds., *Verga e il cinema,* text by Bufalino (Catania: Maimone, 1996);

Maria Teresa Serafini, *Come si scrive un romanzo,* text by Bufalino and others (Milan: Bompiani, 1996).

TRANSLATIONS: Jean Giraudoux, *Susanna e il Pacifico* (Palermo: Sellerio, 1980);

Madame de la Fayette, *L'amor geloso* (Palermo: Sellerio, 1980);

Paul Jean Toulet, *Le Controrime* (Palermo: Sellerio, 1981);

Ernest Renan and Jean Giraudoux, *Due preghiere* (Palermo: Sellerio, 1981);

Charles Baudelaire, *I fiori del male* (Milan: Mondadori, 1983);

Terence, *I due fratelli* (Siracusa: Istituto nazionale del dramma antico, 1983);

Victor Hugo, *Le orientali* (Palermo: Sellerio, 1985);

Ramón Gómez de la Serna, *Sghiribizzi,* selected and translated by Bufalino (Milan: Bompiani, 1997).

Gesualdo Bufalino became an overnight success when at the age of sixty he published his first novel, *Diceria dell'untore* (1981; translated as *The Plague-Sower,* 1988). The novel, one of the masterpieces of twentieth-century Italian fiction, won the prestigious Campiello Prize in 1981. After his sensational appearance on the Italian literary scene, Bufalino became a prolific writer, publishing novels, prose pieces, some poetry, many introductions to the works of others, and translations of French authors.

Bufalino writes from a stance of cosmic pointlessness, a position that reminds one of other great pessimists such as Giacomo Leopardi and Luigi Pirandello. He shares their fatalistic view of life and, paradoxically, their strong creative urge. His fiction bears witness to the ethos of restlessness, ambiguity, and the sense of exhaustion typical of postmodern art. It is precisely his identification with the indecisive postmodernist self that separates Bufalino from a great modernist writer such as Marcel Proust, whom in so many ways he otherwise resembles. While Proust's belief in the Romantic, imperialistic concept of self enabled him to keep his identity strong and intact over the flux of time, for Bufalino, and more generally for any postmodern artist, the pretensions of the self have been greatly lowered. In Bufalino's fiction the impotence of the self is tied to his two other predominant themes, time and death.

Because Bufalino's characters are so enmeshed in chronological time and focus so on their memories, his fiction projects no sense of hope or expectation for the future. The writer's inner imperative of death-oriented linear time is so intense and so disturbing that it ends up pulling his vision inexorably toward the darkness and the void he conceives as winning a universal victory over life. The pathos he achieves in his fiction is the result of the continuous struggle of his characters to wrestle memories and meaning against the relentless and engulfing action of time. The haunting and mournful lyrical quality he imparts to this process is one of the distinctive characteristics of Bufalino's art.

Born on 15 November 1920 in Comiso, a town in southeastern Sicily, Gesualdo Bufalino lived on his beloved native island except for the years of his involvement in World War II. In his autobiographical novel, *Calende greche: ricordi d'una vita immaginaria* (Greek Kalends: Memories of an Imaginary Life, 1992), he draws a splendid portrait of his father as a handsome, humble blacksmith in love with books and talks of his own high school days in nearby Ragusa, where he had as a teacher the Dante scholar Paolo Nicosia.

Bufalino attended the universities of Catania and Palermo, leaving in 1942 to fight with the partisans in northern Italy. Captured by the Germans in 1943, he managed to escape and to hide first in the Friuli and then in the Emilia regions of Italy. Bufalino contracted tuberculosis in one lung at the end of 1944 while fighting at the front and entered the hospital at Scandiano, where a friendly doctor allowed him free rein in his large library. From here he passed to the sanatorium of La Rocca in Sicily, which he was later to make famous in *Diceria dell'untore*.

His health restored, he left the hospital in the fall of 1946, completed his studies, and became a humanities teacher at a teacher-training school in Vittoria. He later became a principal at Comiso. Although he began writing *Diceria dell'untore* in the 1950s, he did not achieve literary success until after he retired from teaching in 1976. The novelist Leonardo Sciascia helped Bufalino find a publisher for his book. Throughout his life he remained attached to his province and his town, which he hardly ever left except for the brief trips that his new literary career and the subsequent, not altogether welcomed, fame required of him. His tranquil life ended tragically on 14 June 1996 in a car accident.

All of Bufalino's novels powerfully illustrate the importance of memory. It is the means through which Bufalino as a writer validates his tenuous sense of self, neutralizes his alienation from others, and establishes a link between ethics and aesthetics. *Diceria dell'untore,* a book that is in large part autobiographical, tells the story of a small group of people in a Sicilian sanitarium near Palermo where the narrator, an obvious stand-in for the author, landed after the war. He writes a lyrical evocation of the last summer he spent there.

As one reads the novel interest centers not so much on the action of the young man then as it does on the inner flow of his memories and on his posture toward them now as a man who has survived into the 1970s. He selects brilliantly realized scenes from that summer, and each face, event, and word seems to have been indelibly recorded in his memory. The narrator repeatedly emphasizes how memory represents a magical place, how he cherishes the experience he calls the ecstasy of reliving:

> Io col passato ho rapporti di tipo vizioso, e lo imbalsamo in me, lo accarezzo senza posa ... non so cavare pensieri, io non ho una testa forte, e il pensiero o mi spaventa o mi stanca. Ma baglori invece ... baglori di luce e ombra, e quell'odore di accaduto, rimasto nascosto con milioni d'altri per anni e anni in un cassone invisibile, quassopra, dietro la fronte....

> (My relations with the past are like a vice in nature; I embalm the past inside of me, caress it incessantly ... I am unable to get thoughts out, I don't have a powerful mind, and thought either frightens me or makes me tired. But the flashes, on the other hand ... flashes of light and shadow, and that smell of what happened, hidden away with millions of others for years and years inside an invisible jewel box, up here, behind my forehead....)

The power of memory is so strong in the narrator that it lets him bring back the past with the quality and intensity of its original sense perceptions as well as the strong emotions associated with them.

The narrator never attempts to escape his memories, including those that bring resentment and remorse. Compassion, however, represents his deepest response toward those who shared his fate at La Rocca. At the end of his story, when his memories have reawakened his pain and guilt at having survived the slaughter of war and disease, he concludes, "Per questo forse m'era stato concesso l'esonero: per questo io solo m'ero salvato, e nessun altro, dalla falcidia: per rendere testimonianza, se non delazione, d'una retorica e d'una pietà" (Perhaps this is why I had been granted the pardon, why I alone, and no one else, had survived the massacre: to bear witness to, if not denounce, a rhetoric and a sense of pity). True to his word he does just that.

The reader is taken back to La Rocca to meet a group of terminally ill men and women awaiting death. The narrator lived in the wing reserved for the veterans and the repatriates, men who exchanged uniforms for pajamas. The old doctor who takes care of these men calls them the war's harvest, but the narrator does not distance himself from any of his companions. His feeling of compassion invests every portrait he draws, including Sebastiano, the young medical student who committed suicide by throwing himself down the stairwell instead of waiting for the inevitable; Father Vittorio, the priest from a rich family in the North, who chose to die alone, doubting and forsaken, in the South; and Adelmo, the pale, young

Dust jacket of the American edition of Bufalino's third novel, in which four condemned men tell the stories of their lives

boy who liked to play messenger between the men's and women's wards. But above all there is Marta, a terminal case whose highly charged portrait, both luminous and doomed, is drawn as she stands poised on the threshold of death.

Bufalino is able to capture the whole personality of his characters through their gestures. With Marta it is her gait, which still shows a trace of the trained ballerina, and which exerted a great sexual allure on the narrator. He remembers seeing her for the first time on stage as she danced a solo at the variety show on Santa Rosalia's Day, a gala organized and directed by the doctor in the recreation hall of the sanitarium. Granting her a lyrical, pictorial redemption, he says that she always seemed "un serafino . . . dalla vita sottile e dalle ali roventi, con occhi come ciottoli d'ebano nel fiero ovale ammansito da una corta chioma di luce!" (a seraph . . . with slender waist and burning wings with eyes like ebony pebbles in the proud oval of her face tamed by a short mane of light hair).

In a pious act of fidelity the narrator also allows Marta to maintain the identity of a mysterious heroine she had forged for herself at La Rocca. They believed she was from somewhere north of the Po, but no one knew exactly; some said that she had danced at La Scala; others gossiped about a cabaret and worse things still. Then there was the version she told to the narrator of the S.S. captain who had saved her from an extermination camp: they had lived together at a villa on a lake. There it was that she had her hair cut off by the townspeople for having remained with him till his end in front of a firing squad. Afterwards she had wandered from one luxury boarding house to the next, finally ending up, sick and dying, at La Rocca. At one point in their relationship Marta admits to the narrator that her love of intrigue and disguise has prompted her to lie, to tell him someone else's story, but he is faithful to whatever story she tells, whether fantasy or truth. When after her death the doctor gives the narrator a wax-sealed packet revealing her Jewish identity and containing the facts of her life, he consigns the whole file to the flames without reading any of it.

The story of Marta will doubtless lead many readers to think of Eugenio Montale's Dora Marcus from *Le occasioni* (The Events, 1949) as well as his image of the visiting angel. It may also bring to mind Dante Alighieri's woman-angel—"la donna angelicata." Bufalino's angel, however, does not bring salvation in any sense of the word. An ironic Beatrice, Marta brings contagion and prefigures the eternal void to which the narrator, her lover at the end of her life, will consign her. Nor is there a single note of hope or of salvation in any part of this love story. The common experience that lovers often share of being delivered, even if momentarily, into a larger dimension of time is denied to these two human beings traumatized by war and disease. Love in Bufalino's fiction is never a means of overcoming the consciousness of time but is instead the very means of pointing to the inexorability of time passing. In general his fiction is not so much heavy with the sense of things past, of things that have been lost, as it is with the anguish of the nothingness that they have become, of the darkness into which they have disappeared.

The similarities between Bufalino's novel and Thomas Mann's *The Magic Mountain* (1924) naturally lead to comparisons. In Mann's work the young engineer from Hamburg, Hans Castorp, who goes to visit his cousin in a Swiss sanitarium for tuberculosis patients, remains there for seven years. His debates with the rationalist Settembrini and the irrationalist Jesuit, Maptha, resemble those that Bufalino's narrator has with the doctor and with Father Vittorio. Castorp also falls in love with a woman, a beautiful and mysterious Russian named Claudia Chauchat. But the ethos of Mann's book remains totally different from that of Bufalino's, and the distance between Mann's narrator and Bufalino's is precisely the distance that divides the modernist from the postmodernist self.

In Mann's novel both the lady and the young man leave the sanitarium in perfectly good health. Castorp's attitude upon leaving is optimistic, full of confidence from the sense of wisdom that he feels he has acquired at Davos. Most important of all, Castorp carries with him the Proustian sense of timelessness and of eternity that he has experienced at the magic mountain. Not so for Bufalino's narrator in *Diceria dell'untore*. His portrait of Marta, rich in brilliant hues as it is, is defined against the ticking of the clock. He makes the reader stare at her—her beauty of face and of movement, her fragility as well as her sophistication—but in the end one realizes that everything about her says something about time, how she is trapped in it, how each elegant step she takes brings her closer to death.

Marta's death finally comes in a modest room of a small seaside hotel where the lovers had escaped from La Rocca on a lark, in a red car with unmatching fenders, which was for them as good as a luxurious Bugatti. Her death is described strictly from a naturalistic perspective in all its concrete and physical horror, a presentation that underscores Bufalino's belief that physical death is a final end. He makes no allowances for the mysteries of the cosmic energy that fuels the universe as well as the human body or for the possible survival of the spirit because he equates death with eternity—the dark, the void, nothingness. "Il buio" (the dark) is one of the most recurrent words in all of Bufalino's writing. Such an imagined reality, for which he can offer no empirical evidence, is nonetheless for him a visceral as well as a metaphysical experience.

The crux of the matter for Bufalino is that death trumps the hope of life after death offered by memory. Marta, along with all the other characters who have been resurrected in *Diceria dell'untore*, is not granted emancipation from time. All the narrator has had to offer her against the encroaching dark are his lyrical outpourings and his sacramental act of compassion. This generosity of soul, which Bufalino grants to all the narrators in his fiction, is what saves him ultimately from the moral anarchy and the aesthetic nihilism of much contemporary art. But in considering consciousness as confined to physical life, in seeing the self totally contained within linear, chronological time, Bufalino shares in the claustrophobia of the postmodern psyche. Neither he nor his characters are able to transcend the modern concept of time that they have accepted. Accordingly, since the characters in Bufalino's fiction harbor no sense of hope or expectation for the future, a certain immobility exists in them as well as in the static situations in which they find themselves. La Rocca is a largely unchanging, enclosed world, a situation typical in Bufalino's fiction, but it is not a Sartrean "huis clos" (no exit) where hell is other people, for Bufalino is never cruel or dismissive of his characters. Compassion, which gives his fiction its moral value and depth, saves him from such arrogance.

A similar somber tone as well as lyrical outpourings can be found in Bufalino's second novel, *Argo il cieco, ovvero i sogni della memoria* (1984; translated as *Blind Argus or The Fables of the Memory*, 1988), the experimental work that ties his fiction most clearly to the practices of postmodern art. Once again Bufalino makes use of his memories in a quasi autobiographical novel, giving momentary resurrection and a pristine luster to figures and events drawn out of his inner self. The story Bufalino tells is again a love story but not his own this time, for here the young narrator, fresh out of the war and teaching in a girls' school in the southeastern Sicilian town of Modica, tells of his unrequited love for Maria Venera, the raven-haired beauty whose heart belongs to another. It belongs—in the best of Sicilian traditions—to her first cousin Rosario Trubia.

Such a topic, so recurrent in Sicilian literature, echoes in particular Elsa Morante's *Menzogna e sortilegio* (1948; translated as *The House of Liars*, 1950), for in both works an impoverished girl pines away for her predatory, eccentric, and elusive cousin. Maria Venera lives with her grandfather Don Alvise Salibba in an old, crumbling baronial "palazzo" (palace). Despite the moss running riot out of the mouths of its baroque gargoyles, the neglected mansion, like its inhabitants, still manages an aura of nobility and hauteur. Written in the vein of the Sicilian Baroque, *Argo il cieco* can also certainly take its place with the works of Federico De Roberto, Luigi Pirandello, Vitalino Brancati, Tommasi di Lampedusa, and Vincenzo Consolo, to name just a few.

Maria Venera is another of the female characters on whom Bufalino invests his lyrical feelings and his compassion. Characteristically forgiving, he allows the narrator to acquit Maria Venera of her reckless behavior in having carried out an affair that has resulted in an unwanted pregnancy and a painful miscarriage. He even lets the narrator forgive the manipulative way in which she has used him as the "amatorial postman" in delivering her good-bye letter to her lover. He absolves her in the name of "quel regalo di bellezza spropositata che spargeva sul mondo; e il suo disarmo del cuore, il modo di porgersi volenterosa e innamorata alla luce" (that gift of inordinate beauty that she spread onto the world, and for the defenselessness of her heart, for her way of giving herself willingly and full of love to the light). He also acquits her in the name of all those who inhabit the earth, suspended as they all are and always will be in danger of falling from their perch of light into the void of darkness.

The story of *Argo il cieco* is told with a proliferation of geographical referents. They are so rampant that they constitute one of its major leitmotifs. The novel, for example, opens with an aerial view of Modica reminiscent of Alessandro Manzoni's in *I promessi sposi* (The Betrothed, 1827): "un paese in figura di melagrana spaccata; vicino al mare ma campagnolo; metà ristretto su uno sprone di roccia, metà sparpagliato ai suoi piedi; con tante scale fra le due metà a far da pacieri" (a town like a split pomegranate; close to the sea yet pastoral; half hanging on a cliff, the other half at its feet; with so many flights of steps joining the two like peacemakers).

The narrator remembers all the dancing that went on at the villas in the outskirts of Modica during the summer months of the year he spent there, but it is the last one, the gala ball of Ferragosto—the mid-August Italian holiday—that turns this elegy to the summer of 1951 into a eulogy. It is during this ball that the beautiful Maria Venera, resplendent in her mother's heirloom dress of Vallarmosa lace, publicly embarrasses her cousin and former lover by slapping him at the end of the snakelike dance of the "conga" that she had been leading. This climactic moment is soon followed by tragedy as the ball turns into a funeral march after Don Alvise suddenly drops dead while giving the commands to the concluding event of the quadrille.

What is new and different in *Argo il cieco* is not the plot and characters of the conventional love story but the way in which the story line fades in and out, interspersed as it is by a series of seven asides through which the author intervenes directly in his work. Revealing something of Bufalino's personality and poetics, these asides call attention to the surface of the text in a postmodern manner. The novelist confesses in one of them to have done his work in the Roman hotel room where he, lonely and alone, resolved to heal himself by writing a happy book. He admits that writing for him is a surrogate for living, even a means to cure his chronic insomnia, given as he is to count characters instead of sheep in the vain attempt to fall asleep. He also quips that writing saves him from the temptation of committing suicide at least every four months. Through his total lack of a grandiose self-image as a man and as a writer, Bufalino in a typical postmodern gesture turns away from the exclusive and heroic individualism of the Romantics, the Symbolists, as well as from the egotism of contemporary modernists. Traces of these sensibilities exist in his writing, but his adoption of a self-parodic, clownish posture subverts them while revealing his postmodernist approach.

Bufalino's third novel, *Le menzogne della notte* (1988; translated as *Night's Lies*, 1990), won the Strega prize. As in *Diceria dell'untore* the story unfolds in a restricted space and, similarly, at a significant moment of a fatal crisis. It fits into the tradition of the frame novel, but the frame is more than a pretext for the tales, for it provides the physical, psychological, and metaphorical setting. While the setting is again Sicily, it is a much more abstract Sicily than that of the previous novels: a forbidding fortress, sitting on a sheer cliff above the sea, the only structure on an uninhabited tiny island off the Sicilian coast. Bufalino's use of the symbolism of the fortress is reminiscent of the work of writers such as Franz Kafka and Dino Buzzati. Bufalino also leaves the time setting vague, allowing the novel to float free of any rigid historical framework. However, from the many clues strewn through the text, the time can be deduced to be that of the Italian Risorgimento in the nineteenth century. More specifically, the historical setting is that of the Bourbon Kingdom of the Two Sicilies right before its final dissolution.

The fortress is a prison where four men have come to die after their failed attempt to assassinate the Bourbon king of Naples. One of them is Conrad Ingafù, the baron of Letojanni, a nobleman turned revolutionary. He joined the band led by "God the Father," a legendary political figure, that has been setting the country aflame. Another is Saglimbeni, a forty-year-old man of uncertain origins, whose love of music and adventure is matched only by his well-known fervor for writing lampoons against the Crown. His sidekick is a young student, Narcissus Lucifora, whose mutinous attitude toward all authority has led him to follow the poet's footsteps all the way to the gallows. No less colorful is the fourth prisoner, thirty-year-old Agesilaos Degli Incerti, of illegitimate birth and a soldier by profession. It is Incerti who had made the bomb that was set off beneath the royal stand, thus causing the massacre for which the four have been condemned to die by the guillotine on the twelfth day of October.

The cell in which the four spend their last night together has only two windows, both of which open into the courtyard where the scaffolding for their morning execution is being erected. To silence the hammering outside as well as to calm the beating of their hearts, they pass the night by telling about their lives, each man relating the one memory he wishes to take to his death. Again, as in all of Bufalino's fiction, human experience is represented through the memories of those who are about to see all hope, illusions, and ideals disappear into the nothingness of death. Against this pessimism, which opens and closes the book, the student's tale stands out because though it too arrives at no conclusion and gives no answers, it is a story of altruistic, selfless love. Narcissus tells it in vivid, quick scenes, which achieve, one after another, an effective intensification of the drama.

Born on the Adriatic coast to a family of wealthy cloth merchants, Narcissus lived a carefree if neglected childhood because of his mother's death at his birth and his father's prolonged absences due to his travels throughout Europe and the Near East. He learned to play music from Gasper, the gardener, who had been a trumpeter for a nobleman in the Veneto region. At thirteen Narcissus left home in the company of Gasper, who had been unjustly accused by Olympia, Narcissus's sister, of trying to seduce her. Wandering with his companion for several years, Narcissus studied, matured, and developed a love for justice and for the cause of the people, which led him finally to join the revolutionary movement. His activities forced his escape to the north where he had become a servant in the house of Gasper's former employer, the liberal Grimaldi. In Grimaldi's Palladian villa on the edge of the Po River, Narcissus resumed his horn playing and joined a band of amateur musicians from the neighboring villas. Meandering along the river banks, they provided the music which, along with fireworks, open-air banquets, and masked balls, formed the entertainment during the summer holidays.

During one of these occasions Narcissus met and fell in love with the beautiful and regal Eunice, a Venetian lady married to Venerio Manin, an aristocrat who was in prison for having admitted his leadership of a Carbonari lodge. In spite of the risk of being discovered, Narcissus helps Eunice free her husband from prison and in their escape accross the Apennines to the retreat of God the Father. While en route through the papal territories, they are questioned by a group of papal soldiers, and Manin cowardly identifies Narcissus as the escaped prisoner for whom they are looking. Because of his nineteen years, his love, his magnanimity, Narcissus goes along with the ruse to facilitate Manin's escape. During the three long years he then spent languishing in a cell in Castel Sant'Angelo in Rome, Eunice often came to visit, declaring her love and devotion to him. During his eventual extradition the band of God the Father attacked the guards escorting Narcissus to the royal prison and effected his escape.

In the countryside Narcissus finds Eunice, who had accompanied the revolutionaries and was anxiously awaiting him, and during a moonlit night they consummate their love. Although their relationship later is a factor leading to his capture and death sentence, he will not speak ill of the dizzying experience that her love had been for him: "Idea di bellezza e di spirito, trionfo di fiamme e di carne, etereo volume calato nel senso, senso rapito oltre i sensi.... Qualcosa che forse due parole, per come le intendo all'ingrosso, saprebbero meglio dilucidare: il magnete e l'elettrico" (Idea of beauty and of spirit, a triumph of flame and flesh, ethereal volume descended into the senses, and sense itself transported beyond its reach. . . . Something that, maybe two words, as I roughly understand them, might better explain it: magnetism and electricity). The images of this night are the ones that Narcissus chooses to hold on to in the morning against the blade's edge that will deliver him to the dark.

In *Calende greche: ricordi d'una vita immaginaria,* Bufalino extends the asides of *Argo il cieco.* Here also the author in his own person directly expresses his anxiety about life and art. The book is written in the form of a confessional autobiography "à la Rousseau," and the emphasis is on his artistic sensibility. Bufalino's past experiences as they come to the periphery of his consciousness are lyrically presented. While the caressing of his own pain and resentment recall the Crepuscolari (Twilight poets) who wrote at the beginning of the twentieth century, Bufalino is more blunt in expressing his feelings and self-deprecatory in a way they never were.

Calende greche presents an interesting picture of the writer's mind at work as well as much of Bufalino's biography as he recapitulates in chronological fragments the various periods of his life from his birth in Comiso in 1920 to 1992, the year the book was published. The novel does not end so much as it winds down in a general sense of defeat as the author gives in to his general state of anxiety and to the feeling of doom he seems incapable or unwilling to stave off. In a way Bufalino may be said to write and rewrite the same book, endlessly returning with each new one to the same questions that obsess him and for which he can find no answers. His discontent seems to have nothing to do with political ideology or class struggle. His is not a rebellion in the name of social justice but an existential one against the human predicament.

In addition to the perpetual tension in Bufalino's work between Eros and Thanatos (Love and Death), there is an equally strong opposition between what he calls his vice of dreaming and daydreaming and his strong need to reason things out. One cannot help but think of Pirandello when Bufalino in *Calende greche* confesses his impulse to give in to the "cavilli del raziocinio" (reason's cavilings) in his attempt to unlock "i codici di un mondo che ancora mi sto affannando di capire" (the codes of a world that still I am anxiously trying to understand). In this he resembles not only Pirandello but also the many characters in his own fiction who never tire of engaging in debates in which they exude what Bufalino calls philosophical vapors.

The formal structure of dialogue, or debate, is present in all of Bufalino's fiction. Characters such as the doctor in *Diceria dell'untore,* the governor in *Le menzogne della notte,* and the narrator's friend, Iaccarino, in *Argo il cieco* are among Bufalino's most unforgettable ones, and each shares with his creator a need to reason things out in order to understand his identity and purpose. Certainty both tempts and eludes these doubters, who have abandoned all the metaphysical assurances that for centuries have cushioned the Western psyche. In the end their debates admit no transcendence and remain mired in uncertainty and profound skepticism.

Bufalino believes that the nature of language itself is as limited as that of the self. In one of the asides in *Argo il cieco* he laments that words have never been enough for him. He continues his lament in *Calende greche:* "Dire che un tempo avrei creduto nella santità del linguaggio e che esso muovesse ogni creatura creata. 'Sia la luce' ordinasti 'ma la luce non fu'" (To say that once I would have believed in the sanctity of language and that it could have moved every creature alive. "Let there be light" you ordered "but there was no light"). His deep language anxiety is always contrasted, though, by the opulence of his prose. Restless vitality, eloquence, and lyricism are the hallmarks of his style. Fully aware of his ability to give a high charge to his language, he typically mocks his power, as when he asserts that at times he writes in a state of hysterical exhilaration.

Bufalino's powerful rhetoric is as evident in the prose pieces gathered in such collections as *Museo d'ombre* (The Museum of Shadows, 1982), which treats Comiso in the 1930s and 1940s, and *Cere perse* (Lost Faces, 1985), which contains pieces written for newspapers, magazines, and journals, as it is in his novels. Such work harkens back to the tradition of the "prosa d'arte" or "frammenti" (fragments) of the first part of the century. The essence of Bufalino's career is perhaps best captured in one of his prose pieces, "Voci di pianto da un lettino di sleeping-car" (The Cry from a Bunk Bed in a Sleeping Car), which he included in the collection *L'uomo invaso e altre invenzioni* (The Possessed Man and Other Stories, 1986).

The space in the story is restricted to the narrow cabin in the sleeping car of a train, where the speaker lies in total darkness on his bunk bed as the train hurtles into the night. His spoken prayer soon turns into a recognition of his true relationship with God: "Da quanti anni duelliamo senza vederci . . . un battibecco da sordo a muto, di parole contro il silenzio. Sebbene poi non siano nemmeno parole, le mie, ma un lagno, un mugghio, un urlo che si confonde col fischio del treno. . . ." (We've been fighting this duel for years without seeing each other . . . a bickering between a deaf and a mute, made of words against silence. Although mine are not even words, but a lament, a mooing, a scream that blends itself with the train's whistle. . . .). As the image of the dark grows into a triumphant presence, so does the voice in prayer become stark and startling in addressing God: "Eccomi dunque qui, sprofondato nella pece della notte . . . al sicuro di tutto fuorchè dal tempo; nascosto a tutti, forchè all'arbitrio della Tua mira e alla Tua distratta veggenza" (Here I am then, sunk in the pitch-dark of night . . . safe from everything except from time; hidden from everybody, except from the arbitrariness of Your aim and of Your indifferent sight).

Nothing placates the inner tension of this uninterrupted monologue, which is both a challenge and a plea. The existential anguish is palpable in the air of the "noche oscura" (dark night) of the soul. In a manner characteristic of Bufalino and reminiscent of Leopardi, the voice arches over from the enclosed space to the cosmic dimension, from "uno stanzino di due metri per due a un abisso di cieli vuoti" (from a square of two meters room to an abyss of empty skies). But Bufalino does not lose himself in the immensity of space as Leopardi does, nor does he take Søren Kierkegaard's "leap into faith." He remains instead closer to Martin Heidegger's position of radical ontological doubt, for like the German philosopher he feels the experience of being "thrown" into the world as if by chance and wonders why "gli uomini non si sentano tutti come io mi sento dai piedi ai capelli, ridondanti sulla terra" (all mankind does not feel as I do from head to toe, redundant on the face of the earth).

The speaker's impulse to prayer remains a frustrated one as no miraculous signs appear. In all of Bufalino, consciousness is a form of torture as the self remains immobilized, captive and exposed to the dark and to the engulfing action of time in this spaceship earth. Bufalino leaves his readers with a gloomy picture of the human condition in which memory and art afford only a small degree of relief but no saving grace. He does not in the end overcome his fatalistic view of human finitude, his naturalistic one of death, and his narrow concept of time. But how much poetry and tenderness there is in this voice that brings in the dark while longing for the light!

Interview:

Conversazione con Gesualdo Bufalino; essere o riessere, edited by Paola Gaglianone and Luciano Tas (Rome: Omicron, 1996).

References:

Giuseppe Amoroso, *Narrativa italiana 1975–1983* (Milan: Mursia, 1983);

Giulio Ferroni, *Storia della letteratura italiana,* volume 4 (Turin: Einaudi, 1991);

Enzo Papa, "Gesualdo Bufalino," *Novecento,* volume 10 (Milan: Marzorati, 1988);

Nunzio Zago, *Gesualdo Bufalino* (Messina: Pungitopo, 1982).

Italo Calvino
(15 October 1923 - 19 September 1985)

Franco Ricci
University of Ottawa

BOOKS: *Il sentiero dei nidi di ragno* (Turin: Einaudi, 1947); translated by Archibald Colquhoun as *The Path to the Nest of Spiders* (Boston: Beacon, 1957);

Ultimo viene il corvo (Turin: Einaudi, 1949);

Il visconte dimezzato (Turin: Einaudi, 1952); translated by Colquhoun as *The Cloven Viscount* in *The Nonexistent Knight and The Cloven Viscount* (New York: Random House, 1962);

L'entrata in guerra (Turin: Einaudi, 1954);

La panchina: Opera in un atto di Italo Calvino; musica di Sergio Liberovici (Turin: Einaudi, 1956);

Il barone rampante (Turin: Einaudi, 1957); translated by Colquhoun as *The Baron in the Trees* (New York: Random House, 1959);

La speculazione edilizia (Turin: Einaudi, 1957); translated by D. S. Carne-Ross as "A Plunge into Real Estate" in *Difficult Loves; Smog; A Plunge into Real Estate* (London: Secker & Warburg, 1983);

La nuvola di smog e La formica argentina (Turin: Einaudi, 1958); translated by William Weaver as "The Smog" and "The Argentine Ant" in *The Watcher and Other Stories* (New York: Harcourt Brace Jovanovich, 1971);

I racconti (Turin: Einaudi, 1958);

Il cavaliere inesistente (Turin: Einaudi, 1959); translated by Colquhoun as *The Nonexistent Knight* in *The Nonexistent Knight and The Cloven Viscount;*

La giornata di uno scrutatore (Turin: Einaudi, 1963); translated as "The Watcher" in *The Watcher and Other Stories;*

Marcovaldo, ovvero le stagioni in città (Turin: Einaudi, 1963; revised edition, 1966); translated by Weaver as *Marcovaldo, or The Seasons in the City* (New York: Harcourt Brace Jovanovich, 1983);

Le cosmicomiche (Turin: Einaudi, 1965); translated by Weaver as *Cosmicomics* (New York: Harcourt, Brace & World, 1968);

Italo Calvino (photograph by Giovanni Giovannetti)

Ti con zero (Turin: Einaudi, 1967); translated by Weaver as *t zero* (New York: Harcourt, Brace & World, 1969);

La memoria del mondo e altre storie cosmicomiche (Milan: Club degli Editori, 1968);

Tarocchi: Il mazzo visconteo di Bergamo e di New York, by Calvino and Sergio Samek Ludovici (Parma: Franco Maria Ricci, 1969); translated by Weaver as *Tarots: The Visconti Pack in Bergamo and New York* (Parma: Franco Maria Ricci, 1976);

Gli amori difficili (Turin: Einaudi, 1970); translated by Weaver, Colquhoun, and Peggy Wright as

Difficult Loves (San Diego: Harcourt Brace Jovanovich, 1984);

Orlando Furioso di Ludovico Arisosto raccontato da Italo Calvino, con una scelta del poema (Turin: Einaudi, 1970);

Le città invisibili (Turin: Einaudi, 1972); translated by Weaver as *Invisible Cities* (New York: Harcourt Brace Jovanovich, 1974; London: Pan Books, 1979);

Il castello dei destini incrociati (Turin: Einaudi, 1973)—includes *La taverna dei destini incrociati*;

Se una notte d'inverno un viaggiatore (Turin: Einaudi, 1979); translated by Weaver as *If on a Winter's Night a Traveler* (New York: Harcourt Brace Jovanovich, 1981);

Una pietra sopra. Discorsi di letteratura e società (Turin: Einaudi, 1980);

Palomar (Turin: Einaudi, 1983); translated by Weaver as *Mr. Palomar* (New York: Harcourt Brace Jovanovich, 1985);

Collezione di sabbia (Milan: Garzanti, 1984);

Sotto il sole giaguaro (Milan: Garzanti, 1986); translated by Weaver as *Under the Jaguar Sun* (New York: Harcourt Brace Jovanovich, 1988);

Lezioni americane: Sei proposte per il prossimo millennio (Milan: Garzanti, 1988); translated by Weaver as *Six Memos for the Next Millennium* (Cambridge, Mass.: Harvard University Press, 1988);

Sulla fiaba, edited by Mario Lavagetto (Turin: Einaudi, 1988);

La strada di San Giovanni (Milan: Mondadori, 1990); translated by Tim Parks as *The Road to San Giovanni* (New York: Pantheon, 1993);

Perchè leggere i classici, edited by Esther Calvino (Milan: Mondadori, 1991);

Prima che tu dica pronto (Milan: Mondadori, 1993); translated by Parks as *Numbers in the Dark and Other Stories* (New York: Pantheon, 1995);

Omaggio a Italo Calvino: autobiografia di uno scrittore, edited by Domenico Ribatti (Manduria: Lacaita, 1995);

Carlo Emilio Gadda e Italo Calvino: scritti di architettura, edited by Gabriella Spizzuoco (Turin: Testo & immagine, 1997).

Collections: *I nostri antenati: Il cavaliere inesistente, Il visconte dimezzato, Il barone rampante* (Turin: Einaudi, 1960);

Cosmicomiche vecchie e nuove (Milan: Garzanti, 1984);

Romanzi e racconti, edited by Barenghi and Bruno Falcetto (Milan: Mondadori, 1991);

Racconti sparsi e altri scritti d'invenzione (Milan: Mondadori, 1994);

Altri romanzi (Milan: CDE, 1994);

Saggi 1945-1985, edited by Barenghi (Milan: Mondadori, 1995);

Tutte le cosmicomiche, edited by Claudio Milanini (Milan: Mondadori, 1997).

Editions in English: *Adam, One Afternoon, and Other Stories*, translated by Archibald Cloquhoun and Peggy Wright (London: Collins, 1957);

The Nonexistent Knight and The Cloven Viscount, translated by Colquhoun (New York: Random House, 1962);

The Watcher and Other Stories, translated by William Weaver (New York: Harcourt Brace Jovanovich, 1971);

The Castle of Crossed Destinies, translated by Weaver (New York: Harcourt Brace Jovanovich, 1977);

Difficult Loves; Smog; A Plunge into Real Estate, translated by Weaver and D. S. Carne-Ross (London: Secker & Warburg, 1983);

The Uses of Literature: Essays, translated by Patrick Creagh (San Diego: Harcourt Brace Jovanovich, 1986); republished as *The Literature Machine: Essays* (London: Secker & Warburg, 1987).

OTHER: *Fiabe italiane*, selected and translated by Calvino (Turin: Einaudi, 1956); translated by Louis Brigante as *Italian Fables* (New York: Collier, 1961); translated by George Martin as *Italian Folktales* (New York: Pantheon, 1980);

I giovani del Po, in *Officina* (January 1957–April 1958);

Cesare Pavese, *Lettere 1926-1950*, edited by Calvino and Lorenzo Mondo (Turin: Einaudi, 1966);

Raymond Queneau, *I fiori blu*, translated by Calvino (Turin: Einaudi, 1967);

Charles Fourier, *Teoria dei quattro movimenti*, selected and introduced by Calvino (Turin: Einaudi, 1971);

L'uccel belverde e altre fiabe italiane, selected and translated by Calvino (Turin: Einaudi, 1972);

Silvina Ocampo, *Porfiria*, edited by Calvino (Turin: Einaudi, 1973);

Il principe granchio e altre fiabe italiane, selected and translated by Calvino (Turin: Einaudi, 1974);

Tommaso Landolfi, *Le piu belle pagine*, selected by Calvino (Milan: Rizzoli, 1982);

Racconti fantastici dell'Ottocento, edited, with an introduction, by Calvino (Milan: Mondadori, 1983); translated as *Fantastic Tales: Visionary and Everyday* (New York: Pantheon, 1997).

Italo Calvino has long been recognized as one of the most prominent writers of the twentieth cen-

Cover for the American edition of two of Calvino's early novels, Il visconte dimezzato *(1952) and* Il cavaliere inesistente *(1959)*

tury. At once experimental and accessible, he is able to fuse sophisticated narrative techniques with pleasurable storytelling. His writing, internationally praised for imagination, humor, and technical virtuosity, is characterized by the interweaving of reality, fantasy, allegory, and fable as well as its treatment of abstract philosophical and scientific ideas and speculation. He has explored subjects ranging from the absurdity of the human condition, to the relationships of time and space and of fantasy and reality, to the nature of writing itself.

Calvino was born in Santiago de Las Vegas, Cuba, on 15 October 1923, where his parents were working as agronomists. Shortly thereafter the family returned to San Remo, Italy, a Ligurian town near France, where Calvino grew up and spent the better part of the next twenty years. He attended public schools, and because his parents were nonreligious he did not receive a religious education, nor was he subjected to the obligatory Fascist indoctrination of the time. A family tradition of devotion to science obliged him to enter the School of Agriculture at the University of Turin, where his father was a distinguished professor of tropical agriculture.

Calvino's studies were interrupted by twenty months of German occupation during World War II. When his parents were abducted by the Germans, their twenty-year-old son joined the Garibaldi Brigade, a partisan resistance group active in the Maritime Alps. His anti-Fascism, though, was due more to his tenaciously liberal upbringing than to political conviction. After the war he returned to the university and, taking advantage of special allowances made to wartime students, enrolled in the faculty of literature, graduating one year later with a thesis on Joseph Conrad.

Calvino began his writing career in the mid 1940s, at a time when Neorealism was becoming the dominant literary movement. The dilemma for the young author coming of age at this moment of cultural flux was whether to follow the accepted standard of social realism promoted by Marxist ideology or move beyond literary convention on his own. For a while Calvino was able to maintain a healthy balance and satisfy both his political commitment and evolving literary aspirations. Sharing an allegiance to socialist ideology with the writers Cesare Pavese and Elio Vittorini, he worked as a militant journalist for the communist newspaper *L'Unità* and also contributed to *Il Politecnico*. Much later, between 1959 and 1966, he served as codirector with Vittorini of the journal *Il menabò*.

Between the summer of 1945 and the spring of 1949 Calvino wrote many short stories. Thirty of them were eventually collected in the volume *Ultimo viene il corvo* (The Crow Comes Last, 1949). Twenty of these stories were translated in *Adam, One Afternoon, and Other Stories* (1957). The subject matter of the stylistically disparate tales is the war and Fascism, often seen through the eyes of unreliable narrators. Evidently having espied a disturbing undercurrent of discontent in postwar Italian society, Calvino examines the ideological fervor of his day and a growing conservative trend among the lower middle class.

A single-minded perspective emerges from these stories of strife and difficulty in postwar Italy. Through the filter of intellectual detachment he dispassionately draws fragments of reality, evoking scenes not so much to portray human passions but to depict a reconstruction of social relationships. It is an approach that privileges superficiality and denies psychological motivations. In the stories, whether one wishes to call them fantastic or realistic, Calvino seems most interested in a speculative realm beyond literature. He would soon turn to literary experiments combining folklore and fantasy with science and philosophy in his search to unveil the hidden syntax of the world and reveal the thread that binds all matter surreptitiously.

The years from 1947 to 1956 were difficult for young Calvino. While he was working as a party operative, dutifully writing a weekly feature called "Gente nel tempo" (People Today) for the communist newspaper as well as serving as editorialist, social commentator, and analyst, the fiery, intelligent writer also sought a different avenue of individual expression. He discharged his creative tension by submitting polemical articles to the cultural review *Il Politecnico,* in which he took his *impegno* (political commitment) into literary criticism.

In the preface to the 1954 edition of *Il sentiero dei nidi di ragno* (1947; translated as *The Path to the Nest of Spiders,* 1957), Calvino gives an invaluable portrait of postwar Italy. The term *Neorealism* first began circulating in Italy in 1945, and the movement, an intellectual response to the excesses of Fascist doctrine, fostered strong political commitment and a passionate interest in social issues. Indeed it was expected that a serious artist bear witness to history and contribute to the reconstruction of the moral fiber of the country. As Calvino notes, at the time the term characterized the collective outburst of heretofore repressed expressionism:

> Il "neorealismo" non fu una scuola.... Fu un insieme di voci, in gran parte periferiche, una molteplice scoperta delle diverse Italie, anche–o specialmente–delle Italie fino allora più inedite per la letteratura.

> ("Neorealism" was not a school.... It was a collection of voices, largely marginal, a multiple discovery of the various Italy, even–or particularly–the Italys previously unknown to literature.)

The passion of the Resistance ignited the Left and inspired many young writers to work for the common good of society.

Although Calvino remained a member of the Italian Communist Party until 1958, the year that Russia's invasion of Hungary drove many disgruntled intellectuals from the party, he was not inclined to accept a politically motivated narrative paradigm. He was at odds with the communist officials who decried what they considered the decadent individualism of unbridled self-expression as well as all literary experimentation dealing with historical issues. Calvino's position is clear in a 1948 article titled "Saremo come Omero," in which he responded to Emilio Sereni, a party officer whose responsibility was to draw clear guidelines for acceptable literature: "Caro Sereni... i linguaggi letterari sono personali come fazzoletti da naso" (Dear Sereni... literary language is as personal as one's handkerchief). Calvino was deeply troubled by the attempt of the leftist intelligentsia to curb artistic expression in order to achieve ideological purity. In the heated debate sparked by the ideologues who desired the programmatic literature and art of socialist realism, Calvino took his stand with those who believed that any form of constraint on the artist would ultimately result in propaganda.

Cover for the American edition of Calvino's 1957 novel, in which Baron Cosimo Piovasco di Rondò observes the French Revolution and the Napoleonic Wars from the trees of his family estate

Calvino's main contribution to the neorealist literature of the Resistance is the novel *Il sentiero dei nidi di ragno,* for which he won the Premio Riccione. The protagonist of the novel is Pin, an orphaned boy enticed by the perilous interests of war and sex. He spends most of his time in a local tavern, where he sings bawdy tavern songs and learns the lewd secrets of adulthood. One day he is taunted by the tavern crowd into stealing the pistol of one of his sister's German clients. He accepts the challenge, seeing this as an opportunity to prove his worth as a "man." At the same time, however, Pin is still a boy and is confused by the often unexplainable habits of these same men. He reacts by discovering a secret haunt where he may hide from the world and remain a child. This is the path where spiders make their nest, and here he hides the stolen gun.

Calvino's youthful political naiveté is mirrored in Pin, who is thrust into a world of incompetent partisans. Pin learns about life through mysterious, magic words (*gap, sim, stem*) and through the dubious behavior of so-called committed individuals. Based partly on Calvino's experiences, *Il sentiero dei nidi di ragno* presents a firsthand account of the historical period and an ingenious analysis of an unprepared populace facing the vicissitudes of war. At the end the young protagonist, much like the rest of Italian society, embarks upon a new life though no clue is given of what the future holds. Calvino's own direction was just as uncertain. Though he shared both the optimism of his mentor Elio Vittorini and the troubled, heartfelt nostalgia of his friend Cesare Pavese, he could not identify with either. He was searching for an approach beyond the commonplace and the popularly successful.

Calvino can also be identified with Kim, the young intellectual of *Il sentiero dei nidi di ragno,* who in the heightened moment of war

> ha un desiderio enorme di logica, di sicurezza sulle cause e gli effetti, eppure la sua mente s'affolla a ogni istante d'interrogative irrisolti. C'è uhn enorme interesse per il genere umano, in lui: per questo studia medicina perchè sa che la spiegazione di tutto è in quella macina di cellule in moto, non nelle categorie della filosofia.

> (has a great yearning for logic, for certainty about cause and effect, otherwise his mind is apt to crowd at every second with unanswered questions. He has an enormous interest in humanity; that is why he is a medical student, for he knows that the explanation of everything is to be found in the grinding moving cells of the human body, and not in philosophic speculation.)

It is not surprising that Calvino dedicated *Il sentiero dei nidi di ragno* to Kim, the inspiration for the most sensitive and rational of his early characters. Although the novel was considered a work of Neorealism, Calvino's investigation of the human condition clearly leaned toward the rational and scientific rather than the psychological and political. While Calvino would eventually substitute remote times and places for the realist settings of his early works, the fundamental positions elaborated through Kim remain constant regardless of the context. These include a concern for the destiny of the individual in society, a preoccupation with the mechanics of narrating, an acute awareness of the limits of philosophy and rationalism, and above all a steadfast belief in the cognitive necessity of fiction.

Calvino's narrative from its beginning is highly personalized, and *Il sentiero dei nidi di ragno* exhibits the enduring duality most critics find in his work. Calvino is both the wayward, wide-eyed daydreamer Pin and the logical, rational Kim. His later works show both extremes as Calvino rationalizes the universe into manageable schemes through the joy of fantasy. In his first book, then, Calvino set himself at the crossroads of his destiny.

After his first novel Calvino found it increasingly difficult to derive interesting stories from his personal experiences. He began a novel in a social realist vein, *I giovani del Po,* but became quickly dissatisfied with its wavering protagonist and left it in a drawer for years. Conceived in the late 1940s and written between January 1950 and July 1951, *I giovani del Po* was belatedly published in serial form in the journal *Officina* from January 1957 to April 1958. In this experiment with the epistolary novel, one of the earliest forms of the genre, Calvino is clearly at a loss for inspiration.

He also tried his hand at another novel, the fruits of which he eventually published as the three-story collection, *L'entrata in guerra* (Entering the War, 1954). The three stories–"L'entrata in guerra," "Gli avangardisti a Mentone" (The Vanguard Reached Menton), and "Le notte dell'UNPA" (The Nights of the UNPA)–were republished in *I racconti* (The Stories, 1958). They and several of the other stories that appeared in *I racconti* are considered Calvino's most autobiographical tales.

Antonio Gramsci, the Marxist critic and cofounder of the Italian Communist Party whose writings were published posthumously in book form in the 1940s, exercised a remarkable influence on Calvino. Gramsci insisted that literature must be viewed in relation to the life of the nation and called for a national popular literature that would be accessible to the people and receptive to their real concerns. It is not difficult to understand why Calvino would see Gramsci as a systematic and innovative intellectual in search of a new culture and a socially inspired conception of the artist's active role in history. If a new literature was possible, it would not concern itself solely with aesthetics but would be vibrant, alive, and rooted in real social values yet laced with a range of contemporary topics, including film, the American novel, music, and comic books.

The debate regarding the role of the intellectual in society became a general point of departure for the generation of post–World War II Italian writers. Calvino's antipathy toward social engineering and a desire to see literature born "da un terreno di non letteratura" (from nonliterary soil) is clear in three articles he published in *Rinascita* around the turn of 1949–"Saremo come Omero," "Ingegneri e demolitori" and "Letteratura, città aperta?" (Literature, An Open City?), all of which were collected in *Saggi 1945–1985* (1995) and discussed by Gian Carlo Ferretti in his *Le capre di Bikini: Calvino giornalista e saggista 1945–1985* (1989). The literary-political essay was one of Calvino's favorite and most prolific vehicles of expression throughout his career. These essentially optimistic pieces demonstrate Calvino's continuous study of fiction and its relationship to cultural, scientific, and historical trends. In "Letteratura, città aperta?," for example, he explores the possible role of cinema as a medium for the masses.

With *Il visconte dimezzato* (1952; translated as *The Cloven Viscount*, 1962) Calvino expressed both his political as well as literary differences with the often dull and tedious perspective of neorealist verisimilitude. The novel may be seen as symbolizing Calvino's difficulty in merging the public and the private spheres of his life, for in this rich fantastic allegory the author explores the idea of division through a man who is literally at war with himself. Set in the seventeenth century, *Il visconte dimezzato* describes an alienated and mutilated man, Viscount Medardo di Terralba, who is cut in half not only physically but also morally when he is struck in battle by a cannonball.

Medado's two halves survive, one decidedly good, the other reprehensibly evil, and everything in the story, which is told by the viscount's young nephew, is based on the scheme of opposites and contrasts. One half of Medardo is compulsive in his attempts to reorder the world in his own malevolent image; the other half is just as obsessed with extirpating evil from all living things. The good Medardo literally kills with kindness, an irony that suggests the complexity Calvino is able to weave into his tale. The schism of Medardo is also reflected in the larger world of the story, as in the contrast between the hedonistic lepers and the moralistic Huguenots or between the unfulfilled male characters, such as Dr. Trelawney and Master Pietrochiodo, and the integrated females, Sebastiana and Pamela. All function as social expressions of psychological divisions. At the end, when the two halves of Medardo are reunited in a climactic moral battle, the thematic balance of the story is restored, but none of the questions concerning the complexities of the true nature of good and evil are resolved. Only the young narrator remains, willing to tell new stories and invent new tales.

As may be surmised from its title, *Il barone rampante* (1957; translated as *The Baron in the Trees*, 1959), is another fantasy. On 15 June 1767 Baron Cosimo Piovasco di Rondò climbs a tree on his family estate and decides never to come down. At the end of the book an old but limber Cosimo catches the rope of a passing hot air balloon and is carried off into the sky, never to be seen again. Despite the fantasy inherent in his novella Calvino takes care with the details of historical characters with whom Cosimo is involved, including Voltaire, Napoleon Bonaparte, and Denis Diderot, and with the historical background. Cosimo is affected by the French Revolution and the Napoleonic Wars and ponders the conflict between the Jesuits and the Freemasons, but he largely remains aloof, uninvolved, an observer of eighteenth-century mores. He possesses an instinctual wisdom that allows him to peer obliquely, like Calvino, at the crises he sights from his perch.

This detached authorial stance is further abstracted in *Il cavaliere inesistente* (1959; translated as *The Nonexistent Knight*, 1962). The protagonist, Agilulfo Emo Bertrandino, is a model, though bodiless, paladin who animates an empty suit of gleaming white armor. Calvino, long an admirer of Ludovico Ariosto and his epic *Orlando furioso* (1516), takes many characters—Astolfo, Roland, Oliver, Charlemagne, and Bradamante—from the poet's tales of chivalry while inventing others—Agilulfo, Gurdulu, Torrismundo, and Sister Teodora. The story is rich in romance and adventure, with each character questing after a personal ideal, but it is much more as well. The unreliable narrator of the tale, Sister Teodora, whose real identity as the amazon Bradamante is finally revealed, creates an account of the past as well as of the present, as she sits writing her tale. She serves as a metaphor for Calvino the writer, the self-conscious extension of his desire to enter the realm of literature by creating and controlling characters.

In the midst of his own writing in the 1950s Calvino was also busy researching, rewriting, and bringing together two hundred folktales as *Fiabe italiane* (1956; translated as *Italian Fables*, 1961, and as *Italian Folktales*, 1980). In the introduction to the collection Calvino discusses the presence of myth in history and of history in myth. His study leads him to conclude that "fables are real" because they record the spiritual aspirations of a period. In this sense they provide a different, though no "less accurate," account of the past than more conventional forms of historiography. As a fruit of the imagination, Calvino argues, fables can reveal the hidden structures and patterns of the collective past. Such a belief doubtless explains why Calvino chose the title *I nostri antenati* (Our Ancestors, 1960) for the volume that includes the three novellas *Il visconte dimezzato*, *Il barone rampante*, and *Il cavaliere inesistente*.

Like *Fiabe italiane*, *I nostri antenati* presents a collective past through a combination of authentic history and fantastic invention. Calvino argues for the vibrancy of his approach in his introduction to *Il barone rampante*: "L'uomo che vive sugli alberi è un'allegoria del poeta, il suo modo di esser nel mondo. È, più in particolare, un'allegoria del 'disempegno'? Oppure, al contrario, dell'impegno?" (The man that lives in the trees is an allegory of the poet, of his way of being in the world. And, in particular, is it an allegory of 'non-engagement'? Or on the contrary, of 'engagement'?"). Maintaining distance offers security and permits calculated participation. The young Calvino finds momentary solace in the Age of Reason, for in the trees he happily explores new worlds and invents social utopias. The danger, represented by Agilulfo, is that of becoming a disembodied rationalist with no ties to reality, emotionally dissociated from everyday life.

Yet even while he was evolving his own aesthetic, Calvino also clung to the neorealist vision. Perhaps to counterbalance his fanciful propensity, he continued writing stories dealing with various social themes. The forty-nine stories and three novellas of *I racconti,* all written between 1946 and 1958, constitute a central text in Calvino's career because they show most clearly the two opposing sides of his soul, reality and fantasy. The eclectic collection includes ten Marcovaldo stories, neorealist treatments of a burdened laborer in an inhospitable city, and juxtaposes tales of youthful optimism with war stories. The three previously published novellas that end the volume—*La formica argentina* (1958; translated as "The Argentine Ant," 1971), *La speculazione edilizia* (1957; translated as "A Plunge into Real Estate," 1983), and *La nuvola di smog* (1958; translated as "The Smog," 1971)—provide a synopsis of Calvino's stylistic and thematic evolution in the 1950s.

Critics have found it difficult to categorize *I racconti* because these stories contain all the variations in content, form, and style that mirror Calvino's shift from a literature that describes the world to one that creates possible worlds. But from the boy Zefferino's surreal underwater antics in the first story of *I racconti,* "Pesci grossi, pesci piccoli" (Big Fish, Little Fish), to the cerebral and detached musings of the withered intellectual "Io" (I) of the last work, *La nuvola di smog,* there runs a vein of subtle irony. Though all fifty-two pieces are memorable, most critics favor those that exhibit stylistic elements that signal an emerging sophistication in the author. These include "Campo di mine" (Mine Field), "Il bosco sull'autostrada" (The Forest on the Superhighway), "Luna e Gnac" (Moon and Gnac), and the poignant social vignettes "L'avventura di un viaggiatore" (The Adventure of a Traveler), "L'avventura di un lettore" (The Adventure of a Reader), and "L'avventura di un poeta" (The Adventure of a Poet).

Some of Calvino's stories of the late 1950s were about the industrial triangle of northern Italy, from Genoa to Turin to Milan. Rather than describing the widespread neurosis, exploitation, fraud, corruption, and chicanery in society, Calvino focuses on dehumanization. His stories revolve around missed appointments, unfulfilled eros, and unrequited desire. He uses subtle humor and gentle irony to elicit the grotesque nature of social relations. In the stories that make up the section of *I racconti* titled "Gli amori difficili"—which in 1970 became a separate volume by the same title (translated as *Difficult Loves,* 1984)—a soldier has a surreptitious rendezvous with a sultry widow; a housewife loses her bikini bottom while swimming on a crowded beach; and an ordinary clerk experiences a passionate night of lovemaking. In each situation the socially prescribed masks worn by the unnamed protagonists prevent true communication with others.

A similar neorealist theme runs through the Marcovaldo stories, which Calvino later revised and enlarged as *Marcovaldo, ovvero le stagioni in città* (1963; translated as *Marcovaldo, or The Seasons in the City,* 1983). Marcovaldo, a Charlie Chaplin–like character whose exploits often turn out to be well-told *barzellette,* or humorous anecdotes, represents every "little man" who attempts to recover that which is his and has been lost in the modern labyrinth. In a story such as "La cura delle vespe" (The Wasp Treatment) a bizarre turn of events can only elicit compassion for the hapless protagonist, but others of these stories are among Calvino's best. In "Il bosco sull'autostrada" the need for firewood causes Marcovaldo's city-wise children to mistake highway billboards for real trees; while chopping them down they are themselves mistaken for advertisements by a policeman. In "Luna e Gnac" a huge, partially burned-out, regularly flashing advertisement causes Marcovaldo's entire family to discover the wonder of nature in the twenty-second intervals. The aesthetic of socialist realism takes on a Chekhov-like twist here and is lifted into the realm of fantasy. The Marcovaldo stories foreshadow the Qfwfq stories in *Le cosmicomiche* (1965; translated as *Cosmicomics,* 1968), for the colors are vivid; the situations are joyfully drawn; the actions are compelling; and the conclusions are animated with hope.

The three novellas that close the collection are a mixture of piquant criticism and calm skepticism. Calvino's penchant for casting moral and social issues into fable is evident in *La formica argentina,* which first appeared in *Botteghe oscure* in 1952, the same year that the satiric *Il visconte dimezzato* was published. Calvino creates a surreal landscape of macabre social relationships centered around the various ways of giving meaning to life in an ant-infested neighborhood. While the agency that is supposed to rid the town of ants actually helps them proliferate by setting out sweet molasses, Captain Brauni, the inventor of false steel teeth, creates fantastic paraphernalia to kill the ants, and others, such as Signora Mauro, bear the inconvenience stoically. Just

Cover for the American edition of Calvino's 1972 novel, in which Kublai Khan learns of the "invisible order" of his kingdom from Marco Polo

as smog affords structure to the lives of the characters of "La nuvola di smog," so too the ants give meaning to the paltry survival of their beleaguered hosts.

The horrors of urban living continue in "La speculazione edilizia," where condominiums and high-rise buildings invade the landscape in a veritable war on the countryside. In these last stories man is caught up in a corrupt web of his own making. There are moments when Calvino seems to be expressing genuine pessimism, others where the hysterical doubts of the protagonists seem only comic.

In his critical essays Calvino shows an ongoing analytical interest in cultural movements and especially the role of the author in the evolving political and social reality of an industrialized Italy. Not content to voice dissatisfaction with the status quo, he invents programs, enters debates, and adopts innovative poetics in his search for a link between literature and society. He collected forty-two of his most important essays on literature and society spanning the years 1955 to 1978 in *Una pietra sopra. Discorsi di letteratura e società* (1980), many of which were translated in *The Uses of Literature* (1986). Calvino asserted that he chose these "dichiarazioni di poetica" (declarations of poetics) in order to "capire il punto in cui mi trovo. Per metterci una pietra sopra" (understand where I'm at. To close a chapter of my life). The essays, which mark moments of personal transition and attest to Calvino's multitude of sources and vibrant range of scholarly interests, stand as revealing signposts to his fiction.

Just as his characters struggle to avoid being engulfed by the menacing realities of a society undergoing structural changes, so too Calvino outlines strategies for survival. In the essay "Il mare dell'oggettività" (The Sea of Objectivity) he attacks the dominance of technology in the modern world and sees the danger of one's human identity becoming overwhelmed:

> Da una cultura basata sul rapporto e contrasto tra due termini, da una parte la coscienza la volontà il giudizio individuali e dell'altra il mondo oggettivo, stiamo passando a una cultura in cui quel primo termine è sommerso dal mare dell'oggettività.

> (From a culture based on the relationship and contrast between two terms, on the one hand, conscience, will, individual judgment, and on the other, the objective world, we are moving toward a culture in which that first term is submerged by the sea of objectivity, by the uninterrupted flux of what exists.)

This essay is complemented by "La sfida al labirinto" (The Challenge to the Labyrinth), where a complete loss of the self in "the sea of things" is seen as the conditioning ethic of modern man. Calvino, though, is cautiously optimistic in seeing literature as an intellectual antidote to modern existence:

> Quel che la letteratura può fare è definire l'atteggiamento migliore per trovare la via d'uscita, anche se questa via d'uscita non sarà altro che il passaggio da un labirinto all'altro. È la sfida al labirinto che vogliamo salvare, è una letteratura della sfida al labirinto che vogliamo enucleare e distinguere dalla letteratura della resa al labirinto.

> (What literature can do is define the best attitude for finding an exit, even if this exit is nothing more that the passage from one labyrinth to another. It is the challenge to the labyrinth that we wish to save, it is a literature that challenges the labyrinth that we wish to explain and distinguish from the literature that succumbs to the labyrinth.)

In another essay, "Il midollo del leone" (The Lion's Marrow), Calvino postulates an important use for literature:

> Le cose che la letteratura può ricercare e insegnare sono poche ma insostituibili: il modo di guardare il prossimo e se stessi, di porre in relazione fatti personali e fatti generali, di attribuire valore a piccole cose o a grandi, di considerare i propri limiti e vizi e gli altrui, di trovare le proporzioni della vita, e il posto dell'amore in essa, e la sua forza e il suo ritmo, e il posto della morte, il modo di pensarci o non pensarci; la letteratura può insegnare la durezza, la pietà, la tristezza, l'ironia, l'umorismo, e tante altre di queste cose necessarie e difficili. Il resto lo si vada a imparare altrove, dalla scienza, dalla storia, dalla vita, come noi tutti dobbiamo continuamente andare ad impararlo.

> (The things that literature can seek and teach are few but irreplaceable: the manner in which one looks at one's fellow man and at oneself, the manner of relating personal and general facts, of attributing value to things small and large, of considering one's own limits and vices and those of others, of finding the proportions of life, and the role that love plays in it, and its force and its rhythm, and the role of death, the manner of thinking about it or not thinking about it; literature can teach harshness, compassion, sadness, irony, humor, and so many other necessary and difficult things. Go learn the rest somewhere else, from science, from history, from life, as we all must constantly go to learn it.)

Calvino thus sees literature as an instrument to penetrate the false rationality of an increasingly complex social order.

Calvino seems to have come to terms with his Neorealism in *La giornata di uno scrutatore* (1963; translated as "The Watcher," 1971), a story about a man's experience as a poll officer during the 1953 elections that critics cite as his last concerted effort to deal explicitly with politics in fiction. A member of the Communist Party, Amerigo Ormea, is assigned the unenviable polling place of Cottolengo Hospital for Incurable Patients in Turin, where he observes that the patients are fraudulently placed on election lists and encouraged by Catholic authorities to vote. The young intellectual is at first horrified by the sight of a deformed humanity; then he is disgusted by the corrupt political machinery that feeds on their helpless condition.

Calvino's subtle analysis not only reveals a personal disenchantment with the blatant manipulation of the infirm by a misguided and opportunistic political system but also signals his rejection of any human action that does not directly address human need. The approval of direct action is plain when Amerigo watches a nun with a patient:

> Ecco, pensò Amerigo, quei due, cosí come sono, sono reciprocamente necessari. E penso ecco, questo modo d'essere è l'amore. E poi l'umano arriva dove arriva l'amore; non ha confini se non quelli che gli diamo.

> ("There," Amerigo thought, "those two, as they are, are necessary to each other." And he thought: "There, this way of being is love." And then "Humanity reaches as far as love reaches, it has no frontiers except those we give it.")

The insight is immediate and indelible. Redemption, Calvino shows, need not be achieved through election returns. Indeed, Calvino's audience in 1963 knew that the 1953 results had brought about no social revolution.

In 1964 Calvino moved to Paris, where he maintained his permanent residence until 1980. Soon after arriving he married Esther (Chichita) Singer, an Argentine translator for UNESCO, and one year later they had a daughter, Abigail, their only child. His long sojourn in Paris was motivated at least in part by the desire for apartness that characterizes many of his protagonists. While in Paris he remained in the employ of Einaudi as an editorial director, continued to write articles for the Milanese daily *Il Corriere della sera,* and traveled to Italy weekly though he confined his employment-related visits to Turin, the headquarters of his publisher. His circle of friends and professional acquaintances in the French capital grew steadily and included Roland Barthes, Jacques Lacan, and A. J. Greimas. In the early 1960s he joined the OuLiPo (Ouvroir de Littèrature Potentielle, or Workshop of Potential Literature), an experimental workshop founded by Raymond Queneau that influenced much of his subsequent work.

The surest mark of Calvino's expanding horizons is his appropriation of new literary models. While Ariosto, Luigi Pirandello, and the Italian tradition remained at the core of his work, it also began to show the influence of writers such as Vladimir Nabakov, James Joyce, and Robert Musil. A reconciliation with his father, which is treated in the short story "La strada di San Giovanni" (1990; translated in *The Road to San Giovanni,* 1993), gave him the freedom to explore and embrace a scientific perspective more vigorously, honing it into an attitude that is a blend of humanist innocence and scientific wonder.

Moved by the impulse to reach a wider audience and to speak to larger issues, Calvino took a great leap forward into the fashionable world of scientific speculation, boldly turning the critical world on its ear with three collections of short stories: *Le cosmicomiche, Ti con zero* (1967; translated as *t zero,* 1969), and *La memoria del mondo e altre storie cosmicomiche* (The Memory of the World and Other Cosmicomics, 1968). This last volume contains stories from the previous two collections as well as eight additional stories. The 1984 collection *Cosmicomiche vecchie e nuove* (Old and New Cosmicomics) brought together all but two of the cosmic tales published in the 1960s. The subjects here are cosmogonic, and the characters remind one of the freewheeling antics of the gods of Ovid. After the semirealistic style and bittersweet taste of *La giornata di uno scrutatore,* Calvino catapulted his reader into an unbounded and airy science fiction of the past.

These witty tales of *Le cosmicomiche* are narrated for the most part by the protean, energy-like particle of matter that is both within and without time, named Qfwfq–characterized by Calvino as "a voice, a point of view, an eye." Each story begins with a scientific theory explaining the universe at the beginning of time and space. Qfwfq is an eyewitness to the cataclysmic events that forged the world. Although Qfwfq is a disembodied consciousness, "he" brings a human sensitivity to what life was like before the sun was born in "Sul far del giorno" (At Daybreak), how it felt to live as a dinosaur in "I dinosauri" (The Dinosaurs), and the subtle inconveniences and niceties of being compressed into a single dot before the universe expanded in "Tutto in un punto" (All in One Point). The poetic conception of scientific principles is augmented by imaginative invention for such matters as the creation of language in "Un segno nello spazio" (A Sign in Space), the origin of the moon in "La distanza della luna" (The Distance of the Moon), and the theory of evolution in "Lo zio aquatico" (The Aquatic Uncle). Calvino is never bogged down by the scientific implications of his stories; instead he revels in the artistic, mystic, and transcendental possibilities that science offers.

The first part of *Ti con zero* is a sort of sequel to the often whimsical tales of *Le cosmicomiche.* Many of the same themes are elaborated as Qfwfq reveals a comic-strip mythology about birds replete with Ariosto-like trips through the air in "L'origine degli uccelli" (The Origin of the Birds), speculates on how the world might have been had it evolved as a crystallized mineral in "I cristalli" (Crystals), and returns to the subject of the moon in "La molle luna" (The Soft Moon). In the second section of the collection, however, Calvino presents a more arcane and less jocular Qfwfq. It is as if having exhausted the playful connotations of science, he must then adopt scientific methodology to conduct his experiments with reality. The metaphysical stakes are much higher as the unpronounceable raconteur wades through lengthy processes of deductive reasoning.

In the Priscilla stories–"Mitosi" (Mitosis), "Meiosi" (Meiosis), and "Morte" (Death), Qfwfq explores the fundamental processes of unicellular reproduction. Inextricably connected to sex, the ingenious analysis implies that the sheer force of human will lies in the chromosomes whose biological functions determine attraction, repulsion, and death—the epic of life. In the last section of the book Qfwfq disappears. In the short story "Ti con zero" a lion hunter deduces his chances for survival against an attacking lion according to the laws of physics. In "Il guidatore notturno" (The Night Driver) the protagonist makes intricate mathematical calculations in order to discover the best possible relationship to maintain with his lover. "Il conte di Monte Cristo" (The Count of Monte Cristo) presents so complex a hypothetical intellectual topology that the reader is certain that Edmond Dantès, prisoner in the infamous Chateau d'If, will never escape. Calvino clearly elevates philosophy over physical science when the conjectured possibility of escape becomes more important than any attempt at actual escape. The second section of the collection shows that Calvino has shifted his gaze inward to the intricacies and paradoxes that characterize the human mind. The almost obsessive analysis in these stories suggests his fascination with the technique of Alain Robbe-Grillet and the *nouveau roman* (new novel).

Il castello dei destini incrociati (The Castle of Crossed Destinies), first published in *Tarocchi: Il mazzo visconteo di Bergamo e di New York* (1969; translated as *Tarots: The Visconti Pack in Bergamo and New York*, 1976), is a book that Calvino worked on periodically for several years. A 1973 edition titled *Il castello dei destini incrociati* also includes the sequel *La taverna dei destini incrociati* (The Tavern of Crossed Destinies). This text and *Le città invisibili* (1972; translated as *Invisible Cities*, 1974) are probably Calvino's most difficult works. The books complement one another since both are concerned with the retelling of the stories of others and the process of storytelling. In the 1973 postscript to *Il castello dei destini incrociati* Calvino writes about the double origin of the work. The idea first came to him in 1968 while attending an international seminar in which one of the participants spoke of fortune-telling with cards. The die was cast when publisher Franco Maria Ricci decided to bring out an art book employing the Visconti tarot cards illustrated by Bonifazio Bembo and asked Calvino to provide the commentary.

In his essay "La sfida al labirinto" Calvino had expressed a faith in the potential of literature as a game or project. In *Il castello dei destini incrociati* his ploy is to enter the realm of storytelling through a cast of mysteriously mute characters. How will they tell their tales? The answer is to use the fifteenth-century Visconti tarot deck, the cards of which are printed in the margins alongside the verbal narration to provide visual stimuli to the reader and iconographical representations of the stories the characters invent. Calvino arranges the spread of cards into a puzzle of intertwined destinies so that the tales they tell can be read forward as well as backward, up and down, left to right, and right to left. The project is a metaphor for the familiar theme of the struggle between order and the unconscious, for Calvino allows the cards to tell their own story, each card acquiring a meaning according to its place in the emerging sequence. The result of formal experimentation growing out of the author's association with OuLiPo, the book shows the influence of Vladimir Propp's studies of the morphology of the folktale as well of Calvino's continuing interest in chivalric romance and readings in structuralism and semiotics. It is a work of infinite possibilities with neither a beginning nor an end.

In *La taverna dei destini incrociati* a similar group of weary and forlorn travelers is isolated in a tavern and must recount their tales using the so-called Marseilles deck of tarot cards. The characters seem doomed to tell their stories over and over again without respite. The mood of the text is somber, melodramatic, almost infernal. Calvino admits in the postscript to having conceived a sequel titled "Il motel dei destini incrociati" (The Motel of Crossed Destinies), in which survivors of a nuclear holocaust tell their tales using comic-strip remnants, but decided to abandon the project.

Calvino's *Le città invisibili*, the first book to bring him international recognition as a major writer, is a work of unquestionable merit and enduring success. Yet it can hardly be called fiction, for it neither resembles a narrative, nor does it tell a story. Calvino's aim is to create an open series of delicate mood pieces that challenge the nature of logic, meaning, and discourse. In the palace of the emperor of the Tartars, the Great Kublai Khan, though old and enfeebled, speaks with his emissary, Marco Polo. Their talk, mediated by the objects Polo exhibits from his recent journey through the empire of the Khan, is a game of signs in which the explorer attempts to describe the basic design of the kingdom by inventing elegant prose poems while the Khan attempts to divine the "invisible order" of his kingdom hidden in Polo's narrative.

The book is divided into nine chapters, each of which includes two dialogues between Kublai Khan and Marco Polo and the descriptions of a set of cities. The first and last sets contain ten cities apiece while the central sets each contain five cities, for a total of fifty-five cities, each having the

Dust jacket for the American edition of Calvino's Charles Eliot Norton lectures at Harvard, on which he was working when he died

name of a woman (Diomira, Zenobia, Laudomia, Tecla, Raissa). With the sets, the cities are grouped as geometrically arranged series that reflect both an internal and external mapping of mathematical correspondences. The palindromic sequencing is rigid. Each of the nine sections begins and ends with an italicized section in which Kublai Khan and the Venetian traveler converse. The catalogue of cities offers no fewer than eleven headings: the cities and *memory,* the cities and *desire,* the cities and *eyes,* the cities and *names,* the cities and *the dead,* the cities and the *sky, continuous* cities, the cities and *signs, thin* cities, *trading* cities, and *hidden* cities.

The key to understanding *Le città invisibili* is the realization that the cities are metaphors for psychological states and poetic possibilities. The themes of the chimerical cities are varied. Some reveal the ills of mankind: Raissa shows the vanity of the pursuit of happiness; Tecla reveals that life is endless toil. In others the theme of the double image takes the reader to an esoteric rhetorical plane. In "Tamara" the eye "non vede cose ma figure di cose che significano altre cose" (does not see things but images of things that mean other things). The city "dice tutto quello che devi pensare, ti fa ripetere il suo discorso, e mentre credi di visitare Tamara non fai che registrare i nomi con cui essa definisce se stessa e tutte le sue parti" (says everything you must think, makes you repeat her discourse, and while you believe you are visiting Tamara you are only recording the names with which she defines herself and all her parts).

Still other cities reveal a deep concern with social issues: the population explosion, garbage, pollution, and the state of the ecology. In the end one realizes that the plot of the cities is in the mind of Kublai Khan and the mind of the reader as he reads them.

Polo has ingeniously created a treatise on the enigma of communication, of imagination, and of life. The real meaning of the book lies in the closing message of this richly powerful narrative:

> L'inferno dei viventi non è qualcosa che sarà; se ce n'è uno, è quello che è già qui, l'inferno che abitiamo tutti i giorni, che formiamo stando insieme. Due modi ci sono per non soffrirne. Il primo riesce facile a molti: accettare l'inferno e diventarne parte fino al punto di non vederlo più. Il secondo è rischioso ed esige attenzione e apprendimento continui: cercare e saper riconoscere chi e cosa, in mezzo al'inferno non è inferno, e farlo durare, e dargli spazio.

> (The inferno of the living is not something that will be; if there is one, it is what is already here, the inferno where we live every day, that we form by being together. There are two ways to escape suffering it. The first is easy for many: accept the inferno and become such a part of it that you can no longer see it. The second is risky and demands constant vigilance and apprehension: seek and learn to recognize who and what in the midst of the inferno are not inferno, then make them endure, give them space.)

While the imaginary journey invaginates Khan and Polo, it liberates the reader, allowing an inner mapping of the soul and a renewed faith in personal strength and courage.

Calvino's readers had to wait seven years for his next book, *Se una notte d'inverno un viaggiatore* (1979; translated as *If on a Winter's Night a Traveler*, 1981). As if to reassure mockingly his public of the authenticity of the book, he begins the work, "Stai per cominciare a leggere il nuovo romanzo *Se una notte d'inverno un viaggiatore* di Italo Calvino" (You are about to begin reading Italo Calvino's new novel, *If on a Winter's Night a Traveler*). The reader is soon pulled into this tour de force that is, in fact, ten separate novels in one, held together by a frame tale that allows "You," the reader, to enter the text: "Rilassati. Raccogliti. Allontana da te ogni altro pensiero. . . . Prendi la posizione più comoda: seduto, sdraiato, raggomitolato, coricato" (Relax. Concentrate. Dispel every other thought. . . . Find the most comfortable position: seated, stretched out, curled up, or lying flat). You will have company, for Calvino's work abounds with eager Readers, Non-Readers, and Other Readers.

The title of the book evokes a hypothetical nineteenth-century dime novel, but what the reader finds is a potpourri of literary styles and themes. One uncompleted book leads to another as You search for the first book You began to read but were interrupted by a printing error in pagination. You have fallen into an endlessly inventive piece of machinery that is a marvelous send-up of reader-response theory. The quest, however, is not without its pleasures. Along the way You encounter Ludmilla, an elusive Other Reader who entices You to continue the playful, though obviously frustrating, perusing and interruption of one novel after another. You also meet her feminist, structuralist sister Lotaria, a shady translator-thief-counterfeiter named Ermes Marana, and even an author who aspires to write just the novel that You are holding.

In *Il barone rampante* Calvino likens his text to a "filo d'inchiostro" (a trace of ink) that runs on for pages and pages, eventually ending in dream. In "Il conte di Monte Cristo," the story that concludes *Ti con zero*, Edmund Dantès's meditation on how to mentally escape the fortress transforms itself into a meditation by Aleksandr Dumas writing his novel *The Count of Monte Cristo* (1844-1845). These self-conscious books within books are taken to the extreme in *Se una notte d'inverno un viaggiatore*. It is first and foremost a detective novel in search of itself. All the variations of novels that Calvino presents—the South American, the Japanese, the Eastern European, the spy, the adventure, and the detective—and the authors he so ably parodies—Barthes, Borges, Marquez, and Nabokov—are used to construct a fantastic wall of books about books. *Se una notte d'inverno un viaggiatore* is an emblematic text of brilliant rigor in which Calvino celebrates the act of reading by providing a book of eleven (including the frame tale) exceptionally pleasurable potential novels. Although it ultimately relies on conventional literary devices, the text raises important questions about the conventional novel and its possible future permutations.

In 1980 Calvino and his family moved back to Italy, settling in Rome. The protagonist of his next work of fiction, *Palomar* (1983; translated as *Mr. Palomar*, 1985), is a visionary quester after knowledge. Named for the telescope at Mount Palomar in Southern California, he is a wise and perceptive scanner of humanity's foibles and mores. In the manner of Marcovaldo, the Baron Cosimo Piovasco di Rondò, and the Watcher, he is a loner, an onlooker who seems to experience life by thinking about it rather than living it. Much more than in earlier works, though, the reflections here are somber and uncompromisingly realistic. It is an aging Palomar who reviews his life and prepares to take that difficult step to act "come se fosse morto, per vedere come va il mondo senza di lui" (as if he were dead, to see how the world gets along without him).

The book is a series of meditations connected to one another by the temperamental logic of Palomar, who wishes to understand and classify every moment of lived or imagined experience. His aspiration is a daunting one which, as he realizes, is doomed to failure: "Solo dopo aver conosciuto la superficie delle cose ci si può spingere a cercare quel che c'è sotto. Ma la superficie delle cose è inesauribile" (It is only after you have come to know the surface of things that you can venture to seek what is underneath. But the surface of things is inexhaustible). The volume has three main sections: "Le vacanze di Palomar" (Mr. Palomar's Vacation), "Palomar in città" (Mr. Palomar in the City), and "I silenzi di Palomar" (The Silences of Mr. Palomar). Each section has three titled subsections, and each subsection has three parts, numbered 1 through 3. The parts numbered 1 in each subsection correspond to a visual experience; those marked 2 contain cultural or anthropological elements; and the parts marked 3 concern speculations on time, infinity, and the relationship between the self and the world. There are twenty-seven short prose passages in all.

While the scheme of *Palomar* is less complex than that of *Le città invisibili,* Calvino again employs ideas borrowed from science, set theory, semiotics, linguistics, and structuralism. The uniqueness of Palomar's observations is apparent in his attempt to read the precise nature of just one individual wave in the first narrative, "Lettura di un'onda" (Reading a Wave):

Un'onda è sempre diversa da un'altra onda; ma è anche vero che ogni onda è uguale a un'altra onda, anche se non immediatamente contigua o successiva; insomma ci sono delle forme e delle sequenze che si ripetono sia pur distribuite irregolarmente nello spazio e nel tempo.

(Each wave is different from another wave, but it also is true that one wave is equal to another wave even if not immediately adjacent or successive: in other words, there are some forms and sequences that are repeated, though irregularly distributed in space and time.)

In "Un kilo e mezzo di grasso d'oca" (Two Pounds of Goose Fat) he muses over the white softness of the world.

Palomar's apartness is emphasized in "Il museo dei formaggi" (The Cheese Museum) when he waxes philosophically on the social context of cheeses in a cheese store:

–Monsieur! Houhou! Monsieur–Una giovane formaggiaia vestita di rosa è davanti a lui, assorto nel suo taccuino. È il suo turno, tocca a lui, nella fila dietro di lui tutti stanno osservando il suo incongruo comportamento e scuotono il capo con l'aria tra ironica e spazientita con cui gli abitanti delle grandi città considerano il numero sempre crescente dei deboli di mente in giro per le strade.

(–Monsieur! Hoo there! Monsieur–A young clerk, dressed in pink, is standing in front of him while he is occupied with his notebook. It is his turn, he is next; in the line behind him, everyone is observing his incongruous behavior, heads are being shaken with those half-ironic, half-exasperated looks which the inhabitants of the big cities consider the ever-increasing number of the mentally retarded wandering about the streets.)

At the end Palomar discovers that there is no escape through ratiocination. He is shackled to his status as philosopher-observer much in the same way that the baron is a prisoner of his trees, Agilulfo is condemned to nonexistence; Qfwfq is saddled with constant mutation; and Edmond Dantès is an eternal prisoner of Chateau d'If.

Calvino had once commented on the impossibility of even attempting to consider a rationalization of reality through literature in the essay "Non darò più fiato alle trombe" (I will no longer blow horns), which was published in *Una pritra sopra:* "Ero anch'io uno che pensava di fare letteratura (romanzo o non romanzo) nell'intento di razionalizzare la realtà di fondare [o scegliere] dei valori" (I too thought I could create literature [novel and non-novel] with the intent of rationalizing reality and establishing [or choosing] ideals). In *Palomar* Calvino seems to return to this belief as he rejects the principles of causation and seems satisfied to merely catalogue the world. Whenever superrationalization and solipsism seem to overwhelm the hapless philosopher-observer, he finds comfort in the natural world and is reminded of his unique role in the evolving universe.

Calvino continued his own inquiry into reality in a series of ongoing newspaper articles describing personal trips and museum visits as well as providing social commentary. In the journalistic essays gathered in *Collezione di sabbia* (Collections of Sand, 1984) he is the restless voyager obsessed by detail, continuously speculating on the philosophical, social, historical, and cosmic implications beneath the surface of the things he describes. He is a real-life Palomar convinced that should he ever miraculously see exactly what is going on in front of his eyes–if he can discover that hidden thread that simultaneously binds and unties the disparate elements of matter–then he will be able to truly un-

Dust jacket for the American edition of Calvino's 1990 collection of "memory exercises"

derstand the universe. The year following the publication of this collection, the sixty-two-year-old Calvino suffered a stroke. He died in Siena on 19 September 1985.

Calvino's personal meditations continued to be published in the form of melancholy fictions in the experimental vignettes posthumously collected by his wife in *Sotto il sole giaguaro* (1986; translated as *Under the Jaguar Sun,* 1988). In 1972 he intended to write five tales as explorations of the five senses but never completed the project, publishing three early versions in journals in 1976, 1982, and 1984. The three revised tales–"Il nome, il naso" (The Name, the Nose), "Sotto il sole giaguaro" (Under the Jaguar Sun), and "Un re in ascolto" (A King Listens)–give vivid presentations of smell, taste, and hearing and reveal a warmer side of the author.

A human and surprisingly vulnerable Calvino is also evident in the five idiosyncratic and previously published stories collected in *La strada di San Giovanni*. An introductory note by Calvino's wife explains his intent to publish a collection of "memory exercises" that would have included these and other, never written, stories. These unabashedly personal evocations include a war battle in "Ricordo di una battaglia" (Memory of a Battle), the youthful thrill of movie matinees in "Autobiografia di uno spettatore" (A Moviegoer's Autobiography), and the sometimes desperate plight of a writer at his desk in "La poubelle agréée" (The Happy Wastebasket). The title story, written in 1962, recounts Calvino's reconciliation with his father and reveals how his decision to be a writer had divided father and son. At the end of the story the son is stunned when he realizes the price he has to pay for his chosen profession.

Because of the increasing recognition Calvino received toward the end of his life, he frequently visited the United States and gave seminars at both Harvard and Columbia Universities. The month he died he was struggling to complete the essays he was to deliver for the prestigious Charles Eliot Norton Lectures at Harvard, a forum for major statements by important living artists. The collected papers for these lectures were published posthumously by his wife. It is a serene, wise, and contemplative author that appears in the unfinished meditations of *Lezioni americane: Sei proposte per il prossimo millennio* (1988; translated as *Six Memos for the Next Millennium,* 1988). The book serves as a legacy of the man and postscript of the author. Each essay explores a particular literary quality: lightness, the ability to maintain a constant balance despite the gravity of life; quickness, a combination of physical agility with mental acrobatics; exactitude, or preciseness of expression; visibility, the awareness that visual imagination may explain reality; and multiplicity, or the necessary disposition toward the infinite possibilities of life. The missing sixth essay was to address consistency. This defense of literature is a fitting close to a career for a writer who viewed the literary arts as a touchstone of man's existence. Calvino—the unpredictable neorealist, fabulator, essayist, semiotician, rationalist, and imagist—capped his formidable past with a strategy for future action.

In *The Hero with a Thousand Faces* (1949) Joseph Campbell speculates that the standard quest of the traditional hero follows a triptych pattern of separation from the world, a stage of purging and initiation to a new life-giving source of energy, and finally an eventual return to enhanced social status. Such a pattern seems to fit Calvino's literary career. From initial hesitation, to persistent, youthful inquiry, to reclusive withdrawal and eventual mature meditation and projection toward the future, he remained heroically faithful to his craft and to his own poetic vision of storytelling. Indeed it is a measure of his greatness and uncommon historical awareness that from his early neorealist tales to the meta-narrative modes of his later fiction he can be said to reflect the major literary trends of the past forty years. He is and will continue to be one of the most important writers of the twentieth century.

Calvino's message points to the creation of a society in which the impediments of convention, taboo, inhibition, and superstition are removed so that the individual can be a contented member of a society of essentially optimistic, uninhibited individuals. He fundamentally believed in the ability of human beings to win despite obstacles. While pushing his readers toward the far reaches of the universe and into ever expanding dimensions, Calvino never lost sight of human nature and never lost the ability to express his faith in the redemptive potential of intelligence. His writings encompass his intellectual and moral ethic and are a lasting memorial to the richness of imaginative possibilities.

Letters:

I libri degli altri. Lettere 1947–1981, edited by Giovanni Tesio (Turin: Einaudi, 1991).

Interviews:

Mario Lunetta, "Italo Calvino dal paese di Kublai Khan," in his *Sintassi dell'altrove. Conversazioni e interviste letterarie* (Florence: Lalli Editore, 1978), pp. 81–84;

Italo Calvino, "Se una sera d'autunno uno scrittore . . . : Autocolloquio di Italo Calvino," *Europeo,* 36 (17 November 1980): 84–91;

Walter Mauro, "Calvino al crocevia fra realtà e favola," *Il Tempo,* no. 48 (20 February 1984): 3;

Gregory Lucente, "An Interview with Italo Calvino," *Contemporary Literature,* 26, no. 3 (1985): 244–253;

Alexander Stille, "An Interview with Italo Calvino," *Saturday Review* (March–April 1985): 36–39;

Maria Corti, "Italo Calvino," *Autografo,* 2 (October 1985): 47–53.

References:

Sara Maria Adler, *Calvino: The Writer as Fablemaker,* (Potomac, Md.: José Porrúa Turanzas, 1979);

Guido Almansi, "Il mondo binario di Italo Calvino," *Paragone,* 258 (1971): 95–110;

Giorgio Baroni, *Italo Calvino: Introduzione e guida allo studio dell'opera calviniana. Storia e antologia della critica* (Florence: Le Monnier, 1988);

Cristina Benussi, *Introduzione a Calvino* (Rome: Laterza, 1989);

Giuseppe Bertone, ed., *Italo Calvino: la letteratura, la scienza, la città* (Genoa: Marietta, 1986);

Andrea Bisacchia, "Dalla letteratura dell'oggettività alla letteratura della coscienza," *Aspetti del secondo Novecento* (Siracusa: Editrice Meridionale, 1973);

Giuseppe Bonura, *Invito alla lettura di Calvino* (Milan: Mursia, 1972);

Germana Pescio Bottino, *Italo Calvino* (Florence: La Nuova Italia, 1967);

Contarda Calligaris, *Italo Calvino* (Milan: Mursia, 1973); revised by Gian Piero Bernasconi (Milan: Mursia, 1985);

JoAnn Cannon, *Italo Calvino: Writer and Critic* (Ravenna: Longo Editore, 1981);

Albert Howard Carter III, *Italo Calvino: Metamorphoses of Fantasy* (Ann Arbor, Mich.: UMI Research, 1987);

Teresa De Lauretis, "Narrative discourse in Calvino: Praxis of Poesis?," *PMLA,* 90, no. 3 (1975): 414-425;

Giovanni Falaschi, "Ritratti critici di contemporanei: Italo Calvino," *Belfagor,* 27 (1972): 530-558;

Falaschi, ed., *Italo Calvino. Atti del convegno internazionale* (Milan: Garzanti, 1988);

Gian Carlo Ferretti, *Le capre di Bikini: Calvino giornalista e saggista 1945-1985* (Rome: Editori Riuniti, 1989);

Joseph Francese, *Narrating Postmodern Time and Space* (Albany: State University of New York Press, 1997);

Aurore Frasson-Marin, *Italo Calvino et l'imaginaire* (Paris: Editions Slatkine, 1986);

Delia Frigessi, *Inchiesta sulle fate: Italo Calvino e la fiaba* (Bergamo: Lubrina, 1988);

Tommasina Gabriele, *Italo Calvino: Eros and Language* (London: Fairleigh Dickinson University Press, 1994);

John Gatt-Rutter, "Calvino Ludens: Literary Play and Its Political Implications," *Journal of European Studies,* 5 (1975): 319-340;

Kathryn Hume, *Calvino's Fictions: Cogito and Cosmos* (Oxford: Clarendon Press, 1992);

Claudio Marabini, "Scrittori negli anni sessanta: Italo Calvino," *Nuova Antologia,* 501 (1967): 374-393;

Antonia Mazza, "Italo Calvino: Uno scrittore dimezzato?," *Letture,* 26 (1971): 3-14;

Claudio Milanini, *L'utopia discontinua. Saggio su Italo Calvino* (Milan: Gazanti, 1990);

Francesca Bernardini Napoletano, *I segni nuovi di Italo Calvino* (Rome: Bulzoni, 1977);

Irene T. Olken, *With Pleated Eye and Garnet Wing: Symmetries of Italo Calvino* (Ann Arbor: University of Michigan Press, 1984);

Sergio Pautasso, "Il filo invisibile di Calvino," in *Il laboratorio dello scrittore* (Florence: La Nuova Italia Editore, 1975), pp. 21-52;

Lorenzo Pellizzari, ed., *L'Avventura di uno spettatore: Italo Calvino e il cinema* (Bergamo: Lubrina Editore, 1990);

Franco Petroni, "Italo Calvino: Dall'impegno all'arcadia neocapitalistica," *Studi Novecenteschi,* 5, nos. 13-14 (1976): 57-101;

Olga Ragusa, "Italo Calvino: The Repeated Conquest of Contemporaneity," *World Literature Today,* 57, no. 2 (1983): 195-201;

Lucia Re, *Calvino and the Age of Neorealism* (Stanford, Calif.: Stanford University Press, 1990);

Franco Ricci, *Difficult Games: A Reading of "I racconti" by Italo Calvino* (Waterloo: Wilfred Laurier University Press, 1990);

Ornella Sobrero, "Calvino scrittore 'rampante,'" *Il caffè,* 12 (1964): 28-42;

Gore Vidal, "Fabulous Calvino," *New York Review of Books,* 21 (20 May 1974): 13-21;

Beno Weiss, *Understanding Italo Calvino* (Columbia: University of South Carolina Press, 1993);

John R. Woodhouse, *Italo Calvino: A Reappraisal and an Appreciation of the Trilogy* (Hull: University of Hull Press, 1968).

Ferdinando Camon
(14 November 1935 -)

Angela M. Jeannet
Franklin and Marshall College

BOOKS: *Il mestiere di poeta* (Milan: Lerici, 1965);
La moglie del tiranno (Milan: Lerici, 1969); enlarged as *Il mestiere di scrittore: conversazioni critiche* (Milan: Garzanti, 1973);
Il quinto stato (Milan: Garzanti, 1970; revised, 1988); translated by John Shepley as *The Fifth Estate* (Marlboro, Vt.: Marlboro Press, 1987);
La vita eterna (Milan: Garzanti, 1972; revised, 1988); translated by Shepley as *Life Everlasting* (Marlboro, Vt.: Marlboro Press, 1987);
Liberare l'animale (Milan: Garzanti, 1973);
Letteratura e classi subalterne (Venice-Padua: Marsilio, 1974);
Occidente (Milan: Garzanti, 1975);
Avanti popolo (Milan: Garzanti, 1977);
Un altare per la madre (Milan: Garzanti, 1978); translated by David Calicchio as *Memorial* (Marlboro, Vt.: Marlboro Press, 1983);
La malattia chiamata uomo (Milan: Garzanti, 1981); translated by Shepley as *The Sickness Called Man* (Marlboro, Vt.: Marlboro Press, 1992);
Storia di Sirio: parabola per la nuova generazione (Milan: Garzanti, 1984); translated by Cassandra Bertea as *The Story of Sirio: A Parable* (Marlboro, Vt.: Marlboro Press, 1985);
La donna dei fili (Milan: Garzanti, 1986);
I miei personaggi mi scrivono (Padua: Nord-Est, 1987);
Il canto delle balene (Milan: Garzanti, 1989);
Il Super-Baby (Milan: Rizzoli, 1991);
Il Santo assassino: dichiarazioni apocrife (Venice: Marsilio, 1991);
Mai visti sole e luna (Milan: Garzanti, 1994);
La Terra é di tutti (Milan: Garzanti, 1996).
Collection: *Romanzi della pianura* (Milan: Garzanti, 1988)—includes revised *Il quinto stato* and *La vita eterna.*

OTHER: Enrico Groppali, *L'ossessione e il fantasma: il teatro di Pasolini e Moravia,* preface by Camon (Venice: Marsilio, 1979);
Primo Levi, *Autoritratto di Primo Levi,* edited by Camon (Padua: Nord-Est, 1987); republished as *Conversazione con Primo Levi* (Milan: Garzanti,

Ferdinando Camon in Paris, 1991

1991); translated by John Shepley as *Conversations with Primo Levi* (Marlboro, Vt.: Marlboro Press, 1989);
Alberto Moravia: io e il mio tempo, edited by Camon (Padua: Nord-Est, 1988).

Ferdinando Camon belongs to the generation of Italians whose early childhood occurred during World War II. His writings are intensely concerned with issues that have tormented and excited his contemporaries: the horrors of living through a war fought on one's own territory and Italy's rapid transition from a predominantly agrarian culture to an industrial society facing such novel phenomena as mass culture, political terrorism, the import of psychoanalysis, and the linguistic and literary issues connected with them. His novels and essays as well as his willingness to explore the most disturbing trends of recent Italian history have made him one of the best-known interpreters of Italian postwar culture.

Camon was born on 14 November 1935 in a small village in the province of Padua, near the town of Montagnana, which is encircled by walls dating from the beginning of the second millennium. The town is also notable as the location where Italian director Renato Castellani filmed *Romeo and Juliet* in the early 1950s. Camon belonged to a peasant family. He was ten years old when World War II ended and remembers well bombings and raids. From the branches of a tree he used to climb he observed the air duels between Allied and German fighter planes and saw Italian Resistance fighters being hunted by Fascists and German troops. One day he saw a relative, who belonged to the Garibaldi guerrilla formations, surrender to the Germans in the middle of a burned-out wheat field. He was holding in his hands his intestines, which were escaping from a massive wound. That scene obsessively reappears in the novel titled *La vita eterna* (1972; translated as *Life Everlasting,* 1987) and in the poem "Occorrono interi millenni," included in *Liberare l'animale* (Freeing the Beast, 1973).

Camon began his schooling in the Montagnana area, then continued his studies at the University of Padua in the humanities. He still lives in Padua with his wife, Gabriella Imperatori, a journalist, whom he married in 1962. They have two sons, Alessandro and Alberto, who hold degrees in philosophy and law, respectively. Tall, dark-haired, and dark-eyed, Camon is an impressive presence in person. He is soft-spoken and eager to establish contact with an interlocutor. This personable demeanor served him well early in his career as an interviewer. In fact his first two books consist of conversations with Italian novelists and poets titled *Il mestiere di poeta* (The Poet's Trade, 1965) and *La moglie del tiranno* (The Wife of the Tyrant, 1969), the latter of which was enlarged with the addition of an interview with Italo Calvino and republished as *Il mestiere di scrittore* (The Writer's Trade, 1973). The subjects interviewed include Alberto Moravia, Vasco Pratolini, Giorgio Bassani, Carlo Cassola, and Pier Paolo Pasolini.

Camon's perceptive and informative interviews show his intense interest in literary matters such as style and theme. He created a new tool for critical analysis, what Camon calls "una critica parlata" (a spoken critic), a true dialogue in which a reader-critic and a writer speak to each other as peers. The ambiance as well as body language are significant factors in the exchange. The conversations focus on the relationships between technique and experience, literature and its social context, and reception and self-evaluation.

The dialogue is doubly revealing, for Camon conveys the sense of his own contribution to the exchange, not only by the aptness of his questions but also by the originality of his views and familiarity with the dilemmas and pleasures inherent in the process of writing. Two themes are particularly prominent: the complexity and determinant function of linguistic factors, and the fundamental significance of the social and cultural changes that have occurred in society. The titles of the two collections exploit the ambiguity of the Italian term "mestiere," which corresponds to "trade" as well as "craft." It is clear that Camon is concerned both with the trade a writer exercises in the world and with the culturally imposed apprenticeship it assumes. In his own career as a novelist he often entertains the same fundamental questions: What is the writer's trade? How does one learn it? Why and for whom does one write?

Camon's initial novel, *Il quinto stato* (1970; translated as *The Fifth Estate,* 1987), was the first of three novels in what he called "il ciclo degli ultimi" (The Saga of Those Who Are Last). The Enlightenment had focused on the "third estate," the bourgeoisie, and in the nineteenth century a "fourth estate," the proletariat, had emerged. Camon, however, refers to a social stratum that had never had a voice, the peasant class. *Il quinto stato* tells the stories of peasants who once lived in the Po Valley, hemmed in by marshy fields, contiguous to but light-years away from the Italian postwar "economic miracle." The protagonist is actually an entire people. Camon in his superb preface for the revised edition of the novel included in *Romanzi della pianura* (Novels of the Plains, 1988) characterizes them as an alien and disappearing presence in the nation.

Camon evokes a harsh country landscape as he chronicles the demise of an entire way of life. The story he tells is neither demagogic, nor sentimental, nor easily associated with the narratives of the peasant-turned-industrial proletariat that were prominent in the nineteenth- and early-twentieth-century fiction. A first-person male narrator recounts his childhood and his discovery of the existence of a world beyond the Po plains. The eye that sees, the voice that narrates are double: they belong

Dust jacket for Camon's 1988 book, revised versions of the first two novels in the series he called "il ciclo degli ultimi" (The Saga of Those Who Are Last)

at the same time to the consciousness that is still rooted in the native land and to that same consciousness after its separation from that world. Such a separation, whether it brings salvation or damnation, implies a transgression, and it has left a wound. Writing is the record of that transgression and the expression of that dislocation.

Camon's style in this novel may be considered in the context of the issue raised by Ignazio Silone at the outset of his *Fontamara* (1931): What is the appropriate linguistic expression for a narrator striving to relate a story lived by people whose language was unknown, or despised, outside of their villages? His solution is original and highly effective as the book is written in the language the narrator learned in school but with a rhythm and images of its own. The result is a medium appropriate to the mature, cultured narrator while it conveys to the outsider the alien worldview of the illiterate, dialect-speaking peasants of the plains. The language is a mixture of incongruous elements welded seamlessly together, incorporating both bits of dialect and some learned terms. The reader can hear in it the voice of a culture that had not been heard before, its silence born of isolation, humiliation, and a fear that has lasted for centuries.

Because everything in the peasant universe is present and the future is nonexistent, the narration is atemporal and presents a world where change is unknown: "Altro mai non avviene perché tutto è immobile" (Nothing ever happens because everything is immobile). However, immobility becomes evident only if confronted by change. Midway through the novel, though, the narrator has a "mirabile visione" (wondrous vision) of the city and its culture, so different from the peasants' world that it requires a different language: "Non sono diverse parole che indicano la stessa cosa ma sono cose diverse indicate giustamente da parole diverse" (They are not different words that indicate the same things, but different things that are rightly indicated by different words). It is through the language and manners of a young city girl who is a guest at his house that the narrator first catches a glimpse of what lies outside his closed universe.

The narrator's rediscovery of that diversity is accompanied by his sense of being nothing and his desire to be reborn within that new world of speaking, the city. He experiences the city as a structure that follows the hierarchical plan of Dante's heavens, with varying degrees of beatitude from periphery to center. The loneliness of Hell, or peasant life, is replaced by streets, buses, and cafés filled with people and by previously unimaginable comforts. Nevertheless, the city remains a foreign world. The narrator of *Il quinto stato* ultimately reveals a long-suppressed and double rage: rage for having been a peasant and rage at being confused in the city.

Pier Paolo Pasolini wrote an enthusiastic preface for this story of emigration and exile, which Camon in a fall 1988 interview for *Italian Quarterly* characterized as "too passionate" for a young writer. Pasolini overlooked a fundamental difference between his own and Camon's vision. Whereas the older writer saw in peasant culture the unspoiled future of humanity and the promise of the subversion of capitalism and consumerism, Camon's narrator does not wish for the survival of the "culture of penury." He speaks of the impossibility of the survival of the peasantry, the foundation of such a culture.

In *La vita eterna,* the second book in the series, Camon examines World War II as seen by the people at the bottom of the social scale. For the peasants of Camon's world all wars are much the same: the armed invader is still and always Lord Ezzelino—the prototypical military conqueror who built the walls around Montagnana in the depths of the Middle Ages—and the gestures of domination and the atrocities differ little through time. Those crushed by history do not imagine the future, for that word is synonymous with hope. Fear is a condition suffered historically by peasants, and it is a fear not of what may happen but of what will necessarily happen again because it has happened before.

The narrator speaks a literary language familiar to the reader, but Camon is able to infuse the narration with a hint of unreality, as though the story were coming through a simultaneous translator with imperceptible pauses. History, readers are told, is an alien construct of a culture that places goals at the end of straight lines and possesses a linguistic medium in which events become a solid structure with a particular meaning. The experience of subordinated people must be translated if they are to be heard at all. Being a victim in Camon's world is to be caught in the labyrinth of history built by a foreign architect; it means becoming imprisoned in other people's versions of historical events. *La vita eterna* was a best-seller in Europe, particularly in Germany where it contributed to the prosecution of an S.S. officer, mentioned by name, whose brutality was described.

Liberare l'animale, which won the Viareggio prize, is Camon's only book of poetry. (He plans to publish a second collection in 1998, "Dal silenzio delle campagne" [From the Silence of the Plains].) It is a slim volume in which he asserts that he is above all a writer by choice or vocation, malediction or grace. In *Avanti popolo* (Onward, the People!, 1977), a collection of his periodical writings, he asserts: "L'orgoglio e la gioia di aver difeso la necessità del discorso poetico . . . può essere la gioia e l'orgoglio di chi ha inteso la condizione nella quale il mondo si trova, e ha temuto che la lingua gli si gelasse in bocca, ma non gli s'è gelata" (the pride and joy of having defended the necessity of poetic discourse . . . may also be the joy and pride of one who has understood the plight of the world and had feared that his voice would die on his lips, but his voice hasn't died).

As a critic Camon often explores the connection between ideology and language. He knows, as Pier Paulo Pasolini remarked in "Il mestiere di poeta," that language is a filter, a "social communicative convention," that the neutrality of language is a fallacy, and that the norm for validating and organizing experience is embodied in the language of the technologically advanced middle class. Camon lives in the universe of that norm and yet is aware of the norms that inform other, nondominant cultures. In *Letteratura e classi subalterne* (Literature and the Subordinate Classes, 1974) he dissects the conflict of classes as it is embedded in the written language and within which the writer is caught. He discusses the issue of writing in local dialects and the various positions taken by contemporary Italian authors such as Pasolini.

In the section titled "Classi subalterne e letteratura: il codice interpretativo umile" (Subordinate Classes and Literature: The Humble Interpretive Code) there is a detailed and uncompromising analysis of the intersection of linguistic and cultural conflict. The reader witnesses the collision of two worlds and the rejection of each by the other. Ca-

Page from the manuscript of Mai visti sole e luna *(Collection of Ferdinando Camon)*

mon publishes and rebuts a critique of *Il quinto stato*—not a review written by a fellow writer or a critic but a letter from one of his country relatives who felt betrayed by the novel and the writer's exposure of a culture both once shared. Ambivalent in his empathy for his relative's feelings, Camon as an artist argues that the critique is alien to the world of autonomous freedom that is literature. The criticism of the novel, he argues, is anchored in an archaic system of values that wishes to control what is said. And yet the urgency of those values is seared in the writer's memory. Pasolini agrees with the peasant author of the letter.

While he maintains his aesthetic argument, Camon allows his readers a rare glimpse into a world that has been made invisible because it is viewed as subordinate. He explicates the interpretive code of this culture, with its folk beliefs and its obeisance to Roman Catholic conventions, mythology, and style. As in any religiously informed universe, no distancing, no detachment, no ambiguity is acceptable: "Il codice 'umile' è principalmente contenutista. Il contenutismo è principalmente realismo. Il suo realismo è esclusivamente moralismo" (The "humble" code is basically content-oriented. Content is interpreted as realism. Realism is interpreted exclusively as moralism). Literature is offensive to the culture of the sacred because it places itself outside that system of values and because it "uses" people for its own ends: "La sottrazione di valori lascia dietro di sè il vuoto ... richiama l'immagine della letteratura come guerra" (The destruction of values leaves behind the void ... it evokes the image of literature as war). The analysis raises important issues, for the conflict between the artistic and religious views is the same that sent author Salman Rushdie into hiding to save his life from fundamentalists.

The first of a two-book sequence that Camon called "il ciclo del terrore" (The Cycle of Terror), *Occidente* (The West, 1975) is about the eruption of a new brand of violence in the region of the Veneto and the western world, neofascist violence. The story is inspired by the actual struggle between an exhausted, discredited bourgeoisie that has lost its hold on power and a poorly organized proletariat that cannot yet rule. Groups of the left and the right are the protagonists, and through them Camon depicts the cycles of birth, development, and internal dissension that characterized Italian political life in the late 1960s and 1970s.

The narration in *Occidente* shifts between the first and the third person. The characters are marionette-like in their compulsive agitation, and the plot they follow, while intricate, is shaped by the larger elementary struggle of two groups vying for control, but Camon is nevertheless able through his first-person narrations to involve the reader in the action. The frequent intervention of the third-person narrating voice ensures detachment, enabling Camon to dissect each moment in the cycle of violence with clinical precision while chronicling events for the reader. In this unique presentation of political rage, centuries-old hatreds between the classes play themselves out, inspiring in the narrator and the reader alike an unsavory attraction.

The chronicle of the collision between the neofascists and the students and workers, accurately reconstructed down to the transcription of political debates and ideological pamphlets, also has a dimension almost of hallucinatory fantasy. The characters, who happen to live at the historical moment when the transition of power from the old rulers to the formerly oppressed begins to take place, are "partoriti da una sconfitta . . . da un'esplosione che ha fatto il vuoto alle loro spalle" (bred by a defeat . . . by an explosion that created a void behind them). Their existence is a daily attempt to forget or avenge that defeat, that explosion. It is not surprising that the last societal convulsion treated in the novel is marked by the decimation of the government and business leaders held hostage by terrorists.

Upon the publication of *Occidente* terrorist groups of the Right threatened Camon's life. When a 1976 film was based on the novel, he and his family had to leave town. Franco Freda, a neofascist leader, believed he saw himself in the protagonist of Camon's novel and filed a complaint against the author, which was dismissed. Freda, who later was condemned to life in prison for his crimes but then was acquitted and released, subsequently had a daylong interview with Camon, which was published in *I miei personaggi mi scrivono* (My Characters Write to Me, 1987). When Camon asked his interlocutor what was the innocence he claimed, the answer was: "È innocente non colui che è incapace di peccare, ma colui che pecca senza rimorso" (innocent is not one who is incapable of sinning, but one who sins without remorse).

Since the 1970s Camon has become one of the major voices in Italian cultural life. Although opposed to punditry and uninterested in fashionable literary circles, Camon has participated intensely in journalistic life, contributing opinion columns to several major Italian dailies, including *Il Corriere della sera*, *Il Giorno*, *L'Unità*, and *La Stampa*. He gathered these writings from between 1972 and 1977 in *Avanti popolo*. The title echoes the first line of a popular song of the Italian Resistance during World War II.

Although Camon was deeply involved in the issues of a rapidly changing Italian society, he was still in his imagination drawn to his former life in the Po Valley and returned to that world with *Un altare per la madre* (1978; translated as *Memorial*, 1983), the last work of his Saga of Those Who Are Last and winner of the prestigious Premio Strega award. Camon tells the story of a man who returns to his native village to attend his mother's funeral. She belonged to a society where no one knew how to write, so its unwritten utterances and its memories are bound to die if they are not remembered or recorded. In attempting to reappropriate the world he has left behind while carrying its burdens inside, the man shows how writing can enter the world of unwritten memories and treat them with dignity and love.

In *Un altare per la madre* Camon depicts the traditions and values of an oral culture, with its gestures, aphorisms, and parables, through a sophisticated literary approach. In contrast to his earlier, more generalized treatments of peasant culture, Camon concentrates here on the individual reality. The mother lives in an "earthen world" that Camon refuses to idealize or subject to tragic transfigurations. There is no idyllic contemplation of nature, and poverty is an enveloping presence. Exhausting work is as unavoidable as the weather, and violence is often experienced in atrocious ways as foreign-speaking armies periodically bring war to an otherwise forgotten land.

And yet the values dear to the mother and her people are deeply held and profound. They include solidarity, the refusal to take human lives, and a humility so profound as to be unaware of itself. The mother is one of the least among those who are last, yet the memory of her and her generous actions will live on in the altar her husband builds by hand out of wood and copper. The pace of the narrative parallels the slow, careful pace of the widower's manual work as the narrator concentrates on realizing the details of peasant culture and builds "un altare di parole" (an altar of words). The two altars perpetuate the memory of an individual without isolating her from the collective context that held and nurtured her. The material altar belongs to her "language," while the altar made of words is, as the narrator explains, a translation of that homage into the medium of another world: "Scrivo queste cose in italiano, cioè le traduco in un'altra lingua" (I am writing these things in Italian, that is to say I am translating them into another language).

Camon makes it clear that writing is an act of translation. It is building anew, using new materials but also a few irreplaceable bits of the old, the most poignant reminders of what is being lost, that could not otherwise be preserved. His book is not only the record of what is passing away but also a homage and a testimonial to the worth of his Saga of Those Who Are Last, a memorial written in the very language that excluded them. In the conclusion to his trilogy on the end of peasant civilization, the transition to the new culture of the written word is concretely consummated and symbolically performed. In this novel and in all his work Camon attempts to be faithful to human experience in all its diversity, especially when he lends a voice to those historically silent groups excluded from the literary tradition.

In *La malattia chiamata uomo* (1981; translated as *The Sickness Called Man,* 1993) Camon turns to the agony of a man coming to terms with his own deep wounds caused by his separation from his native culture, but he also continues to probe the meaning of the act of writing. The novel is the first of a cycle that Camon calls "il ciclo della famiglia" (The Cycle of the Family), for he believes that the family is at the center of the dilemmas that individuals face in a postindustrial context of continuous changes. Camon began his career as a novelist with the exploration of a crisis of culture, continued by exploring the sociopolitical crisis of terrorism, and now he set out to examine the type of crises that cause people to turn to the analysis of the psyche.

In this story of a man's psychoanalysis, told in the first person by the subject of the analysis, the reader becomes privy to the rapport between the analysand and his analyst as well as the narrator's fears, dreams, and obsessions. His abandonment of his native culture has exacted a high price, as pride and shame are mingled in the hurt of having cut off his roots. Paradoxically, he learns that writing, which is a means of "speaking out," also silences the speech that is "Other." The language of rebirth, the language of literature, is also the language of loss and loneliness. Writing brings estrangement and a new imprisonment, a point poignantly made by the narrator of *Un altare per la madre:* "Colui che non gli è permesso di usare la propria lingua non può essere felice e sentirsi libero. Più scrivo e più mi lego" (The one who is not allowed to use his own language cannot be happy and feel free. The more I write, the more I bind myself). Whereas earlier authors had to come to grips with the questions of how to speak of and to the Other, the questions Camon wrestles with are more personal: How can one write of the self that is also the Other? How can one speak the language of the Other and be oneself?

Storia di Sirio: parabola per la nuova generazione (1984; translated as *The Story of Sirio: A Parable,* 1985) brought to completion the Cycle of Terror that Camon began with *Occidente*. Subtitled by Camon as "a parable for a new generation," the novel covers the various stages through which a young man comes to awareness during the 1970s. The protagonist, Sirio, is a representative European youth from the upper middle class. The son of a wealthy and powerful industrialist, he is expected to find his place in the paternalistic, family-centered Italian society. The protagonist begins his maturing alone, as the understudy of his authoritarian father, but is influenced more and more by a close friend and other young people. As Sirio becomes aware of social injustices, he gives up his social position and leaves home, refusing to abide by the conventions of his class. He joins a collective, participates in violent demonstrations, and experiences the failure of revolutionary activities.

Sirio's personal development parallels and enriches his social maturation as he falls in and out of love and experiences the loss of a friend who is betrayed by politics and drug addiction and sentenced to a long jail term. Having witnessed the destructiveness of violence and drugs, he ultimately turns to self-analysis with a group of his peers. Camon shows a keen sensitivity to the atmosphere of the 1970s and the language of the young. In this tale of a rebellious, earnest, and intense generation, with its naiveté and its disastrous experiments, the reader perceives an authentically rendered dramatic moment in Italian history.

In *La donna dei fili* (A Woman Ensnared, 1986), the second volume in the Cycle of the Family, the female protagonist, who suffers the collapse of her family and has no true sense of direction in her life, resorts to psychoanalysis and embarks on a journey within herself. The narrator who observes Michela, the protagonist, asserts that "l'entrata in analisi fa l'uomo più uomo, la donna più donna" (entering analysis makes a man more manly, a woman more womanly). Whereas the male protagonist of *La malattia chiamata uomo* went into analysis as if it were a war and confronted the powerful presences such as his political party, his mother, and the Church that tormented his life, Michela goes inside her own dreams and fantasies.

During each descent Michela unlocks a compartment of symbols and begins a retrieval of meanings. Each relationship Michela has is a long thread that gets tangled with the other threads, until she feels she is suffocating: "Tutti volevano vivere a mie spese. Mio marito, mia figlia, mia madre. Tutti volevano vivere la propria vita, sapendo che potevano sempre contare sulla mia. Io non avevo scampo" (They all wanted to live off me. My husband, my daughter, my mother. They all wanted to live their lives, knowing that they could always count on mine. I was trapped). Through the psychoanalytical experience, however, she finds the strength to live, though precariously, by herself and for herself.

At the end of the 1980s Camon began another two-volume cycle—"il ciclo della coppia" (The Cycle of the Couple)—with *Il canto delle balene* (The Whales' Song, 1989). Camon's characters, particularly the males, seem ill at ease with the changes society is undergoing, particularly with the changing balance of power between men and women. Here, a professional man nearing middle age is asked by his wife and her therapist to participate in one of their sessions. What he discovers to his utter dismay is that his and his wife's sexual activities, which he believed they kept a secret between themselves, have become the subject of the analysis.

The comical fury of the husband makes this the most humorous of Camon's novels. When the hapless protagonist vents his frustration by having an affair, he asserts that he is only attempting to recapture a last glimpse of his youthful fantasies and regain a measure of privacy. While engaged in an adulterous relationship he actually feels as though he is remaining faithful to his wife: "Senza segreti non si può vivere" (Without secrets, one cannot live). In a further commentary on society, this dysfunctional couple is seen against the backdrop of a perpetual search for something elusive and mysterious, whose metaphor is the tourists' pursuit of the sound of whales that cross in the distance off the California shore.

The second novel of the cycle, *Il Super-Baby* (The Super Baby, 1991), treats issues of reproduction, gestation, and birthing in an advanced technological age. The male narrator in a long monologue laments being left out of the drama of childbearing. His early attempts at impregnating his wife having failed, he contemplates the conception and growth of his child from outside the process as modern techniques of fecundation and parturition allow his wife to conceive and prepare for delivery. As grotesque images become more and more frequent in the novel, the foreignness and power of the maternal body is presented as intimidating for the male character and a source of his hostility toward the female. The various moments in the saga of giving birth—says the author in the postscript—can be read by men "come romanzi epici a puntate" (like cantos of epic poems), and it is obvious that the protagonist is disturbed by an epic in which he has no role. Again, Camon focuses on a character who feels lost and is filled with repressed rage in a transformed society.

In the late 1980s and into the 1990s Camon has resumed the interview-dialogue, the activity with which he began his literary career. Edited and produced exclusively by him, the volumes published by *Nord-Est* (Northeast), whose title refers to the geographical area of Italy where he and several other prominent authors operate, give a voice to some of the most interesting of Camon's interlocutors, including a female reader who responds to *La donna dei fili,* Alberto Moravia, and—most movingly—Primo Levi. In *Il Santo assassino: dichiarazioni apocrife* (The Saint Assassin: Apocharyphal Declarations, 1991) the interviewer has disappeared, and the interviewees speak alone. The script, however, is written by the absent interviewer, and readers soon realize that the unusual voices they are listening to are the fictions of a novelist's imagination.

In *Mai visti sole e luna* (They Knew Neither Sun nor Moon, 1994) Camon returns to the land of his beginnings. He speaks again about the encounters that have taken place between the country people of the Po plains, the outsiders who cannot communicate with them, and the armies that throughout history have arrived in successive waves to torture, kill, and destroy. Camon's language is again rich in dialectal inflections, flavorful similes, and aphorisms. The narration flows as in folk recitations and storytelling. Camon strikes a humorous note at the beginning of the book: "Quando le tragedie della storia si confondono, e il ragazzo interrogato a scuola nel datare un avvenimento sbaglia di tre secoli, vuol dire che non fanno più male: che ci siano state o non ci siano state non fa nessuna differenza" (When the tragedies of history get confused with one another, and the students in class are wrong by three centuries, it means that those events don't hurt any more. It doesn't matter any longer if they happened or not). But the reader soon realizes that this is precisely the story of the events that some cannot forget. Camon's black humor, with its horrific details, guarantees that no forgiveness will be granted any tormentors on behalf of the victims. In his postscript Camon asserts that all that happened is destined to sink into silence, and it is this sense of loss and profound injustice that gives the text the raw power of desperate truthfulness. Such was the passion that caused Count Ugolino to tell his tale of inhumanity in Dante's Hell.

Ferdinando Camon is one of the best-known Italian authors of his generation and is well known in the rest of Europe. In 1996 he published the novel *La Terra è di tutti,* about the chaos in Europe resulting from the recent flood of immigration from Africa, Asia, and South America. Television films have been made of *Occidente* and *Un altare per la madre.* In France, Jean-Paul Sartre, to whom *La vita eterna* is dedicated, supported the translation of all of Camon's works in the Gallimard collection. Also in France *La malattia chiamata uomo* has been adapted into a play. For Camon writing is not a marginal, solitary activity but a form of action, a transgressive as well as joyful impulse. He merges the desire to tell a story, to keep alive the memory of human experience, with a writer's passion for craft and a belief in the autonomy of literature. The effort to integrate literature and the great human dilemmas of his times are the vital core of Camon's writing.

Interviews:

Gabriella Imperatori, "Ferdinando Camon," in *Profondo Nord* (Padua: Nord-Est, 1988), pp. 189–214;

Angela M. Jeannet, "Conversazione con Ferdinando Camon," *Italian Quarterly,* 29 (Fall 1988): 59–68;

Sophie Ronsin, "Interview de Ferdinando Camon," *Chroniques italiennes,* 6 (1990): 161–171.

References:

Vittorio Dornetti, "Sociologia e letteratura nel 'Quinto stato' di Camon," *Otto-Novecento,* 3 (March–April 1979): 329–340;

Angela M. Jeannet, "The Worlds of Ferdinando Camon," in *Italiana,* edited by Albert N. Mancini, P. Giordano, and P. R. Baldini (River Forest, Ill: Rosary College, 1988), pp. 347–359;

Carlo A. Madrignani, "Il rosso e il nero del 'cittadino' Camon," *Quaderni piacentini,* 58–59 (1976): 191–195;

Cesare de Michelis, "Ferdinando Camon," *Studi novecenteschi,* 12 (June 1985): 7–35;

Nada Pesetti, "Camon: lingua e narrazione dei 'vilani,'" *L'immagine riflessa,* 1 (May–August 1977): 182–198.

Gianni Celati
(10 January 1937 -   )

Michael Hanne
University of Auckland

BOOKS: *Comiche* (Turin: Einaudi, 1971);
Le avventure di Guizzardi (Turin: Einaudi, 1973);
Il chiodo in testa, by Celati and Carlo Gajani (Pollenza-Macerata: Nuova Foglio, 1975);
Finzioni occidentali: Fabulazioni, comicità e scrittura (Turin: Einaudi, 1975; revised and enlarged, 1986);
La banda dei sospiri (Turin: Einaudi, 1976);
La bottega dei mimi (Pollenza-Macerata: Nuova Foglio, 1977);
Lunario del paradiso (Turin: Einaudi, 1978);
Frasi per narratori (Bologna: C.U.S.L., 1984);
Narratori delle pianure (Milan: Feltrinelli, 1985); translated by Robert Lumley as *Voices from the Plains* (London: Serpent's Tail, 1989);
Quattro novelle sulle apparenze (Milan: Feltrinelli, 1987); translated by Stuart Hood as *Appearances* (London: Serpent's Tail, 1991);
Il profilo delle nuvole, immagini di un paesaggio italiano, text by Celati, photographs by Luigi Ghirri (Milan: Feltrinelli, 1989);
Verso la foce (Milan: Feltrinelli, 1989);
L'Orlando innamorato raccontato in prosa (Turin: Einaudi, 1994);
Recita dell'attore Vecchiatto nel teatro di Rio Saliceto (Milan: Feltrinelli, 1996);
Avventure in Africa (Milan: Feltrinelli, 1997);
Collection: *Parlamenti buffi* (Milan: Feltrinelli, 1989).

TELEVISION: *La strada provinciale delle anime,* written and directed by Celati, Pierrot, and La Rosa, 1991.

OTHER: *Alice disambientata: materiali collettivi (su Alice) per un manuale di sopravvivenza,* edited by Celati (Milan: L'erba voglio, 1978);
Narratori delle riserve, edited by Celati (Milan: Feltrinelli, 1992).

TRANSLATIONS: Jonathan Swift, *Favola della botte* (Bologna: Samptetro, 1966);
Jack London, *Il richiamo della foreste* (Turin: Einaudi, 1986);

Gianni Celati (photograph by Marianne Fleitmann)

Herman Melville, *Bartleby lo scrivano* (Milan: Feltrinelli, 1991);
Stendhal, *La certosa di purma* (Milan: Feltrinelli, 1993);
Friedrich Hölderlin, *Poesie delle Torre* (Milan: Feltrinelli, 1993);
Louis-Ferdinand Céline, *Guignoll's Band I–II* (Turin: Einaudi, 1996);
Swift, *I viaggi di Gulliver* (Milan: Feltrinelli, 1997).

SELECTED PERIODICAL PUBLICATIONS–UNCOLLECTED: "Il sogno senza fondo," *Quindici,* 9 (1968): 6-7;
"Parlato come spettacolo," *Il Verri,* series 4, 26 (1968): 80-88;
"Al bivio della letteratura fantastica," *Periodico ipotetico,* 6 (1972): 10-12;
"Da *Finnegan's Wake* di James Joyce: Elaborazioni sul tema visita al museo Wellington. Traduzioni di linguaggi inventati," *Il Caffé,* 19, no. 3-4 (1972): 26-30;
"Il racconto di superficie," *Il Verri,* series 5, 1 (1973): 93-114;
"Il corpo comico nello spazio," *Il Verri,* series 6, 3 (1976): 22-32;

"Palomar, la prosa nel mondo," *Alfabeta,* 59 (1984): 7-8;

"Finzioni a cui credere," *Alfabeta,* 67 (1984): 13.

Gianni Celati is not a writer whose work can be easily categorized. His fiction divides into two distinct phases, each of which has occupied almost a decade. He established his reputation in the 1970s with a series of four experimental novels—of which the most successful was *Le avventure di Guizzardi* (The Adventures of Guizzardi, 1973)—noted for their comically frenetic energy and stylistic exuberance as well as their representation of the world of individuals on the margins of society: the mentally disturbed, the delinquent, and the foreigner. After a break of six years he returned with another series of books so different that the casual reader would not think they were by the same author. These works—the first of which, *Narratori delle pianure* (1985; translated as *Voices from the Plains,* 1989), received great critical acclaim—are remarkable for their quiet, reflective, fragmentary character; simple style; and specific geographical location in the Po Valley.

Celati is also an essayist whose critical and theoretical work on both narrative and photography has been influential. He is a scholar and university teacher of American and English literature and has written a collection of essays titled *Finzioni occidentali* (Western Fictions, 1975). Among his many translations are works by Louis-Ferdinand Céline, Jack London, Jonathan Swift, and Herman Melville. In recent years he has become increasingly involved in the writing and making of movies and videos. He has one intriguing video, *La strada provinciale delle anime* (The Provincial Road of the Spirits, 1991), to his credit.

Gianni Celati was born on 10 January 1937 in the town of Sondrio, a provincial city in a mountainous part of northern Lombardy near the Swiss border. He grew up in various locations, mostly in the Veneto, as his father, Antonio Celati, and his mother, Dolores Exenia Maztelli, moved frequently in connection with his father's work. His family came from Ferrara, and he has regularly returned throughout his life to that small, beautiful Renaissance city located to the south of Venice in the middle of the flat, agriculturally rich plain on the delta of the River Po. His uncles were skilled craftsmen in Ferrara—one a tailor, another a mason who maintained and restored old buildings—and Celati has often emphasized his respect for their skills and capacity for a lifetime of work as well as his belief that as a writer he too practices a trade and a craft.

As a student in the early 1960s Celati lived in Germany for some months. He then studied philosophy, linguistics and English language and literature at the University of Bologna, writing a thesis on the language of James Joyce. From 1970 to 1972 he taught at Cornell University, and from 1972 to 1978 he taught English and American literature at the University of Bologna. After another two years in the United States he returned to the University of Bologna. Since leaving the university in 1984 he has spent long periods in France, has returned to the United States as a visiting professor at Brown University in 1990, and has in the 1990s been based in Brighton though he makes frequent visits to Italy.

Having published several articles in the late 1960s on Joyce, the implied gesture in the language of Céline, the literary theories of Northrop Frye, and on what he called "il racconto di superficie" (the surface narrative) of Italo Calvino and others, Celati made his debut as a novelist in 1971 with a curious and difficult work titled *Comiche* (Comic Cuts), accompanied by a long postface by Calvino. The focus of the novel is an unstable, paranoid character, apparently a teacher, who lives out his life in an institution that seems part holiday resort, part school, and part insane asylum. He writes a diary that three primary-school teachers try to steal from him in a series of bizarre, surrealistic episodes involving political conspirators, a talking airplane, and a fat woman who is the superintendent of the institution.

An undoubted influence on Celati's experimentation in this and his next two novels is comic silent movies, such as those of Buster Keaton or the Marx Brothers. He seeks in *Comiche* to transfer something of the rapid sequence of absurd visual gags into literary form, adapting for the purpose the creative, ungrammatical language of the semiliterate school pupil. According to Guido Almansi, "the whole book is a precious anthology of inspired linguistic and grammatical idiocies, slyly exploited in the distant clattering echo of the author's typewriter." This novel impressed the critics more perhaps for the promise demonstrated in its cleverly contrived disrespect for traditional "good writing" than as a major work in its own right.

In his next novel, *Le avventure di Guizzardi,* Celati's promise was amply fulfilled. The protagonist, Guizzardi, is a manic, poorly educated, illiterate youth, unloved even by his parents, whose speech impediment makes any kind of communication with others difficult. He recounts in a long monologue his hectic and tormented adventures, including a period as patient and worker in a corruptly administered hospital. Guizzardi—whose nickname "Danci" suggests the traveler through Hell, Purgatory, and Paradise—begins his story with an account of his devotion to Signorina Frizzi, whom he meets regularly in a city park and who, he claims, is his "foreign language teacher" (all language seems frustratingly foreign to Danci). Having assaulted his mother in the course of an argument, he not only misses his appointment with Signorina Frizzi but sets off in search of a more hospitable dwelling.

An unsavory figure, Danci nevertheless invites more sympathy than the host of smarter and more socially competent characters he encounters, who trick, cheat, exploit, and attack him. The nightmarish depiction of the hospital, whose staff oppresses the patients by making entirely arbitrary diagnoses, prognoses, and choices about who will or will not be operated on and also by sexually harassing some of them, is sufficiently close to reality to be read as social satire. It is only by diving out of a window, in classic silent-movie fashion, into a moving rubbish truck that Danci makes his escape.

The picaresque nature of Danci's journey, with its allusions to folktale, the *Decameron*, silent movies, the *Odyssey*, the novels of Franz Kafka, and *La Divina Commedia*, invites the reader to admire Celati's technical skill rather than view his work in terms of psychological or social realism. He requires little or no emotional involvement from the reader in the adventures of his antihero. The darkly grotesque manner of his depiction of humanity recalls something of German expressionism in the visual arts—George Grosz the caricaturist, perhaps—rather than recent Italian cultural works though he captures some of the grim energy of Pier Paolo Pasolini's depiction of the Roman subproletariat in Pasolini's novel *Una vita violenta* (A Violent Life, 1959). Nevertheless, as Stefano Tani has observed, Celati's achievement in *Le avventure di Guizzardi* lies in his capacity to create a character entirely in terms of its voice, "behind which there lies only apparent spontaneity, but in reality a deep culture and control, patient research and innumerable earlier drafts." Guizzardi's lexicon and syntax are a blend of the crudeness and confusion of the language of a young man of low intelligence and no education with the awkwardness of the low-level official such as a police officer or a municipal worker striving for recognition. *Le avventure di Guizzardi* was awarded the Premio Bagutta for 1973.

In his next novel, *La banda dei sospiri* (Band of Sighs, 1976), Celati's narrator and protagonist is a small boy, Garibaldi, who observes and tries unsuccessfully to come to terms with the adult world around him. Whereas Guizzardi was excluded from all family life, Garibaldi is trapped by the demands of his family, not least by the overactive fantasies of his older brother, a great reader of adventure stories with settings such as czarist Russia, the Indian Ocean, and the jungles of Africa. He insists that Garibaldi play every victim role he can think of, to the point where the boy's physical safety is regularly threatened.

Garibaldi's own vision of the various members of his extended family is influenced by his fascination with romantic Hollywood movies. His account of their lives, especially their sexual exploits, mixes soft-focus glamour with a crude desire to get some of the action for himself. In this latter wish he is inhibited by his extreme smelliness. He adores but is ignored by a blonde worker in his mother's sewing workshop, whom he calls "my Veronica Lake," yet finds himself subject to the groping attentions of an older woman, one of his mother's customers. Garibaldi, like Guizzardi, manages somehow to be both innocent and vicious. (In this and other respects the novel recalls the flavor of Günther Grass's *The Tin Drum, 1959*.) While empathy with Guizzardi was virtually impossible, any reader who has had older siblings will identify just a little with Garibaldi's experience.

Despite Celati's later comments about his respect for working-class skills and culture, none of that comes through in this work, in which Garibaldi's adult male relatives, at least, are almost uniformly rogues or fools or both. Only his mother, who works on in spite of the extravagant posturing of the men in her family, is truly admirable. As in the two previous novels, Celati's concern is not to create rounded characters in a realistic social setting, but rather to evoke a set of grotesque, marionette-like figures in a grubby puppet theater. In those terms the novel was recognized by critics as a virtuoso performance.

Lunario del paradiso (Paradise Almanac, 1978) is presented as the confused recollection of a man, Giovanni, who as a young student lived for a time with a family in Germany. The flavor of the novel is nicely captured in its first episode, in which the protagonist comes out of a subway and meets a cyclist who speaks to him in incomprehensible German and waves his bicycle pump menacingly. "Appena arrivato, lingua estera, le parole ostrogote, che cavolo voleva da me? Già, cosa voleva? . . . Me l'ha spiegato in due e due quattro. Mi ha mollato la pompa in testa ea tradimento. Poi è andato via tranquillo, pedalando da gran signore, come ve la racconto" (Just arrived, foreign language, Hunnish words, what the hell did he want with me? Right, what did he want? . . . He explained to me as quick

Dust jacket for the British edition of Celati's 1985 book, which was inspired by his travels in the Po River region

as a flash. Whacked me on the head with the pump, no trouble. Then he went off, calm as anything, just like I'm telling this story"). Whereas Celati's earlier protagonists were alienated from their environments in some metaphorical sense, Giovanni is the literal foreigner, blundering uncomprehendingly from conversation to adventure, unsure whether the people who talk to him and about him are being friendly or not.

Celati plays with national stereotypes, especially in the case of the father of the host family, doubtless a former Nazi, who being a dealer in chandeliers promises "Enlightenment" to his young visitor and slaps the young man's thigh (but is it a sexual approach or just Teutonic jollity?). Giovanni finds himself barred from the house at times when he would be alone with the daughter, Antje, on the basis of a German stereotype about Italian men: "In quanto io italiano, pare c'è poco da fidarsi su cose di competenza intima" (Me being Italian, it seems we're not to be trusted in matters of an intimate nature). Giovani's experience of heterosexual love is another encounter with "otherness" as he faces the problem of reconciling his image of the beloved with the actual person. He had first met Antje on holiday in Italy, where they spoke English, a language belonging to neither of them. As Giovanni comments, their love was "un mezzo sogno che non era né suo né mio, ma come un sogno di prati e alberi" (half a dream which wasn't hers or mine, but like a dream of meadows and trees).

An important feature of the novel, neglected by the few critics who have written about it, is that Giovanni's journey of initiation is sponsored by his student friends on the condition that he write them on the account of his experiences. There is, then, an ongoing tension in the book between Giovanni's frequent unhappiness and incomprehension and the requirement to encapsulate his experiences in an orderly and enjoyable way. Though Giovanni claims the story as his own, it is narrated entirely in the third person. Early in the book Giovanni concludes his acknowledgment of the help received from his friends with the revealing words: "Io ringrazio tutti di cuore, ma la storia deve andare avanti e non posso attardarmi" (I thank you all from the bottom of my heart, but the story must go on and I can't delay).

Critical response to this novel has been mixed. Tani argues interestingly that in *Lunario del paradiso* Celati conveys a measure of the sense of discovery of young people in the early 1960s while ironically undercutting their optimism with an implied acknowledgment of the terrorism of both the Left and the Right to which the student movement contributed in the mid 1970s. Almansi describes it as "un po' legnoso" (a bit of a bore), adding that it was a pity that some savage reviewer did not let Celati know that "the autobiographical road is paved with good intentions but lined with weeping willows."

These three early novels—whose protagonists' names, Guizzardi, Garibaldi, and Giovanni, all suggest a tenuous link to the author—were republished together in 1989 as *Parlamenti buffi* (Comic Parliaments). The collection allowed Celati to reframe the novels and to rewrite substantially *Lunario del paradiso,* tightening up its style and structure. He added a prefatory "Congedo dell'autore al suo libro" (Author's Farewell to his Book) in which he sums up his own feelings toward them in characteristically self-deprecating terms: "Queste recite sono i giochi del parlare, che è comunque un'arte e un gioco di tutti. Toni e spasimi e cadenze e mosse di voce da far sentire, danza della lingua nella bocca e fiato perso" (These performances involve playing with speech, which is nevertheless an art and a game played by everyone. Tones of voice, muscular contractions, cadences, voice shifts making themselves heard, the dance of the tongue in your mouth and wasted breath). His comment is a useful reminder that these works are best appreciated when read aloud.

The collection—packaged with a unifying title, with subtitles added for each work, and featuring a detail from Brueghel's painting *Children Playing* for its cover illustration—suggests a coherence and development among the novels that was not evident when they were published separately. *Le avventure di Guizzardi* is subtitled *Storia di un senza famiglia* (Story of a Boy Without a Family); *La banda dei sospiri* is referred to as *Romanzo d'infanzia* (Novel of Childhood); and *Lunario del paradiso* is described as *Esperienze d'un ragazzo all'estero* (Experiences of a Young Man Abroad). The trilogy as it now appears may be seen to depict Guizzardi's existence as a chaotic hell and Garibaldi's pained but hopeful adolescence as a kind of purgatory, but the realm to which Giovanni journeys must then be seen as a wholly ironic *paradiso*. The stylistic shift registered in the three works seems in retrospect to involve the progressive abandonment of the frenetic wordplay of his earliest fiction in favor of an emphasis on a quieter narrative play that continues in his later work. Encountering the three novels together is likely to make the reader particularly aware of the extreme maleness of these texts, and many women readers find the focus on adolescent male sexual desire, fear, and fantasy repellent. In Celati's defense, it must be said that he nowhere suggests that the mixture of raw testosterone and naive idealism which characterizes each of his protagonists is anything but unattractive nor indeed that it is limited to younger men. *Parlamenti buffi* was awarded the Premio Mondello for 1990.

The cover of *Narratori delle pianure,* the first novel of Celati's second phase, is designed around a photograph of the author taken by the late Luigi Ghirri, his great friend with whom he collaborated on several projects, including *Il profilo delle nuvole, immagini di un paesaggio italiano* (Profile of the Clouds, Images of an Italian Landscape, 1989). Standing a little awkwardly with his back to the reader, Celati looks hesitant and rather vulnerable in the midst of a flat landscape blanketed in snow that is turning to brown slush. This photograph conveys with beautiful simplicity the tone of the book. *Narratori delle pianure* is a collection of stories of several different kinds—urban legends, anecdotes about eccentric individuals, narratives derived from newspaper stories—held together by a succession of references to towns and villages ranged across the great plain formed by the Po River, from Gallarate in the northwest, close to Lago Maggiore and the Alps, to the mouth of the Po in the east, where its waters flow into the Adriatic.

There are many hints, including a sketch map preceding the text, that most of the thirty stories derive from conversations Celati had with people he met in the course of an actual journey from west to east across Lombardy, Emilia-Romagna, and the Veneto. Nevertheless Celati avoids recounting the events of the journey itself and does not claim to have transmitted the stories unaltered. Indeed, the reference in the title to "narrators" is ironic since readers never encounter the people who one supposes might have told Celati their stories. Typically the pieces begin with phrases such as "Ho sentito raccontare la storia di un radioamatore di Gallarate, provincia di Varese" (I was told the story of a radio ham from Gallarate in the province of Varese) or "C'era un uomo che abitava a Ficarolo, in provincia di Ferrara, era un falegname" (There was a man who lived in Ficarolo, in the province of Ferrara, he was a carpenter), though on occasion he credits a particular person—a German friend, his paternal grandfather, his mother. In just a few stories such as "Storia di un apprendistato" (Story of an Apprenticeship), do events from Celati's own life apparently provide the kernel of a story: "Quando era a Los Angeles, il narratore di questa storia ha abitato a lungo nella villa d'un produttore cinematografico greco" (When he was in Los Angeles, the narrator of this story lived for a long time in a villa belonging to a Greek film producer).

The stories of *Narratori delle pianure* are straight forwardly told though some of the events within them are quite bizarre: an Italian radio ham makes contact with a policeman from Glasgow who has settled on a remote Scottish island because he accidentally shot a criminal he was pursuing; a provincial pharmacist dedicates his life to rewriting every book in his large personal library so that they all end happily; a woman tapes shut every orifice of her body before committing suicide; two children scour Milan for an adult who is not boring. As Rebecca West wrote in her review article in the fall 1985 issue of *Forum Italicum*, "These stories, simple as they are, create a strong sense of metaphysical resonance that is both familiar and disturbing. The people who populate his stories are looking for a way of living in a world that is both incomprehensible and hostile."

In the absence of reliable grand narratives Celati depicts individuals trying to construct explanatory narratives on an idiosyncratic, miniature level. The endings of the stories offer few vantage points for contemplating with any certainty or satisfaction the events that have gone before. Several end with the solitary death of the protagonist. Some conclude with philosophical remarks that are wholly pessimistic or even nihilistic. In "Sul valore delle apparenze" (On the Value of Appearances) the comment by the owner of the wrecked-car yard on the obsession of having glossy, new consumer goods suggests a fundamental absurdity about all human aspirations: "Una macchina appena comprata vale meno della metà, e appena succede qualcosa è già da buttar via. Prima o poi finiscono tutte da me in demolizione: tutte in demolizione, perché non hanno durata" (As soon as you buy a new car it loses more than half its value, and once something has happened to it, you might just as well throw it away. Sooner or later they all end up at my wrecker's yard: all wrecks because they're not built to last). As often as not, however, the stories conclude with the protagonist's being reconciled to the narrow limits within which life must be lived.

On the autobiographical level, the descent from the near-Alpine location of the beginning of the book to the featureless Po delta at the end recalls Celati's own shift from his mountainous birthplace to the Veneto. More important, the implied journey down the river suggests that life may be no more than a meandering journey across flat land before one finally reaches the sea. The implied challenge is to construct what one character refers to as "cerimoniali" (ritual ceremonies) that give shape, and so meaning, to daily lives. The moving and thoughtful qualities of this work, which has been awarded the Premio Cinque Scole and the Premio Grinzane-Cavour, have been noted by many critics. As novelist Antonio Tabucchi wrote in the 22 June 1985 issue of *Il manifesto*, "Celati puts himself forward first as listener and then as storyteller . . . He knows how to turn himself into a medium and the secret of his implosive writing comes from this hard-to-achieve openness."

The two long narrative works that followed, *Quattro novelle sulle apparenze* (1987; translated as *Appearances*, 1991) and *Verso la foce* (Toward the Estuary, 1989), continue to explore the same personal and geographical sources as the earlier work. The protagonists of *Quattro novelle sulle apparenze*, which literally means "four stories about appearances," all search for meaning in a world where absolute meanings are no longer to be found. As the title of the collection suggests, their quests for meaning in the everyday world uncover only more surfaces, more appearances.

While commentators have savored the troublesome paradoxes offered by these stories, there is general agreement that as a collection *Quattro novelle sulle apparenze* repeats the themes of *Narratori delle pianure* rather than markedly developing them. Baratto, the eponymous protagonist of the first tale, one day finds himself devoid of thoughts and so gives up speaking. As time passes, though he regains the capacity to think and speak, it is only because he acknowledges that he and by implication everyone else are the products rather

Celati in Palermo, 1990 (photograph by Giovanni Giovannetti)

than the originators of the ideas and the language they speak. This story poses in accessible, narrative form the contemporary philosophical problem of the instability of the "personal subject." The third story, "I lettori di libri sono sempre piú falsi" (Readers of Books are More and More False), recalls Calvino's *Se una notte d'inverno un viaggiatore* (If On a Winter's Night a Traveler, 1979) in its depiction of the intertwining of the lives of a male reader and a female reader. But whereas the couple in Calvino's novel get acquainted in the course of their struggle to locate and read the same book, Celati's pair work out their relationship in terms of their work as door-to-door booksellers. In Celati's story the male reader metamorphoses from idealistic creative writer to being a sad critic.

Verso la foce expands on the geographical and environmental themes of *Narratori delle pianure* more than the philosophical ones. It consists of four travel diaries Celati wrote during journeys across the Po Valley with a group of photographers, including Ghirri. A recurrent motif in the two preceding fictional works is the degradation of the Italian landscape, especially that of the Po Valley, in the period following World War II: the rivers are poisoned with industrial and agricultural runoff; trees are cut down or are dying; the air is thick with fumes from factories and motor vehicles. In *Verso la foce* Celati comments on the economic and political system that has made such degradation possible. Celati also provides an existential rationale for these diaries: "Se hanno qualche rilevanza, almeno per chi li ha scritti, questa dipende dal fatto che un'intensa osservazione del mondo esterno ci rende meno apatici (più pazzi o più savi, più allegri o più disperati)" (If they have any relevance, at any rate for the author, it derives from the fact that close observation of the external world makes us less apathetic—more insane or wiser, happier or more desperate). *Verso la foce* was awarded the Premio Latina for 1992.

The first work Celati created in the 1990s is the hour-long "videoracconto" (videostory) *La strada provinciale delle anime,* which he wrote and directed for Italian television. Its gentle, unemphatic, reflective tone and its depiction of the flat, canal-crossed landscape of the Po delta link it closely to the three preceding literary works. Following Celati and a party of relatives and old friends who set off from Ferrara on a tour by bus of the area between Ferrara and the sea, the video is a documentary that avoids traditional documentary technique. The party does not visit so-called points of interest, and the video does not highlight the architecture of the towns, the crops and methods of cultivation, the fishing industry, local customs, or even the dynamics of the traveling group itself though there is some reference to all of those. Even the view of the landscape seems not to be strongly directed: there are many shots through the bus windows of fields, canals, and sky, all strictly horizontal since the land is so flat.

In general Celati seems intent on trying not to prove a point of any kind, except perhaps that it is worth looking in a sustained way at the apparently unremarkable. These "tourists"—a mixture of young, middle-aged, and elderly—talk to local people, tell stories, refer to their own way of making a living (Celati's two charming old uncles are featured), recite a poem by Giacomo Leopardi, and comment quietly on what they have seen. One member of the group observes that he did not see anything special but that he still enjoyed the tour. Another asks whether it is better to feel lost or only look at the things you have been told to look at. The viewer is invited to agree that there is a value in feeling a bit lost sometimes. If Celati had his way and the available funds he would make more such videos. In the public presentation he gave of *La strada provinciale delle anime* in Ferrara in late 1991, he emphasized that more than movies it is the less grand, less polished, and more low-key medium of videos that attracts him.

Celati has since published two more books, *L'Orlando innamorato raccontato in prosa* (*Orlando Innamorto* Retold in Prose, 1994*)* and *Recita dell'attore Vecchiatto nel teatro di Rio Saliceto* (The Actor Vecchiatto's Performance at the Rio Saliceto Theater, 1996), that are clearly connected to his earlier work though superficially they may seem different from each other and from what he has done before. In *L'Orlando innamorato raccontato in prosa,* a work inspired by Matteo Maria Boiardo's great poem, one is reminded that the literary tradition of the chivalrous epic of which Boiardo's work was an important part had its origins in the same Po Valley region that has provided the setting and source for most of Celati's work. His adaptation of the great Renaissance epic aims to continue the long tradition of popular retellings of the fantastic adventures of Charlemagne and his knights that has manifested itself from the Sicilian marionette theater in the South to the peasant oral performances of the North. In *Recita dell'attore Vecchiatto* Celati reconstructs the last performance of an extraordinary theatrical figure, Attilio Vecchiatto, who gained great fame in both South and North America for his adaptations for Italian migrant audiences of Shakespeare's plays but who remained almost unknown in Italy until his death. This work consists of what Celati calls "un monologo a due voci" (a monologue for two voices) in which Attilio and his wife Carlotta explore the drama of old age.

Now in his sixties, Celati continues to write. He recently published *Avventure in Africa* (1998), a work based on a trip to Africa he took in 1997. In his only other writing about that continent, a brief story in *Narratori delle pianure* titled "La città di Medina Sabah" (The City of Medina Sabah) a young Italian has all of his belongings stolen. Even the truck in which he is traveling is stripped of its salable parts. The man nevertheless returns to Italy richer for the experience, bringing a new wisdom about the origins of human storytelling. One can only anticipate that new works by Gianni Celati, one of Italy's most intriguing modern writers, will similarly enrich his readers by showing how human beings struggle to make even provisional sense of this existence.

Interviews:
Michael Caesar, *Journal of the Association of Teachers of Italian,* 36 (Summer 1982): 28-34;

Nico Orengo, "Celati: racconto la gente che ho ascoltato," *Tuttolibri,* 15 June 1985, p. 5;

Robert Lumley, "The Novella and the New Italian Landscape: An Interview with Gianni Celati," *Edinburgh Review,* 83 (1990): 40-51;

Franco Marenco, "Non fatti, ma parole! Gianni Celati risponde a Franco Marenco," *L'Indice dei libri del mese,* 7 (1991): 17-19;

Manuela Teatini, "Il sentimento dello spazio: conversazione con Gianni Celati," *Cinema e cinema,* 62 (September-December 1991): 25-28.

References:
Guido Almansi, "Il letamaio di Babele," in his *La ragion comica* (Milano: Feltrinelli, 1986), pp. 43-61;

Laura Barile, "Un ostinato inseguimento: linguaggio e immagine in Calvino, Celati, Perec, e l'ultimo Beckett," *Forum Italicum,* 26 (Spring 1992): 188-200;

Mario Boselli, "Finzioni di superficie," *Nuova Corrente,* 33 (1986): 75-88;

Michael Caesar, "Caratteri del comico nelle *Avventure di Guizzardi*," *Nuova Corrente*, 33 (1986): 33–46;

Guido Fink, "Da dove vengono tutte le storie," *Paragone-Letteratura*, 426 (1985): 67–73;

Lino Gabellone, "Quello che sta fermo, quello che cammina: Apologo per Gianni Celati," *Nuova Corrente*, 33 (1986): 27–32;

Michael Hanne, "Narrative Wisdom in Celati's *Narratori delle pianure*," *Rivista di studi italiani*, 14 (June 1996): 133–152;

Franco La Polla, "Comiche letterarie e tecniche cinematografiche," *Paragone-Letteratura*, 272 (1972): 94–98;

Robert Lumley, "Gianni Celati: Fictions to Believe In," in *The New Italian Novel*, edited by Zygmunt Barański and Lino Pertile (Edinburgh: Edinburgh University Press, 1993), pp. 43–58;

Mario Moroni, "Il paradigma dell'osservazione in *Verso la foce* di Gianni Celati," *Romance Languages Annual: RLA*, 4 (1992): 307–313;

Francesco Muzzioli, "Celati e i segreti dell'arte tomatica," *Nuova Corrente*, 33 (1986): 47–64;

Claudia Nocentini, "Celati, artigiano della narrativa," *Civiltà italiana*, 19, no. 1 (1995): 129–139;

Nocentini, "A Short Story about Silence: Celati's 'Baratto,'" in *The Short Story: Structure and Statement*, edited by W. Hunter (Exeter: Elm Bank Publications, 1996), pp. 173–185;

Cecilia Novero, "'Baratto' di Gianni Celati e l'affermazione passiva del pudore," *Romance Languages Annual: RLA*, 4 (1992): 314–318;

Pina Piccolo, "Celati's *Quattro novelle:* On Vacillation and Suspension," *Italian Quarterly*, 30 (Fall 1989): 29–37;

Piccolo, "Gianni Celati's Silence, Space, Motion and Relief," *Gradiva*, 4, no. 2 (1988): 61–65;

Stefano Tani, *Il romanzo di ritorno* (Milano: Mursia, 1990), pp. 42–54, 116–122;

Giorgio Terrone, "Le favole del reale: Il percorso espressivo di Celati," *Nuova Corrente*, 33 (1986): 89–106;

Rebecca West, "Before, Beneath and Around the Text: the Genesis and Construction of Some Postmodern Prose Fictions," *Annali d'italianistica*, 9 (1991): 272–292;

West, "Gianni Celati and Literary Minimalism," *L'anello che non tiene*, 1 (Spring 1989): 11–29;

West, "Gianni Celati's *La strada provinciale delle anime:* A 'Silent' Film about 'Nothing,'" *Romance Languages Annual: RLA*, 4 (1992): 367–374;

West, "*Narratori delle pianure*," *Forum Italicum*, 19 (Fall 1985): 360–362;

West, "Pasolini's Intoxication and Celati's Detoxification," *Romance Languages Annual: RLA*, 9 (1997);

West, "Lo spazio nei *Narratori delle pianure*," *Nuova Corrente*, 33 (1986): 65–74.

Vincenzo Consolo
(18 February 1933 -   )

Tom O'Neill
University of Melbourne

BOOKS: *La ferita dell'aprile* (Milan: Mondadori, 1963);

Il sorriso dell'ignoto marinaio (Turin: Einaudi, 1976); translated by Joseph Farrell as *The Smile of the Unknown Mariner* (Manchester: Carcanet, 1994);

Lunaria (Turin: Einaudi, 1985);

Retablo (Palermo: Sellerio, 1987);

Le pietre di Pantalica. Racconti (Milan: Mondadori, 1988);

La Sicilia passeggiata (Turin: ERI Edizioni Rai, 1991);

Il Barocco in Sicilia. La rinascita del Val di Noto (Milan: Bompiani, 1991);

Nottetempo, casa per casa. Romanzo (Milan: Mondadori, 1992);

Requiem per le vittime della mafia (Palermo: Ila Palma, 1993);

Fuga dall'Etna: la Sicilia e Milano, la memoria e la storia (Rome: Donzelli, 1993);

L'olivo e l'olivastro (Milan: Mondadori, 1994).

OTHER: Giuseppe Corsentino, *Gli arabi paesani: inchiesta sui giovani di oggi,* introduction by Consolo (Trapani: Celebes, 1977);

Carlo Levi, *Le parole sono pietre,* preface by Consolo (Turin: Einaudi, 1979);

Christophe Charle, *Letteratura e potere,* introduction by Consolo (Palermo: Sellerio, 1979);

Giovanni Verga, *Le storie del castello di Trezza,* with a note by Consolo (Palermo: Sellerio, 1982), pp. 75-86;

Sicilia. Immagini del XIX secolo dagli Archivi Alinari, with an essay by Consolo (Florence: Fratelli Alinari, 1985);

"Un uomo di alta dignità," in *'Nfernu veru–Uomini & immagini dei paesi dello zolfo,* edited by Aurelio Grimaldi (Rome: Lavoro, 1985);

Basilio Reale, *Sirene siciliane. L'anima esiliata in "Lighea" di Tomasi di Lampedusa,* preface by Consolo (Palermo: Sellerio, 1986);

La pesca del tonno in Sicilia, edited, with an introduction, by Consolo (Palermo: Sellerio, 1986);

Vincenzo Consolo

Johann Wolfgang von Goethe, *Viaggio in Sicilia,* introduction by Consolo (Siracusa: Ediprint, 1987);

"L'idea della Sicilia," in *La Sicilia dei grandi viaggiatori,* edited by Franco Paloscia (Rome: Edizioni Abete, 1989);

Ruggero Savinio, *Ruggero Savinio: ex Convento di San Francesco, Sciacca, 8 luglio–15 agosto 1989,* with a commentary by Consolo (Palermo: Sellerio, 1989);

"Catarsi," in *Trittico: Bufalino Consolo Sciascia,* edited by Antonio Di Grado and Giuseppe Lazzaro Danzuso (Catania: Domenico Sanfilippo Editore, 1989);

Giuseppe Tornatore, *Nuovo Cinema Paradiso,* with a foreword by Consolo (Palermo: Sellerio, 1990);

"Viaggi dal mare alla terra," in *Museo Mandralisca* (Palermo: Novecento, 1991), pp. 8–13;

"Le foto sul comò," in *Verga fotografo,* edited by Giovanni Garra Agosta (Catania: Maimone, 1991);

Verga, *Novelle,* introduction by Consolo (Milan: Feltrinelli, 1992).

From the time of Giovanni Verga, the celebrated Sicilian novelist of the *verisimo* (realism) school in the nineteenth century, writers have tried through their works to enrich and revitalize Italy's literary-linguistic tradition. If one leaves aside the baroque prose of the Lombard writer Carlo Emilio Gadda, perhaps no Italian writer more than Vincenzo Consolo has so forthrightly challenged the dominance of the Tuscan-based written language that has been the official language of Italy since Unification despite the vibrancy of regional dialects. Through his novels Consolo has celebrated the language of his native Sicily while critically examining paradigmatic moments in Sicily's history since Italy's Unification. His clear intention is to highlight the essentially flawed nature of that history and its quintessentially nonrevolutionary origins which, to adopt the words of Tancredi in Giuseppe Tomasi di Lampedusa's *Il Gattopardo* (1958; translated as *The Leopard,* 1960), have allowed conditions to change so that they would stay the same.

The biographical information available on Consolo is sparse. He was born in Sant'Agata di Militello, a small town on the northern coast of Sicily, west of Messina, on 18 February 1933, the sixth of a family of eight children. After local primary school he attended high school at Barcellona Pozzo di Gotto between Sant'Agata and Messina and then, in keeping with a long-standing tradition, moved to the mainland to pursue his education at the university level. Like many Sicilian writers before him—Giovanni Verga, Luigi Capuana, and Federico De Roberto in the nineteenth century and Elio Vittorini in the twentieth century—he chose Milan, where he studied jurisprudence. Upon completion of his degree and after military service in Rome he returned to Sicily, where he taught in agricultural institutes.

During his five years of teaching Consolo made the acquaintance of two writers who were arguably to have a formative influence on his development as a writer: the novelist Leonardo Sciascia and the poet Lucio Piccolo. Hailing from Capo d'Orlando, a town to the east of Sant'Agata, Piccolo symbolized what Consolo saw as the characteristic qualities of eastern Sicily: "la Natura, l'esistenza, il mito, la memoria" (Nature, existence, myth, memory). He counterbalanced his relationship with Piccolo's "con la contemporanea frequentazione dello 'storico' occidentale e illuminista Sciascia" (by associating at the same time with the enlightened "historian" Sciascia from the island's west) as he asserts in his preface to Basilio Reale's book on Lampedusa. The works he dedicated to Piccolo—the first chapter of *Il sorriso dell'ignoto marinaio* (1976; translated as *The Smile of the Unknown Mariner,* 1994), which originally appeared in the journal *Nuovi Argomenti* in 1969, and his theatrical piece *Lunaria* (1985), which was set in eighteenth-century Sicily—are perhaps best seen as a tribute to poetry itself, the appreciation of which Consolo believes is crucial to the writing of enduring prose.

On New Year's Day 1968 Consolo moved back to Milan, where, having given up teaching, he went to work for RAI, the Italian television network, writing cultural material. Consolo followed in the wake of the mass internal migration from the country to the city, from the South to the North, which effectively signed the death warrant of the peasant world, which in *Le pietre di Pantalica. Racconti* (The Stories of Pantalica, 1988) he characterized as "un mondo di fatica e dolore" (a world of fatigue and suffering). Consolo still lives in Milan with his wife Caterina Pilenga. He now writes full time.

In an interview with the French critic Mario Fusco, Consolo confessed he started writing stories under the influence of Verga while still at school and having much admired Vittorini, but it was, he said, Sciascia's first work, *Le parrocchie di Regalpetra* (Salt in the Wound, 1956), that inspired him to write his first novel. In *Fuga dall'Etna: la Sicilia e Milano, la memoria e la storia* (Flight from Etna: Sicily and Milan, Memory and History, 1993) he widened his field of inspiration to include Carlo Levi and Danilo Dolci as well as historians of the "southern question" such as Gaetano Salvemini and Guido Dorso and the founder and theoretician of the Italian Communist Party, Antonio Gramsci.

Consolo's first novel, *La ferita dell'aprile* (The Wound of April, 1963), met with almost total silence upon publication, and it needed the success of his second novel, *Il sorriso dell'ignoto marinaio,* some thirteen years later to induce its republication and a modicum of critical attention. The story of the "education" of a young Sicilian in a religious institution in the years immediately following World War II,

Dust jacket for Consolo's 1987 novel, a light-hearted fantasy

related in the first person and in part in the dialect of the character, must have seemed dated in the year that saw the launching in Palermo of Gruppo 63, a group of radically and polemically neoavantgarde young literary Turks, including Nanni Balestrini, Antonio Porta, and Edoardo Sanguineti. On the surface Consolo's work appeared to harken back to the Neorealism of the 1950s and such works as Pier Paolo Pasolini's *Ragazzi di vita* (1955; translated as *The Ragazzi,* 1968) and *Una vita violenta* (1959; translated as *A Violent Life,* 1968).

La ferita dell'aprile was, however, more complex than a simple neorealist label suggests, and its genesis was doubtless more intricate than Consolo was prepared to admit. In all probability an important unnamed model was James Joyce's *Portrait of the Artist as a Young Man* (1916), which had been published in an Italian translation by Cesare Pavese in 1933. The parallels are many, not least the education of Consolo's unwilling protagonist in a religious institution which replicates that of Stephen Dedalus at the hands of the Jesuits. Both works mingle religion and politics: Joyce treats the church's condemnation of Charles Stewart Parnell; Consolo presents the conflict between the Christian Democrats and the Communists. Also significant is that in each work the author portrays the growth of artistic consciousness. Dedalus vows to pursue life as an artist: "I will try to express myself in some mode of life or art as freely as I can and as wholly as I can, using for my defence the only arms I allow myself to use—silence, exile, and cunning." Consolo's unnamed protagonist faces doubts as he follows his vocation: "E questa storia che m'intestardo a scrivere, questo fermarmi a pensare, a ricordare, non è segno di babbía, a cangio di saltare da bravo i muri che mi restano davanti?" (And this story that I stubbornly try to write, this stopping myself to think, to remember, is it not a sign of foolishness, instead of courageously leaping over the walls that are still in front of me?).

No less important for both writers is the linguistic expression of a subordinate culture. In his interview with Fusco, Consolo stresses that the mixture of language and dialect in his work is not a result of wishing to imitate Gadda "mais parce que la Sicile est un pays de stratifications linguistiques: j'ai essayé de tenir compte de ces divers vestiges, sur un plan musical" (but because Sicily is a country of linguistic stratification: I have tried to take account of these diverse traces, on a musical plan). The musicality of the text, however, is not to be understood in a primarily decadent sense, for Consolo immediately adds: "Mais c'est aussi une forme d'opposition au nationalisme linguistique italien. On sait que c'est le toscan qui s'est imposé comme langue nationale, mais, pour moi, je revendique cette indépendance linguistique du dialecte sicilien" (But it is also a form of opposition to Italian linguistic nationalism. We know that it is Tuscan which has imposed itself as the national language, but I for my part reassert this linguistic independence of the Sicilian dialect).

In addition to the archetypal model provided by Joyce there were other writers closer in time and place to Consolo and Sicily that almost certainly affected his writing. Fellow Sicilian Elio Vittorini was the undisputed arbiter of Italian literary taste in the 1950s, and his views on the nature and purpose of literature were well known. In the first number of *Il Politecnico,* which came out 29 September 1945, he had advocated: "non più una cultura che consoli nelle sofferenze ma una cultura che protegga dalle sofferenze, che le combatta e le elimini" (no longer a culture which consoles us in our sufferings but a culture that protects us from sufferings, that combats them and eliminates them). The sentiment finds an echo in Consolo's remark in his interview with Fusco that in part the thirteen-year silence between his first and second novel was due to his inability to "faire de l'écriture quelque chose de consolant" (make of writing something consoling).

Vittorini was also the author of *Conversazione in Sicilia* (1941; translated as *In Sicily,* 1947), one of the most original novels to have come out of the fascist period. It was widely admired outside Italy by diverse writers such as Ernest Hemingway, Stephen Spender, and Tennessee Williams. In 1953 a new edition of the work was published, illustrated by photographs taken by Luigi Crocenzi and Vittorini in 1950. Consolo, whose *Il sorriso dell'ignoto marinaio* and *Nottetempo, casa per casa. Romanzo* (Nighttime, House by House: A Novel, 1992) are set in Cefalù, clearly was struck by this edition; he noted in an interview with Grazia Cherchi how photography "può aiutare la scrittura, può anzi sollecitarla" (can help writing, indeed can provoke it). He admitted that he still had a notebook in which he had drawn various maps of Cefalù "percorrendo innumerevoli volte il centro storico di quella cittadina quartiere per quartiere, vicolo per vicolo" (criss-crossing on countless occasions the historic centre of that small town district by district, lane by lane). Two of Consolo's nonfiction works, *La Sicilia passeggiata* (Walking Around Sicily, 1991) and *Il Barocco in Sicilia. La rinascita del Val di Noto* (The Baroque in Sicily. The Rebirth of the Noto Valley, 1991), are beautifully illustrated with Giuseppe Leone's photographs.

Consolo was probably also influenced by *Il menabò,* the journal edited by Vittorini and Italo Calvino, which was first published in June 1959. *Il menabò 1* included a wide-ranging article by Michele Rago on the proliferation of dialect in literature which was followed by two brief notes, one on language and dialect from Gadda to Pasolini by Raffaele Crovi, the other on "Parlato e metafora" (Spoken Language and Metaphor) by Vittorini. In 1962 the journal published *I giorni della fera* (The Days of the Dolphin), a novel by Stefano D'Arrigo, a Sicilian from Alí, south of Messina, which it described as "un testo dotato d'una sua riottosa, grezza ma talora elaboratissima forza, come immagini e come lingua—una lingua ampiamente intrisa . . . di voci dialettali" (a text endowed with its own boisterous, rough but on occasions highly elaborated strength, both in images and language—a language amply larded . . . with dialect voices). It is likely that Consolo, who has since written admiringly of D'Arrigo's work, was as much inspired by his novel as he was by Sciascia's *Le parrocchie di Regalpetra.*

No writer emerges from a vacuum or operates in one. Of the influences mentioned–(Joyce, Gadda, Pasolini, Vittorini, and D'Arrigo)–the first two names indicate how high Consolo had set his sights right from the outset, and the others perhaps are an indication of how his inspiration had need of being buttressed by models. While it is best to approach Consolo's work from the broad context of his intellectual background, the elaboration of the influences evident in his work also suggests that at least in the early stages of his career he was derivative rather than original, somewhat akin to a mannerist painter.

The narrator-protagonist of *La ferita dell'aprile* is certainly a much less memorable character than

Page from the manuscript for a work in progress (Collection of Vincenzo Consolo) the protagonist of *Portrait of the Artist as a Young Man*. This "ragazzo irriverente" (irreverent youngster), as the critic Gian Carlo Ferretti defines him, "con un disincanto e un'ironia [e sarcasmo] già matura" (with an already mature disenchantment and an irony [and sarcasm]), does not really stand out against the choral background of the novel. The sociohistorical canvas of the early postwar years—with its nostalgia for Fascism, fascination with the American dream, fear of communism, and the strong ascendancy of the Christian Democrats—seems less important than was perhaps intended because all experience has equal value for the spongelike adolescent consciousness presented.

"Without empire [. . .] there is no European novel as we know it," claims Edward Said in *Culture and Imperialism* (1993). His contention is that the power to narrate, combined with that of blocking other narratives from forming and emerging, is what imperialism and novel writing have in common. Sicily has been under the yoke of diverse empires through the centuries, Italy being the most recent of these, and it could be argued that *Il sorriso dell'ignoto marinaio*, Consolo's second and arguably most significant novel, is both anti-imperialist in theme and antitraditionalist in structure. Indeed, the antitraditionalism of the latter mirrors and heightens the anti-imperialism of the former.

Il sorriso dell'ignoto marinaio, unlike a straightforward historical novel, is structured with breaks and allusions through which the reader intuits the unfolding of events. The novel's nine chapters, each of which presents varied materials without apparent regard to chronology, range over an eight-year time span (1852–1860) in less than 150 pages. The opening chapter, set in 1852, includes an "Antefatto" (antecedent facts) regarding the provenance of the painting—the portrait of the unknown mariner referred to in the title—which has been purchased by the protagonist, Enrico Pirajno, baron of Mandralisca. It is followed by two appendices, the first a letter from the Mandralisca by way of a preface to a scholarly work on malacology (1840), the other a brief preliminary note to subsequent discoveries in this same field. The appendixes in the novel have an allusive and connective function among the chapters, shedding light on the characters and giving a sense of the time in which the events occur.

During the course of the novel the baron evolves from an inward-looking scientist whose only concern is mollusks to a socially engaged figure as a result of the massacre at Alcara Li Fusi, a small town in the Nebredi Mountain region of Sicily. There, peasants revolted, believing that Garibaldi had brought a social revolution to the island leading to their emancipation. Their uprising was actually put down by Garibaldi, showing the intrinsically repressive, nonrevolutionary nature of his so-called revolution.

In subsequent chapters Consolo continues to make use of local history. Chapter 2 also has two appendices: the first, an extract from a 1907 historical paper on the 1856 uprising in Cefalú; the second, extracts from Giuseppe Cesare Abba's account of his participation in Garibaldi's expedition, *Noterelle d'uno dei Mille* (The Diary of One of Garibaldi's Thousand, 1880). Chapters 3–5 all treat the events of May 1860. Chapter 6, a letter from the baron, serves as a preamble to his memoir of the Alcàra Li Fusi uprising, and chapter 7 presents that memoir.

In the last chapters—Chapter 8, titled "The Prison," and Chapter 9, titled "Writings,"—the baron reflects on the human condition and the events he has witnessed. Chapter 9 is followed by three appendixes; the writings of the chapter proper are in verse of the Lombard dialect of San Fratello, a village in the hinterland of Sant'Agata. Consolo may have chosen this dialect because of the reputation of the poetry of the area. In an essay titled "La Lombardia siciliana" (Sicilian Lombardy) in *La corda pazza* (1970) Sciascia notes its peculiar qualities: "una risentita coscienza delle condizioni sociali, un'aspirazione civile, una attenzione dolorosa e ironica alla vita quotidiana" (an angry awareness of social conditions, an aspiration to citizenship, a painful and ironic attention to daily life).

Il sorriso dell'ignoto marinaio is an historical novel, a genre that has flourished in Italy more than in other European countries. The theoretical key to the work is to be found in the opening two sentences of Karl Marx's *Eighteenth Brumaire of Louis Bonaparte* (1852): "Hegel remarks somewhere that all facts and personages of great importance in world history occur, as it were, twice. He forgot to add: the first time as tragedy, the second as farce." For Consolo Sicilian history since the nineteenth century is farcical because its revolutions begin with radical social aims and invariably end up being co-opted by political conservatives.

The essential question for the peasants, particularly the mountain shepherds who had a permanent sense of injustice against the landlords of the plain, was land. In chapter 2 Consolo alludes to the French philosopher Pierre-Joseph Proudhon and his 1840 book *Qu'est-ce que la propriété?* (What is Property?), with its opening assertion "La propriété c'est le vol" (Property is theft). This is an idea Consolo returns to later in "Il fotografo" (The Photographer), a story collected in *Le pietre di Pantalica* (The Stones of Pantalica, 1988) that concerns the resistence to Fascism in Italy. The currency of such an idea in disparate contexts suggests that for Consolo history has as much to do with his own thinking in the present as it does with the events of the past. Recognizing this, Fusco called *Il sorriso dell'ignoto marinaio* a "faux roman historique mais véritable roman politique" (false historical novel but real political novel). Consolo acknowledged this tendency in a remark about *Nottetempo, casa per casa* in his interview with Roberto Barbolini: "Scrivo del passato per dire del presente" (I write about the past to speak about the present).

What is perhaps most striking in *Il sorriso dell'ignoto marinaio*, however, is not what Consolo has to say but how he says it. In the Fusco interview he asserts: "L'écriture pour moi, c'est une affaire de poésie, même en prose: il faut que j'arrive à une sorte de musicalité, de rythme" (Writing for me is a question of poetry, even in prose: I have to achieve a sort of musicality, of rhythm). It is a style that makes demands on the reader, for Consolo is a writer who always maintains a tension between feeling and form, between story and style. The reader also must contend with the many languages used in the novel: the Latin of the Book of Exodus, the Spanish of Goya, the Greek of Stephen of Byzantium, the dialect of San Fratello, and more. Of all the various non-Italian speech in the novel Consolo translates into standard Italian only the "lingua stramba, forestiera" (strange, foreign tongue) spoken by a prisoner chained in the courtyard of a noble, a language eventually recognized by the novel's protagonist as a "lingua bellissima, romanza o mediolatina, rimasta intatta per un millennio sano" (a most beautiful tongue, Romance or medieval Latin, [which has] remained intact for a full thousand years). The writing is also rich in intertextual allusions to writers such as Dante, Alessandro Manzoni, Giacomo Leopardi, and Luigi Pirandello. In sum the performance shows Consolo to be a consummate stylist with few, if any, equals among the writers of his generation.

The only other work by Consolo that bears comparison to *Il sorriso dell'ignoto marinaio* is *Nottetempo, casa per casa,* which was awarded the 1992 Premio Strega prize. While it does not have the linguistic complexity of the earlier novel, it still encompasses a wide range of styles in its twelve chapters. Right from the howl of the werewolf in the opening chapter Consolo creates a strong sense of time being out of joint. The unifying theme that binds its parts together is the antithesis between nature and history that lies at the heart of much of Consolo's work. The inspiring and inspired model of the world of nature is "Jeli il pastore" (Jeli the Shepherd), a character Consolo draws upon from Verga's collection *Vita dei campi* (Life in the Fields, 1880). As Consolo writes in his 1992 introduction to Verga's *Novelle* (Short Stories), Jeli represents "l'assoluta 'naturalità' dell'intatto mondo ultraliminale, presociale" (the absolute 'naturalness' of an intact, presocial world). Against the natural stands the force of history and progress, represented by the Englishman Crowley and his band of esoteric followers who arrived in Cefalù in 1920. Consolo may well have been drawn to Crowley through Sciascia's short story "Apocrifi sul caso Crowley" (Apocrypha on the Crowley Case), which was collected in *Il mare color del vino* (The Wine-Dark Sea, 1973).

To begin his third chapter Consolo parodies the opening of Gabriele D'Annunzio's first novel *Il piacere* (The Child of Pleasure, 1889), reflecting through style the degradation of history: "Il re possente sopra il piedistallo dispensa panico incubo stupro ebbrezza scioglimento—torna in parola, in immagine, in mito ora il remoto, o viene ricreato in falsità, in rito, in teatrino estetico, in imitazione insana" (The powerful king upon the pedestal dispenses panic nightmare rape drunkenness release—the remote returns in word, in image, in myth, or is re-created in falseness, in rite, in paltry aesthetic theater, in unhealthy imitation). Language, as is always the case in Consolo, represents reality, but he aims no less to make his readers aware that language reflects society and its changes. When society becomes deformed, language reflects its distortion.

Through *Nottetempo, casa per casa* Consolo expresses poetically his idiosyncratic meditation on recent Sicilian and Italian history, employing many allusions culled from his wide and often arcane readings. His work is akin thematically to the contemporary Genovese novelist Sebastiano Vassalli, whose novels such as *La chimera* (The Chimera, 1989) and *Il cigno* (The Swan, 1993) attempt to account for recent Italian history by imaginatively examining episodes from its past. The difficulty of Consolo's style, though, recalls Montale, particularly such volumes of poetry as *Le occasioni* (The Occasions, 1939) and *La bufera e altro* (The Storm and Other Things, 1957). Just as Montale's denseness and obscurity have become clearer thanks to scholarly work, perhaps *Nottetempo, casa per casa* will receive similar scholarly attention and gain greater appreciation in the future.

Meanwhile, a key to the novel may be found in a conversation between the elementary-school teacher Petro, the protagonist, and his old school friend Cicco Paolo that occurs in chapter 8. The conversation highlights a conflict between two ways of dealing with life, the active and the contemplative. The dialectic, articulated initially in terms of the spoken versus the written word, is extended in terms of reason versus imagination to become in the end an argument between extroversion and introspection. Cicco is the rationalist, the activist, the individual whose persuasiveness, enhanced by his ability to define and analyze problems, has become a powerful weapon in his fight for justice. And yet the reader is given the sense that there is something more valuable to be found in the seemingly escapist world of literature in which Petro lives with the great writers of nineteenth-century European realism: "Davano degli uomini, di un luogo e un tempo, l'immagine più vera, più della politica, che a Petro sembrava allontanasse la realtà, come i numeri e le figure della geometria, verso l'astrazione, il generale. Come l'allontanavano gli scrittori privi di verità e rispetto per la vita d'ognuno, per le vicende umane" (They gave of men, place and time, a truer image, truer than that of politics, which to Petro seemed to distance reality, like numbers and figures in geometry, towards abstraction, and the general. In the same way that those writers lacking truth and respect for the life of the individual, for the ups and downs of life, distanced it).

Petro briefly flirts with action but finally decides to search within himself to achieve the "immagine vera" (true image) by attempting to strip away those layers of meaning that have falsified the essence of things, clouded the truth, and taken people down wrong paths. The choice is not, however, clear-cut or simple, as is shown through the figure of the baron Nené. Caught up in the world of D'Annunzian art and intrigued by the arrival of Crowley and his followers, he sees in them an antidote to his own actual world, which may be defined by a catalogued past and a petrified present. Nené's library consists mainly of works of history and science (including those of Mandralisca referred to in *Il sorriso dell'ignoto marinaio*) but not the works of the imagination after which he hankers.

The allusion to Mandralisca's treatises on malacology seems to suggest an ironic awareness on Consolo's own part of the fatal attractions of the world of dusty tomes. How indispensable are such works, Consolo seems to ask himself, for a narrative grounded in the historical reality of Sicily, if they risk blocking up the sources of imagination without which he would not be a writer? It is another means of defining the dilemma between writing and narrating he articulated more than ten years earlier in the story "Un giorno come gli altri" (A Day Like Any Other Day), which appeared in the 17 July 1980 issue of *Il Messaggero*:

È che il narrare, operazione che attinge quasi sempre alla memoria, a quella lenta sedimentazione su cui germina la memoria, è sempre un'operazione vecchia, arretrata, regressiva. Diverso è lo scrivere . . . mera operazione di scrittura, impoetica, estranea alla memoria, che è madre della poesia, come si dice. E allora è questo il dilemma, se bisogna scrivere o narrare. Con lo scrivere si può forse cambiare il mondo, con il narrare non si può, perché il narrare è rappresentare il mondo, cioè ricrearne un altro sulla carta.

(Narrating, an operation that almost always draws on memory, on that slow sedimentation on which memory germinates, is always an old, backward, regressive operation. Writing is different . . . a mere operation, unpoetic, extraneous to memory, which is the mother of poetry, as one says. So that the dilemma is whether to write or narrate. Through writing one can perhaps change the world, through narrating no, because to narrate is to represent the world, that is to create another one on paper.)

The novel does have its victims—notably, Lucia, Petro's sister, and Janu are destroyed by the artifice of society—but it ends on a note of optimism, for Petro with his insight and capacity for self-expression will survive and at some future date will be able to give expression to his grief.

Since the publication of *Nottetempo, casa per casa* Consolo has written three books. He translated the Latin text of the Mass for the dead, published as *Requiem per le vittime della mafia* (Requiem for the Victims of the Mafia, 1993), which Leonetta Bentivoglia described in the 26 March 1993 *La Repubblica* as "versi asciutti e solenni, che in un italiano vivo, dei nostri giorni, introducono elementi originali e specifici in un innesto di linguaggi locali, siciliano arcaico, citazioni greche" (terse, solemn verses, which in a living Italian, that of our times, introduce original and specific elements in a grafting of local spoken tongues, archaic Sicilian, and Greek quotations). Consolo's text accompanied the score written by seven young composers in memory of the two assassinated Sicilian judges, Giovanni Falcone and Paolo Borsellino, which was performed in the cathedral of Palermo on 27 March 1993. He has also published *Fuga dall'Etna: La Sicilia e Milano, la memoria e la storia* and *L'olivo e l'olivastro* (The Olive Tree and the Wild Olive Tree, 1994).

Consolo would see himself as the heir to Sciascia, writing within a realist tradition, primarily concerned with interpreting Sicily's past with an eye to its present. While there is undoubtedly some truth in this assessment, Consolo in his books is far more circumscribed to the insular reality of Sicily than is Sciascia, who frequently took a more comprehensively national viewpoint. But the real difference is not so much in the area of subject matter as of form. Consolo composes with the painstaking care of the poet with the rhythms of verse echoing in his memory, and it is his style that distinguishes him among writers of his generation.

Interviews:

"A colloquio con Vincenso Consolo," *Italienisch: Zeitschrift for Italienische Sprache und Literatur in Wissenschaft und Unterricht* (May 1987): 8–50;

Mario Fusco, "Questions à Vincenzo Consolo," *La Quinzaine Littéraire,* 31 March 1980, pp. 16–17;

"Con la penna e il caffé. Intervista con Vincenzo Consolo di Grazia Cherchi," *Panorama,* 12 March 1989, pp. 138–139;

Roberto Barbolini, *"Cosí nasce la dittatura,"* *Panorama,* 12 January 1992, p. 69;

L'invenzione della realtà. Conversazioni su letteratura e altro, edited by Monica Gemelli and Felice Piemontese (Naples: Guida Editore, 1994), pp. 29–48.

References:

Sebastiano Addamo, "Linguaggio e barocco in Vincenza Consolo," in *Oltre le figure* (Palermo: Sellerio, 1989), pp. 121–125;

Roberto Bertoni, 'Impostura' and 'Verita': A review of Narrative," *Journal of Association of Teachers of Italian,* 46 (Spring 1986): 63–65;

Raimondo Barone, "Verga nella narrativa siciliana del Novecento da Vittorini a Consolo," *Problemi: Periodico quadrimestrale di cultura* (September–December 1983): 252–265;

Sebastiano Burgaretta, "Mito e ragione nell'opera di Vicenzo Consolo," *Otto-Novecento* (January–February 1993): 171–180;

Gaetano Compagnino, "La talpa e la lumaca. Vincenzo Consolo narratore," in *Narratori siciliani del secondo dopoguerra,* edited by Sarah Zappulla Muscarà (Catania: Giuseppe Maimone Editore, 1990) pp. 155–169;

Flora Di Legami, *Vincenzo Consolo* (Messina: Pungitopo, 1990);

Joseph Farrell, "Translator's Afterword," *The Smile of the Unknown Mariner,* by Consolo (Manchester: Carcanet, 1994), pp. 121–131;

Farrell, "Vincenzo Consolo: Metaphors and False History," in *The New Italian Novel,* edited by Zygmunt Baranski and Lino Pertile (Edinburgh: Edinburgh University Press, 1993), pp. 59–74;

Gian Carlo Ferretti, introduction to *La ferita dell'aprile,* by Consolo (Milan: Mondadori, 1989);

G. Finzi, "Strutture metriche nella prosa di Consolo," *Linguistica e letteratura,* 3 (1978): 121–135;

Mario Fusco, "Images et Mirages de I'Immobilisme à propos des Romans Historiques Siciliens," in *Récit et Histoire* (Paris: Presses Universitaires de France, 1984), pp. 179–192;

Fernando Gioviale, "L'isola senza licantropi. 'Regressione' e 'illuminazione' nella scrittura di Vincenzo Consolo," in *Scrivere la Sicilia. Vittorini ed oltre* (Siracusa: Ediprint, 1985);

Tom O'Neill, "Re-Writing the Risorgimento in Sicily: Vincenzo Consolo's *Il sorriso dell'ignoto marinaio,*" in *Literature and Film in the Historical Dimension,* Selected Papers from the 15th Annual Conference on Literature and Film, edited by John Simons (Gainesville: Florida State University Press, 1993);

Massimo Onofri, "Vincenzo Consolo: *Nottetempo, casa per casa.* Considerazioni in margine," *Nuovi Argomenti,* 44 (October–December 1992): 114–118;

Leonardo Sciascia, "L'ignoto marinaio," in *Cruciverba* (Turin: Einaudi, 1983);

Cesare Segre, *Intrecci di voci. La polifonia nella letteratura del Novecento* (Turin: Einaudi, 1991);

Gianni Turchetta, introduction to *Le pietre di Pantalica,* by Consolo (Milan: Mondadori, 1990).

Franco Cordelli
(1943 -)

Simone Casini
University of Florence

Translated by Augustus Pallotta

BOOKS: *Procida* (Milan: Garzanti, 1973);
Fuoco celeste (Milan: Guanda, 1976);
Il poeta postumo; manie, pettegolezzi, rancori (Milan: Rizzoli, 1978);
Le forze in campo (Milan: Garzanti, 1979);
Partenze eroiche (Cosenza: Lerici, 1981);
I puri spiriti (Milan: Rizzoli, 1982);
Proprietà perduta (Milan: Guanda, 1983);
Pinkerton (Milan: Mondadori, 1986);
L'antipasqua, by Cordelli and *Lenz* di Georg Buchner, translated by Rosanna Farinazzo and Renzo Bez (Milan: Mondadori, 1987);
L'Italia di mattina (Milan: Leonardo, 1990);
Guerre lontane (Turin: Einaudi, 1990);
Scipione l'italiano (Milan: Cremese, 1993);
Diderot Dondolero. Quattro commedie (Rome: Edizioni Fondo Pier Paolo Pasolini, 1993);
Arancio (Salerno: Sottotraccia, 1994);
La democrazia magica: il narratore, il romanziere, lo scrittore (Turin: Einaudi, 1997).

OTHER: *Il pubblico della poesia,* by Cordelli and Alfonso Berardinelli (Cosenza: Lerici, 1975);
Pierre Drieu la Rochelle, *L'uomo a cavallo,* introduction by Cordelli (Milan: Guanda, 1980);
I cento romanzi stranieri 1900–1943, edited by Cordelli and Giovanni Raboni (Milan: Europeo, 1986);
La mia America: antologia della letteratura americana dal 1945 a oggi, edited by Cordelli (Milan: Leonardo, 1991);
Teatro moderno, selected with an introduction by Cordelli (Rome: Istituto Poligrafico e Zecca dello Stato, 1995).

TRANSLATIONS: André Gide, *I nutrimenti terrestri,* translated by Cordelli and M. Miglietta Ricci (Milano: Garzanti, 1975);
Henry James, *Principessa Casamassima* (Milan: Garzanti, 1975);
Lewis Carroll, *Sylvie e Bruno* (Milan: Garzanti, 1978);
Virginia Woolf, *Tra un atto e l'altro* (Milan: Guanda, 1979);
Emile Zola, *L'opera* (Milan: Garzanti, 1981);
Stendhal, *Armance, o alcune scene di un salotto parigino nel 1827* (Milan: Garzanti, 1982);
Jacques Cazotte, *Il diavolo innamorato* (Turin: Einaudi, 1992).

Marked by a strong literary consciousness, Franco Cordelli's work engages the important issues of the cultural debate that has been waged in Italy since the 1970s. Guided by a spirit of experimentalism, Cordelli writes in direct opposition to the Gruppo 63, the major avant-garde movement of the post–World War II era. His atypical experimentalism can be identified with Rome's literary tradition, for even though he has little in common with the two writers who are the main exponents of that tradition, Alberto Moravia and Pier Paolo Pasolini, his narratives are closely tied to the city of Rome through setting and themes. As the critic Alberto Asor Rosa points out, Cordelli is one of the few Roman writers to achieve national recognition. He has been criticized, though, for a tendency to over-intellectualize. In addition to being a novelist, Cordelli is a poet, playwright, drama critic, translator, and an organizer of significant cultural events.

Believing that writing is a cultural activity grounded in the author's judgment, will, and superstition, Cordelli views the novel as an arbitrary form that is governed by the construction of a temporal-causal frame. Recognizing the artificiality of the form and accepting the proclamations by critics regarding the death of the author and plot, he argues that it is essential that the narrative maintains at least the appearance of a logical structure. The novel for Cordelli is "il labirinto dell'intertestualità" (the labyrinth of intertextuality), but as a means of connecting the scattered data of human experience it remains nonetheless "un notevole metodo igienico, un metodo di centrifugazione della schizofre-

Franco Cordelli

nia" (a significant hygienic method of evading schizophrenia).

Cordelli's playful superstitiousness is evident, for example, in "la legge segreta del numero otto" (the secret law of the number eight), which dominates his first novel, *Procida* (1973). This law is also present in *Fuoco celeste* (Celestial Fire, 1976), which is made up of eight parts, each consisting of eight poems. Other superstitions are apparent in the recurrence of the letter *P* as the initial letter in the first prominent word of several of his titles–*Procida, Pubblico, Poeta, Pinkerton, Proprietà*–and in the prominence of the initials of his name, F. C., in the titles *Fuoco celeste* and *Le forze in campo*. While he has abandoned these particular devices in his later works, superstition remains a serious matter for Cordelli. Superstition serves as a substitute for faith in providing a constant in an unstable world where traditional truths are always under attack. He uses superstitions in his work as metaphors to explore the difficult connections between life and literature, form and content, and private and collective history.

Cordelli's novel *Procida*, which was published the year he turned thirty, takes the form of a diary written by the main character during Christmas vacation at his home in Procida, a small island in the bay of Naples. The protagonist clearly hopes to purify himself through his written meditations on the present, but the connection between the present and the act of writing is abandoned as the recording of daily events soon becomes laced with past recollections, with letters written to Agata, Amelia, and to his daughter Alice, and with the strange events that occur on the island, including a murder. It becomes difficult for the diarist to write about the present because he has yet to report salient facts of yesterday. In this fashion the diary loses its intended function. Writing turns to history, to chronicle, to document. Fiction and the detective story force their way into the narrative, usurping the space intended for inward reflection.

In *Procida* the present and past are intertwined, and every daily event seems charged with ominous meaning. Factual memories become mixed with projections of fictional episodes involving sex and betrayals. The characters–including the dog Lorenzo renamed Witold (the name of his wife's lover); the young, uninhibited Alberta; and Alice–are often enigmatic and their meanings remain unresolved. The style is at once realistic, abstract, and ambiguous; the abundance of parenthetical clauses and afterthoughts reflects the maniacal temper of the protagonist.

The publication of Cordelli's second book–the anthology *Il pubblico della poesia* (Poetry and its Audience, 1975) that he edited with Alfonso Berardinelli–coincided with a renewed interest in poetry and a relative eclipse in the narrative. As Giulio Ferroni pointed out in the October 1987 issue of *Il Ponte*, the younger generation saw poetry as an avenue to express social and personal problems free of rigid theoretical constraints. In this vein Cordelli and Berardinelli in the anthology present their poets as figures, as characters acting on a stage. In his own poetry, such as *Proprietà perduta* (Lost Property, 1983), Cordelli indicates his difficulty identifying with such a public role for poetry. Addressing the nineteenth-century German poet C. F. Hölderman, he writes:

> Hölderlin: siamo un segno senza significato
> ed ecco, vedi, la frase, il verso
> non è più suo, né qui, bene o male
> ma anche di me che lo riscrivo
> il verso è anche mia proprietà.
>
> (Hölderlin: we are a sign without meaning
> and here, you see, the phrase, the verse
> are no longer his, are not here, good or bad
> and even I rewriting it
> can say the verse is my property.)

The volume is not easy reading as Cordelli intuitively joins together images and ideas, paying little heed to the need to be accessible or to the requirements of a rational or critical mind.

Cordelli's second novel, *Le forze in campo* (The Forces in the Field, 1979), is connected to *Procida*, beginning with Witold, the dog who accompanies the protagonist to Rome and dies there. The protagonist-narrator is a retired boxer and tennis instructor at a sport club, and the central scene takes place at a party in one of Rome's private sport clubs where a sex incident lays bare the interpersonal relationship among the characters. This work continues the diary form, which again borders on becoming a narrative when clues—such as the anonymous postcards pointing to a mysterious event—take over the focus. The mystery, though, remains unresolved, absorbed by the flow of daily life.

The patina of realism hides a strong mysterious force apparent in the events and, more importantly, in the neurotic make-up of the narrator. Ordinary situations take on an air of mystery when they are filtered through the lucid delirium of the main character, who in his mania for orderliness is scrupulously fastidious. His past as a moderately successful boxer, relived through newspaper clippings, is juxtaposed to his present demeanor, which is comparable to someone who seeks to catch his adversary by surprise. The title of the book points to this difficult and despairing struggle against an enemy that cannot be defined. This metaphoric equivalence between sport and war reappears in Cordelli's later works as well.

Much more complex is Cordelli's next novel, *I puri spiriti* (The Pure Spirits, 1982), another work marked by narrative experimentation. The novel is actually made up of four "short stories," which despite their independence of each other are treated as chapters of the work. Cordelli comments on the genesis of the work in his remark on the first story in the volume, "La superstizione" (Superstition): "Questo racconto fu scritto alla fine del settantaquattro. Allora ignoravo che ne sarebbero seguiti altri tre, ad incastro, un poco. Ignoravo insomma che questo era il primo capitolo di un nuovo romanzo" (This short story was written at the end of 1974. At the time I did not know that three other stories would follow, one carried into the next, as it were. In short, I did not know that this would be the first chapter of a new novel.) This first chapter explores Rome's literary world. The setting is the sidewalks of the city on a summer evening, during the course of which the most prominent writers, critics, and linguists of the younger generation come together by accident.

In the story that follows, "Il solista" (The Soloist), the author writes from Palermo to four women, each of whose name begins with an *O*–a clear reference to Pauline Reage's erotic classic *Histoire d'O* (1954; translated as *The Story of O*, 1965). The next story, "La staffetta," (The Relay), relates the love affair that two of the four women in the preceding story have during the author's absence. Finally, in "Il seminario" (The Seminar) the author turns from subject to object in the sense that the characters found in the previous story talk about the author as well as his work *I puri spiriti* at a literary symposium in Venice. The introduction of prominent men of letters virtually identified by name (such as Umberto E. for Umberto Eco) and the disappearance of the author's voice in the last story force the reader to take stock of the extratextual dimension of Cordelli's work rather than to seek the closure of a traditional novel.

I puri spiriti represents an unusual case in Cordelli's intellectual investigation of the novel. It may be said to be constructed without a plot, for the scant materials drawn from real life fall short of telling a story, even in the third part, where such an effort seems most apparent. The novel points to the crux of contemporary narrative, according to Cordelli, who in his 1990 novel *L'Italia di mattina* (Italy in the Morning) states the problem directly: "Come si può scrivere senza fatti? Eppure è una delle prove di nobiltà, se non di destrezza, dello scrivere contem-poraneo" (How can one write without facts? And yet, this is a challenge of nobility, if not of skill, that faces contemporary writing). Moravia called *I puri spiriti* "heroic-comical" because Cordelli tells a story that in the end proves to be nonexistent. But if the title of the work is an ironical or satirical allusion to the metaphysical pretensions of literature and in particular to the pretentious demeanor of the writers living in Rome, the sole referent in the last analysis is Cordelli himself.

In fashioning *I puri spiriti* Cordelli neglected the story, moved mainly by theoretical issues; he escaped this trap in *Pinkerton* (1986) and *Guerre lontane* (Distant Wars, 1990), his most difficult, complex, and substantive novels. These novels mark a turning point in his writing, for he abandons the urge to theorize and to represent the problems facing contemporary narrative and strives instead for a deeper understanding of historical reality. Everything becomes clear and takes on depth: approximations disappear; intellectual irony is softened; and narrative style becomes denser, more somber, reflective. He no longer views the construction of a narrative to penetrate the opaqueness of life as theoretically impossible but as a pressing, tangible problem.

Cordelli's steady and long-standing interest in theater, which is well represented by such experimental plays as *Siberina,* written in 1984 and included in *Diderot Dondolero. Quattro commedie* (Diderot Dondolero. Four Comedies, 1993), *L'antipasqua* (Before Easter, 1987), *Lena,* and *Diderot Dondolero,* is the apparent inspiration for both *Pinkerton* and *Guerre lontane.* At the center of each novel is the staging of an ambitious play by a small group of people. In both cases the productions spark unexpected receptions that culminate in tragedy. Due to the complexity of the situation that Cordelli set himself, his constructed narratives are problematic. The devices he employs to tell his stories include diary entries, witness accounts, historical research, quotations, and the transcription of letters and taped materials—all of which are subjected to close analysis in the course of his novels.

In *Pinkerton* a group of boys living in a home for orphans and the handicapped in Rome is trained in acting and stage production by Teresa, the founder and director of the home. The boys travel to Berlin, where they stage *L'Invasione* (The Invasion), a play by Arthur Adamov that was inspired by the work of the French playwright Antonin Artaud. The play is directed by the group leader, Oscar, whose approach to directing stands in sharp contrast to the classical notion of acting and directing taught by Teresa. The situation becomes tense when a member of the group, Mario Bastiani, is kidnapped by a terrorist organization. The focus of the novel is not the events themselves but the taped comments on the kidnapping given by Agostino, perhaps the least important of the boys engaged in the production of the play. It turns out that Teresa has secretly taped the fourteen boys as they were being questioned by the chief of police, Morioni, several months after the occurrence of the event in Berlin.

A work open to multiple interpretations, *Pinkerton,* from a sociohistorical perspective, suggests the failure of the social utopia promoted by the protest movements of the 1970s. Worthy of note in this regard is Cordelli's interest in the relationship between art and social progress and his belief that a "guerriero," or warlike element, is a fermenting ingredient of enlivened, polemical, and politically conscious discourse. *Pinkerton* alludes clearly, albeit obliquely, to the terrorist groups active in Italy in the 1970s as an "idealistic" degeneration of "war." One finds, for instance, subtle allusions to the kidnapping and murder of Italy's prime minister, Aldo Moro, by the Red Brigades in Cordelli's dating Bastiani's kidnapping in the same month as Moro's, May 1978, and in his locating the boys' home in Monte Mario, not far from Moro's family residence in Via Fani. However, such a connection is complicated by Bastiani's being "a soldier" in the terrorist group and the description of Pinkerton, the sarcastic police chief, as a "malinconico e buio cavaliere senza ideali" (melancholic and somber knight without ideals).

Guerre lontane deals with the staging in 1981 of Sean O'Casey's *Red Roses for Me* (1942), a play depicting labor unrest in Ireland, at Rome's Villa Borghese park. Surrounding the mysterious figure of the director, Bruno, is a group of friends he wants to act in the play. To Bruno, an experimental director, the play means a return to classic drama with a traditional plot. The performance of the drama brings tragedy: aroused by the strike presented in the final scene, the audience reacts violently, and Bruno is killed in the melee that follows.

The nucleus of the novel is the diligent and complex work of the reconstructing of the events leading to Bruno's death. To carry out the task is Lorenzo, a fine-arts student whom Bruno entrusted the task of *cronista* (reporter) of the staging of the play. Because he has lost his notebook, Lorenzo has to rely on memory. His story is affected by the complex relationship that existed between Bruno, the idealistic "warrior," and Lorenzo, which in its intimacy and opposition is suggestive of a split personality. While Bruno attempted to control the forces that were operative in the event-performance, Lorenzo rejects such a course:

La dinamica degli eventi non la so dominare—e poi mi ripugnerebbe farlo: preferisco, il tempo, lasciarlo fluire.... Bruno mi disse: "Mi raccomando, non un diario. Quella è una brutta tentazione. Un fatto dietro l'altro, si finisce per attribuirgli troppa importanza: oppure ciò che se ne pensa." Che era forse la matematica la sua illusione: quella, cioè della simultaneità, della rapidità e della finezza nel percepire i rapporti tra le cose. I "fini amori" dei cavalieri.

I don't know how to control the dynamics of events—and, besides, I would be ashamed to do it. I prefer to let time flow. . . . Bruno told me: "Please don't write a diary: it is a bad idea. When you report one fact after another, you end up lending them too much importance or writing what you think." Perhaps he nurtured the illusion of mathematics: simultaneity, swiftness, and finesse in perceiving the relationship among things. The "fine love" of medieval knights.

In an interview Cordelli suggested an analogy between his work and Elio Vittorini's *Uomini e no.*

Lorenzo is a voracious reader of the diaries of such famous artists and art historians as Johann Joachim Winckelmann, Eugène Delacroix, Paul Klee, Henri Matisse, and, above all, Bernard Berenson. What counts for him is not the work but "il confronto delle opere con la vita dell'autore" (the connection between an artistic work and the life of the artist). Accordingly, Bernini's statue of Apollo and Daphne in Rome's Villa Borghese becomes gradually the ambivalent metaphor of the book, the symbol of Bruno's belief that art captures and immortalizes a moment in time, which contrasts with Lorenzo's position that writing dilutes the eternal through its record of the passage of time.

In 1989 Cordelli worked as a reporter covering the Giro d'Italia, Italy's most important bicycle race, for a major Italian newspaper. Subsequently he set out to condense all the thoughts and emotions sparked by the experience in *L'Italia di mattina,* a novel in which he as the sports reporter-protagonist takes the name Scipione. Cordelli writes like one who has rediscovered something once loved and cherished, who experiences anew what he thought only existed as memory. Such a discovery opens the way to a mode of writing at once affable, realistic, and essaylike. What emerges from this effort is an original analysis of the physical competition of sports, bicycling in particular.

Cordelli explores a less-than-idealistic dimension of the Giro d'Italia and of the sports world in general. He reveals the collective identity of the fans swept by the fever of spectacle and competition, a passion that has deep, immemorial roots. Through bicycling, a sport almost incongruous in the modern technological world, Cordelli is able to find the genuine face of a forgotten Italy, her people and geography. As seen by Cordelli sports are an instrument of mass control by those exercising political power, but his analysis of sports also allows for other insights. He strongly denounces the ecological devastation the country has seen in the last fifty years. He is even able to give fresh meaning to the overwrought theme of war and the battling hero through his analysis of sport champion and the challenges of competition. In the extraordinary use of the metaphor of competition, the champion replaces the traditional hero in literature.

Dust jacket for Cordelli's 1997 book

In 1991 Cordelli edited *La mia America* (My America), an anthology of American writers published to honor the fiftieth anniversary of *Americana* (1941), the anthology edited by Vittorini that introduced American writers to Italian readers. Some argue that this anthology marks the end of an historical cycle of the presence of American culture in Italy. Cordelli chooses selections from forty-nine writers that constitute a sort of ideological map of post–World War II American civilization. In his introduction Cordelli echoes Pasolini's views in returning to his division between "guerrieri" (warriors) and "mercanti" (merchants):

Questa è la guerra in atto: ci sono i mercanti con le armi, gli americani, e i mercanti senza armi, i tedeschi e i giapponesi. Per ora vincono i mercanti con le armi: ma probabilmente è solo l'apparenza, siamo già al "declino dell'impero americano." Del resto, in armi o senza, quella dei mercanti è la specie migliore.... essa è anche la più buona, per così dire: la più umana, appunto: è disposta a trattare. E là dove l'interesse coincide con il bene, la pulsione del singolo con la media delle pulsioni collettive.

This is the ongoing war: there are merchants with arms, the Americans, and merchants without arms, namely Germans and Japanese. For the time being the merchants with arms are winning, but that may be misleading since we have already come to the point of the "decline of the American empire." In any event, with arms or without, the merchants' is the better human species ... better in the sense of being more human and disposed to deal. It is the species where self-interest coincides with the common good, where individual motivation coincides with a large share of collective motivations.

In 1993 Cordelli returned to the world of sports and the protagonist he created in *L'Italia di mattina* in writing *Scipione l'italiano* (The Italian Scipio), the title clearly playing on the successful Roman general known as Scipio Africanus, the African Scipio. Sports here become a sensitive instrument to measure the nature of political tensions in the world. Through his good-natured and experienced protagonist, Cordelli makes his readers feel the pulse of important dynamics in the world of the 1990s by pointing out the social and political realities of individual countries. Understandably, the focus remains on Italy, seen as the original place of the competitive spirit. Cordelli traces this spirit to the *palestrae*, the gyms of ancient Rome, and unfolds it through such great events as the Olympics, bicycling, soccer, and car racing.

In the Rome of the 1990s the sight of sweating wrestlers in a gym elicits in the protagonist both puzzlement and love:

Pochi giorni fa giurammo di non essere più interessati ad alcuna forma di lotta. Perchè, allora, ritrovarci tra tutti questi lottatori, benché piccoli nani, invisibili, inconsapevoli? Perchè ritrovarci in questa palestra, noi, i giuratori? Lo con fermiamo, giuriamo che rifiuteremo ogni forma di lotta. ma volevamo dire, e ora lo ribadiamo, ogni forma di lotta che, accanto al disprezzo per il nemico, escluda la consapevolezza che il nemico non è che una parte di noi, non altro che una emanazione dello stesso sistema, dello stesso dio: in altre parole, un essere che appartiene al secolo, alla storia—ma anche una creatura, qualcuno che non possiamo non abbracciare, non stringere al petto.... —lotte insomma, che sono, grosso modo, un bacio.

A few days ago we swore that we were no longer interested in any form of fights. Why, then, do we find ourselves among these wrestlers, though they are small, midgets, invisible, unconscious? Why do we, who swore otherwise, find ourselves in this gym? We confirm, swear again that we shall reject any such fights. But what we meant to say, and we reiterate now, any forms of fighting which, together with contempt for the enemy, acknowledges that the enemy is part of ourselves, none other than the expression of the system, of the same god. In other words the enemy is part of the century and part of history, a human being, someone whom we cannot but embrace and hold close to our heart... in short, these are fights which, in broad terms, amount to a kiss.

Cordelli has shown himself to be a serious artist whose career has already taken unexpected turns. His work will likely continue to be important to the development of Italian letters.

Interviews:
Giampiero Mughini, "Sono scrittore e me ne vanto," *L'Europeo*, 7 January 1986, pp. 116-121;
Massimo Dini, "L'Italia presa in giro," *L'Europeo*, 15 May 1990, pp. 132-133;
Caludio Toscani, "Intervista a Franco Cordelli per *Guerre lontane*," *Otto/Novecento*, 15 (Spring 1991): 173-176.

References:
Andrea Barbuto, review of *Il pubblico della poesia*, *Prospetti*, 43-44 (September-December 1976): 26-33;
Giulio Ferroni, "Marginalità e deriva," *Il Ponte*, October 1987, pp. 1202-1213;
Vincenzo Pardini, "Gli eroi del pedale," *Nuovi argomenti*, 36 (October-December 1990): 95-97.

Andrea De Carlo
(11 December 1952 -)

Antonella Francini
Syracuse University

BOOKS: *Treno di panna* (Turin: Einaudi, 1981); translated by John Gatt as *Cream Train* (London: Olive Press, 1987);
Uccelli da gabbia e da voliera (Turin: Einaudi, 1982);
Macno (Milan: Bompiani, 1984); translated by William Weaver (San Diego: Harcourt Brace Jovanovich, 1987);
Yucatan (Milan: Bompiani, 1986); translated by Weaver (San Diego: Harcourt Brace Jovanovich, 1990);
Due di due (Milan: Mondadori, 1989);
Tecniche di seduzione (Milan: Bompiani, 1991);
Arcodamore (Milan: Bompiani, 1993);
Uto (Milan: Bompiani, 1995);
Di noi tre (Milan: Mondadori, 1997).

SELECTED PERIODICAL PUBLICATIONS—UNCOLLECTED: "Capitolo I, scena IV," *Esquire* (April 1990): 25-26;
"Oggetti da vetrina," *Furore letterario,* 8 (August-September 1990): 23-28.

MOTION PICTURES: *Le facce di Fellini,* screenplay and direction by De Carlo, Vides, 1983;
Treno di panna, adapted and directed by De Carlo, Italiana Film s.r.l.-Azzura Film-Rete Italia, 1988.

Andrea De Carlo made his literary debut in 1981 with the novel *Treno di panna* (translated as *Cream Train,* 1987), impressing Italian readers as an original, young voice in contrast to the repetitive formulas and provincialism of the "romanzo medio"—a kind of best-selling novel produced in the 1960s and the 1970s that was generally characterized by fine writing and nostalgic returns to the past. Winner of the Giovanni Comisso Prize, this first work defined De Carlo as the precursor of a new generation of writers—a generation that seemed to challenge and renew the elegiac, autobiographic prose that had distinguished Italian fiction for some twenty years. The originality of his writing,

Andrea De Carlo

strongly influenced by the cinema, lies in the dry, antirhetorical language he uses to analyze contemporary scenes, characters, and moods as well as in his peculiar perspective which, much like a camera, focuses and brings his subjects into sharp relief.

De Carlo's photographic eye moves from the urban setting of Los Angeles to metropolitan Milan and Rome, recording, through nine novels, nine different representations of the efforts of a young artist—often patterned after a salient aspect of the author's eclectic personality—to find integration in a society duped by the media and seduced by the elusive dream of personal power and success. The countryside of Umbria, Latin America, Greece, or Australia is juxtaposed to contemporary cities. To such settings De Carlo's characters retreat, escape temporarily, or dream of escaping. These literary settings coincide with the places he has lived or visited: his native Milan; Urbino, where he has established his second home in the mid-1980s; Rome, where he lived in the late 1980s; and the foreign countries he visited as a young man and continues to travel to frequently.

De Carlo's search for alternative means of artistic expression is a distinguishing trait of both his fiction and his life. As a writer, photographer, cineast, painter, and musician De Carlo stands out as a multimedia artist. His main concern, though, is literary language, which in his narrative work draws substantially from other arts and the media.

De Carlo's writing is known for its faithful rendering of the generation that came of age in the 1980s—its ideals, lost illusions, and desire to break loose from traditional roles and the routine of daily life. As the initiator of the so-called *giovane narrativa* (young narrative), De Carlo has earned a literary reputation still largely tied to the success of his first novel even though his style and themes have changed significantly through the years. Since the publication of *Treno di panna,* which was issued under the favorable recommendations of Natalia Ginzburg and Italo Calvino, his books have been translated into eight languages and published in eighteen countries.

Andrea De Carlo was born in Milan on 11 December 1952, the son of the well-known architect Giancarlo De Carlo and the editor and translator Giuliana Baracco. He grew up in the city, pursuing classical studies and attending the state university. He studied history and completed a thesis on the Spanish Civil War before pursuing a degree in modern literature, which he received in 1977. De Carlo's cosmopolitanism, partly a reflection of the taste of his generation, is in some measure traceable to his literary background. He readily admits that writers such as Fyodor Dostoyevski, Leo Tolstoy, Stendhal, Franz Kafka, F. Scott Fitzgerald, J. D. Salinger, and Jack Kerouac played an important role in his literary formation. Only two Italian authors, Italo Svevo and Calvino—two of Italy's least provincial writers—were important to his development. While attending the university he worked as a photographer, an activity that was to shape the technique of his first book.

In presenting *Treno di panna* to readers, Calvino was the first to point to De Carlo's "partico-lare acutezza dello sguardo che afferra e registra un enorme numero di particolari e sfumature" (sharp and distinctive eye which grasps and retains an enormous amount of details and subtleties). He praised his ability to replace "la penna all'obbiettivo fotografico" (his camera lens with a pen). In *Treno di panna* a fictionalized autobiographical narrator, Giovanni Maimeri, relates his experiences in Los Angeles as though he were expressing himself with images rather than words, as though he were assembling a montage of snapshots.

Giovanni is a young Italian photographer who travels to Los Angeles largely by chance. When his money runs out, he takes odd jobs—bicycling around the city to advertise a health food store, waiting in an Italian restaurant, and teaching Italian in a school attended by the rich and famous of Beverly Hills. His experiences afford him the opportunity to observe successful individuals who have realized the American dream. Living in a real or imagined limelight and constantly engaged in unreal competition, they are either recognized as successful or are seen as *squali* (sharks), searching for scraps of fame to snap up so that they can grow into bigger sharks. They have been duped by the American myth that more is better, and they measure happiness and self-worth in terms of money and fame. Too self-satisfied and too ambitious, they are unable to transcend their identies as flat, one-dimensional characters.

The Americans Giovanni encounters—from the couple that hosts him in the initial chapters, to his girlfriend Jill and her parents, to a famous actress named Marsha Mellows and her husband—all seem to play rehearsed roles and deliver scripted monologues. The image of acting a part recurs constantly in the novel: like actors, De Carlo's protagonists play passionate love scenes, weep in tragic tones, or rehearse familiar roles as though they were on stage. The loud voices of radio and television speakers accompany their actions and interfere with their conversations. The characters shout to be heard and whisper clichés on the ever-present telephone—one more device that prevents direct human interaction.

Giovanni is almost speechless as he moves in this world of surfaces, leaving his unblinking eye the task of filling the void that pervades the American metropolis and its inhabitants. Yet, in spite of his apparent detachment, he is drawn to and seduced by the myth of success. He moves in and out of roles, and from scene to scene his actions and thoughts are disconnected, as though his external demeanor was separated from his inner life. Unable to synchronize his body either with his social milieu or his inner self, Giovanni remains an onlooker, an ambiguous and displaced character to the end, a position that condemns him to live on the edge of American society but prevents him from turning into one more human robot.

The novel ends with a Hollywood party: here the narrator realizes that he has finally reached "il centro del mondo" (the world's center). Ironically, Giovanni finds himself in the midst of real actors who, having embraced role-playing as their profession, have erased the distance between acting and living. The title of the book, then, not only refers to a film in which Marsha Mellows has acted but also to the grotesque show offered by De Carlo's characters: the train of their self-absorbed lives runs on a track as foamy and unsubstantial as cream.

Echoes of Nathaniel West's *The Day of the Locust* (1939) are present in *Treno di panna*. The protagonist of West's novel is an artist, the painter Tod Hackett, who also witnesses the American dream of fame and success in an artificial Los Angeles. However, while Tod's criticism eventually leads to a final catharsis, Giovanni's lack of moral judgment suggests his inability to extricate himself from the seduction of a materialistic society.

De Carlo's meticulous and detached descriptions of events and behavior reminds the reader of the French nouveau roman of Alain Robbe-Grillet, perhaps mediated by the experimental novel of the Italian avant-garde of the 1960s and by Calvino's ironic treatment of such writings in *Se una notte d'inverno un viaggiatore* (1979; translated as *If on a Winter's Night a Traveler,* 1981). However, the obsessive description of objects and the minute recording of individual acts often result in an unbridgeable gap between the reader and the text. Even so De Carlo enables the reader to perceive the void that pervades a self-engrossed consumer society dominated by the mechanical forces of the media.

Treno di panna was originally written in English in 1980; that year, De Carlo traveled for extended periods in Australia and the United States, taking on a variety of jobs to support himself. The Italian of the finished novel shows traces of its first version in the anglicized form of certain words and idioms. For instance, the verb forms in the English sentences "she pressed a door opener button" and "Tracy drove off at speed" linger in the Italian: "Ha *pressato* il tasto di un citofono" and "Tracy ha *guidato via* veloce"–doubtless as part of De Carlo's effort to mimic American speech.

In the wake of the success of his first novel De Carlo published *Uccelli da gabbia e da voliera* (Cage and Aviary Birds, 1982). His first work was the product of an inexperienced author even though he had been writing since his early youth and had completed two unpublished novels. *Uccelli da gabbia e da voliera,* on the other hand, was the work of a full-time writer, the result of a long, painstaking revision of its first draft. As he related in an 18 April 1982 interview in *La nazione,* he followed a strict work schedule: writing from nine in the morning to seven in the evening, then some relaxing in the gym or the swimming pool, and, after dinner, spending some time with friends, maybe in a disco. De Carlo has kept faith to this schedule and is a disciplined writer: he corrects, revises, and refines his drafts until he is satisfied with the final product. Then, like many of his characters, he moves on, often traveling extensively before returning to his work.

In *Uccelli da gabbia e da voliera* actions are arranged in sequence and described as though De Carlo were writing a movie script, providing detailed instructions to his imaginary actors and fragmenting scenes to convey a sense of movement. Even the dialogues sound like lines to be recited before the camera, in as much as the narrator's comments and facial expressions appear to be directions on how to achieve, scene after scene, a desirable impact on an imaginary viewer. The use of the present tense throughout the narrative further strengthens the overall cinematic effect.

The first-person narrator and protagonist of the novel, Fiodor Barna, while similar to Giovanni Maimeri in *Treno di panna,* is less interesting and less successful. Like Giovanni, Fiodor is a passive and unpredictable character who travels the roads of the United States, starting in California. He acts on impulse and it is no surprise that he abruptly leaves his American girlfriend at the end of the first chapter. He eventually settles in Milan, reluctantly accepting work in a branch of the family-owned company, and performs routine work in an executive office. His generous salary and credit cards satisfy his whims: a Stratocaster guitar, a powerful stereo, many records, an answering machine, a luxury Fiat. Surrounded by his mechanical gadgets in his huge but empty apartment, Fiodor makes casual friendships, has an affair with the wife of the company director, and falls in love with a mysterious woman, Malaidina, who is probably connected with a terrorist group.

De Carlo's decision to bring his autobiographical character to Milan not only reflects the author's own return to Italy but also suggests his interest in a historically significant setting, for the Milan in the late 1970s of the novel is experiencing the final stage of Italian terrorism. While historical events become more relevant to the action in subsequent books, in *Uccelli da gabbia e da voliera* the focus is on the immature and self-absorbed Fiodor, who is unable to move effectively in a traditional society governed by capitalistic ethics and beset by social and political turmoil. He succumbs to the sterile apathy typical of a spoiled, wealthy child and remains uncertain about what to do with his life. His efforts to evade apathy through an improbable love story with Malaidina or through unlikely projects in Australia, where two acquaintances dream of becoming bird breeders, are too sentimental and too fashionable to be a convincing rebellion against role-playing.

As in *Treno di panna*, *Uccelli da gabbia e da voliera* is permeated with an authentic flavor of contemporaneity. The characters are caught up in the fast-paced rhythm of Milanese life, where the answering machines are always on, and yet they yearn to escape from the urban and mental cages to which the title refers. The language is adapted to the spoken idiom: short, slangy, essential phrases, sometimes modeled after English grammar, record the characters' actions and describe settings in fast sequences.

Having experimented with cinematic techniques in his fiction, De Carlo had his first real experience in motion pictures in 1982-1983 as assistant director to Federico Fellini, one of Italy's greatest filmmakers, in *E la nave va* (And the Ship Goes On, 1983). While shooting the last scenes at Cinecittà studios in Rome, De Carlo directed a documentary on the relationship between Fellini and his actors titled *Le facce di Fellini* (Fellini's Faces, 1983). In 1983 and 1984 he also contributed eleven travel articles to Milan's daily *Il Corriere della Sera* dealing with his trips to Berlin and Australia. Written in a clipped, bare, photographic style, these "block-notes of a young novelist," as the subtitle indicates, remind one of narrated slides. In 1984 De Carlo also worked with Michelangelo Antonioni as scriptwriter for a movie that was never released. In 1988 he adapted, directed, and acted in a minor role in *Treno di panna* (1988). While based on his novel, the film is hardly faithful to it as several parts were omitted or rewritten; the setting was changed from Los Angeles to New York; and the characters are radically different. That same year he and Ludovico Einaudi also wrote an "abstract" script (there are almost no words) for a multimedia ballet, *Time Out—A Journey into the Fourth Dimension,* which was staged by the American group Iso Dance Theater.

De Carlo dedicated his third novel, *Macno* (1984; translated, 1987), to Fellini, whose sets often seem to be appropriate visual referents for the settings of De Carlo's books. *Macno* is a political allegory about a peaceful revolution and its ultimate failure, set in an unnamed country that unmistakably represents contemporary Italy. In contrast to his first two novels, De Carlo writes in the third person, a change that highlights the cinematic qualities of his prose even more. The artificiality of the settings, the variety of walk-on characters, and the ever-present motion-picture cameras, videotapes, speakers, and stage technicians all suggest the atmosphere of moviemaking.

The active, charismatic Macno is a thirty-three-year-old dictator who has overthrown an arrogant and corrupt political regime through shrewd manipulation of television. Interviewing government leaders on a live talk show, Macno unmasks the hypocrisy and corruption that lies behind their empty rhetoric. His popularity enables him to ascend to absolute power. However, as a dictator he recognizes that in order to wield power he must maintain the image that has determined his success. Surrounded by a team of experts in mass communication who manufacture video propaganda, Macno realizes he has become an emblem, a role-player constrained by the limits of the image of himself he has created.

The political machinery of mass media obeys its own rules, and Macno cannot stand up against it. The dichotomy between a stereotyped public image and the mutability of the human mind is at the base of Macno's political and personal crisis. It is even reflected in the architecture of his residence, which is meaningfully divided into two sections—the official facade and his private rooms where he plans his utopia and asserts his basic anarchism. But even in the "corticina pseudorinascimentale" (pseudo-Renaissance little court) that he has created to contrast the decadence of the capital, intellectuals and artists are frozen into stereotypes.

The witness of this crisis is Liza, a journalist from New York who with her colleague Ted manages to get into Macno's palace for a scoop interview. Liza surrenders to Macno's seduction and becomes the docile confidante of his frustrations as well as the companion with whom he can abandon his official role. Walking secretly around a Rome-like capital, Macno confides in her his disappointments with a country of pliable masses who are receptive only to sensational politics while remaining essentially passive. As the third anniversary of his regime approaches, he feels that his utopian dream of real change has collapsed under the ineluctable logic of political power. Like Giovanni Maimeri and Fiodor Barna, Macno chooses physical escape as a solution. Just as he planned his ascent to power, so he plans his way out: an explosion in his apartment apparently ends his life as the scapegoat of a decadent society; in reality he reemerges at the airport as an anonymous passenger about to leave for a faraway tourist resort.

Often defined as a technological fable, *Macno* stands out as the first book in which De Carlo explores a political theme and treats the inability of his own generation to assure political and social continuity. Beyond the allegory De Carlo never loses sight of Italy in the 1980s, marked by the connivance of political parties with industrial leaders and popular distaste for a system that has engendered contempt and indifference for the political process. At the same time, the dictator's failure is not depicted as being due only to his rejection of an established political logic but also to his own collusion with the system. Like Giovanni and Fiodor, he is also a child of consumerism and technology, subject to the seduction of power, success, and comfort. His escape into high-tech privacy and his love story with Liza underline his inability to reform society by becoming its moral leader. However, the private Macno, with his sentimentalism and platitudes, is at odds with the ideological scope of the book and weakens the novel.

In November 1984 De Carlo, Fellini, and the son of a Roman producer took an adventurous journey together through southern California and Mexico. The trip prompted Fellini to write a script and afforded De Carlo a subject for his fourth novel, *Yucatan* (1986; translated, 1990), a comedy in which he returns to an international setting and to first-person narration. Although the main characters have been radically transformed, the plot retains many elements of the actual journey. In reality the group met the writer and anthropologist Carlos Castaneda and traveled south of the border to collect material for a movie based on his books. Fellini did not transform the experience into a movie although a script (which has points in common with De Carlo's work) was readily written and, in 1986, published in six episodes in the *Corriere della sera* as *Viaggio a Tulun* (Journey to Tulun).

Yucatan, winner of the Bancarella Prize, opens at the London airport of Heathrow, where the narrator, Dave Hollis, and a famous director of Yugoslavian origin, Dru Resnik, are about to leave for Los Angeles. There they are supposed to meet the wealthy producer Nick Nesbitt and the mysterious writer Astor Camado, with whom they will discuss a movie project. This setting, much favored by De Carlo's cosmopolitan protagonists, links his fourth novel to the ending of *Macno*. In fact, Dave is a Macno who, having failed as a reformer, has slipped back into the role of critical observer of people's behavior, the same type as the protagonist of *Treno di panna*. Less naive, less passive than Giovanni, Dave nonetheless is like him in his ability to organize his material through a skilled use of perspective and manipulation of details. It is his viewpoint, which is mixed with a short series of diary-like entries reporting Dru's feelings, that creates a compact texture in *Yucatan*.

The book revolves around the eccentric personalities of the four members of the group and their responses to a medium-led presence that keeps interfering with their plans. Strange notes and telephone calls conveying obscure messages and absurd instructions for the group begin to arrive from anonymous senders who, from their first appearance, shape the threads of the plot. Frightened, Camado disappears while the other three, intrigued by the events, pursue the planned trip to the prospective site of the movie in Mexico. Allured by the mystery, Dru, Dave, and Nick succumb to the absurd messages they receive and recite the parts imposed on them by the invisible directors. Thus, following the instructions, they frantically travel back and forth from the shallow technological city of Los Angeles and the mysterious bewitching Mexican milieu until they find themselves among tourists visiting the archeological ruins of the Yucatan.

Camado's vague warning to Dru in the first pages of the book: "È' tutto un giro nel vuoto" (Everything is a turn in the void) turns out to be an apt description of their nonsensical trip as well as a metaphor for their stereotyped social roles. The novel keeps pointing to a revelation that fails to materialize, just as the three men's search for an alternative lifestyle fails in its objectives. Back in Los Angeles at the end of the novel, the protagonists interrupt the game, breaking into collective, derisive laughter—a self-mocking act meant to celebrate the impossibility of evading their official positions which, through the narration, often made them appear to be caricatures of themselves and the cinema world they represent. "Come ci siamo sforzati di entrare nella parte" (How much effort we have made to get into our parts) says Dru, before eating a simple dinner of hamburgers and beers that brings their lives back to normality and puts an end to an unsolvable plot.

Yucatan might be read as the unfinished script of a film the readers have seen in the making. In its postmodern overtones it is a specimen of the Italian fiction of the 1980s where—in the wake of Calvino's books and Eco's two novels—the acts of writing and reading as well as the value of the autonomous text are recurrent motifs. De Carlo's postmodernism is also evident in *Treno di panna,* which can be regarded as the narrator's collage of his snapshots, and in *Macno,* where all of the dictator's guests are reading

Dust jacket for the American edition of the translation of De Carlo's 1984 novel, a politcal allegory in which a talk-show host becomes dictator

a book that proves to be a negative of the novel they inhabit. However, the writer's structural games are never entirely gratuitous as they always serve to denounce patterns of social and personal conduct.

In 1989 De Carlo published *Due di due* (Two of Two), a novel he had been writing since 1984. The title suggests the content, for the story is about a friendship between two young men, two different lives, and two houses in the Umbrian countryside. Upon publication, reviewers saw *Due di due* as a turning point in De Carlo's work because of his new found preference for an Italian setting. There is indeed a thematic and stylistic novelty in this text, where the somewhat covert "Italianism" of the previous works is replaced by an open re-appropriation of the writer's own background. In the "Tottolibri" section of the 7 October 1989 *La Stampa* De Carlo acknowledged this change and spoke of his need, at that point in his career, to tell stories closer to his personal experiences, to explore his youth and its relation to his native town. The period between 1967 and 1987 forms the background of the novel.

In 1968, a time of social and political upheavals, the adolescents Mario and Guido meet in a Milan school. The two boys' initiation into adulthood takes place in a climate of rebellion that provides them the opportunity to vent their undefined dissatisfactions. In the first half of the book the brilliant, charismatic Guido is able to draw Mario out of the security of his middle-class family and out of the industrial and consumer-oriented city of Milan. Mario's eventual retreat to a dwelling called "Le Due Case" (The Two Houses) in the Umbrian hills, where he cultivates the land with traditional methods, constitutes the realization of Guido's utopian dream of an ideal world. It is opposed to the industrial civilization because industry destroys "i ritmi e gli equilibri complessi della vita per adattarli a quelli delle macchine" (a life's rhythm and complex balance, adapting them to the machines).

Guido's personal rebellion, though, only incidentally overlaps with that of his generation. He nurtures an instinctive desire to escape from structures and social roles, as is the case with De Carlo's other major characters. He abandons school, for education appears to him "fuori dalla *vita,* un mondo sotterraneo" (outside *life,* an underground world), and he opts for anarchism and rock music. As an adult he dreams of living in the United States and Australia, writes a book critical of Milan and other industrial cities, challenges the media, and abandons himself to a self-destructive chain of events.

The car accident that ends Guido's life also ends Mario's narration of their lives. The young men gradually define themselves as dichotomous aspects of the same person. At the end of the novel Mario sets fire to the house he has restored for his friend, thus expressing the failure of the purest part of their rebellion. His own utopia is contaminated by the structures of capitalism as soon as machines, the telephone, and a fledgling commercial activity appear on the farm.

A funereal and melancholy tone runs through the book, which is narrated with an unemotional, soft, diary-like voice. It is this polished yet simple prose that conveys an internal tension and a deeply tormented authenticity to *Due di Due,* arguably De Carlo's most personal book. Like Guido, the novelist used to write short stories when he was in high school and used to write long letters to friends in the guise of short tales. Not unlike his characters, De Carlo has often expressed his dislike for Milan despite his parents, his daughter Malina, and his friends all living in the city. There he returns after long journeys abroad or sojourns in the house he has bought in the countryside near Urbino.

Critical reviews of De Carlo's fiction after *Uccelli da gabbia e da voliera* have been uneven. Many critics were displeased when he abandoned the style of *Treno di panna,* which is often considered his best work. *Tecniche di seduzione* (Techniques of Seduction, 1991) again focuses on two main themes: the transformation of human beings into players with prescribed roles and the formative experience of a young artist. The work has met with praise from readers and critics alike. The scene remains Italy and its urban centers of power, filled with characters who resemble contemporary political leaders.

The narrator is Roberto Bata, a young journalist working for a Milanese weekly magazine, where he makes phone interviews and publishes gossip features. When he meets a famous fiction writer, Marco Polidori, his life changes radically. Polidori reads the draft of a novel Roberto is writing and encourages the young man to abandon his dull life in Milan to follow him to Rome. Through the novelist's powerful connections in the capital, Roberto is offered a position on the editorial board of a magazine that is financed by a government ministry. There he revises his novel while ghostwriters produce articles and books bearing Polidori's name.

As the title suggests, De Carlo's book is a sort of manual meant to instruct the innocent Roberto on the techniques of seduction. The instructor is Polidori, who shows to the aspiring writer the mechanisms that assure leadership in politics and culture, guiding him through the Roman labyrinth of legalized corruption and bribery. Attractive, fascinating, successful, even a candidate for the Nobel Prize, Polidori (whose name recalls that of John William Polidori, George Gordon, Lord Byron's physician and author of the first vampire story in literature) seduces his inexperienced protégé with his friendship. Enticed and intrigued by the novelist's attention, Roberto becomes a condescending and almost silent confidant of his mentor's personal secrets and ideas. Bata surrenders to Polidori's will and whims, accompanying him to social and cultural events where the older writer introduces his younger friend to influential politicians and literary critics in order to set the ground for a successful launch of Roberto's first novel and his career. Polidori's character comes into sharp relief: he is a cynical and compromised artist who has built his literary fame by exploiting to his advantage opportunities and connections. Half victim, half hero, his larger-than-life personality dominates the novel, his speeches echoing in each part of the narrative.

Like Roberto, the reader is mesmerized by the seductive Polidori, who moves in and out of his role of internationally successful artist. Publicly he complies with the expectations of his critics and admirers while in the conversations with Roberto he assumes the position of a caustic judge of the people and the institutions that support his fame and wealth. As in a detective story, suspense is maintained until the end, when the truth about Polidori's reasons for befriending Roberto is revealed: a new book by the novelist is published and Bata discovers that it is actually the first draft of his own novel which, under the older man's spell, he had discarded. Roberto has fallen into the trap of Polidori, an expert exploiter of young writers' dreams and De Carlo's contemporary, realistic version of a vampire.

Once the ambiguity that runs throughout the book is thus dispelled, what remains is a world of false relationships. Yet, unlike the protagonists of *Macno* and *Due di due,* the narrator of *Tecniche di seduzione* renounces escapism and remains in Rome, making of his writing a weapon against the social diseases that plague and block intellectual integrity. Although Roberto closes his narration in disillusionment, he comes to the conclusion that the experience he has been relating may become the subject matter of a new book—the one the reader has just finished.

Within the scheme of the novel, De Carlo inserts other forms of seduction, from Roberto's love story with the actress Maria Blini to his wife's subtle response to Polidori's attention. *Tecniche di seduzione* is a complete cycle of lessons on the initiation of an apprentice writer into maturity. On the one hand, integration in contemporary Italy means accepting Polidori's extreme cynicism and compromises. On the other hand, there is Roberto's courageous denunciation of the artificial mechanisms and the corruption existing behind the publishing industry which he unveils through his narration. Thus the reader is presented with two opposite approaches to life, two generations, two frames of mind: Polidori's hypocrisy and opportunism for the sake of success and Roberto's moral integrity and his desire to react against an unbearable status quo.

The novel is divided into four parts in accordance with the four techniques of seduction present in the text: the techniques of approach, conquest, possession, and abandonment. Each corresponds to a stage in Roberto's education. Superimposed on the four parts is the analysis of the two opposite characters of Polidori and Bata and of two cities, the efficient Milan and Rome, defined as "lo stomaco dell'Italia" (the stomach of Italy). Stylistically, a dry and concise language alternates with the more-fluid and captivating words used by Polidori. Coming at what may be the midpoint in De Carlo's career, *Tecniche di seduzione* reaffirmed De Carlo's talent. In this work he redefines his major themes with a new style and a new voice, setting them against the background of corruption and scandal that characterizes Italian life in the early 1990s.

In his subsequent novels De Carlo has appeared intent on revisiting his early subjects in order to analyze them in greater depth and with the maturity of style and perspective that only experience can lend to a writer. Also set in contemporary Italy, *Arcodamore* (Love Bow, 1993) deals with love between a man and woman, a subject the novelist had not previously explored fully. In *Uto* (1995) he returns to the setting of the United States, to Connecticut, where the title character settles temporarily with a family dedicated to transcendental meditation under the guidance of a guru. The novel revolves around Uto's psychological transformation from a cold, cynical young man devoted to music to the spiritual guide of the community. In *Di noi tre* (About the Three of Us, 1997) De Carlo explores anew the terms of love and friendship by retracing the life stories of three friends against the backdrop of the social and political history of Italy during the previous twenty-five years. Despite the continued best-selling success of his novels in the 1990s, many critics still regard De Carlo's early writing as his most significant.

References:

Maria Pia Ammirati, "Andrea De Carlo," in her *Il vizio di scrivere. Letture di Busi, De Carlo, Del Giudice, Pazzi, Tabucchi e Tondelli* (Catanzaro: Rubbettino, 1991), pp. 51–65;

Cesare De Michelis, "Andrea de Carlo," in his *Fiori di carta. La nuova narrativa italiana* (Milan: Bompiani, 1990), pp. 77–83;

Marzia Fontanta, "Andrea De Carlo," thesis, Università degli Studi, Facoltà di lettere e Filosofia (Genoa), 1993;

Stefano Tani, *Il romanzo di ritorno: dal romanzo medio degli anni Sessanta alla giovane narrativa degli anni Ottanta* (Milan: Mursia Editore, 1990), pp. 248–258.

Daniele Del Giudice
(11 July 1949 -)

Christopher Concolino
San Francisco State University

BOOKS: *Lo stadio di Wimbledon* (Turin: Einaudi, 1983);
Atlante occidentale (Turin: Einaudi, 1985); translated by Norman MacAfee and Luigi Fontanella as *Lines of Light* (San Diego: Harcourt, 1988);
Nel museo di Reims (Milan: Mondadori, 1988);
Staccando l'ombra da terra (Turin: Einaudi, 1994); translated by Joseph Farrell as *Takeoff: The Pilot's Lore* (New York: Harcourt, 1996); republished as *Take-off* (London: Harvill, 1996);
Mania (Turin: Einaudi, 1997).

OTHER: "Prendere la parola per prendere il potere" and "Nuova Scena: Storia di un'esperienza," in *La parola nel pugno: Teatro politico di Nuova Scena,* edited by Del Giudice (Rimini: Guaraldi, 1972), pp. 18–23; 135–142;
"Dillon Bay, un racconto militare," in *La metropoli difesa: Architettura militare dell'Ottocento nelle città capitali d'Italia,* by Amelio Fara (Rome: Stato Maggiore dell'Esercito-Ufficio Storico, 1985): vii–xxii.

SELECTED PERIODICAL PUBLICATIONS– UNCOLLECTED: "La cloche fra le nuvole," *Corriere della sera,* 6 November 1988, p. 3;
"Elogio dell'ombra," *Corriere della sera,* cultural insert, 17 February 1991, p. 3.

Daniel Del Giudice (photograph by Bruno Murialdo)

Daniele Del Giudice has been recognized as a novelist of promise since his first novel, *Lo stadio di Wimbledon* (Wimbledon Stadium, 1983), was awarded the Viareggio Prize for literature in 1983. Subsequent works, which show a relationship to developments in late-twentieth-century literature both nationally and internationally, have realized this potential. His fiction is notable for its contribution to a trend within Italian literature that since the 1960s has explored what previously had been considered scientific or technological language and subjects.

The use of scientific culture to further the goals of creative fiction has many precedents and can be traced back at least as far as the works of nineteenth-century writers of science fiction such as Jules Verne. However, Del Giudice's best works differ from science fiction because they do not share its hallmarks: a taste for adventure, the fantastic, settings in the past or the future, and strong plots. Instead they reflect a philosophical shift that has taken place in the late twentieth century: the dissolution of the boundaries that before the 1960s had traditionally separated literature and the humanities from the sciences. Topics once considered the reserve of fields such as biology, astrophysics, sociology, and anthropology figure prominently in modern Italian fiction, especially after the appearance of Italo Calvino's *Le Cosmicomiche* (Cosmicomics, 1965) and *Ti con zero* (t zero, 1967). Later works such as Giorgio Saviane's *Il mare verticale* (The Vertical Sea, 1973) and Primo Levi's *Il sistema periodico* (The Periodic Table, 1975) continued a trend that came to be known in Italy as scientific realism.

While it differs in many respects from Italian Neorealism of the 1940s and 1950s, scientific realism does share one of its primary concerns: the perception and interpretation of physical reality. In the late twentieth century perception has been affected by changing technological means to an unprecedented extent, and for Del Giudice the technological mediation of knowledge becomes the pretext for exploring the ways in which language is and is not suitable for conveying meaning. His protagonists often ponder the nature and meaning of knowledge, a circumstance that enriches rather than undermines his realism since two of the themes found throughout his work are also mainstays of traditional realism: a self-conscious examination of what one sees on the one hand and reflection upon movement and travel on the other. The quality of literary self-examination of his work and the concise essay-like style that he has in common with Calvino, Saviane, and Levi are reminiscent of the French philosophical tale, of which Voltaire's *Candide* (1759) is the most important.

Del Giudice's realism goes beyond the description of exterior reality. Because his analysis of sight, for example, is typically a metaphor for the act of understanding, Del Giudice's work lends itself to multiple interpretations. The reader may choose a particular interpretation or try to acknowledge several or all concurrently. In this sense Paolo Mauri's assertion in the 22 November 1985 issue of *La Repubblica* about Del Giudice's second novel, *Atlante occidentale* (1985; translated as *Lines of Light*, 1988) describes all of his writing: "fortemente allegorica, dove ogni elemento si presta (invita esplicitamente) alla doppia lettura" (strongly allegorical, where every element lends itself to [inviting explicitly] a double reading). In similar fashion the often-used theme of travel transcends its function in conventional realism because, as Del Giudice has noted in his interview in 21 August 1991 issue of *L'Unità*, "[o]ggi il viaggio ha perso, prima di tutto, e definitivamente, la dimensione di conoscenza esterna" (today travel has lost, first of all, and definitively, its capacity to convey knowledge about the outside world).

Despite his reservations about the philosophical significance of the physical journey, Del Giudice is strongly and personally drawn to travel, and his literary treatment of travels is rooted in personal experience. His remarks about his 1990 voyage to the Antarctic in a 1991 interview are emblematic of how travel themes function in his fiction: "Quando usciamo dall'ambiente che abbiamo razionalizzato per la nostra comunità ci accorgiamo di un universo intero che sfugge al nostro controllo. . . . Questo produce un bel ridimensionamento sull'Io" (When we leave the environment that we have rationalized for our community, we become aware of an entire universe that escapes our control. . . . This produces a considerable reorganization of the self). As this statement shows, he is much less interested in presenting a picture of the external world than he is in internal cognitive processes.

Del Giudice was born 11 July 1949 in Rome, where he lived throughout childhood and early adulthood. His literary curiosity led him at first to study for a degree in literature at the University of Rome, but it was a goal he eventually abandoned in order to pursue his interest in the theater. At the age of nineteen he attended the annual summer cultural festival in Spoleto where he met the Polish stage director Jerzy Grotowsky, founder of the influential Polish Laboratory Theater. This encounter was a turning point for him since it prompted his decision six months later to go to Poland, where he remained for nine months to observe Grotowsky's methods firsthand. Later his interest in dramatic theory and his involvement in the experimental theatrical cooperative Nuova Scena (New Scene), founded by playwright and actor Dario Fo in 1968, spawned Del Giudice's first published work: the two political articles, "Prendere la parola per prendere il potere" (Using Words to Take Power) and "Nuova Scena: Storia di un'esperienza" (New Scene: The Story of an Experience), in *La parola nel pugno: Teatro politico di Nuova Scena* (The Word in the Fist: The Political Theater of the New Scene, 1972), a volume of collected writing he edited.

Coming of age during the late 1960s through the mid 1970s when international student political protests and grassroots countercultures were actively challenging established systems of government, Del Giudice followed the events of the Prague Spring in Czechoslovakia and was an eyewitness as Soviet Union forces invaded Wenceslaus Square in 1968 to suppress reforms. But Del Giudice's interest in such events stopped short of full participation due to his reluctance to embrace militant forms of protest, which he suspected of being irresponsible and ideologically incoherent. As he is quoted by Cristina Parodi and Roberto Cotroneo in the June 1987 issue of *Max*, "C'era troppa violenza, troppa superficialità, troppo cinismo, e una preoccupante incapacità di assumersi le proprie responsabilità. E anche se nel '68 avevo vent'anni, seguivo una mia strada personale" (There was too much violence, too much superficiality, too much cynicism and a troubling inability to assume one's own responsibility. And even if I was only twenty years old in '68, I was following my own path in life). Del Giudice's experience of life in Poland did awaken his fascination with non-Italian cultures. He subsequently traveled to Eastern Europe, Africa, and the United States.

Dust jacket for the American edition of Del Giudice's 1985 novel, in which a scientist and a writer discuss the ways time and space condition perception

After his return from Poland, the twenty-year-old Del Giudice found work as a literary critic for the Rome daily *Paese Sera,* where he worked for more than ten years. During his tenure at the newspaper he read widely, including the authors he considers to have had the greatest literary influence on him: "Leggevo di tutto, persino i gialli più commerciali, ma gli autori che mi hanno influenzato maggiormente sono Stevenson, Conrad, Kafka. Forse nella mia scrittura loro hanno contribuito in modo determinante, aiutandomi a rendere lo stile letterario semplice ed essenziale" (I used to read everything, even the most commercial detective mysteries, but the authors that influenced me the most are Stevenson, Conrad, and Kafka. Perhaps they have contributed to my writing in a determinant way, helping to make my literary style simple and essential).

At the age of thirty-three Del Giudice gave up his career as a literary critic to write fiction, to which he has since devoted himself exclusively. A bachelor, Del Giudice lives alone except for the company of his cat. He maintains a nine-hour daily work schedule, from nine in the morning to six in the evening, listening to music as he writes. (He wrote several chapters of *Atlante occidentale* to the accompaniment of recordings by the Doors, an American rock band of the late 1960s, which Del Giudice has pointed to as an influence on the prose style of that work.) He rarely works at night, a time he usually spends with friends. Considered to be a reserved man, Del Giudice is not known for speaking candidly about his private life, but he does participate in lectures and conferences open to the public and has frequently granted interviews.

The result of nearly two years of work, *Lo stadio di Wimbledon* recounts a series of short trips to Trieste and London taken by an unnamed first-person narrator to talk to those who once knew Bobi Bazlen, the catalyst of literary activity in early twentieth-century Trieste. A friend and advocate of writers such as Umberto Saba, Robert Musil, and Eugenio Montale, Bazlen published little of his own work although he was the first to translate works, then unknown in Italy, by major Middle-European thinkers such as Sigmund Freud and Carl Jung; he was also one of the first to champion the works of Italo Svevo and Kafka. Del Giudice's novel centers on the protagonist's quest to understand why Bazlen never wrote a major work even though he led a flourishing intellectual life and is recognized as having sustained almost single-handedly the vitality of Trieste's once-fertile literary community.

The narrator's search is motivated by his own uncertainty about the value of literature and the meaning of the act that creates it. The implication operating in *Lo stadio di Wimbledon* is that the thoughts of the narrator parallel those of Bazlen. The reader is thus in a position to consider such themes as the influence of art on life, the concept of life itself as a work of art, the bearing of the literary past upon the present, and the extent to which the act of writing is a metaphor for contemplation, action, or both. In a 1 June 1988 interview in *L'Unità* Del Giudice argues for the kind of elastic and complex interpretation of fiction proposed by literary reception theory and semiotic analysis: "[N]on è retorica che un libro viene fatto dalle letture. Nel senso che i libri crescono attraverso chi li legge.... [L]o scrittore è soltanto il primo lettore di un libro.... La forza stupenda della letteratura è che io scrivo "sgabello" e penso a un certo "sgabello," uno legge "sgabello" e pensa a un altro sgabello. A me piace vedere che sgabello ha immaginato lui leggendo" (It is not empty rhetoric to say that a book is made up of its readings, in the sense that books grow through those who read them.... [T]he writer is only the first reader of a book.... The stupendous strength of literature is that when I write "stool" I think of a certain "stool," but someone reading "stool" thinks of another stool. I like to see what stool the person reading has imagined).

The major theme Del Giudice explores in *Lo stadio di Wimbledon* is the idea of absence. The intellectual life of the Trieste of the past is accessible in the present only through the remains that have endured from the past, especially the memories of those who survive. The place and time of the present thus constitute a void with respect to the object of the protagonist's quest. As Stefano Tani has pointed out, this is a model of narrative structure akin to the concept of the hole-in-the-middle, which is similar to Jacques Lacan's term *manque* (lack), a psychoanalytic concept referred to widely by literary theorists in the 1980s, as well as to the philosophy of Gianni Vattimo's *pensiero debole* (weak thought). Variations of this theme are explored in other contemporary works such as Giuseppe Pontiggia's *Il giocatore invisibile* (The Invisible Player, 1978), Antonio Tabucchi's *Il filo dell'orizzonte* (The Edge of the Horizon, 1986), Francesca Duranti's *Effetti personali* (Personal Effects, 1988) and Liaty Pisani's *Il falso pretendente* (The False Pretender, 1986).

The six people that the narrator meets all reminisce about Bazlen at length and recount a variety of personal anecdotes. The most developed moments of human intimacy in the novel occur between two of the six, who are also prominently recalled in Montale's poetry: Ljuba Blumenthal and Gerti Tolazzi. The six ultimately reveal more about themselves than about Bazlen even though several of them are able to add to their accounts by bringing out period photographs. The narrator regards their recollections, told by each person in much the same way, as fruitless and increasingly tedious. His dissatisfaction with even their photographs underscores the search for meaning in the novel, according to which knowledge is gained through a process of elimination.

From the narrator's perspective knowledge can only be defined negatively or in terms of what it is not. The last person the narrator goes to see, Ljuba, lives in London near Wimbledon stadium. When the narrator visits the empty stadium, he considers photographing it but then suddenly changes his mind. Were he to take some photos, having images of an empty stadium where Bazlen was never in attendance would strikingly resemble his failure in the present to obtain answers about Bazlen in the past: both provide knowledge about him only by default. His rejection of photography coincides with the end of his literary inquiry, and the two events trigger the conclusion of the novel. The narrator's actions do not signal a rejection of the idea of absence as a cognitive process, though, for he affirms that "s crivere non è importante, però non si può fare altro" (writing is not important; however, one can't do without it).

Del Giudice's negative road to understanding is also supported by his fascination with technology. As with the title *Lo stadio di Wimbledon,* Del Giudice undercuts conventional logic by choosing the image of an airplane for his novel's cover rather than anything associated with Bazlen or Trieste. In the novel he uses the description of airplane travel to suggest the relation of the self to the external world.

In his mid thirties Del Giudice moved into a simply furnished home near the Rialto bridge in Venice, as he told Parodi and Cotroneo:

> Il motivo che mi ha spinto a Venezia è la morbosa passione che ho per l'acqua e che credo risalga ai tempi lontani della mia infanzia. E in realtà Venezia è proprio un giocattolo sull'acqua, è una città dove non esistono nevrosi, perché non si può essere nevrotici quando dal ponte di Rialto si vede tramontare il sole dietro San Tomà. Essere spettatori di eventi simili è un privilegio a cui non ho saputo rinunciare.

(The reason I was compelled to come to Venice is the overriding emotional attachment that I have to water, which I believe goes back to the distant past of my infancy; and, actually, Venice is virtually a toy on the water. It's a city where neuroses don't exist, because one can't be neurotic when one sees the sun set behind [the church of] St. Thomas from the Rialto bridge. Witnessing events of this kind is a privilege that I haven't been able to give up.)

As his first novel demonstrates, Del Giudice attaches great importance to the sense of place, which can take on almost metaphysical meaning.

A novel that opens with references to air travel rather than closes with them as does *Lo stadio di Wimbledon*, *Atlante occidentale* bears on its cover the toy locomotive that is mentioned at the beginning of *Lo stadio di Wimbledon*. This is but one example of the way in which Del Giudice intertwines common themes and imagery across the borders of these novels, showing that the two works are cut from a single block. In *Lo stadio di Wimbledon* chapter 5 opens with a densely technical account of aerial navigation from Italy to England. Showcasing his scientific narrative style, Del Giudice in the passage points out the enormous importance the Mercator projection has had on the history of navigation; the passage thus functions as another anticipatory link to *Atlante occidentale,* which is literally translated as Western Atlas.

The second novel focuses on the friendship between Pietro Brahe, a young Italian physicist conducting research on subatomic particles, and Ira Epstein, an aging German novelist on the brink of being awarded the Nobel Prize. Their names are suggestive of the sixteenth-century Danish astronomer Tycho Brahe and Albert Einstein, and the characters evoke both the historical past and the quest for knowledge. The two men meet after their planes nearly collide in midair when by accident the pilots lose sight of each other's aircraft. This occurrence takes place on the first page of the novel, and the aeronautical near-miss soon takes on an allegorical import because it mirrors Brahe's experiments with subatomic-particle collision. His research involves recording observable evidence of what cannot be seen, which calls attention to the increasing reliance on a highly technological control of physical reality that is inaccessible to direct experience.

The core of the novel is a series of conversations between the scientist who carries on his experiments in a vast particle accelerator beneath Geneva and the writer who has given up writing and passes the time in the garden of the summer house he rents in that city. In their conversations they analyze the ways that time and space condition perception, the same themes found in *Lo stadio di Wimbledon*. Epstein functions as a Bazlen come to life as he contemplates whether or not to write a last book, an "Atlas of Light." A kind of catalogue, it would be a guide to the remaining means of sensory perception that allow an emotional connection to material existence. *Atlante occidentale* traces both men's reflections on the technological changes that Epstein predicts will bring about the gradual devaluation of nonvisual forms of perception.

In the first and last of the conversations the two friends play a kind of parlor game. Its aim is to describe everything within one's field of vision as completely as possible. The first time they play it Epstein critiques Brahe's rendering of the view from Epstein's garden. In the second game Epstein gives a lavish description of a display of fireworks over Lake Geneva. Intended as a stylistic tour de force, Epstein's words form a companion piece to the passage on aerial navigation in *Lo stadio di Wimbledon,* but its catalogue-like list of technical terminology borders on an esoteric, baroque sensibility. Between these two conversations Brahe's experiences show that he perceives historical and cultural analogues to the disjunction in experience caused by technology. In one metaphorical analogue he imagines a variety of fossils that could still be buried in Switzerland's Jura Mountains: undiscovered and hence inaccessible to human experience. When observing passersby he notices that commercial fashion often perpetuates modes of dress associated with activities and behavior long since obsolete.

The novel ends when almost at the same time Brahe's research team achieves positive experimental results and it is announced that Epstein will be awarded the Nobel Prize. About to leave Geneva, he tells Brahe that he will not write about his stay there because "[l]'importante non era scriverla, l'importante era provarne un sentimento" (the important thing was not to write about it, the important thing was to feel emotion for it). This view, plainly in accordance with Epstein's analysis of contemporary sensory perception, is ultimately the explanation of Bazlen's withdrawal from writing. The danger, though, is that Epstein's introspection tends to isolate him from his friend.

This kind of emotional isolation also characterizes the protagonist in *Nel museo di Reims* (In the Reims Museum, 1988), a thirty-eight-page novella that includes sixteen color reproductions of paintings by Del Giudice's friend Marco Nereo Rotelli. It is about the degenerative blindness that afflicts Barnaba, a young former Navy officer, and his study of a few carefully selected museum paintings before the onset of total blindness. One of these is

Jacques-Louis David's *Death of Marat* (1794) in the Reims Museum, where Barnaba unwittingly attracts the attention of Anne, a woman who gives him an oral account of the details of the paintings that his weakening sight misses. Almost immediately Barnaba realizes that her descriptions are generously embellished though he ultimately decides not to let her know this.

Anne's white lies, which resemble Barnaba's own lies to the military doctor about being able to see more than he actually could, suggest to him that he should try to uncover his own motives for lying, which are far from clear to him or to the reader. Barnaba ponders the nature of intentionality, realizing that even his knowledge of his own motives is uncertain. Anne's half-truths seem appropriate to the half-light he now sees by, which is a state of being that serves as a fitting metaphor for his or anyone's life as a thinking person.

As in all of Del Giudice's works the act of seeing in *Nel museo di Reims* encompasses many levels of interpretation. Prior to coming to the Reims Museum Barnaba had studied the historical and biographical contexts of David's portrait of Marat, and thus the painting becomes a point of departure for his thinking. He knows that Marat was a doctor who treated blindness with electrotherapy, and this knowledge underlines the poignancy that the *Death of Marat* has for him. Even though the reader's appreciation of the portrait is wholly dependent on Barnaba's viewpoint and identity, the painting seems to suggest an emotional undercurrent as if by coincidence.

Unexplained motivations and implicit intentions are at the heart of this work. Such concepts are also the interpretive keys to the sixteen reproductions of Rotelli's paintings that follow the text. Dark but colorful, their nonrepresentational character is nonetheless identified in the book's concluding note as "fortemente narrativo" (strongly narrative). Yet aside from their generally dark appearance, which clearly can be associated with the motif of blindness, Del Giudice does not explain how two opposite goals such as nonrepresentation and narration can be reconciled. Instead he characteristically lets his readers draw their own conclusions. To complicate matters he also suggests that the text is tied to "una mia personale esperienza di bugie" (a personal experience of lies) and that "[i] quadri non illustrano il racconto, così come il racconto non accompagna i quadri" (the paintings don't illustrate the story, just as the story doesn't accompany the paintings).

Del Giudice's abiding interest in travel and in the technological mediation of perception as a metaphor for human understanding led him to return to the theme of air travel in his subsequent book, *Staccando l'ombra da terra* (1994; translated as *Takeoff: The Pilot's Lore,* 1996), a collection of eight stories that recounts pilots' experiences from a psychological and existential point of view: "Per l'errore" (All Because of the Mistake), "Tra il secondo 1423 e il secondo 1797" (Between Second 1423 and Second 1797), "E tutto il resto?" (And Everything Else?), "*Pauci sed semper immites*" (Few But Always Tough), "Fino al punto di rugiada" (Reaching Dew Point), "Manovre di volo" (Flight Maneuvers), "Unreported inbound Palermo" and "Doppio decollo all'alba" (Double Takeoff at Dawn). Del Giudice is himself a pilot, and his 1991 reenactment of the flight of Antoine De Saint-Exupéry, the aviator and writer who disappeared in 1944 while flying from Borgo, Corsica, to Nice, is the basis of "Doppio decollo all'alba."

The winner of three Italian literary prizes—the Bagutta, the Flaiano International, and the Campiello—*Staccando l'ombra da terra* deals with issues ranging from the flight student's relationship to his instructor in "Per l'errore" to the kind of self-doubt and crisis of understanding that assail the pilot who loses his bearings. In "Fino al punto di rugiada" the narrator is caught in zero-visibility weather. Knowing that he cannot trust his own senses, the pilot must rely on his flight instruments, yet what they tell him is often directly counter to the perceptions of his own senses. He must therefore mistrust what his own body tells him to be correct, and this means mistrusting the usual means by which one measures reality.

Del Giudice shows a strong interest in aviation history in his stories. In "*Pauci sed semper immites*" he imagines the reminiscences of a former World War II torpedo pilot who flew harrowing bombing missions off the Algerian coast. In "Unreported inbound Palermo" he reconstructs the conversation between pilot and control tower during Itavia flight 870's trip from Bologna to Palermo. This DC-9 never reached Palermo because it fell into the sea near the island of Ustica on 27 June 1980, killing eighty-one passengers as well as the crew. After much investigation no clear cause was ever ascertained, though many Italians believe that the plane was willfully destroyed with the complicity of the Italian government.

Mania (Mania, 1997) is Del Giudice's second volume of short stories. It contains six works—"L'orecchio assoluto" (Perfect Pitch), "Com'è adesso!" (As He Is Now!), "Evil Live," "Fuga" (Escape), "Dillon Bay," and "Come cometa" (Like a Comet)—two of which were previously published separately. These stories depart from the author's novels in that they present situations evoking a sense of mystery, death, and sometimes violence. In this they are reminiscent of the tales of terror and the macabre produced by the writers of the late-nineteenth-century Milanese movement known as Scapigliatura. Their works, however, often mention ghosts and the spirit world while Del Giudice's do not. Some of the stories in *Mania* depict unbalanced personalities preoccupied with a technical topic or specialized field of pursuit. Skewed from the outset, they are compelled to follow their own logic to gruesome conclusions. In "L'orecchio assoluto," for example, a murderer's admiration for a piece of music leads him to kill its composer.

Other stories stand out as displays of stylistic bravura. A type of modern epistolary fiction, "Evil Live" recreates a kind of erotic fiction in the form of E-mail messages. "Dillon Bay" explores the military mind through conversations between a young captain and an older colonel that are reminiscent of those between Brahe and Epstein in *Atlante occidentale*. The two officers share an interest in strategy, fortifications, and ballistics, and their discussions show how these topics are forms of human expression and even objects of emotional attachment.

For some, such as Stefano Giovanardi in his 23 December 1988 review of *Nel museo di Reims* in *La Repubblica,* Del Giudice's highly allusive prose, which raises more questions than it answers, proves to be ultimately disappointing. For others, such as Antonio Tabucchi in the 3 December 1988 issue of *Corriere della sera,* these characteristics are valuable because they are indicative of a seriousness and a dedication to literary goals. Del Giudice's stylistic restraint and concision are similar to that of Jorge Luis Borges, the Argentine writer who is widely known in Italy. Del Giudice's pursuit of traditional literary goals also links him to the aristocratic and elitist conventions of much of Italy's literary past. At the same time, Calvino, a friend and sometime mentor to Del Giudice, suggested in a jacket note for *Lo stadio di Wimbledon* that it signaled "un nuovo approccio alla rappresentazione, al racconto, secondo un nuovo sistema di coordinate" (a new approach to representation and narration according to a new system of coordinates). Although he is not prolific and only now reaching middle age, Del Giudice has already established a reputation in Italian letters. Nonetheless, the significance and reputation of his work will depend to a large degree on his future literary production.

Interviews:

Sergio Bertolucci, Tullia Gaddi, Antonino Postorino, and Gian Luigi Saraceni, eds., "Il tempo del visibile nell'Atlante di Daniele Del Giudice," *Palomar: Quaderni di Porto Venere,* 1 (Spring 1986): 75;

Andrea Liberatori, "A prova di mercato," *L'Unità,* 1 June 1988: 13;

Antonlla Fiori, "Partire e un po' restare," *L'Unità,* 21 August 1991: 24.

References:

Maria Pia Ammirati, *Il vizio di scrivere: Letture su Busi, De Carlo, Del Giudice, Pazzi, Tabucchi e Tondelli* (Soveria Mannelli: Rubbettino, 1991);

Anna Dolfi and C. P. Brand, "Daniele Del Giudice: Planimetry of Sight/Vision in Three Books," in *The New Italian Novel,* edited by Zygumunt G. Baranski and Lino Pertile (Edinburgh: Edinburgh University Press, 1993), pp. 89–98;

Cristina Parodi and Roberto Cotroneo, "Daniele Del Giudice," *Max* (June 1987): 36–38;

Franco Ricci, "Daniele Del Giudice's *New Atlantis,*" *Mosaic,* 23, no. 1 (1990): 45–53;

Filippo Secchieri, "Gli interstizi del visibile: Glosse a *Nel museo di Reims* di Daniele Del Giudice," *Il lettore di Provincia,* 21, no. 76 (1989): 93–95;

Valeria Sperti, "Voyages à la recherche de soi: Yourcenar, Del Giudice, Tabucchi," in *Voyage et conaissance dans l'oeuvre de Marguerite Yourcenar,* edited by Carminella Biondi and Corrado Rosso (Pisa: Goliardica, 1988), pp. 259–272;

Stefano Tani, *Il romanzo di ritorno: Dal romanzo medio degli anni sessanta alla giovane narrativa degli anni ottanta* (Milan: Mursia, 1990), pp. 344–349.

Luca Desiato
(13 November 1941 -)

Nicoletta Tinozzi-Mehrmand
Middlebury College

BOOKS: *Belfagor arcidiavolo ovvero la Nuova Chiesa vista da Satana* (Milan: Massimo, 1969);

Il diario di Luca (Turin: Gribaudi, 1971);

Così pregano i giovani (Alba: Edizioni Paoline, 1973);

Mirella: diario di una studentessa (Turin: Gribaudi, 1973);

Il coraggio si chiama Thomas More: sotto il segno dell'Acquario (Alba: Paoline, 1974);

Il sogno di Papa Asdrubale (Padua: Marsilio, 1974);

Benito e il mostro (Milan: Mondadori, 1976);

La risposta: il problema della fede (Alba: Paoline, 1977);

Marco: diario di un timido (Turin: Gribaudi, 1978);

La marcia su Roma delle amazzoni (Milan: Rusconi, 1979);

Il Marchese del Grillo (Milan: Mondadori, 1981);

Estate romana (Rome: Gremese, 1982);

Galileo mio padre (Milan: Mondadori, 1983);

Come il fuoco (Milan: Mondadori, 1986);

Dialoghi e silenzi (Turin: Paoline, 1988);

Bocca di Leone (Milan: Rizzoli, 1989);

Storie dell'eremo (Turin: Gribaudi, 1990);

Giulioverme e altri racconti (Turin: Paoline, 1990);

Sulle rive del mar Nero (Milan: Rizzoli, 1992);

La notte dell'angelo (Milan: Mondadori, 1994);

Giuliano l'Apostata (Milano: Mondadori, 1997).

OTHER: *Incomunicabilità e comunione,* edited by Desiato (Turin: Paoline, 1974);

Canti dell'impegno, dell'amore, della speranza, edited by Desiato (Turin: Gribaudi, 1974);

Dal dubbio alla fede: Pascal, edited by Desiato (Turin: Gribaudi, 1975).

Luca Desiato (photograph by Tano Citeroni)

Luca Desiato emerged as a novelist of note with the success in 1981 of *Il Marchese del Grillo* (The Marquis Grillo), his third novel. He had been active as a writer since the late 1960s, a few years after he returned from a long sojourn as a student in Argentina. Although his success is to be attributed largely to his historical novels, Desiato also dedicates himself to psychological and philosophical works. The release of the film based on *Il Marchese del Grillo,* starring the beloved actor Alberto Sordi, contributed to the writer's renown.

Born 13 November 1941 in Rome, Desiato in his early twenties went to Argentina, where he lived for nearly four years. In Buenos Aires he studied Hispanic literature, philosophy, and theology, and he met Jorge Luis Borges who, together with other Latin American writers such as Gabriel García Márquez, had a significant influence on the development of his thought and writing style. During his Argentina years Desiato developed a great appreciation for the Spanish language, but his desire to be a writer in his own country convinced him to go back to Rome and "riappropriarsi della madre lingua" (repossess the native language). In 1978 Desiato married a pediatrician and five years later they adopted two Brazilian children.

Desiato's first book shows the influence of the philosophical and especially theological studies in Buenos Aires. *Belfagor arcidiavolo ovvero la Nuova Chiesa vista da Satana* (Belfagor the Archdevil or the New Church Seen by Satan, 1969) was inspired by the consideration that the Christian world is experiencing a period of profound crisis:

> Ora, al livello profondo della stessa coscienza individuale si muove la "presenza del satanico."
> Satana rimane uno dei grandi misteri della vita umana, e, puntualmente, si presenta in tutta la sua virulenza alle varie generazioni di cristiani, nel momento in cui prendono coscienza del loro dovere di maturità.... Assistiamo alla fine di un'epoca ed al nascere di una nuova dai contorni non ancora definiti.
> Il vero pericolo è nella possibilità di "spegnere lo Spirito."
> Satana, dal canto suo, si innesta baldanzoso nel momento storico presente come "male oscuro della divisione."
> L'esito finale però gli è precluso.
> Forse niente di nuovo in questo libretto, tranne il tentativo di dar forma ad alcune idee che circolavano nell'aria.
>
> (Now, at the deep level of individual conscience itself, the "presence of the satanic" is in motion.
> Satan remains one of the great mysteries of human life, and, inevitably, he manifests himself in all his virulence to the various generations of Christians, in the moment in which they recognize their maturity.... We are witnessing the end of an era and the beginning of another with still undefined features.
> The real danger is in the possibility of "annulling the Spirit."
> Satan, on one hand, posits himself, self-confident, in the present historical moment as "obscure evil of the division."
> But the final outcome is precluded to him.
> Perhaps there is nothing new in this booklet, except the attempt to formulate some ideas that circulated in the air.)

The assumption that the latter part of the twentieth century is a time of great change and malaise also inspired Desiato's *Incomunicabilità e comunione* (Incommunicability and Communion, 1974), a series of essays, poems, and dialogues by several young writers, which he selected and edited. The first section is concerned with the lack of communication between human beings, caused by a loss of appreciation for the mystery of life. The pieces lament that in modern society there exists no place for a transcendental view of life. Even love has lost its sentimental connotation and exists only as a physical act. In the second section, which is dedicated to friendship and to the human potential for communication, the book takes on a more optimistic tone. The efforts exhibit the writers' desire to fight for solidarity and justice, for love and friendship.

In a world where people seem to have lost the ability to love, a spiritual leader could easily find himself without followers. In Desiato's first novel, *Il sogno di Papa Asdrubale* (Pope Asdrubale's Dream, 1974), the protagonist, a fictional pope of the future, faces the challenge of regaining control of the Church. Through a process of search and redemption he discovers the connection between his mission and the everyday life of all Christians.

Although Desiato was born during World War II and was much too young to remember anything that happened during that period, his fascination with those tragic years inspired two of his books. The theme of the relations between parents and children, which he examined in many of his later works, begins to develop in *Benito e il mostro* (Benito and the Monster, 1976), a novel set in fascist Italy. Desiato described the book as "una iniziazione alla vita e ai suoi misteri" (an initiation to life and its mysteries). He unravels with great tact and delicacy the frustrations, uncertainties, and emotional fluctuations of the adolescent Benito who is plagued by a love-hate relationship with his mother, Elena:

> Era inspiegabile. Mi paralizzava con la sua bellezza, e la distanza, il rancore.... Sognavo spesso di ucciderla, poi di piangerne lungamente il solare corpo su una tomba adorna di giganteschi crisantemi.
> Elena temeva la morte, ed io l'assassinavo in sogno, per fermarne la bellezza; in un certo senso la salvavo dallo sfacelo: una sua nuova vittoria.
> In questa tensione di rapporto ossequioso, venerazione risentita, e amore-odio, passai gran parte della mia adolescenza.
>
> (It was inexplicable. She paralyzed me with her beauty, her distance and her resentment.... I often dreamed of killing her, and then of weeping for a long time over her luminous body surrounded by gigantic chrysanthemums.
> Elena was afraid of death, and I killed her in my sleep, so as to freeze her beauty. In a way I was saving her from decay: a new victory for her.
> In this tension of respectful relation, resentful veneration, and love-hate, I spent most of my adolescence.)

The interest in Benito's ambiguous relationship with his mother attenuates when the attention of the reader shifts to the tragic love story of Benito and a mysterious Jewish woman, Rachel, whose disfigured face, hidden by a mask, he is never able to see.

Rome always appears in Desiato's books; the city is his observatory, his *luogo dell'anima* (place of the soul), the point of intersection between history, fiction, and reality that inspires him. In *Estate romana*

(Roman Summer, 1982) Desiato's protagonist is again an adolescent, Guido, who, on the great *palcoscenico* (stage) of Rome, experiences life and progresses toward maturity. Desiato skillfully intertwines the July 1943 bombing of Rome by the Allies and the tragic episodes of that summer with the personal lives of the characters such as Guido, his uncle Arcangelo, and Carmela while Italy and its capital, like the boy, face an ambiguous future and an uncertain destiny. In subsequent books Desiato would explore the past, present, and even contemplate the future of the "eternal city."

Although nearly half of his books are set in the present, Desiato's inclination for characters of the past is evident throughout his career. Linguistically, the figurative palette of colors that the past offers to a writer is deeper and more brilliant than that of the limited present. Desiato believes that contemporary man needs to search for his roots and identity in the rich phantasmagoria of history, for it contains examples that personify the courage needed to face the struggles of everyday life and to triumph over the obstacles of a harsh world. Desiato believes that reading an historical novel should present a learning experience for the modern reader because in the splendors, tragedies, and miseries of the past, one can recognize those of our own time.

Il Marchese del Grillo, Desiato's most famous book, is "un grande affresco" (a great fresco) of eighteenth-century Rome, presenting its lights and shadows amid the decadence of the last gleams of the Baroque era. The marquis is a character of great complexity and depth despite the simplicity of his motto:

> Er grillo del Marchese sempre zompa,
> chi zompa allegramente bene campa.
>
> (The Marquis's cricket always jumps;
> he who happily jumps will always live.)

His inclination for jokes is part of an existential malaise. A man who defies the social barriers and conventions of the time, he wishes to change stratified Roman society, which is divided between the rich aristocracy and the poor. This inequality disturbs the marquis, who tries to understand his role in a society that in its turmoil and decadence is comparable to the modern world.

The marquis suffers the ills of his society with a sense of despair that leads him to satire, mockery, and practical jokes. He is also afflicted by a deep melancholy that he dispels by pursuing the pleasures of the flesh. His own death, caused by venereal disease, is the final mockery of his existence. In a conversation with his faithful servant, Arcangelino, who brings words of reverent wisdom to the story of the marquis, he expresses a pessimistic view of life:

> Arcangelì, che fatica vivere! La malinconia, quella che t'assale nel mezzo dell'azione e imbratta com'un peccato d'origine i pensieri luminosi, è una spina, l'orribile pena del vivere impotenti in un mondo che marcisce.
>
> (Arcangelino, how tiring life is! Melancholy, the one that assails you in the midst of the action and taints the luminous thoughts, like an original sin, is a thorn, the horrible pain of living, impotent, in a decaying world.)

The narrative follows the marquis of Grillo in his search for his real father, who may be the Pope, but his quest also becomes a search for happiness.

At the end of the novel the wise Arcangelino and the marquis's lover, Olimpia, agree that happiness can perhaps only be found in the acceptance of reality and the willingness to live with it. Neither believes that one should destroy oneself in the attempt to change it. Olimpia writes to Arcangelino from the monastery of San Sisto, where she has retired following the death of the marquis. She expresses her feelings about her lover and her present life:

> Le sue beffe ... erano una parte di lui, il sogno ribelle d'una realtà diversa, la pazzia momentanea che squarciava i veli più tristi del nostro secolo: l'artifizio e la finzione.... Con il Marchese conobbi più d'una bella primavera. Con lui fui giovane e sazia, e mi rinnovai, respirai mille desideri.... L'autunno è la migliore stagione. Persino i rovi producono dolci e sanguigne bacche. La pace dello spirito, altro non cerco.
>
> (His mockeries ... were a part of himself, the rebellious dream of a different reality, the momentary madness that tore the saddest veils of our century: artifice and falsity.... With the Marquis I knew more than one beautiful spring. With him I was young and satisfied, and I renewed myself, I breathed a thousand desires.... Autumn is the best season. Even thorns produce sweet and sanguine berries. Now I seek nothing but peace of mind.)

Olimpia and Desiato's other female characters are all notable for their sensitivity, intelligence, and realistic views of life.

Desiato published *Galileo mio padre* (My Father Galileo, 1983), an historical novel based on the exchange of letters between Galileo Galilei and his daughter Sister Maria Celeste Galilei between May 1623 and the end of 1633, on the 350th anniversary of Galileo Galilei's abjuration of his *Dialogo sopra i due massimi sistemi* (Dialogue Concerning the Two Chief World Systems, 1633). The author declares that his novel is a homage to one of the most beautiful stories of all times: a passionate tale of filial love.

Desiato suggests that the daughter's letters were so precious to Galileo that he treasured and kept them jealously until his death. (The 127 letters were discovered by a scholar at the end of the nineteenth century.)

Galileo Galilei, who never married, had three children with Marina Gamba, a woman of the lower class. Because his offspring were illegitimate, they could not marry into nobility, but neither could they marry plebeians since at the time Galileo was a man of singular importance, a scientist renowned in Europe who was received by kings and princes. Consequently, Livia and Virginia Galilei were forced to take the veil. The sisters reacted in entirely opposite ways to their lot. Livia as Sister Arcangela became an ambivalent and hypochondriac nun who was destroyed by her undesired profession; Virginia as Sister Maria Celeste proved herself a woman of strong character, intense spirituality, and great intellect.

Desiato poured his own feelings about family relationships, especially the bonds between parents and children, into the affectionate portrait of Galileo and his daughter. This empathy doubtless accounts for the immediacy of the novel. Virginia Galilei's total dedication to her father is evident at the opening of the novel:

> Mia sorella Livia prese il nome di Suor Arcangela. Come protettore scelse l'Arcangelo Gabriele. Io, Virginia, divenni Suor Maria Celeste. Non elessi alcun santo, ché mi sono votata al padre mio.

> (My sister Livia adopted the name of Sister Arcangela. She chose the Archangel Gabriel as her protector. I did not select any saint, because I devoted myself to my father.)

From the Monastery of the Clarisse in Arcetri, Virginia corresponded with her father in the nearby villa Il Gioiello (The Jewel) and became deeply involved in the turbulence caused by his scientific discoveries. She rejoiced and cried with her father and was of great comfort to him until her death on 2 April 1634. Virginia's *lettere luminose* (luminous letters) show moral strength and a belief in the search for truth and justice. Her purity and daintiness, together with the unconditional acceptance of her destiny, provide an example of complete unselfishness and devotion. Beyond her reverence and pride in being the daughter of such a father, she sometimes was bold enough to remind Galileo of what lies beyond this earthly life:

> Ma per maggiormente regalarla gli mando una rosa, la quale, come cosa straordinaria di questa stagione dovrà da lei esser molto gradita, e tanto più che insieme con la rosa potrà accettar le spine, che in essa rappresentano l'acerba passione del nostro Signore; e anco le sue verdi frondi che significheranno la speranza, che mediante questa santa passione possiamo avere, di dover dopo la brevità ed oscurità dell'inverno della vita presente pervenire alla chiarezza e felicità dell'eterna primavera del cielo.

> (But so as to give you more, I am sending you a rose, that, as an extraordinary thing of this season, might be more appreciated by you, and together with the rose you can accept the thorns, which represent the bitter passion of our Lord; and also its green leaves that may mean the hope, which, thanks to his holy passion, we can have, of being able to reach the clarity and happiness of the eternal celestial spring, after the ephemeral obscurity of the winter of our present life.)

Galileo's struggle is an emblematic one because in human history there has always existed the conflict between institutional oppression and the individual's independence and freedom of thought.

Desiato believes that autobiography is not direct but a mediated matter: whatever is autobiographical is poured into a writer's stories through his imagination. Various aspects of his personal life are transposed into the lives of his characters. Some

Dust jacket for Desiato's 1992 novel, in which an old author contemplates Ovid's exile

of Desiato's attitudes toward life can be perceived in the character of Sister Maria Celeste Galilei and likewise in the marquis of Grillo in his rebellion against a flat and hypocritical world. Even in the character of the marquis's servant, Arcangelino, the writer has transposed the wisdom of an old uncle of his own who enriched the memories of his childhood with his enchanting fables. Personal history and fiction as well as real and imaginary characters are constantly intertwined in Desiato's books, and they create the rich amalgam that constitutes the finished work.

The immediacy and tangibility of true life experiences unify *Dialoghi e silenzi* (Dialogues and Silences, 1988), a collection of "frammenti" (fragments) that touch various meaningful stages in the author's life. Desiato admits that his family, with whom he maintains that he has a "dialectic" relationship, occupies a great deal of his energies. The art of writing can cause a writer to become lost in his own fantasy, but a gratifying family life can provide a haven where the mind takes refuge after wandering too freely; the family can prove to be the anchor that holds the writer down to earth and renders him a true human being. The choice to have a family is explored in the first section of *Dialoghi e silenzi*, "Dalla terra del Brasile" (From the Land of Brazil), which recounts the story of Desiato's adoption of two children, Virginia and Marco. He maintains that the decision to adopt was "una scelta fatta prima del matrimonio" (a choice made before our marriage) and not one that was influenced by the loss of his newborn baby girl: "Adottare un bambino non è l'estremo rifugio per coppie sterili, l'azzardo umanitario, ma la fiduciosa accoglienza di una nascita" (Adopting a child is not the last resource for sterile couples, the humanitarian hazard, but it is the confident welcome of a birth).

Desiato includes many other episodes of his personal life in *Dialoghi e silenzi:* from his memories of World War II—which he previously developed in *Estate romana*—to his encounters with Borges, Silone, and Maria Bellonci. The three writers are presented in the simplicity of their everyday lives: Borges scratches his ear with a finger encircled by his great-grandfather's ring; Silone buttons his pajamas top; and Bellonci adjusts her pearl necklace with a delicate hand. From the words of these masters Desiato draws the inspiration that has illuminated his writing career: Borges reminds him that "l'universo non èu nivoco, ma analogico" (the universe is not univocal, but analogical); Silone tells him "sia sincero quando scrive . . . cerchi le verità, le piccole verità, dovunque si trovino" (be sincere when you write . . . look for truths, little truths, wherever they may be); and Bellonci talks to him about "la verità ricostruita sul documento e la fantasia che da questo scaturisce aggiungendogli significato" (the truth re-created in the text, and the fantasy that issues from it, enhancing its significance). *Dialoghi e silenzi* is a key to Desiato's career and contains the basis for his inspiration as it captures his philosophy of human existence.

One of the striking features of Desiato's work is his fascination with the richness of women's emotions. He believes that the archetypical past is for a woman "come un lago dal quale pesca e attinge" (like a lake which she fishes in and draws from) and that her subconscious apprehension of past patterns deepens her involvement in the present. Desiato's interest in female characters, combined with his interest in enigmatic historical personas, led to the creation of a complex protagonist in *Bocca di Leone* (1989).

Vittoria—also known as Tolla—di Bocca di Leone can be regarded as the female counterpart of the marquis of Grillo. Both lived in eighteenth-century Rome under the Pope's rule and neither had a father. But while the marquis spent most of his adult life seeking his roots, Tolla rejected the little she knew about her background in her search for a way to ascend the social ladder. Her mother, Cecilia, introduced Tolla and her sister, Angiola, into prostitution, which seemed the only alternative to hunger and poverty. In Via Bocca di Leone, an ill-famed quarter of Rome that swarmed with harlots, criminals and outcasts, Tolla struggled to survive after the violent death of her mother.

Cecilia, who first understood the potential of Tolla's beauty and intelligence, instilled a sense of morality in the immoral life that she had provided her daughters. Her wise teaching always enlightened the way for Tolla: "Espedienti, smercio di sé ma senza spreco, umori quieti, mirata allegria e il piacere: quando reticente quando esplicito. Ossia il corpo regolato dal bilancino del cervello" (Makeshifts, selling oneself without waste, quiet humor, gaiety with a purpose, and pleasure: at times reserved and at times explicit. That is the body regulated by the balance of the mind). From Via Bocca di Leone, Tolla is able to advance socially with her beauty and intelligence. Following her mother's advice, she is not willing to give herself to "vaccari e tripparoli" (cowherds and tripe sellers). With her "occhi pretenziosi" (pretentious eyes) she waits for the men that "cadranno nel canestro" (will fall into the basket). She eventually becomes a refined and respected *cortigiana* (courtesan). Her charm, iron will, and ambition are enriched by her controlled passions and sincere tenderness and ultimately elevate her to a sphere that would have been unthinkable for a woman of her social position in eighteenth-century Italy. She first becomes the lover of Duke Cesarini Sforza and later that of Prince Sobieski. She ascends to the zenith of high society but in the end falls from it like a meteor.

Desiato's empathy extends to this woman who resists the moral and physical violence exerted by the ruling class and in particular by men. Her parabolic rise and fall mirrors the lives of other famous cortigiane of the time, such as Costanza Maccari, "la sfregiatella" (the disfigured woman), who was brutally punished by an abandoned lover; Angela Voglia, the favorite of the viceroy of Naples; and Nena, the target of several obscene writings. Through his novel Desiato pays homage to such women who, thanks to their beauty, charm, and intelligence, were able to achieve more than their social status and their times would have ever offered them.

Desiato particularly extols Tolla's intelligence, and he seems to value it more than he does her beauty as an important element in this courtesan's career. In an episode that he defined as "un divertimento dell'autore" (a diversion of the author) Tolla meets the marquis of Grillo. The encounter occurs in a crucial moment for the cortigiana, for though she is aware of her beauty and knows that she can have any man at her feet, she wants this legendary libertine to appreciate her for her intellect. She insists that if he wants her to concede her favors to him in a night of love, he must invent something so that her intelligence "vada in carrozza" (may ride in a carriage). In response the marquis composes a poem for her about the various anatomical parts of the female body that evoke the smells of different flowers:

> La sua mano a percorrermi la schiena, che un aggradimento ricevevo all'evocazione del balsamo arcano che si leva dalla rosa al mattino, dal giglio a mezzodì, dalla giunchiglia alla sera. Tremavo, un tantino più convinta, anzi incuriosita. La donna porto di mare, accoglie per non rimanere deserta.
>
> (His hand was going down my back, as I was enjoying the evocation of the arcane balm that is released by the rose in the morning, the lily in the afternoon, by the daffodil at night. I was trembling, a little more convinced, perhaps curious. The woman is a harbor who receives as not to remain deserted.)

Tolla is pleased with the marquis's poetic seduction. She feels flattered and fulfilled, and she loses herself "tra le braccia del piacere" (in the embrace of pleasure).

Desiato continues to explore the past in *Storie dell'eremo* (Stories from the Hermitage, 1990), a collection of short tales that are structured as a medieval *novellino*. The storyteller, a friar of the Eremo delle Carceri of Assisi, tells his friend one story after another. All of the stories are interconnected: one develops into another, which is, according to Desiato, "la quintessenza della letteratura" (the quintessence of literature), the never-ending game of human fantasy. While the stories of the fictional Fra Ginepro may be true or invented, all of them touch situations and feelings that appeal to the modern reader. The stories may be set in a remote and mysterious time, but they have the taste and smell of the ambiguous present.

One of the most striking stories, "La lucertola" (The Lizard), is centered around a young Jesus who is taken by his parents to the temple in Jerusalem so that he may be instructed by the rabbis. The freshness and curiosity of Jesus make him an appealing character. As he notices a lizard warming itself in the sun, he is attracted by that "piccola felicità" (small happiness) and asks the rabbi whether the desire for knowledge is as meritorious as the action of the little animal who merely seeks a ray of sun. The rabbi explains that the lizard does not know that there is a greater happiness, which is the happiness of one who observes and realizes how happy the lizard is. While the lizard is not aware, the human being is; he, therefore, is the most happy. Likewise, men are also cognizant of their unhappiness. Jesus learns that it is the awareness of the inevitability of death that translates into man's most anguished cry of protest.

During his school years, especially those he spent in Argentina, Desiato was deeply influenced by the Scholastic and Tomistic philosophies filtered through the writings of Jacques Maritain, Emmanuel Mounier, and Henri-Louis Bergson. His readings led him to meditate on the *dolore delle cose* (sorrow of the things), the inanity of everyday struggles, and making history: in essence, the absurdity of human existence in which one's attempts to attain happiness clash with inexorable death. Being able to accept the life-death cycle as defining human existence is part of an individual spiritual experience as well as of a universal and existential one. It is also the journey of Saverio, the protagonist in *Sulle rive del mar Nero* (On the Shores of the Black Sea, 1992), a novel set in the present.

Saverio is an elderly writer who lives in the Prati section of Rome; he is working on his final novel, which deals with Ovid. The Latin poet, having been accused of a crime that has remained a mystery, was exiled by the emperor Augustus to the frigid town of Tomi on the shores of the Black

"GIULIANO L'APOSTATA

(SECONDA STESURA)

Capitolo primo

Prego il Sole, il grande Helios.
Prego la Luna, la grande Demetra, Madre di tutti gli Dei, che le sue mammelle nutrano la mia mente. Prego il mio dèmone: nella battaglia che si preannunzia decisiva contro i Persiani mi sia propizio.

Ho fatto un sogno, una di queste notti afose, quando mi rivolto sulla graticola del letto da campo mentre il sudore mi macera. Un fiore d'ornitogalo, la sua spiga di foglie bianche con l'aculeo fosco al centro mi cresceva da una ferita al ventre, l'impeto di quel bianco latte degli uccelli sul rosso della slabbratura. Fioriva, si slargava alla luce, e subito appassiva. In quell'appassire sentivo un dolore putrido. Un soprassalto, e mi sono svegliato. Ho attribuito a un'incordatura del collo l'incontro col malessere. Eppure sapevo. Gli Dei godono a mettere in guardia, a segni, coloro per i quali si sono esaurite le vie del possibile.

Spiriti vagano nello spazio, Aristeo. Presagi lugubri: lamenti notturni di civette, sangue sgorgato da una pianta d'alloro divelta da uno degli elefanti del re Shapur. Quando camminano in fila, quelle gigantesche termiti frantumano e svellono. Dopo il loro passaggio restano solchi come trincee; sono le testuggini viventi di un esercito infido. Shapur, il monocolo dai grandi orecchini di perla, deve rifarsi delle sconfitte con le quali abbiamo ustionato il suo orgoglio. Sono cani vaganti, questi barbari, e dicono di discendere definitiva, e sarà una vittoria romana.

Un indovino armeno dagli occhi d'ossidiana ha preteso di paragonarmi a Gilgamesh, l'antico eroe di questi luoghi, il semidio che aveva affidato le tenebre dell'ignoto passando attraverso prove di fuoco e d'acqua per giungere alla conoscenza. La cognizione del mondo, la pace con gli Dei è forse lo scopo di

Page from the revised typescript for Giuliano l'Apostata *(Collection of Luca Desiato)*

Sea. During the torrid Roman summer Saverio copes with the emptiness left by the death of his wife, Dora. His solitude and the sensation that his life too is coming to an end echo Ovid's story of exile and exclusion. Desiato's fascination with Ovid's experience resonates in the parallel he draws between the spiritual isolation of Saverio and the practical and moral exile of the Latin poet of eros who, at the apex of his artistic and social fortune, was psychologically destroyed by the emperor.

"Senectus ipsa morbus" (Old age is itself a disease): the old Latin saying seems to define Saverio's life. He writes about Ovid and his loneliness as though in the poet's isolation he recognizes the isolation of old age itself. Memories from his past haunt him and remind him of tragedies and mistakes that time has not erased. He imagines Ovid on the cold shores of Scizia, which were covered with "un lastrome di ghiaccio sul quale scorre un vento abrasivo" (a layer of ice over which an abrasive wind blows), longing for his lost Roman triumphs, the warm baths, and the perfume of the quiet villas. The theme of exile is extended to the totality of human life, for all in some way feel exiled: from happiness, health, family, love, or youth. This is a reality that is part of life and must be accepted with humility and faith, with a positive resignation that is a matter of choice.

While Ovid never found this resignation in his spirit and pleaded uselessly until his death for the end of his exile, first with Augustus and later with his successor, Tiberius, Saverio in the end accepts his condition as he writes his final novel:

> "Ti ho rivissuto, Publio Ovidio" gli dice allora Saverio, ... "Per un po' siamo stati compagni. Tu il mio demone, io la tua spiegazione. Eppure mi sto liberando di te, dal momento che posso dire che ognuno ha avuto la sua parte, ognuno la sua pena: sono cose umane." ... L'altro continua a scuotere il capo. Come fargli capire che la vita, l'amore, l'arte stessa sono esilio? Non da una precedente esistenza beata, ma da sé. Esilio è il vivere stesso e il non riconoscerlo.

("I lived in you, Publius Ovidius" Saverio then tells him, ... "For a while we were comrades. You my demon, and I your explanation. And yet I am freeing myself from you, since I can say that each one of us has had his share, each his own pain: such is a man's life." ... The other keeps shaking his head. How can he make him understand that life, love, and art itself are an exile? ... Not from a previous happy existence, but from oneself. Exile is life itself, and not acknowledging it.)

Ovid's and Saverio's are two parallel lives, even if two thousand years apart: a tormenting exile that annuls the barrier of time and manifests itself as "un punto di dolore nella circolarità della vita" (a point of sorrow in the cyclicity of life).

Desiato published two more historical novels: *La notte dell'angelo* (The Night of the Angel, 1994) and *Giuliano l'Apostata* (Julian, the Apostate, 1997). The first novel, whose subtitle is "Vita scellerata di Caravaggio" (Caravaggio's Wicked Life), is a visionary account of the life of genial Baroque painter Caravaggio. The life of the artist is told from his youth in Rome until his death, at age thirty-nine on a beach in Tuscany. His genius and disorderliness drag the painter into a life full of anguish, constantly wandering from Rome to Naples, from Malta to Sicily in search of a peace and serenity that even art cannot grant him. Although it is based on historical facts, this novel is not to be considered a biography. It is instead the author's representation of the timeless, universal themes of the relationship between art and life, artistic creation and individual conscience, between God's saving grace and personal damnation. In Giuliano l'Apostata Desiato revisited the life of the fourth-century emperor Julian, a great political figure, reformer, army leader, and philosopher. The story, which is narrated in first person, traces the short life of the emperor who died at age thirty-two during the Persian war. He is depicted as a major figure who represents the last years of paganism at a time of religious and historical transition. Desiato is presently working on a new novel, tentatively titled *Il bosco di Thomas Mann* (Thomas Mann's Forest). This novel centers on the search for a lost manuscript of Thomas Mann in a small town near Rome where the German writer lived for a few months of his life.

Although praised by many critics, Desiato's works have not gotten the attention that they deserved. His importance as a novelist in contemporary Italian literature is underestimated. According to the writer, this is probably due to his not being affiliated to any particular literary circle. This, at least, is likely not to change for he confesses to a love for independence.

Francesca Duranti
(2 January 1935 –)

Jan Kozma
University of Kansas

BOOKS: *La Bambina* (Milan: La Tartaruga, 1976);
Piazza mia bella piazza (Milan: La Tartaruga, 1978);
La casa sul lago della luna (Milan: Rizzoli, 1984); translated by Stephen Sartarelli as *The House on Moon Lake* (New York: Random House, 1986);
Lieto fine (Milan: Rizzoli, 1987); translated by Annapaola Cancogni as *Happy Ending* (New York: Random House, 1991);
Effetti personali (Milan: Rizzoli, 1988); translated by Sartarelli as *Personal Effects* (New York: Random House, 1993);
Ultima stesura (Milan: Rizzoli, 1991);
Progetto Burlamacchi (Milan: Rizzoli, 1994);
Sogni mancini (Milan: Rizzoli, 1996).

TRANSLATION: Virgina Woolf, Lunedi o martedi: tutti i racconti (Milan: La Tartaruga, 1980).

Francesca Duranti has contributed to post-World War II Italian literature through her close examination of personal experiences, especially her relationships with her mother and husbands, and through her exploration of the dynamics of writing fiction. Duranti's novels show how life affords the material for art and how one's devotion to art can affect one's life. In *La casa sul lago della luna* (1984; translated as *The House on Moon Lake,* 1986), her most famous work, the writer-protagonist becomes so entangled with his creation that he cannot escape it. Duranti often focuses on a woman's desire to free herself from external control and become a whole, independent, functioning person. Her work appeals to a spectrum of readers and has appeared in translation in Finland, Denmark, Sweden, Holland, Germany, France, Bulgaria, Spain, Brazil, and Israel as well as the United States.

Born on 2 January 1935 in Genova as Maria Francesca Rossi, Duranti spent her formative years in a villa near Lucca in Tuscany. She had one younger sister, Marina. Her paternal grandfather was one of the founders of the Italian Socialist Party. Her mother, Giuseppina Bagnara Rossi, came from

Francesca Duranti

the industrialist, upper classes of Genova. Her father, Paolo Rossi, a passionate antifascist who was kept under constant surveillance during World War II, became a member of Parliament after the first elections. He also started to teach jurisprudence at the University of Pisa. While serving as minister of education from 1955 to 1957 Rossi moved the family to Rome. In 1956 Francesca married Enrico Magnani, with whom she had a son, Gregorio Magnani, before they separated in 1960. She lived with Massimo Duranti from 1960 until 1976, marrying him when divorce became legal in the early 1970s. Their daughter, Maddalena Duranti was born in 1962. She earned her law degree from the University of Pisa in 1960 but never practiced law. Francesca

Duranti now divides her writing time between Tuscany and New York.

Duranti's first book, *La Bambina* (The Little Girl, 1976), was enormously successful in Italy and critically acclaimed worldwide. The novel is set in a villa in the Tuscan countryside during the Nazi occupation. A highly autobiographical work, the "little girl" of the title, Francesca Rossi, recounts salient episodes of her childhood from age three to the verge of adolescence. Forced to mature quickly by the advent of Fascism and the implementation of racial laws, Francesca, whose first words are "da sola" (by myself), grows up to be a spunky, endearing child with a wisdom far beyond her years. Her vibrance and courage offer a counterpoint to the physical and moral devastation of war.

Raised in an upper-class family, she is largely isolated from her extraordinary parents—her father is a courageous political activist while her mother asserts her authority with Nazi generals and troops alike—whom she considers permanent visitors of the same house. She perceives early that love is bestowed in proportion to her precociousness, and to please her parents she becomes fluent in German, French, and English by listening to the foreign governesses and household servants. As she grows, Francesca becomes self-sufficient, no longer needing the emotional support of her preoccupied parents. Her independence comes at a price, however, as is particularly evident in Duranti's later works, which also draw from personal experience.

Francesca's mother, a formidable woman devoid of maternal qualities, is cold and sometimes psychologically cruel. While she treats Francesca more as an adult rival than a child of her own, Francesca's love for her mother is unconditional and her admiration constant. The child is unceasing in her efforts to please, but love is always quid pro quo for her mother. After Francesca saves her sister's life, her mother says she will grant her one wish as a reward. But when Francesca wants to be allowed to dress as a youngster rather than as a child, her mother reneges: "Neanche per sogno!" (In your dreams!). The mother-daughter struggle continues in different forms in Duranti's subsequent novels.

Throughout *La Bambina* Francesca's reminiscences create a world in which nearly every experience holds surprise and freshness. Her natural observations often seem humorous to adult readers, as when immediately following a costume party Francesca goes to a baptismal ceremony and wonders why no one at this party, except for the priest, is wearing a costume. The novel consists of similar small adventures that are nevertheless key to a child's development and the adult she will become. Perhaps Duranti's main accomplishment is to recall for the reader the memories of childhood that are at the same time both insignificant and all-important.

With charm and ironic humor Duranti strings together episodes that show the ability of her child protagonist to see things differently from adult perception. In a child's mind all events seem equally significant even though not all are really of the same importance in retrospect. Francesca's nocturnal fishing expeditions are remembered with the same wonder as is the scene of her mother, with the aid of an interpreter, standing up to a Nazi general. Duranti is meticulous in depicting the subtle wit and insights of her protagonist, who is poised enough to deal in the same friendly, intelligent, self-confident way with children and adults, servants and masters, and Nazis and Fascists. At the end of the novel Francesca reaches a transition state—she is no longer a bambina but not yet an adult. She sees the absurdity of adulthood but cannot relinquish her childhood.

To transform memory into art is difficult; the writer must walk a tightrope between lightness and precision. Duranti's reliance on a child as a narrator makes for an interesting narrative in which the reader must sometimes interpret the child's misunderstandings. For example, the reader knows immediately that the woman who delivered Francesca's sister was not an *imperatrice* (empress) but a *levatrice* (midwife), realizing that the similar sound of the Italian words fooled the child. Duranti also includes some engaging doses of adult insight in her story, providing occasional hints that the child-narrator is now a mature bambina looking back on herself. Her use of anachronism, such as a 1960s reference in a World War II setting, jolts the reader from the child's point of view: "Egli, (zio Enzo), infatti, era considerato da tutti, in quel periodo in cui gli hippies non erano ancora di moda, come una persona estremamente sconclusionata" (In fact, Uncle Enzo was considered really frivolous by everyone in those days when hippies were not yet fashionable). Such moments forge a seamless temporal unity, putting the present into the past, and contribute to the artistic success of the novel.

Duranti allowed her second novel, *Piazza mia bella piazza* (My Town Square, My Beautiful Square, 1978), to be republished in 1986 but has since refused to permit its republication. In the novel a first-person narrator, Paola, tells the story of her marriage, which is destroyed by her husband, Marco, because he is threatened by her desire to pursue a writing career seriously. Duranti asserts that *Piazza mia bella piazza* is not among her best work. Even

Dust jacket for Duranti's first novel, about a young girl growing up during World War II

so, the novel is important because it sows the seeds of her later soul-searching, feminist themes.

Paola recounts in painful detail what she learned from her marriage: never again to let anyone destroy her dignity or make mincemeat of her heart. The novel traces Paola's determination to become a writer while Marco, fearful that he will become "the author's husband," threatens to leave her if she persists. He manifests violent mood swings, alternately giving and withdrawing his love to her and their child, Eloisa. Eventually he establishes unreasonable rules as the conditions of their marriage and prohibits all activities beyond the home. He forbids her to earn money, denies her the opportunity to continue her hobby of horseback riding, and bans her friends from the house. Neurotically insecure, he even prevents her from picking up her diploma from the University of Pisa.

The couple's dysfunctional symbiosis continues with minor variations on the same fundamental dispute until she feels suffocated by his manic behavior. Although Paola seems psychologically incapable of leaving him, during an intense period of introspection she realizes that her first husband, Carlo, freed her from her controlling mother, that Marco freed her from Carlo, and that only she can finally free herself from the constraints of others. After she has left Marco, achieved literary success, and acquired self-awareness, Paola continues to feel incomplete without a man: "Essere senza un uomo che si prendesse cura di lei le sembrava come aver perduto i documenti in un paese straniero e ostile, si sentiva privata di ogni diritto, di ogni protezione" (To be without a man to care for her seemed like having lost her papers in a foreign and hostile country; she felt deprived of all rights and protections).

Unsure that she is worthy of love, Paola has yet to learn that she must first love herself in order to be whole. In *Effetti personali* (1988; translated as *Personal Effects,* 1993) Duranti depicts a woman protagonist who is without a man in a hostile foreign country, but Paola, disoriented and insecure after her failed marital experiences, is not ready for such a test. She knows, though, that she is on her way to recovery, having learned from her women friends that all parts of her life will eventually find fulfillment with or without a man.

The title, which refers to a child's rhyming song, provides a telling metaphor for the novel. In singing the song, one caresses a child's hand and describes a rabbit hopping through the piazza formed by the palm. Beginning with the thumb and proceeding to the fingers, the child closes the hand: the thumb sees the rabbit; the index finger seizes it; the middle finger kills it; the ring finger cooks it; and the little finger eats the rabbit. The song thus transforms the piazza into a death trap. The child, like Marco, is pitiless; the rabbit, like Paola, seems caught in an inescapable, life-threatening situation.

The novel has all the seeds of a feminist awakening. It shows the evolution of a woman who comes to the conclusion—prevalent in contemporary feminist discourse—that it is better to be alone, self-sufficient, and happy rather than to be a trapped rabbit imprisoned in a marriage that satisfies only society's expectations of a woman. Yet there is no evidence in this work of programmatic feminism, and Duranti denies any commitment to a feminist agenda. Everything in *Piazza mia bella piazza* unfolds naturally, without ideological constraints. Her writing has a therapeutic frankness, with no filter between feeling and the written word.

Duranti's third novel, *La casa sul lago della luna,* first appeared on the best-seller list of *La Stampa* in December 1984, remaining there for four weeks. Awarded the Bagutta Prize, the Martina Franca Prize, and the City of Milano Prize, it is by far Duranti's most successful novel and has been translated into more than seventeen languages. The protagonist is Fabrizio Garrone, a near penniless translator of novels. Fabrizio's girlfriend, Fulvia, is as capable as Fabrizio is inept, a take-charge, no-nonsense woman who loves Fabrizio but who cannot abide his indecisiveness. At the beginning of the novel Fabrizio is about to begin a translation of Alfred Doeblin's *Berlin Alexanderplatz* (1929), whose protagonist mirrors Fabrizio. Generally unhappy, he like Fabrizio is incapable of making a commitment and has unsatisfactory personal relationships. With self-ironic wit and a charming off-handedness, Duranti pokes fun at the ineffectual Fabrizio, who seems incapable of taking action even to save himself.

Browsing, Fabrizio finds a reference to a novel, *Das Haus am Mondsee* (The House on Moon Lake), by an unknown Viennese author, Fritz Oberhofer. Sensing it will be a best-seller, Fabrizio decides to translate it and make a name in the literary world he despises yet is eager to enter. He journeys to Austria and at Moon Lake locates one of the few extant copies of the work. His translation is a triumph, and to take advantage of the interest in the novel Fabrizio writes a biography of Oberhofer. However, when he finds he is unable to reconstruct the last years of his subject, Fabrizio invents them by concocting the perfect woman for Fritz, a collage of all the qualities that Fabrizio believes are desirable in a woman. He calls her Maria Lettner, imagining her as Fritz's literary inspiration and muse. In a fitting ironic twist Duranti has Fabrizio's view of the perfect Maria Lettner include every stereotypical female trait imaginable. She is beautiful, nurturing, self-sacrificing, and unconditionally supportive.

Fabrizio's biography is a great success, to the point that it brings out people claiming to have gone to school with and known Maria Lettner. There even surfaces a literary critic who ascribes to Maria all the credit for Fritz's last work and can prove it textually. Duranti's wit is especially keen in the passages where Maria takes on a life of her own, even inspiring "the Maria look" in popular fashion. Duranti thus debunks the publishing industry that creates literary icons and feeds the public its own mythology.

When Fabrizio's ideal creation is co-opted by the popular culture he so despises, he in disgust decides to confess publicly that Maria is a hoax. This twentieth-century Pygmalion needs to destroy his invention so no one else can have her. However, before he takes action Maria Lettner's "granddaughter," Petra Ebner, steps forward and claims to have the love letters exchanged by Fritz and Maria. Suspecting blackmail, the curious Fabrizio visits her on Moon Lake. As a guest at her villa, Fabrizio slowly is seduced by this specterlike woman. Eventually they become Fritz and Maria, the personae of the writer and his invented lover overtaking and merging with Fabrizio and Petra. Rejecting his chance to escape from this self-destructive relationship, Fabrizio chooses to stay with Petra presumably to die on Moon Lake.

Duranti's main theme is embodied in Fabrizio, an alienated man who chooses spiritual death instead of a contemporary life he abhors because fiction offers him what life cannot provide. At the point where Fabrizio goes to Moon Lake the satire

Dust jacket for Duranti's 1984 novel, in which a translator loses his grasp on reality when his fraudulent biography becomes a popular success

takes on a dimension of fantasy, and the real dovetails with the surreal. The fablelike quality of the story aids the reader in accepting Fabrizio's fatal choice. Fabrizio predestines his own disaster by failing to act when he can save himself. As he progressively identifies with Fritz, Fabrizio goes from the flesh-and-blood Fulvia to the dream-fulfillment Maria Lettner to the mysterious Petra Ebner. At thirty-eight, the same age that Fritz died, he goes from reality to a moribund unreality.

Like Duranti's other novels, *La casa sul lago della luna* encodes autobiographical clues. Duranti's first name, Francesca, is similar to the names of her characters Fabrizio and Fritz. Like Duranti, Fabrizio was raised in a well-to-do Genoese villa. Like her protagonist, Duranti worked as a translator and knew German well. Yet despite such links there is a much greater distance between Duranti and her protagonist in this book than in her first two novels. Fabrizio grows out of the circumstances of Duranti's life, but he does not resemble her in the same personal way as her earlier protagonists.

Lieto fine (1987; translated as *Happy Ending*, 1991) is the story of the voyeuristic narrator, Aldo, an erstwhile dealer in fake art who has become a middle-aged, respectable art historian. Aldo has purchased social legitimacy by renovating a tower bordering the Santini estate, which is ruled by the manipulative matriarch, Violante Santini. Aldo keeps his snooping telescope trained on Violante's parklike grounds, an oasis of comfort and privilege, that contains three villas: the first is Violante's own; the second is inhabited by her son, Leopoldo, and his neurotic wife, Cynthia, from Columbus, Ohio; and the third is the summer place of her widowed daughter-in-law, Lavinia, a scatterbrained, disorganized, flighty spendthrift. Into this dysfunctional world wanders the mooching Marco, a young, laid-back hippy, who acts as the catalyst. Because of his interaction with the others, Cynthia and Leopoldo find love again; Aldo and Lavinia begin a relationship; and Violante solidifies her dynasty.

Aldo functions as a theatrical voice-over who tells the story. He retreats at intervals to allow others their viewpoints, only to return to weave the threads together into a seamless narrative. *Lieto fine* is structured like a farcical play, for Duranti's chapters are constructed loosely as acts that each have three or four scene changes. As Aldo observes, the title and shifts of perspective mimic a lightweight musical: "Questa è tutta roba che dovrei scrivere. Io so scrivere solo di pittura, altrimenti sarebbe quasi un dovere mettere giù nero su bianco—sotto forma di romanzo, di dramma o, meglio ancora, di commedia musicale—qualcosa che racconti i personaggi del mio teatrino segreto" (This is stuff that I ought to write about. I only know how to write about painting, otherwise it would almost be a duty to write in the form of a novel, a play or better yet a musical comedy—something that would tell the story of my secret theatre).

Much as Fabrizio, who could not assert himself professionally in Milan's complex publishing world, Aldo is an observer rather than an actor. He is the archetypal Peeping Tom who lives through his telescope, heedless of its ability to bend reality. He follows a pattern established in his youth, for then too Aldo was mesmerized by the lifestyle of a wealthy family he spied on from the outside. His perspective of the world is limited to what he sees from his tower, and his values are based on his voyeuristic experience. Through Aldo, Duranti analyzes the alienated male who searches for an identity based on skewed values—an important and recurring theme in Duranti's works. Lavinia, on the other hand, presents the theme of the ungrounded woman, for she is controlled by, rather than being in control of, her world.

In *Effetti personali,* a popular work that won several literary awards, Duranti shows the growth of her protagonist, Valentina. At the beginning of the novel she has no ballast to define her existence. She has worked ten years for her husband, Riccardo, receiving no gratitude or respect, and he has abandoned her for another woman. During the course of the story, though, Valentina gains self-confidence and becomes a woman who has learned to be a whole person. *Effetti personali* thus goes beyond women's issues to broader human concerns.

When Valentina hears a strange sound outside her door, she sees her estranged husband removing his brass nameplate, thus leaving her without an identity, the ultimate "personal effect." The Italian verb *valere* (to be worth something), a play on her name, defines Valentina's quest for self-esteem. She begins her journey with a trip behind the Iron Curtain to interview Milos Jarco, an enigmatic author of international fame whose novel has the translated title "The Answer." It turns out that Milos Jarco is a literary hoax, an invention of the Communist Writers' Union to take advantage of the mistaken perception in the capitalist West that he is a literary giant. Valentina meets instead Ante Radek, a poet, a believer in the antimaterialist tenets of communism and part inventor of Jarco. Eventually she has to choose between a life of her own or sublimating her newly found self for Radek, who is a sharp contrast to her former husband: Riccardo is elegant while Ante is unfashionable; Riccardo is greedy while Ante is ascetic; and Riccardo is lusty while Ante is passive. Ante's name is an example of Duranti's playfulness: he is an anti-Riccardo.

Valentina discovers that finding the antithesis of Riccardo is not necessary to her development. Ante is equally unacceptable precisely because of his abstemiousness and lack of materialism. The title "Personal Effects" suggests the importance of possessions as the means of grounding and defining the individual. Valentina leaves Ante, returns to Italy, and symbolically handwrites a nameplate on her door as she waits for a permanent replacement. The protagonists of Duranti's two most successful novels, Valentina and Fabrizio are both alienated from society, but while Fabrizio never learns to adapt, Valentina readjusts fully. While Fabrizio chooses to die, Valentina chooses rehabilitation, eventually gaining the courage and freedom to eat alone in a restaurant and to drive alone in a foreign country. She acquires her own identity and takes an active role in life.

Ultima stesura (The Last Draft, 1991) is narrated by the diarist Teodora Francia. Printed in italics, the diary portion of the novel spans thirty years and forms a frame for the eight short stories Teodora has published, six of which are narrated by men. The stories are not italicized, thus differentiating the two types of voices in the work. Teodora and her narrators engage progressively in a dialectic. Eventually the italicized diary entries interrupt the storytellers to such an extent—at one point comprising about 50 percent of the story space—that the narration becomes a skein of inextricable voices, a contest between life as chronicled

Dust jackets for Duranti's 1987 novel and its American translation

in the diaries and art as realized in the stories, showing how life intrudes on art and vice versa.

The frame of *Ultima stesura* binds the stories as they allude to and echo one another. The stories become such a part of the chronicle that the two become one, an integrated fiction of multiple perspectives, or "meta novel" as it has been called, and the book must be read as a single piece to be appreciated. At the same time, in a fashion mindful of Luigi Pirandello, one of her favorite authors, Duranti raises the question of whether art and life can ever really blend. Duranti believes that a writer can either live or write, but not both. Writing lies outside of life and is a means of observing the world, much like Aldo's telescope that distorts reality.

Duranti's autobiographical impulse is again clear in her fusion of diary and fiction. She is interested in how individuals try to make sense of chaos, of forces beyond their control, and look to literature for help. Teodora speaks for Duranti when she asserts that she has spent thirty years living a life and writing stories in an effort to impose harmony upon the disorder of her life. When a character in the diary observes that with fiction one never knows where the truth ends and where fiction begins, Teodora answers that it is a bit of this and a bit of that: "Un po' si copia dalla vita e un po' si inventa" (You copy a little from life and you invent a little).

Another recurring issue is the husband's attempt to stifle his wife's talent. Both Duranti and her character Teodora use writing as therapy, and the work of each records her evolution as a self-made writer. For example, Teodora explains how she filled the time between the publication of the first and second volumes of stories by painting, tutoring children, making marmalade, teaching her child to read, and learning to sew. These specific activities hearken back to Paola in *Piazza mia bella piazza,* who was forced by her husband to take up activites other than writing. In the second volume Maria Giulia is like Teodora and Paola in being oppressed by a husband who has turned her into his personal servant. Like Teodora and Paola she is a woman who can only live in symbiosis. Teodora's diary is a mosaic of the tragedies that have befallen the novelist, yet Teodora claims to be a whole person who likes herself enough to keep her own company.

Duranti began her literary career with *La Bambina,* a searching examination of her own childhood; in *Ultima stesura* she seems to arrive at self-acceptance. In an aside that suggests her development as a person as well as a writer, the diarist at the end of *Ultima stesura* reports that she rather regrets no longer having to wait for the book reviews to determine the significance of her works. The ironic observation shows a playful author who continues to entertain readers with questions about the place of fiction in this postmodern era.

Progetto Burlamacchi (The Burlamacchi Project, 1994) is somewhat of a departure from Duranti's previous works. Concerned with Italy's missed opportunities at becoming a modern country, it deals with Francesco Burlamacchi's idea, first promoted in 1548, to unify the cities of Tuscany and to infuse the federation with a new spirit of reform based on moral accountability and the absence of Medici domination. Set in contemporary Italy, the novel depicts a re-creation of the Burlamacchi experiment and more. It begins when Ruggero Pacini finds the original of a venerated religious icon, a statue known as the Volto Santo (Holy Image) of the city of Lucca, hidden in a niche of a medieval tower that was once part of the Burlamacchi estate. Pacini also discovers that the original thief of the statue, Fra Jacopo di Neri, had the notion of a Tuscan league some 250 years before Burlamacchi did and suggested that the "disappearance" of the statue was a sign of divine displeasure with the sorry state of the world during his time. Duranti contrives events to suggest the analogies between the past and the present. Her protagonists, including Pacini, gather in Lucca to shoot a film in which they plan to showcase the long-lost original statue on television, hoping that its appearance will incite the changes in contemporary society that were envisioned by both Fra Jacopo di Neri and Francesco Burlamacchi.

In *Sogni mancini* (Left-Handed Dreams, 1996) Duranti returns to more familiar and personal territory, the story of a woman who chooses to make it on her own. The difference in this work is that her protagonist from the beginning seems to be reasonably happy, well adjusted, and independent. Content to live her life quietly as she carries out her duties as a professor of Italian at New York University, Martina Satriano nevertheless strives to penetrate the layers of her own defenses in order to reach a real sense of her own identity. This quest is fueled by her discovery that she was originally left-handed but was assiduously trained from childhood to be right-handed. She suspects this may account for many contradictions she detects in her life.

Sogni mancini confirms Francesca Duranti's strength as a writer, for from her first work on she delves ever deeper into the psyches of her characters. Her novels show her evolving continually as a writer and as a person. Her fearlessness and honesty as an artist are recognized by critics; the hundreds of reviews of her work contain few, if any, negative evaluations. Clearly she is regarded as one of the most accomplished writers active in Italy today.

Interviews:

Martha Witt, "Incidentalmente antifemminista: Intervista a Francesca Duranti," *Leggere Donna,* new series 34 (September–October 1991): 23–24;

Sharon Wood, "Writing in a Changing World: An Interview with Francesca Duranti," *Italianist,* 12 (1992): 186–195.

References:

Gianfranco Bettini, "Luna spaesata sul lago morente," *Discussione* (Summer 1986): 212–217;

Jan Kozma, "Bio-fictive Conversations and the Uncentered Woman in Francesca Duranti's Novels," *Italianist,* 16 (1996): 176–190;

Carol Lazzaro-Weis, *From Margins to Mainstream: Feminism and Fictional Modes in Italian Women's Writing 1968-90* (Philadelphia: University of Pennsylvania Press, 1993), pp. 180–189;

Stefania Lucamonte, "La geometria nel romanzo: i grafici narrativi di Francesca Duranti," *Forum Italicum 29* (Fall 1995): 313–323;

Shirley W. Vinall, "Francesca Duranti: Reflections and Inventions," in *The New Italian Novel,* edited by Z. G. Baranski and L. Pertile (Edinburgh: Edinburgh University Press, 1993), pp. 99–120;

Rita Wilson, "City and Labyrinth: Theme and Variation in Calvino and Duranti's Cityscapes," *Literator,* 13, no. 2 (1992): 85–95;

Wilson, "Identità revelate: Le speculazioni narrative di Marta Morazzoni e Francesca Duranti," *SIAA,* 7, no. 2 (1994): 50–68;

Wilson, "Writing an Identity: The Case of Francesca Duranti," *SIAA,* 9, no. 2 (1996): 81–98;

Sharon Wood, "Seductions and Brazen Duplications: Two Recent Novels from Italy," *Forum for Modern Language Studies,* 28, no. 4 (1992): 349–362.

Umberto Eco
(5 January 1932 -)

Carl A. Rubino
Hamilton College

BOOKS: *Il problema estetico in San Tommaso* (Turin: Edizioni di Filosofia, 1956); revised and enlarged as *Il problema estetico in Tommaso d'Aquino* (Milan: Bompiani, 1970); translated by Hugh Bredin as *The Aesthetics of Thomas Aquinas* (Cambridge: Harvard University Press, 1988);

Filosofi in libertà (Turin: Taylor, 1958);

Sviluppo dell'estetica medievale, in *Momenti e problemi di storia dell'estetica* (Milan: Marzorati, 1959); translated by Hugh Bredin as *Art and Beauty in the Middle Ages* (New Haven: Yale University Press, 1986); revised and enlarged as *Arte e bellezza nell'estetica medievale* (Milan: Bompiani, 1987);

Opera aperta: forma e indeterminazione nelle poetiche contemporanee (Milan: Bompiani, 1962; revised, 1972); translated by Anna Cancogni as *The Open Work* (Cambridge: Harvard University Press, 1989);

Diario minimo (Milan: Mondadori, 1963; revised, 1975);

Apocalittici e integrati: comunicazioni di massa e teorie della cultura di massa (Milan: Bompiani, 1964; revised, 1977);

Appunti per una semiologia delle comunicazioni visive (Milan: Bompiani, 1967);

La struttura assente: Introduzione alla ricerca semiologica (Milan: Bompiani, 1968; revised, 1983)—includes revised *Appunti per una semiologia delle comunicazioni visive*;

La definizione dell'arte (Milan: Mursia, 1968);

Le forme del contenuto (Milan: Bompiani, 1971);

Ammazza l'uccellino: letture scolastiche per i bambini della maggioranza silenziosa (Milan: Bompiani, 1973);

Eugenio Carmi: una pittura di paesaggio? (Milan: G. Prearo, 1973); enlarged as *Carmi,* by Eco and Duncan Macmillan (Milan: L'agrifoglio, 1996);

Il segno (Milan: ISEDI, 1973; second edition, Milan: Mondadori, 1973);

Il costume di casa: evidenze e misteri dell'ideologia italiana (Milan: Bompiani, 1973);

Beato di Liébana: miniature del Beato de Fernando 1. y Sancha (Milan: F. M. Ricci, 1973);

A Theory of Semiotics (Bloomington: Indiana University Press, 1976);

Il superuomo di massa: studi sul romanzo popolare (Rome: Cooperativa Scrittori, 1976; revised and enlarged edition, Milan: Bompiani, 1978);

Dalla periferia dell'impero (Milan: Bompiani, 1977);

Come si fa una tesi di laurea (Milan: Bompiani, 1977);

Carolina Invernizio, Matilde Serao, Liala, by Eco and others (Florence: La Nuova Italia, 1979);

Informazione: consenso e dissenso, by Eco, Marino Livolsi, and Giovanni Panozzo (Milan: Saggiatore, 1979);

The Role of the Reader: Explorations in the Semiotics of Texts (Bloomington: Indiana University Press, 1979)—includes selections from *Opera aperta, Apocalittici e integrati, Le forme del contenuto, Il superuomo di massa,* and *Lector in fabula*);

Lector in fabula: la cooperazione interpretativa nei testi narrativi (Milan: Bompiani, 1979);

Il nome della rosa (Milan: Bompiani, 1980); translated by William Weaver as *The Name of the Rose* (San Diego: Harcourt Brace Jovanovich, 1983; London: Secker & Warburg, 1984);

De Bibliotheca (Milan: Biblioteca comunale, 1981);

Postille al "Nome della Rosa" (Milan: Bompiani, 1983); translated by Weaver as *Postscript to "The Name of the Rose"* (San Diego: Harcourt Brace Jovanovich, 1984); republished as *Reflections on The Name of the Rose* (London: Secker & Warbury, 1985);

Sette anni di desiderio (Milan: Bompiani, 1983);

Semiotica e filosofia del linguaggio (Turin: Einaudi, 1984); translated by Eco as *Semiotics and the Philosophy of Language* (Bloomington: Indiana University Press, 1984);

Sugli specchi e altri saggi (Milan: Bompiani, 1985);

Arte e bellezza nell'estetica medievale (Milan: Bompiani, 1987);

Il pendolo di Foucault (Milan: Bompiani, 1988); translated by Weaver as *Foucault's Pendulum* (San Diego: Harcourt Brace Jovanovich, 1989; London: Secker & Warburg, 1989);

Lo strano caso della Hanau 1609 (Milan: Bompiani, 1989);

I limiti dell'interpretazione (Milan: Bompiani, 1990); translated by Eco as *The Limits of Interpretation* (Bloomington: Indiana University Press, 1990);

Stelle e stellette: la via lattea mormorò (Turin: Melangolo, 1991);

Vocali, by Eco and Paolo Domenico Malvinni (Naples: Guida, 1991);

Gli gnomi di Gnù, by Eco and Eugenio Carmi (Milan: Bompiani, 1992);

Il secondo diario minimo (Milan: Bompiani, 1992);

Interpretation and Overinterpretation, by Eco, Richard Rorty, Jonathan Culler, and Christine Brooke-Rose, edited by Stefan Collini (Cambridge: Cambridge University Press, 1992);

La ricerca della lingua perfetta nella cultura europea (Rome-Bari: Laterza, 1993); translated by James Fentress as *The Search for the Perfect Language* (Oxford: Blackwell, 1995);

Six Walks in the Fictional Woods (Cambridge, Mass: Harvard University Press, 1994); translated by Eco as *Sei passeggiate nei boschi narrativi* (Milan: Bompiani, 1994);

L'isola del giorno prima (Milan: Bompiani, 1994); translated by Weaver as *The Island of the Day Before* (New York: Harcourt, Brace, 1995; Secker & Warburg, 1995);

In cosa crede chi non crede?, by Eco and Carlo Maria Martini (Rome: Liberal, 1996);

Cinque scritti morali (Milan: Bompiani, 1997);

Kant e l'ornitorinco (Milan: Bompiani, 1997).

Editions in English: *The Aesthetics of Chaosmos: The Middle Ages of James Joyce* translated by Ellen Esrock (Tulsa: University of Tulsa Press, 1982), republished as *The Middle Ages of James Joyce* (Harvard University Press, 1989)–includes selection from *Opera aperta;*

Travels in Hyperreality, translated by William Weaver (San Diego: Harcourt Brace Jovanovich, 1986)republished as *Faith in Fakes: Essays* (London: Secker & Warburg, 1986);–includes selections from *Sette anni di desiderio, Il costume di casa* and *Dalla periferia dell'impero;*

The Open Work, translated by Anna Cancogni (Cambridge: Harvard University Press, 1989)–includes *Opera aperta* and selections from *Apocalittici e integrati, La struttura assente,* and *La definizione dell'arte;*

Misreadings, translated by Weaver (San Diego: Harcourt, Brace, 1993; London: Cape, 1993)–comprised of selections from *Diario minimo;*

How to Travel with a Salmon and Other Essays translated by Weaver (New York: Harcourt, Brace, 1994; Secker & Warburg, 1994)–includes selections from *Il secondo diario minimo;*

Apocalypse Postponed, translated by Robert Lumley and others (Bloomington: Indiana University Press, 1994)–includes selections from *Apocalittici e integrati, Dalla periferia dell'impero,* and *Sette anni di desiderio.*

OTHER: *Storia figurata delle invenzioni,* edited by Eco and G. B. Zorzoli (Milan: Bompiani, 1961); translated by Anthony Lawrence as *The Picture History of Inventions* (New York: Macmillan, 1963);

Il caso Bond, edited by Eco and Oreste Del Buono (Milan: Bompiani, 1965);

L'arte come mestiere, edited by Eco (Milan: Bompiani, 1969);

Cent'anni dopo: il ritorno dell'intreccio, edited by Eco and Cesare Sughi (Milan: Bompiani, 1971);

I fumetti di Mao, edited by Eco, Jean Chesneaux, and Gino Nebiolo (Bari: Laterza, 1971);

Rudolf Arnheim and others, *Estetica e teoria dell'informazione,* edited by Eco (Milan: Bompiani, 1972);

Enrico Baj, *Apocalisse,* edited by Eco (Milan: Mazzotta, 1979);

A Semiotic Landscape, edited by Eco, Seymour Chatman, and Jean-Marie Klinkenberg, Proceedings of the first Congress of the International Association for Semiotic Studies, Milan, June 1974 (The Hague: Mouton, 1979);

"Function and Sign: The Semiotics of Architecture," six chapters revised and translated by David Osmone-Smith and others from *La struttura assente,* in *Signs, Symbols, and Architecture,* edited by Geoffrey Broadbent, Richard Brunt, and Charles Jencks (New York: Wiley, 1980), pp. 11-69;

Raymond Queneau, *Esercizi di stile,* introduced and translated by Eco (Turin, 1983);

Il segno dei tre, edited by Eco and Thomas A. Sebeok (Milan: Bompiani, 1983); translated as *The Sign of Three: Dupin, Holmes, Peirce* (Bloomington: Indiana University Press, 1983);

Trent'anni di costume. Parte prima, edited by Eco (Milan: L'Espresso, 1985);

Meaning and Mental Representations, edited by Eco, Marco Santambrogio, and Patrizia Violi (Bloomington, 1988);

On the Medieval Theory of Signs, edited by Eco and Costantino Marmo (Amsterdam: J. Benjamins, 1989);

Encyclomedia, four CD roms directed by Eco (Milan: Opera multimedia, 1995).

Umberto Eco (photograph by Lucien Clergue and Spadem)

The long list of Umberto Eco's books and publications contains only three novels, *Il nome della rosa* (1980; translated as *The Name of the Rose,* 1983), *Il pendolo di Foucault* (1988; translated as *Foucault's Pendulum,* 1989), and *L'isola del giorno prima* (1994; translated as *The Island of the Day Before,* 1995), but their remarkable international success has made him the most famous Italian novelist writing today. Before the appearance of his first novel, Eco, a man of encyclopedic learning, was already well known for his contributions to the discipline of semiotics, as a prolific author of books and essays on a wide range of scholarly subjects, and as a gifted writer on politics and popular culture. His novels and other writings have been translated into many languages, and he has lectured and taught at universities all over the world.

As one of Italy's most prominent writers Eco remains resolutely Italian. Yet he is also a cosmopolitan intellectual whose personality and work are well known throughout the world. The enormous success of his novels, the first two in particular, has made him perhaps the most influential of contemporary European intellectuals. As such, he has restored Italy and its intellectual tradition to a position of prominence in European cultural life.

Eco's novels represent only a fraction of his output and cannot be separated from his work as a philosopher, historian, literary critic, and aesthetician. His novels issue from and elaborate upon themes that are treated extensively in his other writings. Accordingly, anyone who wishes to study Eco as a novelist cannot afford to ignore his critical and theoretical work.

Umberto Eco was born at Alessandria, in Piemonte, on 5 January 1932. His father was an accountant at a bathtub manufacturer; one grandfather was a typographer and the other a tailor. The first in his family to attend a university, he studied at the University of Turin, graduating in 1954 with a degree in philosophy. At Turin he came under the lasting influence of the philosopher Luigi Pareyson, under whose guidance he wrote his thesis, which became his first published book, *Il problema estetico in San Tommaso* (1956; translated as *The Aesthetics of Thomas Aquinas,* 1988). A substantial essay titled "Sviluppo dell'estetica medievale" (translated as *Art and*

Beauty in the Middle Ages, 1986) appeared in 1959 as a chapter of *Momenti e problemi di storia dell'estetica.* He later revised and enlarged the chapter as *Arte e bellezza nell'estetica medievale* (1987).

In 1961 Eco received his Libera Docenza (a degree that is roughly equivalent to the Ph.D.) in aesthetics, and from that year until 1964 he held the position of lecturer in aesthetics at both the University of Turin and the Politecnico in Milan. He was appointed professor of visual communication at the University of Florence in 1966, and in 1969 he returned to the Politecnico as professor of semiotics. The breadth of his interests was evident in the early stages of his career. Eco's collaborator in editing *Storia figurata delle invenzioni* (1961; translated as *The Picture History of Inventions,* 1963), was not, as one might expect, a historian or philosopher but the physicist Giovanni Battista Zorzoli, one of his colleagues at the Milan Politecnico. *Opera aperta: forma e indeterminazione nelle poetiche contemporanee* (1962; translated as *The Open Work,* 1989), the book that established his reputation in Italy, moves far beyond the medieval focus of his studies at Turin, containing discussions of the music of Karlheinz Stockhausen, Luciano Berio, Pierre Boulez, and Henri Pousseur as well as of the mobile sculptures of Alexander Calder.

Although one might be tempted to associate Eco with the conventional notion of "arts and letters," during his years at Florence and the Politecnico he was in fact a member of the faculty of architecture. *La struttura assente: Introduzione alla ricerca semiologica* (The Absent Structure: Introduction to the Study of Semiotics, 1968) contains an extended treatment of architecture as a medium of communication, a subject to which he has returned throughout his career. Thus his 1975 essay "Nel cuore dell'impero: viaggio nell'iperrealtà," republished in *Dalla periferia dell'impero* (From the Outskirts of the Empire, 1977) and translated as "Travels in Hyperreality" in the 1986 collection bearing the same title, deals with American phenomena such as San Simeon, the Getty Museum, Disneyland, the San Diego Zoo, and Redwood City's Marine World Africa. To take another example, the architectural details of the great monastery that provides the setting for *The Name of the Rose* are so meticulously described that the monastery itself, in particular its labyrinthine library, could almost be regarded as one of the main characters of the novel.

In 1971 Eco became associate professor of semiotics at the University of Bologna, assuming his current position of full professor in 1975 (he holds the first chair of semiotics ever to be established at an Italian university). As his academic distinction and reputation grew, he was invited to lecture and teach at many institutions in Europe and in North and South America. In the United States he was appointed visiting professor at New York University in 1969 and 1976; at Northwestern University in 1972; at the University of California, San Diego in 1975; at Yale University in 1977; and Columbia University in 1978. During these years he also lectured at a wide variety of other American colleges and universities, forging a close association with Indiana University, one of the major American centers of semiotic studies. Eco's reputation in the United States was furthered by his work on Charles Sanders Peirce, the American philosopher, physicist, and mathematician who was a towering figure in the development of semiotics.

Not only did Eco continue to produce books and articles at a rapid pace but also he remained intensely involved in fostering semiotics as an academic discipline. He was active on the editorial boards of several semiotic publications, and in 1971 he founded the semiotic journal (*VS*). From 1972 to 1979 he served as secretary general of the International Association for Semiotic Studies, and in 1979 he became its vice president. In 1976 he was appointed director of the Instituto di Discipline della Comunicazione e dello Spettacolo (Institute for Communication and Performing Arts) at the University of Bologna.

While pursuing this highly successful university career, Eco was not confined by his academic roles. In 1954, the year of his graduation from the University of Turin, he began a five-year stint in Milan working on cultural programming for RAI, the Italian radio and television network. From 1959 to 1965 he held the position of senior nonfiction editor at the Milanese publishing firm of Bompiani, which became the publisher of nearly all of his books. As his blossoming academic career led to appointments elsewhere, he maintained his identification with Milan, where he continues to reside even after assuming his position at Bologna. During the academic year he spends four days a week in Bologna.

A member of the Italian neoavant-garde, Eco became a frequent contributor to *Il Verri,* a progressive literary journal founded in 1956 by the critic Luciano Anceschi. He was one of the founders of the Gruppo '63, a group of avant-garde writers and critics that held its first meeting in Palermo in October 1963 to discuss the function of literature and the role of the intellectual in contemporary Italian society. Eco was also involved

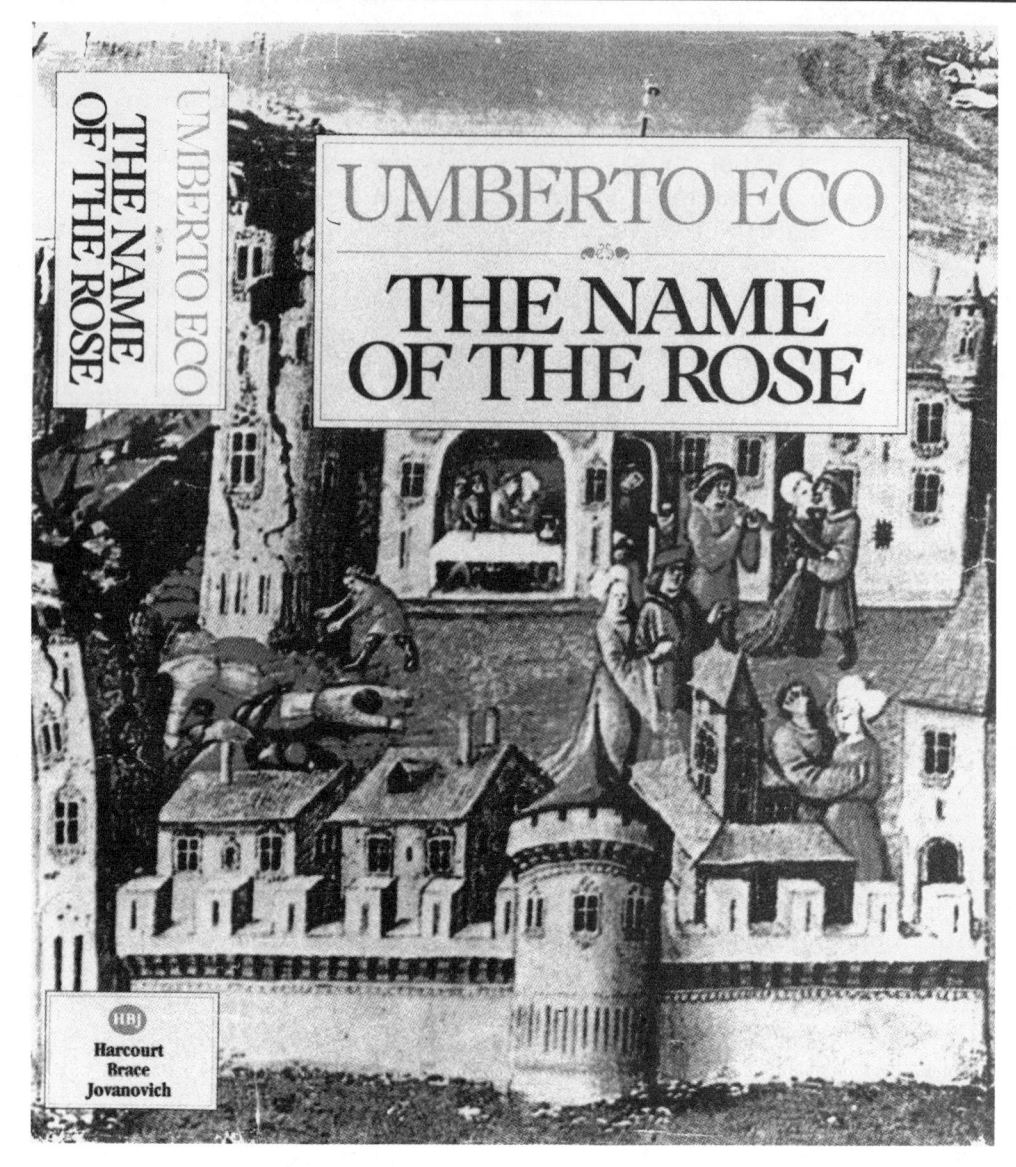

Dust jacket for the American edition of Eco's 1980 novel, which brought him international acclaim

with *Quindici,* the short-lived journal founded by the group in 1967.

In the early 1960s Eco began writing on various aspects of daily life, ranging from sports to politics and culture, for the daily and weekly press. He wrote columns for such widely read publications as *Il Giorno, La Stampa, Il Corriere della sera, La Repubblica, L'Espresso,* and *Il Manifesto.* Several of his books are collections of his writings for newspapers and periodicals.

There are those, Americans in particular, who might see a conflict between Eco's journalistic work—not to mention his involvement in politics and his career as a novelist—and his work as a scholar and university professor. Indeed, in a preface written specifically for American readers of *Travels in Hyperreality* (1986), Eco has recorded his answer to an American interviewer who once asked him how he managed to reconcile his academic career and his habit of writing for newspapers and magazines:

> My answer was that this habit is common to all European intellectuals, in Germany, France, Spain, and, naturally, Italy; all countries where a scholar or a scientist often feels required to speak out in the papers, to comment, if only from the point of view of his own interests and special field, on events that concern all citizens. And I added, somewhat maliciously, that if there was any problem with this it was not my problem as a European intellectual; it was more a problem of American intellectuals, who live in a country where the division of labor between university professors and militant intellectuals is much more strict than in our countries.

Eco might have added that his political concerns have also played a large part in his theoretical and scholarly writings. His words give a clear picture of his conception of himself and his role as an intellectual. In spite of his close ties to the United States, he views himself as a European and, above all, as an Italian intellectual.

By the end of the 1970s Eco was well known as a critic, a journalist, and a politically involved intellectual. No one, however, could have predicted the great leap in his fame—and fortune—that would follow the appearance of *The Name of the Rose* in 1980. Set in a northern Italian monastery of the fourteenth century, the novel is replete with literary, philosophical, theological, and historical arcana, and it is punctuated by many passages in Latin and other languages. There is only one "sex scene" in the book, and it is quite tame by contemporary standards. Such is the book that sold more than a million copies in Italy, where it won several prizes, among them the highly regarded Premio Strega. Translated into French in 1982, it became a best-seller in France, winning the Prix Medicis. *Il nome della rosa* was translated into English in 1983, and in the United States the hardcover edition remained on the best-seller list for forty weeks, ultimately selling over one million copies. The paperback rights brought $550,000, reputed to be the largest sum of money ever paid for a paperback translation; and sales of the paperback edition exceeded eight hundred thousand copies within the first three months after its appearance. *The Name of the Rose* has been translated into more than thirty-six languages, including Japanese, Chinese, Korean, Vietnamese, Turkish, and Arabic. A motion-picture version directed by Jean-Jacques Annaud was released in 1986. Within a few years after the publication of his first novel, Umberto Eco had become one of the most well-known writers in the world.

The Name of the Rose has been described as a medieval murder mystery. That description is accurate, for the novel is set in 1327, at the end of the High Middle Ages, and its plot involves seven spectacular and mysterious murders. In light of his earlier work it is not surprising that Eco chose a medieval setting for his first novel. Offering his own reflections on the genesis of the novel in his *Postille al "Nome della Rosa"* (1983; translated as *Postscript to "The Name of the Rose,"* 1984), Eco writes that he chose the Middle Ages because they are "his day-to-day fantasy." Describing himself as "a medievalist in hibernation," he reminds readers of his early interest in medieval aesthetics, on which he began to publish in the 1950s. He also notes that he returned to the medieval tradition in 1962 for his work on Joyce and again in the early 1970s, when he published a study of the illuminations for an eighth-century commentary on the Apocalypse by the Spanish abbot Beatus of Liébana.

The connection of the novel with the detective story is as clear as its medieval setting. Called upon to solve the murders is the wise Franciscan friar William of Baskerville, whose name recalls Sir Arthur Conan Doyle's great creation, Sherlock Holmes, the master of detection who is the hero of *The Hound of the Baskervilles* (1902) and many other tales. Furthermore, the story of the novel is told by the Benedictine novice Adso of Melk, who describes himself as William's "scribe and disciple," a role that parallels that of Doctor Watson, the admiring narrator of Holmes's exploits.

Charles Sanders Peirce was also on Eco's mind while he was working on the novel. In 1978, two years before the novel's publication, Eco gave a lecture at Columbia University applying Peirce's notion of abductive logic to the methods employed by Holmes and Voltaire's Zadig, and in 1979 he conducted a six-month seminar at Bologna on Peirce and the detective novel. During this period he was also involved in editing a volume of essays dealing with the semiotics of detective fiction: that book, to which Eco contributed the final version of his 1978 Columbia lecture, was published in 1983 as *The Sign of Three: Dupin, Holmes, Peirce*. The Italian version, *Il segno dei tre,* appeared at the same time.

Commenting on Eco's novel in his introduction to the English translation of *Opera aperta*, David Robey notes that passages from Eco's contribution to *The Sign of Three* sometimes appear in *The Name of the Rose* as the words of the purportedly medieval William of Baskerville. Indeed, as Robey observes, William often seems surprisingly well acquainted with semiotic theory, displaying a view of knowledge that Eco would define as characteristically modern. According to Robey, not only do William's acts of detection serve to illustrate Eco's conception of the essential nature of all semiotic processes, but "he also proposes a theory of detection strikingly similar to Eco's and Peirce's." Thus, *The Name of the Rose* is no ordinary detective novel, and it does not offer anything resembling a conventional picture of the Middle Ages.

William's great adversary—his Professor Moriarty, as it were—is a blind Spanish monk, "venerable in age and wisdom," who is the resolute guardian of the abbey's labyrinthine library. As Eco notes in his *Postscript*, "library plus blind man can only equal Borges." Thus the blind monk's name, Jorge of Burgos, echoes that of Jorge Luis Borges, the twentieth-century Argentinean writer, also blind, who was

Sean Connery and F. Murray Abraham in the 1986 movie version of The Name of the Rose

much concerned with libraries and labyrinths and whose work intersects with Eco's at other key points. In many interviews, however, Eco has taken pains to point out that Jorge is not Borges and that the analogies are not ideological but, so to speak, "pictorial." The Jorge of the novel conceives the library as a closed system whose world of meaning remains subject to one absolute truth. "The library," he insists, "is testimony to truth and error." On the other hand, for William as for Eco, libraries and the books they contain constitute an open universe that speaks in many voices and is accessible to the free movement of thought. Detectives must become skillful semioticians: they must learn, in William's words, "to recognize the evidence through which the world speaks to us like a great book."

Jorge's world is a rigidly ordered cosmos in which there is a single path to the truth, but William comes to deny the validity of any such order. When he finally uncovers the solution to the mystery, he realizes that although he arrived at the solution by assuming the existence of a pattern that seemed to underlie all the crimes, in reality his discovery was accidental. He was, he says, pursuing the plan of a perverse and rational mind where there was no real plan. Instead, the planner "was overcome by his own initial design and there began a series of causes, and concauses, and of causes contradicting one another, which proceeded on their own, creating relations that did not stem from any plan." As the novel comes to its end, he informs Adso that "the order our mind imagines is like a net, or like a ladder, built to attain something." Once the goal is reached, he says, in an allusion to Ludwig Wittgenstein, "you must throw the ladder away, because you discover that, even if it was useful, it was meaningless."

In the context of the novel these words may seem elegiac, for they signal the end of the Middle Ages and the arrival of the modern era, the death of one era and the birth of another, the passing from one way of thinking about the universe to another. But when William's words are placed in a modern context, there is nothing melancholy about them at all. In his *Postscript* Eco offers a discussion of the labyrinth as "an abstract model of conjecturality," noting the existence of three kinds of labyrinths. First there is the classical labyrinth, the labyrinth of Theseus, the Minotaur, and Ariadne's thread. In this kind of labyrinth no one is allowed to get lost: the classical labyrinth is "the Ariadne's-thread of itself." Next there is the "mannerist maze," in which there are many blind alleys and it is easy to get lost: this labyrinth, Eco says, is a model of the trial-and-error process. Finally, there is the net, which Eco associates with what the French writers Gilles Deleuze and Félix Guattari call the rhizome:

> The rhizome is so constructed that every path can be connected with every other one. It has no center, no periphery, no exit, because it is potentially infinite. The space of conjecture is a rhizome space. The labyrinth of my library is still a mannerist labyrinth, but the world in which William realizes he is living already has a rhizome structure; that is, it can be structured but is never structured definitively.

The rhizome provides the model for the conception of knowledge joyfully espoused by Eco and discovered by William at the end of the novel. When the abbey's labyrinthine library is destroyed by fire, the old way of knowing perishes along with it, and William is compelled to embark on a new way of thought.

Jorge's orderly universe is a deadly serious place where there is no room for laughter, for which he has contempt. When William raises the issue of laughter, the blind monk argues that a debate about laughter can only be an idle debate, claiming emphatically, against William's objections, that "Christ did not laugh." Laughter, on the other hand, is central to the logic of the open universe. In the world of nature and knowledge as conceived by William and the novelist who created him, laughter becomes, as William says, an eminently suitable instrument for undermining the false authority of absurd propositions. The debate about laughter, far from being idle, is central to the plot of the novel, and the lost second book of Aristotle's *Poetics,* whose subject was comedy, becomes a key element in the story.

Eco's conception of his own role as the author of *The Name of the Rose* remains true to his belief in the open work. He has resisted the temptation to offer interpretations of his novel, telling us in his *Postscript* that narrators should not provide interpretations for their own texts. A novel is "a machine for generating interpretations," and an author should not attempt to interfere with its operation. He goes on to remark, perhaps somewhat facetiously, that an author should die once the writing is finished "so as not to trouble the path of the text." *The Name of the Rose* has been an extremely effective machine, engendering a voluminous amount of interpretation since its appearance in 1980. Far from standing in its way, Eco appears to have taken great pleasure in observing the production of the commentary his novel has generated. He has listened with obvious relish while others delivered papers on his novel, all the while refraining from offering a single interpretation of his own.

In 1988 Eco consolidated his success as a novelist with the publication of *Il pendolo di Foucault* (translated as *Foucault's Pendulum,* 1989). Although his second novel did not enjoy the astonishing level of success attained by *The Name of the Rose,* by normal standards its success was also enormous. Translated into twenty-six languages, it, like its predecessor, also became a worldwide best-seller and inspired a large body of commentary.

Unlike *The Name of the Rose,* Eco's second novel is set in the contemporary world (1970–1984), telling the story of three intellectuals, one of whom—like the author himself—happens to be Piemontese. They work as editors for a press in Milan and are much absorbed with the potential of computers: like the library in *The Name of the Rose,* their computer, named Abulafia, nearly becomes one of the book's principal characters. Yet while *The Name of the Rose* moves forward from the Middle Ages to the intellectual issues of the twentieth century, *Foucault's Pendulum* moves backward, confronting the reader with an avalanche of arcane learning about such subjects as the Knights Templar, the Cabala, and the Rosicrucians.

In his 1990 article "Pendulum Diary," William Weaver, who has translated all three of Eco's novels into English, remarks on the tremendous amount of "sheer information" that Eco puts into his fiction, noting that *Foucault's Pendulum,* like its predecessor, is marked by elaborate and abstruse references, extravagant linguistic play, and a formidable number of quotations. Weaver reflects on one day of work:

> In today's stint–I reached page (or rather, galley) 19 before quitting–there are lists of old cars, planes, machines of all kinds, descriptions of Lavoisier's instruments (I am reminded of those lists of heresies, of precious stones, in *The Name of the Rose*); I have figured some of them out, but have much more investigating to do, and will in the end consult the author. Often even the Brittanica and the Larousse fail me. Who is Gramme, of whom is there a statue in the Conservatoire des Arts et Métiers, the important setting of chapter one? I assume an eighteenth-century scientist. Not terribly important to the novel, but I still must check.

Thus it turns out that Eco's second novel, despite its contemporary setting, is at least as challenging for the reader as his first.

The story told in *The Name of the Rose* is set in one place, the monastery, while the loci of the events depicted in *Foucault's Pendulum* are various. Eco takes his readers from Paris, where the novel begins, to Milan, which provides its main setting, to

Dust jacket for the American edition of Eco's 1988 novel, in which the Diabolicals search for the secret knowledge that will give them absolute power

Piemonte, where it ends, and even to Brazil, the scene of one of its most riveting episodes. This easy movement from place to place, along with many other details, gives the novel a certain autobiographical flavor, for Piemonte, Milan, Paris, and Brazil have been places of great significance in Eco's life and career.

Although many readers have stressed the differences between *Foucault's Pendulum* and *The Name of the Rose,* the two novels are in many ways quite similar. Perhaps the most important likeness is their mutual focus on the ways in which human beings come to understand the world. Like Jorge in *The Name of the Rose,* the Diabolicals of Eco's second novel are obsessed with what they imagine to be the secret of the universe. The Diabolicals are deadly serious, fanatic believers in a debased version of Bacon's assertion that knowledge is power. They hope to gain possession of the secret that will make them masters of the world, searching for the map that will lead them to the hidden source of a power far greater than anything yet discovered.

Eco's narrative exposes the futility—and the mortal danger—of their quest, a quest that puts the Diabolicals at odds with life itself. One of the novel's most arresting passages describes a magic moment of understanding that occurs in Piemontese on a hillside covered with vines and peach trees. It is here that one of the protagonists finds an answer for those who seek to uncover the plan of the universe, who yearn for the secret and go in search of the map that will lead them to it. "There is no Map," he says.

There is no plan: the secret, he has come to see, is that there is no secret; the answer is that there is no answer. There are only the most marvelous and intricate of riddles. In the end, then, Eco's second novel joins with his first in giving a narrative expression to his semiological creed.

Eco's third novel, *L'isola del giorno prima* (The Island of the Day Before), was published in late 1994, and by early 1996 it had already appeared in English, French, Portuguese, Spanish, and German. Its plot, like those of its predecessors, revolves around the search for a secret. In this case the secret is the location of the *Punto Fijo*, the fixed point on the earth from which all other longitudes can be established, making it also the point that divides one day from another. The protagonist, Roberto della Griva, is a young Piemontese from an estate "along the border of the province of Alessandria," Eco's own native region. After passing through a series of plot twists that take him as far as Paris, Roberto is charged by Cardinal Mazarin—né Giulio Mazarini—with finding the *Punto Fijo*, a location vital to the interests of the European colonial powers of the mid seventeenth century, the period in which the novel is set. In Eco's third novel, as in his first two, knowledge, learning, and science are linked to power.

Like his predecessors in *The Name of the Rose* and *Foucault's Pendulum*, Roberto discovers the secret, assuming there really is a secret, by mistake. He survives a shipwreck only to end up on yet another ship. This second ship, the *Daphne,* lies deserted, resting at anchor in the bay of a mysterious and beautiful island in the South Seas. Roberto's journey to this point has already been a marvelous one, involving war, love, and the prodigious bursts of learning to which all of Eco's protagonists—and all his readers—are routinely exposed. His time aboard the *Daphne,* however, provides the climax of his tale. It is then that he meets Father Caspar Wanderdrossel, an old Jesuit who is one of Eco's most endearing characters, and comes to grips with Ferrante, the seemingly imaginary half brother who has haunted him the whole of his life.

The end of the novel provides one of its most powerful moments. Roberto has left Europe forever, setting out for the New World at a time when the old Europe is about to disappear. Yet at the end, when he finally learns to swim and leaves the *Daphne* for the mysterious island, he is heading toward the past, for the island is the *island of the day before*—when Roberto crosses over to it it will be yesterday. *The Island of the Day Before* is a novel that is meticulous about matters of time, and this marvelously appropriate conflation of past and future brings it to a satisfying conclusion.

Readers know from the novel's beginning, when they learn that Roberto's father "spoke French with his wife, the local dialect with his peasants, and Italian with foreigners," that Eco is going to offer another multinational and multilingual romp. Leaving Piemonte, Roberto travels to Spain and France, and from there he embarks on his fateful sea voyage. Along the way he and the reader encounter a dizzying variety of languages—not only all the languages of southern Europe, but also German, Dutch, English, Latin, and ancient Greek.

The *Island of the Day Before* is perhaps the most literary of Eco's novels. It is, of course, full of allusions. The references to Daniel Defoe's *Robinson Crusoe* (1719) are obvious, but readers will also detect traces, among many others, of William Shakespeare's *The Tempest* (1623) as well as the work of Dante Alighieri, Jonathan Swift, Voltaire, Jules Verne, Alexandre Dumas, Eugène Sue, and Victor Hugo. The novel also directs a great deal of attention to the problem of the narrator. *The Name of the Rose* is presented as Adso's narrative, discovered in manuscript and provided with a preface, while *Foucault's Pendulum* comes in the form of a conventional first-person narrative. The narrative of Eco's third novel is far more complex. The unnamed narrator has found Roberto's diary, written during his days aboard the *Daphne,* cast as a series of letters to his beloved back in Paris. Why would Roberto write such letters, the narrator asks, when "he knows, assumes, fears that these letters will never arrive and that he is writing them only for his own torment?" The narrator gives a simple answer: "Roberto was writing for himself." He then comes to the obvious conclusion: "The situation is the stuff of a novel."

Where *The Name of the Rose* purports to present the manuscript containing Adso's narrative, Eco's third novel gives the narrator's version of Roberto's story. Readers do get a fair dose of Roberto's own writing, but for the most part the story is told in the narrator's words, not Roberto's. The narrator is also an unabashed interpreter of Roberto's narrative, sorting out facts, commenting on the significance of events, and offering observations on the characters. In short, the narrator, whose identity remains mysterious to the end, becomes a player who intervenes in Roberto's story. Such qualities make *The Island of the Day Before* more obviously literary than the two novels that preceded it.

The success of his novels and the steady progress of his scholarly work throughout the 1980s brought Eco the highest academic and public distinctions. In 1983 the Rotary Club of Florence hon-

Dust jacket for the American edition of Eco's 1994 novel, in which the protagonist searches for Punto Fijo, *the fixed point that divides one day from another*

ored him with its Columbus Award, and in 1985 he was made a commander of France's Ordre des Arts et des Lettres. In the same year he also received the Marshall McLuhan Award from UNESCO Canada and Teleglobe. Since 1985 universities throughout the world have awarded him twenty-four honorary degrees. In 1990 he was Tanner Lecturer at the University of Cambridge, and in the following year he was named an Honorary Fellow of Rewley House at Oxford. In 1992 he was appointed Professeur Étranger at the College de France, and in 1993 he gave the Charles Eliot Norton Lectures at Harvard, which were published in 1994 as *Six Walks in the Fictional Woods*. Since 1992 he has been a member of the International Forum of UNESCO and of the Académie Universelle des Cultures in Paris.

All the while, Eco has remained fully involved in the academic pursuits to which he was devoted before he became famous. His scholarly and theoretical writing continues unabated, as does his commitment to the progress of semiotics. He remains the editor of *Versus* and continues to serve on the editorial boards of other journals. At the same time, the enormous success of Eco's novels has greatly intensified academic interest in his work. His fame as a novelist has led to an exponential increase in invitations to lecture and teach at institutions all over the world. Likewise, in the years since 1985 there has been an explosion in the number of doctoral dissertations written on his work, with the novels being their principal concern.

At the end of the 1980s, acting partly in response to some of the excesses to which his work has been subjected, Eco turned his attention to the ways in which the act of interpretation is constrained. In *I limiti dell'interpretazione* (1990; translated as *The Limits of Interpretation*), he emphasizes that the open-ended reading he advocated in *Opera aperta* remains "an activity elicited by (and aiming at interpreting) a *work*." What he was considering there was "the dialectics between the rights of texts and the rights of their interpreters." He goes on to define two extremes of "epistemological fanaticism." One assumes that "to interpret a text means to find out the meaning intended by its original author or—in any case—its objective nature an essence, an essence which, as such, is independent of our interpretation." The other extreme is "to assume that texts can be interpreted in infinite ways," to say that interpretation has no object, that there are no unacceptable interpretations, that every act of interpretation will have a "happy ending." "The limits of interpretation," Eco concludes, "coincide with the rights of the text." He is careful to note, however, that by the rights of the text he does not mean the rights of its author. In asserting that texts, like the universe itself, can impose limitations on their interpreters even if their authors cannot and by continuing resolutely to oppose all forms of intellectual fanaticism, Eco remains faithful to the conception of knowledge advanced in his novels as well as in his previous theoretical work.

This fidelity to his work as a whole can also be found in *La ricerca della lingua perfetta nella cultura europea* (1993; translated as *The Search for the Perfect Language*, 1995), an immensely learned book that joins *The Name of the Rose* and *The Island of the Day Before* as Eco's joyful affirmations of the irreducibility of linguistic pluralism. The *confusio linguarum*, Eco suggests, did not result from the invention of new languages but from the fragmentation of a unique language that existed from the beginning and in which all the other languages were already contained. In whatever language they speak, people can find "the spirit, the breath, the perfume, the traces of the original polylingualism." Thus "our mother tongue," the language given by God to Adam, "was not a single language but rather a complex of all languages." Adam's successors, Eco argues, must embark on the long and arduous path of apprenticeship necessary to recover the marvelous gift of language that God has promised.

Personal acquaintances of Eco often speak of his zest for life, his devotion to laughter, and his unquenchable sense of humor. These characteristics emerge in the portrait of the author that William Weaver paints in his "Pendulum Diary." Eco is depicted during the course of a day in Bologna: returning to his apartment after a morning spent teaching, eating lunch, bargaining at an antiquarian bookstore, working with Weaver in the afternoon on some of the problems he has encountered in translating *Foucault's Pendulum,* and ending the day, quite late, at a lively party given by students. Weaver gives a vivid picture of Eco's appetite for work. Before the party, while Weaver is in his hotel room, resting after their afternoon's work, Eco, who would be leaving for Palermo in the morning and for New York only a few days later, writes four of his weekly columns for *L'Espresso!*

Four weeks later Weaver spends a morning working with Eco at his home in Milan:

> Umberto, though he had arrived from New York (and London) only the night before last, was up and dressed, full of pep, eager to show me his Christmas present from his son Stefano: a Casio saxophone. He immediately played "As Time Goes By" on it for me, in about eight different keys.

When they set to work Eco is "immediately helpful, jumping up constantly from the table, to rush from the dining room into the study, returning with an armful of books." Weaver reports that, although nearly all his problems are solved, sometimes Eco so swamps him with erudition that he becomes more bewildered than before. At one point, as they discuss the *genis,* the musical instrument played by one of the characters in the novel—and which Eco himself once had to play as a member of his parish band, Eco "stood up, grabbed the instrument and demonstrated, marching smartly up and down the apartment." Later, out for a "wonderful, relaxed evening" in the city with the author and his German-born wife, Renate, Weaver takes note of Eco's irrepressible energy. While his companions become exhausted, Eco, a true "noctambule," remains "keyed-up, reluctant to end the evening."

The energy, zest for life, and love of laughter that mark Eco as a person are all central features of all his writings, his novels included. In *The Name of the Rose* laughter becomes an instrument for exposing the vanity of human wishes for absolute knowledge and perfect order. "Perhaps the mission of those who love mankind," William suggests, "is to make people laugh at the truth, *to make truth laugh,* because the only truth lies in learning to free ourselves from the insane passion for the truth." It is the boundless energy of life itself that emerges in triumph at the end of *Foucault's Pendulum,* where the joke is on the Diabolicals, who remain insanely obsessed with the notion that they can capture the secret truth of the universe—but they will never get the joke and will never laugh.

Now in his sixties, Eco will likely continue to produce a wealth of writing—including, perhaps, a few more novels—in the years left to him. He and his work stand as convincing testimony against intellectual arrogance in all its forms. That one cannot know everything, he argues, does not mean that one knows nothing; if one cannot say everything, neither is one permitted to say just anything. His is a plea for sanity in an age given to ruinous extremes.

References:

Michael Caesar and Peter Hainsworth, "The Transformation of Postwar Italy," in their *Writers and Society in Contemporary Italy* (New York: St. Martin's Press, 1984), pp. 1-34;

JoAnn Cannon, *Postmodern Italian Fiction: The Crises of Reason in Calvino, Eco, Sciascia, Malerba* (Rutherford, N.J.: Fairleigh Dickinson University Press, 1989);

Rocco Capozzi, ed., *Reading Eco. An Anthology* (Bloomington & Indianapolis: Indiana University Press, 1997);

Theresa Coletti, *Naming the Rose: Eco, Medieval Signs, and Modern Theory* (Ithaca, N.Y.: Cornell University Press, 1988);

Teresa de Lauretis, *Umberto Eco* (Florence: La Nuova Italia, 1981);

Margherita Ganeri, *Il "Caso" Eco* (Palermo: Palumbo, 1991);

Renato Giovannoli, ed., *Saggi su "Il Nome della Rosa"* (Milan: Bompiani, 1985);

Adele Haft, Jane G. White, and Robert J. White, *The Key to "The Name of the Rose"* (Harrington Park, N.J.: Ampersand, 1987);

"In Search of Eco's Roses," Special Issue *SubStance*, 47 (1985): 2-101;

M. Thomas Inge, ed., *Naming the Rose: Essays on Eco's "The Name of the Rose"* (Jackson: University Press of Mississippi, 1988);

Patrizia Magli, Giovanni Manetti, Patrizia Violi, eds., *Semiotica: storia, teoria, interpretazione. Saggi intorno a Umberto Eco* (Milan: Bompiani, 1992);

Costantino Marmo, introduction, *Il nome della rosa*, by Eco (Milan: Bompiani, 1990);

David Robey, "Umberto Eco," in *Writers and Society in Contemporary Italy,* edited by Caesar and Hainsworth (New York: St. Martin's Press, 1984), pp. 63-87; revised as introduction, *The Open Work,* translated by Anna Cancogni (Cambridge, Mass.: Harvard University Press, 1989);

Robey, "Umberto Eco: Theory and Practice in the Analysis of the Media," in *Culture and Conflict in Postwar Italy,* edited by Zygmunt G. Baranski and Robert Lumley (New York: St. Martin's Press, 1990), pp. 160-177;

Carl A. Rubino, "'To Make Truth Laugh': Umberto Eco and the Power of Laughter," in *Laughter Down the Centuries,* volume 3 edited by Siegfried Jäkel, Asko Timonen, and Veli-Matti Rissanen (Turku: Turen Yliopisto, 1997), pp. 257-263;

Rubino, "Joyous Entropy: The Phenomenon of Laughter and the Science of Thermodynamics," in *Laughter Down the Centuries,* volume 1, edited by Siegfried Jäkel, and Asko Timonen (Turku: Turen Yliopisto, 1994), pp. 134-144;

Walter E. Stephens, "Ec[h]o in Fabula," *Diacritics,* 13 (1983): 51-64;

"Swinging *Foucault's Pendulum,*" *MLN,* 107 (1992): v-vi, 819-904;

Christopher Wagstaff, "The Neo-avantgarde," in *Writers and Society in Contemporary Italy,* edited by Caesar and Hainsworth (New York: St. Martin's Press, 1984), pp. 35-61;

William Weaver, "Pendulum Diary," *Southwest Review,* 75 (Spring 1990): 150-178;

Weaver, "A Translator's Journey," *The New York Times Book Review,* 19 November 1995, pp. 16-20.

Franco Ferrucci
(20 September 1936 -)

Tommasina Gabriele
Wheaton College

BOOKS: *Addio al Parnaso* (Milan: Bompiani, 1971);
L'anatra nel cortile (Milan: Rizzoli, 1971);
Il cappello di Panama (Milan: Rizzoli, 1973);
L'assedio e il ritorno (Milan: Bompiani, 1974);
A sud di Santa Barbara (Milan: Rizzoli, 1976);
Il giardino simbolico: modelli letterari e autobiografia dell'opera (Rome: Bulzoni, 1980); translated by Ann Dunnigan as *The Poetics of Disguise: The Autobiography of the Work in Homer, Dante and Shakespeare* (Ithaca, N.Y.: Cornell University Press, 1980);
Lettera a un ragazzo sulla felicità (Milan: Bompiani, 1982); republished as *Lettera a me stesso ragazzo* (Milan: Bompiani, 1989);
Il mondo creato (Milan: Mondadori, 1986); translated by Ferrucci and Raymond Rosenthal as *The Life of God (As Told by Himself)* (Chicago: University of Chicago Press, 1996);
I satelliti di Saturno (Milan: Leonardo, 1989);
Il poema del desiderio: poetica e passione in Dante (Milan: Leonardo, 1990);
Boundaries: On Poets and Territory in Romantic Literature, edited by Luigi Ballerini (New York: Arts and Science Publications Office, New York University, 1991);
Fuochi (Turin: Einaudi, 1993);
Nuovo discorso sugli italiani and *Discorso sopra lo stato presente dei costumi degl'italiani di Giacomo Leopardi* (Milan: Mondadori, 1993);
Ars poetica (Turin: Il Melangolo, 1993);
Lontano da casa (Turin: Einaudi, 1996).

TRANSLATIONS: Michel Foucault, *Storia della follia nell'età classica* (Milan: Rizzoli, 1963);
Lyall Watson, *Supernatura* (Milan: Rizzoli, 1974);
Irving Shaw, *Lavoro di notte* (Milan: Rizzoli, 1977);
Oscar Wilde, *Il ritratto di Dorian Gray* (Turin: Einaudi, 1996).

Franco Ferrucci published his first novel, *L'anatra nel cortile* (The Duck in the Courtyard) in 1971. Yet even in his native Italy, Ferrucci was better known for his literary criticism and essays than

Franco Ferrucci (photograph by John Foley)

his novels until the late 1980s. As Furio Colombo notes in the 20 September 1986 *La Stampa,* Ferrucci "è stato subito riconosciuto come il miglior saggista letterario della sua generazione" (was quickly identified as the best literary critic of his generation). His recognition as a novelist surged forward with Umberto Eco's praise of Ferrucci's ambitious and original novel *Il mondo creato* (1986; translated as *The Life of God (as Told by Himself)*, 1996). This work was presented at the prestigious Frankfurt Book Fair in 1988, resulting in the republication of it as well as Ferrucci's earlier novels and essays, sometimes in paperback editions, such as the 1991 Mondadori's Oscar edition of *L'assedio e il ritorno* (The Seige and the Return, 1974). Regarding Ferrucci's importance as a novelist, a journalist for *Epoca* wrote, "Ce l'avevamo davanti agli occhi, ma non siamo stati capaci di vederlo" (He was before our very eyes, but we were not capable of seeing him).

Ferrucci was born 20 September 1936 in Pisa and attended the University of Pavia. Upon graduation he immigrated to France before moving to California in 1963 and finally settling in New York City, where he lived for many years. *Settling* is perhaps a misleading term for this author-professor-critic, who is reticent when it comes to the details of his personal life. Like his wandering characters, from the questing young narrator-protagonist of his first novel to his timeless and homeless God in *Il mondo creato,* Ferrucci is always on the move. He still splits his time between the three countries—and the three major literatures—that constitute his literary and professional formation: Italy, the United States, and France. Each year he divides his time between New York City and Rome and makes occasional trips to Paris.

L'anatra nel cortile, a modern, existential bildungsroman, traces the protagonist from his childhood in Pisa, rendered with vivid metaphorical force, to college in Pavia, to the failure of his great love affair with Lina. The first section, titled "Nuvole" (Clouds), presents the pivotal themes of the novel: metamorphosis, exile, and imprisonment. The narrator traces the family's move from his home near the warm sea—a lost paradise—to a cold northern city. This wrench from the warm and aqueous womb to the urban world symbolizes the first archetypal exile, for which the father is blamed.

The Oedipal antagonism between father and son, which recurs throughout Ferrucci's works, is evident in the first paragraph, where the father is seen as moody and omnipotent, like an ancient Greek god. The son perceives his father's nature as extremely changeable: "nuvola a forma d'orso poi di drago o serpente infine d'anguilla" (a cloud in the form of a bear, then of a dragon or serpent, and finally of an eel). However, the oedipal complex and the existential crisis are portrayed in a parodic vein, for an essential characteristic of Ferrucci's narrative is his sense of humor, the light touch with which he handles his characters and their crises. The fight for primacy between father and son, for example, includes a melodramatic moment at the dinner table when the mother decides whom to serve first. The existential, oedipal ropes tighten dramatically around father and son on a freezing day; they turn to a church, which offers no refuge from the poverty and cold or from their social, economic, and spiritual rootlessness. As is often the case in Ferrucci's work, both religion and the church fail the individual in need. Soon after, the father apparently commits suicide by throwing himself (or does he fall?) into the freezing river.

The adolescent protagonist-narrator—often the central figure in Ferrucci's work—initiates the archetypal separation from his father by beginning a journey of his own. Detaching himself as well from his companion Marco, the first of many he will abandon in the course of the novel, this young Ulysses travels to Pisa and wanders around the countryside. The tension between his need for roots and his desire for freedom compels the narrator to keep moving. However, his search for roots coexists uneasily with a Pavesian fear of being tied to these very roots. As long as he is without ties, in a state of nonbelonging, with a still uncertain identity, everything is possible. His solitude and detachment from others—two other traits shared by many of Ferrucci's characters—weigh on him but also guarantee his inexhaustible opportunities to change, escape, and disguise himself successfully. He returns home only to learn of his father's terminal illness. Thus the first section, which depicts a stage of paternal reign, of childhood, and of transformations, ends with the death of the father and the end of the narrator's adolescence.

In the second section the narrator enrolls at the university in Pavia and earns his keep while attending school. He believes he can be sufficient unto himself and maintains his independence by excluding others. The city functions as a sort of limbo, providing a place and time for him to resist the truth of his nature. The fog in Pavia helps him "a nascondermi, a sparire" (to hide, to disappear).

At the university the narrator meets Professor Ferrante, the most provocative character in the novel because he is the most false, the most complex, and the most adept at wearing masks. Ferrante is crucial to the narrator's literary formation, both as reader and as writer, and the novel can be read as the bildungsroman of a writer in the making. As a child the narrator first became interested in his brother's books, then in the books "caged" in bookshop windows, and later in the books studied in school. But books, like people, can be false, mediocre, good, or dangerous. Significantly, Ferrante's books have all been tamed and organized while the narrator's books "make war."

Books provide a central topos in Ferrucci's novels and of course have great autobiographical and professional significance for the author. His first novel contains allusions to one of the authors Ferrucci has most studied, Dante Alighieri, as is evident in his play on Dante's famous opening lines of the *Inferno*—"nel bel mezzo della mia corsa nel labirinto, avevo avuto una visione" (in the middle of my

Dust jacket for the 1996 American edition of Ferrucci's 1986 novel, in which a forgetful God reconstructs His memories through writing

run in the labyrinth, I had had a vision). There are allusions as well to Elio Vittorini and also the Russian painter Marc Chagall. Books in *L'anatra nel cortile* along with the season of spring—echoing T. S. Eliot's cruel April in *The Waste Land* (1922)—flush the narrator out of his hiding place in Pavia. When the narrator finally leaves the city, he takes nothing of his experience except "i fogli su cui avevo ripreso a scrivere" (the pages on which I had resumed writing).

Also significant is the sea, archetypal symbol of life, death, and the unconscious. "Mare" (The Sea), the title of the third section, is about the protagonist's relationship with Lina, a character who obstinately refuses to disguise herself in falsehood. The catalyst for the narrator's ultimately coming to grips with his own nature, she refuses to become trapped in the games of camouflage at which most of the characters in the novel excel. When his Pygmalion-like attempt to change her is unsuccessful, the protagonist concedes: "Non potevo mascherare Lina" (I could not mask Lina). He admits that "tutto il mio castello di laboriose menzogne" (all of my castle of laborious lies) crumbles in the face of Lina's "quieta inafferabile essenza" (quiet, elusive essence).

Unable to bring his relationship with Lina to a breaking point through jealousies and tantrums, he discovers a way out through illness, whose symptoms include difficulty in breathing and claustrophobia. In his 1992 interview with Francesco Guardiani, the author remarks, "I cannot stay long in a room without windows or in an elevator. . . . I am claustrophobic, and every form of 'closed' life in itself gives me a sense of oppression." For the protagonist the cure, naturally, will necessitate his separation from Lina and his return to the sea, where the burgeoning writer in him abandons "l'illusione che scrivere fosse come parlare con qualcuno" (the illusion that writing is like talking to someone). He begins to write for himself and to understand his need as a writer and as an individual for "il star solo" (being alone).

The narrator confronts the image of death at Marina, the city of his convalescence, in the figure of his landlord, a sour old man filled with rage who with a hatchet cleaves the head of a duck from its body in the courtyard. In this scene that gives the novel its title, the headless body of the bird continues to run around within the enclosed yard. The horrifying image of unequal struggle, of senseless end, and of imprisonment reactivates the protagonist's existential anxiety.

Lured back to Pisa, he discovers that everything has changed. Lina has left without a trace. However, the image of his mother and his brother growing fat together like an old married couple reassures him that he escaped the matrimonial trap when he fled Lina. In Ferrucci's work marriage repeatedly assumes the negative form of a closed life. The protagonist's words to Lina before he leaves for the sea are reminiscent of Cesare Pavese: "Sono capace di stancarmi fino a odiare tutto quello che mi sta intorno, te compresa, e me ne vado perché questo non avvenga. . . . Essere sempre quello, ci pensi?, uguale a ieri, uguale a domani" (I am capable of growing so tired as to hate everything around me, you included, and I am leaving so that it won't happen. . . . To always be the same, can you imagine? The same as yesterday, the same as tomorrow). The narrator's ultimate reaction to Lina's departure is happiness. Having safely crossed the river of love and emerged safe and sound—that is, at liberty—the protagonist has achieved a certain self-sufficiency and the freedom to flee continuously.

Ferrucci's next two novels are *Il cappello di Panama* (The Panama Hat, 1973) and *A sud di Santa Barbara* (South of Santa Barbara, 1976). Published within five years of his first novel, they are written in third, rather than first, person; the characters are treated with amused detachment; and the narrative center moves continuously as the focus changes from one character to another. These works offer the reader fewer opportunities than the first for identifying and empathizing with the characters. Instead they demand the reader's awareness of the dissimilarity of the text to the everyday world while suggesting provocative parallels as regards the meaning of life and the nature of human destiny.

Despite these fundamental differences, Ferrucci's second and third novels share with his first the common element of movement. The characters seem to appear and speak only to vanish. Like puppets, they seem to be players in a game in which their "destinies will cross." In all three the catalyst for constant physical motion is a deep existential crisis that broadly can be defined as the tension between the consciousness that life is absurd and the relentless need to extract some meaning from it. What differentiates Ferrucci from other existential writers is the treatment of individual crisis in a light and humorous fashion.

Ferrucci's longest and most important novel to date and the first to be translated into English is *Il mondo creato,* a work that is a significant departure from his previous novels. Written in the first person like *L'anatra nel cortile,* it is a more mature work with a more mature protagonist. Ambitious in its scope, dense and lyrical in language, *Il mondo creato* features God as the protagonist and cosmic history as its subject.

The differences notwithstanding, *Il mondo creato* develops such familiar themes as metamorphosis, wandering in exile, and existential crisis. But the crisis takes on a uniquely comic, though poignant, dimension since it is God who cannot make sense of his own creation. The use of the first-person singular is employed in an unexpected and ingenious way. Since God is speaking in the first person, one might expect the answers to the deepest philosophical problems; however, Ferrucci's God, far from the omniscient, omnipotent figure of the major Western religions, is a fallible being. He says of himself, "Non ero affatto onnisciente" (I was not at all omniscient). God suffers anthropomorphically from colds, from a sense of isolation from his own creation, especially human beings, and from the inability of making himself understood and understanding in turn. In short, he is one of Ferrucci's most likable, engaging creations.

Il mondo creato subverts traditional conceptions of God, offering the reader a new myth grounded on the demythologization of myths, accomplished by God's self-deprecating humor: "Essere Dio non è male, mi dissi; se solo fossi un po' più sicuro di me" (Being God is not bad, I told myself; if only I were a little more sure of myself). In fact, Ferrucci strips the great Western myths as God continues to change but never into a great historical or religious figure; he never appears as Moses, Christ, St. Thomas, or Freud but always as a humble, unknown observer. God is actually revolted by some of his so-called followers. Moses, for example, driven by an arrogant thirst for power, pits himself against God in an unexpected episode in which Moses excites a mob to a pitch of hysteria. God is always suspect of such excesses, even when it takes the form of St. Augustine's mystical ecstasy. The result is that God and his lover Asca are stoned. While she is killed, God is propelled into the oblivion of forgetfulness.

One of God's major defects is that he is prone to forgetfulness, especially to forgetting that he is God. He forgets what his own nature is as well as what he created and its purpose. Over and over God loses touch with himself and loses his memory; again and again, he must rediscover himself and his creation. "A lungo mi dimentico d'essere Dio," he says at the very start of the book, "Ma la mia memoria non è il mio forte e devo aiutarla in ogni modo" (For long periods I forget that I am God. But memory is not my forte, and I have to help it along in any way that I can). It is within this context that the topos of the Book of God is introduced—but it is not the Bible. Using Galileo's famous metaphor, God says that before the advent of man "il mio libro era il cosmo" (my book was the cosmos). It is the advent of man that makes possible the writing of the autobiography of God—the "memorie di Dio" (the memories of God)—which is also the memory of the world. But in order to write, God must remember, and documenting his memories helps him remember once and for all.

The underlying theme of God as writer is connected to the larger theme of the world as created, rediscovered, and re-created through memory and writing; in this regard the novel is uniquely self-referential and self-conscious. In the end God looks for someone to write the Book; when he finds that the unfinished diary has been stolen, he sits down to write the book himself in the figure of Roland around the time of World War II. Roland writes: "Nel mio libro mi sovvenni di tutto, da Mosè al Cristo, giù per i secoli fino alla mia ultima dimora sullo specchio chiaro del lago. In poche settimane giunsi a due terzi dell'opera" (In my book I remembered everything, from Moses to Christ, down through the centuries to my last home on the crystal-clear lake. In a few weeks I finished two-thirds of the work). But Roland's book is never completed. It is never clear whether the book God intended to write is *Il mondo creato,* which connects the process of memory with that of writing.

Inspired by the lapsed condition of the human race, Ferrucci's novels are never mere divertissements. Clearly his exhortation to memory is directed at his readers, and *Il mondo creato* can be best read as an examination of the collective conscience, inspired by the turning of the millennium. At the end of the novel God, fed up with cruelty and war, prepares to leave, though he is loathe to wrench himself from the beauty that is his creation. The question of whether he will actually leave or not is not answered. The unmistakable message, as critic Alessandro Carrera points out, is that humanity must take some responsibility for its own survival and that of the planet.

Il mondo creato further delineates two themes of Ferrucci's narrative that are present in his first novel and also apparent in his subsequent works. One of his main concerns involves the nature of evil, which comes to the fore in God's final permutation into a lizard. Earlier in the novel God feared that "la creazione stessa—e non soltanto i difetti della creazione—fosse opera delle forze del male" (creation itself—and not merely the defects of creation—might be the work of the forces of evil). God's metamorphosis into a lizard occurs just after he encounters Benito Mussolini, witnesses World War II, and explodes in the atomic bomb on Japan. The episode, in which God the lizard is tortured and mutilated at the hands of children for sport, functions as a meditation on the nature of war, cruelty, and destruction as well as on the nature of humanity. It is a parable, an exhortation against the cruelty that can in the smallest creature target God the life force. War and destruction, recurring concerns of Ferrucci, first surfaced in a despondent meditation in *L'anatra nel cortile* and are part of the thematic core of *Lontano da casa* (Far from Home, 1996).

The other theme Ferrucci explores in *Il mondo creato,* the main concern of his first novel, revolves around the necessity of being or becoming an orphan while searching for roots and a sense of belonging. This separation, the crisis of adolescence, appears in *Fuochi* (1993) but is best developed in Ferrucci's finely structured *I satelliti di Saturno* (Saturn's Moon, 1989). The paradoxical nature of existence as defined by the contradictory desires for independence and belonging is revealed in *Il mondo creato* by one of those disconcerting moments in which God remembers that he is, in fact, God. In such a moment he realizes he must embrace his solitary condition as creator and, ultimately, as an orphan: "Si, sono Dio, pensai: non ho più padre, non ho più madre, ho perduto la sposa, ho perduto il figlio" (Yes, I am God, I thought: I no longer have a father, or a mother. I have lost my wife, I have lost my son). The orphan, by circumstance or by choice, is thus the privileged figure in Ferrucci's narrative. Of his favorite characters, he says in the interview with Guardiani: "A destiny of solitude (of triumphant solitude at times) awaits them." Inspired by a noble calling, "they are led to contemplation and creation at the same time."

The twenty-year-old narrator of *I satelliti di Saturno* shares some important similarities to the God of *Il mondo creato*. The deliberate connection between the two novels is reinforced by such comments in the latter work as the speculation that "Dio fosse in partenza verso un altro mondo, dopo essersi stancato di questo" (Having tired of this one, God was on his way to another world). This narrator, like God, is "vecchio-giovane" (young-old) and is consumed by the task of discovering his beginnings through the unearthing of memories. He, too, is an orphan and must invent himself by reconstructing his past before he was born: "Non avendo mai conosciuto mio padre e mia madre, i ricordi mi hanno dominato con la forza dell'ignoto" (Never having known my father or mother, memories have dominated me with the force of the unknown). The protagonist observes: "Si fa di tutto, pur di non nascere dal nulla" (One tries everything in order not to be born from nothing).

The novel traces the narrator's origins and genealogy going back several generations. The separate lives of the narrator's parents are treated alternately until their paths finally join. The successful orchestration of the anticipated encounter of two fascinating and fated lovers who are the narrator's parents adds dramatic suspense to the narrative. Each of the parents meets Ferrucci's criteria of noble solitude and detachment, creativity, and meditation. They have made the right choices, and the narrator, as critic Alessandro Carrera points out, discovers his own noble heritage in resurrecting their lives.

The narrator's talented mother inherited the drive to pursue excellence from her own father, Alessio, who was in love with the skies, first as a flyer in the war and then as an astronomer. Maintaining a dignified solitude in a family of detached individuals, she is a brilliant pianist but will not perform in public lest her ability be wasted on the masses. Self-sufficient, she supports herself by giving piano lessons in Paris.

The narrator's father, on the other hand, is the son of Augusto, a mediocre, embarrassing man employed as a postal worker. Mediocrity is a particularly galling failure for Ferrucci, who declares in his interview with Guardiani that it "is the poison of the world." The narrator's father asks himself, "Come posso fare a non avere padre?" (What can I do in order not to have a father?). He chooses another Master, as he occasionally refers to him, in the person of Augusto's eccentric cousin, Marco Bru. In the manner of the apostle-disciple relationship of Greek times, Marco becomes his real father, guiding him as a teacher in his readings and meditations and taking him fishing. Marco engages the young man in philosophical discussions on the nature of man, specifically about the self-destructive instinct in human beings. The main point of the discussion is to determine how to reverse this self-destructive bent.

Deeply influenced by Marco, the narrator's father takes as his main goals the transformation of man's nature through architectural design and being as "free" as possible in the life he lives. The final advice he receives from his mentor regards methodology: "Fa' da solo! Fa' sempre da solo, perché questa sarà l'unica via di rifondare il mondo" (Do it on your own! Always do it on your own, because this is the only way to remake the world). It is worthy of note that the father considers himself—like many of Ferrucci's protagonists—an "esule volontario" (voluntary exile). He seeks, in words identical to those used by Ferrucci's protagonist in *L'anatra nel cortile,* to be sufficient unto himself.

The young narrator is of course proud of his distinctive ancestors and their legacy of talent, thought, and passion: "Egli ardeva del fuoco che io sento discendere per i rami della mia famiglia. Per lui l'architettura era composta della stessa fiamma che bruciava l'anima di mia madre sotto forma di armonia musicale" (He [my father] burned with the fire that I feel descend along the branches of my family. For him architecture was composed of the same flame that burned in my mother's soul in the form of musical harmony). This passion explains his father's "entry" into the world; otherwise, father and son ask, "Perché mai saremmo nati?" (What need was there for us to be born?).

In his journey of self-discovery the son retraces his parents' footsteps along paths familiar to Ferrucci: Pisa is mentioned briefly; then Paris, where the mother gives piano lessons; then Manhattan, where the two lovers finally meet for the first time in a hotel. Such is Ferrucci's skill that the reader rarely questions the narrator's unusual memory that allows him to see into the past and into the minds of his dead parents. The implicit explanation for this perfect "remembering" is suggested by Plato's notion of ideal forms. Toward the end of the novel, when the narrator discovers his father's drawings, he notes a building that is neither residence, municipal building, nor church. With its "classical" lines it resembles a gymnasium, and the narrator hazards the guess that "esprimesse la concezione del sapere e della conoscenza . . . di chi l'aveva vergata: la vera chiesa, il vero palazzo, il vero stadio nel cuore dell'umanità contenta" (it expressed the notion of knowledge and familiarity of the person who had drawn it: the true church, the true building, the true stadium in the heart of a happy humanity). In this drawing of the Platonic ideal, of the quintessential form that awaits remembering in each individual, man's self-destructive nature has been transcended. As in all great love stories the two lovers die—the man by falling off a funicular and the grieving woman by falling into a deep, deathly sleep—but their son is born: "La nascita era finita" (the birth was finished).

In many ways Ferrucci's novel *Lontano da casa* functions as a counterpoint to *I satelliti di Saturno.* While the author approves of the values of the impassioned artist parents in *I satelliti di Saturno,* he just as obviously deplores those of the money grabbers in *Lontano da casa.* Most of the characters in *I satelliti di Saturno* are on the right road, for they have made the right choices; most of those in *Lontano da casa* are on the path to a self-inflicted hell.

While the young male narrator of *I satelliti di Saturno* is bent on remembering where he came from, Dana Scott, the twenty-year-old heiress introduced in the second section of *Lontano da casa*, is just as determined to forget her past. She leaves her Long Island home after she is raped on the beach by a black man, stowing away on a train that takes her to a warehouse in Connecticut overseen by the protagonist of the novel, Gregorio Pane. Dana is not the only one who would forget the past, for before he meets her Gregorio had lived nearly a lifetime on another continent—a life driven by an obsession for money inherited from his grandfather.

At the beginning of the novel Gregorio is peeking in on his rich, avaricious grandfather, who dies shortly thereafter. The year is 1897; Gregorio's father promptly squanders the family riches, dies, and leaves his family in poverty. Determined to restore the family's fortunes, Gregorio scrimps and saves, hiding his money about the house as his grandfather had done. Just as he is about to harvest his labors and reinstate the family fortune, creditors appear to throw the family out of their home before Gregorio can take his money. Like his grandfather, Gregorio had not anticipated that the nature of making money has changed, that investing is becoming more important than saving, and that money was no longer secure under a mattress. Having lost everything, Gregorio faces the twentieth century and World War I.

Continuing to define his life in terms of money without recognizing its ephemeral and unsatisfactory—not to mention dangerous—nature, Gregorio contracts a bland marriage to a rich woman named Lidia. Soon after, he sells his soul to Kurt, a modern-day Mephistopheles, in exchange for wealth by agreeing to work in Berlin on the transfer of weapons between Italy and Germany on the eve of World War I. Gregorio's figurative nearsightedness is evident as he works diligently amassing wealth in a room without windows, having no contact with anyone except his advisor, Kurt, and his secretary, Hanna. In time, Gregorio comes to see war as "uno scontro economico" (an economic clash). The exchange of weapons presumes that Germany and Italy will be allies, so when Italy takes the "wrong" side, Gregorio barely survives. Upon his return to Italy his wife and her patriotic lover almost turn him in as a traitor. Gregorio then realizes he has no choice but to forget: "Non dev'esserci più passato per te. Non più Italia né Bologna né Europa; non più moglie né altro. Comportati da esule, se ti riesce. E così fece" (There must be no more past for you. Neither Italy nor Bologna nor Europe; neither wife nor other. Behave like an exile, if you can manage it. And that he did).

Like scores of Europeans before him who were pursuing a new beginning by trying to forget the past, Gregorio departs for the United States. Through Gregorio's travels and experiences Ferrucci explores the world of money, with all of the violence, destruction, and egoism that accompany it. After depicting the indifference in marriage based on economic stability, he targets the lottery, Wall Street, and the chasm that divides the destitute from the affluent. In Dana's father, Rosco Scott, he presents a modern-day Midas whose drive for amassing wealth and power is unquenchable. All he touches turns to gold, but all his wealth ultimately cannot save his daughter.

Like Gregorio, Dana is a semivoluntary exile. She is the goddess Diana who has lost her innocence. She and Gregorio meet and cohabit as if they were reinventing themselves and the world. Like the innocent children they would once again wish to be, they set up house in a warehouse with borrowed objects. They then travel through the virgin territory, the pre-Edenic wilderness that is America, the pregnant Dana resembling a gentle, glowing Madonna. All along, though, her past is catching up to her in the figure of the detective Reymo, hired by her father, and more compellingly through her own body as she goes into labor. Dana's life ends in the violent rent that is creation: giving birth. The life Gregorio, an archetypal immigrant-exile, has constructed is once again destroyed when Dana dies and he is deported from the United States because he entered on a false visa. He leaves without ever knowing who Dana was, and the narrator, engagingly nonomniscient at this point, loses track of him in Genova.

The novel ends with a short summary of Dana's son, who is the offspring of the rapist rather than Gregorio's. Since the Scott family is anonymous in its financial support of him, Dana's son never solves the mystery of his origins. In time he marries a white woman and has two dark sons and a blue-eyed daughter. A tangle of family genealogies and a muddle of legacies converge in this dark-skinned progeny.

Ferrucci's novels are extraordinarily philosophical. Like the poets Edmund Spenser and Emily Dickinson, Ferrucci in his fiction often makes use of allegorical personifications, including five—Life, Death, Love, Time, and the Void ("il Nulla")—that recur in his novels. The use of personification reveals both the poetic and the philosophical nature of the author's imagination. As does Spenser, Ferrucci uses personifications to tell lyrical parables. As in Dickinson—whom Ferrucci often quotes in the classroom—the moral weight is tempered by light humor, as when God huffs and puffs after St. Augustine.

It is essential to point out that Ferrucci's literary criticism serves as a valuable complement to his novels. While the novels are philosophical in nature, his critical work is lyrical and imaginative. In his interview with Guardiani, Ferrucci notes the interdependence of his dual careers:

> For me there has always been an uncommon dialectical interaction between my philosophical and literary readings: philosophy stimulates me to narrate, while literature to meditate in philosophical terms. If I read poetry or fiction, my first reaction is to rationalize and interpret; if I read philosophy I get the urge to write.

Ferrucci loves to tell stories as he analyzes stories or ponders the nature of literature through time, a tendency he exhibits in all his critical works.

In his 1993 study, *Ars poetica,* a paradigmatic example of his penchant for personification, Ferrucci classifies writers into six categories: Efesto, Orfeo, Narciso, Selene, Ariel, and Glauco, each representing the essential nature of a writer and his or her work that he discusses in the essays. The book begins with the sort of extended metaphor—a story-within-a-story that is a fundamental substructure of his narrative—which could easily be found in the pages of one of his novels: "Il nostro corpo è una casa, e al suo interno c'è uno spazio che è stato variamente denominato nel corso del tempo" (Our body is a house and inside it is a space that has been given various names through the course of time). In that space Ferrucci discovers the landlady Persona, who receives as a guest the traveler Ermes, the "io creativo che coabita, assieme a Persona, in ogni individuo che viene alla luce" (the creative I who cohabits, along with Persona, in every individual who sees the light of day).

Interview:

Francesco Guardiani, "Franco Ferrucci," *Review of Contemporary Fiction,* 12 (Fall 1992): 46–56.

References:

Alessandro Carrera, "La nascita del creatore. Un'interpretazione dell'opera narrativa di Franco Ferrucci," *Studi novecenteschi,* 20 (June-December 1993): 7–53;

Rosemarie La Valva, "Il narratore errante di Franco Ferruci," *Forum Italicum,* 30 (Fall 1996): 351–367.

Raffaele La Capria
(8 October 1922 -)

Monica Cristina Storini
University of Rome "La Sapienza"

Translated by Augustus Pallotta

BOOKS: *Un giorno d'impazienza* (Milan: Bompiani, 1952; revised edition, 1973); translated by William Weaver as *A Day of Impatience* (New York: Farrar, Straus & Young, 1954);

Ferito a morte (Milan: Bompiani, 1961); translated by Marguerite Waldman as *The Mortal Wound* (London: Collins, 1964; New York: Farrar, Straus, 1964);

Amore e psiche (Milan: Bompiani, 1973);

Colapesce: favola italiana (Milan: Mondadori, 1974);

False partenze: frammenti per una biografia letteraria (Milan: Bompiani, 1974);

Variazioni sopra una sola nota. Lettere a Francesca (Rome: Cooperativa Scrittori, 1977);

Fiori giapponesi (Milan: Bompiani, 1979);

Il bambino che non volle sparire (Teramo: Lisciani & Giunti, 1980);

L'armonia perduta (Milan: Mondadori, 1986);

La neve del Vesuvio (Milan: Mondadori, 1988);

Letteratura e salti mortali (Milan: Mondadori, 1990);

Capri e non più Capri (Milan: Mondadori, 1991);

L'occhio di Napoli (Milan: Mondadori, 1994);

I "Sillabari" di Goffredo Parise (Naples: Guida, 1994);

La mosca nella bottiglia: elogio del senso comune (Milan: Rizzoli, 1996);

Il sentimento della letteratura (Milan: Mondadori, 1997).

Collection: *Tre romanzi di una giornata* (Turin: Einaudi, 1982)–includes *Un giorno d'impazienza, Ferito a morte,* and *Amore e psiche.*

MOTION PICTURES: *Le mani sulla città,* screenplay by La Capria, 1963;

Uomini contro, screenplay by La Capria, 1973;

Il genio, screenplay by La Capria, 1984;

La piovra, screenplay by La Capria, 1984.

TRANSLATIONS: J. M. Barrie, *Peter Pan,* in *Fiabe teatrali* (Turin: E.R.I., 1958), pp. 409–480;

Thierry Maulnier, *Giovanna e i giudici,* in *Teatro francese contemporaneo di autori cattolici* (Turin: E.R.I., 1959), pp. 422–464;

Thomas S. Eliot, *Assassinio nella cattedrale* (Milan: Bompiani, 1985).

The reader of Raffaele La Capria's work can not fail to recognize his constant attention to style and language that prompted Geno Pampaloni in 1961 to call him "scrittore gentile, elegante e complicato" (a gentle, elegant yet difficult writer). In each of his novels La Capria focuses on an individual life that is always on the breaking point; when the fracture occurs escapist daydreams usually yield to the unpleasant realities of life. In his short stories he examines different forms of discovery, from the wonder of childhood to the confusion of adult daily experiences, often yielding surprises that are extraordinary or horrific.

In *Fiori giapponesi* (Japanese Flowers, 1979) La Capria calls normality "a state of emergency," especially when one happens to spend his early youth in Naples, the impenetrable forest that "ti ferisce a morte o ti addormenta" (wounds you to death or puts you to sleep). The presence of La Capria's native Naples in his work, especially in his essays, is pervasive to the point of assuming the function of "a mythical place" that marks the destiny of the novelist's generation—a generation that was born in the shadow of Benito Mussolini's rise to power and was engulfed in World War II, that once read Gabriele D'Annunzio and Giovanni Verga but was soon drawn to foreign authors such as Arthur Rimbaud, Stéphane Mallarmé, T. S. Eliot, Federico García Lorca, Fyodor Dostoyevsky, and Franz Kafka.

Born in Naples to Augusto and Dora La Capria on 8 October 1922, La Capria attended school in the city. His background is similar to that of Candido, the main character in his *False partenze: frammenti per una biografia letteraria* (False Starts: Fragments of a Literary Biography, 1974), a child born in "una famiglia di media borghesia, in un ambiente di media cultura, in una città di media importanza" (a middle-class family, in an average environment, in a city of average importance). In the novel Candido identifies with a group of young men that included the playwright Giuseppe Patroni Griffi and the film director Francesco Rosi. Like them, La Capria was catapulted into World War II; he shared with them and many other leftist intellectuals between 1945 and 1948 the dream of renewing Italian society, which waned in the 1950s.

In the immediate postwar period, La Capria graduated from law school in 1947 and moved to Rome. There he found employment as scriptwriter and producer with RAI, the Italian radio and television network. At the same time, he initiated what proved to be a long career as contributor to major Italian newspapers and magazines such as *Il Mattino, Il Corriere della sera, L'Espresso,* and *Nuovi argomenti.* In spite of his continuous residence in Rome and his frequent trips abroad, Naples has remained the main point of reference in his work throughout his career. In 1994 the mayor of Naples, Antonio Bassolino, appointed La Capria to head an effort aimed at developing a fresh relationship between Neapolitan writers and their native city.

La Capria's first novel, *Un giorno d'impazienza* (translated as *A Day of Impatience,* 1954), was first published in 1952 and substantially revised in 1973. In the revision the initial division in chapters is abandoned in favor of a continuous monologue in which the protagonist and first-person narrator betrays a state of restlessness seemingly tied to his date with a young woman, Mira, but actually rooted in his inability to connect with reality and to identify with the one-dimensional character of his peers. The exception is Enrico, the narrator's childhood friend, a young man described as "proprio il contrario dei personaggi che avevano sempre bisogno di decidersi per fare qualcosa, e quando poi la facevano non era per farla, ma per fare come gli altri, per non essere da meno" (exactly the opposite of the characters who constantly needed to do something, and when they did it, it wasn't because they wanted to do it, but to imitate others and not feel inferior to them).

Impatient and doubtful for reasons unknown to him, the protagonist remains an inconsequential presence to Mira, her parents, and to his friends, Walter and Gina. His experience cannot but end in the manner it started: with the same inner feelings, the same desires and anxiety, and the same unresolved relationship with reality. Accordingly the novel begins with Mira saying, "Domani alle sei a casa tua" (Tomorrow at six at your house) and ends with a slight variation as Mira remarks, "Domani alle sei a casa sua" (Tomorrow at six at his house)—a repetition that underscores the narrator's inability to act.

The main character's passive disposition is characterized by his indecision, impatience, and fixed vision of the world around him. He has no desire to experience life in spite of his expressed need to live from one day to the next. But it is not a question of ineptitude. He suffers from a paralysis of the will stemming from his inability to decode the signs that convey reality. He also is paralyzed by his refusal to pretend. He asks at one point: "Ma come si fa a stabilre la differenza tra voler provare un sentimento e provarlo di fatto?" (How does one draw the difference between wanting to experience a certain feeling and actually experiencing it?). The inability to answer this simple, perhaps trivial, question generates a sense of impatience and urgency that underlie the protagonist's actions.

The narrator's relationship with Mira should help him to solve his crisis, for she is one who accepts what life has to offer her without question. Yet the potential solution is not sought, because the narrator allows Mira to determine the terms of their relationship, even the hour and the place they will meet. Juxtaposed to Mira's personality, the protagonist's unfolds in all its debilitating weakness: "Lei, Mira, non faceva tante storie, agiva d'impulso. Il mio primo impulso, invece, era di non averne" (Mira was a woman of few words and acted impulsively. My first impulse was not to be impulsive at all). What prevents him from having real problems and pain is his inability to experience true feelings and sensations. Stated differently, the narrator suffers from apathy: he perceives every aspect of life exactly the same, without any qualitative difference.

The indifference of the mirrors the narrator looks into offers an eloquent metaphor for his existential condition: "Tutto quanto cadeva entro il falso riverbero degli specchi, compreso me stesso, pareva fermo, sospeso, un aspetto illusorio della vita. E la realtà rimaneva sempre, ostinatamente, al di fuori del mio sguardo" (Everything that fell in the false reflection of a mirror, including myself, seemed lifeless, suspended, an illusory image of life. And reality remained, obstinately, outside my field of vision). More than any other, it is the images the narrator finds in the mirror that link La Capria's novel to Alberto Moravia's *Gli indifferenti* (1929; translated as *The Indifferent Ones,* 1932). The mirror reflects an "image of death." When he tries on a suit, shaves, or desperately seeks Mira in a nightclub, the mirror is a distorting glass. In the eyes of the protagonist it transforms people into kafkaesque insects: "Dai divani, azzurri e non verdi, come avevo creduto, veniva

Raffaele La Capria (photograph by Giovanni Giovannetti)

un brusio d'insetti" (From the sofas, which were blue and not green, as I thought, came a buzzing of insects).

The protagonist's impatience toward people and objects as well as his self-hatred allow him to separate himself from the world. Thus, the sexual initiation that the protagonist undertakes unwillingly with Mira does not lead him to cognizance or to adulthood in a world of adults: "Tra ciò che si vuol provare e ciò che si prova di fatto c'era solo la trasparenza di un vetro. Io mi trovavo al di qua di quel vetro, per me ancora invalicabile" (Between what one wishes to experience and what is experienced, there is, in fact, only the transparency of a glass. I found myself on this side of the glass, unable to go beyond). The narrator is prevented from overcoming this obstacle because of his excessive self-questioning, which is tied to his adolescent doubts.

In a larger sense the protagonist's self-questioning challenges those of his generation who seek reform in society without first entertaining the need for individual change. In this light Mira's accusation that such obsessive questioning is fundamentally narcissistic is a serious criticism, for it threatens the reassuring pretense of seeing oneself outside of history. The city—its name never explicitly mentioned but clearly identifiable with Naples—is left in physical and spiritual ruin by the departure of American troops. The setting seems to prove the impossibility of living beyond the pull of events. Like the protagonist the city is now in a state of "wintry lethargy." Compared to the helpless young men who during the occupation watched as Italian women danced the boogie-woogie with American soldiers, the characters of Mira, Gina, and even the violent Walter (who lives by his wits and homosexual acts), while morally compromised, represent a vitality that is far healthier than the protagonist's sterile view of life.

La Capria's second novel, *Ferito a morte* (1961; translated as *The Mortal Wound,* 1964), differs drastically from his first in that it covers a period of more than fifteen years rather than just a day. On a muggy summer morning of 1954, Massimo De Luca, the novel's protagonist and first-person narrator, lies half awake in bed thinking about his imminent departure for Rome where he has found employment. As he prepares himself psychologically to leave Naples, his native city, Massimo thinks back to the summer of 1943 and to his relationship with Carla Boursier. The painful love for this woman, with whom he had an embarrassing experience of impotence, takes up the first seven chapters.

As he relives the past during the siesta that same afternoon, Massimo brings to life the salient episodes of the last ten years: his aborted suicide while deep-sea fishing, which has left a persistent piercing pain in his ear; the relationship with his brother Nini; his experiences at the exclusive Naples Sail Club, which is patronized by rich, parasitic young men; and a meal with his family as recounted by Gaetano, one of his friends. The last three chapters of the novel deal mainly with Massimo's return trips to Naples from 1957 to 1960 and the time spent with old friends: Gaetano, Sasa, Guidino, Niní, and Glauco.

Massimo and his friends nurture the illusion that they are living in an unending adolescence: "Si tratta d'immaturità . . . : non quella, palese, di un individuo, ma quella più incomprensibile e sconcertante di una generazione . . . che si è messa fuori della storia" (It is a question of immaturity . . . : not that of an individual, but the more puzzling and disconcerting immaturity of a generation . . . which has divorced itself from history). They are a generation without meaningful experiences and without a distinctive mark: "quel segno che ti fa capire che qualunque cosa ti è successa è veramente successa a te, perchè tu, vuoi o non vuoi, te la porti appresso anche dopo che te ne sei dimenticato, e anche se non lo sai ti ha cambiato" (a mark which makes you understand that whatever happened to you, it really happened to you because, whether you like it or not, you carry it with you even after you have forgotten about it, and even if you don't know it has changed you). In this light *Ferito a morte* records the failure of a generation that could have saved itself only through a critical and dispassionate acceptance of life—in the case of these men their acceptance of the life lived in the city of Naples. La Capria presents his theme by alternating episodes showing the private dimension of characters and the social and collective dimension of the community.

In *Un giorno d'impazienza* La Capria fuses present, past, and future into a single day—a pioneering effort in the early 1950s—but with *Ferito a morte* he reaches a new stage of narrative innovation by coupling existentialist questions with the formal experimentation of the French *nouveau roman* (new novel). Massimo rebels against the absurdity of the human condition and his own abulic torpor, seeing himself as a victim of the stagnant life in his city that is exemplified by "l'anestesia della siesta" (the anesthesia of the siesta):

> Il sonno della ragione. Il cervello, un re detronizzato nella rocca della testa. L'insonnia del ventre. Nella penombra della stanza, anche il tuo corpo, estraneo. Primo esibito sulle spiagge, poi mette pancia. La mente prigioniera dell'apparato digerente. Bastava sapersi controllare a tavola, fermarsi in tempo.
>
> (The mind asleep. The brain, a dethroned king in its skull fortress. A sleepless belly. In the dimly lit bedroom even your body is a stranger. First exhibited on the beaches, then heavy from overeating. The mind a captive of the digestive system. It would have sufficed to be moderate at the dinner table, to stop on time.)

Massimo is imprisoned by his habits, by the ties between the mind and the body, by the questions that have no answer in an irrational universe: "Possibile che tutto sia uguale e tutto sia cambiato? Sì, è possibile. Possibile che nessun segno preannunci il cambiamento?" (Is it possible that everything is the same and everything has changed? Yes, it is possible. Why is it that there is no sign announcing the change?).

Such questions bring to mind the works of Albert Camus, especially *La peste* (1947; translated as *The Plague,* 1948) and *La chute* (1956; translated as *The Fall,* 1957), but La Capria's work does not just denounce the moral and social bonds that tie one to repeating the same scenario endlessly. Massimo's inclination is to flee, to free himself from the paralysis of daily existence and build a life for himself, to confront what Cesare Pavese called "il mestiere del vivere" (the business of living). His seeking a timely maturity in order to avoid a stifling bourgeois life makes him seem closer in disposition to the characters created by Camus and Jean-Paul Sartre than to those fashioned by such southern Italian writers as Carlo Bernari and Michele Prisco. The protagonist finds in his return visits to Naples that the middle class carries on its stable, abulic existence without him. In spite of apparent change, the life he led before has remained virtually intact thanks to the painless substitution of his brother Niní for Massimo. The social rituals of parties, the small talk at the espresso bar, and the taking advantage of tourists continue. Despite Massimo's escape, the reader is left with a melancholic disenchantment toward the business of the living in the Naples described in the novel.

In La Capria's third novel, *Amore e psiche* (Love and Psyche, 1973), an average man who works with the Italian television network lives with his wife's unfaithfulness as though it were of no concern to him. He does so to the point of confusing his reality with the fictional reality of the novel he is writing: "Il mio corpo è quello-che-c'è, che è sempre lí dove si trova, mentre io non sempre ci sono, non sempre sono lí dove mi trovo" (My body is that-which-is-there, it is always where it happens to be, whereas I am not always there, not always where I happen to be). His fundamental problem is one of identity: where is one when he realizes that he is separated from his body that acts like a ghost, like an intermediary?

The protagonist divides his time between the novel he is writing and his job, which requires him to produce scripts for television programs; the two creative efforts are juxtaposed and often linked. Moreover, the narrator retraces his wife's adultery, examines and seeks to understand it as if only through the act of writing is he able to put together the pieces of their relationship, to discover that "è un anno che la parola Amore è scomparsa dal loro vocabolario" (it has been a year that the word *love* has disappeared from their lexicon).

René Magritte's painting *The Human Condition* becomes a central image in the novel and the protagonist's search for understanding: "Un quadro nel quadro, ma sovrapposti parzialmente completano lo stesso soggetto. Sembra un solo paesaggio e invece sono due: quello di fuori, reale, e quello di dentro dipinto sulla tela davanti alla finestra, rappresentato" (A picture within a picture but, partially superimposed, they frame the same subject matter. There seems to be one landscape and yet there are two: the real landscape outside and the one painted on the canvas facing the window).

The protagonist experiences a nagging doubt as he wonders what the painting within the painting might conceal:

> Sulla tela c'è un albero, ma lí, fuori, nel punto corrispondente del paesaggio, al posto dell'albero potrebbe anche esserci—niente: un buco, una lacuna, un tassello mancante. La tela sarebbe stata messa a bella posta sul cavalletto, davanti alla finestra, per coprire questa magagna della realtà, con l'immagine dell'albero per nascondere l'assenza dell'albero. Una specie di rattoppo, insomma, escogitato dal pittore per riempire un vuoto, una falla, una macchia di assenza che si apre laggiù e sfonda lo scenario del visibile oltre il quale si presume qualcosa che non si può né pensare né rappresentare. Sarebbe questa "la condizione umana"?

(On the canvas there is a tree, but outside, on the corresponding spot of the landscape, in place of the tree there could be—nothing: a hole, a gap, a missing dowel. The canvas could have been placed deliberately on the easel, facing the window, to cover a flaw of reality, the image of the tree meant to hide the missing tree. In short, a sort of patch devised by the painter to fill in a void, a hole, a black spot denoting absence which opens up down there and breaks through the scenery of visible reality beyond which there presumably lies something that one can neither imagine nor represent. Is that "the human condition"?)

There cannot be, of course, an answer to the question. And like the painting, La Capria's novel—a juxtaposition of various forms including diary entries, letters, and dialogue—also points to what is absent. The task of arranging the pieces into a unified whole is left to the reader.

Perhaps the most congenial measure of La Capria's writing is the short form of the anecdote and the aphorism, as contained in *Fiori giapponesi*. Consisting of contracted narratives, these "easy pieces"—as the author calls them—treat in a nearly obsessive fashion the theme of appearance and reality in such stories as "Fotoromanzo", "La Bella e la Bestia" (The Beauty and the Beast), "L'indifferenza" (Indifference), and "Incontri" (Meetings). Compiled from 1973 to 1977, *Fiori giapponesi,* according to critic Giuseppe Amoroso, offers the reader all the diverse pleasures of "la novella esemplare, l'apologo, l'elzeviro, il taccuino, il racconto rarefatto fino al coagulo di un'idea, la favola e l'album fotografico, l'appunto da meditare e il dissodato apparato della didascalia . . . il raffinato concettismo simbolico e il taglio un po' scientifico dell'operetta morale" (the exemplary novel, the apologue, the literary article, the notebook, the short story rarified until an idea coalesces, the fable and the photo album, a point to meditate, the cultivated apparatus of the note . . . the refined symbolical conceptualism, and the somewhat scientific elaboration of a moral essay).

In his novella on adolescence titled *La neve del Vesuvio* (The Snow on Mount Vesuvius, 1988) La Capria focuses on a child, Tonino, whose gradual discovery of the world around him and his often uneasy initiation to life are recounted in a fluid, simple narrative. These are, as the author writes in his foreword, "capitoli di un breve romanzo che inizia

Cover for a 1997 edition of La Capria's 1961 novel, in which the protagonist relives his life through daydreams

nell'età in cui si conoscono solo poche parole e non si è nemmeno tanto sicuri di essere uno e distinto, e finisce intorno ai dieci anni, quando per la prima volta si prende coscienza del mondo in cui si vive e della storia che ci condiziona" (chapters of a short novel that begins at an age when a person only knows a few words and one is not even sure of being an individual, and it ends around ten when for the first time one becomes aware of the world in which we live and of history that conditions us).

In the chapter "Il tempo e il risveglio" (Time and Awakening) Tonino learns to appreciate the value of time, recognizes himself in a mirror, and begins to identify with the world around him. But the child still identifies mostly with his mother whom "sentiva intorno, inseparata, sempre" (he felt around him, constantly, inseparable). Indeed "la madre era il suo spazio e il suo tempo, un tempo che si misurava dalla presenza e dalle assenze" (his mother was space and time to him, a time measured by her presence and her absence).

Toward the middle of the book Tonino begins to gain an awareness of language: "Stava imparando a scrivere correttamente, ma ogni parola appresa lo stava separando dalla sua infanzia" (He was learning to write, but every word he learned was separating him from his childhood). The learning process, La Capria shows, generates the rupture between one's individuality and the code that defines it. It is in this light that Tonino develops a relationship with his father, who is insincere, fearful, and unsure of himself.

In the chapter titled "La bella giornata" (The Beautiful Day) La Capria re-creates a carefree summer day "dell'infanzia e della primissima giovinezza" (of infancy and very early youth), impossible to relive except as memory. The short narrative contains a cogent existential metaphor conveyed through a seemingly insignificant incident. While deep-sea fishing one day, Tonino aims his spear gun at what he deems to be a large crustacean; instead

> si accorse che non era un granchio grosso come aveva creduto. Era un cosino da nulla, su cui aveva infierito. L'aveva fatto a pezzi, dilaniato, smembrato, e perché? *Perché?* Ebbe uno scatto d'ira contro se stesso, contro lo stupido impassibile azzurro che avvolgeva il mondo come un guscio trasparente, e buttò via lo spiedo tra gli scogli e il resto del granchio a mare. Mentre affondavano, tanti pesciolini velocissimi corsero a divorarli.
>
> (he realized that it was not the large crab he expected. It was a little, insignificant thing he had shot. It was torn to pieces and dismembered, but why? *Why?* He had a fit of anger against himself, against the stupid, indifferent blue sky that covered the earth like a transparent shell; he threw the spear away, amidst the reefs and the floating pieces of the crab. As they moved downward, they were devoured rapidly by numerous little fish.)

Meaningful as it was to Tonino, to the mature author's point of view the "beautiful day" remained "indifferente come la Natura al destino dell'uomo" (indifferent, like Nature, to man's destiny).

In *L'armonia perduta* (The Lost Harmony, 1986), a collection of articles published in dailies and magazines between 1980 and 1985, the prominent theme is La Capria's relationship to Naples. It is instructive to note that as the epigraph for his collection he chose a passage from Italo Calvino's *Le citta invisibili* (1972; translated as *Invisible Cities*, 1974), in which Marco Polo advises the khan not to confuse the city with the language that describes it. The work draws heavily upon La Capria's recollections of personal experiences, but it addresses as well the historical image of Naples. He discusses the Neapolitan dialect, the lifeblood of the culture, and the important cultural role the city has played in

Europe. He also treats the negative facets of daily life in Naples and the peculiar habits of her people that have earned them the questionable honor of national stereotypes. The book represents a key to La Capria's work, for Naples here is far more than a place or a city: it is history, civilization, a people with a particular identity. Reading about Naples one is challenged to penetrate the core of La Capria's symbolic discourse and glimpse the essence of his writing.

Another collection of personal observations, *L'occhio di Napoli* (Naples' Eyes, 1994), consists of notes and observations regarding Naples that are varied, disparate, even contradictory, reflecting the city and her people. The author sees the book as a challenge to readers and invites them to accept or reject any parts of it, but he also urges them to find "la connessione tra le cose che appaiono disparate e più spesso contradditorie (the connection between matters that appear disparate and quite often contradictory). More than *L'armonia perduta* this book shows a greater pessimism regarding Naples, which extends to a southern Italy afflicted by corruption, crimes, violence, and general deterioration. Neapolitan culture, La Capria argues, has become provincial, which is to say, irrelevant and insignificant compared to the European-minded culture of the past. He worries that Naples has become "per tanti aspetti solo l'esempio di una sopravvivenza indebita del passato" (in so many ways only an example of unworthy survival of the past).

La Capria considers *L'armonia perduta* and *L'occhio di Napoli* to be unsuccessful books, but they show his moral courage. In them he rejects "il comodo rifugio dello stile, la comoda tana della forma, e avventurarsi fuori nel vasto e scomodo e periglioso mondo dei fatti e degli eventi" (the comfortable refuge given by style, the comfortable cave provided by form, and venture outside, into the vast, uncomfortable and dangerous world of facts and events).

The critic Giorgio Luti has referred to La Capria's career as "work in progress" and compares his production to that of William Faulkner. Other critics have alluded to such writers as James Joyce, F. Scott Fitzgerald, Dylan Thomas, and Luigi Pirandello in discussing La Capria's work. As an artist, though, La Capria stands on his own, sustained by the conviction that only language can deal effectively with the complexity of reality, that only writing—when it eschews naturalism and pedantic philosophy—can yield fresh, albeit provisional, meaning to human existence.

Interview:

Conversazione con Raffaele La Capria: letteratura e sentimento del tempo, edited by Paolo Gaglianone (Rome: Omicron, 1995).

References:

Giuseppe Amoroso, *Narrativa italiana, 1975–1983* (Milan: Mursia, 1983), pp. 136–185;

Luigi Baldacci, "Narrativa," *Letteratura,* 25 (1961): 133–142;

Eleonora Canè, "Il racconto su piani diversi: Raffaele La Capria," in her *Il discorso indiretto libero nella narrativa italiana del Novecento* (Rome: Silva, 1969), pp. 133–155;

Carmine Di Biase, *L'altra Napoli: scrittori napoletani d'oggi* (Naples: Società Editrice Napoletana, 1978), pp. 95–105;

Enzo Golino, "La patria napoletana," *Paragone,* 37 (1986): 104–108;

Massimo Grillandi, "Raffaele La Capria," in *Letteratura italiana. I contemporanei,* volume 8 (Milan: Marzorati, 1979), pp. 1399–1415;

Geno Pampaloni, "Raffaele La Capria," *Terzo programma,* 1 (1961): 238–245;

Sergio Pautasso, Introduction, *Un giorno d'impazienza,* by La Capria (Milan: Mondadori, 1989);

Aldo Rossi, "Le vie del 'nuovo' romanzo italiano," *Paragone,* 12 (1961): 87–98.

Gina Lagorio
(6 January 1922 -)

Maria Rosaria Vitti-Alexander
Nazareth College of Rochester

BOOKS: *Il polline* (Milan: Mondadori, 1966);
Un ciclone chiamato Titti (Bologna: Cappelli, 1969);
Fenoglio (Florence: La Nuova Italia, 1970);
Approssimato per difetto (Bologna: Cappelli, 1971);
Cultura e letteratura ligure del '900 (Genoa: Sabatelli, 1972);
Angelo Barile e la poesia dell'intima trasparenza (Capua: Centro d'arte e di cultura L'airone, 1973);
Sui racconti di Sbarbaro (Parma: Guanda, 1973);
Sbarbaro controcorrente (Parma: Guanda, 1973);
Beppe Fenoglio (Florence: La Nuova Italia, 1975);
La spiaggia del lupo (Milan: Garzanti, 1977);
Fuori scena (Milan: Garzanti, 1979);
Sbarbaro: un modo spoglio di esistere (Milan: Garzanti, 1981);
Tosca dei gatti (Milan: Garzanti, 1983);
Penelope senza tela: argomenti e testi, edited by Franco Mollia (Ravenna: Longo, 1984);
Golfo del Paradiso (Milan: Garzanti, 1987);
Russia oltre l'URSS: taccuini di viaggio ottobre 1988, giugno 1977 (Rome: Riuniti, 1989);
Freddo al cuore e altri testi teatrali (Milan: Mondadori, 1989);
Tra le mura stellate (Milan: Mondadori, 1991);
Il silenzio: racconti di una vita (Milan: Mondadori, 1993);
Il bastardo (Milan: Rizzoli, 1996);
Inventario (Milan: Rizzoli, 1997).

OTHER: Beppe Fenoglio, *La malora e altri racconti,* edited by Lagorio (Turin: Einaudi, 1971);
Fenoglio, *Una questione privata,* edited by Lagorio (Milan: Garzanti, 1981);
Camillo Sbarbaro, *L'opera in versi e in prosa,* edited by Lagorio and Vanni Scheiwiller (Milan: Garzanti, 1985).

The restlessness that has characterized the artistic world of the twentieth century is reflected by the proliferation of many schools, movements, and currents in all creative fields but, most prominently, in cinema and literature. It is, however, difficult if not impossible to bring certain artists under a specific "ism," especially when they have developed a particu-

Gina Lagorio

lar voice and style to explore and express the fundamental experiences of living and dying. One such artist is Gina Lagorio.

Lagorio has established her reputation during a career of more than thirty years, and her works range from fiction to drama, from literary criticism to essays of general interest. She has contributed to major newspapers, magazines, and radio broadcasts. Her important criticism includes work on Camillo Sbarbaro, Beppe Fenoglio, Renato Serra, and Angelo Barile. Her writings for the theater are collected in *Freddo al cuore e altri testi teatrali* (Cold at Heart and Other Theatrical Texts, 1989). Lagorio is a steadfast writer who strives for clarity and incisiveness, objectivity and substantive meaning. Her writing reveals an artist sure of her individual identity, seeking through her work to overcome inner constraints and to free herself from traditional roles and limitations imposed by society. Her strong female characters, who never falter in their quest for self-knowledge and personal understanding, are reflections of their author.

Gina Lagorio was born Luigina Bernocco on 6 January 1922 in the Langhe region of Piedmont, the only child of Giovanni Battista Bernocco and Pierina Picollo Bernocco. After World War I the family moved to Savona, in Liguria, where her father traded in the wines produced on the family's estate. Lagorio studied at the Istituto Magistrale Giuliano Della Rovere, a teachers' college in Savona, and at the University of Turin, where in 1943 she received a degree in Italian literature with a thesis on English sepulchral poetry. In 1945 she married Emilio Lagorio, a businessman, and had two daughters, Simonetta (1946) and Silvia (1960).

As early as 1950 Lagorio began contributing to cultural magazines and newspapers. In 1954, having won various *concorsi statali* (state competitions), she was appointed professor of history and Italian literature at the Instituto Magistrale di Mondovi, a teachers' college in Cuneo. From 1955 to 1973 she taught at the Istituto Tecnico Commerciale in Savona. In 1973 she abandoned teaching to devote more time to writing. After the death of her first husband in 1963, Lagorio moved to Milan, where she works as an editorial consultant to the Garzanti publishing house. She is also a contributor to the dailies *Corriere della sera, Società civile,* and *L'Unità*. She was elected to the Italian Parliament in 1987 and served for five years as a member of the Independent Left. Lagorio married the publisher Livio Garzanti in 1981.

In her literary development Lagorio drew inspiration from the two geographical areas where she grew up and from the writers associated with them. Her work shows strong affinities with the novelists Cesare Pavese and Beppe Fenoglio, who are also natives of the Langhe region. In Liguria, to which she became attached during her adolescence and early married life, she developed close relationships with Camillo Sbarbaro and Angelo Barile, who contributed decisively to her sensitivity to nature and its transformation in remarkable images. When discussing her literary formation, Lagorio never fails to mention these regions and writers.

Il polline (The Pollen, 1966), Lagorio's first important work, is a tribute to her beloved Langhe. The twelve short stories that comprise the volume evoke images of Piedmont, with its range of colors, tones and shadings, scents, and textures. In these stories one can even see reflections of Pavese's treatment of specific themes, such as one's attachment to the native region, peasant customs, and rural folklore. But unlike Pavese, Lagorio creates characters who when they return to their native towns find the strength they need to transform sorrows and pains into learning experiences. Not unlike some of her fictional characters, Lagorio says of her native land: "Scoprivo la mia terra vivendone lontana: certi ricordi affioravano e li rielaboravo secondo un filo fantastico" (I discovered my land living away from it: certain memories would surface and I would re-elaborate them through a fantastic thread). These early stories already show the marks of Lagorio's distinctive style: agile expression, absence of euphemisms, immediacy of feelings and ideas, and vivid images of places and people.

Liguria provides the backdrop for the short novel *Un ciclone chiamato Titti* (A Cyclone Called Titti, 1969), Lagorio's second book. The narrator, Gina, discloses her feelings about the arduous yet enchanting development of her relationship with her second child, Titti, who was born rather late in her life. The daughter creates a "cyclone" in her mother's life, bringing confusion and upsetting the routine of family life. The text abounds with spirited confrontations between mother and daughter as the latter goes from youthful obstinacy to independence. The intensity and fluent style of the novel recall the richness of the tones and rhythms of the spoken language. It is Lagorio's first serious exploration of the love theme that is central to her fiction: "Il nocciolo delle cose umane resta sempre l'amore . . . le violenze più profonde, quelle che straziano, perché non sai come combatterle, ci vengono dall'amore" (Love remains the center of human action . . . the most violent acts, those that tug at your heart because you don't know how to fight them, come from love).

In Lagorio's literary development these first two books are of fundamental importance, for they reveal the critical premises for the novels that follow. Together they underscore Lagorio's commitment to fiction, her belief that through imaginative writing one can probe complex relationships and diverse psychological states. They also establish the cultural and geographical foci for her career.

Approssimato per difetto (Approximation by Default, 1971) is considered by many critics to be Lagorio's most important work. It deals with sorrow, joy, illness, death, love, and the search for truth–themes that are filtered through the sentimental and psychological portraits of the characters. The novel, narrated in the first person, begins with an account by Renzo, the main character, who is dying from a brain tumor, and is then concluded by his wife, Valeria. As the illness increasingly isolates Renzo, he begins to fill the silences and the immobility of his days with long soliloquies in an effort to draw a full account of his life and achieve an understanding of his relationship with his wife. The result is a process of deconstruction and reconstruction of his life as he tries to give meaning to the choices he has made and the events that have marked his existence: his active opposition to Fascism, his political disillusionment after the war, his love for Valeria and his children, and the awful present.

Renzo is moved to self-analysis, above all, by the realization that it has been both painful and difficult for him to communicate with Valeria, a problem that has been conveniently hidden behind their mutual respect and a facade of matrimonial devotion:

> Vicini, come estranei, sentivo che la sua sofferenza veniva incontro alla mia, a onde sempre più larghe, e noi ciechi a opporle la nostra resistenza, di orgoglio, di pudore chissà di che.... Chi può dire perchè si sciupino tante parole per cose che non contano e si taccia di quello che ci preme di più, e ci soffoca se non riusciamo a tirarlo fuori.

> (Next to each other, like strangers, I felt that her suffering was moving toward mine in ever larger waves, and we, blind, were opposing resistance, made up of pride, of reserve, who knows what. Who can say why we waste so many words on things that do not count but keep silent on what matters the most, something that suffocates us if we don't succeed in pulling it out.)

The novel treats Renzo's death through its long and painful agony, yet one soon realizes that the real focus is Valeria. It is Valeria who begins to punctuate her husband's long silences with actions, thoughts, and words, closing the gaps in understanding his existence as her husband's illness progresses and death comes ever closer. Valeria's identification with him becomes a meeting point of parallel suffering converging in Renzo's death, a meeting of souls never achieved before. The rhythm of the narrative is tight and free of diversions. The action of the novel unfolds through a close interlacing of the two characters' points of view and recollections of the past rendered through juxtaposed monologues.

Since Valeria shared the stage with Renzo in *Approssimato per difetto*, *La spiaggia del lupo* (Wolf's Beach, 1977), Lagorio's next novel, may be said to feature her first female protagonist. Angela is followed through the stages of adolescence to young adulthood and on to full maturity—acquiring at each stage an inner strength that gives her self-reliance and determination. In the first part of the novel, dealing with Angela's adolescence, she leads a fanciful life, with long swims and endless walks along the beach. The images of the sun, seagulls' flights, and swimming are framed by immense expanses of blue skies and a waving sea. The title was suggested by "uno scoglio grande scavato in alto, come una testa su un corpo di bestia accovacciata ma pronta a scattare" (a large sea rock, with an erosion at the top, such as resembles the head of a crouched animal, ready to leap forward).

Angela's dreamy innocence is brought to a halt by the arrival of Vladi, a handsome married man of thirty from Milan with whom she falls in love. Her first clash with mature life is painful, and her first stay in Milan proves to be a disappointment. When she has a child with Vladi and realizes his unwillingness to leave the comfort of his married life, Angela is thrust into a world of responsibility, class struggle, and social engagement. The harshness of real life forces her to reexamine her actions and to gain fresh insights until in the end she finds the inner strength needed to remain faithful to herself and to her roots. The Angela that returns to Milan at the close of the novel is a fully mature woman ready to take responsibility for herself as well as for her son:

> Alzò gli occhi al finestrino: si accorse che il mare non accompagnava più la corsa del treno. Con una stretta al cuore pensò a Carlo.... Si alzò. Aveva la sua forza e la sua gioventù, per lui e per sè: insieme, a Milano, avrebbero costruito la loro casa. Milano era una città ferita, ma viva. Anche lei lo era.

> (She looked up to the train window: she realized the view of the sea was gone. With a constricted heart she thought of Carlo.... She got up. She had strength and she had her youth, for him and for herself; in Milan, together they would build their home. Milan was a wounded city but alive. So was she.)

As Lagorio told Claudio Toscani in a 1977 interview, Angela is the image of the modern woman because she fights to gain her own dignity and individual identity: "Senza inutili nostalgie o regressioni di convenienza, accetta fino in fondo la realtà sua e del suo tempo e del suo ambiente" (Without useless nostalgia, or regressions of convenience, she accepts to the end her reality, the reality of her time and her environment).

In *Fuori scena* (Away from the Spotlight, 1979) Lagorio shows that love is both impossible to achieve and impossible to forsake. In a strong vein of Pirandellian existential thought, Lagorio elaborates on the inability to communicate between individuals, be it mother and daughter, husband and wife, or lovers. Incomprehension, cold barriers of silence, and strained dialogues seem to rise between people, couples in particular, while a frantic search for meaning motivates individual actions and behavior.

Like Angela in *La spiaggia del lupo*, the protagonist, Elena, asks questions dealing with life, love, and existential meaning. Unlike Angela, Elena is a mature woman at the twilight of life, not discovering love as a youthful emotion but reeling from the crisis of a painful experience with a younger man, Marco, who is unfaithful. While Angela's interior monologues afford her the strength to face the future, Elena's thoughts revert to the past. The return to the safety of the hometown brings Elena back, spiritually and emotionally, to her youth, with its idealism and dreams.

Fuori scena elaborates an important theme in Lagorio's works: the significance of one's tie to birthplace, a relationship that can be envisioned as an uncut umbilical cord connecting individuals to their native roots. Young and old, Lagorio's characters find in the return to their origins the strength needed to reorder their lives. It is in the town of her youth, Cherasco, a place of solitude, silence, and memories, that Elena is finally able to comprehend herself. Here she expresses her anguish and in so doing acquires a perspective that had eluded her. As in a mythical world, Elena feels the town's fresh air anew; recognizes its ancient churches, old walls, ramparts, and trees; and becomes aware of the town as a silent witness to other times and other dreams. Submerging herself in her memory enables her to face her daughter, free herself from Marco, and find the courage to accept a life of solitude: "Se la solitudine è una scelta, non è angoscia, ma è maturità" (If loneliness is a choice, it is not anguish, but maturity).

In the works examined thus far, Lagorio's female protagonist through personal suffering is able to develop an emancipatory awareness, an autonomy of judgment and will that parallels the author's own *voglia di chiarezza* (desire for clarity). Angela's words could be spoken by Elena and seem representative of the courageous quintessential female imagined by Lagorio: "Essere sola non mi fa paura: mi fa paura sentirmi divisa, vivere a metà. Sono forte e mi basto; di questo soffro: che mi sono accorta di bastarmi" (To be alone does not scare me: what scares me is to feel divided, to live in half. I am strong and I am self-sufficient; I suffer for this: I have become aware of being self-sufficient).

In *Tosca dei gatti* (Tosca of the Cats, 1983) Lagorio creates a protagonist who is not as strong as her predecessors. The novel tells the sad story of a fifty-year-old woman who finds herself widowed, childless, and alone. She reacts by withdrawing into a closed world where cats are her only companions. Lagorio renders Tosca's solitude even more desolate by contrasting it with the beauty of her surroundings, the secluded beaches with luxuriant slopes and shimmering sea. Like many of Luigi Pirandello's characters, Tosca in her anguish searches for meaning in her life. And like Pirandello's humble characters, Tosca's vain attempts to communicate with others are met with scorn and indifference to the point of moving her to an irrational solution: a maniacal love and dedication to cats.

Gigi Moncalieri, a writer and journalist, and Toni, his girlfriend, become interested in Tosca's solitary existence to the point where Gigi decides to write about Tosca. In getting to know her, he comes to understand not only Tosca's life but also the reality of so many other displaced women who are condemned to lives of miserable solitude. The intellectual Gigi is so taken by Tosca's life that he grows to commiserate with her and to feel the pain and the isolation of Tosca's world. Despite Gigi's and Toni's friendship, Tosca finds little reason to alter her life of alienation. Their befriending her does not suffice to fill the void. Slowly but inexorably, Tosca poisons her body as she seeks the oblivion wine can provide.

Tosca's final night at the beach exemplifies the beauty of shared lives and the misfortune of being alone. In this scene the celebration for Italy's World Cup victory is over; the last bonfires are reduced to ashes; and everyone has gone home. Tosca is left alone, with nowhere to go and no one waiting for her:

> Con il freddo, la nausea la riafferrò al pensiero delle ore che sarebbero venute, nella serie dei giorni che l'aspettava . . . la festa, la breve inebriante prova che si può essere felici con gli altri, insieme, era davvero finita. Doveva rientrare in casa, incontrare gli stessi fantasmi, senza nessuna voce a salutare con lei un altro sole.

> (With the cold air, the nausea took hold of her again at the thought of the coming hours, of the days waiting for her . . . the celebration, the brief exhilarating proof that it is possible to be happy with others, together had indeed come to an end. She had to return home, meet the same ghosts, and without a voice to greet with her another dawn.)

Tosca lacks the courage and the ability to learn from suffering that characterizes Valeria, Angela, and Elena. For Tosca the only triumph is death, as Gigi recognizes:

> Se fosse, che so, più colta, o forse no, solo più forte, o avesse una fede sicura, raggiungerebbe uno stato di perfetta autonomia nella sua solitudine. Ma per riuscirci bisogna essere santi, o un genio, o un artista. Lei è solo una donna che non ha avuto una buona sorte.

> (If she were, what should I say, more educated, or perhaps only stronger, or if she had a strong faith, she would reach a state of perfect autonomy in her loneliness. But to succeed one must be a saint, or a genius, or an artist. She is only a woman who has not been lucky in life.)

Tosca's life affords Lagorio the opportunity to explore the ultimate failure of communication and the existential condition of solitude.

Dust jackets for two of Lagorio's books published in the 1990s

Golfo del Paradiso (Paradise Gulf, 1987) brought Lagorio the coveted Rapallo Prize. Even though the novel reexamines themes presented in other works, such as the problems of women and their quest for self-identity, and in particular the theme of solitude, it must be seen as a pause in Lagorio's existential search for meaning and self-understanding. The rhythm of the narration is less dramatic and less intense. Giulia, the protagonist, hardly resembles the women of earlier novels. Her sweet, docile personality contrasts with the complex spirits of the other Lagorian protagonists, all engaged in the battle of self-discovery.

Giulia, still beautiful and in love with her husband, Michele, is lonely and frustrated in her childlessness and feeling some distance from him. Michele, though a loving husband, is a famous painter and labors under a host of pressures and professional demands. He views Giulia as a passive yet necessary presence for his inspiration. The plot of the novel revolves around the search for one of Michele's early oil paintings, *Silenzio a Pareggi,* which he sold when he was young but now wants to find it for his personal collection. She is especially jealous of Michele's female students and his admirers. The importance of the novel, though, lies in Lagorio's fine observations on the meanderings of the human mind as the protagonists and two other characters, Paolo and Margherita, search for Michele's missing paintings. The novelist uses this search to explore the convoluted folds of the human psyche, unknown and often threatening, and shows how a common experience can affect personal growth in different ways.

Lagorio's *Tra le mura stellate* (Within the Stellar Walls, 1991) is a return to the mythical town of Cherasco, the setting of *Fuori scena*. The novel tells the tale of the town through incidents and stories related to entire families and single individuals, from all social classes, economic backgrounds, and religious faiths. The work was inspired by the unpublished "Annali di Cherasco," an account of annual events in Cherasco, written by Gian Francesco Damilano between 1731 and 1806, an era that spans from the middle of the eighteenth century to the Napoleonic period. Lagorio extends the time frame to the end of World War II, covering the years from 1731 to 1945.

Weaving historical events and plausible facts, Lagorio creates vivid sketches of past life in Cherasco: the rise and fall of noble families, happy and unfortunate love episodes, births of legitimate and illegitimate children—the representative events of a bygone era.

There are stories of legendary madness, such as that of Count Ernesto Del Melle, who, in order to offer his beloved Russian wife a taste of her native land, had his whole estate covered with sugar during a snowless winter. There are unforgettable images of women, such as the young wife of the Conte della Torre, Margherita Giacinta Colli, who suffered death at the hands of her rejected lover; and Marietta, a humble embroideress, who, young and untamable, fought relentlessly to keep her illegitimate son. The novel recounts the visit of the legendary poet Countess Lara, who found in Cherasco a brief but intense love affair with the handsome and aristocratic Ratti. Finally there are stories of proud Cherasco citizens who offered shelter to the Jews persecuted during the dark years of Fascism.

The structure of *Tra le mura stellate* is a cyclical one. It opens and closes with the same image—"La nebbia, tanto fitta che oltre i bastioni il mondo non esiste più" (A fog so thick that the world beyond the city walls no longer exists). This framing device suggests an understanding of life as a recurrence of cycles, of natural seasons and of the stages of human existence spanning from birth to death. A gentle yet ironic tone pervades the novel, which Lagorio uses to remind the reader that historical events leave room for interpretation, for in most instances truth proves elusive. Thus she prefers to leave a veil of mystery over the characters and events that mark Cherasco's past.

Il silenzio: racconti di una vita (The Silence: Stories and a Life, 1993) is a collection of twenty-four short stories, some written as early as 1963. Only one, "Natale a Serre Chevalier"- (Christmas at Serre Chevalier), was previously unpublished. *Il silenzio* moves from images of small towns to larger cities, from country to mountains, always revealing a deep, objective understanding of the places visited and the individuals and situations presented, combining a distinctive style with vivid and meaningful images. From the first to the last, these stories spanning much of Lagorio's career show her as an intrepid woman, always striving to know and understand herself.

New concerns surface in the collection as Lagorio often focuses on the feeling of abandonment that comes with the departure of children and advancing age. Her characters neither fear nor hide from the natural process of aging. Shedding their illusions, they face the future with renewed faith in themselves. The author shows that denial is sometimes a necessary mechanism in the struggle for survival. In "Il signor Pietro" a dying old man denies to others, and most of all to himself, the pain caused by his son's abandonment so he can die with dignity. A mother in "Il tramonto" (Sunset) denies her solitude, filling the silence of her home created by the departure of her youngest daughter with music from the radio. The character remains simply "a mother," her anonymity suggesting the universality of her situation.

With *Il bastardo* (The Bastard, 1996) Lagorio continues her fictional exploration of history. When asked if her work is historical fiction or a real historical novel, Lagorio answered: "Credo che ci sia più verità storica nel mio bastardo reinventato che non in una serie di documenti messi uno accanto all'altro" (I believe there is more historical truth in my reinvented bastard than in a series of manuscripts placed next to one another). The novel is centered on the sad story of Don Emanuel, the illegitimate son of Carlo Emanuele I of Savoy. Emanuel, though beloved by his father, lived all his life at the margins of the European courts. He was looked down upon and ridiculed by all, not only for his illegitimate birth but also for the "diversity" of his sexuality. Don Emanuel was a homosexual, an unacceptable condition in the furiously religious seventeenth century.

Lagorio studied the character of Don Emanuel for five years, poring over his 270 extant letters. She presents a man who pursues an impossible search for acceptance, not only from others but also from himself. Always lonely and desperately afraid of the hostile world in which he lives, Emanuel attempts to find solace in ephemeral affairs with many young men that he encounters during his roaming life. Even his long-lasting relationship with his beloved footman, Vercellone, brings him unhappiness. Emanuel, continuously feeling the irreconcilable chasm between his learned religiosity and his sexual desires, cannot appease the restlessness of his soul. At his death in October 1652, the penniless Emanuel was denied a burial due one of his class. Lagorio writes, "Fu sepolto miseramente: talis vita similis exitus" (He was buried miserably: such was his life, such his death).

In her next work, *Inventario* (Inventory, 1997), as suggested by its title, Lagorio takes stock of her full life, not only of her career as an artist but also of her experiences as woman, wife, mother, and grandmother:

> Ora, con i pensieri della sera, mi pare di giocare ancora "a vendere": meglio, tento l'inventario delle merci. L'inventario è per un magazzino che si è riempito in così lungo tempo di cose, e alcune preziose, questo è vero, ma che potrebbe chiudere i battenti da un momento all'altro. E senza preavviso.

> (Now, my thoughts turned to the evening of my life, I feel as though I am still playing the "selling" game: better yet, I am offering an inventory of my merchandise. It is the inventory of a warehouse filled with objects over a long time, some truly precious, but the place could close its doors at any moment. And without notice.)

Reading *Inventario*, one encounters faces and places, voices and characters present in Lagorio's earlier prose.

The overall tone is one of melancholy, for time that has gone by too fast and for a body that has aged while the spirit has remained young. Lagorio asserts, "non si spengono con l'età i desideri, la curiosità, l'impegno per le cose in cui si crede" (age does not stifle desires, curiosity, obligations for those things one believes in). The book closes with an observation about love: "L'amore, già. Senza, niente si dovrebbe fare e se si fa, ha la gravezza della roccia che ti schiaccia il petto in un ascensione sfortunata" (Love, indeed. Without it, nothing should be done, and if one does anything, it has the heaviness of a mountain that crushes your breasts in an unfortunate ascending). The love that Lagorio brings to her conclusion, intended here for her granddaughter, is key to her entire corpus.

Gina Lagorio is a writer of intelligence and tenderness, interested in probing the mysterious folds of the human mind so to better understand the inescapable realities of modern lives: the inability to communicate, the rupture of relationships, the continual need for love. Her works are notable for their complex portraits of women and reflect both traditional and modern perspectives. Her modern woman develops strength in order to learn, to find within herself what is necessary to break away from internal and external boundaries. Courage keeps such women moving, even if it means isolation within a resisting society accustomed to a different image of womanhood. But Lagorio's woman is traditional in the ties she has to her familial origins, which help her to live fully in the present.

Interviews:

Claudio Toscani, "Incontro con Gina Lagorio," *Il Ragguaglio librario*, no. 5 (1977): 128–129;

Maria Grazia Bevilacqua, "Intervista a Lagorio," *Famiglia cristiana*, 27 January 1980, pp. 45–54;

Edgarda Ferri, "Scrivo e scrivo, taglio e sento dolore," *Millelibri* (1989): 52–60;

Pasquale Maffeo, "Gina Lagorio," in *Le scritture narrative. Interviste a scrittori italiani* (Napoli: Italibri, 1992), pp. 53–64;

Brenda Webster, "Interview with Gina Lagorio," *Pen American Center Newsletter*, 79 (October 1992): 31–32.

References:

Alberto Bertoni, "Autocoscienza e sensibilità d'artista," *Il lettore di provincia*, 71 (April 1988): 45–54;

Gualtiero De Santi, "Il cerchio della vita," *Si scrive. Rivista semestrale di letteratura*, 25 (February 1993): 209–212;

Lorenza Farina, "Gina Lagorio, scrittrice di sentimenti e di personaggi," *Letture*, 40 (1985): 691–708;

Lucio Felici, "Gina Lagorio," *Otto/Novecento*, 4 (March–April 1980): 121–147;

Rosario Fisichella, "Condizione femminile e solitudine nei romanzi di Gina Lagorio," *Atti e Memorie dell'Accademia Petrarca di Lettere, Arti e Scienze*, new series 52 (1990): 57–74;

Silvana Folliero, "Approssimato per difetto," *Il Ponte*, no. 2–3 (February–March 1973): 413–419;

Pietro Frassica, "Gina Lagorio and Tosca's Solitude," *Italica*, 65 (Winter 1988): 329–343;

Elio Gianola, "La divisione, la morte, l'amore: strutture profonde dei romanzi di Gina Lagorio," *Letteratura italiana contemporanea*, 14 (1984): 215–232;

Dante Maffia, *Forme espressive e radici nella narrativa di Gina Lagorio* (Acireale: Lunarionuovo, 1985);

Silvio Riolfo Marengo, "*Approssimato per difetto*, Gina Lagorio," *Ausonia*, no. 5–6 (September–December 1971): 89–92;

Franco Mollia, "La condizione di Penelope," in *Penelope senza tela* (Ravenna: Longo, 1984), pp. 333–370;

Mark F. Pietralunga, "Gina Lagorio and the Courage of Women," in *Contemporary Women Writers in Italy: A Modern Renaissance*, edited by Santo L. Arico (Amherst: University of Massachusetts Press, 1990), pp. 77–88;

Paolo Ruffilli, "La scrittura al femminile," *Il lettore di provincia*, no. 49–50 (September 1982): 82–87;

Guido Sommavilla, "Fuori scena di Gina Lagorio," *Letture*, no. 13 (February 1980): 127–130;

Maria Luisa Vecchi, "Ritratti critici di contemporanei: Gina Lagorio," *Il lettore di provincia*, 65–66 (June–September 1986): 48–58.

Luigi Malerba
(11 November 1927 –   )

Francesco Guardiani
University of Toronto

BOOKS: *La scoperta dell'alfabeto* (Milan: Bompiani, 1963);

Il serpente (Milan: Bompiani, 1966); translated by William Weaver as *The Serpent* (New York: Farrar Straus Giroux, 1968; London: Hamilton, 1968);

Salto mortale (Milan: Bompiani, 1968); translated by Weaver as *What Is This Buzzing, Do You Hear It Too?* (New York: Farrar Straus Giroux, 1969);

Il protagonista (Milan: Bompiani, 1973);

Le rose imperiali (Milan: Bompiani, 1974);

Mozziconi (Turin: Einaudi, 1975);

Le parole abbandonate. Un repertorio dialettale emiliano (Milan: Bompiani, 1977);

Pinocchio con gli stivali (Rome: Cooperativa Scrittori, 1977);

Storiette (Turin: Einaudi, 1977);

Il pataffio (Milan: Bompiani, 1978);

Dopo il pescecane (Milan: Bompiani, 1979);

Le galline pensierose (Turin: Einaudi, 1980; enlarged edition, Milan: Mondadori, 1994);

Diario di un sognatore (Turin: Einaudi, 1981);

Storiette tascabili (Turin: Einaudi, 1984);

Cina Cina (Lecce: Piero Manni, 1985);

Nuove storie dell'anno Mille, by Malerba and Tonino Guerra, edited by Gaetano Sansone (Milan: Bompiani, 1986);

Il pianeta azzurro (Milan: Garzanti, 1986);

I cani di Gerusalemme, by Malerba and Fabio Carpi (Rome: Theoria, 1988);

Testa d'argento (Milan: Mondadori, 1988);

Il fuoco greco (Milan: Mondadori, 1990);

Le pietre volanti (Milan: Rizzoli, 1992);

Il viaggiatore sedentario (Milan: Rizzoli, 1993);

Le maschere (Milan: Mondadori, 1995);

Itaca per sempre (Milan: Mondadori, 1997).

Collection: *Storie dell'anno Mille,* by Malerba and Tonino Guerra (Milan: Bompiani, 1977).

OTHER: *Cinquanta anni di cinema italiano,* edited by Malerba and Carmine Siniscalaco (Rome: Bestetti, 1954); translated as *Fifty Years of Italian Cinema,* edited by Herman G. Weinberg (Rome: Bestetti, 1955).

Luigi Malerba (photograph by Giovanni Giovannetti)

Widely read and translated, Luigi Malerba published the first of his more than twenty books of fiction in 1963. Working as a young screenwriter in Cinecittà, the large motion-picture studio outside of Rome, Malerba met and was encouraged to write *La scoperta dell'alfabeto* (The Discovery of the Alphabet), a collection of short stories about the peasants of his native Emilia, by Ennio Flaiano, the multifaceted author of novels, plays, films, and documentaries. Malerba's early experience in film, television, and advertising undoubtedly influenced his vivid prose style, especially his use of fast-paced dialogue, in his subsequent career. While this first collection was well received critically, it was *Il serpente* (1966; translated as *The Serpent,* 1968) and especially *Salto mortale* (1968; translated as *What Is This Buzzing, Do You Hear It Too?,* 1969) that established Malerba's reputation as one of the major Italian writers of the time both nationally, on account of the novelty of his style in responding to the expectations for renewal expressed by the Gruppo 63, and internationally, thanks also to the brilliant English translations by William Weaver.

Malerba was born 11 November 1927 in Berceto, a small town in the Emilia region of northern central Italy, where his family owned a farm. He lived there until 1950 when, having satisfied the expectations of his family with a law degree from the University of Parma, he moved to Rome eager to change his life radically and become a scriptwriter in the motion-picture industry. In the early 1950s he collaborated with screenwriter Cesare Zavattini and movie directors such as Alberto Lattuada, Marco Ferreri, and Mario Monicelli. In 1953 he and Antonio Marchi codirected the movie *Donne e soldati* (Women and Soldiers). He continued to take an interest in the family farm, and when circumstances demanded his presence there, he divided his time between Rome and Berceto. He married Anna Lapenna in 1962 and the couple has two children.

Malerba played an active role in the intellectual renewal of the 1960s. He was a member of the Gruppo 63 avant-garde movement. With Walter Pedullà, Angelo Guglielmi, and Alfredo Giuliani he founded the Cooperativa Scrittori, a publishing company intended as a risk-taking alternative to the established publishing houses. The first book brought out by Cooperativa Scrittori was *Relazione parlamentare antimafia* (Report of the Parliamentary Commission on the Mafia), a document that proved to be crucial for subsequent investigations regarding the Mafia and its connections with political institutions.

In addition to his novels Malerba is an important writer in other venues. From 1972 until 1982 he wrote regularly for the cultural section of *Il Corriere della sera,* and since then he has collaborated steadily with another national newspaper, *La Repubblica*. Other occasional writings, short fiction, and criticism appeared regularly for more than two decades in various periodicals in Italy and abroad in Germany, France, Russia, England, and the United States. Malerba's social commitment and literary achievements won him an honorary degree from the University of Palermo in 1990. He has also won several literary prizes, including the Viareggio, Selezione Campiello, Prix Medicis, Mondello, and Flaiano. He presently spends his time between Rome and in a farmhouse near Orvieto.

Il serpente, Salto mortale, and *Il protagonista* (The Protagonist, 1973), in which he refined the experimental language of the first two novels, established Malerba's identity as a writer not only in the market of ideas that was the Italian literary milieu of the 1960s and early 1970s but especially in the writer's own consciousness. Malerba has never written a novel to demonstrate or rationalize something he acquired through philosophical speculation; as he once remarked, every new book is an adventure as well as a gamble, a statement that indicates how the act of writing enables him to make new discoveries.

Because of his background Malerba's development cannot be said to be the result of a writer-to-writer influence. His answer to a question about his sources, which was published in Francesco Guardiani's article "New Italian Fiction" in the fall 1992 issue of *The Review of Contemporary Fiction,* was telling:

> This is a thorny subject. I have said many times that my literature teacher is Buster Keaton, but if I have to mention a writer not too far back in time, I would cite Italo Svevo, a real source of inspiration for the Italian literature of this century. On a wider perspective, I would recall *Notes from Underground* by Dostoyevski. Another debt that I can recognize without problems is to scientific publications, physics texts specifically, which for me are the real avant-garde of literature.

Especially in view of Malerba's declared debt to a silent-movie artist, it seems that his peculiar style is primarily dependent on a perceptual attitude, at the same time quixotic and scientific.

Malerba's writing reveals an uncompromising desire to probe even the most remote aspects of a given experience and to verify them without any physical, intellectual, or spiritual help from outside, as is suggested by a reflection in *Il serpente:*

> Tieni presente che nessuno vorrà aiutarti, che molti cercheranno anzi di ostacolarti. Ti converrà lavorare in silenzio e in segreto perché solo cosí si portano a termine le grandi imprese. E non chiedere aiuto all'Architetto perche l'Architetto ha molto da fare.
>
> (Keep in mind that nobody will want to help you, will try rather, to obstruct you. It will be better to work in silence and in secret because that is the only way great deeds are achieved. And don't ask The Architect for any help because He is very busy.)

The object of Malerba's quest is to make sense of reality, and this can only be done with painstaking attention to detail. Occasionally he interrupts the narration to emphasize this point: "Racconto tutto per precisione, perche mi piace essere preciso" (I tell everything for the sake of precision, because I like to be precise).

Dust jacket for the American edition of Malerba's 1966 novel, in which a storekeeper claims to have murdered and devoured his lover

Malerba's characters are often alienated human beings, troubled by an imbalance between their inner vision of the world and the actual situations in which they find themselves. It is from the dynamics created by this conflict that the plot develops. He often narrates in the first person, which means that the text comes out as if uttered by his alienated protagonists. Francesco Muzzioli, author of a lucid essay on Malerba, presents him as "an educational writer" to signify that he forces readers to think, to verify "the facts" from many perspectives before coming to conclusions about what is real and what is not. Malerba's practical lesson is one of tolerance in the face of experiences that do not fit the heretofore accepted vision of the world. This in part explains the writer's attraction for unusual or exotic settings–from the Far East to the Middle Ages, from hallucinations to fairy tales.

The storekeeper of *Il serpente* is a lucid narrator of his own alienation. He is believable when he asserts that he has killed his lover and devoured her still warm body. The reader's first inkling of doubt comes with his confession to the police; they cannot identify the victim and there is no trace of her other than the words of the confessed murderer. Further investigations lead the reader to question the reality of the murder and, with it, the entire tale of the novel. One is forced to conclude that the storekeeper's story was fiction, fiction within a work of fiction, which is Malerba's way of approaching reality.

In *Salto mortale* the central gap between reality and imagination widens and becomes more problematic since the events are presented from a multiplicity of viewpoints and make one suspect Gadda's

Quer pasticciaccio brutto de via Merulana (1957; translated as *That Awful Mess on Via Merulana*, 1965) as a source of inspiration. The mystery story (a character sees a leg lying in the grass, and then the rest of a dead body—every perceptual "frame" counts) fascinates Malerba for the variety of possibilities (and impossibilities) offered by the analytical attempt to reconstruct what really happened.

Less problematic on a narrative level but more overtly experimental in terms of language, *Il protagonista* has as its protagonist a penis, to which a body and a mind are attached. The narration of this story, which is built around a psychological case of threatened identity, is again in the first person. The most disquieting reality of the protagonist's situation is that he becomes impotent in normal sexual circumstances. He can only have a sexual relationship with his lover through the electromagnetic waves of their amateur radio sets. Technology, then, has altered the normal channels of communication. At the end of the novel, after a crescendo of dramatic attempts to make love with the world—with the embalmed corpse of a gigantic whale, a bronze statue of Garibaldi, and an Egyptian mummy in the Vatican museum—the amateur radio operator is presented as trying to sodomize himself. Such a disturbing image allegorically represents the psychological disaster looming over a self-centered society unable to maintain its human dimension in a technologically altered environment.

With *Le rose imperiali* (Imperial Roses, 1974) Malerba embraces the realm of the exotic, for the stories that make up this loosely assembled novel are all set in the Far East of ancient times. This variation in setting is a consequence of Malerba's systematic questioning of the principles that make up the reality of his characters. His frequent use of the first-person narrator intensifies and dramatizes his protagonists' ever anxious and often frustrated quest for a stable order of social and psychological structures where imagination and factual reality may coexist in balanced harmony. Assuming the mental framework and dispositions of his chosen characters, Malerba tries to explain from within the unusual contexts he imagines.

In 1975 Malerba published *Mozziconi* (Cigarette Butts), a book for children that is of interest to adults as well. Other such books include *Pinocchio con gli stivali* (Pinocchio with Boots, 1977), in which he mixes up familiar fairy tales, giving them surprising twists; *Nuove storie dell'anno Mille* (New Stories of the Year One Thousand, 1986), a collaboration with Tonino Guerra where survival becomes the dramatic subject; and *Storiette* (Little Stories, 1977) and *Storiette tascabili* (Little Pocket Stories, 1984), in which he uses the rhetorical device of personification to allow objects and animals to explain their points of view. *Le galline pensierose* (Thoughtful Chickens, 1980), in which the protagonists come up with 131 bizarre propositions or short anecdotes, provides a good example of Malerba's ability to write for audiences of all ages:

> Una gallina enciclopedica aveva imparato a memoria più di mille parole. A questo punto credeva di essere diventata sapiente e quando stava con le compagne ogni tanto diceva "rombo" oppure "cratere" oppure "ortica." A chi le domandava che cosa significassero quelle parole rispondeva che il mondo è fatto di parole e che se non ci fossero le parole non ci sarebbe nemmeno il mondo, comprese le galline.
>
> (An encyclopedic chicken had memorized more than a thousand words. At this point she thought she had become learned and when she was with her friends, every now and then she would say "rhombus" or "crater" or "nettle." To those who asked her what those words meant she answered that the world is made of words, and that without words there would be no world, and no chickens either.)

While verging on nonsense, these propositions often have existential significance.

Malerba's fundamental concern with language is manifest in his nonfiction work *Le parole abbandonate. Un repertorio dialettale emiliano* (Forgotten Words. A Repertoire of Emilian Dialect, 1977). As the subtitle indicates, the book contains a repertoire of words belonging to the oral tradition of the Emilia region. Malerba, who has often listed farming as among his favorite activities, reconstructs a community that flourished for centuries and is now rapidly heading for extinction. With chapter headings "House," "Land," "Work," "Animals," "Humans," and "Food," the culture is examined through the words the people used everyday.

Malerba returned to the Middle Ages, which he had used as the setting for *Nuove storie dell'anno Mille,* for the major novel *Il pataffio* (The Epitaph, 1978), a work that also shows his central concern with language and style. Quoting Erich Auerbach, Malerba asserts in "New Italian Fiction" that ideally a story should be told in the language in which it occurred, and in *Il pataffio* the characters speak in an old dialect of the Lazio region where the action is set. A group of hunger-stricken soldiers who speak an improbable mixture of dialects attempt the conquest of a remote fiefdom in the interior of the region; they claim to have a "mandate," but the peasants are convinced they are there only to disturb their way of life and steal their food. The tone varies from the antiheroic to the grotesque, taken to the extreme in an episode depicting cannibalism. The most striking quality of the novel, though, is the language concocted by the resourceful author.

Malerba began the 1980s with *Diario di un sognatore* (Diary of a Dreamer, 1981), in which a thin line separates reality from fiction. By collecting in chronological order one year of his dreams, Malerba suggests that one must become aware of the subconscious level of existence. The dreams, which he refuses to interpret or to reduce to a mere reflection of the supposedly more important reality of waking life, create a setting that is similar to those in his novels. In Marlerba's dreams, as in his fiction, the reader joins the author in the attempt to decipher human constructs.

Malerba contends that the reality of dreams is not inferior to that of waking life. The dream, as he explains in the "Prologo del sognatore" (Prologue of the Dreamer), seems to him a purer form of imagination:

> I sogni diventano di per sé stessi esperienze reali senza per questo dover rendere conto alla realtà delle loro strutture e forme. Il rapporto tra *la cosa* e *l'immagine* che rende concrete le nostre percezioni nell'ambito del reale, decade nel sogno per *assenza della cosa*. Per quanto il sogno si presenti spesso come prolungamento e digressione della realtà, le sue immagini sono dunque senza fondamento e non si dispongono secondo un ordine, ma lo creano a posteriori, lo inventano.

> (Dreams in themselves become real experiences without needing to account for their structures and forms to reality. The relationship between *the thing* and *the image*, which solidifies our perceptions in the realm of reality, declines in the dreams because of *the absence of the thing*. Although dreams present themselves as extensions and digressions of reality, their images are without foundation and do not align themselves according to an order; rather, they create it, they invent it.)

One of Malerba's most acclaimed novels, *Il pianeta azzurro* (The Blue Planet, 1986) is undoubtedly his most overtly political work. It deals with the decay of the ruling political class in Italy, represented by the malignant figure of the Professore (Professor), a master of treacherous plots involving Freemasons, the Catholic Church, and a horde of corrupt collaborators, who has always been able to escape justice. The novel is structured as an upside-down mystery, with the murder of the Professore taking place at the end and the would-be assassin identified from the beginning. And yet the long-planned assassination is far from being logically explained by the punctiliously exact and fact-oriented narration. The story unfolds through a set of notebooks the author pretends to have found; the notes, however, appear to have been examined and retouched by a second hand. Readers, then, follow a plot (with commentary by the principal narrator, the author himself, at the beginning and then at the end of each chapter) taken from a story that has already been filtered through a first "reviewer." It is a Chinese box structure in which the question of what is real soon becomes central and disquieting. Malerba thus again leads his readers into a territory of verbal camouflage in which reality coincides with, or is actually made by, fiction.

More than his earlier collections of short stories, *Testa d'argento* (Silver Head, 1988) is a true writing laboratory for Malerba in which he experiments with old approaches and tests new ideas. In the title story "Testa d'argento" he explores ideas and imagery that he returns to in the novel *Le pietre volanti* (Flying Rocks, 1992). The title of the story refers to a silver prosthesis that because of an accident the first-person narrator has had installed to replaced part of his cranium. The silver head makes him proud since he feels that the metal makes him better equipped to face the hardness of the world.

The unnatural satisfaction of the protagonist, who has two other metal prostheses in his body, serves as the basis for the reflections found in the story. He would evidently trade in his humanity for a sense of invulnerability:

> Voglio essere esplicito: mi piacerebbe essere tutto di metallo, dalla testa ai piedi ... In realtà ho una maledetta paura delle parole perché dovrei dire con chiarezza: desidero diventare un robot e credo che in un futuro nemmeno tanto lontano molti uomini riusciranno a diventare dei robot.

> (I want to be explicit: I would like to be all metal, from head to foot ... The truth is that I have a bloody fear of the right words, since I should say clearly: I wish I could become a robot, and I believe that in the not too distant future many people will be able to become robots.)

When his wife learns of his unusual desire, she brings him back to reality by remarking that even his penis would then be made of steel. He has only a moment of uncertainty, however, before returning to his dream:

> Non ho smesso di perfezionare la mia idea, di rimuginare il mio sogno. Se è vero che la natura produce analogie, l'uomo che fa parte della natura deve incominciare a produrre qualcosa di analogo a sé stesso, però più semplice e sopratutto più duro ... Lo dice anche la Bibbia che la carne è fragile, non soltanto in senso figurato e dice inoltre che si riduce in polvere come niente. Io non voglio essere ridotto in polvere. Voglio essere

Io non voglio essere ridotto in polvere. Voglio essere tutto di metallo, una macchina metallica, lucente, per far fronte alla durezza del mondo.

(I haven't stopped perfecting my idea, ruminating over my dream. If it is true that nature produces analogies, man, who is part of nature, should start producing something analogous to himself, simpler though, and harder... Even the Bible says that the flesh is weak, not only in a figurative sense, and that it can turn into ashes in a flash. I don't want to be turned into ashes. I want to be all metal, a shining metallic machine, to face the hardness of the world.)

Ultimately, though, it is only through language that the narrator can attempt to solve his existential crisis. Malerba regards language as an extension of man that creates all problems and can, therefore, also solve them.

Set in the imperial court of Byzantium, *Il fuoco greco* (The Greek Fire, 1990) treats a deadly struggle for power involving multileveled conspiracies. All vie for possession of the precious scroll containing the secret formula for the Greek fire–a weapon that enabled Byzantine forces to dominate the Mediterranean. Malerba creates a court in which intriguing characters communicate with calculated and ambiguous messages. The novel has been interpreted as an allegory of sociopolitical life in the bureaucratic milieu of Rome, but more generally it is again about the power of language itself. In a key passage translated here by Antonio Ricci, a scribe encapsulates Malerba's faith in the autonomous power of the word and the writer:

Una storia, dal momento che è stata scritta, esiste. Non importa quante persone la leggeranno, non importa se le sue parole verranno dimenticate, a me basta un solo lettore che ne assorba il senso e che lo trasmetta ad altri. Quel lettore posso essere io stesso che l'ho scritta. Non occorre che lavorino schiere di copisti e di traduttori, le storie scritte continuano a viaggiare per il mondo e nella mente degli uomini che si fanno loro messaggeri senza saperlo.

(A story, from the moment that it is written down, exists. It is not important how many people will read it, it is not important if its words will be forgotten; for me, just one reader that absorbs its meaning and that passes it to others is enough. I myself, the person who wrote it, can be that reader. Legions of copyists and translators need not work–written stories continue to travel through the world and in the minds of men who become their messengers without knowing it.)

Le pietre volanti, Malerba's most ambitious work, treats the anxieties of the planet as the third millennium approaches. "Fra due mesi," writes the first-person narrator, painter Ovidio Romer, "comincerà il nuovo Millennio. Non sarà una scadenza facile" (In two months the next Millennium will begin. It won't be an easy deadline). He writes in his diary to clarify his own thoughts on the personal and social implications of what he sees as the "Grande Transizione" (the Great Transition):

Nel momento in cui scrivo queste parole mi rendo conto di stare a cavallo di due millenni, sofferente protagonista della Grande Transizione, e di non aver abbandonato del tutto le vecchie illusioni pur avendo gli occhi aperti verso il futuro. Una condizione ambigua che appartiene a questa congiuntura temporale e della quale non soffriranno i miei posteri che vivranno nel felice caos del nuovo Millennio.

(I realize, as I write these words, that I am straddling two millennia, a suffering protagonist of the Great Transition, and have never completely abandoned the old illusions although my eyes are open to the future. It is an ambiguous condition, belonging to this particular temporal circumstance, which will not cause suffering to posterity since they will live in the happy chaos of the new Millennium.)

In this novel Malerba's analyses and denunciations seem to reach a point of no return. The message is that there is nothing more to adjust or salvage from the old world since the breakup of the entire social and cultural system is imminent and inevitable. Beyond the turn of the millennium there is only chaos, ironically labeled as "happy" or "blissful."

The "flying rocks" of the title come from the subject of one of Romer's paintings in which rocks detach themselves from the side of a mountain and are caught in midair before plunging into the abyss. Although the painter, who is drawn to arid, inorganic landscapes just as the protagonist of *Testa d'argento* was obsessed with the inhumanity of metal, fears the change he sees approaching, he unexpectedly finds himself developing an imagery of rebirth and renewal and begins to paint flowers and roses as though the organic humors of the Earth were flowing through his hand. To the Earth, symbolically feminine, Romer opposes the imperious masculine figure of the departed father that he has always kept "al centro del mio Palazzo della Memoria" (at the center of my Palace of Memory).

After the father is finally dead and buried, Romer is left with the burden and the responsibility of reinventing life. There is no optimism in this conclusion since the anguish for the loss of a guiding father prevails and with it the fear of great calamities to come. Some mysterious coincidences and events, however, that Romer discovers in his own works and life indicate new sources of energy and a sense of hope for the future: an ancient stone that Romer sees only after having painted it in the most minute detail gives him consciousness of his creative powers, and his encounter with an Egyptian girl "innamorata dell'elettronica" (in love with electronics), an apparent bridge between the distant past and the near future, seems a good omen. The dust-jacket illustration for the novel reproduces a painting by Fabrizio Clerici titled *Speranza* (Hope).

Malerba's *Il viaggiatore sedentario* (The Sedentary Traveler, 1993) combines the previously published *Cina Cina* (China China, 1985) with a new series of short pieces on the Orient in which he makes observations and reflects on the comparision between Eastern and Western customs. The title indicates the disquieting image of a contemporary traveler, displaced from one corner of the world to another by sitting through thousands of blank miles in the anonymous space of an airplane. Throughout his career Malerba has brought his readers along on many such journeys, which though unsettling have always been rewarding.

Interviews:

JoAnn Cannon, "Intervista con Luigi Malerba," *MLN,* 104 (January 1989): 226-237;

Grazia Menechella, "Intervista a Luigi Malerba," *Quaderni d'italianistica,* 13, no. 1 (1992): 133-138.

References:

Guido Almansi, *La ragion comica* (Milan: Feltrinelli, 1986), pp. 63-110;

Rosalaura Ballerini, *Malerba e la topografia del vuoto* (Chieti: Vecchio Faggio, 1988);

Sabine Brocher, *Abenteurliche Elemente in modernen Roman* (München: Hanser 1981), pp. 85-116;

JoAnn Cannon, *Postmodern Italian Fiction: The Crisis of Reason in Calvino, Eco, Sciascia and Malerba* (Rutherford, N.J.: Fairleigh Dickinson University Press, 1989);

Maria Corti, "Luigi Malerba: Una scommessa con il reale," *Autografo,* 13 (February 1988): 3-21;

Corti, *Il viaggio testuale* (Turin: Einaudi, 1978), pp. 137-143;

Alfredo Giuliani, *Autunno del Novecento* (Milan: Feltrinelli, 1984), pp. 130-136;

Enzo Golino, *La distanza culturale* (Bologna: Cappelli, 1980), pp. 233-238;

Francesco Guardiani, "Luigi Malerba e la 'Grande Transizione,'" *Italienisch,* 28 (November 1992): 2-16;

Guardiani, "New Italian Fiction," *Review of Contemporary Fiction,* 12 (Fall 1992): 7-24;

Angelo Guglielmi, *Carta stampata* (Rome: Cooperativa Scrittori, 1978), pp. 113-115;

Guglielmi, *Vero e falso* (Milan: Feltrinelli, 1968), pp. 157-160;

Armando La Torre, *La mania della scrittura: Moravia, Malerba, Sanguineti* (Rome: Bulzoni, 1987);

Giuliano Manacorda, *La letteratua italiana d'oggi 1965-1985* (Rome: Editori Riuniti, 1987);

Paolo Mauri, *Corpi estranei* (Palermo: Sellerio, 1984), pp. 84-92;

Mauri, *Luigi Malerba* (Florence: La Nuova Italia, 1977);

J. Mitchell Morse, "Masters and Innocents," *Hudson Review,* 3 (Fall 1968): 522-529;

Francesco Muzzioli, *Malerba. La materialità dell'immaginazione* (Rome: Bagatto, 1988);

Walter Pedullà, *Miti, finzioni e buone maniere di fine millennio* (Milan: Rusconi, 1983), pp. 291-304;

Pedulla, *Il morbo di Basedow* (Cosenza: Lerici, 1975), pp. 93-114;

Marilyn Schneider, "To Know Is to Eat: A Reading of *Il Serpente, Yale Italian Studies,* 2 (Winter 1978): 71-84;

Enzo Siciliano, *La Boheme del mare. Dieci anni di letteratura. 1972-1982* (Milan: Mondadori, 1983), pp. 127-131;

Sandra Sora, *Modalitaten des Komischen: Eine Studie zu Luigi Malerba* (Heidelberg: Gottfried Egert Verlag, 1988);

Natale Tedesco, *L'occhio e la memoria: interventi sulla letteratura contemporanea* (Marina di Patti: Pungitopo, 1988), pp. 115-120;

Rebecca West, "The Poetics of Plenitude: Malerba's *Diario di un sognatore,*" *Italica,* 3 (1985): 201-213.

Gianfranco Manfredi
(26 November 1948 -)

Anna Nelli

Translated by Augustus Pallotta

BOOKS: *1992: Zombie di tutto il mondo unitevi a Nervi,* by Manfredi and Ricky Gianco (Milano: Mazzotta, 1978);
L'amore e gli amori in J. J. Rousseau (1735-1755): teorie della sessualità (Milan: Mazzotta, 1979);
La strage delle innocenti (Rome: Lato side, 1982);
Piange il grammofono: la canzone-feuilleton dal primo Novecento ai giorni nostri, by Manfredi and Clara Manfredi (Rome: Lato side, 1982);
Magia rossa (Milan: Feltrinelli, 1983);
Cromantica (Milan: Feltrinelli, 1985);
Ultimi vampiri (Milan: Feltrinelli, 1987);
Trainspotter (Milan: Feltrinelli, 1989);
Il peggio deve venire (Milan: Mondadori, 1992);
La fuga del cavallo morto (Milan: Anabasi, 1993).

OTHER: "Gianfranco Manfredi," in *Autodizionario degli scrittori italiani,* edited by Felice Piemontese (Milan: Leonardo, 1989), pp. 213-215.

In the early 1980s, when Gianfranco Manfredi's first novels were published, they were seen in part as the expression of a general movement of rejuvenation in Italian fiction, which had experienced a long period of stasis in the 1970s. With Manfredi a new generation of novelists was coming into its own. These mostly young writers sought to distance themselves from the introspective, often lyrical works of the recent past. Manfredi's work in particular marked a return to an emphasis on plot, frequently disregarded in postwar Italian fiction in favor of character analysis and psychological and social issues.

Manfredi, one of the few contemporary Italian writers interested in the fantastic, uses time-tested formulas such as quest, adventure, mystery, and horror to create dynamic narratives unburdened by digressions that stand in the way of building a climax and a resolution. His fiction is generally dark, ranging from a focus on obsessions and nightmares, which can be explained in psychological terms, to the introduction of cosmic forces or creatures that

Gianfranco Manfredi (photograph by Nivo Maseardi)

are impervious, even hostile, to reason and human control. Interested in popular culture, Manfredi is attentive to the myths, rituals, and ideology of the consumer society, often connecting and juxtaposing popular and highbrow culture through an appealing and suggestive syncretism.

Manfredi was born on 26 November 1948 in Senigallia, a provincial city in central Italy, but as a youngster he moved to Milan with his family. Raised a Protestant in a predominantly Catholic country, he learned what it means to be part of a religious minority that is both proud and fully cognizant of its own tradition. His experiences led to an important thread in his work, for he explores such themes as predestination, alienation, and persecution. Manfredi points to his early exposure to the Bible as one of his formative experiences. Also decisive in his educational growth were the short stories of Edgar Allan Poe, to which one can trace his penchant for mystery, perversion, and horror.

Educated at the University of Milan, Manfredi graduated in philosophy with a thesis titled "Jean Jacques Rousseau and Social Classes." At this time he acquired substantial experience as a translator, rendering in Italian works by Poe, the Marquis de Sade, Brian Aldiss, and Cronin. Following his graduation he was appointed adjunct professor of philosophy at his alma mater. Using unpublished texts by the French philosopher, he wrote *L'amore e gli amori in J. J. Rousseau (1735-1755): teorie della sessualità* (Love and Love Experiences in Rousseau's Work: Theories of Sexuality, 1979), focusing on Rousseau's youth.

Some of Manfredi's other activities were anything but typical of the background of an Italian novelist, for in the late 1970s he also achieved success as a singer and songwriter. His work in this area echoes the yearnings for profound social change that moved thousands of young people to join protest demonstrations. In the 1980s, having left teaching and cut back on his musical engagements, Manfredi devoted most of his energies to the cinema, working as an actor, music composer, and scriptwriter. He took part as well in several television productions. More recently Manfredi's manifold and evolving interests have shifted to the theater, where he has worked as an actor, and to writing scripts for cartoons. Not surprisingly, some influential critics of the traditional literary establishment view Manfredi's novels skeptically.

Magia rossa (Red Magic, 1983), Manfredi's first novel, is a fluid thriller rich in clues and dramatic turns of events that have ideological and cultural reverberations. The action is set in Milan, the emblematic city of postindustrial life. To underscore the point, the Museum of Science and Technology, which boasts an impressive display commemorating the first Italian Industrial Fair held in Milan in 1881 and patterned after the Paris Expo organized ten years earlier, figures prominently. The curator of the exhibit is Mario Montrese, an expert in the history of industry and avid builder of miniature machinery. He is so fascinated by the early, utopian years of industry that he has chosen to live in what used to be a printing house, redecorated more as an annex to the museum than as an apartment.

A man with a murky personality and a maniacal devotion to research, Montrese in his studies comes across the historical figure of Tommaso Reiner, a mysterious character in the Milan of the end of the nineteenth century who patronized anarchist and avant-garde circles. An opium smoker endowed with disturbing psychic powers, Reiner is depicted as the prophet of bloody revenge against technology by those who have been its victims throughout history. Montrese's obsessive effort to reconstruct Reiner's life and political project takes the story through a chain of discoveries and coincidences increasingly resistant to rational explanations, and the rising tension leads to a dramatic and supernatural denouement. Partaking in the research are his companions Marisa, who has abandoned Etruscan history in favor of experimental theater, and Alberto Bellini, a historian now working freelance, a close friend of Montrese and Marisa's former lover. The three, with their starkly different personalities, engage in a triangle of emotional and intellectual relationships.

The story, which unfolds mainly through dialogue and action, is told through a third-person narration that involves various minor characters. The narrating voice reflects the characters' language and points of view, enabling them to relate their discoveries as secondary narrators. To reconstruct Reiner's story in a documentary fashion, Manfredi introduces genuine historical documents; at the same time he selects literary and philosophical passages, including the epigraphs that orient the reader to the three parts of the novel, which function as a commentary on the action from within and outside the plot. The novel, then, includes a variety of registers, from modern colloquial speech, to the nineteenth-century language of Reiner's contemporaries found in letters and diaries, to the formal tone and diction of academic writing, to the regional speech of minor characters, who serve as reminders of common sense and pragmatism and as a counterweight to the magical forays of the novel.

Noteworthy too is the variety of settings that Manfredi brings to life with great accuracy. Milan appears less as a metropolis than as a series of interiors. The ill-kept apartments of the young adults who led the protests against the establishment in the 1970s; the large, silent halls of the Museum of Science and Technology; an old library in the suburbs, its books collecting dust; a tiny theater animated by mechanical puppets—all seem to hold secrets that lie outside the fast pace of life in the city. Juxtaposed to modern-day Milan is the fin de siècle Milan as it appears in early films, with its first electrical plants, its séances in middle-class living rooms, and its clashes

Cover for Manfredi's 1989 novel, in which a maniacal narrator is goaded to action when he observes a crime on a train

between special army units and factory workers. The remnants of this older city still exist in depressing working-class buildings and antiquated factories, not far from the impressive structures of the modern metropolis—a warning to a civilization grounded in technology and too optimistic about its future.

To counterbalance what he sees as the myth of progress, science, and technology, Manfredi points to supernatural powers that expand gradually until they culminate in macabre and horrific events. He creates an intensive crescendo that includes the spilling of bloody guts, the summoning of infernal powers and hellish winds, and the uncovering of tombs. Such are the images, worthy of a horror movie, with which the novelist portrays the irrepressible forces raised by the experiments of modern civilization overly confident about its capacities to dominate nature and history. Written with an awareness of Karl Marx and early-nineteenth-century utopian socialism as well as the conflict between Enlightenment ideals and the proclivity of Romanticism for the supernatural, *Magia rossa* is a work of ideas smartly concealed as a popular novel.

In the self-portrait published in *Autodizionario degli scrittori italiani* (Dictionary of Italian Writers Written by Themselves, 1989), Manfredi asserts that the idea for his first novel came from the eighteenth-century philosophical novel, which he defines as a study in personal relationships issuing from a problematic core and unfolding through a play of unveilings and discoveries. He claims that the dynamics at work in such relationships connect the premodern novel, largely immune from the self-conscious analysis of characters and milieus, to the postmodern novel, with its ludic and skeptical attitude. Manfredi points out that an interest in sociohistorical or psychological analysis becomes the focus of nineteenth- and early- to mid-twentieth-century novels, be they dependent on general theories of society and the individual or committed to signal the failure of such theories.

In the inner contrasts of the eighteenth century—the century of Enlightenment but also of the Gothic novels of Horace Walpole, Matthew Gregory Lewis, and Ann Radcliffe—one finds the genesis of Manfredi's next novel, *Cromantica* (1985). The work follows the formula of *Magia rossa* by depicting an obscure event of the past that comes to permeate the present and spurs events forward in a climate of expectation and discovery. The catalyst is provided by a few black paintings that appear mysteriously in Milan at an exhibit titled "Dark-light," devoted to eighteenth-century Italian art. To discover their origin and what lies under the crust of the black paint, art critics and detectives are mobilized. Around their investigations swirl the private interests and the passions of a large number of characters, who move in the lively and cynical background of Milanese cultural life in the 1980s.

What comes to light, through the gradual piecing together of disparate documentary evidence, is an event in the libertine lifestyle of the eighteenth century which is rooted back in the previous century, a time marked by the wars of religion and the persecution of witches. It is a story of lonesome and tenacious passions for knowledge dealing with the northern Italian region of Valtellina, barely affected by the great intellectual currents of the time. Separated by two centuries, two noblemen from the region travel the paths of rationalism and alchemy, each in his own way challenging traditional sources of knowledge and the power structures of the time. Through his plot Manfredi is able to weave aspects of eighteenth-century history into the naration of twentieth-century events, especially the struggle against Fascism which aroused strong passions together with fresh episodes of violence and intolerance.

As in *Magia rossa* Manfredi focuses on the connection between magic and science, between delusion and truth. The unfolding of present events as well as those of the past points to a continual relationship among opposites, such as the one suggested by the contrasts in light and darkness of the paintings shown at the exhibition. In *Autodizionario degli scrittori italiani* (1989) Manfredi refers to the principle in alchemy of harmony between opposites. The quest for knowledge, then, can be both demonic and freeing, a tyrannical idol that sets one apart from the rest of humanity or a cherished value capable of inspiring genuine brotherhood. In the same fashion every action can be ambivalent, and every intention carries the seed of its opposite.

An emblematic episode showing the yoking of opposites centers on a carnival in Bormio, which is related by an Englishman traveling through the turmoil that is Europe at the end of the eighteenth century. The carnival presents a grotesque revolution which through its eversion of the social order momentarily frees the individual from dogmas and fears, bringing together for one day the elite, who participate in the hope of forestalling the social revolution the carnival foreshadows, and the ruled, joining the freethinking intellectuals with the uninhibited masses. In a similar fashion Manfredi, with his inspired use of popular forms, hopes to encourage the hedonistic consumption of his literary product.

Fashioned after the detective story, the plot of the novel has plenty of action and suspense, but in *Cromantica*, more than *Magia rossa*, Manfredi posits many documents that are presented without any mediation and intended to tell their share of truth. He clearly enjoys devising plausible forgeries of the past that offer him the opportunity to utilize his professional training as an academic researcher. To dissipate the doubts of readers, he offers notes and bibliographical sources. His interest in using history and the tools of historical research was shared by other Italian novelists of the period. All of them to greater or lesser degrees were obliged to a new narrative form of historiography suggested by Carlo Ginsburg in his book *Il formaggio e i vermi* (The Cheese and the Worms, 1976).

In Manfredi's next work, a collection of short stories titled *Ultimi vampiri* (The Last Vampires, 1987), the image of the vampire lends legendary substance to the notion of a life that resists the normalization of morality. Vampires live in the interstices of history, persecuted yet free, ferocious yet peculiarly playful, nurtured by the obsessiveness of dreams and the anarchy of the imagination. With this perspective Manfredi revisits milieus and events of the modern era, drawing skillfully from the reservoir of folklore and the cinema. His vampires love, hunt, suffer, and fight in such places as sixteenth-century Moravia, the Spain of the Inquisition, the Versailles of Louis XIV, and the snowy steppes of the Baltic region at the end of the nineteenth century, down to contemporary times when vampires are assured of survival in the factory of dreams of Hollywood. The mythology of vampires is at the center of the tradition of prejudices and intolerance, of violence and stupidities that spans European civilization. The men that vampires find along the way share with them a thirst for blood, but unlike vampires they hide it behind fanaticism and the tyranny of their principles. Next to humans given to exorcising the fear of evil and death, Manfredi's vampires emerge as pure and sensitive creatures, attuned to a chaotic universe in which good and evil cannot be separated.

Narrated in the first person by the vampires who are the protagonists, the stories intertwine the darkness of reality and the imagination. The most original is the last, "Il metodo Vago" (The Vago Method), where cinema, the last locus of fantasy and legend, not only gives life to ghosts by sucking from the actors the life of their characters but also lives vampirelike in the dreams of spectators, feeding the human need for darkness. The longest story, "Limpieza" (Cleanliness, in Spanish) is set in seventeenth-century Spain at the time the Holy See is engaged in persecuting Jews, Moors, gypsies, and atheists in a futile quest for purity of blood and religious faith, a quest that finally leads to self-purging. At the end Manfredi enlarges the meaning of his story with the suggestion that such attempts at cleansing are not confined to a place or time: "Ogni popolo a turno si proclama Eletto, ma questa è superstizione. L'unica vera, grande superstizione" (In time every nation calls itself the chosen one, which is a superstition. The one and only superstition). Through his story Manfredi shows that the self-righteous inevitably discover within themselves vampires that live in darkness. In short, between the vampire and his persecutor, blinded by fanaticism and intolerance, there is a substantial affinity: the "other" is the mirror of what is unacceptably cast aside. It is in this mirror, Manfredi suggests, that mankind must look at itself.

Ultimi vampiri concludes Manfredi's trilogy of the supernatural clothed with history. In these works he uses history and traditions as a network of signs, in which one does not find linear interpretations but reversible relationships between ideas and intertwined meanings—as one character in *Magia rossa* puts it: "La storia è una ragnatela senza centro" (History is a cobweb without a center). Manfredi skillfully exploits setting, images, and language, but his emphasis is always on fashioning a compelling plot, with revelations and unexpected turns that afford the reader pleasure.

As Manfredi points out, plot is the absolute master of his third novel, *Trainspotter* (1989), which shares with his previous work a somber, melancholic tone. Yet here one does not find Gothic or fantastic ingredients, and the action is set in a realistic present, a domain of cold, cynical individuals who live in a setting almost devoid of historical and social context. Although the background is recognizably European—perhaps a compression or synthesis of several countries—in this disturbing vision the reader enters a world marked by individual alienation, violence, and the rejection of one's roots. It is a projection of a future Europe destined to resemble the America of many Hollywood movies, with rundown cities and faceless suburbs.

The action revolves around a lucidly maniacal character, Sacha Dozier, a remarkably intelligent man who loves trains, has a history of repressed emotions, and finds it difficult to communicate with others. He is also kind, attractive, educated, and professionally successful; he leads a life above reproach in a provincial town, the sole occupant of an isolated villa he rented for the summer, near the railroad. One day, after witnessing a crime in a train he was watching, Dozier yields to the disease—which he perceives as a form of destiny—lurking in his inner self.

Dozier injects himself into the crime scene with a meticulously calculated plan of action, for the situation presents the opportunity he seems to have wanted in order to give creative expression, as in a work of art, to the filth that obsesses him. Hoping to achieve a long-sought control of his life, he behaves like a movie director and tries to manipulate people and subject them to his will. He is surrounded by four people who represent a degraded world: a rebellious but vulnerable young woman; a confused and sensual young woman who feels the need to be dominated; a tough, low-class drug addict, violent by nature and determined to maintain his habit; and a tired policeman, disenchanted with his private life and professional milieu in which "metà dei poliziotti [sembrano] delinquenti, l'altra metà agenti di borsa" (half of the police force look like hoodlums, the other half like stockbrokers). These four are a foil for Dozier's perverse genius and imperious personality.

Despite flashbacks designed to give depth to the characters, the narrative is fast paced, with the action shifting from one character to another, till the end when it reaches an even higher pitch of intensity. The language used by the third-person narrator and by Dozier is analytical and intentionally neutral, while the other characters often use colloquialisms. Their attitudes and the places of which they speak—a world that might be characterized as existing midway between the street life found in Pasolini's neorealistic novels and the hard-boiled social settings of Hollywood films, with smoke-filled bars, thunderous jukebox music, motorcycles, guns, and black jackets—suggest humanity gone adrift.

Manfredi's passion for cinema is reflected throughout the novel. The text has allusions to Alfred Hitchcock's psychological thrillers, such as the glass of milk that figured prominently in *Suspicion* (1941) and the fear of heights featured in *Vertigo* (1958). Dozier owns a collection of films, including a series in which much of the action takes place aboard trains. Indeed, Dozier is fascinated by the perfect functional role assigned to every object in James Bond movies and in general by the relentlessness of film narratives.

As in *Magia rossa* the effort to control events rationally ends in failure, for the ending here goes counter to the traditional detective novel and to the dominion of reason alleged in the story. Dozier's apparent ability to control events is undermined by their accidental nature. Through his books Manfredi shows that real life has no plot, no intentional design. Life is chaos, with events determined by chance and the clash of blind forces. An artful plot is only to be found in a novel or in actual events reconstructed a posteriori, which also in a sense is a fiction.

Il peggio deve venire (The Worst Has Yet to Come, 1992) also has gloomy settings and fast-paced action, but its plotline is linear and its themes less problematic than those of *Trainspotter*. The main character, a young terrorist from a totalitarian Eastern European country, successfully removes the head of state, but his accomplices are killed and he alone manages to escape. An orphan who has lost his family to ethnic persecutions, he is a Jew in name only. He has led a lonesome and dangerous life, including bloody encounters with violent rivals. Counting on his sharp reflexes and the speed of a stolen car, he heads for the border while a few prominent government officials are plotting to take the place of the dead tyrant and hold on to their power. In his encounter with hostile people in distant and desolate places, the experiences of the fugitive become increasingly surreal. He finally reaches an abandoned military area, a monstrous site of electronic gadgets with a life of their own, and the site as well of horrible atomic experiments that have resulted in genetic mutations of animal and plant life.

At this point the narrative takes on chivalric and Gothic overtones. The central quarter of the compound, which is inhabited by strange individuals functioning as prisoners and guards, seems akin to a forest with an enchanted castle and the evil wizard. As in the traditional romance the adventurous knight held prisoner can only escape by overcoming a series of hurdles placed in his path. In Manfredi's postmodern version the obstacles take the form and the rhythm of a video game: an extremely dangerous road to be traveled at high speed while the driver is being attacked on all sides by electronic weapons.

As in his previous novel Manfredi is able to create an atmosphere of disturbing squalor in his representation of a modern civilization that has regressed to a barbaric state because of its inherent pride and arrogance. The totalitarian regime in *Il peggio deve venire,* with stolid popular acquiescence, is as natural an expression of such reversion as is the exasperating individualism of the "free" Europe in *Trainspotter*. But though the simple plot of *Il peggio deve venire,* wedded to the protagonist's continuing escape, allows a clear presentation of theme, it is inherently more superficial and less interesting than *Trainspotter,* with its web of resonating relationships.

After the duet of *Trainspotter* and *Il peggio deve venire* Manfredi changed direction with *La fuga del cavallo morto* (The Flight of the Dead Horse, 1993), the memoir of a comedian published after his suicide by an editor with the same initials as Manfredi. In his introduction the editor, after bemoaning the loss of the subject, Antonio Zeppa (whose last name, meaning patch or plug, is evocative of a poor mending or playing a secondary role), comments on his elusive character, his promising career, and his years lived in a limbo of mediocrity and uneven performances. The editor is struck by the text, which seems to him to have been written by someone who is very much alive. This detail is clarified in the course of the narrative.

The novel is especially notable for the self-deprecating irony of a comedian who strives to continue amusing his public even while deconstructing and rejecting the conventional machinery of his own work. His is the experience of a mediocre individual, naturally funny to the public, who is transformed into a personality by the stratagems of show business. In relating his life Zeppa lays bare, with caustic and grotesque humor, the frivolous and neurotic life behind the scenes in the theater and on television. The background is again Milan, with its obsessive drive for success which Manfredi brought to life in the first two novels. But Zeppa goes beyond Milan: he brings into focus the mythical Hollywood, a land of credulity, cynicism, and institutionalized transgression. Next to Hollywood, the model and ultimate destiny of Western culture, Italy emerges as a provincial little country given to imitation and hopelessly affected by an inferiority complex.

This part too is funny, but it is a bitter and self-denigrating laughter.

Zeppa's rapport with his public, dictated by the formula of success, gradually robs him of his identity. His initial spontaneity turns into routine work, into a necessity to meet the expectations of his audience; in short the necessity to make people laugh clashes with his notion of a comedy based on intelligence. He discovers that when a comedian, an anomalous social being, functions as a valve to ease the restrictions of society, show business packages him as a successful product, thus removing the transgressive and critical thrust of his work. In an age that sees even intelligence as a consumer product, the structure of mass communication becomes a large digestive apparatus that transforms everything into a homogenous mass and expels any form of originality. When someone refuses to play the game by opposing conformity, he is excluded from the process or banished to oblivion; such is the fate of Antonio Zeppa, who, much like Luigi Pirandello's Mattia Pascal, chooses death by remaining alive. *La fuga del cavallo morto* depicts show business from within, free of ponderous ruminations, through a light, brilliant monologue dressed with humorous lines and situations.

Manfredi's novels are not milestones of literary history, for they are patterned after well-known formulas of narration, but they do comprise an original contribution to literature because of his ability to combine enjoyable, popular means of expression with a critical view of mass culture. He is able to present a gloomy and bankrupt modernity while lending his stories the rhythm and suspense of a horror or science-fiction movie. He supports his historical plots with research, sophisticated knowledge, and intellectual depth; but it must be noted that his narration underscores the morbid and the sensational. He is willing to treat subjects popularized by the movies, but he does so by injecting in his work a vein of anxiety and pessimism. The success of Manfredi's conjunction of opposites depends on the sensitivity of the reader's response: on a superficial level his work can be read as pulp fiction, but he also offers much more.

Manfredi makes no attempt to dictate the way in which his novels should be read. Indeed he ends his self-portrait for *Autodizionario degli scrittori italiani* with these words: "La [mia] somma e insieme minima aspirazione resta quella di non tediare il lettore con le [mie] motivazioni e di non arrecare disturbo al piacere (o al disagio) della libera e personale lettura" (Both my highest and minimal aspiration is to not bore the reader with my own motivations and to not interfere with the pleasure, or the unease, of a free and personal reading). In other words, any clarification on the part of the author and, likewise, any interpretation on the part of the critics are limitations on the potentialities offered by the text.

References:

Silvia Albertazzi, *Bugie sincere. Narratori e narrazioni 1970-1990* (Rome: Riuniti, 1992), pp. 45-47, 49-50;

Daniela Marcheschi, "La fuga di Atalanta," *Stazione di posta,* 36/37 (1990): 1-32;

Stefano Tani, *Il romanzo di ritorno. Dal romanzo degli anni sessanta alla giovane narrativa degli anni ottanta* (Milan: Mursia, 1991), pp. 297-304.

Giorgio Manganelli

(15 November 1922 – 28 May 1990)

Rebecca West
University of Chicago

BOOKS: *Hilarotragoedia* (Milan: Feltrinelli, 1964);
La letteratura come menzogna (Milan: Feltrinelli, 1967);
Nuovo commento (Turin: Einaudi, 1969);
Agli dèi ulteriori (Turin: Einaudi, 1972);
Lunario dell'orfano sannita (Turin: Einaudi, 1973);
Cina e altri orienti (Milan: Bompiani, 1974);
A e B (Milan: Rizzoli, 1975);
Ex voto. Storie di miracoli e di miracolati (Parma: Franco Maria Ricci, 1975);
Sconclusione (Milan: Rizzoli, 1976);
Pinocchio. Un libro parallelo (Turin: Einaudi, 1977);
Cassio governa a Cipro (Milan: Rizzoli, 1977);
Centuria. Cento piccoli romanzi fiume (Milan: Rizzoli, 1979);
Amore (Milan: Rizzoli, 1981);
Angosce di stile (Milan: Rizzoli, 1981);
Danimarca, Islanda, by Manganelli and Giorgio Zampa, photography by Francesco Radino (Milan: Touring club italiano, 1982);
Discorso dell'ombra e dello stemma, o, Del lettore e dello scrittore considerati come dementi (Milan: Rizzoli, 1982);
Dall'inferno (Milan: Rizzoli, 1985);
Laboriose inezie (Milan: Garzanti, 1986);
Tutti gli errori (Milan: Rizzoli, 1986); translated by Henry Martin as *All the Errors* (Kingston, N.Y.: McPherson, 1990);
Rumori o voci (Milan: Rizzoli, 1987);
Salons (Milan: Franco Maria Ricci, 1987);
Scialoja a Gibellina, by Manganelli and Giuseppe Appella (Rome: Edizioni della cometa, 1987);
Antologia privata (Milan: Rizzoli, 1989);
Improvvisi per macchina da scrivere (Milan: Leonardo, 1989);
Encomio del tiranno. Scritto all'unico scopo di fare dei soldi (Milan: Adelphi, 1990);
La palude definitiva, edited by Ebe Flamini (Milan: Adelphi, 1991);
Esperimento con l'India, edited by Flamini (Milan: Adelphi, 1992);
Il presepio, edited by Flamini (Milan: Adelphi, 1992);
Il rumore sottile della prosa, edited by Paola Italia (Milan: Adelphi, 1994);

Giorgio Manganelli (photograph by Jerry Bauer/G. Neri)

La notte, edited by Salvatore Nigro (Milan: Adelphi, 1996).

OTHER: Edgar Allan Poe, *Opere scelte,* edited by Manganelli (Milan: Mondadori, 1971);
Giulia Niccolai, *Harry's Bar e altre poesie 1969–1980,* preface by Manganelli (Milan: Feltrinelli, 1981);
Torquato Accetto, *Della dissimulazione onesta,* introduction by Manganelli (Genoa: Costa & Nolan, 1983);

Graziella Pulce, ed., *Il monarca delle Indie: corrispondenza fra Giacomo e Monaldo Leopardi,* introduction by Manganelli (Milan: Adelphi, 1988);

"Il libro e la lettura," in *Il cammino della lettura: come leggere un testo letterario,* edited by Maria Corti (Milan: Bompiani, 1993): pp. 91-93.

TRANSLATIONS: Cecil Sprigge, *Benedetto Croce: l'uomo e il pensatore* (Milan, 1956);

O. Henry, *Memorie di un cane giallo e altri racconti* (Milan: Feltrinelli, 1962);

Edgar Allan Poe, *I racconti, 3 volumes* (Turin: Einaudi, 1983).

SELECTED PERIODICAL PUBLICATIONS—
UNCOLLECTED: "Manganelli disse," *Tuttolibri* (9 June 1990): 3;

"Ars satirica," *Panorama* (15 September 1991): 100-103;

"Due racconti inediti: 'Giovanna d'Arco giudicata' e 'Di Circe e di Penelope,'" *La Rivista dei libri* (April 1992): 4-5;

"Scrivere storie umane," *La Rivista dei libri,* 5 (May 1992): 21-24.

Giorgio Manganelli is remarkable for the rich variety, marked eccentricity, and absolute originality of his contributions to letters. He is celebrated for the depth of his creative and critical talents, his journalistic flare, his multilingual translating abilities, and his abiding expansion of the boundaries of contemporary Italian literature. A man whose writing has often been called bizarre and esoteric, the inimitable Manganelli is a genuine man of letters who dedicated his life to the written word.

It is inaccurate to label Manganelli a novelist in the usual sense, for his creative writings go beyond even the most experimental or avant-garde conceptions of this genre—he is an antinovelist par excellence. In 1986 critic Pietro Citati wrote in his "Ritratto di Manganelli" (Portrait of Manganelli) that "tra gli scrittori italiani di oggi, Manganelli è l'unico che possieda una vocazione metafisica" (among today's Italian writers, Manganelli is the only one who possesses a metaphysical vocation). Like Edgar Allan Poe or Franz Kakfa, Manganelli plumbs the depths of human emotions that arise out of an awareness of mortality and of the ultimate mystery of existence, creating from those emotions unique verbal universes filled with anguish, fear, and obsessive visions of nothingness.

Yet, like other great metaphysical writers, Manganelli is also a master of formal, rhetorical control and elaboration, the artificer of unworldly landscapes built on pure abstractions: ideas, sounds, and language itself. In *Il viaggio testuale. Le ideologie e le strutture semiotiche* (The Textual Voyage: Ideologies and Semiotic Structures, 1978) Maria Corti, one of the best critics of Manganelli's work, rightly defines him as "prolifero archetipo della passione formale stessa della neoavanguardia" (the prolific archetype of that very formalistic passion of the neoavantgarde). Marked by sharp wit, acute intelligence, and a dark sense of the absurd, Manganelli's writing reveals as well a blackly humorous and pungently satirical bent unmatched in contemporary Italian literature.

Born 15 November 1922 in Milan of a liberal Jewish father and a Catholic mother who adhered to the newly installed Fascist regime, Manganelli was no doubt troubled in childhood by the tensions that arose out of his parents' differing backgrounds and beliefs. In his 1993 article "Fu il difensore degli aggettivi" (He was the Defender of Adjectives), critic Giulio Nascimbeni quotes the writer's own synthesis of his youthful years:

> Sono milanese, ma non di stirpe. I miei erano di Roccabianca, in provincia di Parma. . . . A Milano ho fatto le elementari, il ginnasio e il liceo classico. Per l'università sono andato a Pavia, facoltà di scienze politiche. Mi sono laureato con una tesi su Tommaso Campanella. Ho avuto la gloria di essere l'ultimo della classe e il primo. Sono stato l'ultimo in quarta ginnasio, classe che ho ripetuto, e il primo durante un anno di liceo.

> (I am Milanese, but not by origin. My people were from Roccabianca, in the province of Parma. . . . In Milan I went to elementary, junior and senior high school. For university studies I went to Pavia, in the Department of political science. I got my degree with a thesis on Tommaso Campanella. I have had the glory of being both the last and first in my class. I was the last in my fourth year of junior high school, which I had to repeat, and first during one of my senior high school years.)

During World War II, Manganelli was assigned to an infantry unit and spent time in sedentary activities such as compiling by hand the roll-call list for the unit. His handwriting was so bad, however, that the list was unreadable, and he was saved from disciplinary action only by the end of the war in September 1943. With his characteristically self-deprecating style, Manganelli told Nascimbeni that he "contributed to the defeat of Italy." According to Corti, however, he was active as a partisan in the region of Emilia-Romagna.

After the war Manganelli taught in high schools near Milan and married Fausta Preschern, a woman of Yugoslavian descent, with whom he had a daughter, Lietta. The marriage was not a happy one, and the couple was together only from 1946 to

Dust jackets for two of Manganelli's books

1948. In 1947 the writer had already begun a passionate liaison with a young poet, Alda Merini, whose *Il tormento delle figure* (The Torment of Figures, 1990) is dedicated to Manganelli. According to Corti in the 29 May 1990 issue of *La Repubblica,* from 1947 to 1949 Manganelli oscillated "tra un amore assoluto, caparbio e il sospetto della follia incombente sulla giovane poetessa amata" (between an absolute, obstinate love and the suspicion of the beloved young poet's encroaching madness). Corti attributes the oxymoronic title of Manganelli's first book *Hilarotragoedia* (1964), the coined combination of *hilarious* and *tragedy,* as well as its anguished content to this turbulent affair of great joy and equally great despair. Manganelli tried to save his beloved and to cure her with the help of trustworthy caretakers, but her madness was too profound.

One day, Corti writes, the overwhelmed Manganelli simply took off on a Lambretta, a motorscooter, toward Rome. He was hired at the University of Rome in 1953 as an assistant to the noted Anglo-American scholar Gabriele Baldini, the husband of the writer Natalia Ginzburg. Manganelli taught English literature in the Magistero, then the teachers' college, but never became a full-fledged professor. His deep knowledge of English and American literature was influential in his future critical and creative work.

Milan and Rome were the two major centers for Manganelli's professional activities for the rest of his career. Although he lamented in print and in person the foggy, damp, and lugubrious atmosphere that often characterizes life in Milan and led a solitary existence in the most colorless residential area of Rome—near the street made famous by Carlo Emilio Gadda in the novel *Quer pasticciaccio brutto de via Merulana* (1957; translated as *That Awful Mess on Via Merulana,* 1965)—Manganelli actually thrived on city life, for it was only in these urban centers that he could find the culture, the concerts, and the books and journals that nourished him.

In the years immediately following World War II Manganelli had begun to write for Milanese newspapers, especially *Corriere della sera,* and he would continue to contribute book reviews, travel pieces, and meditations on various topics to Roman and Milanese newspapers and journals through the course of his writing career. Many of these brief pieces as well as prefaces and introductions to the works of other writers were gathered in collections: *La letteratura come menzogna* (Literature as Lie, 1967), *Lunario dell'orfano sannita* (Almanac of the Samnite Orphan, 1973), *Angosce di stile* (Agonies of Style, 1981), *Laboriose inezie* (Laborious Inanities, 1986), *Antologia privata* (Private Anthology, 1989), *Improvvisi per macchina da scrivere* (Improvisations for Typewriter, 1989), and *Il rumore sottile della prosa* (The Subtle Sound of Prose, 1994). From the late 1950s until his death he also worked as an editor, translator, and advisor for many publishing houses, including Garzanti and Adelphi.

It was with the 1964 publication of *Hilarotragoedia* that Manganelli gained serious critical notice as a writer of extraordinary originality and importance. Before that, although Manganelli disdained participation in groups, public debates on the status of literature, and any other activity in which writers were called upon to represent collective cultural and intellectual trends or directions, he had contributed a short theatrical piece, "Iperipotesi" (Hyperhypothesis) to the 1964 volume *Gruppo 63*, a collection of works from the 1963 convention of writers and critics held in Palermo that marked the height of the neoavantgarde movement of the late 1950s and early 1960s. Moreover, Manganelli's critical contributions to the important neoavantgarde journal *Quindici* and his cofounding of the short-lived journal *Grammatica* attest to his presence among the writers and critics of the 1960s now known as the experimental neoavantgarde.

Manganelli's association with Gruppo 63 was at best informal and peripheral. Neither he nor the full-fledged "members" of this loose coalition of young cultural lions ever considered him to be an insider of the group's theoretical, ideological, and literary debates. In "Manganelli, la regola e l'eccezione" (Manganelli, the Rule and the Exception), a piece published shortly after the author's death in the 10 June 1990 issue of *L'Espresso*, Umberto Eco characterizes the Gruppo 63 as "un poco come le assemblee studentesche: per farne parte basta entrarvi per caso" (a little like student assemblies: to be a part of them all you need to do is to come in by chance). Eco adds that Manganelli was one who "came in by chance," already quite a bit older than most of the core group and already well along on a defined path or "destiny" as far as his interests and his style were concerned. Nevertheless, Eco does believe that Manganelli took some inspiration from the group's literary and cultural debates.

At the least one can say that Manganelli shared many of the convictions of those who were out to renew Italian culture and letters with a definitive move away from the Neorealism of the 1940s and the bourgeois writing that had dominated the 1950s. Manganelli's emphasis on the pure literariness of literature, on rhetoric and style, suited the antirealist mood of young writers in the early 1960s, much as Gadda's neobaroque works captured their admiration. Certainly the writer's interest in form and in language rather than in content or "message" rightly allies him with the directions followed by many other writers of the neoavantgarde. Also, his rejection of the traditional novel, his love of baroque and foreign models—especially eighteenth- and nineteenth-century English and American novels—and his open disdain for literature of and for the middle class all connect him to the intellectual climate of the 1960s. Manganelli is unique, however, in his continued insistence on the asocial, amoral, and metaphysical nature of literature as well as in the rich inventiveness of his fictions.

In an eloquent essay titled "Giorgio, malinconico tapiro" (Giorgio, Melancholy Tapir) in the 29 May 1990 issue of *La Repubblica* Citati discusses the transformation of a shy and even apparently somewhat stodgy English teacher and editor into a writer of amazing genius. Citati recalls that in the late 1950s they both worked for the Garzanti publishing house in Rome while Manganelli also taught English in technical schools in the city. The critic saw him as "un professore più intelligente degli altri" (a professor [who was] more intelligent than other professors), but he did not think that he was a particularly talented writer. Citati goes on to relate the "metamorphosis":

> Niente mi meravigliò più di quello che accadde una sera del 1964. Stavo in ufficio . . . quando Manganelli venne molto lentamente verso di me. Sembrava più che mai cauto, timoroso, diffidente di se stesso . . . e mi porse un libro, scusandosi e vergognandosi per un atto così insensato: "Sì, l'ho proprio scritto io." Era *l'Hilarotragoedia*: un libro bellissimo. L'onesto professore era diventato all'improvviso uno scrittore di genio.
>
> (Nothing surprised me more than what happened one evening in 1964. I was in the office . . . when Manganelli came very slowly toward me. He seemed even more cautious, timid, diffident of himself . . . and he handed me a book, excusing himself and showing embarrassment for such a crazy act: "Yes, I wrote it myself." It was *Hilarotragoedia*, a very beautiful book. The stolid professor had become a writer of genius.)

Citati attributes Manganelli's discovery of his vocation as a writer to the psychoanalysis that he had undergone under the guidance of Ernst Bernhard, during which the repressed and desperately unhappy Manganelli had been able to free the ghosts of his unconscious and to use them as fuel for his writing. However it came about, Manganelli's "cure" was literature itself; Citati states flatly that "analysis had woken up the hidden writer in him; literature saved him from desperation."

Throughout his career Manganelli was evidently uncomfortable with the concept of authorship. The blurb on the dust jacket of the first edition of *Hilarotragoedia* describes the book as the "monologue of a fool"—the words *fool* or *clown* being his favorite and constant definition of a writer. In an unpublished 1985 letter, written in his serviceable English, Manganelli bristled at the term *author:* "You tell me very kind words about 'my books,' but I don't think there is such a thing, an author. Books do happen, quite as dreams do . . . and of course the dreams we dream are not 'ours.'"

Falling as it does somewhere between the novel and the essay, the ludic and the serious, *Hilarotragoedia,* like the books that followed, is unclassifiable. It details what Manganelli calls the "natura discenditiva" or descending nature of humankind, as all endlessly fall towards a Hell or "Ade." The universe, made up of the dispersed bits and pieces of a dead God, is itself a place of death in which all tends toward a Hell that is never reached and cannot be known. Within this somber frame, the sheer exuberance of rhetorical and lexical elaboration erupts to create a kind of "hilarity," albeit darkly tinged with metaphysical anguish.

While the blurb to the first edition was a fairly traditional attempt at a description of the book—"As the title, which repeats the name of an old heroic-comic play, indicates, a crazy hilarity runs through the structure of this book filled with tragic material"—the blurb to the second edition in 1972 inaugurates Manganelli's important practice of describing his own work. From the anodyne remarks of the first edition, Manganelli moved to the exhilarating self-irony that characterizes this and subsequent blurbs. The "libretto" is called a "manualetto teorico-pratico" (little theoretical-practical manual), a "*do it yourself,*" written by an "umile pedagogo" (humble pedagogue) who has provided "esempi di quel realismo, moralmente e socialmente significativo, di cui il raccoglitore vuol essere ossequioso seguace" (examples of that realism, morally and socially meaningful, of which the anthologizer seeks to be an obsequious follower). The blurb further informs the reader that the book teaches about death and includes such useful items as a "classification of different sorts of anguish" and an "insert on farewells." The pseudo-scholarly tone and exaggerated earnestness of his description make clear Manganelli's abhorrence of humanistic and "useful" definitions of literary texts.

In addition to their entertainment value Manganelli's blurbs underline his belief in the decidedly asocial, amoral nature of literature, which is for him the pure elaboration of language in service of nothing other than the "God" of all writers: rhetoric itself. Furthermore, blurbs are a form of *paratextual* writing—a term defined by Gérard Genette in *Palimpsestes: la littérature au second degré* (1982; translated as *Palimpsests: Literature in the Second Degree,* 1997) as "titles, subtitles, prefaces, postfaces, blurbs, marginal notes, epigraphs, illustrations, book jackets, and all sorts of other accessory signs that form an entourage around and at times a commentary to the main text"—and are therefore ideal for a writer such as Manganelli who often seems to prefer appendages and accessories to the main text. In addition to writing many prefaces and introductions to books penned by others, Manganelli has played with reader expectations in his own books: *Nuovo commento* (New Comment, 1969) consists entirely of commentary on a missing main text, and *Pinocchio: un libro parallelo* (Pinocchio: A Parallel Book, 1977) presents Manganelli's rewritten version of the original book. Genette has further defined paratext as a "flexible space . . . all those things . . . which contribute to present—or to 'presentify'—the text by making it into a book." This "flexible space" is Manganelli's natural habitat, for he has always been dedicated to presenting literature as literature.

In "La letteratura come menzogna," the famous title essay of his second book, Manganelli forthrightly argues the "lying" nature of literature with no holds barred. Openly antihumanistic, his position is that literature is cynical, indifferent to human suffering, useless, corrupt, scandalous, and anarchic. The writer is a fool and a clown who must be asocial, must refuse all myths of a good conscience such as collective wisdom, progress, and justice. Manganelli's proclamations reveal his absolutism: "L'oggetto letterario è oscuro, denso, direi pingue, opaco, fitto di pieghe casuali . . . proietta attorno a sé un alone di significati, vuol dire tutto e dunque niente" (The literary object is obscure, dense, I would say corpulent, thick with accidental folds . . . it projects around itself a halo of meanings, it means everything and therefore nothing), and "La letteratura si organizza come una pseudoteologia, in cui si celebra un intero universo, la sua fine e il suo inizio, i suoi riti e le sue gerarchie, i suoi esseri mortali e immortali: tutto è esatto, e tutto è mentito" (Literature is organized like a pseudotheology, in which is celebrated an entire universe with its end and its beginning, its rites and its hierarchies, its mortal and immortal beings: all is exact and all is sham). In all the fiction and essays he would write in the more than two decades before his death, Manganelli never swerved from his conviction that literature is nothing other than rhetorical organization of itself and, ultimately, of nothingness.

By the late 1970s Manganelli had published several more books and had developed a loyal following of readers, many of them writers or literary critics. As critic Giulio Ferroni notes in *Storia della letteratura italiana: il Novecento* (The History of Italian Literature: The Twentieth Century, 1991) Manganelli had become known as a "detached observer," a "touchy moralist," a "critic of contemporary vulgarity." Although he wrote copiously of both literary texts and contemporary culture, when Antonio Debenedetti of the *Corriere della sera* asked him in 1985 if he could be called a "critico-scrittore" (critic-writer), Manganelli was uninterested in taking up the mantle: "L'unica possibile critica letteraria credo che sia quella che fa della letteratura sulla letteratura. Se la letteratura è menzogna, la critica deve essere una menzogna di secondo grado" (I believe that the only literary criticism possible is the sort that creates literature out of literature. If literature is a lie, criticism must be a second-level lie).

Criticism or not, Manganelli's writing on other writers generally equals, and often surpasses, that of his subjects. He is especially good on minor writers, whom he always preferred to the so-called classic authors. In a 1986 interview with Guido Almansi, Manganelli admitted that even when he wrote on the hallowed greats of the classical and Italian tradition–Vergil, Dante Alighieri, Vittorio Alfieri, Ugo Foscolo, and Alessandro Manzoni–he tried to transform them into minor writers so as "impedire al maggiore di coagularsi definitivamente in monumento" (to stop major critics from coagulating definitively into monuments).

Although the essay-novel remained Manganelli's preferred structure, he did experiment with other forms. He emphasizes dialogue in several works: his reworking of William Shakespeare's *Othello* (1622) titled *Cassio governa a Cipro* (Cassius Is Governing in Cyprus, 1977), *Amore* (Love, 1981), *Pinocchio: un libro parallelo,* and *Centuria: cento piccoli romanzi fiume* (One-Hundred Short Novels, 1979). In the interview with Almansi, Manganelli admitted to having become a "graphomaniac," writing ever more copiously and continuously in the final years of his life. Since his death on 28 May 1990 in Milan, several of the many unpublished pieces he left behind have been retrieved and published in journals.

The 1994 collection of meditations on literature, *Il rumore sottile della prosa,* includes several previously unpublished pieces. Many of his earlier works have been republished by Adelphi, and there are plans to print even more of his unpublished work.

Critical interest in Manganelli has not waned with his passing. Graziella Pulce's *Bibliografia degli scritti di Giorgio Manganelli* (Bibliography of Manganelli's Writings, 1996) is an invaluable and exhaustive listing of Manganelli's published work, including books, translations, journalistic pieces, art catalogues, and interviews. In addition Pulce has written four essays analyzing Manganelli's writing. She investigates his debt to Jungian thought and provides close readings of selected fictional works, including the posthumous *La palude definitiva* (The Definitive Swamp, 1991). On 17 and 18 December 1997 his former colleagues at the University of Rome organized a conference on his writing at the Teatro Argentina in the city.

Posthumous publications seem particularly suited to Manganelli, given his belief in the ghostly essence of literary texts, which he viewed as not connected in any way to concrete reality or to fixable individual or collective meanings. According to Manganelli the basic building blocks of literary texts–words–are themselves "dead." In a piece titled "Manganelli disse" (Manganelli Said), published in *Tuttolibri* just a few days after his death, the writer meditates on dictionaries, asserting that they are "dove le parole si riposano, stanno ferme, cioè celebrano la loro qualità suprema che è quella di essere parole morte" (where words rest, are fixed, that is to say, they celebrate their supreme quality which is that of being dead). He believed that as soon as words are used by a writer they "die," insisting that James Joyce knew this when he wrote that "a writer writes only in a dead language." He argues that creative writers use words in such a way as to make them lose any communicative capacity, any connection with lived life, and the literature they create is ultimately only "suono" (sound) or "sudore larvale" (shadowy excretion). The writer is even more ghostly than the words on the page, for at least they have a material presence in print, but their author is nowhere to be found. Alive or dead Manganelli was and remains, in his conception of literature, as insubstantial and ungraspable as the meanings of his texts.

For all of Giorgio Manganelli's antihumanistic, anticommunicative, and anti-institutional views and practices, he cared deeply about literature and about its place and significance in human experience. This concern, implicit in his fiction and essays, is made explicit from time to time and no more directly than in one of his last writings, left on his desk until passed on by his companion and editor Ebe Flamini to critic Maria Corti, who published it in a book for high school students titled *Il cammino della lettura: Come leggere un testo letterario* (Reading's Path: How to Read a Literary Text, 1993). The short essay, "Il libro e la lettura" (The Book and Reading), was written specifically for a series of seminars in Rome directed at high school students and pertaining to school libraries.

Manganelli begins by referring to a commemorative plaque affixed to a wall in the Piazza del Popolo in Rome. The plaque honors two members of the Risorgimento Secret Society for the unification of Italy known as the Carbonari who were executed. Manganelli writes that the plaque is something like the page of a book in the sense that the words inscribed on it "appartengono a tutti coloro che vogliono leggerle" (belong to all those who wish to read them). These words contrast sharply with the many ephemeral "messaggi scritti" (written messages) that assail us every day, such as posters announcing upcoming events or newspapers that are "parole destinate a scomparire insieme a ciò di cui parlano" (words destined to disappear along with that about which they speak). Manganelli grants that these messages are useful and that they are worth paying attention to, but, returning to the plaque, he writes that it is "diversa" (different) in that it does not announce anything or give practical instructions, but rather "racconta, celebra" (it recounts, celebrates).

The great difference is that the words of the plaque endure and are destined to be read by future generations. Like a book, the plaque is "una lettera che non ha busta, né indirizzo" (a letter that has neither an envelope nor an address); it is meant to be read by anyone wishing to do so, and it thus belongs to each reader individually and collectively to all readers, past, present, and future. The eccentric and solitary Manganelli then writes words that belie his anguished and ironic solipsism, revealing his genuine love for literature: "Nulla più di un libro ci fa consapevoli di appartenere ad una comune umanità, illuminata e tormentata dalle medesime speranze e angosce" (There is nothing better than a book to make us aware that we belong to a common humanity, illuminated and tormented by the very same hopes and anxieties). He then highlights the mystery of literature's endurance, the ways in which certain books wax and wane, are read and then disappear, only to reemerge decades or centuries later.

No matter how fragile the endurance of literature is, however, Manganelli writes that not to have access to great books is equivalent to not having access to ourselves, "alle zone più oscure, magiche, enigmatiche; a ciò che in noi sogna, ama, teme, crede e dispera" (to the most obscure, magical, enigmatic zones; to all that dreams, loves, fears, believes and despairs in us). Reading only the ephemera of the mass media is, for Manganelli, the same as being illiterate; reading literature, on the other hand, gives one entry into the human condition and experience "della vastità e della drammaticità della sorte dell'uomo" (of the vastness and dramatic quality of human destiny). In a short but beautifully forceful hymn Manganelli describes the library as "molte, strane, inquietanti cose: è un circo, una balera, una ceremonia, un incantesimo, una magheria, un viaggio per la terra, un viaggio al centro della terra, un viaggio per i cieli" (many strange, disquieting things: it is a circus, a dance hall, a ceremony, an enchantment, a bewitchment, a voyage around the world, a voyage to the center of the world, a voyage to heaven).

Above all, Manganelli concludes, a library is a labyrinth and an enigma that he has no wish to solve, "perché la sua misteriosa grandezza dà un oscuro senso alla nostra vita–quel senso che la pubblicità va cercando di cancellare" (because its mysterious greatness gives some obscure meaning to our life–a meaning that mass media are trying to nullify). He thus comes full circle back to his opening comparison between the enduring plaque and the evanescent posters in the Piazza del Popolo, between, implicitly, the value of literature and the insignificance and even danger of lived ephemera. For Manganelli, whatever is great in humanity is to be found in books that, like his own, address the mysterious afterlife. The metaphysical anguish generated by mortality fuels the quest for immortality, one of the forms of which is the writing of literature. Such is the rich legacy of the work of Giorgio Manganelli.

Interviews:

Antonio Debenedetti, "La critica? Una menzogna di secondo grado," *Corriere dei Libri,* 18 December 1985, p. 17;

Sandra Petrignani, *Fantasia e fantastico* (Brescia: Camunia, 1985), pp. 125–133;

Guido Almansi, "Nulla più che un'inezia," *Panorama,* 16 February 1986, pp. 114–121;

Graziella Pulce, *Lettura d'autore: conversazioni di critica e di letteratura con Giorgio Manganelli, Pietro Citati e Alberto Arbasino* (Rome: Bulzoni, 1988).

Bibliographies:

Ebe Flamini, "Ricordo di Giorgio Manganelli," *La Rivista dei Libri,* 5 (May 1992): 25–26;

Graziella Pulce, *Bibliografia degli scritti di Giorgio Manganelli* (Florence: Titivillus Editore, 1996).

References:
Pietro Citati, "Ritratto di Manganelli," in his *Il sogno della camera rossa* (Milan: Rizzoli, 1986), pp. 223–226;

Maria Corti, *Il viaggio testuale. Le ideologie e le strutture semiotiche* (Turin: Einaudi, 1978), pp. 147–159;

Umberto Eco, "Manganelli, la regola e l'eccezione," *L'Espresso,* 10 June 1990, p. 190;

Ernesto Ferrero, "C'è del metodo nel terrore di Edgar Poe," *Tuttolibri,* 24 December 1983, p. 5;

Giulio Ferroni, "Giorgio Manganelli: Lo spazio assoluto della iperletteratura divina, meraviglia, magia, mistificazione, artificio. Astrazione, fantasia, irrealtà, arbitrio, menzogna, congegno, gioco, giocattolo, manipolazione, evvia dicendo," in *Novecento: I contemporanei* (Milan: Marzorati, 1979), pp. 10057–10081;

Ferroni, *Storia della letteratura italiana: il Novecento* (Turin: Einaudi, 1991), pp. 544–545;

Gianfranco Galliano, *Letteratura e cultura in Giorgio Manganelli* (Florence: Firenze Libri, 1986);

Angelo Guglielmi, "Hilarotragoedia," in his *Vero e falso* (Milan: Feltrinelli, 1968), pp. 161–164;

Guglielmi, "Nuovo commento," in *La letteratura del risparmio* (Milan: Bompiani, 1973), pp. 131–139;

Guglielmi, "Una polemica," in *Carta stampata* (Rome: Cooperativa Scrittori, 1978), pp. 123–132;

Ludovica Koch, "La palude, indecorosa preghiera," in *La Rivista dei libri,* November 1991, pp. 37–40;

Gregory L. Lucente, "Giorgio Manganelli. The World of the Word: Fool's Truth," in his *Beautiful Fables: Self-consciousness in Italian Narrative from Manzoni to Calvino* (Baltimore & London: Johns Hopkins University Press, 1986), pp. 312–322;

Grazia Menechella, "La distanza ironica in Giorgio Manganelli," in *Scrittori, tendenze letterarie e conflitto delle poetiche in Italia (1960–1990),* edited by Rocco Capozzi and Massimo Ciavolella (Ravenna: Longo Editore, 1992), pp. 143–150;

Menechella, "Moravia/Manganelli: la querelle tra leggibilità," in *Homage to Moravia,* edited by Capozzi and Mario B. Mignone, Moravia supplement, *Forum Italicum* (5 February 1993): 125–139;

Alda Merini, *Il tormento delle figure* (Genoa: Il Melangolo, 1990);

Giuseppe Ottone, "Barocco di Manganelli," in *Novecento: I contemporanei* (Milan: Marzorati, 1979), pp. 10081–10089;

Rebecca West, "Before, Beneath, and Around the Text: The Genesis and Construction of Some Postmodern Prose Fictions," *Annali d'italianistica,* 9 (1991): 272–292;

West, review-essay on *La letteratura come menzogna, Dall'inferno, Laboriose inezie* and *tutti gli errori, Annali d'italianistica,* 4 (1986): 307–311;

West, "Toward the Millennium: Update on Celati, Malerba, Manganelli," *L'Anello che non tiene* (1993): 57–70.

Papers:
Manganelli's papers, library, and bookshelves are housed at the Fondo Manoscritti di Autori Contemporanei at the University of Pavia.

Dacia Maraini
(11 November 1936 -)

Augustus Pallotta
Syracuse University

BOOKS: *La vacanza* (Milan: Lerici, 1962); translated by Stuart Hood as *The Holiday* (London: Weidenfeld, 1966);

L'età del malessere (Turin: Einaudi, 1963); translated by Frances Frenaye as *The Age of Malaise* (New York: Grove, 1963); republished as *The Age of Discontent* (London: Weidenfeld & Nicolson, 1963);

Crudeltà all'aria aperta (Milan: Feltrinelli, 1966);

A memoria (Milan: Bompiani, 1967);

Mio marito (Milan: Bompiani, 1968; enlarged, 1974);

Cuore di mamma, by Maraini and Salvatore Samperi (Milan: Forum, 1969);

Il ricatto a teatro e altre commedie (Turin: Einaudi, 1970);

Memorie di una ladra (Milan: Bompiani, 1972); translated by Nina Rootes as *Memoirs of a Female Thief* (London: Abelard-Schuman, 1973; Levittown, N.Y.: Transatlantic Arts, 1974);

E tu chi eri? Interviste sull'infanzia (Milan: Bompiani, 1973);

Viva l'Italia (Turin: Einaudi, 1973);

Donne mie (Turin: Einaudi, 1974);

Fare teatro. Materiali, testi, interviste (Milan: Bompiani, 1974);

Donna in guerra (Turin: Einaudi, 1975); translated by Mara Benetti and Elspeth Spottiswood as *Women at War* (London: Lighthouse Books, 1984);

La donna perfetta, seguito da Il cuore di una vergine (Turin: Einaudi, 1975);

Don Juan (Turin: Einaudi, 1976);

Dialogo di una prostituta con un suo cliente (Padua: Mastrogiacomo, 1978);

Mangiami pure (Turin: Einaudi, 1978); translated by Genni Donati Gunn as *Devour Me Too* (Toronto: Guernica, 1987);

Storia di Piera, by Maraini and Piera degli Espositi (Milan: Bompiani, 1980);

Lettere a Marina (Milan: Bompiani, 1981); translated by Dick Kitto and Spottiswood as *Letters to Marina* (Freedom, Cal.: Crossing Press, 1981);

I sogni di Clitennestra e altre commedie (Milan: Bompiani, 1981);

Dacia Maraini (photograph by Gerhard Jaeger)

Lezioni d'amore e altre commedie (Milan: Bompiani, 1982);

Dimenticato di dimenticare (Turin: Einaudi, 1982);

Il treno per Helsinki (Turin: Einaudi, 1984); translated by Kitto and Spottiswood as *The Train* (London: Camden, 1989);

Isolina: la donna tagliata a pezzi (Milan: Mondadori, 1985); translated by Siân Williams as *Isolina* (London & Chester Springs, Pa.: Peter Owens, 1993);

Il bambino Alberto (Milan: Bompiani, 1986);

Stravaganza (Rome: Sercangeli, 1987);

La bionda, la bruna e l'asino (Milan: Rizzoli, 1987);
Maraini Stein (Rome: Il ventaglio, 1987);
Delitto (Lungro di Cosenza: Marco, 1990);
La lunga vita di Marianna Ucría (Milan: Rizzoli, 1990); translated by Kitto and Spottiswood as *The Silent Duchess* (London: Flamingo, 1993);
L'uomo tatuato (Naples: Guida, 1990);
Erzbeth Bathory; Il geco; Norma 44 (Rome: Editori & Associati, 1991);
Viaggiando con passo di volpe: poesie, 1983–1991 (Milan: Rizzoli, 1991); translated by Genni Donati Gunn as *Traveling in the Gait of a Fox* (Kingston, Ontario: Quarry Press, 1992);
Veronica, meretrice e scrittora (Milan: Bompiani, 1992);
Bagheria (Milan: Rizzoli, 1993); translated by Kitto and Spottiswood as *Bagheria* (London & Chester Springs, Pa.: Peter Owens, 1994);
Cercando Emma (Milan: Rizzoli, 1993);
Il sommacco: piccolo inventario dei teatri parlermitani trovati e persi (Palermo: Flaccovio, 1993);
Mulino, Orlov e Il gatto che si crede pantera (Roma: Stampa alternativa, 1994);
Voci (Milan: Rizzoli, 1994);
La casa tra due palme (Salerno: Sottotraccia, 1995);
Silvia (Ravenna: Edizioni del girasole, 1995);
Un clandestino a bordo (Milan: Rizzoli, 1996);
Storie di cani per una bambina (Milan: Bompiani, 1996);
Dolce per sé (Milan: Rizzoli, 1997);
Dizionarietto quotidiano. Da "amare" a "zonzo": 229 voci raccolte da Gioconda Marinelli. (Milan: Bompiani, 1997).

Edition in English: *Only Prostitutes Marry in May. Four Plays,* edited, with an introduction, by Rhoda Helfman Kaufman (Toronto: Guernica, 1994).

OTHER: *La protesta poetica del Giappone. Antologia di cent'anni di poesia giapponese,* edited by Maraini and Michiko Nojiri (Rome: Officina, 1968);
"Suor Juana," in Juana Inés de la Cruz's *Risposta a suor Filotea,* edited by Angelo Morino (Turin: La Rosa, 1980);
Joseph Conrad, *Il compagno segreto,* translated, with an introduction by Maraini (Milan: Biblioteca Universale Rizzoli, 1996).

A timid and insecure young writer in the early 1960s, Dacia Maraini established herself as a significant novelist, poet, and playwright in the 1970s. She is closely identified with feminism, but it would be a mistake to view her work only through a feminist lens. She is a contemporary writer committed to feminism who offers a socially provoking view of the human condition, often focusing on but not limited to women.

Dacia Maraini was born in Florence on 11 November 1936 into a cultured and aristocratic family that had lost much of its wealth and social prestige. Her father, Fosco Maraini, was a well-known ethnographer who published several successful books on Japan. Maraini's mother, Topazia Alliata, was a Sicilian noblewoman from Bagheria whose family flourished in the eighteenth century. Both parents were nonconformists, as Maraini relates in *Bagheria* (1993), an engaging book of autobiographical recollections centering on the coastal town near Palermo:

> Mia madre [era] bionda e splendente, insofferente di ogni imposizione materna, sprezzante verso i "grandi matrimoni" che le volevano imporre. Difatti, abbandonando tutti i nobili principi siciliani, era partita, da sola, per Firenze dove aveva incontrato mio padre, ragazzo burbero e allegro, ribelle e solitario, sportivo, inquieto, introverso e imprevedibile. Si sposarono subito, e senza una lira andarono ad abitare a Fiesole, in una stanza in cima a una torre, mangiando patate bollite e uova sode.

> (My mother was blonde, a splendid young woman who resisted impositions from her mother, and looked with scorn to the "great marriages" that the family sought to impose on her. In fact, forsaking all the norms of Sicilian aristocracy, she left, all alone, for Florence and there she met my father, who was both surly and good-natured, a lone and rebellious youngster, athletic and restless, introverted and unpredictable. They were married within a short time; pennyless, they went to live in Fiesole, in a single room atop a tower, with nothing to eat but eggs and boiled potatoes.)

From 1938 to 1945 Maraini lived in Japan with her parents. The move was prompted initially by a research project that her father carried out at the University of Sapporo. When the stay was extended and war broke out, the family, which by 1943 included two other girls, was arrested by Japanese authorities and sent to a concentration camp because of the parents' opposition to fascism. In the camp the family suffered hunger and other physical deprivations.

In 1946 they returned to Italy, settling in Bagheria. They lived in three small, uncomfortable rooms—not a designed living space—in the eighteenth-century villa owned by Maraini's maternal grandmother. The family's financial means were quite limited, which had prompted the decision to live in Bagheria in the first place. In an interview published in *Panorama* on 15 December 1980, Maraini looks back on the mixed experience of her childhood: "In casa ho sempre respirato cultura e fame. Per anni non ho avuto soldi per comprarmi un paio di scarpe o andare dal dentista" (At home I was exposed to culture and hunger. For years I did not have the money to buy a pair of shoes or to go to the dentist).

From 1947 to 1950 she attended a private school, the Collegio Santissima Annunziata in Florence, and in 1950 she returned to Bagheria to continue her studies. Four years later her parents separated, and she chose to live with her father in Rome. Regarding her parents' influence on her upbringing, Maraini told Giosuè Calciura of *Il Giornale di Sicilia* on 11 November 1986: "Mio padre era anarchico, mia madre una libertaria. Non avevo nessuno dei complessi che di solito pesano all'interno delle famiglie cattoliche tradizionali" (My father was anarchic, my mother a libertarian. I did not have any of the complexes that usually carry a weight within traditional Catholic families).

In Rome in the late 1950s Maraini gained access to the literary world through her acquaintance with several writers, among them Alberto Moravia, Pier Paolo Pasolini, Giorgio Manganelli, Goffredo Parise, and Enzo Siciliano. During the same period she met Lucio Pozzi, whom she married in 1959. The marriage lasted a short time. Following her separation in 1961 Maraini began a long relationship with Moravia, which was to last until 1978. In Alain Alkann's *Vita di Moravia* (Moravia's Life, 1990) Moravia remembers his years with Maraini fondly: "Ricordo quei diciotto anni come tra i migliori della mia vita" (I remember those eighteen years as among the best of my life).

Maraini's first book, *La vacanza* (1962; translated as *The Holiday*, 1966) was published at a time of deep uncertainties for Italian writers. The economic boom of the late 1950s had fostered industrial expansion and a newly found prosperity, but economic growth had also given rise to a new reality, the consumer society, which had a decisive impact on cultural and intellectual life. In the review *Il menabò* Elio Vittorini urged young writers to take cognizance of a new social order in which progressive ideas were being obscured by the materialism that was overtaking Italian society. Among the works that reflect such concerns is Elémire Zolla's *L'eclisse dell'intellettuale* (The Eclipse of the Intellectual, 1962). It is in this climate that Maraini wrote her initial novel, a work that carries the seeds of discontent toward the traditional values of a conservative society and, in particular, toward a sociopolitical order dominated by patriarchy.

As a young female writer Maraini found herself at a disadvantage in a literary environment dominated by men. For the republication of *La vacanza*

Dust jacket for Maraini's 1963 novel, in which a naive young woman allows herself to be exploited

in 1976, she recalls the unpleasant experience of seeking a publisher: "Avevo offerto *La vacanza* a vari editori.... Avvertivo, per il fatto di essere donna, di mancare di credibilità. Sentivo che non mi prendevano sul serio, che non credevano in quel che facevo, e ne ero molto mortificata" (I had sent *La vacanza* to various publishers.... I noticed that, for the simple reason I was a woman, I lacked credibility. I felt they did not take me seriously, they did not believe in what I was doing, and that hurt me very much). Lerici, the publisher, accepted *La vacanza* with the proviso that she secure an introduction by Moravia, the most popular Italian writer at the time. She did, but later regretted it.

In her first novel and in most of her subsequent work, Maraini chose to write about female protagonists. Clearly the most important reason for this decision is her desire to reverse the longstanding practice in society and in literature of regarding women as subordinate agents reacting to the actions of men. In *The Irish Times* of Dublin, 16 June 1984, Maraini justifies her practice: "In my writing, I attempt to mold women characters as instances of subjectivity. I present the woman as subject, thus neutralizing the prevailing image of the woman as object." However, Maraini did not from the beginning create assertive women characters fully conscious of their identities. Her protagonists evolved gradually over the course of the first fifteen years of her career.

In the early fiction the distinctive trait of Maraini's female characters is their lack of self-consciousness. Probably the most interesting feature of *La vacanza* and *L'età del malessere* (1963; translated as *The Age of Malaise,* 1963)—both youthful, to some extent derivative efforts—is the dormant consciousness betrayed by the female protagonist's point of view. Both works focus on adolescent women who move aimlessly from one experience to the next, subjecting themselves, often with masochistic condescension, to sexual and emotional exploitation by older men as well as youngsters of their own age. Their sense of alienation, accentuated by the lack of interpersonal relationships within the family, expresses a social and psychological disorientation rooted in a subconscious refusal to come to terms with reality. Embedded in these works is a despairing view of woman's inaction in the face of far-reaching external changes stimulated by the economic prosperity of the late 1950s.

Although Maraini's reputation is based largely on her novels, nearly all of which have been translated in various foreign languages, her plays and collections of poetry are also integral to the organic body of her work. Her first book of verses, *Crudeltà all'aria aperta* (Cruelty in the Open Air, 1966), is marked by an insistent return to childhood and its central figure: a youthful, handsome father to whom the child is drawn irresistibly and with immeasurable devotion. A good share of the volume re-creates fleeting moments of closeness and intense joy that become etched in memory: "Father, in quella villa barocca / m'insegnavi a non soffrire e a pedalare in fretta" (Father, in that baroque villa / you taught me not to suffer and to pedal fast). The father image is crucial to Maraini's work, for hidden between the folds of her creative forms, behind the invention of various characters, is a father who did not, or could not, grasp what he meant to his child:

Insomma tu non sai
quanto di te è germogliato in me
e come se la memoria è un sentimento
io odio te stesso in me.

(In short, you don't know
how much of you opened in me like a bud
and, if memory is feeling, how
I hate you in me.)

In *Bagheria* Maraini writes of her father as an enduring presence: "Per tutta la mia infanzia, l'ho amato senza essere ricambiata. È stato un amore solitario il mio" (Throughout my childhood, I loved him without ever being loved in return. My love was one-sided). The one-sided relationship was due to her father's frequent departures, often to the Far East, occasioned by professional and personal interests. As a result, the magic spell of closeness was broken, replaced by hurt and confusion in a child deeply attached to her father. Still in *Bagheria,* she writes: "Poi tutto si è guastato, non so come, non so perché. Lui è sparito lasciandosi dietro un cuore di bambina innamorato e molti pensieri gravi" (Then everything was ruined. I don't know how or why he disappeared leaving behind the enamored heart of a child and many grave thoughts).

Maraini's lifelong interest in the theater led her to take the important step in 1967 of founding with Moravia and Siciliano the theatrical company Il Porcospino for the express purpose of staging works by modern and contemporary writers. When the troupe disbanded the following year for lack of funds, she continued to stage and often direct plays in a lower-class section of Rome called Centocelle. Believing theater to be an appropriate sociological tool for raising class and gender consciousness, she encouraged local people to take on minor roles. Sometimes the performance of a play was interrupted once or twice to allow the director, actors, and audience to discuss its ideas and relevance to society. "Il teatro," she says in a 1990 interview with Sumeli Weinberg, "è un fatto sociale, legato alla società in cui si vive" (Theater is a social matter, tied to the society in which one lives). Virtually all social questions engaged by feminists, from abortion to patriarchy, are present in her plays, given voice by assertive women on stage.

In Maraini's earliest play, *La famiglia normale* (The Normal Family), which was staged in Rome in January 1967, she takes on the bedrock of society, the site where values are inculcated and assimilated. But the "normal" family of which Maraini writes lacks a mother and includes a handicapped father, a gay son who is an aspiring playwright, and a neurotic daughter who defends traditional bourgeois values in which she does not really believe. This play and three others were collected in *Il ricatto a teatro e altre commedie* (Blackmail on the Stage and Other Plays, 1970). The theme of women's liberation is treated in *Il manifesto* (The Manifesto) whose protagonist is a rebellious young woman who defies all behavioral codes expected of her, only to find herself, in the end, crushed by the superior forces of what was then called the Establishment. In *Recitare* (To Perform), Maraini attempts to revitalize the improvisation of the commedia dell'arte and the Pirandellian resources of a play within a play with loosely

Dust jacket for the British edition of Maraini's 1993 book of recollections

connected dramatic sketches in which actors with interchangeable roles enact and interpret various facets of bourgeois life. The result is only partially successful, for the sketches improvised on stage are rarely a credible representation of reality. What stands out is the writer's searching mind striving, through experimentation, to give texture and meaning to overpowering social questions: capitalist exploitation; racial, gender, and class discrimination; the bourgeois aspirations of the proletariat; and the war in Vietnam.

The most significant phase of Maraini's life began in the late 1960s with her growing involvement in the women's movement, which in the next twenty years would become the main force of her creative work. In 1969 she joined Rivolta Femminile (Women's Revolt), the first feminist group established in Rome, and in 1973 she was instrumental in forming the Associazione La Maddalena, a feminist organization whose activities evolved around its theater and cultural center. For several years La Maddalena served as an important site for the personal growth and enrichment of many Italian women.

Maraini's third novel, *A memoria* (From Memory, 1967), attests to a transitional stage marked by a search for innovative means of expression. One of the more-interesting experimental efforts of the post–World War II avant-garde in Italy, this work shows the influence of the French *nouveau roman* (new novel) pioneered by Alain Robbe-Grillet. Maraini uses three levels of narration, each drawing the existential consciousness of the fictional personae through a resourceful treatment of the following elements: diary entries in which Maria, the narrator, records her experiences with cold objectivity; extended dialogues in which Maria's difficulty in relating to her husband is shown through the repetition of the same point, each time with a different twist; and a series of letters from a friend to Maria, written in a fragmented, highly elliptical style that requires the reader's intuition for interpretation.

The novel's tripartite structure is loosely held together by the strands of the peculiar and complex relationships involving Maria; her husband, Pietro, a schoolteacher in his thirties; and Giacomo, a family friend in love with Maria. A disillusioned Marxist, Pietro is *consapevole* (aware), *consenziente* (consentient), and *consecutivo* (stable)—where the prefix *con* underlies the complementary nature of the marriage. Maria, on the other hand, is pictured as "free, independent, frantically active."

Maria's strength—the self-conscious strength she identifies superficially with an active and assertive personality—is juxtaposed to Pietro's aloofness and sterile intellectualism in a series of vivid images inspired by the seventeenth-century Spanish playwright Pedro Calderón de la Barca's *La vida es sueño* (Life Is a Dream), as when Maraini writes, "Qui si rappresenta un uomo che va sognando e cavalcando fra le rocce della desolazione. Qui si rappresenta una donna che taglia con una spada le proprie debolezze" (This scene will show a man who daydreams as he rides through the stones of desolation. This scene will show a woman who with a sword severs her frailties). Among the narrative strains that echo Calderón's drama, the conflict between reason and instinct points to a dichotomous analogy with Pietro's and Maria's existential outlook: his faith in the intellect to understand life and her reliance on instinctive behavior to experience life. Equally relevant is the analogy between Pietro and Segismundo, the protagonist of Calderón's play, an analogy that, as perceived by Maria, throws light on Pietro's wasteful existence in the stifling confinement of his ivory tower.

But Maria's freedom proves illusory outside the sphere of her impulsive, erotic adventures with younger men, who react to her advances with uneasy consent to the inversion of sexual roles. Reflection and contemplation—the existential models that identify Pietro and Giacomo through selective references to Petrarch and Leopardi—are discarded by Maria as insufficient means of maintaining a rapport with reality. In time, however, the young woman realizes that her propensity to associate reality with sexual possession is equally insufficient.

Maria's problem, as explained by a psychiatrist at the end of the novel, is that she suffers from a loss of "social" memory that has impaired her ability to function rationally within society. The doctor believes her behavior is an expression of uninhibited sexual impulses, a condition he claims to be able to treat:

> "La memoria è la coscienza e la coscienza è la totale unità della persona. In te la coscienza è malata, non morta, non credo, ma in grave pericolo."
> "Da dove comincio?"
> "Questo lavoro, se mai, lo faremo insieme. Tua madre e il signor Giacomo . . . mi hanno incaricato di curarti e guarirti."

> ("Memory is consciousness, and consciousness is the total unity of the person. Your consciousness is impaired, not totally inactive, I believe, but in great danger."
> "Where do I begin?"
> "This is a task that, if you want, we will work on together. Your mother and signor Giacomo . . . have asked me to take care of you and to cure you.")

From a feminist viewpoint *A memoria* is a disturbing, ambivalent work permeated with contradictory notions. On the surface the portrait of an assertive and independent woman who has shed the lethargy of her counterparts in *La vacanza* and *L'età del malessere* seems to point to feminist awareness.

Moreover, Maria's sense of initiative and her appropriation of masculine traits unfold in the context of persistent, competitive analogies with Pietro's disposition. Yet Maria is hardly a positive character. The veneer of independence and sexual freedom hides a disturbed young woman incapable of giving her life structure and a purposeful direction.

In the collection *Mio marito* (My Husband, 1968) most of the stories focus on the marital experiences of young couples coping with misunderstandings and hypocrisy. As revealed through the eyes of women, the modes of behavior that define marital relationships are marked by a stifling sense of ill feeling. The men are the more pathetic figures, for once the initial euphoria of conjugal life fades away, they are unable to withstand the boredom of daily life and turn to sexual deviations or find the ultimate solution in suicide.

Maraini also gives considerable attention to the lonely life of the single working woman in a large city. Moving from her tiny apartment to a menial job, such a woman goes through her daily routine with a sense of resignation, her dreary existence sustained solely by a constant yearning for a sexual outlet. In the story "Il letargo" (Lethargy) the propensity to dissociate the self from reality through a complacent indulgence in daydreaming leads to a split between the fantasizing mind absorbed in wish fulfillment and the body that reacts mechanically to external stimuli. The female narrator expresses the abulia that is the consequence of such a life:

> Il fatto è che mi sto allenando a dormire, anche quando lavoro e devo dire che ci sono quasi riuscita. Alle volte il risveglio è improvviso e penoso; soprattutto se qualche compagna mi tocca una spalla o mi urta senza volere o mi ride nell'orecchio per farmi dispetto. Allora sussulto e vengo presa da una febbre che dura per fortuna pochi secondi ma che mi lascia spossata e fiacca.
>
> Quando non lavoro, sto a casa, seduta su una sedia in cucina e dormo. I mei occhi restano aperti e potrei anche parlare e muovermi o eseguire qualche semplice lavoro manuale, mentre le mie pupille risucchiano in sé tutto il vigore del mio corpo e lo trattengono sospeso come in un limbo sonnolento e immobile.

> (The truth of the matter is that I am training myself to fall asleep even while I work, and I must say that I have nearly succeeded. At times the awakening is sudden, especially when a coworker touches me on the shoulder or bumps into me or laughs in my ear out of spite. At that moment I wake up with a start, and I am overtaken by a fever which luckily only lasts a few seconds but leaves me weak and exhausted.

>   When I am not working, I stay home and sleep on a chair in the kitchen. My eyes remain open and I could talk, move about, or perform a simple task while the pupils of my eyes absorb all the strength of my body and hold it in suspense as in a limbo of dormant immobility.)

Several of Maraini's books seem to lie midway between journalism and fiction, for they are based on the type of inquisitive and documentary effort associated with investigative journalism. *Memorie di una ladra* (1972; translated as *Memoirs of a Female Thief*, 1973) bears some similarities to the Spanish picaresque novel in that the experiences that unfold in the course of its protagonist's itinerant life are used to unveil social ills and injustices. The book is an extraordinary tour de force dominated by the central character, Teresa Numa, social outcast and incorrigible swindler.

Raised on a farm by unloving parents, Teresa runs away from home as a youngster and after a brief, unhappy marriage is introduced to the Roman underworld, teeming with thieves, pimps, prostitutes, petty criminals, pickpockets, and black marketeers. Under their influence she embarks on a life of risky adventures that take her across the Italian peninsula, from the small towns to the large cities where duping people becomes perforce a refined skill of ingenuity and sophistication. But most of the time Teresa spends in prison, exposed to hunger and filth and subjected to punishment. It is in this regard that the book takes on complementary significance as an exposé of inhumane conditions found in Italian detention centers for women. Much of the criticism implicit in the text is based on Maraini's substantial research, including visits to the prisons she describes.

A new tack for Maraini, *Memorie di una ladra* seems to harken back to nineteenth-century naturalism, for it represents her appreciation of the novel as a sociological expression. In an interview with Adele Cambria published in *Quotidiano donna* on 17 April 1981, Maraini remarks on how her feminism led her to a new understanding: "Col femminismo è stato possibile un'identificazione tra letteratura e vita" (Feminism made it possible to identify literature with life); as a result, she continued, "È finito per me un certo modo di vedere la letteratura come separata, come esterna" (My way of seeing literature as separate from and external to life came to an end).

In *E tu chi eri? Interviste sull'infanzia* (And Who Were You? Interviews on Childhood, 1973) Maraini conducts interviews with prominent individuals regarding their childhood experiences. It is the first of three culturally significant books in which she uses the medium of the interview to explore questions of general interest. *Storia di Piera* (Piera's Story, 1980), which brings to light the troubled life of the stage actress Piera degli Esposti, presents a sustained and absorbing dialogue, especially interesting for the light it sheds on the actress's relationship with her assertive mother, whose unconventional ideas and social conduct left a deep impression on her daughter. In *Il bambino Alberto* (The Child Alberto, 1986) Maraini analyzes Moravia, whom she also interviewed for *E tu chi eri?* Despite a long relationship with him, in both books Moravia comes across as a reticent man, resistant to revealing much about his private life. Maraini regards him as a complex person with ambivalent feelings about sexuality, the ever-present subject of Moravia's fiction. According to Maraini, deep down Moravia views sexuality in moral terms, as a sin, and "il peccato è quasi sempre attribuito alla donna" (the sin is almost invariably attributed to the woman).

Maraini concentrated most intensely on the stage during the 1970s. In *Viva l'Italia* (Long Live Italy, 1973), the first of her plays to explore the place of women in history and myth, Maraini brings together, with overtly critical overtones, two historical events: Italy's political unification and the consequent expectations of social justice on one hand and on the other the bloody revolt of southern Italian peasants in which a young proletarian woman plays a leading role. In 1975 she published *La donna perfetta* (The Perfect Woman), whose title, like *La famiglia normale,* is charged with mocking irony. Nina, the protagonist, is naive, gentle, and submissive to a strong and decisive man. Tragedy brings to an end Nina's transparently contrived traditional role when she dies as a result of a botched abortion. In *Don Juan* (1976) Maraini revisits with mixed results the classical figure of the seducer immortalized first by the Spanish playwright Gabriel Téllez, known by the pseudonym Tirso de Molina. To feminist critic Grazia Sumeli Weinberg the merit of the play lies in stressing that for Don Juan "la conquista e non il possesso è il simbolo del potere" (seduction and not lovemaking is the symbol of power), which makes the mythical lover "l'incarnazione più spietata della logica patriarcale del potere" (the most merciless embodiment of the patriarchal logic of power).

Maraini's second book of poetry, *Donne mie* (Oh, My Women, 1974), is in a sense a feminist manifesto in verse, containing a passionate appeal to women to break free from the centuries-old stereotypes fashioned by men and assert themselves as independent beings. The tone is didactic, meant to awaken and educate:

Vi siete identificate con l'uomo
per sfiducia in voi stesse, avete seguito il
modello maschile del forte, virile, sicuro
e con questo avete tradito le vostre compagne
le donne di tutti i tempi.

(You have identified yourselves with man
because you lacked faith in yourselves, you have followed
the male model, strong, virile, self-assured
and thus you have betrayed your companions
the women of all ages.)

For the woman attached to tradition, the poet has nothing but scorn, addressing her as "guardiana feroce e impura / della tua servitù storica" (ferocious and impure guardian / of your history of servitude).

The contradictions apparent in *A memoria* are resolved in Maraini's first fully coherent feminist novel, *Donna in guerra* (1975; translated as *Women at War*, 1984). The title itself is noteworthy: the noun *woman* is accompanied by a militant qualifier that immediately directs the reader's attention to the Italian feminist movement, which coalesced in 1968 amid widespread and often violent protests by students, factory workers, and groups of women. No doubt the work is the outgrowth of Maraini's association with the movement, but, examined closely, it contains few traces of the militancy suggested by the title. *Donna in guerra* is, rather, a thought-provoking narrative in which a woman's individual consciousness and her yearning for self-fulfillment are probed with calm objectivity.

Written in the form of a diary, the story documents the gradual disaffection in the relationship of a young couple. Essentially the difficulty arises from a clash of attitudes involving Giacomo, a kind but inflexible man whose traditional perception of marriage attaches little value to a woman's needs, and his wife, Vannina, who grows weary of feigning happiness while accepting her gray existence with resigned indifference. The resolution of the crisis that comes at the end takes the form of an open break with tradition: the woman leaves her husband to start a new life.

Much more significant than the inversion of roles found in *A memoria* is the emergence, in this work, of a woman who relies on reasoning and reflection rather than instinct, not only to solve her predicament but also to take cognizance of social injustices, especially the injustices perpetrated against women. Attracted for a short time to the revolutionary ideals of an underground organization, Vannina takes part in a series of investigative reports designed to expose the *lavoro nero,* piecework done at home, for a pittance, by proletarian women living in the squalid back streets of Naples.

The transition from *A memoria* to *Donna in guerra* is also marked by the question of "the total unity of the person" identified by the psychiatrist of the earlier novel with a healthy consciousness. Indeed, unity characterizes Vannina's quest for coherence and purpose as she makes responsible individual choices rather than acting to appease social expectations. Vannina's painful decision to end her marriage is self-perceived as an act of courage stemming from her moral conviction that she has the right to grow as an independent being and to do so outside the sphere of an institution that has proven unresponsive to her aspirations.

From a feminist viewpoint *Donna in guerra* is significant not only because of Vannina's decision to pursue an independent life but also because of her gradual realization that her disaffection with life stems from the institution of marriage, not just from her husband's unresponsiveness. Indeed, the criticism of marriage as an institution is the compelling subtext of the novel. Calling *Donna in guerra* "il mio romanzo più coscientemente femminista" (the most conscientiously feminist novel I have written), Maraini, in an interview published on 18 November 1975 in Bologna's *Il Resto del Carlino,* stresses the complexity of the political vision: "La coscienza femminista consiste nel riconoscere ciò che vi è di comune nei mali che affliggono le donne, consiste nel capire la natura politica dei rapporti fra uomo e donna, fra donna e istituzioni, fra donna e cultura" (Feminist consciousness consists in recognizing what is common to the social ills that afflict women; it consists in understanding the political nature of the rapports between women and men, between women and institutions, between women and culture).

Mariani's next collections of verse, *Mangiami pure* (1978; translated as *Devour Me Too,* 1987) and *Dimenticato di dimenticare* (Forgot to Forget, 1982), contain a markedly different perspective on women than the view evident in her previous collection, *Donne mie*. The change in part reflects the vicissitudes of the Italian feminism as the realization of limited gains at high costs replaced the idealistic expectations of the early movement. The relationships of women with each other are shown to include reservations and misapprehensions while the feasibility of dialogues with men, even cautious trust in the opposite sex, is posited, albeit with ambivalent feelings. Later in *Viaggiando con passo di volpe* (1991; translated as *Traveling in the Gait of a Fox,* 1992), the rancor and tension between the sexes has dissipated; what is left is the realization that in the dissensions and contentious among human beings the only winner is time, which flattens, blurs, and erases the experiences of women and men alike, linking them together in a single, shared destiny.

In the 1980s and after, Maraini's writings for the stage have continued to explore myth and history that have special relevance for women. In *I sogni di Clitennestra* (Clytemnestra's Dreams, 1981) she examines the dynamics of power from a feminist perspective that sees patriarchy as an abusive and oppressive institution. The play is based on the figure of Clytemnestra, Agamemnon's wife, who, with the aid of her lover, Aegisthus, murders her husband and is later killed by their son Orestes. Two other plays feature extraordinary women with quite different professions. *Sor Juana* is based on the life of the seventeeth-century Mexican nun named Sor Juana Inés de la Cruz, and it was included in the Italian edition of her work, *Risposta a suor Filotea* (1980). On the other hand *Veronica, meretrice e scrittora* (Veronica, Prostitute and Writer, 1992) focuses on the Renaissance courtesan Veronica Franco. Both works celebrate exemplary individuals who ran against the grain of their times through their writing, an activity almost wholly the reserve of men.

In *Isolina: la donna tagliata a pezzi* (1985; translated as *Isolina*, 1993), a work closer to investigative writing than to the novel, Maraini offers a careful reconstruction of the gruesome murder of Isolina Canuti, a nineteen-year-old woman from Verona whose mutilated body was found in the waters of the river Adige in January 1900. Tried for the murder was Carlo Trivulzio, an army officer whose relationship with Isolina led to her pregnancy. Isolina wanted to keep the baby, but Trivulzio was opposed to it, believing the circumstances of the affair would have an adverse effect on his career. At the time of the murder Isolina had not had an abortion. Trivulzio was cleared after a lengthy trial, and the identity of the murderer remained a mystery.

Maraini offers a comprehensive and largely objective account of the case by drawing from the reportage of five local newspapers and Milan's daily, *Il Corriere della sera*. The book takes on a subjective vein through the author's clear identification with Isolina, whose transgressive behavior scandalized Verona's middle class. Based on her close examination of the trial proceedings reported in the press, Maraini intimates that the district attorney's prosecution of the case was more attentive to the reputation of the army than to justice.

The publication of *La lunga vita di Marianna Ucría* (1990; translated as *The Silent Duchess,* 1993) marks, in several aspects, a new stage in Maraini's work. The book proved to be her most popular, but that alone would not account for its significance. It is a remarkable novel because of Maraini's technical and stylistic mastery of the narrative craft, fully matured after a long season of innovation and experimentation. The text also reflects the author's quest to reach beyond feminism while remaining essentially faithful to its tenets. She views the human condition in individual terms, no longer—or at least not exclusively, as had been the case heretofore—through the prism of the male-female dichotomy.

Set in the early part of the eighteenth century, the narrative begins with a long and arresting account of a young bandit's final hours before he is brought to the gallows amid a large and festive crowd gathered for the occasion in a central square in Palermo. The scene, drawn in a clearly cinematic fashion, holds crucial significance because the spectacle of a thirteen-year old hanging in a public square is being closely followed, from the cavernous jail to the gallows, by the watchful eye of Marianna Ucría, the deaf-mute child of an aristocratic family on the island. The father has brought little Marianna to see the hanging in the hope that the shock of the experience would prompt her to speak. But later, through reminiscences, the reader learns that the event was also used by her father to block a painful and psychologically scarring experience: Marianna's memory of her being molested by an uncle—the same uncle to whom she is given in marriage as soon as she reaches the age of puberty. As an agreeable wife and a devoted mother, Marianna gives birth to five children, communicating with them and other members of the family by writing short notes on a tablet she carries, hanging from her waist, at all times.

The figure of Marianna is loosely based on one of Maraini's noble ancestors. There are several autobiographical echoes in the book, which become apparent to the reader of *Bagheria*. As is the case with her poetry and other works, Maraini pauses anew on the fleeting image of Fosco Maraini, her beloved father, appearing here in the semblance of Marianna's parent:

Le sembra di scorgere da lontano la figura piacevole del signor padre. Il solo "cavalliere candido come neve" che si sia proposto al suo amore. Fin da quando aveva sei anni il "cavalliere" l'aveva ammaliata col suo "pennacchio di bianco pavoncello" e poi quando lei si era messa ad inseguirlo, lui se n'era andato ad ammaliare altri cuori, altri occhi inquieti.

(She seems to notice from a distance the pleasant figure of her father. The only "knight, white as snow" with whom she fell in love. Since she was six, the "knight" had enchanted her with his "plume of white feathers," and when she set out to pursue him, he had left to bewitch other hearts, other restless eyes.)

Not an historical novel in a traditional sense, *La lunga vita di Marianna Ucría* offers nonetheless an accurate and valuable picture of life within the home of an aristocratic family in eighteenth-century Sicily, from the daily routine and constant contacts with servants, to architectural details of palaces and urban centers, to the formal party at Marianna's palace that includes the highest ranking nobility of Palermo. There are echoes, in this regard, of Lampedusa's *Il Gattopardo* (1958; translated as *The Leopard*, 1960), but they are echoes betraying a careful and pleasurable reading of the work, not any sort of imitation, for Maraini's self-assured hand can hold its own.

In her *Invito alla lettura di Dacia Maraini* Sumeli Weinberg characterizes Marianna's condition as symbolic of "il mutismo storico della donna" (the historical silence of women) in the sense that the work "è la storia di tutte le donne che non hanno potuto parlare, che sono dovute rimanere mute" (is the story of all the women who have been unable to speak, who have had to remain silent). Marianna never regains her speech, but she is able to speak through her life—through sustained courageous efforts to overcome her disability by educating herself, raising a family, and, after her husband's death, running a large estate and household efficiently and benignly.

In terms of overcoming obstacles, individual assertion, and self-fulfillment, *La lunga vita di Marianna Ucría* reflects familiar feminist values treated in most of Maraini's works. Yet one is struck by the transformation of feminism implicit in the comparison of this work and *Donna in guerra,* published fifteen years before. The most apparent of such changes is Maraini's attitude toward motherhood, which, in *Donna in guerra* and other earlier works, is devalued and at times scorned as an impediment in women's struggle for full emancipation. Admittedly *La lunga vita di Marianna Ucría* is set in an historical period that, socially, has few similarities with the modern world, but it is nonetheless significant that Maraini's Marianna values and cultivates her role as a mother with the same unselfish devotion with which she pursues her own education. In the description of four-year-old Signoretto, her firstborn lying on his death bed, the reader is offered one of the most tender expressions of a mother's interaction with her baby in Italian literature:

È stato il più precoce nel riconoscerla e non c'erano balie ... che potessero acquietarlo: finché non tornava in collo a sua madre non smetteva di strillare.

Un bambino allegro e intelligente che sembrava avere intuito la sordità della madre e aveva inventato lì per lì un linguaggio per farsi capire da lei e solo da lei. Le parlava scalciando, mimando, ridendo, tempestandola di baci appiccicosi. Le incollava la grande bocca senza denti sulla faccia, le lambiva gli occhi chiusi con la lingua, le stringeva con le gengive i lobi delle orecchie, ma senza farle male, come un cagnolino che conosce le sue forze e sa dosarle per giocare.

(He was the most precocious in recognizing her, and no wet nurse could quiet him down: he would not stop crying until he was in his mother's arms.

He was a happy and intelligent child who seemed to have intuited his mother's deafness and invented right there and then a language so she and she alone could understand him. He spoke to her by kicking, miming, laughing, smothering her with sticky kisses. He glued his large and toothless mouth on to her face, he rubbed gently his mouth on her closed eyes, and with his gums he squeezed, without hurting, her ear lobes, like a puppy who knows its strength and how to temper it to play.)

Further, the hostility and acrimonious spirit that mark the female-male rapport in so many of Maraini's works are surprisingly attenuated in *La lunga vita di Marianna Ucría*. The woman who has been "punished" by an accident of birth and by her own father has also suffered more than anyone around her. Yet rather than hardening her heart, suffering has opened it to forgiveness and compassion, even toward her father and her husband—the two men most responsible for her predicament. Such are Marianna's feelings as, in her bedroom, she thinks about her husband shortly after she has found the strength not to yield to his uncouth sexual advances:

Questa stanza pare volerle dire qualcosa che lei non ha mai voluto ascoltare: una povertà di un uomo solitario che nell'ignoranza di sé ha messo tutto il suo terrorizzato sentimento d'orgoglio. Proprio nel momento in cui ha trovato la forza di negarsi prova una dolcezza sfinita per lui e per la sua vita di vecchio brusco e abbruttito dalla timidezza.

(This room seems to tell her something she never wanted to hear: the misery of a lonely man who placed in the ignorance of his self all his frightful pride. Right at the moment she found the strength not to yield to him, she felt an exhausted sense of gentleness for him and his life of an old gruff marred by timidity.)

Despite the focus on Marianna, Maraini curiously chooses to keep her readers from having full and unmediated access to the character's thoughts by eschewing first-person narration or the generous use of a personal diary. Although most reviewers have stressed the significance of *La lunga vita di Marianna Ucría* as a text in which writing is privileged as a means of communication, Marianna's writing is only used to communicate with her servants and her family members. As readers admire her efforts to enter the intellectual domain of ideas and philosophical speculation and follow her interest in Hume and the French philosophes, their attention continues to be focused outside, and not within, Marianna's mind.

La lunga vita di Marianna Ucría is Maraini's most important work because it stands out as a feminist novel unhampered by the risk of becoming "dated" and in time shunted to the margins of Italian literature. During her writing of the novel Maraini made a statement that throws considerable light on the significance of the work. In an interview with Lidia Ravera published in *Il Corriere della sera* on 7 April 1987, she pointed out that women should, of course, continue to pursue a wide range of professional choices; then she added: "E intanto contribuire ad essere donne, il che ha, tutto sommato, ben poco a vedere con ciò che si fa, bensí con ciò che si è" (And all along continue being women, which, in the last analysis, has little to do with what a woman does, but with what she is).

Maraini's most recent novels follow well-established trends in structure and thematic concerns, showing her mastery of the detective story and the narrative of remembrance. In *Voci* (Voices, 1994) she returns to the problem of violence against women, already explored in *Isolina,* and in other works as well, though in a subtler and less graphic fashion. Here Michela Cova, a radio journalist, sets out to investigate the murder of Angela Bari, a young woman found dead in her apartment. The investigation takes Michela on a tortuous path leading in the end to Angela's dysfunctional family and to the revelation of violence and sexual abuse facilitated by the complicity of a family member. It is a well-constructed detective story combining the concern for a serious social problem with suspense.

Veined with bittersweet recollections of the past, *Dolce per sé* (Sweet by Itself, 1997) consists of a series of letters written from 1988 to 1995 by a middle-aged woman writer to the young niece of a successful violinist with whom the writer has had a close relationship. In relating the central experiences of her life, marked by the separation from her husband and his eventual death, the writer bares her heart and soul. In a captivating fashion she touches on elemental forces of life: fleeting moments of joy and satisfaction along with daily travails, fears, anxieties, dashed hopes, and tragedy. Reflective, intense, and smoothly calibrated, the narrative rings true, in part because some of the experiences seem to spring from the author's personal life. The writer makes use of Leopardi's verses from the first page, and they blend well with the delicate, fluent, and often poetic prose that echoes other writers fascinated with the past, Proust and Lampedusa among them.

Maraini has enjoyed a long and productive career. She will likely continue to write to find strength and renewal through writing. Her work is distinguished by experimentation with nearly all literary genres—a long-standing effort carried out earnestly and in several instances quite successfully. There is little doubt that she has earned an important place in contemporary Italian literature and that some of her works, such as *Donna in guerra* and *La lunga vita di Marianna Ucría,* will stand the test of time.

Interviews:

Paolo Ruffilli, "Tre domande a Dacia Maraini," *Il Resto del Carlino,* 18 November 1975;

Antonio Debenedetti, "Donna guerriera," *Corriere della sera,* 23 November 1975;

Edith Bruck, "Si vende per libera scelta la prostituta filosofa," *Il Messaggero,* 21 June 1976;

Nicola Garrone, "Don Juan, seduttore sedotto dal potere," *La Repubblica,* 29 November 1977;

Ileana Montini, *Parlare con Dacia Maraini* (Verona: Bertani, 1977);

Giovanna De Carli, "Due donne di provincia, anime innocenti in una garconnière," *La Repubblica,* 10 October 1979;

Livia Giustolisi, "Circo e teatro alla Maddalena, un musical di Dacia Maraini," *Paese sera,* 19 February, 1981;

Adele Cambria, "Le confidenze si fanno romanzo," *Quotidiano donna,* 17 April 1981;

Dario Bellezza, "Questo libro sulla memoria di una donna," *Paese sera,* 22 April 1981;

Carla Stampa, "Scrivo inebriandomi con il basilico," *Epoca,* 2 May 1981;

Edera Ciambellotti, "Una stanza tutta per sé: Intorno a *L'età del malessere* di Dacia Maraini" and "Parlando con Dacia Maraini. Intorno a *L'età del malessere,*" in *Nel passato presente degli anni sessanta* (Urbino: Montefeltro, 1981), pp. 69–84;

Garrone, "Vergine e malmaritata, la sovrana non è felice," *La Repubblica,* 18 December 1982;

Liberato Santoro, "Female Person Singular," *Irish Times,* 16 June 1984;

Debenedetti, "Con Pasolini e altri amici in una città amata e odiata," *Corriere della sera,* 15 July 1984;

Simonetta Robiony, "Prima delle femministe c'erano i sentimenti," *La Stampa,* 4 August 1984;

Anna Villa, "Un poesia immersa nella realtà," *Litteraria: incontri e commenti,* 2 (1986): 4–5;

Lidia Ravera, "Siamo sempre state donne," *Corriere della sera,* 7 April 1987;

Ada Testaferri, "Interview with an Italian Feminist Writer, Dacia Maraini," *Resources for Feminist Research,* 16 (1987): 60–63;

Francesca Pansarella, "Looking Back: Interview with Dacia Maraini," *New Observations*, no. 69 (July-August 1989): 2-3;

M. Grazia Sumeli Weinberg, "An Interview with an Italian Feminist Writer," *Sojourner: The Women's Forum*, 15 (1990): 21-23;

Serena Anderlini, "Interview with Dacia Maraini: Prolegomena for a Feminist Dramaturgy of the Feminine," *Diacritics*, 21 (1991): 148-160;

Rocco Capozzi, "Incontro con Dacia Maraini," in *Homage to Moravia*, edited by Capozzi and Mario B. Mignone (Stony Brook, N.Y.: Forum Italicum Filibrary, 1993), pp. 57-61;

Paola Gaglianone, ed., *Conversazione con Dacia Maraini* (Rome: Omicron, 1995);

Simona Wright, "Intervista a Dacia Maraini," *Italian Quarterly*, 34 (1997): 71-91.

References:

JoAnn Cannon, "Rewriting the Female Destiny: Dacia Maraini's *La lunga vita di Marianna Ucría*," *Symposium*, 47 (1995): 136-146;

Daniela Cavallaro, "*I sogni di Clitennestra*: The *Oresteia* According to Dacia Maraini," *Italica*, 72 (1995): 340-355;

Luisa Chiavola Birnbaum, *Liberazione della donna. Feminism in Italy* (Middletown, Conn.: Wesleyan University Press, 1986);

Pauline Dagnino, "*Fra madre e marito:* The Mother/Daughter Relationship in Dacia Maraini's *Lettere a Marina*," in *Visions and Revisions. Women in Italian Culture,* edited by Mirna Ciccioni and Nicole Prunster (Providence: Berg, 1993), pp. 183-198;

Gualtiero De Santi, "La poesia d'amore in Italia, 1966-1983," *Testuale*, 3 (1985): 11-35;

Marco Forti, "Dacia Maraini 'siciliana': romanzo storico familiare e memoria," *Nuova antologia*, 547 (January-March 1995): 191-216; (April-June 1995): 136-159;

Angelica Forti-Lewis, "Virginia Woolf, Dacia Maraini e *Una stanza per noi:* L'autocoscienza politica e il testo," *Rivista di studi italiani*, 12 (1994): 29-47;

Bruce Merry, *Women in Modern Italian Literature. Four Studies Based on the Work of Grazia Deledda, Alba De Cespedes, Natalia Ginzburg, and Dacia Maraini* (Townsville, Australia: James Cook University of North Queensland, 1990), pp. 193-229;

Ryoji Nakamura and Rene de Ceccaty, "La Nuit de Tempaku-Ryo: Entretien avec Dacia Maraini," *Europe: Revue Litteraire Mensuelle* (1987): 140-154;

Aine O'Healy, "Filming Female 'Autobiography.' Maraini, Ferreri, and Piera's Own Story," in *Feminine Feminists. Cultural Practices,* edited by Giovanna Miceli Jeffries (Minneapolis: University of Minnesota Press, 1994), pp. 190-206;

Augustus Pallotta, "Dacia Maraini: From Alienation to Feminism," *World Literature Today*, 58 (1984): 359-362;

Robin Pickering-Iazzi, "Designing Mothers: Images of Motherhood in Novels by Aleramo, Morante, Maraini, Fallaci," *Annali d'italianistica*, 7 (1989): 325-340;

Tonia Caterina Riviello, "The Motif of Entrapment in Elsa Morante's *L'isola di Arturo* and Dacia Maraini's *L'età del malessere*," *Rivista di studi italiani*, 8 (1990): 70-87;

Maria Serena Sapegno, "Oltre e dietro il pudore" in *Conversazione con Dacia Maraini*, edited by Paola Gaglione (Rome: Omicron, 1995), pp. 41-60;

Anthony Tamburri, "Dacia Maraini's *Donna in guerra:* Victory or Defeat?," in *Contemporary Women Writers in Italy: A Modern Renaissance,* edited by Santo L. Aricò (Amherst: University of Massachusetts Press, 1990), pp. 138-151;

M. Grazia Sumeli Weinberg, "Dacia Maraini e il teatro femminista come modello di trasgressione," *Italian Studies in Southern Africa*, 3 (1990): 20-31;

Weinberg, *Invito alla lettura di Dacia Maraini* (Pretoria: University of South Africa, 1993);

Weinberg, "All'ombra del padre: la poesia di Dacia Maraini in *Crudeltà all'aria aperta*," *Italica*, 68 (1990): 453-465;

Sharon Wood, "Women and Theater in Italy: Natalia Ginzburg, Franca Rame, and Dacia Maraini," *Romance Languages Annual*, 5 (1993): 343-348;

Simona Wright, "Dacia Maraini: Charting the Female Experience in the Quest-Plot: *Marianna Ucría*," *Italian Quarterly*, 34 (1997): 59-70;

Giuseppe Zagarrio, "Dacia Maraini ovvero dell'*amore* e del *rancore*," in his *Febbre, furore, fiele. Repertorio della poesia italiana contemporanea, 1970-1980* (Milan: Mursia, 1983).

Stanislao Nievo
(30 June 1928 -   )

Gabriele Erasmi
McMaster University

BOOKS: *Il prato in fondo al mare* (Milan: Mondadori, 1974);
Il padrone della notte (Milan: Mondadori, 1976);
Aurora (Milan: Mondadori, 1979);
Il palazzo del silenzio (Milan: Mondadori, 1985);
La foresta di Tarvisio (Rome: Autostrade gruppo I.R.I.-Italstat, 1986);
Le isole del paradiso (Milan: Mondadori, 1987);
Canto di pietra (Milan: Mondadori, 1989);
La balena azzurra (Milan: Mondadori, 1990);
Il cavallo nero e altre storie (Milan: Edizioni Paoline, 1990);
La Voragine, by Nievo and Maria Clelia Cardona (Naples: Guida, 1991);
Il tempo del sogno (Milan: Mondadori, 1993);
Il sorriso degli dei (Venice: Marsilio, 1997).

OTHER: Rudyard Kipling, *Capitani coraggiosi,* translated by Nievo (Florence: Giunti Marzocco, 1988);
I parchi letterari, edited by Nievo (Rome: Abete, 1990);
E Dio creò le grandi balene, edited by Nievo and Greg Gatenby (Milan: Mondadori, 1991);
Daniel Defoe, *Robinson Crusoe,* translated by Nievo (Florence: Giunti Marzocco, 1991).

Stanislao Nievo (photograph by Rosella Gori)

Stanislao Nievo is a direct descendant of Ippolito Nievo, the author of *Le confessioni di un italiano* (1867; translated as *The Castle of Fratta,* 1958), the most important novel written in Italy between Alessandro Manzoni's *I promessi sposi* (1840; translated as *The Betrothed,* 1845) and Giovanni Verga's *I Malavoglia* (1881; translated as *The House by the Medlar Tree,* 1890). The figure of his famous great-granduncle has loomed large in Stanislao Nievo's career, for his first novel evolved as a result of his research into the life of the ancestor who had written one of the most important works of the Romantic period. In his subsequent career Nievo has established his own reputation as a significant figure in Italian letters.

Born 30 June 1928 in Milan to Saveria Nasalli Rocca and Antonio Nievo, Stanislao Nievo spent his early life in the northern region of Friuli where his aristocratic family lived in the same Colloredo Castle where Ippolito, had written his great work. This castle served as the model for the fictional Castle of Fratta in *Le confessioni di un italiano*. Nievo attended the University of Rome intending to pursue a degree in science. In 1953 he participated in a scientific expedition in the Indian Ocean, an event that was to change his future, for he discovered his attraction to distant places where people live in close proximity to nature.

Nievo maintained a keen interest in science but abandoned his studies and pursued traveling. At first he supported himself by working in different capacities as the situation required. He was in turn a seaman and a dock worker, a teacher of Italian, a waiter, a gardener, and a laborer. He later became a correspondent for various Italian dailies: *Il Giornale d'Italia,* from 1954 to 1962; *Il Piccolo* (Trieste), 1959 to 1964; *La Stampa,* 1978; *Il Gazzettino* (Venezia), beginning in 1980; and *Il Tempo,* from 1987 to 1990. He was a photographer on the side, producing illustrated reports from all over the world for weeklies such as *Epoca.* He also directed documentaries and other programs for Italian television. During the course of his life he has visited more than eighty nations on all five continents. Nievo now lives in Rome with his wife, Consuelo.

Nievo had been writing for magazines and newspapers for twenty years when in 1974 he burst on the Italian literary scene with the novel *Il prato in fondo al mare* (The Meadow at the Bottom of the Sea). It became an immediate best-seller, was well received by critics, and was awarded the Campiello Prize. His sudden acclaim and subsequent sustained literary achievement were the results of a long period of preparation and meditation.

For Nievo, becoming a fiction writer meant breaking with the literary models and trends set by the generation of writers who preceded him. It meant breaking away from the academic and ideological confines of a literature concerned mainly with the historical evolution of Italy between and after the two world wars, its social problems and contradictions, and the alienation of the individual in society. Because of his background as an international reporter, photographer, and documentary film director, he looked to the wider world beyond the circumscribed concerns of Italian intellectuals for inspiration. He saw that while the Italian literary world continued to look at Marxism as the solution for the problems of the country, a new Italian class of entrepreneurs was bent on changing the Italian economy, modernizing its industrial structures, and integrating it into an international system. By the 1970s the contradiction between the inward-looking concerns of Italian intellectuals and the adventurous forward-looking attitudes of Italian businessmen should have been apparent, but it was not.

Nievo began his literary career, however, not by reporting on the present but by exploring the past to come to grips with himself as a writer. He did not originally set out to write a novel but became engrossed in his personal research into the character of his great-granduncle Ippolito Nievo, who died at the age of twenty-nine in the waters of the Tyrrhenian Sea in mysterious circumstances after a short, adventurous life, before the publication of his classic novel. Ippolito had been a young colonel in Garibaldi's army in Sicily and had distinguished himself not only for his valor at the battle of Calatafimi but also for a tough-minded attitude that led Garibaldi to entrust him with the costs of the expedition.

At once a realist and a romantic idealist, Ippolito depicted in *Le confessioni di un italiano* the transformation of the old Italian world at the end of the nineteenth century, provincial and self-contained, into a people conscious of their past and aspiring to a place in the society of nations. The irony was that his message was received at the time the book appeared by a united Italy that was turning again to provincial concerns. In a short story in *Gli zii di Sicilia* (The Uncles of Sicily, 1958) Leonardo Sciascia convincingly recreated Ippolito's character, presenting his conviction that the author's sudden disappearance at a crucial time in Italian history represented a spirit of change that unfortunately had died with him. Stanislao Nievo believed that his country was facing a period of transition that was similar to the one his great uncle had depicted.

Despite his fascination with the historical and technical circumstances that brought about the sinking of the *Hercules* on 4 March 1861, with all its cargo, crew, and passengers, Ippolito among them, Nievo did not feel compelled to write a learned monograph. His book was based on assiduous research, including the characterization of Ippolito, so much so that it could be used as a source of biographical and historical information. However, *Il prato in fondo al mare* crossed over into fiction because of the author's subjective treatment of his involvement in the search for the ship.

Ippolito and Stanislao are both protagonists of the tale: the first is a well-defined character who remains elusive, the latter seeks his own identity and definition through his search. But unlike Stanley's expedition in search of Livingstone, Stanislao's quest for his ancestor seems to end in a presumption of failure. Still the tale told in *Il prato in fondo al mare* is as much the story of Stanislao's attempt to come to terms with his ancestor as it is the record of how, while searching for the objective truth about the life and death of his great-granduncle, he could only discover the subjective reality of his commitment to the search. Just as St. Augustine set out to achieve an objective definition of God only to discover the subjective dimension of his faith, so Stanislao's obsessive search for Ippolito becomes a process of progressive identification with him and in the end, through the reluctant acceptance of his ancestor's elusiveness, he achieves a tentative definition of himself.

Struck by coincidences, Nievo bases much of the structure of his novel around a key one. As it happens *Hercules,* the name of the ship that took Ippolito to his death, is also the namesake for Hercu-

Postcard featuring sketches of Ippolito Nievo and his grand-nephew, Stanislao Nievo

les's Meadows, the area where the ship may have sunk. In his search for answers in those meadows at the bottom of the sea Nievo portrays his search as a reenactment of the twelve labors of Hercules. Just as the twelve labors eventually defined Hercules as a hero, so Stanislao's compulsive research defines him as a writer in his own right. Through a score of details Stanislao's search closely parallels Hercules's twelve labors, suggesting his belief in the importance of myth as a cultural archetype.

In addition to echoing the myth of Hercules in his narrative, Nievo seeks to establish a channel of communication with his ancestor and live in his own psyche the events that led to Ippolito's death. As M. Jeuland-Meynaud notes in his review of the novel in *Revue des études italiennes* in 1976, "Tout le livre baigne dans un climat mystérieux, labyrintique, magique" (the whole book is immersed in a mysterious, labyrinthine, magic atmosphere). In the course of his investigations Nievo does not hesitate to explore the irrational by seeking out the help of mediums and psychics, a course that likely puzzled many of his readers.

The first two chapters of *Il prato in fondo al mare* reiterate what is known about the fate of the *Hercules*. In chapters 3 and 4 Nievo provides a tentative, document-based reconstruction of the sinking of the ship and the death of its passengers. It is in chapter 5 that the author's research begins to take on the systematic references to Hercules's labors. In that chapter as well as in chapters 6 and 7 he offers an account of his archival research of the experts he interviewed. From then on Nievo combines in an interdisciplinary way all sorts of information, coming in turn from mediums and psychics as well as from actual explorations of the bottom of the sea in which he participated. In chapter 7 Nievo begins to subjectively identify with Ippolito; in chapter 18, the last chapter, he admits his failure to penetrate the mystery of the past.

As Gianfranco de Turris notes in "Stanislao Nievo o il ritorno del Mito" (Stanislao Nievo or the Return of Myth, 1988), Nievo has a passionate desire to find the door that connects the known with the unknown, the present with the past, the contingent with the eternal, the finite with the infinite. But Nievo does not presume to find such a door. All his novels seek to reconcile the inevitable failure of the search with its necessity. What is left, as for Dante at the end of his search, is the vague impression of finding a light that for a brief moment fires the mind. In the chapter "Gli uomini sono soli" (Men are Alone) Nievo relates the anecdote of a medium who was once able to divine Ippolito's thoughts. His great-granduncle had attributed the event to chance and dismissed it. When Ippolito later met with the woman again and she offered to divine his mind once more, he refused the experiment, fearing that she might repeat the feat. One suspects that had Stanislao been shown such a door, he would have knocked.

When *Il prato in fondo al mare* appeared, one of the favorable reviews it garnered was from Pier Paolo Pasolini, who thought that it might be the only novel Nievo would write. While providing valuable observations, such as noting how Nievo first approaches his subject objectively and then subjectively, Pasolini offers an essentially Freudian interpretation. He sees the historical investigation culminating in a descent to the bottom of the sea as something of a clinical case, the expression of a desire to return to the womb, the sea being an image of the amniotic fluid enveloping the fetus.

Although Nievo claims that his first novel was written under a compulsion and hence not representative of his work, *Il prato in fondo al mare* in important respects does predict his future approach to fiction. As was the case with the first book, the starting point of each of Nievo's subsequent novels is always an event that triggers research. At first his methods are scholarly and objective as he culls documents and quotes from them extensively. But in each work he mixes the objective with the subjective, for the past is first described and reconstructed from actual data and then vividly and imaginatively represented as Nievo comes to identify himself with the object he seeks. His narrative is sustained by a prose that can be simple, straightforward, and scholarly precise while always rich with metaphorical and mythical suggestions. The reader thus willingly follows Nievo from the reassuring domain of reality to the haunting, disturbing realm of the imagination.

Five years separate Nievo's first novel from his second, *Aurora* (Dawn, 1979). Such gaps, necessary for the research and preparation that go into each novel, have marked his career. Between the first and second novel Nievo gathered a collection of stories, *Il padrone della notte* (Lord of the Night, 1976), which includes several tales that one could single out as preparatory work for *Aurora* as well as others that anticipate the following novels. To Nievo this collection (though the title story still deals with the world of Ippolito) and *Aurora* are the works in which he sets himself free from the overwhelming presence of his ancestor. Indeed, as the successor to *Il prato in fondo al mare*, *Aurora* is surprising for the novelty of its contents and the range of its themes.

From a world solidly grounded in the relatively recent history of Italy and based on a familiar literary figure, Nievo moves to a remote past where historical memory, ritual, and myth blend with the mystery of the origin of society. As in *Il prato in fondo al mare* the novel revolves around a search for something that has been lost, but here the protagonist, Alessandro, an archaeologist and anthropologist, searches not for the clues to a person's character but for a dimension of humanity, the original feminine component that has been repressed historically through the development of a patriarchal society. Nievo suggests the extent of the loss through the powerful episode of a peasant woman who takes her retarded son, bathes him in a brook, and then in an act of terrible resignation and unspeakable love calms his unrestrainable sexual urge by submitting to him. *Aurora* is a novel about primeval love that may explode in uncontrollable forms, leading to murder and destruction because the male is too afraid of according his feminine counterpart the understanding she needs.

The novel is set in the Agro Pontino, south of Rome, an area where Nievo lived as a youngster and the site of the epic legends of Circe and Ulysses as well as the destination of Aeneas after an oracle impelled him to look for the "ancient mother." While the mythical allusions in his first novel seemed a bit artificial, propelled as they were by a coincidence of names, Nievo in *Aurora* conjures places where the references are natural and unavoidable. From the beginning he creates the suggestion of a world where it may be possible to perceive and uncover the traces of primeval events.

Nievo uses the word *aurora* as a leitmotiv in the first chapter, which takes place with Venus still visible as the sun breaks over the mystical landscape. He reinforces the mythological associations through his descriptions of the ancient traditions of the common folk and alludes to a comet whose mysterious revolution around the sun accompanies the events in the novel. Astronomy and archaeology come more concretely together as the plot begins to focus on the search for a lost temple–the Satricum temple of the Mater Matuta–destroyed by the Romans in 204 B.C. Scrupulous in his research, Nievo even indicates a few of the standard books on the cult of the Mater Matuta, which the great Roman poet Lucretius associated with the goddess Aurora.

As in *Il prato in fondo al mare* Nievo presents his archival research, the result of his consultations in university libraries and Roman museums of antiquities. Instead of a descent to the bottom of the sea, he explores the foundations of the temple. Nievo also links his second novel to the first by symbolically associating Hercules with the Greek incarnation of the Mater Matuta. He notes that a well-known temple in Rome was dedicated to Hercules or Matuta at different times. Also, he has Alessandro refer to Hercules as his favorite constellation.

In *Aurora* Nievo investigates the mysterious rites of Matuta that were seemingly obliterated with the temple; he suggests, on the basis of the little that is actually known, that such rites were related to those of the Greek Maenads and presented women's need for freedom in the expression of love that came

Dust jacket for Nievo's 1993 book, which includes stories that show the close relationship of women with animals

in conflict with the possessiveness of males, who sought to suppress it. A feminist novel written by a male, *Aurora* presents the conflicting needs of men and women and identifies in the figure of the Earth Mother a lost human potential that may still be realized if man would manage to open his mind to a fresh understanding of the other sex.

During his research Alessandro becomes involved with a mysterious woman, passionate but elusive. He discovers that she is devoted to her invalid spouse but needs Alessandro as a lover to feel alive and to find the strength to continue loving her husband. She is, like the peasant woman, another paradigm of Matuta, where the erotic and the maternal coexist and balance each other. When Alessandro cannot return such love, the woman disappears from his life, and once again the quest at the heart of Nievo's novel apparently ends in failure. The closest Alessandro can get to the mythical dimension he seeks is through dreams and drug-induced visions. Nievo leaves his reader with an acute sense of loss, the enduring, poetic longing for a Paradise lost.

Echoing the narrative schemes of *Aurora*, Nievo explores another myth in *Il palazzo del silenzio* (The Halls of Silence, 1985), a work he considers to be the conclusion of a trilogy. The premise of the novel is that man lives on the surface of the earth largely unaware that the soil underneath him contains the mysterious record of his past. The darkness below is both the primeval womb from which humans emerge and the nothingness to which they will return, leaving only faint archaeological traces of having once lived on the earth. But Nievo, who has the same Romantic faith in the enduring essence of literature as his great-granduncle, in this novel makes the claim that words are more enduring than stones and that names endure as echoes of the past presence of others who bore them and thus link past and present to a common destiny.

Nievo's interest in exploring the point of contact between past and present led him to conflate myths of the underworld. Remembering that three times a year the ancient Romans opened the *mundus Cereris* to let the lower world emerge into the world of the living, Nievo mentions the proper dates for the ritual. He was especially interested in the myth that explains the origin of the *Lacus Curtius,* the pond in the Forum that was said to form after the Roman Citizen Marcus Curtius descended on his horse into the chasm that opened there in 362 B.C., never to return. Drawing on such myths and on the complex archaeology of Rome with its still partly functioning ancient *cloacae* (underground sewers), Nievo imagines a labyrinth of obscure passageways populated by smugglers and thieves, rats, ancient stones, and images of death. In such an environment the mind becomes open to arcane fears and suggestions. Ditties heard as a child seem to harbor meanings that haunt a mind easily deceived by echoes in the darkness. But the darkness is the darkness of the mind that forever seeks something that has been lost.

The protagonist of *Il palazzo del silenzio* is Nievo, but the name *Stanislao* is stated only toward the end as a result of a series of coincidences in which names variously connected with history and myth become names in the mythology of the author's family. The notion of something that has been lost is proposed again: Rome, the city of stones, mythically derives from Albalonga, its ancient rival. There, where Aeneas died and Ascanius ruled, no stones testify to the existence of the lost city, only a name, air that sounds in the human throat, wind that echoes the past on forlorn hills and crevices, a name that continues to express the maternal myth of dawn presented in *Aurora.* In Italian *Albalonga* (the long dawn) refers to the coming of the first white light of the day; it announces the rosy light of the dawn. The novel also presents a love story between the protagonist and Merope, an itinerant beekeeper, free and enigmatic, a creature of light and eros who cannot be possessed. She seems to have emerged from an archaic world that can be seen only dimly, as is suggested by her mythical name, connected with the dimmest star of the Pleiades, *méros* (part) and *ops* (vision).

In 1987 Nievo received the most coveted Italian literary award, the Strega Prize, for *Le isole del paradiso* (Islands of Paradise, 1987), the first of what he regards as a second trilogy of novels. In important respects Nievo's fourth novel seems a continuation of the first three, for the examination of the relationship between man and nature is key to all of his work. The recurring idea of a search for what was lost has been all along a search for a lost Eden, a golden age whose memory survives in myth and tradition. The difference here is that the quest no longer seems a compulsive personal search whose original motivations remain obscure but instead is an historical account of the need and the attempts of modern man to begin anew and establish a society in harmony with nature.

Through the first part of *Le isole del paradiso* Nievo's research, which spanned a period of twenty-five years and included three long voyages to the South Seas, is not mentioned at all. He unfolds his narrative objectively, painstakingly reconstructing through his interdisciplinary method the obscure story of the failed colonization of New Ireland, an island in the Bismarck Archipelago. In 1879 a group of French and Italian emigrants began the attempt, which ended at the beginning of 1882.

The novel begins with the discovery of the island and its beautiful falls in 1699; it retraces the various reports of subsequent explorations and continues to follow the characters involved. Following his pattern, Nievo in the second part turns his seemingly objective story of the past into a personal search, which he conducts in Europe, Australia, New Guinea, and New Ireland. And while the quest for paradise of course fails, Nievo creates an astonishing achievement. Though the narrative methods and devices are the same as the ones employed in Nievo's previous novels, they are deployed with an even greater skill, and the interweaving of the historical, personal, and fictional elements is seamless. Nievo explores the difference between civilized and primitive man by setting them against the mythical background of an immutable nature. The former, for all his knowledge and technology, is not in harmony with it; the latter, for all his irrational superstition, is strangely attuned to it because his behavior is grounded on instinct. The story is an apologue intended to show that society can survive and endure only if man recovers or rediscovers his natural instincts.

Having moved from the personal concerns of the first three novels to social and ecological ones, Nievo took the next logical step in his evolving outlook with *La balena azzurra* (The Blue Whale, 1990), a novel in which he again makes use of extensive research, this time about the habitat, traveling patterns, mating, and nurturing habits of the largest creature on earth. In the course of the novel Nievo identifies with and humanizes these mysterious animals. The protagonists are a woman and a whale nicknamed "The Mother." Working with the premise that the human female is closer to nature than the male, Nievo suggests here and in some of the tales in his story collection *Il tempo del sogno* (When Time Becomes a Dream, 1993) that women have a privileged relationship with animals.

The female protagonist of *La balena azzurra,* a researcher in the field of marine mammals, follows the path of a particular blue whale from Sri Lanka to Antarctica and establishes with her an unusual friendship. She goes beyond the statistical attempts to decipher the communicative patterns of whales and in the end achieves identification with the whale through the animal's act of giving birth. The contact between the human and the animal is momentary, and their communication is more a feeling or the impression of a feeling than an actual exchange. As he wrote at the conclusion of his book of poetry, *Canto di pietra* (A Song Written on Stone, 1989), Nievo tries to go back to "l'origine delle parole dove gli impulsi diventano coscienza" (the beginning of words where impulses become consciousness).

Nievo's work is rooted in the Romantic religion of nature. He believes that sensitivity and emotions, rather than a system of rational principles, are the keys to understanding the human condition. As with many Romantics, Nievo's flaw may be in his propensity to excess. In all his works there are moments when his pursuit of the irrational may leave the reader disconcerted. On the other hand Nievo has the ability to endow fragmentary historical information with narrative vitality. His writing looks back to authors such as Herman Melville and Edgar Allan Poe, but inevitably issues from the realistic and neorealistic tradition. However, whereas in the works of his immediate predecessors one can usually distinguish the historical and the autobiographical from the fictional, such is the thoroughness of Nievo's research that one is tempted to say that the main task of his students in the future will be that of separating objective facts from fictional elaboration.

It is too early to place so singular a writer as Stanislao Nievo in any well-defined literary perspective. What can be said safely is that the consistency, coherence, and originality of his work place Nievo among the most distinguished Italian writers at the close of the twentieth century.

References:

Giuseppe Amoroso, *Narrativa italiana 1975–1983* (Milan: Mursia, 1983), pp. 56–56, 155–156, 182;

Anna De Stefano, "Stanislao Nievo," *La realtà e il sogno. Narratori italiani del Novecento,* edited by Gaetano Mariani and Mario Petrucciani (Rome: Lucarini, 1987), pp. 441–448;

Gianfranco de Turris, "Stanislao Nievo o il ritorno del Mito" in *Il padrone della notte,* by Nievo (Milan: Mondadori, 1988), pp. 5–24;

Carmine Di Biase, "Realtà, e Inconscio," in his *Linea surreale in scrittori d'oggi* (Naples: Società Editrice Napoletana, 1981), pp. 135–142;

Marco Forti, "Stanislao Nievo, cronista fantasmatico," *Nuova antologia* (1988): 306–318;

Claudio Marabini, introduction to *Aurora,* by Nievo (Milan: Mondadori, 1981);

M. Jeuland-Meynaud, review of *Il prato in fondo al mare,* in *Revue des études italiennes,* 3 (1976), pp. 274–275;

Pier Paolo Pasolini, "Negli abissi del mare come nell'utero materno," in his *Descrizione di descrizioni* (Turin: Einaudi, 1979), pp. 446–451;

Carlo Sgorlon, introduction to *Le isole del paradiso,* by Nievo (Milan: Mondadori, 1989);

Claudio Toscani, introduction to *La balena azzurra,* by Nievo (Milan: Mondadori, 1993).

Roberto Pazzi
(18 August 1946 -)

Franco Ricci
University of Ottawa

BOOKS: *Le ultime notizie e altre poesie* (Rome: De Luca, 1969);
L'esperienza anteriore (Milan: I dispari, 1973);
Versi occidentali (Quarto d'Altino: Rebellato, 1976);
Poesie scelte (1966-1979) (Quarto d'Altino: Rebellato, 1979);
Il re, le parole (Manduria: Lacaita, 1980);
Mida: dieci poesie (Milan: Mondadori, 1982);
Cercando l'imperatore: storia di un reggimento russo disperso nella Siberia durante la Rivoluzione in cerca dello Zar prigioniero (Casale Monferato: Marietti, 1985); translated by M. J. Fitzgerald as *Searching for the Emperor: The Story of a Russian Regiment Lost in Siberia during the Revolution, in Search of the Imprisoned Tsar* (New York: Knopf, 1988; London: Deutsch, 1989);
La principessa e il drago (Milan: Garzanti, 1986); translated by Fitzgerald as *The Princess and the Dragon* (New York: Knopf, 1990; London: Duetsch, 1990);
Calma di vento (Milan: Garzanti, 1987);
La malattia del tempo (Genoa: Marietti, 1987); translated by Vivien Sinott as *Adrift in Time* (London: Deutsch, 1991);
Il vangelo di Giuda (Milan: Garzanti, 1989);
La stanza sull'acqua (Milan: Garzanti, 1991);
Il bambino (Naples: Guida, 1991);
Le città del dottor Malaguti (Milan: Garzanti, 1993);
Il filo delle bugie. Poesie edite ed inedite 1966-1994 (Rome: Gabriele Corbo, 1994);
Le acque della Nena e L'Aquila (Cento: Cooperativa Culturale Centoggi, 1995);
Incerti di viaggio (Milan: Longanesi, 1996);
Domani sarò "re"' (Milan: Longanesi, 1997).

Roberto Pazzi is the best known and most prolific of the so-called new generation of writers who came to the fore in the 1970s and 1980s. He was an established poet before he turned to narrative, having published three books of poetry. Since the publication of his first novel in 1985, Pazzi has received increasing critical attention. Renowned as a master storyteller, he weaves tales that incorporate memory, history, fantasy, mysticism, and religion. The well-known critic Giorgio Bárberi Squarotti called Pazzi's work "probably the finest and most luminous prose of Italian twentieth century narrative" in the 31 October 1987 issue of *La Stampa*.

Pazzi was born in Ameglia, a town in Liguria near La Spezia, on 18 August 1946. He spent his formative years in Ferrara, a city that was to mark both his temperament as a man and his intellectual growth as an artist. He attended Liceo classico Lodovice Ariosto, the secondary school that was also attended by two famous writers associated with the city, Giorgio Bassani and Lanfranco Caretti. In

Roberto Pazzi (photograph by Jerry Bauer)

Ameglia, where he spent his summer holidays, he met the poet Vittorio Sereni, who would introduce the young writer to the Italian public by writing a complimentary preface to Pazzi's first book of verse.

Attracted to literature at a young age, Pazzi attended the University of Bologna, graduating in classical literature. His thesis on Umberto Saba was directed by Luciano Anceschi. After graduating, he returned to Ferrara and was employed as a secondary-school teacher of Italian literature at the V. Monti Institute, where he stayed for nineteen years. He then taught at the University of Urbino for three years, before becoming a professor of cultural anthropology at the University of Ferrara. Pazzi's first poems were published in poetry journals, among them *Contrappunto,* which he eventually directed as editor (1984–1985). In 1985 he also founded the journal *Sinopia.*

Pazzi has distinguished himself from his contemporaries by embracing a "high style" and condemning the "culture of the masses." He has sought to revive the possibilities of literary language in the novel by moving the genre beyond descriptive realism. First and foremost a poet, Pazzi has translated the subliminal, indeed divinatory, capacity of his poetic language into his fiction, balancing the reader's expectations of clarity with his own search for meaning. Offering his own psyche as an intensely subjective starting point, Pazzi seeks to tap archetypal imagery. He views life not as a progression but as a mandala—a circle of reciprocal relationships. His holistic thinking runs counter to the hierarchy and depersonalization of contemporary society.

Pazzi's influences are many. He is fond of the literature of memory as practiced by Marcel Proust and Rainer Maria Rilke, shares the same existential angst of Torquato Tasso and Giacomo Leopardi, and finds peace in the mysticism of Antonio Rosmini and the youthful poetry of Alessandro Manzoni. Yet he is also a student of the transcendental philosophies of Arthur Schopenhauer and Friedrich Nietzsche. He is interested in a wide range of literary and visual art forms but is most interested in Romantic and Gothic manifestations of the macabre. Because of the breadth of influences upon his work, his aesthetic concerns move beyond direct political meanings. He is able to scrutinize seemingly casual details with an eye for the subtlety that leads to epiphany. For Pazzi, then, meaning lies in the noumena of intuitive experience, not in the phenomena of surface reality.

Leopardi was convinced that "la prosa nutre la poesia" (prose nourished poetry). For Pazzi, however, the reverse may be said to be the case. His poetry is born from his need to fill the void of daily existence with the eternal nature of words. In "Mida," a poem included in the collection *Calma di vento* (Calm Wind, 1987), a melancholic poet explains what is both the gift and curse of his existence:

Vivo come re Mida
nel mio museo di sole parole ...
A me la memoria non potrà più
giocare brutti scherzi,
tutto quello che tocco
è diventato nome.

(I live like King Midas
in my museum of words ...
To me memory will no longer
play ugly tricks,
everything I touch
has become a name.)

This dedication to the solitude of the artist reveals Pazzi as a restless, questing, even an obsessed author.

Pazzi's varied poetry exhibits an intensity that is missing in much modern poetry. In his work he transforms ordinary objects into symbols of evanescence and mystery, as in "La casa" (The Home) from *Calma di vento:*

Divinità domestiche in mia assenza
restano a custodia delle stanze, aprono armadi, provano vestiti. ...

(Domestic divinities in my absence
remain to watch over the rooms, open closets, try on clothes. ...)

His imagery is that of dreams and unconscious perceptions freed from time. The real easily slides into the surreal. In his novels Pazzi's imagination, while influenced by the events of history, is similarly unrestrained by reality or time.

In his first novel, *Cercando l'imperatore: storia di un reggimento russo disperso nella Siberia durante la Rivoluzione in cerca dello Zar prigioniero* (1985; translated as *Searching for the Emperor: The Story of a Russian Regiment Lost in Siberia during the Revolution, in Search of the Imprisoned Tsar,* 1988), Pazzi places the reader in the midst of a world where everything that is familiar is dissolving. The novel, which garnered several prizes including the coveted Premio Campiello, was hailed by critics such as Angelo Guglielmi, Alfredo Giuliani, and Ottavio Cecchi. Although it is organized in a conventional manner as a third-person sequential narrative and based on historical circumstance, Pazzi tells two tales that alternate in episodic fashion and allows his imagination to supersede historical fact.

Dust jacket for the American edition of Pazzi's 1985 novel, which focuses on the last days of Czar Nicholas II and his family

Pazzi reconstructs the last days of Czar Nicholas II and his family under house arrest in Ekaterinbury, Siberia, focusing on the maddening psychological isolation of the monarchs, who fill their desperate final hours with disquieting idiosyncrasies. The czar, the divinely ordained ruler of Russia and once one of the most powerful men in the world, finds solace chopping wood; the young hemophiliac Czarevich Aleksei, his nephew and heir to the throne, hallucinates cryptic dreams while his sister, Tatiana, probes the cabala attempting to invoke Rasputin, the enigmatic and evil monk considered responsible for their downfall.

The second tale concerns the Preobrajensky regiment led by Prince Ypsilanti, which is marching across the frozen tundra in order to rescue the doomed czar. Unusual events, however, hound the expedition. In the midst of the treacherous Siberian winter, summer suddenly appears. When the soldiers head into the forest to hunt a tiger led by the peasant Kaigar, a curious Mongol that is able to speak the languages of wolves, elks, and birds, they do not find the tiger but are caught up in a multidimensional reality where forms are magically conjured. The mission, of course, is doomed to failure: the regiment does not arrive in time to save the czar. Spinning beautifully away into imagination, the lost regiment is symbolically transformed into a flock of strange birds that arrive at Ekaterinbury at the moment of the imperial family's impending death:

Da oriente si levò allora un vento cosí spaventoso da sradicare gli alberi del giardino dove Alessio aveva giocato tante volte. La serra, la palizzata con le guardiole, i cancelli e le panchine di ferro, le siepi di sicomori e i pali della luce, gli attrezzi usati da Nicola per segare la legna, tutto fu travolto dalla furia di quel vortice. Sulla parte più alta della casa riapparve l'aquila: solo Jurovsky la vide guidare quel reggimento alato che prendeva il volo, riparandosi a stento il volto dagli ultimi uccelli.

(From the west there arose a wind so terrible as to uproot the trees in the garden where Alessio had played many times. The greenhouse, the palisade with its guardhouses, the gates and the iron benches, the sycamore bushes and the light poles, the tools used by Nicholas to saw wood, all was swept up by the fury of that whirlwind. On the uppermost part of the house the eagle reappeared: only Jurovsky saw it guide the winged regiment that was taking flight, shielding his face as best he could from the last birds.)

Pazzi thus takes the real historical figure of the czar and introduces him into a magical-historical context.

Pazzi's fascination with the imperial family of Russia arises from the childhood memory of a portrait of Nicholas and Alexandra seen at the home of a neighbor. The idea of an aristocracy fascinated the urban apartment dweller as he fantasized their royal existence in the midst of palatial opulence. Imagination helped the youth assuage his loneliness and led to his vocation as a writer. Through writing Pazzi is able to confer life on the dead, as metaphor vanquishes the restrictions of time and logic.

Pazzi's interest naturally gravitates to characters in history to whom he can personally relate. Through such characters he explores his own subjective memories and experiences. Indeed, in all of his novels Pazzi embraces forgotten historical figures the same way one holds on to the memory of a beloved grandfather. When asked by Franco Ricci in 1989 why he preferred singing the praises of the outcasts instead of the winners, the Trojans instead of the Greeks, he responded:

> È diverso che cantare i vincenti come fanno tanti oggi, quelli che amano più il lato vitalistico dell'esistenza che non il lato nascosto o misterioso dell'esistenza. Quindi, penso che la mia sia una preoccupazione per il futuro nel senso di chiedersi problematicamente cosa verrà fra venti, trent'anni.

> (It's different from singing the praises of winners like everyone does today, those that love the vital side of existence and not the hidden or mysterious side of existence. Therefore, I think that mine is a preoccupation with the future in the sense of asking oneself problematically about what will happen in twenty or thirty years.)

Pazzi is constantly falling in love with the weak and the helpless victims of history. In contrast to the traditional historical novel that extols the exemplary virtues of great men for the national psyche, Pazzi recuperates those who have fallen through the cracks of historical memory.

One such figure in need of rehabilitation is the subject of his next novel, *La principessa e il drago* (1986; translated as *The Princess and the Dragon*, 1990). This is the story of the little-known Granduke Giorgio Alexandrovich Romanov, brother of Czar Nicholas, who died of tuberculosis at the age of twenty-eight in 1899. As in his first novel Pazzi focuses on a marking trait—what he calls the "dono," or gift—of the young granduke, in this case his tuberculosis, to weave a tale of magic realism.

Using a technique he would employ in subsequent novels, Pazzi begins his story artificially with a purely literary and fictitious private letter, written by a cardinal to the Pope. In the letter, recommendations are made to restore order in the Polish republic by placing the young granduke on the vacant Polish throne. The Pope refuses to bestow the honorific title on the granduke who is madly scouring the Caucacus Mountains in search of a hidden valley where legend has it that death never enters. The granduke, like all of Pazzi's protagonists, is maniacally consumed by all-encompassing passions. One of them is his love for his wife, Elena, the princess of the title, who happens to be his cousin.

The reader also learns that an expedition has departed from the imperial court of China in search of the same legendary valley. As in the first novel a doubling occurs as the two expeditions are bound for a climactic rendezvous that is never realized. Pazzi mixes his themes of illness and death, forced isolation and impotence, and the supernatural to create an air of exotic surrealism. For example, during one of his fits the granduke is visited by his sinister counselor Ourousov—actually a demon in disguise—who accompanies him on a Faustian voyage of self-discovery. By entering a baroque mirror Giorgio travels to the past and visits Napoleon on the island of St. Helena, witnesses the execution of Louis XVI, is a guest at the court of the emperor of China, confers with Cardinal Ercole Consalvi (secretary of state for Pius VII), and finally visits a future Bolshevik Russia in 1917. The granduke's death at the end of the novel is not the result of his illness but a willed refusal to enter a future Russia he abhors. It is a mark of Pazzi's ability as a writer that he is able to convince us of the phantasmagoric elements while maintaining a patina of historical fact.

Pazzi's exploration of the past continues with his third novel, *La malattia del tempo* (1987; translated as *Adrift in Time*, 1991). Once again the author disorients the reader. Critic Giuliano Gramigna in his review in the 15 March 1986 issue of *Corriere della sera* suggests that Pazzi's belief is that "Il lettore non dovrebbe mai capire dove è" (The reader must never know where he is). The plot twists and turns on itself like a Proustian corkscrew. The protagonist, Aiku, a Mongolian prince, assumes different historical roles. As an avatar Aiku is at once Napoleon, Genghis Khan, Julius Caesar, Attila the Hun, Tamerlane, and even a bit of St. Francis of Assisi. His daughter, Lilith, is a reincarnation of Eve. Other characters also assume diverse historical double roles. The real protagonist of the novel, however, is time itself, the "figlio malvagio" (malevolent son) from which there is no escape.

Pazzi imagines that Aiku conquers the world in the final days of the second millennium. After sweeping through Europe he stops his army in northern Italy on the banks of the Po River, thus fulfilling the prophecy of his birth that he would reclaim the world for the Asians but stop at a great river:

> Suo nonno, quel giorno, gli aveva afferrato la mano sinistra... l'aveva sfiorata con la plama rugosa della destra, come a voler riconoscere un paesaggio scritto in quella mano infantile, un paesaggio di stelle e cammini vasto come una vita....
>
> —Aiku, ti fermerai a un fiume, quando la città sprofonderà davanti a te. Ricordalo....
>
> (His grandfather, that day, had taken his left hand... he had touched it with the wrinkled palm of his right hand, as if to recognize a written landscape in the infant hand, a landscape of stars and paths as vast as a lifetime....
>
> —Aiku, you will stop at a river where a city plunges before you. Remember....)

It was also prophesied that he would one day become a new Adam, spawning a new race of man and a new order for mankind.

To fulfill his destiny Aiku holds a peace conference with the president of the United States at Waterloo (a new Yalta), and after deciding to divide the world in two with Japan and the United States—the perpetrators of the rise of satanic technology—he drops an atomic device on Germany, catapulting the entire European continent back to the year 1815. The world is trapped in the breach of time he has created. Aiku, the new Napoleon, now declares himself "Alto Protettore" (Supreme Protector). Not wishing to repeat the mistakes of past conquerors, he abolishes technology, especially computers and television, and begins a holistic "culto e venerazione della Natura" (cult and veneration of Nature). He marries the heir to the Habsburg throne, Maria Christina, and eventually disappears to an island in the Atlantic.

Meanwhile the world is suffering from a "malattia del tempo" (sickness of time). This "sindrome 1815" (1815 syndrome) causes time to swing between the years 2000 and 1815. A sort of wave effect is created as kings of the past are seen sitting on their thrones; the living visit their own long-forgotten tombs; and the United States disappears and reappears. Present, past, and future commingle in temporal cacophony. Because Chronos (Time) no longer dictates the rhythm of man's existence, man may choose to live his own destiny in whatever time he wishes. Indeed, in the final pages of the novel, the secretary of state of the United States elects to leave the present for a more promising future dimension.

In *La malattia del tempo* Pazzi uses the disjunction of time to explore the alienation of man from nature by technology, the reincarnation of spirit, social insanity, collective memory, and the relationship of historical fact to the imagination. He believes that since history and fiction may both be considered selective orderings of reality, their different patterns—which may or may not be true—can mutually influence each other to create a new world vision. Through Aiku (his name means "man") the author imagines hypothetical possibilities in space and time.

Pazzi continues his experiments in narrative space and time in *Il vangelo di Giuda* (The Gospel of Judas, 1989). He takes his cues from a literary text, Tertullian's *Apologeticum,* which reports that Tiberius, having heard that a prophet was stirring the multitudes in Palestine and realizing the political consequences, asked the Roman senate to sanction the divinity of the so-called Christ. In Pazzi's version of the story, a tired and politically spent Tiberius has retired to the island of Capri, where he awaits death in stoic solitude. Far from Rome and the tribulations of imperial power, he is preoccupied with the personal concerns of eternity, fate, and his role in history as emperor of a dying empire.

Tiberius's antagonist in the novel is Cornelio Gallo, a real though enigmatic Latin poet of whom little is known. In Pazzi's story Cornelio, unlike his friend Virgil, refused to sing the praises of the empire in verse and was condemned to death by Augustus Caesar. Because of the decree of "Damnatio memoriae" (Destruction of Memory), all traces of his existence were destroyed, and the poet committed suicide. Before his death in exile, Cornelio wrote a politically provocative epic that prophesied the end of the Roman Empire and entrusted the poem to his daughter Cornelia. Herself in peril for possessing the heretical text, she commits the work to memory and then destroys the written text. All that remains, then, of Cornelio Gallo is memory incarnated in the figure of his daughter Cornelia, who mysteriously arrives one day on the island of Capri.

Over a period of nights and in a series of interrupted episodes resembling the nights of Scheherazade, Cornelia re-creates the patterns of prophecy her father so carefully designed. He had shrewdly dedicated his epic to Jeshua, a real prophet he had met during his exile in Palestine. He pretends, though, to have found a manuscript written by one of Jeshua's disciples, Judas Iscariot, who under the cloak of darkness had copied down his master's words without his knowledge. The epic not only reveals the fate of the empire but also records the teachings of Jeshua. After hearing the epic related by Cornelia, Tiberius in an effort to save the empire and his own faltering reputation decides to dictate his own fictitious gospel. His story is about a prophet named Jesus, a governor named Pontius Pilate, and a crucifixion—the accepted story of Christianity that sets history in motion. Once again Pazzi makes his reader conscious of the creative and conditioning potential of accepted fictions.

One of the most obscure of Pazzi's protagonists is the focus of *La stanza sull'acqua* (The Room on the Water, 1991): Cesarione, son of Julius Caesar and Cleopatra, who is mentioned in Plutarch's *Life of Antony*. In the novel Cesarione escapes the plots of Ottavian Augustus Caesar, the adopted son of Julius Caesar, by fleeing by boat up the Nile and into Ethiopia, hoping to reach India eventually. The crew, which is faithful to Ottavian, is about to mutiny against Cesarione when they meet a mysterious black boat traveling in the opposite direction. Now begins a typically Pazzian game of mirrors as it turns out the black boat is carrying the Ethiopian princess Afra, who is escaping similar political circumstances. The two outcasts meet, recognize their symbiotic "otherness," and exchange places and roles by disguising themselves. However, both remain victims of the cruel treachery of power. Afra is killed in her sleep by agents of the emperor who mistake her for the Roman heir while Cesarione vanishes into the wilderness, never to be heard from again.

Pazzi can be described as the most reluctant postmodern Italian author of his generation. In contrast to his contemporaries, he wishes to overcome the widespread sense of isolation and fragmentation by invoking permanence, eternity, and history. Yet by treating history as fiction he essentially construes all written texts as fiction. For Pazzi, history is a story with a visionary span that extends from creation and is moving, deterministically, chapter by chapter, like life, toward its prophesied conclusion:

> Io sento la presenza di un destino, di qualcosa che è stato impegnato sulla mia testa, a nome mio senza consultarmi. Noi veniamo al mondo con degli impegni presi per noi da qualcuno che noi non conosciamo; tutta la vita passa nel riconoscimento di questo destino.... Credo come dice Federico Nietzsche, nell'*amor fati,* cioè nell'amore del proprio destino.

> (I feel the presence of a destiny, of something that has been placed on my head, in my name without consulting me. We come to the world with duties chosen for us by someone that we do not know; life passes in the discovery of this destiny.... I believe, as Fredrick Nietzsche says, in *amor fati,* that is in the love of one's own destiny.)

Pazzi thus integrates his belief in transcendental Truth in a postmodern narrative framework.

In Pazzi's novels history becomes a general text, a geography of the mind rather than a privileged authority. His novels defy historical fact, detaching characters from their chronological straitjackets. But beneath the fluid and frenetically sensuous imagery and the captivating rhythms of his prose there lies the author's apprehensive knowledge of the here and now. Pazzi's narrative is thus a quest not so much for form as it is for meaning, for lost horizons. His novels are important because he strives to go beyond the debilitating anxiety of postmodernism without resorting to a naive return to the past.

Interviews:

"Il romanzo metafisico. Intervista con Roberto Pazzi," *Mondo operaio* (November 1985): 143–146;

Francesco Monini, "Dopo l'imperatore la principessa," *L'Unità,* 2 April 1986, p. 3;

Franco Ricci, "Intervista con Roberto Pazzi," *Italian Quarterly,* 30 (Summer 1989): 55–66.

References:

Franco Ricci, "Beyond Tautology: The Cosmoconception of Time in *La malattia del tempo* by Roberto Pazzi," *Italaica,* 68, no. 1 (1991): 13–28.

Giuseppe Pontiggia

(25 September 1934 -   )

Daniela Marcheschi

Translated by Augustus Pallotta

BOOKS: *La morte in banca: Cinque racconti e un romanzo breve* (Milan: Rusconi e Paolazzi, 1959); enlarged as *La morte in banca: Un romanzo breve e undici racconti* (Milan: Mondadori, 1979); enlarged as *La morte in banca: un romanzo breve e sedici racconti* (Milan: Mondadori, 1991);

L'arte della fuga (Milan: Adelphi, 1968; enlarged edition, 1990);

Il giocatore invisibile (Milan: Mondadori, 1978); translated by Annapaola Cancogni as *The Invisible Player* (Hygiene, Colo.: Eridanos Press, 1988);

Chichita la scimmia parlante (Teramo: Lisciani & Zampetti, 1979);

Il raggio d'ombra (Milan: Mondadori, 1983; enlarged edition, 1988);

Il giardino delle Esperidi (Milan: Adelphi, 1984);

La grande sera (Milan: Mondadori, 1989; enlarged and revised, 1995);

Le sabbie immobili (Bologna: Il Mulino, 1991);

Vite di uomini non illustri (Milan: Mondadori, 1993);

L'isola volante (Milan: Mondadori, 1996).

OTHER: Bonvesin de la Riva, *De magnalibus Mediolani,* translated by Pontiggia (Milan: Bompiani, 1974);

Leonardo Sinisgalli, *L'ellisse: poesie 1932–1972,* edited by Pontiggia (Milan: Mondadori, 1974);

Decimus Magnus Ausonius, *La Mosella,* translated by Pontiggia (Milan: Verba, 1984);

Manzoni europeo, edited by Pontiggia (Milan: CARIPLO, 1985);

I volti di Hermann Hesse. Atti del Convegno, Milano, 27 marzo 1992, edited by Pontiggia and Marco Manzoni (Milan: Fondazione Arnoldo & Alberto Mondadori, 1993).

Giuseppe Pontiggia's most significant contribution to Italian letters lies in his fashioning a narrative apart from Neorealism and the other currents of the post–World War II period. While close to the circle of avant-garde writers of Gruppo 63, he yet holds a strong belief in literature as a repository of significant values. More than language and ideology, Pontiggia believes that the quest for truth sustains literature. Even in an experimental work such as *L'arte della fuga* (The Art of Fleeing, 1968), which lacks a conventional plot or account of events, he never allows the pleasure of the text to become an evasion, a ludic exercise, or a self-gratifying experience.

With *Il giocatore invisibile* (1978; translated as *The Invisible Player,* 1988) Pontiggia began to emphasize readability and the importance of plotline, seeking a middle road between simplicity and complexity, between clarity and enigma. In all of his novels he shows a tenacious rationality and is unafraid to deal with troubling existential questions. Unwilling to yield to fashion, Pontiggia writes prose marked by terse, precise language. He was influenced by the French writer René Daumal—to whom he dedicated the initial essay in *Il giardino delle Esperidi* (The Garden of the Hesperides, 1984)—to use "transparent" language that seeks to illuminate rather than obscure its object. Such language is the antithesis of the language of mass communication and pseudoinformation, which is often intended to do just the opposite.

Pontiggia is hardly a prolific writer; each of his works represents a unique personal and intellectual experience born of a compelling need to explore the human condition. Concerned with fundamental issues, he wonders at the human propensity for hatred, betrayal, wanton violence, and deception and boldly points out evil and its perpetrators. Pontiggia shows a deep compassion for the common destiny of men—a feeling of solidarity that comes from a personal vision of human existence and a deep attachment to classical culture.

Giuseppe Pontiggia was born 25 September 1934 into a petit bourgeois family from Erba, a town north of Como that traditionally has served as a resort for the vacationing Milanese aristocracy. His fa-

Giuseppe Pontiggia (photograph by Giovanni Giovannetti)

ther was a bank clerk; his mother was an amateur actress. In November 1943 his childhood was scarred by the murder of his father, who was killed by two young men for unknown reasons during the civil strife that raged toward the end of World War II. After the war Pontiggia's mother moved her family first to Santa Margherita Ligure, then to Varese, and finally to Milan, where Pontiggia finished secondary school. In 1955 a second tragedy struck his family as his sister, Elena, committed suicide for no apparent reason.

Pontiggia attended the Catholic University of Milan, graduating in 1959 with a thesis on Italo Svevo's work. He had worked in a bank while going to school, and his first book, *La morte in banca: Cinque racconti e un romanzo breve* (Death in a Bank: Five Stories and a Short Novel, 1959), was inspired by this experience. During his university years he developed a stronger relationship with his brother, Giampiero, a well-known poet who writes under the pseudonym Giampiero Neri. The two shared interests in art, music, and the works of Herman Melville, Mark Twain, Henry James, and Ernest Hemingway. Their circle of friends included scene designer Ezio Frigerio, novelist Nanni Balestrini, poet Antonio Porta, and critic Luciano Anceschi, who invited Pontiggia to contribute to his influential review, *Il Verri*. After receiving his degree Pontiggia remained in Milan and taught Italian language and literature in secondary schools for some twenty years. In 1963 he married Lucia Magnocavallo. In 1969 their child, Andrea, was born handicapped.

La morte in banca, the first draft of which dates back to 1952, is the story of a young man, Carabba, who gains growth, insights, and maturity in the anxiety-ridden environment of a central bank. The bank is shown to be an eminent locus of hypocrisy, alienation, aggressiveness, and human degradation—a disturbing symbol of a society governed by profit as its sole rationale of life. These negative qualities can be ascribed to burgeoning industrial development, which leads to too rapid changes in social life and economic activities.

There surface in this work two important themes of Pontiggia's narrative: the prevalence of insidious and merciless violence and the evasion of the individual who refuses to deal with reality and accept life as a mystery. Carabba matures as a man when he can accept his "death" as a human being in the dehumanizing milieu of the bank. This acceptance is necessary for him to be born again as a new person.

Although Pontiggia's use of third-person narration is typical of the realistic novel, he undercuts the conventional realism of his work in other ways. His autonomous narrative sequences not only erode Carabba's personality through psychological probing but also have a symbolic referent in the game of chess. Pontiggia, who has written articles on the game, here and in other works uses chess as a metaphor, creating individual actions and relationships that lead to checkmate. The analogy is often explicit, as in his description of the urban landscape: "La città si riempiva, in quelle sere di settembre i grattacieli, oltre il parco, parevano scacchiere illuminate" (The city was getting crowded, and on those September evenings the skyscrapers beyond the park looked like lighted chessboards).

Appearing nearly ten years after Pontiggia's first book, *L'arte della fuga* has begun to be reevaluated critically after being virtually ignored for two decades. One of the most successful of Pontiggia's works, it was written from 1961 to 1968, at a time of intense debate surrounding the avant-garde. Containing language charged with fresh symbolic connotation, *L'arte della fuga* reflects Pontiggia's search for new narrative forms, a search that echoes a yearning for innovation in literary expression widely felt in the 1960s and 1970s and in a more general sense the desire for change and renewal in society. The largely plotless book—whose title might be translated as "The Art of the Fugue" as easily as "The Art of Fleeing"—centers on violent crime.

The protagonists are a clerk, a man enclosed in an artificial world of dogma and certainties, and a writer, an intellectual who views reality as an enigma and is intent on criticizing contemporary culture. The conflict is also in the twofold delineation of the word *palazzo*: on the one hand as a political site in which civil order is constituted and legislation is enacted and on the other hand as the site that corrodes a rigid and pseudorational vision of reality. Both the clerk and the writer interact with many other characters in a dramatic course of action marked by murders and flights. The anonymity of many characters suggests the serious efforts by society to collectivize the individual. "La specie," Pontiggia asserts at one point, "è il personaggio" (The human species is the individual character). He also writes: "La specie non è la vittima soltanto ... ma è anche l'assassino" (The human species is both the victim and the assassin). Any effort to eschew individual destiny, according to Pontiggia, is not only vain but also tragic and absurd because it has to end inevitably in death.

Inspired by the ideas of Martin Heidegger in *Being and Time* (1927), Pontiggia regards the contemplation of death as the means of achieving a more authentic consciousness of the self and life. In "Sequenza Undicesima" (Sequence Eleven) he suggests in verse the importance of facing the prospect of death:

Vivere-per-la-morte per sentirci vivi,
poi morire fu falso come vivere.
Poi, per sentirci morti, la vita: il capo
di una lucertola improvvisa, una frana gialla.

(Living with death in order to feel alive,
then dying became as false as living.
Then, to feel dead, life: the head
Of an unexpected lizard, a yellow landslide.)

Death sheds a new light on the meaning of existence.

Il giocatore invisibile, on which Pontiggia worked from 1971 to 1978, can be described as an effort to revisit the issues raised in *L'arte della fuga*. It is noteworthy that the novel came out at a time of political and cultural upheaval in Italy, for it manifests Pontiggia's clear intent to point to ethics as the necessary foundation of intellectual experience. The start of the action of *Il giocatore invisibile* is etymological as a middle-aged college professor is attacked in a professional journal for having validated an imprecise origin of the word *hypocrite*. Who is his anonymous enemy? Why does he hate the professor, as his article shows?

Il giocatore invisibile is also a psychological thriller suggestive of Carlo Emilio Gadda. The victimized professor leads an investigation to identify his antagonist. Before finding the villain the professor comes to realize the petty pretenses that color his relationships with coworkers, his wife, and his young mistress. An assortment of moral transgressions renders the victim "the murderer" and the murderer the "victim" in a complex world in which,

Dust jacket for Pontiggia's 1996 book

as in the writing of Franz Kafka, every individual's fate is sealed. Because the signs offered in this world in which "la nostra libertà è solo immaginaria" (our freedom is only imagined) defy definition, Pontiggia suggests the opposite: that true rationality requires the bold perception of such signs and a recognition of a "convergenza tra vivere e conoscere" (convergence between living and knowing). During his search for the villain, the professor follows the wrong leads, identifies possible foes, and rejects the truth when he discovers it because the solution to the crime appears to him "troppo facile, troppo banale" (too easy, too trivial).

Pontiggia, acting as an invisible chess player, lays bare the mediocrity and pettiness of his characters who speak hypocritically of truth and sincerity even though they are contradicted at every turn by events around them. Concerned with how the characters look from the outside, he offers a precise description of their gestures, even those that seem insignificant. While he does not analyze the psychology of his characters in depth, Pontiggia skillfully uses dialogue and language to bring to the fore their inner makeup.

Pontiggia alludes to the chessboard several times in the course of his novel and clearly regards the game as a metaphor for human experience. In chess the element of surprise is crucial because while the player must always consider moves aimed at counteracting or neutralizing his opponent's strategies, he must go beyond his foe's thinking in order to control the game. Accordingly a game of chess can become a powerful symbol, suggesting one's effort to control one's destiny—even to escape responsibilities and to evade death—as well as the illusion that one can exert such control, for the game shows the tragic consequences that follow from mistakes and wrong choices. The suicide committed by Daverio, the professor's "enemy," can be understood through the symbolism of the game, for his death is tragically absurd—as useless as sacrificing a valuable piece for no advantage.

In this context it makes little sense to speak of victims or guilt because the game in which one engages with the invisible player is marked by the sign of death. Indeed one can say that death is one of the protagonists of the story—the black hole to which Pontiggia's universe, sketched in this and other books, is inevitably drawn. Many characters in the story appear spiritually dead. Yet the climate of death, devastation, and deception in which they move also elicits a sense of compassion for their destinies. Such is the disposition shared by the professor at the end of the novel: "Fissò, con gli occhi umidi, la cupola scintillante del palazzo, in attesa del verde per passare. Dove aveva letto che, quando ci si commuove degli altri, si pensa anche a se stessi" (With tears in his eyes, he stared at the building's shining cupola as he awaited for the green light. He wondered where he had read that when we feel sorry for others, we think of ourselves as well).

As in *L'arte della fuga* Pontiggia is particularly concerned with language in *Il giocatore invisibile*. He reflects on the semantic equivalence of particular words and comments on how words interact. Pontiggia writes that every word "è un mondo e non ci si può permettere distrazioni" (is a world and we can not afford distractions). As usual the novelist draws from simple, everyday language and expressions, but such language is used in a context pregnant with expressive power, tension, and pathos. In the novel words are used as a battering ram to bring down the walls of pseudolearning and false language erected by the professor, a man who wears the mask of learning to hide his hollowness.

Il raggio d'ombra (A Ray of Shadow, 1983) is based on an incident that occurred in 1927. In the novel a man named Losi manages to escape from prison, where he was ostensibly serving time for political reasons. As a fugitive he seeks help from his party. It turns out, however, that he is an informer and is instrumental in getting several party members arrested. Among them is Mariano, who is not politically active but who made the mistake of sheltering Losi when he identified himself as an antifascist fugitive. There follows a search for Losi not so much to seek retribution as to learn the motives of his betrayal. The search ends in the cemetery where Losi is buried to underscore the elusive nature of truth. Pontiggia here elaborates what is already present in his previous works, the Pirandellian proposition that the individual decides what truth is, accepting only what he or she chooses to believe. He suggests that human beings are "precluded" from reaching or even from coming close to the truth or the appearance of truth. Clearly, Pontiggia seeks to underscore, with caustic irony, the significance of a human incident that ended in death but did not achieve closure.

With *La grande sera* (The Big Evening, 1989) Pontiggia offers an approach to narrative that is unfailingly antirealistic. He is indifferent to the development of the character of the protagonist, a man like Luigi Pirandello's protagonist in *Il fu Mattia Pascal* (1904; translated as *The Late Mattia Pascal*, 1923) who, because he is tired of his responsibilities and relationships, disappears with the intention of building a new life for himself elsewhere. Pontiggia is interested instead in probing, often with detachment and irony, the inner lives, motives, and reactions to neglect and unexpected betrayal of the characters who are involved with the protagonist. As a consequence readers are able to have but a vague, abstract idea of the character in whom they are most interested. This technique leaves a void, an empty space; it brings to mind a carousel with strange figures rotating around a hidden pivot. Even the secondary characters at times are introduced obliquely in the course of a dialogue and lack an individual personality, each being a slight variation of another. They share a gray, unhappy life devoid of meaning and purpose.

Pontiggia often digresses to comment on the narrative with sarcasm and merciless irony. Moreover, he employs laughter to unmask the inanities and the pseudovalues of Italian consumer society in the 1980s. Emblematic in this regard is the police detective Bonghi's view of human behavior:

> I suini cercano, rotolandosi nel fango, di pulirsi e il modello gli rendeva più comprensibili certi esami di coscienza in pubblico, certe esibizioni di visceri non richieste da nessuno, o certe confessioni che gli facevano i suoi nemici, non capiva se per apparire meno sordidi o per diventarlo di più. Non era facile capire neanche l'anima dei suini e questo era un altro insegnamento.

> (By rolling into the mud, pigs try to clean themselves; this model made it easier for him to understand certain public confessions, certain unwanted displays of entrails, or certain confessions made by his enemies to appear less sordid than they were or to become more so, he did not know. Then again it was not easy to understand the pigs' inner motives either, and this too was very instructive.)

Vite di uomini non illustri (Lives of Nonillustrious Persons, 1993) provides incisive, ironic portraits of eighteen individuals. It is one of Pontiggia's most accomplished books, demonstrating his erudition and creative talent as he revises the classical model of depicting famous lives associated with Plutarch. Informed by a caustic intent, which is skillfully effected by parody, the book tells the story of ordinary men and women, their gray and unhappy lives, their illusions and self-deceptions, and their brief moments of extraordinary happiness. The book contains sarcasm, levity, sadness, tragedy, pathos, and compassion for man's destiny, consistent with George Santayana's words, chosen as the epigraph of the work: "Everything in nature has a lyrical essence, a tragic destiny, and a comic existence."

Pontiggia's created characters and settings range from the late nineteenth century to the years just after 2000. He follows a narrative structure patterned after the format of a biographical dictionary. Noteworthy events, such as birth and death, are related with precision and often in minute detail but with an underlying ironic vein that in places reaches the point of comic relief. A good example is provided by a short excerpt from the Premoli Giovanna entry, her last name given first as in many biographical dictionaries:

> Le visite al cimitero diventeranno quotidiane dall'autunno del 1995, anche con la pioggia o la neve. Da sola senza più la compagnia dei nipoti, continuerà con indefettibile minuzia la pulizia della tomba matrimoniale, le due lastre adagiate una accanto all'altra, la spalliera di porfido che le accoglie come allargando le braccia. Qui verrà sepolta, dopo breve malattia sopportata con cristiana rassegnazione, il 6 giugno 2002.

> (In autumn 1995 the visits to the cemetery will become daily, even with rain or snow. Alone, without her grandchildren, she will continue to clean, with indefatigable care, the tombstones built for her and her husband, placed next to each other, the head piece of porphyry marble connecting them like outstretched arms. Here she will be buried on 6 June 2002 after a brief illness, borne with Christian resignation.)

The woman portrayed here is faithful to her husband even after his death; to the very end of her life she will cling to the "semplicità lineare del suo matrimonio" (linear simplicity of her marriage).

One can feel Pontiggia's pleasure in imagining the climate and the time in which his characters move, and he does so with a multifaceted style that ranges from playful realism to the precise reproduction of specialized speech, such as that associated with bureaucracy and medicine. He takes full advantage of the latitude, the formal invention permitted by these "pomeriggi di radiose incursioni tra le tombe" (afternoons of radiant incursions amidst the tombstones), capturing such vivid images as a slightly handicapped gentleman who

> a viso alto, con la sua andatura, lenta e ritmica di nobile claudicante, tra i raggi che scendono dalle bifore, percorre il tappeto rosso che porta all'altare, lungo la commozione dei presenti.

> (head high, the pace slow and rhythmic of a limping nobleman, bathed in the sunlight shining through the church windows, goes forward on the red carpet leading to the altar, along the sympathy of those present.)

In such a passage Pontiggia asserts himself as a singularly talented writer. During the course of his career he has shown the ability to reach a balance between fresh creativity and intellectual depth, between irony and emotion, humor and sadness, elegant prose and wealth of meanings. Unmoved by the trends of ideology and sociology that have attracted many of his contemporaries, Pontiggia has given his readers a significant picture of Italian society in the twentieth century.

Interviews:

Franco Zangrilli, *Canadian Journal of Italian Studies,* 15 (1992);

Monica Gemelli and Felice Piemontesi, *L'invenzione della realtà. Conversazioni su letteratura e altro* (Naples: Guida, 1994).

References:

Giuseppe Amoroso, *Narrativa italiana 1975–1983, con vecchie e nuove varianti* (Milan: Mursia, 1983), pp. 102–104, 339–341;

Gianfranco Bettin, "La narrazione invisibile di Giuseppe Pontiggia," *Linea d'ombra,* 2 (1983);

Gian Carlo Ferretti, *Il best seller all'italiana* (Bari: Laterza, 1983);

Marco Forti, "Il romanziere Pontiggia," *Nuova antologia* (January–March 1984);

Alfredo Giuliani, *Autunno del Novecento* (Milan: Feltrinelli, 1983);

Giuliano Manacorda, *Letteratura italiana d'oggi* (Rome: Riuniti, 1987);

Daniela Marcheschi, "Uno scrittore contemporaneo: Giuseppe Pontiggia," *Rassegna lucchese,* 6 (1981): 18–29;

Gennaro Mercogliano, *Un mondo senza parole. Saggio sull'opera di Giuseppe Pontiggia* (Manduria: Licata, 1991);

Alberto Moravia, *Diario europeo* (Milan: Bompiani, 1993), pp. 212–214;

Walter Pedullà, *Le caramelle di Musil* (Milan: Rizzoli, 1993);

Paolo Ruffilli, "La narrativa di Giuseppe Pontiggia," *Il lettore di provincia,* 12 (1981): 72–75;

Enzo Siciliano, *Racconti italiani del Novecento* (Milan: Mondadori, 1983), pp. 1443–1451.

Francesca Sanvitale
(17 May 1928 -   )

Simona Wright
College of New Jersey

BOOKS: *Il cuore borghese* (Florence: Vallecchi, 1972);

Madre e figlia (Turin: Einaudi, 1980);

L'uomo del parco (Milan: Mondadori, 1984);

La realtà è un dono (Milan: Mondadori, 1987);

Mettendo a fuoco: pagine di letteratura e realtà (Rome: Gremese, 1988);

Verso Paola (Turin: Einaudi, 1991);

Il figlio dell'impero (Turin: Einaudi, 1993);

Tre favole dell'ansia e dell'ombra (Genoa: Il Melangolo, 1994);

Il canto di una vita: Francesco Paolo Tosti, by Sanvitale and Andreina Manzo (Turin: EDT, 1996);

Separazioni (Turin: Einaudi, 1997);

Le scrittrici italiane dell'800: da Eleonora de Fonseca Pimentel a Matilde Serao (Rome: Istituto Poligrafico e Zacca di Stato, 1997).

Editions in English: "Nostalgia per Admont," translated by Niccolò Vivarelli, in *Nuovi Argomenti,* edited by Jonathan Galassi and Manfredi Piccolomini (New York: Muovi Argomenti, 1988), pp. 205-232;

"The Electric Typewriter," translated by Martha King, in *New Italian Women* (New York: Ithaca Press, 1989), pp. 176-186;

"Jolly e Poker," translated by Katherine Jason, in *Name and Tears* (St. Paul: Greywolf Press, 1990), pp. 181-188;

"La bella principessa Rosalinda," translated by Umberto Mariani, in *Marvels and Tales,* special issue on "The Italian Tale," edited by Giuseppe di Scipio (Boulder: University of Colorado Press, 1993): 221-287.

OTHER: *Pier Paolo Pasolini: una vita futura,* edited by Sanvitale, Laura Betti, and Giovanni Raboni (Cernusco: Garzanti, 1985);

Raymond Radiguet, *Il diavolo in corpo,* translated by Sanvitale (Turin: Einaudi, 1989).

Francesca Sanvitale, one of Italy's most renowned contemporary authors, was born in Milan on 17 May 1928 into an aristocratic but impoverished family from Emilia-Romagna. At the age of twelve her family moved to Florence, where she attended school and subsequently the university. In 1952 she graduated with a degree in Italian literature under her mentor, Giuseppe de Robertis, a prominent literary critic of the time. After graduation Sanvitale worked as a journalist in Florence and as a reader and editor for various publishing houses, among them Bompiani and Mondadori. She was also a manuscript reader for Elio Vittorini, an influential writer who worked for the publisher Einaudi. This demanding apprenticeship forged Sanvitale's literary experience in two ways: it provided her with an extensive knowledge of European and world cultures and it helped her to refine her writing.

In 1961 Sanvitale moved to Rome, where she worked for RAI, the national television network until she retired in the 1980s. The experience proved to be rewarding, for it provided an opportunity to use television as a cultural and educational tool. As she stated in an interview with Simona Wright in 1996, television as a means of communication captivated the attention of many Italian writers and critics, who took part in the development of original programs: "Questi intellettuali, Umberto Eco, Furio Colombo, Angelo Guglielmi, Raffaele La Capria, Renzo Rosso, erano attirati dalla possibilità di usare un nuovo mezzo espressivo e poterlo condizionare, renderlo originale" (These intellectuals, Umberto Eco, Furio Colombo, Angelo Guglielmi, Raffaele La Capria, and Renzo Rosso were attracted by the possibility of using the new medium in a creative way).

While she was employed at RAI, Sanvitale wrote her first novel, *Il cuore borghese* (The Bourgeois Heart, 1972). After working in the evening hours for seven years the author completed a narrative that was structured as a compact succession of situations, marked not by a consequential or chronological story line but rather by the main characters' streams of thought, considerations, and observations. The work is clearly a personal response to the crisis of the traditional novel, which had been at the center of critical scrutiny in the 1960s, particularly from the French *Ecole du regard* and the Italian Gruppo

Francesca Sanvitale in 1973

63. The criticism focused mainly on the obsolescent structure of the nineteenth-century novel, which many deemed unsuited to reflect the dynamic transformations taking place in society. Modern culture and civilization called for more complex and heterogeneous modes of aesthetic expression and the novel was to conform to the tenets of this new philosophy or to succumb to inevitable decline. The literary turmoil of the 1960s prompted many writers, among them Sanvitale, to devise original solutions in order to revitalize the narrative.

Influenced in part by contemporary movements and in part by authors such as Robert Musil and Robert Walser, Sanvitale lent *Il cuore borghese* a philosophical dimension together with a strong cultural and intellectual foundation. Following no clear chronological pattern, the plot is a sequence of disconnected episodes and scenarios that depict an individual's inability to act in the external world and to react to the dilemmas and challenges that it poses. Every chapter in this mosaic is frozen in time, a fragment of life where there seems to be no recognizable beginning or end, no discernible cause-and-effect progression.

There are five main characters: Julius and Olimpia; and Claretine, Tullio, and their child, Fatï. In the course of the story they cross each other's paths while their daily existence is scrutinized. By creating several protagonists, Sanvitale seeks to introduce different perspectives and points of view, which make up the comprehensive fresco of *Il cuore borghese*. Here the human heart is not empty or shallow; on the contrary, as Antonio Porta points out in the introduction to the 1987 edition of the novel, it is "semmai troppo ricco, dunque inappagabile. Infiniti progetti lo percorrono e lo devastano: finisce sempre con la sconfitta" (if anything, too abounding, and therefore insatiable. It is crossed by endless projects which end in defeat and ultimately destroy it).

The two couples are the emblems of a generation of upper-middle-class intellectuals who grew up during World War II and the Resistance against Fascism. They are now adults, facing the inconsistencies of their relationships, constantly oscillating between intensifying and relaxing their emotional ties. Julius works for a national television channel; completely entrenched in his professional life, he seems incapable of translating his political ideology into concrete action. Olimpia, who is neglected by her husband, searches unsuccessfully for new stimulation, a relationship or a passion that will enable her to recover and regenerate her disarranged self.

Tullio and Claretine represent the mirror image of the first couple; their relationship is gradually being destroyed by Tullio's failure as a husband and by Claretine's shallowness. She is in love with her husband, but she never ceases to betray him. Tullio's indecision contributes to the crisis. When the marital problems come to the fore, he returns to his native town, where he becomes entangled in projects that never materialize. Sanvitale does not reveal much of the characters' backgrounds and activities; there are few facts and only a series of scenes isolated in time that suggest solitude and hopelessness.

The story is set in bourgeois Rome in the late 1950s, a time of unprecedented economic growth and prosperity as well as social uncertainty and ideological conflicts. The crises experienced by the characters mirror the social and political crises of the country. To dramatize this period in Italian life Sanvitale abandons conventional plot and the customary notion of time, pointing only to the characters' inability to make simple decisions and carry out inconsequential actions. This passive, static demeanor is reflected in Olympia's game:

> Olimpia sta persistendo nel suo gioco, ha buttato per la decima volta le tre monete. Ritenta nuove combinazioni e gli ideogrammi si mescolano come i numeri per i dadi. Anche il numero è un ideogramma, ciò che lei cerca ha qualcosa in comune con i risultati meccanico-magici della matematica. Nel numero si supera il caos per entrare nelle combinazioni dell'eterno: lo spazio si libera dal tempo, il mondo si rappresenta simultaneamente–cause ed effetti–per concetti sintetici; si abolisce la convenzione del futuro.
>
> (Olimpia persists in her game, she tosses the three coins for the tenth time. She tries new combinations as the ideograms blend like numbers on the dice. The number is an ideogram as well, what she is searching for has something in common with the mechanical and magical mathematical sequences. Numbers defeat chaos and enter the combination of eternity: space frees itself of time, the world is represented contemporaneously–cause and effects–in synthetical concepts; the convention of the future is abolished.)

Il cuore borghese marks both a starting point in Sanvitale's career as well as the culmination of a labor that took years to come to fruition. By the time of its publication she had come to have strong views concerning the key components of a successful narrative. She believed it was necessary to convey a "sense of reality," for the reader must believe in the characters and circumstances of a fiction in order for its events to be defined, comprehended, and interpreted and for its actions and emotions to carry a spiritual meaning or a compelling message. Sanvitale also believed that the characters must be represented as wholly human, their depiction encompassing not only their intellects but also their emotions. Both the rational and the emotional sides play a significant role in shaping human experience, and literary works must portray their interaction.

Published eight years after her first work, Sanvitale's second novel, *Madre e figlia* (Mother and Daughter), appeared in 1980. The intervening years led to a drastic change in the author's approach to the novel. Sanvitale became convinced that writing emanates from the exploration of the most secret and concealed spheres of the subconscious. Most significantly, she learned that the process of invention cannot be dissociated from the search for self-identity and self-conceptualization.

The story of the complex and passionate relationship between a mother and her daughter, *Madre e figlia* is Sanvitale's response to feminist ideology. In the 1960s and 1970s, influenced by the political manifesto of the women's movement that emphasized the necessity of self-analysis, many Italian women began a strenuous process of self-scrutiny. As a result more women took part in social debates, leading to changes in what was a traditionally male-dominated society. Sanvitale's dramatization of an individual woman's courageous attempt to examine her cryptic self attains historical as well as personal significance. Through Sonia, her complex female protagonist, Sanvitale creates a narrative that connects to the experience of Fascism, World War II, the war against French colonization in Algeria, Italy's postwar years, and the advent of economic prosperity.

In her 1996 interview Sanvitale stated that her intent was primarily to write "un racconto fantastico, ricostruzione di un'infanzia e di una giovinezza primi Novecento, ricuperare cioè attraverso un gioco le favole storiche dell'infanzia" (a fiction centered in the reconstruction of a childhood and a youth set in the early twentieth century in order to recover, through a game, the historical tales of childhood). The memory game that the narrator initiates at the inception of the novel soon turns into the story of her personal evolution. The reader meets Sonia, one of the two main characters, as she tries to reorganize her life, struggling with the death and memory of her mother, Marianna, whose childlike behavior still perplexes her. The attempt to recover and understand the past evolves gradually into an elaborate lattice of emotional relationships in which the narrator through meticulous scrutiny of her memory realizes her quest for self-discovery. As in *Il cuore borghese,* Sanvitale eschews a rigid chronological ordering of events, favoring instead an open, inclusive approach in which occurrences from the past and the present join through dreams, visions, and memories.

The novel consists of two narrative planes, one of the imagined past and one of the near present. In the first, the daughter attempts to reconstruct the mother's past through old photos, fragments of conversations, and objects that give rise to imaginary settings. She creates a composite canvas of mental images in which young Marianna's life is portrayed as innocent and uncomplicated. The past is the magic realm where the human being connects harmoniously with fantasy and myth; it is a dreamlike world devoid of anguish, laden with yet unfulfilled promises of happiness.

A letter sent to little Marianna by her father captures the idyllic past through the metaphor of an imaginary garden.

> La primavera è arrivata. Ieri il sole è apparso sorridente, mi ha ricordato il tuo sorriso . . . Oggi, prima di dedi-

carmi ai miei studi, ho inventato per te questo giardino che è il più bello che ci sia perchè è fatto con tutti i fiori del mondo. Chiudi gli occhi, Mariannina, e dammi la mano: andiamo insieme in questo parco incantato.

(Spring has come. Yesterday the sun arose, beaming, and reminded me of your smile . . . Today, before returning to my studies, I imagined this garden, the most beautiful one because it contains all the flowers in the world. Close your eyes, Mariannina, and give me your hand: let us enter together this enchanted forest.)

The father's death and the start of World War I mark the beginning of the family's reversal of fortunes; these events force Marianna to confront the hardships of reality. Her life takes a negative turn when she becomes pregnant and gives birth to an illegitimate child, Sonia, the unexpected consequence of a secret and much romanticized liaison with an army officer. A married man, Sonia's father chooses not to compromise his career by divorcing his wife. His sentimental relationship with Marianna progressively deteriorates, and later feelings of alienation and estrangement prevail between father and daughter.

On the second narrative plane Sonia narrates in the first and third person a journey that is diametrically opposed to the fantasized past: a daily existence characterized by ordinary struggles as mother and daughter experience the adversities of living without social recognition and financial stability. The desolate reality of the present she knows and the indignities she endured compel Sonia to look back to her mother's past and her own. The mother's life and eventually her death lead Sonia to analyze her own suffering and to complete her search for a separate identity. As Sharon Wood has stated, Sonia's journey into her mother's past is also an "impassioned search for freedom," a freedom that is carried out through the writing process.

In *Madre e figlia* Sanvitale favors the circular discourse of autobiography, where there is no sequential ordering of cause and effect but a juxtaposition of facts and impressions from the subconscious. Sanvitale suggests in the 1996 interview that every writer must embark on self-examination and explore the dark regions of the psyche: "A volte il silenzio, scendere nel silenzio, oltre ad essere rischioso come tentare caverne sotterranee, può essere una estrema esperienza. Se l'istinto e il caso ci guidano, ci guidano anche verso complete metamorfosi" (Sometimes silence, the descent into silence, besides being risky like exploring subterranean caves, can be an extreme experience. If instinct and chance guide us, they also lead us to a complete change).

The search for identity continues to concern Sanvitale in her third novel, *L'uomo del parco* (The Man

Cover for Sanvitale's 1993 book, which chronicles the life of Napoleon Bonaparte's son

in the Park, 1984). Here too a female character is the main protagonist. Abandoned by an abusive husband, Giulia has fallen prey to hallucinatory states in which she confuses a tormented inner reality with her fragmentary perception of the external world. Despondent and alienated, she floats in a space devoid of social and historical coordinates. Sanvitale departs from the description of Giulia's delirium to take the reader through the most crucial phases of her life: chronic depression; bizarre psychic activities; her encounters with Tommaso, a man she occasionally sees during her wanderings in the Villa Doria Pamphili Park; and the agonizing process of restoring her rationality. The author mixes third- and first-person narration throughout, especially at the end.

Giulia's deranged condition is gradually intertwined with events occurring in the external world. As the novel progresses, Sanvitale unveils salient facts and historical circumstances, allowing the reader to learn that Giulia lives and works in Rome, has been left by her husband, and has two children. Tommaso's attentive demeanor activates Giulia's desire to analyze the sources of her crisis. She returns home from one of their meetings in the park to retrieve from an old trunk long-forgotten objects, significant fragments of her past. The fairy-tale book given to Giulia by her father and other relics become fetishes through which she relives the trauma of her father's abrupt departure and her mother's disaffection while becoming conscious of her own alienation from her mother.

On the path to self-recovery, Giulia travels to Greece and the island of Crete. At Knossos, Giulia explores the ancient myth of the labyrinth—an obvious metaphor for her mental state—while she seeks her personal objective:

> Voleva strapparsi da questi sentimenti senza interlocutore, strappare il velo che le impediva di vedere gli altri esseri umani e arrivare ad affrontare il loro tempo sempre a portata di mano e sempre in fuga: come un viaggiatore nella nebbia che viaggia, che viaggia e tenta di raggiungere una nitida città che sta alle spalle facendo il giro del mondo.
>
> (She wanted to tear herself from these feelings without interlocutor; she wanted to tear the veil that hindered the sight of other human beings; she wanted to confront herself with their time, a time that was always at a hand's reach and yet always fleeting. She was like a traveler in the haze, a traveler that attempts to come to a clearly outlined city that lies behind him by circumnavigating the world.)

Giulia experiences the descent into the labyrinth of her life and crisis as a suspension from reality, isolation, and death, but ultimately she conquers the maze. She does so by attaining the wisdom of self-acceptance that allows her to treasure life and its inevitable transformations.

Giulia's contact with Greek civilization inspires her to see in her dreams the celebration of a passage, the ritual of purification that brings coherence out of emotional derangement. In this light her visions and dreams turn from apparitions of an aberrant mental landscape to curative remedies that chart the course of self-analysis. Her return to Rome marks the final chapter in Giulia's recovery as she is able to face the present rationally. The rapprochement with reality is narrated in a heartfelt and often painful first-person confession. In the final page of the novel the protagonist sees her image reflected in the mirror: "Si ritrovò allo specchio, mentre per un gesto consueto allargava le dita nei capelli: erano candidi come la spuma sulla cresta dell'onda, e ancora marezzati di grigio e di castano, qua e là. Le piacevano, le ricordavano il cambiamento e la novità" (Once again she stood in front of the mirror, while with usual motion she spread her fingers in her hair: it was white like the foam on the crest of a wave, and still marbled here and there with grey and brown. She found it pleasing, it reminded her of transformation and newness).

L'uomo del parco is certainly one of Sanvitale's most complex and courageous novels. Rich in themes and symbolic language, its baroque structure is marked by remarkable juxtapositions of times, real and unreal settings, and subjective and objective realities. Through Giulia's self-investigation Sanvitale gives expression to a new conception of narrative, one that emphasizes segmented narratives and dreamlike scenarios.

The style of *L'uomo del parco* is largely the result of Sanvitale's distrust of conventions and traditional ideas. Ideologically close to the tenets of the postmodernism and feminism, Sanvitale views writing as the best means to render the fragmented reality of the individual in a modern society that is subject to continuous transformations. Moreover, Sanvitale believes that literature's fundamental objective is to help to bring order to the chaotic inner self in its struggle with the ever-changing world. She would agree with Jean François Lyotard who asserts in *The Postmodern Condition. A Report on Knowledge* (1984) that "the artist and the writer . . . are working without rules in order to formulate the rules of what *will have been done*." Speaking of the aim of creative artists, Lyotard states: "It is our business not to supply reality but to invent allusions to the conceivable which cannot be presented."

Sanvitale's fourth book, *La realtà è un dono* (Reality is a Gift, 1987), is a collection of short stories. While seeing no substantive difference between the novel and the short story, Sanvitale asserts in her 1996 interview that she actually prefers the shorter form:

> Per me il racconto è più divertente, ha una immediatezza e una concentrazione che stimolano alla creatività, che liberano la fantasia. Si è più spericolati nei racconti, poichè in essi si devono creare emozioni più forti per arrivare al lettore.
>
> (To me, the short story is more fun, since it has an immediacy and a concentration that stimulate creativity and free the imagination. The writer is more daring in writing short stories, because he or she must create stronger emotions in order to reach the reader.)

In her stories Sanvitale investigates the entry into adulthood and the solitude experienced by the human being. She particularly focuses on relationships between the sexes, on the inadequacy of communication and its consequent emotional failure. Every story is an inner search; the characters are entangled in conflicts with the most secret and sometimes enigmatic forces of the subconscious. Sanvitale's reality is thus not comforting and harmonious but grinding and difficult to endure. Surviving and accepting it means to recognize that a constant struggle is operative within every individual, an agonizing examination of the self and its surroundings.

In stories such as "L'ultima notte di Shahrazad" (Sheherazade's Last Night) Sanvitale depicts the isolation and feeling of abandonment that often result from a sexual encounter. Longing to regain her weary lover's attention, the female protagonist, Shahrazad, tells him an enigmatic story, hoping to entice him with her ability to invent and dramatize. At last recognizing the hopelessness of her undertaking, she leaves him and the next morning is found dead on a Roman thoroughfare. Her suicide is the consequence of her inability to participate naturally, without pretenses and simulations, in her partner's emotional life. Falsification and make-believe destroy Shahrazad, who is too much of a pretender to be able to see herself as an individual.

In "L'età dell'oro" (The Golden Age) the first-person narrator uses the confidentiality offered by a diary to revisit a trip to England and the emotions of an intense but brief love affair. The narration opens into a vivid recollection of a time of restlessness, a season brimming with anxiety and suffering but also saturated with expectations and beautiful encounters. In looking back the protagonist recognizes the isolation and despondency of the present, marred by a hypocritical marital relationship and his own poisonous inertia. But he also becomes aware that experiencing this oscillation between past and present constitutes an exceptional aesthetic moment, his mind finely discerning its poetic implications: "Lo sguardo allora si volta indietro e si fissa in immagini di sé, del mondo, di altri esseri umani. È' il momento dei ricordi. No, meglio si potrebbe dire: è il momento in cui tutti raccontano a se stessi bellissime storie" (Our mind turns back and focuses on images of the self, of the world and of other human beings. It is time for memories. No, it is better to say: it is the time in which we tell ourselves very beautiful stories).

"La realtà è un dono," the last story in the book, defines Sanvitale's notion of literature, which is based on seemingly insignificant accidents or events that have unexpected consequences. Irma, the protagonist, celebrates her fifty-eighth birthday by reading a book on catastrophes that shows how little events can have extraordinary consequences. She easily finds similarities between her life and the theories posited in the book:

> L'autore sosteneva che piccole variazioni nelle cause possono produrre variazioni enormi negli effetti. Infatti il viaggio a Vienna di più di dieci anni primi, anzi tredici, era stato una variazione minuscola nel suo sistema di vita e aveva prodotto grandi variazioni sugli effetti. Da un microscopico forellino la realtà era entrata con un sibilo. Si erano creati a catena fatti sconvolgenti che a loro volta avevano portato imprevedibili atteggiamenti psichici.

> (The author maintained that small variations in causes could produce enormous variations in effects. In fact, her trip to Vienna, more than ten years, actually thirteen years earlier, had been a minuscule variation in her way of life, but had produced substantial variations in results. From a microscopic hole reality had entered with a hiss. A chain of momentous facts had followed and had determined unexpected psychological dispositions.)

The narration of Irma's long-anticipated vacation in Vienna shows how the short trip created a cleft, modifying her existence in unforeseen ways. Her trip produced a chain of brief romantic encounters whose meaning is only now becoming clear as Irma looks back and reflects. Reality, she thinks, is a gift: every event is an enigma and every action an extraordinary source of self-knowledge.

Mettendo a fuoco (Being Focused, 1988)—is a collection of articles originally published in newspapers and literary magazines such as *L'Unità, Il Messaggero,* and *Nuovi Argomenti* in which Sanvitale addresses a variety of issues, including Italy's political situation, the condition of women in postindustrial society, and the malaise affecting the younger generation. In 1991 Sanvitale returned to the novel with *Verso Paola* (On the Road to Paola), which like many of her short stories features a male protagonist. This short novel marks a turning point in Sanvitale's approach, for here she views her protagonist more objectively than in her preceding works and is more concerned with issues that transcend the individual.

The novel is based on the chronicle of a journey taken by Alessandro, a professor of linguistics. He has decided to visit his wife, who is on vacation in the southern village of Paola. Returning himself from a mountain holiday, he boards the train that will take him from the north to the south of Italy. The trip sets the stage for a variety of disparate encounters, conversations, and personal considerations that evolve into a traumatic and unsuccessful struggle for transformation.

The middle-aged Alessandro experiences a psychological crisis as he vacillates between two women.

Sanvitale at the Villa Borghese in Rome, 1989

On one hand he is fascinated by his wife, Matilde, and the intricacy of her linguistic games; he is seduced by the theatrical transformations that she performs before and during every sexual act as she invents and acts out different roles. Through language the uninhibited Matilde attains the attributes of a female ruler who reigns by imposing her discourse as a supernatural instrument of knowledge: "Matilde non aveva altre abilità oltre a questa nell'amore. Era pigra e senza iniziative ma senza frustrazioni. A lui sembrava un essere più divino che umano, perché lo strumento che usava, il linguaggio, era lo strumento della conoscenza, un talismano che la trasformava in una regina" (Matilde did not have other abilities except that of lovemaking. She was lazy and had no initiative but also no frustrations. To him she was more divine than human, because the device that she used, language, was the instrument of knowledge, a talisman that transformed her into a queen).

While Matilde represents the creative but supremely artificial burst of invention, Evelina, Alessandro's university assistant who has followed him on his alpine vacation, seems to embody an opposite disposition. Her impenetrable nature and monosyllabic answers inspire Alessandro to contemplate the eloquence of silence. For Evelina language is a simple but dangerous system of signs that one should use sparingly, always conscious of its possible distortions and falsifications: "Con fortunato intuito aveva trovato l'opposto ... ma soprattutto il silenzio dal quale le parole uscivano lavate dalle scorie, formule esatte e a volte inattese ... Pareva che in questa parsimonia Evelina fosse arrivata ad uno stadio espressivo superiore ... La lingua diventava un sistema di segni semplice e criptico insieme" (With happy intuition he had found the opposite ... but most of all he had found silence, from which words would come out cleansed of dross, in exact and sometimes unexpected formulas ... It seemed that Evelina had come to a superior expressive stage ... [Her] language had become a simple and yet cryptic system of signs).

Alessandro's search for an ideal language, an absolute means of expression, is emblematic of his search for order as he tries to fend off a perplexing reality. He believes that reorganizing reality through language will help him to find a justification and a meaning for the complicating experiences of his life. As he boards the train to Paola, Alessandro is still confronting the questions that the brief liaison with Evelina was unable to answer. His own vacation has produced no solution, and he finds himself returning to his wife's captivating tales that efface her individuality.

Traveling allows Alessandro to separate himself from both expressive worlds, Matilde's and Evelina's. He has the chance to meditate about the purpose of language and to explore its relationship to reality. The course of his meditations is interrupted, however, by the interference of the objective world that surrounds him in the train's compartment. As the journey progresses, Alessandro acquires two different perspectives: the first is centered on the external environment, where he perceives the gradual degradation of Italy's natural, historical, and cultural landscape; the second is focused on the conflict that threatens to erase his identity, the conflict between self and language, self and objective world.

The novel follows the protagonist until the end of his journey a few kilometers outside Paola, where the train stops because of a strike. Exhausted and depressed by his day of self-reflection, Alessandro will reach his destination, returning to Matilde only to be engulfed once again in her erratic contrivances. The metaphor of travel and discovery, a recurring theme in Sanvitale's narrative, here dramatizes larger issues as well as Alessandro's psychological quest. To travel means to change, to face challenges at the personal and social level; on his journey Alessandro contemplates problems that range from the private to the public domain, from the fear of losing his individual identity to the degeneration produced by capitalism.

Perhaps the most insightful question Sanvitale broaches in her novel concerns language and its loss of significance, its devaluation and semantic crisis. She believes that in the cultural and political arenas

> la parola perde sempre più di significato. Essa dovrebbe avere tante valenze, ma oggi non vuole dire più niente. . . . E mi pare che per gli intellettuali e per gli scrittori non dare un significato importante alla parola significa anche usarla con grande distrazione, significa non credere più che la scrittura abbia un senso profondo, per se stessa, ma che sia soltanto un gioco, una utilizzazione, e questo può solo portare alla morte della letteratura.
>
> (words are losing meaning more and more every day. They should possess a plurality of connotations, but today they do not mean anything any longer. . . . I think that depriving the word of its meaning implies, for today's intellectuals and writers, to employ it with great distraction, not to believe in its profound import and consequently to use it as a utilitarian game. This can only lead to the death of literature).

Sanvitale suggests that the anxiety experienced by Alessandro is symptomatic of a crisis that affects society as a whole. She contends that the default of language cannot be interpreted merely as an individual's failure to communicate but must be analyzed in its wider social consequences. The loss of language invalidates history, culture, and civilization. In his search for linguistic meaning Alessandro aims to counter such a possibility.

Il figlio dell'impero (The Son of the Empire, 1993) chronicles the largely neglected story of the son of Napoleon Bonaparte. Working with historical documents, Sanvitale reconstructs François and his mother's prolonged travels through a war-ravaged Europe, following Napoleon's final defeat. Through the novelist's compassionate eyes readers follow their arrival in Vienna, the boy's conservative tutelage in the Hapsburgs' imperial palace, his unsuccessful attempts to obtain formal recognition as his father's successor, his military detachment in a removed province of the empire, and his devastating illness and premature death at the age of twenty-one. François was kept at a distance from the momentous historical transformations of his time by a powerful monarchy, watchfully shielded by Metternich's masterful diplomacy. Set in Paris and Vienna, the two capitals that dominated political and cultural life, the narrative yields a penetrating analysis of an epoch and the individuals who played significant roles in shaping it.

Sanvitale in her 1996 interview traces the inspiration of her novel to the image of little François clinging to the balustrade and tearfully refusing to leave on the tragic day of his departure from the Tuileries palace:

> Mi decisi a scrivere un lungo racconto, del tipo di *Verso Paola,* pensando di ritrovare la storia di questo bambino e, se fosse stato necessario, di ricostruire la sua vita dalla sua partenza da questo palazzo fino alla morte. Mi sono messa a leggere dei libri, ma sempre con un'idea leggera di quello che volevo fare, e leggendo nei libri, cercando di trovare il gesto di un bambino, mi è crollato addosso un impero.
>
> (I decided to write a short novel, like *Verso Paola,* thinking of recovering the child's story, and if it had been necessary, I would have retraced his life from the day he left the palace to his death. I began to read books, but always with an uncertain idea as to what I wanted to do, and in reading books and in trying to recover a child's gesture, a whole empire came crushing down on me.)

Although her original idea was to follow one individual, Sanvitale soon recognized the complexity of her project. To accompany François from French heir to Napoleon's short-lived empire to his days in Vienna meant adopting a wide-angle lens that would capture both historical events and the child's private life.

Sanvitale decided to bear witness to history through her protagonist's eyes. After his arrival in Vienna, François undergoes a dramatic transformation: his identity is molded in accordance with the values and ideals championed by the house of Hapsburg—ideals that contrasted with the political convictions of his father. In Vienna even his name is changed: François is called Franz. Caught in the middle of two opposing cultures and two contrasting visions, Franz becomes the designated victim. Embodying the conflict between tradition and modernity, he searches throughout his life for an identity but ultimately succumbs to the weight of history.

In writing this novel Sanvitale had to come to terms with notions of the history, historical reality, and historical truth. Well aware of ideological entrapments, she chose to be faithful to the presence of historical characters and to rely as much as possible on factual documentation. Historical narrative, maintains Sanvitale, is based on facts and cannot be altered by invention; facts can only be analyzed with a critical disposition: "Io non ho inserito, in questo romanzo di seicento pagine, una sola parola di dialogo che sia stata inventata . . . in me è così forte il senso di una persona che c'è stata che mi impedisce di superarla e cancellarla con la mia presenza" (I did not include, in this novel of six hundred pages, any invented word or dialogue . . . I feel strongly the presence of a person who really existed, and I cannot go beyond it and erase it with my presence).

The dichotomy between facts and invention leads to another important issue, the conflict between historical reality and historical truth. Documents, Sanvitale insists, are the only reference, the only source of information on the past:

> Ma il documento non è la verità, è il dubbio. Allora noi non possiamo ricostruire la storia se non attraverso un insieme di dubbi che noi dobbiamo onestamente riferire a chi legge. E il romanzo storico non può più essere impostato come un romanzo in cui siamo sicuri di tutto . . . ma piuttosto in cui dobbiamo cercare i possibili documenti e lasciare che chi legge decida, presentando i dubbi, offrendo ciò che non è consacrato, anzi dissacrare, per scoprire.
>
> (The document does not represent truth, but doubt. We should reconstruct history through a series of doubts and honestly submit them to the reader. The historical novel cannot be structured like a narrative in which we are sure about everything . . . but as something in which we have to search for the documents and let the reader decide, by presenting doubts, by offering what is not sacred, and to desecrate in order to discover.)

Sanvitale also questions impartiality and reliability of historical documentation, aiming to create a nonideological account. She does not view history as offering definite lessons or conclusive interpretations but as a fragmented, heterogeneous, and fluctuating reality. Finding the truth, Sanvitale asserts, is not the writer's responsibility since its elusiveness would occasion only illusory quests. The author's primary goal is to synthesize the multiplicity and opposition of events in a narrative system.

Sanvitale's *Tre favole dell'ansia e dell'ombra* (Three Tales of Anxiety and Shadows, 1994) is a collection of three stories in which she presents the agony that characterizes the writing process. In "Fanciulla e il gran vecchio" (Little Girl and the Old Man) the writing of fiction symbolizes man's eternal search for immortality, a search that penetrates into the most private realms of the subconscious but often causes anxiety and grief.

In "La principessa Rosalinda" (Princess Rosalinda) Sanvitale depicts the protagonist's gradual detachment from reality and her subsequent descent into an unreal world of hallucinations. Like Giulia of *L'uomo del parco,* the once-happy Rosalinda separates herself from her surroundings physically and mentally, undertaking a long journey of self-discovery and self-reconstruction. Traveling inward to the intimate regions of the self, she experiences the darkness of intricate forests and the cruelty of wild animals but also perceives the complexity of the world. Her encounter with the old weaver who creates extraordinary patterns symbolizes the purpose and extent of Rosalinda's search, for like the old woman she hopes to fuse self-discovery with the representation of the external world, though on paper rather than with fabric: "La vecchina fece una carezza. 'Cara bambina, le cose che un tempo hanno visto gli uomini sono rimaste nella memoria dei più vecchi e con loro spariranno. Per questo io tesso la tela, perchè diventino favole'" (The old lady caressed her. "Dear child, the things that men have seen have remained in the memory of the oldest among them and will disappear with them. For this reason I weave, so that they will become tales").

In "Bambina," the last tale, Sanvitale analyzes the tension and failure to communicate between the sexes. Her mythical iconography proposes two children who, by the gods' desire, were given the gift to remain forever young. But because of a fatal mistake, only one of the two, Bambina, will preserve her childlike senses, while the boy will grow to experience the pains and desires of adolescence. The ensuing contrast destroys their perfectly harmonious relationship as the introduction of lust brings suffering and pain, feelings and passions that Bambina cannot assimilate or admit. Incomprehension, misunderstandings, and alienation produce an atmosphere of hostility and recrimination that divide the two. By tracing the origin of misunderstanding between man and woman to a distant and mythical source, Sanvitale suggests that the passions cause an inextricable entanglement that ultimately falsifies and destroys human intimacy.

Sanvitale's *Separazioni* (Separations, 1997) is a collection that includes a selection of previously published stories and an additional five new short narratives written in the 1980s. The stories turn on the disconnections, separations, and dissolutions often hidden in even the most insignificant events: the renovation of one's residence in "Una nuova vita" (A New Life), the unexpected promotion of a colleague in "La promozione" (The Promotion), the tale of a dinner party and the search for the solution to a riddle in "Il pensionante" (The Guest), and the son's experience at summer camp in "La corsa del ragazzo sotto la luna." The smooth surface of human relations is subverted and invalidated, revealed in its vacuous inconsistency. What first appeared as the permanent facade of life, the author perceptively suggests, is but an evanescent mirage, since even the most trivial event can lead to its disruption.

One of the best new stories, "Orient Express," is a tale of memory, youth, friendship, and loss. The two protagonists meet after several years in a restaurant, the "Orient Express," to exchange old photographs, talk about their present lives, and reminisce about the past. It becomes immediately clear though that the death of their friend Umberto six months before has contaminated their lives, leaving an emotional scar that cannot be removed. Although the lives of the three friends had taken different paths, this loss constitutes an absolute separation, moving the two that are left, to confront the reality of a loss that is chiefly internal. Death did not in fact take away only a friend, it also erased all those images that belong to the past and can no longer be retrieved. In the restaurant background a mythical train, the Orient Express, emblematizes the long journey through life, with its mysterious and unknown stations, its exotic tastes and flavors reproduced in the dishes that the protagonists have savored. Life is made of separations, maintains Sanvitale, events that force the individual to delve into his/her reality and to reject its superficial appearance. However, separations do not exclusively mean destruction and dissolution, they may guide the self toward a better understanding of the objective world, of humanity and its tormented history.

Never comforting or simplistic, Sanvitale's work focuses on the search for self-knowledge and meaning. She views writing as offering the satisfaction of creation and the possibility for self-liberation. But Sanvitale believes that writing is much more than personal expression. Her efforts to renew the narrative stem from her belief that an evolving literature is fundamental to the progress of civilization.

Interviews:

Elisabetta Rasy, "Dal cuore al sesso," *Panorama*, 20 September 1987, pp. 183–185;

Giuseppe di Scipio, "Ten Questions for Francesca Sanvitale," *Italian Journal*, 7 (1993): 33–36;

Simona Wright, "Intervista a Francesca Sanvitale," *Italian Quarterly*, 33 (1996): 87–110.

References:

Luigi Baldacci, introduction to *Il cuore borghese* (Milan: Mondadori, 1986);

Paola Blelloch, "Francesca Sanvitale's *Madre e figlia:* From Self-Reflection to Self-Invention," in *Contemporary Women Writers in Italy. A Modern Renaissance,* edited by Santo L. Aricò (Amherst: University of Massachussetts Press, 1990), pp. 128–137;

Alba della Fazia Amoia, *Women on the Italian Literary Scene: A Panorama* (New York: Whitston, 1992), pp. 113–117, 124;

Ann Hallamore Ceaser, "Investigating the Self and the World," in *The New Italian Novel,* edited by G. Baranski and Lino Pertile (Cambridge: The University Press, 1993), pp. 184–199;

Margherita di Fazio, "Narratori a confronto," in *Narrare: percorsi possibili* (Ravenna: Longo, 1989), pp. 69–81;

Maria Teresa Giuffrè, "Francesca Sanvitale e il romanzo di idee al femminile," *Tempo presente,* 167 (November 1994): 45–49;

Raffaele Manica, "Francesca Sanvitale, Storia e verità," *Nuovi argomenti,* 50 (April–June 1994): 125–127;

Geno Pampaloni, introduction to *Madre e figlia* (Milan: Mondadori, 1986);

Antonio Porta, introduction to *L'uomo del parco* (Milan: Mondadori, 1987);

Sharon Wood, *Italian Women's Writing 1860–1994* (London: Athlone, 1995): 237–245;

Simona Wright, "In viaggio *Verso Paola* tra identità individuale e storia," *Italian Quarterly,* 33 (1996): 61–75.

Carlo Sgorlon
(26 July 1930 -   )

Mario Aste
University of Massachusetts at Lowell

BOOKS: *Un'aurora per Penelope* (Milan: Gastaldi, 1958);
Kafka narratore (Vicenza: Neri Pozzi, 1961);
La poltrona (Milan: Mondadori, 1968);
La notte del ragno mannaro (Udine: Nuova Base, 1970);
Prime di sere (Udine: Società Filologica Friulana, 1971);
Invito alla lettura di Elsa Morante (Milan: Mursia, 1972);
La luna color ametista (Padua: Rebellato, 1972);
Il trono di legno (Milan: Mondadori, 1973); translated by Jessie Bright as *The Wooden Throne* (New York: Italica Press, 1988);
Il vento nel vigneto (Rome: Gremese, 1973);
Il quarto re mago (Ravenna: Girasole, 1974);
La stanchezza di Mosè (Trieste: Asterisco, 1974);
Regina di Saba (Milan: Mondadori, 1975);
I racconti di Nord-Est (Rome: Gremese, 1976);
Gli dei torneranno (Milan: Mondadori, 1977);
La carrozza di rame (Milan: Mondadori, 1979);
La fuga di Istaar (Lugano: Mazzucconi, 1979);
Il paria dell'universo (Rome: Gremese, 1979);
La contrada (Milan: Mondadori, 1981);
Il dolfin (Udine: Panarie, 1982);
Gli affreschi del Tiepolo nel Veneto (Novara: De Agostini, 1982);
La conchiglia di Anataj (Milan: Mondadori, 1983);
Terra d'elegie, by Sgorlon, Antonio Azzano, and Italo Zannier (Ferrara: Belborgo, 1984);
L'armata dei fiumi perduti (Milan: Mondadori, 1985);
Il quarto re mago. Racconti (Pordenone: Studio Tesi, 1986);
I sette veli (Milan: Mondadori, 1986);
L'ultima valle (Milan: Mondadori, 1987);
Il Caldèras (Milan: Mondadori, 1988);
Racconti della terra di Canaan (Milan: Mondadori, 1989);
La fontana di Lorena (Milan: Mondadori, 1990);
La tribù (Milan: Paoline, 1990);
Il patriarcato della luna (Milan: Mondadori, 1991);
La foiba grande (Milan: Mondadori, 1992);
Il guaritore (Milan: Mondadori, 1993);
Marco d'Europa (Milan: Paoline, 1993);
Il regno dell'uomo (Milan: Mondadori, 1994);
Il costruttore (Milan: Mondadori, 1995);

Carlo Sgorlon (photograph by Giovanni Giovannetti)

La malga di Sîr (Milan: Mondadori, 1997).

Carlo Sgorlon's contribution to post–World War II Italian narrative can be traced to his strong interest in the popular traditions of Friuli, his native region in northern Italy that borders Austria and Slovenia. The magic and mystery in his work are tied to his appreciation of the fables, folklore, and tales of Friuli, and he has written some of his many short stories in the language of the region. He thus can be counted among such contemporary Italian writers as Cesare Pavese, Giuseppe Dessì, Gina Lagorio, and Fulvio Tomizza, who draw on their native regions for inspiration. Sgorlon is much more than a regional writer, however, for the values and ideas of his work transcend regional interest.

Sgorlon was born on 26 July 1930 in Casacco, a village near Udine. He spent much of his childhood with his grandparents and came into contact with the life of Friulan peasants. The experience instilled in him a sense of reverence for ancient traditions together with a desire to preserve the language and folklore of the region. His first teachers were his grandfather, a retired schoolmaster, and his grandmother, a practicing midwife.

Sgorlon attended secondary schools in Udine and from 1948 to 1953 continued his education at the University of Pisa, where he studied modern literature. His thesis on Franz Kafka was published as *Kafka narratore* (On Kafka's Narrative) in 1961. In addition to fiction Sgorlon has continued to write criticism in such works as *Invito alla lettura di Elsa Morante* (Introduction to the Work of Elsa Morante, 1972) and *Gli affreschi dei Tiepolo nel Veneto* (Tiepolo's Frescoes in the Veneto Region, 1982).

A scholarship enabled Sgorlon to continue his studies in Germany at the University of Munich. Upon his return to Italy he taught Italian and history at a technical institute in Udine. In 1980 he quit teaching to devote himself to writing. He has been a contributor to the daily *Il Gazzettino* and the review *Nuova antologia*. He has also been a consultant for cultural matters to RAI, the Italian radio and television network.

Sgorlon's early fiction shows the influence of Kafka. Written in a style that reflects the neurosis of its protagonist, *La poltrona* (The Sofa, 1968) tells the story of a man intent on writing an ambitious treatise he never brings to conclusion. Kafka's imprint is also apparent in *La notte del ragno mannaro* (The Night of the Crazed Spider, 1970), which is marked by oneiric, surrealistic images and constantly blurs the line between wakefulness and sleep, reality and illusion.

Sgorlon's narrative attests to a broad range of intellectual interests. While Kafka is a significant point of reference, Sgorlon is also inspired by authors such as Dino Buzzati, Elsa Morante, Herman Melville, Leo Tolstoy, Jorge Luis Borges, and Gabriel García Márquez. He draws from philosophical and psychological sources as well as from the Bible, particularly the Book of Ecclesiastes. From Benedict de Spinoza, Sgorlon derives his philosophical attachment to nature and from Arthur Schopenhuer, his bitter vision of life. He also incorporates Carl Jung's archetype theories and his notion of the "collective unconscious" into his fiction.

Sgorlon's first novels to deal with life in Friuli are *La luna di color ametista* (A Moon the Color of Amethyst, 1972) and *Il vento nel vigneto* (The Wind in the Vineyard, 1973). Expanded from *Prime di sere*, a much shorter version he wrote in Friulan two years before, *Il vento nel vigneto* offers a realistic picture of peasants and artisans toiling in a world in which the people are in synchrony with nature and the eternal cycles of the seasons. In *La luna di color ametista* a mysterious character named Rabal appears suddenly in a sleepy village of the Veneto. Rabal brings confusion as he encourages local people to accept traditional life while affirming individual growth to a level of which they never dreamed before.

The search for a fulfilling life through the acceptance of customs and traditions handed down by past generations is also the focus of *Il trono di legno* (1973; translated as *The Wooden Throne*, 1988), widely regarded as one of Sgorlon's most successful novels. Relying heavily on myth and magic, he depicts the life of a Friulan community attempting to hold onto its past. The recovery of local folklore transforms the characters, enriching their lives through enhanced consciousness of their communal traditions. The theme and narrative approach are consistent with what Sgorlon told Fiora Vincenti in a 1973 interview published in *Uomini e libri*:

> Mi affido alla fantasia, alla mia capacità di vedere il mondo come un immenso baraccone delle meraviglie ... ed anche alla mia capacità di primitivo di rimitizzare il mondo, per quanto i miti e le fiabe siano stati esorcizzati da secoli dalla scienza e dalla tecnologia.
>
> (I place my trust in imagination, in my ability to see the world as a huge carnival tent filled with wonders ... and my ability as a rustic to re-create a mythical world despite the fact that myths and fables have been exorcised for centuries by the advent of science and technology.)

Sgorlon believes in the importance of fables and folklore, particularly for the imaginative development of children. Used to explain the mysteries and the origin of human life, old tales introduce young listeners to the domain of fantasy, magic, and the imagination.

Blessed with a fertile imagination, Giuliano, the protagonist of *Il trono di legno,* embarks on a quest to unravel the mystery surrounding his birth and his family. As a child Giuliano is especially interested in his elusive grandfather nicknamed the Dane. His curiosity later evolves into a great desire to travel around the world. In the end the Dane proves to be less than mysterious; he was a simple man, attracted to such things as voices, sounds, birds in flight, and train whistles.

Fantasy is important to Giuliano because it enables him to reach a reality "piena di vaghi enigmi e sorprese" (full of vague enigmas and surprises). After he learns how to read, he discovers countless new

Dust jacket for Sgorlon's 1997 novel

worlds. In his fantasy he becomes an adventurer who travels through time and space to meet Julius Caesar, Marc Anthony, Hannibal, Genghis Khan, Christopher Columbus, and Ishmael of *Moby-Dick*. He may visit the Shepherd Kings of Greece, as well as Denmark, New York, and the tundra in Alaska. Yet this is not enough for him: he wants to have a place in history and embody the collective memory of humanity. In his travels he goes from the village of Ontans, where he was born, to Cretis, where he chooses to spend the rest of his life. The story evolves around Giuliano's reminiscences as he grows old in Cretis. Readers, much like the listeners of fables and stories who used to sit around a fireplace, are carried from the particular to the universal.

Il trono di legno is the story of Giuliano's development from a restless adolescent to a man of knowledge, experience, and wisdom. His quest is interwoven with his relationship with two sisters, Flora and Lia, respectively his mistress and his wife. Giuliano abandons Lia, the embodiment of innocence, to follow Flora, the image of a primordial Eve, a woman exuding vitality and sensuality who yearns for the excitement of city life. In time, though, he recognizes his wayward ways and returns to his adopted village of Cretis only to find that the gentle Lia has died. Faithful to him to the end, Lia left him a child, who is cared for by Pietro, the patriarch of the village. Pietro's house is a rustic "court" where everyone gathers to listen to him, seated on a wooden chair as he tells stories. His stories are based on events of his life, a rich life spent in the remotest places on earth before settling in Cretis. Giuliano relives in his fertile imagination the stories he hears from Pietro. Still a young man, he begins to discover the magic in the words of the storyteller. He comes to realize that magic is not ethereal, that it can be hidden in the very texture of reality.

Giuliano's journey through life is marked by sadness, sorrow, disappointment, and the discovery of fresh truths. He makes mistakes, and he learns to accept the consequences of his actions. Maturity imparts to him humility and wisdom. As he returns to his occupation as a woodcarver, he reaches a full understanding that he belongs to a peasant and artisan culture. When Pietro dies, he will inherit the wooden "throne."

In *Il trono di legno* Sgorlon shows not only that everything in life carries a price but also that everything has a purpose and a meaning. At the end of his journey Giuliano understands what Pietro has taught him, especially the power of love and the foolish illusions nurtured by Flora. It is significant that the child Lia has given Giuliano, now three years old, will eventually succeed him as storyteller. Through this legacy

Sgorlon points to a fantastic world where human life, by a constant renewal and a deepening sense of knowledge, is elevated to a dimension that oscillates between everyday reality and the realm of symbols. Through this interplay between fantasy and reality Sgorlon realizes his vocation as a writer.

In his next novel, *Regina di Saba* (The Queen of Sheba, 1975), Sgorlon continues to explore the dichotomy between fantasy and reality. More than any other of Sgorlon's protagonists, Silvano is able to avoid the pitfalls of illusions and face the concreteness of everyday life. The novel evolves around the relationship between Silvano and Isabella, a woman absorbed by lofty ideals. Often accompanied by Silvano, Isabella splits her life between the city of Trieste and the Friuli region. The two are parted when Isabella succumbs to the harsh reality of life; Silvano finds himself alone in a world jolted by the death and destruction of World War II.

In *Gli dei torneranno* (The Return of the Gods, 1977) Sgorlon again evokes the ancient land of Friuli. The protagonist, Simone, returns to his native village of Jalmis after an extended stay in Peru. On his arrival, taken by the desire to preserve the culture of his people, he sets out to record the verbal accounts of those inhabitants who have heard stories or have witnessed the memorable events of the past. He discovers that the heart and soul of Friuli is among peasants and craftsmen—their memories hearken back to the Venetians, who invaded the region and ended its independence in 1420; the Austrians, who ruled Friuli in the nineteenth century; and in more recent times the Germans, who occupied it during World War II. The narrative is informed by Sgorlon's desire to preserve Friuli's centuries-old culture and to rescue it from the passing of time and the corrosive effects of a post–World War II society marked by materialism and consumerism.

Sgorlon shows how the Friulan world of farmers and artisans survives calamity in *La carrozza di rame* (The Copper Coach, 1979). The history of the people is revealed in the context of natural disasters and the human passions nurtured within a patriarchal family for six generations. The reader witnesses the physical collapse of a Friulan community as a result of the tragic earthquake of 1976. The pessimism and despair brought by the natural catastrophe is overcome by the inhabitants' tenacious efforts of reconstruction. Through his sense of dignity and love for the past Emilio, the protagonist, inspires others to continue the traditions of old while accepting the present.

In two works of the early 1980s—*La contrada* (The Village, 1981) and *La conchiglia di Anataj* (Anataj's Shell, 1983)—Sgorlon elaborates the memories of those who leave and those who return to an agricultural region such as Friuli. *La contrada* points to the decline and eventual disappearance of the peasant and artisan ways of life. Matteo, a Friulan, has just returned from Alaska. As a gift to his native land he organizes a large festival in a poor and neglected road in Udine. The event, with various types of entertainment for young and old, proves to be a memorable occasion. When the festival is over the only thing left is the memory, soon to be overshadowed by Matteo's illness and death. On the other hand, *La conchiglia di Anataj* centers on the experiences of a group of Friulan railroad workers who take part in building the Transiberian Railroad. The problems affecting these former peasants are those endured by all immigrants. But there are also joys and expanded knowledge of other cultures to be experienced in a voluntary exile. Indeed Sgorlon emphasizes the spirit of brotherhood that forms among workers with a common peasant background, their common transcultural identity and the potential of keener kinship among them and their respective families.

A quite different theme is explored in *L'armata dei fiumi perduti* (The Lost Rivers' Army, 1985), which describes the desperate plight of a contingent of Cossack soldiers who joined the Germans during World War II to fight the Bolshevicks. Promised land in Friuli, the Cossacks were abandoned by the Nazis. Sgorlon graphically depicts the penetration of the German and Cossack army into northeastern Italy and the shedding of Cossack and Friulan blood. The novelist draws from personal recollections of the war but is not partisan in his account; instead his tone is compassionate, for both oppressed and misguided oppressors are seen as victims of history.

Sgorlon's treatment of war and peace echoes that of Tolstoy, especially with regard to the conflicts between occupying forces and the people under occupation. The Cossacks rejoice at first, thinking they have found a new homeland, but their joy turns into tragedy when they and the Friulans become victims of the war. The memory of lost rivers, such as the Volga and the Don, serves as the counterpoint to the land of Friuli, which the Germans hand to the Cossacks under false pretense. Initially the Friulans welcome the disinherited children of "Mother Russia," but the tide of history turns against the Cossacks. A few survive as naturalized Italians; others are executed as Nazi collaborators after their forced return to the Soviet Union; still others find death fighting the Italian partisans opposed to Fascism.

The protagonist of the novel is Marta, a compassionate woman who is able to love both the partisans and their enemies, the Cossacks. She embodies the ideals of coexistence and tolerance among people as she displays her love for a Jewish youth, an Italian soldier, the Cossack Urvan, and the leader of the underground partisans fighting the Germans and the Cossacks, Ivos. Her boundless capacity to love is contrasted by the feelings of hatred and violence harbored by the men in her life, and Sgorlon details the intolerance of the local inhabitants toward foreigners, the provocations amid different ethnic groups, followed by retaliation and violence. Marta, for whom the word *enemy* does not exist, becomes the pivot around whom events, both private and public, turn.

On a symbolic level Marta represents a source of life and healing. She provides a glimpse into the powers of rejuvenation and survival amid war and destruction. In commenting on the novel Claudio Toscani describes Marta's relationship with men:

> La sua è l'insensata freschezza di una energia che travalica la vita contigente: è la rigenerante saggezza dell'universo spirituale che agisce tra istinto, intuito, amore, e pietà. Lei come donna, non si pensa, non si cura: ha in consegna l'uomo, "braccio" di divenire, ma vittima del tempo.

> (She possesses the carefree freshness of an energy that goes beyond contingent life: it is the regenerating wisdom of the spiritual universe which mediates instinct, intuition, love, and compassion. As a woman, she does not look at herself, does not think nor take care of herself: she is the custodian of man, seen as an "arm" of the future, but victim of time.)

In *L'armata dei fiumi perduti* Sgorlon shows a peasant culture neglected by history but constantly renewing itself with surprising and original vitality.

L'ultima valle (The Last Valley, 1987) attests to Sgorlon's deep concern for ecology, a concern present in part or implicitly in many of his works. The novel was inspired by the horror and the destruction caused by a landslide that damaged the recently constructed Vaiont Dam and killed more than 2,500 people in 1963. The setting is a mountain village nestled in the emerald green of a valley at the extreme border of Friuli. The construction of a new dam brings not only technological progress to the village but also the gradual decline of traditional ways of life. According to Sgorlon the promises of progress and technology carry a heavy price, which in many cases is tantamount to the severe deterioration, if not the destruction, of the environment.

The characters of the novel are divided into two groups: the villagers and the outsiders. The villagers include Siro, who is concerned with preserving the ecological balance in the area and hence is opposed to the dam; Giovanni, who works for a construction company building the dam but has reservations about the project; Rachele, Giovanni's barren, bedridden wife; Caterina, an attractive widow who owns the village tavern and is now Giovanni's lover; and Isaia, the patriarch of the village. The main outsiders are Meroj Valbruno, a construction engineer and tireless voice of progress, and his faithful shadow, Augusto, who tries to convince the villagers to believe in the new myths of progress and financial well-being. The townspeople are immediately confronted with the choice between preserving their way of life and accepting a new industrial culture, which many villagers identify with moral decay and the ultimate destruction of the valley's pristine beauty. Only the offended spirits of the mountain will, at the end of the novel, restore traditional values. Through his involving plot and characters Sgorlon suggests that man must learn to live in harmony with nature.

In *Il patriarcato della luna* (The Patriarchy of the Moon, 1991) Sgorlon suggests that history and fantasy are the anchors of all human experiences. The novel treats issues that are crucial to contemporary society: the physical impoverishment of the planet as a result of the feverish search for new raw materials and resources, mass tourism, and the culture of consumer-oriented societies. The protagonist, Morvan; his adopted parents; and a few friends are deeply conscious of these problems and are intent on counteracting what to them is the underlying cause: the pursuit of individual gratification at the expense of the community. Sgorlon is especially keen to bring out the general lack of awareness in regard to the critical erosion of natural resources, a point he makes emphatically in his 1991 interview with Toscani: "Oggi la moda conta più della sopravvivènza. E dopo di me il diluvio" (Today what is fashionable is more important than survival. After me, the deluge).

Sgorlon believes that literature must deal with the most important issues that affect not only contemporary society but also the planet. He would find it absurd to write as though he were oblivious to the fact that man is destroying the earth. Sgorlon concludes the interview on this pessimistic note:

> La terra sta agonizzando, ma gli appetiti degli uomini continuano ad aumentare. Di questo passo la distruzione della natura è inevitabile. La specie umana finirà. Si salveranno le forme più elementari di vita animale e vegetativa. E il ciclo della vita ricomincerà, fino alla morte del sole.

> (The earth is dying, but human appetites continue to rise. At this rate the destruction of nature is inevitable. The human race will cease to exist. Only the elementary forms of animal and plant life will survive. The cycle of life will begin anew until the sun burns out.)

In *Il regno dell'uomo* (Man's Kingdom, 1994) Sgorlon's protagonist is Basilio Arvenis, the son of a bricklayer and a woman of Russian and Rumanian extraction, who returns to his native village of Torralta after he completes his studies at the University of Milan. The novel is set in the late 1960s and early 1970s, the so-called *anni di piombo* (years of lead), in which terrorism and sociopolitical turmoil endangered the stability of Italian society. Not interested in politics, Basilio seems unaware of what is happening in the country. He foregoes participation in the political struggle in favor of an introspective search for self-fulfillment, which he seeks in his homeland. Much of the story concerns his stormy relationship with Patrizia, who is attracted to him but is unwilling to offer a commitment because she wants to abandon her life as a peasant and become an independent woman.

Set in the nineteenth century *Il Costruttore* (The Builder, 1995) evolves around the life of Francesco Falconara, the illegitimate son of a Sicilian nobleman, Gregorio Dayala. Detesting his position and his birthplace, Francesco leaves Sicily and adopts his father's name. But he carries with him the outdated ideas of the island that continue to condition his judgment. He finds refuge in northeastern Italy, where he studies law to please his father though his desire is to become an architect and a master builder. At a party he meets Giuditta, a niece of a countess, whom he soon marries.

After his marriage Francesco becomes a powerful contractor courted by the town's most influential business owners and politicians. His friendship with a high government official involves him in kickbacks and payoffs. At the same time Francesco's effort to build high-rise buildings and housing complexes arouses the ire of ecological groups. During an economic downturn his business ventures begin to suffer to the point that eventually he is left in a state of near poverty. Adding to his sorrow is the estrangement of his children: his older son, Daniele, was part of the ecological group that had a role in Francesco's downfall; his younger son, Luciano, after initial interest in his father's business, goes through a personal crisis and leaves him.

The collapse of the old socioeconomic order, in which Francesco has played an important part, is suggested by the fire that at the end of the novel destroys the castle of Leopoldo, a wealthy capitalist. The fire is the purifying element needed to save society from greed and corruption, but nothing in the novel suggests the birth of a new society. As in earlier works, Sgorlon tries to use his writing to educate people and raise their civic consciousness; yet his lengthy ideological discussions get in the way of characterization and the masterful description of landscapes that are often the strengths of his narrative.

A sensitive and reflective observer of his time, Sgorlon writes about some of the most important questions that concern the human condition, dwelling especially on what the industrialized world has lost and what it risks losing. He understands that in embracing an industrial-consumer society human beings frequently destroy their sense of the sacred. A writer committed to a humane vision of society, Sgorlon makes a case for restoring the values of community and imagination, convinced that the preservation of the best traditions of the past will hold the human family together.

Interviews:
Fiora Vincenti, "Intervista a Sgorlon," *Uomini e libri*, June–July 1973;
Claudio Toscani, "Intervista a Carlo Sgorlon," *Otto-Novecento*, 15 (1991): 165–168.

References:
M. Brandolini, "Italian Self-Analysis. Concise Survey of Contemporary Italian Folkloric and Regional Literature," *Europe. Revue littéraire Mensuelle*, 58 (1980): 202–203;
Roberto Damiani, *Carlo Sgorlon narratore* (Rome: Gremese, 1979);
Carmine Di Biase, "L'età dei sogni e degli eroi in Carlo Sgorlon," *Studium*, 82 (1987): 938–941;
F. Lanza, "The Apocalypse as Setting for Some Contemporary Italian Novels," *Otto-Novecento*, 12 (1988): 193–199;
Bruno Maier, *Sgorlon* (Florence: La Nuova Italia, 1984);
Matteo Nazzaio, "Biblical Archetypes in Carlo Sgorlon's Novels," *Otto-Novecento*, 12 (1988): 83–123;
Liana Nissim, *Sgorlon teste insolente* (Como: Quaderni di Gamajum, 1985);
Claudio Toscani, preface to *L'ultima valle*, by Sgorlon (Milan: Mondadori, 1989).

Antonio Tabucchi
(1943 -)

Augustus Pallotta
Syracuse University

BOOKS: *Piazza d'Italia* (Milan: Bompiani, 1975);
Il teatro portoghese del dopoguerra (Rome: Abete, 1976);
Il piccolo naviglio (Milan: Mondadori, 1978);
Il gioco del rovescio (Milan: Il Saggiatore, 1981); translated by Janice M. Tresher as *Letter from Casablanca* (New York: New Directions, 1986);
Donna di Porto Pim e altre storie (Palermo: Sellerio, 1983);
Notturno indiano (Palermo: Sellerio, 1984); translated by Tim Parks as *Indian Nocturne* (London: Chatto & Windus, 1988; New York: New Directions, 1989);
Pessoana minima: escritos sobre Fernando Pessoa (Lisbon: Nacional-Casa da Moeda, 1984);
Piccoli equivoci senza importanza (Milan: Feltrinelli, 1985); translated by Frances Frenaye as *Little Misunderstandings of No Importance* (London: Chatto & Windus, 1988; New York: New Directions, 1987);
Il filo dell'orizzonte (Milan: Feltrinelli, 1986); translated by Tim Parks as *The Edge of the Horizon* (New York: New Direction, 1990);
I volatili del Beato Angelico (Palermo: Sellerio, 1987);
I dialoghi mancati (Milan: Feltrinelli, 1988);
Un baule pieno di gente: scritti su Fernando Pessoa (Milan: Feltrinelli, 1990);
L'angelo nero (Milan: Feltrinelli, 1991);
Requiem, uma alucinação (1991); translated by Sergio Vecchio into Italian as *Requiem: un'allucinazione* (Milan: Feltrinelli, 1992); translated by Margaret Jull Costa as *Requiem: A Hallucination* (London: Harvill Press, 1994; New York: New Directions, 1994);
Sogni di sogni (Palermo: Sellerio, 1992);
Gli ultimi tre giorni di Fernando Pessoa. Un delirio. (Palermo: Sellerio, 1994);
Sostiene Pereira. Una testimonianza (Milan: Feltrinelli, 1994); translated by Patrick Creagh as *Pereira Declares. A True Account* (London: Harvill Press, 1995); republished as *Pereira Declares. A Testimony* (New York: New Directions, 1995);
La testa perduta di Damasceno Monteiro (Milan: Feltrinelli, 1997);

Antonio Tabucchi (photograph by Michele Tabucchi)

Un fiammifero Minerva; considerazioni a caldo sulla figura dell'intellettuale indirizzate ad Adriano Sofri (Rome: Tip. Città Nuova, 1997);
Marconi, se ben mi ricordo; una piece radiofonica (Rome: Rai-ERI, 1997);

Editions in English: *Short Stories,* translated by Tim Parks (London: Chatto & Windus, 1991).

OTHER: *La parola interdetta. Poeti surrealisti portoghesi,* translated and edited by Tabucchi (Turin: Einaudi, 1971);
Fernando Pessoa, *Una sola moltitudine,* 2 volumes, edited by Tabucchi and Marie Jose de Lancastre (Milan: Adelphi, 1979);
Il poeta e la finzione: scritti su Fernando Pessoa, edited by Tabucchi (Genoa: Tilgher-Genova, 1983);
Carlos Drummond de Andrade, *Sentimento del mondo,* selected and translated by Tabucchi (Turin: Einaudi, 1987);

Fernado Pessoa, *Il poeta è un fingitore,* selected and translated by Tabucchi (Milan: Feltrinelli, 1988);

Giampaolo Barbieri, *Pomellato. Le mappe del desiderio. Un viaggio,* text by Tabucchi (Milan: Idea Books, 1989);

Piccole finzioni con importanza: valori della narrativa italiana contemporanea: convegno internazionale, maggio 1991, Università di Anversa, edited by Nathalie Roelens and Inge Lanslots, with the participation of Tabucchi (Ravenna: Longo, 1993).

Since Italo Calvino's death in 1985, Antonio Tabucchi has emerged as the novelist that best exemplifies Italian narrative at the turn of the century. Tabucchi in some measure follows in the path blazed by Calvino in that his writing continues in the nonideological vein of the postneorealist novel. Also, the qualities that Calvino singles out in his *Lezioni americane: Sei proposte per il prossimo millennio* (1988; translated as *Six Memos for the Next Millennium,* 1988) as befitting postmodern narrative—quickness and lightness—are also distinctive traits of Tabucchi's work.

Born in 1943 in Vecchiano, a small town in the Tuscan countryside, Tabucchi studied at the University of Pisa and at the prestigious Scuola Normale. In the late 1960s, as part of his studies in Portuguese literature, Tabucchi was introduced to the work of Fernando Pessoa (1888-1935), the Portuguese writer who is widely regarded as one of this century's most original poets. Pessoa wrote poetry under his name and under three other names, or "heteronyms" as he called them, each with a different style and point of view. The fact that these heteronyms were regarded by Pessoa not as pseudonyms but as three autonomous beings was so singular and was carried out so credibly that these works had an enormous influence on the perception of an author's relationship to his characters. The notion, also found partly in Luigi Pirandello's work, that an individual's personality is made up of different expressions and characteristics has had a noticeable impact on Tabucchi's writing.

Tabucchi's interest in Portuguese literature led to a strong attachment to Portugal, a country he considers his second homeland and in which he regularly spends part of the year. In 1995 he told Paola Gaglianone in an interview: "Amo il Portogallo proprio perché è un paese del sud, un paese di grande luce, di grande sole, di giornate lunghissime che finiscono alle dieci di sera: è un paese in cui provo un costante senso di benessere" (I love Portugal precisely because it is a country of the South, a land of bright light and bright sun, of very long days that end at ten o'clock at night: it is a country where I experience a constant sense of well-being). Tabucchi is married to a Portuguese woman, María de José de Lancastre, with whom he has had two children. He is a professor of Portuguese at the University of Siena, and his publications on the literature of his second country include *La parola interdetta. Poeti surrealisti portoghesi* (1971), an anthology in Italian of Portuguese poets, and *Una sola moltitudine* (1979), a two-volume translation of Pessoa's works that he edited with his wife. As a novelist he has received the coveted Viareggio and Campiello prizes, the Prix Européen Jean Monnet and, in France, the Prix Médicis Etranger.

Tabucchi's first novel, *Piazza d'Italia* (A Town Square in Italy, 1975), created a stir with the novelty of its structure, which contemporary critics noted owes much to Columbian author Gabriel García Márquez's *Cien años de soledad* (1967; translated as *One Hundred Years of Solitude,* 1970). Like a play, the novel is divided into three acts, each consisting of generally short narrative scenes, some as short as a few lines. It chronicles the vicissitudes of a humble family in a Tuscan village during a span of one hundred years, from the unification of Italy in 1860 to the post–World War II period. The narrator is keenly aware of the continuous historical struggle of peasants and artisans against the forces of a central government that, through the years, changes name and political stripe but remains essentially unsympathetic to the needs and modest aspirations of the proletarian classes. In fluent, nimble prose Tabucchi combines history and fiction, skillfully incorporating swift dialogue and historically accurate descriptions.

After publishing a second novel, *Il piccolo naviglio* (The Small Naval Craft, 1978), in which he portrays everyday life in a Tuscan town in the Apuan Alps, Tabucchi brought out a more successful collection of stories, *Il gioco del rovescio* (1981; translated as *Letter from Casablanca,* 1986). The title of the English translation is taken from one of the stories in the volume, "Lettera da Casablanca," whereas in the Italian original the first story lends the title to the volume. Partly autobiographical (as the author points out in the preface), "Il gioco del rovescio" (The Backwards Game) deals with the ambiguous relationship between an Italian university student who often travels to Lisbon to work in the city libraries and Maria do Carmo, a middle-aged woman unhappily married to a considerably older gentleman.

One summer afternoon, during a short stop in Madrid to visit the Prado museum, the student learns that Maria do Carmo has died. He decides to

Dust jacket for the American edition of Tabucchi's 1985 book, in which he often depicts indecisive disoriented characters

attend the funeral and reserves a seat on the first train to Lisbon. Tabucchi effectively structures his story, smoothly alternating the night journey on the train and the narrator's conversation with a Spanish passenger with his recollections of his first acquaintance with Maria do Carmo, their subsequent encounters, and his tense meeting with her husband, who tells him that his wife was not the unhappy and destitute child she led him to believe but was "figlia di grandi proprietari, ha avuto un'infanzia dorata, quindici anni fa, quando l'ho conosciuta, aveva ventisette anni ed era la donna più corteggiata di Lisbona" (the daughter of large landowners who had a golden childhood, and, fifteen years ago, when I met her, she was the most courted woman in Lisbon).

This last revelation brings to mind the title of the story, for everything the student has believed is turned around. Maria do Carmo foreshadows the reversal of roles and identities when after she tells the student of her unhappy childhood in a poor neighborhood of Buenos Aires she becomes emotionally involved with him: "Senti, viviamo questa vita come se fosse un revés, per esempio stanotte, tu devi pensare che sei me e che stai stringendo te fra le tue braccia, io penso di essere te che sto stringendo me fra le mie braccia" (Listen, let us live this life as though it were reversed; for instance, tonight you must think that you are me and that you are squeezing yourself in your arms, and I think I am you squeezing myself in my arms).

Tabucchi plays his "gioco del rovescio" in other stories to varying degrees. Such ingenious ways of constructing stories carry risks but can achieve distinctive success. In purposely leaving out or merely suggesting key details, Tabucchi requires the participation of his readers, their creative power to respond to the author's entreaty to fill in the missing gaps, to complete as well as to complement. Such is the case with the story "Dolores Ibarruri versa lacrime amare" (Dolores Ibarrurri Sheds Bitter Tears), whose title highlights the legendary revolutionary who fought against Franco in the Spanish Civil War and came to be called La Pasionaria (The Passionflower).

The story takes the form of a long monologue in which a grieving mother, seemingly responding to a reporter's queries, recounts her son's childhood, alluding only in passing to his membership in a 1970s revolutionary group and his death at the hands of the police. The other thread of her recollection is the husband Rodolfo, who fought in the Spanish Civil War and stood side by side with La Pasionaria as members of the International Brigades. The ideological center of the story, the figure of La Pasionaria underscores the passion of individual convictions and the price one must be willing to pay to uphold them.

The figure of La Pasionaria reappears in a collection of what Tabucchi calls "quasi-racconti" (near-stories), *I volatili del Beato Angelico* (The Flying Creatures of Beato Angelico, 1987). Here, from an imaginary "Lettera di Mademoiselle Lenormand, cartomante, a Dolores Ibarruri, rivoluzionaria" (Letter of Mademoiselle Lenormand, [Napoleon's] fortuneteller, to Dolores Ibarruri, revolutionary) emerges the idealized sketch of a woman who in spite of the failure of Marxism is elevated to an emblem of suffering and persecution, indeed to a splendid image of hope to those who have endured poverty and persecution. In this light the letter complements the ideological consciousness of *Piazza d'Italia* and the short story in *Il gioco del rovescio*. In part, it reads as follows:

> Crescerai con la giusta rabbia che hanno i poveri quando non sono rassegnati; parlerai a coloro che i potenti considerano strame e insegnerai loro a non diventare come era tua madre. Accenderai in loro la speranza, ed essi ti seguiranno, perché i poveri come vivrebbero senza speranza? Conoscerai le minacce dei giudici, le percosse dei gendarmi, la volgarità dei carcerieri, il disprezzo dei servi. Ma sarai bella, furente, intrepida, infiammata dallo sdegno. Ti chiameranno la Pasionaria, per indicare il fuoco che ti brucia nel cuore.
>
> (You will grow up with the righteous anger of poor people that are not resigned; you will speak to those the powerful regard as litter and you will teach them not to become like your mother. You will kindle in them hope, and they will follow you, because how would the poor live without hope?
> You will know threats from judges, beatings from the police, the coarseness of prison guards, the contempt of those that serve. But you will be beautiful, furious, fearless, enflamed with wrath. They will call you Pasionaria to indicate the fire that burns in your heart.)

Between 1983 and 1984 Tabucchi published two books that grew out of his travels to the Azores and to India and marked a turning point in his work. In both works travel takes on metaphorical meanings, especially as an intellectual quest beyond an accustomed cultural environment intended to stretch one's cognitive boundaries. Underlying both works as well is the implicit effort, shared by many postmodern writers, to move outside the domain of European culture.

Donna di Porto Pim e altre storie (Woman of Porto Pim and Other Stories, 1983) is a collection of travel accounts and short stories set in the Azores. Tabucchi often refers to bigger and more important books of travel to the Azores and elsewhere, such as René Chateaubriand's *Les Natchez* (1826), which, says the author, "mi affascinò, prese per mano la mia immaginazione e la trascinò con prepotenza fra le quinte dell'avventura" (fascinated me, took my imagination by the hand and led it forcefully on the wings of adventure). The composite nature of the Tabucchi book is suggested by the piece titled "Antero de Quental. Una vita" (Antero de Quental. A Life), in which a biographical account of the native poet Quental is juxtaposed to a fictional recreation of his suicide in 1891. Tabucchi's conscious duality of visitor-writer is marked by a constant desire to transform travel into a narrative experience.

In "Una caccia" (A Hunting), a story included in the section titled "Di balene e balenieri" (Of Whales and Whale Hunters), Tabucchi offers a chilling account of sperm-whale hunting. He describes the aftermath of the first strike:

> La balena, fischiando, solleva completamente il capo e respira; e il getto che sibila per aria è rosso di sangue, sul mare si allarga una pozza vermiglia e un pulviscolo di gocce rosse, portato dalla brezza, arriva fino a noi e ci sporca il viso e i vestiti.
>
> (The whale, whistling, raises fully the head and breathes; and the jet of water that hisses in the air is red with blood; a red spot on the waters becomes larger while a cluster of tiny red drops, carried by the wind, reaches our boat and it dirties our faces and our clothes.)

A second, much sharper and heart-shaped harpoon is then thrown at the wounded whale:

Questa volta lo strumento di morte cala dall'alto verso il basso, scagliato obliquamente, e trafigge la carne molle come se fosse burro. Un tuffo: la grossa mole sparisce agitandosi sott'acqua. Poi affiora di nuovo la coda, impotente e penosa, come una vela nera. E infine il grosso capo emerge e ora sento il grido di morte, un lamento acuto come un sibilo, stridente, struggente, insostenibile.

(This time the instrument of death falls with a downward motion, thrown obliquely, and it cuts through the soft flesh as though it were butter. A dive: the large frame disappears stirring under the water. Then the tail reappears above water, impotent and painful, like a black sail. Lastly the large head appears, and at this point I hear the outcry of death, a lament as sharp as a hissing, screeching, distressing, unbearable.)

The last story in the collection, "Donna di Porto Pim. Una storia" (Woman of Porto Pim. A Story) is based on a tale told to the writer by an older Azorian man who works in a tavern entertaining tourists with native folk songs. It deals with the relationship between a young fisherman from one of the nearby islands and a somewhat older but attractive woman who comes to the town of Porto Pim as the new owner of a tavern. When the woman asks her lover to sever the relationship because she is expecting another man (as it turns out, a much older man, possibly her father), the islander goes home, fetches a harpoon, and returns to the tavern to kill her. This apparently emancipated woman from the modern world ignored or was unaware that she had entered a different order of society governed by a primitive code of desire, transgression, and retribution.

The second work inspired by Tabucchi's travels is *Notturno indiano* (1984; translated as *Indian Nocturne*, 1988), a short novel structured like a detective story. An Italian writer named Roux seeks out a friend, Xavier Janata Pinto, who has been missing for a year and is believed to be in India. In the course of the search, which takes him from Bombay to Madras to Goa, the reader encounters characters much like a casual tourist comes upon landmarks: they appear unexpectedly, are afforded a glance, and then disappear. An example is the attractive woman who comes from nowhere to reclaim a bundle of stock certificates in the hotel room occupied by the narrator. She and other such characters contribute to the atmosphere of mystery and suspicion.

The exception is a European-trained cardiologist, Dr. Ganesh, a practitioner in the Breach Candy Hospital of Bombay, who engages Roux in a lengthy conversation. In this instructive talk he invites Roux to "forget [his] European notions" because in India they are taken as "an arrogant luxury." Tabucchi presents the reader with the tableau of a visitor from Italy facing an Indian doctor with "a sad smile." The differences that separate the two men, as Roux realizes, are written in the doctor's eyes: "Poi io lo guardai e anche lui mi guardò con un'aria assente da preoccupazioni, come se fosse lí per caso e tutto fosse per caso, perché cosí dovesse essere" (And then I looked at him and he looked at me with a trace of concern on his face, as if he were there by chance and everything else were where it was by chance, because that was how it had to be).

The detective story takes a peculiar turn in its final two chapters. After realizing that Xavier may have changed his name to Mr. Nightingale, Roux recognizes him from a distance at the luxurious Oberoi Hotel in Goa. At this point Tabucchi passes the task of narration from Roux to Xavier-Nightingale, who is having dinner at the Oberoi with an attractive photographer named Christine. Following a Pessoa-like strategy, Tabucchi intimates to the reader that Roux, Xavier, and Nightingale are one person—none other than the writer's (or the narrator's) alter ego. The shell game is revealed when the narrator tells Christine that he is writing a novel in which the main character is lost in India:

"Ma lei chi è? voglio dire nel libro?"
"Questo non viene detto," risposi, "sono uno che non vuole farsi trovare, dunque non fa parte del gioco dire chi è."
"E quello che la cerca e che lei sembra conoscere cosi bene," chiese ancora Christine, "costui la conosce?"
"Una volta mi conosceva, supponiamo che siamo stati grandi amici un tempo. Ma questo succedeva molto tempo fa, fuori della cornice del libro."
"E lui perchè la sta cercando con tanta insistenza?"
"Chi lo sa," dissi io, "è difficile saperlo, questo non lo so neppure io che scrivo. Forse cerca un passato, una risposta a qualcosa. In qualche modo sta cercando se stesso cercando me: nei libri succede spesso cosi, è letteratura."

("But who are you?" asked Christine. "In the book I mean."
"That's never revealed," I answered. "I am someone who doesn't want to be found, so it's not part of the game to say who."
"And the person looking for you who you seem to know so well," Christine asked again, "does he know you?"
"Once he knew me, let's suppose that we were great friends, once. But this was a long time ago, outside the frame of the book."
"And why is he looking for you with such determination?"
"Who knows?" I said. "It's hard to tell, I don't even know that and I am writing the book. Perhaps he is looking for a past, for an answer to something. In a way he is looking for himself. I mean, it's as if he were look-

ing for himself, looking for me: that often happens in books, it's literature.")

Tabucchi's detective game, as he calls it, is a ludic literary exercise with a serious component, for the players in the game are disoriented individuals searching for identity and meaning in a world marked by confusion and anonymity. Viewed in historical perspective, Tabucchi's work, featuring the crisis of the individual in a complex and dehumanizing world, is the reiteration of a pervasive, century-long concern that can be traced to the early part of the century in the works of Italo Svevo, Luigi Pirandello, and Alberto Moravia.

Both *Notturno indiano* and *Donna di Porto Pim* are like travel literature in their emphasis on visual representation, a trait that generally is not found in other works by Tabucchi and that harkens back to postwar Neorealism or even late-nineteenth-century Verismo. Often in *Notturno indiano* Tabucchi draws the reader's attention to the squalor evident in parts of the cities, such as the shacks that house prostitutes and little shops in the Cage District of Bombay. They are "made of ill-fitting boards," and some are "not much larger than sentry boxes." Tabucchi's focus on the inhabitants is equally arresting. While at the hospital Roux accompanies Dr. Ganesh on his round in the hope of finding Xavier among the patients; as he crosses a room "as big as a hangar" with about one hundred patients, his eyes fall on an old man:

> Era completamente nudo e molto magro. Sembrava morto, ma teneva gli occhi spalancati e ci guardò senza nessuna espressione. Aveva un pene enorme che gli stava accartocciato sul ventre. Il medico gli si avvicinò e gli toccò la fronte. Mi parve che gli infilasse una medicina in bocca, ma non capii bene perché stavo ai piedi del giaciglio. "È un *sadhu*," disse il medico, "i suoi organi genitali sono consacrati al dio, una volta era adorato dalle donne sterili, ma non ha mai procreato in vita sua."

(He was completely naked and very thin. He looked dead, but kept his eyes wide open and looked at us without any trace of expression, he had an enormous penis curled up on his abdomen. The doctor went to him and touched his forehead. I thought he slipped a pill into his mouth, but I couldn't be sure because I was standing at the foot of the mattress. "He is a *sadhu*," said the doctor. "His genital organs are consecrated to God; once he was worshiped by infertile women, but he has never procreated in his life.")

The eleven stories that make up *Piccoli equivoci senza importanza* (1985; *Little Misunderstandings of No Importance,* 1988) constitute a high point in Tabucchi's work, for they attest to his full mastery of the short narrative. As the author points out in his introductory note, the stories, as in *Il gioco del rovescio,* are grouped under a general theme indicated by his title: "malintesi, incertezze, comprensioni tardive, inutili rimpianti, ricordi forse ingannevoli, errori sciocchi e irrimediabili" (misunderstandings, uncertainties, belated understandings, useless regrets, potentially deceptive recollections, stupid and irreparable mistakes). The slim volume contains an impressive array of characters, settings, situations, and historical periods, but what lends them unity is not a common theme but Tabucchi's refined mastery of the craft of storytelling coupled with his ambivalent, often negative attitude toward life.

The title story which leads the volume, is steeped in pessimism. Four young people become friends in high school and remain close in college; then they go their separate ways only to experience the chasm between the dreamy expectations of youth and the painful realities of adult life. Tabucchi echoes Pirandello's existential pessimism in his presentation of life as "gioco delle parti"—the notion that one plays a role on the stage of life without ever fully understanding who one is or the ultimate meaning of existence. As one of the characters fatalistically asserts, "Ormai le parti erano assegnate ed era impossibile non recitarle" (By that time, the parts had been assigned and it was impossible not to play them). In the same vein, "Aspettando l'inverno" (Waiting for Winter) deals with the futility of life, death being the act that seals a confused collection of fleeting memories whose real meaning remains elusive. Here life is the road to ultimate oblivion and nothing more.

In the introduction to *Piccoli equivoci senza importanza* Tabucchi points out that the writers of the Baroque period loved *equivoci*—a term that in Italian denotes both misunderstandings and deliberate ambiguity. Although it is less prevalent than in other postmodern writers who manipulate language to suggest a thought process, externalized through writing, marked by ambiguity and indecision, there is a strain of the neo-baroque in Tabucchi's narrative, as when the shy young man in the first story describes his relationship to the attractive Maddalena: "C'era una ragazza dai capelli rossi che si chiamava Maddalena della quale ero innamorato, però ero convinto che fosse innamorata del Leo, o meglio, lo sapevo che era innamorata di me, pero avevo paura che fosse innamorata del Leo" (There was a red-head named Maddalena with whom I was in love, but I was convinced she loved Leo, rather, I knew she loved

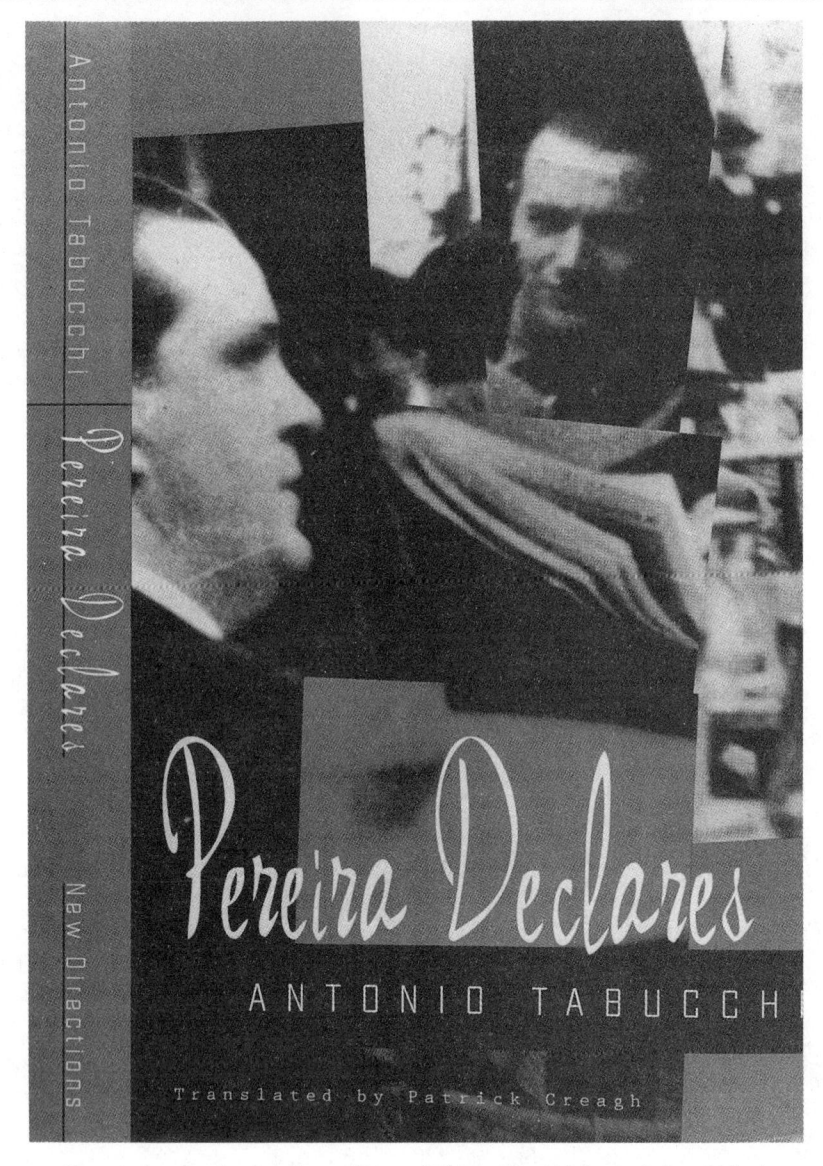

Dust jacket for the American edition of Tabucchi's 1994 novel, in which the protagonist takes a stand against dictatorship in Portugal

me, but I was afraid that she might be in love with Leo). In the English-titled "Anywhere out of the World" the relationship between a man and a woman is expressed in these terms: "Ma lui non se lo meritava. Certo. E anche lei sapeva che lui non se lo meritava. Anche questo è certo. E tu sapevi che lei sapeva che lui non se lo meritava, ma non te ne importò" (But he didn't deserve it. Of course. And she knew he didn't deserve it. True. And you knew that she knew he didn't deserve it, but you didn't care.) Against a background of gray landscapes faceless characters, abulic and disoriented, interact with similarly disposed individuals lacking convictions, indeed devoid of faith in anything. From a philosophical standpoint the blurring of semantic meaning is tantamount to the blurring of certainty and absolutes in nearly every form of intellectual expression and moral consciousness.

Il filo dell'orizzonte (1986; translated as *The Edge of the Horizon,* 1990) is a short detective story that unfolds in an eerie atmosphere of unreality. There are several allusions to films, including *The Battleship Potemkin* (1925) and *Strictly Confidential* (1934), and to actors such as Humphrey Bogart and Myrna Loy. Cinema references are woven into the fabric of the narrative to the point that the main character, Spino, imagines that he is actually in a movie: "Per un attimo gli è parso che anche lui stesse vivendo la scena di un film" (For an instant, he too felt he was living the scene in a film).

The plot of the story is easily outlined. A young man is killed in a downtown apartment during an exchange of fire between the police and several gunmen thought to be terrorists or drug dealers. The body is taken to the city morgue, where the attendant, Spino, having noticed that the victim carries no papers, sets out to ascertain his identity, spurred in part by a friend who is a local reporter. The long search takes him to a tailor, to the city cemetery, to an import-export office, and to a night club—all to no avail. All he is able to discover is that the young man's name was Carlo Nobodi, a name contrived to emphasize the lack of an identity.

If the story is read symbolically, the search for identity leads, ironically, to a person who is nobody. Tabucchi thus carries the theme of *Notturno indiano* a step further in *Il filo dell'orizzonte*. Spino's fruitless efforts suggest that one can find self-definition only in relation to what can be empirically known. Therein lies the existential problem, for Spino—who, Tabucchi asserts in a prefatory note, is short for Spinoza—recognizes that there is purpose and meaning in life but believes that the misguided self prevents one from finding a nexus between two objects, much less between one individual and another. Tabucchi seems to echo Moravia's existential outlook when he describes Spino's epiphany:

[Spino] ha pensato alla forza che hanno le cose di tornare a quanto di noi stessi vediamo negli altri.... E ha pensato che c'è un ordine delle cose e che niente succede per caso; e il caso è proprio questo: la nostra impossibilità di cogliere i veri nessi delle cose che sono, e ha sentito la volgarità e la superbia con cui uniamo le cose che ci circondano.

(He thought of the power things have to come back to us and of how much of ourselves we see in others.... And he thought that things do follow an order and nothing happens by chance, that chance in fact is just this: our incapacity to grasp the true connections between things. And he sensed the vulgarity and the arrogance with which we link the objects that surround us.)

The edge of the horizon, the invisible line that joins the physical and ethereal worlds, suggests transcendence, the ability to find meaning and purpose. In his postscript Tabucchi writes: "Il filo dell'orizzonte è un luogo geometrico, perché si sposta mentre noi ci spostiamo" (The horizon is a geometrical location since it moves as we move). What the novelist perhaps is saying here is that the meaning one finds in living does not depend on a fixed perspective or an outside source but instead depends on one's abllility to look within with discernment. Tabucchi asserts that the actual Spinoza "era sefardita, e come molti della sua gente il filo dell'orizzonte se lo portava dentro gli occhi" (was a Sephardic Jew, and like many of his people carried the horizon with him in his eyes).

While the middle-aged Spino does learn more about himself in his search for another man's identity, he ultimately has limited success. His age and exhaustion may well have hindered from solving the riddle of Carlo Nobodi's identity:

Lui ha sentito una stanchezza opprimente come se gli pesasse sulle spalle la stanchezza di tutto ciò che lo circondava, è uscito nel cortile e ha sentito che anche il cortile era stanco e le mura di quel vecchio ospedale erano stanche, e anche le finestre, e la città e tutto; ha guardato in alto e gli è parso che anche le stelle fossero stanche, e ha desiderato che ci fosse un'eccezione per tutto ciò che è, come un differimento o una dimenticanza.

(He felt an oppressive tiredness, as though the tiredness of everything around him were bearing down on his shoulders. He went outside and sensed that even the courtyard was tired, and the walls were tired, the windows, and the city, and everything. He looked up and had the impression that even the stars were tired, and he wished there were an exception for this condition, like a postponement or forgetfulness.)

His search for meaning and identity is halted by "an oppressive tiredness"—the weariness of mind and spirit whose objective correlative is found in the dreary atmosphere of the decrepit city.

Tabucchi wrote *Requiem, uma alucinação* (1991; translated as *Requiem: A Hallucination,* 1994) in Portuguese; it was translated into Italian as *Requiem: un'allucinazione* (1992) by Sergio Vecchio. In his 1995 interview with Paola Gaglianone, Tabucchi explained his decision not to translate the work himself: "Ho provato a tradurre *Requiem* in italiano io stesso, ma non ci sono riuscito perchè mi sono reso conto che inevitabilmente scrivevo un altro libro" (I tried to translate *Requiem* into Italian myself, but I could not do it because I realized that unavoidably I was writing a different book). The title is partly explained by the remark made by a character named Vecchia Zingara (Old Gypsy): "Non si può vivere da due parti, dalla parte della realtà e dalla parte del sogno. Cosí ti vengono le allucinazioni" (One cannot live on two sides, on the side of reality and on the side of daydreaming. Doing so one develops hallucinations). While there is a realistic dimension in this work, the line of demarcation between reality and fantasy more often than not collapses on the side of the imaginary, the surreal, and the subconscious.

In a sense *Sostiene Pereira. Una testimonianza* (1994; translated as *Pereira Declares. A True Account,* 1995) marks Tabucchi's return to his starting point as a novelist though this is not to discount the maturity and the mastery of the craft he accrued in the interim. After experimenting for twenty years with various narrative forms, including the detective novel and travel literature, and probing the possibilities offered by the subconscious, dreams, multiple perspectives, and the splintering of the self, Tabucchi returns to a narrative with linear development, a well-defined protagonist, and well-developed minor characters. No less important, Tabucchi again explores history and ideology, his main concerns in *Piazza d'Italia*.

The story is set in and around Lisbon in the summer of 1938; the strongman Antonio de Oliveira Salazar rules Portugal while Spain is in the throes of a bloody civil war that will see the rise to power of a second dictator, Francisco Franco. The protagonist, Pereira, is the lonesome director of the cultural section of one of the afternoon dailies in Lisbon. At the start of the novel he is mourning the passing of his wife and is thus absorbed by the thought of death and the afterlife. His emotional state is hardly alleviated by his work, which in part entails preparing the obituaries for writers who are yet living. When Pereira hires a young man named Monteiro Rossi to write obituaries on a freelance basis, the ideological tinge of his submissions to Pereira leave no doubt about his opposition to the Salazar regime. But rather than firing the young man, Pereira is drawn to his idealism even when he realizes that Monteiro, helped by his cousin and his girlfriend, Marta, is involved in underground activities. Caught falsifying passports, Monteiro manages to find cover in Pereira's apartment. Hours later, three men posing as members of the "political police" break into the apartment, submit him to questioning, and torture him to death. Horrified, Pereira chooses one of the passports he finds in Monteiro's briefcase and takes the first train to exile in France. Before he leaves, however, he writes an account of Monteiro's death together with a caustic indictment of Salazar's dictatorship, which he arranges to have published in the next issue of his paper.

The immediate and substantial success of *Sostiene Pereira* in Italy and abroad is due in large part to its structural leanness, for it has none of the digressions, superfluities, and circuitous pathways of such works as *Il filo dell'orizzonte*, *Piccoli equivoci senza importanza*, and *Notturno indiano*. The narrative, carried largely by dialogue, moves forward smoothly and at an unrelenting pace. In the interview with Gaglianone, Tabucchi calls *Sostiene Pereira* "un romanzo estremamente dialogato, che sembra quasi un testo teatrale o una sceneggiatura cinematografica" (a novel with profuse dialogue which resembles a play or a movie script).

In part the success of this novel in Italy is also due to the resonance of Portugal's history. Italians, especially of the older generations, could read the novel as a transposed image of their own country's experience with Fascism. Tabucchi explicitly links the two countries in Monteiro's introduction of himself to Pereira:

L'anno scorso è morto mio padre, che era italiano e che lavorava come navale nei bacini del porto di Lisbona, mi ha lasciato qualcosa, ma questo qualcosa è già finito, ho ancora una nonna che vive in Italia, ma non la vedo da quando avevo dodici anni, e non ho voglia di andare in Italia, mi pare che la situazione sia ancora peggio della nostra, di morire sono stufo, dottor Pereira, scusi se sono franco con lei.

(Last year my father died; he was Italian and worked as a naval engineer on the docks of Lisbon's harbor. He left me something, but it is gone now; I also have a grandmother who lives in Italy, but I have no desire to travel to Italy because apparently the situation over there is worse than ours. I am tired of death, Mr. Pereira, forgive me if I am honest with you.)

Indeed, death permeates the novel from the first to the last page, for a despotic regime such as Salazar's feeds on death and the acquiescent silence it brings. Pereira, a sickly elderly man contemplating his own death after he loses his wife, is gradually transformed by the idealism and unselfishness of two young people, Monteiro and Marta. It is Monteiro's death that leads Pereira to oppose Fascism and to discover a new order of values.

La testa perduta di Damasceno Monteiro (The Missing Head of Damasceno Monteiro, 1997) is an unusual detective story for Tabucchi in that the perpetrator of the crime is arrested, tried, and convicted, though on a lesser charge. At the end of the novel the attorney representing the victim is seeking a retrial of the case. The setting is contemporary Portugal, a late member of the European Union and a newcomer to the race for prosperity and material well being. Tabucchi depicts a society in which all social classes seek wealth through various means, legitimate and otherwise.

The main action occurs in Oporto, Portugal's second-largest city, where a young reporter for one of the newspapers in Lisbon comes to cover the story. He is befriended by Don Fernando Mello Sequeira, a tall and obese lawyer known in the city as Loton because he a bears a resemblance to the British actor Charles Laughton. Sequeira is the dominant figure of the book, a compassionate man as conversant in history, philosophy, and literature as he is in jurisprudence. As the descendant of Oporto's aristocracy, he is a man of the past, the kindly exponent of a moribund social class historically unresponsive to the needs of their subordinates yet refined, highly cultured, and, more important, discerning enough to recognize and adapt to social changes. However, the felicitous portrait of Sequeira is not enough to raise this novel to the level of *Sostiene Pereira*.

With *Sostiene Pereira* Tabucchi came full circle in his writing, and *La testa perduta di Damasceno Monteiro* continues in this more traditional vein. Given the path described by Tabucchi's career, it is impossible to predict what direction his narrative will take in the future. What one can say with a reasonable degree of certainty is that Tabucchi likely will be regarded as the most original Italian writer at the turn of the century.

Interviews:

Joseph Francese, "Tabucchi: una conversazione plurivoca," *Spunti e ricerche*, 6 (1990): 19–34;

Andrea Borsari, "Cos'è una vita se non viene raccontata? Conversazione con Antonio Tabucchi," *Italiensche-Zeitschrift für Italienische Sparache und Literatur* (November 1991): 2–23;

El siglo XX, balance y perspectivas; seguido de La novela, el problema: una conversación con Antonio Tabucchi (Las Palmas: Viceconsejería de Cultura y Deportes, Gobierno de Canarias, 1991);

Paola Gaglianone, "Conversazione con Antonio Tabucchi," in *Dove va il romanzo?*, edited by Gaglianone and Marco Cassini (Rome: Omicron, 1995): 5–34.

References:

Gian Paolo Biasin, *Le periferie della letteratura. Da Verga a Tabucchi* (Ravenna: Longo, 1997), pp. 139–146;

Joseph Francese, "L'eteronimia di Antonio Tabucchi," *Stanford Italian Review*, 11 (1992): 123–138;

Francese, *Narrating Postmodern Time and Space* (Albany: State University of New York Press, 1997), pp. 138–154;

Francese, "The Postmodern Discourses of Doctorow's *Billy Bathgate* and Tabucchi's *Dialoghi mancati*," *Annali d'italianistica*, 9 (1991): 182–197;

Riccardo Scrivano, "L'orizzonte narrativo di Antonio Tabucchi," in *Dove va il romanzo?*, edited by Paola Gaglianone and Marco Cassini (Rome: Omicron, 1995), pp. 35–52;

Stefano Tani, "Il filo del silenzio," *Il Ponte*, 43, no. 6 (1987): 174–177;

Tani, *Il romanzo di ritorno. Dal romanzo medio degli anni sessanta alla giovane narrativa degli anni ottanta* (Milan: Mursia, 1990), pp. 154–163.

Pier Vittorio Tondelli
(14 September 1955 – 16 January 1991)

Christopher Concolino
San Francisco State University

BOOKS: *Altri libertini* (Milan: Feltrinelli, 1980);
Pao Pao (Milan: Feltrinelli, 1982);
Rimini (Milan: Bompiani, 1985);
Biglietti agli Amici (Bologna: Baskerville, 1986);
Camere separate (Milan: Bompiani, 1989); translated by Simon Pleasance as *Separate Rooms* (London & New York: Serpent's Tail, 1992);
Un weekend postmoderno: Cronache dagli anni ottanta (Milan: Bompiani, 1990);
L'abbandono: racconti dagli anni ottanta, edited by Fulvio Panzeri (Milan: Bompiani, 1993);
Dinner Party, edited by Panzeri (Milan: Bompiani, 1994).

MOTION PICTURE: *Sabato italiano,* treatment by Tondelli and Luciano Mannuzzi, Numero Uno Cinematografica, 1992.

PLAY PRODUCTION: *La notte della vittoria,* Cesano Boscone, La Monaca Auditorium, 25 January 1986; revised as *Dinner Party,* Rome, Sala Umberto, 1991.

OTHER: *Giovani Blues: Under 25 I,* edited, with an introduction, by Tondelli (Ancona: Il lavoro editoriale, 1986);
Belli e perversi: Under 25 II, edited, with an afterward, by Tondelli (Ancona: Transeuropa, 1987);
Gianni De Martino, *Hotel Oasis,* edited by Tondelli, Mouse to Mouse series (Milan: Mondadori, 1988);
Elisabetta Valentini, *Fotomodella,* edited by Tondelli, Mouse to Mouse series (Milan: Mondadori, 1988);
"L'Influence de Kerouac sur la littérature italienne des années quatre-vingt," in *Un Homme grand: Jack Kerouac à la confluence des cultures,* edited by Pierre Anctil, Louis Dupont, Remi Ferland, and Eric Waddell. (Ottawa: Carleton University Press, 1990), pp. 217–222;
Papergang: Under 25 III, edited by Tondelli (Ancona: Transeuropa, 1990).

Pier Vittorio Tondelli (photograph by Giovanni Giovannetti)

Pier Vittorio Tondelli's writings mirror many of the changes that occurred in Italian popular culture, particularly among the young, during the 1970s and 1980s. The protagonists of his four novels belong to Tondelli's generation, which came of age in the 1970s. Showing a commitment to realism Tondelli, in his first two novels, mimics the spoken language of the young as he presents the cultural milieus of Italy's exuberant counterculture in great detail. His realistic depiction of society is tempered in his last two novels, which tend more toward psychological introspection.

In his works Tondelli often organizes his narratives according to the conventions of journalistic travel literature, but he may also unite the traits of two or more distinct literary genres, an intermingling that is a salient feature of his writing. For example, in *Rimini* (1985), Tondelli's third book, aspects of the psychological novel coexist with a plot usually associated with detective fiction. Although in the posthumous collection *L'abbandono: racconti dagli anni ottanta* (Departure: Stories From the Eighties, 1993), he describes his works as "materiale più o meno autobiografico" (more or less autobiographical material), Tondelli was not a confessional writer. Reserved and retiring by nature, he disclosed little about his own life directly.

A homosexual, Tondelli wrote of both homosexual and heterosexual love, especially in the context of youthful experimentation. One of his key contributions as a writer, though, is his treatment of homosexuality in his novels. While literature on such subjects has been written primarily in the United States, Tondelli's fiction adds to a growing body of homosexual literature in Italian, which has increased in size since the liberalization of social attitudes toward homosexuality at the end of the 1960s and has experienced a significant growth in the 1980s. This literature encompasses fiction on AIDS but also addresses themes that predate the AIDS crisis and raises issues that are unrelated to questions of mortality.

The corpus of Tondelli's narrative can perhaps best be likened to a bildungsroman, for his novels show how youthful experience gives way to maturity. In his first novels Tondelli depicts his generation's search for experience and identity; his later novels represent the attempts of young adults to come to terms with the inherent limitations on human life—irreversible change, emotional unfulfillment, and death—that one must confront in order to reach maturity. Each novel has different characters, so one cannot point to the development of a single character's life over the course of all four books, but because each protagonist is older than the one in the novel preceding it, what results is nonetheless a chronological sequence of development.

Tondelli was born in Correggio, near Reggio Emilia, on 14 September 1955. One of many small communities spread across the intensely cultivated Po River valley, Correggio exemplifies the kind of close-knit social fabric typical of life in small town Italy. Its solid provincial customs and the agrarian traditions of its hinterland undoubtedly influenced Tondelli's largely uneventful and happy childhood.

Later, recalling fond memories of these traditions in his essay "Un racconto sul vino" (A Tale About Wine) collected in *L'abbandono,* Tondelli recounts wistfully how his parents had abandoned most of the agrarian traditions to which they and many of their generation had been born. Brenno Tondelli, a shopkeeper, and his wife, Marta, who assumed the traditional responsibilities of domestic family life, raised their sons Giulio and Pier Vittorio at the center of Correggio. Tondelli writes that he spent his childhood as an urban dweller: "nato in paese, praticamente in piazza, e cresciuto in un cinema" (born in town, practically in the town square, and raised in a cinema). He and Giulio, two years older, grew up in "un modesto appartamento al sesto piano di un grigio, brutto palazzo," (a modest apartment on the sixth floor of an ugly gray building).

Tondelli studied Latin and Greek classics in secondary school, from which he graduated in 1974, and then went on to study at the University of Bologna from 1975 to 1979. There, in the wake of pan-European countercultural movements at the end of the 1960s, Tondelli came directly into contact with the popular culture spawned by the ideologies of social protest. He enrolled in the Department of Dance, Art, Music and Theater, where he studied American literature under Gianni Celati, semiotics under Umberto Eco, and wrote a thesis titled "Il romanzo epistolare come problema di teoria del romanzo" (The Epistolary Novel as a Problem in the Theory of the Novel).

Emblematic of Tondelli's interest in popular culture as an object of literary study is the term paper "La cultura del vino" (The Culture of Wine) that Tondelli submitted to Umberto Eco at the end of his course in semiotics during the 1976-1977 academic year. Dense with literary and historical references, the paper nonetheless failed to meet the eminent professor's highest standards of intellectual rigor—even though Eco reportedly initiated a lively series of questions about a bibliographical reference in the paper to Raymond Chandler, the American writer of hard-boiled detective novels. At least a decade later, Tondelli's interests in drink and literature had remained constant. According to a friend, during his first trip to New York, Tondelli searched Manhattan for the perfect "martini cocktail," of which he had knowledge only through literary sources.

The style, characters, and settings in Tondelli's first book, *Altri libertini* (Other Libertines, 1980), were influenced by the works of Henry Miller, Jack Kerouac, and Louis-Ferdinand Céline. Miller's groundbreaking candor in portraying sexual behavior and his use of a lexicon traditionally considered vulgar or obscene in order to disarm the rhetorical authority of literary language at the same time that he intensified its expressive potential are historical antecedents whose importance cannot be underestimated. Like Miller's work, *Altri libertini* was charged with obscenity upon publication and confiscated though Tondelli was later absolved of the charges.

Although Tondelli always acknowledged his indebtedness to Miller's works and his admiration for Kerouac, *Altri libertini* does not in any way represent the transposition of American literary themes onto an Italian reality, since Tondelli identified other influences that contributed to his literary education. These influences included other foreign authors such as Christopher Isherwood and W. H. Auden but also range from sources as diverse as the cinema (for the most part American and European movies from the 1970s and 1980s) and the lyrics of rock-and-roll songs to experimental theater, contemporary painting, and comic book art.

In addition to foreign influences Tondelli also read and admired Italian writers such as Giovanni Testori, Alberto Arbasino, and Carlo Coccioli. *Altri libertini* may be seen as continuing the work of these three writers: Testori's portrayals of Milan's working-class suburbs and his experiments with dialect and colloquial language; Arbasino's use of catalogue-like lists to describe settings; and Coccioli's treatment of homosexual themes in his fiction. But despite such influences and precedents *Altri libertini* is an original creation. Its language reproduces Italian slang from the 1970s and is attuned to reflect both the physical conditions and the cultural niche of the speaker.

The heterogenous nature of Tondelli's interests, though, ultimately confirmed his strong attachment to his native culture, a point he makes in *L'abbandono:*

> È occorso del tempo per capire, dentro di me, che pur essendo figlio di una più vasta cultura occidentale, pur essendo un inguaribile estimatore di musica pop e rock, pur essendo un consumatore di cinema americano e di letteratura della beat generation, sono anche profondamente emiliano.

> (In spite of being a child of a larger Western culture, an incurable fan of pop and rock music and a consumer of American films and beat generation literature, it has taken me time to understand deep down inside that I am also profoundly Emilian.)

His interest in the contemporary cultural world at large, coupled with a strong sense of his own cultural origins, make Tondelli one of the keenest observers of popular culture among Italian writers of his generation.

At the center of *Altri libertini,* a collection of six loosely connected chapters that can also be read as separate stories, is the honest and unapologetic depiction of various homosexual subcultures. "Postoristoro" (Snack Bar), the first chapter, is set in the train station in Reggio Emilia, a city which, like other cities in *Altri libertini* such as Bologna, Modena, and Milano, is along the Po River valley's Via Emilia. As in all of his fiction, Tondelli in his initial chapter—with its vivid depiction of addicts and drug peddlers, alcoholics and prostitutes, the urban indigent and the less important gang members of local organized crime—writes about a reality with which he was personally familiar.

Other parts of Tondelli's reality are represented in the subsequent chapters. The second chapter, "Mimi e istrioni" (Mimes and Actors), features four sexually liberated members of a communal household. Filled with culturally naive aspirations, they participate in activities organized by a cultural cooperative and those of an independent radio station. Distanced by comic irony, the escapades of the four embody the kind of sexual experimentation and search for self-definition that typify the youthful mind. These same themes are further developed in the third chapter, "Viaggio" (Travel), where the reader follows teenage hitchhikers across northern Europe and around Italy as they enroll in university studies, find employment, and seek emotional as well as sexual intimacy with kindred spirits. Kerouac's celebration of transcontinental automobile travel, the exhilaration of speed, and new sensory experiences are reflected as a conscious imitative choice in chapters four and six of *Altri libertini:* "Senso contrario" (Wrong Way) and "Autobahn" (Superhighway). In chapter five, which provides the book with its title, Tondelli recounts the comical sexual misadventures of a group of university students during the Christmas holidays.

After he completed his university studies, Tondelli lived in Bologna with his friend Mauro Rotini. He was inducted into the army at the age of twenty-four and completed his one year of military service in Orvieto and Rome, an experience that informed his second novel, *Pao Pao* (1982). In the early 1980s he began traveling regularly throughout Eastern Europe, Great Britain, the Mediterranean countries, and North Africa. Evidence of his travels appears everywhere in his fiction; and it is present in his journalistic and travel writing, where his attraction to cross-cultural movements led him to write about such ephemeral sociological phenomena as the "skinhead" and "new romantic" fashions in

Cover for the 1996 edition of Tondelli's 1982 novel, an account of a draftee's military experiences

London during the 1980s. In particular, the years between the end of Tondelli's university studies and his move to Milan in 1985 were devoted to fairly frequent travel. He got to know Berlin, London, Amsterdam, and Barcelona, and he deepened his familiarity with Paris.

During the same period, Tondelli was also increasingly attracted to the popular music, night life, theater, and figurative arts then associated with the artistic community in Florence. At the time, Tondelli was working as a freelance journalist, although he didn't earn enough to support himself. He accepted hospitality in the homes of friends and acquaintances—often at a different address each night—and he was aided by the occasional financial support of a patron seeking to encourage budding literary talent. But in spite of these difficulties, Tondelli was eventually able to establish an address in Florence, where he lived intermittently for about two years, from the time he was twenty-seven. In fact, Tondelli's Florentine circle of friends is the basis for the Florentine characters and settings later found in *Rimini*, while many of his excursions throughout Europe are presented in fictionalized form in *Camere separate* (1989; translated as *Separate Rooms*, 1992).

Many of the same linguistic and stylistic traits found in *Altri libertini* are also evident in *Pao Pao*, a repetition of the abbreviation for *picchetto armato ordinario* (ordinary armed troop). Unlike *Altri libertini*, this novel follows the same first-person narrator from beginning to end and recounts a draftee's year of military service. In addition to style *Pao Pao* is quite similar to *Altri libertini* in its emphasis on new experiences and the exploration of sex. As in his first book, Tondelli bases his fiction on his own experiences and presents events at a frenzied pace—piling up rather than unfolding—to express the intensity of youthful consciousness.

Tondelli's principal means of support was provided by his career as a journalist, which necessitated his move in April 1985 to Milan, where he shared an apartment until the end of his life with Rotini. Journalism also provided raw material for the novel *Rimini*, in which the protagonist, Marco Bauer, is assigned to cover a seaside resort city as a special correspondent.

With a sale of one hundred thousand copies soon after publication, *Rimini* was Tondelli's largest commercial success. However, it failed to impress Italian critics such as Oreste Del Buono, who saw it as a "romanzo di consumo" (light reading produced for the mass market). This characterization is doubtless due to the mystery of Attilio Lughi's murder that forms the backbone of the novel. Stefano Tani has pointed out in this regard that Tondelli's two characters Marco Bauer and Bruno May constitute latter-day renditions of Chandler's detective Philip Marlowe and the blocked writer Roger Wade, who appeared in *The Long Goodbye* (1954). Since Tondelli also alludes to other Chandler novels, from *Farewell, My Lovely* (1940) to *Playback* (1958), *Rimini* is certainly in part a literary homage to Chandler's hard-boiled detective fiction.

A multifaceted work, *Rimini* presents various interwoven subplots, some of which mimic elements of the modern romance novel. The account of the ill-fated homosexual liaison between the novelist Bruno May and the young English artist Aelred is representative in this sense because Bruno's affairs of the heart are experienced as existential crises while, in contrast, Marco's less sentimental heterosexual encounters are depicted in indulgently graphic terms. Other subplots, such as Renato's story and that of his parents' family-run hotel, serve to provide a sketch of the tourist industry and its growth along the Italian Adriatic since the 1960s. From this point of view, Renato offers a glimpse of Rimini's seasonal economy from within, while journalist Marco provides an external look at the texture of life put on display by mass-marketed tourism.

A unique suburban sprawl, Tondelli's Rimini is a kind of way station crisscrossed by an international clientele who are beset by the diverse concerns that define the late twentieth century. These concerns include the drug abuse that affects Claudia, the teenage sister of a German antiquarian; Renato's desperate and irrational act of urban terrorism; and Robby and Tony's successful struggle in realizing their lifelong dream of producing an independent film. Enlarging the panorama of flawed urban leisure is the story of Alberto, the lonely nightclub saxophonist. His brief trysts with a married woman add texture to Tondelli's picture of private life in the city. News releases reporting predictions of the end of the world heighten the narrative tension.

Unlike the linguistic experiments present in the first two novels, the language in *Rimini* is much closer to standard Italian prose because Tondelli employs an omniscient third-person narrative voice (used extensively for the first time), which he deploys as an alternate register to his habitual first-person narrators. These two narrative voices mimic the conventional realism often associated with commercially successful fiction. Tondelli offers an ambivalent and therefore critical depiction of popular culture. On the one hand, Marco is surrounded by the middle-class lifestyle of the average vacationer at an Adriatic beach resort—the bars, restaurants, sports events, discotheques, hotels, amusement parks, and nightclubs—and to the extent that he is immersed in that culture he signifies a celebration of it as well. On the other hand, Marco's professional status as a journalist means that he is responsible for the interpretation, manipulation, and transmission of that culture to the public.

The outcome of the investigation into Lughi's murder is ultimately ambiguous and disquieting. With an ironic twist, Tondelli moves his novel beyond the rigid conventions of the murder mystery genre. The events at the end of *Rimini* lead Marco to question the accuracy and sources of all the information he has received and to realize that he has little control over the public's interpretation of what it reads in his newspaper. Because of these considerations, *Rimini* is a work that questions the function of writers and writing in relation to popular culture. Working with the director Luciano Mannuzzi, Tondelli hoped to make *Rimini* into a film; but this project was never realized. Instead, he collaborated with Mannuzzi on an original story for the latter's film *Sabato italiano* (Italian Saturday), released in 1992.

When *Rimini* was published in 1985, Tondelli had also completed a play, *La notte della vittoria* (Victory Night), later revised as *Dinner Party* and published posthumously in 1994. The play was written at the beginning of 1984 as an entry for the 1985 Riccione-Ater Prize for Theater, which it won. A two-act black comedy, Tondelli referred to *La notte della vittoria* as a "commedia borghese di conversazione" (bourgeois conversation play). It depicts the frivolous and consumer-oriented lifestyles of jet-setting urban professionals in the 1980s: an alcoholic author with writer's block, his lawyer brother and sister-in-law, a commercially successful painter, and a fashion journalist. Tondelli knew this social milieu well, and the first act's repartee mimics its language and mannerisms. The second act, in which there are sudden revelations about the characters' pasts, aims at unmasking their hypocrisy, which is represented by the infidelity and lack of love in the lawyer's bourgeois marriage and by his own homosexuality, which he keeps secret. The lawyer's duplicity is also implicitly compared to a character who is revealed to be a male transvestite. The latter, brutally unmasked and attacked, is far less hypocritical than his attackers.

The writer's purpose and responsibility within a social context were issues that Tondelli addressed personally during the 1980s, when he accepted editorial responsibility for two initiatives: an anthology series titled *Under 25 I* (1986), consisting of new fiction by unpublished young writers; and *Mouse to Mouse* (1988), fiction by emerging writers concerned with extra-literary cultural fields, such as fashion and advertising, theater, rock music, and the figurative arts. *Under 25* eventually appeared in three volumes, while *Mouse to Mouse* brought forth only two books, *Hotel Oasis* (1988) and *Fotomodella* (1988). These initiatives attest to Tondelli's interest in the youth culture as a wellspring of new literary stimuli and his perception of literature as an integral part of the larger framework of popular culture.

Tondelli sought contacts with the generation that followed his own, and he sought to observe and stimulate its cultural grassroots. He published regular articles in the magazine *Linus*, which he considered one of the few magazines in Italy that addressed adequately the needs of a young readership. He also wrote a monthly column titled "Culture Club" for the magazine *Rockstar*, in which he responded to the readers' interests.

As a thematic and a structural component, travel is an important part of *Biglietti agli Amici* (Notes to Friends, 1986), published in a limited printing originally intended only for close friends. Slim enough to be called a pamphlet, this short work meant a great deal to Tondelli. It is divided into twenty-four sections, corresponding to the hours of the day (each one further identified by a representative angel and astrological sign), and the short and somewhat cryptic notes are addressed to an equal number of friends. Many of the short texts cite or make explicit reference to some of Tondelli's favorite prose and poetry; they range from Ingeborg Bachmann's *The Thirtieth Year* (1961), G. K. Chesterton's early detective stories and Alfred de Vigny's *Servitude et Grandeur Militaires* (Military Service and Grandeur, 1835) to lyrics from North American and British rock songs, such as Joe Jackson's "Big World," Leonard Cohen's "Love and Hate," and The Smith's "The Queen is Dead."

In "Nota Numero Uno" (Note Number One) travel is recognized as the ordering principle not just of *Biglietti agli Amici* as a text but more generally of the self's relationship to the outside world and to one's livelihood, which for Tondelli was the act of writing:

> In treno, dopo Amiens, quando la nebbia e i grigi lo riportano alla stagione d'autunno, e al freddo, si chiede perché sta fuggendo. Lui lo sa. Ma sono ragioni che all'esterno appaiono esili e misteriose, mentre per Lui sono totali e assolute. Va a Londra–sa–perché deve ritrovare la sua terza persona, un fantasma che deve incontrare per continuare a scrivere. Va a Londra per incontrarsi con il suo libro.

> (On the train, after Amiens, when the fog and the greyness bring him back to the season of autumn, and to the cold, he wonders why he is fleeing. He knows. But they are reasons that seem trivial and mysterious from the outside, while for Him they are total and absolute. He is going to London–he knows–because he must find his third person, a ghost that he must meet to continue writing. He is going to London to meet his book.)

The narrative voice is ostensibly directed towards the friends it addresses, but it also reflects on past personal, professional, and amorous experiences.

While some of the notes are musings over creative decisions made during the writing of Tondelli's previously published fiction, others invoke the concept of "fading" that Roland Barthes introduced in his *Fragments d'un discours amoureux* (1977; translated as *A Lover's Discourse: Fragments*, 1978). This notion is explicitly mentioned in the eighteenth note and refers to the waning of emotional intensity within a couple. In reference to the relationship between friends, Tondelli's borrowing of Barthes' notion is certainly not without meaning, but fading acquires a particular poignancy when it indicates the death of one's partner, as it does in "Nota Numero Ventiuno" (Note Number Twenty-One). Hence fading comes to indicate a progressive sequence leading from a state of withdrawal to one of absence and, eventually, to death. For these reasons, *Biglietti agli Amici* can be considered a stylized and formal codification of Tondelli's thoughts about the death of one's partner, and how these thoughts affected him while traveling. Tondelli's travel notes were included in *Un weekend postmoderno: Cronache dagli anni ottanta* (A Postmodern Weekend: Reports from the Eighties, 1990).

Those who knew Tondelli consistently characterize him as kind, shy, and withdrawn, almost to the point that he may have appeared aloof. This description is clearly at odds with the aggressive vitality displayed by the narrative voices in all of Tondelli's novels except his last, *Camere separate* (Separate Rooms). In this novel Tondelli explores further the themes of emotional intimacy and the definition of self in relation to a lover. Organized according to flashbacks that portray the depth and nature of the love between Leo and Thomas, the novel examines Leo's sensibilities before he had met Thomas and his state of mind following Thomas's death at the age of twenty-five from an unnamed disease. This event, especially when considered in the light of the novel's last page, where Leo alludes to his own future death, suggests that the disease is AIDS, which devastated much of the international homosexual community during the 1980s. The wider significance of the story is further emphasized by its international settings, which span Europe and North America. Thomas's death, then, raises issues pertinent not only to the protagonist Leo/Tondelli but also to homosexual identity in the age of AIDS, especially the redefinition of individual identity when faced with the loss of a partner and the necessity of finding meaning in life when confronted with the danger of imminent death.

The novel also deals with themes that are unrelated to mortality, such as the conflict between Thomas and Leo in regard to a desirable domestic arrangement. Leo rejects cohabitation and marriage as models for his homosexuality—a point of view reflected in the title of the novel. The title may also be taken to indicate a homosexual's permanent state of psychological separation from heterosexuality, since homosexual identity often results in estrangement from a biological family. Homosexuality precludes the future survival of one's own biological heredity and, in another sense, denies the biological future of a hypothetical mate of the opposite sex; hence Tondelli's homosexual couples live in "camere separate" in a biological sense as well.

The separation from the family raises the question of the meaning of homosexuality within the social context. If homosexuality is more than just a question of sexual identity or orientation, as Tondelli implies, then homosexuals comprise a recognizable group within society. However, Leo in *Camere separate* explicitly realizes that his definition of self and that of others like him is an identity denied a social status according to familial, ecclesiastic, and legal definitions. Faced with his lover's impending death, Leo feels excluded from and unrecognized by Thomas's family, since it has no place for him as a family member nor a name for him as a relative:

> Leo capisce che deve andarsene. Thomas è restituito, nel momento finale, alla famiglia, alle stesse persone che l'hanno fatto nascere e che ora, con il cuore devastato dalla sofferenza, stanno cercando di aiutarlo a morire. Non c'è posto per lui in questa ricomposizione parentale. Lui non ha sposato Thomas, non ha avuto figli con lui, nessuno dei due porta per l'anagrafe il nome dell'altro e non c'è un solo registro canonico sulla faccia della terra su cui siano vergate le firme dei testimoni della loro unione.
>
> (Leo understands that he has to go. At the final moment Thomas is given back to his family, to the same people who bore him; who are now, with hearts ravaged by suffering, trying to help him face death. There is no place for him in this parental regrouping. He didn't marry Thomas; didn't have children with him; neither of them legally bears the other's name, and there's not a single church registry on the face of the earth holding the signatures of those who witnessed their union.)

Camere separate also contributes to contemporary homosexual literature in its serious treatment of Leo's homosexual friendships and the social settings where he and his friends meet—the bar, the nightclub, and the dinner party. Tondelli's depiction of homosexual society makes visible what had been hidden from view, implicitly asserting that social relations among homosexuals are more complex and highly developed than the scant portrayals that literature historically has accorded them and advancing homosexuality as a cultural construct. This is also the vantage point from which to consider Tondelli's references to the history of homosexual literature and writers such as Walt Whitman, Auden, Isherwood, and Allen Ginsberg. References such as these indicate that Tondelli meant to position his own work within an evolving tradition.

As in *Biglietti agli Amici* changes of physical settings in *Camere separate* often lead to an evocation of past experiences or a reflection on death. According to one of Tondelli's friends, Filippo Betto, Leo's travel, bereavement, and acceptance of imminent death directly reflect and intentionally foretell the events that concluded Tondelli's own life:

> Credo che il viaggio a Klagenfurt, come il viaggio a Kirchstetten e quello a Grasse, sia stato per Pier uno dei passaggi attraverso cui, faticosamente, in silenzio,

Tondelli (front, left) with friends in his apartment in Milan in the 1980s

si compiva il "tentativo di colmare il vuoto della morte e del fallimento": la sofferta elaborazione del dolore per il proprio imminente, ingiusto e precoce distacco dal mondo, oltre che per quello, già avvenuto, della persona che Pier aveva amato.

(I believe that the trip to Klagenfurt, like the trip to Kirchstetten and the one to Grasse, was one of the channels through which Pier silently and laboriously completed his "effort to fill the void of death and failure": the painful encounter with sorrow over his imminent, unjust and premature separation from the world—and this beyond his suffering over the earlier death of the person Pier had loved.)

Un weekend postmoderno: Cronache dagli anni ottanta, the last work published during Tondelli's life, includes his notes on these trips as well as others. It is a compendium of his nonfiction and journalistic work and amounts to a volume of 622 pages divided into twelve sections. Tracing the development of Italian popular culture in the 1980s, these articles exhibit an energetic and polished style, tailored to the taste of young readers. The large collection shows that the breadth of Tondelli's knowledge and cultural interests was far wider than what is evident in his fiction.

The remainder of Tondelli's career is represented in *L'abbandono: racconti dagli anni ottanta* (1993), which brings together fiction and nonfiction that Tondelli had written for the newspapers *Corriere della sera, Il Resto del Carlino, Il Mattino, L'Unità,* and *Il Manifesto,* and the periodicals *L'Espresso, L'Illustrazione italiana, Uomo Harper's Bazaar, Per Lui,* and *Max.* Half of the volume is comprised of short fiction and assorted journalistic work, but large sections are grouped around three central themes: "Il mestiere dello scrittore" (The Writer's Craft), offering reflections on writing; "Il diario del soldato Acci" (Soldier Acci's Diary), an account of life in the army; and articles on concerts, recordings, performances, and broadcasts of rock music, headed by the title "Quarantacinque giri per dieci anni" (Forty-fives for Ten Years).

Intended to be a complementary second half of *Un weekend postmoderno, L'abbandono* differs from its companion volume in that it includes generous endnotes for each selection. These notes are especially useful for the nine previously uncollected stories published under the rubric "Racconti" (Stories), which are among the most important works in the volume. The notes indicate, for example, that "La casa! . . . La casa! . . ." (A Home! . . . A Home! . . . , 1981) is an attempt to recreate speech in the way Céline did and that "Pier a gennaio" (Pier's January, 1986) was written as a stylistic exercise in the technique of inserting autobiographical characters into a short story—an exercise that Tondelli undertook after reading Isherwood's *Christopher and His Kind* (1976) and *October* (1980).

Tondelli did not live to see the final version of *L'abbandono,* but he did approve the contents and the sequence before he became too ill to concern himself with it personally. Until August 1990, when he first became ill with AIDS, Tondelli continued to travel and write as he always had. He died at his parents' home in Correggio on 16 January 1991 and is buried in the church cemetery at nearby Cànolo. The fact that bilateral pneumonia was announced as his cause of death is an indication of the reserve maintained by Tondelli and his family regarding his homosexuality and AIDS. When his actual cause of death was exposed in the national press it shocked much of Italy because Tondelli was one of the first Italians of prominence to die of the disease. Tondelli's death by AIDS also meant that his last novel was reread as an autobiographical work, and as a result *Camere separate* was perceived as its author's thinly veiled swan song.

While all of Tondelli's works assert a positive affirmation of homosexuality, many regretted that he chose not to affirm his solidarity with others suffering from AIDS while he lived. Such an act would have been perceived as an overtly political statement, and hence, many Italians, given the stigma attached to AIDS, defended Tondelli's right to have kept the truth about his disease from the public. His silence, perhaps the result of his inablility to resolve the personal conflict between his homosexuality and his Catholicism, is consistent with his career choice never to write about homosexuality from an explicitly political orientation.

There is as yet no consensus of critical opinion on Tondelli's work, and some critics describe it as limited to the concerns of the writer's own generation. During a decade when most writers avoided contemporary reality in favor of traditional forms such as the historical novel, Tondelli chose to delve into the complex and murky world in which he lived. While in his last two novels he abandoned his earlier experimentalism for more commercially viable writing, he succeeded in offering a complex interpretation of middle-class culture together with a multifaceted treatment of sexuality and an honest portrayal of homosexual life in the 1980s. Arising within a culture burdened by the authority of tradition and history, Tondelli with his small body of work contributed to the nascent literature of homosexuality in Italy through a renewed commitment to realism.

Bibliography:

Fulvio Panzeri, ed., "Bibliografia degli scritti di Pier Vittorio Tondelli," in *L'abbandono: racconti dagli anni ottanta* (Milan: Bompiani, 1993), pp. 315–331.

References:

Maria Pia Ammirati, "Pier Vittorio Tondelli," in *Il vizio di scrivere: Letture su Busi, De Carlo, Del Giudice, Pazzi, Tabucchi e Tondelli* (Soveria Mannelli: Rubbettino, 1991), pp. 123–131;

Renato Barilli, "Dal leggibile all'illegibile," in *Letteratura tra consumo e ricerca,* edited by Luigi Russo (Bologna: Mulino, 1984), pp. 9–22;

Sonia Basili, "Morte e rinascita nelle esperienze erratiche di Pier Vittorio Tondelli," *Narrativa* (8 July 1995): 19–40;

Neil Campbell, "Altri libertini: A Glossary," *Bulletin of the Society of Italian Studies: A Journal for Teachers of Italian in Higher Education,* 20 (1987): 52–57;

Giovanni Dall'Orto, "Con le ali tarpate," *Babilonia,* 97 (February 1992): 21–23;

Mario Fortunato, "Aids/Vita e morte di Pier Vittorio Tondelli: Due anni di solitudine," *L'Espresso,* 1 (5 January 1992): 10–14;

Joachim Meinert, "Von Aussteigern und Aufsteigern: Leseeindrucke von drei jungen italienischen Erzahlern: Pier Vittorio Tondelli, Andrea De Carlo, Daniele Del Giudice," *Weimarer Beitrage: Zeitschrift fur Literaturwissenschaft, Asthetik und Kulturwissenschaften,* 32, no. 2 (1987): 236–255;

Elisabetta Sgarbi, ed., *Pier Vittorio Tondelli,* special issue, *Panta: I nuovi narratori,* 9 (1992): 371;

Wilhelm Snyman, "Politics and Power in Giovanni Comisso's *Giorni di guerra* and Pier Vittorio Tondelli's *Pao Pao,*" *Studi d'Italianistica nell'Africa Australe,* 9, no. 1 (1996): 19–34;

Stefano Tani, "Gli accumulatori e l'autoritratto generazionale," in his *Il romanzo di ritorno: Dal romanzo medio degli anni sessanta alla giovane narrativa degli anni ottanta* (Milan: Mursia, 1990), pp. 197–207;

Diego Zancani, "Pier Vittorio Tondelli: The Calm After the Storm," in *The New Italian Novel,* edited by Zygmunt G. Baranski & Lino Pertile (Edinburgh: Edinburgh University Press, 1993), pp. 219–238.

Dante Troisi
(21 April 1920 – 2 January 1989)

Patricia M. Gathercole
Roanoke College

Augustus Pallotta
Syracuse University

BOOKS: *L'ulivo nella sabbia* (Florence: Macchia, 1951);
La gente di Sidaien e altri racconti (Milan: Feltrinelli, 1957);
La strada della perfezione (Venice: Sodalizio del Libro, 1958);
Innocente delitto (Venice: Sodalizio del Libro, 1960);
Chiamata in giudizio (1960);
Diario di un giudice (Turin: Einaudi, 1962);
L'odore dei cattolici (Rome: Canesi, 1963);
I bianchi e i neri (Bari: Laterza, 1965);
Viaggio scomodo (Bari: Laterza, 1967);
Voci di Vallea (Milan: Rizzoli, 1969);
Tre storie di teatro (Milan: Rizzoli, 1972);
La sopravvivenza (Milan: Rusconi, 1981);
La finta notte (Milan: Rusconi, 1984);
L'inquisitore dell'interno sedici (Pordenone: Edizioni Studio Tesi, 1986);
La sera del concerto (Venice: Marsilio, 1991).

Dante Troisi

Among the most intellectually engaging writers to emerge after World War II, Dante Troisi has used his novels, plays, and short stories to draw a disturbing picture of social and cultural life in southern Italy after the war. In the tradition of Elio Vittorini, Ignazio Silone, and Carlo Levi, Troisi confronts many of the prejudices and traditional attitudes that have retarded social and economic progress in the South. His work shows a constant interest in the human condition as represented by insecure, alienated individuals who embody the modern moral and spiritual crisis. Troisi's dry style has been likened to that of Albert Camus and Anton Checkov; yet it would be more accurate to see him as a worried moralist deeply concerned with the social and ideological tensions.

The roots of Troisi's disillusionment with Italian society stem from the expectations that the writers of his generation nurtured in the wake of World War II, the hope that the fall of Fascism would be followed by a profound social transformation, by a new order bearing the imprint of socialism. Troisi never lost faith in the ideals of equality and social renewal; his works bear witness to such faith, but they also point to the erosion of the individual values nurtured during the struggle against

Fascism. In his 29 April 1984 interview in *Il Mattino* Troisi admitted that "lo sfondo delle mie storie è sempre il grigiore del presente succeduto alle speranze del dopoguerra" (The background of my novels is always marked by the grayness of present times which followed the hopes of the postwar period).

Troisi was born on 21 April 1920 in Tufo, a small southern town in the province of Avellino. He completed the secondary schools in Avellino and graduated from the University of Bari with a degree in law. Drafted during World War II, he took part in the military campaigns in Libya and Tunisia. He was captured by Allied forces in May 1943 and sent to the prison camp in Heredford, Texas, where he remained until the end of the war. Upon his return to Italy in 1947 he was named judge in Mede Lomellina (Pavia) and then magistrate in the district courts, first in Cassino and then in Rome.

Troisi's work is permeated by his judicial experience. He constantly probes the consciences of his characters and at times betrays a mistrust of Italian judicial and political systems. The cynicism he acquired as a judge is counterbalaced, though, by the broad social consciousness he developed as a writer. In an October 1981 interview with Claudio Toscani he emphasized this point: "Per me scrivere è un sentire la propria voce e quella del prossimo" (To me writing means hearing my voice and that of my neighbors). No doubt the ideals of socialism and the existential thought of postwar French writers, especially the work of Camus, played a large part in shaping his consciousness.

Most of Troisi's novels are marked by thin plots, brief descriptions of physical settings, and a heavy reliance on dialogue. Character interactions occasionally assume the form of debates, as in a courtroom. He uses narrative devices such as flashbacks and diaries but is more interested in ideas than style: he employs unrefined everyday language and is indifferent to the symbolic functions of the landscape and the forces of Nature. Troisi's main focus is on psychological and spiritual matters, and he delves deeply into the complex psyche of his characters, many of whom feel anxiety or guilt in one form or another. He barely mentions the physical traits of his protagonists, who often take on symbolic significance. Given to thought and introspection, they are frustrated, filled with doubts, and too weak to act. Much like Luigi Pirandello's characters, Troisi's protagonists are restless and alienated and seek certainties that constantly elude them.

In Troisi's first book *L'ulivo nella sabbia* (The Olive Tree in the Sand, 1951) Giovanni Tenda, the main character, is arrested for hiding a cachet of firearms. Detained for security reasons, he is tried and found guilty by the presiding judge, his former military comrade in northern Africa during the war. The tale turns into a psychological study of contrasting individuals: Judge Crani, whose successful career in the judiciary seems to satisfy both his professional ambitions and his duty to society, and Tenda, who, unable to overcome the psychological burden of his war experiences, channels his energies and anxieties toward the Italian Communist Party, which he regards as an effective mechanism to promote social justice. The novel revolves around the juxtaposition of the two men: Crani, self-assured and at peace with himself; Tenda, insecure and afflicted by deep-seated unrest.

In prison, influenced in part by his cell mate, Tenda begins to have second thoughts about communism and eventually comes to the conclusion that "la lotta del partito è inadeguata al male che si propone di combattere" (the struggle of the party is inadequate to the evils it seeks to attack). As is often the case in Troisi's work, the novel ends in irresolution: Tenda begins to think that, rather than the party ideology, it may be his flawed character that is the real source of his anxieties. It is worth noting that Troisi, never a member of the Communist Party, was among the first to dwell on its wide-ranging social significance and to discern the symptoms of a crisis that was to culminate with the substantial restructuring of the party in 1992. In in his volume *Vent'anni di pazienza* (Twenty Years of Patience, 1972) critic Giuliano Manacorda comments on Troisi's relationship to communism:

> Troisi è stato a lungo dominato dal problema dei comunisti nella nostra società. Sentiva lí il punto dolente, il limite di rottura di certi valori accettati e contemporaneamente subiva il fascino di quella carica di energia e di umanità che premeva ai confini di un mondo in procinto di rispecchiarsi compiaciuto nelle proprie colpe.

> (Troisi was preoccupied for a long time with the problem of communists in our society. To him they represented a sensitive issue, the breaking point of certain traditional values; at the same time he felt the attraction of that charge of energy and humanity which pressed forward from the boundaries of a self-satisfied world about to recognize itself in its own sins.)

In 1957 Troisi published *La gente di Sidaien e altri racconti* (The People of Sidaien and Other Stories), a collection of four novellas based in large measure on his war experiences. The stories emphasize a collective struggle for survival and are marked by a lack of character development. The collection is unified by its protagonists' broken spirits and dashed hopes. Troisi presents soldiers coping with the military defeat suffered in Libya; young people and their adventurous experiences during the war; and the interaction between two Italian intellectuals concerned with political ideology. The title story takes place at the oasis of Sidaien and elsewhere in Africa. Against a desolate and alien background, Troisi paints poignant scenes of loneliness and demoralization that are compounded by many casualties suffered in battle. A common anxiety binds the soldiers together; their fears and anxieties convey a sense of the fragility of human existence that moves individuals closer to God.

Innocente delitto (Innocent Crime, 1960) pits the postwar generation, represented by a young man, Renato, against the generation represented by his parents, which is blamed for the ills that beset Italian society. When Renato kills a police officer during a strike and is subsequently tried for the crime, he is assailed by contradictory feelings about himself and his community, which he sees as mired in superstitions and conservative traditions. The resentful and contradictory feelings toward his father continue unabated even when the father assumes responsibility for the crime in the appellate court. There is hardly anything in this novel that escapes Troisi's pessimism, which is inclusive of both generations, the political class, the Church, and Italy's economic system. Indeed, the book is marked by an aura of fatalism that concerns the human condition as much as it does the South, which Troisi depicts as deeply entrenched in century-old traditions and incapable of renewing itself.

Diario di un giudice (Diary of a Judge, 1962), one of Troisi's most significant novels, is based on the author's experiences as a magistrate and the people that appeared before him. At times Troisi steps outside the courtroom, offering the reader memorable scenes of daily life among southern Italians. The characters move in a social setting marked by prejudice, superstition, the scars of war, and a deep mistrust in the judicial system. The most frequent cases brought before the judge involve robbery, family disputes, and violence. The litigants often manifest excessive emotions and show a lack of education. The judge, tired from overwork, is forced to neglect his family and other personal interests. He feels unappreciated by the townspeople and fears that he may become the target of a fanatical individual he has sent to prison. When he is among lawyers, he senses a mixture of envy and mistrust, and he is shocked by the earnings lawyers can accumulate from a single case.

The book offers a close portrait of the judiciary as a profession. Troisi shows that being a judge is a difficult life, marked by the fear of laboring uselessly in the face of popular mistrust in the processes of justice. Like priests at the confessional, judges enter into the lives of people and are privy to their problems and difficulties. Through their experiences judges learn to become pessimistic about human nature: the courts are filled with misery and pain, which cannot but affect judges in a negative fashion. But Troisi is also caustically critical of his profession. He calls his peers "zeppi di difetti, di dolori, di noia, di ambizioni, di desideri meschini" (full of flaws, sorrows, boredom, ambitions, and petty desires), and he offers disconcerting admissions, such as the observation that "fra tutti gli uomini, noi siamo i meno liberi e perciò odiamo la libertà degli altri" (among social beings, we are the least free and thus hate the freedom that others have).

Ultimately the merits of the book rest on Troisi's earnest effort as a writer, judge, and man of the South to understand the complex and elusive character of his people, their centuries-old habits, their virtues and prejudices, their unchanging way of life, and their deep mistrust of the law. But it should be noted that Troisi's criticism of peasant culture does not at all imply his admiration for the materialistic values of the postwar industrial society. In *I bianchi e i neri* (Blacks and Whites, 1965) he writes of the inequities brought by economic prosperity: "Abbiamo inventato il benessare per nasconderci, per rassegnarci. Non abbiamo neppure atteso che prendesse consistenza, che arrivasse a un livello decente per tutti e subito ne abbiamo approfittato per giustificare la nostra piccola angoscia" (We have invented material prosperity to hide, to grow resigned. We haven't even waited until it became stable, until it reached a decent level for all; we took advantage of it to justify our little anxieties).

In *L'odore dei cattolici* (The Odor of Catholics, 1963) Troisi is harshly critical of the Catholicism practiced in the provincial communities of southern Italy. The protagonist is Martino Ferri, a man who chose to leave the priesthood. Although he has married, fathered a child, and found employment with the town, he still faces the resentment

Cover for a 1978 edition of Troisi's 1962 novel, in which he depicts the life of a judge in Southern Italy

of the townspeople who want him to return to the priesthood. He is abandoned by nearly everyone, including his wife, who yields to the pressures of her mother and leaves him. She says to him: "Siamo come pecore in mezzo ai lupi" (We are like sheep surrounded by wolves). To no avail he pleads with her not to yield to the narrow-mindedness of the community: "Resta con me, Irene. . . . Crederanno che non siamo stati felici, diranno che è una sconfitta del nostro amore, e invece è un ricatto della superstizione" (Don't leave me, Irene. . . . People will believe that we were not happy together, they will say that our love failed, when, in fact, it is an act of blackmail motivated by superstition).

After he is tempted to take his life, Martino regains self-confidence and decides to stand by the choice he has made. When the pressure from the townspeople increases, he contemplates immigrating to the United States, where he is told that catholics are more understanding toward individuals in his situation. A doctor tells him that in a Southern town it is impossible to dispel "l'odore di secoli, che un prete alita intorno" (the odor of centuries that emanates from a priest). Taking exception to Catholic thought, the doctor tells the former priest that the solution lies in seeking collective, not individual, salvation and in promoting the awareness that people ought to fight evil together, as brothers and sisters. Martino, echoing Troisi, offers an unflattering assessment of the Italian character: "Noi italiani non conosciamo atteggiamenti positivi ed eccelliamo nelle negazioni; non ci piace costruire, ma distruggere" (We Italians do not know positive attitudes and excel in negations: we like to destroy rather than build). Clearly Troisi attacks the conformity of conservative Catholicism and its inability to adjust to the realities of a changing world.

Troisi's *I bianchi e i neri* is set during the final days of World War II, a time when downtrodden people were yearning for a new order, for economic opportunities in a society free of prejudices. The title has symbolic meaning: the whites are the elite class and other privileged members of society; the blacks are the impoverished classes, the urban proletariat and the peasants. The protagonist senses that he is different from his neighbors in that he does not submit easily to the will of political leaders who are fanatical in their adherence to tradition. Anxious about social and economic conditions in southern Italy, he attempts nonetheless to understand why people discriminate on the basis of color and social status; he reaches the conclusion that evil in the world stems, in large measure, from individual moral laziness.

In this novel Troisi again draws from his experience as a judge who has seen people misrepresent the truth because it is easier or more convenient to do so. The novel can be seen, in part, as a defense of a judge's predicament in a society whose laws are not always just. Troisi is particularly critical of lawyers who only care about fashioning rewarding careers: "Ogni problema che li riguarda diventa astratto, oggetto di dispute cavillose e infruttose" (Every problem that concerns them becomes abstract, an object of detailed and unproductive arguments).

The life in a southern town as depicted by Troisi is marked by conformity and suffering in silence. Tolerance is confused with weakness; passivity breeds conformity. In such a climate individuals live in stoic solitude even though they naturally turn to a neighbor for assistance when adversity strikes.

Countering the myth of social community in the rural South as protective and close-knit, Troisi points to the isolation, indeed the alienation, of the individual from his community in everyday life.

Voci di Vallea (Voices from Vallea, 1969), a collection of short stories whose characters are haunted by and become victims of their past, is notable among Troisi's lesser works. The stories offer another picture of southern Italy as a society subject to apathy and age-old customs which often carry prejudices and stereotypes with them. The author longs for change, yet he knowingly reiterates customary themes of his work. The collection is pervaded by an air of discouragement, "una anonima opaca mestizia dell'anima" (a nameless, opaque sadness of the soul).

In *Tre storie di teatro* (Three Stories for the Stage, 1972) Troisi adapted two of his novels for the stage with considerable success. The reduction of descriptions and dialogue yields texts of heightened emotional and intellectual intensity. As in the original novels, the characters are weak and indecisive, at times even "unpleasant," as Manacorda has pointed out. On stage there is, as one might expect, little action and much soul-searching by alienated individuals who have come to realize how deficient or far-fetched were the ideals of their youthful years. The plays are also critical of society and the role of religion. In *Il vizio dell'innocenza* (The Habit of Innocence), for example, Troisi attacks the influential role the priest exercises in small rural communities, especially among naive and ignorant people.

The title *La finta notte* (The Feigned Night, 1984) draws its meaning from the disposition of the protagonist, Cosimo, who is unable to face reality, choosing instead to live in a state of "finta notte," a semiconscious state of rationalizations and daydreaming. Cosimo's attitude is questioned by his companion, Nora, but she is part of the problem in that she has been with other men, a reality Cosimo attempts to dispel by identifying with and mentally playing the role of one of her former lovers. The work is set in the couple's bedroom in the hours preceding dawn. Through intense arguments, mutual accusations, and self-exculpations, Cosimo and Nora, like many of Troisi's characters, end up resolving nothing and only hurting themselves.

In *La finta notte* Troisi explores what the writer Cesare Pavese calls "il mestiere di vivere," the business of living—the strenuous effort that individuals such as Cosimo have to make as they carry on, unwillingly, the painful exercise of daily life. The indulgent Cosimo is disposed to *dormiveglia* (semiwakefulness) because the alternative of wakefulness requires a choice between two uneasy alternatives: contemplating death or facing unpleasant realities. *La finta notte* is a painfully honest book of introspection and self-analysis mirroring, at least in part, the novelist's persona and his quest to comprehend his being, the reasons for his existence, and the ultimate purpose of his life and the life of others. There is little doubt that Troisi was influenced by the French philosopher Blaise Pascal, as evidenced by the following meditative passage attributed to the protagonist:

Quando considero la breve durata della mia vita, sommersa nell'eternità che la precede e la segue ... io mi spavento e stupisco di trovarmi qui piuttosto che là, oggi piuttosto che domani. Chi mi ci ha messo? Per opera e per ordine di chi questo luogo e questo tempo furono destinati a me?

(When I think about the short span of my life, submerged in the eternity that precedes and follows it ... I am frightened and amazed that I am here rather than there, today rather than tomorrow. Who put me here? By virtue of whom and by whose order were this time and this place destined to me?)

The protagonist is on a spiritual quest and in his moments of highest tension calls upon God to solve the mystery of life. Turning to a priest for an answer is no consolation, for the question is always met with silence: "il silenzio eterno alla domanda di quel che siamo e quel che dobbiamo fare" (the eternal silence to the question of what we are and what we must do). As Di Biase points out, Cosimo "ha paura del mistero della vita perchè teme di scoprirvi, al fondo, il nulla, di trovarsi senza il riparo di una tenda" (fears the mystery of life because he fears, in the end, to find nothing, to find himself without the protection of a tent). Troisi's existential view that life is a struggle and evil is an integral part of the human condition is clear in the novel.

Troisi suggests that each human being harbors a two-fold "Dio-Diavolo" (God-Devil) force representing, the expressions of good and evil in constant clash with each other. He believes that the same twofold force is present in the course of history. In a peculiar mixture of Marxist and religious thought Troisi intimates that the individual quest for salvation, though commendable, cannot be divorced from, or pursued independently of, the individual quest for the freedom from injustice, hunger, and suffering.

L'inquisitore dell'interno sedici (The Inquisitor in Apartment Sixteen, 1986) is a philosophical novel that again addresses questions of good and evil. Here Troisi advances the idea that individuals must develop their own convictions and values, independent of external superstitions and fears. Echoing an important theme from the previous novel, the novelist suggests that wisdom is the capacity to pursue good and avoid evil in daily life. Further, he makes a distinction between an active and an unexamined life, the latter represented by a knife-sharpener who accepts his lot in life passively. Using a judge as a character and alter ego, Troisi argues that one must not be satisfied or become complacent but instead must seek answers to the complexities of one's individual being, for "Dio ha fatto dell'uomo un abisso di taglienti e indecifrabili contradizioni che rendono l'anima un oscuro campo di morte" (God has made of man an abyss of sharp and indecipherable contradictions which render the soul a dark cemetery). Many anxieties stem, according to Troisi, from the inability to comprehend the complex and problematic nature of the human condition.

La sera del concerto (The Night of the Concert) was published in 1991 after a serious illness that lasted nearly two years claimed Troisi in Rome on 2 January 1989. It was during this gray period of silent suffering and reflection that the judge-turned-novelist wrote his last piece. He became committed to it and was assailed by the fear of being unable to bring it to completion. It is a poignant homage to the craft of fiction, lyrical in parts, meditative and introspective in others, but always engaging.

The writer imagines attending a concert where he spots an attractive woman. He knows she is married, but he is taken by her and decides he must court her by writing her letters. With the passage of time she becomes more attractive, and he courts her with greater devotion until he asks her to join him in his final voyage. It becomes evident that the lady sought by the narrator is the image of Death, a narrative ploy that is found frequently in Romantic literature. But Troisi, fully aware of literary antecedents, did not strive to be original. He meant to be strikingly emulative and, in this regard, was no doubt mindful of the memorable episode of Prince Salina's courtship of Death, disguised as a young woman, in Tomasi di Lampedusa's novel *Il Gattopardo* (1958; translated as *The Leopard*, 1960).

In a comprehensive essay on Troisi's work Giuseppe Neri offers a succinct and enlightening assessment of the novelist-judge:

> Pochi autori come Troisi sanno darci l'esatta misura della profondità della crisi che travaglia l'uomo e la società contemporanea, comunicarci quella sensazione di acuto disagio di fronte al progressivo sfaldamento, al quotidiano svilimento di certi ideali che pure, in un determinato periodo storico, ci avevano dato l'illusione di poter cambiare il corso delle cose, di poter imprimere una sterzata brusca e salutare agli avvenimenti.

(Few authors are as capable as Troisi of giving us the exact dimensions of the deep crisis that besets contemporary man and his society, of communicating to us the sense of keen uneasiness we feel vis-à-vis the gradual collapse, the daily erosion of those ideals which, at a given historical moment, had given us the illusion that we could change things, that we could bring an abrupt and healthy swerve to human events.)

Indeed, Troisi's contributions to Italian culture grew from his commitment to make use of his judicial profession and narrative talent to examine the moral temper of his time. His work suggests strongly that it is the responsibility of everyone to erase evil in the world and improve the human lot by opposing such destructive forces as religious bigotry, social stereotypes, and all forms of prejudice. His thought-provoking work transcends the boundaries of southern Italy in the twentieth century, which constitute only the external structure of his narrative.

Interviews:

Claudio Toscani, *Il ragguaglio librario,* October 1981, p. 334;

A. Gnoli, *Il mattino,* 29 April 1984.

References:

Salvatore Battaglia, "*I bianchi e i neri* di Dante Troisi," *Filologia e letteratura,* 11 (1965): 348–353;

Rocco Capozzi, "Inquietudine e denuncia ne *La finta notte*," *Forum Italicum,* 20 (Fall 1986): 245–251;

Giuseppe d'Errico, "*L'inquisitore dell'interno sedici* di Dante Troisi," *Riscontri,* 9 (July–September 1987): 124–128;

Carmine Di Biase, "Il notturno di Dante Troisi," *Italian Quarterly,* 27 (1986): 63–69;

Di Biase, "*La sopravvivenza* di Dante Troisi," *Studium,* 78 (July–August 1982): 514–518;

Renzo Frattarolo, "Due profili: Cesare Pavese e Dante Troisi," *Baretti,* 7 (1966): 34–39;

Peppino Grossi, "L'inquisitore," *Studium,* 84 (July–August 1988): 616–624;

Giuliano Manacorda, "Dante Troisi," in his *Vent'anni di pazienza. Saggi sulla letteratura italiana contemporanea* (Florence: Nuova Italia, 1972), pp. 419–427;

Giuseppe Neri, "Un giudice scomodo," *Nuova antologia,* 517 (1973): 370–384.

Ferruccio Ulivi
(10 September 1912 -)

Salvatore Cappelletti
Providence College

BOOKS: *Federigo Tozzi* (Brescia: Morcelliana, 1946; revised edition, 1973);
Il romanticismo di Ippolito Nievo (Rome: A.V.E., 1947);
Il Manzoni lirico e la poetica del Rinnovamento (Rome: Gismondi, 1950);
Galleria di scrittori d'arte (Florence: Sansoni, 1953);
Settecento neoclassico (Pisa: Nistri-Lischi, 1957);
Il primo Carducci (Florence: Le Monnier, 1957);
L'imitazione nella poetica del Rinascimento (Milan: Marzorati, 1957);
Gian Vincenzo Gravina; I Minori (Milan: Marzorati, 1958);
Dal Manzoni ai decadenti (Rome: Caltanissetta, 1963);
Il Canto XX del "Purgatorio" (Florence: Le Monnier, 1964);
Il romanticismo e Alessandro Manzoni (Bologna: Cappelli, 1965);
Il manierismo del Tasso ed altri studi (Florence: Olschki, 1966);
Figure e protagonisti dei "Promessi Sposi" (Torino: ERI-RAI, 1967);
La lirica del Manzoni (Bari: Adriatica, 1967);
La lirica del Carducci dai primi versi a "Levia gravia:" saggio e antologia (Bari: Adriatica, 1968);
Poesia come pittura (Bari: Adriatica, 1969);
Stile e critica: Avviamento allo studio della letteratura italiana (Bari: Adriatica, 1969);
Le origini e il Duecento, by Ulivi and Rodolfo Macchioni Jodi (Florence-Messina, D'Anna, 1971);
Prospettive e problemi; antologia della critica letteraria e della civiltà italiana, by Ulivi and Jodi (Florence-Messina: D'Anna, 1971);
La civiltà comunale, by Ulivi and Jodi (Florence-Messina: D'Anna, 1971);
L' Umanesimo, by Ulivi and Jodi (Florence-Messina: D'Anna, 1971);
Rinascimento e Manierismo, by Ulivi and Jodi (Florence-Messina: D'Anna, 1971);
Il Barocco, by Ulivi and Jodi (Florence-Messina: D'Anna, 1971);
Dall'Arcadia al Neoclassicismo, by Ulivi and Jodi (Florence-Messina: D'Anna, 1971);
Dal Romanticismo al Verismo, by Ulivi and Jodi (Florence-Messina: D'Anna, 1971);
Dal Decadentismo alle esperienze contemporanee, by Ulivi and Jodi (Florence-Messina: D'Anna, 1971);
La letteratura verista (Torino: Eri, 1972);
La letteratura artistica dal manierismo al classicismo secentesco (Rome: Elia, 1972);
Acquarelli di Marino (Caltanisetta: Sciascia, 1972);
Alberto Chiari (Brescia: Paideia, 1973);
Manzoni: Storia e Provvidenza (Rome: Bonacci, 1974);
Antologia tassiana: testi e commento (Rome: Elia, 1974);
Racconto siciliano di Carpinteri (Rome-Caltanissetta: Sciascia, 1974);
Salvator Rosa: pittore e poeta (Rome: Accademia Nazionale, 1975);
E le ceneri al vento (Milan: Mondadori, 1977);
Il visibile parlare: saggi sui rapporti fra lettere e arti (Caltanissetta: Sciascia, 1978);
Le mani pure (Milan: Rizzoli, 1979);
Le mura del cielo (Milan: Rizzoli, 1981);
L'alba del terzo giorno (Rome: Edizioni del Tornese, 1982);
La notte di Toledo (Milan: Rusconi, 1983);
Manzoni (Milan: Rusconi, 1984);
Trenta denari (Milan: Rusconi, 1986);
D'Annunzio (Milan: Rusconi, 1988);
Linee per un ritratto di Manzoni (Naples: Edizioni scientifiche italiane, 1988);
La maschera senza il volto (Naples: Edizioni scientifiche italiane, 1989);
L'anello (Milan: Rusconi, 1990);
La parola pittorica (Rome-Caltanissetta: Sciascia, 1990);
Storie bibliche d'amore e di morte (Cinisello Balsamo: Edizioni Paoline, 1990);
Vita e opere di Gabriele D'Annunzio (Modena: Mucchi, 1990);
Da Leopardi a Montale: aggiornamenti di letteratura ottonovecentesca e testimonianze di scrittori contemporanei, by Ulivi, P. Paganuzzi, and P. Rabuzzi (Brescia: Grafo, 1990);
La straniera (Milan: Mondadori, 1991);
L'angelo rosso (Casale Monferrato: Piemme, 1992);

Tempesta di marzo (Casale Monferrato: Piemme, 1993);

Torquato Tasso: l'anima e l'avventura (Casale Monferrato: Piemme, 1995);

Come il tragitto di una stella; Giuseppe di Nazareth: sogno, amore e solitudine (Cinisello Balsamo: Edizioni Paoline, 1997).

OTHER: Eugenio Cirese, *Poesie molisane,* edited by Ulivi and A. M. Cirese (Caltanissetta: Sciascia, 1955);

I poeti della scuola romana dell'Ottocento, edited by Ulivi (Bologna: Cappelli, 1964);

Il Conte di Carmagnola, edited by Ulivi (Rome: 1966);

Lirici pugliesi del Novecento, edited by Ulivi and Elio Filippo Accrocca (Bari: Adriatica, 1967);

Gianna Manzini, *Un' altra cosa: con una scelta di prose,* edited by Ulivi (Milan: Edizioni scolastiche Mondadori, 1969);

Alessandro Manzoni, *I promessi sposi,* edited by Ulivi (Padua: RADAR, 1969);

Prosatori e narratori pugliesi, edited by Ulivi and Accrocca (Bari: Adriatica, 1969);

Pompeo Bettini, *Poesie e prose,* edited by Ulivi (Bologna: Cappelli, 1970);

Gaetano Giangrandi, *Giangrandi, i gatti, il surreale,* edited by Ulivi (Rome-Caltanissetta: Sciascia, 1971);

Alessandro Manzoni, *Poesie: Inni sacri, odi, poesie non approvate o postume,* edited by Ulivi (Milan: Mondadori, 1985);

Matteo Maria Boiardo, *Opere di Matteo Maria Boiardo,* edited by Ulivi (Milan: Mursia, 1986);

Francesco Petrarca, *Poesie d'amore,* edited by Ulivi (Rome: Newton Compton, 1989);

Le più belle poesie d'amore della letteratura italiana: dalle origini al Novecento, edited by Ulivi and Marta Savini (Rome: Newton Compton, 1990);

Alessandro Manzoni, *Storia della colonna infame,* edited, with an introduction, by Ulivi (Rome: TEN, 1993);

Poesia religiosa italiana: dalle origini al '900, edited by Ulivi and Savini (Casale Monferrato: Piemme, 1994);

Gli scrittori d'arte, selected and introduced by Ulivi (Rome: Istituto Poligrafico e Zecca dello Stato, 1995).

Renowned literary critic, essayist, biographer, and recipient of many literary prizes for fiction, Ferruccio Ulivi published his first book of fiction, *E le ceneri al vento* (Ashes in the Wind) in 1977 at the age of sixty-five. Despite his late start he has become a prolific novelist, widely read and highly regarded. His narrative is known for its character development and stimulating intellectual content. The structure of much of Ulivi's fiction emerges from what critic Franco Lanza calls "la fenomenologia della solitudine" (the phenomenology of solitude); he explores such issues as conscience and consciousness, freedom and destiny, and the presence and absence of God in human existence.

Born on 10 September in Borgo San Lorenzo near Florence, Ulivi graduated from the University of Florence in 1934. He has been living in Rome since 1941. Ulivi's activity as a writer dates back to the 1930s, when he was actively involved in Florentine cultural life. It was at this time that he began to contribute to such periodicals as *Campo di Marte, Corrente,* and *Letteratura.* In a 1960 self-profile published in Elio Filippo Accrocca's *Ritratti su misura* (Custom-Made Portraits) he recalls: "La mia prima formazione risale al periodo fiorentino di *Campo di Marte;* più tardi ho scritto su altre riviste di allora" (My formative years date back to the Florentine time of *Campo di Marte;* later, I published in other journals of that period).

Prior to devoting himself to writing fiction, Ulivi was a professor of Italian at the University of Bari, where he began his career in 1934; in the 1960s he taught at the University of Perugia; and he spent the last years of his teaching career at the University of Rome. He is one of Italy's most prominent literary scholars, an expert on Alessandro Manzoni, the Renaissance, and the eighteenth century. In addition to his areas of specialization, he has published on various other writers and topics, spanning the breadth of Italian literature. His work has appeared in leading journals such as *Convivium, Nuova Antologia, Paragone,* and *Rassegna della letteratura italiana.*

Manzoni has held a privileged place in Ulivi's professional life; to him he has devoted major studies, biographies, short stories, and two novels, *La straniera* (The Foreigner, 1991) and *Tempesta di marzo* (March Storm, 1993). Moreover, through Manzoni, Ulivi discovered several minor Italian writers of the nineteenth century. In the 1960 self-profile he wrote of the value of his scholarship: "Imparai a riconoscere nelle fibre più sottili il tessuto poetico-letterario di un periodo storico. Fin d'allora mi interessarono profondamente i motivi di gusto, i rapporti culturali, i rapporti tra estetiche e poetiche, i rapporti tra le arti" (I learned how to recognize the most delicate fibers in the poetic and literary texture of an historical period. Ever since, I have been keenly interested in questions of taste, cultural relationships, the relationship between aesthetic and poetic theories, and the connections among the arts).

As a result of his long study of literature Ulivi's fiction is dotted with the sensation-awaken-

Ferruccio Ulivi at eighty-five

ing images common to art and poetry. Horace's precept "ut pictura poesis" (poetry is like painting) is the cornerstone to Ulivi's long-standing research into the relationship between art and poetry. His writings on this subject include *Il manierismo del Tasso ed altri studi* (Tasso's Mannerism and Other Studies, 1966), which includes essays on the relationship between art and literary criticism; the integration of Franciscan, Romanesque, and Gothic culture; the art of natural figuration in Manzoni; and *Poesia come pittura* (Poetry as Painting, 1969).

Ulivi laid the foundation of his narrative in *E le ceneri al vento,* which proved to be a major success with readers. The work consists of four short stories inspired by four major writers: Giacomo Leopardi, Oscar Wilde, Alessandro Manzoni, and Torquato Tasso. The unifying link of the stories is the theme of solitude, which reveals the temperament and the folds of the characters' inner lives. In this collection, as well as in the works that follow, Ulivi brings the reader close to the mysterious truths and tragedies that lie at the core of the human condition.

Ulivi is able to successfully probe the souls of human beings at critical stages of their existence in part because he learned from Manzoni the intimate connection between historical and poetical truth. Although Ulivi is known as humble, kind, and courteous, he lost his customary calmness when in March 1993 left-leaning politicians proposed to remove Manzoni's classic historical novel *I Promessi Sposi* (1827; translated as *The Betrothed,* 1828), from the school curriculum. Ulivi did not hesitate to call these politicians "imbecilli" (idiots) because he regards Manzoni as the creator of modern Italian. He is convinced that Manzoni and Dante Alighieri are as seminal figures to Italian culture as William Shakespeare is to the English and Johann Wolfgang von Goethe to the Germans.

The critic Italo A. Chiusano has observed that Ulivi's style is classical, clear, and penetrating. As a scholar Ulivi wrote a major essay on eighteenth-century Neoclassicism, but his outlook as a novelist is existential. His style reflects smoothness, swiftness, accuracy, visibility, and multiplicity, the essential qualities of good writing. Characteristic of Ulivi's fiction is its atmosphere of mystery and suspense. Though each journey begins with clear historical references, used essentially as points of de-

Ulivi as a young man

parture, the action soon moves into a web of poetic truth. Unexpected situations bend and tangle in all directions, creating, in a narrative vein reminiscent of Edgar Allan Poe, a sense of increasing and disquieting suspense. Ulivi does not consider himself a realistic writer; in fact, in an interview with Chiusano he stated: "Non credo in un'arte realista" (I do not believe in realistic art). Reality, as well as life and truth, he added, can be grasped only "di scorcio"—that is to say, through a foreshortened perspective.

Ulivi believes that an author's intention is neither to discover nor to distort historical truth. He chooses not to shed light on dark areas of history but to the contrary, as the poet Mario Luzi has observed, he purposely colors gray even those events that are clear to historians. Thus, Ulivi offers the reader a new perspective that highlights the complexity, ambiguity, and tormenting doubts marking human events.

Ulivi's Brutus in *Le mani pure* (Pure Hands, 1979) is neither a tyrant nor a hero. He is, as Lanza has pointed out, an individual caught in a moral dilemma in which he must assume individual responsibility. Brutus is overwhelmed by forces generated by the clash between ideas and emotion; he must choose between political duty and impulses veiled as a desire for justice. Brutus cannot turn back and kills Caesar for the same reasons that he will kill himself: love for his wife, Portia (to vindicate the suicide of her father Cato); the Oedipal bond; and, ultimately, his identification with the dead father.

At Philippi, as the decisive moment of Brutus's final decision draws near, Ulivi's language becomes succinct. Brief sentences contribute to highlight Brutus's state of solitude and dismay, suggesting the gradual erosion of his world: "Di fronte, e alle spalle, non c'era che l'abisso" (Ahead of him, to the back of him, there was nothing but the abyss); "Dei, mostri o fantasmi l'avevano abbandonato" (Gods, monsters or ghosts had abandoned him); "Si era abbuiato" (It had become dark); "Il giorno, oramai, declinava" (the sun, by then, was setting); "Si avvicinava un'ora. Quale ora?" (An hour was approaching. What hour?); and "Il silenzio era totale: immenso" (There was total silence: immense). Brutus, adds the narrator, "era rimasto completamente solo" (was left completely alone); even hate, his driving force, had finally left him. In a 1991 interview Ulivi explained that Brutus committed suicide, having realized the "suprema altezza del Tradito" (the supreme nobility of the Betrayed).

Unlike Brutus, Ulivi's Francesco d'Assisi (Francis of Assisi), the protagonist of *Le mura del cielo* (The Boundary Walls of Heaven, 1981) looks to God for the answer to the riddle of his existence. Francesco is portrayed as a man of action, a hero driven by an irresistible desire to reach God. The traditional image of St. Francis talking with animals is not present in Ulivi's novel; however, that truth is not distorted, either. Ulivi was inspired by Dante's St. Francis, seen in the *Divine Comedy* as a new "sun that rose on the world," the herald of a new dawn, a new age. In his search for God, Francesco is like a knight in the quest for the Holy Grail. Francesco believes that God is the Absolute and the Unknown; he is without name and without face: "Qualcuno sta là, certamente. Ma quale è il suo nome? Qualche volta, in sogno, ho creduto di ravvisarlo. Altre volte . . . non ho visto che il cielo puro, il cielo infinito (Someone is there, certainly. But, what is his name? At times, in my dreams, I thought I recognized him. Other times . . . I saw nothing but the pure sky, the infinite sky).

God, to Francesco, is an ambiguous Lord: He is there and he is not there. The same attitude is evident in the preface to the novel as the narrator describes how he was taken by Delacroix's *Jacob Wrestling with Angel,* which he had seen in the church of Saint-Sulpice in Paris. As he observed the painting, the narrator realized that the angel was only a screen: "un qualcosa tra luce e ombra che avrebbe potuto esserci e no" (something between light and shadow that could have been there or not). Yet the important thing for Francesco is to continue his quest, for to stop searching would give way to desperation, to hopelessness; it would mean giving up freedom. Mindful of Dante's image of St. Francis as the new sun, Ulivi portrays Francesco as being always surrounded by the light that emanates from beyond the walls of heaven, from the mystery of God.

In general Ulivi's central characters must strive to survive and cope with anguish and hopelessness in a world gone astray. In *La notte di Toledo* (Toledo Night, 1983) the ship on which the passengers travel is guided by a "bussola impazzita" (a wild compass).

Diego, the main character, is overwhelmed by the cruelty of the Spanish Inquisition and reflects on his times: "I tempi dirottavano verso esiti oscuri, mossi da forze ineluttabili' dirottavano, di sicuro, verso altri lutti, altre guerre" (Times were headed for somber consequences, steered by ineluctable forces; surely, times were heading towards more deaths, more wars). To Diego the world is overtaken by madness.

Ulivi dwells on life lived, on the experiences the individual characters make in exercising their free will and in making choices, particularly when they find themselves on the threshold of life and death, in a strange and murky area, in a spiritual wasteland. Free will is the interconnecting thread in Ulivi's works. It is seen as power and responsibility, which causes anguish but only because one must regard himself the arbiter of his own hope. One of the characters in *La notte di Toledo* can be seen as a spokesman for Ulivi's religious thought:

> Se qualcosa o Qualcuno ci fosse . . . bisognerebbe ammettere che ha svolto il suo lavoro in modo ineccepibile: fino a lasciar credere di non esserci affatto. . . . Vuol dire, se sei *homo religiosus*, che il tuo Dio ti lascia la libertà di determinarti: ti lascia solo; se invece non credi a nulla, che è la tua volontà, la forza, l'intelligenza personale o collettiva, a farlo.
>
> (If there were something or Someone . . . one would have to admit that he carried out his work in a way which was above reproach: to the point of letting us believe his being not there, at all. . . . If you are *homo religiosus*, it means that God allows you the freedom to define yourself: God leaves you alone; on the other hand, if you don't believe in anything, it means that it is your free will, your power, your individual or collective intelligence to do so.)

Here Ulivi seems to echo Italian humanists, especially Pico della Mirandola's observations on the question of free will. The novelist suggests that it is up to the individual to decide "quando nasca l'alba" (when dawn shall rise). In this image the individual is seen as having the Godlike ability to create light out of the darkness of existence.

In another passage in *La notte di Toledo* one of the characters wakes up during the night with the revelation that he has led a sterile and meaningless life:

> Soffro al punto che vorrei cessare di vivere. . . . Nello stesso tempo, capisco che solo a questa condizione posso avvicinarmi all meta, all'Unico. . . . La contraddizione è tremenda. . . . Mi trovo sospeso tra il nulla che mi incalza, e ciò di cui spero, o mi angoscio . . . mi costringo a vivere, a riprendere interesse, e così vengo osservando chi mi circonda, amici e nemici. Forse ho trovato un modo per conciliarmi con l'esistenza.
>
> (My suffering is such that I would rather stop living. . . . At the same time, however, I realize that only on this condition will I be able to approach the end: the Only One. . . . It is a tremendous contradiction. . . . I find myself hovering between nothingness (pressing hard on my heels) and what I wish for, or anguish about . . . I force myself to live, to take interest in life again, thus I go on observing those who surround me, friends and enemies. Perhaps, I have found a way to come to terms with existence.)

Woven into this passage are allusions to the poems of two contemporary poets: Salvatore Quasimodo's "Ed è subito sera" (And Suddenly It Is Dark), written at a time when the poet saw no alternative to man's solitude, and Giuseppe Ungaretti's "Sono una creatura" (I Am a Human Being), whose message is that one must pay in advance through living and suffering for the benefit of death.

Questions about the nature of existence are also at the heart of Judas's dilemma, the protagonist of the novel *Trenta denari* (Thirty Pieces of Silver, 1986). Ulivi's Judas acquires depth and ambiguity as a result of doubts that slowly seem to change the way he feels and thinks. Ulivi presents Judas as struggling with questions of freedom and destiny: Had he been chosen by God to betray Christ? Would someone else take his place if he chose not to betray Christ? Why was he chosen to betray Christ? To betray so as to love him, was that his vocation?

The development of Judas's character reaches its most dramatic stage in Gethsemane. As Judas looks at Christ, he is moved by anguish and overwhelmed with mixed feelings of retaliation, suffering, and affection: "Ti amo" (I love you) is what he wanted to say to Christ; however, looking into Christ's eyes, he realized that he could not breathe a single word. A feeling of love veined with hopelessness nearly brought him down on his knees to kiss Christ's hands: "E, con un moto irresistibile, reprimendo insieme all'orrore la forza ehe lo lacerava, mirò, anzi contemplò di nuovo, a lungo, il volto;

Dust jacket for Ulivi's 1986 novel, which depicts a complex, tortured Judas

porse le labbra verso quelle labbra pallide, e le baciò" (And, with an irresistible feeling, repressing, together with the horror, the force which was harrowing him, he aimed, or rather he contemplated again, at length, Christ's face, held his lips out to Christ's pale lips, and kissed them). Judas's kiss seems to take on a meaning of love: the kiss as the ultimate revelation of Judas's love for the indecipherable and irresistible Christ.

In *L'angelo rosso* (The Red Angel, 1992) Ulivi focuses on such figures as Ulysses, Pontius Pilate, and Rembrandt, each caught at the decisive moment of facing death. In the retelling of Pilate's story, Pilate became aware of a truth, conveyed to him by his wife Claudia Procula, who, in a dream learned that God had decided to respect man's free will. Pilate sees in Claudia's dream a hidden message of horror, because he finds himself, for the first time in his life, entangled within the questions of freedom, destiny, responsibility, and judgment.

In a 1992 interview with Chiusano, Ulivi explained that his prose owes everything to the art of light and color. Indeed, by integrating the aesthetics of art into his writing, he creates portraits, such as that of Saul and Rembrandt in *L'angelo rosso*, that vibrate with dramatic tension arising from the complexities in the characters' lives and their quest for truth. The interweaving of dialogue and flashbacks and the juxtaposition of images and ideas create a web of interconnections that captivate the reader. Ulivi spins his web to slow the pace of his readers as the plot comes to an end in order to involve them more deeply in interactions with the characters. He thus makes his readers pause and stimulates them intellectually. There is a definite dramatic aspect in all of Ulivi's novels that would make them suitable for the stage.

A dominant dilemma shared by Ulivi's fictional characters—particularly in *L'angelo rosso*—is "la presenza-assenza del divino" (the presence-absence of the divine), as the author indicated in an unpublished 12 April 1993 letter. With respect to *L'angelo rosso,* Ulivi writes that the vanishing image of the red angel—which in the novel appears in a painting supposedly damaged by fire—symbolizes the disappearance of transcendency and beauty during the trauma of World War II, in which people failed to exercise the values of goodness and charity associated with angels. The idea for the novel came to Ulivi years ago in Sicily, after he had seen "un quadro straordinario" (an extraordinary painting) by Antonello da Messina or one his followers; later he learned that the painting had been stolen, found, and stolen a second time, and never found again.

Through Giuseppe di Nazareth, the main character of *Come il tragitto di una stella; Giuseppe di Nazareth: sogne amore e solitudine* (As the Journey of a Star; Joseph of Nazareth: Dream, Love and Solitude, 1997), Ulivi again reflects poetically on human destiny. Joseph of Nazareth, like Francis of Assisi of *Le mura del cielo* is seen on a journey searching for God. However, unlike the faceless and barely visible Joseph of the Matthew Gospel, Ulivi's Giuseppe is omnipresent, vigorous, speculative, and complex; further, he bears little, if any, resemblance to the traditional image of the old carpenter, as depicted by artists.

Ulivi descends into the heart of Christ's putative father, exploring his innermost silences, shadows, dreams, feelings, desires, and dilemmas. If on one hand Joseph renounces his virility for the love of Mary and God; on the other, he accepts the mystery of his God, with whom he shares a reciprocal need, an intentional and indissoluble relation for mutual existence. As Joseph gains awareness of his ontological relationship with Christ (toward and from whom he would often feel concurrently close and distant), he also finds in Christ the source and stimulus of the search for truth. Accordingly, as unalterable as the life journey of a star. Joseph's path for truth is an immutable journey toward salvation.

Chiusano has remarked that Ferruccio Ulivi's novels are like pure diamonds: at first they appear as hardened water without color, but, as one rotates them with the fingers, they sparkle with all the colors in the rainbow. Indeed, just one journey in Ulivi's world is a valuable experience: past, present, and future come together into an harmonious whole. His novels, though, do not appeal to those who are looking for reinforcement of absolute truths, to those who have a static view of the world, or to those who believe that all the questions about our existence have been answered. Ulivi offers a new perspective on the human condition: a perspective that is dynamic and intellectually provoking, for he sows the seeds of doubt into truths that are taken for granted. Ulivi offers readers the opportunity to view the world from a perspective that does not distort the facts. His narrative strategy can be likened to a telescope: from one end it makes actions and events appear closer in time and space; from the opposite end it distances readers from them, so as to allow time to pause and reflect.

Ulivi, now well into his eighties, is in good health and continues to write. It is to be hoped that his works will soon be translated into English, for he is a writer who merits recognition outside of his native country. As a novelist and as a critic he occupies a unique place among major Italian authors. Students and scholars, no matter what period of Italian literature they study, will surely encounter his works.

Interviews:

Elio Filippo Accrocca, "Ferruccio Ulivi," in *Rittratti su misura* (Venezia: Sodalizio del Libro, 1960), pp. 415–416;

Claudio Toscani, *La voce e il testo–Colloqui con Bassami, Benari, Berto, Brignetti, Dessi, Levi, Moretti, Pomilio, Prisco, Silone, Strati, Tombari, Ulivi* (Milan: Istituto Propaganda Libraria, 1985);

Toscani, "Intervista a Ferruccio Ulivi per *Storie bibliche e d'amore e L'anello*," *Otto-Novecento*, no. 1 (January–February 1991): 103–108;

Toscani, "Intervista a Ferruccio Ulivi per La straniera," *Otto-Novecento*, no. 5 (September–October 1991): 109–113;

Italo A. Chiusano, "Parla l'autore: 'Non credo in un'arte realista,'" *Il nostro tempo*, 26 July 1992;

Piero Lazzarin, "Non toccate Manzoni," *Messaggero di Sant'Antonio* (March 1993): 68–70.

References:

Giuseppe Amoroso, "E le ceneri al vento," *Humanitas* (October 1977): 773–774;

Amoroso, "Ferruccio Ulivi," in *Narrativa italiana 1975–1983* (Milan: Mursia, 1983);

Amoroso, "Ferruccio Ulivi," in *Narratori italiani del secondo Novecento,* edited by Giorgio Luti (Rome: Nuova Italia Scientifica, 1985);

Amoroso, "Ferruccio Ulivi," in *La realtà e il sogno: Narratori italiani del Novecento* (Rome: Lucarini, 1987);

Giorgio Barberi-Squarotti, "Gli eroi di Ulivi in lotta col sacro," *La Stampa, Tutto Libri* (6 June 1992);

Carlo Betocchi, Giulio Cattaneo, and Claudio Varese, "Testo della presentazione di *Le mani pure*," *Antologia Vieusseux,* no. 56 (October–December 1979): 9–17;

Ettore Bonora, "Un intellettuale di fronte a San Francesco: Tra storia e romanzo," *Letteratura italiana contemporanea,* 3 (1982): 59–69;

Umberto Bosco, "L'eredità del neorealismo," *Rassegna di cultura e vita scolastica* (November–December 1977);

A. T. Romano Cervone, "Ulivi e le vite integrali," *Studi latini e italiani,* 4 (1960);

Elio Chinol, "Ferruccio Ulivi: *E le ceneri al vento,*" *Interventi sulla narrativa italiana contemporanea 1975–1977* (Treviso: Matteo, 1978), pp. 88–89;

Franco Lanza, "La narrativa di Ferruccio Ulivi," *Otto-Novecento,* no. 1 (January–February 1982): 243–257;

Lorenzo Mondo, "Un certo Leopardi," *La Stampa, Tutto Libri* (8 July 1977);

Angelo R. Pupino, "*Le mura del cielo,*" *Letteratura italiana contemporanea,* 2 (1981): 105–109;

Giovanni Scarsi, "Il francescanesimo nella letteratura contemporanea e Ferruccio Ulivi fra storia e romanzo," *Studium,* 78 (November–December 1982): 737–746.

Paolo Valesio
(14 October 1939 -   )

Paul Colilli
Laurentian University

BOOKS: *Strutture dell'alliterazione. Grammatica, retorica e folklore verbale* (Bologna: Zanichelli, 1968);

Between Italian and French: The Fine Semantics of Active Versus Passive (Lisse: Peter de Ridder Press, 1976);

L'ospedale di Manhattan (Rome: Editori Riuniti, 1978);

Prose in poesia (Milan: Guanda, 1979);

Novantiqua: Rhetorics as a Contemporary Theory (Bloomington: Indiana University Press, 1980); enlarged and revised, translated by Assunta Pelli as *Ascoltare il silenzio: la retorica come teoria* (Bologna: Mulino, 1986);

Il regno doloroso (Milan: Spirali, 1983);

La rosa verde (Padova: Editoriale Clessidra, 1987);

Dialogo del falco e dell'avvoltoio (Milan: Editrice Nuovi Autori, 1987);

Le isole del lago (Venice: Edizioni del Leone, 1990);

La campagna dell'ottantasette: poesie e prose-in-poesia (Milan: Scheiwiller, 1990);

Analogia del mondo (Udine: Campanotto, 1992);

Gabriele D'Annunzio: The Dark Flame, translated by Marilyn Migiel (New Haven: Yale University Press, 1992);

S'incontrano gli amanti: tre storie interoceaniche (Rome: Empiria, 1993);

Tradimenti (Bologna: Quaderni del Masaorita, 1994);

Dialogo coi volanti (Naples: Cronogio, 1997).

Edition in English: *Nightchant,* translated by Graziella Sidoli and Vanna Tessier (Edmonton: Snowapple Press, 1995).

OTHER: Edward Sapir, *Il linguaggio. Introduzione alla linguistica,* edited by Valesio (Turin: Einaudi, 1969);

Nicola Zingarelli, *Vocabolario della lingua italiana,* tenth edition, edited by Valesio and others (Bologna: Zanichelli, 1970);

Quaderni dannunziani: D'Annunzio a Yale: atti del Convegno, Yale University, 26–29 marzo 1988, edited by Valesio (Milan: Garzanti, 1988);

Paolo Valesio (photograph by Arturo Patten)

Paesaggio: poeti italiani d'America, edited by Valesio and Peter Carravetta (Treviso: Pagus, 1993).

Paolo Valesio, professor of Italian at Yale University, is a widely known scholar in the fields of linguistics, literary criticism, critical theory, and rhetoric. He is also a novelist, poet, and short story writer. A good point of departure for a critical assessment of his writings is the word *between* as a geographical as well as a critical and aesthetic preposition. Valesio, who calls himself an "Atlantic witness," is both Italian and American; metaphorically his work may be located between the poles of Italy and the United States. Valesio also operates between the poles of prose and verse, between the mind-sets of critical-theoretical writing and creative writing. The result of these geographic and cognitive scissions is not a cultural pathology but instead the enriching "contamination" of all of his writing. In particular, his two novels—*L'ospedale di Manhattan* (The Hospital in Manhattan, 1978) and *Il regno doloroso* (The Kingdom of Pain, 1983)—show the influence of his work as a poet and a theoretician.

Born in Bologna on 14 October 1939, Valesio is the son of Germano Valesio and Maria Galletti. After graduating from the Liceo Classico Luigi Galvani of his native city, he obtained a degree in the humanities from the University of Bologna in 1961. He won the Antonio Canova Prize for art criticism in 1957 and the Premio Marzotto in 1963. Valesio's research interests in linguistic, stylistic, and rhetorical analysis are evident in his dissertation, "Contributo ad un'analisi stilistica della lingua aristofanea" (Contribution to a Stylistic Analysis of the Language of Aristophanes). Beginning in 1963 Valesio won a series of scholarships that allowed him the opportunity to spend time in the department of linguistics at Harvard.

Valesio steadily climbed the academic ladder. Between 1968 and 1973 he rose from lecturer to become an associate professor of Romance languages at Harvard. During this period he published many articles, as well as the book *Strutture dell'allitterazione. Grammatica, retorica e folklore verbale* (Structure of Alliteration. Grammar, Rhetoric and Verbal Folklore, 1968), in which he attempted to unify rhetoric, linguistics, and stylistics. Valesio has continued to publish in the area of theory and criticism, but he did not regularly produce creative works until 1977. After a short stint at New York University, Valesio became a professor of Italian at Yale in 1974. He has since been a visiting professor at many universities, including the University of California at Santa Cruz in 1982, Stanford University in 1984, New York University in 1986, Brown University 1987, the University of Calabria in 1987, the University of Arizona in 1988, the University of Sao Paulo in 1989, the University of Alberta in 1990, the University of Venice in 1991, and the University of Basilicata in 1991.

In his works Valesio seeks to bridge the division between knowing and creating by using a style that moves across boundaries and seeks the contamination of differing modes of linguistic and intellectual expression. *Prose in poesia* (Prose Poems, 1979) is a testament to such a poetic and philosophical dissolution of the barriers and literary genre. In prose poems such as "Effare l'infame" (To Be Infamous), "Esame per l'ammissione alla scuola per terapisti della riabilitazione" (Test for Admission to the School for Rehabilitation Therapy), and "Performanza," Valesio explicitly refers to the alchemical tradition, in which reality is viewed as the product of perception, a mind-set that informs his writing and is especially evident in *Il regno doloroso* and the poetry collection *La rosa verde* (The Green Rose, 1987).

As the title suggests, *Prose in poesia* is characterized by an interplay between prose and verse forms. The outcome is a poetic reflection on the possibilities that living between things has to offer. The interplay between disparate things is evident in "Effare l'infame." Its opening words "Passer delicia della mia puella"—a macaronic version of Catullus's "Passer, deliciae meae puellae"—anticipate the mixture of Italian and Latin found throughout the poem. This poem provides a powerful example of Valesio's yoking together what is thought to be incompatible, for he combines the heated eroticism of the first part of the piece with meditations on Christ in its latter part.

In the prose poem "Pregando a Manhattan" (Praying in Manhattan) Valesio treats some of the major themes found in *L'ospedale di Manhattan*. The main issue in the poem is that of estrangement from the rest of the world, a feeling often experienced by the immigrant and the traveler as well as by the city dweller. Valesio immediately makes the reader aware of the brutal sense of inauthenticity—the feeling that one lacks genuine purpose or meaning—and estrangement that sometimes overwhelms people living in modern metropolises such as New York. The narrator of the poem listens attentively to the spiritual squalor that surrounds him as he seeks a means to ease his oppressive feelings. He soon comes to the realization that the alternative to the state of alienation is re-familiarization with the world, for estrangement is the result of not being able to recognize the world. Valesio thus suggests that one overcomes inauthenticity by means of a total immersion into and acceptance of the banal and the mundane. Such immersion allows one to make every place a sacred place.

In *L'ospedale di Manhattan,* a book that is as much critical theory as it is prose fiction, Valesio relies on the narrator's voice in order to disclose the intellectual territory that rests between the critic and the novelist. The novel is about the narrator's attempt to fathom the depths of his intellectual state while he waits in a hospital. One can surmise that the narrator is a university professor whose lover had entered the hospital to undergo routine surgery.

The work, which has no conventional plot as such, is made up of reminiscences, such as what the narrator was doing the day Kennedy was assassinated; his lover's checking into the hospital and going to her room; and flashes of images, such as his lover's body and the urban wolfman. What stands out is the author's imagination, manifested in both critical meta-language and poetic image-making, which roams freely throughout the novel. From the opening chapter it is clear that Valesio intends his novel to deal with the act of meditating between disparate ideas, to create a discourse that is both critical and poetic.

In the initial pages of the novel the narrator is concerned with finding a place where he can think with tranquillity. His choice for the ideal place of meditation is both logical and banal: "Il solo loco rimasto che possa adempiere alcune delle funzioni di una cappella privata, è la stanzetta del bagno" (the only place which can fulfil some of the functions of a private chapel is the bathroom). With this decision the narrator wishes to dislodge thinking from the lofty summits of elitism to the "puro rumore della tosse e del catarro" (pure noise of coughing and of catarrh). The meaning of such an assertion becomes clear as the narrator addresses his alter ego:

> Io voglio dunque, o mio altro io, afferarti per la collottola e piegarti giù, giù, fino a farti soffregare il naso e tutto il volto contro il fango della madre comune ... ti metterò la cavezza e ti farò curvare il collo; camminerai lento e ti pascerai in campi meno aprichi, il cui forte odore è quello del concime e della stalla.
>
> (I want, oh my other I, to grab you by the neck, lower your head and rub your nose and your face against the mud of the common mother ... I will put a halter on you and I will make you curve your neck; you will walk slowly and you will graze in fields which are less sunny, whose strong odor is that of fertilizer and of the barn.)

The narrator's strategy is to transfer critical thinking from the abstract realm of stable dialectics to the fluid impurities of everyday life. By doing so he celebrates the instability and provisional nature of daily life. For most of *L'ospedale di Manhattan* the narrator spends time thinking to himself, seeking solutions to vexing problems. But even with this emphasis on the mind, the narrator and the events he describes are presented in the most concrete and realistic terms. It is the interplay between abstraction and concreteness that inspires the novel.

While he was writing *L'ospedale di Manhattan* Valesio was entertaining the possibility of using Marxism as an ideological means to deal with a host of thorny social, intellectual, and cultural issues while also seeking to connect Marxist thought to Christian tenets. Valesio's first novel, then, juxtaposes a materialistic worldview with a spiritual one:

> La piú alta sfida che il pensiero il quale voglia cercare un senso serio dell'attributo "materialista" deve affrontare oggi non è lo studio di ciò che è più chiaramente materiale, bensì l'indagine di quelle umane produzioni sulle quali da sempre è stato inciso il motto "spiritualità"–prima fra tutte queste produzioni, il sistema della parola divina, ovvero teologia.
>
> (The greatest challenge facing an intellectual who wishes to find a serious attribute for materialism is not the study of that which is clearly material, but rather an investigation into those human productions on which the word "spirituality" has always been inscribed–foremost of all of these productions, the system of the divine word, namely, theology.)

Later on Valesio indicates that one of the tasks of his novel is to outline a systematic critique of the figure of Christ. The conclusion Valesio reaches, however, is one that reconfirms the originality of Christ's philosophy of being in, but not of, the world. Valesio's approach to Marx and Christ was to evolve into a dynamic form of spiritual listening that characterizes his later work.

Valesio does not limit the term *theology* to a purely religious context. In *L'ospedale di Manhattan* it also refers to the study of what is overlooked or forgotten, of the banal as well as the apocalyptic. One of the narrator's most provocative thoughts arises from his observation of how his lover, lying in the hospital bed, is dressed. His meditation on how women deal with everyday details leads to his formulation of a "theology of the minimal," which in this case refers to a way of selecting clothes that is not tentative and slow but "un susseguirsi nervoso e staccato di gesti rapidi–o meglio, un alternarsi di ritmi diversi" (a nervous and staccato succession of rapid gestures–better still, an alternation of different rhythms). The woman chooses her clothes "senza analisi: dico, senza soffermarsi verbalmente sui gesti, senza elucubrare, senza ostentare erudizione archeologica" (without analysis; I mean without lucubration, without showing off archaeological erudition). Just as knowledge is to be found in those acts that are traditionally ignored, so too is art to be discovered in the sublime nature of those acts.

The novel also offers a series of evocative images and events, such as the detailed description of the human body and the narrator's account of the day that Malcolm X was assassinated. The final pages, which include a reference to what appears to be Judgement Day, have a biblical and apocalyptic aura. On that day, the narrator relates, an angel will direct a confusing gaze at a host of people who do not know what to expect. Voices of angels will then ask each person to explain why they deserve resurrection. The narrator claims he already knows what he will say in response to the angels. With his mind focused on the afterlife, the narrator envisions his own painful death and is consoled by his belief that his lover will be there to provide comfort, to allow him to suck on her finger tips "senza vergogna, oltre il tempo" (without shame, beyond time). It is at this point that the narrator discovers the intersection of materialism and spirituality, where love dominates the experiences of life, death, and the afterlife.

Il regno doloroso, Valesio's second novel, traces the everyday life of three characters, Aurelio, Leo, and Doriana, as they move freely between Europe and North America. Structurally, the work is marked by an experimental effort to combine prose and verse forms, an effort Valesio had already made in *Prose in poesia* and would return to in *La campagna dell'ottantasette: poesie e prose-in-poesia* (The Campaign of 1987: Poetry and Prose Poems, 1990).

The choice of genre conditions the unfolding of *Il regno doloroso*. The second novel, much more than the first, reflects Valesio's philosophical notion that "una non materialistica microanalisi di tutto ciò ch'è materiale mostra . . . che ciò che noi effettivamente vediamo sono sequenze di minimi segmenti di gesti oggetti parole, oppure altri testi" (a nonmaterialist microanalysis of all that which is material shows . . . that what we actually see are sequences of minimal segments of gestures objects words, or other texts). The poetic prosing genre allows the author flexibility when dealing with a microphysics of reality.

The continuity between the first novel and *Il regno doloroso* rests on two motifs: living between two worlds and the theology of the minimal. Readers achieve a greater understanding of the characters when they learn how they approach living in the world they inhabit:

> Vi è, nel vivere di costoro, una sola ma significativa differenza: l'acuità (che arriva ad essere dolorosa) con cui essi osservano le cose e gli eventi anche minimi.
> Ogni prolungata e acuminata contemplazione delle cose del mondo nei loro particolari dettagli dà un misto di piacere e dolore. "Doloroso," dunque, non nel senso di un'assenza o aridità, ma al contrario: nel senso di un mondo gremito, affollato—che trasmette un affanno, e insieme una specie particolare di gioia. Il sacro si manifesta nel mondo d'oggi in modo frammentario e in forma degradata. Questo romanzo—che é stato definito come una serie di epifanie soffocate—descrive la miseria e l'inseparabile bellezza (la peculiare nobiltà disperata) di questa presenza del sacro. Che é indissolubilmente legato alla materia, alla fenomenologia della carne e dei sensi.

> (In their life, there is one albeit significant difference: the acuity [which turns out to be painful] with which they observe the minimal things and events.
> Any prolonged and pointed contemplation of the things of the world in their particular details provides a mixture of pleasure and pain. "Painful" then, not in the sense of an absence or of lack of feeling, but on the contrary: in the sense of a crammed and crowded world—that transmits anxiety together with a particular kind of joy. The sacred manifests itself in today's world in a fragmentary way and in a degraded form. This novel—which has been defined as a series of suffocated epiphanies—describes the misery and inseparable beauty [the peculiar despaired nobility] of this presence of the sacred. Which is indissolubly linked to matter, to a phenomenology of the flesh and the senses.)

The passage indicates the salient points that inform the text: the theme of the detailed observation of the ordinary; the interplay between joy and pain that results from such observation; the idea of "painful" being defined as a fullness, a crowdedness that, again, leads to both joy and anguish; the presence of the sacred, however degraded; the novel conceived as a series or collection of framed revelations or images; and the indelible link between the sacred and the material. These are the themes around which Valesio constructs this novel.

The opening of *Il regno doloroso*—the narrator's retelling of the biblical story of the Angel Raphael, Tobias, and Sarah against the background of modern Rome—shows that Valesio is seeking to show how sacred history and the banality of everyday life intersect. To further this theme he refers to the life of the German mystic Jakob Böhme, who was awakened to the pursuit of occult truths when he observed sunlight striking a pewter plate. Not a work of surreal imagination, Valesio's novel is an aesthetic transcription of images and sequences of events that can be experienced in the world.

Precisely because it is a staple ingredient in Valesio's own life, an important theme in the second novel is the incessant movement between Italy and the United States. For example, chapter four, "Le grammatiche" (The Grammars), might be characterized as a grammar of betweenness, where Valesio attempts to define the distinctiveness in the linguistic and cultural expressions of the two countries. He describes the differences from another perspective in chapter seven, "Le maniere" (Manners). The world that dominates the novel, though, is the one that exists in between Italy and the United States. Indeed, *Il regno doloroso* is not so much about Italy or the United States as it is about the existential netherworld that is inhabited by those individuals who ground their being in the geographic and cultural divide that separates the two countries.

It requires a particular gaze on the part of the observer in order to perceive in ordinary daily existence the dynamic intersecting of the banal and the apocalyptic. At the end of the first chapter, Valesio indicates that all Aurelio has in order to confront the threats of the world is the ability to gaze at whatever he is faced with; Valesio qualifies the gaze as "il

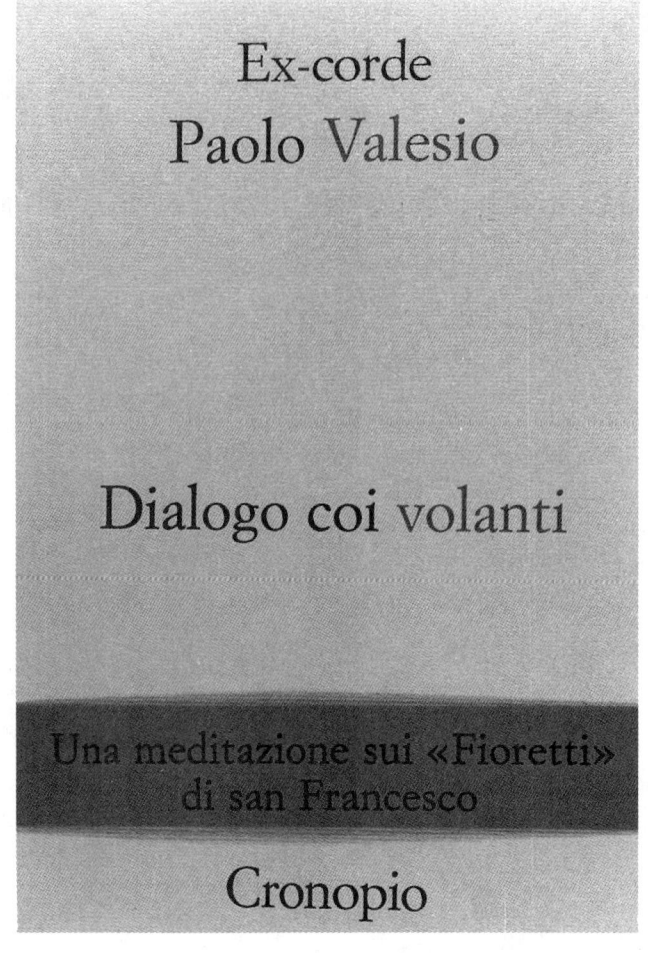

Cover for Valesio's 1997 book

vuoto riflettente di occhi aperti" (the reflective emptiness of open eyes), a phrase that suggests not so much a passive state as a state of continuous thought. The highly sensitive gaze of Valesio and that of his characters allows readers to see into what is taking place. (A distinctive aspect of *Il regno doloroso* is that it resembles the hermetic memory theatre described by Frances A. Yates.)

The reference to the gaze at the conclusion of the first chapter serves to introduce the idea of a form of thought that is rooted in the visual perception of images:

> voci, dentro; sguardi, fuori.
> No:
> anche lo sguardo é impossibile, se non dentro
>
> (voices, inside; gazes, outside.
> No:
> even the gaze is impossible, if not inside.)

Here Valesio asserts that gazing is of value only if the gaze is internalized. The object that is so perceived has the potential to be both the "thing" itself as well as a sign that directs the mind to a source of knowledge and thought, a "pensiero delle immagini," a thought-by-figures.

Chapter two, appropriately titled "Le viste" (The Vistas), consists of a series of images briefly described—a gallery of everyday portraits of everyday people. But the manner in which Valesio portrays this gallery echoes the Renaissance practice of employing emblems as a means to allegorically express sublime philosophical truths. Emblems had a key role in orienting the mind to perceive the external world. The forgotten meaning of alchemy within the Renaissance tradition is precisely this: the alchemical imagination sought to transform the material world not by physically altering it but by altering how it was perceived. At one point in *Il regno doloroso* the reader is confronted with an image—the black egg of alchemy, which appears in a discussion concerning the Holy Spirit—that contaminates Christianity with the esoteric tradition.

To understand the value of Valesio's formal contamination of prose, verse, and themes, one needs to keep in mind that critical and creative language have in common the ability to transform the way the world is perceived. The singular strength of Valesio's writing is that he transforms the ordinariness of everyday life by revealing the strangeness that is hidden within it. In this second chapter Valesio fashions a perspective that is necessary in order to understand the remainder of the novel. Readers learn they must seek what is hidden behind the images constructed by words and transform what is present on the page into something else by means of their inner eyes. It is this alchemy of the creative and the critical imagination—nourished by the theology of the minimal—that constitutes the basis of Valesio's narrative art.

In one of his essays Valesio notes that "Al suo livello più profondo, lo scrivere è una coltivazione del silenzio; e il silenzio, che apparentemente è causa di isolamento, risulta invece spesso essere un modo di approfondire i legami tra gli esseri umani" (At its deepest level, writing is the cultivation of silence; and silence, which apparently is the cause of isolation, often turns out to be a way of deepening the ties between human beings). In *Il regno doloroso* Valesio collapses the barrier that separates theory from practice, for the author's cultivation of silence by way of writing is one and the same with Aurelio's construction of his private world:

> Aurelio ha preso ad ascoltare il silenzio—e si è preso di questo ascolto. . . .
> Il perfetto silenzio nell'appartamento piccolo si costruisce da solo come fosse tutto un paesaggio di montagna:
> i secondi, i minuti si erigono l'uno sull'altro come strati di roccia o alture, cancellando l'altro-
>
> (Aurelio began listening to the silence—he was taken by the listening. . . .
> The perfect silence in the small apartment builds itself on its own, as if everything were a mountain landscape: the seconds, the minutes elevate themselves one on top of the other like strata of rock or of heights).

The knowledge of silence allows for the joyful construction of possible worlds. The perfect silence builds itself "come fosse tutto un paesaggio di montagna" (as if anything were a mountain landscape). Silence as edification is not a gratuitous or simplistic metaphoric formulation on Valesio's part. Aurelio realizes that he is not so much listening to silence as he is contemplating it as it "eleva scaffalature di roccia, erba, terra nella mente" (raises shelves of rock, grass, and earth in the mind). The implication here is that Aurelio' appreciation of silence brings him closer to the first silence, which arose the moment darkness and light were juxtaposed.

In the collection *La rosa verde* many of Valesio's poems have themes that directly involve the botanical world, including "Primavera d'autunno" (Autumn Spring), "Floresta," "Sovra un mazzo di fiori, inviati dopo un pranzo" (On a Bouquet of Flowers, Sent After Supper), "Porta del sole" (Gate of the Sun), "Ancora un volta, il fiore" (Once Again, the Flower), and "Foglie cadute dentro un diario" (Leaves Fallen in a Diary). In his descriptions of flowers, trees, and blades of grass Valesio shows that such flora are living ideas whose silent voice must be attended. They are post-allegorical as they stand not for something else but for themselves as specimens of life on earth.

The sense of a phase of transition is evident throughout *Dialogo del falco e dell'avvoltoio* (Dialogue of the Hawk and the Vulture, 1987) The opening poem, "Il pasto dell'avvoltoio" (The Vulture's Meal), plays on the idea of a destruction that is necessary for the creation of any new world. In the introduction to the collection Valesio makes explicit the critical framework of his verse: "Il lavoro di poesia che qui si presenta è stato costruito sulle rovine di ogni percezione sistematica, e di ogni maneggio funzionale del mondo" (The poetic work here presented was constructed on the ruins of all systematic perceptions, and on all functional handlings of the world). This statement is important in that it seems to signal the point of discontinuity between the early Marxist-influenced Valesio with the later poet-philosopher who looks to the future in order to see the past.

The systems of understanding alluded to by Valesio certainly include Marxist ideology but also the totalizing interpretative system with which Valesio experimented in *Novantiqua: Rhetorics as a Contemporary Theory* (1980). It should be noted that there is a significant difference between *Novantiqua* and the revised Italian version published six years later, *Ascoltare il silenzio: La retorica come teoria* (Listening to Silence: Rhetoric as Theory). While the English version is rooted in a materialist critique of metaphysics, the Italian version, which includes an extra chapter, instead elaborates an interpretative mind-set that can best be characterized as a form of spiritual listening.

Le isole del lago (Islands of the Lake, 1990) is a narrative in the form of poems. In "Nota ai testi" (Note on the Text), Valesio tells us that the story concerns Nerio and Nilio. Nerio attempts to find ways to be able to go on living, and he wants to get over his tempestuous past. In the preface to Valesio's collection of poems, Mario Lunetta characterizes *Le isole del lago* as a descent into the hell of everyday life. Lunetta observes that the poems often are rooted in what could be called cultural memory, where the present is placed into relation with an historical moment. In essence Valesio presents the interplay between the painful banality of everyday life and the intuitive awe one feels when faced with something that is chronologically remote. The contamination of the present moment with the past is characteristic to the Valesian poetic voice.

Valesio has also written collections of short stories whose dominant themes are the sacred observation of the ordinary, and listening to silence. For example, in "S'incontrano gli amanti" (Where Lovers Meet), in the 1993 collection bearing the same title, the character Vittore suggests that "il mistero della vita si coglie nelle sue banalità: cioè si sente . . . quando ci si rende ben conto di come 'banale' raramente sia sinonimo di 'semplice'" (the mystery of life is grasped in its banalities; that is, it is sensed when we realize very well how "banal" is rarely synonymous with "simple"). It is passages such as this that underscore the thematic congruency of Valesio's creative writing. Harold Bloom, in his introduction to the collection, asserts that Valesio is an ironist in the classical sense of the term, but that he is spiritually affected by a nostalgia for the romantic precisely because he pivots his rhetorical strategies on the ironical mode.

The novella *Tradimenti* (Betrayals, 1994) deals with the love affair of Larissa and Nuccio. In his postface to the story, Salvatore Jemma points out how Valesio takes care in describing for the reader the "minimi particolari nei rapporti quotidiani" (the smallest particulars in everyday relationships). Jemma also notes that Larissa appears to be a guide who accompanies Nuccio through an otherworldly voyage. This insightful observation sheds light on the existential frame that supports Valesio's story. In its most important respects, *Tradimenti* is a subtle reading of Dante's *Divine Comedy* as it explores the physical and spiritual spaces that define the real and the unreal.

Valesio is distinguished from other novelists by the great extent to which his creative writing is contaminated by his critical writing. He practices a variation of self-exegesis, not so much in that he directly explains what he writes about but in the sense that his creative works and his critical writings are two sides of the same coin. Since *L'ospedale di Manhattan* and *Il regno doloroso,* Valesio's writing has undergone a transformation dictated by his own changing philosophical and religious worldviews. The Marxist materialist of the first novel has evolved into a writer-thinker who is fascinated by the world of the sacred and of silence. In the experiments found in *L'ospedale di Manhattan* and *Il regno doloroso,* though, he produced convincing and original insights into the fleeting and often ignored dimensions of human experience by taking the quotidian existence as his main object of reflection.

One can place Valesio's aesthetic in historical perspective by considering his studies of Gabriele D'Annunzio, which include *Gabriele D'Annunzio: The Dark Flame* (1992), selected as book of the year by the American Association for Italian Studies in 1993. According to Valesio, D'Annunzio is the last Italian writer to articulate a totalizing and joyous vision of Italy. In fact, Valesio is convinced that there exists a spiritual genealogy linking Dante with D'Annunzio. To D'Annunzio the greatest truth is beauty, which is known mainly through the reelaboration of the mythopoeic material in Antiquity, the Middle Ages, and the Renaissance. However, D'Annunzio also believed that beauty could be known through the acute observation of everyday life. His *Notturno* (Nocturne) is a case in point, for there the poet details the most minute particulars of his daily existence. It is the same sort of documentation of the "minimal segments" of reality found in Valesio's novels and other creative works. This spiritual link to D'Annunzio emphasizes the optimistic tenor of Valesio's writing. While he focuses in his art on the fragments of life, his conclusion is not that existence is made up of disconnected particulars, which would lead to dark nihilism. Instead, Valesio's fragments reflect a vision of the world that celebrates its beauty.

Sebastiano Vassalli
(25 October 1941 -)

Deborah L. Contrada
University of Iowa

See also the Vassalli entry in *DLB 128: Twentieth-Century Italian Poets, Second Series.*

BOOKS: *Lui (egli)* (Florence: Rebellato, 1965);
Narcisso (Turin: Einaudi, 1968);
Disfaso (Rome: Trevi, 1969);
Tempo di màssacro: Romanzo di centramento & sterminio (Turin: Einaudi, 1970);
La poesia oggi (Novara: Ant, 1971);
Il millennio che muore (Turin: Einaudi, 1972);
AA. Il libro dell'utopia ceramica (Ravenna: Longo, 1974);
L'arrivo della lozione (Turin: Einaudi, 1976);
Brindisi (Bergamo: El Bagatt, 1979);
Abitare il vento (Turin: Einaudi, 1980);
La distanza (Bergamo: El Bagatt, 1980);
Mareblù (Milan: Mondadori, 1982; revised and enlarged, Milan: Mondadori, 1990);
Manuale di corpo (Siena: Barbablu, 1982);
Vani e servizi (Alessandria: Piombino, 1983);
Arkadia: Carriere, caratteri, confraternite degli impoeti d'Italia (Bergamo: El Bagatt, 1983);
Ombre e destini: Poesie 1977–1981 (Naples: Guida, 1983);
Il finito (Bergamo: El Bagatt, 1984);
La notte della cometa: il romanzo di Dino Campana (Turin: Einaudi, 1984); translated by John Gatt as *The Night of the Comet* (Manchester: Carcanet, 1989);
L'antica Pieve di Casalvolone in provincia di Novara (secoli XI–XII) (Bergamo: Bagatt, 1984);
Sangue e suolo: Viaggio fra gli italiani trasparenti (Turin: Einaudi, 1985);
L'alcova elettrica (Turin: Einaudi, 1986);
L'oro del mondo (Turin: Einaudi, 1987);
Marradi, by Vassalli and Attilio Lolini (Brescia: L'Obliquo, 1988);
Il neoitaliano: Le parole degli anni ottanta (Bologna: Zanichelli, 1989; enlarged edition, 1991);
La chimera (Turin: Einaudi, 1990); translated by Patrick Creagh as *The Chimera* (London: Harvill, 1993; New York: Scribners, 1995);

Sebastiano Vassalli (photograph by C. Marco Sorrentino)

Marco e Mattio (Turin: Einaudi, 1992);
Il Cigno (Turin: Einaudi, 1993); translated by Emma Rose as *The Swan* (London; Harvill, 1999);
3012: L'anno del Piofecta (Turin: Einaudi, 1995);
Cuore di pietra (Turin: Einaudi, 1996);
La notte del lupo (Milan: Baldini & Castoldi, 1998).

OTHER: Leonardo Sciascia, *Il giorno della civetta,* edited by Vassalli (Turin: Einaudi Edizioni Scolastiche, 1972);

Sciascia, *La scomparsa di Majorana,* edited by Vassalli (Turin: Einaudi Edizioni Scolastiche, 1981);

Dino Campana, *Opere,* edited by Vassalli and Carlo Fini (Milan: Editori Associati, 1989);

Novara: storia arte ambiente tradizione, introduction by Vassalli (Novara: Istituto Geografico De Agostini, 1994);

Roero Monferrato Langhe: le quattro stagioni, text by Vassalli, photographs by Claudio Penna (Turin: Umberto Allemandi, 1995).

One of the most articulate and influential writers of his generation, Sebastiano Vassalli endured twenty years in literary limbo before achieving widespread critical success in 1990 with *La chimera* (translated as *The Chimera,* 1993). No stranger to controversy, the outspoken Vassalli refused to conform to the expectations of the editorial and academic establishments. Indeed, if his predilection for protagonists trapped in perilous moments in history are any indication, he has probably derived inspiration from his position as a black sheep of the Italian literary world. He belongs to the *generazione di mezzo* (middle generation), those writers caught in time between the so-called death of Italian literature in the late 1960s and its tentative rebirth in the late 1980s.

Despite their critical dismissal, Vassalli's early works, born of the rebellious 1960s and designed to accentuate a split with traditional narrative, define the emotions and frustrations of a defiant generation. He and his contemporaries refused to follow blindly the dictates of their elders; many of them, failing to achieve the desired societal changes, abandoned idealism for cynicism and despair. The mature Vassalli chooses persuasion over anarchism and realism (some would argue cynicism) over nihilism. His successful revival of the historical novel, first with *La chimera* and then with *Marco e Mattio* (1992), betrays Vassalli's doubts that man is capable of learning from history, given his propensity for rewriting it, while demonstrating his unique ability to take a moment in time and make it come alive.

Sebastiano Vassalli was born in Genoa on 25 October 1941. His mother, Falaschi Alfreda, was Tuscan; his father, Luciano, was Lombardian. Vassalli earned a degree from the University of Milan with a thesis on contemporary art and psychoanalysis before settling into a teaching position in a *liceo* (secondary school) in Novara. During the 1960s and 1970s he was active in the so-called neoavantgarde movement promoted by Gruppo 63 and produced works of experimental prose, including *Narcisso* (Narcissus, 1968) and *Tempo di màssacro: Romanzo di centramento & sterminio* (Time of Slaughter: A Novel of Centralization and Extermination, 1970).

In order to appreciate the Vassalli of the 1990s, it is necessary to examine the evolution that brought the author from the linguistically complex and structurally difficult works of his early period to the spellbinding and highly readable prose of his maturity. Typical of the earliest Vassalli, strongly under the influence of the tenets of the Gruppo 63 and determined to subvert the expectations of the status quo, is *AA. Il libro dell'utopia ceramica* (AA. The Book of Ceramic Utopia, 1974). Here Vassalli suggests the infinite and indescribable storytelling possibilities inherent in the universe through a series of brief chapters, or "ceramic tiles," presented in no particular order.

The unusual title forewarns the reader of the stylistic peculiarities that follow: *AA* is not a familiar abbreviation, nor is it a borrowing of the attention-getting device of the newspaper personal ads (although it serves the same purpose). The letters, Vassalli explains in a note at the end of his text, are inspired by a work by medieval Provençal poet Jaufré Rudel. Each stanza of Rudel's verse concludes with the repetition of the final vowel sound of the final word of the stanza, creating what Vassalli describes as "un effetto davvero indefinibile, tra il riso aperto, spiegato, e la pura e semplice cadenza" (a truly indefinable effect somewhere between outright open laughter and rhythm pure and simple). Vassalli appropriates this phonetic poetic device—"l'eco di una risata antica, a, a" (the echo of an ancient laughter, ha, ha)—throughout his book at the conclusion of selected tiles, almost as a reminder to himself and to the reader not to take his proposals too seriously.

According to Vassalli every story he will later relate (and indeed every story ever written by any author in any time or any place) must be born of one of the ceramic tiles of *AA;* in addition, many of his favorite literary devices and ploys can be observed here. His experimentation with various forms of authorial voice, a fascination that continues even in Vassalli's mature works, is discussed in the preface as he explains the premise of *AA* and describes "la sopraffazione dell'Io sul mondo" (the I's overpowering of the world).

The vastness of Vassalli's purpose in *AA* renders it impossible. Despite the plethora of ideas, his rhetoric proves unequal to the task, and as the book develops, the language used to articulate each tile becomes redundant and monotonous. Vassali's awareness of this contradiction is revealed by increasing numbers of brackets that indicate details omitted as well as by an outrageous yet amusing reliance on *et cetera* at the conclusion of ceramic tiles where the singsong closing refrains have been repeated so often that it is scarcely necessary to com-

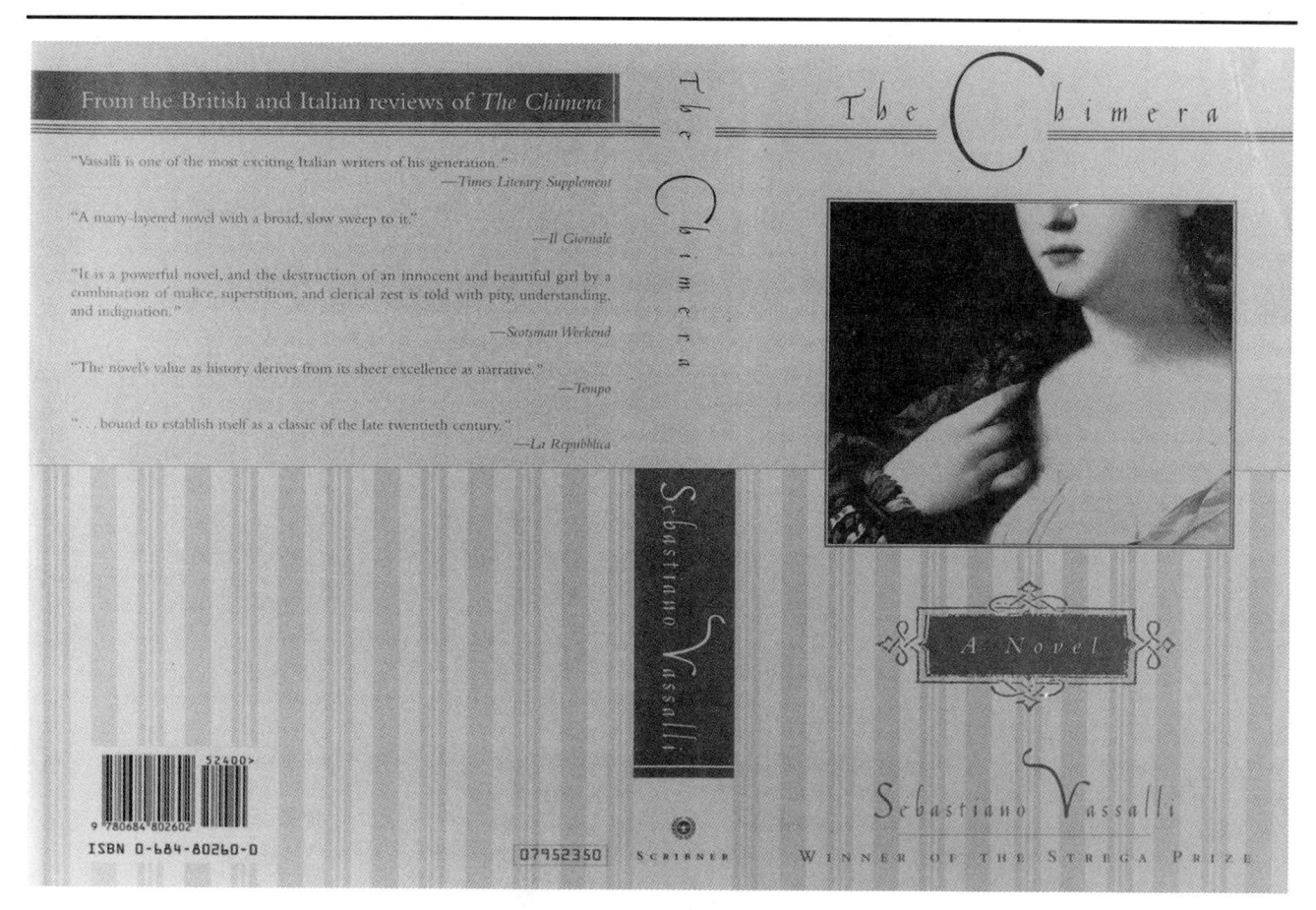

Dust jacket for the American edition of Vassalli's 1990 novel, about the fate of a woman reputed to be a witch

plete the lines; the reader has come to anticipate the recurring doggerel.

Amusing as it may be in small doses, however, in the long run *AA* does not offer the reader the substantial food for thought as do the later Vassalli works although it does provide a fecund starting point on which to build, particularly in its emphasis on rhetorical strategies that in modified form become identifying trademarks of Vassalli's later work.

The all-encompassing and oddly impersonal world of *AA* evolves into novels that, rather than alienating readers, involve them in the lives and day-to-day experiences of individual characters. The situations evoke many of the same emotions found in Vassalli's earlier prose: alienation, isolation, madness, political and social dissatisfaction, and sardonic humor.

Together with *L'arrivo della lozione* (The Arrival of the Lotion, 1976)—the title is the militant Right's phonetic corruption of *la rivoluzione*—*Abitare il vento* (To Inhabit the Wind, 1980) and *Mareblù* (Blue Sea, 1982) represent Vassalli's next literary stage, in which rebellious experimentation gives way to novels of political anarchism gone awry. In *Abitare il vento* and *Mareblù* one can find the germs of themes that become hallmarks of Vassalli's more critically successful later novels: the manic, obsessive behavior of the protagonists; their inability to survive or interact productively in the real world; and their ultimate self-destruction foreshadow the tragic circumstances of the protagonists of *La chimera* and *Marco e Mattio*.

Alternately hilarious and exasperating, tragic and provocative, *Abitare il vento* is the first-person narrative of Antonio Cristiano Rigotti—Cris for short—an incompetent but enthusiastic aspiring terrorist whose performance never seems to live up to his grandiose fantasies and expectations. Inevitably the story Cris relates and the reader's interpretation of his adventures are quite different: the narrator's words reveal far more than he intends to betray. This occurs in large part because he uses a colloquial spoken language replete with dialect, jargon, and wordplay. His manner of expression exhibits all the linguistic traits that separate spoken from written language—repetition, interjections, rambling sentences, nonstandard grammar, and abrupt changes of tone, style, and subject. Cris's voice ranges from gutter slang to literary allusion. He explains his erudite philosphical and literary digressions by frequently reminding his audience, "Ho fatto il liceo classico prima del sessantotto, io" (I completed the liceo before '68, I did).

Cris's identity crisis reflects the social and political crises of his generation (and of his author), and his distorted self-image denotes their unsatisfactory and shortsighted resolution. Despite Cris's vision of himself as the heroic loner of an old Western roaming from town to town in the service of a just cause, his actions are dictated more by the urges of lust than by political conviction. The alternating references to his penis—with whom he seems to interact more meaningfully than with any of the other characters of the novel, either with pride as "il Grande Proletario" (the Great Proletarian) or in ever-increasing moments of frustration and impotence as "il piccolo borghese" (the little bourgeois)—invite speculation on possible metaphoric interpretations and contribute an element of comic erotic pathos to Cris's tale while belying through the revelation of his single-minded narcissism his insistence that he is "cavaliere errante amico di tanti e di tante" (a wandering knight, friend of many, both men and women). Cris's bravado is inevitably revealed for the facade it is as sexual impotence and social isolation drive him to announce and plan his imminent suicide, a final gesture that will free him once and for all to "inhabit the wind," to achieve his ideal of "vivere via, dal tempo o dall'ideologia, a scelta" (living away from time or from ideology, choose one). He then is forced to turn his story back over to the author.

Vassalli's narrative strategy permits him an extended opportunity to explore the roles of narrator and author and to test the limits of narrative voice. Cris, the protagonist-narrator, makes the author, Vassalli, a character in this farce, a character with certain obligations to the narrator, who laments the author's attempts to control and manipulate him. In the end, of course, the narrator's deferral to his author, a surrender necessitated by his suicide, reminds readers that the two voices are indeed one. As for the delicate question of exactly how much of Vassalli is in his character, or vice versa, he provides an answer in his remarks on the novel in the *Autodizionario degli scrittori italiani* (Autobiographical Dictionary of Italian Authors, 1989):

> Vi si narrano le vicende del personaggio che l'autore stesso avrebbe potuto esser e non fu, mosso dall'illusione di poter cambiare il mondo e finito a margine di un "movimento armato" contro qualcosa di non ben individuato: forse il Destino, o lo Stato, o chissà che altro.

> (Therein are related the fortunes of a character which the author himself could have been, but wasn't, driven by the illusion of being able to change the world and winding up on the fringes of an "armed movement" against something not very well-defined: maybe Destiny, or the State, or who knows what.)

Augusto Ricci, the protagonist of *Mareblù*, is the embodiment of what Cris might have become had he survived. A self-proclaimed "rivoluzionario individualista" (individualist revolutionary), the sixty-year-old Ricci, for thirty years custodian of the Mareblù campground, is another of Vassalli's alienated loners, isolated from the real world and caught up in the militant fervor of decades past, forced to earn a living that condemns him to be a part of the system he has sworn to overthrow. Ricci is like Cris in that his closest confidants are not the people who surround him: he openly resents his employers and amuses himself by spying on and tormenting the campers he is hired to assist. Instead he engages in lengthy discussions with Marx, Lenin, Stalin, and Mao, the four "Giganti della storia" (giants of history) whose images adorn the wall of his camper, and takes comfort in his pets—a parrot called Spartacus, a hen named Elizabeth VIII, and dogs Winston (Churchill) and Charles (De Gaulle).

Augusto is also like Cris in choosing not to live in a world from which he feels hopelessly alienated. In *Abitare il vento* Vassalli allowed Cris the interference of an author-character and a surfeit of distracting word games to provide him a measure of detachment from the disillusionments of reality; in *Mareblù* Vassalli uses a different stylistic device to permit his character a degree of disassociation with the negative realities of his existence. Augusto isolates himself from his surroundings by viewing events, both real and imagined, through the lens of a camera. He is bent on capturing for posterity the action unfolding before his eyes, a feature-film production in which he is at once producer, director, author, and leading man with full creative control of all cinematographic options.

The discovery that the owners of the campground are planning to close it down and force him into retirement sends Ricci over the deep end into antiestablishment plotting that is both hilarious and alarming. He is convinced that "la rivoluzione è una cosa che si fa con passione o non si fa" (revolution is something you either undertake with passion or not at all) but is largely ignored by those around him, who already consider him a madman. Ricci's dreams of single-handedly masterminding the downfall of his capitalist oppressors literally and figuratively go up in smoke, as does the Mareblù campground—not, as he had fantasized, in the guise of a bourgeois apocalypse, but rather, at the hands of less than loftily motivated juvenile arsonists.

The destruction of Mareblù (the novel was written to coincide with the sixtieth anniversary of the foundation of the Italian Communist Party in 1920) is also the devastation of Ricci's utopian visions, and the dizzying spiral into madness is intensified by one final irony: as his world lies in ashes around him, the self-styled individualistic revolutionary finds himself pressured to testify—for financial remuneration—on behalf of the men he has sworn to overthrow. A defeated Ricci, stricken by the perception of the proletariat and capitalists working side by side to create a world not much different from that with which they began, lets loose with a tragic yet liberating peal of laughter as he slips into insanity:

> E io Augusto Ricci per la prima volta dopo sessant'anni di vita seria finalmente rido di gusto, sghignazzo: ah ah ah ah ah ah ah ah ah. Oh oh oh oh oh oh oh oh oh. Ah ah ah ah ah ah ah ah ah. Rido come un pazzo, ah, ah.

> (And I Augusto Ricci for the first time in sixty years of serious living at long last laugh with gusto, I roar: ha ha ha ha ha ha ha ha ha ha. Ho ho ho ho ho ho ho ho ho. Ha ha ha ha ha ha ha ha ha. I laugh like a madman, ha ha.)

The chilling echo of Ricci's laughter, reminiscent of the "a, a, a" (ha ha ha) that permeates *AA,* is a final bitter reminder of the motto of the creative forces of the political movement of 1977: "Ah, ah, ah, sarà una risata che vi seppellirà" (Ha, ha, ha, it will be laughter that buries you).

In the chain of literary works leading up to *La chimera,* *Mareblù* is distinguished from its predecessors by its readability. Vassalli puts aside the heavy-handed use of linguistic and stylistic verbal ploys that characterized even *Abitare il vento* and instead concentrates on the allegorical aspects of his tale. The result is a prose that engages the reader in the story while still documenting and probing the vicissitudes of the Communist Party in Italy. *Mareblù* is the last of Vassalli's political novels and propels him to confront a new adversary: history.

In the concluding phase of his journey toward *La chimera*—represented by *La notte della cometa: il romanzo di Dino Campana* (1984; translated as *The Night of the Comet,* 1989), *L'alcova elettrica* (The Electric Alcove, 1986), and *L'oro del mondo* (The Gold of the World, 1987)—Vassali explores the investigative novel. In *La notte della cometa,* subtitled "The Novel about Dino Campana," Vassalli presents his research into the life of the tormented poet as a means of examining the art of poetry. He regards Campana, known primarily as the author of the *Canti orfici* (Orphic Cantos, 1914), as the last of the true Italian poets. Campana spent most of his adult life in and out of institutions and at his death in 1932 had been institutionalized continuously for fourteen years.

Written in an almost journalistic style and composed of many short chapters just two or three pages long, *La notte della cometa* juxtaposes fact and speculation, but Vassalli is careful to distinguish between the two. The reader becomes intimately involved in the details of Campana's life through Vassalli's ongoing explanation of how his fourteen years of research unfolded. The author uses the historical present to lend immediacy to his tale and directly includes the reader in the course of events by the use of the first-person plural subject: "Entriamo con Dino nel manicomio di Imola. . . . Immaginiamo l'ambiente coi corridoi, gli stanzoni, le inferriate a tutte le finestre, le catenelle a tutti i letti" (Let's enter the Imola mental asylum with Dino. . . . Imagine the inside with its corridors, large rooms, bars on all the windows, chains on all the beds). The result is not a traditional novel nor a typical biography written in the manner of a novel but a reconstructed documentary, all the more convincing for the disruption in narrative flow brought about by rapid-fire alternations between the present, the historical present, and authorial conjecture.

Campana is revealed as a misunderstood and mistreated victim of his family and his times, a misfit unable to live in a world he cannot control—in short, a character dear to his author's heart. Vassalli acknowledges the felicity of his choice of Campana as a biographical subject in the conclusion of the novel:

> Io cercavo un personaggio con certi particolari connotati. Il caso me l'ha fatto trovare nella realtà storica e da lí l'ho tirato fuori. . . . Ma se anche Dino non fosse esistito io ugualmente avrei scritto questa storia e avrei inventato quest'uomo meraviglioso e "mostruoso," ne sono assolutamente certo. L'avrei inventato cosí.

> (I was searching for a character who fit a certain description. By chance I found him in historical reality and so I drew him out of there. . . . But even if Dino had not existed, I would have written this story anyway, and I would have invented this wonderful and "monstrous" man, I'm absolutely positive. I would have invented him exactly this way.)

The last step to *La chimera* is *L'oro del mondo*. Here Vassalli blends fact and fiction not in the staccato method of *La notte della cometa* but in a smooth-flowing narrative. He alternates three essentially separate but interrelated stories throughout the novel: the narrator-author's obsessive efforts to convince his editor of the validity and viability of his proposed novel about Italy emerging from Fascism, which allows Vassalli the pleasure of satirizing current editorial and academic foibles with a zeal mitigated only by a generous dose of accompanying self-mockery; the text of the proposed historical novel, which, ironically, is the smallest segment of the actual novel; and the predominant narration, which traces the coming-of-age of the first-person narrator, a character named Sebastiano Vassalli, whose tormented relationship with his father, repeatedly referred to as "l'infame autore dei miei giorni" (the infamous author of my days), is a focal point of the fictional biography.

In *L'oro del mondo*, which is as much the story of the genesis of a novel as it is the description of the creation of a nation, Vassalli treats a specific period in history and delves into the everyday lives of characters who would appear to include Vassalli's closest relatives. As in the novels that follow he reveals the folly of history while attempting to unravel the misconceptions that are at its roots. *L'oro del mondo* is a story of adolescence, both of a young boy and of a nation as they must come to terms with past and present in order to face the future. Vassalli's conclusion—placed in the mouths of deposed monarchs—reminds a generation of Italians of a history they prefer to revise: "'Les italiens, maintenant, ne se contentent pas de n'être plus fascistes; ils exigent de n'avoir jamais été fascistes.' 'Ils sont un drôle de peuple, les italiens!'" ("The Italians aren't satisfied with no longer being fascist; they want never to have been fascist." "A strange people, the Italians!").

In 1989 Vassali published *Il neoitaliano: le parole degli anni ottanta* (The New Italian: The Words of the 1980s), a work that is valuable as a study of neologisms as well as for what it reveals of its author. While the volume may at first appear to be merely a dictionary of the words that were invented, reinvented, or redefined during the 1980s, a close reading reveals the nontraditional, almost parodic nature of Vassalli's endeavor and his incorrigible efforts to indoctrinate and entertain while educating. Characteristic of Vassalli's approach is his labeling of the various decades to which he refers: the 1980s are invariably and repetitively classified as *banali* (banal) while the decades of Vassalli's youth are provided with more favorable descriptions: the 1970s are *folli* (crazy); the 1960s, *favolosi* (fabulous); and the 1950s, *miracolosi* (miraculous). His approach yields a portrayal of the 1980s that goes beyond the confines of a traditional vocabulary and explores the vagaries of a decade.

While the first stages of Vassalli's literary life were marked by polemics with publishers and critical neglect—he chronicled his disdain for the Italian literary scene in *Arkadia: Carriere, caratteri, confraternite degli impoeti d'Italia* (Arkadia: Careers, Characters, Fraternities of Italy's Unwriters, 1983)—he has enjoyed unprecedented success in the 1990s. The much-praised historical novel *La chimera*, which chronicles the alleged events leading up to and surrounding the trial for witchcraft against Antonia Spagnolini, "witch of Zardino," during the Counter Reformation, captured prominent literary prizes including the Premio Strega, Premio Napoli, and the Premio Selezione Campiello. *La chimera* demonstrates Vassalli's ability to examine historical events from a variety of perspectives simultaneously: readers share the thoughts, fears, and beliefs of the characters within the framework of the seventeenth century world; at the same time Vassalli never allows his readers to forget that the tale is being related in a twentieth century that has learned little from history. Vassalli makes sure that readers witness Antonia's death at the stake in 1610 with the awareness that such ignorance and brutality continues to claim victims.

La chimera has been unremittingly compared to Alessandro Manzoni's *I promessi sposi* (1827; translated as *The Betrothed*, 1828), the exemplar of the traditional Italian novel, with a preponderance of critics discussing its blatantly anti-Manzonian aspects. But in the 1992 article "Intertextual Patterns: *I promessi sposi* in *La chimera*" Verina R. Jones goes further, maintaining that Vassalli's debt to Manzoni is far more complex and scholarly than the conspicuous oppositions may make it appear. Jones offers many examples to demonstrate how Vassalli has manipulated the text of *I promessi sposi* to convey the message of *La chimera* while concurrently making a comment on the text and message of Manzoni's masterpiece. As had *I promessi sposi*, *La chimera* probes "history from below," but the sceptic and unbeliever Vassalli can venture far beyond the self-imposed boundaries of the Christian Manzoni, thus paying homage to the earlier novel while betraying its limitations.

With *La chimera* Vassalli makes ambiguity a vital part of his prose. The title suggests the multiple interpretations the reader is invited to explore during the course of the novel. The Chimera is the fire-breathing she-wolf of Greek mythology and by extension any imaginary monster constructed of incongruous parts; a chimera is also an illusion, a fantasy, or an unrealizable dream. The chimera of Vassalli's novel may be its protagonist, Antonia; the town of Zardino; the villagers and clergy who bring about Antonia's destruction; the events the author relates; all of these; or something else. In contrast to the precise distinctions between fact and fantasy that characterize *La notte della cometa,* with *La chimera* it is never clear if the story—or indeed the town of Zardino itself—is real or imagined, if the documents the author takes pains to cite are genuine or fabricated. The line between truth and fiction is blurred and unimportant as the author weaves a spell that makes the reader believe the characters are real, the events true. An air of authenticity is conferred by the characters' use of their native dialect rather than an artificial language imposed on them. Typical of his style, Vassalli feels free to comment and criticize his characters' actions, occasionally even pointing out situations in which he would have behaved quite differently.

Strong female characters in Vassalli's writings are essentially nonexistent prior to Antonia (although Lory Ferrero-Barbero in *Mareblù* shows potential as a fitting match for its manic narrator, Augusto Ricci), serving more as objects of convenience for self-serving male protagonists than as real people, as necessary plot devices rather than as thinking individuals. But while Antonia, a foundling adopted by kindhearted farmers of Zardino, is ostensibly the heroine of *La chimera,* she may also be viewed primarily as a catalyst that allows Vassalli to explore in detail the events and people that conspire to destroy her. Although her actions contribute to her problems, it is Antonia's exceptional beauty—too remarkable and unacceptable "per la sua condizione e per i gusti dell'epoca" (for her social condition and for the tastes of the times)—and her adopted status that are at the heart of the superstition and fear of her contemporaries.

In *Marco e Mattio,* dedicated "to the insane," Vassali further explores the boundaries of the historical novel. He presents the intertwined lives of the two title characters, focusing on the recurring themes of insanity and isolation by once again dissecting a crucial moment in Italian history—the years of the Enlightenment and the Napoleonic invasions at the end of the eighteenth and beginning of the nineteenth centuries—through the eyes of the impoverished and the neglected. Within the eloquently portrayed microcosm of the declining years of the Republic of Venice, the novel recounts the story of Mattio Lovat, impoverished but honest son of a shoemaker of Zoldo, a village of the upper valley of the Piave River. In 1805, the victim of madness brought about by malnutrition, he attempts to crucify himself as a second Christ, convinced that his sacrifice will save his world from destruction, and is then institutionalized. From the age of fourteen to his death by self-imposed starvation in 1806, Mattio frequently encounters the mysterious Marco, an ambiguous and equivocal character, the moral opposite of Mattio, who appears in different guises and under different names. Vassalli thus counterbalances a realistic, morally clear-cut historical saga with the mercurial yet pervasive presence of evil.

Man's aversion to change, his fear of the unknown, and his suspicion of all that is different are also revealed as constants that transcend time and space. The reluctance of the poverty-stricken residents of the Piave Valley to break with the traditions of the Old World and accept new alternatives is nowhere more compellingly evoked than in the reaction of the famished villagers to the arrival of the potato, the miracle food from the New World. The townspeople are suspicious and scornful of what appears to them to be food for hogs, not for men. The potatoes, distributed one to a village and intended to alleviate the polenta famine, are carefully cut up and planted; that same night in every village the potato sprouts are dug up and consumed raw—not by animals, but by men. The citizens of the Republic of Venice, as Mattio discovers, are not yet ready for salvation.

Whether the religious and superstitious catalysts that lead to the destruction of Antonia in *La chimera* or the physical condition that propels Mattio into insanity, the powerlessness of Vassalli's later characters, like their earlier counterparts, has its origins in their inability to counter the outside forces that govern them. There is, however, a crucial difference in Vassalli's characterization of these sets of protagonists: in their vulnerability to destructive powers acting from outside, Antonia and Mattio represent the emarginated in a losing struggle against the mighty, and their choices are based on the limited options reality offers them; the helplessness of Cris in *Abitare il vento* and Augusto in *Mareblù,* while their original goals may have been lofty, seems to derive as much from within as from without, rendering them less ideally sympathetic.

In *Il Cigno* (The Swan, 1993), at once timely and controversial with its theme of Mafia political machinations and murder, Vassalli writes of the years between 1893 and 1920, a period that by its proximity to the present renders the task of weaving truth and invention both more delicate and more complex. As in his previous two books, Vassalli convincingly blends reality and fiction, as he relates the story of the assassination in Sicily of Emanuele Notabartolo, sent to Palermo by the Italian government in order to investigate financial irregularities at the Bank of Sicily. Notabartolo's violent death is arranged by Raffaele Palizzolo, known as "il Cigno" (the Swan) for his glibness and his penchant of reciting his own awful poetry. Palizzolo, despite considerable evidence to the contrary, is absolved of all charges after a ten-year legal battle and returns to Sicily a hero to the Sicilian people, who resent the interference of outsiders in their affairs and who staunchly claim that the Mafia is naught but the vicious invention of a meddling "foreign" government. The publication of *Il Cigno* at a moment in which the Italian people seem determined to declare war on Mafia political and economic control led many to recall the early, bitterly political Vassalli, who now seemed to be employing subtlety and wile where before he preferred hyperbole and heavy-handed sarcasm.

While *La chimera* had prompted comparisons to Manzoni's work, *Il Cigno* led many to think of Leonardo Sciascia. The connection is inevitable and the debt unsurprising: Vassalli, in fact, edited the scholastic editions of two of Sciascia's works. And in his own inimitable fashion Vassalli tossed down the gauntlet to critics, comparing his achievement to that of Sciascia in an interview reported in the 19 December 1993 issue of *Corriere della Sera*:

> I suoi mafiosi hanno una oscura e contraddittoria grandezza. I mafiosi veri, i Liggio e i Riina, sono lontanissimi dall'idealizzazione che ne ha fatto Sciascia.... I mafiosi raccontati da Sciascia ... sono avvolgenti, sono un po' Totò Riina, un po' Sciascia stesso. Per questo mi sembra indiscutibile la sua compromissione letteraria. Nel mio *Cigno,* al contrario, non c'è niente di Sebastiano Vassalli. Niente.

> (His mafiosi have a vague but contradictory greatness. The real mafiosi, the Liggios and the Riinas, are a far cry from the idealization which Sciascia has made of them.... The mafiosi that Sciascia writes about ... are deceptive, part Totò Riina, part Sciascia himself. For this reason I consider the compromise of his literary works indisputable. In my *Swan,* on the other hand, there's nothing of Sebastiano Vassalli. Nothing.)

In addition to his work as a novelist, Vassalli is known as a poet and as an artist. He has published several volumes of poetry, including *Brindisi* (Toasts, 1979), *La distanza* (Distance, 1980), and *Ombre e destini* (Shadow and Destiny, 1983). In the early 1960s he explored plastic arts and had several shows of pop art to his credit. His continuing appreciation for the visual arts is evident in his prose contributions to photographic collections: *Novara: storia, arte ambience tradizione* (Novara; History, Art Ambience, Tradition, 1994) and *Roero Monferrato Langhe: le quattro stagioni* (Roero Monferrato Langhe: The Four Seasons, 1995). He is an active contributor to literary periodicals, and he also founded and edited the periodicals *Ant Ed* and *Pianura*. Since the early 1980s Vassalli has lived in the countryside between Novara and Vercelli, where, he maintains, he has distanced himself from literary trends and fashions and pursues his own intellectual ambitions undeterred by critical or editorial disapproval. He remains, however, a frequent and vocal participant in current literary controversies.

Letters:
Belle lettere, by Vassalli and Giovanni Bianchi (Bergamo: El Bagatt, 1979).;
Belle lettere, by Vassalli and Attilio Lolini (Turin: Einaudi, 1991).

Biography:
Felice Piemontese, ed., *Autodizionario degli scrittori italiani* (Milan: Leonardo, 1989).

References:
Zygmunt G. Baranski, "Sebastiano Vassalli: Literary Lives," in *The New Italian Novel,* edited by Baranski and Lino Pertile (Edinburgh: Edinburgh University Press, 1993), pp. 239–257;
Paolo Di Stefano, "La mafia e il letterato: fascino della dimensione oscura," *Corriere della Sera,* 19 December 1993;
Susanne Knaller, "Un ponte sull'infinito'–Literatur als Formel? Intersuchungen zu Sebastiano Vassalli," *Sprachkunst,* 24, no. 1 (1993): 127–143;
Verina R. Jones, "Intertextual Patterns: *I Promessi Sposi* in *La Chimera*," *Italian Studies,* 47 (1992): 51–67;
Anna Laura Lepschy, "Intolerance Prevails," *Times Literary Supplement,* 5–11 October 1990, p. 1074;
Stefano Tani, *Il Romanzo di ritorno* (Milano: Mursia, 1990).

Elémire Zolla
(9 July 1926 -)

Anna Botta
Smith College

BOOKS: *Saggi di etica e di estetica* (Turin: Spaziana, 1947);

Minuetto all'inferno (Turin: Einaudi, 1956);

Eclissi dell'intellettuale (Milan: Bompiani, 1959); translated by Raymond Rosenthal as *The Eclipse of the Intellectual* (New York: Funk & Wagnalls, 1968);

Cecilia o la disattenzione (Milan: Garzanti, 1961);

Volgarità e dolóre (Milan: Bompiani, 1962);

Le origini del trascendentalismo (Rome: Edizioni di Storia e Letteratura, 1963);

Storia del fantasticare (Milan: Bompiani, 1964);

Le potenze dell'anima (Milan: Bompiani, 1968);

I letterati e lo sciamano (Milan: Bompiani, 1969); translated by Rosenthal as *The Writer and the Shaman. A Morphology of the American Indian* (New York: Harcourt Brace Jovanovich, 1973);

Che cos'è la tradizione (Milan: Bompiani, 1971);

Le meraviglie della natura. Introduzione all'alchimia (Milan: Bompiani, 1975);

Archetypes. The Persistence of Unifying Patterns (New York: Harcourt Brace Jovanovich, 1981; London: Allen & Unwin, 1981);

The Androgyne: The Creative Tension of Male and Female (New York: Crossroad, 1981); republished as *The Androgyne: Fusion of the Sexes* (London: Thames & Hudson, 1981);

Aure, i luoghi e i riti. (Venice: Marsilio, 1985);

L'amante invisibile. L'erotica sciamanica nelle religioni, nella letteratura e nella legittimazione politica (Venice: Marsilio, 1986);

Verità segrete esposte in evidenza. Sincretismo e fantasia. Contemplazione e esotericità (Venice: Marsilio, 1990);

Tre discorsi metafisici (1989-1990) (Naples: Guida, 1991);

Il Bosco sacro (Foggia: Bastogi, 1992);

Uscite dal mondo (Milan: Adelphi, 1992);

Lo stupore infantile (Milan: Adelphi, 1994);

Le tre vie (Milan: Adelphi, 1995);

La nube del telaio. Ragione e irrazionalità tra Oriente e Occidente (Milan: Mondadori, 1996).

OTHER: *I moralisti moderni,* edited by Zolla and Alberto Moravia (Milan: Garzanti, 1959);

La psicanalisi, edited by Zolla (Milan: Garzanti, 1960);

Emily Dickinson. Selected Poems and Letters, edited by Zolla (Milan: University Mursia, 1961);

Antologia di Sade, edited by Zolla (Milan: Longanesi, 1962);

I mistici, edited by Zolla (Milan: Garzanti, 1963); enlarged as *I mistici dell'Occidente,* four volumes (Milan: Rizzoli, 1978-1981);

Herman Melville, *Clarel,* translated into Spanish by Zolla (Turin: Einaudi, 1965);

Novecento americano, three volumes, edited by Zolla (Rome: Lucarini, 1980-1981);

L'esotismo nelle letterature moderne, edited by Zolla (Naples: Liguori, 1987).

Elémire Zolla is a scholar, a critic, and a novelist whose wide-ranging oeuvre is characterized by an interdisciplinary approach, originality, and an impressive knowledge of both Western and Eastern cultures. Zolla, who taught Anglo-American and comparative literature at La Sapienza University in Rome and at the University of Genoa, has written essays on such wide-ranging topics as late capitalist culture, sociology, anthropology, philosophy, ethics, psychoanalysis, mysticism, alchemy, shamanism, esoteric doctrines, and orientalism. Early in his career, Zolla also published two novels, *Minuetto all'inferno* (Minuet in Hell, 1956) and *Cecilia o la disattenzione* (Cecilia or Inattentiveness, 1961). He subsequently abandoned the novel to become an internationally known essayist. In the 1990s he published collections of short texts, *Uscite dal mondo* (Exits from the World, 1992) and *Lo stupore infantile* (The Child's Wonder, 1994), that can be characterized as metaphysical travel narratives since they present meditative forays into a variety of cultures interspersed with actual travel memoirs. Zolla has also translated a few of his favorite writers (Herman Melville, Marquis de Sade, J. R. R. Tolkien, Gustav Meyrink) and has written critical articles dealing with Italian, French, British, American, and Russian authors.

Elémire Zolla (photograph © Giovanni Giovannetti)

Zolla is a comparatist in the broadest definition of the term. In 1956 he won the prestigious Premio Strega literary prize with his *Minuetto all'inferno*. In the 1970s he achieved worldwide renown for his studies on shamanism and esoteric doctrines. In the 1980s and the 1990s his mystical-religious quest has matured: his is a distinctive voice that proposes the syncretism of Eastern and Western philosophies as a way of saving Western civilization from decadence. His 1995 book-length interview with Doriano Fasoli, which is as close as Zolla has come to writing an autobiography, bears the title: *Un destino itinerante. Conversazioni fra Occidente e Oriente* (An Itinerant Destiny. Conversations Between West and East).

Zolla was born in Turin on 9 July 1926 but spent the first ten years of his life traveling between London and Paris. He grew up in an international and artistic milieu; his father, Venanzio Zolla, was an Italian painter born in England; his mother, Blanche Smith, was an English pianist, and he had a French grandmother from Alsace. He remembers his childhood as an "earthly paradise" during which he developed an early interest in painting, music, adult conversations, and books. Yet that joyful world came to an abrupt end in the mid 1930s. Like Lotario, the protagonist of *Minuetto all'inferno,* the young Zolla had to come to terms with being Jewish within the all-encompassing reality of European Fascism. Zolla describes his encounter with Fascism in a self-portrait found in *Ritratti su misura di scrittori italiani* (Custom-made Portraits of Italian Writers, 1960), edited by Elio Filippo Accrocca:

> Poi di colpo, un giorno orrendo, fui cacciato dal paradiso, anche se in apparenza tutto restava intatto. Mi portarono a vivere, stavolta definitivamente, a Torino, un giorno della guerra di Etiopia. Ricordo l'uscita dalla stazione, mi trovavo in una città dove tutto procedeva tetramente a rilento, dove a ogni passo s'incrociavano uomini in divise stravaganti e per giunta armati....
>
> (Then, suddenly, an awful day, I was banished from paradise, even if everything apparently stayed the same. During the Ethiopian war they took me to Turin, this time to live there permanently. I remember coming out of the train station and finding myself in a city where everything unfolded very slowly and in a gloomy fashion, where, at each step, one would come across men in eccentric uniforms who were also armed....)

In his fiction Zolla tried to exorcise these two demons, the city of Turin with its desolation and sense of unreality and the collective tragicomedy of Fascism.

More important, from that traumatic experience Zolla derived a feeling of alienation and dark pessimism that has consistently characterized his thought, becoming the trademark of both his narrative and his essays. As he wrote in *Ritratti su misura:* "Allora mi scese addosso una nube nera che non s'è più dissipata." (From that moment on, a black cloud came upon me which has never dispersed).

In the December 1959 issue of *Paragone* Pietro Citati writes that Zolla's double origin (his English ancestors and his youth spent in Turin) reflects the contradictions that characterized Turin during its Liberty period. At that time the city was as much attracted by the British aestheticism of John Ruskin, William Morris, and Oscar Wilde as it was by mathematics and the Oriental occult. "Assurdamente razionalista e lunaticamente irrazionalista" (absurdly rationalist and whimsically irrationalist) like his city, Zolla is depicted by Citati as a modern encyclopedist who uses his vast rationalistic culture against itself, denouncing its aberrations and its limitations in relation to Oriental spiritual doctrines.

Zolla's interest in spiritualism can be traced to his early years in Turin, a city that has long been associated with Satanism and the occult. While he lived there from 1934 to 1957, Zolla claims to have come in contact with the cult teachers, both the serious and the charlatans. The impact of such experience is unmistakable, for Zolla decided to devote his life to the study of myths and religions. As to the "unreal city" of Turin, its irrational and contradictory image comes to signify, in Zolla's thought, nothing less than contemporary Western civilization.

Zolla's first novel, *Minuetto all'inferno,* narrates the separate stories of two characters, Giulia and Lotario. It is a kind of double bildungsroman of two children growing up separately to become self-absorbed young adults, contemptuous of society and its morality, whose stories converge when they meet. Although at the time of their meeting Giulia is already married to Edmeo–"un uomo dai voluti modi d'ipocrita" (a man with affected hypocritical manners)–the two protagonists fall in love, or, to be more precise, each recognizes a worldly indifference in the other. Their encounter takes place when Turin is liberated by the partisans; Giulia and Lotario live out their story, under Edmeo's benevolent eyes, during the intense days of the immediate postwar period.

In the second part of the novel the action is suddenly transposed onto a metaphysical stage. Here "due personaggi rimasti fin'ora mell'ombra" (two characters who had remained until now in the shadows) reveal themselves in a scene that Italo Calvino, then working as editor at Einaudi, particularly liked. In one of the few comic scenes of the novel a challenge takes place in Heaven between the Dictator (also called God or the Demiurge) and Satan, the two principles of good and evil, who are described in terms as realistic as the earthly beings they manipulate. At stake in their challenge are the souls of Lotario and Edmeo. Subsequently both the Dictator and Satan actively intervene into the lives of the two men: the Dictator wins the soul of Lotario, who becomes a creature of God, fully immersed in a life of work and sufferance, while Satan wins his bet with Edmeo, who grows increasingly disgusted with the nothingness and boredom of his existence and ends up willfully killing his wife, Giulia, and two friends, as well as himself, in a car accident.

Zolla depicts a decadent bourgeois society against the surreal setting of Turin, drawn as a city of illusions. While the other characters live fully immersed in their roles, the three protagonists are singled out as being fully conscious of their existence as fiction and spectacle. Lotario, who looks at the world with "svelenito distacco" (unpoisoned detachment), recognizes a kindred soul in Giulia when he sees her for the first time; he reads in her face "un modo di esprimere il rifiuto senza la teatralità della macerazione" (a way of expressing refusal without theatrical sufferance). Edmeo openly professes his amorality and rejoices in being superior to what the others call pleasure, which is for him merely a covert form of duty.

The unreal city of Turin becomes an emblem of reality viewed from the perspective of these cynical characters. The suggestive beauty of the city's landscape with its soft hills proves to be an illusion hiding the ubiquitous squalor of human lives. Such illusion has been with Lotario since his childhood, when he sensed that "sotto la fungaia di comignoli non avrebbe mai trovato altro che laidezza, inganno, aridità, vuoto e lussuria, o vuoto e follia" (under the medley of chimneys, he would only find ugliness, deception, aridity, emptiness and lust, or emptiness and madness).

Lotario, Giulia, and Edmeo are powerful because they are conscious hypocrites, proud witnesses to the common farcical comedy of life that others tolerate. What they disdain most is faith and trust; in Lotario's words: "È una parola che detesto, fiducia: la usano i governi bacati, gli avvocati incapaci, le amanti infedeli" (Trust is a word I detest; it is used by corrupt governments, inept lawyers, unfaithful lovers).

The turning point of Lotario's formation is his encounter with Fascism during his high-school years. When confronted with the collective hypocrisy of fascist indoctrination his natural propensity for acting is transformed into an act of rebellion against the blind faith of others who cannot read through fascist mystifications. "Ritirato nel guscio della sua schifata e annoiata solitudine" (withdrawn into the tower of his disgusted and bored solitude), he utterly despises everyone. Edmeo, on the contrary, is an opportunist; his strategy during the fascist years is to conform to the general trend as he intends to be waiting "by the fireside" until the situation clears out. Giulia enjoys watching others with "una strana crudeltà" (a strange cruelty) and is steadily searching for some complication, some new turn of events that might break the boredom of her life.

This theatrical vision is also shared by God and Satan, whom Zolla imagines observing human beings with a "diletto misto di noia" (amusement mixed with boredom) and constantly intervening to create new complications for them as an antidote to their own divine spleen. The two decide to humiliate Lotario and Edmeo, whom they deem guilty of hubris since neither seems to feel the misery of being human or to suffer from his emotions. God wants them to view the world as inimical to man's happiness while Satan wants them to despair at the sense of emptiness that permeates their lives.

The novel closes with two images of Turin's rivers, which represent metaphorically the results of the heavenly challenge to the souls of the two characters. Lotario, after a long descent into Hell—he becomes poor, sick, and leaves Giulia—finds work in a factory. He is singing as he watches the Po River from a bridge; the river is swollen by recent rainfalls, and Lotario inhales its "greyness" with pleasure. The Po's "rigoglio sporco e maestoso" (dirty and majestic billowing) is emblematic of life's abjection, a burden that Lotario has learned to accept as his own. On the other hand Edmeo has his epiphanic moment walking over the bridge of a small canal in the suburbs; a drought has bared the bottom of the canal, which has rubbish strewn about. Suddenly he is overcome by a sense of unbearable solitude stemming from the consciousness he is inhabiting a world as fictitious as a stage set: "Tornò a casa dissecato, svuotato, com'egli diceva: 'disidratato,' deciso a sfracellarsi quella domenica sulla strada del Sestriere" (He went back home dried up, emptied, 'dehydrated,' as he would say, determined to kill himself that Sunday in a car accident on the road to Sestriere).

In sum Zolla's characters go through life as though they were performing a controlled and manneristic dance, "un minuetto all'inferno," as the title of the novel suggests. At one point Edmeo is said to be dancing "un minuetto canzonatorio" (a mocking minuet) while Giulia's demeanor is compared to a skilled dancer always in control of her body: "Eppure quella sua vigilanza su se stessa era perfettamente dissimulata, era lo studio ormai inconsapevole, fatto abitudine inavvertita di danzatrice" (Yet her attentiveness towards herself was perfectly concealed, it was by now an unconscious discipline which had become an unnoticed habit, as though she were a dancer). The dance metaphor unites two tropes—bodily control and spectacle—which are recurrently negative in Zolla's early writing. The characters of Zolla's second novel, *Cecilia o la disattenzione* exhibit those same behaviors as their lives are also marked by boredom, indifference, and dissimulation.

Zolla's two novels reflect the ideology developed at length in *Eclissi dell'intellettuale* (1959; translated as *The Eclipse of the Intellectual*, 1968), the theoretical work Zolla published between the two works of fiction. The volume addresses two timely topics: mass civilization and the alienation of modern intellectuals from society. Although Zolla does not acknowledge his influences, his work is greatly indebted to the Frankfurt School, especially to Theodor W. Adorno and Max Horkheimer's analysis of modern culture present in *Dialectic of Enlightenment* (1944) and Walter Benjamin's 1936 essay on "The Work of Art in the Age of Mechanical Reproduction." Zolla's book has the merit, nonetheless, of being one of the first works of this sort in Italy where the debate about mass culture found its concrete expression only years later, in works such as Umberto Eco's *Apocalittici e integrati. Comunicazioni di massa e teorie della cultura di massa* (Apocalyptical and Integral Writers. Mass Communications and Theories of Mass Culture, 1964).

The masses, according to Zolla, are not defined by numbers of people but rather by a type of social relationship: "Si ha una massa laddove l'indifferenza profonda regna fra persona e persona e i movimenti generali e particolari sono coordinati da forze esterne, per lo più anonime" (The masses are to be found wherever the greatest indifference reigns between individuals and where general and particular movements are determined by external, mainly anonymous, forces). For Zolla "l'uomo massa" (the man of the masses) is a modern, decadent Prospero who has employed all his powers only to become a brute—to eschew the dangerous emotions of joy and sorrow and to regress into a pet-

Cover for Zolla's 1994 book, in which he argues that the West has "murdered" the childlike bliss of learning

rified stupor. In this regard Zolla likens modern man to an opossum that fakes being dead when it is attacked—an image that can also be found in *Cecilia*, relative to the protagonist. In their state of solitude and constant boredom men and women of the masses thus become easy prey for the culture industry, which under the pretext of supplying a means to mitigate boredom, feeds on it.

To boredom Zolla opposes the concept of "festività" (festivity). He asserts that the masses lack the ability to raise their lives to a higher level through festivity:

> Festività è una disposizione non necessariamente allegra o felice: ci sono feste funebri, di cordoglio e di pena. . . . Eppure nella festa sono insiti una certa giocosità e un certo distacco, perchè vi si è singoli, ma non individui. . . . Nelle feste l'uomo impara a portare la sua gioia o il suo dolore con dignità, con grazia a trasformarli in bellezza.

> (Festivity is a disposition which is not necessarily joyful or happy: there are funereal feasts, feasts of grief and pain. . . . Yet in one the feast, a sort of jocularity and detachment are present, because one is a single person, not an individual. . . . During feasts, human beings learn how to endure their joy and their grief with dignity, to transform them gracefully into beauty.)

According to Zolla modern intellectuals are responsible for not denouncing the evils in society on time and for being co-opted by the culture industry.

Zolla argues that the culture industry threatens intellectuals with extinction and seeks to replace them with technical experts. Only irony and reprobation can make "la festa del narrare" (the feast of narration) still possible. Intellectuals must acknowledge the disease which weakens society and denounce it vehemently. They must not pretend to offer advice and precepts but only *sképsis,* a vigilant and critical attitude toward reality. In order for the feast of narration to continue, explains Zolla, it is necessary for the artist to have felt fully the horror of the general corruption of the age. Yet Zolla's "progressive intellectual" is not involved in practical solutions as was Gramsci's organic intellectual, otherwise the individual would run the risk of being confused with the expert.

> Soltando contemplando il reale senza lasciarsi distrarre dalle ragioni dell'utile personale o collettivo ci si mette in una condizione che detterà l'azione buona, senza necessità di deliberazione. Guardare dev'essere *sképsis* e *theorèin* (*theoria* è festa).

> (Only by contemplating the real without letting oneself be distracted by reasons such as personal or collective gain, can one be put in a condition which will move one to a good action, without any decision having been necessary. To observe must be both *sképsis* and *theorèin* [*theoria* is feast].)

Zolla refers here to the meaning of the Greek word *theoria,* the acts of observation and examination. For him skepticism and festivity as well as theoretical speculation and involved participation must be intimately connected. As Citati comments in *Paragone,* Zolla "si accontenta di proporre come ideale del vivere il puro, autentico fatto di vivere" (is satisfied with proposing the pure, authentic fact of life as an ideal for living).

Eclissi dell'intellettuale presents a powerful criticism of modern culture; indeed, the function of "negative anthropology" the author advocates for the intellectuals reminds one of Herbert Marcuse's concept of "negative thought" expressed in *One-Dimensional Man* (1964). Yet Zolla seems less concerned with a positive program, which remains vague and unattended. Angelo Guglielmi writes in the *Belfagor* of March 1960: "Azzeccato il disegno dell'uomo massa, [l'autore] ne manca clamorosamente la trascrizione logica" (Having succeeded in portraying man as expression of the masses, [the author] fails conspicuously to give a rational account of such an individual). And in *Paragone* Citati admires Zolla's ability to invent his subject yet asserts that "il suo sguardo è sempre deformante e con la realtà ha pochissima consuetudine" (his viewpoint is always deformed, and it has very little to do with reality).

When he took part in the debate on the novel organized by the review *Nuovi Argomenti* in May-August 1959, Zolla, like Alberto Moravia and other well-known Italian writers interviewed, agreed that the novel must distinguish itself from other forms of industrialized culture. He proposed an essaylike narrative in which the author indulges in forceful attacks upon society. Italo Calvino aptly describes Zolla's position in a 1958 letter to him: "Capisco quel che vuoi fare, immettere nella letteratura italiana, che non lo ha mai conosciuto, l'inferno swiftiano, l'elemento dello schifo generale, una nozione dell'umanità basata sulla ripugnanza" (I understand what you want to do, you seek to inject into Italian literature Swift's hell, which it has never known, that is to say, an element of general disgust, a notion of man based on repugnance). Calvino criticizes this attitude, arguing that repulsion ends up perpetuating immorality in society:

> Tu invece cosa dici? Che i brutti sono brutti. Che gli sporchi sono sporchi. Che gli ignoranti sono ignoranti. E quindi, implicitamente, per converso, che i belli sono belli che i puliti sono puliti, che i colti sono colti. Sulla tua narrativa grava dunque a mio avviso un sospetto di tautologia.

> (What do you say instead? That ugly people are ugly. That dirty people are dirty. That ignorant people are ignorant. Therefore, conversely, that beautiful people are beautiful, clean people are clean, learned people are learned. Thus I believe that a suspicion of tautology weighs on your fiction.)

In *Cecilia o la disattenzione* Zolla depicts a group of middle-class youths; the resulting portrait is as pitiless and squalid as in his first novel. This time the protagonists are the children of the generation that lived through Fascism and the war years. Cecilia is a young woman in her twenties who teaches advertising courses and leads an unusually independent life although she still lives with her rich parents. At the beginning of the novel Cecilia finds out that she is pregnant and contemplates the possibility of an abortion. The other two protagonists are Dionigi, her boyfriend; Matteo, his best friend, who is also Cecilia's former boyfriend; and Ninon, the rebellious daughter of a countess who is thought to be mentally ill.

The dust jacket of the novel reads, in part: "In questo romanzo i personaggi hanno già perduto notizia di essere stati un giorno trasformati in bruchi.... Questa incapacità di peccato è la loro dannazione o massificazione" (In this novel the characters have already lost the memory that one day they were transformed into worms.... Such inability to sin is their damnation and massification). The subtitle, "La disattenzione" (Inattentiveness), refers precisely to the trait of indifference that is the way of life of young people in Zolla's work. The characters in *Cecilia,* like those in *Minuetto all'inferno,* are the products of a mass society that turns women and men into automatons, always intent on mastering their emotional reactions as though their body were a defective machine to be kept under check. Bored with the daily routine of facts and feelings, Cecilia and her friends need a constant diet of violence to relieve their boredom.

Zolla blames both his characters and contemporary society for a nonchalant attitude toward life that leads individuals to yield to evil by not adopting a questioning attitude:

> Perché il male non sta nel rappresentarsi ciò che degrada (e nemmeno nel compierlo), ma nel consentire ad esso, nel vederlo senza guardarlo, con distrazione, sicchè, non tutelandoci più lo schermo del nostro acume, che lo osserva senz'odio e senza amore, esso ci avvolge e ci avvelena.
>
> (Evil does not consist in representing what is degrading [nor does it consist in committing it], but in consenting to it, in looking at it with distraction and without seeing it. Once evil is no longer screened out by our acumen, which observes it without hate or love, evil takes hold of us and poisons us.)

The most cynical character in the novel is Dionigi, "un fannullone presuntuoso" (a conceited idler) who spends his time commenting on the farcical nature of human behavior, his own as well as that of others:

> Dionigi Pauta, sta a ridosso di costoro come un pesce parassita attorno alle balene, pronto a fuggire, ma solo per entrare in bocca ad altre balene, a divorarne le scorie, guizzando, schiavo torvo e impazzito.
>
> (Dionigi Pauta stays close to those people like a parasite fish around whales; ready to flee, but only to enter the mouth of other whales; ready to devour their dregs, swimming like a wild and enraged captive.)

The inability to view life other than a spectacle even in the most intimate moments eventually leads Dionigi to cynical withdrawal. He tells Matteo, his faithful friend and disciple: "Pentiamoci d'aver mai avuto a che fare con Cecilia o Ninon, accettiamo come prova l'orrore che salutarmente ne proviamo.... Ci aspettano l'attesa e la rassegnazione" (Let's repent for being involved with Cecilia or Ninon, let's accept as a trial the healthy horror we are experiencing.... Waiting and resignation are in store for us).

The novel begins and ends with descriptions of Cecilia asleep. Particularly effective is the contrast in the first scene between a dream world in which Cecilia's unconscious reestablishes contact with "l'antica saggezza del sangue" (the ancient wisdom of blood) and Cecilia's awakening when she automatically puts on her everyday mask, a grimace at times of indifference and at times of disgust hiding her inner void.

When confronted with a problematic reality—in this case her unwanted pregnancy—Cecilia knows that the secret is to avoid dramatizing. She must remain "sgombra di pena e di gioia, contratta e inerte, astratta bellezza come corazza d'insetto, distesa di ali di tarma che si confonde con la corteccia dove riposa" (free from pain and joy, taut and inert, a beauty as abstract as an insect's carapace, the open wings of a moth which mingles with the bark where it lays). In order to achieve such a result she has learned "to break up hell into endurable fragments," to think of one moment and never to anticipate the next. Any sort of pain can be anesthetized as long as she keeps perfect control of herself. In this she is assisted by Dr. Bertrame, who, like all experts, knows how to give practical solutions and thus restore efficiency to the flawed human machine. By taking care of her abortion he is able to give back to her that sense of superiority over human life that enables her to watch it as though it were a Hollywood movie.

Recognizable here, in narrative form, is the polemic from *Eclissi dell'intellettuale* in which Zolla opposed the expert to the intellectual. Anticipating Daniel Bell's influential thesis in *The Coming of Post-Industrial Society* (1973), Zolla believes that contemporary society is enslaved by experts. People delegate their responsibility in decision-making without realizing that the experts' solutions contribute to the objectification of the individual. Intellectuals, on the other hand, are hated by society because their function is to denounce the moral degeneration of mass culture. They cannot, however, claim to occupy an antithetical position since they too are victims of the same invisible gods that have subsumed the human libido to the principle of productivity. The last pages of *Cecilia*, in fact, contain an invective against such "dei inafferrabili" (elusive gods) although the author also acknowledges the inability of modern artists to supply an appropriate—and most importantly redeeming—representation of the evils that beset society. To Zolla literature has moved far away from its classical roots.

Both of Zolla's novels must be viewed in the light of the debate waged in Italy during the late 1950s and early 1960s regarding the crisis that marked the relationship between artists and reality. The outcome resulted in works often featuring characters who lead emotionally and intellectually sterile lives. Thus the main character in Alberto Moravia's novel *La noia* (1960; translated as *The Empty Canvas*, 1961)—a title that has become emblematic of that period—is a painter affected by a paralyzing boredom that prevents him from painting. Michelangelo Antonioni's movies of the time—such as *L'avventura* (The Adventure, 1960) and *L'eclisse* (The Eclipse, 1962)—portray neurotic female characters as victims of solitude and alienation.

Zolla's fiction distinguishes itself by virtue of its unusual blend of lyrical tones and philosophical, often apocalyptic, argumentation. His style is unmistakable: his sentences are elaborate, carefully wrought, and unusually rich in uncommon vocabulary, paratactical constructions, parenthetical phrases, and Latinate constructs. Yet his most distinctive trait remains the vindictive passion of his polemics. As he writes in *Eclissi dell'intellettuale,* and as the characters Lotario and Dionigi reiterate in his novels, Zolla believes that the sine qua non of narrating is a sense of horror for the corruption of the modern world. Such a poetics ties the author so intimately to the subject matter that he finds himself defenseless before the civilization he loathes. In his review of *Cecilia* in *I libri degli altri* (1991), after praising the novel as "una narrativea lirico-saggistica di prim'ordine" (a first-rate lyrical and essaylike narrative), Calvino urges Zolla to distance himself from the characters he condemns: "Distaccati in una prospettiva più cosmica, fa' del tuo disprezzo e della tua collera una catapulta per ignorarli, per cancellarli dal mondo, rappresentaci solo la parte salva o salvabile dell'umanità" (Detach yourself through a more cosmic perspective, use your contempt and rage as a trigger to ignore [your characters], to erase them from the world; represent only the saved or salvageable part of humanity).

In 1962, after publishing *Volgarità e dolóre* (Vulgarity and Pain) that year, another virulent attack against the "black magic" of the invisible agents of mass culture, Zolla became increasingly interested in researching mystical and transcendental movements. Studies published in the years that followed led him to explore manifestations of the sacred in non-European civilizations. This quest enabled him to complete, with a more positive alternative, his condemnation of modern civilization in the West, which he views as alienated from its spiritual values. He is persuaded that "nell'era nostra è puerile imprigionarsi nel mondo nato dalla Grecia e da Roma" (in our era it is naive to become captive of the world born from Greece and Rome) and that only a systematic syncretism drawn from different religious experiences can restore modern individuals to the authenticity of their being. With a Jamesian eclecticism Zolla examines Renaissance scholarship, Carl Jung's archetypes, and Christian cults of initiation as well as alchemy, cabal, and spirit trance with the intent of constructing unifying patterns across traditions.

Thus, at the age of forty, by his own admission, Zolla moved away from "i grandi precettori dell'Italia" (the great masters of Italy)—Benedetto Croce, Gentile and Gramsci, who, in his view, had subsumed religion to their political ideology. In an interview with Doriano Fasoli he stated:

[Croce, Gentile e Gramsci] non hanno informazioni da darmi, non mi offrono suggerimenti per affrontare un'epoca. Inoltre essi mi bloccherebbero completamente l'accesso a tutto il mondo—senza il quale non ci si può orientare nell'era nostra: vale a dire il mondo sciamanico, che ignorano totalmente.

([Croce, Gentile, and Gramsci] do not have information to give me, they do not offer any ideas on how to deal with an historical period. Moreover, they would completely prevent me from entering the world of shamanism, a world which is necessary for anyone to orient oneself in our times, a world they ignore totally.)

Zolla is particularly interested in the figure of the shaman insofar as he is reputed to possess powers of healing. In this regard he finds a similarity between the shaman and the artist, given that the art of both is based on representation. According to Zolla the artist should imitate the shaman's curative method: modifying the sentiments of the patients by putting them on stage.

Zolla's essays written after *Volgarità e dolóre* document journeys which the author often made, both intellectually and literally, into other cultures with the intent of extending his limited, Western perspective. Through the 1960s and 1970s he traveled extensively either alone or with his longtime companion, the poet Cristina Campo (whose real name was Vittoria Guerrini), with whom he lived in Rome from 1957 until her death in 1978. When free from his professional duties at the University of Rome, Zolla liked to journey to the East and Far East as well as North America, where he is widely known in academic circles for his studies on shamanism and orientalism. Two of his works, *Archetypes. The Persistence of Unifying Patterns* (1981) and *The Androgyne: The Creative Tension of Male and Female* (1981), were first published in English in the United States; these scholarly studies were written after the author attended an American symposium in 1979 where he witnessed, for the first time, a dialogue between Oriental esoteric schools and Western therapeutical practices.

The publication of *Aure, i luoghi e i riti* (Auras, The Places and the Rites) in 1985 marks an important moment in Zolla's intellectual development, especially if one is mindful of the fact that he began his scholarly career as a student of Anglo-American letters. Zolla himself acknowledged as much in his interview with Fasoli:

> La svolta di *Aure* fu decisiva perché mi portò fuori di una falsità cui avevo in parte aderito per debolezza o confusione, non so: la sudditanza al pensiero europeo. Tutta la storia che da Kant porta a Hegel e si dirama quindi nelle tante scuole europee o americane scoprii che si poteva semplicemente rigettare, in un esodo che metteva in libero rapporto con le tradizioni dell'India, della Cina, del Giappone o anche con la tradizione universale dello sciamanesimo che già Herder aveva nitidamente individuato.
>
> (*Aure* was a decisive turning point because it liberated me from my subjection to European thought, a falsehood to which I had partially adhered due to either weakness or confusion, I don't know. I discovered that one could simply ignore all history which goes from Kant to Hegel and subsequently branches out to the many European and American schools. After such an exodus, one could then be free to come in contact with the traditions from India, China, Japan as well as the universal tradition of shamanism which Herder had already clearly singled out.)

Like Walter Benjamin, Zolla in *Aure* regrets the death of the concept of "aura" in the Western world. In a series of essays Zolla shows how the concept gradually disappeared from Western culture but suggests that it is still possible to be initiated to its influence by coming in contact with certain Oriental places and rites.

Zolla's *Uscite dal mondo* (Exits from the World, 1992) and *Lo stupore infantile* (The Wondering Child, 1994) continue his attempt at reconciling Western culture with its forgotten primordial roots and mystical cults. Like the previous work, *Aure,* these books alternate philosophical reflections with travel narratives. However, whereas *Aure* was still structured around a central argument, the last two works are collections of essays only loosely tied to their titular subjects. On the dust jacket of *Lo stupore infantile* Zolla is called correctly "un maestro del vagabondaggio metafisico" (a master of metaphysical wandering). In *Uscite dal mondo* Zolla offers, as a way to cure the polluted psyche, a "fourth dimension" as a means of experiencing reality. In order to illustrate this alternative dimension he presents examples of artists and scholars who introduced the West to manifestations of the sacred in different countries and at different times. The book also offers scholarly investigations of zodiac signs, Indo-European etymologies, and various cosmogonies as well as Zolla's own prediction about the future of society.

The subjects of *Lo stupore infantile* vary from human migratory patterns to Goethe's theories on comparative botany, from a treatise on light as spiritual presence to a critique of North American society in the 1970s and 1980s, from Lorenzo il Magnifico to virtual reality. As he states in the introduction, Zolla's purpose is to give a sense of that blissed state of attentive learning that only the children of a few eastern cultures still know and that Western civilization has "murdered." Indeed, the first essay of the volume is titled "Infanzia assassinata" (Childhood Murdered). The essays are at once remarkable for the diversity and the breadth of the author's scholarship and for the negative moral judgment with which he views Western technology and culture. For instance, the discussion of the influence of such new developments as virtual reality and cyberspace on the human condition becomes a pretext for Zolla to show his scorn for Western science and its inability to cure moral debasement. It is not surprising that such positions have provoked the ire of scientists—the historian of physics Ruggero Pierantoni wrote a satirical review of *Lo stupore infantile* which appeared in *Leggere* of February 1995. In an ironic reference to Zolla's title, Pierantoni writes that he is "stupefied" by the author's refusal to recognize that both theologians and scientists are engaged in the common endeavor of broadening empirical knowledge.

In the 1990s Zolla has become the prophet of a new type of indistinct religiosity, a sort of Italian "New Ageism," which searches for alternatives to the moral disarray of advanced industrialized society. He lives in Montepulciano, a small town in the Tuscan countryside, but he still makes frequent trips to the East. He considered moving to Japan, a country whose literature and religious practices he finds particularly interesting, but decided against it because he has yet to master the Japanese language.

Zolla is a modern moralist, a Cato who judges contemporary Western society not with an ironic smile but with the sternest condemnation. Like Molière's misanthrope, Zolla is uncompromising towards a civilization he never tires of castigating in the most dire apocalyptic tones. In *La narrativa italiana del dopoguerra* (Postwar Italian Narrative, 1965) Giorgio Barberi-Squarotti calls Zolla "un secco, essenziale predicatore" (a dry, minimalist preacher) who has "una visione lucida, sulfurea, disperata dell'inferno, senza salvezza politica o religiosa" (a lucid, sulphureous, desperate vision of hell, without political or religious salvation). In the August 1961 issue of *Paragone* Aldo Rossi referred to him as "un testimone piuttosto scomodo del nostro tempo" (a rather disturbing witness of our time), one who speaks "con il tono di 'profeta disarmato elettissimo'" (with the tone of a "chosen, yet unarmed, prophet"). Citati in that same journal detected some decadent overtones in Zolla's severe judgments, depicting him as an angel of the Last Judgment whose ascetic indifference was similar to the indifference of an aesthete who takes pleasure in "affondare il dito in quelle orribili piaghe" (putting his finger in those awful wounds).

Through his forty years of research into mystical and religious experiences Zolla has gained a unique and controversial position within the circle of Italian literati. He is credited with opening up Italian culture to cosmopolitan influences while also providing a powerful jeremiad against its invisible machinations. Although his two early novels, as well as *Eclissi dell'intellettuale* and *Volgarità e dolóre,* are exclusively engaged in a condemnation of Western materialism, the later works offer a much wider perspective from which to contemplate the West and, eventually, to find a cure for its ills. In his writings Zolla teaches his readers how knowledge is the result of the human capacity to investigate everything that comes under one's scrutiny and that an adequate vision of reality must encompass the spiritual and the sacred.

Interview:

Elémire Zolla and Doriano Fasoli, *Un destino itinerante. Conversazioni fra Occidente e Oriente* (Venezia: Marsilio, 1995).

Bibliography:

Grazia Marchianò, ed., *La religione della Terra. Vie sciamaniche, universi immaginali, iperspazi virtuali nell'esperienza sacrale della vita* (Como: Red, 1991).

References:

Elio Filippo Accrocca, *Ritratti su misura di scrittori italiani* (Venice: Sodalizio del Libro, 1960), pp. 442–443;

Giorgio Barberi-Squarotti, *La narrativa italiana del dopoguerra* (Bologna: Cappelli, 1965);

Italo Calvino, *I libri degli altri. Lettere 1947–1981* (Turin: Einaudi, 1991);

Pietro Citati, "Eclissi dell'intellettuale," *Paragone. Letteratura,* 10 (December 1959): 98–100;

Angelo Guglielmi, "Elémire Zolla, *Eclissi dell'intellettuale,*" *Belfagor,* 15 (March 1960): 250–253;

Ruggero Pierantoni, "Fermate il mondo, voglio scendere," *Leggere* (February 1995): 5–11;

Aldo Rossi, "Narrativa," *Paragone. Letteratura,* 12 (August 1961): 83–98.

Books for Further Reading

Aricò, Sante, ed. *Contemporary Women Writers in Italy.* Amherst: University of Massachusetts Press, 1990.

Balduino, Armando. *Messaggi e problemi della lettaratura italiana contemporanea.* Venice: Marsilio, 1976.

Balestrini, Nanni. *Il romanzo sperimentale.* Milan: Feltrinelli, 1966.

Baranski, Zygmunt G. and Robert Lumley. *Culture and Conflict in Postwar Italy. Essays on Mass and Popular Culture.* New York: St. Martin's Press, 1990.

Bàrberi-Squarotti, Giorgio. *La narrativa italiana dal '45 ad oggi.* Palermo: Centro Pitré, 1981.

Barilli, Renato and Angelo Guglielmi. *Gruppo 63: critica e teoria.* Milan: Feltrinelli, 1976.

Barilli. *Tra presenza e assenza. Due ipotesi per l'età postmoderna.* Milan: Bompiani, 1991.

Benussi Frandoli, Cristina. *Il romanzo d'esordio tra immaginario e mercato.* Venice: Marsilio, 1986.

Bertacchini, Renato. *Cultura e società nel romanzo del Novecento.* Turin: Società Editrice Italiana, 1974.

Biondi, Marino. *Il sogno e altro: note di letteratura e psicanalisi.* Verona: Gutenberg, 1988.

Birnbaum, Lucia Chiavola, ed. *Liberazione della donna. Feminism in Italy.* Middletown, Conn.: Wesleyan University Press, 1986.

Blelloch, Paola. *Quel mondo dei guanti e delle stoffe. Profili di scrittrici italiane del '900.* Verona: Essedue, 1987.

Cadioli, Alberto. *L'industria del romanzo. L'editoria letteraria in Italia dal 1945 agli anni ottanta.* Rome: Editori Riuniti, 1981.

Calvino, Italo. *Lezioni americane. Sei proposte per il prossimo millennio.* Milan: Mondadori, 1993.

Calvino. *Una pietra sopra. Discorsi di letteratura e società.* Turin: Einaudi, 1980.

Camon, Ferdinando. *Letteratura e classi subalterne.* Venice: Marsilio, 1974.

Cannon, JoAnn. *Postmodern Italian Fiction: The Crisis of Reason in Calvino, Eco, Sciasca, Malerba.* Rutherford, N.J.: Farleigh Dickinson University Press, 1989.

Capozzi, Rocco. *Scrittori, critici e industria culturale dagli anni '60 ad oggi.* Lecce: Manni, 1991.

Cervigni, Dino, ed. *Italy 1991: The Modern and the Postmodern,* special issue of *Annali d'italianistica,* 9 (1991).

Cicioni, Mirna and Nicole Prunster, eds. *Visions and Revisions. Women in Italian Culture.* Providence: Berg, 1993.

De Michelis, Cesare. *Fiori di carta: la nuova narrativa italiana.* Milan: Bompiani, 1990.

D'Oria Anna Grazia, ed. *Gruppo 93. Le tendenze attuali della poesia e della narrativa.* Lecce: Manni, 1993.

Eco, Umberto. *Lector in fabula. La cooperazione nei testi narrativi.* Milan: Bompiani, 1979.

Books for Further Reading

Ferraris, Maurizio. *Tracce. Nichilismo, moderno, postmodernismo*. Milan: Multhipla, 1983.

Ferretti, Giancarlo. *L'autocritica dell'intellettuale*. Padova: Marsilio, 1970.

Ferretti. *Il best seller all'italiana*. Milan: Masson, 1993.

Ferretti. *Il mercato delle lettere*. Turin: Einaudi, 1979.

Ginsborg, Paul. *A History of Contemporary Italy. Society and Politics, 1943–1988*. London: Penguin, 1990.

Golino, Enzo. *Letteratura e classi sociali*. Bari: Laterza, 1976.

Gramigna, Giuliano. *La menzogna del romanzo*. Milan: Garzanti, 1980.

Granese, Alberto. *La leggenda del Nilo: l'immaginario e il sociale nella narrativa italiana degli anni settanta*. Naples: Conte, 1984.

Guardiani, Francesco, ed. *New Italian Fiction*, special issue of *The Review of Contemporary Fiction* (Fall 1992).

Guglielmi, Guido. *La prosa italiana del Novecento: umorismo, metafisica, grottesco*. Turin: Einaudi, 1986.

Guglielminetti, Marziano. *Il romanzo del Novecento italiano*. Rome: Riuniti, 1986.

Harvey, David. *The Condition of Postmodernity*. London: Blackwell, 1989.

Kaplan, Ann, ed. *Postmodernism and Its Discontents*. London: Verso, 1988.

La Porta, Filippo. *La nuova narrativa italiana. Travestimenti e stili di fine secolo*. Turin: Bollati Boringhieri, 1995.

Lazzaro-Weiss, Carol. *From the Margins to the Mainstream: Feminist and Fictional Modes in Italian Women's Writings, 1968–1990*. Philadelphia: University of Pennsylvania Press, 1993.

Luperini, Romano and Vanna Gozzoli Stecchini, *Letteratura e cultura dell'età presente* (Bari: Laterza, 1980).

Luperini. *Il Novecento*, 2 volumes. Turin: Loescher, 1981.

Luperini, ed. *Teoria e critica letteraria oggi*. Milan: Angeli, 1991.

Lyotard, Jean François. *The Postmodern Condition*. Minneapolis: University of Minnesota Press, 1984.

Manacorda, Giuliano. *Vent'anni di pazienza. Saggi sulla letteratura italiana contemporanea*. Florence: La Nuova Italia, 1972.

Marchese, Angelo. *Officina del racconto. Semiotica della narrativa*. Milan: Mondadori, 1983.

Mari, Giovanni, ed. *Moderno postmoderno. Soggetto, tempo, sapere nella società attuale*. Milan: Feltrinelli, 1987.

Mariani, Gaetano and Mario Petrucciani, eds. *Letteratura italiana contemporanea*. Rome: Lucarini, 1979.

Mauro, Walter. *Realtà, mito e favola nella narrativa italiana del Novecento*. Milan: Sugar, 1974.

Merry, Bruce. *Women in Italian Literature: Four Studies Based on the Works of Grazia Deledda, Alba de Céspedes, Natalia Ginzburg, and Dacia Maraini*. Townsville, Australia: James Cook University Press, 1990.

Miceli Jeffries, Giovanna, ed. *Feminine Feminists. Cultural Practices.* Minneapolis: University of Minnesota Press, 1994.

Mignone, Mario B. *Italy Today. A Country in Transition.* New York: Peter Lang, 1995.

Nozzoli, Ann. *La parete di carta: scritture al femminile nel Novecento italiano.* Verona: Gutenberg, 1989.

Nozzoli. *Tabù e coscienza. La condizione femminile nella letteratura italiana del Novecento.* Florence: La Nuova Italia, 1978.

Passeri Pignoni, Vera. *Panorama della narrativa italiana del dopoguerra.* Bologna: Istituto Carlo Tincani, 1986.

Paternostro, Rocco. *Poetica dell'assenza.* Rome: Bulzoni, 1990.

Piccioni, Leone. *Proposte di letture.* Milan: Rusconi, 1985.

Pullini, Giorgio. *Tra esistenza e coscienza: narrativa e teatro del '900.* Milan: Mursia, 1986.

Raimondi, Ezio. *Le poetiche della modernità in Italia.* Milan: Garzanti, 1990.

Romano, Massimo. *Gli stregoni della fantacultura.* Turin: Pavia, 1978.

Tani, Stefano. *Il romanzo di ritorno. Dal romanzo medio degli anni sessanta alla giovane narrativa degli anni ottanta.* Milan: Mursia, 1990.

Tanturri, Riccardo. *La linea del conformismo.* Padua: CEDAM, 1973.

Vattimo, Gianni. *La fine della modernità.* Milan: Garzanti, 1985.

West, Rebecca and Dino Cervigni, eds. *Women's Voices in Italian Literature,* special issue of *Annali d'italianistica,* 7 (1989).

Wood, Sharon. *Italian Women's Writings: 1860–1994.* Manchester: Manchester University Press, 1994.

Zangrilli, Franco. *Linea pirandelliana nella narrativa contemporanea.* Ravenna: Longo, 1990.

Contributors

Mario Aste	*University of Massachusetts at Lowell*
Anna Botta	*Smith College*
Salvatore Cappelletti	*Providence College*
Simone Casini	*University of Florence*
Paul Colilli	*Laurentian University*
Christopher Concolino	*San Francisco State University*
Deborah L. Contrada	*University of Iowa*
Rosetta di Pace	*University of Oklahoma*
Gabriele Erasmi	*McMaster University*
Antonella Francini	*Syracuse University*
Tommasina Gabriele	*Wheaton College*
Patricia M. Gathercole	*Roanoke College*
Francesco Guardiani	*University of Toronto*
Michael Hanne	*University of Auckland*
Angela M. Jeannet	*Franklin and Marshall College*
Jan Kozma	*University of Kansas*
Ernesto Livorni	*Yale University*
Daniela Marcheschi	*Lucca, Italy*
Anna Nelli	*Lucca, Italy*
Tom O'Neill	*University of Melbourne*
Augustus Pallotta	*Syracuse University*
Eugenio Ragni	*University of Rome "Roma Tre"*
Franco Ricci	*University of Ottawa*
Carl A. Rubino	*Hamilton College*
Monica Cristina Storini	*University of Rome "La Sapienza"*
Nicoletta Tinozzi-Mehrmand	*Middlebury College*
Maria Rosaria Vitti-Alexander	*Nazareth College of Rochester*
David Ward	*Wellesley College*
Rebecca West	*University of Chicago*
Simona Wright	*College of New Jersey*

Cumulative Index

Dictionary of Literary Biography, Volumes 1-196
Dictionary of Literary Biography Yearbook, 1980-1997
Dictionary of Literary Biography Documentary Series, Volumes 1-17

Cumulative Index

DLB before number: *Dictionary of Literary Biography*, Volumes 1-196
Y before number: *Dictionary of Literary Biography Yearbook*, 1980-1997
DS before number: *Dictionary of Literary Biography Documentary Series*, Volumes 1-17

A

Abbey, Edwin Austin 1852-1911 .... DLB-188

Abbey Press DLB-49

The Abbey Theatre and Irish Drama, 1900-1945 .... DLB-10

Abbot, Willis J. 1863-1934 .... DLB-29

Abbott, Jacob 1803-1879? DLB-1

Abbott, Lee K. 1947- DLB-130

Abbott, Lyman 1835-1922 .... DLB-79

Abbott, Robert S. 1868-1940 .... DLB-29, 91

Abe, Kōbō 1924-1993 .... DLB-182

Abelard, Peter circa 1079-1142 ..... DLB-115

Abelard-Schuman DLB-46

Abell, Arunah S. 1806-1888 ...... DLB-43

Abercrombie, Lascelles 1881-1938 .... DLB-19

Aberdeen University Press Limited DLB-106

Abish, Walter 1931- DLB-130

Ablesimov, Aleksandr Onisimovich 1742-1783 .... DLB-150

Abraham à Sancta Clara 1644-1709 .... DLB-168

Abrahams, Peter 1919- DLB-117

Abrams, M. H. 1912- DLB-67

Abrogans circa 790-800 .... DLB-148

Abschatz, Hans Aßmann von 1646-1699 .... DLB-168

Abse, Dannie 1923- DLB-27

Academy Chicago Publishers DLB-46

Accrocca, Elio Filippo 1923- DLB-128

Ace Books DLB-46

Achebe, Chinua 1930- DLB-117

Achtenberg, Herbert 1938- DLB-124

Ackerman, Diane 1948- DLB-120

Ackroyd, Peter 1949- DLB-155

Acorn, Milton 1923-1986 .... DLB-53

Acosta, Oscar Zeta 1935?- DLB-82

Actors Theatre of Louisville DLB-7

Adair, Gilbert 1944- DLB-194

Adair, James 1709?-1783? DLB-30

Adam, Graeme Mercer 1839-1912 .... DLB-99

Adam, Robert Borthwick II 1863-1940 .... DLB-187

Adame, Leonard 1947- DLB-82

Adamic, Louis 1898-1951 .... DLB-9

Adams, Alice 1926- Y-86

Adams, Brooks 1848-1927 .... DLB-47

Adams, Charles Francis, Jr. 1835-1915 .... DLB-47

Adams, Douglas 1952- Y-83

Adams, Franklin P. 1881-1960 ...... DLB-29

Adams, Henry 1838-1918 ... DLB-12, 47, 189

Adams, Herbert Baxter 1850-1901 .... DLB-47

Adams, J. S. and C. [publishing house] DLB-49

Adams, James Truslow 1878-1949 .... DLB-17; DS-17

Adams, John 1735-1826 .... DLB-31, 183

Adams, John 1735-1826 and Adams, Abigail 1744-1818 ..... DLB-183

Adams, John Quincy 1767-1848 ..... DLB-37

Adams, Léonie 1899-1988 .... DLB-48

Adams, Levi 1802-1832 .... DLB-99

Adams, Samuel 1722-1803 ...... DLB-31, 43

Adams, Thomas 1582 or 1583-1652 .... DLB-151

Adams, William Taylor 1822-1897 ..... DLB-42

Adamson, Sir John 1867-1950 ...... DLB-98

Adcock, Arthur St. John 1864-1930 .... DLB-135

Adcock, Betty 1938- DLB-105

Adcock, Fleur 1934- DLB-40

Addison, Joseph 1672-1719 .... DLB-101

Ade, George 1866-1944 .... DLB-11, 25

Adeler, Max (see Clark, Charles Heber)

Adonias Filho 1915-1990 .... DLB-145

Advance Publishing Company DLB-49

AE 1867-1935 .... DLB-19

Ælfric circa 955-circa 1010 .... DLB-146

Aeschines circa 390 B.C.-circa 320 B.C. DLB-176

Aeschylus 525-524 B.C.-456-455 B.C. DLB-176

Aesthetic Poetry (1873), by Walter Pater DLB-35

After Dinner Opera Company Y-92

Afro-American Literary Critics: An Introduction DLB-33

Agassiz, Elizabeth Cary 1822-1907 ... DLB-189

Agassiz, Jean Louis Rodolphe 1807-1873 .... DLB-1

Agee, James 1909-1955 ...... DLB-2, 26, 152

The Agee Legacy: A Conference at the University of Tennessee at Knoxville Y-89

Aguilera Malta, Demetrio 1909-1981 .... DLB-145

Ai 1947- DLB-120

Aichinger, Ilse 1921- DLB-85

Aidoo, Ama Ata 1942- DLB-117

Aiken, Conrad 1889-1973 .... DLB-9, 45, 102

Aiken, Joan 1924- DLB-161

Aikin, Lucy 1781-1864 .... DLB-144, 163

Ainsworth, William Harrison 1805-1882 .... DLB-21

Aitken, George A. 1860-1917 ...... DLB-149

Aitken, Robert [publishing house] DLB-49

Akenside, Mark 1721-1770 .... DLB-109

Akins, Zoë 1886-1958 .... DLB-26

Akutagawa, Ryūnosuke 1892-1927 .... DLB-180

Alabaster, William 1568-1640 ..... DLB-132

Alain-Fournier 1886-1914 .... DLB-65

Alarcón, Francisco X. 1954- ... DLB-122

Alba, Nanina 1915-1968 .... DLB-41

Albee, Edward 1928- DLB-7

Albert the Great circa 1200-1280 .... DLB-115

Alberti, Rafael 1902- DLB-108

Albertinus, Aegidius circa 1560-1620 .... DLB-164

Alcaeus born circa 620 B.C. DLB-176

Alcott, Amos Bronson 1799-1888 ..... DLB-1

Alcott, Louisa May 1832-1888 .... DLB-1, 42, 79; DS-14

Alcott, William Andrus 1798-1859 .... DLB-1

Alcuin circa 732-804 .... DLB-148

Alden, Henry Mills 1836-1919 ..... DLB-79

Alden, Isabella 1841-1930 .... DLB-42

301

Alden, John B. [publishing house] DLB-49
Alden, Beardsley and Company DLB-49
Aldington, Richard
  1892-1962 . . . . DLB-20, 36, 100, 149
Aldis, Dorothy 1896-1966 . . . . DLB-22
Aldis, H. G. 1863-1919 . . . . DLB-184
Aldiss, Brian W. 1925- DLB-14
Aldrich, Thomas Bailey
  1836-1907 . . . . DLB-42, 71, 74, 79
Alegría, Ciro 1909-1967 . . . . DLB-113
Alegría, Claribel 1924- DLB-145
Aleixandre, Vicente 1898-1984 . . . . . DLB-108
Aleramo, Sibilla 1876-1960 . . . . DLB-114
Alexander, Charles 1868-1923 . . . . . . DLB-91
Alexander, Charles Wesley
  [publishing house] DLB-49
Alexander, James 1691-1756 . . . . . . DLB-24
Alexander, Lloyd 1924- DLB-52
Alexander, Sir William, Earl of Stirling
  1577?-1640 . . . . DLB-121
Alexie, Sherman 1966- DLB-175
Alexis, Willibald 1798-1871 . . . . DLB-133
Alfred, King 849-899 . . . . DLB-146
Alger, Horatio, Jr. 1832-1899 . . . . . . DLB-42
Algonquin Books of Chapel Hill DLB-46
Algren, Nelson 1909-1981 . . . . DLB-9; Y-81, Y-82
Allan, Andrew 1907-1974 . . . . DLB-88
Allan, Ted 1916- DLB-68
Allbeury, Ted 1917- DLB-87
Alldritt, Keith 1935- DLB-14
Allen, Ethan 1738-1789 . . . . DLB-31
Allen, Frederick Lewis 1890-1954 . . . . DLB-137
Allen, Gay Wilson
  1903-1995 . . . . DLB-103; Y-95
Allen, George 1808-1876 . . . . DLB-59
Allen, George [publishing house] DLB-106
Allen, George, and Unwin
  Limited DLB-112
Allen, Grant 1848-1899 . . . . . DLB-70, 92, 178
Allen, Henry W. 1912- Y-85
Allen, Hervey 1889-1949 . . . . DLB-9, 45
Allen, James 1739-1808 . . . . DLB-31
Allen, James Lane 1849-1925 . . . . . . DLB-71
Allen, Jay Presson 1922- DLB-26
Allen, John, and Company DLB-49
Allen, Paula Gunn 1939- DLB-175
Allen, Samuel W. 1917- DLB-41
Allen, Woody 1935- DLB-44
Allende, Isabel 1942- DLB-145
Alline, Henry 1748-1784 . . . . DLB-99
Allingham, Margery 1904-1966 . . . . . DLB-77
Allingham, William 1824-1889 . . . . . . DLB-35

Allison, W. L.
  [publishing house] DLB-49
The *Alliterative Morte Arthure* and
  the *Stanzaic Morte Arthur*
  circa 1350-1400 . . . . DLB-146
Allott, Kenneth 1912-1973 . . . . DLB-20
Allston, Washington 1779-1843 . . . . . DLB-1
Almon, John [publishing house] DLB-154
Alonzo, Dámaso 1898-1990 . . . . DLB-108
Alsop, George 1636-post 1673 . . . . . . DLB-24
Alsop, Richard 1761-1815 . . . . DLB-37
Altemus, Henry, and Company DLB-49
Altenberg, Peter 1885-1919 . . . . DLB-81
Altolaguirre, Manuel 1905-1959 . . . . . DLB-108
Aluko, T. M. 1918- DLB-117
Alurista 1947- DLB-82
Alvarez, A. 1929- DLB-14, 40
Amadi, Elechi 1934- DLB-117
Amado, Jorge 1912- DLB-113
Ambler, Eric 1909- DLB-77
*America: or, a Poem on the Settlement of the
  British Colonies* (1780?), by Timothy
  Dwight DLB-37
American Conservatory Theatre DLB-7
American Fiction and the 1930s DLB-9
American Humor: A Historical Survey
  East and Northeast
  South and Southwest
  Midwest
  West DLB-11
The American Library in Paris Y-93
American News Company DLB-49
The American Poets' Corner: The First
  Three Years (1983-1986) Y-86
American Proletarian Culture:
  The 1930s DS-11
American Publishing Company DLB-49
American Stationers' Company DLB-49
American Sunday-School Union DLB-49
American Temperance Union DLB-49
American Tract Society DLB-49
The American Trust for the
  British Library Y-96
The American Writers Congress
  (9-12 October 1981) Y-81
The American Writers Congress: A Report
  on Continuing Business Y-81
Ames, Fisher 1758-1808 . . . . DLB-37
Ames, Mary Clemmer 1831-1884 . . . . DLB-23
Amini, Johari M. 1935- DLB-41
Amis, Kingsley
  1922-1995 . . . . DLB-15, 27, 100, 139, Y-96
Amis, Martin 1949- DLB-194
Ammons, A. R. 1926- DLB-5, 165
Amory, Thomas 1691?-1788 . . . . DLB-39

Anania, Michael 1939- DLB-193
Anaya, Rudolfo A. 1937- DLB-82
Ancrene Riwle circa 1200-1225 . . . . . DLB-146
Andersch, Alfred 1914-1980 . . . . DLB-69
Anderson, Alexander 1775-1870 . . . . . DLB-188
Anderson, Margaret 1886-1973 . . . . DLB-4, 91
Anderson, Maxwell 1888-1959 . . . . . . DLB-7
Anderson, Patrick 1915-1979 . . . . . . DLB-68
Anderson, Paul Y. 1893-1938 . . . . . . DLB-29
Anderson, Poul 1926- DLB-8
Anderson, Robert 1750-1830 . . . . . . DLB-142
Anderson, Robert 1917- DLB-7
Anderson, Sherwood
  1876-1941 . . . . DLB-4, 9, 86; DS-1
Andreae, Johann Valentin
  1586-1654 . . . . DLB-164
Andreas-Salomé, Lou 1861-1937 . . . . . DLB-66
Andres, Stefan 1906-1970 . . . . DLB-69
Andreu, Blanca 1959- DLB-134
Andrewes, Lancelot
  1555-1626 . . . . DLB-151, 172
Andrews, Charles M. 1863-1943 . . . . . DLB-17
Andrews, Miles Peter ?-1814 . . . . DLB-89
Andrian, Leopold von 1875-1951 . . . . DLB-81
Andrić, Ivo 1892-1975 . . . . DLB-147
Andrieux, Louis (see Aragon, Louis)
Andrus, Silas, and Son DLB-49
Angell, James Burrill 1829-1916 . . . . . DLB-64
Angell, Roger 1920- DLB-171, 185
Angelou, Maya 1928- DLB-38
Anger, Jane flourished 1589 . . . . DLB-136
Angers, Félicité (see Conan, Laure)
Anglo-Norman Literature in the
  Development of Middle English
  Literature DLB-146
The *Anglo-Saxon Chronicle*
  circa 890-1154 . . . . DLB-146
The "Angry Young Men" DLB-15
Angus and Robertson (UK)
  Limited DLB-112
Anhalt, Edward 1914- DLB-26
Anners, Henry F.
  [publishing house] DLB-49
Annolied between 1077
  and 1081 . . . . DLB-148
Anselm of Canterbury
  1033-1109 . . . . DLB-115
Anstey, F. 1856-1934 . . . . DLB-141, 178
Anthony, Michael 1932- DLB-125
Anthony, Piers 1934- DLB-8
Anthony Burgess's *99 Novels*:
  An Opinion Poll Y-84
Antin, David 1932- DLB-169
Antin, Mary 1881-1949 . . . . Y-84

Anton Ulrich, Duke of Brunswick-Lüneburg
    1633-1714 . . . . DLB-168
Antschel, Paul (see Celan, Paul)
Anyidoho, Kofi 1947- DLB-157
Anzaldúa, Gloria 1942- DLB-122
Anzengruber, Ludwig
    1839-1889 . . . . DLB-129
Apess, William 1798-1839. . . . . . . DLB-175
Apodaca, Rudy S. 1939- DLB-82
Apollonius Rhodius third century B.C.
    . . . . DLB-176
Apple, Max 1941- DLB-130
Appleton, D., and Company DLB-49
Appleton-Century-Crofts. DLB-46
Applewhite, James 1935- DLB-105
Apple-wood Books DLB-46
Aquin, Hubert 1929-1977. . . . . . . DLB-53
Aquinas, Thomas 1224 or
    1225-1274 . . . . DLB-115
Aragon, Louis 1897-1982. . . . . . . DLB-72
Aralica, Ivan 1930- DLB-181
Aratus of Soli circa 315 B.C.-circa 239 B.C.
    . . . . DLB-176
Arbasino, Alberto 1930- DLB-196
Arbor House Publishing
    Company DLB-46
Arbuthnot, John 1667-1735 . . . . . DLB-101
Arcadia House. DLB-46
Arce, Julio G. (see Ulica, Jorge)
Archer, William 1856-1924 . . . . . . DLB-10
Archilochhus mid seventh century B.C.E.
    . . . . DLB-176
The Archpoet circa 1130?-? DLB-148
Archpriest Avvakum (Petrovich)
    1620?-1682. . . . . DLB-150
Arden, John 1930- DLB-13
Arden of Faversham DLB-62
Ardis Publishers. Y-89
Ardizzone, Edward 1900-1979. . . . DLB-160
Arellano, Juan Estevan 1947- DLB-122
The Arena Publishing Company. . . DLB-49
Arena Stage. DLB-7
Arenas, Reinaldo 1943-1990. . . . . . DLB-145
Arensberg, Ann 1937- Y-82
Arguedas, José María 1911-1969 . . . DLB-113
Argueta, Manlio 1936- DLB-145
Arias, Ron 1941- DLB-82
Arishima, Takeo 1878-1923 . . . . . . DLB-180
Aristophanes
    circa 446 B.C.-circa 386 B.C. . . . DLB-176
Aristotle 384 B.C.-322 B.C. DLB-176
Ariyoshi, Sawako 1931-1984 . . . . . DLB-182
Arland, Marcel 1899-1986 . . . . DLB-72

Arlen, Michael
    1895-1956 . . . . DLB-36, 77, 162
Armah, Ayi Kwei 1939- DLB-117
Armantrout, Rae 1947- DLB-193
Der arme Hartmann
    ?-after 1150 . . . . DLB-148
Armed Services Editions DLB-46
Armstrong, Richard 1903- DLB-160
Arndt, Ernst Moritz 1769-1860. . . . DLB-90
Arnim, Achim von 1781-1831 . . . . DLB-90
Arnim, Bettina von 1785-1859 . . . . DLB-90
Arno Press. DLB-46
Arnold, Edwin 1832-1904. . . . . DLB-35
Arnold, Edwin L. 1857-1935 . . . . . DLB-178
Arnold, Matthew 1822-1888 . . . . DLB-32, 57
Arnold, Thomas 1795-1842. . . . . . . DLB-55
Arnold, Edward
    [publishing house] DLB-112
Arnow, Harriette Simpson
    1908-1986. . . . . DLB-6
Arp, Bill (see Smith, Charles Henry)
Arpino, Giovanni 1927-1987 . . . . . DLB-177
Arreola, Juan José 1918- DLB-113
Arrian circa 89-circa 155 . . . . DLB-176
Arrowsmith, J. W.
    [publishing house] DLB-106
The Art and Mystery of Publishing:
    Interviews Y-97
Arthur, Timothy Shay
    1809-1885 . . . . DLB-3, 42, 79; DS-13
The Arthurian Tradition and Its European
    Context. DLB-138
Artmann, H. C. 1921- DLB-85
Arvin, Newton 1900-1963 . . . . DLB-103
As I See It, by
    Carolyn Cassady DLB-16
Asch, Nathan 1902-1964. . . . . . . DLB-4, 28
Ash, John 1948- DLB-40
Ashbery, John 1927- DLB-5, 165; Y-81
Ashburnham, Bertram Lord
    1797-1878 . . . . DLB-184
Ashendene Press DLB-112
Asher, Sandy 1942- Y-83
Ashton, Winifred (see Dane, Clemence)
Asimov, Isaac 1920-1992 . . . . . DLB-8; Y-92
Askew, Anne circa 1521-1546. . . . . DLB-136
Asselin, Olivar 1874-1937. . . . . DLB-92
Asturias, Miguel Angel
    1899-1974 . . . . DLB-113
Atheneum Publishers DLB-46
Atherton, Gertrude 1857-1948 . . DLB-9, 78, 186
Athlone Press. DLB-112
Atkins, Josiah circa 1755-1781 . . . . DLB-31
Atkins, Russell 1926- DLB-41

The Atlantic Monthly Press DLB-46
Attaway, William 1911-1986 . . . . . DLB-76
Atwood, Margaret 1939- DLB-53
Aubert, Alvin 1930- DLB-41
Aubert de Gaspé, Phillipe-Ignace-François
    1814-1841 . . . . DLB-99
Aubert de Gaspé, Phillipe-Joseph
    1786-1871 . . . . DLB-99
Aubin, Napoléon 1812-1890 . . . . . DLB-99
Aubin, Penelope 1685-circa 1731. . . DLB-39
Aubrey-Fletcher, Henry Lancelot
    (see Wade, Henry)
Auchincloss, Louis 1917- DLB-2; Y-80
Auden, W. H. 1907-1973 . . . . . . DLB-10, 20
Audio Art in America: A Personal
    Memoir Y-85
Audubon, John Woodhouse
    1812-1862 . . . . DLB-183
Auerbach, Berthold 1812-1882 . . . . DLB-133
Auernheimer, Raoul 1876-1948. . . . DLB-81
Augier, Emile 1820-1889 . . . . DLB-192
Augustine 354-430 . . . . DLB-115
Austen, Jane 1775-1817 . . . . DLB-116
Austin, Alfred 1835-1913 . . . . DLB-35
Austin, Mary 1868-1934. . . . . DLB-9, 78
Austin, William 1778-1841 . . . . DLB-74
Author-Printers, 1476–1599 . . . . . . DLB-167
Author Websites Y-97
The Author's Apology for His Book
    (1684), by John Bunyan DLB-39
An Author's Response, by
    Ronald Sukenick Y-82
Authors and Newspapers
    Association DLB-46
Authors' Publishing Company DLB-49
Avalon Books DLB-46
Avancini, Nicolaus 1611-1686 . . . . . DLB-164
Avendaño, Fausto 1941- DLB-82
Averroëö 1126-1198 . . . . DLB-115
Avery, Gillian 1926- DLB-161
Avicenna 980-1037. . . . . DLB-115
Avison, Margaret 1918- DLB-53
Avon Books DLB-46
Awdry, Wilbert Vere 1911- DLB-160
Awoonor, Kofi 1935- DLB-117
Ayckbourn, Alan 1939- DLB-13
Aymé, Marcel 1902-1967 . . . . DLB-72
Aytoun, Sir Robert 1570-1638 . . . . DLB-121
Aytoun, William Edmondstoune
    1813-1865 . . . . DLB-32, 159

B

B. V. (see Thomson, James)

Babbitt, Irving 1865-1933 .... DLB-63

Babbitt, Natalie 1932- DLB-52

Babcock, John [publishing house] DLB-49

Babrius circa 150-200 .... DLB-176

Baca, Jimmy Santiago 1952- DLB-122

Bache, Benjamin Franklin
 1769-1798 .... DLB-43

Bachmann, Ingeborg 1926-1973 ..... DLB-85

Bacon, Delia 1811-1859 .... DLB-1

Bacon, Francis 1561-1626 .... DLB-151

Bacon, Roger circa
 1214/1220-1292 .... DLB-115

Bacon, Sir Nicholas
 circa 1510-1579 .... DLB-132

Bacon, Thomas circa 1700-1768 .... DLB-31

Badger, Richard G.,
 and Company DLB-49

Bage, Robert 1728-1801 .... DLB-39

Bagehot, Walter 1826-1877 .... DLB-55

Bagley, Desmond 1923-1983 .... DLB-87

Bagnold, Enid 1889-1981 ... DLB-13, 160, 191

Bagryana, Elisaveta 1893-1991 .... DLB-147

Bahr, Hermann 1863-1934 ..... DLB-81, 118

Bailey, Alfred Goldsworthy
 1905- DLB-68

Bailey, Francis
 [publishing house] DLB-49

Bailey, H. C. 1878-1961 .... DLB-77

Bailey, Jacob 1731-1808 .... DLB-99

Bailey, Paul 1937- DLB-14

Bailey, Philip James 1816-1902 .... DLB-32

Baillargeon, Pierre 1916-1967 ..... DLB-88

Baillie, Hugh 1890-1966 .... DLB-29

Baillie, Joanna 1762-1851 .... DLB-93

Bailyn, Bernard 1922- DLB-17

Bainbridge, Beryl 1933- DLB-14

Baird, Irene 1901-1981 .... DLB-68

Baker, Augustine 1575-1641 ...... DLB-151

Baker, Carlos 1909-1987 .... DLB-103

Baker, David 1954- DLB-120

Baker, Herschel C. 1914-1990 ..... DLB-111

Baker, Houston A., Jr. 1943- DLB-67

Baker, Samuel White 1821-1893 .... DLB-166

Baker, Walter H., Company
 ("Baker's Plays") DLB-49

The Baker and Taylor
 Company DLB-49

Balaban, John 1943- DLB-120

Bald, Wambly 1902- DLB-4

Balde, Jacob 1604-1668 .... DLB-164

Balderston, John 1889-1954 .... DLB-26

Baldwin, James
 1924-1987 .... DLB-2, 7, 33; Y-87

Baldwin, Joseph Glover
 1815-1864 .... DLB-3, 11

Baldwin, Richard and Anne
 [publishing house] DLB-170

Baldwin, William
 circa 1515-1563 .... DLB-132

Bale, John 1495-1563 .... DLB-132

Balestrini, Nanni 1935- DLB-128, 196

Balfour, Arthur James 1848-1930 ... DLB-190

Ballantine Books DLB-46

Ballantyne, R. M. 1825-1894 ..... DLB-163

Ballard, J. G. 1930- DLB-14

Ballerini, Luigi 1940- DLB-128

Ballou, Maturin Murray
 1820-1895 .... DLB-79, 189

Ballou, Robert O.
 [publishing house] DLB-46

Balzac, Honoré de 1799-1855 ..... DLB-119

Bambara, Toni Cade 1939- DLB-38

Bamford, Samuel 1788-1872 ...... DLB-190

Bancroft, A. L., and
 Company DLB-49

Bancroft, George
 1800-1891 .... DLB-1, 30, 59

Bancroft, Hubert Howe
 1832-1918 .... DLB-47, 140

Bandelier, Adolph F. 1840-1914 .... DLB-186

Bangs, John Kendrick
 1862-1922 .... DLB-11, 79

Banim, John
 1798-1842 .... DLB-116, 158, 159

Banim, Michael 1796-1874 ..... DLB-158, 159

Banks, Iain 1954- DLB-194

Banks, John circa 1653-1706 ...... DLB-80

Banks, Russell 1940- DLB-130

Bannerman, Helen 1862-1946 ..... DLB-141

Bantam Books DLB-46

Banti, Anna 1895-1985 .... DLB-177

Banville, John 1945- DLB-14

Baraka, Amiri
 1934- DLB-5, 7, 16, 38; DS-8

Barbauld, Anna Laetitia
 1743-1825 ...... DLB-107, 109, 142, 158

Barbeau, Marius 1883-1969 .... DLB-92

Barber, John Warner 1798-1885 ..... DLB-30

Bàrberi Squarotti, Giorgio
 1929- DLB-128

Barbey d'Aurevilly, Jules-Amédée
 1808-1889 .... DLB-119

Barbour, John circa 1316-1395 ..... DLB-146

Barbour, Ralph Henry
 1870-1944 .... DLB-22

Barbusse, Henri 1873-1935 .... DLB-65

Barclay, Alexander
 circa 1475-1552 .... DLB-132

Barclay, E. E., and Company DLB-49

Bardeen, C. W.
 [publishing house] DLB-49

Barham, Richard Harris
 1788-1845 .... DLB-159

Barich, Bill 1943- DLB-185

Baring, Maurice 1874-1945 .... DLB-34

Baring-Gould, Sabine
 1834-1924 .... DLB-156, 190

Barker, A. L. 1918- DLB-14, 139

Barker, George 1913-1991 .... DLB-20

Barker, Harley Granville
 1877-1946 .... DLB-10

Barker, Howard 1946- DLB-13

Barker, James Nelson 1784-1858 ..... DLB-37

Barker, Jane 1652-1727 .... DLB-39, 131

Barker, Lady Mary Anne
 1831-1911 .... DLB-166

Barker, William
 circa 1520-after 1576 .... DLB-132

Barker, Arthur, Limited DLB-112

Barkov, Ivan Semenovich
 1732-1768 .... DLB-150

Barks, Coleman 1937- DLB-5

Barlach, Ernst 1870-1938 ..... DLB-56, 118

Barlow, Joel 1754-1812 .... DLB-37

Barnard, John 1681-1770 .... DLB-24

Barne, Kitty (Mary Catherine Barne)
 1883-1957 .... DLB-160

Barnes, Barnabe 1571-1609 .... DLB-132

Barnes, Djuna 1892-1982 ..... DLB-4, 9, 45

Barnes, Jim 1933- DLB-175

Barnes, Julian 1946- DLB-194; Y-93

Barnes, Margaret Ayer 1886-1967 ..... DLB-9

Barnes, Peter 1931- DLB-13

Barnes, William 1801-1886 .... DLB-32

Barnes, A. S., and Company DLB-49

Barnes and Noble Books DLB-46

Barnet, Miguel 1940- DLB-145

Barney, Natalie 1876-1972 .... DLB-4

Barnfield, Richard 1574-1627 ..... DLB-172

Baron, Richard W.,
 Publishing Company DLB-46

Barr, Robert 1850-1912 .... DLB-70, 92

Barral, Carlos 1928-1989 .... DLB-134

Barrax, Gerald William
 1933- DLB-41, 120

Barrès, Maurice 1862-1923 .... DLB-123

Barrett, Eaton Stannard
 1786-1820 .... DLB-116

Barrie, J. M. 1860-1937 .... DLB-10, 141, 156

Barrie and Jenkins DLB-112	Beacon Press. DLB-49	Behrman, S. N. 1893-1973 . . . . . . DLB-7, 44
Barrio, Raymond 1921- DLB-82	Beadle and Adams DLB-49	Belaney, Archibald Stansfeld (see Grey Owl)
Barrios, Gregg 1945- DLB-122	Beagle, Peter S. 1939- Y-80	Belasco, David 1853-1931 . . . . DLB-7
Barry, Philip 1896-1949 . . . . DLB-7	Beal, M. F. 1937- Y-81	Belford, Clarke and Company DLB-49
Barry, Robertine (see Françoise)	Beale, Howard K. 1899-1959. . . . . . . DLB-17	Belitt, Ben 1911- DLB-5
Barse and Hopkins DLB-46	Beard, Charles A. 1874-1948. . . . . . . DLB-17	Belknap, Jeremy 1744-1798. . . . . . DLB-30, 37
Barstow, Stan 1928- DLB-14, 139	A Beat Chronology: The First Twenty-five Years, 1944-1969 . . . . DLB-16	Bell, Adrian 1901-1980 . . . . DLB-191
Barth, John 1930- DLB-2	Beattie, Ann 1947- Y-82	Bell, Clive 1881-1964 . . . . DS-10
Barthelme, Donald 1931-1989 . . . . DLB-2; Y-80, Y-89	Beattie, James 1735-1803 . . . . DLB-109	Bell, Gertrude Margaret Lowthian 1868-1926 . . . . DLB-174
Barthelme, Frederick 1943- Y-85	Beauchemin, Nérée 1850-1931 . . . . . DLB-92	Bell, James Madison 1826-1902 . . . . DLB-50
Bartholomew, Frank 1898-1985 . . . . . DLB-127	Beauchemin, Yves 1941- DLB-60	Bell, Marvin 1937- DLB-5
Bartlett, John 1820-1905 . . . . DLB-1	Beaugrand, Honoré 1848-1906 . . . . . DLB-99	Bell, Millicent 1919- DLB-111
Bartol, Cyrus Augustus 1813-1900 . . . . DLB-1	Beaulieu, Victor-Lévy 1945- DLB-53	Bell, Quentin 1910- DLB-155
Barton, Bernard 1784-1849 . . . . DLB-96	Beaumont, Francis circa 1584-1616 and Fletcher, John 1579-1625 . . . . DLB-58	Bell, Vanessa 1879-1961 . . . . DS-10
Barton, Thomas Pennant 1803-1869 . . . . DLB-140	Beaumont, Sir John 1583?-1627. . . . . DLB-121	Bell, George, and Sons DLB-106
Bartram, John 1699-1777 . . . . DLB-31	Beaumont, Joseph 1616–1699 . . . . . DLB-126	Bell, Robert [publishing house]. DLB-49
Bartram, William 1739-1823 . . . . . . DLB-37	Beauvoir, Simone de 1908-1986. . . . . DLB-72; Y-86	Bellamy, Edward 1850-1898 . . . . . . DLB-12
Basic Books DLB-46	Becher, Ulrich 1910- DLB-69	Bellamy, John [publishing house] DLB-170
Basille, Theodore (see Becon, Thomas)	Becker, Carl 1873-1945 . . . . DLB-17	Bellamy, Joseph 1719-1790 . . . . DLB-31
Bass, T. J. 1932- Y-81	Becker, Jurek 1937- DLB-75	Bellezza, Dario 1944- DLB-128
Bassani, Giorgio 1916- DLB-128, 177	Becker, Jurgen 1932- DLB-75	La Belle Assemblée 1806-1837 . . . . . . DLB-110
Basse, William circa 1583-1653 . . . . . DLB-121	Beckett, Samuel 1906-1989 . . . . DLB-13, 15; Y-90	Belloc, Hilaire 1870-1953 . . . . . DLB-19, 100, 141, 174
Bassett, John Spencer 1867-1928 . . . . . DLB-17	Beckford, William 1760-1844 . . . . . . DLB-39	Bellonci, Maria 1902-1986. . . . . . . DLB-196
Bassler, Thomas Joseph (see Bass, T. J.)	Beckham, Barry 1944- DLB-33	Bellow, Saul 1915- DLB-2, 28; Y-82; DS-3
Bate, Walter Jackson 1918- DLB-67, 103	Becon, Thomas circa 1512-1567 . . . . DLB-136	Belmont Productions DLB-46
Bateman, Christopher [publishing house] DLB-170	Becque, Henry 1837-1899 . . . . DLB-192	Bemelmans, Ludwig 1898-1962. . . . . DLB-22
Bateman, Stephen circa 1510-1584 . . . . DLB-136	Bećković, Matija 1939- DLB-181	Bemis, Samuel Flagg 1891-1973 . . . . . DLB-17
Bates, H. E. 1905-1974 . . . . . DLB-162, 191	Beddoes, Thomas 1760-1808 . . . . . DLB-158	Bemrose, William [publishing house] DLB-106
Bates, Katharine Lee 1859-1929 . . . . . DLB-71	Beddoes, Thomas Lovell 1803-1849 . . . . DLB-96	Benchley, Robert 1889-1945 . . . . . . DLB-11
Batsford, B. T. [publishing house] DLB-106	Bede circa 673-735. . . . . DLB-146	Benedetti, Mario 1920- DLB-113
Battiscombe, Georgina 1905- DLB-155	Beecher, Catharine Esther 1800-1878 . . . . DLB-1	Benedictus, David 1938- DLB-14
The Battle of Maldon circa 1000 . . . . . DLB-146	Beecher, Henry Ward 1813-1887 . . . . DLB-3, 43	Benedikt, Michael 1935- DLB-5
Bauer, Bruno 1809-1882. . . . . DLB-133	Beer, George L. 1872-1920. . . . . . . DLB-47	Benét, Stephen Vincent 1898-1943. . . . . DLB-4, 48, 102
Bauer, Wolfgang 1941- DLB-124	Beer, Johann 1655-1700 . . . . DLB-168	Benét, William Rose 1886-1950 . . . . . DLB-45
Baum, L. Frank 1856-1919 . . . . DLB-22	Beer, Patricia 1919- DLB-40	Benford, Gregory 1941- Y-82
Baum, Vicki 1888-1960 . . . . DLB-85	Beerbohm, Max 1872-1956 . . . . . DLB-34, 100	Benjamin, Park 1809-1864 . . . . DLB-3, 59, 73
Baumbach, Jonathan 1933- Y-80	Beer-Hofmann, Richard 1866-1945 . . . . DLB-81	Benjamin, S. G. W. 1837-1914 . . . . . DLB-189
Bausch, Richard 1945- DLB-130	Beers, Henry A. 1847-1926. . . . . . . DLB-71	Benlowes, Edward 1602-1676 . . . . . DLB-126
Bawden, Nina 1925- DLB-14, 161	Beeton, S. O. [publishing house] DLB-106	Benn, Gottfried 1886-1956 . . . . DLB-56
Bax, Clifford 1886-1962. . . . . . . DLB-10, 100	Bégon, Elisabeth 1696-1755 . . . . . . DLB-99	Benn Brothers Limited DLB-106
Baxter, Charles 1947- DLB-130	Behan, Brendan 1923-1964 . . . . DLB-13	Bennett, Arnold 1867-1931. . . . . . DLB-10, 34, 98, 135
Bayer, Eleanor (see Perry, Eleanor)	Behn, Aphra 1640?-1689 . . . . DLB-39, 80, 131	Bennett, Charles 1899- DLB-44
Bayer, Konrad 1932-1964. . . . . DLB-85	Behn, Harry 1898-1973 . . . . DLB-61	Bennett, Gwendolyn 1902- DLB-51
Baynes, Pauline 1922- DLB-160		Bennett, Hal 1930- DLB-33
Bazin, Hervé 1911- DLB-83		Bennett, James Gordon 1795-1872 . . . . DLB-43
Beach, Sylvia 1887-1962 . . . . . DLB-4; DS-15		Bennett, James Gordon, Jr. 1841-1918 . . . . DLB-23

Bennett, John 1865-1956 . . . . DLB-42
Bennett, Louise 1919- DLB-117
Benni, Stefano 1947- DLB-196
Benoit, Jacques 1941- DLB-60
Benson, A. C. 1862-1925. . . . . DLB-98
Benson, E. F. 1867-1940. . . . . DLB-135, 153
Benson, Jackson J. 1930- DLB-111
Benson, Robert Hugh
 1871-1914 . . . . DLB-153
Benson, Stella 1892-1933 . . . . . . DLB-36, 162
Bent, James Theodore 1852-1897. . . . DLB-174
Bent, Mabel Virginia Anna ?-? DLB-174
Bentham, Jeremy
 1748-1832. . . . . DLB-107, 158
Bentley, E. C. 1875-1956. . . . . DLB-70
Bentley, Phyllis 1894-1977. . . . . . . DLB-191
Bentley, Richard
 [publishing house] DLB-106
Benton, Robert 1932- and Newman,
 David 1937- DLB-44
Benziger Brothers DLB-49
Beowulf circa 900-1000
 or 790-825. . . . . DLB-146
Beresford, Anne 1929- DLB-40
Beresford, John Davys
 1873-1947 . . . . DLB-162; 178
Beresford-Howe, Constance
 1922- DLB-88
Berford, R. G., Company DLB-49
Berg, Stephen 1934- DLB-5
Bergengruen, Werner 1892-1964. . . . DLB-56
Berger, John 1926- DLB-14
Berger, Meyer 1898-1959 . . . . DLB-29
Berger, Thomas 1924- DLB-2; Y-80
Berkeley, Anthony 1893-1971 . . . . . . DLB-77
Berkeley, George 1685-1753 . . . . DLB-31, 101
The Berkley Publishing
 Corporation DLB-46
Berlin, Lucia 1936- DLB-130
Bernal, Vicente J. 1888-1915 . . . . . . DLB-82
Bernanos, Georges 1888-1948 . . . . . DLB-72
Bernard, Harry 1898-1979 . . . . DLB-92
Bernard, John 1756-1828 . . . . DLB-37
Bernard of Chartres
 circa 1060-1124?. DLB-115
Bernari, Carlo 1909-1992 . . . . DLB-177
Bernhard, Thomas
 1931-1989 . . . . DLB-85, 124
Bernstein, Charles 1950- DLB-169
Berriault, Gina 1926- DLB-130
Berrigan, Daniel 1921- DLB-5
Berrigan, Ted 1934-1983 . . . . . . DLB-5, 169
Berry, Wendell 1934- DLB-5, 6

Berryman, John 1914-1972 . . . . DLB-48
Bersianik, Louky 1930- DLB-60
Berthelet, Thomas
 [publishing house] DLB-170
Berto, Giuseppe 1914-1978 . . . . . . DLB-177
Bertolucci, Attilio 1911- DLB-128
Berton, Pierre 1920- DLB-68
Besant, Sir Walter 1836-1901 . . . DLB-135, 190
Bessette, Gerard 1920- DLB-53
Bessie, Alvah 1904-1985 . . . . DLB-26
Bester, Alfred 1913-1987 . . . . DLB-8
The Bestseller Lists: An Assessment Y-84
Betham-Edwards, Matilda Barbara (see Edwards,
 Matilda Barbara Betham-)
Betjeman, John 1906-1984 . . . . . DLB-20; Y-84
Betocchi, Carlo 1899-1986. . . . . . . DLB-128
Bettarini, Mariella 1942- DLB-128
Betts, Doris 1932- Y-82
Beveridge, Albert J. 1862-1927 . . . . . DLB-17
Beverley, Robert
 circa 1673-1722. . . . . DLB-24, 30
Bevilacqua, Alberto 1934- DLB-196
Beyle, Marie-Henri (see Stendhal)
Bianco, Margery Williams
 1881-1944 . . . . DLB-160
Bibaud, Adèle 1854-1941 . . . . DLB-92
Bibaud, Michel 1782-1857 . . . . DLB-99
Bibliographical and Textual Scholarship
 Since World War II. Y-89
The Bicentennial of James Fenimore
 Cooper: An International
 Celebration Y-89
Bichsel, Peter 1935- DLB-75
Bickerstaff, Isaac John
 1733-circa 1808 . . . . DLB-89
Biddle, Drexel [publishing house] DLB-49
Bidermann, Jacob
 1577 or 1578-1639 . . . . DLB-164
Bidwell, Walter Hilliard
 1798-1881 . . . . DLB-79
Bienek, Horst 1930- DLB-75
Bierbaum, Otto Julius 1865-1910. . . . DLB-66
Bierce, Ambrose
 1842-1914?. . . DLB-11, 12, 23, 71, 74, 186
Bigelow, William F. 1879-1966. . . . . DLB-91
Biggle, Lloyd, Jr. 1923- DLB-8
Bigiaretti, Libero 1905-1993 . . . . . . DLB-177
Bigland, Eileen 1898-1970 . . . . DLB-195
Biglow, Hosea (see Lowell, James Russell)
Bigongiari, Piero 1914- DLB-128
Billinger, Richard 1890-1965 . . . . . . DLB-124
Billings, Hammatt 1818-1874 . . . . . DLB-188
Billings, John Shaw 1898-1975 . . . . . DLB-137
Billings, Josh (see Shaw, Henry Wheeler)

Binding, Rudolf G. 1867-1938 . . . . . DLB-66
Bingham, Caleb 1757-1817 . . . . . . DLB-42
Bingham, George Barry
 1906-1988 . . . . DLB-127
Bingley, William
 [publishing house] DLB-154
Binyon, Laurence 1869-1943 . . . . . . DLB-19
Biographia Brittanica DLB-142
Biographical Documents I Y-84
Biographical Documents II Y-85
Bioren, John [publishing house] DLB-49
Bioy Casares, Adolfo 1914- DLB-113
Bird, Isabella Lucy 1831-1904. . . . . . DLB-166
Bird, William 1888-1963. . . . . . DLB-4; DS-15
Birken, Sigmund von 1626-1681 . . . . DLB-164
Birney, Earle 1904- DLB-88
Birrell, Augustine 1850-1933 . . . . . . DLB-98
Bisher, Furman 1918- DLB-171
Bishop, Elizabeth 1911-1979 . . . . . DLB-5, 169
Bishop, John Peale 1892-1944 . . . DLB-4, 9, 45
Bismarck, Otto von 1815-1898 . . . . . DLB-129
Bisset, Robert 1759-1805 . . . . DLB-142
Bissett, Bill 1939- DLB-53
Bitzius, Albert (see Gotthelf, Jeremias)
Black, David (D. M.) 1941- DLB-40
Black, Winifred 1863-1936 . . . . DLB-25
Black, Walter J.
 [publishing house]. DLB-46
The Black Aesthetic: Background DS-8
The Black Arts Movement, by
 Larry Neal DLB-38
Black Theaters and Theater Organizations in
 America, 1961-1982:
 A Research List. DLB-38
Black Theatre: A Forum
 [excerpts] DLB-38
Blackamore, Arthur 1679-? DLB-24, 39
Blackburn, Alexander L. 1929- Y-85
Blackburn, Paul 1926-1971 . . . . DLB-16; Y-81
Blackburn, Thomas 1916-1977 . . . . . DLB-27
Blackmore, R. D. 1825-1900 . . . . . . DLB-18
Blackmore, Sir Richard
 1654-1729 . . . . DLB-131
Blackmur, R. P. 1904-1965. . . . . . . DLB-63
Blackwell, Basil, Publisher. DLB-106
Blackwood, Algernon Henry
 1869-1951. . . . . DLB-153, 156, 178
Blackwood, Caroline 1931- DLB-14
Blackwood, William, and
 Sons, Ltd. DLB-154
Blackwood's Edinburgh Magazine
 1817-1980 . . . . DLB-110
Blades, William 1824-1890 . . . . DLB-184
Blair, Eric Arthur (see Orwell, George)

Blair, Francis Preston 1791-1876 . . . . . DLB-43

Blair, James circa 1655-1743 . . . . DLB-24

Blair, John Durburrow 1759-1823 . . . . DLB-37

Blais, Marie-Claire 1939- DLB-53

Blaise, Clark 1940- DLB-53

Blake, George 1893-1961 . . . . DLB-191

Blake, Nicholas 1904-1972 . . . . DLB-77
(see Day Lewis, C.)

Blake, William
1757-1827 . . . . DLB-93, 154, 163

The Blakiston Company DLB-49

Blanchot, Maurice 1907- DLB-72

Blanckenburg, Christian Friedrich von
1744-1796 . . . . DLB-94

Blaser, Robin 1925- DLB-165

Bledsoe, Albert Taylor
1809-1877 . . . . DLB-3, 79

Blelock and Company DLB-49

Blennerhassett, Margaret Agnew
1773-1842 . . . . DLB-99

Bles, Geoffrey
[publishing house] DLB-112

Blessington, Marguerite, Countess of
1789-1849 . . . . DLB-166

The Blickling Homilies
circa 971 . . . . DLB-146

Blish, James 1921-1975 . . . . DLB-8

Bliss, E., and E. White
[publishing house] DLB-49

Bliven, Bruce 1889-1977 . . . . DLB-137

Bloch, Robert 1917-1994 . . . . DLB-44

Block, Rudolph (see Lessing, Bruno)

Blondal, Patricia 1926-1959 . . . . DLB-88

Bloom, Harold 1930- DLB-67

Bloomer, Amelia 1818-1894 . . . . DLB-79

Bloomfield, Robert 1766-1823 . . . . . . DLB-93

Bloomsbury Group DS-10

Blotner, Joseph 1923- DLB-111

Bloy, Léon 1846-1917 . . . . DLB-123

Blume, Judy 1938- DLB-52

Blunck, Hans Friedrich 1888-1961 . . . . DLB-66

Blunden, Edmund
1896-1974 . . . . DLB-20, 100, 155

Blunt, Lady Anne Isabella Noel
1837-1917 . . . . DLB-174

Blunt, Wilfrid Scawen
1840-1922 . . . . DLB-19, 174

Bly, Nellie (see Cochrane, Elizabeth)

Bly, Robert 1926- DLB-5

Blyton, Enid 1897-1968 . . . . DLB-160

Boaden, James 1762-1839 . . . . DLB-89

Boas, Frederick S. 1862-1957 . . . . . . DLB-149

The Bobbs-Merrill Archive at the
Lilly Library, Indiana University Y-90

The Bobbs-Merrill Company DLB-46

Bobrov, Semen Sergeevich
1763?-1810 . . . . DLB-150

Bobrowski, Johannes 1917-1965 . . . . . DLB-75

Bodenheim, Maxwell 1892-1954 . . . DLB-9, 45

Bodenstedt, Friedrich von
1819-1892 . . . . DLB-129

Bodini, Vittorio 1914-1970 . . . . DLB-128

Bodkin, M. McDonnell
1850-1933 . . . . DLB-70

Bodley Head DLB-112

Bodmer, Johann Jakob 1698-1783 . . . . DLB-97

Bodmershof, Imma von 1895-1982 . . . DLB-85

Bodsworth, Fred 1918- DLB-68

Boehm, Sydney 1908- DLB-44

Boer, Charles 1939- DLB-5

Boethius circa 480-circa 524 . . . . . . DLB-115

Boethius of Dacia circa 1240-? DLB-115

Bogan, Louise 1897-1970 . . . . . . DLB-45, 169

Bogarde, Dirk 1921- DLB-14

Bogdanovich, Ippolit Fedorovich
circa 1743-1803 . . . . DLB-150

Bogue, David [publishing house] DLB-106

Böhme, Jakob 1575-1624 . . . . DLB-164

Bohn, H. G. [publishing house] DLB-106

Bohse, August 1661-1742 . . . . DLB-168

Boie, Heinrich Christian
1744-1806 . . . . DLB-94

Bok, Edward W. 1863-1930 . . . DLB-91; DS-16

Boland, Eavan 1944- DLB-40

Bolingbroke, Henry St. John, Viscount
1678-1751 . . . . DLB-101

Böll, Heinrich 1917-1985 . . . . . DLB-69; Y-85

Bolling, Robert 1738-1775 . . . . DLB-31

Bolotov, Andrei Timofeevich
1738-1833 . . . . DLB-150

Bolt, Carol 1941- DLB-60

Bolt, Robert 1924- DLB-13

Bolton, Herbert E. 1870-1953 . . . . . . DLB-17

Bonaventura DLB-90

Bonaventure circa 1217-1274 . . . . . . DLB-115

Bonaviri, Giuseppe 1924- DLB-177

Bond, Edward 1934- DLB-13

Bond, Michael 1926- DLB-161

Boni, Albert and Charles
[publishing house] DLB-46

Boni and Liveright DLB-46

Bonner, Paul Hyde 1893-1968 . . . . . . DS-17

Robert Bonner's Sons DLB-49

Bonnin, Gertrude Simmons (see Zitkala-Ša)

Bonsanti, Alessandro 1904-1984 . . . . DLB-177

Bontemps, Arna 1902-1973 . . . . . DLB-48, 51

The Book Arts Press at the University
of Virginia Y-96

The Book League of America DLB-46

Book Reviewing in America: I Y-87

Book Reviewing in America: II Y-88

Book Reviewing in America: III Y-89

Book Reviewing in America: IV Y-90

Book Reviewing in America: V Y-91

Book Reviewing in America: VI Y-92

Book Reviewing in America: VII Y-93

Book Reviewing in America: VIII Y-94

Book Reviewing in America and the
Literary Scene Y-95

Book Reviewing and the
Literary Scene Y-96, Y-97

Book Supply Company DLB-49

The Book Trade History Group Y-93

The Booker Prize Y-96

The Booker Prize
Address by Anthony Thwaite,
Chairman of the Booker Prize Judges
Comments from Former Booker
Prize Winners Y-86

Boorde, Andrew circa 1490-1549 . . . . DLB-136

Boorstin, Daniel J. 1914- DLB-17

Booth, Mary L. 1831-1889 . . . . DLB-79

Booth, Franklin 1874-1948 . . . . DLB-188

Booth, Philip 1925- Y-82

Booth, Wayne C. 1921- DLB-67

Booth, William 1829-1912 . . . . DLB-190

Borchardt, Rudolf 1877-1945 . . . . . . DLB-66

Borchert, Wolfgang
1921-1947 . . . . DLB-69, 124

Borel, Pétrus 1809-1859 . . . . DLB-119

Borges, Jorge Luis
1899-1986 . . . . DLB-113; Y-86

Börne, Ludwig 1786-1837 . . . . DLB-90

Borrow, George
1803-1881 . . . . DLB-21, 55, 166

Bosch, Juan 1909- DLB-145

Bosco, Henri 1888-1976 . . . . DLB-72

Bosco, Monique 1927- DLB-53

Boston, Lucy M. 1892-1990 . . . . . . DLB-161

Boswell, James 1740-1795 . . . . DLB-104, 142

Botev, Khristo 1847-1876 . . . . DLB-147

Bote, Hermann
circa 1460-circa 1520 . . . . DLB-179

Botta, Anne C. Lynch 1815-1891 . . . . . DLB-3

Bottomley, Gordon 1874-1948 . . . . . DLB-10

Bottoms, David 1949- DLB-120; Y-83

Bottrall, Ronald 1906- DLB-20

Bouchardy, Joseph 1810-1870 . . . . . DLB-192

Boucher, Anthony 1911-1968 . . . . . . DLB-8

Boucher, Jonathan 1738-1804 . . . . . . DLB-31

Cumulative Index

Boucher de Boucherville, George
    1814-1894 . . . . DLB-99

Boudreau, Daniel (see Coste, Donat)

Bourassa, Napoléon 1827-1916 . . . . . . DLB-99

Bourget, Paul 1852-1935 . . . . DLB-123

Bourinot, John George 1837-1902 . . . . DLB-99

Bourjaily, Vance 1922- DLB-2, 143

Bourne, Edward Gaylord
    1860-1908 . . . . DLB-47

Bourne, Randolph 1886-1918 . . . . DLB-63

Bousoño, Carlos 1923- DLB-108

Bousquet, Joë 1897-1950 . . . . DLB-72

Bova, Ben 1932- Y-81

Bovard, Oliver K. 1872-1945 . . . . DLB-25

Bove, Emmanuel 1898-1945 . . . . DLB-72

Bowen, Elizabeth 1899-1973 . . . . DLB-15, 162

Bowen, Francis 1811-1890 . . . . DLB-1, 59

Bowen, John 1924- DLB-13

Bowen, Marjorie 1886-1952 . . . . DLB-153

Bowen-Merrill Company DLB-49

Bowering, George 1935- DLB-53

Bowers, Claude G. 1878-1958 . . . . . . DLB-17

Bowers, Edgar 1924- DLB-5

Bowers, Fredson Thayer
    1905-1991 . . . . DLB-140; Y-91

Bowles, Paul 1910- DLB-5, 6

Bowles, Samuel III 1826-1878 . . . . . . DLB-43

Bowles, William Lisles 1762-1850 . . . . DLB-93

Bowman, Louise Morey
    1882-1944 . . . . DLB-68

Boyd, James 1888-1944 . . . . . . DLB-9; DS-16

Boyd, John 1919- DLB-8

Boyd, Thomas 1898-1935 . . . . . DLB-9; DS-16

Boyesen, Hjalmar Hjorth
    1848-1895 . . . . DLB-12, 71; DS-13

Boyle, Kay
    1902-1992 . . . . . DLB-4, 9, 48, 86; Y-93

Boyle, Roger, Earl of Orrery
    1621-1679 . . . . DLB-80

Boyle, T. Coraghessan 1948- Y-86

Božić, Mirko 1919- DLB-181

Brackenbury, Alison 1953- DLB-40

Brackenridge, Hugh Henry
    1748-1816 . . . . DLB-11, 37

Brackett, Charles 1892-1969 . . . . DLB-26

Brackett, Leigh 1915-1978 . . . . DLB-8, 26

Bradburn, John
    [publishing house] DLB-49

Bradbury, Malcolm 1932- DLB-14

Bradbury, Ray 1920- DLB-2, 8

Bradbury and Evans DLB-106

Braddon, Mary Elizabeth
    1835-1915 . . . . DLB-18, 70, 156

Bradford, Andrew 1686-1742 . . . . DLB-43, 73

Bradford, Gamaliel 1863-1932 . . . . . . DLB-17

Bradford, John 1749-1830 . . . . DLB-43

Bradford, Roark 1896-1948 . . . . DLB-86

Bradford, William 1590-1657 . . . . DLB-24, 30

Bradford, William III
    1719-1791 . . . . DLB-43, 73

Bradlaugh, Charles 1833-1891 . . . . . . DLB-57

Bradley, David 1950- DLB-33

Bradley, Marion Zimmer 1930- DLB-8

Bradley, William Aspenwall
    1878-1939 . . . . DLB-4

Bradley, Ira, and Company DLB-49

Bradley, J. W., and Company DLB-49

Bradshaw, Henry 1831-1886 . . . . . . DLB-184

Bradstreet, Anne
    1612 or 1613-1672 . . . . DLB-24

Bradwardine, Thomas circa
    1295-1349 . . . . DLB-115

Brady, Frank 1924-1986 . . . . DLB-111

Brady, Frederic A.
    [publishing house] DLB-49

Bragg, Melvyn 1939- DLB-14

Brainard, Charles H.
    [publishing house] DLB-49

Braine, John 1922-1986 . . . . . . DLB-15; Y-86

Braithwait, Richard 1588-1673 . . . . . DLB-151

Braithwaite, William Stanley
    1878-1962 . . . . DLB-50, 54

Braker, Ulrich 1735-1798 . . . . DLB-94

Bramah, Ernest 1868-1942 . . . . DLB-70

Branagan, Thomas 1774-1843 . . . . . . DLB-37

Branch, William Blackwell
    1927- DLB-76

Branden Press DLB-46

Brant, Sebastian 1457-1521 . . . . DLB-179

Brassey, Lady Annie (Allnutt)
    1839-1887 . . . . DLB-166

Brathwaite, Edward Kamau
    1930- DLB-125

Brault, Jacques 1933- DLB-53

Braun, Volker 1939- DLB-75

Brautigan, Richard
    1935-1984 . . . . . . DLB-2, 5; Y-80, Y-84

Braxton, Joanne M. 1950- DLB-41

Bray, Anne Eliza 1790-1883 . . . . DLB-116

Bray, Thomas 1656-1730 . . . . DLB-24

Braziller, George
    [publishing house] DLB-46

The Bread Loaf Writers'
    Conference 1983 . . . . Y-84

The Break-Up of the Novel (1922),
    by John Middleton Murry DLB-36

Breasted, James Henry 1865-1935 . . . . DLB-47

Brecht, Bertolt 1898-1956 . . . . . . DLB-56, 124

Bredel, Willi 1901-1964 . . . . DLB-56

Breitinger, Johann Jakob
    1701-1776 . . . . DLB-97

Bremser, Bonnie 1939- DLB-16

Bremser, Ray 1934- DLB-16

Brentano, Bernard von
    1901-1964 . . . . DLB-56

Brentano, Clemens 1778-1842 . . . . . . DLB-90

Brentano's DLB-49

Brenton, Howard 1942- DLB-13

Breslin, Jimmy 1929- DLB-185

Breton, André 1896-1966 . . . . DLB-65

Breton, Nicholas
    circa 1555-circa 1626 . . . . DLB-136

The Breton Lays
    1300-early fifteenth century DLB-146

Brewer, Luther A. 1858-1933 . . . . . . DLB-187

Brewer, Warren and Putnam DLB-46

Brewster, Elizabeth 1922- DLB-60

Bridge, Ann (Lady Mary Dolling Sanders
    O'Malley) 1889-1974 . . . . DLB-191

Bridge, Horatio 1806-1893 . . . . DLB-183

Bridgers, Sue Ellen 1942- DLB-52

Bridges, Robert 1844-1930 . . . . . DLB-19, 98

Bridie, James 1888-1951 . . . . DLB-10

Brieux, Eugene 1858-1932 . . . . DLB-192

Bright, Mary Chavelita Dunne
    (see Egerton, George)

Brimmer, B. J., Company DLB-46

Brines, Francisco 1932- DLB-134

Brinley, George, Jr. 1817-1875 . . . . . DLB-140

Brinnin, John Malcolm 1916- DLB-48

Brisbane, Albert 1809-1890 . . . . DLB-3

Brisbane, Arthur 1864-1936 . . . . DLB-25

British Academy DLB-112

The British Library and the Regular
    Readers' Group Y-91

The British Critic 1793-1843 . . . . DLB-110

*The British Review and London
    Critical Journal* 1811-1825 . . . . . . DLB-110

Brito, Aristeo 1942- DLB-122

Brittain, Vera 1893-1970 . . . . DLB-191

Broadway Publishing Company DLB-46

Broch, Hermann 1886-1951 . . . . . DLB-85, 124

Brochu, André 1942- DLB-53

Brock, Edwin 1927- DLB-40

Brockes, Barthold Heinrich
    1680-1747 . . . . DLB-168

Brod, Max 1884-1968 . . . . DLB-81

Brodber, Erna 1940- DLB-157

Brodhead, John R. 1814-1873 . . . . . . DLB-30

Brodkey, Harold 1930- DLB-130

Brodsky, Joseph 1940-1996 . . . . Y-87

Broeg, Bob 1918- DLB-171

Brome, Richard circa 1590-1652 ..... DLB-58

Brome, Vincent 1910- DLB-155

Bromfield, Louis 1896-1956 .... DLB-4, 9, 86

Bromige, David 1933- DLB-193

Broner, E. M. 1930- DLB-28

Bronk, William 1918- DLB-165

Bronnen, Arnolt 1895-1959 .... DLB-124

Brontë, Anne 1820-1849 .... DLB-21

Brontë, Charlotte 1816-1855 .... DLB-21, 159

Brontë, Emily 1818-1848 .... DLB-21, 32

Brooke, Frances 1724-1789 ..... DLB-39, 99

Brooke, Henry 1703?-1783 .... DLB-39

Brooke, L. Leslie 1862-1940 ...... DLB-141

Brooke, Margaret, Ranee of Sarawak
1849-1936 .... DLB-174

Brooke, Rupert 1887-1915 ...... DLB-19

Brooker, Bertram 1888-1955 ..... DLB-88

Brooke-Rose, Christine 1926- DLB-14

Brookner, Anita 1928- DLB-194; Y-87

Brooks, Charles Timothy
1813-1883 .... DLB-1

Brooks, Cleanth 1906-1994 ..... DLB-63; Y-94

Brooks, Gwendolyn
1917- DLB-5, 76, 165

Brooks, Jeremy 1926- DLB-14

Brooks, Mel 1926- DLB-26

Brooks, Noah 1830-1903..... DLB-42; DS-13

Brooks, Richard 1912-1992 ...... DLB-44

Brooks, Van Wyck
1886-1963 .... DLB-45, 63, 103

Brophy, Brigid 1929- DLB-14

Brophy, John 1899-1965 .... DLB-191

Brossard, Chandler 1922-1993 ..... DLB-16

Brossard, Nicole 1943- DLB-53

Broster, Dorothy Kathleen
1877-1950 .... DLB-160

Brother Antoninus (see Everson, William)

Brotherton, Lord 1856-1930 .... DLB-184

Brougham and Vaux, Henry Peter
Brougham, Baron
1778-1868 .... DLB-110, 158

Brougham, John 1810-1880 .... DLB-11

Broughton, James 1913- DLB-5

Broughton, Rhoda 1840-1920 ...... DLB-18

Broun, Heywood 1888-1939 .... DLB-29, 171

Brown, Alice 1856-1948 .... DLB-78

Brown, Bob 1886-1959 .... DLB-4, 45

Brown, Cecil 1943- DLB-33

Brown, Charles Brockden
1771-1810 .... DLB-37, 59, 73

Brown, Christy 1932-1981 .... DLB-14

Brown, Dee 1908- Y-80

Brown, Frank London 1927-1962 .... DLB-76

Brown, Fredric 1906-1972 .... DLB-8

Brown, George Mackay
1921- DLB-14, 27, 139

Brown, Harry 1917-1986 .... DLB-26

Brown, Marcia 1918- DLB-61

Brown, Margaret Wise
1910-1952 .... DLB-22

Brown, Morna Doris (see Ferrars, Elizabeth)

Brown, Oliver Madox
1855-1874 .... DLB-21

Brown, Sterling
1901-1989 .... DLB-48, 51, 63

Brown, T. E. 1830-1897 .... DLB-35

Brown, William Hill 1765-1793 ..... DLB-37

Brown, William Wells
1814-1884 .... DLB-3, 50, 183

Browne, Charles Farrar
1834-1867 .... DLB-11

Browne, Francis Fisher
1843-1913 .... DLB-79

Browne, Michael Dennis
1940- DLB-40

Browne, Sir Thomas 1605-1682 .... DLB-151

Browne, William, of Tavistock
1590-1645 .... DLB-121

Browne, Wynyard 1911-1964 ...... DLB-13

Browne and Nolan DLB-106

Brownell, W. C. 1851-1928 .... DLB-71

Browning, Elizabeth Barrett
1806-1861 .... DLB-32

Browning, Robert
1812-1889 .... DLB-32, 163

Brownjohn, Allan 1931- DLB-40

Brownson, Orestes Augustus
1803-1876 .... DLB-1, 59, 73

Bruccoli, Matthew J. 1931- DLB-103

Bruce, Charles 1906-1971 .... DLB-68

Bruce, Leo 1903-1979 .... DLB-77

Bruce, Philip Alexander
1856-1933 .... DLB-47

Bruce Humphries
[publishing house] DLB-46

Bruce-Novoa, Juan 1944- DLB-82

Bruckman, Clyde 1894-1955 ...... DLB-26

Bruckner, Ferdinand 1891-1958 .... DLB-118

Brundage, John Herbert (see Herbert, John)

Brutus, Dennis 1924- DLB-117

Bryan, C. D. B. 1936- DLB-185

Bryant, Arthur 1899-1985 .... DLB-149

Bryant, William Cullen
1794-1878 .... DLB-3, 43, 59, 189

Bryce Echenique, Alfredo
1939- DLB-145

Bryce, James 1838-1922 ..... DLB-166, 190

Brydges, Sir Samuel Egerton
1762-1837 .... DLB-107

Bryskett, Lodowick 1546?-1612 ..... DLB-167

Buchan, John 1875-1940 .... DLB-34, 70, 156

Buchanan, George 1506-1582 ...... DLB-132

Buchanan, Robert 1841-1901 ..... DLB-18, 35

Buchman, Sidney 1902-1975 ...... DLB-26

Buchner, Augustus 1591-1661 ...... DLB-164

Büchner, Georg 1813-1837 .... DLB-133

Bucholtz, Andreas Heinrich
1607-1671 .... DLB-168

Buck, Pearl S. 1892-1973 .... DLB-9, 102

Bucke, Charles 1781-1846 .... DLB-110

Bucke, Richard Maurice
1837-1902 .... DLB-99

Buckingham, Joseph Tinker 1779-1861 and
Buckingham, Edwin
1810-1833 .... DLB-73

Buckler, Ernest 1908-1984 .... DLB-68

Buckley, William F., Jr.
1925- DLB-137; Y-80

Buckminster, Joseph Stevens
1784-1812 .... DLB-37

Buckner, Robert 1906- DLB-26

Budd, Thomas ?-1698 .... DLB-24

Budrys, A. J. 1931- DLB-8

Buechner, Frederick 1926- Y-80

Buell, John 1927- DLB-53

Bufalino, Gesualdo 1920-1996 ..... DLB-196

Buffum, Job [publishing house] DLB-49

Bugnet, Georges 1879-1981 .... DLB-92

Buies, Arthur 1840-1901 .... DLB-99

Building the New British Library
at St Pancras Y-94

Bukowski, Charles
1920-1994 .... DLB-5, 130, 169

Bulatović, Miodrag 1930-1991 ..... DLB-181

Bulger, Bozeman 1877-1932 ...... DLB-171

Bullein, William
between 1520 and 1530-1576 .... DLB-167

Bullins, Ed 1935- DLB-7, 38

Bulwer-Lytton, Edward (also Edward Bulwer)
1803-1873 .... DLB-21

Bumpus, Jerry 1937- Y-81

Bunce and Brother DLB-49

Bunner, H. C. 1855-1896 ...... DLB-78, 79

Bunting, Basil 1900-1985 .... DLB-20

Buntline, Ned (Edward Zane Carroll Judson)
1821-1886 .... DLB-186

Bunyan, John 1628-1688 .... DLB-39

Burch, Robert 1925- DLB-52

Burciaga, José Antonio 1940- DLB-82

Bürger, Gottfried August
1747-1794 .... DLB-94

Burgess, Anthony 1917-1993 . . . . DLB-14, 194
Burgess, Gelett 1866-1951 . . . . DLB-11
Burgess, John W. 1844-1931 . . . . . . DLB-47
Burgess, Thornton W.
 1874-1965 . . . . DLB-22
Burgess, Stringer and Company DLB-49
Burick, Si 1909-1986 . . . . DLB-171
Burk, John Daly circa 1772-1808 . . . . DLB-37
Burke, Edmund 1729?-1797 . . . . . . DLB-104
Burke, Kenneth 1897-1993 . . . . . DLB-45, 63
Burlingame, Edward Livermore
 1848-1922 . . . . DLB-79
Burnet, Gilbert 1643-1715 . . . . DLB-101
Burnett, Frances Hodgson
 1849-1924 . . . . . DLB-42, 141; DS-13, 14
Burnett, W. R. 1899-1982 . . . . DLB-9
Burnett, Whit 1899-1973 and
 Martha Foley 1897-1977 . . . . . . DLB-137
Burney, Fanny 1752-1840 . . . . DLB-39
Burns, Alan 1929- DLB-14, 194
Burns, John Horne 1916-1953 . . . . Y-85
Burns, Robert 1759-1796 . . . . DLB-109
Burns and Oates DLB-106
Burnshaw, Stanley 1906- DLB-48
Burr, C. Chauncey 1815?-1883 . . . . . DLB-79
Burroughs, Edgar Rice 1875-1950 . . . . DLB-8
Burroughs, John 1837-1921 . . . . DLB-64
Burroughs, Margaret T. G.
 1917- DLB-41
Burroughs, William S., Jr.
 1947-1981 . . . . DLB-16
Burroughs, William Seward
 1914- DLB-2, 8, 16, 152; Y-81, Y-97
Burroway, Janet 1936- DLB-6
Burt, Maxwell Struthers
 1882-1954 . . . . DLB-86; DS-16
Burt, A. L., and Company DLB-49
Burton, Hester 1913- DLB-161
Burton, Isabel Arundell
 1831-1896 . . . . DLB-166
Burton, Miles (see Rhode, John)
Burton, Richard Francis
 1821-1890 . . . . DLB-55, 166, 184
Burton, Robert 1577-1640 . . . . DLB-151
Burton, Virginia Lee 1909-1968 . . . . . DLB-22
Burton, William Evans
 1804-1860 . . . . DLB-73
Burwell, Adam Hood 1790-1849 . . . . . DLB-99
Bury, Lady Charlotte
 1775-1861 . . . . DLB-116
Busch, Frederick 1941- DLB-6
Busch, Niven 1903-1991 . . . . DLB-44
Bushnell, Horace 1802-1876 . . . . DS-13
Bussieres, Arthur de 1877-1913 . . . . . DLB-92

Butler, Josephine Elizabeth
 1828-1906 . . . . DLB-190
Butler, Juan 1942-1981 . . . . DLB-53
Butler, Octavia E. 1947- DLB-33
Butler, Pierce 1884-1953 . . . . DLB-187
Butler, Robert Olen 1945- DLB-173
Butler, Samuel 1613-1680 . . . . DLB-101, 126
Butler, Samuel 1835-1902. . . . DLB-18, 57, 174
Butler, William Francis
 1838-1910 . . . . DLB-166
Butler, E. H., and Company DLB-49
Butor, Michel 1926- DLB-83
Butter, Nathaniel
 [publishing house] DLB-170
Butterworth, Hezekiah 1839-1905 . . . . DLB-42
Buttitta, Ignazio 1899- DLB-114
Buzzati, Dino 1906-1972 . . . . DLB-177
Byars, Betsy 1928- DLB-52
Byatt, A. S. 1936- DLB-14, 194
Byles, Mather 1707-1788 . . . . DLB-24
Bynneman, Henry
 [publishing house] DLB-170
Bynner, Witter 1881-1968 . . . . DLB-54
Byrd, William circa 1543-1623 . . . . . DLB-172
Byrd, William II 1674-1744 . . . . DLB-24, 140
Byrne, John Keyes (see Leonard, Hugh)
Byron, George Gordon, Lord
 1788-1824 . . . . DLB-96, 110
Byron, Robert 1905-1941 . . . . DLB-195

C

Caballero Bonald, José Manuel
 1926- DLB-108
Cabañero, Eladio 1930- DLB-134
Cabell, James Branch
 1879-1958 . . . . DLB-9, 78
Cabeza de Baca, Manuel
 1853-1915 . . . . DLB-122
Cabeza de Baca Gilbert, Fabiola
 1898- DLB-122
Cable, George Washington
 1844-1925 . . . . DLB-12, 74; DS-13
Cable, Mildred 1878-1952 . . . . DLB-195
Cabrera, Lydia 1900-1991 . . . . DLB-145
Cabrera Infante, Guillermo
 1929- DLB-113
Cadell [publishing house] DLB-154
Cady, Edwin H. 1917- DLB-103
Caedmon flourished 658-680 . . . . . . DLB-146
Caedmon School circa 660-899 . . . . . DLB-146
Cafés, Brasseries, and Bistros DS-15
Cage, John 1912-1992 . . . . DLB-193

Cahan, Abraham
 1860-1951 . . . . DLB-9, 25, 28
Cain, George 1943- DLB-33
Caldecott, Randolph 1846-1886 . . . . . DLB-163
Calder, John
 (Publishers), Limited DLB-112
Calderón de la Barca, Fanny
 1804-1882 . . . . DLB-183
Caldwell, Ben 1937- DLB-38
Caldwell, Erskine 1903-1987 . . . . DLB-9, 86
Caldwell, H. M., Company DLB-49
Caldwell, Taylor 1900-1985 . . . . DS-17
Calhoun, John C. 1782-1850 . . . . . . DLB-3
Calisher, Hortense 1911- DLB-2
A Call to Letters and an Invitation
 to the Electric Chair,
 by Siegfried Mandel DLB-75
Callaghan, Morley 1903-1990 . . . . . . DLB-68
Callahan, S. Alice 1868-1894 . . . . . . DLB-175
Callaloo Y-87
Callimachus circa 305 B.C.-240 B.C.
 . . . . DLB-176
Calmer, Edgar 1907- DLB-4
Calverley, C. S. 1831-1884 . . . . DLB-35
Calvert, George Henry
 1803-1889 . . . . DLB-1, 64
Calvino, Italo 1923-1985 . . . . DLB-196
Cambridge Press DLB-49
Cambridge Songs (Carmina Cantabrigensia)
 circa 1050 . . . . DLB-148
Cambridge University Press DLB-170
Camden, William 1551-1623 . . . . . . DLB-172
Camden House: An Interview with
 James Hardin Y-92
Cameron, Eleanor 1912- DLB-52
Cameron, George Frederick
 1854-1885 . . . . DLB-99
Cameron, Lucy Lyttelton
 1781-1858 . . . . DLB-163
Cameron, William Bleasdell
 1862-1951 . . . . DLB-99
Camm, John 1718-1778 . . . . DLB-31
Camon, Ferdinando 1935- DLB-196
Campana, Dino 1885-1932 . . . . DLB-114
Campbell, Gabrielle Margaret Vere
 (see Shearing, Joseph, and Bowen, Marjorie)
Campbell, James Dykes
 1838-1895 . . . . DLB-144
Campbell, James Edwin
 1867-1896 . . . . DLB-50
Campbell, John 1653-1728 . . . . DLB-43
Campbell, John W., Jr.
 1910-1971 . . . . DLB-8
Campbell, Roy 1901-1957 . . . . DLB-20
Campbell, Thomas
 1777-1844 . . . . DLB-93, 144

Campbell, William Wilfred 1858-1918 . . . . DLB-92	Carnero, Guillermo 1947- DLB-108	Castellanos, Rosario 1925-1974 . . . . . DLB-113
Campion, Edmund 1539-1581 . . . . . DLB-167	Carossa, Hans 1878-1956. . . . . DLB-66	Castillo, Ana 1953- DLB-122
Campion, Thomas 1567-1620 . . . . DLB-58, 172	Carpenter, Humphrey 1946- DLB-155	Castlemon, Harry (see Fosdick, Charles Austin)
	Carpenter, Stephen Cullen ?-1820? . . . DLB-73	Čašule, Kole 1921- DLB-181
Camus, Albert 1913-1960. . . . . DLB-72	Carpentier, Alejo 1904-1980. . . . . . . DLB-113	Caswall, Edward 1814-1878 . . . . DLB-32
The Canadian Publishers' Records Database Y-96	Carrier, Roch 1937- DLB-53	Catacalos, Rosemary 1944- DLB-122
	Carrillo, Adolfo 1855-1926 . . . . DLB-122	Cather, Willa 1873-1947. . . . . . . DLB-9, 54, 78; DS-1
Canby, Henry Seidel 1878-1961 . . . . . DLB-91	Carroll, Gladys Hasty 1904- DLB-9	
Candelaria, Cordelia 1943- DLB-82	Carroll, John 1735-1815 . . . . DLB-37	Catherine II (Ekaterina Alekseevna), "The Great," Empress of Russia 1729-1796 . . . . DLB-150
Candelaria, Nash 1928- DLB-82	Carroll, John 1809-1884 . . . . DLB-99	
Candour in English Fiction (1890), by Thomas Hardy DLB-18	Carroll, Lewis 1832-1898 . . . . DLB-18, 163, 178	Catherwood, Mary Hartwell 1847-1902 . . . . DLB-78
Canetti, Elias 1905-1994 . . . . . DLB-85, 124	Carroll, Paul 1927- DLB-16	Catledge, Turner 1901-1983 . . . . DLB-127
Canham, Erwin Dain 1904-1982 . . . . DLB-127	Carroll, Paul Vincent 1900-1968 . . . . DLB-10	Catlin, George 1796-1872 . . . . DLB-186, 189
	Carroll and Graf Publishers DLB-46	Cattafi, Bartolo 1922-1979. . . . . DLB-128
Canitz, Friedrich Rudolph Ludwig von 1654-1699 . . . . DLB-168	Carruth, Hayden 1921- DLB-5, 165	Catton, Bruce 1899-1978 . . . . DLB-17
	Carryl, Charles E. 1841-1920 . . . . . . DLB-42	Causley, Charles 1917- DLB-27
Cankar, Ivan 1876-1918 . . . . DLB-147	Carson, Anne 1950- DLB-193	Caute, David 1936- DLB-14
Cannan, Gilbert 1884-1955. . . . . DLB-10	Carswell, Catherine 1879-1946 . . . . . DLB-36	Cavendish, Duchess of Newcastle, Margaret Lucas 1623-1673 . . . . DLB-131
Cannan, Joanna 1896-1961 . . . . DLB-191	Carter, Angela 1940-1992. . . . . DLB-14	
Cannell, Kathleen 1891-1974. . . . . . . DLB-4	Carter, Elizabeth 1717-1806 . . . . DLB-109	Cawein, Madison 1865-1914 . . . . DLB-54
Cannell, Skipwith 1887-1957 . . . . . . DLB-45	Carter, Henry (see Leslie, Frank)	The Caxton Printers, Limited DLB-46
Canning, George 1770-1827 . . . . DLB-158	Carter, Hodding, Jr. 1907-1972 . . . . . DLB-127	Caxton, William [publishing house] DLB-170
Cannon, Jimmy 1910-1973 . . . . DLB-171	Carter, Landon 1710-1778 . . . . DLB-31	
Cantwell, Robert 1908-1978 . . . . DLB-9	Carter, Lin 1930- Y-81	Cayrol, Jean 1911- DLB-83
Cape, Jonathan, and Harrison Smith [publishing house]. DLB-46	Carter, Martin 1927- DLB-117	Cecil, Lord David 1902-1986 . . . . . . DLB-155
	Carter and Hendee DLB-49	Cela, Camilo José 1916- Y-89
Cape, Jonathan, Limited. DLB-112	Carter, Robert, and Brothers. DLB-49	Celan, Paul 1920-1970 . . . . DLB-69
Capen, Joseph 1658-1725. . . . . DLB-24	Cartwright, John 1740-1824 . . . . DLB-158	Celati, Gianni 1937- DLB-196
Capes, Bernard 1854-1918. . . . . DLB-156	Cartwright, William circa 1611-1643 . . . . DLB-126	Celaya, Gabriel 1911-1991. . . . . DLB-108
Capote, Truman 1924-1984 . . . . . . DLB-2, 185; Y-80, Y-84		Céline, Louis-Ferdinand 1894-1961 . . . . DLB-72
	Caruthers, William Alexander 1802-1846. . . . . DLB-3	
Caproni, Giorgio 1912-1990. . . . . DLB-128		The Celtic Background to Medieval English Literature. DLB-146
Cardarelli, Vincenzo 1887-1959 . . . . . DLB-114	Carver, Jonathan 1710-1780 . . . . DLB-31	
Cárdenas, Reyes 1948- DLB-122	Carver, Raymond 1938-1988. . . . . DLB-130; Y-84, Y-88	Celtis, Conrad 1459-1508 . . . . DLB-179
Cardinal, Marie 1929- DLB-83		Center for Bibliographical Studies and Research at the University of California, Riverside Y-91
Carew, Jan 1920- DLB-157	Cary, Joyce 1888-1957 . . . . DLB-15, 100	
Carew, Thomas 1594 or 1595-1640 . . . . DLB-126	Cary, Patrick 1623?-1657 . . . . DLB-131	
	Casey, Juanita 1925- DLB-14	The Center for the Book in the Library of Congress. Y-93
Carey, Henry circa 1687-1689-1743 . . . . DLB-84	Casey, Michael 1947- DLB-5	
	Cassady, Carolyn 1923- DLB-16	Center for the Book Research. Y-84
Carey, Mathew 1760-1839 . . . . . DLB-37, 73	Cassady, Neal 1926-1968 . . . . DLB-16	Centlivre, Susanna 1669?-1723 . . . . . . DLB-84
Carey and Hart. DLB-49	Cassell and Company DLB-106	The Century Company. DLB-49
Carey, M., and Company DLB-49	Cassell Publishing Company DLB-49	Cernuda, Luis 1902-1963 . . . . DLB-134
Carlell, Lodowick 1602-1675 . . . . DLB-58	Cassill, R. V. 1919- DLB-6	"Certain Gifts," by Betty Adcock. . . . DLB-105
Carleton, William 1794-1869 . . . . . . DLB-159	Cassity, Turner 1929- DLB-105	Cervantes, Lorna Dee 1954- DLB-82
Carleton, G. W. [publishing house]. DLB-49	Cassius Dio circa 155/164-post 229 . . . . DLB-176	Chacel, Rosa 1898- DLB-134
		Chacón, Eusebio 1869-1948 . . . . DLB-82
Carlile, Richard 1790-1843 . . . . DLB-110, 158	Cassola, Carlo 1917-1987 . . . . DLB-177	Chacón, Felipe Maximiliano 1873-? DLB-82
Carlyle, Jane Welsh 1801-1866 . . . . . . DLB-55	*The Castle of Perseverance* circa 1400-1425 . . . . DLB-146	
Carlyle, Thomas 1795-1881. . . . DLB-55, 144		Chadwyck-Healey's Full-Text Literary Data-bases: Editing Commercial Databases of Primary Literary Texts Y-95
Carman, Bliss 1861-1929 . . . . DLB-92	Castellano, Olivia 1944- DLB-122	
Carmina Burana circa 1230 . . . . DLB-138		Challans, Eileen Mary (see Renault, Mary)

311

Cumulative Index

Chalmers, George 1742-1825 . . . . . . DLB-30
Chaloner, Sir Thomas
   1520-1565 . . . . DLB-167
Chamberlain, Samuel S.
   1851-1916 . . . . DLB-25
Chamberland, Paul 1939- DLB-60
Chamberlin, William Henry
   1897-1969 . . . . DLB-29
Chambers, Charles Haddon
   1860-1921 . . . . DLB-10
Chambers, W. and R.
   [publishing house] DLB-106
Chamisso, Albert von
   1781-1838 . . . . DLB-90
Champfleury 1821-1889 . . . . DLB-119
Chandler, Harry 1864-1944 . . . . . . DLB-29
Chandler, Norman 1899-1973 . . . . . DLB-127
Chandler, Otis 1927- DLB-127
Chandler, Raymond 1888-1959 . . . . . DS-6
Channing, Edward 1856-1931 . . . . . DLB-17
Channing, Edward Tyrrell
   1790-1856 . . . . DLB-1, 59
Channing, William Ellery
   1780-1842 . . . . DLB-1, 59
Channing, William Ellery, II
   1817-1901 . . . . DLB-1
Channing, William Henry
   1810-1884 . . . . DLB-1, 59
Chaplin, Charlie 1889-1977 . . . . . . DLB-44
Chapman, George
   1559 or 1560 - 1634 . . . . . DLB-62, 121
Chapman, John DLB-106
Chapman, Olive Murray
   1892-1977 . . . . DLB-195
Chapman, William 1850-1917 . . . . . DLB-99
Chapman and Hall DLB-106
Chappell, Fred 1936- DLB-6, 105
Charbonneau, Jean 1875-1960 . . . . . DLB-92
Charbonneau, Robert 1911-1967 . . . . DLB-68
Charles, Gerda 1914- DLB-14
Charles, William
   [publishing house] DLB-49
The Charles Wood Affair:
   A Playwright Revived Y-83
Charlotte Forten: Pages from
   her Diary DLB-50
Charteris, Leslie 1907-1993 . . . . . . DLB-77
Charyn, Jerome 1937- Y-83
Chase, Borden 1900-1971 . . . . DLB-26
Chase, Edna Woolman
   1877-1957 . . . . DLB-91
Chase-Riboud, Barbara 1936- DLB-33
Chateaubriand, François-René de
   1768-1848 . . . . DLB-119
Chatterton, Thomas 1752-1770 . . . . DLB-109
Chatto and Windus DLB-106

Chatwin, Bruce 1940-1989 . . . . . . DLB-194
Chaucer, Geoffrey 1340?-1400 . . . . DLB-146
Chauncy, Charles 1705-1787 . . . . . DLB-24
Chauveau, Pierre-Joseph-Olivier
   1820-1890 . . . . DLB-99
Chávez, Denise 1948- DLB-122
Chávez, Fray Angélico 1910- DLB-82
Chayefsky, Paddy
   1923-1981 . . . . DLB-7, 44; Y-81
Cheesman, Evelyn 1881-1969 . . . . . DLB-195
Cheever, Ezekiel 1615-1708 . . . . . . DLB-24
Cheever, George Barrell
   1807-1890 . . . . DLB-59
Cheever, John
   1912-1982 . . . . . . DLB-2, 102; Y-80, Y-82
Cheever, Susan 1943- Y-82
Cheke, Sir John 1514-1557 . . . . . DLB-132
Chelsea House DLB-46
Cheney, Ednah Dow (Littlehale)
   1824-1904 . . . . DLB-1
Cheney, Harriet Vaughn
   1796-1889 . . . . DLB-99
Chénier, Marie-Joseph 1764-1811 . . . DLB-192
Cherry, Kelly 1940- Y-83
Cherryh, C. J. 1942- Y-80
Chesnutt, Charles Waddell
   1858-1932 . . . . DLB-12, 50, 78
Chesney, Sir George Tomkyns
   1830-1895 . . . . DLB-190
Chester, Alfred 1928-1971 . . . . . . DLB-130
Chester, George Randolph
   1869-1924 . . . . DLB-78
The Chester Plays circa 1505-1532;
   revisions until 1575 . . . . DLB-146
Chesterfield, Philip Dormer Stanhope,
   Fourth Earl of 1694-1773 . . . . . DLB-104
Chesterton, G. K. 1874-1936
   . . . . DLB-10, 19, 34, 70, 98, 149, 178
Chettle, Henry
   circa 1560-circa 1607 . . . . . . DLB-136
Chew, Ada Nield 1870-1945 . . . . . DLB-135
Cheyney, Edward P. 1861-1947 . . . . DLB-47
Chiara, Piero 1913-1986 . . . . DLB-177
Chicano History DLB-82
Chicano Language DLB-82
Child, Francis James
   1825-1896 . . . . DLB-1, 64
Child, Lydia Maria
   1802-1880 . . . . DLB-1, 74
Child, Philip 1898-1978 . . . . DLB-68
Childers, Erskine 1870-1922 . . . . . . DLB-70
Children's Book Awards
   and Prizes DLB-61
Children's Illustrators,
   1800-1880 . . . . DLB-163
Childress, Alice 1920-1994 . . . . . . DLB-7, 38

Childs, George W. 1829-1894 . . . . . DLB-23
Chilton Book Company DLB-46
Chinweizu 1943- DLB-157
Chitham, Edward 1932- DLB-155
Chittenden, Hiram Martin
   1858-1917 . . . . DLB-47
Chivers, Thomas Holley
   1809-1858 . . . . DLB-3
Chopin, Kate 1850-1904 . . . . DLB-12, 78
Chopin, Rene 1885-1953 . . . . DLB-92
Choquette, Adrienne 1915-1973 . . . . DLB-68
Choquette, Robert 1905- DLB-68
The Christian Publishing
   Company DLB-49
Christie, Agatha 1890-1976 . . . . . DLB-13, 77
Christus und die Samariterin
   circa 950 . . . . DLB-148
Christy, Howard Chandler 1873-1952 . DLB-188
Chulkov, Mikhail Dmitrievich
   1743?-1792 . . . . DLB-150
Church, Benjamin 1734-1778 . . . . . DLB-31
Church, Francis Pharcellus
   1839-1906 . . . . DLB-79
Church, Richard 1893-1972 . . . . . DLB-191
Church, William Conant
   1836-1917 . . . . DLB-79
Churchill, Caryl 1938- DLB-13
Churchill, Charles
   1731-1764 . . . . DLB-109
Churchill, Sir Winston
   1874-1965 . . . . DLB-100; DS-16
Churchyard, Thomas
   1520?-1604 . . . . DLB-132
Churton, E., and Company DLB-106
Chute, Marchette 1909-1994 . . . . . DLB-103
Ciardi, John 1916-1986 . . . . DLB-5; Y-86
Cibber, Colley 1671-1757 . . . . DLB-84
Cima, Annalisa 1941- DLB-128
Čingo, Živko 1935-1987 . . . . DLB-181
Cirese, Eugenio 1884-1955 . . . . . . DLB-114
Cisneros, Sandra 1954- DLB-122, 152
City Lights Books DLB-46
Cixous, Hélène 1937- DLB-83
Clampitt, Amy 1920-1994 . . . . . . DLB-105
Clapper, Raymond 1892-1944 . . . . . DLB-29
Clare, John 1793-1864 . . . . DLB-55, 96
Clarendon, Edward Hyde, Earl of
   1609-1674 . . . . DLB-101
Clark, Alfred Alexander Gordon
   (see Hare, Cyril)
Clark, Ann Nolan 1896- DLB-52
Clark, C. E. Frazer Jr. 1925- DLB-187
Clark, C. M., Publishing
   Company DLB-46

DLB 196   **Cumulative Index**

Clark, Catherine Anthony 1892-1977 . . . . DLB-68
Clark, Charles Heber 1841-1915 . . . . DLB-11
Clark, Davis Wasgatt 1812-1871 . . . . . DLB-79
Clark, Eleanor 1913- DLB-6
Clark, J. P. 1935- DLB-117
Clark, Lewis Gaylord 1808-1873 . . . . DLB-3, 64, 73
Clark, Walter Van Tilburg 1909-1971 . . . . DLB-9
Clark, William (see Lewis, Meriwether)
Clark, William Andrews Jr. 1877-1934 . . . . DLB-187
Clarke, Austin 1896-1974 . . . . . . DLB-10, 20
Clarke, Austin C. 1934- DLB-53, 125
Clarke, Gillian 1937- DLB-40
Clarke, James Freeman 1810-1888 . . . . DLB-1, 59
Clarke, Pauline 1921- DLB-161
Clarke, Rebecca Sophia 1833-1906 . . . . DLB-42
Clarke, Robert, and Company DLB-49
Clarkson, Thomas 1760-1846 . . . . . . DLB-158
Claudel, Paul 1868-1955 . . . . DLB-192
Claudius, Matthias 1740-1815 . . . . . . DLB-97
Clausen, Andy 1943- DLB-16
Clawson, John L. 1865-1933 . . . . . . DLB-187
Claxton, Remsen and Haffelfinger DLB-49
Clay, Cassius Marcellus 1810-1903 . . . . DLB-43
Cleary, Beverly 1916- DLB-52
Cleaver, Vera 1919- and Cleaver, Bill 1920-1981 . . . . DLB-52
Cleland, John 1710-1789 . . . . DLB-39
Clemens, Samuel Langhorne (Mark Twain) 1835-1910 . . . . . DLB-11, 12, 23, 64, 74, 186, 189
Clement, Hal 1922- DLB-8
Clemo, Jack 1916- DLB-27
Cleveland, John 1613-1658 . . . . DLB-126
Cliff, Michelle 1946- DLB-157
Clifford, Lady Anne 1590-1676 . . . . . DLB-151
Clifford, James L. 1901-1978 . . . . . . DLB-103
Clifford, Lucy 1853?-1929 . . . . DLB-135, 141
Clifton, Lucille 1936- DLB-5, 41
Clines, Francis X. 1938- DLB-185
Clode, Edward J. [publishing house] DLB-46
Clough, Arthur Hugh 1819-1861 . . . . DLB-32
Cloutier, Cécile 1930- DLB-60
Clutton-Brock, Arthur 1868-1924 . . . . DLB-98
Coates, Robert M. 1897-1973 . . . . DLB-4, 9, 102

Coatsworth, Elizabeth 1893- DLB-22
Cobb, Charles E., Jr. 1943- DLB-41
Cobb, Frank I. 1869-1923 . . . . DLB-25
Cobb, Irvin S. 1876-1944 . . . . DLB-11, 25, 86
Cobbe, Frances Power 1822-1904 . . . DLB-190
Cobbett, William 1763-1835 . . . . DLB-43, 107
Cobbledick, Gordon 1898-1969 . . . . . DLB-171
Cochran, Thomas C. 1902- DLB-17
Cochrane, Elizabeth 1867-1922 . . . DLB-25, 189
Cockerill, John A. 1845-1896 . . . . . . DLB-23
Cocteau, Jean 1889-1963 . . . . DLB-65
Coderre, Emile (see Jean Narrache)
Coffee, Lenore J. 1900?-1984 . . . . . . DLB-44
Coffin, Robert P. Tristram 1892-1955 . . . . DLB-45
Cogswell, Fred 1917- DLB-60
Cogswell, Mason Fitch 1761-1830 . . . . DLB-37
Cohen, Arthur A. 1928-1986 . . . . . . DLB-28
Cohen, Leonard 1934- DLB-53
Cohen, Matt 1942- DLB-53
Colden, Cadwallader 1688-1776 . . . . DLB-24, 30
Cole, Barry 1936- DLB-14
Cole, George Watson 1850-1939 . . . . DLB-140
Colegate, Isabel 1931- DLB-14
Coleman, Emily Holmes 1899-1974 . . . . DLB-4
Coleman, Wanda 1946- DLB-130
Coleridge, Hartley 1796-1849 . . . . . . DLB-96
Coleridge, Mary 1861-1907 . . . . DLB-19, 98
Coleridge, Samuel Taylor 1772-1834 . . . . DLB-93, 107
Colet, John 1467-1519 . . . . DLB-132
Colette 1873-1954 . . . . DLB-65
Colette, Sidonie Gabrielle (see Colette)
Colinas, Antonio 1946- DLB-134
Coll, Joseph Clement 1881-1921 . . . . DLB-188
Collier, John 1901-1980 . . . . DLB-77
Collier, John Payne 1789-1883 . . . . . DLB-184
Collier, Mary 1690-1762 . . . . DLB-95
Collier, Robert J. 1876-1918 . . . . . . DLB-91
Collier, P. F. [publishing house] DLB-49
Collin and Small DLB-49
Collingwood, W. G. 1854-1932 . . . . . DLB-149
Collins, An floruit circa 1653 . . . . . . DLB-131
Collins, Merle 1950- DLB-157
Collins, Mortimer 1827-1876 . . . DLB-21, 35
Collins, Wilkie 1824-1889 . . . DLB-18, 70, 159
Collins, William 1721-1759 . . . . DLB-109

Collins, William, Sons and Company DLB-154
Collins, Isaac [publishing house] DLB-49
Collis, Maurice 1889-1973 . . . . DLB-195
Collyer, Mary 1716?-1763? DLB-39
Colman, Benjamin 1673-1747 . . . . . DLB-24
Colman, George, the Elder 1732-1794 . . . . DLB-89
Colman, George, the Younger 1762-1836 . . . . DLB-89
Colman, S. [publishing house] DLB-49
Colombo, John Robert 1936- DLB-53
Colquhoun, Patrick 1745-1820 . . . . . DLB-158
Colter, Cyrus 1910- DLB-33
Colum, Padraic 1881-1972 . . . . DLB-19
Colvin, Sir Sidney 1845-1927 . . . . . . DLB-149
Colwin, Laurie 1944-1992 . . . . Y-80
Comden, Betty 1919- and Green, Adolph 1918- DLB-44
Comi, Girolamo 1890-1968 . . . . DLB-114
The Comic Tradition Continued [in the British Novel] DLB-15
Commager, Henry Steele 1902- DLB-17
The Commercialization of the Image of Revolt, by Kenneth Rexroth DLB-16
Community and Commentators: Black Theatre and Its Critics DLB-38
Compton-Burnett, Ivy 1884?-1969 . . . . DLB-36
Conan, Laure 1845-1924 . . . . DLB-99
Conde, Carmen 1901- DLB-108
Conference on Modern Biography Y-85
Congreve, William 1670-1729 . . . . DLB-39, 84
Conkey, W. B., Company DLB-49
Connell, Evan S., Jr. 1924- DLB-2; Y-81
Connelly, Marc 1890-1980 . . . . . DLB-7; Y-80
Connolly, Cyril 1903-1974 . . . . DLB-98
Connolly, James B. 1868-1957 . . . . . DLB-78
Connor, Ralph 1860-1937 . . . . DLB-92
Connor, Tony 1930- DLB-40
Conquest, Robert 1917- DLB-27
Conrad, Joseph 1857-1924 . . . . DLB-10, 34, 98, 156
Conrad, John, and Company DLB-49
Conroy, Jack 1899-1990 . . . . Y-81
Conroy, Pat 1945- DLB-6
The Consolidation of Opinion: Critical Responses to the Modernists DLB-36
Consolo, Vincenzo 1933- DLB-196
Constable, Henry 1562-1613 . . . . . . DLB-136
Constable and Company Limited DLB-112

313

Cumulative Index

Constable, Archibald, and
  Company DLB-154
Constant, Benjamin 1767-1830 . . . . . DLB-119
Constant de Rebecque, Henri-Benjamin de
  (see Constant, Benjamin)
Constantine, David 1944- DLB-40
Constantin-Weyer, Maurice
  1881-1964 . . . . DLB-92
Contempo Caravan: Kites in
  a Windstorm Y-85
A Contemporary Flourescence of Chicano
  Literature Y-84
"Contemporary Verse Story-telling,"
  by Jonathan Holden DLB-105
The Continental Publishing
  Company DLB-49
A Conversation with Chaim Potok Y-84
Conversations with Editors Y-95
Conversations with Publishers I: An Interview
  with Patrick O'Connor Y-84
Conversations with Publishers II: An Interview
  with Charles Scribner III Y-94
Conversations with Publishers III: An Interview
  with Donald Lamm Y-95
Conversations with Publishers IV: An Interview
  with James Laughlin Y-96
Conversations with Rare Book Dealers I: An
  Interview with Glenn Horowitz Y-90
Conversations with Rare Book Dealers II: An
  Interview with Ralph Sipper Y-94
Conversations with Rare Book Dealers
  (Publishers) III: An Interview with
  Otto Penzler Y-96
The Conversion of an Unpolitical Man,
  by W. H. Bruford DLB-66
Conway, Moncure Daniel
  1832-1907 . . . . DLB-1
Cook, Ebenezer
  circa 1667-circa 1732 . . . . DLB-24
Cook, Edward Tyas 1857-1919 . . . . . DLB-149
Cook, Michael 1933- DLB-53
Cook, David C., Publishing
  Company DLB-49
Cooke, George Willis 1848-1923 . . . . . DLB-71
Cooke, Increase, and Company DLB-49
Cooke, John Esten 1830-1886 . . . . . . DLB-3
Cooke, Philip Pendleton
  1816-1850 . . . . DLB-3, 59
Cooke, Rose Terry
  1827-1892 . . . . DLB-12, 74
Cook-Lynn, Elizabeth 1930- DLB-175
Coolbrith, Ina 1841-1928 . . . . DLB-54, 186
Cooley, Peter 1940- DLB-105
Coolidge, Clark 1939- DLB-193
Coolidge, Susan (see Woolsey, Sarah Chauncy)
Coolidge, George
  [publishing house] DLB-49

Cooper, Giles 1918-1966 . . . . DLB-13
Cooper, James Fenimore
  1789-1851 . . . . DLB-3, 183
Cooper, Kent 1880-1965 . . . . DLB-29
Cooper, Susan 1935- DLB-161
Cooper, William
  [publishing house] DLB-170
Coote, J. [publishing house] DLB-154
Coover, Robert 1932- DLB-2; Y-81
Copeland and Day DLB-49
Ćopić, Branko 1915-1984 . . . . DLB-181
Copland, Robert 1470?-1548 . . . . . . DLB-136
Coppard, A. E. 1878-1957 . . . . DLB-162
Coppel, Alfred 1921- Y-83
Coppola, Francis Ford 1939- DLB-44
Copway, George (Kah-ge-ga-gah-bowh)
  1818-1869 . . . . DLB-175, 183
Corazzini, Sergio 1886-1907 . . . . . . DLB-114
Corbett, Richard 1582-1635 . . . . . . DLB-121
Corcoran, Barbara 1911- DLB-52
Cordelli, Franco 1943- DLB-196
Corelli, Marie 1855-1924 . . . . . DLB-34, 156
Corle, Edwin 1906-1956 . . . . Y-85
Corman, Cid 1924- DLB-5, 193
Cormier, Robert 1925- DLB-52
Corn, Alfred 1943- DLB-120; Y-80
Cornish, Sam 1935- DLB-41
Cornish, William
  circa 1465-circa 1524 . . . . DLB-132
Cornwall, Barry (see Procter, Bryan Waller)
Cornwallis, Sir William, the Younger
  circa 1579-1614 . . . . DLB-151
Cornwell, David John Moore
  (see le Carré, John)
Corpi, Lucha 1945- DLB-82
Corrington, John William 1932- DLB-6
Corrothers, James D. 1869-1917 . . . . . DLB-50
Corso, Gregory 1930- DLB-5, 16
Cortázar, Julio 1914-1984 . . . . DLB-113
Cortez, Jayne 1936- DLB-41
Corvinus, Gottlieb Siegmund
  1677-1746 . . . . DLB-168
Corvo, Baron (see Rolfe, Frederick William)
Cory, Annie Sophie (see Cross, Victoria)
Cory, William Johnson
  1823-1892 . . . . DLB-35
Coryate, Thomas
  1577?-1617 . . . . DLB-151, 172
Ćosić, Dobrica 1921- DLB-181
Cosin, John 1595-1672 . . . . DLB-151
Cosmopolitan Book Corporation DLB-46
Costain, Thomas B. 1885-1965 . . . . . DLB-9
Coste, Donat 1912-1957 . . . . DLB-88

Costello, Louisa Stuart 1799-1870 . . . DLB-166
Cota-Cárdenas, Margarita
  1941- DLB-122
Cotten, Bruce 1873-1954 . . . . DLB-187
Cotter, Joseph Seamon, Sr.
  1861-1949 . . . . DLB-50
Cotter, Joseph Seamon, Jr.
  1895-1919 . . . . DLB-50
Cottle, Joseph [publishing house] DLB-154
Cotton, Charles 1630-1687 . . . . DLB-131
Cotton, John 1584-1652 . . . . DLB-24
Coulter, John 1888-1980 . . . . DLB-68
Cournos, John 1881-1966 . . . . DLB-54
Courteline, Georges 1858-1929 . . . . . DLB-192
Cousins, Margaret 1905- DLB-137
Cousins, Norman 1915-1990 . . . . . . DLB-137
Coventry, Francis 1725-1754 . . . . . . DLB-39
Coverdale, Miles
  1487 or 1488-1569 . . . . DLB-167
Coverly, N. [publishing house] DLB-49
Covici-Friede DLB-46
Coward, Noel 1899-1973 . . . . DLB-10
Coward, McCann and
  Geoghegan DLB-46
Cowles, Gardner 1861-1946 . . . . . . DLB-29
Cowles, Gardner ("Mike"), Jr.
  1903-1985 . . . . DLB-127, 137
Cowley, Abraham
  1618-1667 . . . . DLB-131, 151
Cowley, Hannah 1743-1809 . . . . DLB-89
Cowley, Malcolm
  1898-1989 . . . . . DLB-4, 48; Y-81, Y-89
Cowper, William
  1731-1800 . . . . DLB-104, 109
Cox, A. B. (see Berkeley, Anthony)
Cox, James McMahon
  1903-1974 . . . . DLB-127
Cox, James Middleton
  1870-1957 . . . . DLB-127
Cox, Palmer 1840-1924 . . . . DLB-42
Coxe, Louis 1918-1993 . . . . DLB-5
Coxe, Tench 1755-1824 . . . . DLB-37
Cozzens, James Gould
  1903-1978 . . . . DLB-9; Y-84; DS-2
Cozzens's *Michael Scarlett* Y-97
Crabbe, George 1754-1832 . . . . DLB-93
Crackanthorpe, Hubert
  1870-1896 . . . . DLB-135
Craddock, Charles Egbert
  (see Murfree, Mary N.)
Cradock, Thomas 1718-1770 . . . . . . DLB-31
Craig, Daniel H. 1811-1895 . . . . . . DLB-43
Craik, Dinah Maria
  1826-1887 . . . . DLB-35, 136
Cramer, Richard Ben 1950- DLB-185

Cranch, Christopher Pearse
  1813-1892 . . . . DLB-1, 42
Crane, Hart 1899-1932 . . . . DLB-4, 48
Crane, R. S. 1886-1967. . . . . DLB-63
Crane, Stephen 1871-1900. . . . DLB-12, 54, 78
Crane, Walter 1845-1915 . . . . DLB-163
Cranmer, Thomas 1489-1556. . . . . . DLB-132
Crapsey, Adelaide 1878-1914. . . . . . . DLB-54
Crashaw, Richard
  1612 or 1613-1649 . . . . DLB-126
Craven, Avery 1885-1980 . . . . DLB-17
Crawford, Charles
  1752-circa 1815. . . . . DLB-31
Crawford, F. Marion 1854-1909 . . . . . DLB-71
Crawford, Isabel Valancy
  1850-1887 . . . . DLB-92
Crawley, Alan 1887-1975. . . . . DLB-68
Crayon, Geoffrey (see Irving, Washington)
Creamer, Robert W. 1922- DLB-171
Creasey, John 1908-1973 . . . . DLB-77
Creative Age Press DLB-46
Creech, William
  [publishing house]. DLB-154
Creede, Thomas
  [publishing house]. DLB-170
Creel, George 1876-1953 . . . . DLB-25
Creeley, Robert
  1926- DLB-5, 16, 169; DS-17
Creelman, James 1859-1915 . . . . DLB-23
Cregan, David 1931- DLB-13
Creighton, Donald Grant
  1902-1979 . . . . DLB-88
Cremazie, Octave 1827-1879 . . . . DLB-99
Crémer, Victoriano 1909?- DLB-108
Crescas, Hasdai
  circa 1340-1412?. DLB-115
Crespo, Angel 1926- DLB-134
Cresset Press DLB-112
Cresswell, Helen 1934- DLB-161
Crèvecoeur, Michel Guillaume Jean de
  1735-1813 . . . . DLB-37
Crews, Harry 1935- DLB-6, 143, 185
Crichton, Michael 1942- Y-81
A Crisis of Culture: The Changing Role
  of Religion in the New Republic
  . . . . DLB-37
Crispin, Edmund 1921-1978 . . . . DLB-87
Cristofer, Michael 1946- DLB-7
"The Critic as Artist" (1891), by
  Oscar Wilde DLB-57
"Criticism In Relation To Novels" (1863),
  by G. H. Lewes DLB-21
Crnjanski, Miloš 1893-1977 . . . . . . DLB-147
Crockett, David (Davy)
  1786-1836. . . . . DLB-3, 11, 183

Croft-Cooke, Rupert (see Bruce, Leo)
Crofts, Freeman Wills
  1879-1957 . . . . DLB-77
Croker, John Wilson
  1780-1857 . . . . DLB-110
Croly, George 1780-1860 . . . . DLB-159
Croly, Herbert 1869-1930 . . . . DLB-91
Croly, Jane Cunningham
  1829-1901 . . . . DLB-23
Crompton, Richmal 1890-1969 . . . . . DLB-160
Cronin, A. J. 1896-1981. . . . . DLB-191
Crosby, Caresse 1892-1970. . . . . DLB-48
Crosby, Caresse 1892-1970 and Crosby,
  Harry 1898-1929. . . . . DLB-4; DS-15
Crosby, Harry 1898-1929. . . . . DLB-48
Cross, Gillian 1945- DLB-161
Cross, Victoria 1868-1952 . . . . DLB-135
Crossley-Holland, Kevin
  1941- DLB-40, 161
Crothers, Rachel 1878-1958 . . . . DLB-7
Crowell, Thomas Y., Company DLB-49
Crowley, John 1942- Y-82
Crowley, Mart 1935- DLB-7
Crown Publishers DLB-46
Crowne, John 1641-1712 . . . . DLB-80
Crowninshield, Edward Augustus
  1817-1859 . . . . DLB-140
Crowninshield, Frank 1872-1947 . . . . . DLB-91
Croy, Homer 1883-1965 . . . . DLB-4
Crumley, James 1939- Y-84
Cruz, Victor Hernández 1949- DLB-41
Csokor, Franz Theodor
  1885-1969 . . . . DLB-81
Cuala Press. DLB-112
Cullen, Countee
  1903-1946 . . . . DLB-4, 48, 51
Culler, Jonathan D. 1944- DLB-67
The Cult of Biography
  Excerpts from the Second Folio Debate:
  "Biographies are generally a disease of
  English Literature" – Germaine Greer,
  Victoria Glendinning, Auberon Waugh,
  and Richard Holmes. Y-86
Cumberland, Richard 1732-1811 . . . . . DLB-89
Cummings, Constance Gordon
  1837-1924 . . . . DLB-174
Cummings, E. E. 1894-1962 . . . . . DLB-4, 48
Cummings, Ray 1887-1957 . . . . DLB-8
Cummings and Hilliard. DLB-49
Cummins, Maria Susanna
  1827-1866 . . . . DLB-42
Cundall, Joseph
  [publishing house]. DLB-106
Cuney, Waring 1906-1976 . . . . DLB-51
Cuney-Hare, Maude 1874-1936 . . . . . DLB-52

Cunningham, Allan 1784-1842 . . DLB-116, 144
Cunningham, J. V. 1911- DLB-5
Cunningham, Peter F.
  [publishing house]. DLB-49
Cunqueiro, Alvaro 1911-1981. . . . . . DLB-134
Cuomo, George 1929- Y-80
Cupples and Leon DLB-46
Cupples, Upham and Company DLB-49
Cuppy, Will 1884-1949. . . . . DLB-11
Curll, Edmund
  [publishing house]. DLB-154
Currie, James 1756-1805. . . . . DLB-142
Currie, Mary Montgomerie Lamb Singleton,
  Lady Currie (see Fane, Violet)
Cursor Mundi circa 1300 . . . . DLB-146
Curti, Merle E. 1897- DLB-17
Curtis, Anthony 1926- DLB-155
Curtis, Cyrus H. K. 1850-1933 . . . . . DLB-91
Curtis, George William
  1824-1892 . . . . DLB-1, 43
Curzon, Robert 1810-1873 . . . . DLB-166
Curzon, Sarah Anne
  1833-1898 . . . . DLB-99
Cushing, Harvey 1869-1939. . . . . . . DLB-187
Cynewulf circa 770-840 . . . . DLB-146
Czepko, Daniel 1605-1660. . . . . DLB-164

D

D. M. Thomas: The Plagiarism
  Controversy. Y-82
Dabit, Eugène 1898-1936. . . . . DLB-65
Daborne, Robert circa 1580-1628 . . . . DLB-58
Dacey, Philip 1939- DLB-105
Dach, Simon 1605-1659 . . . . DLB-164
Daggett, Rollin M. 1831-1901 . . . . . . DLB-79
D'Aguiar, Fred 1960- DLB-157
Dahl, Roald 1916-1990 . . . . DLB-139
Dahlberg, Edward 1900-1977. . . . . . . DLB-48
Dahn, Felix 1834-1912. . . . . DLB-129
Dale, Peter 1938- DLB-40
Daley, Arthur 1904-1974 . . . . DLB-171
Dall, Caroline Wells (Healey)
  1822-1912. . . . . DLB-1
Dallas, E. S. 1828-1879. . . . . DLB-55
The Dallas Theater Center DLB-7
D'Alton, Louis 1900-1951. . . . . DLB-10
Daly, T. A. 1871-1948 . . . . DLB-11
Damon, S. Foster 1893-1971 . . . . . . DLB-45
Damrell, William S.
  [publishing house]. DLB-49
Dana, Charles A. 1819-1897 . . . . . DLB-3, 23

Cumulative Index

Dana, Richard Henry, Jr. 1815-1882 .... DLB-1, 183
Dandridge, Ray Garfield DLB-51
Dane, Clemence 1887-1965 .... DLB-10
Danforth, John 1660-1730 .... DLB-24
Danforth, Samuel, I 1626-1674 ..... DLB-24
Danforth, Samuel, II 1666-1727 .... DLB-24
Dangerous Years: London Theater, 1939-1945 .... DLB-10
Daniel, John M. 1825-1865 .... DLB-43
Daniel, Samuel 1562 or 1563-1619 .... DLB-62
Daniel Press DLB-106
Daniells, Roy 1902-1979 .... DLB-68
Daniels, Jim 1956- DLB-120
Daniels, Jonathan 1902-1981 ..... DLB-127
Daniels, Josephus 1862-1948 ..... DLB-29
Danis Rose and the Rendering of *Ulysses* Y-97
Dannay, Frederic 1905-1982 and Manfred B. Lee 1905-1971 ..... DLB-137
Danner, Margaret Esse 1915- DLB-41
Danter, John [publishing house] DLB-170
Dantin, Louis 1865-1945 .... DLB-92
Danzig, Allison 1898-1987 .... DLB-171
D'Arcy, Ella circa 1857-1937 ..... DLB-135
Darley, Felix Octavious Carr 1822-1888 .... DLB-188
Darley, George 1795-1846 .... DLB-96
Darwin, Charles 1809-1882 ..... DLB-57, 166
Darwin, Erasmus 1731-1802 .... DLB-93
Daryush, Elizabeth 1887-1977 ..... DLB-20
Dashkova, Ekaterina Romanovna (née Vorontsova) 1743-1810 .... DLB-150
Dashwood, Edmée Elizabeth Monica de la Pasture (see Delafield, E. M.)
Daudet, Alphonse 1840-1897 ..... DLB-123
d'Aulaire, Edgar Parin 1898- and d'Aulaire, Ingri 1904- DLB-22
Davenant, Sir William 1606-1668 .... DLB-58, 126
Davenport, Guy 1927- DLB-130
Davenport, Marcia 1903-1996 ..... DS-17
Davenport, Robert ?-? DLB-58
Daves, Delmer 1904-1977 .... DLB-26
Davey, Frank 1940- DLB-53
Davidson, Avram 1923-1993 .... DLB-8
Davidson, Donald 1893-1968 ...... DLB-45
Davidson, John 1857-1909 .... DLB-19
Davidson, Lionel 1922- DLB-14
Davidson, Sara 1943- DLB-185
Davie, Donald 1922- DLB-27
Davie, Elspeth 1919- DLB-139

Davies, Sir John 1569-1626 ...... DLB-172
Davies, John, of Hereford 1565?-1618 .... DLB-121
Davies, Rhys 1901-1978 ..... DLB-139, 191
Davies, Robertson 1913- DLB-68
Davies, Samuel 1723-1761 .... DLB-31
Davies, Thomas 1712?-1785 .... DLB-142, 154
Davies, W. H. 1871-1940 ..... DLB-19, 174
Davies, Peter, Limited DLB-112
Daviot, Gordon 1896?-1952 ..... DLB-10 (see also Tey, Josephine)
Davis, Charles A. 1795-1867 ...... DLB-11
Davis, Clyde Brion 1894-1962 ..... DLB-9
Davis, Dick 1945- DLB-40
Davis, Frank Marshall 1905-? DLB-51
Davis, H. L. 1894-1960 .... DLB-9
Davis, John 1774-1854 .... DLB-37
Davis, Lydia 1947- DLB-130
Davis, Margaret Thomson 1926- DLB-14
Davis, Ossie 1917- DLB-7, 38
Davis, Paxton 1925-1994 .... Y-94
Davis, Rebecca Harding 1831-1910 .... DLB-74
Davis, Richard Harding 1864-1916 ...... DLB-12, 23, 78, 79, 189; DS-13
Davis, Samuel Cole 1764-1809 ..... DLB-37
Davison, Peter 1928- DLB-5
Davys, Mary 1674-1732 .... DLB-39
DAW Books DLB-46
Dawn Powell, Where Have You Been All Our lives? Y-97
Dawson, Ernest 1882-1947 .... DLB-140
Dawson, Fielding 1930- DLB-130
Dawson, William 1704-1752 ...... DLB-31
Day, Angel flourished 1586 ...... DLB-167
Day, Benjamin Henry 1810-1889 ..... DLB-43
Day, Clarence 1874-1935 .... DLB-11
Day, Dorothy 1897-1980 .... DLB-29
Day, Frank Parker 1881-1950 ..... DLB-92
Day, John circa 1574-circa 1640 ..... DLB-62
Day, John [publishing house] DLB-170
Day Lewis, C. 1904-1972 ..... DLB-15, 20 (see also Blake, Nicholas)
Day, Thomas 1748-1789 .... DLB-39
Day, The John, Company DLB-46
Day, Mahlon [publishing house] DLB-49
Dazai, Osamu 1909-1948 .... DLB-182
Deacon, William Arthur 1890-1977 .... DLB-68
Deal, Borden 1922-1985 .... DLB-6
de Angeli, Marguerite 1889-1987 ..... DLB-22
De Angelis, Milo 1951- DLB-128

De Bow, James Dunwoody Brownson 1820-1867 .... DLB-3, 79
de Bruyn, Günter 1926- DLB-75
de Camp, L. Sprague 1907- DLB-8
De Carlo, Andrea 1952- DLB-196
The Decay of Lying (1889), by Oscar Wilde [excerpt] DLB-18
Dechert, Robert 1895-1975 .... DLB-187
Dedication, *Ferdinand Count Fathom* (1753), by Tobias Smollett DLB-39
Dedication, *The History of Pompey the Little* (1751), by Francis Coventry DLB-39
Dedication, *Lasselia* (1723), by Eliza Haywood [excerpt] DLB-39
Dedication, *The Wanderer* (1814), by Fanny Burney DLB-39
Dee, John 1527-1609 .... DLB-136
Deeping, George Warwick 1877-1950 .... DLB 153
Defense of *Amelia* (1752), by Henry Fielding DLB-39
Defoe, Daniel 1660-1731 .... DLB-39, 95, 101
de Fontaine, Felix Gregory 1834-1896 .... DLB-43
De Forest, John William 1826-1906 .... DLB-12, 189
DeFrees, Madeline 1919- DLB-105
DeGolyer, Everette Lee 1886-1956 ... DLB-187
de Graff, Robert 1895-1981 .... Y-81
de Graft, Joe 1924-1978 .... DLB-117
De Heinrico circa 980? DLB-148
Deighton, Len 1929- DLB-87
DeJong, Meindert 1906-1991 ...... DLB-52
Dekker, Thomas circa 1572-1632 .... DLB-62, 172
Delacorte, Jr., George T. 1894-1991 .... DLB-91
Delafield, E. M. 1890-1943 .... DLB-34
Delahaye, Guy 1888-1969 .... DLB-92
de la Mare, Walter 1873-1956 .... DLB-19, 153, 162
Deland, Margaret 1857-1945 ..... DLB-78
Delaney, Shelagh 1939- DLB-13
Delano, Amasa 1763-1823 .... DLB-183
Delany, Martin Robinson 1812-1885 .... DLB-50
Delany, Samuel R. 1942- DLB-8, 33
de la Roche, Mazo 1879-1961 ..... DLB-68
Delavigne, Jean François Casimir 1793-1843 .... DLB-192
Delbanco, Nicholas 1942- DLB-6
De León, Nephtal 1945- DLB-82
Delgado, Abelardo Barrientos 1931- DLB-82
Del Giudice, Daniele 1949- DLB-196

De Libero, Libero 1906-1981 . . . . . . DLB-114

DeLillo, Don 1936- DLB-6, 173

de Lisser H. G. 1878-1944 . . . . . . DLB-117

Dell, Floyd 1887-1969 . . . . DLB-9

Dell Publishing Company DLB-46

delle Grazie, Marie Eugene
1864-1931 . . . . DLB-81

Deloney, Thomas died 1600 . . . . . DLB-167

Deloria, Ella C. 1889-1971 . . . . . . DLB-175

Deloria, Vine, Jr. 1933- DLB-175

del Rey, Lester 1915-1993 . . . . DLB-8

Del Vecchio, John M. 1947- DS-9

de Man, Paul 1919-1983 . . . . DLB-67

Demby, William 1922- DLB-33

Deming, Philander 1829-1915 . . . . . DLB-74

Demorest, William Jennings
1822-1895 . . . . DLB-79

De Morgan, William 1839-1917 . . . . DLB-153

Demosthenes 384 B.C.-322 B.C. DLB-176

Denham, Henry
[publishing house] DLB-170

Denham, Sir John
1615-1669 . . . . DLB-58, 126

Denison, Merrill 1893-1975 . . . . DLB-92

Denison, T. S., and Company DLB-49

Dennery, Adolphe Philippe 1811-1899 . . . DLB-192

Dennie, Joseph
1768-1812 . . . . . . DLB-37, 43, 59, 73

Dennis, John 1658-1734 . . . . DLB-101

Dennis, Nigel 1912-1989 . . . . . DLB-13, 15

Denslow, W. W. 1856-1915 . . . . . . DLB-188

Dent, Tom 1932- DLB-38

Dent, J. M., and Sons DLB-112

Denton, Daniel circa 1626-1703 . . . . . DLB-24

DePaola, Tomie 1934- DLB-61

Department of Library, Archives, and Institutional Research, American Bible Society Y-97

De Quille, Dan 1829-1898 . . . . DLB-186

De Quincey, Thomas
1785-1859 . . . . DLB-110, 144

Derby, George Horatio
1823-1861 . . . . DLB-11

Derby, J. C., and Company DLB-49

Derby and Miller DLB-49

Derleth, August 1909-1971 . . . . DLB-9; DS-17

The Derrydale Press DLB-46

Derzhavin, Gavriil Romanovich
1743-1816 . . . . DLB-150

Desaulniers, Gonsalve
1863-1934 . . . . DLB-92

Desbiens, Jean-Paul 1927- DLB-53

des Forêts, Louis-Rene 1918- DLB-83

Desiato, Luca 1941- DLB-196

Desnica, Vladan 1905-1967 . . . . DLB-181

DesRochers, Alfred 1901-1978 . . . . . DLB-68

Desrosiers, Léo-Paul 1896-1967 . . . . . DLB-68

Dessì, Giuseppe 1909-1977 . . . . DLB-177

Destouches, Louis-Ferdinand
(see Céline, Louis-Ferdinand)

De Tabley, Lord 1835-1895 . . . . DLB-35

"A Detail in a Poem,"
by Fred Chappell DLB-105

Deutsch, Babette 1895-1982 . . . . DLB-45

Deutsch, Niklaus Manuel (see Manuel, Niklaus)

Deutsch, André, Limited DLB-112

Deveaux, Alexis 1948- DLB-38

The Development of the Author's Copyright
in Britain DLB-154

The Development of Lighting in the Staging
of Drama, 1900-1945 . . . . DLB-10

The Development of Meiji Japan DLB-180

De Vere, Aubrey 1814-1902 . . . . DLB-35

Devereux, second Earl of Essex, Robert
1565-1601 . . . . DLB-136

The Devin-Adair Company DLB-46

De Vinne, Theodore Low
1828-1914 . . . . DLB-187

De Voto, Bernard 1897-1955 . . . . DLB-9

De Vries, Peter 1910-1993 . . . . DLB-6; Y-82

Dewdney, Christopher 1951- DLB-60

Dewdney, Selwyn 1909-1979 . . . . . . DLB-68

DeWitt, Robert M., Publisher DLB-49

DeWolfe, Fiske and Company DLB-49

Dexter, Colin 1930- DLB-87

de Young, M. H. 1849-1925 . . . . DLB-25

Dhlomo, H. I. E. 1903-1956 . . . . DLB-157

Dhuoda circa 803-after 843 . . . . DLB-148

The Dial Press DLB-46

Diamond, I. A. L. 1920-1988 . . . . . . DLB-26

Dibdin, Thomas Frognall
1776-1847 . . . . DLB-184

Di Cicco, Pier Giorgio 1949- DLB-60

Dick, Philip K. 1928-1982 . . . . DLB-8

Dick and Fitzgerald DLB-49

Dickens, Charles
1812-1870 . . . . . DLB-21, 55, 70, 159, 166

Dickinson, Peter 1927- DLB-161

Dickey, James 1923-1997
. . . . DLB-5, 193; Y-82, Y-93, Y-96; DS-7

Dickey, William 1928-1994 . . . . DLB-5

Dickinson, Emily 1830-1886 . . . . DLB-1

Dickinson, John 1732-1808 . . . . DLB-31

Dickinson, Jonathan 1688-1747 . . . . . DLB-24

Dickinson, Patric 1914- DLB-27

Dickinson, Peter 1927- DLB-87

Dicks, John [publishing house] DLB-106

Dickson, Gordon R. 1923- DLB-8

Dictionary of Literary Biography
Yearbook Awards Y-92, Y-93

The Dictionary of National Biography
. . . . DLB-144

Didion, Joan
1934- DLB-2, 173, 185; Y-81, Y-86

Di Donato, Pietro 1911- DLB-9

Die Fürstliche Bibliothek Corvey Y-96

Diego, Gerardo 1896-1987 . . . . DLB-134

Digges, Thomas circa 1546-1595 . . . . DLB-136

Dillard, Annie 1945- Y-80

Dillard, R. H. W. 1937- DLB-5

Dillingham, Charles T.,
Company DLB-49

The Dillingham, G. W.,
Company DLB-49

Dilly, Edward and Charles
[publishing house] DLB-154

Dilthey, Wilhelm 1833-1911 . . . . DLB-129

Dimitrova, Blaga 1922- DLB-181

Dimov, Dimitŭr 1909-1966 . . . . . . DLB-181

Dimsdale, Thomas J. 1831?-1866 . . . . DLB-186

Dingelstedt, Franz von
1814-1881 . . . . DLB-133

Dintenfass, Mark 1941- Y-84

Diogenes, Jr. (see Brougham, John)

Diogenes Laertius circa 200 . . . . DLB-176

DiPrima, Diane 1934- DLB-5, 16

Disch, Thomas M. 1940- DLB-8

Disney, Walt 1901-1966 . . . . DLB-22

Disraeli, Benjamin 1804-1881 . . . . DLB-21, 55

D'Israeli, Isaac 1766-1848 . . . . DLB-107

Ditzen, Rudolf (see Fallada, Hans)

Dix, Dorothea Lynde 1802-1887 . . . . . DLB-1

Dix, Dorothy (see Gilmer,
Elizabeth Meriwether)

Dix, Edwards and Company DLB-49

Dixie, Florence Douglas
1857-1905 . . . . DLB-174

Dixon, Paige (see Corcoran, Barbara)

Dixon, Richard Watson
1833-1900 . . . . DLB-19

Dixon, Stephen 1936- DLB-130

Dmitriev, Ivan Ivanovich
1760-1837 . . . . DLB-150

Dobell, Bertram 1842-1914 . . . . DLB-184

Dobell, Sydney 1824-1874 . . . . DLB-32

Döblin, Alfred 1878-1957 . . . . DLB-66

Dobson, Austin
1840-1921 . . . . DLB-35, 144

Doctorow, E. L.
1931- DLB-2, 28, 173; Y-80

Documents on Sixteenth-Century
Literature DLB-167, 172

Cumulative Index   DLB 196

Dodd, William E. 1869-1940 . . . . . . DLB-17
Dodd, Anne [publishing house] DLB-154
Dodd, Mead and Company DLB-49
Doderer, Heimito von 1896-1968 . . . . DLB-85
Dodge, Mary Mapes
    1831?-1905 . . . . DLB-42, 79; DS-13
Dodge, B. W., and Company DLB-46
Dodge Publishing Company DLB-49
Dodgson, Charles Lutwidge
    (see Carroll, Lewis)
Dodsley, Robert 1703-1764 . . . . DLB-95
Dodsley, R. [publishing house] DLB-154
Dodson, Owen 1914-1983 . . . . DLB-76
Doesticks, Q. K. Philander, P. B.
    (see Thomson, Mortimer)
Doheny, Carrie Estelle
    1875-1958 . . . . DLB-140
Doherty, John 1798?-1854 . . . . DLB-190
Domínguez, Sylvia Maida
    1935- DLB-122
Donahoe, Patrick
    [publishing house] DLB-49
Donald, David H. 1920- DLB-17
Donaldson, Scott 1928- DLB-111
Doni, Rodolfo 1919- DLB-177
Donleavy, J. P. 1926- DLB-6, 173
Donnadieu, Marguerite (see Duras,
    Marguerite)
Donne, John 1572-1631 . . . . . . DLB-121, 151
Donnelley, R. R., and Sons
    Company DLB-49
Donnelly, Ignatius 1831-1901 . . . . . DLB-12
Donohue and Henneberry DLB-49
Donoso, José 1924- DLB-113
Doolady, M. [publishing house] DLB-49
Dooley, Ebon (see Ebon)
Doolittle, Hilda 1886-1961 . . . . . . DLB-4, 45
Doplicher, Fabio 1938- DLB-128
Dor, Milo 1923- DLB-85
Doran, George H., Company DLB-46
Dorgelès, Roland 1886-1973 . . . . . . DLB-65
Dorn, Edward 1929- DLB-5
Dorr, Rheta Childe 1866-1948 . . . . . DLB-25
Dorris, Michael 1945-1997 . . . . . . DLB-175
Dorset and Middlesex, Charles Sackville,
    Lord Buckhurst,
    Earl of 1643-1706 . . . . DLB-131
Dorst, Tankred 1925- DLB-75, 124
Dos Passos, John
    1896-1970 . . . . . DLB-4, 9; DS-1, DS-15
John Dos Passos: A Centennial
    Commemoration Y-96
Doubleday and Company DLB-49
Dougall, Lily 1858-1923 . . . . DLB-92

Doughty, Charles M.
    1843-1926 . . . . DLB-19, 57, 174
Douglas, Gavin 1476-1522 . . . . DLB-132
Douglas, Keith 1920-1944 . . . . DLB-27
Douglas, Norman 1868-1952 . . . . DLB-34, 195
Douglass, Frederick
    1817?-1895 . . . . DLB-1, 43, 50, 79
Douglass, William circa
    1691-1752 . . . . DLB-24
Dourado, Autran 1926- DLB-145
Dove, Arthur G. 1880-1946 . . . . . . DLB-188
Dove, Rita 1952- DLB-120
Dover Publications DLB-46
Doves Press DLB-112
Dowden, Edward 1843-1913 . . DLB-35, 149
Dowell, Coleman 1925-1985 . . . . . . DLB-130
Dowland, John 1563-1626 . . . . DLB-172
Downes, Gwladys 1915- DLB-88
Downing, J., Major (see Davis, Charles A.)
Downing, Major Jack (see Smith, Seba)
Dowriche, Anne
    before 1560-after 1613 . . . . DLB-172
Dowson, Ernest 1867-1900 . . . . DLB-19, 135
Doxey, William
    [publishing house] DLB-49
Doyle, Sir Arthur Conan
    1859-1930 . . . . . . DLB-18, 70, 156, 178
Doyle, Kirby 1932- DLB-16
Doyle, Roddy 1958- DLB-194
Drabble, Margaret 1939- DLB-14, 155
Drach, Albert 1902- DLB-85
Dragojević, Danijel 1934- DLB-181
Drake, Samuel Gardner 1798-1875 . . . DLB-187
The Dramatic Publishing
    Company DLB-49
Dramatists Play Service DLB-46
Drant, Thomas
    early 1540s?-1578 . . . . DLB-167
Draper, John W. 1811-1882 . . . . . . DLB-30
Draper, Lyman C. 1815-1891 . . . . . DLB-30
Drayton, Michael 1563-1631 . . . . . . DLB-121
Dreiser, Theodore
    1871-1945 . . . . DLB-9, 12, 102, 137; DS-1
Drewitz, Ingeborg 1923-1986 . . . . . DLB-75
Drieu La Rochelle, Pierre
    1893-1945 . . . . DLB-72
Drinkwater, John 1882-1937
    . . . . DLB-10, 19, 149
Droste-Hülshoff, Annette von
    1797-1848 . . . . DLB-133
The Drue Heinz Literature Prize
    Excerpt from "Excerpts from a Report
    of the Commission," in David
    Bosworth's *The Death of Descartes*
    An Interview with David
    Bosworth Y-82

Drummond, William Henry
    1854-1907 . . . . DLB-92
Drummond, William, of Hawthornden
    1585-1649 . . . . DLB-121
Dryden, Charles 1860?-1931 . . . . . . DLB-171
Dryden, John 1631-1700 . . . DLB-80, 101, 131
Držić, Marin circa 1508-1567 . . . . . DLB-147
Duane, William 1760-1835 . . . . DLB-43
Dubé, Marcel 1930- DLB-53
Dubé, Rodolphe (see Hertel, François)
Dubie, Norman 1945- DLB-120
Du Bois, W. E. B.
    1868-1963 . . . . DLB-47, 50, 91
Du Bois, William Pène 1916- DLB-61
Dubus, Andre 1936- DLB-130
Ducange, Victor 1783-1833 . . . . . . DLB-192
Du Chaillu, Paul Belloni
    1831?-1903 . . . . DLB-189
Ducharme, Réjean 1941- DLB-60
Dučić, Jovan 1871-1943 . . . . DLB-147
Duck, Stephen 1705?-1756 . . . . DLB-95
Duckworth, Gerald, and
    Company Limited DLB-112
Dudek, Louis 1918- DLB-88
Duell, Sloan and Pearce DLB-46
Duerer, Albrecht 1471-1528 . . . . . . DLB-179
Dufief, Nicholas Gouin 1776-1834 . . . DLB-187
Duff Gordon, Lucie 1821-1869 . . . . . DLB-166
Duffield and Green DLB-46
Duffy, Maureen 1933- DLB-14
Dugan, Alan 1923- DLB-5
Dugard, William
    [publishing house] DLB-170
Dugas, Marcel 1883-1947 . . . . DLB-92
Dugdale, William
    [publishing house] DLB-106
Duhamel, Georges 1884-1966 . . . . . DLB-65
Dujardin, Edouard 1861-1949 . . . . . DLB-123
Dukes, Ashley 1885-1959 . . . . DLB-10
du Maurier, Daphne 1907-1989 . . . . DLB-191
Du Maurier, George
    1834-1896 . . . . DLB-153, 178
Dumas, Alexandre *fils* 1824–1895 . . . . DLB-192
Dumas, Alexandre *père*
    1802-1870 . . . . DLB-119, 192
Dumas, Henry 1934-1968 . . . . DLB-41
Dunbar, Paul Laurence
    1872-1906 . . . . DLB-50, 54, 78
Dunbar, William
    circa 1460-circa 1522 . . . . . DLB-132, 146
Duncan, Norman 1871-1916 . . . . . . DLB-92
Duncan, Quince 1940- DLB-145
Duncan, Robert 1919-1988 . . . DLB-5, 16, 193
Duncan, Ronald 1914-1982 . . . . . . DLB-13

Duncan, Sara Jeannette
 1861-1922 . . . . DLB-92
Dunigan, Edward, and Brother DLB-49
Dunlap, John 1747-1812 . . . . DLB-43
Dunlap, William
 1766-1839. . . . . DLB-30, 37, 59
Dunn, Douglas 1942- DLB-40
Dunn, Harvey Thomas 1884-1952 . . . DLB-188
Dunn, Stephen 1939- DLB-105
Dunne, Finley Peter
 1867-1936. . . . . DLB-11, 23
Dunne, John Gregory 1932- Y-80
Dunne, Philip 1908-1992 . . . . DLB-26
Dunning, Ralph Cheever
 1878-1930. . . . . DLB-4
Dunning, William A.
 1857-1922 . . . . DLB-17
Duns Scotus, John
 circa 1266-1308 . . . . DLB-115
Dunsany, Lord (Edward John Moreton
 Drax Plunkett, Baron Dunsany)
 1878-1957 . . . . . DLB-10, 77, 153, 156
Dunton, John [publishing house] DLB-170
Dunton, W. Herbert 1878-1936 . . . . DLB-188
Dupin, Amantine-Aurore-Lucile (see Sand, George)
Durand, Lucile (see Bersianik, Louky)
Duranti, Francesca 1935- DLB-196
Duranty, Walter 1884-1957. . . . . DLB-29
Duras, Marguerite 1914- DLB-83
Durfey, Thomas 1653-1723. . . . . DLB-80
Durrell, Lawrence
 1912-1990 . . . . DLB-15, 27; Y-90
Durrell, William
 [publishing house]. DLB-49
Dürrenmatt, Friedrich
 1921-1990 . . . . DLB-69, 124
Dutton, E. P., and Company DLB-49
Duvoisin, Roger 1904-1980. . . . . DLB-61
Duyckinck, Evert Augustus
 1816-1878 . . . . DLB-3, 64
Duyckinck, George L. 1823-1863 . . . . DLB-3
Duyckinck and Company DLB-49
Dwight, John Sullivan 1813-1893 . . . . DLB-1
Dwight, Timothy 1752-1817 . . . . DLB-37
Dybek, Stuart 1942- DLB-130
Dyer, Charles 1928- DLB-13
Dyer, George 1755-1841 . . . . DLB-93
Dyer, John 1699-1757. . . . . DLB-95
Dyer, Sir Edward 1543-1607 . . . . . . DLB-136
Dylan, Bob 1941- DLB-16

E

Eager, Edward 1911-1964 . . . . DLB-22

Eames, Wilberforce 1855-1937 . . . . . DLB-140
Earle, James H., and Company DLB-49
Earle, John 1600 or 1601-1665 . . . . DLB-151
Early American Book Illustration,
 by Sinclair Hamilton DLB-49
Eastlake, William 1917- DLB-6
Eastman, Carol ?- DLB-44
Eastman, Charles A. (Ohiyesa)
 1858-1939 . . . . DLB-175
Eastman, Max 1883-1969. . . . . DLB-91
Eaton, Daniel Isaac 1753-1814 . . . . DLB-158
Eberhart, Richard 1904- DLB-48
Ebner, Jeannie 1918- DLB-85
Ebner-Eschenbach, Marie von
 1830-1916 . . . . DLB-81
Ebon 1942- DLB-41
Ecbasis Captivi circa 1045. . . . . . . DLB-148
Ecco Press DLB-46
Eckhart, Meister
 circa 1260-circa 1328 . . . . DLB-115
The Eclectic Review 1805-1868 . . . . . DLB-110
Eco, Umberto 1932- DLB-196
Edel, Leon 1907- DLB-103
Edes, Benjamin 1732-1803 . . . . DLB-43
Edgar, David 1948- DLB-13
Edgeworth, Maria
 1768-1849. . . . . DLB-116, 159, 163
The Edinburgh Review 1802-1929. . . . . DLB-110
Edinburgh University Press DLB-112
The Editor Publishing Company DLB-49
Editorial Statements DLB-137
Edmonds, Randolph 1900- DLB-51
Edmonds, Walter D. 1903- DLB-9
Edschmid, Kasimir 1890-1966 . . . . . DLB-56
Edwards, Amelia Anne Blandford
 1831-1892 . . . . DLB-174
Edwards, Edward 1812-1886 . . . . . . DLB-184
Edwards, Jonathan 1703-1758 . . . . . DLB-24
Edwards, Jonathan, Jr. 1745-1801 . . . DLB-37
Edwards, Junius 1929- DLB-33
Edwards, Matilda Barbara Betham-
 1836-1919 . . . . DLB-174
Edwards, Richard 1524-1566 . . . . . . DLB-62
Edwards, James
 [publishing house] DLB-154
Effinger, George Alec 1947- DLB-8
Egerton, George 1859-1945 . . . . . . DLB-135
Eggleston, Edward 1837-1902 . . . . . DLB-12
Eggleston, Wilfred 1901-1986. . . . . . DLB-92
Ehrenstein, Albert 1886-1950 . . . . . DLB-81
Ehrhart, W. D. 1948- DS-9
Eich, Günter 1907-1972 . . . . . . DLB-69, 124

Eichendorff, Joseph Freiherr von
 1788-1857 . . . . DLB-90
1873 Publishers' Catalogues DLB-49
Eighteenth-Century Aesthetic
 Theories DLB-31
Eighteenth-Century Philosophical
 Background DLB-31
Eigner, Larry 1926-1996 . . . . . . DLB-5, 193
Eikon Basilike 1649 . . . . DLB-151
Eilhart von Oberge
 circa 1140-circa 1195 . . . . DLB-148
Einhard circa 770-840 . . . . DLB-148
Eiseley, Loren 1907-1977. . . . . DS-17
Eisenreich, Herbert 1925-1986 . . . . . DLB-85
Eisner, Kurt 1867-1919 . . . . DLB-66
Eklund, Gordon 1945- Y-83
Ekwensi, Cyprian 1921- DLB-117
Eld, George
 [publishing house] DLB-170
Elder, Lonne III 1931- DLB-7, 38, 44
Elder, Paul, and Company. DLB-49
Elements of Rhetoric (1828; revised, 1846),
 by Richard Whately [excerpt] DLB-57
Elie, Robert 1915-1973 . . . . DLB-88
Elin Pelin 1877-1949. . . . . DLB-147
Eliot, George 1819-1880 . . . . . DLB-21, 35, 55
Eliot, John 1604-1690 . . . . DLB-24
Eliot, T. S. 1888-1965 . . . . DLB-7, 10, 45, 63
Eliot's Court Press. DLB-170
Elizabeth I 1533-1603 . . . . DLB-136
Elizabeth of Nassau-Saarbrücken
 after 1393-1456 . . . . DLB-179
Elizondo, Salvador 1932- DLB-145
Elizondo, Sergio 1930- DLB-82
Elkin, Stanley 1930- DLB-2, 28; Y-80
Elles, Dora Amy (see Wentworth, Patricia)
Ellet, Elizabeth F. 1818?-1877 . . . . . DLB-30
Elliot, Ebenezer 1781-1849 . . . . . DLB-96, 190
Elliot, Frances Minto (Dickinson)
 1820-1898 . . . . DLB-166
Elliott, George 1923- DLB-68
Elliott, Janice 1931- DLB-14
Elliott, William 1788-1863 . . . . DLB-3
Elliott, Thomes and Talbot DLB-49
Ellis, Alice Thomas (Anna Margaret Haycraft)
 1932- DLB-194
Ellis, Edward S. 1840-1916 . . . . DLB-42
Ellis, Frederick Staridge
 [publishing house] DLB-106
The George H. Ellis Company DLB-49
Ellis, Havelock 1859-1939 . . . . DLB-190
Ellison, Harlan 1934- DLB-8
Ellison, Ralph Waldo
 1914-1994 . . . . DLB-2, 76; Y-94

Ellmann, Richard 1918-1987 . . . . DLB-103; Y-87

The Elmer Holmes Bobst Awards in Arts and Letters Y-87

Elyot, Thomas 1490?-1546 . . . . DLB-136

Emanuel, James Andrew 1921- DLB-41

Emecheta, Buchi 1944- DLB-117

The Emergence of Black Women Writers DS-8

Emerson, Ralph Waldo 1803-1882 . . . . DLB-1, 59, 73, 183

Emerson, William 1769-1811 . . . . DLB-37

Emerson, William 1923-1997 . . . . Y-97

Emin, Fedor Aleksandrovich circa 1735-1770 . . . . DLB-150

Empedocles fifth century B.C. DLB-176

Empson, William 1906-1984 . . . . DLB-20

Enchi, Fumiko 1905-1986 . . . . DLB-182

Encounter with the West DLB-180

The End of English Stage Censorship, 1945-1968 . . . . DLB-13

Ende, Michael 1929- DLB-75

Endō, Shūsaku 1923-1996 . . . . DLB-182

Engel, Marian 1933-1985 . . . . DLB-53

Engels, Friedrich 1820-1895 . . . . DLB-129

Engle, Paul 1908- DLB-48

English Composition and Rhetoric (1866), by Alexander Bain [excerpt] DLB-57

The English Language: 410 to 1500 . . . . DLB-146

The English Renaissance of Art (1908), by Oscar Wilde DLB-35

Enright, D. J. 1920- DLB-27

Enright, Elizabeth 1909-1968 . . . . DLB-22

L'Envoi (1882), by Oscar Wilde DLB-35

Epictetus circa 55-circa 125-130 . . . . . DLB-176

Epicurus 342/341 B.C.-271/270 B.C. DLB-176

Epps, Bernard 1936- DLB-53

Epstein, Julius 1909- and Epstein, Philip 1909-1952 . . . . DLB-26

Equiano, Olaudah circa 1745-1797 . . . . DLB-37, 50

Eragny Press DLB-112

Erasmus, Desiderius 1467-1536 . . . . . DLB-136

Erba, Luciano 1922- DLB-128

Erdrich, Louise 1954- DLB-152, 178

Erichsen-Brown, Gwethalyn Graham (see Graham, Gwethalyn)

Eriugena, John Scottus circa 810-877 . . . . DLB-115

Ernest Hemingway's Toronto Journalism Revisited: With Three Previously Unrecorded Stories Y-92

Ernst, Paul 1866-1933 . . . . DLB-66, 118

Erskine, Albert 1911-1993 . . . . Y-93

Erskine, John 1879-1951 . . . . . . DLB-9, 102

Erskine, Mrs. Steuart ?-1948 . . . . . . DLB-195

Ervine, St. John Greer 1883-1971 . . . . DLB-10

Eschenburg, Johann Joachim 1743-c1820 . . . DLB-97

Escoto, Julio 1944- DLB-145

Eshleman, Clayton 1935- DLB-5

Espriu, Salvador 1913-1985 . . . . DLB-134

Ess Ess Publishing Company DLB-49

Essay on Chatterton (1842), by Robert Browning DLB-32

Essex House Press DLB-112

Estes, Eleanor 1906-1988 . . . . DLB-22

Eszterhas, Joe 1944- DLB-185

Estes and Lauriat DLB-49

Etherege, George 1636-circa 1692 . . . . DLB-80

Ethridge, Mark, Sr. 1896-1981 . . . . . DLB-127

Ets, Marie Hall 1893- DLB-22

Etter, David 1928- DLB-105

Ettner, Johann Christoph 1654-1724 . . . . DLB-168

Eudora Welty: Eye of the Storyteller Y-87

Eugene O'Neill Memorial Theater Center DLB-7

Eugene O'Neill's Letters: A Review Y-88

Eupolemius flourished circa 1095 . . . . DLB-148

Euripides circa 484 B.C.-407/406 B.C. DLB-176

Evans, Caradoc 1878-1945 . . . . DLB-162

Evans, Charles 1850-1935 . . . . DLB-187

Evans, Donald 1884-1921 . . . . DLB-54

Evans, George Henry 1805-1856 . . . . DLB-43

Evans, Hubert 1892-1986 . . . . DLB-92

Evans, Mari 1923- DLB-41

Evans, Mary Ann (see Eliot, George)

Evans, Nathaniel 1742-1767 . . . . DLB-31

Evans, Sebastian 1830-1909 . . . . DLB-35

Evans, M., and Company DLB-46

Everett, Alexander Hill 1790-1847 . . . . DLB-59

Everett, Edward 1794-1865 . . . . . . DLB-1, 59

Everson, R. G. 1903- DLB-88

Everson, William 1912-1994 . . . . . . DLB-5, 16

Every Man His Own Poet; or, The Inspired Singer's Recipe Book (1877), by W. H. Mallock DLB-35

Ewart, Gavin 1916- DLB-40

Ewing, Juliana Horatia 1841-1885 . . . . DLB-21, 163

The Examiner 1808-1881 . . . . DLB-110

Exley, Frederick 1929-1992 . . . . DLB-143; Y-81

Experiment in the Novel (1929), by John D. Beresford DLB-36

von Eyb, Albrecht 1420-1475 . . . . . DLB-179

"Eyes Across Centuries: Contemporary Poetry and 'That Vision Thing,'" by Philip Dacey DLB-105

Eyre and Spottiswoode DLB-106

Ezzo ?-after 1065 . . . . DLB-148

F

"F. Scott Fitzgerald: St. Paul's Native Son and Distinguished American Writer": University of Minnesota Conference, 29-31 October 1982 . . . . Y-82

Faber, Frederick William 1814-1863 . . . . DLB-32

Faber and Faber Limited DLB-112

Faccio, Rena (see Aleramo, Sibilla)

Fagundo, Ana María 1938- DLB-134

Fair, Ronald L. 1932- DLB-33

Fairfax, Beatrice (see Manning, Marie)

Fairlie, Gerard 1899-1983 . . . . DLB-77

Fallada, Hans 1893-1947 . . . . DLB-56

Falsifying Hemingway Y-96

Fancher, Betsy 1928- Y-83

Fane, Violet 1843-1905 . . . . DLB-35

Fanfrolico Press DLB-112

Fanning, Katherine 1927 . . . . DLB-127

Fanshawe, Sir Richard 1608-1666 . . . . DLB-126

Fantasy Press Publishers DLB-46

Fante, John 1909-1983 . . . . . . DLB-130; Y-83

Al-Farabi circa 870-950 . . . . DLB-115

Farah, Nuruddin 1945- DLB-125

Farber, Norma 1909-1984 . . . . DLB-61

Farigoule, Louis (see Romains, Jules)

Farjeon, Eleanor 1881-1965 . . . . . . DLB-160

Farley, Walter 1920-1989 . . . . DLB-22

Farmer, Penelope 1939- DLB-161

Farmer, Philip José 1918- DLB-8

Farquhar, George circa 1677-1707 . . . . DLB-84

Farquharson, Martha (see Finley, Martha)

Farrar, Frederic William 1831-1903 . . . . DLB-163

Farrar and Rinehart DLB-46

Farrar, Straus and Giroux DLB-46

Farrell, James T. 1904-1979 . . . . DLB-4, 9, 86; DS-2

Farrell, J. G. 1935-1979 . . . . DLB-14

Fast, Howard 1914- DLB-9

Faulkner and Yoknapatawpha Conference, Oxford, Mississippi Y-97

"Faulkner 100–Celebrating the Work," University of South Carolina, Columbia Y-97

Faulkner, William 1897-1962
. . . . . . DLB-9, 11, 44, 102; DS-2; Y-86

Faulkner, George [publishing house] DLB-154

Fauset, Jessie Redmon 1882-1961 . . . . DLB-51

Faust, Irvin 1924- DLB-2, 28; Y-80

Fawcett Books DLB-46

Fawcett, Millicent Garrett 1847-1929 . . DLB-190

Fearing, Kenneth 1902-1961 . . . . DLB-9

Federal Writers' Project DLB-46

Federman, Raymond 1928- Y-80

Feiffer, Jules 1929- DLB-7, 44

Feinberg, Charles E. 1899-1988 . . . . DLB-187; Y-88

Feind, Barthold 1678-1721 . . . . DLB-168

Feinstein, Elaine 1930- DLB-14, 40

Feiss, Paul Louis 1875-1952 . . . . DLB-187

Feldman, Irving 1928- DLB-169

Felipe, Léon 1884-1968 . . . . DLB-108

Fell, Frederick, Publishers DLB-46

Felltham, Owen 1602?-1668 . . . . DLB-126, 151

Fels, Ludwig 1946- DLB-75

Felton, Cornelius Conway 1807-1862 . . . . DLB-1

Fenn, Harry 1837-1911 . . . . DLB-188

Fennario, David 1947- DLB-60

Fenno, John 1751-1798 . . . . DLB-43

Fenno, R. F., and Company DLB-49

Fenoglio, Beppe 1922-1963 . . . . DLB-177

Fenton, Geoffrey 1539?-1608 . . . . . . DLB-136

Fenton, James 1949- DLB-40

Ferber, Edna 1885-1968 . . . . . DLB-9, 28, 86

Ferdinand, Vallery III (see Salaam, Kalamu ya)

Ferguson, Sir Samuel 1810-1886 . . . . . DLB-32

Ferguson, William Scott 1875-1954 . . . . DLB-47

Fergusson, Robert 1750-1774 . . . . . . DLB-109

Ferland, Albert 1872-1943 . . . . DLB-92

Ferlinghetti, Lawrence 1919- DLB-5, 16

Fern, Fanny (see Parton, Sara Payson Willis)

Ferrars, Elizabeth 1907- DLB-87

Ferré, Rosario 1942- DLB-145

Ferret, E., and Company DLB-49

Ferrier, Susan 1782-1854 . . . . DLB-116

Ferrini, Vincent 1913- DLB-48

Ferron, Jacques 1921-1985 . . . . DLB-60

Ferron, Madeleine 1922- DLB-53

Ferrucci, Franco 1936- DLB-196

Fetridge and Company DLB-49

Feuchtersleben, Ernst Freiherr von 1806-1849 . . . . DLB-133

Feuchtwanger, Lion 1884-1958 . . . . . . DLB-66

Feuerbach, Ludwig 1804-1872 . . . . . DLB-133

Feuillet, Octave 1821-1890 . . . . DLB-192

Feydeau, Georges 1862-1921 . . . . . . DLB-192

Fichte, Johann Gottlieb 1762-1814 . . . . DLB-90

Ficke, Arthur Davison 1883-1945 . . . . DLB-54

Fiction Best-Sellers, 1910-1945 . . . . . . DLB-9

Fiction into Film, 1928-1975: A List of Movies Based on the Works of Authors in *British Novelists*, 1930-1959 . . . . . . DLB-15

Fiedler, Leslie A. 1917- DLB-28, 67

Field, Edward 1924- DLB-105

Field, Eugene 1850-1895 . . . . . DLB-23, 42, 140; DS-13

Field, John 1545?-1588 . . . . DLB-167

Field, Marshall, III 1893-1956 . . . . . . DLB-127

Field, Marshall, IV 1916-1965 . . . . . . DLB-127

Field, Marshall, V 1941- DLB-127

Field, Nathan 1587-1619 or 1620 . . . . DLB-58

Field, Rachel 1894-1942 . . . . DLB-9, 22

A Field Guide to Recent Schools of American Poetry Y-86

Fielding, Henry 1707-1754 . . . . DLB-39, 84, 101

Fielding, Sarah 1710-1768 . . . . DLB-39

Fields, James Thomas 1817-1881 . . . . . DLB-1

Fields, Julia 1938- DLB-41

Fields, W. C. 1880-1946 . . . . DLB-44

Fields, Osgood and Company DLB-49

Fifty Penguin Years Y-85

Figes, Eva 1932- DLB-14

Figuera, Angela 1902-1984 . . . . DLB-108

Filmer, Sir Robert 1586-1653 . . . . . . DLB-151

Filson, John circa 1753-1788 . . . . DLB-37

Finch, Anne, Countess of Winchilsea 1661-1720 . . . . DLB-95

Finch, Robert 1900- DLB-88

"Finding, Losing, Reclaiming: A Note on My Poems," by Robert Phillips DLB-105

Findley, Timothy 1930- DLB-53

Finlay, Ian Hamilton 1925- DLB-40

Finley, Martha 1828-1909 . . . . DLB-42

Finn, Elizabeth Anne (McCaul) 1825-1921 . . . . DLB-166

Finney, Jack 1911- DLB-8

Finney, Walter Braden (see Finney, Jack)

Firbank, Ronald 1886-1926 . . . . DLB-36

Firmin, Giles 1615-1697 . . . . DLB-24

Fischart, Johann 1546 or 1547-1590 or 1591 . . . . DLB-179

First Edition Library/Collectors' Reprints, Inc. Y-91

First International F. Scott Fitzgerald Conference Y-92

First Strauss "Livings" Awarded to Cynthia Ozick and Raymond Carver
An Interview with Cynthia Ozick
An Interview with Raymond Carver Y-83

Fischer, Karoline Auguste Fernandine 1764-1842 . . . . DLB-94

Fish, Stanley 1938- DLB-67

Fishacre, Richard 1205-1248 . . . . . . DLB-115

Fisher, Clay (see Allen, Henry W.)

Fisher, Dorothy Canfield 1879-1958 . . . . DLB-9, 102

Fisher, Leonard Everett 1924- DLB-61

Fisher, Roy 1930- DLB-40

Fisher, Rudolph 1897-1934 . . . . . DLB-51, 102

Fisher, Sydney George 1856-1927 . . . . DLB-47

Fisher, Vardis 1895-1968 . . . . DLB-9

Fiske, John 1608-1677 . . . . DLB-24

Fiske, John 1842-1901 . . . . DLB-47, 64

Fitch, Thomas circa 1700-1774 . . . . . . DLB-31

Fitch, William Clyde 1865-1909 . . . . . . DLB-7

FitzGerald, Edward 1809-1883 . . . . . . DLB-32

Fitzgerald, F. Scott 1896-1940
. . . . . DLB-4, 9, 86; Y-81; DS-1, 15, 16

F. Scott Fitzgerald Centenary Celebrations Y-96

Fitzgerald, Penelope 1916- DLB-14, 194

Fitzgerald, Robert 1910-1985 . . . . Y-80

Fitzgerald, Thomas 1819-1891 . . . . . . DLB-23

Fitzgerald, Zelda Sayre 1900-1948 . . . . . . Y-84

Fitzhugh, Louise 1928-1974 . . . . DLB-52

Fitzhugh, William circa 1651-1701 . . . . DLB-24

Flagg, James Montgomery 1877-1960 . . DLB-188

Flanagan, Thomas 1923- Y-80

Flanner, Hildegarde 1899-1987 . . . . . DLB-48

Flanner, Janet 1892-1978 . . . . DLB-4

Flaubert, Gustave 1821-1880 . . . . . . DLB-119

Flavin, Martin 1883-1967 . . . . DLB-9

Fleck, Konrad (flourished circa 1220) DLB-138

Flecker, James Elroy 1884-1915 . . . DLB-10, 19

Fleeson, Doris 1901-1970 . . . . DLB-29

Fleißer, Marieluise 1901-1974 . . . . DLB-56, 124

Fleming, Ian 1908-1964 . . . . DLB-87

Fleming, Paul 1609-1640 . . . . DLB-164

Fleming, Peter 1907-1971 . . . . DLB-195

The Fleshly School of Poetry and Other Phenomena of the Day (1872), by Robert Buchanan DLB-35

The Fleshly School of Poetry: Mr. D. G. Rossetti (1871), by Thomas Maitland (Robert Buchanan) DLB-35

Fletcher, Giles, the Elder
  1546-1611 . . . . DLB-136
Fletcher, Giles, the Younger
  1585 or 1586-1623 . . . . DLB-121
Fletcher, J. S. 1863-1935 . . . . DLB-70
Fletcher, John (see Beaumont, Francis)
Fletcher, John Gould 1886-1950 . . . DLB-4, 45
Fletcher, Phineas 1582-1650 . . . . . . DLB-121
Flieg, Helmut (see Heym, Stefan)
Flint, F. S. 1885-1960 . . . . DLB-19
Flint, Timothy 1780-1840 . . . . . DLB-73, 186
Florio, John 1553?-1625 . . . . DLB-172
Fo, Dario 1926- Y-97
Foix, J. V. 1893-1987 . . . . DLB-134
Foley, Martha (see Burnett, Whit, and Martha Foley)
Folger, Henry Clay 1857-1930 . . . . . DLB-140
Folio Society DLB-112
Follen, Eliza Lee (Cabot) 1787-1860 . . . DLB-1
Follett, Ken 1949- DLB-87; Y-81
Follett Publishing Company DLB-46
Folsom, John West
  [publishing house] DLB-49
Folz, Hans
  between 1435 and 1440-1513 . . . . DLB-179
Fontane, Theodor 1819-1898 . . . . . . DLB-129
Fonvisin, Denis Ivanovich
  1744 or 1745-1792 . . . . DLB-150
Foote, Horton 1916- DLB-26
Foote, Mary Hallock 1847-1938 . . DLB-186, 188
Foote, Samuel 1721-1777 . . . . DLB-89
Foote, Shelby 1916- DLB-2, 17
Forbes, Calvin 1945- DLB-41
Forbes, Ester 1891-1967 . . . . DLB-22
Forbes, Rosita 1893?-1967 . . . . DLB-195
Forbes and Company DLB-49
Force, Peter 1790-1868 . . . . DLB-30
Forché, Carolyn 1950- DLB-5, 193
Ford, Charles Henri 1913- DLB-4, 48
Ford, Corey 1902-1969 . . . . DLB-11
Ford, Ford Madox
  1873-1939 . . . . DLB-34, 98, 162
Ford, Jesse Hill 1928- DLB-6
Ford, John 1586-? DLB-58
Ford, R. A. D. 1915- DLB-88
Ford, Worthington C. 1858-1941 . . . . DLB-47
Ford, J. B., and Company DLB-49
Fords, Howard, and Hulbert DLB-49
Foreman, Carl 1914-1984 . . . . DLB-26
Forester, C. S. 1899-1966 . . . . DLB-191
Forester, Frank (see Herbert, Henry William)
"Foreword to *Ludwig of Bavaria*," by
  Robert Peters DLB-105

Forman, Harry Buxton 1842-1917 . . . DLB-184
Fornés, María Irene 1930- DLB-7
Forrest, Leon 1937- DLB-33
Forster, E. M.
  1879-1970 DLB-34, 98, 162, 178, 195; DS-10
Forster, Georg 1754-1794 . . . . DLB-94
Forster, John 1812-1876 . . . . DLB-144
Forster, Margaret 1938- DLB-155
Forsyth, Frederick 1938- DLB-87
Forten, Charlotte L. 1837-1914 . . . . . DLB-50
Fortini, Franco 1917- DLB-128
Fortune, T. Thomas 1856-1928 . . . . . DLB-23
Fosdick, Charles Austin
  1842-1915 . . . . DLB-42
Foster, Genevieve 1893-1979 . . . . . . DLB-61
Foster, Hannah Webster
  1758-1840 . . . . DLB-37
Foster, John 1648-1681 . . . . DLB-24
Foster, Michael 1904-1956 . . . . DLB-9
Foster, Myles Birket 1825-1899 . . . . . DLB-184
Foulis, Robert and Andrew / R. and A.
  [publishing house] DLB-154
Fouqué, Caroline de la Motte
  1774-1831 . . . . DLB-90
Fouqué, Friedrich de la Motte
  1777-1843 . . . . DLB-90
Four Essays on the Beat Generation,
  by John Clellon Holmes DLB-16
Four Seas Company DLB-46
Four Winds Press DLB-46
Fournier, Henri Alban (see Alain-Fournier)
Fowler and Wells Company DLB-49
Fowles, John 1926- DLB-14, 139
Fox, John, Jr. 1862 or 1863-1919 . DLB-9; DS-13
Fox, Paula 1923- DLB-52
Fox, Richard Kyle 1846-1922 . . . . . . DLB-79
Fox, William Price 1926- DLB-2; Y-81
Fox, Richard K.
  [publishing house] DLB-49
Foxe, John 1517-1587 . . . . DLB-132
Fraenkel, Michael 1896-1957 . . . . . . DLB-4
France, Anatole 1844-1924 . . . . DLB-123
France, Richard 1938- DLB-7
Francis, Convers 1795-1863 . . . . DLB-1
Francis, Dick 1920- DLB-87
Francis, Jeffrey, Lord 1773-1850 . . . . DLB-107
Francis, C. S. [publishing house] DLB-49
François 1863-1910 . . . . DLB-92
François, Louise von 1817-1893 . . . . DLB-129
Franck, Sebastian 1499-1542 . . . . . . DLB-179
Francke, Kuno 1855-1930 . . . . DLB-71
Frank, Bruno 1887-1945 . . . . DLB-118
Frank, Leonhard 1882-1961 . . . . . DLB-56, 118

Frank, Melvin (see Panama, Norman)
Frank, Waldo 1889-1967 . . . . DLB-9, 63
Franken, Rose 1895?-1988 . . . . Y-84
Franklin, Benjamin
  1706-1790 . . . . DLB-24, 43, 73, 183
Franklin, James 1697-1735 . . . . DLB-43
Franklin Library DLB-46
Frantz, Ralph Jules 1902-1979 . . . . . DLB-4
Franzos, Karl Emil 1848-1904 . . . . . DLB-129
Fraser, G. S. 1915-1980 . . . . DLB-27
Fraser, Kathleen 1935- DLB-169
Frattini, Alberto 1922- DLB-128
Frau Ava ?-1127 . . . . DLB-148
Frayn, Michael 1933- DLB-13, 14, 194
Frederic, Harold
  1856-1898 . . . . DLB-12, 23; DS-13
Freeling, Nicolas 1927- DLB-87
Freeman, Douglas Southall
  1886-1953 . . . . DLB-17; DS-17
Freeman, Legh Richmond
  1842-1915 . . . . DLB-23
Freeman, Mary E. Wilkins
  1852-1930 . . . . DLB-12, 78
Freeman, R. Austin 1862-1943 . . . . . DLB-70
Freidank circa 1170?-circa 1233 . . . . DLB-138
Freiligrath, Ferdinand 1810-1876 . . . DLB-133
Frémont, John Charles 1813-1890 . . . DLB-186
Frémont, John Charles 1813-1890
  and Frémont, Jessie Benton
  1834-1902 . . . . DLB-183
French, Alice 1850-1934 . . . . . . DLB-74; DS-13
French, David 1939- DLB-53
French, Evangeline 1869-1960 . . . . . DLB-195
French, Francesca 1871-1960 . . . . . . DLB-195
French, James [publishing house] DLB-49
French, Samuel [publishing house] . . . DLB-49
Samuel French, Limited DLB-106
Freneau, Philip 1752-1832 . . . . . . DLB-37, 43
Freni, Melo 1934- DLB-128
Freshfield, Douglas W.
  1845-1934 . . . . DLB-174
Freytag, Gustav 1816-1895 . . . . DLB-129
Fried, Erich 1921-1988 . . . . DLB-85
Friedman, Bruce Jay 1930- DLB-2, 28
Friedrich von Hausen
  circa 1171-1190 . . . . DLB-138
Friel, Brian 1929- DLB-13
Friend, Krebs 1895?-1967? DLB-4
Fries, Fritz Rudolf 1935- DLB-75
Fringe and Alternative Theater
  in Great Britain DLB-13
Frisch, Max 1911-1991 . . . . DLB-69, 124
Frischlin, Nicodemus 1547-1590 . . . . DLB-179

Frischmuth, Barbara 1941- DLB-85

Fritz, Jean 1915- DLB-52

Fromentin, Eugene 1820-1876...... DLB-123

From *The Gay Science,* by
    E. S. Dallas DLB-21

Frost, A. B. 1851-1928 ..... DLB-188; DS-13

Frost, Robert 1874-1963...... DLB-54; DS-7

Frothingham, Octavius Brooks
    1822-1895................. DLB-1

Froude, James Anthony
    1818-1894.......... DLB-18, 57, 144

Fry, Christopher 1907- DLB-13

Fry, Roger 1866-1934........... DS-10

Frye, Northrop 1912-1991 ..... DLB-67, 68

Fuchs, Daniel
    1909-1993........ DLB-9, 26, 28; Y-93

Fuentes, Carlos 1928- DLB-113

Fuertes, Gloria 1918- DLB-108

The Fugitives and the Agrarians:
    The First Exhibition Y-85

Fulbecke, William 1560-1603?...... DLB-172

Fuller, Charles H., Jr. 1939- DLB-38

Fuller, Henry Blake 1857-1929...... DLB-12

Fuller, John 1937- DLB-40

Fuller, Margaret (see Fuller, Sarah Margaret,
    Marchesa D'Ossoli)

Fuller, Roy 1912-1991 .... DLB-15, 20

Fuller, Samuel 1912- DLB-26

Fuller, Sarah Margaret, Marchesa
    D'Ossoli 1810-1850 ... DLB-1, 59, 73, 183

Fuller, Thomas 1608-1661. .... DLB-151

Fullerton, Hugh 1873-1945 .... DLB-171

Fulton, Alice 1952- DLB-193

Fulton, Len 1934- Y-86

Fulton, Robin 1937- DLB-40

Furbank, P. N. 1920- DLB-155

Furman, Laura 1945- Y-86

Furness, Horace Howard
    1833-1912 .... DLB-64

Furness, William Henry 1802-1896 .... DLB-1

Furnivall, Frederick James
    1825-1910 .... DLB-184

Furthman, Jules 1888-1966 .... DLB-26

Furui, Yoshikichi 1937- DLB-182

Futabatei, Shimei (Hasegawa Tatsunosuke)
    1864-1909 .... DLB-180

The Future of the Novel (1899), by
    Henry James DLB-18

Fyleman, Rose 1877-1957 .... DLB-160

G

The G. Ross Roy Scottish Poetry
    Collection at the University of
    South Carolina Y-89

Gadda, Carlo Emilio 1893-1973 .... DLB-177

Gaddis, William 1922- DLB-2

Gág, Wanda 1893-1946........... DLB-22

Gagnon, Madeleine 1938- DLB-60

Gaine, Hugh 1726-1807........... DLB-43

Gaine, Hugh [publishing house] DLB-49

Gaines, Ernest J.
    1933- DLB-2, 33, 152; Y-80

Gaiser, Gerd 1908-1976........... DLB-69

Galarza, Ernesto 1905-1984 ...... DLB-122

Galaxy Science Fiction Novels DLB-46

Gale, Zona 1874-1938......... DLB-9, 78

Galen of Pergamon 129-after 210 ... DLB-176

Gall, Louise von 1815-1855...... DLB-133

Gallagher, Tess 1943- DLB-120

Gallagher, Wes 1911- DLB-127

Gallagher, William Davis
    1808-1894 .... DLB-73

Gallant, Mavis 1922- DLB-53

Gallico, Paul 1897-1976 .... DLB-9, 171

Gallup, Donald 1913- DLB-187

Galsworthy, John
    1867-1933 ... DLB-10, 34, 98, 162; DS-16

Galt, John 1779-1839 .... DLB-99, 116

Galton, Sir Francis 1822-1911...... DLB-166

Galvin, Brendan 1938- DLB-5

Gambit..................... DLB-46

Gamboa, Reymundo 1948- DLB-122

Gammer Gurton's Needle.......... DLB-62

Gannett, Frank E. 1876-1957....... DLB-29

Gaos, Vicente 1919-1980 .... DLB-134

García, Lionel G. 1935- DLB-82

García Lorca, Federico
    1898-1936 .... DLB-108

García Márquez, Gabriel
    1928- DLB-113; Y-82

Gardam, Jane 1928- DLB-14, 161

Garden, Alexander
    circa 1685-1756............ DLB-31

Gardiner, Margaret Power Farmer (see
    Blessington, Marguerite, Countess of)

Gardner, John 1933-1982...... DLB-2; Y-82

Garfield, Leon 1921- DLB-161

Garis, Howard R. 1873-1962....... DLB-22

Garland, Hamlin
    1860-1940....... DLB-12, 71, 78, 186

Garneau, Francis-Xavier
    1809-1866 .... DLB-99

Garneau, Hector de Saint-Denys
    1912-1943 .... DLB-88

Garneau, Michel 1939- DLB-53

Garner, Alan 1934- DLB-161

Garner, Hugh 1913-1979 .... DLB-68

Garnett, David 1892-1981 .... DLB-34

Garnett, Eve 1900-1991 .... DLB-160

Garnett, Richard 1835-1906...... DLB-184

Garrard, Lewis H. 1829-1887...... DLB-186

Garraty, John A. 1920- DLB-17

Garrett, George
    1929- DLB-2, 5, 130, 152; Y-83

Garrett, John Work 1872-1942 .... DLB-187

Garrick, David 1717-1779 .... DLB-84

Garrison, William Lloyd
    1805-1879 .... DLB-1, 43

Garro, Elena 1920- DLB-145

Garth, Samuel 1661-1719.......... DLB-95

Garve, Andrew 1908- DLB-87

Gary, Romain 1914-1980 .... DLB-83

Gascoigne, George 1539?-1577 ..... DLB-136

Gascoyne, David 1916- DLB-20

Gaskell, Elizabeth Cleghorn
    1810-1865 .... DLB-21, 144, 159

Gaspey, Thomas 1788-1871........ DLB-116

Gass, William Howard 1924- DLB-2

Gates, Doris 1901- DLB-22

Gates, Henry Louis, Jr. 1950- DLB-67

Gates, Lewis E. 1860-1924........ DLB-71

Gatto, Alfonso 1909-1976 .... DLB-114

Gaunt, Mary 1861-1942.......... DLB-174

Gautier, Théophile 1811-1872...... DLB-119

Gauvreau, Claude 1925-1971 ...... DLB-88

The *Gawain*-Poet
    flourished circa 1350-1400 ..... DLB-146

Gay, Ebenezer 1696-1787........ DLB-24

Gay, John 1685-1732......... DLB-84, 95

The Gay Science (1866), by E. S. Dallas [excerpt]
    .... DLB-21

Gayarré, Charles E. A. 1805-1895.... DLB-30

Gaylord, Edward King
    1873-1974 .... DLB-127

Gaylord, Edward Lewis 1919- DLB-127

Gaylord, Charles
    [publishing house].......... DLB-49

Geddes, Gary 1940- DLB-60

Geddes, Virgil 1897- DLB-4

Gedeon (Georgii Andreevich Krinovsky)
    circa 1730-1763 .... DLB-150

Geibel, Emanuel 1815-1884 ...... DLB-129

Geiogamah, Hanay 1945- DLB-175

Geis, Bernard, Associates DLB-46

323

Cumulative Index

Geisel, Theodor Seuss
    1904-1991. . . . . DLB-61; Y-91

Gelb, Arthur 1924- DLB-103

Gelb, Barbara 1926- DLB-103

Gelber, Jack 1932- DLB-7

Gelinas, Gratien 1909- DLB-88

Gellert, Christian Füerchtegott
    1715-1769 . . . . DLB-97

Gellhorn, Martha 1908- Y-82

Gems, Pam 1925- DLB-13

A General Idea of the College of Mirania (1753),
    by William Smith [excerpts] DLB-31

Genet, Jean 1910-1986 . . . . . . DLB-72; Y-86

Genevoix, Maurice 1890-1980 . . . . . DLB-65

Genovese, Eugene D. 1930- DLB-17

Gent, Peter 1942- Y-82

Geoffrey of Monmouth
    circa 1100-1155 . . . . DLB-146

George, Henry 1839-1897 . . . . DLB-23

George, Jean Craighead 1919- DLB-52

Georgslied 896? DLB-148

Gerhardie, William 1895-1977 . . . . . DLB-36

Gerhardt, Paul 1607-1676 . . . . DLB-164

Gérin, Winifred 1901-1981 . . . . DLB-155

Gérin-Lajoie, Antoine 1824-1882 . . . . DLB-99

German Drama 800-1280 . . . . DLB-138

German Drama from Naturalism
    to Fascism: 1889-1933 . . . . DLB-118

German Literature and Culture from
    Charlemagne to the Early Courtly
    Period DLB-148

German Radio Play, The DLB-124

German Transformation from the Baroque
    to the Enlightenment, The DLB-97

The Germanic Epic and Old English Heroic
    Poetry: *Widseth, Waldere,* and *The
    Fight at Finnsburg.* DLB-146

Germanophilism, by Hans Kohn DLB-66

Gernsback, Hugo 1884-1967 . . . . DLB-8, 137

Gerould, Katharine Fullerton
    1879-1944 . . . . DLB-78

Gerrish, Samuel [publishing house] . . . DLB-49

Gerrold, David 1944- DLB-8

The Ira Gershwin Centenary Y-96

Gersonides 1288-1344 . . . . DLB-115

Gerstäcker, Friedrich 1816-1872 . . . . DLB-129

Gerstenberg, Heinrich Wilhelm von
    1737-1823 . . . . DLB-97

Gervinus, Georg Gottfried
    1805-1871 . . . . DLB-133

Geßner, Salomon 1730-1788 . . . . . . DLB-97

Geston, Mark S. 1946- DLB-8

"Getting Started: Accepting the Regions You
    Own–or Which Own You," by Walter
    McDonald DLB-105

Al-Ghazali 1058-1111. . . . . DLB-115

Gibbings, Robert 1889-1958 . . . . DLB-195

Gibbon, Edward 1737-1794 . . . . DLB-104

Gibbon, John Murray 1875-1952 . . . . DLB-92

Gibbon, Lewis Grassic (see Mitchell,
    James Leslie)

Gibbons, Floyd 1887-1939 . . . . DLB-25

Gibbons, Reginald 1947- DLB-120

Gibbons, William ?-? DLB-73

Gibson, Charles Dana 1867-1944 . . . . DS-13

Gibson, Charles Dana
    1867-1944 . . . . DLB-188; DS-13

Gibson, Graeme 1934- DLB-53

Gibson, Margaret 1944- DLB-120

Gibson, Margaret Dunlop
    1843-1920 . . . . DLB-174

Gibson, Wilfrid 1878-1962 . . . . DLB-19

Gibson, William 1914- DLB-7

Gide, André 1869-1951 . . . . DLB-65

Giguère, Diane 1937- DLB-53

Giguère, Roland 1929- DLB-60

Gil de Biedma, Jaime 1929-1990 . . . . DLB-108

Gil-Albert, Juan 1906- DLB-134

Gilbert, Anthony 1899-1973 . . . . DLB-77

Gilbert, Michael 1912- DLB-87

Gilbert, Sandra M. 1936- DLB-120

Gilbert, Sir Humphrey
    1537-1583 . . . . DLB-136

Gilchrist, Alexander
    1828-1861 . . . . DLB-144

Gilchrist, Ellen 1935- DLB-130

Gilder, Jeannette L. 1849-1916 . . . . . DLB-79

Gilder, Richard Watson
    1844-1909 . . . . DLB-64, 79

Gildersleeve, Basil 1831-1924 . . . . . . DLB-71

Giles, Henry 1809-1882 . . . . DLB-64

Giles of Rome circa 1243-1316 . . . . . DLB-115

Gilfillan, George 1813-1878 . . . . DLB-144

Gill, Eric 1882-1940 . . . . DLB-98

Gill, William F., Company DLB-49

Gillespie, A. Lincoln, Jr.
    1895-1950 . . . . DLB-4

Gilliam, Florence ?-? DLB-4

Gilliatt, Penelope 1932-1993 . . . . DLB-14

Gillott, Jacky 1939-1980 . . . . DLB-14

Gilman, Caroline H. 1794-1888 . . . . DLB-3, 73

Gilman, W. and J.
    [publishing house] DLB-49

Gilmer, Elizabeth Meriwether
    1861-1951 . . . . DLB-29

Gilmer, Francis Walker
    1790-1826 . . . . DLB-37

Gilroy, Frank D. 1925- DLB-7

Gimferrer, Pere (Pedro) 1945- DLB-134

Gingrich, Arnold 1903-1976 . . . . DLB-137

Ginsberg, Allen 1926- DLB-5, 16, 169

Ginzburg, Natalia 1916-1991 . . . . . . DLB-177

Ginzkey, Franz Karl 1871-1963 . . . . . DLB-81

Gioia, Dana 1950- DLB-120

Giono, Jean 1895-1970 . . . . DLB-72

Giotti, Virgilio 1885-1957 . . . . DLB-114

Giovanni, Nikki 1943- DLB-5, 41

Gipson, Lawrence Henry
    1880-1971 . . . . DLB-17

Girard, Rodolphe 1879-1956 . . . . . . DLB-92

Giraudoux, Jean 1882-1944 . . . . DLB-65

Gissing, George 1857-1903 . . DLB-18, 135, 184

Giudici, Giovanni 1924- DLB-128

Giuliani, Alfredo 1924- DLB-128

Glackens, William J. 1870-1938 . . . . DLB-188

Gladstone, William Ewart
    1809-1898 . . . . DLB-57, 184

Glaeser, Ernst 1902-1963 . . . . DLB-69

Glancy, Diane 1941- DLB-175

Glanville, Brian 1931- DLB-15, 139

Glapthorne, Henry 1610-1643? DLB-58

Glasgow, Ellen 1873-1945 . . . . DLB-9, 12

Glasier, Katharine Bruce 1867-1950 . . DLB-190

Glaspell, Susan 1876-1948 . . . . . DLB-7, 9, 78

Glass, Montague 1877-1934 . . . . DLB-11

The Glass Key and Other Dashiell Hammett
    Mysteries Y-96

Glassco, John 1909-1981 . . . . DLB-68

Glauser, Friedrich 1896-1938 . . . . . . DLB-56

F. Gleason's Publishing Hall DLB-49

Gleim, Johann Wilhelm Ludwig
    1719-1803 . . . . DLB-97

Glendinning, Victoria 1937- DLB-155

Glover, Richard 1712-1785 . . . . DLB-95

Glück, Louise 1943- DLB-5

Glyn, Elinor 1864-1943 . . . . DLB-153

Gobineau, Joseph-Arthur de
    1816-1882 . . . . DLB-123

Godbout, Jacques 1933- DLB-53

Goddard, Morrill 1865-1937 . . . . DLB-25

Goddard, William 1740-1817 . . . . . . DLB-43

Godden, Rumer 1907- DLB-161

Godey, Louis A. 1804-1878 . . . . DLB-73

Godey and McMichael DLB-49

Godfrey, Dave 1938- DLB-60

Godfrey, Thomas 1736-1763 . . . . DLB-31

Godine, David R., Publisher DLB-46

Godkin, E. L. 1831-1902 . . . . DLB-79

Godolphin, Sidney 1610-1643 . . . . . DLB-126

Godwin, Gail 1937- DLB-6

Godwin, Mary Jane Clairmont
  1766-1841 . . . . DLB-163
Godwin, Parke 1816-1904 . . . . . . DLB-3, 64
Godwin, William
  1756-1836. . . . DLB-39, 104, 142, 158, 163
Godwin, M. J., and Company DLB-154
Goering, Reinhard 1887-1936 . . . . . . DLB-118
Goes, Albrecht 1908- DLB-69
Goethe, Johann Wolfgang von
  1749-1832 . . . . DLB-94
Goetz, Curt 1888-1960 . . . . DLB-124
Goffe, Thomas circa 1592-1629 . . . . . DLB-58
Goffstein, M. B. 1940- DLB-61
Gogarty, Oliver St. John
  1878-1957 . . . . DLB-15, 19
Goines, Donald 1937-1974 . . . . DLB-33
Gold, Herbert 1924- DLB-2; Y-81
Gold, Michael 1893-1967 . . . . DLB-9, 28
Goldbarth, Albert 1948- DLB-120
Goldberg, Dick 1947- DLB-7
Golden Cockerel Press DLB-112
Golding, Arthur 1536-1606 . . . . DLB-136
Golding, Louis 1895-1958 . . . . DLB-195
Golding, William 1911-1993 . DLB-15, 100; Y-83
Goldman, William 1931- DLB-44
Goldsmith, Oliver
  1730?-1774 . . . . DLB-39, 89, 104, 109, 142
Goldsmith, Oliver 1794-1861 . . . . . . DLB-99
Goldsmith Publishing Company DLB-46
Goldstein, Richard 1944- DLB-185
Gollancz, Victor, Limited DLB-112
Gómez-Quiñones, Juan 1942- DLB-122
Gomme, Laurence James
  [publishing house] DLB-46
Goncourt, Edmond de 1822-1896 . . . DLB-123
Goncourt, Jules de 1830-1870 . . . . . DLB-123
Gonzales, Rodolfo "Corky"
  1928- DLB-122
González, Angel 1925- DLB-108
Gonzalez, Genaro 1949- DLB-122
Gonzalez, Ray 1952- DLB-122
González de Mireles, Jovita
  1899-1983 . . . . DLB-122
González-T., César A. 1931- DLB-82
"The Good, The Not So Good," by
  Stephen Dunn DLB-105
Goodbye, Gutenberg? A Lecture at
  the New York Public Library,
  18 April 1995 . . . . Y-95
Goodison, Lorna 1947- DLB-157
Goodman, Paul 1911-1972 . . . . DLB-130
The Goodman Theatre DLB-7
Goodrich, Frances 1891-1984 and
  Hackett, Albert 1900- DLB-26

Goodrich, Samuel Griswold
  1793-1860 . . . . DLB-1, 42, 73
Goodrich, S. G. [publishing house] . . . DLB-49
Goodspeed, C. E., and Company DLB-49
Goodwin, Stephen 1943- Y-82
Googe, Barnabe 1540-1594 . . . . DLB-132
Gookin, Daniel 1612-1687 . . . . DLB-24
Gordimer, Nadine 1923- Y-91
Gordon, Caroline
  1895-1981 . . . . DLB-4, 9, 102; DS-17; Y-81
Gordon, Giles 1940- DLB-14, 139
Gordon, Helen Cameron, Lady Russell
  1867-1949 . . . . DLB-195
Gordon, Lyndall 1941- DLB-155
Gordon, Mary 1949- DLB-6; Y-81
Gordone, Charles 1925- DLB-7
Gore, Catherine 1800-1861 . . . . DLB-116
Gorey, Edward 1925- DLB-61
Gorgias of Leontini circa 485 B.C.-376 B.C.
  . . . . DLB-176
Görres, Joseph 1776-1848 . . . . DLB-90
Gosse, Edmund 1849-1928 . . DLB-57, 144, 184
Gosson, Stephen 1554-1624 . . . . . . DLB-172
Gotlieb, Phyllis 1926- DLB-88
Gottfried von Straßburg
  died before 1230 . . . . DLB-138
Gotthelf, Jeremias 1797-1854 . . . . . . DLB-133
Gottschalk circa 804/808-869 . . . . . . DLB-148
Gottsched, Johann Christoph
  1700-1766 . . . . DLB-97
Götz, Johann Nikolaus
  1721-1781 . . . . DLB-97
Goudge, Elizabeth 1900-1984 . . . . . DLB-191
Gould, Wallace 1882-1940 . . . . DLB-54
Govoni, Corrado 1884-1965 . . . . . . DLB-114
Gower, John circa 1330-1408 . . . . . DLB-146
Goyen, William 1915-1983 . . . . . DLB-2; Y-83
Goytisolo, José Augustín 1928- DLB-134
Gozzano, Guido 1883-1916 . . . . . . DLB-114
Grabbe, Christian Dietrich
  1801-1836 . . . . DLB-133
Gracq, Julien 1910- DLB-83
Grady, Henry W. 1850-1889 . . . . . . DLB-23
Graf, Oskar Maria 1894-1967 . . . . . . DLB-56
Graf Rudolf between circa 1170
  and circa 1185 . . . . DLB-148
Grafton, Richard
  [publishing house] DLB-170
Graham, George Rex
  1813-1894 . . . . DLB-73
Graham, Gwethalyn 1913-1965 . . . . . DLB-88
Graham, Jorie 1951- DLB-120
Graham, Katharine 1917- DLB-127
Graham, Lorenz 1902-1989 . . . . . . DLB-76

Graham, Philip 1915-1963 . . . . DLB-127
Graham, R. B. Cunninghame
  1852-1936 . . . . DLB-98, 135, 174
Graham, Shirley 1896-1977 . . . . DLB-76
Graham, Stephen 1884-1975 . . . . . . DLB-195
Graham, W. S. 1918- DLB-20
Graham, William H.
  [publishing house] DLB-49
Graham, Winston 1910- DLB-77
Grahame, Kenneth
  1859-1932 . . . . DLB-34, 141, 178
Grainger, Martin Allerdale
  1874-1941 . . . . DLB-92
Gramatky, Hardie 1907-1979 . . . . . . DLB-22
Grand, Sarah 1854-1943 . . . . DLB-135
Grandbois, Alain 1900-1975 . . . . . . DLB-92
Grange, John circa 1556-? DLB-136
Granich, Irwin (see Gold, Michael)
Grant, Duncan 1885-1978 . . . . DS-10
Grant, George 1918-1988 . . . . DLB-88
Grant, George Monro 1835-1902 . . . . DLB-99
Grant, Harry J. 1881-1963 . . . . DLB-29
Grant, James Edward 1905-1966 . . . . DLB-26
Grass, Günter 1927- DLB-75, 124
Grasty, Charles H. 1863-1924 . . . . . . DLB-25
Grau, Shirley Ann 1929- DLB-2
Graves, John 1920- Y-83
Graves, Richard 1715-1804 . . . . DLB-39
Graves, Robert
  1895-1985 . . . . . . DLB-20, 100, 191; Y-85
Gray, Alasdair 1934- DLB-194
Gray, Asa 1810-1888 . . . . DLB-1
Gray, David 1838-1861 . . . . DLB-32
Gray, Simon 1936- DLB-13
Gray, Thomas 1716-1771 . . . . DLB-109
Grayson, William J. 1788-1863 . . . . DLB-3, 64
The Great Bibliographers Series Y-93
The Great War and the Theater, 1914-1918
  [Great Britain] DLB-10
The Great War Exhibition and Symposium at the
  University of South Carolina Y-97
Greeley, Horace 1811-1872 . . . DLB-3, 43, 189
Green, Adolph (see Comden, Betty)
Green, Duff 1791-1875 . . . . DLB-43
Green, Elizabeth Shippen 1871-1954 . . DLB-188
Green, Gerald 1922- DLB-28
Green, Henry 1905-1973 . . . . DLB-15
Green, Jonas 1712-1767 . . . . DLB-31
Green, Joseph 1706-1780 . . . . DLB-31
Green, Julien 1900- DLB-4, 72
Green, Paul 1894-1981 . . . . DLB-7, 9; Y-81
Green, T. and S.
  [publishing house] DLB-49

Green, Thomas Hill 1836-1882 . . . . . DLB-190

Green, Timothy
[publishing house] DLB-49

Greenaway, Kate 1846-1901 . . . . . . DLB-141

Greenberg: Publisher DLB-46

Green Tiger Press DLB-46

Greene, Asa 1789-1838 . . . . DLB-11

Greene, Belle da Costa 1883-1950 . . . DLB-187

Greene, Benjamin H.
[publishing house] DLB-49

Greene, Graham 1904-1991
. . . DLB-13, 15, 77, 100, 162; Y-85, Y-91

Greene, Robert 1558-1592 . . . . . DLB-62, 167

Greene Jr., Robert Bernard (Bob)
1947- DLB-185

Greenhow, Robert 1800-1854 . . . . . . DLB-30

Greenlee, William B. 1872-1953 . . . . DLB-187

Greenough, Horatio 1805-1852 . . . . . DLB-1

Greenwell, Dora 1821-1882 . . . . DLB-35

Greenwillow Books DLB-46

Greenwood, Grace (see Lippincott, Sara Jane Clarke)

Greenwood, Walter 1903-1974 . . . DLB-10, 191

Greer, Ben 1948- DLB-6

Greflinger, Georg 1620?-1677 . . . . . DLB-164

Greg, W. R. 1809-1881 . . . . DLB-55

Gregg, Josiah 1806-1850 . . . . . DLB-183, 186

Gregg Press DLB-46

Gregory, Isabella Augusta
Persse, Lady 1852-1932 . . . . . . DLB-10

Gregory, Horace 1898-1982 . . . . . . DLB-48

Gregory of Rimini
circa 1300-1358 . . . . DLB-115

Gregynog Press DLB-112

Greiffenberg, Catharina Regina von
1633-1694 . . . . DLB-168

Grenfell, Wilfred Thomason
1865-1940 . . . . DLB-92

Greve, Felix Paul (see Grove, Frederick Philip)

Greville, Fulke, First Lord Brooke
1554-1628 . . . . DLB-62, 172

Grey, Sir George, K.C.B.
1812-1898 . . . . DLB-184

Grey, Lady Jane 1537-1554 . . . . . . DLB-132

Grey Owl 1888-1938 . . . . . . DLB-92; DS-17

Grey, Zane 1872-1939 . . . . DLB-9

Grey Walls Press DLB-112

Grier, Eldon 1917- DLB-88

Grieve, C. M. (see MacDiarmid, Hugh)

Griffin, Bartholomew
flourished 1596 . . . . DLB-172

Griffin, Gerald 1803-1840 . . . . DLB-159

Griffith, Elizabeth 1727?-1793 . . . DLB-39, 89

Griffith, George 1857-1906 . . . . . . DLB-178

Griffiths, Trevor 1935- DLB-13

Griffiths, Ralph
[publishing house] DLB-154

Griggs, S. C., and Company DLB-49

Griggs, Sutton Elbert
1872-1930 . . . . DLB-50

Grignon, Claude-Henri 1894-1976 . . . DLB-68

Grigson, Geoffrey 1905- DLB-27

Grillparzer, Franz 1791-1872 . . . . . DLB-133

Grimald, Nicholas
circa 1519-circa 1562 . . . . DLB-136

Grimké, Angelina Weld
1880-1958 . . . . DLB-50, 54

Grimm, Hans 1875-1959 . . . . DLB-66

Grimm, Jacob 1785-1863 . . . . DLB-90

Grimm, Wilhelm 1786-1859 . . . . DLB-90

Grimmelshausen, Johann Jacob Christoffel von
1621 or 1622-1676 . . . . DLB-168

Grimshaw, Beatrice Ethel
1871-1953 . . . . DLB-174

Grindal, Edmund
1519 or 1520-1583 . . . . DLB-132

Griswold, Rufus Wilmot
1815-1857 . . . . DLB-3, 59

Grosart, Alexander Balloch
1827-1899 . . . . DLB-184

Gross, Milt 1895-1953 . . . . DLB-11

Grosset and Dunlap DLB-49

Grossman, Allen 1932- DLB-193

Grossman Publishers DLB-46

Grosseteste, Robert
circa 1160-1253 . . . . DLB-115

Grosvenor, Gilbert H. 1875-1966 . . . . DLB-91

Groth, Klaus 1819-1899 . . . . DLB-129

Groulx, Lionel 1878-1967 . . . . DLB-68

Grove, Frederick Philip 1879-1949 . . . . DLB-92

Grove Press DLB-46

Grubb, Davis 1919-1980 . . . . DLB-6

Gruelle, Johnny 1880-1938 . . . . . . DLB-22

von Grumbach, Argula
1492-after 1563? DLB-179

Grymeston, Elizabeth
before 1563-before 1604 . . . . . . DLB-136

Gryphius, Andreas 1616-1664 . . . . . DLB-164

Gryphius, Christian 1649-1706 . . . . . DLB-168

Guare, John 1938- DLB-7

Guerra, Tonino 1920- DLB-128

Guest, Barbara 1920- DLB-5, 193

Guèvremont, Germaine
1893-1968 . . . . DLB-68

Guidacci, Margherita 1921-1992 . . . . DLB-128

Guide to the Archives of Publishers, Journals, and Literary Agents in North American Libraries
. . . . Y-93

Guillén, Jorge 1893-1984 . . . . DLB-108

Guilloux, Louis 1899-1980 . . . . DLB-72

Guilpin, Everard
circa 1572-after 1608? DLB-136

Guiney, Louise Imogen 1861-1920 . . . . DLB-54

Guiterman, Arthur 1871-1943 . . . . . DLB-11

Günderrode, Caroline von
1780-1806 . . . . DLB-90

Gundulić, Ivan 1589-1638 . . . . DLB-147

Gunn, Bill 1934-1989 . . . . DLB-38

Gunn, James E. 1923- DLB-8

Gunn, Neil M. 1891-1973 . . . . DLB-15

Gunn, Thom 1929- DLB-27

Gunnars, Kristjana 1948- DLB-60

Günther, Johann Christian
1695-1723 . . . . DLB-168

Gurik, Robert 1932- DLB-60

Gustafson, Ralph 1909- DLB-88

Gütersloh, Albert Paris 1887-1973 . . . . DLB-81

Guthrie, A. B., Jr. 1901- DLB-6

Guthrie, Ramon 1896-1973 . . . . . . DLB-4

The Guthrie Theater DLB-7

Guthrie, Thomas Anstey (see Anstey, FC)

Gutzkow, Karl 1811-1878 . . . . DLB-133

Guy, Ray 1939- DLB-60

Guy, Rosa 1925- DLB-33

Guyot, Arnold 1807-1884 . . . . DS-13

Gwynne, Erskine 1898-1948 . . . . . . DLB-4

Gyles, John 1680-1755 . . . . DLB-99

Gysin, Brion 1916- DLB-16

H

H. D. (see Doolittle, Hilda)

Habington, William 1605-1654 . . . . . DLB-126

Hacker, Marilyn 1942- DLB-120

Hackett, Albert (see Goodrich, Frances)

Hacks, Peter 1928- DLB-124

Hadas, Rachel 1948- DLB-120

Hadden, Briton 1898-1929 . . . . DLB-91

Hagedorn, Friedrich von
1708-1754 . . . . DLB-168

Hagelstange, Rudolf 1912-1984 . . . . . DLB-69

Haggard, H. Rider
1856-1925 . . . . . DLB-70, 156, 174, 178

Haggard, William 1907-1993 . . . . . . Y-93

Hahn-Hahn, Ida Gräfin von
1805-1880 . . . . DLB-133

Haig-Brown, Roderick 1908-1976 . . . DLB-88

Haight, Gordon S. 1901-1985 . . . . . DLB-103

Hailey, Arthur 1920- DLB-88; Y-82

Haines, John 1924- DLB-5

Hake, Edward
　　flourished 1566-1604 . . . . DLB-136
Hake, Thomas Gordon 1809-1895. . . . DLB-32
Hakluyt, Richard 1552?-1616 . . . . . . DLB-136
Halbe, Max 1865-1944 . . . . DLB-118
Haldone, Charlotte 1894-1969. . . . . . DLB-191
Haldane, J. B. S. 1892-1964. . . . . . . DLB-160
Haldeman, Joe 1943- DLB-8
Haldeman-Julius Company DLB-46
Hale, E. J., and Son DLB-49
Hale, Edward Everett
　　1822-1909 . . . . DLB-1, 42, 74
Hale, Janet Campbell 1946- DLB-175
Hale, Kathleen 1898- DLB-160
Hale, Leo Thomas (see Ebon)
Hale, Lucretia Peabody
　　1820-1900 . . . . DLB-42
Hale, Nancy
　　1908-1988 . . . . DLB-86; DS-17; Y-80, Y-88
Hale, Sarah Josepha (Buell)
　　1788-1879 . . . . DLB-1, 42, 73
Hales, John 1584-1656. . . . . DLB-151
Halévy, Ludovic 1834-1908 . . . . DLB-192
Haley, Alex 1921-1992 . . . . DLB-38
Haliburton, Thomas Chandler
　　1796-1865. . . . . DLB-11, 99
Hall, Anna Maria 1800-1881 . . . . . DLB-159
Hall, Donald 1928- DLB-5
Hall, Edward 1497-1547. . . . . DLB-132
Hall, James 1793-1868 . . . . DLB-73, 74
Hall, Joseph 1574-1656. . . . . DLB-121, 151
Hall, Radclyffe 1880-1943 . . . . DLB-191
Hall, Samuel [publishing house] DLB-49
Hallam, Arthur Henry 1811-1833 . . . DLB-32
Halleck, Fitz-Greene 1790-1867 . . . . . DLB-3
Haller, Albrecht von 1708-1777. . . . . DLB-168
Halliwell-Phillipps, James Orchard
　　1820-1889 . . . . DLB-184
Hallmann, Johann Christian
　　1640-1704 or 1716?. DLB-168
Hallmark Editions. DLB-46
Halper, Albert 1904-1984 . . . . DLB-9
Halperin, John William 1941- DLB-111
Halstead, Murat 1829-1908. . . . . . . DLB-23
Hamann, Johann Georg 1730-1788 . . . DLB-97
Hamburger, Michael 1924- DLB-27
Hamilton, Alexander 1712-1756 . . . . . DLB-31
Hamilton, Alexander 1755?-1804. . . . DLB-37
Hamilton, Cicely 1872-1952 . . . . DLB-10
Hamilton, Edmond 1904-1977 . . . . . DLB-8
Hamilton, Elizabeth 1758-1816 . . . DLB-116, 158
Hamilton, Gail (see Corcoran, Barbara)
Hamilton, Ian 1938- DLB-40, 155

Hamilton, Patrick 1904-1962 . . . . DLB-10, 191
Hamilton, Virginia 1936- DLB-33, 52
Hamilton, Hamish, Limited DLB-112
Hammett, Dashiell 1894-1961 . . . . DS-6
Dashiell Hammett:
　　An Appeal in TAC Y-91
Hammon, Jupiter 1711-died between
　　1790 and 1806. . . . . DLB-31, 50
Hammond, John ?-1663 . . . . DLB-24
Hamner, Earl 1923- DLB-6
Hampson, John 1901-1955 . . . . . . DLB-191
Hampton, Christopher 1946- DLB-13
Handel-Mazzetti, Enrica von
　　1871-1955 . . . . DLB-81
Handke, Peter 1942- DLB-85, 124
Handlin, Oscar 1915- DLB-17
Hankin, St. John 1869-1909 . . . . . . DLB-10
Hanley, Clifford 1922- DLB-14
Hanley, James 1901-1985 . . . . DLB-191
Hannah, Barry 1942- DLB-6
Hannay, James 1827-1873 . . . . DLB-21
Hansberry, Lorraine 1930-1965 . . . . DLB-7, 38
Hapgood, Norman 1868-1937 . . . . . DLB-91
Happel, Eberhard Werner
　　1647-1690 . . . . DLB-168
Harcourt Brace Jovanovich. DLB-46
Hardenberg, Friedrich von (see Novalis)
Harding, Walter 1917- DLB-111
Hardwick, Elizabeth 1916- DLB-6
Hardy, Thomas 1840-1928. . . . DLB-18, 19, 135
Hare, Cyril 1900-1958 . . . . DLB-77
Hare, David 1947- DLB-13
Hargrove, Marion 1919- DLB-11
Häring, Georg Wilhelm Heinrich (see Alexis,
　　Willibald)
Harington, Donald 1935- DLB-152
Harington, Sir John 1560-1612 . . . . . DLB-136
Harjo, Joy 1951- DLB-120, 175
Harlow, Robert 1923- DLB-60
Harman, Thomas
　　flourished 1566-1573 . . . . DLB-136
Harness, Charles L. 1915- DLB-8
Harnett, Cynthia 1893-1981. . . . . . . DLB-161
Harper, Fletcher 1806-1877. . . . . . . DLB-79
Harper, Frances Ellen Watkins
　　1825-1911 . . . . DLB-50
Harper, Michael S. 1938- DLB-41
Harper and Brothers DLB-49
Harraden, Beatrice 1864-1943. . . . . DLB-153
Harrap, George G., and Company
　　Limited. DLB-112
Harriot, Thomas 1560-1621 . . . . . . DLB-136
Harris, Benjamin ?-circa 1720 . . . . DLB-42, 43

Harris, Christie 1907- DLB-88
Harris, Frank 1856-1931. . . . . DLB-156
Harris, George Washington
　　1814-1869 . . . . DLB-3, 11
Harris, Joel Chandler
　　1848-1908 . . . . . . DLB-11, 23, 42, 78, 91
Harris, Mark 1922- DLB-2; Y-80
Harris, Wilson 1921- DLB-117
Harrison, Charles Yale
　　1898-1954 . . . . DLB-68
Harrison, Frederic 1831-1923 . . . . DLB-57, 190
Harrison, Harry 1925- DLB-8
Harrison, Jim 1937- Y-82
Harrison, Mary St. Leger Kingsley
　　(see Malet, Lucas)
Harrison, Paul Carter 1936- DLB-38
Harrison, Susan Frances
　　1859-1935 . . . . DLB-99
Harrison, Tony 1937- DLB-40
Harrison, William 1535-1593 . . . . . . DLB-136
Harrison, James P., Company DLB-49
Harrisse, Henry 1829-1910 . . . . DLB-47
Harryman, Carla 1952- DLB-193
Harsdörffer, Georg Philipp
　　1607-1658 . . . . DLB-164
Harsent, David 1942- DLB-40
Hart, Albert Bushnell 1854-1943 . . . . . DLB-17
Hart, Julia Catherine 1796-1867 . . . . DLB-99
The Lorenz Hart Centenary. Y-95
Hart, Moss 1904-1961 . . . . DLB-7
Hart, Oliver 1723-1795 . . . . DLB-31
Hart-Davis, Rupert, Limited. DLB-112
Harte, Bret
　　1836-1902 . . . . DLB-12, 64, 74, 79, 186
Harte, Edward Holmead 1922- DLB-127
Harte, Houston Harriman 1927- DLB-127
Hartlaub, Felix 1913-1945 . . . . DLB-56
Hartlebon, Otto Erich
　　1864-1905 . . . . DLB-118
Hartley, L. P. 1895-1972 . . . . . DLB-15, 139
Hartley, Marsden 1877-1943 . . . . . . DLB-54
Hartling, Peter 1933- DLB-75
Hartman, Geoffrey H. 1929- DLB-67
Hartmann, Sadakichi 1867-1944 . . . . DLB-54
Hartmann von Aue
　　circa 1160-circa 1205 . . . . DLB-138
Harvey, Gabriel 1550?-1631. . . . . . . DLB-167
Harvey, Jean-Charles 1891-1967 . . . . . DLB-88
Harvill Press Limited DLB-112
Harwood, Lee 1939- DLB-40
Harwood, Ronald 1934- DLB-13
Haskins, Charles Homer
　　1870-1937 . . . . DLB-47

Hass, Robert 1941- DLB-105

The Hatch-Billops Collection DLB-76

Hathaway, William 1944- DLB-120

Hauff, Wilhelm 1802-1827 .... DLB-90

A Haughty and Proud Generation (1922), by Ford Madox Hueffer DLB-36

Haugwitz, August Adolph von 1647-1706 .... DLB-168

Hauptmann, Carl 1858-1921 .... DLB-66, 118

Hauptmann, Gerhart 1862-1946 .... DLB-66, 118

Hauser, Marianne 1910- Y-83

Hawes, Stephen 1475?-before 1529 .... DLB-132

Hawker, Robert Stephen 1803-1875 .... DLB-32

Hawkes, John 1925- DLB-2, 7; Y-80

Hawkesworth, John 1720-1773 ..... DLB-142

Hawkins, Sir Anthony Hope (see Hope, Anthony)

Hawkins, Sir John 1719-1789. .... DLB-104, 142

Hawkins, Walter Everette 1883-? DLB-50

Hawthorne, Nathaniel 1804-1864. .... DLB-1, 74, 183

Hawthorne, Nathaniel 1804-1864 and Hawthorne, Sophia Peabody 1809-1871 .... DLB-183

Hay, John 1835-1905 ...... DLB-12, 47, 189

Hayashi, Fumiko 1903-1951 .... DLB-180

Haycraft, Anna Margaret (see Ellis, Alice Thomas)

Hayden, Robert 1913-1980 ...... DLB-5, 76

Haydon, Benjamin Robert 1786-1846 .... DLB-110

Hayes, John Michael 1919- DLB-26

Hayley, William 1745-1820 ..... DLB-93, 142

Haym, Rudolf 1821-1901 .... DLB-129

Hayman, Robert 1575-1629 .... DLB-99

Hayman, Ronald 1932- DLB-155

Hayne, Paul Hamilton 1830-1886 .... DLB-3, 64, 79

Hays, Mary 1760-1843 ..... DLB-142, 158

Haywood, Eliza 1693?-1756 .... DLB-39

Hazard, Willis P. [publishing house] DLB-49

Hazlitt, William 1778-1830 .... DLB-110, 158

Hazzard, Shirley 1931- Y-82

Head, Bessie 1937-1986 .... DLB-117

Headley, Joel T. 1813-1897 .... DLB-30, 183; DS-13

Heaney, Seamus 1939- DLB-40; Y-95

Heard, Nathan C. 1936- DLB-33

Hearn, Lafcadio 1850-1904... DLB-12, 78, 189

Hearne, John 1926- DLB-117

Hearne, Samuel 1745-1792 .... DLB-99

Hearst, William Randolph 1863-1951 .... DLB-25

Hearst, William Randolph, Jr 1908-1993 .... DLB-127

Heartman, Charles Frederick 1883-1953. .... DLB-187

Heath, Catherine 1924- DLB-14

Heath, Roy A. K. 1926- DLB-117

Heath-Stubbs, John 1918- DLB-27

Heavysege, Charles 1816-1876 ...... DLB-99

Hebbel, Friedrich 1813-1863. .... DLB-129

Hebel, Johann Peter 1760-1826. ...... DLB-90

Heber, Richard 1774-1833. .... DLB-184

Hébert, Anne 1916- DLB-68

Hébert, Jacques 1923- DLB-53

Hecht, Anthony 1923- DLB-5, 169

Hecht, Ben 1894-1964
.... DLB-7, 9, 25, 26, 28, 86

Hecker, Isaac Thomas 1819-1888 ..... DLB-1

Hedge, Frederic Henry 1805-1890 .... DLB-1, 59

Hefner, Hugh M. 1926- DLB-137

Hegel, Georg Wilhelm Friedrich 1770-1831 .... DLB-90

Heidish, Marcy 1947- Y-82

Heißenbüttel 1921- DLB-75

Hein, Christoph 1944- DLB-124

Heine, Heinrich 1797-1856 .... DLB-90

Heinemann, Larry 1944- DS-9

Heinemann, William, Limited. DLB-112

Heinlein, Robert A. 1907-1988 .... DLB-8

Heinrich Julius of Brunswick 1564-1613 .... DLB-164

Heinrich von dem Türlîn flourished circa 1230 .... DLB-138

Heinrich von Melk flourished after 1160 .... DLB-148

Heinrich von Veldeke circa 1145-circa 1190 .... DLB-138

Heinrich, Willi 1920- DLB-75

Heiskell, John 1872-1972 .... DLB-127

Heinse, Wilhelm 1746-1803 .... DLB-94

Heinz, W. C. 1915- DLB-171

Hejinian, Lyn 1941- DLB-165

Heliand circa 850. .... DLB-148

Heller, Joseph 1923- DLB-2, 28; Y-80

Heller, Michael 1937- DLB-165

Hellman, Lillian 1906-1984 ..... DLB-7; Y-84

Hellwig, Johann 1609-1674 .... DLB-164

Helprin, Mark 1947- Y-85

Helwig, David 1938- DLB-60

Hemans, Felicia 1793-1835 .... DLB-96

Hemingway, Ernest 1899-1961. DLB-4, 9, 102; Y-81, Y-87; DS-1, DS-15, DS-16

Hemingway: Twenty-Five Years Later Y-85

Hémon, Louis 1880-1913. .... DLB-92

Hemphill, Paul 1936- Y-87

Hénault, Gilles 1920- DLB-88

Henchman, Daniel 1689-1761 .... DLB-24

Henderson, Alice Corbin 1881-1949 .... DLB-54

Henderson, Archibald 1877-1963 .... DLB-103

Henderson, David 1942- DLB-41

Henderson, George Wylie 1904- DLB-51

Henderson, Zenna 1917-1983 .... DLB-8

Henisch, Peter 1943- DLB-85

Henley, Beth 1952- Y-86

Henley, William Ernest 1849-1903 .... DLB-19

Henniker, Florence 1855-1923. ...... DLB-135

Henry, Alexander 1739-1824 .... DLB-99

Henry, Buck 1930- DLB-26

Henry VIII of England 1491-1547 .... DLB-132

Henry, Marguerite 1902- DLB-22

Henry, O. (see Porter, William Sydney)

Henry of Ghent circa 1217-1229 - 1293 .... DLB-115

Henry, Robert Selph 1889-1970 ..... DLB-17

Henry, Will (see Allen, Henry W.)

Henryson, Robert 1420s or 1430s-circa 1505 ...... DLB-146

Henschke, Alfred (see Klabund)

Hensley, Sophie Almon 1866-1946. .... DLB-99

Henson, Lance 1944- DLB-175

Henty, G. A. 1832?-1902. ..... DLB-18, 141

Hentz, Caroline Lee 1800-1856 ...... DLB-3

Heraclitus flourished circa 500 B.C.
.... DLB-176

Herbert, Agnes circa 1880-1960..... DLB-174

Herbert, Alan Patrick 1890-1971 .. DLB-10, 191

Herbert, Edward, Lord, of Cherbury 1582-1648. .... DLB-121, 151

Herbert, Frank 1920-1986 .... DLB-8

Herbert, George 1593-1633 .... DLB-126

Herbert, Henry William 1807-1858 .... DLB-3, 73

Herbert, John 1926- DLB-53

Herbert, Mary Sidney, Countess of Pembroke (see Sidney, Mary)

Herbst, Josephine 1892-1969 .... DLB-9

Herburger, Gunter 1932- DLB-75, 124

Èercules, Frank E. M. 1917- DLB-33

Herder, Johann Gottfried 1744-1803 .... DLB-97

Herder, B., Book Company DLB-49

Herford, Charles Harold
   1853-1931 . . . . DLB-149

Hergesheimer, Joseph
   1880-1954 . . . . DLB-9, 102

Heritage Press DLB-46

Hermann the Lame 1013-1054 . . . . . DLB-148

Hermes, Johann Timotheus
   1738-1821 . . . . DLB-97

Hermlin, Stephan 1915- DLB-69

Hernández, Alfonso C. 1938- DLB-122

Hernández, Inés 1947- DLB-122

Hernández, Miguel 1910-1942 . . . . . DLB-134

Hernton, Calvin C. 1932- DLB-38

"The Hero as Man of Letters: Johnson,
   Rousseau, Burns" (1841), by Thomas
   Carlyle [excerpt] DLB-57

The Hero as Poet. Dante; Shakspeare (1841),
   by Thomas Carlyle DLB-32

Herodotus circa 484 B.C.-circa 420 B.C.
   . . . . DLB-176

Heron, Robert 1764-1807 . . . . DLB-142

Herr, Michael 1940- DLB-185

Herrera, Juan Felipe 1948- DLB-122

Herrick, Robert 1591-1674 . . . . DLB-126

Herrick, Robert 1868-1938 . . . . DLB-9, 12, 78

Herrick, William 1915- Y-83

Herrick, E. R., and Company DLB-49

Herrmann, John 1900-1959 . . . . DLB-4

Hersey, John 1914-1993 . . . . DLB-6, 185

Hertel, François 1905-1985 . . . . DLB-68

Hervé-Bazin, Jean Pierre Marie (see Bazin, Hervé)

Hervey, John, Lord 1696-1743 . . . . . DLB-101

Herwig, Georg 1817-1875 . . . . DLB-133

Herzog, Emile Salomon Wilhelm (see Maurois, André)

Hesiod eighth century B.C. DLB-176

Hesse, Hermann 1877-1962 . . . . DLB-66

Hessus, Helius Eobanus
   1488-1540 . . . . DLB-179

Hewat, Alexander
   circa 1743-circa 1824 . . . . DLB-30

Hewitt, John 1907- DLB-27

Hewlett, Maurice 1861-1923 . . . . DLB-34, 156

Heyen, William 1940- DLB-5

Heyer, Georgette 1902-1974 . . . . DLB-77, 191

Heym, Stefan 1913- DLB-69

Heyse, Paul 1830-1914 . . . . DLB-129

Heytesbury, William
   circa 1310-1372 or 1373 . . . . DLB-115

Heyward, Dorothy 1890-1961 . . . . . . DLB-7

Heyward, DuBose
   1885-1940 . . . . DLB-7, 9, 45

Heywood, John 1497?-1580? DLB-136

Heywood, Thomas
   1573 or 1574-1641 . . . . DLB-62

Hibbs, Ben 1901-1975 . . . . DLB-137

Hichens, Robert S. 1864-1950 . . . . . . DLB-153

Hickman, William Albert
   1877-1957 . . . . DLB-92

Hidalgo, José Luis 1919-1947 . . . . . . DLB-108

Hiebert, Paul 1892-1987 . . . . DLB-68

Hieng, Andrej 1925- DLB-181

Hierro, José 1922- DLB-108

Higgins, Aidan 1927- DLB-14

Higgins, Colin 1941-1988 . . . . DLB-26

Higgins, George V. 1939- DLB-2; Y-81

Higginson, Thomas Wentworth
   1823-1911 . . . . DLB-1, 64

Highwater, Jamake 1942?- DLB-52; Y-85

Hijuelos, Oscar 1951- DLB-145

Hildegard von Bingen
   1098-1179 . . . . DLB-148

Das Hildesbrandslied circa 820 . . . . . DLB-148

Hildesheimer, Wolfgang
   1916-1991 . . . . DLB-69, 124

Hildreth, Richard
   1807-1865 . . . . DLB-1, 30, 59

Hill, Aaron 1685-1750 . . . . DLB-84

Hill, Geoffrey 1932- DLB-40

Hill, "Sir" John 1714?-1775 . . . . DLB-39

Hill, Leslie 1880-1960 . . . . DLB-51

Hill, Susan 1942- DLB-14, 139

Hill, Walter 1942- DLB-44

Hill and Wang DLB-46

Hill, George M., Company DLB-49

Hill, Lawrence, and Company,
   Publishers DLB-46

Hillberry, Conrad 1928- DLB-120

Hilliard, Gray and Company DLB-49

Hills, Lee 1906- DLB-127

Hillyer, Robert 1895-1961 . . . . DLB-54

Hilton, James 1900-1954 . . . . . . DLB-34, 77

Hilton, Walter died 1396 . . . . DLB-146

Hilton and Company DLB-49

Himes, Chester
   1909-1984 . . . . DLB-2, 76, 143

Hindmarsh, Joseph
   [publishing house] DLB-170

Hine, Daryl 1936- DLB-60

Hingley, Ronald 1920- DLB-155

Hinojosa-Smith, Rolando
   1929- DLB-82

Hippel, Theodor Gottlieb von
   1741-1796 . . . . DLB-97

Hippocrates of Cos flourished circa 425 B.C.
   . . . . DLB-176

Hirabayashi, Taiko 1905-1972 . . . . . . DLB-180

Hirsch, E. D., Jr. 1928- DLB-67

Hirsch, Edward 1950- DLB-120 The History of the
   Adventures of Joseph Andrews
   (1742), by Henry Fielding
   [excerpt] DLB-39

Hoagland, Edward 1932- DLB-6

Hoagland, Everett H., III 1942- DLB-41

Hoban, Russell 1925- DLB-52

Hobbes, Thomas 1588-1679 . . . . DLB-151

Hobby, Oveta 1905- DLB-127

Hobby, William 1878-1964 . . . . DLB-127

Hobsbaum, Philip 1932- DLB-40

Hobson, Laura Z. 1900- DLB-28

Hoby, Thomas 1530-1566 . . . . DLB-132

Hoccleve, Thomas
   circa 1368-circa 1437 . . . . DLB-146

Hochhuth, Rolf 1931- DLB-124

Hochman, Sandra 1936- DLB-5

Hocken, Thomas Morland
   1836-1910 . . . . DLB-184

Hodder and Stoughton, Limited DLB-106

Hodgins, Jack 1938- DLB-60

Hodgman, Helen 1945- DLB-14

Hodgskin, Thomas 1787-1869 . . . . . . DLB-158

Hodgson, Ralph 1871-1962 . . . . DLB-19

Hodgson, William Hope
   1877-1918 . . . . . . DLB-70, 153, 156, 178

Hoe, Robert III 1839-1909 . . . . DLB-187

Hoffenstein, Samuel 1890-1947 . . . . . DLB-11

Hoffman, Charles Fenno
   1806-1884 . . . . DLB-3

Hoffman, Daniel 1923- DLB-5

Hoffmann, E. T. A. 1776-1822 . . . . . DLB-90

Hoffman, Frank B. 1888-1958 . . . . . . DLB-188

Hoffmanswaldau, Christian Hoffman von
   1616-1679 . . . . DLB-168

Hofmann, Michael 1957- DLB-40

Hofmannsthal, Hugo von
   1874-1929 . . . . DLB-81, 118

Hofstadter, Richard 1916-1970 . . . . . DLB-17

Hogan, Desmond 1950- DLB-14

Hogan, Linda 1947- DLB-175

Hogan and Thompson DLB-49

Hogarth Press DLB-112

Hogg, James 1770-1835 . . . . DLB-93, 116, 159

Hohberg, Wolfgang Helmhard Freiherr von
   1612-1688 . . . . DLB-168

von Hohenheim, Philippus Aureolus
   Theophrastus Bombastus (see Paracelsus)

Hohl, Ludwig 1904-1980 . . . . DLB-56

Holbrook, David 1923- DLB-14, 40

Holcroft, Thomas
   1745-1809 . . . . DLB-39, 89, 158

Holden, Jonathan 1941- DLB-105

Cumulative Index

Holden, Molly 1927-1981 . . . . DLB-40
Hölderlin, Friedrich 1770-1843 . . . . . . DLB-90
Holiday House DLB-46
Holinshed, Raphael died 1580 . . . . . DLB-167
Holland, J. G. 1819-1881 . . . . DS-13
Holland, Norman N. 1927- DLB-67
Hollander, John 1929- DLB-5
Holley, Marietta 1836-1926 . . . . DLB-11
Hollingsworth, Margaret 1940- DLB-60
Hollo, Anselm 1934- DLB-40
Holloway, Emory 1885-1977 . . . . . . DLB-103
Holloway, John 1920- DLB-27
Holloway House Publishing
  Company DLB-46
Holme, Constance 1880-1955 . . . . . . DLB-34
Holmes, Abraham S. 1821?-1908 . . . . DLB-99
Holmes, John Clellon 1926-1988 . . . . DLB-16
Holmes, Oliver Wendell
  1809-1894 . . . . DLB-1, 189
Holmes, Richard 1945- DLB-155
Holmes, Thomas James 1874-1959 . . . DLB-187
Holroyd, Michael 1935- DLB-155
Holst, Hermann E. von
  1841-1904 . . . . DLB-47
Holt, John 1721-1784 . . . . DLB-43
Holt, Henry, and Company DLB-49
Holt, Rinehart and Winston DLB-46
Holtby, Winifred 1898-1935 . . . . . . DLB-191
Holthusen, Hans Egon 1913- DLB-69
Hölty, Ludwig Christoph Heinrich
  1748-1776 . . . . DLB-94
Holz, Arno 1863-1929 . . . . DLB-118
Home, Henry, Lord Kames (see Kames, Henry Home, Lord)
Home, John 1722-1808 . . . . DLB-84
Home, William Douglas 1912- DLB-13
Home Publishing Company DLB-49
Homer circa eighth-seventh centuries B.C.
  . . . . DLB-176
Homer, Winslow 1836-1910 . . . . . . DLB-188
Homes, Geoffrey (see Mainwaring, Daniel)
Honan, Park 1928- DLB-111
Hone, William 1780-1842 . . . . DLB-110, 158
Hongo, Garrett Kaoru 1951- DLB-120
Honig, Edwin 1919- DLB-5
Hood, Hugh 1928- DLB-53
Hood, Thomas 1799-1845 . . . . DLB-96
Hook, Theodore 1788-1841 . . . . . . DLB-116
Hooker, Jeremy 1941- DLB-40
Hooker, Richard 1554-1600 . . . . DLB-132
Hooker, Thomas 1586-1647 . . . . DLB-24
Hooper, Johnson Jones
  1815-1862 . . . . DLB-3, 11

Hope, Anthony 1863-1933 . . . . DLB-153, 156
Hopkins, Ellice 1836-1904 . . . . DLB-190
Hopkins, Gerard Manley
  1844-1889 . . . . DLB-35, 57
Hopkins, John (see Sternhold, Thomas)
Hopkins, Lemuel 1750-1801 . . . . . . DLB-37
Hopkins, Pauline Elizabeth
  1859-1930 . . . . DLB-50
Hopkins, Samuel 1721-1803 . . . . . . DLB-31
Hopkins, John H., and Son DLB-46
Hopkinson, Francis 1737-1791 . . . . . DLB-31
Hoppin, Augustus 1828-1896 . . . . . . DLB-188
Horgan, Paul 1903- DLB-102; Y-85
Horizon Press DLB-46
Horne, Frank 1899-1974 . . . . DLB-51
Horne, Richard Henry (Hengist)
  1802 or 1803-1884 . . . . DLB-32
Hornung, E. W. 1866-1921 . . . . DLB-70
Horovitz, Israel 1939- DLB-7
Horton, George Moses
  1797?-1883? DLB-50
Horváth, Ödön von
  1901-1938 . . . . DLB-85, 124
Horwood, Harold 1923- DLB-60
Hosford, E. and E.
  [publishing house] DLB-49
Hoskyns, John 1566-1638 . . . . DLB-121
Hotchkiss and Company DLB-49
Hough, Emerson 1857-1923 . . . . DLB-9
Houghton Mifflin Company DLB-49
Houghton, Stanley 1881-1913 . . . . . DLB-10
Household, Geoffrey 1900-1988 . . . . DLB-87
Housman, A. E. 1859-1936 . . . . DLB-19
Housman, Laurence 1865-1959 . . . . . DLB-10
Houwald, Ernst von 1778-1845 . . . . . DLB-90
Hovey, Richard 1864-1900 . . . . DLB-54
Howard, Donald R. 1927-1987 . . . . . DLB-111
Howard, Maureen 1930- Y-83
Howard, Richard 1929- DLB-5
Howard, Roy W. 1883-1964 . . . . . . DLB-29
Howard, Sidney 1891-1939 . . . . . DLB-7, 26
Howe, E. W. 1853-1937 . . . . . . DLB-12, 25
Howe, Henry 1816-1893 . . . . DLB-30
Howe, Irving 1920-1993 . . . . DLB-67
Howe, Joseph 1804-1873 . . . . DLB-99
Howe, Julia Ward 1819-1910 . . . . DLB-1, 189
Howe, Percival Presland
  1886-1944 . . . . DLB-149
Howe, Susan 1937- DLB-120
Howell, Clark, Sr. 1863-1936 . . . . . . DLB-25
Howell, Evan P. 1839-1905 . . . . DLB-23
Howell, James 1594?-1666 . . . . DLB-151

Howell, Warren Richardson
  1912-1984 . . . . DLB-140
Howell, Soskin and Company DLB-46
Howells, William Dean
  1837-1920 . . . . . DLB-12, 64, 74, 79, 189
Howitt, William 1792-1879 and
  Howitt, Mary 1799-1888 . . . . . . DLB-110
Hoyem, Andrew 1935- DLB-5
Hoyers, Anna Ovena 1584-1655 . . . . DLB-164
Hoyos, Angela de 1940- DLB-82
Hoyt, Palmer 1897-1979 . . . . DLB-127
Hoyt, Henry [publishing house] DLB-49
Hrabanus Maurus 776?-856 . . . . . . DLB-148
Hrotsvit of Gandersheim
  circa 935-circa 1000 . . . . DLB-148
Hubbard, Elbert 1856-1915 . . . . DLB-91
Hubbard, Kin 1868-1930 . . . . DLB-11
Hubbard, William circa 1621-1704 . . . DLB-24
Huber, Therese 1764-1829 . . . . DLB-90
Huch, Friedrich 1873-1913 . . . . DLB-66
Huch, Ricarda 1864-1947 . . . . DLB-66
Huck at 100: How Old Is
  Huckleberry Finn? Y-85
Huddle, David 1942- DLB-130
Hudgins, Andrew 1951- DLB-120
Hudson, Henry Norman
  1814-1886 . . . . DLB-64
Hudson, W. H.
  1841-1922 . . . . DLB-98, 153, 174
Hudson and Goodwin DLB-49
Huebsch, B. W.
  [publishing house] DLB-46
Hughes, David 1930- DLB-14
Hughes, John 1677-1720 . . . . DLB-84
Hughes, Langston
  1902-1967 . . . . . . DLB-4, 7, 48, 51, 86
Hughes, Richard 1900-1976 . . . . DLB-15, 161
Hughes, Ted 1930- DLB-40, 161
Hughes, Thomas 1822-1896 . . . . DLB-18, 163
Hugo, Richard 1923-1982 . . . . DLB-5
Hugo, Victor 1802-1885 . . . . . . DLB-119, 192
Hugo Awards and Nebula Awards DLB-8
Hull, Richard 1896-1973 . . . . DLB-77
Hulme, T. E. 1883-1917 . . . . DLB-19
Humboldt, Alexander von
  1769-1859 . . . . DLB-90
Humboldt, Wilhelm von
  1767-1835 . . . . DLB-90
Hume, David 1711-1776 . . . . DLB-104
Hume, Fergus 1859-1932 . . . . DLB-70
Hummer, T. R. 1950- DLB-120
Humorous Book Illustration DLB-11
Humphrey, William 1924- DLB-6
Humphreys, David 1752-1818 . . . . . DLB-37

Humphreys, Emyr 1919- DLB-15
Huncke, Herbert 1915- DLB-16
Huneker, James Gibbons
    1857-1921 . . . . DLB-71
Hunold, Christian Friedrich
    1681-1721 . . . . DLB-168
Hunt, Irene 1907- DLB-52
Hunt, Leigh 1784-1859 . . . . DLB-96, 110, 144
Hunt, Violet 1862-1942 . . . . DLB-162
Hunt, William Gibbes 1791-1833 . . . . DLB-73
Hunter, Evan 1926- Y-82
Hunter, Jim 1939- DLB-14
Hunter, Kristin 1931- DLB-33
Hunter, Mollie 1922- DLB-161
Hunter, N. C. 1908-1971 . . . . DLB-10
Hunter-Duvar, John 1821-1899. . . . . DLB-99
Huntington, Henry E.
    1850-1927 . . . . DLB-140
Hurd and Houghton DLB-49
Hurst, Fannie 1889-1968 . . . . DLB-86
Hurst and Blackett. DLB-106
Hurst and Company DLB-49
Hurston, Zora Neale
    1901?-1960 . . . . DLB-51, 86
Husson, Jules-François-Félix (see Champfleury)
Huston, John 1906-1987 . . . . DLB-26
Hutcheson, Francis 1694-1746 . . . . . . DLB-31
Hutchinson, R. C. 1907-1975 . . . . . DLB-191
Hutchinson, Thomas
    1711-1780 . . . . DLB-30, 31
Hutchinson and Company
    (Publishers) Limited DLB-112
von Hutton, Ulrich 1488-1523 . . . . . DLB-179
Hutton, Richard Holt 1826-1897. . . . . DLB-57
Huxley, Aldous
    1894-1963 . . . . . . DLB-36, 100, 162, 195
Huxley, Elspeth Josceline 1907- DLB-77
Huxley, T. H. 1825-1895. . . . . DLB-57
Huyghue, Douglas Smith
    1816-1891 . . . . DLB-99
Huysmans, Joris-Karl 1848-1907 . . . . DLB-123
Hyde, Donald 1909-1966 and
    Hyde, Mary 1912- DLB-187
Hyman, Trina Schart 1939- DLB-61

I

Iavorsky, Stefan 1658-1722 . . . . . . DLB-150
Ibn Bajja circa 1077-1138 . . . . DLB-115
Ibn Gabirol, Solomon
    circa 1021-circa 1058 . . . . DLB-115
Ibuse, Masuji 1898-1993 . . . . DLB-180

The Iconography of Science-Fiction
    Art DLB-8
Iffland, August Wilhelm
    1759-1814 . . . . DLB-94
Ignatow, David 1914- DLB-5
Ike, Chukwuemeka 1931- DLB-157
Iles, Francis (see Berkeley, Anthony)
The Illustration of Early German
    Literary Manuscripts,
    circa 1150-circa 1300 . . . . DLB-148
"Images and 'Images,'" by
    Charles Simic DLB-105
Imbs, Bravig 1904-1946 . . . . DLB-4
Imbuga, Francis D. 1947- DLB-157
Immermann, Karl 1796-1840 . . . . . DLB-133
Impressions of William Faulkner Y-97
Inchbald, Elizabeth 1753-1821 . . . . DLB-39, 89
Inge, William 1913-1973 . . . . DLB-7
Ingelow, Jean 1820-1897 . . . . . DLB-35, 163
Ingersoll, Ralph 1900-1985 . . . . . . DLB-127
The Ingersoll Prizes Y-84
Ingoldsby, Thomas (see Barham, Richard
    Harris)
Ingraham, Joseph Holt 1809-1860. . . . . DLB-3
Inman, John 1805-1850. . . . . DLB-73
Innerhofer, Franz 1944- DLB-85
Innis, Harold Adams 1894-1952 . . . . . DLB-88
Innis, Mary Quayle 1899-1972. . . . . . DLB-88
Inoue, Yasushi 1907-1991 . . . . . . DLB-181
International Publishers Company DLB-46
An Interview with David Rabe Y-91
An Interview with George Greenfield,
    Literary Agent Y-91
An Interview with James Ellroy. Y-91
Interview with Norman Mailer Y-97
An Interview with Peter S. Prescott. . . . Y-86
An Interview with Russell Hoban. Y-90
Interview with Stanley Burnshaw Y-97
An Interview with Tom Jenks. Y-86
"Into the Mirror," by
    Peter Cooley DLB-105
Introduction to Paul Laurence Dunbar,
    Lyrics of Lowly Life (1896),
    by William Dean Howells DLB-50
Introductory Essay: Letters of Percy Bysshe
    Shelley (1852), by Robert
    Browning DLB-32
Introductory Letters from the Second Edition
    of Pamela (1741), by Samuel
    Richardson DLB-39
Irving, John 1942- DLB-6; Y-82
Irving, Washington 1783-1859
    . . . . DLB-3, 11, 30, 59, 73, 74, 183, 186
Irwin, Grace 1907- DLB-68
Irwin, Will 1873-1948. . . . . DLB-25

Isherwood, Christopher
    1904-1986. . . . . DLB-15, 195; Y-86
Ishiguro, Kazuo 1954- DLB-194
Ishikawa, Jun 1899-1987. . . . . DLB-182
The Island Trees Case: A Symposium on
    School Library Censorship
    An Interview with Judith Krug
    An Interview with Phyllis Schlafly
    An Interview with Edward B. Jenkinson
    An Interview with Lamarr Mooneyham
    An Interview with Harriet
        Bernstein Y-82
Islas, Arturo 1938-1991 . . . . DLB-122
Ivanišević, Drago 1907-1981 . . . . . . DLB-181
Ivers, M. J., and Company DLB-49
Iwano, Hōmei 1873-1920 . . . . DLB-180
Iyayi, Festus 1947- DLB-157
Izumi, Kyōka 1873-1939. . . . . DLB-180

J

Jackmon, Marvin E. (see Marvin X)
Jacks, L. P. 1860-1955. . . . . DLB-135
Jackson, Angela 1951- DLB-41
Jackson, Helen Hunt
    1830-1885 . . . . . . DLB-42, 47, 186, 189
Jackson, Holbrook 1874-1948. . . . . . DLB-98
Jackson, Laura Riding 1901-1991 . . . . DLB-48
Jackson, Shirley 1919-1965 . . . . DLB-6
Jacob, Naomi 1884?-1964 . . . . DLB-191
Jacob, Piers Anthony Dillingham (see Anthony,
    Piers)
Jacobi, Friedrich Heinrich
    1743-1819 . . . . DLB-94
Jacobi, Johann Georg 1740-1841 . . . . DLB-97
Jacobs, Joseph 1854-1916 . . . . DLB-141
Jacobs, W. W. 1863-1943. . . . . DLB-135
Jacobs, George W., and Company . . . DLB-49
Jacobson, Dan 1929- DLB-14
Jaggard, William
    [publishing house] DLB-170
Jahier, Piero 1884-1966 . . . . DLB-114
Jahnn, Hans Henny
    1894-1959 . . . . DLB-56, 124
Jakes, John 1932- Y-83
James, C. L. R. 1901-1989 . . . . . . DLB-125
James Dickey Tributes Y-97
James, George P. R. 1801-1860. . . . . DLB-116
James Gould Cozzens—A View from
    Afar. Y-97
James Gould Cozzens Case Re-opened . . . Y-97
James Gould Cozzens: How to Read
    Him. Y-97
James, Henry
    1843-1916 . . . DLB-12, 71, 74, 189; DS-13

James, John circa 1633-1729 . . . . . . DLB-24	Jhabvala, Ruth Prawer 1927- . . DLB-139, 194	Johnston, Basil H. 1929- DLB-60
The James Jones Society Y-92	Jiménez, Juan Ramón 1881-1958 . . . . DLB-134	Johnston, Denis 1901-1984 . . . . DLB-10
James Laughlin Tributes Y-97	Joans, Ted 1928- DLB-16, 41	Johnston, George 1913- DLB-88
James, M. R. 1862-1936. . . . . DLB-156	John, Eugenie (see Marlitt, E.)	Johnston, Sir Harry 1858-1927 . . . . . DLB-174
James, P. D. 1920- DLB-87; DS-17	John of Dumbleton circa 1310-circa 1349 . . . . DLB-115	Johnston, Jennifer 1930- DLB-14
James, Will 1892-1942 . . . . DS-16	John Edward Bruce: Three Documents DLB-50	Johnston, Mary 1870-1936. . . . . DLB-9
James Joyce Centenary: Dublin, 1982. . . . Y-82	John O'Hara's Pottsville Journalism Y-88	Johnston, Richard Malcolm 1822-1898 . . . . DLB-74
James Joyce Conference Y-85	John Steinbeck Research Center Y-85	Johnstone, Charles 1719?-1800? DLB-39
James VI of Scotland, I of England 1566-1625. . . . . DLB-151, 172	John Updike on the Internet Y-97	Johst, Hanns 1890-1978 . . . . DLB-124
James, U. P. [publishing house] DLB-49	John Webster: The Melbourne Manuscript Y-86	Jolas, Eugene 1894-1952 . . . . DLB-4, 45
Jameson, Anna 1794-1860. . . . . DLB-99, 166	Johns, Captain W. E. 1893-1968 . . . . DLB-160	Jones, Alice C. 1853-1933 . . . . DLB-92
Jameson, Fredric 1934- DLB-67	Johnson, B. S. 1933-1973 . . . . . . DLB-14, 40	Jones, Charles C., Jr. 1831-1893 . . . . . DLB-30
Jameson, J. Franklin 1859-1937. . . . . . DLB-17	Johnson, Charles 1679-1748 . . . . . . DLB-84	Jones, D. G. 1929- DLB-53
Jameson, Storm 1891-1986 . . . . DLB-36	Johnson, Charles R. 1948- DLB-33	Jones, David 1895-1974 . . . . DLB-20, 100
Jančar, Drago 1948- DLB-181	Johnson, Charles S. 1893-1956. . . . DLB-51, 91	Jones, Diana Wynne 1934- DLB-161
Janés, Clara 1940- DLB-134	Johnson, Denis 1949- DLB-120	Jones, Ebenezer 1820-1860 . . . . DLB-32
Janevski, Slavko 1920- DLB-181	Johnson, Diane 1934- Y-80	Jones, Ernest 1819-1868. . . . . DLB-32
Jaramillo, Cleofas M. 1878-1956 . . . . DLB-122	Johnson, Edgar 1901- DLB-103	Jones, Gayl 1949- DLB-33
Jarman, Mark 1952- DLB-120	Johnson, Edward 1598-1672 . . . . . . DLB-24	Jones, George 1800-1870 . . . . DLB-183
Jarrell, Randall 1914-1965 . . . . . DLB-48, 52	Johnson E. Pauline (Tekahionwake) 1861-1913 . . . . DLB-175	Jones, Glyn 1905- DLB-15
Jarrold and Sons DLB-106	Johnson, Fenton 1888-1958. . . . . DLB-45, 50	Jones, Gwyn 1907- DLB-15, 139
Jarry, Alfred 1873-1907 . . . . DLB-192	Johnson, Georgia Douglas 1886-1966 . . . . DLB-51	Jones, Henry Arthur 1851-1929 . . . . . DLB-10
Jarves, James Jackson 1818-1888 . . . . DLB-189	Johnson, Gerald W. 1890-1980 . . . . . DLB-29	Jones, Hugh circa 1692-1760 . . . . . . DLB-24
Jasmin, Claude 1930- DLB-60	Johnson, Helene 1907- DLB-51	Jones, James 1921-1977 . . . DLB-2, 143; DS-17
Jay, John 1745-1829. . . . . DLB-31	Johnson, James Weldon 1871-1938 . . . . DLB-51	Jones, Jenkin Lloyd 1911- DLB-127
Jefferies, Richard 1848-1887. . . . . DLB-98, 141	Johnson, John H. 1918- DLB-137	Jones, LeRoi (see Baraka, Amiri)
Jeffers, Lance 1919-1985 . . . . DLB-41	Johnson, Linton Kwesi 1952- DLB-157	Jones, Lewis 1897-1939 . . . . DLB-15
Jeffers, Robinson 1887-1962 . . . . . . DLB-45	Johnson, Lionel 1867-1902 . . . . DLB-19	Jones, Madison 1925- DLB-152
Jefferson, Thomas 1743-1826 . . . . DLB-31, 183	Johnson, Nunnally 1897-1977 . . . . . . DLB-26	Jones, Major Joseph (see Thompson, William Tappan)
Jelinek, Elfriede 1946- DLB-85	Johnson, Owen 1878-1952 . . . . Y-87	Jones, Preston 1936-1979 . . . . DLB-7
Jellicoe, Ann 1927- DLB-13	Johnson, Pamela Hansford 1912- DLB-15	Jones, Rodney 1950- DLB-120
Jenkins, Elizabeth 1905- DLB-155	Johnson, Pauline 1861-1913 . . . . DLB-92	Jones, Sir William 1746-1794 . . . . . . DLB-109
Jenkins, Robin 1912- DLB-14	Johnson, Ronald 1935- DLB-169	Jones, William Alfred 1817-1900 . . . . . DLB-59
Jenkins, William Fitzgerald (see Leinster, Murray)	Johnson, Samuel 1696-1772. . . . . . . DLB-24	Jones's Publishing House DLB-49
Jenkins, Herbert, Limited DLB-112	Johnson, Samuel 1709-1784 . . . . . DLB-39, 95, 104, 142	Jong, Erica 1942- DLB-2, 5, 28, 152
Jennings, Elizabeth 1926- DLB-27	Johnson, Samuel 1822-1882 . . . . DLB-1	Jonke, Gert F. 1946- DLB-85
Jens, Walter 1923- DLB-69	Johnson, Uwe 1934-1984 . . . . DLB-75	Jonson, Ben 1572?-1637 . . . . . . DLB-62, 121
Jensen, Merrill 1905-1980 . . . . DLB-17	Johnson, Benjamin [publishing house] DLB-49	Jordan, June 1936- DLB-38
Jephson, Robert 1736-1803 . . . . DLB-89	Johnson, Benjamin, Jacob, and Robert [publishing house] DLB-49	Joseph, Jenny 1932- DLB-40
Jerome, Jerome K. 1859-1927 . . . . DLB-10, 34, 135	Johnson, Jacob, and Company DLB-49	Joseph, Michael, Limited DLB-112
Jerome, Judson 1927-1991 . . . . DLB-105	Johnson, Joseph [publishing house] . . . DLB-154	Josephson, Matthew 1899-1978 . . . . . . DLB-4
Jerrold, Douglas 1803-1857 . . . . DLB-158, 159	Johnston, Annie Fellows 1863-1931 . . . DLB-42	Josephus, Flavius 37-100 . . . . DLB-176
Jesse, F. Tennyson 1888-1958 . . . . . . DLB-77	Johnston, David Claypole 1798?-1865 . DLB-188	Josiah Allen's Wife (see Holley, Marietta)
Jewett, Sarah Orne 1849-1909 . . . . DLB-12, 74		Josipovici, Gabriel 1940- DLB-14
Jewett, John P., and Company. DLB-49		Josselyn, John ?-1675 . . . . DLB-24
The Jewish Publication Society DLB-49		Joudry, Patricia 1921- DLB-88
Jewitt, John Rodgers 1783-1821 . . . . . DLB-99		Jovine, Giuseppe 1922- DLB-128
Jewsbury, Geraldine 1812-1880 . . . . . DLB-21		Joyaux, Philippe (see Sollers, Philippe)
		Joyce, Adrien (see Eastman, Carol)

A Joyce (Con)Text: Danis Rose and the Remaking of *Ulysses* Y-97

Joyce, James 1882-1941 . . . . DLB-10, 19, 36, 162

Judd, Sylvester 1813-1853 . . . . DLB-1

Judd, Orange, Publishing Company DLB-49

Judith circa 930 . . . . DLB-146

Julian of Norwich 1342-circa 1420 . . . . DLB-1146

Julian Symons at Eighty Y-92

June, Jennie (see Croly, Jane Cunningham)

Jung, Franz 1888-1963 . . . . DLB-118

Jünger, Ernst 1895- DLB-56

Der jüngere Titurel circa 1275 . . . . . . DLB-138

Jung-Stilling, Johann Heinrich 1740-1817 . . . . DLB-94

Justice, Donald 1925- Y-83

The Juvenile Library (see Godwin, M. J., and Company)

K

Kacew, Romain (see Gary, Romain)

Kafka, Franz 1883-1924 . . . . DLB-81

Kahn, Roger 1927 . . . . DLB-171

Kaikō, Takeshi 1939-1989 . . . . DLB-182

Kaiser, Georg 1878-1945 . . . . DLB-124

Kaiserchronik circca 1147 . . . . DLB-148

Kaleb, Vjekoslav 1905- DLB-181

Kalechofsky, Roberta 1931- DLB-28

Kaler, James Otis 1848-1912 . . . . . . DLB-12

Kames, Henry Home, Lord 1696-1782 . . . . DLB-31, 104

Kandel, Lenore 1932- DLB-16

Kanin, Garson 1912- DLB-7

Kant, Hermann 1926- DLB-75

Kant, Immanuel 1724-1804 . . . . DLB-94

Kantemir, Antiokh Dmitrievich 1708-1744 . . . . DLB-150

Kantor, Mackinlay 1904-1977 . . . . DLB-9, 102

Kaplan, Fred 1937- DLB-111

Kaplan, Johanna 1942- DLB-28

Kaplan, Justin 1925- DLB-111

Kapnist, Vasilii Vasilevich 1758?-1823 . . . . DLB-150

Karadžić, Vuk Stefanović 1787-1864 . . . . DLB-147

Karamzin, Nikolai Mikhailovich 1766-1826 . . . . DLB-150

Karsch, Anna Louisa 1722-1791 . . . . DLB-97

Kasack, Hermann 1896-1966 . . . . . . DLB-69

Kasai, Zenzō 1887-1927 . . . . DLB-180

Kaschnitz, Marie Luise 1901-1974 . . . . DLB-69

Kaštelan, Jure 1919-1990 . . . . DLB-147

Kästner, Erich 1899-1974 . . . . DLB-56

Kattan, Naim 1928- DLB-53

Katz, Steve 1935- Y-83

Kauffman, Janet 1945- Y-86

Kauffmann, Samuel 1898-1971 . . . . . DLB-127

Kaufman, Bob 1925- DLB-16, 41

Kaufman, George S. 1889-1961 . . . . . DLB-7

Kavanagh, P. J. 1931- DLB-40

Kavanagh, Patrick 1904-1967 . . . . DLB-15, 20

Kawabata, Yasunari 1899-1972 . . . . . DLB-180

Kaye-Smith, Sheila 1887-1956 . . . . . . DLB-36

Kazin, Alfred 1915- DLB-67

Keane, John B. 1928- DLB-13

Keary, Annie 1825-1879 . . . . DLB-163

Keating, H. R. F. 1926- DLB-87

Keats, Ezra Jack 1916-1983 . . . . DLB-61

Keats, John 1795-1821 . . . . . . DLB-96, 110

Keble, John 1792-1866 . . . . DLB-32, 55

Keeble, John 1944- Y-83

Keeffe, Barrie 1945- DLB-13

Keeley, James 1867-1934 . . . . DLB-25

W. B. Keen, Cooke and Company DLB-49

Keillor, Garrison 1942- Y-87

Keith, Marian 1874?-1961 . . . . DLB-92

Keller, Gary D. 1943- DLB-82

Keller, Gottfried 1819-1890 . . . . . . DLB-129

Kelley, Edith Summers 1884-1956 . . . . DLB-9

Kelley, William Melvin 1937- DLB-33

Kellogg, Ansel Nash 1832-1886 . . . . . DLB-23

Kellogg, Steven 1941- DLB-61

Kelly, George 1887-1974 . . . . DLB-7

Kelly, Hugh 1739-1777 . . . . DLB-89

Kelly, Robert 1935- DLB-5, 130, 165

Kelly, Piet and Company DLB-49

Kelman, James 1946- DLB-194

Kelmscott Press DLB-112

Kemble, E. W. 1861-1933 . . . . DLB-188

Kemble, Fanny 1809-1893 . . . . DLB-32

Kemelman, Harry 1908- DLB-28

Kempe, Margery circa 1373-1438 . . . . DLB-146

Kempner, Friederike 1836-1904 . . . . . DLB-129

Kempowski, Walter 1929- DLB-75

Kendall, Claude [publishing company] . . DLB-46

Kendell, George 1809-1867 . . . . DLB-43

Kenedy, P. J., and Sons DLB-49

Kennan, George 1845-1924 . . . . . . DLB-189

Kennedy, Adrienne 1931- DLB-38

Kennedy, John Pendleton 1795-1870 . . . . DLB-3

Kennedy, Leo 1907- DLB-88

Kennedy, Margaret 1896-1967 . . . . . DLB-36

Kennedy, Patrick 1801-1873 . . . . . . DLB-159

Kennedy, Richard S. 1920- DLB-111

Kennedy, William 1928- DLB-143; Y-85

Kennedy, X. J. 1929- DLB-5

Kennelly, Brendan 1936- DLB-40

Kenner, Hugh 1923- DLB-67

Kennerley, Mitchell [publishing house] DLB-46

Kenneth Dale McCormick Tributes Y-97

Kenny, Maurice 1929- DLB-175

Kent, Frank R. 1877-1958 . . . . DLB-29

Kenyon, Jane 1947- DLB-120

Keough, Hugh Edmund 1864-1912 . . . DLB-171

Keppler and Schwartzmann DLB-49

Kerlan, Irvin 1912-1963 . . . . DLB-187

Kern, Jerome 1885-1945 . . . . DLB-187

Kerner, Justinus 1776-1862 . . . . DLB-90

Kerouac, Jack 1922-1969 . . . DLB-2, 16; DS-3

The Jack Kerouac Revival Y-95

Kerouac, Jan 1952- DLB-16

Kerr, Orpheus C. (see Newell, Robert Henry)

Kerr, Charles H., and Company DLB-49

Kesey, Ken 1935- DLB-2, 16

Kessel, Joseph 1898-1979 . . . . DLB-72

Kessel, Martin 1901- DLB-56

Kesten, Hermann 1900- DLB-56

Keun, Irmgard 1905-1982 . . . . DLB-69

Key and Biddle DLB-49

Keynes, John Maynard 1883-1946 . . . . . DS-10

Keyserling, Eduard von 1855-1918 . . . DLB-66

Khan, Ismith 1925- DLB-125

Khaytov, Nikolay 1919- DLB-181

Khemnitser, Ivan Ivanovich 1745-1784 . . . . DLB-150

Kheraskov, Mikhail Matveevich 1733-1807 . . . . DLB-150

Khristov, Boris 1945- DLB-181

Khvostov, Dmitrii Ivanovich 1757-1835 . . . . DLB-150

Kidd, Adam 1802?-1831 . . . . DLB-99

Kidd, William [publishing house] DLB-106

Kidder, Tracy 1945- DLB-185

Kiely, Benedict 1919- DLB-15

Kieran, John 1892-1981 . . . . DLB-171

Kiggins and Kellogg DLB-49

Kiley, Jed 1889-1962 . . . . DLB-4

Kilgore, Bernard 1908-1967 . . . . . . DLB-127

Killens, John Oliver 1916- DLB-33

Killigrew, Anne 1660-1685 . . . . . . DLB-131

Killigrew, Thomas 1612-1683 . . . . . . DLB-58	Klabund 1890-1928 . . . . DLB-66	Koeppen, Wolfgang 1906- DLB-69
Kilmer, Joyce 1886-1918 . . . . DLB-45	Klaj, Johann 1616-1656 . . . . DLB-164	Koertge, Ronald 1940- DLB-105
Kilwardby, Robert circa 1215-1279 . . . . DLB-115	Klappert, Peter 1942- DLB-5	Koestler, Arthur 1905-1983 . . . . Y-83
Kincaid, Jamaica 1949- DLB-157	Klass, Philip (see Tenn, William)	Kohn, John S. Van E. 1906-1976 and Papantonio, Michael 1907-1978 . . . DLB-187
King, Charles 1844-1933 . . . . DLB-186	Klein, A. M. 1909-1972 . . . . DLB-68	Kokoschka, Oskar 1886-1980 . . . . . . DLB-124
King, Clarence 1842-1901 . . . . DLB-12	Kleist, Ewald von 1715-1759 . . . . . . DLB-97	Kolb, Annette 1870-1967 . . . . DLB-66
King, Florence 1936 . . . . Y-85	Kleist, Heinrich von 1777-1811 . . . . . DLB-90	Kolbenheyer, Erwin Guido 1878-1962 . . . . DLB-66, 124
King, Francis 1923- DLB-15, 139	Klinger, Friedrich Maximilian 1752-1831 . . . . DLB-94	Kolleritsch, Alfred 1931- DLB-85
King, Grace 1852-1932 . . . . . . DLB-12, 78	Klopstock, Friedrich Gottlieb 1724-1803 . . . . DLB-97	Kolodny, Annette 1941- DLB-67
King, Henry 1592-1669 . . . . DLB-126	Klopstock, Meta 1728-1758 . . . . DLB-97	Komarov, Matvei circa 1730-1812 . . . . DLB-150
King, Stephen 1947- DLB-143; Y-80	Kluge, Alexander 1932- DLB-75	Komroff, Manuel 1890-1974 . . . . DLB-4
King, Thomas 1943- DLB-175	Knapp, Joseph Palmer 1864-1951 . . . . DLB-91	Komunyakaa, Yusef 1947- DLB-120
King, Woodie, Jr. 1937- DLB-38	Knapp, Samuel Lorenzo 1783-1838 . . . . DLB-59	Koneski, Blaže 1921-1993 . . . . DLB-181
King, Solomon [publishing house] DLB-49	Knapton, J. J. and P. [publishing house] DLB-154	Konigsburg, E. L. 1930- DLB-52
Kinglake, Alexander William 1809-1891 . . . . DLB-55, 166	Kniazhnin, Iakov Borisovich 1740-1791 . . . . DLB-150	Konrad von Würzburg circa 1230-1287 . . . . DLB-138
Kingsley, Charles 1819-1875 . . . . DLB-21, 32, 163, 178, 190	Knickerbocker, Diedrich (see Irving, Washington)	Konstantinov, Aleko 1863-1897 . . . . . DLB-147
Kingsley, Mary Henrietta 1862-1900 . . . . DLB-174	Knigge, Adolph Franz Friedrich Ludwig, Freiherr von 1752-1796 . . . . . . DLB-94	Kooser, Ted 1939- DLB-105
Kingsley, Henry 1830-1876 . . . . DLB-21	Knight, Damon 1922- DLB-8	Kopit, Arthur 1937- DLB-7
Kingsley, Sidney 1906- DLB-7	Knight, Etheridge 1931-1992 . . . . . . DLB-41	Kops, Bernard 1926?- DLB-13
Kingsmill, Hugh 1889-1949 . . . . . . DLB-149	Knight, John S. 1894-1981 . . . . DLB-29	Kornbluth, C. M. 1923-1958 . . . . DLB-8
Kingston, Maxine Hong 1940- DLB-173; Y-80	Knight, Sarah Kemble 1666-1727 . . . . DLB-24	Körner, Theodor 1791-1813 . . . . DLB-90
Kingston, William Henry Giles 1814-1880 . . . . DLB-163	Knight, Charles, and Company DLB-106	Kornfeld, Paul 1889-1942 . . . . DLB-118
Kinnell, Galway 1927- DLB-5; Y-87	Knight-Bruce, G. W. H. 1852-1896 . . . . DLB-174	Kosinski, Jerzy 1933-1991 . . . . . . DLB-2; Y-82
Kinsella, Thomas 1928- DLB-27	Knister, Raymond 1899-1932 . . . . . . DLB-68	Kosmač, Ciril 1910-1980 . . . . DLB-181
Kipling, Rudyard 1865-1936 . . . . . . DLB-19, 34, 141, 156	Knoblock, Edward 1874-1945 . . . . . . DLB-10	Kosovel, Srečko 1904-1926 . . . . DLB-147
Kipphardt, Heinar 1922-1982 . . . . . DLB-124	Knopf, Alfred A. 1892-1984 . . . . Y-84	Kostrov, Ermil Ivanovich 1755-1796 . . . . DLB-150
Kirby, William 1817-1906 . . . . DLB-99	Knopf, Alfred A. [publishing house] DLB-46	Kotzebue, August von 1761-1819 . . . . DLB-94
Kircher, Athanasius 1602-1680 . . . . . DLB-164	Knorr von Rosenroth, Christian 1636-1689 . . . . DLB-168	Kotzwinkle, William 1938- DLB-173
Kirk, John Foster 1824-1904 . . . . . . DLB-79	"Knots into Webs: Some Autobiographical Sources," by Dabney Stuart DLB-105	Kovačić, Ante 1854-1889 . . . . DLB-147
Kirkconnell, Watson 1895-1977 . . . . . DLB-68	Knowles, John 1926- DLB-6	Kovič, Kajetan 1931- DLB-181
Kirkland, Caroline M. 1801-1864 . . . . DLB-3, 73, 74; DS-13	Knox, Frank 1874-1944 . . . . DLB-29	Kraf, Elaine 1946- Y-81
Kirkland, Joseph 1830-1893 . . . . DLB-12	Knox, John circa 1514-1572 . . . . . . DLB-132	Kramer, Jane 1938- DLB-185
Kirkman, Francis [publishing house] DLB-170	Knox, John Armoy 1850-1906 . . . . . . DLB-23	Kramer, Mark 1944- DLB-185
Kirkpatrick, Clayton 1915- DLB-127	Knox, Ronald Arbuthnott 1888-1957 . . . . DLB-77	Kranjčević, Silvije Strahimir 1865-1908 . . . . DLB-147
Kirkup, James 1918- DLB-27	Knox, Thomas Wallace 1835-1896 . . . DLB-189	Krasna, Norman 1909-1984 . . . . DLB-26
Kirouac, Conrad (see Marie-Victorin, Frère)	Kobayashi, Takiji 1903-1933 . . . . . . DLB-180	Kraus, Hans Peter 1907-1988 . . . . . . DLB-187
Kirsch, Sarah 1935- DLB-75	Kober, Arthur 1900-1975 . . . . DLB-11	Kraus, Karl 1874-1936 . . . . DLB-118
Kirst, Hans Hellmut 1914-1989 . . . . . DLB-69	Kocbek, Edvard 1904-1981 . . . . DLB-147	Krauss, Ruth 1911-1993 . . . . DLB-52
Kiš, Danilo 1935-1989 . . . . DLB-181	Koch, Howard 1902- DLB-26	Kreisel, Henry 1922- DLB-88
Kita, Morio 1927- DLB-182	Koch, Kenneth 1925- DLB-5	Kreuder, Ernst 1903-1972 . . . . DLB-69
Kitcat, Mabel Greenhow 1859-1922 . . . . DLB-135	Kōda, Rohan 1867-1947 . . . . DLB-180	Kreymborg, Alfred 1883-1966 . . . . DLB-4, 54
Kitchin, C. H. B. 1895-1967 . . . . . . DLB-77	Koenigsberg, Moses 1879-1945 . . . . . DLB-25	Krieger, Murray 1923- DLB-67
Kizer, Carolyn 1925- DLB-5, 169		Krim, Seymour 1922-1989 . . . . DLB-16
		Krleža, Miroslav 1893-1981 . . . . DLB-147
		Krock, Arthur 1886-1974 . . . . DLB-29
		Kroetsch, Robert 1927- ‰DLB-53

Krutch, Joseph Wood 1893-1970 .... DLB-63
Krylov, Ivan Andreevich 1769-1844 .... DLB-150
Kubin, Alfred 1877-1959 .... DLB-81
Kubrick, Stanley 1928- DLB-26
Kudrun circa 1230-1240 .... DLB-138
Kuffstein, Hans Ludwig von 1582-1656 .... DLB-164
Kuhlmann, Quirinus 1651-1689 .... DLB-168
Kuhnau, Johann 1660-1722 .... DLB-168
Kumin, Maxine 1925- DLB-5
Kunene, Mazisi 1930- DLB-117
Kunikida, Doppo 1869-1908 ...... DLB-180
Kunitz, Stanley 1905- DLB-48
Kunjufu, Johari M. (see Amini, Johari M.)
Kunnert, Gunter 1929- DLB-75
Kunze, Reiner 1933- DLB-75
Kupferberg, Tuli 1923- DLB-16
Kurahashi, Yumiko 1935- DLB-182
Kureishi, Hanif 1954- DLB-194
Kürnberger, Ferdinand 1821-1879 .... DLB-129
Kurz, Isolde 1853-1944 .... DLB-66
Kusenberg, Kurt 1904-1983 .... DLB-69
Kuttner, Henry 1915-1958 .... DLB-8
Kyd, Thomas 1558-1594 .... DLB-62
Kyffin, Maurice circa 1560?-1598 .... DLB-136
Kyger, Joanne 1934- DLB-16
Kyne, Peter B. 1880-1957 .... DLB-78

L

L. E. L. (see Landon, Letitia Elizabeth)
Laberge, Albert 1871-1960 .... DLB-68
Laberge, Marie 1950- DLB-60
Labiche, Eugène 1815-1888 .... DLB-192
La Capria, Raffaele 1922- DLB-196
Lacombe, Patrice (see Trullier-Lacombe, Joseph Patrice)
Lacretelle, Jacques de 1888-1985 ..... DLB-65
Lacy, Sam 1903- DLB-171
Ladd, Joseph Brown 1764-1786 ..... DLB-37
La Farge, Oliver 1901-1963 .... DLB-9
Lafferty, R. A. 1914- DLB-8
La Flesche, Francis 1857-1932 ..... DLB-175
Lagorio, Gina 1922- DLB-196
La Guma, Alex 1925-1985 .... DLB-117
Lahaise, Guillaume (see Delahaye, Guy)
Lahontan, Louis-Armand de Lom d'Arce, Baron de 1666-1715? DLB-99
Laing, Kojo 1946- DLB-157

Laird, Carobeth 1895- Y-82
Laird and Lee DLB-49
Lalić, Ivan V. 1931-1996 .... DLB-181
Lalić, Mihailo 1914-1992 .... DLB-181
Lalonde, Michèle 1937- DLB-60
Lamantia, Philip 1927- DLB-16
Lamb, Charles 1775-1834 .... DLB-93, 107, 163
Lamb, Lady Caroline 1785-1828 .... DLB-116
Lamb, Mary 1764-1874 .... DLB-163
Lambert, Betty 1933-1983 .... DLB-60
Lamming, George 1927- DLB-125
L'Amour, Louis 1908?- Y-80
Lampman, Archibald 1861-1899 .... DLB-92
Lamson, Wolffe and Company DLB-49
Lancer Books DLB-46
Landesman, Jay 1919- and Landesman, Fran 1927- DLB-16
Landolfi, Tommaso 1908-1979 ..... DLB-177
Landon, Letitia Elizabeth 1802-1838 ... DLB-96
Landor, Walter Savage 1775-1864 .... DLB-93, 107
Landry, Napoléon-P. 1884-1956 ..... DLB-92
Lane, Charles 1800-1870 .... DLB-1
Lane, Laurence W. 1890-1967 ..... DLB-91
Lane, M. Travis 1934- DLB-60
Lane, Patrick 1939- DLB-53
Lane, Pinkie Gordon 1923- DLB-41
Lane, John, Company DLB-49
Laney, Al 1896-1988 .... DLB-4, 171
Lang, Andrew 1844-1912 ... DLB-98, 141, 184
Langevin, André 1927- DLB-60
Langgässer, Elisabeth 1899-1950 .... DLB-69
Langhorne, John 1735-1779 ...... DLB-109
Langland, William circa 1330-circa 1400 .... DLB-146
Langton, Anna 1804-1893 .... DLB-99
Lanham, Edwin 1904-1979 .... DLB-4
Lanier, Sidney 1842-1881 .... DLB-64; DS-13
Lanyer, Aemilia 1569-1645 ...... DLB-121
Lapointe, Gatien 1931-1983 .... DLB-88
Lapointe, Paul-Marie 1929- DLB-88
Lardner, John 1912-1960 .... DLB-171
Lardner, Ring 1885-1933 ... DLB-11, 25, 86, 171; DS-16
Lardner, Ring, Jr. 1915- DLB-26
Lardner 100: Ring Lardner Centennial Symposium Y-85
Larkin, Philip 1922-1985 .... DLB-27
La Roche, Sophie von 1730-1807 .... DLB-94
La Rocque, Gilbert 1943-1984 ..... DLB-60
Laroque de Roquebrune, Robert (see Roquebrune, Robert de)

Larrick, Nancy 1910- DLB-61
Larsen, Nella 1893-1964 .... DLB-51
Lasker-Schüler, Else 1869-1945 .... DLB-66, 124
Lasnier, Rina 1915- DLB-88
Lassalle, Ferdinand 1825-1864 ..... DLB-129
Lathrop, Dorothy P. 1891-1980 .... DLB-22
Lathrop, George Parsons 1851-1898 .... DLB-71
Lathrop, John, Jr. 1772-1820 ...... DLB-37
Latimer, Hugh 1492?-1555 .... DLB-136
Latimore, Jewel Christine McLawler (see Amini, Johari M.)
Latymer, William 1498-1583 ...... DLB-132
Laube, Heinrich 1806-1884 .... DLB-133
Laughlin, James 1914- DLB-48
Laumer, Keith 1925- DLB-8
Lauremberg, Johann 1590-1658 .... DLB-164
Laurence, Margaret 1926-1987 .... DLB-53
Laurentius von Schnüffis 1633-1702 .... DLB-168
Laurents, Arthur 1918- DLB-26
Laurie, Annie (see Black, Winifred)
Laut, Agnes Christiana 1871-1936 .... DLB-92
Lauterbach, Ann 1942- DLB-193
Lavater, Johann Kaspar 1741-1801 .... DLB-97
Lavin, Mary 1912- DLB-15
Lawes, Henry 1596-1662 .... DLB-126
Lawless, Anthony (see MacDonald, Philip)
Lawrence, D. H. 1885-1930 ... DLB-10, 19, 36, 98, 162, 195
Lawrence, David 1888-1973 ...... DLB-29
Lawrence, Seymour 1926-1994 ...... Y-94
Lawrence, T. E. 1888-1935 ...... DLB-195
Lawson, John ?-1711 .... DLB-24
Lawson, Robert 1892-1957 .... DLB-22
Lawson, Victor F. 1850-1925 ..... DLB-25
Layard, Sir Austen Henry 1817-1894 .... DLB-166
Layton, Irving 1912- DLB-88
LaZamon flourished circa 1200 ..... DLB-146
Lazarević, Laza K. 1851-1890 ..... DLB-147
Lea, Henry Charles 1825-1909 ..... DLB-47
Lea, Sydney 1942- DLB-120
Lea, Tom 1907- DLB-6
Leacock, John 1729-1802 .... DLB-31
Leacock, Stephen 1869-1944 ..... DLB-92
Lead, Jane Ward 1623-1704 ...... DLB-131
Leadenhall Press DLB-106
Leapor, Mary 1722-1746 .... DLB-109
Lear, Edward 1812-1888 ... DLB-32, 163, 166
Leary, Timothy 1920-1996 .... DLB-16

Leary, W. A., and Company DLB-49
Léautaud, Paul 1872-1956 . . . . DLB-65
Leavitt, David 1961- DLB-130
Leavitt and Allen DLB-49
Le Blond, Mrs. Aubrey
  1861-1934 . . . . DLB-174
le Carré, John 1931- DLB-87
Lécavelé, Roland (see Dorgeles, Roland)
Lechlitner, Ruth 1901- DLB-48
Leclerc, Félix 1914- DLB-60
Le Clézio, J. M. G. 1940- DLB-83
Lectures on Rhetoric and Belles Lettres (1783),
  by Hugh Blair [excerpts] DLB-31
Leder, Rudolf (see Hermlin, Stephan)
Lederer, Charles 1910-1976 . . . . . . DLB-26
Ledwidge, Francis 1887-1917 . . . . . DLB-20
Lee, Dennis 1939- DLB-53
Lee, Don L. (see Madhubuti, Haki R.)
Lee, George W. 1894-1976 . . . . . . DLB-51
Lee, Harper 1926- DLB-6
Lee, Harriet (1757-1851) and
  Lee, Sophia (1750-1824) DLB-39
Lee, Laurie 1914- DLB-27
Lee, Li-Young 1957- DLB-165
Lee, Manfred B. (see Dannay, Frederic, and
  Manfred B. Lee)
Lee, Nathaniel circa 1645 - 1692 . . . DLB-80
Lee, Sir Sidney 1859-1926 . . . . DLB-149, 184
Lee, Sir Sidney, "Principles of Biography," in
  Elizabethan and Other Essays DLB-149
Lee, Vernon
  1856-1935 . . . . DLB-57, 153, 156, 174, 178
Lee and Shepard DLB-49
Le Fanu, Joseph Sheridan
  1814-1873 . . . . DLB-21, 70, 159, 178
Leffland, Ella 1931- Y-84
le Fort, Gertrud von 1876-1971 . . . . DLB-66
Le Gallienne, Richard 1866-1947 . . . . DLB-4
Legaré, Hugh Swinton
  1797-1843 . . . . DLB-3, 59, 73
Legaré, James M. 1823-1859 . . . . . . DLB-3
The Legends of the Saints and a Medieval
  Christian Worldview DLB-148
Léger, Antoine-J. 1880-1950 . . . . . . DLB-88
Le Guin, Ursula K. 1929- DLB-8, 52
Lehman, Ernest 1920- DLB-44
Lehmann, John 1907- DLB-27, 100
Lehmann, Rosamond 1901-1990 . . . . DLB-15
Lehmann, Wilhelm 1882-1968 . . . . . DLB-56
Lehmann, John, Limited DLB-112
Leiber, Fritz 1910-1992 . . . . DLB-8
Leibniz, Gottfried Wilhelm
  1646-1716 . . . . DLB-168

Leicester University Press DLB-112
Leigh, W. R. 1866-1955 . . . . DLB-188
Leinster, Murray 1896-1975 . . . . . . DLB-8
Leisewitz, Johann Anton
  1752-1806 . . . . DLB-94
Leitch, Maurice 1933- DLB-14
Leithauser, Brad 1943- DLB-120
Leland, Charles G. 1824-1903 . . . . . DLB-11
Leland, John 1503?-1552 . . . . DLB-136
Lemay, Pamphile 1837-1918 . . . . . . DLB-99
Lemelin, Roger 1919- DLB-88
Lemercier, Louis-Jean-Népomucène
  1771-1840 . . . . DLB-192
Lemon, Mark 1809-1870 . . . . DLB-163
Le Moine, James MacPherson
  1825-1912 . . . . DLB-99
Le Moyne, Jean 1913- DLB-88
Lemperly, Paul 1858-1939 . . . . DLB-187
L'Engle, Madeleine 1918- DLB-52
Lennart, Isobel 1915-1971 . . . . DLB-44
Lennox, Charlotte
  1729 or 1730-1804 . . . . DLB-39
Lenox, James 1800-1880 . . . . DLB-140
Lenski, Lois 1893-1974 . . . . DLB-22
Lenz, Hermann 1913- DLB-69
Lenz, J. M. R. 1751-1792 . . . . DLB-94
Lenz, Siegfried 1926- DLB-75
Leonard, Elmore 1925- DLB-173
Leonard, Hugh 1926- DLB-13
Leonard, William Ellery
  1876-1944 . . . . DLB-54
Leonowens, Anna 1834-1914 . . . . DLB-99, 166
LePan, Douglas 1914- DLB-88
Leprohon, Rosanna Eleanor
  1829-1879 . . . . DLB-99
Le Queux, William 1864-1927 . . . . . DLB-70
Lerner, Max 1902-1992 . . . . DLB-29
Lernet-Holenia, Alexander
  1897-1976 . . . . DLB-85
Le Rossignol, James 1866-1969 . . . . . DLB-92
Lescarbot, Marc circa 1570-1642 . . . . DLB-99
LeSeur, William Dawson
  1840-1917 . . . . DLB-92
LeSieg, Theo. (see Geisel, Theodor Seuss)
Leslie, Doris before 1902-1982 . . . . . DLB-191
Leslie, Frank 1821-1880 . . . . . . DLB-43, 79
Leslie, Frank, Publishing House DLB-49
Lesperance, John 1835?-1891 . . . . . . DLB-99
Lessing, Bruno 1870-1940 . . . . DLB-28
Lessing, Doris 1919- DLB-15, 139; Y-85
Lessing, Gotthold Ephraim
  1729-1781 . . . . DLB-97
Lettau, Reinhard 1929- DLB-75

Letter from Japan Y-94
Letter from London Y-96
Letter to [Samuel] Richardson on Clarissa
  (1748), by Henry Fielding DLB-39
A Letter to the Editor of The Irish
  Times Y-97
Lever, Charles 1806-1872 . . . . DLB-21
Leverson, Ada 1862-1933 . . . . DLB-153
Levertov, Denise 1923- DLB-5, 165
Levi, Peter 1931- DLB-40
Levi, Primo 1919-1987 . . . . DLB-177
Levien, Sonya 1888-1960 . . . . DLB-44
Levin, Meyer 1905-1981 . . . . DLB-9, 28; Y-81
Levine, Norman 1923- DLB-88
Levine, Philip 1928- DLB-5
Levis, Larry 1946- DLB-120
Levy, Amy 1861-1889 . . . . DLB-156
Levy, Benn Wolfe
  1900-1973 . . . . DLB-13; Y-81
Lewald, Fanny 1811-1889 . . . . DLB-129
Lewes, George Henry
  1817-1878 . . . . DLB-55, 144
Lewis, Agnes Smith 1843-1926 . . . . . DLB-174
Lewis, Alfred H. 1857-1914 . . . . DLB-25, 186
Lewis, Alun 1915-1944 . . . . DLB-20, 162
Lewis, C. Day (see Day Lewis, C.)
Lewis, C. S. 1898-1963 . . . . DLB-15, 100, 160
Lewis, Charles B. 1842-1924 . . . . . . DLB-11
Lewis, Henry Clay 1825-1850 . . . . . . DLB-3
Lewis, Janet 1899- Y-87
Lewis, Matthew Gregory
  1775-1818 . . . . DLB-39, 158, 178
Lewis, Meriwether 1774-1809 and
  Clark, William 1770-1838 . . . DLB-183, 186
Lewis, R. W. B. 1917- DLB-111
Lewis, Richard circa 1700-1734 . . . . DLB-24
Lewis, Sinclair
  1885-1951 . . . . DLB-9, 102; DS-1
Lewis, Wilmarth Sheldon
  1895-1979 . . . . DLB-140
Lewis, Wyndham 1882-1957 . . . . . . DLB-15
Lewisohn, Ludwig
  1882-1955 . . . . DLB-4, 9, 28, 102
Leyendecker, J. C. 1874-1951 . . . . . . DLB-188
Lezama Lima, José 1910-1976 . . . . . DLB-113
The Library of America DLB-46
The Licensing Act of 1737 . . . . DLB-84
Lichfield, Leonard I
  [publishing house] DLB-170
Lichtenberg, Georg Christoph
  1742-1799 . . . . DLB-94
The Liddle Collection Y-97
Lieb, Fred 1888-1980 . . . . DLB-171
Liebling, A. J. 1904-1963 . . . . . . DLB-4, 171

Lieutenant Murray (see Ballou, Maturin Murray)

Lighthall, William Douw 1857-1954 .... DLB-92

Lilar, Françoise (see Mallet-Joris, Françoise)

Lillo, George 1691-1739 .... DLB-84

Lilly, J. K., Jr. 1893-1966 .... DLB-140

Lilly, Wait and Company DLB-49

Lily, William circa 1468-1522 ...... DLB-132

Limited Editions Club DLB-46

Lincoln and Edmands DLB-49

Lindsay, Alexander William, Twenty-fifth Earl of Crawford 1812-1880 .... DLB-184

Lindsay, Jack 1900- Y-84

Lindsay, Sir David circa 1485-1555 .... DLB-132

Lindsay, Vachel 1879-1931 .... DLB-54

Linebarger, Paul Myron Anthony (see Smith, Cordwainer)

Link, Arthur S. 1920- DLB-17

Linn, John Blair 1777-1804 .... DLB-37

Lins, Osman 1924-1978 .... DLB-145

Linton, Eliza Lynn 1822-1898 ..... DLB-18

Linton, William James 1812-1897 ... DLB-32

Lintot, Barnaby Bernard [publishing house] DLB-170

Lion Books DLB-46

Lionni, Leo 1910- DLB-61

Lippincott, Sara Jane Clarke 1823-1904 .... DLB-43

Lippincott, J. B., Company DLB-49

Lippmann, Walter 1889-1974 ..... DLB-29

Lipton, Lawrence 1898-1975 ...... DLB-16

Liscow, Christian Ludwig 1701-1760 .... DLB-97

Lish, Gordon 1934- DLB-130

Lispector, Clarice 1925-1977 ..... DLB-113

The Literary Chronicle and Weekly Review 1819-1828 .... DLB-110

Literary Documents: William Faulkner and the People-to-People Program Y-86

Literary Documents II: *Library Journal* Statements and Questionnaires from First Novelists Y-87

Literary Effects of World War II [British novel] DLB-15

Literary Prizes [British] DLB-15

Literary Research Archives: The Humanities Research Center, University of Texas Y-82

Literary Research Archives II: Berg Collection of English and American Literature of the New York Public Library Y-83

Literary Research Archives III: The Lilly Library Y-84

Literary Research Archives IV: The John Carter Brown Library Y-85

Literary Research Archives V: Kent State Special Collections Y-86

Literary Research Archives VI: The Modern Literary Manuscripts Collection in the Special Collections of the Washington University Libraries Y-87

Literary Research Archives VII: The University of Virginia Libraries Y-91

Literary Research Archives VIII: The Henry E. Huntington Library Y-92

"Literary Style" (1857), by William Forsyth [excerpt] DLB-57

Literatura Chicanesca: The View From Without DLB-82

Literature at Nurse, or Circulating Morals (1885), by George Moore DLB-18

Littell, Eliakim 1797-1870 .... DLB-79

Littell, Robert S. 1831-1896 ...... DLB-79

Little, Brown and Company DLB-49

Little Magazines and Newspapers DS-15

The Little Review 1914-1929 .... DS-15

Littlewood, Joan 1914- DLB-13

Lively, Penelope 1933- DLB-14, 161

Liverpool University Press DLB-112

The Lives of the Poets DLB-142

Livesay, Dorothy 1909- DLB-68

Livesay, Florence Randal 1874-1953 .... DLB-92

"Living in Ruin," by Gerald Stern ... DLB-105

Livings, Henry 1929- DLB-13

Livingston, Anne Howe 1763-1841 .... DLB-37

Livingston, Myra Cohn 1926- DLB-61

Livingston, William 1723-1790 .... DLB-31

Livingstone, David 1813-1873 ..... DLB-166

Liyong, Taban lo (see Taban lo Liyong)

Lizárraga, Sylvia S. 1925- DLB-82

Llewellyn, Richard 1906-1983 .... DLB-15

Lloyd, Edward [publishing house] DLB-106

Lobel, Arnold 1933- DLB-61

Lochridge, Betsy Hopkins (see Fancher, Betsy)

Locke, David Ross 1833-1888 .... DLB-11, 23

Locke, John 1632-1704 ...... DLB-31, 101

Locke, Richard Adams 1800-1871 ... DLB-43

Locker-Lampson, Frederick 1821-1895 .... DLB-35, 184

Lockhart, John Gibson 1794-1854 .... DLB-110, 116 144

Lockridge, Ross, Jr. 1914-1948 .... DLB-143; Y-80

Locrine and *Selimus* DLB-62

Lodge, David 1935- DLB-14, 194

Lodge, George Cabot 1873-1909 .... DLB-54

Lodge, Henry Cabot 1850-1924 .... DLB-47

Lodge, Thomas 1558-1625 .... DLB-172

Loeb, Harold 1891-1974 .... DLB-4

Loeb, William 1905-1981 .... DLB-127

Lofting, Hugh 1886-1947 .... DLB-160

Logan, James 1674-1751 ...... DLB-24, 140

Logan, John 1923- DLB-5

Logan, William 1950- DLB-120

Logau, Friedrich von 1605-1655 .... DLB-164

Logue, Christopher 1926- DLB-27

Lohenstein, Daniel Casper von 1635-1683 .... DLB-168

Lomonosov, Mikhail Vasil'evich 1711-1765 .... DLB-150

London, Jack 1876-1916 ..... DLB-8, 12, 78

The London Magazine 1820-1829 .... DLB-110

Long, Haniel 1888-1956 .... DLB-45

Long, Ray 1878-1935 .... DLB-137

Long, H., and Brother DLB-49

Longfellow, Henry Wadsworth 1807-1882 .... DLB-1, 59

Longfellow, Samuel 1819-1892 ..... DLB-1

Longford, Elizabeth 1906- DLB-155

Longinus circa first century DLB-176

Longley, Michael 1939- DLB-40

Longman, T. [publishing house] DLB-154

Longmans, Green and Company DLB-49

Longmore, George 1793?-1867 ..... DLB-99

Longstreet, Augustus Baldwin 1790-1870 .... DLB-3, 11, 74

Longworth, D. [publishing house] ... DLB-49

Lonsdale, Frederick 1881-1954 ..... DLB-10

A Look at the Contemporary Black Theatre Movement DLB-38

Loos, Anita 1893-1981 ..... DLB-11, 26; Y-81

Lopate, Phillip 1943- Y-80

López, Diana (see Isabella, Ríos)

Loranger, Jean-Aubert 1896-1942 .... DLB-92

Lorca, Federico García 1898-1936 ... DLB-108

Lord, John Keast 1818-1872 ...... DLB-99

The Lord Chamberlain's Office and Stage Censorship in England DLB-10

Lorde, Audre 1934-1992 .... DLB-41

Lorimer, George Horace 1867-1939 .... DLB-91

Loring, A. K. [publishing house] DLB-49

Loring and Mussey DLB-46

Lossing, Benson J. 1813-1891 ..... DLB-30

Lothar, Ernst 1890-1974 .... DLB-81

Lothrop, Harriet M. 1844-1924 .... DLB-42

Lothrop, D., and Company DLB-49

Loti, Pierre 1850-1923 . . . . DLB-123

Lotichius Secundus, Petrus 1528-1560 . . . . DLB-179

Lott, Emeline ?-? DLB-166

The Lounger, no. 20 (1785), by Henry Mackenzie DLB-39

Louisiana State University Press Y-97

Lounsbury, Thomas R. 1838-1915 . . . . DLB-71

Louÿs, Pierre 1870-1925 . . . . DLB-123

Lovelace, Earl 1935- DLB-125

Lovelace, Richard 1618-1657 . . . . . . DLB-131

Lovell, Coryell and Company DLB-49

Lovell, John W., Company DLB-49

Lover, Samuel 1797-1868 . . . . . DLB-159, 190

Lovesey, Peter 1936- DLB-87

Lovingood, Sut (see Harris, George Washington)

Low, Samuel 1765-? DLB-37

Lowell, Amy 1874-1925 . . . . . . DLB-54, 140

Lowell, James Russell 1819-1891 . . . . . DLB-1, 11, 64, 79, 189

Lowell, Robert 1917-1977 . . . . . DLB-5, 169

Lowenfels, Walter 1897-1976 . . . . DLB-4

Lowndes, Marie Belloc 1868-1947 . . . . DLB-70

Lowndes, William Thomas 1798-1843 . . . . DLB-184

Lownes, Humphrey [publishing house] DLB-170

Lowry, Lois 1937- DLB-52

Lowry, Malcolm 1909-1957 . . . . DLB-15

Lowther, Pat 1935-1975 . . . . DLB-53

Loy, Mina 1882-1966 . . . . DLB-4, 54

Lozeau, Albert 1878-1924 . . . . DLB-92

Lubbock, Percy 1879-1965 . . . . DLB-149

Lucas, E. V. 1868-1938 . . . . DLB-98, 149, 153

Lucas, Fielding, Jr. [publishing house] DLB-49

Luce, Henry R. 1898-1967 . . . . DLB-91

Luce, John W., and Company DLB-46

Lucian circa 120-180 . . . . DLB-176

Lucie-Smith, Edward 1933- DLB-40

Lucini, Gian Pietro 1867-1914 . . . . . DLB-114

Luder, Peter circa 1415-1472 . . . . . . DLB-179

Ludlum, Robert 1927- Y-82

Ludus de Antichristo circa 1160 . . . . . DLB-148

Ludvigson, Susan 1942- DLB-120

Ludwig, Jack 1922- DLB-60

Ludwig, Otto 1813-1865 . . . . DLB-129

Ludwigslied 881 or 882 . . . . DLB-148

Luera, Yolanda 1953- DLB-122

Luft, Lya 1938- DLB-145

Luke, Peter 1919- DLB-13

Lummis, Charles F. 1859-1928 . . . . . DLB-186

Lupton, F. M., Company DLB-49

Lupus of Ferrières circa 805-circa 862 . . . . DLB-148

Lurie, Alison 1926- DLB-2

Luther, Martin 1483-1546 . . . . DLB-179

Luzi, Mario 1914- DLB-128

L'vov, Nikolai Aleksandrovich 1751-1803 . . . . DLB-150

Lyall, Gavin 1932- DLB-87

Lydgate, John circa 1370-1450 . . . . . DLB-146

Lyly, John circa 1554-1606 . . . . DLB-62, 167

Lynch, Patricia 1898-1972 . . . . DLB-160

Lynch, Richard flourished 1596-1601 . . . . DLB-172

Lynd, Robert 1879-1949 . . . . DLB-98

Lyon, Matthew 1749-1822 . . . . DLB-43

Lysias circa 459 B.C.-circa 380 B.C. DLB-176

Lytle, Andrew 1902-1995 . . . . . DLB-6; Y-95

Lytton, Edward (see Bulwer-Lytton, Edward)

Lytton, Edward Robert Bulwer 1831-1891 . . . . DLB-32

M

Maass, Joachim 1901-1972 . . . . DLB-69

Mabie, Hamilton Wright 1845-1916 . . . . DLB-71

Mac A'Ghobhainn, Iain (see Smith, Iain Crichton)

MacArthur, Charles 1895-1956 . . . . DLB-7, 25, 44

Macaulay, Catherine 1731-1791 . . . . DLB-104

Macaulay, David 1945- DLB-61

Macaulay, Rose 1881-1958 . . . . DLB-36

Macaulay, Thomas Babington 1800-1859 . . . . DLB-32, 55

Macaulay Company DLB-46

MacBeth, George 1932- DLB-40

Macbeth, Madge 1880-1965 . . . . . . DLB-92

MacCaig, Norman 1910- DLB-27

MacDiarmid, Hugh 1892-1978 . . . . . DLB-20

MacDonald, Cynthia 1928- DLB-105

MacDonald, George 1824-1905 . . . . DLB-18, 163, 178

MacDonald, John D. 1916-1986 . . . . DLB-8; Y-86

MacDonald, Philip 1899?-1980 . . . . DLB-77

Macdonald, Ross (see Millar, Kenneth)

MacDonald, Wilson 1880-1967 . . . . . DLB-92

Macdonald and Company (Publishers) DLB-112

MacEwen, Gwendolyn 1941- DLB-53

Macfadden, Bernarr 1868-1955 . . . . DLB-25, 91

MacGregor, John 1825-1892 . . . . . . DLB-166

MacGregor, Mary Esther (see Keith, Marian)

Machado, Antonio 1875-1939 . . . . . DLB-108

Machado, Manuel 1874-1947 . . . . . DLB-108

Machar, Agnes Maule 1837-1927 . . . . DLB-92

Machen, Arthur Llewelyn Jones 1863-1947 . . . . DLB-36, 156, 178

MacInnes, Colin 1914-1976 . . . . . . DLB-14

MacInnes, Helen 1907-1985 . . . . . . DLB-87

Mack, Maynard 1909- DLB-111

Mackall, Leonard L. 1879-1937 . . . . DLB-140

MacKaye, Percy 1875-1956 . . . . . . DLB-54

Macken, Walter 1915-1967 . . . . . . DLB-13

Mackenzie, Alexander 1763-1820 . . . . DLB-99

Mackenzie, Alexander Slidell 1803-1848 . . . . DLB-183

Mackenzie, Compton 1883-1972 . . . . DLB-34, 100

Mackenzie, Henry 1745-1831 . . . . . DLB-39

Mackenzie, William 1758-1828 . . . . DLB-187

Mackey, Nathaniel 1947- DLB-169

Mackey, William Wellington 1937- DLB-38

Mackintosh, Elizabeth (see Tey, Josephine)

Mackintosh, Sir James 1765-1832 . . . . DLB-158

Maclaren, Ian (see Watson, John)

Macklin, Charles 1699-1797 . . . . . . DLB-89

MacLean, Katherine Anne 1925- DLB-8

MacLeish, Archibald 1892-1982 . . . . DLB-4, 7, 45; Y-82

MacLennan, Hugh 1907-1990 . . . . . DLB-68

Macleod, Fiona (see Sharp, William)

MacLeod, Alistair 1936- DLB-60

Macleod, Norman 1906-1985 . . . . . . DLB-4

Mac Low, Jackson 1922- DLB-193

Macmillan and Company DLB-106

The Macmillan Company DLB-49

Macmillan's English Men of Letters, First Series (1878-1892) DLB-144

MacNamara, Brinsley 1890-1963 . . . . DLB-10

MacNeice, Louis 1907-1963 . . . . DLB-10, 20

MacPhail, Andrew 1864-1938 . . . . . DLB-92

Macpherson, James 1736-1796 . . . . DLB-109

Macpherson, Jay 1931- DLB-53

Macpherson, Jeanie 1884-1946 . . . . . DLB-44

Macrae Smith Company DLB-46

Macrone, John [publishing house] DLB-106

MacShane, Frank 1927- DLB-111

Macy-Masius DLB-46

Madden, David 1933- DLB-6
Madden, Sir Frederic 1801-1873 .... DLB-184
Maddow, Ben 1909-1992 .... DLB-44
Maddux, Rachel 1912-1983 .... Y-93
Madgett, Naomi Long 1923- DLB-76
Madhubuti, Haki R.
    1942- DLB-5, 41; DS-8
Madison, James 1751-1836 .... DLB-37
Maeterlinck, Maurice 1862-1949 .... DLB-192
Magee, David 1905-1977 .... DLB-187
Maginn, William 1794-1842 .... DLB-110, 159
Mahan, Alfred Thayer 1840-1914 .... DLB-47
Maheux-Forcier, Louise 1929- DLB-60
Mafūz, Najīb 1911- Y-88
Mahin, John Lee 1902-1984 .... DLB-44
Mahon, Derek 1941- DLB-40
Maikov, Vasilii Ivanovich
    1728-1778 .... DLB-150
Mailer, Norman 1923- ....
    DLB-2, 16, 28, 185; Y-80, Y-83; DS-3
Maillart, Ella 1903-1997 .... DLB-195
Maillet, Adrienne 1885-1963 .... DLB-68
Maimonides, Moses 1138-1204 ..... DLB-115
Maillet, Antonine 1929- DLB-60
Maillu, David G. 1939- DLB-157
Main Selections of the Book-of-the-Month
    Club, 1926-1945 .... DLB-9
Main Trends in Twentieth-Century Book Clubs
    .... DLB-46
Mainwaring, Daniel 1902-1977 ..... DLB-44
Mair, Charles 1838-1927 .... DLB-99
Mais, Roger 1905-1955 .... DLB-125
Major, Andre 1942- DLB-60
Major, Clarence 1936- DLB-33
Major, Kevin 1949- DLB-60
Major Books DLB-46
Makemie, Francis circa 1658-1708 .... DLB-24
The Making of a People, by
    J. M. Ritchie DLB-66
Maksimović, Desanka 1898-1993 .... DLB-147
Malamud, Bernard
    1914-1986 .... DLB-2, 28, 152; Y-80, Y-86
Malerba, Luigi 1927- DLB-196
Malet, Lucas 1852-1931 .... DLB-153
Malleson, Lucy Beatrice (see Gilbert, Anthony)
Mallet-Joris, Françoise 1930- DLB-83
Mallock, W. H. 1849-1923 ...... DLB-18, 57
Malone, Dumas 1892-1986 .... DLB-17
Malone, Edmond 1741-1812 ...... DLB-142
Malory, Sir Thomas
    circa 1400-1410 - 1471 .... DLB-146
Malraux, André 1901-1976 .... DLB-72

Malthus, Thomas Robert
    1766-1834 .... DLB-107, 158
Maltz, Albert 1908-1985 .... DLB-102
Malzberg, Barry N. 1939- DLB-8
Mamet, David 1947- DLB-7
Manaka, Matsemela 1956- DLB-157
Manchester University Press DLB-112
Mandel, Eli 1922- DLB-53
Mandeville, Bernard 1670-1733 .... DLB-101
Mandeville, Sir John
    mid fourteenth century DLB-146
Mandiargues, André Pieyre de
    1909- DLB-83
Manfred, Frederick 1912-1994 ...... DLB-6
Manfredi, Gianfranco 1948- DLB-196
Mangan, Sherry 1904-1961 .... DLB-4
Manganelli, Giorgio 1922-1990 ... DLB-196
Mankiewicz, Herman 1897-1953 ... DLB-26
Mankiewicz, Joseph L. 1909-1993 .... DLB-44
Mankowitz, Wolf 1924- DLB-15
Manley, Delarivière
    1672?-1724 .... DLB-39, 80
Mann, Abby 1927- DLB-44
Mann, Heinrich 1871-1950 ..... DLB-66, 118
Mann, Horace 1796-1859 .... DLB-1
Mann, Klaus 1906-1949 .... DLB-56
Mann, Thomas 1875-1955 .... DLB-66
Mann, William D'Alton
    1839-1920 .... DLB-137
Mannin, Ethel 1900-1984 .... DLB-191, 195
Manning, Marie 1873?-1945 ...... DLB-29
Manning and Loring DLB-49
Mannyng, Robert
    flourished 1303-1338 .... DLB-146
Mano, D. Keith 1942- DLB-6
Manor Books DLB-46
Mansfield, Katherine 1888-1923 ..... DLB-162
Manuel, Niklaus circa 1484-1530 .... DLB-179
Manzini, Gianna 1896-1974 ...... DLB-177
Mapanje, Jack 1944- DLB-157
Maraini, Dacia 1936- DLB-196
March, William 1893-1954 ...... DLB-9, 86
Marchand, Leslie A. 1900- DLB-103
Marchant, Bessie 1862-1941 ..... DLB-160
Marchessault, Jovette 1938- DLB-60
Marcus, Frank 1928- DLB-13
Marden, Orison Swett
    1850-1924 .... DLB-137
Marechera, Dambudzo
    1952-1987 .... DLB-157
Marek, Richard, Books DLB-46
Mares, E. A. 1938- DLB-122
Mariani, Paul 1940- DLB-111

Marie-Victorin, Frère 1885-1944 .... DLB-92
Marin, Biagio 1891-1985 .... DLB-128
Marincović, Ranko 1913- DLB-147
Marinetti, Filippo Tommaso
    1876-1944 .... DLB-114
Marion, Frances 1886-1973 ...... DLB-44
Marius, Richard C. 1933- Y-85
The Mark Taper Forum DLB-7
Mark Twain on Perpetual Copyright Y-92
Markfield, Wallace 1926- DLB-2, 28
Markham, Edwin 1852-1940 .... DLB-54, 186
Markle, Fletcher 1921-1991 .... DLB-68; Y-91
Marlatt, Daphne 1942- DLB-60
Marlitt, E. 1825-1887 .... DLB-129
Marlowe, Christopher 1564-1593 .... DLB-62
Marlyn, John 1912- DLB-88
Marmion, Shakerley 1603-1639 .... DLB-58
Der Marner
    before 1230-circa 1287 ...... DLB-138
The Marprelate Tracts 1588-1589 .... DLB-132
Marquand, John P. 1893-1960 .... DLB-9, 102
Marqués, René 1919-1979 ...... DLB-113
Marquis, Don 1878-1937 ...... DLB-11, 25
Marriott, Anne 1913- DLB-68
Marryat, Frederick 1792-1848 .... DLB-21, 163
Marsh, George Perkins
    1801-1882 .... DLB-1, 64
Marsh, James 1794-1842 .... DLB-1, 59
Marsh, Capen, Lyon and Webb DLB-49
Marsh, Ngaio 1899-1982 .... DLB-77
Marshall, Edison 1894-1967 ..... DLB-102
Marshall, Edward 1932- DLB-16
Marshall, Emma 1828-1899 ..... DLB-163
Marshall, James 1942-1992 ...... DLB-61
Marshall, Joyce 1913- DLB-88
Marshall, Paule 1929- DLB-33, 157
Marshall, Tom 1938- DLB-60
Marsilius of Padua
    circa 1275-circa 1342 .... DLB-115
Marson, Una 1905-1965 .... DLB-157
Marston, John 1576-1634 ..... DLB-58, 172
Marston, Philip Bourke 1850-1887 .... DLB-35
Martens, Kurt 1870-1945 .... DLB-66
Martien, William S.
    [publishing house] DLB-49
Martin, Abe (see Hubbard, Kin)
Martin, Charles 1942- DLB-120
Martin, Claire 1914- DLB-60
Martin, Jay 1935- DLB-111
Martin, Johann (see Laurentius von Schnüffis)
Martin, Violet Florence (see Ross, Martin)

Martin du Gard, Roger
  1881-1958 . . . . DLB-65

Martineau, Harriet 1802-1876
  . . . . . DLB-21, 55, 159, 163, 166, 190

Martínez, Eliud 1935- DLB-122

Martínez, Max 1943- DLB-82

Martyn, Edward 1859-1923 . . . . DLB-10

Marvell, Andrew 1621-1678 . . . . . . DLB-131

Marvin X 1944- DLB-38

Marx, Karl 1818-1883 . . . . DLB-129

Marzials, Theo 1850-1920 . . . . DLB-35

Masefield, John
  1878-1967 . . . . . DLB-10, 19, 153, 160

Mason, A. E. W. 1865-1948 . . . . . . DLB-70

Mason, Bobbie Ann
  1940- DLB-173; Y-87

Mason, William 1725-1797 . . . . . . DLB-142

Mason Brothers DLB-49

Massey, Gerald 1828-1907 . . . . DLB-32

Massey, Linton R. 1900-1974 . . . . . DLB-187

Massinger, Philip 1583-1640 . . . . . . DLB-58

Masson, David 1822-1907 . . . . DLB-144

Masters, Edgar Lee 1868-1950 . . . . . DLB-54

Mastronardi, Lucio 1930-1979 . . . . DLB-177

Matevski, Mateja 1929- DLB-181

Mather, Cotton
  1663-1728 . . . . DLB-24, 30, 140

Mather, Increase 1639-1723 . . . . . . DLB-24

Mather, Richard 1596-1669 . . . . . . DLB-24

Matheson, Richard 1926- . . . DLB-8, 44

Matheus, John F. 1887- DLB-51

Mathews, Cornelius
  1817?-1889 . . . . DLB-3, 64

Mathews, John Joseph
  1894-1979 . . . . DLB-175

Mathews, Elkin
  [publishing house] DLB-112

Mathias, Roland 1915- DLB-27

Mathis, June 1892-1927 . . . . DLB-44

Mathis, Sharon Bell 1937- DLB-33

Matković, Marijan 1915-1985 . . . . . DLB-181

Matoš, Antun Gustav 1873-1914 . . . . DLB-147

Matsumoto, Seichō 1909-1992 . . . . . DLB-182

The Matter of England
  1240-1400 . . . . DLB-146

The Matter of Rome
  early twelfth to late fifteenth
  century DLB-146

Matthews, Brander
  1852-1929 . . . . DLB-71, 78; DS-13

Matthews, Jack 1925- DLB-6

Matthews, William 1942- DLB-5

Matthiessen, F. O. 1902-1950 . . . . . DLB-63

Maturin, Charles Robert
  1780-1824 . . . . DLB-178

Matthiessen, Peter 1927- DLB-6, 173

Maugham, W. Somerset
  1874-1965 . . DLB-10, 36, 77, 100, 162, 195

Maupassant, Guy de 1850-1893 . . . . DLB-123

Mauriac, Claude 1914- DLB-83

Mauriac, François 1885-1970 . . . . . . DLB-65

Maurice, Frederick Denison
  1805-1872 . . . . DLB-55

Maurois, André 1885-1967 . . . . DLB-65

Maury, James 1718-1769 . . . . DLB-31

Mavor, Elizabeth 1927- DLB-14

Mavor, Osborne Henry (see Bridie, James)

Maxwell, William 1908- Y-80

Maxwell, H. [publishing house] DLB-49

Maxwell, John [publishing house] . . . DLB-106

May, Elaine 1932- DLB-44

May, Karl 1842-1912 . . . . DLB-129

May, Thomas 1595 or 1596-1650 . . . . DLB-58

Mayer, Bernadette 1945- DLB-165

Mayer, Mercer 1943- DLB-61

Mayer, O. B. 1818-1891 . . . . DLB-3

Mayes, Herbert R. 1900-1987 . . . . . DLB-137

Mayes, Wendell 1919-1992 . . . . . . DLB-26

Mayfield, Julian 1928-1984 . . . . DLB-33; Y-84

Mayhew, Henry 1812-1887 . . DLB-18, 55, 190

Mayhew, Jonathan 1720-1766 . . . . . DLB-31

Mayne, Jasper 1604-1672 . . . . DLB-126

Mayne, Seymour 1944- DLB-60

Mayor, Flora Macdonald
  1872-1932 . . . . DLB-36

Mayrocker, Friederike 1924- DLB-85

Mazrui, Ali A. 1933- DLB-125

Mažuranić, Ivan 1814-1890 . . . . . . DLB-147

Mazursky, Paul 1930- DLB-44

McAlmon, Robert
  1896-1956 . . . . DLB-4, 45; DS-15

McArthur, Peter 1866-1924 . . . . . . DLB-92

McBride, Robert M., and
  Company DLB-46

McCabe, Patrick 1955- DLB-194

McCaffrey, Anne 1926- DLB-8

McCarthy, Cormac 1933- DLB-6, 143

McCarthy, Mary 1912-1989 . . . . . DLB-2; Y-81

McCay, Winsor 1871-1934 . . . . DLB-22

McClane, Albert Jules 1922-1991 . . . DLB-171

McClatchy, C. K. 1858-1936 . . . . . . DLB-25

McClellan, George Marion
  1860-1934 . . . . DLB-50

McCloskey, Robert 1914- DLB-22

McClung, Nellie Letitia 1873-1951 . . . DLB-92

McClure, Joanna 1930- DLB-16

McClure, Michael 1932- DLB-16

McClure, Phillips and Company DLB-46

McClure, S. S. 1857-1949 . . . . DLB-91

McClurg, A. C., and Company DLB-49

McCluskey, John A., Jr. 1944- DLB-33

McCollum, Michael A. 1946- Y-87

McConnell, William C. 1917- DLB-88

McCord, David 1897- DLB-61

McCorkle, Jill 1958- Y-87

McCorkle, Samuel Eusebius
  1746-1811 . . . . DLB-37

McCormick, Anne O'Hare
  1880-1954 . . . . DLB-29

McCormick, Robert R. 1880-1955 . . . DLB-29

McCourt, Edward 1907-1972 . . . . . . DLB-88

McCoy, Horace 1897-1955 . . . . DLB-9

McCrae, John 1872-1918 . . . . DLB-92

McCullagh, Joseph B. 1842-1896 . . . . DLB-23

McCullers, Carson
  1917-1967 . . . . DLB-2, 7, 173

McCulloch, Thomas 1776-1843 . . . . . DLB-99

McDonald, Forrest 1927- DLB-17

McDonald, Walter
  1934- DLB-105, DS-9

McDougall, Colin 1917-1984 . . . . . . DLB-68

McDowell, Obolensky DLB-46

McEwan, Ian 1948- DLB-14, 194

McFadden, David 1940- DLB-60

McFall, Frances Elizabeth Clarke
  (see Grand, Sarah)

McFarlane, Leslie 1902-1977 . . . . . . DLB-88

McFee, William 1881-1966 . . . . . . DLB-153

McGahern, John 1934- DLB-14

McGee, Thomas D'Arcy
  1825-1868 . . . . DLB-99

McGeehan, W. O. 1879-1933 . . . DLB-25, 171

McGill, Ralph 1898-1969 . . . . DLB-29

McGinley, Phyllis 1905-1978 . . . . DLB-11, 48

McGinniss, Joe 1942- DLB-185

McGirt, James E. 1874-1930 . . . . . . DLB-50

McGlashan and Gill DLB-106

McGough, Roger 1937- DLB-40

McGraw-Hill DLB-46

McGuane, Thomas 1939- DLB-2; Y-80

McGuckian, Medbh 1950- DLB-40

McGuffey, William Holmes
  1800-1873 . . . . DLB-42

McIlvanney, William 1936- DLB-14

McIlwraith, Jean Newton
  1859-1938 . . . . DLB-92

McIntyre, James 1827-1906 . . . . . . DLB-99

McIntyre, O. O. 1884-1938 . . . . . . DLB-25

McKay, Claude
1889-1948 . . . . DLB-4, 45, 51, 117

The David McKay Company DLB-49

McKean, William V. 1820-1903 . . . . DLB-23

The McKenzie Trust Y-96

McKinley, Robin 1952- DLB-52

McLachlan, Alexander 1818-1896 . . . . DLB-99

McLaren, Floris Clark 1904-1978 . . . . DLB-68

McLaverty, Michael 1907- DLB-15

McLean, John R. 1848-1916 . . . . . . DLB-23

McLean, William L. 1852-1931 . . . . . DLB-25

McLennan, William 1856-1904 . . . . . DLB-92

McLoughlin Brothers DLB-49

McLuhan, Marshall 1911-1980 . . . . . DLB-88

McMaster, John Bach 1852-1932 . . . . DLB-47

McMurtry, Larry
1936- DLB-2, 143; Y-80, Y-87

McNally, Terrence 1939- DLB-7

McNeil, Florence 1937- DLB-60

McNeile, Herman Cyril
1888-1937 . . . . DLB-77

McNickle, D'Arcy 1904-1977 . . . . . DLB-175

McPhee, John 1931- DLB-185

McPherson, James Alan 1943- DLB-38

McPherson, Sandra 1943- Y-86

McWhirter, George 1939- DLB-60

McWilliams, Carey 1905-1980 . . . . . DLB-137

Mead, L. T. 1844-1914 . . . . DLB-141

Mead, Matthew 1924- DLB-40

Mead, Taylor ?- DLB-16

Meany, Tom 1903-1964 . . . . DLB-171

Mechthild von Magdeburg
circa 1207-circa 1282 . . . . DLB-138

Medill, Joseph 1823-1899 . . . . DLB-43

Medoff, Mark 1940- DLB-7

Meek, Alexander Beaufort
1814-1865 . . . . DLB-3

Meeke, Mary ?-1816? DLB-116

Meinke, Peter 1932- DLB-5

Mejia Vallejo, Manuel 1923- DLB-113

Melanchthon, Philipp 1497-1560 . . . . DLB-179

Melançon, Robert 1947- DLB-60

Mell, Max 1882-1971 . . . . DLB-81, 124

Mellow, James R. 1926- DLB-111

Meltzer, David 1937- DLB-16

Meltzer, Milton 1915- DLB-61

Melville, Elizabeth, Lady Culross
circa 1585-1640 . . . . DLB-172

Melville, Herman 1819-1891 . . . . DLB-3, 74

Memoirs of Life and Literature (1920),
by W. H. Mallock [excerpt] DLB-57

Menander 342-341 B.C.-circa 292-291 B.C.
. . . . DLB-176

Menantes (see Hunold, Christian Friedrich)

Mencke, Johann Burckhard
1674-1732 . . . . DLB-168

Mencken, H. L.
1880-1956 . . . . . . DLB-11, 29, 63, 137

Mencken and Nietzsche: An Unpublished Excerpt
from H. L. Mencken's My Life
as Author and Editor Y-93

Mendelssohn, Moses 1729-1786 . . . . DLB-97

Méndez M., Miguel 1930- DLB-82

Mens Rea (or Something) Y-97

The Mercantile Library of
New York Y-96

Mercer, Cecil William (see Yates, Dornford)

Mercer, David 1928-1980 . . . . DLB-13

Mercer, John 1704-1768 . . . . DLB-31

Meredith, George
1828-1909 . . . . . . DLB-18, 35, 57, 159

Meredith, Louisa Anne
1812-1895 . . . . DLB-166

Meredith, Owen (see Lytton, Edward Robert Bulwer)

Meredith, William 1919- DLB-5

Mergerle, Johann Ulrich
(see Abraham ä Sancta Clara)

Mérimée, Prosper 1803-1870 . . . DLB-119, 192

Merivale, John Herman
1779-1844 . . . . DLB-96

Meriwether, Louise 1923- DLB-33

Merlin Press DLB-112

Merriam, Eve 1916-1992 . . . . DLB-61

The Merriam Company DLB-49

Merrill, James
1926-1995 . . . . DLB-5, 165; Y-85

Merrill and Baker DLB-49

The Mershon Company DLB-49

Merton, Thomas 1915-1968 . . . . DLB-48; Y-81

Merwin, W. S. 1927- DLB-5, 169

Messner, Julian [publishing house] . . . DLB-46

Metcalf, J. [publishing house] DLB-49

Metcalf, John 1938- DLB-60

The Methodist Book Concern DLB-49

Methuen and Company DLB-112

Mew, Charlotte 1869-1928 . . . . DLB-19, 135

Mewshaw, Michael 1943- Y-80

Meyer, Conrad Ferdinand 1825-1898 . . . DLB-129

Meyer, E. Y. 1946- DLB-75

Meyer, Eugene 1875-1959 . . . . . . DLB-29

Meyer, Michael 1921- DLB-155

Meyers, Jeffrey 1939- DLB-111

Meynell, Alice 1847-1922 . . . . . DLB-19, 98

Meynell, Viola 1885-1956 . . . . . . DLB-153

Meyrink, Gustav 1868-1932 . . . . . . DLB-81

Michael M. Rea and the Rea Award for the
Short Story Y-97

Michaels, Leonard 1933- DLB-130

Micheaux, Oscar 1884-1951 . . . . . . DLB-50

Michel of Northgate, Dan
circa 1265-circa 1340 . . . . DLB-146

Micheline, Jack 1929- DLB-16

Michener, James A. 1907?- DLB-6

Micklejohn, George
circa 1717-1818 . . . . DLB-31

Middle English Literature:
An Introduction DLB-146

The Middle English Lyric DLB-146

Middle Hill Press DLB-106

Middleton, Christopher 1926- DLB-40

Middleton, Richard 1882-1911 . . . . DLB-156

Middleton, Stanley 1919- DLB-14

Middleton, Thomas 1580-1627 . . . . . DLB-58

Miegel, Agnes 1879-1964 . . . . DLB-56

Mihailović, Dragoslav 1930- DLB-181

Mihalić, Slavko 1928- DLB-181

Miles, Josephine 1911-1985 . . . . . . DLB-48

Miliković, Branko 1934-1961 . . . . . DLB-181

Milius, John 1944- DLB-44

Mill, James 1773-1836 . . . . . . DLB-107, 158

Mill, John Stuart 1806-1873 . . . . DLB-55, 190

Millar, Kenneth
1915-1983 . . . . DLB-2; Y-83; DS-6

Millar, Andrew
[publishing house] DLB-154

Millay, Edna St. Vincent
1892-1950 . . . . DLB-45

Miller, Arthur 1915- DLB-7

Miller, Caroline 1903-1992 . . . . DLB-9

Miller, Eugene Ethelbert 1950- DLB-41

Miller, Heather Ross 1939- DLB-120

Miller, Henry 1891-1980 . . . . . DLB-4, 9; Y-80

Miller, Hugh 1802-1856 . . . . DLB-190

Miller, J. Hillis 1928- DLB-67

Miller, James [publishing house] DLB-49

Miller, Jason 1939- DLB-7

Miller, Joaquin 1839-1913 . . . . . . DLB-186

Miller, May 1899- DLB-41

Miller, Paul 1906-1991 . . . . DLB-127

Miller, Perry 1905-1963 . . . . . . DLB-17, 63

Miller, Sue 1943- DLB-143

Miller, Vassar 1924- DLB-105

Miller, Walter M., Jr. 1923- DLB-8

Miller, Webb 1892-1940 . . . . DLB-29

Millhauser, Steven 1943- DLB-2

Millican, Arthenia J. Bates
1920- DLB-38

Mills and Boon DLB-112

Milman, Henry Hart 1796-1868 . . . . . DLB-96
Milne, A. A.
   1882-1956 . . . . . . DLB-10, 77, 100, 160
Milner, Ron 1938- DLB-38
Milner, William
   [publishing house] DLB-106
Milnes, Richard Monckton (Lord Houghton)
   1809-1885 . . . . DLB-32, 184
Milton, John 1608-1674 . . . . . DLB-131, 151
Minakami, Tsutomu 1919- DLB-182
The Minerva Press DLB-154
Minnesang circa 1150-1280 . . . . DLB-138
Minns, Susan 1839-1938 . . . . DLB-140
Minor Illustrators, 1880-1914 . . . . . . DLB-141
Minor Poets of the Earlier Seventeenth
   Century DLB-121
Minton, Balch and Company DLB-46
Mirbeau, Octave 1848-1917 . . . . DLB-123, 192
Mirk, John died after 1414? DLB-146
Miron, Gaston 1928- DLB-60
A Mirror for Magistrates DLB-167
Mishima, Yukio 1925-1970 . . . . DLB-182
Mitchel, Jonathan 1624-1668 . . . . . . DLB-24
Mitchell, Adrian 1932- DLB-40
Mitchell, Donald Grant
   1822-1908 . . . . DLB-1; DS-13
Mitchell, Gladys 1901-1983 . . . . DLB-77
Mitchell, James Leslie 1901-1935 . . . . DLB-15
Mitchell, John (see Slater, Patrick)
Mitchell, John Ames 1845-1918 . . . . . DLB-79
Mitchell, Joseph 1908-1996 . . . . DLB-185; Y-96
Mitchell, Julian 1935- DLB-14
Mitchell, Ken 1940- DLB-60
Mitchell, Langdon 1862-1935 . . . . . . DLB-7
Mitchell, Loften 1919- DLB-38
Mitchell, Margaret 1900-1949 . . . . . . DLB-9
Mitchell, W. O. 1914- DLB-88
Mitchison, Naomi Margaret (Haldane)
   1897- DLB-160, 191
Mitford, Mary Russell
   1787-1855 . . . . DLB-110, 116
Mitford, Nancy 1904-1973 . . . . DLB-191
Mittelholzer, Edgar 1909-1965 . . . . . . DLB-117
Mitterer, Erika 1906- DLB-85
Mitterer, Felix 1948- DLB-124
Mitternacht, Johann Sebastian
   1613-1679 . . . . DLB-168
Miyamoto, Yuriko 1899-1951 . . . . . . DLB-180
Mizener, Arthur 1907-1988 . . . . DLB-103
Mo, Timothy 1950- DLB-194
Modern Age Books DLB-46
"Modern English Prose" (1876),
   by George Saintsbury DLB-57

The Modern Language Association of America
   Celebrates Its Centennial Y-84
The Modern Library DLB-46
"Modern Novelists – Great and Small" (1855), by
   Margaret Oliphant DLB-21
"Modern Style" (1857), by Cockburn
   Thomson [excerpt] DLB-57
The Modernists (1932),
   by Joseph Warren Beach DLB-36
Modiano, Patrick 1945- DLB-83
Moffat, Yard and Company DLB-46
Moffet, Thomas 1553-1604 . . . . . . DLB-136
Mohr, Nicholasa 1938- DLB-145
Moix, Ana María 1947- DLB-134
Molesworth, Louisa 1839-1921 . . . . . DLB-135
Möllhausen, Balduin 1825-1905 . . . . DLB-129
Momaday, N. Scott 1934- DLB-143, 175
Monkhouse, Allan 1858-1936 . . . . . . DLB-10
Monro, Harold 1879-1932 . . . . DLB-19
Monroe, Harriet 1860-1936 . . . . . DLB-54, 91
Monsarrat, Nicholas 1910-1979 . . . . . DLB-15
Montagu, Lady Mary Wortley
   1689-1762 . . . . DLB-95, 101
Montague, John 1929- DLB-40
Montale, Eugenio 1896-1981 . . . . . . DLB-114
Monterroso, Augusto 1921- DLB-145
Montgomerie, Alexander
   circa 1550?-1598 . . . . DLB-167
Montgomery, James
   1771-1854 . . . . DLB-93, 158
Montgomery, John 1919- DLB-16
Montgomery, Lucy Maud
   1874-1942 . . . . DLB-92; DS-14
Montgomery, Marion 1925- DLB-6
Montgomery, Robert Bruce (see Crispin, Edmund)
Montherlant, Henry de 1896-1972 . . . . DLB-72
The Monthly Review 1749-1844 . . . . . DLB-110
Montigny, Louvigny de 1876-1955 . . . DLB-92
Montoya, José 1932- DLB-122
Moodie, John Wedderburn Dunbar
   1797-1869 . . . . DLB-99
Moodie, Susanna 1803-1885 . . . . . . DLB-99
Moody, Joshua circa 1633-1697 . . . . . DLB-24
Moody, William Vaughn
   1869-1910 . . . . DLB-7, 54
Moorcock, Michael 1939- DLB-14
Moore, Catherine L. 1911- DLB-8
Moore, Clement Clarke 1779-1863 . . . DLB-42
Moore, Dora Mavor 1888-1979 . . . . . DLB-92
Moore, George
   1852-1933 . . . . . . DLB-10, 18, 57, 135
Moore, Marianne
   1887-1972 . . . . DLB-45; DS-7
Moore, Mavor 1919- DLB-88

Moore, Richard 1927- DLB-105
Moore, T. Sturge 1870-1944 . . . . . . DLB-19
Moore, Thomas 1779-1852 . . . . DLB-96, 144
Moore, Ward 1903-1978 . . . . DLB-8
Moore, Wilstach, Keys and
   Company DLB-49
The Moorland-Spingarn Research
   Center DLB-76
Moorman, Mary C. 1905-1994 . . . . . DLB-155
Moraga, Cherríe 1952- DLB-82
Morales, Alejandro 1944- DLB-82
Morales, Mario Roberto 1947- DLB-145
Morales, Rafael 1919- DLB-108
Morality Plays: *Mankind* circa 1450-1500 and
   Everyman circa 1500 . . . . DLB-146
Morante, Elsa 1912-1985 . . . . DLB-177
Morata, Olympia Fulvia
   1526-1555 . . . . DLB-179
Moravia, Alberto 1907-1990 . . . . . . DLB-177
Mordaunt, Elinor 1872-1942 . . . . . . DLB-174
More, Hannah
   1745-1833 . . . . . DLB-107, 109, 116, 158
More, Henry 1614-1687 . . . . DLB-126
More, Sir Thomas
   1477 or 1478-1535 . . . . DLB-136
Moreno, Dorinda 1939- DLB-122
Morency, Pierre 1942- DLB-60
Moretti, Marino 1885-1979 . . . . . . DLB-114
Morgan, Berry 1919- DLB-6
Morgan, Charles 1894-1958 . . . . DLB-34, 100
Morgan, Edmund S. 1916- DLB-17
Morgan, Edwin 1920- DLB-27
Morgan, John Pierpont
   1837-1913 . . . . DLB-140
Morgan, John Pierpont, Jr.
   1867-1943 . . . . DLB-140
Morgan, Robert 1944- DLB-120
Morgan, Sydney Owenson, Lady
   1776?-1859 . . . . DLB-116, 158
Morgner, Irmtraud 1933- DLB-75
Morhof, Daniel Georg
   1639-1691 . . . . DLB-164
Mori, Ōgai 1862-1922 . . . . DLB-180
Morier, James Justinian
   1782 or 1783?-1849 . . . . DLB-116
Mörike, Eduard 1804-1875 . . . . . . DLB-133
Morin, Paul 1889-1963 . . . . DLB-92
Morison, Richard 1514?-1556 . . . . . DLB-136
Morison, Samuel Eliot 1887-1976 . . . . DLB-17
Moritz, Karl Philipp 1756-1793 . . . . . DLB-94
Moriz von Craûn
   circa 1220-1230 . . . . DLB-138
Morley, Christopher 1890-1957 . . . . . DLB-9
Morley, John 1838-1923 . . . . DLB-57, 144, 190

Morris, George Pope 1802-1864 . . . . . DLB-73
Morris, Lewis 1833-1907 . . . . DLB-35
Morris, Richard B. 1904-1989 . . . . . . DLB-17
Morris, William
   1834-1896 . . DLB-18, 35, 57, 156, 178, 184
Morris, Willie 1934- Y-80
Morris, Wright 1910- DLB-2; Y-81
Morrison, Arthur 1863-1945 . . . . DLB-70, 135
Morrison, Charles Clayton
   1874-1966 . . . . DLB-91
Morrison, Toni
   1931- DLB-6, 33, 143; Y-81, Y-93
Morrow, William, and Company DLB-46
Morse, James Herbert 1841-1923 . . . . DLB-71
Morse, Jedidiah 1761-1826 . . . . DLB-37
Morse, John T., Jr. 1840-1937 . . . . . . DLB-47
Morselli, Guido 1912-1973 . . . . DLB-177
Mortimer, Favell Lee 1802-1878 . . . . DLB-163
Mortimer, John 1923- DLB-13
Morton, Carlos 1942- DLB-122
Morton, H. V. 1892-1979 . . . . DLB-195
Morton, John P., and Company DLB-49
Morton, Nathaniel 1613-1685 . . . . . . DLB-24
Morton, Sarah Wentworth
   1759-1846 . . . . DLB-37
Morton, Thomas
   circa 1579-circa 1647 . . . . DLB-24
Moscherosch, Johann Michael
   1601-1669 . . . . DLB-164
Moseley, Humphrey
   [publishing house] DLB-170
Möser, Justus 1720-1794 . . . . DLB-97
Mosley, Nicholas 1923- DLB-14
Moss, Arthur 1889-1969 . . . . DLB-4
Moss, Howard 1922-1987 . . . . DLB-5
Moss, Thylias 1954- DLB-120
The Most Powerful Book Review in America
   [*New York Times Book Review*] Y-82
Motion, Andrew 1952- DLB-40
Motley, John Lothrop
   1814-1877 . . . . DLB-1, 30, 59
Motley, Willard 1909-1965 . . . . DLB-76, 143
Motte, Benjamin Jr.
   [publishing house] DLB-154
Motteux, Peter Anthony
   1663-1718 . . . . DLB-80
Mottram, R. H. 1883-1971 . . . . DLB-36
Mouré, Erin 1955- DLB-60
Mourning Dove (Humishuma)
   between 1882 and 1888?-1936 . . . . DLB-175
Movies from Books, 1920-1974 . . . . . DLB-9
Mowat, Farley 1921- DLB-68
Mowbray, A. R., and Company,
   Limited DLB-106

Mowrer, Edgar Ansel 1892-1977 . . . . DLB-29
Mowrer, Paul Scott 1887-1971 . . . . . DLB-29
Moxon, Edward
   [publishing house] DLB-106
Moxon, Joseph
   [publishing house] DLB-170
Mphahlele, Es'kia (Ezekiel)
   1919- DLB-125
Mtshali, Oswald Mbuyiseni
   1940- DLB-125
Mucedorus DLB-62
Mudford, William 1782-1848 . . . . . . DLB-159
Mueller, Lisel 1924- DLB-105
Muhajir, El (see Marvin X)
Muhajir, Nazzam Al Fitnah (see Marvin X)
Mühlbach, Luise 1814-1873 . . . . . . DLB-133
Muir, Edwin 1887-1959 . . . . DLB-20, 100, 191
Muir, Helen 1937- DLB-14
Muir, John 1838-1914 . . . . DLB-186
Mukherjee, Bharati 1940- DLB-60
Mulcaster, Richard
   1531 or 1532-1611 . . . . DLB-167
Muldoon, Paul 1951- DLB-40
Müller, Friedrich (see Müller, Maler)
Müller, Heiner 1929- DLB-124
Müller, Maler 1749-1825 . . . . DLB-94
Müller, Wilhelm 1794-1827 . . . . DLB-90
Mumford, Lewis 1895-1990 . . . . DLB-63
Munby, Arthur Joseph 1828-1910 . . . DLB-35
Munday, Anthony 1560-1633 . . . . DLB-62, 172
Mundt, Clara (see Mühlbach, Luise)
Mundt, Theodore 1808-1861 . . . . . . DLB-133
Munford, Robert circa 1737-1783 . . . . DLB-31
Mungoshi, Charles 1947- DLB-157
Munonye, John 1929- DLB-117
Munro, Alice 1931- DLB-53
Munro, H. H. 1870-1916 . . . . . DLB-34, 162
Munro, Neil 1864-1930 . . . . DLB-156
Munro, George
   [publishing house] DLB-49
Munro, Norman L.
   [publishing house] DLB-49
Munroe, James, and Company DLB-49
Munroe, Kirk 1850-1930 . . . . DLB-42
Munroe and Francis DLB-49
Munsell, Joel [publishing house] DLB-49
Munsey, Frank A. 1854-1925 . . . . DLB-25, 91
Murakami, Haruki 1949- DLB-182
Munsey, Frank A., and
   Company DLB-49
Murav'ev, Mikhail Nikitich
   1757-1807 . . . . DLB-150
Murdoch, Iris 1919- DLB-14, 194

Murdoch, Rupert 1931- DLB-127
Murfree, Mary N. 1850-1922 . . . . DLB-12, 74
Murger, Henry 1822-1861 . . . . DLB-119
Murger, Louis-Henri (see Murger, Henry)
Murner, Thomas 1475-1537 . . . . . . DLB-179
Muro, Amado 1915-1971 . . . . DLB-82
Murphy, Arthur 1727-1805 . . . . . DLB-89, 142
Murphy, Beatrice M. 1908- DLB-76
Murphy, Emily 1868-1933 . . . . DLB-99
Murphy, John H., III 1916- DLB-127
Murphy, John, and Company DLB-49
Murphy, Richard 1927-1993 . . . . . . DLB-40
Murray, Albert L. 1916- DLB-38
Murray, Gilbert 1866-1957 . . . . DLB-10
Murray, Judith Sargent 1751-1820 . . . DLB-37
Murray, Pauli 1910-1985 . . . . DLB-41
Murray, John [publishing house] DLB-154
Murry, John Middleton
   1889-1957 . . . . DLB-149
Musäus, Johann Karl August
   1735-1787 . . . . DLB-97
Muschg, Adolf 1934- DLB-75
The Music of *Minnesang* DLB-138
Musil, Robert 1880-1942 . . . . . . DLB-81, 124
Muspilli circa 790-circa 850 . . . . DLB-148
Musset, Alfred de 1810-1857 . . . . . . DLB-192
Mussey, Benjamin B., and
   Company DLB-49
Mutafchieva, Vera 1929- DLB-181
Mwangi, Meja 1948- DLB-125
Myers, Frederic W. H. 1843-1901 . . . DLB-190
Myers, Gustavus 1872-1942 . . . . DLB-47
Myers, L. H. 1881-1944 . . . . DLB-15
Myers, Walter Dean 1937- DLB-33
Myles, Eileen 1949- DLB-193

N

Nabl, Franz 1883-1974 . . . . DLB-81
Nabokov, Vladimir
   1899-1977 . . . . . DLB-2; Y-80, Y-91; DS-3
Nabokov Festival at Cornell Y-83
The Vladimir Nabokov Archive
   in the Berg Collection Y-91
Nafis and Cornish DLB-49
Nagai, Kafū 1879-1959 . . . . DLB-180
Naipaul, Shiva 1945-1985 . . . . DLB-157; Y-85
Naipaul, V. S. 1932- DLB-125; Y-85
Nakagami, Kenji 1946-1992 . . . . . . DLB-182
Nancrede, Joseph
   [publishing house] DLB-49
Naranjo, Carmen 1930- DLB-145

Narrache, Jean 1893-1970 . . . . DLB-92	Neumeister, Erdmann 1671-1756 . . . . DLB-168	Newsome, Effie Lee 1885-1979 . . . . . DLB-76
Nasby, Petroleum Vesuvius (see Locke, David Ross)	Nevins, Allan 1890-1971 . . . . . DLB-17; DS-17	Newspaper Syndication of American Humor DLB-11
Nash, Ogden 1902-1971 . . . . DLB-11	Nevinson, Henry Woodd 1856-1941 . . . . DLB-135	Newton, A. Edward 1864-1940 . . . . . DLB-140
Nash, Eveleigh [publishing house] DLB-112	The New American Library DLB-46	Ngugi wa Thiong'o 1938- DLB-125
Nashe, Thomas 1567-1601? DLB-167	New Approaches to Biography: Challenges from Critical Theory, USC Conference on Literary Studies, 1990 . . . . Y-90	Niatum, Duane 1938- DLB-175
Nast, Conde 1873-1942 . . . . DLB-91		The *Nibelungenlied* and the *Klage* circa 1200 . . . . DLB-138
Nast, Thomas 1840-1902 . . . . DLB-188	New Directions Publishing Corporation DLB-46	Nichol, B. P. 1944- DLB-53
Nastasijević, Momčilo 1894-1938 . . . . DLB-147	A New Edition of *Huck Finn* Y-85	Nicholas of Cusa 1401-1464 . . . . . . DLB-115
Nathan, George Jean 1882-1958 . . . . DLB-137	New Forces at Work in the American Theatre: 1915-1925 . . . . DLB-7	Nichols, Beverly 1898-1983 . . . . . . DLB-191
Nathan, Robert 1894-1985 . . . . DLB-9		Nichols, Dudley 1895-1960 . . . . . . DLB-26
The National Jewish Book Awards Y-85	New Literary Periodicals: A Report for 1987 . . . . Y-87	Nichols, Grace 1950- DLB-157
The National Theatre and the Royal Shakespeare Company: The National Companies DLB-13	New Literary Periodicals: A Report for 1988 . . . . Y-88	Nichols, John 1940- Y-82
	New Literary Periodicals: A Report for 1989 . . . . Y-89	Nichols, Mary Sargeant (Neal) Gove 1810-1884 . . . . DLB-1
Natsume, Sōseki 1867-1916 . . . . DLB-180		Nichols, Peter 1927- DLB-13
Naughton, Bill 1910- DLB-13	New Literary Periodicals: A Report for 1990 . . . . Y-90	Nichols, Roy F. 1896-1973 . . . . DLB-17
Naylor, Gloria 1950- DLB-173	New Literary Periodicals: A Report for 1991 . . . . Y-91	Nichols, Ruth 1948- DLB-60
Nazor, Vladimir 1876-1949 . . . . DLB-147		Nicholson, Edward Williams Byron 1849-1912 . . . . DLB-184
Ndebele, Njabulo 1948- DLB-157	New Literary Periodicals: A Report for 1992 . . . . Y-92	
Neagoe, Peter 1881-1960 . . . . DLB-4	New Literary Periodicals: A Report for 1993 . . . . Y-93	Nicholson, Norman 1914- DLB-27
Neal, John 1793-1876 . . . . DLB-1, 59		Nicholson, William 1872-1949 . . . . . DLB-141
Neal, Joseph C. 1807-1847 . . . . DLB-11	The New Monthly Magazine 1814-1884 . . . . DLB-110	Ní Chuilleanáin, Eiléan 1942- DLB-40
Neal, Larry 1937-1981 . . . . DLB-38	The New *Ulysses* Y-84	Nicol, Eric 1919- DLB-68
The Neale Publishing Company DLB-49	The New Variorum Shakespeare Y-85	Nicolai, Friedrich 1733-1811 . . . . . . DLB-97
Neely, F. Tennyson [publishing house] DLB-49	A New Voice: The Center for the Book's First Five Years Y-83	Nicolay, John G. 1832-1901 and Hay, John 1838-1905 . . . . DLB-47
Negri, Ada 1870-1945 . . . . DLB-114		Nicolson, Harold 1886-1968 . . . . DLB-100, 149
"The Negro as a Writer," by G. M. McClellan DLB-50	The New Wave [Science Fiction] DLB-8	Nicolson, Nigel 1917- DLB-155
	New York City Bookshops in the 1930s and 1940s: The Recollections of Walter Goldwater Y-93	Niebuhr, Reinhold 1892-1971 . . DLB-17; DS-17
"Negro Poets and Their Poetry," by Wallace Thurman DLB-50		Niedecker, Lorine 1903-1970 . . . . . . DLB-48
Neidhart von Reuental circa 1185-circa 1240 . . . . DLB-138	Newbery, John [publishing house] DLB-154	Nieman, Lucius W. 1857-1935 . . . . . DLB-25
		Nietzsche, Friedrich 1844-1900 . . . . . DLB-129
Neihardt, John G. 1881-1973 . . . . . DLB-9, 54	Newbolt, Henry 1862-1938 . . . . DLB-19	Nievo, Stanislao 1928- DLB-196
Neledinsky-Meletsky, Iurii Aleksandrovich 1752-1828 . . . . DLB-150	Newbound, Bernard Slade (see Slade, Bernard)	Niggli, Josefina 1910- Y-80
	Newby, P. H. 1918- DLB-15	Nightingale, Florence 1820-1910 . . . . DLB-166
Nelligan, Emile 1879-1941 . . . . DLB-92	Newby, Thomas Cautley [publishing house] DLB-106	Nikolev, Nikolai Petrovich 1758-1815 . . . . DLB-150
Nelson, Alice Moore Dunbar 1875-1935 . . . . DLB-50		
Nelson, Thomas, and Sons [U.S.] . . . DLB-49	Newcomb, Charles King 1820-1894 . . . . DLB-1	Niles, Hezekiah 1777-1839 . . . . DLB-43
Nelson, Thomas, and Sons [U.K.] . . . DLB-106	Newell, Peter 1862-1924 . . . . DLB-42	Nims, John Frederick 1913- DLB-5
Nelson, William 1908-1978 . . . . DLB-103	Newell, Robert Henry 1836-1901 . . . . DLB-11	Nin, Anaïs 1903-1977 . . . . . . DLB-2, 4, 152
Nelson, William Rockhill 1841-1915 . . . . DLB-23	Newhouse, Samuel I. 1895-1979 . . . . DLB-127	1985: The Year of the Mystery: A Symposium Y-85
	Newman, Cecil Earl 1903-1976 . . . . . DLB-127	
Nemerov, Howard 1920-1991 . . . DLB-5, 6; Y-83	Newman, David (see Benton, Robert)	The 1997 Booker Prize Y-97
Nesbit, E. 1858-1924 . . . . . DLB-141, 153, 178	Newman, Frances 1883-1928 . . . . Y-80	Nissenson, Hugh 1933- DLB-28
Ness, Evaline 1911-1986 . . . . DLB-61	Newman, Francis William 1805-1897 . . . . DLB-190	Niven, Frederick John 1878-1944 . . . . DLB-92
Nestroy, Johann 1801-1862 . . . . DLB-133		Niven, Larry 1938- DLB-8
Neukirch, Benjamin 1655-1729 . . . . . DLB-168	Newman, John Henry 1801-1890 . . . . DLB-18, 32, 55	Nizan, Paul 1905-1940 . . . . DLB-72
Neugeboren, Jay 1938- DLB-28		Njegoš, Petar II Petrović 1813-1851 . . . . DLB-147
Neumann, Alfred 1895-1952 . . . . . . DLB-56	Newman, Mark [publishing house] DLB-49	
Neumark, Georg 1621-1681 . . . . DLB-164	Newnes, George, Limited DLB-112	Nkosi, Lewis 1936- DLB-157

"The No Self, the Little Self, and the Poets,"
by Richard Moore DLB-105

Nobel Peace Prize

The 1986 Nobel Peace Prize:
Elie Wiesel Y-86

The Nobel Prize and Literary Politics ... Y-86

Nobel Prize in Literature

The 1982 Nobel Prize in Literature:
Gabriel García Márquez......... Y-82

The 1983 Nobel Prize in Literature:
William Golding Y-83

The 1984 Nobel Prize in Literature:
Jaroslav Seifert Y-84

The 1985 Nobel Prize in Literature:
Claude Simon Y-85

The 1986 Nobel Prize in Literature:
Wole Soyinka Y-86

The 1987 Nobel Prize in Literature:
Joseph Brodsky............. Y-87

The 1988 Nobel Prize in Literature:
Najīb Mahfūz.............. Y-88

The 1989 Nobel Prize in Literature:
Camilo José Cela............ Y-89

The 1990 Nobel Prize in Literature:
Octavio Paz............... Y-90

The 1991 Nobel Prize in Literature:
Nadine Gordimer Y-91

The 1992 Nobel Prize in Literature:
Derek Walcott Y-92

The 1993 Nobel Prize in Literature:
Toni Morrison Y-93

The 1994 Nobel Prize in Literature:
Kenzaburō Ōe Y-94

The 1995 Nobel Prize in Literature:
Seamus Heaney Y-95

The 1996 Nobel Prize in Literature:
Wisława Szymborsha........... Y-96

The 1997 Nobel Prize in Literature:
Dario Fo Y-97

Nodier, Charles 1780-1844 .... DLB-119
Noel, Roden 1834-1894.......... DLB-35
Nogami, Yaeko 1885-1985......... DLB-180
Nogo, Rajko Petrov 1945- DLB-181
Nolan, William F. 1928- DLB-8
Noland, C. F. M. 1810?-1858 .... DLB-11
Noma, Hiroshi 1915-1991......... DLB-182
Nonesuch Press DLB-112
Noonday Press DLB-46
Noone, John 1936- DLB-14
Nora, Eugenio de 1923- DLB-134
Nordhoff, Charles 1887-1947 .... DLB-9
Norman, Charles 1904- DLB-111
Norman, Marsha 1947- Y-84
Norris, Charles G. 1881-1945 ...... DLB-9
Norris, Frank 1870-1902 .... DLB-12, 71, 186
Norris, Leslie 1921- DLB-27

Norse, Harold 1916- DLB-16
North, Marianne 1830-1890........ DLB-174
North Point Press............ DLB-46
Nortje, Arthur 1942-1970 .... DLB-125
Norton, Alice Mary (see Norton, Andre)
Norton, Andre 1912- DLB-8, 52
Norton, Andrews 1786-1853........ DLB-1
Norton, Caroline 1808-1877 .... DLB-21, 159
Norton, Charles Eliot 1827-1908 ... DLB-1, 64
Norton, John 1606-1663 .... DLB-24
Norton, Mary 1903-1992 .... DLB-160
Norton, Thomas (see Sackville, Thomas)
Norton, W. W., and Company DLB-46
Norwood, Robert 1874-1932....... DLB-92
Nosaka, Akiyuki 1930- DLB-182
Nossack, Hans Erich 1901-1977..... DLB-69
A Note on Technique (1926), by
Elizabeth A. Drew [excerpts]..... DLB-36
Notker Balbulus circa 840-912 ..... DLB-148
Notker III of Saint Gall
circa 950-1022............ DLB-148
Notker von Zweifalten ?-1095 ..... DLB-148
Nourse, Alan E. 1928- DLB-8
Novak, Slobodan 1924- DLB-181
Novak, Vjenceslav 1859-1905...... DLB-147
Novalis 1772-1801............ DLB-90
Novaro, Mario 1868-1944........ DLB-114
Novás Calvo, Lino 1903-1983 ..... DLB-145
"The Novel in [Robert Browning's] 'The Ring
and the Book'" (1912), by
Henry James DLB-32
The Novel of Impressionism,
by Jethro Bithell DLB-66
Novel-Reading: The Works of Charles Dickens,
The Works of W. Makepeace Thackeray
(1879), by Anthony Trollope.... DLB-21
Novels for Grown-Ups........... Y-97
The Novels of Dorothy Richardson (1918),
by May Sinclair........... DLB-36
Novels with a Purpose (1864), by
Justin M'Carthy........... DLB-21
Noventa, Giacomo 1898-1960...... DLB-114
Novikov, Nikolai Ivanovich
1744-1818............. DLB-150
Nowlan, Alden 1933-1983 .... DLB-53
Noyes, Alfred 1880-1958 .... DLB-20
Noyes, Crosby S. 1825-1908....... DLB-23
Noyes, Nicholas 1647-1717 .... DLB-24
Noyes, Theodore W. 1858-1946.... DLB-29
N-Town Plays circa 1468 to early
sixteenth century DLB-146
Nugent, Frank 1908-1965......... DLB-44
Nugent, Richard Bruce 1906- DLB-151
Nušić, Branislav 1864-1938 ...... DLB-147

Nutt, David [publishing house] DLB-106
Nwapa, Flora 1931- DLB-125
Nye, Bill 1850-1896 .... DLB-186
Nye, Edgar Wilson (Bill)
1850-1896............. DLB-11, 23
Nye, Naomi Shihab 1952- DLB-120
Nye, Robert 1939- DLB-14

O

Oakes, Urian circa 1631-1681 ...... DLB-24
Oakley, Violet 1874-1961 .... DLB-188
Oates, Joyce Carol
1938- DLB-2, 5, 130; Y-81
Ōba, Minako 1930- DLB-182
Ober, Frederick Albion 1849-1913 ... DLB-189
Ober, William 1920-1993 .... Y-93
Oberholtzer, Ellis Paxson
1868-1936............. DLB-47
Obradović, Dositej 1740?-1811 ..... DLB-147
O'Brien, Edna 1932- DLB-14
O'Brien, Fitz-James 1828-1862 ..... DLB-74
O'Brien, Kate 1897-1974 .... DLB-15
O'Brien, Tim
1946- DLB-152; Y-80; DS-9
O'Casey, Sean 1880-1964......... DLB-10
Occom, Samson 1723-1792....... DLB-175
Ochs, Adolph S. 1858-1935 ...... DLB-25
Ochs-Oakes, George Washington
1861-1931............. DLB-137
O'Connor, Flannery
1925-1964 .... DLB-2, 152; Y-80; DS-12
O'Connor, Frank 1903-1966 ...... DLB-162
Octopus Publishing Group DLB-112
Oda, Sakunosuke 1913-1947 ...... DLB-182
Odell, Jonathan 1737-1818....... DLB-31, 99
O'Dell, Scott 1903-1989.......... DLB-52
Odets, Clifford 1906-1963........ DLB-7, 26
Odhams Press Limited DLB-112
O'Donnell, Peter 1920- DLB-87
O'Donovan, Michael (see O'Connor, Frank)
Ōe, Kenzaburō 1935- DLB-182; Y-94
O'Faolain, Julia 1932- DLB-14
O'Faolain, Sean 1900- DLB-15, 162
Off Broadway and Off-Off Broadway .. DLB-7
Off-Loop Theatres DLB-7
Offord, Carl Ruthven 1910- DLB-76
O'Flaherty, Liam
1896-1984........ DLB-36, 162; Y-84
Ogilvie, J. S., and Company...... DLB-49
Ogot, Grace 1930- DLB-125
O'Grady, Desmond 1935- DLB-40

Ogunyemi, Wale 1939- DLB-157	Ondaatje, Michael 1943- DLB-60	Oswald von Wolkenstein 1376 or 1377-1445 .... DLB-179
O'Hagan, Howard 1902-1982 ...... DLB-68	O'Neill, Eugene 1888-1953 .... DLB-7	Otero, Blas de 1916-1979 .... DLB-134
O'Hara, Frank 1926-1966 .... DLB-5, 16, 193	Onetti, Juan Carlos 1909-1994 .... DLB-113	Otero, Miguel Antonio 1859-1944 .... DLB-82
O'Hara, John 1905-1970 .... DLB-9, 86; DS-2	Onions, George Oliver 1872-1961 .... DLB-153	Otero Silva, Miguel 1908-1985 ..... DLB-145
Okara, Gabriel 1921- DLB-125	Onofri, Arturo 1885-1928 .... DLB-114	Otfried von Weißenburg circa 800-circa 875? DLB-148
O'Keeffe, John 1747-1833 .... DLB-89	Opie, Amelia 1769-1853 ..... DLB-116, 159	Otis, James (see Kaler, James Otis)
Okes, Nicholas [publishing house] DLB-170	Opitz, Martin 1597-1639 .... DLB-164	Otis, James, Jr. 1725-1783 .... DLB-31
Okigbo, Christopher 1930-1967 .... DLB-125	Oppen, George 1908-1984 ...... DLB-5, 165	Otis, Broaders and Company DLB-49
Okot p'Bitek 1931-1982 .... DLB-125	Oppenheim, E. Phillips 1866-1946 .... DLB-70	Ottaway, James 1911- DLB-127
Okpewho, Isidore 1941- DLB-157	Oppenheim, James 1882-1932 ..... DLB-28	Ottendorfer, Oswald 1826-1900 ..... DLB-23
Okri, Ben 1959- DLB-157	Oppenheimer, Joel 1930-1988 .... DLB-5, 193	Ottieri, Ottiero 1924- DLB-177
Olaudah Equiano and Unfinished Journeys: The Slave-Narrative Tradition and Twentieth-Century Continuities, by Paul Edwards and Pauline T. Wangman DLB-117	Optic, Oliver (see Adams, William Taylor)	Otto-Peters, Louise 1819-1895 ..... DLB-129
	Oral History Interview with Donald S. Klopfer Y-97	Otway, Thomas 1652-1685 .... DLB-80
	Orczy, Emma, Baroness 1865-1947 .... DLB-70	Ouellette, Fernand 1930- DLB-60
		Ouida 1839-1908 .... DLB-18, 156
Old English Literature: An Introduction DLB-146	Origo, Iris 1902-1988 .... DLB-155	Outing Publishing Company DLB-46
Old English Riddles eighth to tenth centuries DLB-146	Orlovitz, Gil 1918-1973 .... DLB-2, 5	Outlaw Days, by Joyce Johnson DLB-16
	Orlovsky, Peter 1933- DLB-16	Overbury, Sir Thomas circa 1581-1613 .... DLB-151
Old Franklin Publishing House DLB-49	Ormond, John 1923- DLB-27	
Old German Genesis and Old German Exodus circa 1050-circa 1130 .... DLB-148	Ornitz, Samuel 1890-1957 ..... DLB-28, 44	The Overlook Press DLB-46
	O'Rourke, P. J. 1947- DLB-185	Overview of U.S. Book Publishing, 1910-1945 .... DLB-9
Old High German Charms and Blessings DLB-148	Ortese, Anna Maria 1914- DLB-177	
	Ortiz, Simon J. 1941- DLB-120, 175	Owen, Guy 1925- DLB-5
The Old High German Isidor circa 790-800 .... DLB-148	Ortnit and Wolfdietrich circa 1225-1250 .... DLB-138	Owen, John 1564-1622 .... DLB-121
Older, Fremont 1856-1935 .... DLB-25		Owen, John [publishing house]..... DLB-49
Oldham, John 1653-1683 .... DLB-131	Orton, Joe 1933-1967 .... DLB-13	Owen, Robert 1771-1858 ..... DLB-107, 158
Olds, Sharon 1942- DLB-120	Orwell, George 1903-1950 ... DLB-15, 98, 195	Owen, Wilfred 1893-1918 .... DLB-20
Olearius, Adam 1599-1671 .... DLB-164	The Orwell Year Y-84	Owen, Peter, Limited DLB-112
Oliphant, Laurence 1829?-1888 .... DLB-18, 166	Ory, Carlos Edmundo de 1923- ... DLB-134	The Owl and the Nightingale circa 1189-1199 .... DLB-146
	Osbey, Brenda Marie 1957- DLB-120	
Oliphant, Margaret 1828-1897 ... DLB-18, 190	Osbon, B. S. 1827-1912 .... DLB-43	Owsley, Frank L. 1890-1956 ...... DLB-17
Oliver, Chad 1928- DLB-8	Osborne, John 1929-1994 .... DLB-13	Oxford, Seventeenth Earl of, Edward de Vere 1550-1604 .... DLB-172
Oliver, Mary 1935- DLB-5, 193	Osgood, Herbert L. 1855-1918 ..... DLB-47	
Ollier, Claude 1922- DLB-83	Osgood, James R., and Company DLB-49	Ozerov, Vladislav Aleksandrovich 1769-1816 .... DLB-150
Olsen, Tillie 1913?- DLB-28; Y-80		
Olson, Charles 1910-1970 ..... DLB-5, 16, 193	Osgood, McIlvaine and Company DLB-112	Ozick, Cynthia 1928- DLB-28, 152; Y-82
Olson, Elder 1909- DLB-48, 63	O'Shaughnessy, Arthur 1844-1881 .... DLB-35	**P**
Omotoso, Kole 1943- DLB-125		
"On Art in Fiction "(1838), by Edward Bulwer DLB-21	O'Shea, Patrick [publishing house] DLB-49	Pace, Richard 1482?-1536 .... DLB-167
		Pacey, Desmond 1917-1975 .... DLB-88
On Learning to Write Y-88	Osipov, Nikolai Petrovich 1751-1799 .... DLB-150	Pack, Robert 1929- DLB-5
On Some of the Characteristics of Modern Poetry and On the Lyrical Poems of Alfred Tennyson (1831), by Arthur Henry Hallam DLB-32		Packaging Papa: The Garden of Eden Y-86
	Oskison, John Milton 1879-1947 .... DLB-175	Padell Publishing Company DLB-46
	Osler, Sir William 1849-1919 ...... DLB-184	Padgett, Ron 1942- DLB-5
	Osofisan, Femi 1946- DLB-125	Padilla, Ernesto Chávez 1944- DLB-122
"On Style in English Prose" (1898), by Frederic Harrison DLB-57	Ostenso, Martha 1900-1963 .... DLB-92	Page, L. C., and Company DLB-49
"On Style in Literature: Its Technical Elements" (1885), by Robert Louis Stevenson DLB-57	Ostriker, Alicia 1937- DLB-120	Page, P. K. 1916- DLB-68
	Osundare, Niyi 1947- DLB-157	Page, Thomas Nelson 1853-1922 .... DLB-12, 78; DS-13
"On the Writing of Essays" (1862), by Alexander Smith DLB-57	Oswald, Eleazer 1755-1795 .... DLB-43	

Page, Walter Hines 1855-1918 . . . . DLB-71, 91

Paget, Francis Edward 1806-1882 . . . . DLB-163

Paget, Violet (see Lee, Vernon)

Pagliarani, Elio 1927- DLB-128

Pain, Barry 1864-1928 . . . . DLB-135

Pain, Philip ?-circa 1666 . . . . DLB-24

Paine, Robert Treat, Jr. 1773-1811 . . . DLB-37

Paine, Thomas 1737-1809 . . . . DLB-31, 43, 73, 158

Painter, George D. 1914- DLB-155

Painter, William 1540?-1594 . . . . . . DLB-136

Palazzeschi, Aldo 1885-1974 . . . . . . DLB-114

Paley, Grace 1922- DLB-28

Palfrey, John Gorham 1796-1881 . . . . DLB-1, 30

Palgrave, Francis Turner 1824-1897 . . . . DLB-35

Palmer, Joe H. 1904-1952 . . . . DLB-171

Palmer, Michael 1943- DLB-169

Paltock, Robert 1697-1767 . . . . DLB-39

Pan Books Limited DLB-112

Panama, Norman 1914- and Frank, Melvin 1913-1988 . . . . . . DLB-26

Pancake, Breece D'J 1952-1979 . . . . DLB-130

Panero, Leopoldo 1909-1962 . . . . . . DLB-108

Pangborn, Edgar 1909-1976 . . . . . . DLB-8

"Panic Among the Philistines": A Postscript, An Interview with Bryan Griffin Y-81

Panizzi, Sir Anthony 1797-1879 . . . . . DLB-184

Panneton, Philippe (see Ringuet)

Panshin, Alexei 1940- DLB-8

Pansy (see Alden, Isabella)

Pantheon Books DLB-46

Papantonio, Michael (see Kohn, John S. Van E.)

Paperback Library DLB-46

Paperback Science Fiction DLB-8

Paquet, Alfons 1881-1944 . . . . DLB-66

Paracelsus 1493-1541 . . . . DLB-179

Paradis, Suzanne 1936- DLB-53

Pareja Diezcanseco, Alfredo 1908-1993 . . . . DLB-145

Pardoe, Julia 1804-1862 . . . . DLB-166

Parents' Magazine Press DLB-46

Parise, Goffredo 1929-1986 . . . . DLB-177

Parisian Theater, Fall 1984: Toward A New Baroque Y-85

Parizeau, Alice 1930- DLB-60

Parke, John 1754-1789 . . . . DLB-31

Parker, Dorothy 1893-1967 . . . . DLB-11, 45, 86

Parker, Gilbert 1860-1932 . . . . DLB-99

Parker, James 1714-1770 . . . . DLB-43

Parker, Theodore 1810-1860 . . . . DLB-1

Parker, William Riley 1906-1968 . . . . DLB-103

Parker, J. H. [publishing house] DLB-106

Parker, John [publishing house] DLB-106

Parkman, Francis, Jr. 1823-1893 . . . . DLB-1, 30, 183, 186

Parks, Gordon 1912- DLB-33

Parks, William 1698-1750 . . . . DLB-43

Parks, William [publishing house] DLB-49

Parley, Peter (see Goodrich, Samuel Griswold)

Parmenides late sixth-fifth century B.C. DLB-176

Parnell, Thomas 1679-1718 . . . . DLB-95

Parr, Catherine 1513?-1548 . . . . . . DLB-136

Parrington, Vernon L. 1871-1929 . . . . DLB-17, 63

Parrish, Maxfield 1870-1966 . . . . . . DLB-188

Parronchi, Alessandro 1914- DLB-128

Partridge, S. W., and Company DLB-106

Parton, James 1822-1891 . . . . DLB-30

Parton, Sara Payson Willis 1811-1872 . . . . DLB-43, 74

Parun, Vesna 1922- DLB-181

Pasinetti, Pier Maria 1913- DLB-177

Pasolini, Pier Paolo 1922- DLB-128, 177

Pastan, Linda 1932- DLB-5

Paston, George 1860-1936 . . . . DLB-149

The Paston Letters 1422-1509 . . . . . . DLB-146

Pastorius, Francis Daniel 1651-circa 1720 . . . . DLB-24

Patchen, Kenneth 1911-1972 . . . . . DLB-16, 48

Pater, Walter 1839-1894 . . . . . DLB-57, 156

Paterson, Katherine 1932- DLB-52

Patmore, Coventry 1823-1896 . . . . DLB-35, 98

Paton, Alan 1903-1988 . . . . DS-17

Paton, Joseph Noel 1821-1901 . . . . . DLB-35

Paton Walsh, Jill 1937- DLB-161

Patrick, Edwin Hill ("Ted") 1901-1964 . . . . DLB-137

Patrick, John 1906- DLB-7

Pattee, Fred Lewis 1863-1950 . . . . . DLB-71

Pattern and Paradigm: History as Design, by Judith Ryan DLB-75

Patterson, Alicia 1906-1963 . . . . . . DLB-127

Patterson, Eleanor Medill 1881-1948 . . . . DLB-29

Patterson, Eugene 1923- DLB-127

Patterson, Joseph Medill 1879-1946 . . . . DLB-29

Pattillo, Henry 1726-1801 . . . . DLB-37

Paul, Elliot 1891-1958 . . . . DLB-4

Paul, Jean (see Richter, Johann Paul Friedrich)

Paul, Kegan, Trench, Trubner and Company Limited DLB-106

Paul, Peter, Book Company DLB-49

Paul, Stanley, and Company Limited DLB-112

Paulding, James Kirke 1778-1860 . . . . DLB-3, 59, 74

Paulin, Tom 1949- DLB-40

Pauper, Peter, Press DLB-46

Pavese, Cesare 1908-1950 . . . . . DLB-128, 177

Pavić, Milorad 1929- DLB-181

Pavlov, Konstantin 1933- DLB-181

Pavlović, Miodrag 1928- DLB-181

Paxton, John 1911-1985 . . . . DLB-44

Payn, James 1830-1898 . . . . DLB-18

Payne, John 1842-1916 . . . . DLB-35

Payne, John Howard 1791-1852 . . . . DLB-37

Payson and Clarke DLB-46

Paz, Octavio 1914-1998 . . . . Y-90

Pazzi, Roberto 1946- DLB-196

Peabody, Elizabeth Palmer 1804-1894 . . . . DLB-1

Peabody, Elizabeth Palmer [publishing house] DLB-49

Peabody, Oliver William Bourn 1799-1848 . . . . DLB-59

Peace, Roger 1899-1968 . . . . DLB-127

Peacham, Henry 1578-1644? DLB-151

Peacham, Henry, the Elder 1547-1634 . . . . DLB-172

Peachtree Publishers, Limited DLB-46

Peacock, Molly 1947- DLB-120

Peacock, Thomas Love 1785-1866 . . . . DLB-96, 116

Pead, Deuel ?-1727 . . . . DLB-24

Peake, Mervyn 1911-1968 . . . . . DLB-15, 160

Peale, Rembrandt 1778-1860 . . . . . . DLB-183

Pear Tree Press DLB-112

Pearce, Philippa 1920- DLB-161

Pearson, H. B. [publishing house] DLB-49

Pearson, Hesketh 1887-1964 . . . . . . DLB-149

Peck, George W. 1840-1916 . . . . . DLB-23, 42

Peck, H. C., and Theo. Bliss [publishing house] DLB-49

Peck, Harry Thurston 1856-1914 . . . . DLB-71, 91

Peele, George 1556-1596 . . . . . DLB-62, 167

Pegler, Westbrook 1894-1969 . . . . . DLB-171

Pekić, Borislav 1930-1992 . . . . DLB-181

Pellegrini and Cudahy DLB-46

Pelletier, Aimé (see Vac, Bertrand)

Pemberton, Sir Max 1863-1950 . . . . DLB-70

Penfield, Edward 1866-1925 . . . . . . DLB-188

Cumulative Index

Penguin Books [U.S.] DLB-46	Petrović, Rastko 1898-1949 . . . . . . DLB-147	Pickthall, Marjorie 1883-1922 . . . . . . DLB-92
Penguin Books [U.K.] DLB-112	*Petruslied* circa 854? DLB-148	Pictorial Printing Company DLB-49
Penn Publishing Company DLB-49	Petry, Ann 1908- DLB-76	Piercy, Marge 1936- DLB-120
Penn, William 1644-1718 . . . . DLB-24	Pettie, George circa 1548-1589 . . . . DLB-136	Pierro, Albino 1916- DLB-128
Penna, Sandro 1906-1977 . . . . DLB-114	Peyton, K. M. 1929- DLB-161	Pignotti, Lamberto 1926- DLB-128
Pennell, Joseph 1857-1926 . . . . DLB-188	Pfaffe Konrad flourished circa 1172 . . . . DLB-148	Pike, Albert 1809-1891 . . . . DLB-74
Penner, Jonathan 1940- Y-83		Pike, Zebulon Montgomery 1779-1813 . . DLB-183
Pennington, Lee 1939- Y-82	Pfaffe Lamprecht flourished circa 1150 . . . . DLB-148	Pilon, Jean-Guy 1930- DLB-60
Pepys, Samuel 1633-1703 . . . . DLB-101	Pforzheimer, Carl H. 1879-1957 . . . . DLB-140	Pinckney, Josephine 1895-1957 . . . . . DLB-6
Percy, Thomas 1729-1811 . . . . DLB-104	Phaer, Thomas 1510?-1560 . . . . . . DLB-167	Pindar circa 518 B.C.-circa 438 B.C. DLB-176
Percy, Walker 1916-1990 . . . DLB-2; Y-80, Y-90	Phaidon Press Limited DLB-112	
Percy, William 1575-1648 . . . . DLB-172	Pharr, Robert Deane 1916-1992 . . . . DLB-33	Pindar, Peter (see Wolcot, John)
Perec, Georges 1936-1982 . . . . DLB-83	Phelps, Elizabeth Stuart 1844-1911 . . . . DLB-74	Pinero, Arthur Wing 1855-1934 . . . . . DLB-10
Perelman, Bob 1947- DLB-193		Pinget, Robert 1919- DLB-83
Perelman, S. J. 1904-1979 . . . . . DLB-11, 44	Philander von der Linde (see Mencke, Johann Burckhard)	Pinnacle Books DLB-46
Perez, Raymundo "Tigre" 1946- DLB-122		Piñon, Nélida 1935- DLB-145
	Philby, H. St. John B. 1885-1960 . . . . DLB-195	Pinsky, Robert 1940- Y-82
Peri Rossi, Cristina 1941- DLB-145	Philip, Marlene Nourbese 1947- DLB-157	Pinter, Harold 1930- DLB-13
Periodicals of the Beat Generation DLB-16		Piontek, Heinz 1925- DLB-75
Perkins, Eugene 1932- DLB-41	Philippe, Charles-Louis 1874-1909 . . . . DLB-65	Piozzi, Hester Lynch [Thrale] 1741-1821 . . . . DLB-104, 142
Perkoff, Stuart Z. 1930-1974 . . . . . . DLB-16		
Perley, Moses Henry 1804-1862 . . . . . DLB-99	Phillipps, Sir Thomas 1792-1872 . . . . DLB-184	Piper, H. Beam 1904-1964 . . . . DLB-8
Permabooks DLB-46	Philips, John 1676-1708 . . . . DLB-95	Piper, Watty DLB-22
Perrin, Alice 1867-1934 . . . . DLB-156	Philips, Katherine 1632-1664 . . . . . . DLB-131	Pirckheimer, Caritas 1467-1532 . . . . . DLB-179
Perry, Bliss 1860-1954 . . . . DLB-71	Phillips, Caryl 1958- DLB-157	Pirckheimer, Willibald 1470-1530 . . . . DLB-179
Perry, Eleanor 1915-1981 . . . . DLB-44	Phillips, David Graham 1867-1911 . . . . DLB-9, 12	
Perry, Matthew 1794-1858 . . . . DLB-183		Pisar, Samuel 1929- Y-83
Perry, Sampson 1747-1823 . . . . DLB-158	Phillips, Jayne Anne 1952- Y-80	Pitkin, Timothy 1766-1847 . . . . DLB-30
"Personal Style" (1890), by John Addington Symonds DLB-57	Phillips, Robert 1938- DLB-105	The Pitt Poetry Series: Poetry Publishing Today Y-85
	Phillips, Stephen 1864-1915 . . . . DLB-10	
Perutz, Leo 1882-1957 . . . . DLB-81	Phillips, Ulrich B. 1877-1934 . . . . . . DLB-17	Pitter, Ruth 1897- DLB-20
Pesetsky, Bette 1932- DLB-130	Phillips, Willard 1784-1873 . . . . DLB-59	Pix, Mary 1666-1709 . . . . DLB-80
Pestalozzi, Johann Heinrich 1746-1827 . . . . DLB-94	Phillips, William 1907- DLB-137	Pixerécourt, René Charles Guilbert de 1773-1844 . . . . DLB-192
	Phillips, Sampson and Company DLB-49	
Peter, Laurence J. 1919-1990 . . . . . . DLB-53	Phillpotts, Adelaide Eden (Adelaide Ross) 1896-1993 . . . . DLB-191	Plaatje, Sol T. 1876-1932 . . . . DLB-125
Peter of Spain circa 1205-1277 . . . . . DLB-115		The Place of Realism in Fiction (1895), by George Gissing DLB-18
Peterkin, Julia 1880-1961 . . . . DLB-9	Phillpotts, Eden 1862-1960 . . . . . . DLB-10, 70, 135, 153	
Peters, Lenrie 1932- DLB-117		Plante, David 1940- Y-83
Peters, Robert 1924- DLB-105	Philo circa 20-15 B.C.-circa A.D. 50 . . . . DLB-176	Platen, August von 1796-1835 . . . . . . DLB-90
Petersham, Maud 1889-1971 and Petersham, Miska 1888-1960 . . . . . DLB-22		Plath, Sylvia 1932-1963 . . . . . DLB-5, 6, 152
	Philosophical Library DLB-46	Plato circa 428 B.C.-348-347 B.C. DLB-176
Peterson, Charles Jacobs 1819-1887 . . . . DLB-79	"The Philosophy of Style" (1852), by Herbert Spencer DLB-57	
		Platon 1737-1812 . . . . DLB-150
Peterson, Len 1917- DLB-88	Phinney, Elihu [publishing house] DLB-49	Platt and Munk Company DLB-46
Peterson, Louis 1922- DLB-76	Phoenix, John (see Derby, George Horatio)	Playboy Press DLB-46
Peterson, T. B., and Brothers DLB-49	PHYLON (Fourth Quarter, 1950), The Negro in Literature: The Current Scene DLB-76	Playford, John [publishing house] DLB-170
Petitclair, Pierre 1813-1860 . . . . DLB-99		
Petrov, Aleksandar 1938- DLB-181	*Physiologus* circa 1070-circa 1150 . . . . DLB-148	Plays, Playwrights, and Playgoers DLB-84
Petrov, Gavriil 1730-1801 . . . . DLB-150		Playwrights and Professors, by Tom Stoppard DLB-13
Petrov, Vasilii Petrovich 1736-1799 . . . . DLB-150	Piccolo, Lucio 1903-1969 . . . . DLB-114	
	Pickard, Tom 1946- DLB-40	Playwrights on the Theater DLB-80
Petrov, Valeri 1920- DLB-181	Pickering, William [publishing house] DLB-106	Der Pleier flourished circa 1250 . . . . DLB-138
		Plenzdorf, Ulrich 1934- DLB-75

Plessen, Elizabeth 1944- DLB-75

Plievier, Theodor 1892-1955 . . . . DLB-69

Plimpton, George 1927- DLB-185

Plomer, William 1903-1973 . . DLB-20, 162, 191

Plotinus 204-270 . . . . DLB-176

Plumly, Stanley 1939- DLB-5, 193

Plumpp, Sterling D. 1940- DLB-41

Plunkett, James 1920- DLB-14

Plutarch circa 46-circa 120 . . . . DLB-176

Plymell, Charles 1935- DLB-16

Pocket Books DLB-46

Poe, Edgar Allan
   1809-1849 . . . . DLB-3, 59, 73, 74

Poe, James 1921-1980 . . . . DLB-44

The Poet Laureate of the United States
   Statements from Former Consultants
   in Poetry Y-86

"The Poet's Kaleidoscope: The Element of Surprise
   in the Making of the Poem," by Madeline De-
   Frees DLB-105

"The Poetry File," by
   Edward Field DLB-105

Pohl, Frederik 1919- DLB-8

Poirier, Louis (see Gracq, Julien)

Polanyi, Michael 1891-1976 . . . . DLB-100

Pole, Reginald 1500-1558 . . . . DLB-132

Poliakoff, Stephen 1952- DLB-13

Polidori, John William
   1795-1821 . . . . DLB-116

Polite, Carlene Hatcher 1932- DLB-33

Pollard, Edward A. 1832-1872 . . . . . . DLB-30

Pollard, Percival 1869-1911 . . . . DLB-71

Pollard and Moss DLB-49

Pollock, Sharon 1936- DLB-60

Polonsky, Abraham 1910- DLB-26

Polotsky, Simeon 1629-1680 . . . . . . DLB-150

Polybius circa 200 B.C.-118 B.C. DLB-176

Pomilio, Mario 1921-1990 . . . . DLB-177

Ponce, Mary Helen 1938- DLB-122

Ponce-Montoya, Juanita 1949- DLB-122

Ponet, John 1516?-1556 . . . . DLB-132

Poniatowski, Elena 1933- DLB-113

Ponsard, François 1814-1867 . . . . . . DLB-192

Ponsonby, William
   [publishing house] DLB-170

Pontiggia, Giuseppe 1934- DLB-196

Pony Stories DLB-160

Poole, Ernest 1880-1950 . . . . DLB-9

Poole, Sophia 1804-1891 . . . . DLB-166

Poore, Benjamin Perley
   1820-1887 . . . . DLB-23

Popa, Vasko 1922-1991 . . . . DLB-181

Pope, Abbie Hanscom
   1858-1894 . . . . DLB-140

Pope, Alexander 1688-1744 . . . . DLB-95, 101

Popov, Mikhail Ivanovich
   1742-circa 1790 . . . . DLB-150

Popović, Aleksandar 1929-1996 . . . . DLB-181

Popular Library DLB-46

Porlock, Martin (see MacDonald, Philip)

Porpoise Press DLB-112

Porta, Antonio 1935-1989 . . . . DLB-128

Porter, Anna Maria
   1780-1832 . . . . DLB-116, 159

Porter, David 1780-1843 . . . . DLB-183

Porter, Eleanor H. 1868-1920 . . . . . . DLB-9

Porter, Gene Stratton (see Stratton-Porter, Gene)

Porter, Henry ?-? DLB-62

Porter, Jane 1776-1850 . . . . . . DLB-116, 159

Porter, Katherine Anne
   1890-1980 . . . . DLB-4, 9, 102; Y-80; DS-12

Porter, Peter 1929- DLB-40

Porter, William Sydney
   1862-1910 . . . . DLB-12, 78, 79

Porter, William T. 1809-1858 . . . DLB-3, 43

Porter and Coates DLB-49

Portis, Charles 1933- DLB-6

Posey, Alexander 1873-1908 . . . . . . DLB-175

Postans, Marianne
   circa 1810-1865 . . . . DLB-166

Postl, Carl (see Sealsfield, Carl)

Poston, Ted 1906-1974 . . . . DLB-51

Postscript to [the Third Edition of] *Clarissa*
   (1751), by Samuel Richardson DLB-39

Potok, Chaim 1929- DLB-28, 152; Y-84

Potter, Beatrix 1866-1943 . . . . DLB-141

Potter, David M. 1910-1971 . . . . DLB-17

Potter, John E., and Company DLB-49

Pottle, Frederick A.
   1897-1987 . . . . DLB-103; Y-87

Poulin, Jacques 1937- DLB-60

Pound, Ezra 1885-1972 . . DLB-4, 45, 63; DS-15

Povich, Shirley 1905- DLB-171

Powell, Anthony 1905- DLB-15

Powell, John Wesley 1834-1902 . . . . DLB-186

Powers, J. F. 1917- DLB-130

Pownall, David 1938- DLB-14

Powys, John Cowper 1872-1963 . . . . DLB-15

Powys, Llewelyn 1884-1939 . . . . DLB-98

Powys, T. F. 1875-1953 . . . . . . DLB-36, 162

Poynter, Nelson 1903-1978 . . . . DLB-127

The Practice of Biography: An Interview
   with Stanley Weintraub Y-82

The Practice of Biography II: An Interview
   with B. L. Reid Y-83

The Practice of Biography III: An Interview
   with Humphrey Carpenter Y-84

The Practice of Biography IV: An Interview with
   William Manchester Y-85

The Practice of Biography V: An Interview
   with Justin Kaplan Y-86

The Practice of Biography VI: An Interview with
   David Herbert Donald Y-87

The Practice of Biography VII: An Interview with
   John Caldwell Guilds Y-92

The Practice of Biography VIII: An Interview
   with Joan Mellen Y-94

The Practice of Biography IX: An Interview
   with Michael Reynolds Y-95

Prados, Emilio 1899-1962 . . . . DLB-134

Praed, Winthrop Mackworth
   1802-1839 . . . . DLB-96

Praeger Publishers DLB-46

Praetorius, Johannes 1630-1680 . . . . DLB-168

Pratolini, Vasco 1913–1991 . . . . DLB-177

Pratt, E. J. 1882-1964 . . . . DLB-92

Pratt, Samuel Jackson 1749-1814 . . . . DLB-39

Preface to *Alwyn* (1780), by
   Thomas Holcroft DLB-39

Preface to *Colonel Jack* (1722), by
   Daniel Defoe DLB-39

Preface to *Evelina* (1778), by
   Fanny Burney DLB-39

Preface to *Ferdinand Count Fathom* (1753), by
   Tobias Smollett DLB-39

Preface to *Incognita* (1692), by
   William Congreve DLB-39

Preface to *Joseph Andrews* (1742), by
   Henry Fielding DLB-39

Preface to *Moll Flanders* (1722), by
   Daniel Defoe DLB-39

Preface to *Poems* (1853), by
   Matthew Arnold DLB-32

Preface to *Robinson Crusoe* (1719), by
   Daniel Defoe DLB-39

Preface to *Roderick Random* (1748), by
   Tobias Smollett DLB-39

Preface to *Roxana* (1724), by
   Daniel Defoe DLB-39

Preface to *St. Leon* (1799), by
   William Godwin DLB-39

Preface to Sarah Fielding's *Familiar Letters*
   (1747), by Henry Fielding
   [excerpt] DLB-39

Preface to Sarah Fielding's *The Adventures of
   David Simple* (1744), by
   Henry Fielding DLB-39

Preface to *The Cry* (1754), by
   Sarah Fielding DLB-39

Preface to *The Delicate Distress* (1769), by
   Elizabeth Griffin DLB-39

Preface to *The Disguis'd Prince* (1733), by
   Eliza Haywood [excerpt] DLB-39

Preface to *The Farther Adventures of Robinson Crusoe* (1719), by Daniel Defoe . . . DLB-39

Preface to the First Edition of *Pamela* (1740), by Samuel Richardson DLB-39

Preface to the First Edition of *The Castle of Otranto* (1764), by Horace Walpole DLB-39

Preface to *The History of Romances* (1715), by Pierre Daniel Huet [excerpts] DLB-39

Preface to *The Life of Charlotta du Pont* (1723), by Penelope Aubin DLB-39

Preface to *The Old English Baron* (1778), by Clara Reeve DLB-39

Preface to the Second Edition of *The Castle of Otranto* (1765), by Horace Walpole DLB-39

Preface to *The Secret History, of Queen Zarah, and the Zarazians* (1705), by Delariviere Manley DLB-39

Preface to the Third Edition of *Clarissa* (1751), by Samuel Richardson [excerpt] DLB-39

Preface to *The Works of Mrs. Davys* (1725), by Mary Davys DLB-39

Preface to Volume 1 of *Clarissa* (1747), by Samuel Richardson DLB-39

Preface to Volume 3 of *Clarissa* (1748), by Samuel Richardson DLB-39

Préfontaine, Yves 1937- DLB-53

Prelutsky, Jack 1940- DLB-61

Premisses, by Michael Hamburger DLB-66

Prentice, George D. 1802-1870 . . . . . DLB-43

Prentice-Hall DLB-46

Prescott, Orville 1906-1996 . . . . Y-96

Prescott, William Hickling 1796-1859 . . . . DLB-1, 30, 59

The Present State of the English Novel (1892), by George Saintsbury DLB-18

Prešeren, Francè 1800-1849 . . . . . . DLB-147

Preston, May Wilson 1873-1949 . . . . . DLB-188

Preston, Thomas 1537-1598 . . . . . . DLB-62

Price, Reynolds 1933- DLB-2

Price, Richard 1723-1791 . . . . DLB-158

Price, Richard 1949- Y-81

Priest, Christopher 1943- DLB-14

Priestley, J. B. 1894-1984
. . . . . . DLB-10, 34, 77, 100, 139; Y-84

Primary Bibliography: A Retrospective Y-95

Prime, Benjamin Young 1733-1791 . . . DLB-31

Primrose, Diana floruit circa 1630 . . . . DLB-126

Prince, F. T. 1912- DLB-20

Prince, Thomas 1687-1758 . . . . DLB-24, 140

The Principles of Success in Literature (1865), by George Henry Lewes [excerpt] . . . DLB-57

Printz, Wolfgang Casper 1641-1717 . . . . DLB-168

Prior, Matthew 1664-1721 . . . . DLB-95

Prisco, Michele 1920- DLB-177

Pritchard, William H. 1932- DLB-111

Pritchett, V. S. 1900- DLB-15, 139

Procter, Adelaide Anne 1825-1864 . . . . DLB-32

Procter, Bryan Waller 1787-1874 . . . . DLB-96, 144

Proctor, Robert 1868-1903 . . . . DLB-184

Producing *Dear Bunny, Dear Volodya: The Friendship and the Feud* Y-97

The Profession of Authorship: Scribblers for Bread Y-89

The Progress of Romance (1785), by Clara Reeve [excerpt] DLB-39

Prokopovich, Feofan 1681?-1736 . . . . DLB-150

Prokosch, Frederic 1906-1989 . . . . . DLB-48

The Proletarian Novel DLB-9

Propper, Dan 1937- DLB-16

The Prospect of Peace (1778), by Joel Barlow DLB-37

Protagoras circa 490 B.C.-420 B.C.
. . . . DLB-176

Proud, Robert 1728-1813 . . . . DLB-30

Proust, Marcel 1871-1922 . . . . DLB-65

Prynne, J. H. 1936- DLB-40

Przybyszewski, Stanislaw 1868-1927 . . . . DLB-66

Pseudo-Dionysius the Areopagite floruit circa 500 . . . . DLB-115

Public Domain and the Violation of Texts Y-97

The Public Lending Right in America Statement by Sen. Charles McC. Mathias, Jr. PLR and the Meaning of Literary Property Statements on PLR by American Writers Y-83

The Public Lending Right in the United Kingdom Public Lending Right: The First Year in the United Kingdom Y-83

The Publication of English Renaissance Plays DLB-62

Publications and Social Movements [Transcendentalism] DLB-1

Publishers and Agents: The Columbia Connection Y-87

A Publisher's Archives: G. P. Putnam . . . Y-92

Publishing Fiction at LSU Press Y-87

Pückler-Muskau, Hermann von 1785-1871 . . . . DLB-133

Pufendorf, Samuel von 1632-1694 . . . . DLB-168

Pugh, Edwin William 1874-1930 . . . . DLB-135

Pugin, A. Welby 1812-1852 . . . . . . DLB-55

Puig, Manuel 1932-1990 . . . . DLB-113

Pulitzer, Joseph 1847-1911 . . . . . . DLB-23

Pulitzer, Joseph, Jr. 1885-1955 . . . . . DLB-29

Pulitzer Prizes for the Novel, 1917-1945 . . . . DLB-9

Pulliam, Eugene 1889-1975 . . . . . . DLB-127

Purchas, Samuel 1577?-1626 . . . . . . DLB-151

Purdy, Al 1918- DLB-88

Purdy, James 1923- DLB-2

Purdy, Ken W. 1913-1972 . . . . . . DLB-137

Pusey, Edward Bouverie 1800-1882 . . . . DLB-55

Putnam, George Palmer 1814-1872 . . . . DLB-3, 79

Putnam, Samuel 1892-1950 . . . . . . DLB-4

G. P. Putnam's Sons [U.S.] DLB-49

G. P. Putnam's Sons [U.K.] DLB-106

Puzo, Mario 1920- DLB-6

Pyle, Ernie 1900-1945 . . . . DLB-29

Pyle, Howard 1853-1911 . . . . DLB-42, 188; DS-13

Pym, Barbara 1913-1980 . . . . . DLB-14; Y-87

Pynchon, Thomas 1937- DLB-2, 173

Pyramid Books DLB-46

Pyrnelle, Louise-Clarke 1850-1907 . . . . DLB-42

Pythagoras circa 570 B.C.-? DLB-176

Q

Quad, M. (see Lewis, Charles B.)

Quaritch, Bernard 1819-1899 . . . . . DLB-184

Quarles, Francis 1592-1644 . . . . . . DLB-126

The Quarterly Review 1809-1967 . . . . DLB-110

Quasimodo, Salvatore 1901-1968 . . . . DLB-114

Queen, Ellery (see Dannay, Frederic, and Manfred B. Lee)

The Queen City Publishing House . . . DLB-49

Queneau, Raymond 1903-1976 . . . . . DLB-72

Quennell, Sir Peter 1905-1993 . . . DLB-155, 195

Quesnel, Joseph 1746-1809 . . . . . . DLB-99

The Question of American Copyright in the Nineteenth Century
Headnote
Preface, by George Haven Putnam
The Evolution of Copyright, by Brander Matthews
Summary of Copyright Legislation in the United States, by R. R. Bowker
Analysis oæ the Provisions of the Copyright Law of 1891, by George Haven Putnam
The Contest for International Copyright, by George Haven Putnam
Cheap Books and Good Books, by Brander Matthews DLB-49

Quiller-Couch, Sir Arthur Thomas 1863-1944 . . . . DLB-135, 153, 190

Quin, Ann 1936-1973 . . . . DLB-14

Quincy, Samuel, of Georgia ?-? DLB-31

Quincy, Samuel, of Massachusetts
1734-1789 . . . . DLB-31

Quinn, Anthony 1915- DLB-122

Quinn, John 1870-1924 . . . . DLB-187

Quintana, Leroy V. 1944- DLB-82

Quintana, Miguel de 1671-1748
A Forerunner of Chicano
Literature DLB-122

Quist, Harlin, Books DLB-46

Quoirez, Françoise (see Sagan, Françoise)

R

Raabe, Wilhelm 1831-1910 . . . . DLB-129

Rabe, David 1940- DLB-7

Raboni, Giovanni 1932- DLB-128

Rachilde 1860-1953 . . . . DLB-123, 192

Racin, Kočo 1908-1943 . . . . DLB-147

Rackham, Arthur 1867-1939 . . . . . . DLB-141

Radcliffe, Ann 1764-1823 . . . . . . DLB-39, 178

Raddall, Thomas 1903- DLB-68

Radichkov, Yordan 1929- DLB-181

Radiguet, Raymond 1903-1923 . . . . . DLB-65

Radishchev, Aleksandr Nikolaevich
1749-1802 . . . . DLB-150

Radványi, Netty Reiling (see Seghers, Anna)

Rahv, Philip 1908-1973 . . . . DLB-137

Raičković, Stevan 1928- DLB-181

Raimund, Ferdinand Jakob
1790-1836 . . . . DLB-90

Raine, Craig 1944- DLB-40

Raine, Kathleen 1908- DLB-20

Rainolde, Richard
circa 1530-1606 . . . . DLB-136

Rakić, Milan 1876-1938 . . . . DLB-147

Rakosi, Carl 1903- DLB-193

Ralegh, Sir Walter 1554?-1618 . . . . . DLB-172

Ralin, Radoy 1923- DLB-181

Ralph, Julian 1853-1903 . . . . DLB-23

Ralph Waldo Emerson in 1982 . . . . . . Y-82

Ramat, Silvio 1939- DLB-128

Rambler, no. 4 (1750), by Samuel Johnson
[excerpt] DLB-39

Ramée, Marie Louise de la (see Ouida)

Ramírez, Sergío 1942- DLB-145

Ramke, Bin 1947- DLB-120

Ramler, Karl Wilhelm 1725-1798 . . . DLB-97

Ramon Ribeyro, Julio 1929- DLB-145

Ramous, Mario 1924- DLB-128

Rampersad, Arnold 1941- DLB-111

Ramsay, Allan 1684 or 1685-1758 . . . . DLB-95

Ramsay, David 1749-1815 . . . . DLB-30

Ranck, Katherine Quintana
1942- DLB-122

Rand, Avery and Company DLB-49

Rand McNally and Company DLB-49

Randall, David Anton
1905-1975 . . . . DLB-140

Randall, Dudley 1914- DLB-41

Randall, Henry S. 1811-1876 . . . . . . DLB-30

Randall, James G. 1881-1953 . . . . . . DLB-17

The Randall Jarrell Symposium: A Small
Collection of Randall Jarrells
Excerpts From Papers Delivered at
the Randall Jarrel Symposium Y-86

Randolph, A. Philip 1889-1979 . . . . . DLB-91

Randolph, Anson D. F.
[publishing house] DLB-49

Randolph, Thomas 1605-1635 . . . DLB-58, 126

Random House DLB-46

Ranlet, Henry [publishing house] DLB-49

Ransom, Harry 1908-1976 . . . . DLB-187

Ransom, John Crowe
1888-1974 . . . . DLB-45, 63

Ransome, Arthur 1884-1967 . . . . . . DLB-160

Raphael, Frederic 1931- DLB-14

Raphaelson, Samson 1896-1983 . . . . DLB-44

Raskin, Ellen 1928-1984 . . . . DLB-52

Rastell, John 1475?-1536 . . . . . . DLB-136, 170

Rattigan, Terence 1911-1977 . . . . . . DLB-13

Rawlings, Marjorie Kinnan
1896-1953 . . . . . DLB-9, 22, 102; DS-17

Raworth, Tom 1938- DLB-40

Ray, David 1932- DLB-5

Ray, Gordon Norton
1915-1986 . . . . DLB-103, 140

Ray, Henrietta Cordelia
1849-1916 . . . . DLB-50

Raymond, Ernest 1888-1974 . . . . . . DLB-191

Raymond, Henry J. 1820-1869 . . . DLB-43, 79

Raymond Chandler Centenary Tributes
from Michael Avallone, James Elroy, Joe
Gores,
and William F. Nolan Y-88

Reach, Angus 1821-1856 . . . . DLB-70

Read, Herbert 1893-1968 . . . . . . DLB-20, 149

Read, Herbert, "The Practice of Biography," in
*The English Sense of Humour and Other
Essays* DLB-149

Read, Opie 1852-1939 . . . . DLB-23

Read, Piers Paul 1941- DLB-14

Reade, Charles 1814-1884 . . . . DLB-21

Reader's Digest Condensed
Books DLB-46

Readers Ulysses Symposium Y-97

Reading, Peter 1946- DLB-40

Reading Series in New York City Y-96

Reaney, James 1926- DLB-68

Rebhun, Paul 1500?-1546 . . . . DLB-179

Rèbora, Clemente 1885-1957 . . . . . . DLB-114

Rechy, John 1934- DLB-122; Y-82

The Recovery of Literature: Criticism in the
1990s: A Symposium Y-91

Redding, J. Saunders
1906-1988 . . . . DLB-63, 76

Redfield, J. S. [publishing house] DLB-49

Redgrove, Peter 1932- DLB-40

Redmon, Anne 1943- Y-86

Redmond, Eugene B. 1937- DLB-41

Redpath, James [publishing house] . . . DLB-49

Reed, Henry 1808-1854 . . . . DLB-59

Reed, Henry 1914- DLB-27

Reed, Ishmael
1938- DLB-2, 5, 33, 169; DS-8

Reed, Rex 1938- DLB-185

Reed, Sampson 1800-1880 . . . . DLB-1

Reed, Talbot Baines 1852-1893 . . . . . DLB-141

Reedy, William Marion 1862-1920 . . . DLB-91

Reese, Lizette Woodworth
1856-1935 . . . . DLB-54

Reese, Thomas 1742-1796 . . . . DLB-37

Reeve, Clara 1729-1807 . . . . DLB-39

Reeves, James 1909-1978 . . . . DLB-161

Reeves, John 1926- DLB-88

"Reflections: After a Tornado,"
by Judson Jerome DLB-105

Regnery, Henry, Company DLB-46

Rehberg, Hans 1901-1963 . . . . DLB-124

Rehfisch, Hans José 1891-1960 . . . . . DLB-124

Reid, Alastair 1926- DLB-27

Reid, B. L. 1918-1990 . . . . DLB-111

Reid, Christopher 1949- DLB-40

Reid, Forrest 1875-1947 . . . . DLB-153

Reid, Helen Rogers 1882-1970 . . . . . DLB-29

Reid, James ?-? DLB-31

Reid, Mayne 1818-1883 . . . . DLB-21, 163

Reid, Thomas 1710-1796 . . . . DLB-31

Reid, V. S. (Vic) 1913-1987 . . . . DLB-125

Reid, Whitelaw 1837-1912 . . . . DLB-23

Reilly and Lee Publishing
Company DLB-46

Reimann, Brigitte 1933-1973 . . . . . . DLB-75

Reinmar der Alte
circa 1165-circa 1205 . . . . DLB-138

Reinmar von Zweter
circa 1200-circa 1250 . . . . DLB-138

Reisch, Walter 1903-1983 . . . . DLB-44

Remarque, Erich Maria 1898-1970 . . . DLB-56

Cumulative Index

"Re-meeting of Old Friends": The Jack Kerouac Conference Y-82

Reminiscences, by Charles Scribner Jr. . . . DS-17

Remington, Frederic 1861-1909 . . . . DLB-12, 186, 188

Renaud, Jacques 1943- DLB-60

Renault, Mary 1905-1983 . . . . Y-83

Rendell, Ruth 1930- DLB-87

Representative Men and Women: A Historical Perspective on the British Novel, 1930-1960 . . . . DLB-15

(Re-)Publishing Orwell Y-86

Research in the American Antiquarian Book Trade Y-97

Responses to Ken Auletta Y-97

Rettenbacher, Simon 1634-1706 . . . . . DLB-168

Reuchlin, Johannes 1455-1522 . . . . . . DLB-179

Reuter, Christian 1665-after 1712 . . . . DLB-168

Reuter, Fritz 1810-1874 . . . . DLB-129

Reuter, Gabriele 1859-1941 . . . . DLB-66

Revell, Fleming H., Company DLB-49

Reventlow, Franziska Gräfin zu 1871-1918 . . . . DLB-66

Review of Reviews Office DLB-112

Review of [Samuel Richardson's] *Clarissa* (1748), by Henry Fielding DLB-39

The Revolt (1937), by Mary Colum [excerpts] DLB-36

Rexroth, Kenneth 1905-1982 . . . . . . DLB-16, 48, 165; Y-82

Rey, H. A. 1898-1977 . . . . DLB-22

Reynal and Hitchcock DLB-46

Reynolds, G. W. M. 1814-1879 . . . . . . DLB-21

Reynolds, John Hamilton 1794-1852 . . . . DLB-96

Reynolds, Mack 1917- DLB-8

Reynolds, Sir Joshua 1723-1792 . . . . . DLB-104

Reznikoff, Charles 1894-1976 . . . . DLB-28, 45

"Rhetoric" (1828; revised, 1859), by Thomas de Quincey [excerpt] DLB-57

Rhett, Robert Barnwell 1800-1876 . . . . DLB-43

Rhode, John 1884-1964 . . . . DLB-77

Rhodes, James Ford 1848-1927 . . . . . DLB-47

Rhodes, Richard 1937- DLB-185

Rhys, Jean 1890-1979 . . . . DLB-36, 117, 162

Ricardo, David 1772-1823 . . . . DLB-107, 158

Ricardou, Jean 1932- DLB-83

Rice, Elmer 1892-1967 . . . . DLB-4, 7

Rice, Grantland 1880-1954 . . . . . DLB-29, 171

Rich, Adrienne 1929- DLB-5, 67

Richards, David Adams 1950- DLB-53

Richards, George circa 1760-1814 . . . . DLB-37

Richards, I. A. 1893-1979 . . . . DLB-27

Richards, Laura E. 1850-1943 . . . . . . DLB-42

Richards, William Carey 1818-1892 . . . . DLB-73

Richards, Grant [publishing house] DLB-112

Richardson, Charles F. 1851-1913 . . . . DLB-71

Richardson, Dorothy M. 1873-1957 . . . . DLB-36

Richardson, Jack 1935- DLB-7

Richardson, John 1796-1852 . . . . DLB-99

Richardson, Samuel 1689-1761 . . . . DLB-39, 154

Richardson, Willis 1889-1977 . . . . . . DLB-51

Riche, Barnabe 1542-1617 . . . . DLB-136

Richepin, Jean 1849-1926 . . . . DLB-192

Richler, Mordecai 1931- DLB-53

Richter, Conrad 1890-1968 . . . . DLB-9

Richter, Hans Werner 1908- DLB-69

Richter, Johann Paul Friedrich 1763-1825 . . . . DLB-94

Rickerby, Joseph [publishing house] DLB-106

Rickword, Edgell 1898-1982 . . . . DLB-20

Riddell, Charlotte 1832-1906 . . . . . . DLB-156

Riddell, John (see Ford, Corey)

Ridge, John Rollin 1827-1867 . . . . . . DLB-175

Ridge, Lola 1873-1941 . . . . DLB-54

Ridge, William Pett 1859-1930 . . . . . DLB-135

Riding, Laura (see Jackson, Laura Riding)

Ridler, Anne 1912- DLB-27

Ridruego, Dionisio 1912-1975 . . . . . . DLB-108

Riel, Louis 1844-1885 . . . . DLB-99

Riemer, Johannes 1648-1714 . . . . . . DLB-168

Riffaterre, Michael 1924- DLB-67

Riggs, Lynn 1899-1954 . . . . DLB-175

Riis, Jacob 1849-1914 . . . . DLB-23

Riker, John C. [publishing house] DLB-49

Riley, James 1777-1840 . . . . DLB-183

Riley, John 1938-1978 . . . . DLB-40

Rilke, Rainer Maria 1875-1926 . . . . . . DLB-81

Rimanelli, Giose 1926- DLB-177

Rinehart and Company DLB-46

Ringuet 1895-1960 . . . . DLB-68

Ringwood, Gwen Pharis 1910-1984 . . . . DLB-88

Rinser, Luise 1911- DLB-69

Ríos, Alberto 1952- DLB-122

Ríos, Isabella 1948- DLB-82

Ripley, Arthur 1895-1961 . . . . DLB-44

Ripley, George 1802-1880 . . . . DLB-1, 64, 73

The Rising Glory of America: Three Poems DLB-37

The Rising Glory of America: Written in 1771 (1786), by Hugh Henry Brackenridge and Philip Freneau DLB-37

Riskin, Robert 1897-1955 . . . . DLB-26

Risse, Heinz 1898- DLB-69

Rist, Johann 1607-1667 . . . . DLB-164

Ritchie, Anna Mowatt 1819-1870 . . . . . DLB-3

Ritchie, Anne Thackeray 1837-1919 . . . . DLB-18

Ritchie, Thomas 1778-1854 . . . . DLB-43

Rites of Passage [on William Saroyan] Y-83

The Ritz Paris Hemingway Award Y-85

Rivard, Adjutor 1868-1945 . . . . DLB-92

Rive, Richard 1931-1989 . . . . DLB-125

Rivera, Marina 1942- DLB-122

Rivera, Tomás 1935-1984 . . . . DLB-82

Rivers, Conrad Kent 1933-1968 . . . . . DLB-41

Riverside Press DLB-49

Rivington, James circa 1724-1802 . . . . DLB-43

Rivington, Charles [publishing house] DLB-154

Rivkin, Allen 1903-1990 . . . . DLB-26

Roa Bastos, Augusto 1917- DLB-113

Robbe-Grillet, Alain 1922- DLB-83

Robbins, Tom 1936- Y-80

Roberts, Charles G. D. 1860-1943 . . . . DLB-92

Roberts, Dorothy 1906-1993 . . . . DLB-88

Roberts, Elizabeth Madox 1881-1941 . . . . DLB-9, 54, 102

Roberts, Kenneth 1885-1957 . . . . DLB-9

Roberts, William 1767-1849 . . . . . . DLB-142

Roberts Brothers DLB-49

Roberts, James [publishing house] . . . DLB-154

Robertson, A. M., and Company DLB-49

Robertson, William 1721-1793 . . . . . DLB-104

Robinson, Casey 1903-1979 . . . . DLB-44

Robinson, Edwin Arlington 1869-1935 . . . . DLB-54

Robinson, Henry Crabb 1775-1867 . . . . DLB-107

Robinson, James Harvey 1863-1936 . . . . DLB-47

Robinson, Lennox 1886-1958 . . . . . . DLB-10

Robinson, Mabel Louise 1874-1962 . . . . DLB-22

Robinson, Mary 1758-1800 . . . . DLB-158

Robinson, Richard circa 1545-1607 . . . . DLB-167

Robinson, Therese 1797-1870 . . . . DLB-59, 133

Robison, Mary 1949- DLB-130

Roblès, Emmanuel 1914- DLB-83

Roccatagliata Ceccardi, Ceccardo 1871-1919 . . . . DLB-114	Rosenwald, Lessing J. 1891-1979 . . . . DLB-187	Royde-Smith, Naomi 1875-1964 . . . . . DLB-191
Rochester, John Wilmot, Earl of 1647-1680 . . . . DLB-131	Ross, Alexander 1591-1654 . . . . DLB-151	Royster, Vermont 1914- DLB-127
Rock, Howard 1911-1976 . . . . DLB-127	Ross, Harold 1892-1951 . . . . DLB-137	Royston, Richard [publishing house] DLB-170
Rockwell, Norman Perceval 1894-1978 . . . . DLB-188	Ross, Leonard Q. (see Rosten, Leo)	Ruark, Gibbons 1941- DLB-120
Rodgers, Carolyn M. 1945- DLB-41	Ross, Lillian 1927- DLB-185	Ruban, Vasilii Grigorevich 1742-1795 . . . . DLB-150
Rodgers, W. R. 1909-1969 . . . . DLB-20	Ross, Martin 1862-1915 . . . . DLB-135	Rubens, Bernice 1928- DLB-14
Rodríguez, Claudio 1934- DLB-134	Ross, Sinclair 1908- DLB-88	Rudd and Carleton DLB-49
Rodriguez, Richard 1944- DLB-82	Ross, W. W. E. 1894-1966 . . . . DLB-88	Rudkin, David 1936- DLB-13
Rodríguez Julia, Edgardo 1946- DLB-145	Rosselli, Amelia 1930- DLB-128	Rudolf von Ems circa 1200-circa 1254 . . . . DLB-138
Roethke, Theodore 1908-1963 . . . . . . DLB-5	Rossen, Robert 1908-1966 . . . . DLB-26	Ruffin, Josephine St. Pierre 1842-1924 . . . . DLB-79
Rogers, Jane 1952- DLB-194	Rossetti, Christina Georgina 1830-1894 . . . . DLB-35, 163	Ruganda, John 1941- DLB-157
Rogers, Pattiann 1940- DLB-105	Rossetti, Dante Gabriel 1828-1882 . . . . DLB-35	Ruggles, Henry Joseph 1813-1906 . . . . DLB-64
Rogers, Samuel 1763-1855 . . . . DLB-93	Rossner, Judith 1935- DLB-6	Rukeyser, Muriel 1913-1980 . . . . . . DLB-48
Rogers, Will 1879-1935 . . . . DLB-11	Rostand, Edmond 1868-1918 . . . . . . DLB-192	Rule, Jane 1931- DLB-60
Rohmer, Sax 1883-1959 . . . . DLB-70	Rosten, Leo 1908- DLB-11	Rulfo, Juan 1918-1986 . . . . DLB-113
Roiphe, Anne 1935- Y-80	Rostenberg, Leona 1908- DLB-140	Rumaker, Michael 1932- DLB-16
Rojas, Arnold R. 1896-1988 . . . . DLB-82	Rostovsky, Dimitrii 1651-1709 . . . . . . DLB-150	Rumens, Carol 1944- DLB-40
Rolfe, Frederick William 1860-1913 . . . . DLB-34, 156	Bertram Rota and His Bookshop Y-91	Runyon, Damon 1880-1946 . . DLB-11, 86, 171
Rolland, Romain 1866-1944 . . . . DLB-65	Roth, Gerhard 1942- DLB-85, 124	Ruodlieb circa 1050-1075 . . . . DLB-148
Rolle, Richard circa 1290-1300 - 1340 . . . . DLB-146	Roth, Henry 1906?- DLB-28	Rush, Benjamin 1746-1813 . . . . DLB-37
Rölvaag, O. E. 1876-1931 . . . . DLB-9	Roth, Joseph 1894-1939 . . . . DLB-85	Rushdie, Salman 1947- DLB-194
Romains, Jules 1885-1972 . . . . DLB-65	Roth, Philip 1933- DLB-2, 28, 173; Y-82	Rusk, Ralph L. 1888-1962 . . . . DLB-103
Roman, A., and Company DLB-49	Rothenberg, Jerome 1931- DLB-5, 193	Ruskin, John 1819-1900 . . . . DLB-55, 163, 190
Romano, Lalla 1906- DLB-177	Rothschild Family DLB-184	Russ, Joanna 1937- DLB-8
Romano, Octavio 1923- DLB-122	Rotimi, Ola 1938- DLB-125	Russell, B. B., and Company DLB-49
Romero, Leo 1950- DLB-122	Routhier, Adolphe-Basile 1839-1920 . . . . DLB-99	Russell, Benjamin 1761-1845 . . . . . . DLB-43
Romero, Lin 1947- DLB-122	Routier, Simone 1901-1987 . . . . DLB-88	Russell, Bertrand 1872-1970 . . . . . . DLB-100
Romero, Orlando 1945- DLB-82	Routledge, George, and Sons DLB-106	Russell, Charles Edward 1860-1941 . . . . DLB-25
Rook, Clarence 1863-1915 . . . . DLB-135	Roversi, Roberto 1923- DLB-128	Russell, Charles M. 1864-1926 . . . . . DLB-188
Roosevelt, Theodore 1858-1919 . . DLB-47, 186	Rowe, Elizabeth Singer 1674-1737 . . . . DLB-39, 95	Russell, George William (see AE)
Root, Waverley 1903-1982 . . . . DLB-4	Rowe, Nicholas 1674-1718 . . . . DLB-84	Russell, R. H., and Son DLB-49
Root, William Pitt 1941- DLB-120	Rowlands, Samuel circa 1570-1630 . . . . DLB-121	Rutherford, Mark 1831-1913 . . . . . . DLB-18
Roquebrune, Robert de 1889-1978 . . . . DLB-68	Rowlandson, Mary circa 1635-circa 1678 . . . . DLB-24	Ruxton, George Frederick 1821-1848 . . . . DLB-186
Rosa, João Guimarães 1908-1967 . . . . DLB-113	Rowley, William circa 1585-1626 . . . . DLB-58	Ryan, Michael 1946- Y-82
Rosales, Luis 1910-1992 . . . . DLB-134	Rowse, A. L. 1903- DLB-155	Ryan, Oscar 1904- DLB-68
Roscoe, William 1753-1831 . . . . DLB-163	Rowson, Susanna Haswell circa 1762-1824 . . . . DLB-37	Ryga, George 1932- DLB-60
Rose, Reginald 1920- DLB-26	Roy, Camille 1870-1943 . . . . DLB-92	Rylands, Enriqueta Augustina Tennant 1843-1908 . . . . DLB-184
Rose, Wendy 1948- DLB-175	Roy, Gabrielle 1909-1983 . . . . DLB-68	
Rosegger, Peter 1843-1918 . . . . DLB-129	Roy, Jules 1907- DLB-83	Rylands, John 1801-1888 . . . . DLB-184
Rosei, Peter 1946- DLB-85	The Royal Court Theatre and the English Stage Company DLB-13	Rymer, Thomas 1643?-1713 . . . . . . DLB-101
Rosen, Norma 1925- DLB-28	The Royal Court Theatre and the New Drama DLB-10	Ryskind, Morrie 1895-1985 . . . . DLB-26
Rosenbach, A. S. W. 1876-1952 . . . . DLB-140	The Royal Shakespeare Company at the Swan Y-88	Rzhevsky, Aleksei Andreevich 1737-1804 . . . . DLB-150
Rosenbaum, Ron 1946- DLB-185		
Rosenberg, Isaac 1890-1918 . . . . DLB-20	Royall, Anne 1769-1854 . . . . DLB-43	
Rosenfeld, Isaac 1918-1956 . . . . DLB-28	The Roycroft Printing Shop DLB-49	
Rosenthal, M. L. 1917- DLB-5		

S

The Saalfield Publishing
    Company DLB-46
Saba, Umberto 1883-1957 . . . . DLB-114
Sábato, Ernesto 1911- DLB-145
Saberhagen, Fred 1930- DLB-8
Sabin, Joseph 1821-1881 . . . . DLB-187
Sacer, Gottfried Wilhelm
    1635-1699 . . . . DLB-168
Sachs, Hans 1494-1576 . . . . DLB-179
Sack, John 1930- DLB-185
Sackler, Howard 1929-1982 . . . . DLB-7
Sackville, Thomas 1536-1608 . . . . . . DLB-132
Sackville, Thomas 1536-1608
    and Norton, Thomas
    1532-1584 . . . . DLB-62
Sackville-West, Edward 1901-1965 . . . DLB-191
Sackville-West, V. 1892-1962 . . . . DLB-34, 195
Sadlier, D. and J., and Company DLB-49
Sadlier, Mary Anne 1820-1903 . . . . . . DLB-99
Sadoff, Ira 1945- DLB-120
Saenz, Jaime 1921-1986 . . . . DLB-145
Saffin, John circa 1626-1710 . . . . DLB-24
Sagan, Françoise 1935- DLB-83
Sage, Robert 1899-1962 . . . . DLB-4
Sagel, Jim 1947- DLB-82
Sagendorph, Robb Hansell
    1900-1970 . . . . DLB-137
Sahagún, Carlos 1938- DLB-108
Sahkomaapii, Piitai (see Highwater, Jamake)
Sahl, Hans 1902- DLB-69
Said, Edward W. 1935- DLB-67
Saiko, George 1892-1962 . . . . DLB-85
St. Dominic's Press DLB-112
Saint-Exupéry, Antoine de
    1900-1944 . . . . DLB-72
St. John, J. Allen 1872-1957 . . . . DLB-188
St. Johns, Adela Rogers 1894-1988 . . . DLB-29
The St. John's College Robert
    Graves Trust Y-96
St. Martin's Press DLB-46
St. Omer, Garth 1931- DLB-117
Saint Pierre, Michel de 1916-1987 . . . . DLB-83
Saintsbury, George
    1845-1933 . . . . DLB-57, 149
Saki (see Munro, H. H.)
Salaam, Kalamu ya 1947- DLB-38
Šalamun, Tomaž 1941- DLB-181
Salas, Floyd 1931- DLB-82
Sálaz-Marquez, Rubén 1935- DLB-122
Salemson, Harold J. 1910-1988 . . . . . . DLB-4
Salinas, Luis Omar 1937- DLB-82

Salinas, Pedro 1891-1951 . . . . DLB-134
Salinger, J. D. 1919- DLB-2, 102, 173
Salkey, Andrew 1928- DLB-125
Salt, Waldo 1914- DLB-44
Salter, James 1925- DLB-130
Salter, Mary Jo 1954- DLB-120
Salustri, Carlo Alberto (see Trilussa)
Salverson, Laura Goodman
    1890-1970 . . . . DLB-92
Sampson, Richard Henry (see Hull, Richard)
Samuels, Ernest 1903- DLB-111
Sanborn, Franklin Benjamin
    1831-1917 . . . . DLB-1
Sánchez, Luis Rafael 1936- DLB-145
Sánchez, Philomeno "Phil"
    1917- DLB-122
Sánchez, Ricardo 1941- DLB-82
Sanchez, Sonia 1934- DLB-41; DS-8
Sand, George 1804-1876 . . . . . . DLB-119, 192
Sandburg, Carl 1878-1967 . . . . . . DLB-17, 54
Sanders, Ed 1939- DLB-16
Sandoz, Mari 1896-1966 . . . . DLB-9
Sandwell, B. K. 1876-1954 . . . . DLB-92
Sandy, Stephen 1934- DLB-165
Sandys, George 1578-1644 . . . . . DLB-24, 121
Sangster, Charles 1822-1893 . . . . DLB-99
Sanguineti, Edoardo 1930- DLB-128
Sansom, William 1912-1976 . . . . DLB-139
Santayana, George
    1863-1952 . . . . DLB-54, 71; DS-13
Santiago, Danny 1911-1988 . . . . DLB-122
Santmyer, Helen Hooven 1895-1986 . . . . Y-84
Sanvitale, Francesca 1928- DLB-196
Sapidus, Joannes 1490-1561 . . . . DLB-179
Sapir, Edward 1884-1939 . . . . DLB-92
Sapper (see McNeile, Herman Cyril)
Sappho circa 620 B.C.-circa 550 B.C.
    . . . . DLB-176
Sardou, Victorien 1831-1908 . . . . . . DLB-192
Sarduy, Severo 1937- DLB-113
Sargent, Pamela 1948- DLB-8
Saro-Wiwa, Ken 1941- DLB-157
Saroyan, William
    1908-1981 . . . . DLB-7, 9, 86; Y-81
Sarraute, Nathalie 1900- DLB-83
Sarrazin, Albertine 1937-1967 . . . . . . DLB-83
Sarris, Greg 1952- DLB-175
Sarton, May 1912- DLB-48; Y-81
Sartre, Jean-Paul 1905-1980 . . . . DLB-72
Sassoon, Siegfried 1886-1967 . . . . DLB-20, 191
Sata, Ineko 1904- DLB-180
Saturday Review Press DLB-46

Saunders, James 1925- DLB-13
Saunders, John Monk 1897-1940 . . . . . DLB-26
Saunders, Margaret Marshall
    1861-1947 . . . . DLB-92
Saunders and Otley DLB-106
Savage, James 1784-1873 . . . . DLB-30
Savage, Marmion W. 1803?-1872 . . . . DLB-21
Savage, Richard 1697?-1743 . . . . DLB-95
Savard, Félix-Antoine 1896-1982 . . . . . DLB-68
Saville, (Leonard) Malcolm
    1901-1982 . . . . DLB-160
Sawyer, Ruth 1880-1970 . . . . DLB-22
Sayers, Dorothy L.
    1893-1957 . . . . DLB-10, 36, 77, 100
Sayle, Charles Edward 1864-1924 . . . DLB-184
Sayles, John Thomas 1950- DLB-44
Sbarbaro, Camillo 1888-1967 . . . . . . DLB-114
Scalapino, Leslie 1947- DLB-193
Scannell, Vernon 1922- DLB-27
Scarry, Richard 1919-1994 . . . . DLB-61
Schaeffer, Albrecht 1885-1950 . . . . . . DLB-66
Schaeffer, Susan Fromberg 1941- DLB-28
Schaff, Philip 1819-1893 . . . . DS-13
Schaper, Edzard 1908-1984 . . . . DLB-69
Scharf, J. Thomas 1843-1898 . . . . DLB-47
Schede, Paul Melissus 1539-1602 . . . . DLB-179
Scheffel, Joseph Viktor von
    1826-1886 . . . . DLB-129
Scheffler, Johann 1624-1677 . . . . DLB-164
Schelling, Friedrich Wilhelm Joseph von
    1775-1854 . . . . DLB-90
Scherer, Wilhelm 1841-1886 . . . . DLB-129
Schickele, René 1883-1940 . . . . DLB-66
Schiff, Dorothy 1903-1989 . . . . DLB-127
Schiller, Friedrich 1759-1805 . . . . DLB-94
Schirmer, David 1623-1687 . . . . DLB-164
Schlaf, Johannes 1862-1941 . . . . DLB-118
Schlegel, August Wilhelm
    1767-1845 . . . . DLB-94
Schlegel, Dorothea 1763-1839 . . . . . . DLB-90
Schlegel, Friedrich 1772-1829 . . . . . . DLB-90
Schleiermacher, Friedrich
    1768-1834 . . . . DLB-90
Schlesinger, Arthur M., Jr. 1917- DLB-17
Schlumberger, Jean 1877-1968 . . . . . . DLB-65
Schmid, Eduard Hermann Wilhelm (see
    Edschmid, Kasimir)
Schmidt, Arno 1914-1979 . . . . DLB-69
Schmidt, Johann Kaspar (see Stirner, Max)
Schmidt, Michael 1947- DLB-40
Schmidtbonn, Wilhelm August
    1876-1952 . . . . DLB-118
Schmitz, James H. 1911- DLB-8

Schnabel, Johann Gottfried 1692-1760 .... DLB-168
Schnackenberg, Gjertrud 1953- DLB-120
Schnitzler, Arthur 1862-1931 .... DLB-81, 118
Schnurre, Wolfdietrich 1920- DLB-69
Schocken Books DLB-46
Scholartis Press DLB-112
The Schomburg Center for Research in Black Culture DLB-76
Schönbeck, Virgilio (see Giotti, Virgilio)
Schönherr, Karl 1867-1943 ..... DLB-118
Schoolcraft, Jane Johnston 1800-1841 .... DLB-175
School Stories, 1914-1960 .... DLB-160
Schopenhauer, Arthur 1788-1860 ..... DLB-90
Schopenhauer, Johanna 1766-1838 .... DLB-90
Schorer, Mark 1908-1977 .... DLB-103
Schottelius, Justus Georg 1612-1676 .... DLB-164
Schouler, James 1839-1920 .... DLB-47
Schrader, Paul 1946- DLB-44
Schreiner, Olive 1855-1920 .. DLB-18, 156, 190
Schroeder, Andreas 1946- DLB-53
Schubart, Christian Friedrich Daniel 1739-1791 .... DLB-97
Schubert, Gotthilf Heinrich 1780-1860 .... DLB-90
Schücking, Levin 1814-1883 .... DLB-133
Schulberg, Budd 1914- .. DLB-6, 26, 28; Y-81
Schulte, F. J., and Company DLB-49
Schulze, Hans (see Praetorius, Johannes)
Schupp, Johann Balthasar 1610-1661 .... DLB-164
Schurz, Carl 1829-1906 .... DLB-23
Schuyler, George S. 1895-1977 ... DLB-29, 51
Schuyler, James 1923-1991 ...... DLB-5, 169
Schwartz, Delmore 1913-1966 .... DLB-28, 48
Schwartz, Jonathan 1938- Y-82
Schwarz, Sibylle 1621-1638 ..... DLB-164
Schwerner, Armand 1927- DLB-165
Schwob, Marcel 1867-1905 .... DLB-123
Sciascia, Leonardo 1921-1989 ..... DLB-177
Science Fantasy DLB-8
Science-Fiction Fandom and Conventions DLB-8
Science-Fiction Fanzines: The Time Binders DLB-8
Science-Fiction Films DLB-8
Science Fiction Writers of America and the Nebula Awards DLB-8
Scot, Reginald circa 1538-1599 ..... DLB-136
Scotellaro, Rocco 1923-1953 ...... DLB-128
Scott, Dennis 1939-1991 .... DLB-125

Scott, Dixon 1881-1915 .... DLB-98
Scott, Duncan Campbell 1862-1947 ... DLB-92
Scott, Evelyn 1893-1963 .... DLB-9, 48
Scott, F. R. 1899-1985 .... DLB-88
Scott, Frederick George 1861-1944 .... DLB-92
Scott, Geoffrey 1884-1929 .... DLB-149
Scott, Harvey W. 1838-1910 .... DLB-23
Scott, Paul 1920-1978 .... DLB-14
Scott, Sarah 1723-1795 .... DLB-39
Scott, Tom 1918- DLB-27
Scott, Sir Walter 1771-1832 .... DLB-93, 107, 116, 144, 159
Scott, William Bell 1811-1890 ..... DLB-32
Scott, Walter, Publishing Company Limited DLB-112
Scott, William R. [publishing house] DLB-46
Scott-Heron, Gil 1949- DLB-41
Scribe, Eugene 1791-1861 .... DLB-192
Scribner, Arthur Hawley 1859-1932 .... DS-13, 16
Scribner, Charles 1854-1930 ...... DS-13, 16
Scribner, Charles, Jr. 1921-1995 ...... Y-95
Charles Scribner's Sons DLB-49; DS-13, 16, 17
Scripps, E. W. 1854-1926 .... DLB-25
Scudder, Horace Elisha 1838-1902 .... DLB-42, 71
Scudder, Vida Dutton 1861-1954 .... DLB-71
Scupham, Peter 1933- DLB-40
Seabrook, William 1886-1945 ...... DLB-4
Seabury, Samuel 1729-1796 .... DLB-31
Seacole, Mary Jane Grant 1805-1881 .... DLB-166
The Seafarer circa 970 .... DLB-146
Sealsfield, Charles (Carl Postl) 1793-1864 .... DLB-133, 186
Sears, Edward I. 1819?-1876 ...... DLB-79
Sears Publishing Company DLB-46
Seaton, George 1911-1979 .... DLB-44
Seaton, William Winston 1785-1866 .... DLB-43
Secker, Martin, and Warburg Limited DLB-112
Secker, Martin [publishing house] DLB-112
Second-Generation Minor Poets of the Seventeenth Century DLB-126
Sedgwick, Arthur George 1844-1915 .... DLB-64
Sedgwick, Catharine Maria 1789-1867 .... DLB-1, 74, 183
Sedgwick, Ellery 1872-1930 ...... DLB-91
Sedley, Sir Charles 1639-1701 ..... DLB-131
Seeger, Alan 1888-1916 .... DLB-45

Seers, Eugene (see Dantin, Louis)
Segal, Erich 1937- Y-86
Šegedin, Petar 1909- DLB-181
Seghers, Anna 1900-1983 .... DLB-69
Seid, Ruth (see Sinclair, Jo)
Seidel, Frederick Lewis 1936- Y-84
Seidel, Ina 1885-1974 .... DLB-56
Seifert, Jaroslav 1901- Y-84
Seigenthaler, John 1927- DLB-127
Seizin Press DLB-112
Séjour, Victor 1817-1874 .... DLB-50
Séjour Marcou et Ferrand, Juan Victor (see Séjour, Victor)
Selby, Hubert, Jr. 1928- DLB-2
Selden, George 1929-1989 .... DLB-52
Selected English-Language Little Magazines and Newspapers [France, 1920-1939] DLB-4
Selected Humorous Magazines (1820-1950) DLB-11
Selected Science-Fiction Magazines and Anthologies DLB-8
Selenić, Slobodan 1933-1995 ..... DLB-181
Self, Edwin F. 1920- DLB-137
Seligman, Edwin R. A. 1861-1939 .... DLB-47
Selimović, Meša 1910-1982 ...... DLB-181
Selous, Frederick Courteney 1851-1917 .... DLB-174
Seltzer, Chester E. (see Muro, Amado)
Seltzer, Thomas [publishing house] DLB-46
Selvon, Sam 1923-1994 .... DLB-125
Semmes, Raphael 1809-1877 ..... DLB-189
Senancour, Etienne de 1770-1846 .... DLB-119
Sendak, Maurice 1928- DLB-61
Senécal, Eva 1905- DLB-92
Sengstacke, John 1912- DLB-127
Senior, Olive 1941- DLB-157
Šenoa, August 1838-1881 .... DLB-147
"Sensation Novels" (1863), by H. L. Manse DLB-21
Sepamla, Sipho 1932- DLB-157
Seredy, Kate 1899-1975 .... DLB-22
Sereni, Vittorio 1913-1983 ...... DLB-128
Seres, William [publishing house] DLB-170
Serling, Rod 1924-1975 .... DLB-26
Serote, Mongane Wally 1944- DLB-125
Serraillier, Ian 1912-1994 ...... DLB-161
Serrano, Nina 1934- DLB-122
Service, Robert 1874-1958 ..... DLB-92
Sessler, Charles 1854-1935 ..... DLB-187
Seth, Vikram 1952- DLB-120

Seton, Ernest Thompson 1860-1942 . . . . DLB-92; DS-13	Sheckley, Robert 1928- DLB-8	Shorthouse, Joseph Henry 1834-1903 . . . . DLB-18
Setouchi, Harumi 1922- DLB-182	Shedd, William G. T. 1820-1894 . . . DLB-64	Showalter, Elaine 1941- DLB-67
Settle, Mary Lee 1918- DLB-6	Sheed, Wilfred 1930- DLB-6	Shulevitz, Uri 1935- DLB-61
Seume, Johann Gottfried 1763-1810 . . . . DLB-94	Sheed and Ward [U.S.] DLB-46	Shulman, Max 1919-1988. . . . . DLB-11
Seuse, Heinrich 1295?-1366 . . . . . . DLB-179	Sheed and Ward Limited [U.K.] DLB-112	Shute, Henry A. 1856-1943 . . . . DLB-9
Seuss, Dr. (see Geisel, Theodor Seuss)	Sheldon, Alice B. (see Tiptree, James, Jr.)	Shuttle, Penelope 1947- DLB-14, 40
The Seventy-fifth Anniversary of the Armistice: The Wilfred Owen Centenary and the Great War Exhibit at the University of Virginia Y-93	Sheldon, Edward 1886-1946 . . . . . . DLB-7	Sibbes, Richard 1577-1635. . . . . DLB-151
	Sheldon and Company DLB-49	Sidgwick and Jackson Limited DLB-112
	Shelley, Mary Wollstonecraft 1797-1851 . . . . . DLB-110, 116, 159, 178	Sidney, Margaret (see Lothrop, Harriet M.)
		Sidney, Mary 1561-1621. . . . . DLB-167
Sewall, Joseph 1688-1769 . . . . DLB-24	Shelley, Percy Bysshe 1792-1822 . . . . DLB-96, 110, 158	Sidney, Sir Philip 1554-1586 . . . . . . DLB-167
Sewall, Richard B. 1908- DLB-111		Sidney's Press DLB-49
Sewell, Anna 1820-1878 . . . . DLB-163	Shelnutt, Eve 1941- DLB-130	Siegfried Loraine Sassoon: A Centenary Essay Tributes from Vivien F. Clarke and Michael Thorpe Y-86
Sewell, Samuel 1652-1730 . . . . DLB-24	Shenstone, William 1714-1763 . . . . . DLB-95	
Sex, Class, Politics, and Religion [in the British Novel, 1930-1959] DLB-15	Shepard, Ernest Howard 1879-1976 . . . . DLB-160	
		Sierra, Rubén 1946- DLB-122
Sexton, Anne 1928-1974 . . . . DLB-5, 169	Shepard, Sam 1943- DLB-7	Sierra Club Books DLB-49
Seymour-Smith, Martin 1928- DLB-155	Shepard, Thomas I, 1604 or 1605-1649 . . . . DLB-24	Siger of Brabant circa 1240-circa 1284 . . . . DLB-115
Sgorlon, Carlo 1930- DLB-196		
Shaara, Michael 1929-1988. . . . . Y-83	Shepard, Thomas II, 1635-1677 . . . . . DLB-24	Sigourney, Lydia Howard (Huntley) 1791-1865 . . . . DLB-1, 42, 73, 183
Shadwell, Thomas 1641?-1692 . . . . . DLB-80	Shepard, Clark and Brown. DLB-49	
Shaffer, Anthony 1926- DLB-13	Shepherd, Luke flourished 1547-1554 . . . . DLB-136	Silkin, Jon 1930- DLB-27
Shaffer, Peter 1926- DLB-13		Silko, Leslie Marmon 1948- DLB-143, 175
Shaftesbury, Anthony Ashley Cooper, Third Earl of 1671-1713 . . . . . . DLB-101	Sherburne, Edward 1616-1702 . . . . . DLB-131	
	Sheridan, Frances 1724-1766 . . . . DLB-39, 84	Silliman, Benjamin 1779-1864 . . . . . . DLB-183
Shairp, Mordaunt 1887-1939 . . . . . . DLB-10	Sheridan, Richard Brinsley 1751-1816 . . . . DLB-89	Silliman, Ron 1946- DLB-169
Shakespeare, William 1564-1616 . . . . DLB-62, 172		Silliphant, Stirling 1918- DLB-26
	Sherman, Francis 1871-1926 . . . . . . DLB-92	Sillitoe, Alan 1928- DLB-14, 139
The Shakespeare Globe Trust Y-93	Sherriff, R. C. 1896-1975 . . . . . . DLB-10, 191	Silman, Roberta 1934- DLB-28
Shakespeare Head Press DLB-112	Sherry, Norman 1935- DLB-155	Silva, Beverly 1930- DLB-122
Shakhovskoi, Aleksandr Aleksandrovich 1777-1846 . . . . DLB-150	Sherwood, Mary Martha 1775-1851 . . . . DLB-163	Silverberg, Robert 1935- DLB-8
		Silverman, Kenneth 1936- DLB-111
Shange, Ntozake 1948- DLB-38	Sherwood, Robert 1896-1955 . . . . DLB-7, 26	Simak, Clifford D. 1904-1988 . . . . DLB-8
Shapiro, Karl 1913- DLB-48	Shiel, M. P. 1865-1947 . . . . DLB-153	Simcoe, Elizabeth 1762-1850 . . . . . . DLB-99
Sharon Publications DLB-46	Shiels, George 1886-1949 . . . . DLB-10	Simcox, Edith Jemima 1844-1901 . . . . DLB-190
Sharp, Margery 1905-1991 . . . . DLB-161	Shiga, Naoya 1883-1971 . . . . DLB-180	Simcox, George Augustus 1841-1905 . . . . DLB-35
Sharp, William 1855-1905 . . . . DLB-156	Shiina, Rinzō 1911-1973 . . . . DLB-182	
Sharpe, Tom 1928- DLB-14	Shillaber, B.[enjamin] P.[enhallow] 1814-1890 . . . . DLB-1, 11	Sime, Jessie Georgina 1868-1958 . . . . . DLB-92
Shaw, Albert 1857-1947 . . . . DLB-91		Simenon, Georges 1903-1989. . . . . DLB-72; Y-89
Shaw, Bernard 1856-1950 . . . DLB-10, 57, 190	Shimao, Toshio 1917-1986 . . . . DLB-182	
Shaw, Henry Wheeler 1818-1885 . . . . DLB-11	Shimazaki, Tōson 1872-1943 . . . . . . DLB-180	Simic, Charles 1938- DLB-105
Shaw, Joseph T. 1874-1952 . . . . DLB-137	Shine, Ted 1931- DLB-38	Simmel, Johannes Mario 1924- DLB-69
Shaw, Irwin 1913-1984 . . . . DLB-6, 102; Y-84	Ship, Reuben 1915-1975 . . . . DLB-88	Simmes, Valentine [publishing house] DLB-170
Shaw, Robert 1927-1978 . . . . DLB-13, 14	Shirer, William L. 1904-1993 . . . . . . DLB-4	
Shaw, Robert B. 1947- DLB-120	Shirinsky-Shikhmatov, Sergii Aleksandrovich 1783-1837 . . . . DLB-150	Simmons, Ernest J. 1903-1972 . . . . . DLB-103
Shawn, William 1907-1992 . . . . DLB-137		Simmons, Herbert Alfred 1930- DLB-33
Shay, Frank [publishing house] DLB-46	Shirley, James 1596-1666 . . . . DLB-58	Simmons, James 1933- DLB-40
Shea, John Gilmary 1824-1892 . . . . . DLB-30	Shishkov, Aleksandr Semenovich 1753-1841 . . . . DLB-150	Simms, William Gilmore 1806-1870 . . . . DLB-3, 30, 59, 73
Sheaffer, Louis 1912-1993 . . . . DLB-103		
Shearing, Joseph 1886-1952 . . . . DLB-70	Shockley, Ann Allen 1927- DLB-33	Simms and M'Intyre DLB-106
Shebbeare, John 1709-1788 . . . . DLB-39	Shōno, Junzō 1921- DLB-182	Simon, Claude 1913- DLB-83; Y-85
	Short, Peter [publishing house] DLB-170	Simon, Neil 1927- DLB-7

Simon and Schuster..........DLB-46
Simons, Katherine Drayton Mayrant
   1890-1969...............Y-83
Simović, Ljubomir 1935-........DLB-181
Simpkin and Marshall
   [publishing house].........DLB-154
Simpson, Helen 1897-1940.......DLB-77
Simpson, Louis 1923-..........DLB-5
Simpson, N. F. 1919-..........DLB-13
Sims, George 1923-...........DLB-87
Sims, George Robert
   1847-1922.........DLB-35, 70, 135
Sinán, Rogelio 1904-..........DLB-145
Sinclair, Andrew 1935-.........DLB-14
Sinclair, Bertrand William
   1881-1972..............DLB-92
Sinclair, Catherine
   1800-1864..............DLB-163
Sinclair, Jo 1913-............DLB-28
Sinclair Lewis Centennial
   Conference..............Y-85
Sinclair, Lister 1921-..........DLB-88
Sinclair, May 1863-1946......DLB-36, 135
Sinclair, Upton 1878-1968.......DLB-9
Sinclair, Upton [publishing house]....DLB-46
Singer, Isaac Bashevis
   1904-1991........DLB-6, 28, 52; Y-91
Singer, Mark 1950-...........DLB-185
Singmaster, Elsie 1879-1958.......DLB-9
Sinisgalli, Leonardo 1908-1981....DLB-114
Siodmak, Curt 1902-...........DLB-44
Siringo, Charles A. 1855-1928....DLB-186
Sissman, L. E. 1928-1976........DLB-5
Sisson, C. H. 1914-...........DLB-27
Sitwell, Edith 1887-1964........DLB-20
Sitwell, Osbert 1892-1969....DLB-100, 195
Skármeta, Antonio 1940-........DLB-145
Skeat, Walter W. 1835-1912.....DLB-184
Skeffington, William
   [publishing house]..........DLB-106
Skelton, John 1463-1529........DLB-136
Skelton, Robin 1925-........DLB-27, 53
Skinner, Constance Lindsay
   1877-1939..............DLB-92
Skinner, John Stuart 1788-1851....DLB-73
Skipsey, Joseph 1832-1903.......DLB-35
Slade, Bernard 1930-..........DLB-53
Slamnig, Ivan 1930-...........DLB-181
Slater, Patrick 1880-1951.......DLB-68
Slaveykov, Pencho 1866-1912....DLB-147
Slaviček, Milivoj 1929-.........DLB-181
Slavitt, David 1935-.........DLB-5, 6

Sleigh, Burrows Willcocks Arthur
   1821-1869..............DLB-99
A Slender Thread of Hope: The Kennedy
   Center Black Theatre Project....DLB-38
Slesinger, Tess 1905-1945.......DLB-102
Slick, Sam (see Haliburton, Thomas Chandler)
Sloan, John 1871-1951..........DLB-188
Sloane, William, Associates.......DLB-46
Small, Maynard and Company.....DLB-49
Small Presses in Great Britain and Ireland,
   1960-1985..............DLB-40
Small Presses I: Jargon Society.......Y-84
Small Presses II: The Spirit That Moves
   Us Press...............Y-85
Small Presses III: Pushcart Press......Y-87
Smart, Christopher 1722-1771.....DLB-109
Smart, David A. 1892-1957......DLB-137
Smart, Elizabeth 1913-1986......DLB-88
Smellie, William
   [publishing house].........DLB-154
Smiles, Samuel 1812-1904........DLB-55
Smith, A. J. M. 1902-1980.......DLB-88
Smith, Adam 1723-1790.........DLB-104
Smith, Adam (George Jerome Waldo Goodman)
   1930-................DLB-185
Smith, Alexander 1829-1867....DLB-32, 55
Smith, Betty 1896-1972...........Y-82
Smith, Carol Sturm 1938-.........Y-81
Smith, Charles Henry 1826-1903....DLB-11
Smith, Charlotte 1749-1806....DLB-39, 109
Smith, Chet 1899-1973.........DLB-171
Smith, Cordwainer 1913-1966......DLB-8
Smith, Dave 1942-.............DLB-5
Smith, Dodie 1896-............DLB-10
Smith, Doris Buchanan 1934-.....DLB-52
Smith, E. E. 1890-1965..........DLB-8
Smith, Elihu Hubbard 1771-1798....DLB-37
Smith, Elizabeth Oakes (Prince)
   1806-1893..............DLB-1
Smith, F. Hopkinson 1838-1915.....DS-13
Smith, George D. 1870-1920.....DLB-140
Smith, George O. 1911-1981.......DLB-8
Smith, Goldwin 1823-1910........DLB-99
Smith, H. Allen 1907-1976.....DLB-11, 29
Smith, Harry B. 1860-1936......DLB-187
Smith, Hazel Brannon 1914-.....DLB-127
Smith, Henry
   circa 1560-circa 1591.......DLB-136
Smith, Horatio (Horace)
   1779-1849..............DLB-116
Smith, Horatio (Horace) 1779-1849 and
   James Smith 1775-1839.......DLB-96
Smith, Iain Crichton
   1928-..............DLB-40, 139

Smith, J. Allen 1860-1924........DLB-47
Smith, Jessie Willcox 1863-1935....DLB-188
Smith, John 1580-1631........DLB-24, 30
Smith, Josiah 1704-1781.........DLB-24
Smith, Ken 1938-.............DLB-40
Smith, Lee 1944-..........DLB-143; Y-83
Smith, Logan Pearsall 1865-1946....DLB-98
Smith, Mark 1935-.............Y-82
Smith, Michael 1698-circa 1771....DLB-31
Smith, Red 1905-1982......DLB-29, 171
Smith, Roswell 1829-1892........DLB-79
Smith, Samuel Harrison
   1772-1845..............DLB-43
Smith, Samuel Stanhope
   1751-1819..............DLB-37
Smith, Sarah (see Stretton, Hesba)
Smith, Seba 1792-1868........DLB-1, 11
Smith, Sir Thomas 1513-1577.....DLB-132
Smith, Stevie 1902-1971.........DLB-20
Smith, Sydney 1771-1845........DLB-107
Smith, Sydney Goodsir 1915-1975....DLB-27
Smith, Wendell 1914-1972.......DLB-171
Smith, William
   flourished 1595-1597........DLB-136
Smith, William 1727-1803........DLB-31
Smith, William 1728-1793........DLB-30
Smith, William Gardner
   1927-1974..............DLB-76
Smith, William Henry
   1808-1872..............DLB-159
Smith, William Jay 1918-.........DLB-5
Smith, Elder and Company......DLB-154
Smith, Harrison, and Robert Haas
   [publishing house]..........DLB-46
Smith, J. Stilman, and Company....DLB-49
Smith, W. B., and Company......DLB-49
Smith, W. H., and Son..........DLB-106
Smithers, Leonard
   [publishing house]..........DLB-112
Smollett, Tobias 1721-1771....DLB-39, 104
Smythe, Francis Sydney
   1900-1949..............DLB-195
Snellings, Rolland (see Touré, Askia
   Muhammad)
Snodgrass, W. D. 1926-..........DLB-5
Snow, C. P. 1905-1980....DLB-15, 77; DS-17
Snyder, Gary 1930-........DLB-5, 16, 165
Sobiloff, Hy 1912-1970..........DLB-48
The Society for Textual Scholarship and
   TEXT..................Y-87
The Society for the History of Authorship, Reading and Publishing............Y-92
Soffici, Ardengo 1879-1964......DLB-114
Sofola, 'Zulu 1938-...........DLB-157

Cumulative Index

Solano, Solita 1888-1975 .... DLB-4
Soldati, Mario 1906- DLB-177
Šoljan, Antun 1932-1993 .... DLB-181
Sollers, Philippe 1936- DLB-83
Solmi, Sergio 1899-1981 .... DLB-114
Solomon, Carl 1928- DLB-16
Solway, David 1941- DLB-53
Solzhenitsyn and America Y-85
Somerville, Edith Œnone
   1858-1949 .... DLB-135
Song, Cathy 1955- DLB-169
Sono, Ayako 1931- DLB-182
Sontag, Susan 1933- DLB-2, 67
Sophocles 497/496 B.C.-406/405 B.C.
   .... DLB-176
Šopov, Aco 1923-1982 .... DLB-181
Sorge, Reinhard Johannes
   1892-1916 .... DLB-118
Sorrentino, Gilbert
   1929- DLB-5, 173; Y-80
Sotheby, William 1757-1833 .... DLB-93
Soto, Gary 1952- DLB-82
Sources for the Study of Tudor and Stuart Drama
   DLB-62
Souster, Raymond 1921- DLB-88
The *South English Legendary*
   circa thirteenth-fifteenth
   centuries DLB-146
Southerland, Ellease 1943- DLB-33
Southern Illinois University Press Y-95
Southern, Terry 1924- DLB-2
Southern Writers Between the
   Wars DLB-9
Southerne, Thomas 1659-1746 .... DLB-80
Southey, Caroline Anne Bowles
   1786-1854 .... DLB-116
Southey, Robert
   1774-1843 .... DLB-93, 107, 142
Southwell, Robert 1561?-1595 .... DLB-167
Sowande, Bode 1948- DLB-157
Sowle, Tace
   [publishing house] DLB-170
Soyfer, Jura 1912-1939 .... DLB-124
Soyinka, Wole 1934- DLB-125; Y-86, Y-87
Spacks, Barry 1931- DLB-105
Spalding, Frances 1950- DLB-155
Spark, Muriel 1918- DLB-15, 139
Sparke, Michael
   [publishing house] DLB-170
Sparks, Jared 1789-1866 .... DLB-1, 30
Sparshott, Francis 1926- DLB-60
Späth, Gerold 1939- DLB-75
Spatola, Adriano 1941-1988 .... DLB-128
Spaziani, Maria Luisa 1924- DLB-128

The Spectator 1828- DLB-110
Spedding, James 1808-1881 .... DLB-144
Spee von Langenfeld, Friedrich
   1591-1635 .... DLB-164
Speght, Rachel 1597-after 1630 .... DLB-126
Speke, John Hanning 1827-1864 .... DLB-166
Spellman, A. B. 1935- DLB-41
Spence, Thomas 1750-1814 .... DLB-158
Spencer, Anne 1882-1975 .... DLB-51, 54
Spencer, Elizabeth 1921- DLB-6
Spencer, George John, Second Earl Spencer
   1758-1834 .... DLB-184
Spencer, Herbert 1820-1903 .... DLB-57
Spencer, Scott 1945- Y-86
Spender, J. A. 1862-1942 .... DLB-98
Spender, Stephen 1909- DLB-20
Spener, Philipp Jakob 1635-1705 .... DLB-164
Spenser, Edmund circa 1552-1599 .... DLB-167
Sperr, Martin 1944- DLB-124
Spicer, Jack 1925-1965 .... DLB-5, 16, 193
Spielberg, Peter 1929- Y-81
Spielhagen, Friedrich 1829-1911 .... DLB-129
"*Spielmannsepen*"
   (circa 1152-circa 1500) DLB-148
Spier, Peter 1927- DLB-61
Spinrad, Norman 1940- DLB-8
Spires, Elizabeth 1952- DLB-120
Spitteler, Carl 1845-1924 .... DLB-129
Spivak, Lawrence E. 1900- DLB-137
Spofford, Harriet Prescott
   1835-1921 .... DLB-74
Spring, Howard 1889-1965 .... DLB-191
Squier, E. G. 1821-1888 .... DLB-189
Squibob (see Derby, George Horatio)
Stacpoole, H. de Vere
   1863-1951 .... DLB-153
Staël, Germaine de 1766-1817 .... DLB-119, 192
Staël-Holstein, Anne-Louise Germaine de
   (see Staël, Germaine de)
Stafford, Jean 1915-1979 .... DLB-2, 173
Stafford, William 1914- DLB-5
Stage Censorship: "The Rejected Statement"
   (1911), by Bernard Shaw
   [excerpts] DLB-10
Stallings, Laurence 1894-1968 .... DLB-7, 44
Stallworthy, Jon 1935- DLB-40
Stampp, Kenneth M. 1912- DLB-17
Stanev, Emiliyan 1907-1979 .... DLB-181
Stanford, Ann 1916- DLB-5
Stanković, Borisav ("Bora")
   1876-1927 .... DLB-147
Stanley, Henry M. 1841-1904 .... DLB-189; DS-13
Stanley, Thomas 1625-1678 .... DLB-131

Stannard, Martin 1947- DLB-155
Stansby, William
   [publishing house] DLB-170
Stanton, Elizabeth Cady 1815-1902 .... DLB-79
Stanton, Frank L. 1857-1927 .... DLB-25
Stanton, Maura 1946- DLB-120
Stapledon, Olaf 1886-1950 .... DLB-15
Star Spangled Banner Office DLB-49
Stark, Freya 1893-1993 .... DLB-195
Starkey, Thomas circa 1499-1538 .... DLB-132
Starkie, Walter 1894-1976 .... DLB-195
Starkweather, David 1935- DLB-7
Starrett, Vincent 1886-1974 .... DLB-187
Statements on the Art of Poetry DLB-54
The State of Publishing Y-97
Stationers' Company of
   London, The DLB-170
Stead, Robert J. C. 1880-1959 .... DLB-92
Steadman, Mark 1930- DLB-6
The Stealthy School of Criticism (1871), by
   Dante Gabriel Rossetti DLB-35
Stearns, Harold E. 1891-1943 .... DLB-4
Stedman, Edmund Clarence
   1833-1908 .... DLB-64
Steegmuller, Francis 1906-1994 .... DLB-111
Steel, Flora Annie 1847-1929 .... DLB-153, 156
Steele, Max 1922- Y-80
Steele, Richard 1672-1729 .... DLB-84, 101
Steele, Timothy 1948- DLB-120
Steele, Wilbur Daniel 1886-1970 .... DLB-86
Steere, Richard circa 1643-1721 .... DLB-24
Stefanovski, Goran 1952- DLB-181
Stegner, Wallace 1909-1993 .... DLB-9; Y-93
Stehr, Hermann 1864-1940 .... DLB-66
Steig, William 1907- DLB-61
Stein, Gertrude
   1874-1946 .... DLB-4, 54, 86; DS-15
Stein, Leo 1872-1947 .... DLB-4
Stein and Day Publishers DLB-46
Steinbeck, John 1902-1968 .... DLB-7, 9; DS-2
Steiner, George 1929- DLB-67
Steinhoewel, Heinrich
   1411/1412-1479 .... DLB-179
Steloff, Ida Frances 1887-1989 .... DLB-187
Stendhal 1783-1842 .... DLB-119
Stephen Crane: A Revaluation Virginia
   Tech Conference, 1989 .... Y-89
Stephen, Leslie 1832-1904 .... DLB-57, 144, 190
Stephen Vincent Benét Centenary Y-97
Stephens, Alexander H. 1812-1883 .... DLB-47
Stephens, Alice Barber 1858-1932 .... DLB-188
Stephens, Ann 1810-1886 .... DLB-3, 73

Stephens, Charles Asbury
1844?-1931 .... DLB-42

Stephens, James
1882?-1950 .... DLB-19, 153, 162

Stephens, John Lloyd 1805-1852 .... DLB-183

Sterling, George 1869-1926 .... DLB-54

Sterling, James 1701-1763 .... DLB-24

Sterling, John 1806-1844 .... DLB-116

Stern, Gerald 1925- DLB-105

Stern, Madeleine B. 1912- DLB-111, 140

Stern, Richard 1928- Y-87

Stern, Stewart 1922- DLB-26

Sterne, Laurence 1713-1768 .... DLB-39

Sternheim, Carl 1878-1942 ..... DLB-56, 118

Sternhold, Thomas ?-1549 and
John Hopkins ?-1570 .... DLB-132

Stevens, Henry 1819-1886 .... DLB-140

Stevens, Wallace 1879-1955 .... DLB-54

Stevenson, Anne 1933- DLB-40

Stevenson, D. E. 1892-1973 .... DLB-191

Stevenson, Lionel 1902-1973 ...... DLB-155

Stevenson, Robert Louis 1850-1894
..... DLB-18, 57, 141, 156, 174; DS-13

Stewart, Donald Ogden
1894-1980 .... DLB-4, 11, 26

Stewart, Dugald 1753-1828 .... DLB-31

Stewart, George, Jr. 1848-1906 ..... DLB-99

Stewart, George R. 1895-1980 ...... DLB-8

Stewart and Kidd Company DLB-46

Stewart, Randall 1896-1964 .... DLB-103

Stickney, Trumbull 1874-1904 ..... DLB-54

Stieler, Caspar 1632-1707 .... DLB-164

Stifter, Adalbert 1805-1868 ...... DLB-133

Stiles, Ezra 1727-1795 .... DLB-31

Still, James 1906- DLB-9

Stirner, Max 1806-1856 .... DLB-129

Stith, William 1707-1755 .... DLB-31

Stock, Elliot [publishing house] DLB-106

Stockton, Frank R.
1834-1902 .... DLB-42, 74; DS-13

Stoddard, Ashbel
[publishing house] DLB-49

Stoddard, Charles Warren
1843-1909 .... DLB-186

Stoddard, Richard Henry
1825-1903 .... DLB-3, 64; DS-13

Stoddard, Solomon 1643-1729 ..... DLB-24

Stoker, Bram 1847-1912 .... DLB-36, 70, 178

Stokes, Frederick A., Company DLB-49

Stokes, Thomas L. 1898-1958 ...... DLB-29

Stokesbury, Leon 1945- DLB-120

Stolberg, Christian Graf zu
1748-1821 .... DLB-94

Stolberg, Friedrich Leopold Graf zu
1750-1819 .... DLB-94

Stone, Herbert S., and Company DLB-49

Stone, Lucy 1818-1893 .... DLB-79

Stone, Melville 1848-1929 .... DLB-25

Stone, Robert 1937- DLB-152

Stone, Ruth 1915- DLB-105

Stone, Samuel 1602-1663 .... DLB-24

Stone and Kimball DLB-49

Stoppard, Tom 1937- DLB-13; Y-85

Storey, Anthony 1928- DLB-14

Storey, David 1933- DLB-13, 14

Storm, Theodor 1817-1888 .... DLB-129

Story, Thomas circa 1670-1742 .... DLB-31

Story, William Wetmore 1819-1895 .... DLB-1

Storytelling: A Contemporary
Renaissance Y-84

Stoughton, William 1631-1701 ..... DLB-24

Stow, John 1525-1605 .... DLB-132

Stowe, Harriet Beecher
1811-1896 ...... DLB-1, 12, 42, 74, 189

Stowe, Leland 1899- DLB-29

Stoyanov, Dimitŭr Ivanov (see Elin Pelin)

Strabo 64 or 63 B.C.-circa A.D. 25
.... DLB-176

Strachey, Lytton
1880-1932 .... DLB-149; DS-10

Strachey, Lytton, Preface to *Eminent
Victorians* DLB-149

Strahan and Company DLB-106

Strahan, William
[publishing house] DLB-154

Strand, Mark 1934- DLB-5

The Strasbourg Oaths 842 .... DLB-148

Stratemeyer, Edward 1862-1930 .... DLB-42

Strati, Saverio 1924- DLB-177

Stratton and Barnard DLB-49

Stratton-Porter, Gene 1863-1924 .... DS-14

Straub, Peter 1943- Y-84

Strauß, Botho 1944- DLB-124

Strauß, David Friedrich
1808-1874 .... DLB-133

The Strawberry Hill Press DLB-154

Streatfeild, Noel 1895-1986 ...... DLB-160

Street, Cecil John Charles (see Rhode, John)

Street, G. S. 1867-1936 .... DLB-135

Street and Smith DLB-49

Streeter, Edward 1891-1976 .... DLB-11

Streeter, Thomas Winthrop
1883-1965 .... DLB-140

Stretton, Hesba 1832-1911 .... DLB-163, 190

Stribling, T. S. 1881-1965 .... DLB-9

Der Stricker circa 1190-circa 1250 ... DLB-138

Strickland, Samuel 1804-1867 ..... DLB-99

Stringer and Townsend DLB-49

Stringer, Arthur 1874-1950 .... DLB-92

Strittmatter, Erwin 1912- DLB-69

Strniša, Gregor 1930-1987 .... DLB-181

Strode, William 1630-1645 ...... DLB-126

Strong, L. A. G. 1896-1958 ...... DLB-191

Strother, David Hunter 1816-1888 .... DLB-3

Strouse, Jean 1945- DLB-111

Stuart, Dabney 1937- DLB-105

Stuart, Jesse
1906-1984 .... DLB-9, 48, 102; Y-84

Stuart, Lyle [publishing house] DLB-46

Stubbs, Harry Clement (see Clement, Hal)

Stubenberg, Johann Wilhelm von
1619-1663 .... DLB-164

Studio DLB-112

The Study of Poetry (1880), by
Matthew Arnold DLB-35

Sturgeon, Theodore
1918-1985 .... DLB-8; Y-85

Sturges, Preston 1898-1959 .... DLB-26

"Style" (1840; revised, 1859), by
Thomas de Quincey [excerpt] DLB-57

"Style" (1888), by Walter Pater DLB-57

Style (1897), by Walter Raleigh
[excerpt] DLB-57

"Style" (1877), by T. H. Wright
[excerpt] DLB-57

"Le Style c'est l'homme" (1892), by
W. H. Mallock DLB-57

Styron, William 1925- DLB-2, 143; Y-80

Suárez, Mario 1925- DLB-82

Such, Peter 1939- DLB-60

Suckling, Sir John 1609-1641? DLB-58, 126

Suckow, Ruth 1892-1960 ...... DLB-9, 102

Sudermann, Hermann 1857-1928 .... DLB-118

Sue, Eugène 1804-1857 .... DLB-119

Sue, Marie-Joseph (see Sue, Eugène)

Suggs, Simon (see Hooper, Johnson Jones)

Sukenick, Ronald 1932- DLB-173; Y-81

Suknaski, Andrew 1942- DLB-53

Sullivan, Alan 1868-1947 .... DLB-92

Sullivan, C. Gardner 1886-1965 .... DLB-26

Sullivan, Frank 1892-1976 .... DLB-11

Sulte, Benjamin 1841-1923 .... DLB-99

Sulzberger, Arthur Hays
1891-1968 .... DLB-127

Sulzberger, Arthur Ochs 1926- DLB-127

Sulzer, Johann Georg 1720-1779 .... DLB-97

Sumarokov, Aleksandr Petrovich
1717-1777 .... DLB-150

Summers, Hollis 1916- DLB-6

Sumner, Henry A.
 [publishing house]............DLB-49

Surtees, Robert Smith 1803-1864.....DLB-21

Surveys: Japanese Literature,
 1987-1995................DLB-182

A Survey of Poetry Anthologies,
 1879-1960................DLB-54

Surveys of the Year's Biographies

A Transit of Poets and Others: American
 Biography in 1982............Y-82

The Year in Literary Biography....Y-83–Y-96

Survey of the Year's Book Publishing

The Year in Book Publishing.........Y-86

Survey of the Year's Children's Books

The Year in Children's Books
 ....Y-92–Y-96

Surveys of the Year's Drama

The Year in Drama
 ....Y-82–Y-85, Y-87–Y-96

The Year in London Theatre.........Y-92

Surveys of the Year's Fiction

The Year's Work in Fiction:
 A Survey..................Y-82

The Year in Fiction: A Biased View....Y-83

The Year in
 Fiction......Y-84–Y-86, Y-89, Y-94–Y-96

The Year in the
 Novel..........Y-87, Y-88, Y-90–Y-93

The Year in Short Stories...........Y-87

The Year in the
 Short Story..........Y-88, Y-90–Y-93

Survey of the Year's Literary Theory

The Year in Literary Theory.....Y-92–Y-93

Surveys of the Year's Poetry

The Year's Work in American
 Poetry....................Y-82

The Year in Poetry....Y-83–Y-92, Y-94–Y-96

Sutherland, Efua Theodora
 1924-..................DLB-117

Sutherland, John 1919-1956........DLB-68

Sutro, Alfred 1863-1933...........DLB-10

Swados, Harvey 1920-1972..........DLB-2

Swain, Charles 1801-1874..........DLB-32

Swallow Press..................DLB-46

Swan Sonnenschein Limited........DLB-106

Swanberg, W. A. 1907-............DLB-103

Swenson, May 1919-1989............DLB-5

Swerling, Jo 1897-...............DLB-44

Swift, Graham 1949-.............DLB-194

Swift, Jonathan 1667-1745...DLB-39, 95, 101

Swinburne, A. C. 1837-1909....DLB-35, 57

Swineshead, Richard floruit
 circa 1350...............DLB-115

Swinnerton, Frank 1884-1982.......DLB-34

Swisshelm, Jane Grey 1815-1884.....DLB-43

Swope, Herbert Bayard 1882-1958....DLB-25

Swords, T. and J., and Company....DLB-49

Swords, Thomas 1763-1843 and
 Swords, James ?-1844........DLB-73

Sykes, Ella C. ?-1939............DLB-174

Sylvester, Josuah
 1562 or 1563 - 1618........DLB-121

Symonds, Emily Morse (see Paston, George)

Symonds, John Addington
 1840-1893.............DLB-57, 144

Symons, A. J. A. 1900-1941.......DLB-149

Symons, Arthur 1865-1945...DLB-19, 57, 149

Symons, Julian 1912-1994..DLB-87, 155; Y-92

Symons, Scott 1933-.............DLB-53

A Symposium on *The Columbia History of
 the Novel*..................Y-92

Synge, John Millington
 1871-1909..............DLB-10, 19

Synge Summer School: J. M. Synge and the Irish
 Theater, Rathdrum, County Wiclow, Ireland
 ....Y-93

Syrett, Netta 1865-1943..........DLB-135

Szymborska, Wisława 1923-..........Y-96

T

Taban lo Liyong 1939?-..........DLB-125

Tabucchi, Antonio 1943-.........DLB-196

Taché, Joseph-Charles 1820-1894....DLB-99

Tachihara, Masaaki 1926-1980....DLB-182

Tadijanović, Dragutin 1905-......DLB-181

Tafolla, Carmen 1951-...........DLB-82

Taggard, Genevieve 1894-1948......DLB-45

Taggart, John 1942-.............DLB-193

Tagger, Theodor (see Bruckner, Ferdinand)

Tait, J. Selwin, and Sons.........DLB-49

Tait's Edinburgh Magazine
 1832-1861................DLB-110

The Takarazaka Revue Company.......Y-91

Talander (see Bohse, August)

Talese, Gay 1932-..............DLB-185

Talev, Dimitŭr 1898-1966.........DLB-181

Tallent, Elizabeth 1954-.........DLB-130

TallMountain, Mary 1918-1994....DLB-193

Talvj 1797-1870.............DLB-59, 133

Tan, Amy 1952-................DLB-173

Tanizaki, Jun'ichirō 1886-1965....DLB-180

Tapahonso, Luci 1953-..........DLB-175

Taradash, Daniel 1913-..........DLB-44

Tarbell, Ida M. 1857-1944........DLB-47

Tardivel, Jules-Paul 1851-1905....DLB-99

Targan, Barry 1932-............DLB-130

Tarkington, Booth 1869-1946....DLB-9, 102

Tashlin, Frank 1913-1972.........DLB-44

Tate, Allen 1899-1979..DLB-4, 45, 63; DS-17

Tate, James 1943-.............DLB-5, 169

Tate, Nahum circa 1652-1715......DLB-80

Tatian circa 830..............DLB-148

Taufer, Veno 1933-............DLB-181

Tauler, Johannes circa 1300-1361....DLB-179

Tavčar, Ivan 1851-1923..........DLB-147

Taylor, Ann 1782-1866..........DLB-163

Taylor, Bayard 1825-1878......DLB-3, 189

Taylor, Bert Leston 1866-1921......DLB-25

Taylor, Charles H. 1846-1921......DLB-25

Taylor, Edward circa 1642-1729....DLB-24

Taylor, Elizabeth 1912-1975.....DLB-139

Taylor, Henry 1942-.............DLB-5

Taylor, Sir Henry 1800-1886......DLB-32

Taylor, Jane 1783-1824.........DLB-163

Taylor, Jeremy circa 1613-1667....DLB-151

Taylor, John 1577 or 1578 - 1653...DLB-121

Taylor, Mildred D. ?-...........DLB-52

Taylor, Peter 1917-1994.......Y-81, Y-94

Taylor, William, and Company....DLB-49

Taylor-Made Shakespeare? Or Is
 "Shall I Die?" the Long-Lost Text
 of Bottom's Dream?...........Y-85

Teasdale, Sara 1884-1933.........DLB-45

The Tea-Table (1725), by Eliza Haywood [excerpt]
 DLB-39

Telles, Lygia Fagundes 1924-.....DLB-113

Temple, Sir William 1628-1699....DLB-101

Tenn, William 1919-.............DLB-8

Tennant, Emma 1937-............DLB-14

Tenney, Tabitha Gilman 1762-1837...DLB-37

Tennyson, Alfred 1809-1892......DLB-32

Tennyson, Frederick 1807-1898....DLB-32

Terhune, Albert Payson 1872-1942...DLB-9

Terhune, Mary Virginia
 1830-1922.............DS-13, DS-16

Terry, Megan 1932-..............DLB-7

Terson, Peter 1932-............DLB-13

Tesich, Steve 1943-..............Y-83

Tessa, Delio 1886-1939..........DLB-114

Testori, Giovanni 1923-1993...DLB-128, 177

Tey, Josephine 1896?-1952........DLB-77

Thacher, James 1754-1844.........DLB-37

Thackeray, William Makepeace
 1811-1863......DLB-21, 55, 159, 163

Thames and Hudson Limited......DLB-112

Thanet, Octave (see French, Alice)

Thatcher, John Boyd 1847-1909....DLB-187

The Theater in Shakespeare's Time ... DLB-62

The Theatre Guild DLB-7

Thegan and the Astronomer
 flourished circa 850 .... DLB-148

Thelwall, John 1764-1834 ...... DLB-93, 158

Theocritus circa 300 B.C.-260 B.C.
 .... DLB-176

Theodulf circa 760-circa 821 ...... DLB-148

Theophrastus circa 371 B.C.-287 B.C.
 .... DLB-176

Theriault, Yves 1915-1983 .... DLB-88

Thério, Adrien 1925- DLB-53

Theroux, Paul 1941- DLB-2

They All Came to Paris DS-16

Thibaudeau, Colleen 1925- DLB-88

Thielen, Benedict 1903-1965 ...... DLB-102

Thiong'o Ngugi wa (see Ngugi wa Thiong'o)

Third-Generation Minor Poets of the
 Seventeenth Century DLB-131

This Quarter 1925-1927, 1929-1932 ..... DS-15

Thoma, Ludwig 1867-1921 .... DLB-66

Thoma, Richard 1902- DLB-4

Thomas, Audrey 1935- DLB-60

Thomas, D. M. 1935- DLB-40

Thomas, Dylan
 1914-1953 .... DLB-13, 20, 139

Thomas, Edward
 1878-1917 .... DLB-19, 98, 156

Thomas, Gwyn 1913-1981 .... DLB-15

Thomas, Isaiah 1750-1831 ... DLB-43, 73, 187

Thomas, Isaiah [publishing house] DLB-49

Thomas, Johann 1624-1679 .... DLB-168

Thomas, John 1900-1932 .... DLB-4

Thomas, Joyce Carol 1938- DLB-33

Thomas, Lorenzo 1944- DLB-41

Thomas, R. S. 1915- DLB-27

The Thomas Wolfe Collection at the University of
 North Carolina at Chapel Hill Y-97

The Thomas Wolfe Society Y-97

Thomasîn von Zerclære
 circa 1186-circa 1259 .... DLB-138

Thomasius, Christian 1655-1728 .... DLB-168

Thompson, David 1770-1857 ...... DLB-99

Thompson, Dorothy 1893-1961 .... DLB-29

Thompson, Francis 1859-1907 ..... DLB-19

Thompson, George Selden (see Selden, George)

Thompson, Henry Yates 1838-1928 .. DLB-184

Thompson, Hunter S. 1939- DLB-185

Thompson, John 1938-1976 .... DLB-60

Thompson, John R. 1823-1873 .... DLB-3, 73

Thompson, Lawrance 1906-1973 ... DLB-103

Thompson, Maurice 1844-1901 ... DLB-71, 74

Thompson, Ruth Plumly
 1891-1976 .... DLB-22

Thompson, Thomas Phillips
 1843-1933 .... DLB-99

Thompson, William 1775-1833 .... DLB-158

Thompson, William Tappan
 1812-1882 .... DLB-3, 11

Thomson, Edward William
 1849-1924 .... DLB-92

Thomson, James 1700-1748 .... DLB-95

Thomson, James 1834-1882 .... DLB-35

Thomson, Joseph 1858-1895 ...... DLB-174

Thomson, Mortimer 1831-1875 .... DLB-11

Thoreau, Henry David
 1817-1862 .... DLB-1, 183

Thornton Wilder Centenary at Yale Y-97

Thorpe, Thomas Bangs
 1815-1878 .... DLB-3, 11

Thoughts on Poetry and Its Varieties (1833),
 by John Stuart Mill DLB-32

Thrale, Hester Lynch (see Piozzi, Hester
 Lynch [Thrale])

Thucydides circa 455 B.C.-circa 395 B.C.
 .... DLB-176

Thulstrup, Thure de 1848-1930 .... DLB-188

Thümmel, Moritz August von
 1738-1817 .... DLB-97

Thurber, James
 1894-1961 .... DLB-4, 11, 22, 102

Thurman, Wallace 1902-1934 ..... DLB-51

Thwaite, Anthony 1930- DLB-40

Thwaites, Reuben Gold
 1853-1913 .... DLB-47

Ticknor, George
 1791-1871 .... DLB-1, 59, 140

Ticknor and Fields DLB-49

Ticknor and Fields (revived) DLB-46

Tieck, Ludwig 1773-1853 .... DLB-90

Tietjens, Eunice 1884-1944 .... DLB-54

Tilney, Edmund circa 1536-1610 ... DLB-136

Tilt, Charles [publishing house] DLB-106

Tilton, J. E., and Company DLB-49

Time and Western Man (1927), by Wyndham
 Lewis [excerpts] DLB-36

Time-Life Books DLB-46

Times Books DLB-46

Timothy, Peter circa 1725-1782 .... DLB-43

Timrod, Henry 1828-1867 .... DLB-3

Tinker, Chauncey Brewster
 1876-1963 .... DLB-140

Tinsley Brothers DLB-106

Tiptree, James, Jr. 1915-1987 ...... DLB-8

Tišma, Aleksandar 1924- DLB-181

Titus, Edward William
 1870-1952 .... DLB-4; DS-15

Tlali, Miriam 1933- DLB-157

Todd, Barbara Euphan
 1890-1976 .... DLB-160

Tofte, Robert
 1561 or 1562-1619 or 1620 .... DLB-172

Toklas, Alice B. 1877-1967 .... DLB-4

Tokuda, Shūsei 1872-1943 .... DLB-180

Tolkien, J. R. R. 1892-1973 .... DLB-15, 160

Toller, Ernst 1893-1939 .... DLB-124

Tollet, Elizabeth 1694-1754 .... DLB-95

Tolson, Melvin B. 1898-1966 .... DLB-48, 76

Tom Jones (1749), by Henry Fielding
 [excerpt] DLB-39

Tomalin, Claire 1933- DLB-155

Tomasi di Lampedusa,
 Giuseppe 1896-1957 .... DLB-177

Tomlinson, Charles 1927- DLB-40

Tomlinson, H. M. 1873-1958
 .... DLB-36, 100, 195

Tompkins, Abel [publishing house] ... DLB-49

Tompson, Benjamin 1642-1714 .... DLB-24

Tondelli, Pier Vittorio 1955-1991 .... DLB-196

Tonks, Rosemary 1932- DLB-14

Tonna, Charlotte Elizabeth
 1790-1846 .... DLB-163

Tonson, Jacob the Elder
 [publishing house] DLB-170

Toole, John Kennedy 1937-1969 .... Y-81

Toomer, Jean 1894-1967 .... DLB-45, 51

Tor Books DLB-46

Torberg, Friedrich 1908-1979 ..... DLB-85

Torrence, Ridgely 1874-1950 ..... DLB-54

Torres-Metzger, Joseph V.
 1933- DLB-122

Toth, Susan Allen 1940- Y-86

Tottell, Richard
 [publishing house] DLB-170

Tough-Guy Literature DLB-9

Touré, Askia Muhammad 1938- ... DLB-41

Tourgée, Albion W. 1838-1905 .... DLB-79

Tourneur, Cyril circa 1580-1626 .... DLB-58

Tournier, Michel 1924- DLB-83

Tousey, Frank [publishing house] ... DLB-49

Tower Publications DLB-46

Towne, Benjamin circa 1740-1793 ... DLB-43

Towne, Robert 1936- DLB-44

The Townely Plays
 fifteenth and sixteenth
 centuries DLB-146

Townshend, Aurelian
 by 1583 - circa 1651 .... DLB-121

Tracy, Honor 1913- DLB-15

Traherne, Thomas 1637?-1674 .... DLB-131

Traill, Catharine Parr 1802-1899 .... DLB-99

Train, Arthur 1875-1945 . . . . . DLB-86; DS-16

The Transatlantic Publishing
   Company DLB-49

The Transatlantic Review 1924-1925 . . . . . DS-15

Transcendentalists, American DS-5

transition 1927-1938 . . . . DS-15

Translators of the Twelfth Century:
   Literary Issues Raised and Impact
   Created DLB-115

Travel Writing, 1837-1875 . . . . DLB-166

Travel Writing, 1876-1909 . . . . DLB-174

Traven, B.
   1882? or 1890?-1969? DLB-9, 56

Travers, Ben 1886-1980 . . . . DLB-10

Travers, P. L. (Pamela Lyndon)
   1899- DLB-160

Trediakovsky, Vasilii Kirillovich
   1703-1769 . . . . DLB-150

Treece, Henry 1911-1966 . . . . DLB-160

Trejo, Ernesto 1950- DLB-122

Trelawny, Edward John
   1792-1881 . . . . DLB-110, 116, 144

Tremain, Rose 1943- DLB-14

Tremblay, Michel 1942- DLB-60

Trends in Twentieth-Century
   Mass Market Publishing DLB-46

Trent, William P. 1862-1939 . . . . . . DLB-47

Trescot, William Henry
   1822-1898 . . . . DLB-30

Trevelyan, Sir George Otto
   1838-1928 . . . . DLB-144

Trevisa, John
   circa 1342-circa 1402 . . . . DLB-146

Trevor, William 1928- DLB-14, 139

Trierer Floyris circa 1170-1180 . . . . . . DLB-138

Trillin, Calvin 1935- DLB-185

Trilling, Lionel 1905-1975 . . . . . DLB-28, 63

Trilussa 1871-1950 . . . . DLB-114

Trimmer, Sarah 1741-1810 . . . . DLB-158

Triolet, Elsa 1896-1970 . . . . DLB-72

Tripp, John 1927- DLB-40

Trocchi, Alexander 1925- DLB-15

Troisi, Dante 1920-1989 . . . . DLB-196

Trollope, Anthony
   1815-1882 . . . . DLB-21, 57, 159

Trollope, Frances 1779-1863 . . . . DLB-21, 166

Troop, Elizabeth 1931- DLB-14

Trotter, Catharine 1679-1749 . . . . . . DLB-84

Trotti, Lamar 1898-1952 . . . . DLB-44

Trottier, Pierre 1925- DLB-60

Troupe, Quincy Thomas, Jr. 1943- . . DLB-41

Trow, John F., and Company DLB-49

Truillier-Lacombe, Joseph-Patrice
   1807-1863 . . . . DLB-99

Trumbo, Dalton 1905-1976 . . . . DLB-26

Trumbull, Benjamin 1735-1820 . . . . . DLB-30

Trumbull, John 1750-1831 . . . . DLB-31

Trumbull, John 1756-1843 . . . . DLB-183

Tscherning, Andreas 1611-1659 . . . . DLB-164

T. S. Eliot Centennial Y-88

Tsubouchi, Shōyō 1859-1935 . . . . . . DLB-180

Tucholsky, Kurt 1890-1935 . . . . DLB-56

Tucker, Charlotte Maria
   1821-1893 . . . . DLB-163, 190

Tucker, George 1775-1861 . . . . . DLB-3, 30

Tucker, Nathaniel Beverley
   1784-1851 . . . . DLB-3

Tucker, St. George 1752-1827 . . . . . DLB-37

Tuckerman, Henry Theodore
   1813-1871 . . . . DLB-64

Tunis, John R. 1889-1975 . . . . . DLB-22, 171

Tunstall, Cuthbert 1474-1559 . . . . . DLB-132

Tuohy, Frank 1925- DLB-14, 139

Tupper, Martin F. 1810-1889 . . . . . . DLB-32

Turbyfill, Mark 1896- DLB-45

Turco, Lewis 1934- Y-84

Turnball, Alexander H. 1868-1918 . . . DLB-184

Turnbull, Andrew 1921-1970 . . . . . . DLB-103

Turnbull, Gael 1928- DLB-40

Turner, Arlin 1909-1980 . . . . DLB-103

Turner, Charles (Tennyson)
   1808-1879 . . . . DLB-32

Turner, Frederick 1943- DLB-40

Turner, Frederick Jackson
   1861-1932 . . . . DLB-17, 186

Turner, Joseph Addison
   1826-1868 . . . . DLB-79

Turpin, Waters Edward
   1910-1968 . . . . DLB-51

Turrini, Peter 1944- DLB-124

Tutuola, Amos 1920- DLB-125

Twain, Mark (see Clemens, Samuel Langhorne)

Tweedie, Ethel Brilliana
   circa 1860-1940 . . . . DLB-174

The 'Twenties and Berlin, by
   Alex Natan DLB-66

Tyler, Anne 1941- DLB-6, 143; Y-82

Tyler, Moses Coit 1835-1900 . . . . DLB-47, 64

Tyler, Royall 1757-1826 . . . . DLB-37

Tylor, Edward Burnett 1832-1917 . . . DLB-57

Tynan, Katharine 1861-1931 . . . . . . DLB-153

Tyndale, William
   circa 1494-1536 . . . . DLB-132

U

Udall, Nicholas 1504-1556 . . . . DLB-62

Ugrešić, Dubravka 1949- DLB-181

Uhland, Ludwig 1787-1862 . . . . DLB-90

Uhse, Bodo 1904-1963 . . . . DLB-69

Ujević, Augustin ("Tin")
   1891-1955 . . . . DLB-147

Ulenhart, Niclas
   flourished circa 1600 . . . . DLB-164

Ulibarrí, Sabine R. 1919- DLB-82

Ulica, Jorge 1870-1926 . . . . DLB-82

Ulivi, Ferruccio 1912- DLB-196

Ulizio, B. George 1889-1969 . . . . . . DLB-140

Ulrich von Liechtenstein
   circa 1200-circa 1275 . . . . DLB-138

Ulrich von Zatzikhoven
   before 1194-after 1214 . . . . DLB-138

Ulysses, Reader's Edition Y-97

Unamuno, Miguel de 1864-1936 . . . . DLB-108

Under the Microscope (1872), by
   A. C. Swinburne DLB-35

Unger, Friederike Helene
   1741-1813 . . . . DLB-94

Ungaretti, Giuseppe 1888-1970 . . . . . DLB-114

United States Book Company DLB-49

Universal Publishing and Distributing
   Corporation DLB-46

The University of Iowa Writers' Workshop
   Golden Jubilee Y-86

The University of South Carolina
   Press Y-94

University of Wales Press DLB-112

"The Unknown Public" (1858), by
   Wilkie Collins [excerpt] DLB-57

Uno, Chiyo 1897-1996 . . . . DLB-180

Unruh, Fritz von 1885-1970 . . . . DLB-56, 118

Unspeakable Practices II: The Festival of
   Vanguard Narrative at Brown
   University Y-93

Unsworth, Barry 1930- DLB-194

Unwin, T. Fisher
   [publishing house] DLB-106

Upchurch, Boyd B. (see Boyd, John)

Updike, John
   1932- . . . DLB-2, 5, 143; Y-80, Y-82; DS-3

Upton, Bertha 1849-1912 . . . . DLB-141

Upton, Charles 1948- DLB-16

Upton, Florence K. 1873-1922 . . . . . DLB-141

Upward, Allen 1863-1926 . . . . DLB-36

Urista, Alberto Baltazar (see Alurista)

Urzidil, Johannes 1896-1976 . . . . . . DLB-85

Urquhart, Fred 1912- DLB-139

The Uses of Facsimile Y-90

Usk, Thomas died 1388 . . . . DLB-146

Uslar Pietri, Arturo 1906- DLB-113

Ustinov, Peter 1921- DLB-13

Uttley, Alison 1884-1976 . . . . DLB-160

Uz, Johann Peter 1720-1796 ...... DLB-97

V

Vac, Bertrand 1914- DLB-88
Vail, Laurence 1891-1968 .... DLB-4
Vailland, Roger 1907-1965 .... DLB-83
Vajda, Ernest 1887-1954 .... DLB-44
Valdés, Gina 1943- DLB-122
Valdez, Luis Miguel 1940- DLB-122
Valduga, Patrizia 1953- DLB-128
Valente, José Angel 1929- DLB-108
Valenzuela, Luisa 1938- DLB-113
Valeri, Diego 1887-1976 .... DLB-128
Valesio, Paolo 1939- DLB-196
Valgardson, W. D. 1939- DLB-60
Valle, Víctor Manuel 1950- DLB-122
Valle-Inclán, Ramón del
  1866-1936 .... DLB-134
Vallejo, Armando 1949- DLB-122
Vallès, Jules 1832-1885 .... DLB-123
Vallette, Marguerite Eymery (see Rachilde)
Valverde, José María 1926- DLB-108
Van Allsburg, Chris 1949- DLB-61
Van Anda, Carr 1864-1945 ...... DLB-25
Van Dine, S. S. (see Wright, Williard Huntington)
Van Doren, Mark 1894-1972 ..... DLB-45
van Druten, John 1901-1957 .... DLB-10
Van Duyn, Mona 1921- DLB-5
Van Dyke, Henry
  1852-1933 .... DLB-71; DS-13
Van Dyke, John C. 1856-1932 ... DLB-186
Van Dyke, Henry 1928- DLB-33
van Gulik, Robert Hans 1910-1967 .... DS-17
van Itallie, Jean-Claude 1936- DLB-7
Van Loan, Charles E. 1876-1919 .... DLB-171
Van Rensselaer, Mariana Griswold
  1851-1934 .... DLB-47
Van Rensselaer, Mrs. Schuyler (see Van
  Rensselaer, Mariana Griswold)
Van Vechten, Carl 1880-1964 .... DLB-4, 9
van Vogt, A. E. 1912- DLB-8
Vanbrugh, Sir John 1664-1726 ... DLB-80
Vance, Jack 1916?- DLB-8
Vane, Sutton 1888-1963 .... DLB-10
Vanguard Press DLB-46
Vann, Robert L. 1879-1940 ..... DLB-29
Vargas, Llosa, Mario 1936- DLB-145
Varley, John 1947- Y-81
Varnhagen von Ense, Karl August
  1785-1858 .... DLB-90

Varnhagen von Ense, Rahel
  1771-1833 .... DLB-90
Vásquez Montalbán, Manuel
  1939- DLB-134
Vassa, Gustavus (see Equiano, Olaudah)
Vassalli, Sebastiano 1941- DLB-128, 196
Vaughan, Henry 1621-1695 ...... DLB-131
Vaughan, Thomas 1621-1666 ..... DLB-131
Vaux, Thomas, Lord 1509-1556 .. DLB-132
Vazov, Ivan 1850-1921 .... DLB-147
Vega, Janine Pommy 1942- DLB-16
Veiller, Anthony 1903-1965 .... DLB-44
Velásquez-Trevino, Gloria
  1949- DLB-122
Veloz Maggiolo, Marcio 1936- .. DLB-145
Venegas, Daniel ?-? DLB-82
Vergil, Polydore circa 1470-1555 .. DLB-132
Veríssimo, Erico 1905-1975 .... DLB-145
Verne, Jules 1828-1905 .... DLB-123
Verplanck, Gulian C. 1786-1870 . DLB-59
Very, Jones 1813-1880 .... DLB-1
Vian, Boris 1920-1959 .... DLB-72
Vickers, Roy 1888?-1965 .... DLB-77
Victoria 1819-1901 .... DLB-55
Victoria Press DLB-106
Vidal, Gore 1925- DLB-6, 152
Viebig, Clara 1860-1952 .... DLB-66
Viereck, George Sylvester
  1884-1962 .... DLB-54
Viereck, Peter 1916- DLB-5
Viets, Roger 1738-1811 .... DLB-99
Viewpoint: Politics and Performance, by
  David Edgar DLB-13
Vigil-Piñon, Evangelina 1949- . DLB-122
Vigneault, Gilles 1928- DLB-60
Vigny, Alfred de 1797-1863 .... DLB-119, 192
Vigolo, Giorgio 1894-1983 ..... DLB-114
The Viking Press DLB-46
Villanueva, Alma Luz 1944- DLB-122
Villanueva, Tino 1941- DLB-82
Villard, Henry 1835-1900 ...... DLB-23
Villard, Oswald Garrison
  1872-1949 .... DLB-25, 91
Villarreal, José Antonio 1924- . DLB-82
Villegas de Magnón, Leonor
  1876-1955 .... DLB-122
Villemaire, Yolande 1949- DLB-60
Villena, Luis Antonio de 1951- . DLB-134
Villiers de l'Isle-Adam, Jean-Marie
  Mathias Philippe-Auguste, Comte de
  1838-1889 .... DLB-123, 192
Villiers, George, Second Duke
  of Buckingham 1628-1687 ..... DLB-80

Vine Press DLB-112
Viorst, Judith ?- DLB-52
Vipont, Elfrida (Elfrida Vipont Foulds,
  Charles Vipont) 1902-1992 ... DLB-160
Viramontes, Helena María
  1954- DLB-122
Vischer, Friedrich Theodor
  1807-1887 .... DLB-133
Vivanco, Luis Felipe 1907-1975 . DLB-108
Viviani, Cesare 1947- DLB-128
Vizenor, Gerald 1934- DLB-175
Vizetelly and Company DLB-106
Voaden, Herman 1903- DLB-88
Voigt, Ellen Bryant 1943- DLB-120
Vojnović, Ivo 1857-1929 .... DLB-147
Volkoff, Vladimir 1932- DLB-83
Volland, P. F., Company DLB-46
Vollbehr, Otto H. F. 1872?-
  1945 or 1946 .... DLB-187
Volponi, Paolo 1924- DLB-177
von der Grün, Max 1926- DLB-75
Vonnegut, Kurt
  1922- DLB-2, 8, 152; Y-80; DS-3
Voranc, Prežihov 1893-1950 .... DLB-147
Voß, Johann Heinrich 1751-1826 . DLB-90
Vroman, Mary Elizabeth
  circa 1924-1967 .... DLB-33

W

Wace, Robert ("Maistre")
  circa 1100-circa 1175 .... DLB-146
Wackenroder, Wilhelm Heinrich
  1773-1798 .... DLB-90
Wackernagel, Wilhelm
  1806-1869 .... DLB-133
Waddington, Miriam 1917- DLB-68
Wade, Henry 1887-1969 .... DLB-77
Wagenknecht, Edward 1900- DLB-103
Wagner, Heinrich Leopold
  1747-1779 .... DLB-94
Wagner, Henry R. 1862-1957 .... DLB-140
Wagner, Richard 1813-1883 ..... DLB-129
Wagoner, David 1926- DLB-5
Wah, Fred 1939- DLB-60
Waiblinger, Wilhelm 1804-1830 . DLB-90
Wain, John
  1925-1994 .... DLB-15, 27, 139, 155
Wainwright, Jeffrey 1944- DLB-40
Waite, Peirce and Company DLB-49
Wakeman, Stephen H. 1859-1924 . DLB-187
Wakoski, Diane 1937- DLB-5
Walahfrid Strabo circa 808-849 . DLB-148

Cumulative Index

Walck, Henry Z. DLB-46

Walcott, Derek 1930- . . . DLB-117; Y-81, Y-92

Waldegrave, Robert
[publishing house] DLB-170

Waldman, Anne 1945- DLB-16

Waldrop, Rosmarie 1935- DLB-169

Walker, Alice 1944- DLB-6, 33, 143

Walker, George F. 1947- DLB-60

Walker, Joseph A. 1935- DLB-38

Walker, Margaret 1915- DLB-76, 152

Walker, Ted 1934- DLB-40

Walker and Company DLB-49

Walker, Evans and Cogswell
Company DLB-49

Walker, John Brisben 1847-1931 . . . . DLB-79

Wallace, Alfred Russel 1823-1913 . . . DLB-190

Wallace, Dewitt 1889-1981 and
Lila Acheson Wallace
1889-1984 . . . . DLB-137

Wallace, Edgar 1875-1932 . . . . DLB-70

Wallace, Lila Acheson (see Wallace, Dewitt,
and Lila Acheson Wallace)

Wallant, Edward Lewis
1926-1962. . . . . DLB-2, 28, 143

Waller, Edmund 1606-1687 . . . . . . DLB-126

Walpole, Horace 1717-1797 . . . . DLB-39, 104

Walpole, Hugh 1884-1941 . . . . DLB-34

Walrond, Eric 1898-1966 . . . . DLB-51

Walser, Martin 1927- DLB-75, 124

Walser, Robert 1878-1956 . . . . DLB-66

Walsh, Ernest 1895-1926 . . . . . . DLB-4, 45

Walsh, Robert 1784-1859 . . . . DLB-59

Waltharius circa 825 . . . . DLB-148

Walters, Henry 1848-1931 . . . . . . DLB-140

Walther von der Vogelweide
circa 1170-circa 1230 . . . . DLB-138

Walton, Izaak 1593-1683 . . . . DLB-151

Wambaugh, Joseph 1937- DLB-6; Y-83

Waniek, Marilyn Nelson 1946- DLB-120

Warburton, William 1698-1779 . . . . . DLB-104

Ward, Aileen 1919- DLB-111

Ward, Artemus (see Browne, Charles Farrar)

Ward, Arthur Henry Sarsfield
(see Rohmer, Sax)

Ward, Douglas Turner 1930- DLB-7, 38

Ward, Lynd 1905-1985. . . . . DLB-22

Ward, Lock and Company DLB-106

Ward, Mrs. Humphry 1851-1920 . . . . DLB-18

Ward, Nathaniel circa 1578-1652 . . . . DLB-24

Ward, Theodore 1902-1983 . . . . . . DLB-76

Wardle, Ralph 1909-1988 . . . . DLB-103

Ware, William 1797-1852 . . . . DLB-1

Warne, Frederick, and
Company [U.S.] DLB-49

Warne, Frederick, and
Company [U.K.] DLB-106

Warner, Charles Dudley
1829-1900 . . . . DLB-64

Warner, Marina 1946- DLB-194

Warner, Rex 1905- DLB-15

Warner, Susan Bogert
1819-1885 . . . . DLB-3, 42

Warner, Sylvia Townsend
1893-1978 . . . . DLB-34, 139

Warner, William 1558-1609 . . . . . . DLB-172

Warner Books DLB-46

Warr, Bertram 1917-1943 . . . . DLB-88

Warren, John Byrne Leicester
(see De Tabley, Lord)

Warren, Lella 1899-1982 . . . . Y-83

Warren, Mercy Otis 1728-1814 . . . . . DLB-31

Warren, Robert Penn
1905-1989 . . . DLB-2, 48, 152; Y-80, Y-89

Warren, Samuel 1807-1877 . . . . . . DLB-190

Die Wartburgkrieg
circa 1230-circa 1280 . . . . DLB-138

Warton, Joseph 1722-1800 . . . . DLB-104, 109

Warton, Thomas 1728-1790 . . . . DLB-104, 109

Washington, George 1732-1799 . . . . . DLB-31

Wassermann, Jakob 1873-1934 . . . . . DLB-66

Wasson, David Atwood 1823-1887 . . . . DLB-1

Waterhouse, Keith 1929- DLB-13, 15

Waterman, Andrew 1940- DLB-40

Waters, Frank 1902- Y-86

Waters, Michael 1949- DLB-120

Watkins, Tobias 1780-1855 . . . . DLB-73

Watkins, Vernon 1906-1967 . . . . . . DLB-20

Watmough, David 1926- DLB-53

Watson, James Wreford (see Wreford, James)

Watson, John 1850-1907 . . . . DLB-156

Watson, Sheila 1909- DLB-60

Watson, Thomas 1545?-1592 . . . . . . DLB-132

Watson, Wilfred 1911- DLB-60

Watt, W. J., and Company DLB-46

Watten, Barrett 1948- DLB-193

Watterson, Henry 1840-1921 . . . . . . DLB-25

Watts, Alan 1915-1973 . . . . DLB-16

Watts, Franklin [publishing house] . . . DLB-46

Watts, Isaac 1674-1748 . . . . DLB-95

Waugh, Alfred Rudolph 1828-1891 . . . DLB-188

Waugh, Alec 1898-1981 . . . . DLB-191

Waugh, Auberon 1939- DLB-14, 194

Waugh, Evelyn 1903-1966 . . DLB-15, 162, 195

Way and Williams DLB-49

Wayman, Tom 1945- DLB-53

Weatherly, Tom 1942- DLB-41

Weaver, Gordon 1937- DLB-130

Weaver, Robert 1921- DLB-88

Webb, Beatrice 1858-1943 and
Webb, Sidney 1859-1947 . . . . . DLB-190

Webb, Frank J. ?-? DLB-50

Webb, James Watson 1802-1884 . . . . . DLB-43

Webb, Mary 1881-1927 . . . . DLB-34

Webb, Phyllis 1927- DLB-53

Webb, Walter Prescott 1888-1963 . . . DLB-17

Webbe, William ?-1591 . . . . DLB-132

Webster, Augusta 1837-1894 . . . . . . DLB-35

Webster, Charles L.,
and Company DLB-49

Webster, John
1579 or 1580-1634? DLB-58

Webster, Noah
1758-1843 . . . . . . DLB-1, 37, 42, 43, 73

Weckherlin, Georg Rodolf
1584-1653 . . . . DLB-164

Wedekind, Frank 1864-1918 . . . . . . DLB-118

Weeks, Edward Augustus, Jr.
1898-1989 . . . . DLB-137

Weeks, Stephen B. 1865-1918 . . . . . DLB-187

Weems, Mason Locke
1759-1825 . . . . DLB-30, 37, 42

Weerth, Georg 1822-1856 . . . . DLB-129

Weidenfeld and Nicolson DLB-112

Weidman, Jerome 1913- DLB-28

Weigl, Bruce 1949- DLB-120

Weinbaum, Stanley Grauman
1902-1935 . . . . DLB-8

Weintraub, Stanley 1929- DLB-111

Weise, Christian 1642-1708 . . . . . . DLB-168

Weisenborn, Gunther
1902-1969 . . . . DLB-69, 124

Weiß, Ernst 1882-1940 . . . . DLB-81

Weiss, John 1818-1879 . . . . DLB-1

Weiss, Peter 1916-1982 . . . . . . DLB-69, 124

Weiss, Theodore 1916- DLB-5

Weisse, Christian Felix 1726-1804 . . . DLB-97

Weitling, Wilhelm 1808-1871 . . . . . DLB-129

Welch, James 1940- DLB-175

Welch, Lew 1926-1971? DLB-16

Weldon, Fay 1931- DLB-14, 194

Wellek, René 1903- DLB-63

Wells, Carolyn 1862-1942 . . . . DLB-11

Wells, Charles Jeremiah
circa 1800-1879 . . . . DLB-32

Wells, Gabriel 1862-1946 . . . . DLB-140

Wells, H. G.
1866-1946 . . . . . . DLB-34, 70, 156, 178

Wells, Robert 1947- DLB-40

Wells-Barnett, Ida B. 1862-1931 . . . . DLB-23

Welty, Eudora
    1909- DLB-2, 102, 143; Y-87; DS-12
Wendell, Barrett 1855-1921......... DLB-71
Wentworth, Patricia 1878-1961...... DLB-77
Werder, Diederich von dem
    1584-1657 .... DLB-164
Werfel, Franz 1890-1945 .... DLB-81, 124
The Werner Company........... DLB-49
Werner, Zacharias 1768-1823........ DLB-94
Wersba, Barbara 1932- DLB-52
Wescott, Glenway 1901- DLB-4, 9, 102
We See the Editor at Work......... Y-97
Wesker, Arnold 1932- DLB-13
Wesley, Charles 1707-1788.......... DLB-95
Wesley, John 1703-1791.......... DLB-104
Wesley, Richard 1945- DLB-38
Wessels, A., and Company DLB-46
Wessobrunner Gebet
    circa 787-815............. DLB-148
West, Anthony 1914-1988 .... DLB-15
West, Dorothy 1907- DLB-76
West, Jessamyn 1902-1984 ..... DLB-6; Y-84
West, Mae 1892-1980........... DLB-44
West, Nathanael 1903-1940 .... DLB-4, 9, 28
West, Paul 1930- DLB-14
West, Rebecca 1892-1983 ..... DLB-36; Y-83
West, Richard 1941- DLB-185
West and Johnson DLB-49
Western Publishing Company DLB-46
The Westminster Review 1824-1914 .... DLB-110
Weston, Elizabeth Jane
    circa 1582-1612........... DLB-172
Wetherald, Agnes Ethelwyn
    1857-1940 .... DLB-99
Wetherell, Elizabeth (see Warner, Susan Bogert)
Wetzel, Friedrich Gottlob
    1779-1819 .... DLB-90
Weyman, Stanley J. 1855-1928 .. DLB-141, 156
Wezel, Johann Karl 1747-1819...... DLB-94
Whalen, Philip 1923- DLB-16
Whalley, George 1915-1983 .... DLB-88
Wharton, Edith
    1862-1937... DLB-4, 9, 12, 78, 189; DS-13
Wharton, William 1920s?- Y-80
Whately, Mary Louisa
    1824-1889 .... DLB-166
Whately, Richard 1787-1863 ...... DLB-190
What's Really Wrong With Bestseller
    Lists.................. Y-84
Wheatley, Dennis Yates
    1897-1977................ DLB-77
Wheatley, Phillis
    circa 1754-1784........... DLB-31, 50

Wheeler, Anna Doyle
    1785-1848?............... DLB-158
Wheeler, Charles Stearns
    1816-1843................. DLB-1
Wheeler, Monroe 1900-1988........ DLB-4
Wheelock, John Hall 1886-1978 ..... DLB-45
Wheelwright, John
    circa 1592-1679 .... DLB-24
Wheelwright, J. B. 1897-1940 .... DLB-45
Whetstone, Colonel Pete (see Noland, C. F. M.)
Whetstone, George 1550-1587 ..... DLB-136
Whicher, Stephen E. 1915-1961 .... DLB-111
Whipple, Edwin Percy 1819-1886 .. DLB-1, 64
Whitaker, Alexander 1585-1617 ..... DLB-24
Whitaker, Daniel K. 1801-1881 ..... DLB-73
Whitcher, Frances Miriam
    1814-1852................. DLB-11
White, Andrew 1579-1656 .... DLB-24
White, Andrew Dickson
    1832-1918................. DLB-47
White, E. B. 1899-1985 .... DLB-11, 22
White, Edgar B. 1947- DLB-38
White, Ethel Lina 1887-1944........ DLB-77
White, Henry Kirke 1785-1806 ..... DLB-96
White, Horace 1834-1916......... DLB-23
White, Phyllis Dorothy James
    (see James, P. D.)
White, Richard Grant 1821-1885 .... DLB-64
White, T. H. 1906-1964......... DLB-160
White, Walter 1893-1955......... DLB-51
White, William, and Company DLB-49
White, William Allen 1868-1944 ... DLB-9, 25
White, William Anthony Parker
    (see Boucher, Anthony)
White, William Hale (see Rutherford, Mark)
Whitechurch, Victor L. 1868-1933.... DLB-70
Whitehead, Alfred North
    1861-1947 .... DLB-100
Whitehead, James 1936- Y-81
Whitehead, William 1715-1785... DLB-84, 109
Whitfield, James Monroe 1822-1871... DLB-50
Whitgift, John circa 1533-1604 ..... DLB-132
Whiting, John 1917-1963 .... DLB-13
Whiting, Samuel 1597-1679......... DLB-24
Whitlock, Brand 1869-1934........ DLB-12
Whitman, Albert, and Company.... DLB-46
Whitman, Albery Allson
    1851-1901 .... DLB-50
Whitman, Alden 1913-1990 .... Y-91
Whitman, Sarah Helen (Power)
    1803-1878................. DLB-1
Whitman, Walt 1819-1892 ...... DLB-3, 64
Whitman Publishing Company..... DLB-46

Whitney, Geoffrey
    1548 or 1552?-1601......... DLB-136
Whitney, Isabella
    flourished 1566-1573 ...... DLB-136
Whitney, John Hay 1904-1982 ..... DLB-127
Whittemore, Reed 1919- DLB-5
Whittier, John Greenleaf 1807-1892.... DLB-1
Whittlesey House............ DLB-46
Who Runs American Literature?...... Y-94
Whose *Ulysses?* The Function of
    Editing Y-97
Wideman, John Edgar 1941- DLB-33, 143
Widener, Harry Elkins 1885-1912 .... DLB-140
Wiebe, Rudy 1934- DLB-60
Wiechert, Ernst 1887-1950 .... DLB-56
Wied, Martina 1882-1957......... DLB-85
Wiehe, Evelyn May Clowes (see Mordaunt,
    Elinor)
Wieland, Christoph Martin
    1733-1813 .... DLB-97
Wienbarg, Ludolf 1802-1872 ...... DLB-133
Wieners, John 1934- DLB-16
Wier, Ester 1910- DLB-52
Wiesel, Elie 1928- DLB-83; Y-86, Y-87
Wiggin, Kate Douglas 1856-1923 .... DLB-42
Wigglesworth, Michael 1631-1705 .... DLB-24
Wilberforce, William 1759-1833..... DLB-158
Wilbrandt, Adolf 1837-1911........ DLB-129
Wilbur, Richard 1921- DLB-5, 169
Wild, Peter 1940- DLB-5
Wilde, Oscar 1854-1900
    ..... DLB-10, 19, 34, 57, 141, 156, 190
Wilde, Richard Henry
    1789-1847 .... DLB-3, 59
Wilde, W. A., Company.......... DLB-49
Wilder, Billy 1906- DLB-26
Wilder, Laura Ingalls 1867-1957...... DLB-22
Wilder, Thornton 1897-1975 .... DLB-4, 7, 9
Wildgans, Anton 1881-1932....... DLB-118
Wiley, Bell Irvin 1906-1980 .... DLB-17
Wiley, John, and Sons DLB-49
Wilhelm, Kate 1928- DLB-8
Wilkes, Charles 1798-1877 .... DLB-183
Wilkes, George 1817-1885 .... DLB-79
Wilkinson, Anne 1910-1961 .... DLB-88
Wilkinson, Sylvia 1940- Y-86
Wilkinson, William Cleaver
    1833-1920 .... DLB-71
Willard, Barbara 1909-1994 ..... DLB-161
Willard, L. [publishing house]..... DLB-49
Willard, Nancy 1936- DLB-5, 52
Willard, Samuel 1640-1707........ DLB-24
William of Auvergne 1190-1249 .... DLB-115

William of Conches
 circa 1090-circa 1154 . . . . DLB-115

William of Ockham
 circa 1285-1347 . . . . DLB-115

William of Sherwood
 1200/1205 - 1266/1271 . . . . DLB-115

The William Chavrat American Fiction
 Collection at the Ohio State University
 Libraries. Y-92

William Faulkner Centenary. Y-97

Williams, A., and Company DLB-49

Williams, Ben Ames 1889-1953. . . . . DLB-102

Williams, C. K. 1936- DLB-5

Williams, Chancellor 1905- DLB-76

Williams, Charles
 1886-1945. . . . . DLB-100, 153

Williams, Denis 1923- DLB-117

Williams, Emlyn 1905- DLB-10, 77

Williams, Garth 1912- DLB-22

Williams, George Washington
 1849-1891 . . . . DLB-47

Williams, Heathcote 1941- DLB-13

Williams, Helen Maria
 1761-1827 . . . . DLB-158

Williams, Hugo 1942- DLB-40

Williams, Isaac 1802-1865 . . . . DLB-32

Williams, Joan 1928- DLB-6

Williams, John A. 1925- DLB-2, 33

Williams, John E. 1922-1994 . . . . DLB-6

Williams, Jonathan 1929- DLB-5

Williams, Miller 1930- DLB-105

Williams, Raymond 1921- DLB-14

Williams, Roger circa 1603-1683. . . . . DLB-24

Williams, Rowland 1817-1870. . . . . . DLB-184

Williams, Samm-Art 1946- DLB-38

Williams, Sherley Anne 1944- DLB-41

Williams, T. Harry 1909-1979 . . . . . DLB-17

Williams, Tennessee
 1911-1983. . . . . DLB-7; Y-83; DS-4

Williams, Ursula Moray 1911- DLB-160

Williams, Valentine 1883-1946 . . . . . DLB-77

Williams, William Appleman
 1921- DLB-17

Williams, William Carlos
 1883-1963 . . . . DLB-4, 16, 54, 86

Williams, Wirt 1921- DLB-6

Williams Brothers DLB-49

Williamson, Henry 1895-1977. . . . . . DLB-191

Williamson, Jack 1908- DLB-8

Willingham, Calder Baynard, Jr.
 1922- DLB-2, 44

Williram of Ebersberg
 circa 1020-1085 . . . . DLB-148

Willis, Nathaniel Parker
 1806-1867 . . . DLB-3, 59, 73, 74, 183; DS-13

Willkomm, Ernst 1810-1886. . . . . . . DLB-133

Wilmer, Clive 1945- DLB-40

Wilson, A. N. 1950- DLB-14, 155, 194

Wilson, Angus
 1913-1991 . . . . DLB-15, 139, 155

Wilson, Arthur 1595-1652 . . . . DLB-58

Wilson, Augusta Jane Evans
 1835-1909 . . . . DLB-42

Wilson, Colin 1931- DLB-14, 194

Wilson, Edmund 1895-1972 . . . . DLB-63

Wilson, Ethel 1888-1980 . . . . DLB-68

Wilson, Harriet E. Adams
 1828?-1863? DLB-50

Wilson, Harry Leon 1867-1939 . . . . . DLB-9

Wilson, John 1588-1667 . . . . DLB-24

Wilson, John 1785-1854 . . . . DLB-110

Wilson, Lanford 1937- DLB-7

Wilson, Margaret 1882-1973 . . . . DLB-9

Wilson, Michael 1914-1978 . . . . DLB-44

Wilson, Mona 1872-1954 . . . . DLB-149

Wilson, Romer 1891-1930. . . . . DLB-191

Wilson, Thomas
 1523 or 1524-1581 . . . . DLB-132

Wilson, Woodrow 1856-1924 . . . . . . DLB-47

Wilson, Effingham
 [publishing house] DLB-154

Wimsatt, William K., Jr.
 1907-1975 . . . . DLB-63

Winchell, Walter 1897-1972 . . . . DLB-29

Winchester, J. [publishing house]. . . . DLB-49

Winckelmann, Johann Joachim
 1717-1768 . . . . DLB-97

Winckler, Paul 1630-1686. . . . . DLB-164

Wind, Herbert Warren 1916- DLB-171

Windet, John [publishing house] DLB-170

Windham, Donald 1920- DLB-6

Wing, Donald Goddard 1904-1972. . . DLB-187

Wing, John M. 1844-1917 . . . . DLB-187

Wingate, Allan [publishing house] . . . DLB-112

Winnemucca, Sarah 1844-1921 . . . . . DLB-175

Winnifrith, Tom 1938- DLB-155

Winsloe, Christa 1888-1944 . . . . DLB-124

Winsor, Justin 1831-1897 . . . . DLB-47

John C. Winston Company DLB-49

Winters, Yvor 1900-1968 . . . . DLB-48

Winthrop, John 1588-1649 . . . . . DLB-24, 30

Winthrop, John, Jr. 1606-1676 . . . . . DLB-24

Wirt, William 1772-1834 . . . . DLB-37

Wise, John 1652-1725. . . . . DLB-24

Wise, Thomas James 1859-1937 . . . . DLB-184

Wiseman, Adele 1928- DLB-88

Wishart and Company DLB-112

Wisner, George 1812-1849 . . . . DLB-43

Wister, Owen 1860-1938 . . . . DLB-9, 78, 186

Wither, George 1588-1667 . . . . DLB-121

Witherspoon, John 1723-1794 . . . . . . DLB-31

Withrow, William Henry 1839-1908. . . . DLB-99

Wittig, Monique 1935- DLB-83

Wodehouse, P. G.
 1881-1975 . . . . DLB-34, 162

Wohmann, Gabriele 1932- DLB-75

Woiwode, Larry 1941- DLB-6

Wolcot, John 1738-1819. . . . . DLB-109

Wolcott, Roger 1679-1767 . . . . DLB-24

Wolf, Christa 1929- DLB-75

Wolf, Friedrich 1888-1953. . . . . DLB-124

Wolfe, Gene 1931- DLB-8

Wolfe, John [publishing house] DLB-170

Wolfe, Reyner (Reginald)
 [publishing house] DLB-170

Wolfe, Thomas
 1900-1938. . DLB-9, 102; Y-85; DS-2, DS-16

Wolfe, Tom 1931- DLB-152, 185

Wolff, Helen 1906-1994 . . . . Y-94

Wolff, Tobias 1945- DLB-130

Wolfram von Eschenbach
 circa 1170-after 1220 . . . . DLB-138

Wolfram von Eschenbach's *Parzival:*
 Prologue and Book 3 . . . . DLB-138

Wollstonecraft, Mary
 1759-1797 . . . . DLB-39, 104, 158

Wondratschek, Wolf 1943- DLB-75

Wood, Benjamin 1820-1900 . . . . DLB-23

Wood, Charles 1932- DLB-13

Wood, Mrs. Henry 1814-1887 . . . . . . DLB-18

Wood, Joanna E. 1867-1927 . . . . DLB-92

Wood, Samuel [publishing house] DLB-49

Wood, William ?-? DLB-24

Woodberry, George Edward
 1855-1930 . . . . DLB-71, 103

Woodbridge, Benjamin 1622-1684 . . . . DLB-24

Woodcock, George 1912- DLB-88

Woodhull, Victoria C. 1838-1927 . . . . DLB-79

Woodmason, Charles circa 1720-? DLB-31

Woodress, Jr., James Leslie 1916- . . . DLB-111

Woodson, Carter G. 1875-1950 . . . . . DLB-17

Woodward, C. Vann 1908- DLB-17

Woodward, Stanley 1895-1965 . . . . . DLB-171

Wooler, Thomas
 1785 or 1786-1853 . . . . DLB-158

Woolf, David (see Maddow, Ben)

Woolf, Leonard 1880-1969 . . . . DLB-100; DS-10

Woolf, Virginia
 1882-1941 . . . . . DLB-36, 100, 162; DS-10

Woolf, Virginia, "The New Biography," *New York Herald Tribune,* 30 October 1927
 . . . . DLB-149

Woollcott, Alexander 1887-1943 . . . . . DLB-29
Woolman, John 1720-1772 . . . . DLB-31
Woolner, Thomas 1825-1892 . . . . DLB-35
Woolsey, Sarah Chauncy 1835-1905 . . . DLB-42
Woolson, Constance Fenimore
   1840-1894 . . . . DLB-12, 74, 189
Worcester, Joseph Emerson
   1784-1865 . . . . DLB-1
Worde, Wynkyn de
   [publishing house] DLB-170
Wordsworth, Christopher 1807-1885 . . DLB-166
Wordsworth, Dorothy 1771-1855 . . . . DLB-107
Wordsworth, Elizabeth 1840-1932 . . . . DLB-98
Wordsworth, William 1770-1850 . . DLB-93, 107
Workman, Fanny Bullock 1859-1925 . . DLB-189
The Works of the Rev. John Witherspoon
   (1800-1801) [excerpts] DLB-31
A World Chronology of Important Science
   Fiction Works (1818-1979) DLB-8
World Publishing Company DLB-46
World War II Writers Symposium at the
   University of South Carolina,
   12–14 April 1995 . . . . Y-95
Worthington, R., and Company DLB-49
Wotton, Sir Henry 1568-1639 . . . . . . DLB-121
Wouk, Herman 1915- Y-82
Wreford, James 1915- DLB-88
Wren, Percival Christopher 1885-1941 . . . DLB-153
Wrenn, John Henry 1841-1911 . . . . . DLB-140
Wright, C. D. 1949- DLB-120
Wright, Charles 1935- DLB-165; Y-82
Wright, Charles Stevenson 1932- DLB-33
Wright, Frances 1795-1852 . . . . DLB-73
Wright, Harold Bell 1872-1944 . . . . . . DLB-9
Wright, James 1927-1980 . . . . . . DLB-5, 169
Wright, Jay 1935- DLB-41
Wright, Louis B. 1899-1984 . . . . DLB-17
Wright, Richard 1908-1960 . . DLB-76, 102; DS-2
Wright, Richard B. 1937- DLB-53
Wright, Sarah Elizabeth 1928- DLB-33
Wright, Willard Huntington ("S. S. Van Dine")
   1888-1939 . . . . DS-16
Writers and Politics: 1871-1918,
   by Ronald Gray DLB-66
Writers and their Copyright Holders:
   the WATCH Project Y-94
Writers' Forum Y-85
Writing for the Theatre, by
   Harold Pinter DLB-13
Wroth, Lady Mary 1587-1653 . . . . . DLB-121
Wroth, Lawrence C. 1884-1970 . . . . DLB-187
Wurlitzer, Rudolph 1937- DLB-173

Wyatt, Sir Thomas
   circa 1503-1542 . . . . DLB-132
Wycherley, William 1641-1715 . . . . . . DLB-80
Wyclif, John
   circa 1335-31 December 1384 . . . DLB-146
Wyeth, N. C.
   1882-1945 . . . . DLB-188; DS-16
Wylie, Elinor 1885-1928 . . . . DLB-9, 45
Wylie, Philip 1902-1971 . . . . DLB-9
Wyllie, John Cook
   1908-1968 . . . . DLB-140
Wynne-Tyson, Esmé 1898-1972 . . . . DLB-191

X

Xenophon circa 430 B.C.-circa 356 B.C.
   . . . . DLB-176

Y

Yasuoka, Shōtarō 1920- DLB-182
Yates, Dornford 1885-1960 . . . . DLB-77, 153
Yates, J. Michael 1938- DLB-60
Yates, Richard 1926-1992 . . DLB-2; Y-81, Y-92
Yavorov, Peyo 1878-1914 . . . . DLB-147
Yearsley, Ann 1753-1806 . . . . DLB-109
Yeats, William Butler
   1865-1939 . . . . DLB-10, 19, 98, 156
Yep, Laurence 1948- DLB-52
Yerby, Frank 1916-1991 . . . . DLB-76
Yezierska, Anzia 1885-1970 . . . . DLB-28
Yolen, Jane 1939- DLB-52
Yonge, Charlotte Mary
   1823-1901 . . . . DLB-18, 163
The York Cycle
   circa 1376-circa 1569 . . . . DLB-146
A Yorkshire Tragedy DLB-58
Yoseloff, Thomas
   [publishing house] DLB-46
Young, Al 1939- DLB-33
Young, Arthur 1741-1820 . . . . DLB-158
Young, Dick
   1917 or 1918 - 1987 . . . . DLB-171
Young, Edward 1683-1765 . . . . DLB-95
Young, Francis Brett 1884-1954 . . . . DLB-191
Young, Stark 1881-1963 . . DLB-9, 102; DS-16
Young, Waldeman 1880-1938 . . . . . DLB-26
Young, William [publishing house] DLB-49
Young Bear, Ray A. 1950- DLB-175
Yourcenar, Marguerite
   1903-1987 . . . . DLB-72; Y-88

"You've Never Had It So Good," Gusted by
   "Winds of Change": British Fiction in the
   1950s, 1960s, and After DLB-14
Yovkov, Yordan 1880-1937 . . . . DLB-147

Z

Zachariä, Friedrich Wilhelm
   1726-1777 . . . . DLB-97
Zajc, Dane 1929- DLB-181
Zamora, Bernice 1938- DLB-82
Zand, Herbert 1923-1970 . . . . DLB-85
Zangwill, Israel 1864-1926 . . . . . DLB-10, 135
Zanzotto, Andrea 1921- DLB-128
Zapata Olivella, Manuel 1920- DLB-113
Zebra Books DLB-46
Zebrowski, George 1945- DLB-8
Zech, Paul 1881-1946 . . . . DLB-56
Zepheria DLB-172
Zeidner, Lisa 1955- DLB-120
Zelazny, Roger 1937-1995 . . . . DLB-8
Zenger, John Peter 1697-1746 . . . . DLB-24, 43
Zesen, Philipp von 1619-1689 . . . . . DLB-164
Zieber, G. B., and Company DLB-49
Zieroth, Dale 1946- DLB-60
Zigler und Kliphausen, Heinrich Anshelm von
   1663-1697 . . . . DLB-168
Zimmer, Paul 1934- DLB-5
Zingref, Julius Wilhelm
   1591-1635 . . . . DLB-164
Zindel, Paul 1936- DLB-7, 52
Zinnes, Harriet 1919- DLB-193
Zinzendorf, Nikolaus Ludwig von
   1700-1760 . . . . DLB-168
Zitkala-Ša 1876-1938 . . . . DLB-175
Zola, Emile 1840-1902 . . . . DLB-123
Zolla, Elémire 1926- DLB-196
Zolotow, Charlotte 1915- DLB-52
Zschokke, Heinrich 1771-1848 . . . . . DLB-94
Zubly, John Joachim 1724-1781 . . . . DLB-31
Zu-Bolton II, Ahmos 1936- DLB-41
Zuckmayer, Carl 1896-1977 . . . . DLB-56, 124
Zukofsky, Louis 1904-1978 . . . . . DLB-5, 165
Zupan, Vitomil 1914-1987 . . . . DLB-181
Župančič, Oton 1878-1949 . . . . . . DLB-147
zur Mühlen, Hermynia 1883-1951 . . . DLB-56
Zweig, Arnold 1887-1968 . . . . DLB-66
Zweig, Stefan 1881-1942 . . . . . . DLB-81, 118

ISBN 0-7876-1851-9

90000